W9-AUK-344

What Reviewers Are Saying About
The Online User's Encyclopedia: Bulletin Boards and Beyond

"This book is expertly done, technically flawless, and written in a superb and thoroughly original style.... Our highest recommendation."
– **Jack Rickard**, *Boardwatch*

"A splendid job of creating a comprehensive and thorough reference."
– **Deborah Branscum**, *MacWorld*

"A priceless collection of online information that deserves a place in your home."
– *ModemNews*

"A helpful, comprehensive effort that won't collect dust on a shelf, because you'll be using it."
– **Bill Gram-Reefer**, *MicroTimes*

"If you're already an experienced traveler, you're still going to discover in the book lots of things you didn't know, and at the very least you'll find it a useful reference to consult.... If you're a budding sysop, you'll find it priceless."
– *Mad Mac News*

"The first book for the Mac that covers what the world of telecommunications is really like... It'll take you from the most beginner of terms and definitions to the most advanced of techniques to navigate the world of cyberspace.... It's been rated as one of the best telecom books ever by experts everywhere, and we can't help but to agree."
– *BMUG Newsletter*

"Far and away the best specifically-BBS book I've seen yet."
– **Tom Jennings**, *FidoNews*

"This is one GREAT book! I highly recommend it to all Mac sysops. There has never been such a work available before that covers BBSing and BBS networking in such exhaustive detail. Buy a copy of it. Recommend that new users to your BBS buy a copy of it. It will answer just about every question they'll ever have about BBSing. Needless to say, I am VERY impressed with this book."
– **Michael Connick, author of Tabby, the Macintosh FidoNet mailer**

"A well-managed compendium of material not previously found in a single source, it gives the larger picture we need.... It covers both Internet and FidoNet. I know of no other book that does this.... In spite of the vast amount of information, I found it easy to navigate this book.... Though the book will make a novice feel comfortable, there are also numerous details that will broaden the horizons of seasoned cyberspace voyagers."
– **Boston Computer Society**, *Online Connection*

"This guide is useful for those interested in grass roots networks such as FidoNet, RIME, and FrEdMail as well as the communications and networking software for DOS, Windows, UNIX, and Macintosh users. If you are thinking of hooking up a site in some way, this is a good place to start exploring options."
– *Electronic Networking*

THE ONLINE USER'S ENCYCLOPEDIA:

BULLETIN BOARDS AND BEYOND

BERNARD ABOBA

Addison-Wesley Publishing Company
Reading, Massachusetts • Menlo Park, California • New York
Don Mills, Ontario • Wokingham, England • Amsterdam • Bonn
Sydney • Singapore • Tokyo • Madrid • San Juan
Paris • Seoul • Milan • Mexico City • Taipei

Throughout this book, trademarks of some products and companies have been used, and no such uses are intended to convey endorsements of or other affiliations with this book or MailCom. Rather than put a trademark symbol in every occurrence of a trademarked name, we are using the names only in an editorial fashion and to the benefit of the trademark owner, with no intention of infringement of the trademark.

The authors, editors and publishers have taken care in preparation of this book, and the programs contained in it, but make no expressed or implied warranty of any kind and assume no responsibility for errors or ommissions. In addition the authors, editors, and publisher shall not assume liability for incidental or consequential damages in connection with or arising out of the use of the information or programs contained herein or arising out of the furnishing, performance, or use of the programs, associated instructions, and/or claims of productivity. In addition, the author, editors, and publisher shall not be liable for the actions of others carried out using the information contained in this book.

The Online User's Encyclopedia is the successor to *Bulletin Boards and Beyond,* published by BMUG, Inc., in 1992.

Library of Congress Cataloging-in-Publication Data

```
Aboba, Bernard.
    The online user's encyclopedia : bulletin boards and beyond /
  Bernard Aboba.
        p.   cm.
    Includes bibliographical references and index.
    ISBN 0-201-62214-9
    1. Computer bulletin boards.   I. Title.
QA76.9.B84A26  1993
004.6'16--dc20
```
                                                              93-13304
                                                              CIP

Copyright © 1993 by Bernard Aboba
The following articles are copyrighted by others:
"International Connectivity," pp. 191-193, © 1993 Lawrence H. Landweber and the Internet Society
"TCP/IP," pp. 279-328 © 1993 MailCom
Map of the BITNET Core, pp. 360 © 1992 Board of Trustees, Princeton University
"A Guide to K12Net," pp. 481-484 © 1992 K12Net
"Home Control," pp. 489-496 © 1992 Bernard Aboba
"Free as Air, Free as Water, Free as Knowledge," pp. 499-502 © 1992 Bruce Sterling
"The Politics of the Electronic Communications Privacy Act," pp. 509-514 © 1990 Bernard Aboba
"Free-Neting," pp. 517-519 © 1991 Tom Grundner
"How the NPTN Came To Be," pp. 521-526 © 1992 Tom Grundner
"How the Internet Came To Be," pp. 527-534 © 1993 Vinton Cerf
"How FidoNet Came to Be," pp. 535-538 © 1984, 1985 Tom Jennings, Ken Kaplan, and Ben Baker
"How PCRelay (and PostLink) Came To Be," pp. 545-548 © 1993 Kip Compton
"How FrEdMail Came To Be," pp. 549-553 © 1993 Al Rogers
"UNIX Tips and Tricks," pp. 713-734 © 1993 Bernard Aboba

All rights reserved. No part of this publication may be reproduced, stored in a retrieval system, or transmitted, in any form or by any means, electronic, mechanical, photocopying, recording, or otherwise without the prior written permission of the publisher and author. Printed in the United States of America. Published simultaneously in Canada.

1 2 3 4 5 6 7 8 9 -CRK- 9796959493
First Printing, November 1993

Sponsoring editor: Keith Wollman
Project Editor: Joanne Clapp Fullagar
Production Coordinator: Gail McDonald Jordan
Cover design: Chad Kubo
Text design: Bernard Aboba
Set in Stone series fonts by MailCom, Oakland CA

Addison-Wesley books are available for bulk purchases by corporations, institutions, and other organizations. For more information please contact the Corporate, Government and Special Sales Department at (617)944-3700 x 2915.

The body of Benjamin Franklin, Printer (like the cover of an old book, its contents torn out and stripped of its lettering and gilding), lies here, food for worms; but the work shall not be lost, for it will (as he believed) appear once more in a new and more elegant edition, revised and corrected by the Author.

– Epitaph of Benjamin Franklin (1706 – 1790)

I know no safe depository of the ultimate powers of the society but the people themselves; and if we think them not enlightened enough to exercise their control with a wholesome discretion, the remedy is not to take it from them, but to inform their discretion by education.

– Thomas Jefferson, letter to William C. Jarvis, Sept. 28, 1820

Dedicated to my parents, Evelyn and Joseph Aboba

TRADEMARK INFORMATION

The following are trademarks of the companies or persons named below:

AppleLink®, Finder™, Macintosh®, MultiFinder™ – Apple Computer, Inc.
Alice – Michael Keller
ARC™, SEAdog™, SEAlink, XlatList, ARCmail, GroupMail – Thom Henderson, System
    Enhancement Associates, Inc.
ArcPop, ZipPop – D. G. Gilbert
ARJ – Robert K. Jung
Call Bonus™ – Pacific Bell
Callers Plus™ – Sprint
Carbon Copy™, Carbon Copy Plus™ – Microcom Systems, Inc.
Compact Pro – Bill Goodman
Copernicus Point System, Copernicus Point System II – Michael Connick and Michael
    Pester
COUNTERPoint – Mike Lininger, Lininger Technologies
Echomail – Jeff Rush
Fido®, FidoNet® – Tom Jennings, Fido Software
FirstClass™ – SoftArc, Inc.
Freddie™ – Kemal Tekinay
GIF™, Graphics Interchange Format™, QuickB™ – CompuServe
Hayes® – Hayes Microcomputer Products, Inc.
HiJaak – INSET Systems, Inc.
LapLink™, LapLink Mac™ – Traveling Software, Inc.
MacWoof™ – Craig Vaughan
MicroPhone II™ – Software Ventures Corp.
MS-DOS® – Microsoft Corporation
NREN – National Science Foundation
IBM®, PC-DOS® – International Business Machines Corporation
Kermit – Columbia University
Opus-CBCS™, ZedZap™, YooHoo™, WaZOO™, OpusNode™ – Wynn Wagner III
OneNet™ Member – Scott Converse
PC-Pursuit™ – GTE/Telenet
PD-ROM™ – BMUG, Inc.
PICTure This™ – FGM, Inc.
Reach Out America™, Select Saver™ – AT&T
StuffIt™, StuffIt™ Classic, StuffIt™ Deluxe, Magic Menu™ – Aladdin Systems, Inc.
Tabby – Michael Connick
TBBS™ – Phil Becker, eSoft, Inc.
Timbuktu™, Timbuktu Remote™ – Farallon Computing, Inc.
UNIX™ – AT&T
USRobotics®, HST™ – US Robotics, Inc.
VT–100®, DEC®, VAX®, VMS® – Digital Equipment Corporation
WAIS – WAIS, Inc.
White Knight, Second Sight – The Freesoft Company
ZMODEM – Chuck Forsberg, Omen Technologies
ZTerm – David P. Alverson

All other names are trademarks of their respective owners.

ACKNOWLEDGMENTS

The writing and production of this guide was an enormous undertaking, one that would have been inconceivable without the help of many people. In particular I would like to thank the folks at Addison-Wesley: editors Keith Wollman and Joanne Clapp Fullagar, production manager Gail McDonald Jordan, and copy editors Tema Goodwin and Mark Duran.

Many of the changes in the second edition were based on the comments of readers of the first edition. Their comments were instrumental in deciding what articles to add and what coverage to expand. I would also like to thank those who have reviewed portions of the second edition before it went to press: J. Allard, Dave Alverson, Alan Bryant, Kip Compton, Ira Fuchs, Beryl Hauser, Tom Jennings, John S. Quarterman, Jack Rickard, and Laurie Sefton. Other reviewers included Roz Ault, Wolfgang Henke, David Morgenstern, Ted Silviera and Edward Vielmetti. With help like this, I might as well state the obvious: any remaining errors of omission or commission are the sole responsibility of the author.

I would also like to thank the following individuals for granting reprint permission: Ira Fuchs of Princeton University for the map of the BITNET core, Tom Jennings for "How FidoNet Came to Be," Bruce Sterling for "Free as Air, Free as Water, Free as Knowledge," Tom Grunder for "Free-Neting," and Rob Reilly of the K12Net Council for "A Guide to K12Net." I would also like to thank those who granted interviews and shared their recollections of the early years with me: Sparky Herring for "How QMAIL Came To Be," Al Rogers for "How FrEdMail Came To Be," Vint Cerf for "How Internet Came to Be," Tom Grundner for "How NPTN Came to Be," Tim Pozar for "How UFGATE Came to Be," Kip Compton for "How PCRelay (and PostLink) Came to Be," and Tim Pozar, Leo Laporte, Vernon Keenan, Michael Connick, and Richard Bollar for their history of the EchoMac Network.

Finally, I would like to acknowledge Kelly Schwarzhoff, who prepared the material on minor BBS networks, MUDs, HoloNet and FidoNet utilities; and Betsy Kennedy of Farallon Computing who contributed many of the questions at the end of the chapters.

PREFACE

What it's all about

Why should I care?

Just as the automobile transformed the workplace, homestead, and landscape, so too will the communications revolution influence our lives in unknowable ways.

Today, activities such as visiting a library, mailing a letter or trading securities no longer need to be carried out in person; they can be handled using a computer and a modem. These tasks, along with many others, have been *virtualized*.

This is only the beginning. In the decades ahead more and more of our daily activities will find electronic analogs, until our lives are fully mirrored in the cavities of electronic networks. Virtual cities, virtual supermarkets, virtual concert halls; almost anything is possible.

Telecommunications technology will influence the way we are governed; where we live; what jobs we perform; what companies will falter, survive, and prosper; how and what we will be paid. Even if you have never used a computer and can't imagine why you'd want to, these changes will affect you, possibly in ways you won't like.

The premise of this guide is that only an educated public can ensure that this technology will be used appropriately. Unlike conventional media, the new telecommunications technologies make it as easy to provide information as to consume it; as easy to communicate with politicians and to demand change, as to sit back and let their words wash over us; as easy to explore places thousands of miles away as to say hello to someone next door. However, all these possibilities do not come without responsibilities: to an extent greater than with any other medium, global computer networks depend on the contributions of people such as yourself.

People are needed to do research and provide their findings; to write software and offer it for use by others; to create and moderate conferences; to set up their own electronic fruit stands; to tutor others in the possibilities and responsibilities of the new media. More than anything else, the idea of "giving back" has made global networks what they are today.

The objective of this guide is to train responsible electronic citizens, people who ask not only "What can telecommunications do for me?" but also "What can we do together to ensure that this technology fulfills its promise?" That is why this guide discusses not only accessing information, but providing it; why we touch on many technologies and networks, rather than just one; why we talk about the past and the future rather than solely about the present; why we sometimes lecture as well as entertain.

If I did not believe that the addition of more educated contributors would add vitality and energy to global networks, I would not have written this guide. I believe that it will be possible not only to settle the Electronic Frontier, but to civilize it; not only to build a new information infrastructure, but in the process to retain the principles that have brought us this far.

Building the global communications infrastructure

As far as I can tell, two feeder roads lead to the information infrastructure of the future.

One road is the Internet, developed over more than 20 years by computer scientists. The Internet architects began as graduate students waiting for the "network geniuses" to show up and tell them what to do (they never did). Today they are middle aged, distinguished, perhaps even celebrated, as close to "network geniuses" as we are likely to find. As the Internet moves into the 90s, their work merits recognition along with the most significant scientific advances of the twentieth century.

The Internet Protocols (TCP/IP) were designed to support a wide variety of networking technologies, and have been ported to many computers and operating systems. With an estimated 2 million hosts, over 15,000 networks, and an estimated 5 to 20 million users in more than 60 countries (as of August, 1993), the Internet is the world's largest computer network. It is doubling in networks, hosts, and traffic every year. While the development of the Internet has been partially funded by government, volunteers have also played an important role by developing much of the underlying software.

On the other road are store and forward networks such as UUCP and BITNET, as well as a plethora of bulletin board networks: FidoNet, RIME, FrEdMail, ILINK, Intelec, OneNet, InfoLink, SmartNet, North AmeriNet, WWIVNet, Alternet, Eggnet and RBBSNet, to name a few. These networks were typically created to provide networking functionality for a particular brand of computer, operating system, or bulletin board software. These networks now also connect millions of people and reach to the farthest corners of the globe, including countries that for economic or political reasons are not connected to the Internet.

Communications at the crossroads

It appears that these two roads are converging, and therein lies the tale. It is possible that this convergence will occur by the Internet supplanting the bulletin board networks. More likely (and desirable) is a marriage that will combine the best features of both: the reliability and economy of the Internet with the grass roots participation and ease of use of the bulletin board networks.

To continue to handle the exploding demand and provide for new services such as multimedia, bulletin board networks need the global connectivity and cost effectiveness of the Internet. What is not quite as widely appreciated is that the Internet also needs the bulletin board networks.

This is not solely because of the potential for technology interchange. Innovations such as ZMODEM, QWK, ARC, ZIP and Remote Imaging Protocol (RIP) first appeared in the bulletin board world, and were later ported to UNIX. With development of TCP/IP compatible bulletin board packages, there are signs that the bulletin board world is warming up to TCP/IP. In time it is likely that the backbones of the bulletin board networks, which currently rely on store and forward technology, will make the transition to running over TCP/IP, much as BITNET and USENET have.

The importance of bulletin board networks lies more in their culture, a movement for the sharing of information much like the public library movement fathered by Benjamin Franklin. Global data highways are interesting largely because people have set up electronic fruit stands along the side of the road: databases, file archives, mailing lists, and conferences created and maintained in the spirit of enterprise and public service. The purpose of the bulletin board networks, which will survive no matter what technology they eventually choose, is to deliver the benefits of the telecommunications revolution to local communities.

In providing links to the Internet as well as access that is responsive to community needs and standards, bulletin board operators serve a role analogous to that of local newspapers, TV, or radio stations. With governments setting up bulletin boards to better serve the public, it is only a matter of time before bulletin boards become as important a fixture in our cities and towns as the public library.

As a vehicle of the telecommunications revolution, bulletin boards are the Model-T. They may not be as flexible, elegant, or powerful as we'd like, but the features and price are right, so they'll do until we understand the medium well enough to build something better. First, we've got to get people on the road.

Of course, before we can do that to any appreciable extent, we've got to have affordable local roads. This is the objective of the ToasterNet movement, which is catching on across the country. By pooling the purchasing power of local citizens, ToasterNets such as The Little Garden (TLG) and the New England Community Internet (NECI) are bringing about a revolution in the pricing of low-speed Internet connections. As ToasterNets spring up and begin to interconnect, they will constitute a power center rivaling that of the commercial service providers. Without ToasterNets, many bulletin boards could not afford Internet access, so it can be argued that ToasterNets are a vital part of the bulletin board movement. It is even conceivable that during the next several years, ToasterNets will cooperate to fund construction of a backbone.

Of course, computer networks are not perfect. Their governance is frequently anarchic, and the messages they carry are at times uncultured, ignorant, or even rude. In these respects they resemble eighteenth century pampleteers such as Thomas Paine. Since exposure to objectionable material is the price of freedom, we shall have to live with these limitations, using law and good sense to restore order when necessary.

More serious are the long-range problems that we cannot foresee. Just as the original automobile makers did not envisage smog-ridden Los Angeles, so too may we now find it hard to imagine the future discomforts of the Information Age, such as information overload, CyberPorn, CyberScams and CyberSmog.

Whatever the outcome, I can think of no better way to ensure the future of our society than by educating the public about the art and science of telecommunications. I can only hope that in the rush to build the global information infrastructure, the roadside fruit stands will not be hastily bulldozed to make way for information supermarkets.

INTRODUCTION

How to use this guide

This is not a book!
(Had you fooled, didn't I?)

This is a guide. Guides are written for people who want to participate and try things out for themselves. This is your guide to bulletin boards and the computer networks they are connected to. Like a guide to an exotic country, there may be places you're intent on visiting and getting to know on an intimate basis; there may be other areas that you'd just as soon avoid. With this guide you can choose where you want to go and what you want to learn.

Who was this guide written for?

You don't have to be a computer expert, or even like computers very much, to get something out of this guide. You just have to have a problem to solve, or a group of people (or a special someone) with whom you'd like to communicate.

As its comprehensive name suggests, this guide offers something for everyone. It accepts you as you are, so reading it will not make you a nerd, although it will not make you less of one either. If you have never used a modem, this guide will teach you about telecommunications and get you up and running. If you already own a modem, but do not understand what a bulletin board is, or how it could be useful to you, this guide will help you teach yourself how to use bulletin boards. If you are already using a bulletin board, but have not made use of the advanced features such as FidoNet, Internet, ILink, UUCP, BITNET, OneNet or RIME networking, this guide will show you how to telecommunicate more efficiently and harness the power of those networks. If you are an advanced communications user who wants a look "under the hood," this guide will provide an introduction to how things work. If you are looking to connect to global networks, this guide offers information on the resources necessary to get started, and tutorials on the debugging tools to get things working. If you aren't interested in running a bulletin board but want to provide information to other people, this guide will show you how to do this without having to run your own system.

This guide is balanced between itsy bitsy details and **The Big Picture.** As I make it out, The Big Picture is that telecommunications is so useful that in a decade lots of ordinary people will be using it to do ordinary (and some extraordinary) things. We will have the online town hall, home-entertainment center, public library, government spokesperson, educator, and talk show host. Maybe by then the press will have outgrown its fascination with Cyberspace as the province of computer weenies with shady backgrounds, but you never know.

What are the goals of this guide?

This guide is about accessing a wealth of information to enrich your personal and professional life. It is also about becoming an information provider. After reading this guide I hope that you will gain an understanding of what computer communications can and cannot do. I also hope to get you using the technology in ways that will save time, improve productivity, or provide recreation. Finally, I hope that many of you will come to see computer communications as I do - as but another useful tool of the modern age, requiring (as all tools do) a certain artisanship in its proper application.

I wrote this guide to show people the easy way to access global networks. An easy way was needed because:

• The software is frequently unfriendly.
• The documentation is often skimpy or excessively technical.
• The software is "self-documenting." (This means that only people who already know how to use the unfriendly software will be able to retrieve the skimpy documentation.)

One of the goals of this book is to help you teach yourself how to telecommunicate using a graphical user interface. Although setting up a graphical connection does involve more work at the beginning, the superior ease of use more than compensates for the increased setup time. This book describes many varieties of graphical connections, from bulletin board links to direct Internet connections, so that you can choose one that is right for your budget and goals.

I have included beginning, intermediate, and advanced material in this guide because, in my experience, beginners don't stay that way for long. Even if you think you only want to learn how to perform a few specific tasks, telecommunications is powerful, and people are naturally curious. You probably won't be able to stop yourself from wanting to learn more, and while you learn, this guide will continue to have something to offer.

What do you need?

To make the best use of this guide, you will need to select a commercial online service, networked bulletin board system or Internet service provider. Many of the vendors listed in Appendix B: Choice Products, and the Chapter 8: Access to the Internet will serve quite well. These include the World, Netcom, HoloNet and MSEN Internet services, and the Planet BMUG, BMUG Boston, MAGIC, ExecNet, AMUG, EXEC-PC, Windows Online, MacCircles, Twilight Clone, and Channel 1 bulletin board systems. Each of these services requires payment of a subscription fee, which is not included in the price of this guide.

If you would like to make use of the graphical Internet applications described in the Internet part of this guide, you will need a SLIP or PPP account. They can be obtained from the ToasterNets described in Chapter 15, or the service providers listed in Appendix B: Choice Products. You will also need a TCP/IP networking package. Choices include MacTCP from Apple, or for the PC, KA9Q or a Windows Sockets-compatible TCP/IP stack such as NetManage Chameleon or Frontier SuperTCP.

Changes from the first edition

The first edition of *Bulletin Boards and Beyond* started out as a manual for the BMUG BBS and grew into a 560-page reference covering everything under the sun. At the time I wrote the first edition, I did not imagine that it would appeal to many people outside the BMUG membership. As a result, much of the book was BMUG and Macintosh-specific, and the book was not designed for wide distribution. The tremendous success of the first edition surprised me. While the initial print run of 2500 copies sold out in only four months, with the switchover from the BMUG TBBS system to FirstClass, the BMUG BBS section of the book became outdated. As a result of this the book went out of print.

Since I so badly misjudged the audience for the first edition, a lot of thinking went into how to better serve the readership. The changes in this, the second edition, reflect that thinking.

Since the inclusion of material on a specific bulletin board system caused the first edition to date rapidly, I decided to separate out the rapidly dating material by splitting the manuscript into two books. The first book, *The Online User's Encyclopedia: Bulletin Boards and Beyond*, you have in your hands right now. It has been written as a general guide to bulletin boards and global networks, without any specific assumptions about the systems you will be using.

The second book, *The BMUG Online Services Reference*, has been published separately by BMUG, Inc. It contains the specific information needed to access global networks such as the Internet, FidoNet, and OneNet from the Planet BMUG and BMUG Boston systems. It also includes a guide to the Macintosh and Windows versions of the FirstClass client software, information on the OneNet and MacUnion networks, and lists of FirstClass BBSes. *The BMUG Online Services Reference* is available on the Internet, as well as via commercial services such as AOL (BMUG forum) and CompuServe, and the Planet BMUG and BMUG Boston systems. For those looking for a paper copy, it is also available directly from BMUG, by calling (510)549-2684.

Another major change was that I selected a commercial publisher with a global presence to take care of the printing and distribution of the second edition. Since I did not plan for the wide distribution of the first edition, many people were unable to obtain it. With the selection of Addison-Wesley as publisher, this book should be available in many more places.

In order to allow for the marketing and distribution expenses of making this guide available worldwide, the retail price has risen substantially. However, in order to continue to serve the community that has nurtured this book, Addison-Wesley has agreed to provide special discounts on volume purchases of this guide by computer users groups. For information, contact Addison-Wesley Special Markets at (800)358-4566 or (617)944-3700, extension 2915.

Organization? In Berkeley?

This guide is divided into six major sections. The first, Quickstart, is designed to give the beginner enough basic information to get started. It demystifies modem and telecommunications jargon, and it discusses how to purchase a modem and choose a bulletin board system (BBS). If you are unfamiliar with any of the following words, you should begin with the Quickstart: modem, RS-232, virus, bulletin board, BBS, baud, bits/parity/stop bits, download, upload, StuffIt, MacBinary.

The way the QuickStart section was organized in the first edition was one of the most frequent complaints we received, so I have tried to transform it from a stream-of-consciousness narrative into a logical progression of ideas. Let me know how well I've done.

The second section, The Internet, is devoted to the Internet. This section discusses how to send mail, transfer files, converse in real time, and access the treasure troves of information in databases and Online Public Access Catalogs (OPACs). Finally, it discusses establishing and debugging Internet connections and creating your own Internet bulletin board or ToasterNet. Since many of you asked for information on SLIP and PPP, I've included quite a bit of information on this.

The third section, the Store and Forward Network Guide, is devoted to store and forward networks such as UUCP, BITNET, FidoNet, RIME, and ILink. It discusses features of these networks such as mail, conferencing, and file transfer. This section also includes chapters on how to use "message readers" to read and post messages, and how to use "point software" to connect your computer to the FidoNet network.

The fourth section, the Tutorial, is designed for the intermediate telecommunicator who is generally proficient but needs detailed information on one or more aspects of telecommunications. The tutorial includes chapters on saving money on your phone bill, compression programs, file format conversion, file transfer methods, and home control. If you are a beginner or intermediate user, you should consult this section as needed, but don't feel obliged to read it all the way through.

The Memories and Visions section is new to the second edition. It was added to provide some perspective on where global networks have been and where they are going. It contains both the histories of networks as told by their creators, as well as visions for the future of global computing. It was a great pleasure to interview network luminaries and publish their stories.

The sixth section, the Appendix, contains reference material that should be consulted as needed. Included within this section are chapters on choice products and cable construction, as well as lists of online resources and bulletin board system phone numbers.

Additions and revisions

In addition to splitting the first edition into two books, this edition contains major changes in organization and content. More than 19 chapters have been added, with 10 chapters undergoing major revisions. Changes include a rewritten Quickstart, expanded coverage of the Internet, updated and expanded versions of the Tutorial and Appendices, and a new section, Memories and Visions.

Another change in this edition is the addition of PC and UNIX coverage. To my surprise, the first edition was quite popular among PC owners, and therefore I have added material of interest to them. Since I've used PCs in my work for many years, and have run several PC-based bulletin boards, that wasn't hard to do. Since I also use a UNIX workstation (NeXT), information on UNIX networking has inevitably crept in, although that is by no means a major focus of this guide. Computer communications is about linking computers of all types, so I think these changes are in keeping with the subject matter.

Of course, balancing the interests of Mac and PC owners in a single volume is probably impossible. Since I couldn't cover everything, I have concentrated on adding PC coverage in areas that I am familiar with, such as material on UUCP software for the PC and the expanded coverage of PC-based bulletin board software and utilities. My apologies to the PC owners for primarily including Mac screen shots of cross-platform applications such as Eudora, Microphone II, or FirstClass client. To make it up to PC owners, I am providing a comprehensive supplementary listing of TCP/IP applications for the PC, along with installation hints. You can retrieve your prize from the MailCom FTP archive, `ftp netcom1.netcom.com`, `get /pub/mailcom/IBMTCP/ibmtcp.zip`.

Design and layout

In order to keep this guide from going over 900 pages, a number of design changes have been made. These include a two-column layout, use of smaller type in the Appendices, and moving material to the electronic updates. For more on this, see the heading "Electronic Updates" that follows. Even with all of these changes, and splitting the first edition into two books, the second edition is still more than 270 pages longer than the first.

Typographic conventions

In order to make clear what is computerese and what is English, and what you type versus what the computer types back at you, we have adopted some typographic conventions. Throughout this guide:

In a text screen dump, `what the computer types is in light courier;` **`what the user types is in bold courier.`** `Filenames, machine names, and email addresses appear in courier light type.`

Program names will use the normal font (Stone Sans Serif). Macintosh names will use upper and lowercase; IBM PC names will be in uppercase only; UNIX names will be in lowercase only.

Electronic updates

The online world is changing so quickly that books go out of date between when they are written and when they are printed. In order to keep you up to date, I will be making additional information available in electronic form from time to time. In order to receive information on updates and special offers, you must complete and mail the registration form at the back of this guide.

In order to make it easy for you to obtain the updates, MailCom maintains an FTP archive on the Internet. Currently, the updates are available via anonymous FTP, although we may at some point support other methods as well, such as retrieval via mail, Gopher, World Wide Web or WAIS.

You can reach the MailCom archive by typing the following commands to your Internet host: `ftp netcom1.netcom.com`, `login:` **`anonymous`**`, cd /pub/mailcom`**`.`**

Available files and directories include:

README	Basic information, including a list of files
BBB_Updates/	Updates to the first edition
BBSONE/	Papers from the BBSONE Conference
BMUG_Online_Reference/	BMUG Online Services Reference
Discounts/	Special markets discounts on this book
Filter/	Information on the filter contest
IBMTCP/	Updated PC TCP/IP Supplement
OUE_Updates/	Updates to this edition
Toaster/	Information on ToasterNets

Updates stored in /pub/mailcom/BBB_Updates include:

bbb1.cpt.hqx — This update to the first edition included information on CD-ROMs, Internet services, home control, K12Net, sysop resources, and commercial online services. Most of that information has made it into this edition, so you won't need this update. This file has been compressed with Compact Pro and then converted to ASCII by BinHex 4.0.

bbb1.zip — This is a version of update 1 in Word for Windows format, compressed with PKZIP 2.04.

bbb2.cpt.hqx — This update includes information on MUDs, TCP/IP on the PC, FrEdMail, and UNIX. Since some of this material (such as the TCP/IP chapter and sendmail.cf files) have not made it into this edition, it is recommended that readers interested in this material obtain this update. This file has been compressed with Compact Pro and then converted to ASCII by BinHex 4.0.

bbb2.zip — This is a version of update 2 in Word for Windows format, compressed with PKZIP 2.04.

Files in /pub/mailcom/BMUG_Online_Reference include:

online.sea.hqx — The latest version of *The BMUG Online Services Reference*. This file has been stored as a self-extracting archive, and then converted to ASCII by BinHex 4.0.

online.zip — The latest version of *The BMUG Online Services Reference*, in Word for Windows format, compressed with PKZIP 2.04.

Files in /pub/mailcom/IBMTCP include:

ibmtcp.zip — Updated information on TCP/IP software for IBM PC compatibles, compressed with PKZIP 2.04.

How to contact the author

The author does not pretend that this guide will answer all questions, or even that it will be comprehensible to everyone. However, he will listen to all suggestions for improving it. If this guide is sufficiently popular, there will be a third edition in which those suggestions will be incorporated.

If for any reason you find this guide unsatisfactory or unclear on some point, want to suggest coverage of a topic or product, or even if you like it a lot and have nothing but good things to say, please drop me a line via the Internet by `mail aboba@world.std.com`, `subject`: `suggestions`.

Filter contest

As described in the Internet section of this guide, the Internet is both the world's greatest information resource and an incredible waste of time. It is the author's opinion that better tools are needed to filter out the InfoNuggets from the InfoChaff. In the spirit of encouraging the development of filters, I will be awarding a $250 prize to the best filter program, as determined by a panel of experts. Rules for the filter contest are obtainable via `mail aboba@world.std.com`, `subject`: `contest.`

If you are interested in volunteering as a judge in the contest, please `mail aboba@world.std.com`, `subject`: `judge`, stating your qualifications. In all matters relating to the contest, my arbitrary and capricious judgement will be final.

Review policy

This guide contains information about many products, and MailCom is always looking for information on new hardware or software that may be of interest to readers. However, since we do not review products in the same manner as do major computer magazines, we ask that vendors understand our review policies before sending us products for review.

Since a book remains on the shelves for a long period of time, we do not focus on feature comparisons, which often go out of date a few weeks after the review is printed. Instead, we focus on longer-term issues such as overall product design and architecture, reliability, and customer support. As a result, product reviews may take as long as six months to write.

We do not review products shipped without printed documentation, or products in beta test, although we do provide feedback on such products. We prefer that all products be sent to us exactly as they are to be sold to the customer, or if there is a difference, that the differences be included in writing along with the product. If you send us a nonfunctioning network adapter, we will assume that you are also shipping a nonfunctioning adapter to customers.

Please send electronic mail to `aboba@world.std.com`, `subject`: `reviews` prior to sending any products. We will make arrangements for the review and will prepare to accept the shipment. Please do not send products to people representing themselves as acting on our behalf. We cannot be responsible for products sent without contacting us first. We recommend that all shipments be insured to guard against loss.

Warning from the Librarian General

One of the great forces shaping our world is the freer movement of ideas and people across national boundaries. Today we know more about other peoples and they more about us than has ever previously been possible. The information glut of yesterday has grown into the information tsunami of today.

This has created the problem of information overload. The symptoms are similar to the problems experienced after a large Thanksgiving dinner: drowsiness, lethargy, headaches, disorientation. Like a coach who counts pitches before pulling the pitcher from the ball game, there is only so much information you can ingest before you start losing it.

This guide contains so much information that it should be ingested only in moderation. Several readers have reported that they have lost entire days, even weekends of their lives, reading this guide from cover to cover. One reader even reported taking it into the shower.

Please read safely. In particular, there is one thing you should never do while reading this guide. Do not read and drive. After all, the Internet is a data highway, not a real highway, and reading this guide while driving on the freeways won't get you anywhere you want to go.

Readers are also warned of the dangers of the flame wars, torrential tirades prevalent on distributed conferencing systems. Participants in these wars have suffered injuries from singed hair to egos burned to a crisp. Even innocent bystanders are not immune; many now suffer the effects of CyberSmog, a form of mental pollution resulting from flame wars. Symptoms are similar to those experienced in a smog alert: burning eyes, parched throat, shortness of breath. A message from Smokey the CyberBear: *Only You Can Prevent Flame Wars*. Thank you.

Disclaimer

Much of the information contained in this guide, such as bulletin board phone numbers or software version numbers, goes out of date very quickly. As a result, please exercise caution when dialing phone numbers that appear in this book. Manually dial only during daytime hours until you verify that the bulletin board you want to reach is still in service. After you have verified that the service is operating, you can switch to automated dialing.

Unless otherwise noted, the opinions in this guide are those of the author. Last time I checked, I had not been appointed the official spokesperson of any of the following:

The Planet Earth
The Internet
The U.S. Government
The State of California (not so good at the moment)
IBM, Compaq, or Dell
Apple Computer, Inc.
The University of California, Berkeley
The City of Berkeley (bringing you *Riot of the Week*[SM])
BMUG, Inc.
The BMUG cat, Megabyte (*Meow*[SM])
Any major or minor breakfast cereal (not even oatmeal!)

Table Of Contents

Table of Contents

Table of Contents

Part I

QuickStart

"To be proud of knowledge is to be blind with light."

– Benjamin Franklin, *Poor Richard's Almanack*

CHAPTER 1:
INTRODUCTION TO
COMMUNICATIONS

Getting prepared

What can I do online?

Some of the things you can do online are to:

• Search for employment
• Do academic, professional, or financial research
• Inform yourself about current events
• Get support for computer hardware or software
• Buy or sell goods and services, including computer hardware and software
• Play games or chat interactively

I've had a computer since 1985, and by now I don't even much think about "using a computer" when I go online. I'm as comfortable with my computer as I am with my toaster, and more comfortable than with the VCR. When I have things to do, I often find that using a computer is the easiest way to go about it.

What can I not do online?

For many people, going online is more than just an activity; it's a lifestyle choice. While computers can make things easier, they are not a substitute for reality (sorry!). While online you cannot:

• Give someone a hug
• Smell a rose
• Climb Mt. Kilamanjaro

No matter how miraculous and neat the online world may seem, if used to excess, it can be harmful. Don't forget to get (or keep) a life!

How do I accomplish things online?

If you are reading this book, the chances are that you are interested in learning about what communications can do for you. To accomplish things online, you need to understand how to match what you want to do (the ends) to the modes of computer communications (the means).

To accomplish a task online, you will need to choose:

• The type of online service or computer to connect to
• The type of connection with that computer or service

Modes of computer communications

Here are some of the ways in which you can communicate with another computer or fax machine:

∇ Mac or PC to fax machine

With addition of a peripheral known as a fax modem, you can send or receive faxes on your computer. This is useful when the document you wish to fax is already on the computer, when you have multiple recipients, when you have a long document, or when you want to do something with an incoming fax, such as converting it to text in order to edit it.

Fax modems are much better at sending than receiving. If your computer is turned off, or is busy doing other things, incoming faxes may be lost or may interrupt ongoing tasks. Incoming faxes also take up lots of disk space and are too large to easily view on a computer screen. In some lines of work you will require a hard copy of incoming faxes, or you will need to send a copy of a paper document. This is why organizations that receive many more faxes than they send usually prefer a fax machine.

▽ Mac to Mac or PC to PC – file transfer

The simplest way of communicating with another computer is to send a file to another machine of the same type. Assuming that both machines have the appropriate software to interpret the file, you will be able to transfer and use reports, databases, or anything else you can create. To transfer a file to another computer, that computer will need to be turned on and running software that will allow for the transfer. You will also need to pay for the phone call or cable to connect one machine to the other.

▽ Mac to PC or PC to Mac – transfer and conversion

The story gets more complicated when you attempt to transfer a file to a different type of computer. In order for the other machine to be able to use the file, you will have to convert it to a format the other machine will understand, usually **before** sending it. The conversion process can be complex, and is discussed in detail in Chapter 23: File Conversion. Efforts towards a "lingua franca" for document exchange are discussed later in this chapter.

▽ Mac or PC to bulletin board

A bulletin board is a computer that functions as an electronic intermediary, allowing other computers to send files and messages to each other by storing them on the bulletin board machine. One big advantage of communicating this way is that the two communicating computers do not need to be available at the same time. You can send a message early in the day and have the recipient call to retrieve it later that night. Since many different computers access bulletin boards,

communicating this way may raise file conversion issues. With this method of communication, each computer pays for the cost of a phone call to the bulletin board service. The bulletin board may also have susbscription or connect fees.

▽ Mac or PC to commercial online service

Commercial online services (e.g. CompuServe, Prodigy or America Online) offer access to a wide variety of information, from investment analyst reports to weather forecasts. These services allow users to communicate with each other using the service as a go-between. As with a bulletin board service, both parties need not be available at the same time. In addition, since many commercial online services have nationwide access networks, you may be able to reach the service with a local call. However, you will have to pay for use of the commercial online service, usually on an hourly basis.

▽ Mac or PC to computer network via a host

Connecting to a computer network (such as the Internet) allows you to communicate worldwide with people who may not be available when you are, often by a local call.

The most common way to get network access is to purchase an account with an online service provider or bulletin board that is connected to the network. Your service provider or BBS (also called the "network host") will do all the work in keeping the network connection functioning, while your personal computer just displays the results, usually by pretending that it is a dumb terminal connected to the host.

Since the host is connected to the network, not your personal computer, transferring information is a two-step process: first getting it to the host, and then having the host transfer it to your machine.

Since the host is usually a workstation or mini-computer that operates via a command-line interface, accessing networks this way involves *typing* in commands. This can be difficult for those who are used using a mouse to select commands.

Online services offer several levels of access to global networks. *Mail* or *gateway* access usually means that the service only supports transfer of messages to other network users and that services such as file transfer or database access are not supported. For this reason *mail access* represents the lowest level of service.

▽ Mac or PC directly to computer network

More advanced users may want to put their personal computers directly on the network. This offers a higher level of service because the personal computer uses its own interface and network capabilities rather than just acting as an appendage to a host. As a result, transferring information to the personal computer is a one-step process: directly from the network to your machine. Although direct network connections offer more flexibility and are easier to use, they are more complicated to set up, and are usually more expensive as well. For more information, please consult Chapter 15: TCP/IP, and Chapter 18: Points.

Types of online activities

Once you have selected the method of communications, you will then need to select the kinds of services to access. Here are some of the major types:

▽ Electronic mail

Using your communications software and modem, you can send messages to other people across the street or across the globe. This includes the capability of sending a fax or telex without requiring any additional equipment. For more information on electronic mail, consult Chapter 9: Electronic Mail.

▽ Computer-mediated conferencing

Through computer-mediated conferencing, a group can discuss a topic of interest, such as skiing, professional interests, or use of a particular software package or brand of hardware. People come and go at different times, reading what has been said to date and adding their own two bits worth for the next participant to read.

One of the largest conferencing systems is network news (also known as USENET), which is available on 100,000 machines worldwide. Network newsgroups (such as news.answers) are denoted by words separated by periods. For more information on conferencing, consult Chapter 12: USENET, Chapter 18: Introduction to FidoNet, Chapter 19: PCBoard Networks, and Appendix J: Conference Listings.

▽ Database searching

Online services offer access to bibliographic, scientific, and business databases, with retrieval by subject, title, author, or key words. Commercial services are typically expensive, but they are well worth it if used wisely. Inexpensive or free searching is also available over global computer networks such as the Internet. For a sampling of available databases, consult Appendix C: Online Resources.

▽ News

News wires such as NewsBytes are now available online. For more information on online news wires, consult Appendix B: Choice Products.

▽ Software

Software releases or updates are often distributed or sold online. For more information on software archives, consult Chapter 10: File Transfer.

▽ Games

Several services offer the ability to compete against other users in games of skill or chance. For more information on games, consult Chapter 13: Playing in the MUDs.

▽ Shopping

It is possible to obtain information about products or to order merchandise online.

▽ Chatting

Using your computer you can hold a conversation by reading and typing replies to other users. Although this mode of communication is often regarded with scorn by advanced users ("Why don't they just pick up the phone?"), it is nevertheless very popular, possibly because it involves live interaction. For information on chatting, consult Chapter 13: Internet Relay Chat.

Choosing appropriate tools

After trying out one or two services and their respective activities, novices usually choose the service and activities that most interest them, and settle into a routine. Unfortunately, they often reach for familiar activities when more appropriate solutions may be available.

In particular, novice users may use mail when a conferencing system might be more appropriate, or use a conferencing system when their needs would be more appropriately met by CD-ROM, file transfer, or database access. For example, if you were looking for a rare claw foot for your 19th century bathtub, you could send mail to everyone on a general BBS, hoping a few plumbers will answer. A better idea would be to post your message in the plumbing conference of a BBS for contractors. It might be smarter yet to go to a CD-ROM put out by a plumbing parts distributor.

To broaden your perspective, I encourage you to at least skim most of the chapters in this book, whether you think you'll use the material or not. Pay particular attention to Chapter 14: Information Servers, which includes information on searching tools such as WAIS and VERONICA.

The advantages of doing it online

In at least a few areas, accomplishing things online is easier and faster than handling it any other way.

Online databases and Online Public Access Catalogs (OPACs) are card catalog, book puller, and stacks all rolled into one. Electronic mail lets you communicate at a distance more quickly and less expensively than using the post office. Computer-mediated conferencing is generally more informative than (though potentially as contentious as) "Geraldo."

Online news services (such as ClariNet) offer news in both more breadth and depth than the average newspaper.

The advantage of the online world in providing entertainment or offering conversational opportunities is less clearcut, but effectiveness is likely to improve over time.

The CD-ROM alternative

In reading about telecommunications it is hard to keep from getting excited, but it would be incorrect to conclude that all your information needs can be satisfied this way. Online services are best at providing small quantities of current information, but there are times when you will be interested in accessing large databases or archives. This is where CD-ROM excels.

Since 1987, people have been touting CD-ROM, but only recently have CD-ROM prices declined enough for many individuals and libraries to purchase CDs and players. With the odds improving that CD-ROM will be coming to a library near you, now is the time to familiarize yourself with the technology.

Telecommunications versus CD-ROM

In order to understand whether your question is appropriate for telecommunications or CD-ROM, ask yourself: How much data am I looking for? How recent is the data?

Question: How has IBM stock performed **over the last 20 years?**
Answer: CD-ROM

Question: What was IBM stock trading at **yesterday**?
Answer: general purpose online service or newspaper

Question: What is IBM stock trading at **now?**
Answer: quotation service, radio terminal, or specialized information service

The figure on the next page shows which sources of information are most appropriate for which uses. Beginning telecommunicators often start out by accessing small amounts of recent data on general or specialized information services. As they become more experienced, they learn how to access large amounts of information on archival databases. Unfortunately, they often continue to use general or specialized information services to do this, when instead they should be migrating to CD-ROM.

Since CD-ROM has become such an important competitor to telecommunications technology, a listing of important CD-ROMs is included in Appendix B: Choice Products. Current CDs include complete snapshots of Internet archives and USENET on CD.

Quantity of Data

	Small	Medium	Large
Now	Specialized information service	Data broadcast service	High speed dedicated network
Yesterday	General information service	High speed store and forward network	Medium speed dedicated network
Last quarter	Books or periodicals	Reference books	CD-ROM

Timeliness (vertical axis label)

Accessing CD-ROMs

One of the best ways to access CD-ROMs is through a corporate or university library, which now frequently carry periodical, financial, and statistical databases on CD-ROM. If you are eligible for borrowing privileges, you will find this much more economical than purchasing your own player and CD-ROMs.

A day in the life of a commercial service user

To give you an idea of what a session on a commercial online service is like, I've included two "day in the life" examples on the following pages, one from CompuServe, and another from America Online. While the screen shots are from a Macintosh, both

services offer Windows versions with similar capabilities.

In both examples, I log on to the service, and then send a mail message via a global computer network known as the Internet. How this works is not important for now, except to know that by using the Internet you can send mail to millions of other online users, including users of other commercial online services. For more information, consult Chapter 9: Electronic Mail.

In the CompuServe session, I then move on to downloading weather maps, and asking a question in the Macintosh Communications Forum. As with many other vendors, Microsoft has established a strong presence on CompuServe, and so I navigate to Microsoft Developer Services to get a technical question answered.

In the America Online session, after sending a mail message, I search for some health-related information (cures for writer's exhaustion), and check out unique America Online forums such as SeniorNet and National Public Radio outreach. I then browse for information on nearby vacation spots in the San Jose Mercury News Center forum, Bay Area Living section. America Online also offers similar services for other cities, such as Chicago Online. Since the Mercury Center forum offers restaurant listings, I search for places to eat in Sonoma, my chosen vacation spot.

What are bulletin boards?

What is a bulletin board? How is it different from an online service? Many of the services offered on bulletin boards and online services are similar, so how do we distinguish them?

Here is my best shot:

• An electronic bulletin board is an electronic information service that (taken by itself) is limited in either scope or depth.

• In contrast, a general online service offers services of considerable breadth **and** depth.

A Day in the Life of a CompuServe User
CompuServe Information Manager (CIM)

Initial splash screen

Overview menu

Basic Services

Creating a mail message

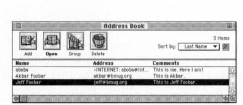

Address book

Sending a message

Mac Communications Forum

MicroSoft Developer Services

Looking for a weather report

Choosing a radar map

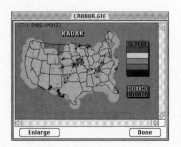

Here's the radar map!

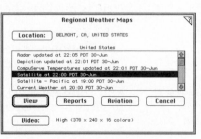

Looking for a satellite photo

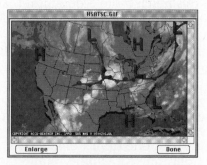

Here's the satellite photo!

A Day in the Life of an America Online User

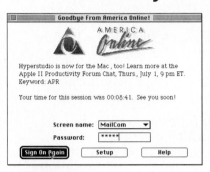

Signing on

Dialing

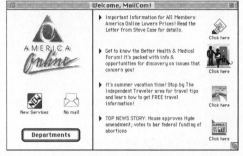

Service overview screen

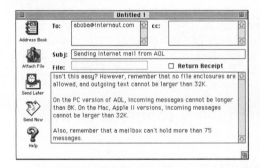

Sending a mail message

Online departments

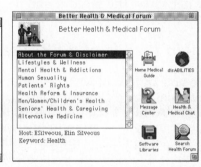

Better Health and Medical Forum

National Public Radio

SeniorNet

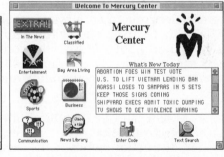

San Jose Mercury Center

Bay Area Living section

Boy do I need a vacation!

Let's find a Sonoma restaurant

Note that I have not mentioned the size or orientation of the service (commercial or noncommercial). The WELL is partially owned by the nonprofit Point Foundation, and is smaller in user base or phone lines than EXEC-PC, a commercially operated system. Yet The WELL is a general online service because of the scope of its services and the depth of treatment in many areas. In contrast, EXEC-PC is a bulletin board, concentrating largely on computing issues for IBM owners.

Like many things in the online world, this definition may not remain valid for long. With more and more bulletin boards connecting to global networks, the breadth and depth of services they offer is increasing.

A day in the life of a BBS user

To give you an idea of what a session on a bulletin board is like, on the next page I have included a session from the MAGIC bulletin board in Canada, a large multi-line system sponsored by Apple Computer. While the screen shots are from the Windows version of the FirstClass client software, a Macintosh version of the software is also available.

In the session, I log on to MAGIC, send an Internet electronic mail message, then search for help, transferring one of the help files to my computer. I then browse the conference areas, which include news wires, technical conferences, and local community areas.

Since CompuServe, America Online, and BBSes such as MAGIC all offer graphical interfaces, Internet electronic mail, conferences, and files, the distinction between the sessions on the commercial services and the BBS session is subtle. While the MAGIC service offers a community area analogous to the Mercury Center section on America Online, it only serves a single community. In contrast, America Online has several such areas for different cities. It is this difference in breadth that distinguishes a BBS from a commercial service.

What are global computer networks?

Computer networks are created by the linking of individual computers. The whole is more than the sum of its parts—a network of bulletin boards, each limited in scope, can together form a whole of enormous power.

There are two major forms of networking technology: one in which commands are executed immediately, and another in which a requested action is queued for later execution. Networks in which actions are carried out immediately include local area networks such as Novell or AppleShare, as well as the global network known as the Internet. Networks in which commands are stored and carried out later are called store and forward networks and include UUCP, BITNET, FidoNet, ILink, WWIVNet, RBBSNet, OneNet and RIME.

What are global computer networks NOT?

Since global networks are so powerful and impressive, it is easy to wax philosophical. Unfortunately, whenever I do this, I have a tendency to trip over my shoelaces and land flat on my face, so let's review some basic facts:

▽ Networks are not your parents

Although computers regularly spawn processes, and the family of networks is continually adding more members, not one computer network has ever given birth to a human being, although they may have contributed to humans doing so.

Since networks are not your parents, please do not:

• Ask them to send money
• Blame them for your looks, personality, or upbringing
• Invite them to your wedding

In return, the network will not:

• Ask who you're dating
• Tell you you've gained weight
• Ask when you're going to get a real job, have grandchildren, or take your vitamins

A Day in the Life of a BBS User – MAGIC

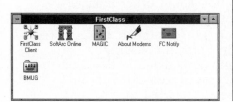

FirstClass Folder   **Logging on**   **Desktop**   **Master Menu**

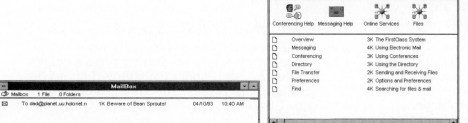

Sending mail via the Internet   **Help area**   **Conference folder**

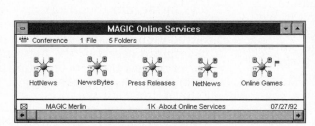

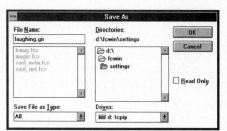

USENET   **MAGIC Online Services**   **Downloading a file**

▽ **Networks are not your doctor, psychiatrist, lawyer, or spiritual leader.**

While accessing global networks may provide certain therapeutic benefits, only a minority of people online have the professional qualifications to provide assistance with a serious problem. If you need professional help, seek it out promptly.

Even if you can find appropriate assistance online, you should consider the risks. Many societies recognize certain relationships as deserving of special protections. Your relationship with your doctor, shrink, lawyer, or spiritual leader may be governed by notions of privileged information that do not apply in public conferences on global networks.

By disclosing personal information about yourself in a public conference, you are putting that information where anyone can read it. Therefore you should not expect it to be kept in confidence.

Since conferences on global computer networks are often archived onto hard disks or pressed onto CD-ROMs, it is possible that your conversations may become part of the permanent record, open to reexamination at any time. The potential for misuse is worth considering.

▽ **Access to global networks is not the same as access to information.**

Access to global networks brings with it no more right to information than access to a car gives you the right to free food at roadside restaurants. The irony of the communications revolution is that as access to data highways becomes more and more common, the outposts along the road are more coming to resemble walled cities than inns with open doors.

With the Internet commercializing at a rapid pace, many useful resources are now commercial information services (such as Dow Jones, Dialog, Lexis, Nexis, and ClariNet), or services partially or completely restricted to members of an academic community (Online Library Catalogs such as CARL, OCLC, or the University of California's Melvyl and Gladis services).

As a result of the Internet Worm incident and an alarming rise in attempted breakins, many corporations are installing "firewalls" against intruders. These security measures are coming to form a complex patchwork which has the potential to make the network harder to use, *at any fee level.*

For example, it is now becoming difficult to find out information about other Internet users using the `finger` command, because many machines no longer support `finger`. The C.A.R.L. library in Colorado recently passworded a periodicals database based on the terms of a site license agreement with a vendor. Since I was interested in obtaining access, I inquired how much I would have to pay to get in. The answer was that C.A.R.L. did not sell access to individuals. Access to a similar database at the University of California is restricted to students, staff, and faculty, with no way for alumni or members of the general community to gain access.

Part of the problem is that many information service vendors and publishing firms have not yet developed a model for selling their services over global networks. The same issues arose with CD-ROM, and as a result it took nearly five years for issues of electronic rights, network licensing, and consumer acceptance to be worked out so that a wide selection of titles could be developed and sold profitably. I expect that a similar period will elapse before a wide variety of information services become available over global networks.

Yet our vision of Information Nirvana must be broader than a future with more high-priced toys in the global network toystore. While organizations such as the Electronic Frontier Foundation are concerned with ensuring widespread access to the network, little attention has been focused on the commodification of information.

As Bruce Sterling notes in Chapter 28: Free as Water, Free as Air, Free as Knowledge, Benjamin Franklin's vision of a public library system is in danger of being brushed aside in the rush toward a Brave New Information World. Ultimately it matters little if we all have universal access to a network in which the individual books are under lock and key.

▽ Networks are not our salvation

Fewer technologies carry with them heavier baggage of hopefulness than does the global networking revolution. I call it baggage because technology alone cannot create an environment in which networks can reach their full potential. For this to happen, we need:

• Extension of fundamental freedoms to the electronic domain. Being able to converse over a global network is of limited value without the right to freedom of speech or protection from government harassment.

• A commitment to public access. The National Public Telecomputing Network (NPTN) project, by encouraging the deployment of free public access bulletin boards (Free-Nets) with terminals available in public libraries, has demonstrated how bulletin boards can be an asset to the community. We need to go further in providing public accessibility.

• Technological diversity. Networks should welcome a variety of software and hardware. Who is to say that an Apple II running FrEdMail (a networking package designed for use in Kindergarten through High School, also known as K-12) isn't a more appropriate educational tool than a Sun workstation on the Internet?

• Common sense, restraint, and discipline. Just because something can be done or said electronically doesn't mean that it should be. And just because something can be distributed globally at the press of a button doesn't mean that it should be accessible to everyone from kindergartners to grandmothers. We will determine how well global networks serve us by how wisely we govern their use.

Lifestyles of the online and infamous

Using a modem can change your life in small or large ways. By not going to the library to search the catalogs and doing it online instead, you may save time and become more productive. If your friends also hung out at the library, you will not be bumping into them, and if you traveled there by bicycle, you will also not be getting the exercise and fresh air.

Although many "experts" have trumpeted the advantages of online services over more primitive media such as TV, excessive use of online services seems to have much the same effect on lifestyle as sitting in front of the boob tube.

In some cases, the excessive use of online services results in the warping of personalities in predictable ways. The pages that follow outline a few of the online "types" you may encounter in conferences or chat areas:

▽ The Ingenue

Ingenues never pay for software and believe that all software and information is available free, if only they could figure out where to look for it. Ingenues believe that everyone in the entire world has an electronic mail address, since all their friends have one. The Ingenue can be spotted asking questions like, "Where can I download a copy of Lotus 1-2-3?" or "Why didn't the Vice President respond to my electronic mail?"

▽ The Anarchist

Anarchists think that all software, hardware, and information should be free, although, unlike Ingenues, they realize that this is not actually the case. The Anarchist is usually an embittered graduate student in the eleventh year of a Ph.D. program and can be found asking for donations of hardware and software "to a good cause" that happens to reside at their home address. The Anarchist also can be spotted accusing anyone trying to sell something for more than 49 cents of "ripping people off." This attitude does not extend to their own labor, for which they expect to extract a premium price.

▽ The Armchair Programmer

Armchair Programmers completed two or three courses in computer science before dropping out of school and declaring themselves an Expert. Found in developer conferences, the Armchair Programmer spends his or her time analyzing software from other programmers and then announcing to the world how braindead it is.

∇ The Expert

The Expert is someone with expertise in some field, which he or she refuses to discuss online. Instead, they use their qualifications in that field to buttress opinions in areas they know nothing about. The Expert can usually be found correcting a mistake with even more erroneous information. Recently, Experts have banded together to bolster their frail egos by creating a newsgroup called alt.newbie. This group consists of quoting messages from beginners and then making fun of them. Of course, no real Expert would stoop to actually answering a question from a beginner. Most writers or pundits are Experts. For further information on the alt conferences (and why they're called that), please consult Chapter 12.

∇ The Adolescent

The adolescent is found logging into bulletin boards using assumed names such as The Avenger. Since they spend most of their time online, they may be unaware that their country is involved in a civil war, or that their parents have been swept away in a flash flood. The Adolescent types messages IN ALL CAPS LIKE THIS BECAUSE THEY HAVE NOT YET FIGURED OUT HOW TO USE THE SHIFT KEY. Luckily for the rest of us, they post few messages since they spend most of their waking hours playing games.

∇ The Cyberpunk

The Cyberpunk specializes in pioneering new ways to annoy bulletin board system operators. If an online service has a security hole, they will find it. Unlike the Adolescent (who excels in school, although he or she has no friends), their behavior cannot be corrected by instruction; a visit by a SWAT team is required. Cyberpunks create newgroups with names like alt.spleen or alt.enya.puke.puke.puke.

∇ The Harried Parent

The Harried Parent is so worn out by a day of taking care of the kids (Adolescents or

Cyberpunks, no doubt) that he or she is near collapse. Since the TV and computer are commandeered by the children during normal waking hours, the Harried Parent is most often found logging on at 3 AM to forums on "How to Have a Thirty-Second Nervous Breakdown," or "The Teenage Years: Psychotic Episode or Passing Phase?"

∇ The Addict

An Addict is someone whose computer equipment is worth more than their car. The Addict owns at least three computers: a Macintosh, a PC, and maybe an Amiga for games, a NeXT for UNIX, or an old Apple II. The Addict typically owns a name brand modem such as one from US Robotics or Telebit, which they studiously trade in for the newest model as soon as it becomes available. Addicts often work with computers, are involved in administering a local or global computer network, and when choosing a home, look first at the size of the basement and the electrical capacity of the house to see if it can hold all their computer paraphernalia.

∇ Stars, Starlets, and Groupies

Now that the computer industry is on its way to becoming as glamorous as Hollywood, it has its own share of Stars, Starlets, and Groupies. A Star or Starlet is someone who once made a contribution to the industry but is now wealthy enough to spend his or her time on quixotic projects or telling other people how it should be done. A Groupie is someone who worships Stars and Starlets.

∇ The Mensch

Mensches are true experts, although you will never discover what a big shot they are except by asking a third party, since they are too modest to blow their own horn. Usually the Mensch has written a major software package, runs his or her own company, or holds a managerial position at a major firm. They are under no obligation to answer questions, but they genuinely like helping people. The Mensch is almost never a writer or pundit.

The Mensch is the lifeblood of whatever conferences they participate in; people will brave dozens of messages from Ingenues, Anarchists, Experts, Armchair Programmers, Adolescents, and Cyberpunks to encounter a posting from a Mensch.

Mensches have a real life outside of the computer industry, which helps them avoid the extremes exhibited by the other types. One of the goals of this guide is to get you further along the road toward Online Menschood.

Exchanging documents

Once you get online you will discover that people are using different types of computers as well different word processing, graphics, spreadsheet, and database programs, each with their own file format.

How can you exchange documents with someone if you don't both have the same type of computer and software? One possibility is to use conversion software to convert from your format to theirs and back. This approach is discussed in Chapter 23: File Conversion. This seems a complicated approach to a problem looking for an easy solution. Wouldn't life would be simpler if there were a universal format that could be read by everybody?

Recently, it seems that every other software company has decided to take a shot at the problem. If things go on this way, pretty soon we'll have as many incompatible "solutions" as we have file formats, and we'll be back to square one! Here are some of your options:

• **ASCII text.** The American Standard Code for Information Interchange (ASCII) is a standard 7-bit format for representing characters. Documents in this format can be pulled into almost any word processing program and further manipulated with only minor conversion problems. However, this format does not allow for fonts, typestyles, graphics or color.

• **PostScript.** PostScript is a page description language created by Adobe that is supported by many software packages and operating systems.

PostScript supports graphics as well as text, and because of its generality, can be used to represent virtually any document. Both Windows and Macintosh OS allow you to print to PostScript. A free PostScript viewer, called GNU Ghostscript, is available for UNIX, Windows (`ftp fatty.law.cornell.edu`) and the Mac (`ftp mac.archive.umich.edu`). As a result, PostScript can be produced by an application on one computer, and then viewed on another machine without needing the original application.

Mac users can print out PostScript files using the LaserWriter Font Utility, which is available via `ftp ftp.apple.com, cd /dts/mac/sys.soft/imaging`. Under UNIX, typing `lpr postscript.ps` ought to print out a PostScript file. If you don't have a PostScript printer, the commercial program Freedom of the Press will allow you to print PostScript files on non-PostScript printers.

Since it is resolution-independent, and capable of reproducing documents of great complexity, including fonts, typestyles, graphics and color, PostScript is among the more flexible forms of electronic documentation. Unfortunately, PostScript files are often huge. For example, the Quickstart section of this book generated more than 40 megabytes of PostScript! Also, there are minor incompatibilities among the PostScript files generated by different programs and computers, which can result in major headaches.

• **Adobe Acrobat.** Acrobat is Adobe's proprietary document exchange format, which is supported on the Mac, DOS, and UNIX. Acrobat documents are resolution independent, and are more compact than Common Ground or PostScript files, due to use of compression. To create files using the Windows or Macintosh printer driver, Acrobat Exchange ($195) is required. To create .PDF files involving embedded Encapsulated PostScript (EPSF), you will need the Acrobat Distiller ($695). To read Acrobat files, you will need to purchase the Acrobat Reader, which is available for $35-$50 per user, depending on volume. No freely distributable reader is available, although the Reader is now being bundled with packages such as The Guide. This was a big mistake on Adobe's part, since few people are interested in creating electronic documents without the assurance that many people will be able to read the files they produce. Hopefully Adobe will see the light and bundle Acrobat Reader with their own software or packages from other vendors. Another problem with the Reader is that it only supports single word searches, although it does support hypertext links and bookmarks.

Adobe Systems, Inc.; 1585 Charleston Rd., P.O. Box 7900, Mountain View, CA 94039; (800)833-6687, (415)961-4400, fax: (415)961-3769.

• **Farallon Replica.** Replica is a document exchange format from Farallon Computing that has been released for Windows, and is due to be ported to the Macintosh. While Replica documents are resolution independent, only TrueType fonts are supported, not Adobe Type 1. However, Replica does have one major advantage: the document viewer can be embedded within the document, so that users wanting to read it don't need to purchase any software. This makes it my pick for exchanging documents under Windows.

Farallon Computing; 2470 Mariner Square Loop, Alameda, CA 94501; (510)814-5100 (main office), (510)814-5000 (customer service), fax: (510)814-5020

• **Common Ground.** Common Ground is a document exchange program from No Hands Software that is currently available for the Mac ($189.95) and due to be ported to Windows. Common Ground can handle fonts, typestyles, graphics, and color, but it currently only supports resolutions up to 300 DPI. The package includes a reader application that can print, search, and annotate. However, this reader may not be freely distributed, and the semi-freely distributable reader (only 100 copies per document allowed) cannot print or search. Also, complex Common Ground documents can be as much as five times larger that Acrobat files, which is a big disadvantage for distribution of large documents.

No Hands Software; 1301 Shoreway Rd., Suite 220, Belmont, CA 94002; (800)598-3821, (415)802-5800, fax: (415)593-6868

• **TeX documents or DVI files.** TeX is a typesetting system developed by Prof. Donald Knuth, that has been implemented on a variety of computers, sometimes called "platforms". DVI files are the device independent output of the typesetting process. While TeX and DVI viewers are common on UNIX platforms, the DVI format was not really created for electronic document exchange, and I am not aware of viewers that support searching.

For more information

Below and at the end of every chapter you'll find conference listings. For an explanation of how to access FidoNet, see Chapter 18: Introduction to FidoNet. For information on USENET, please consult Chapter 12: USENET.

FidoNet conferences

CDROM	General CD-ROM forum

USENET conferences

alt.cd-rom	General CD-ROM forum
alt.cyberspace	The future of Cyberspace
alt.dcom.telecom	General telephony

CHAPTER 2:
PROVISIONS FOR THE ONLINE
EXPEDITION

Hardware, software, wetware

To get online you will need a computer, an account with an online service or BBS, telecommunications software, and a modem.

First came computer

Any Macintosh can drive the fastest modems available today. Any PC compatible faster than the original PC XT should also be fine, although you may need to replace the serial port chip, as we'll discuss. While all the considerations in buying a computer are too complicated to get into here, help is available from books and user groups. The Edwin Rusch guides are excellent sources of information on PC compatible machines. BMUG, the largest Macintosh User Group, has recently published a booklet entitled *Which Macintosh Should I Buy?* that covers the important issues for Mac owners-to-be.

Then come online services

Although it is difficult to know all the uses you will find for telecommunications before you get started, chances are that you have a major motivating force for getting online. Perhaps you need to access your university's Online Public Access Catalog (OPAC). Maybe there is an online service or bulletin board oriented toward your profession or hobby. Maybe you'd like to be able to correspond with your children or parents. Or maybe you want to get online just to see what's out there.

Even if you don't have a clear idea of what you're looking for, the chances are that somewhere in the online universe there is a service that will meet your needs.

To wit:

• If you are looking for business information, you will probably want to consult a business-oriented online service such as Dow Jones News Retrieval. Consult Chapter 11: Online Libraries for some brief information on Dow Jones commands.

• If you are looking for information relating to science and engineering, then the Internet is probably where you should focus your efforts. Consult Chapters 7–15 for more information on the Internet.

• If you are an educator, then you may also be interested in the Internet, as well as store and forward networks such as FrEdMail, or K12Net. For information on these networks, consult Chapter 26: A Guide to K12Net, and Chapter 38: How FrEdMail Came To Be.

• If you are looking to download publicly distributable software, or if you are working for help with a computer or software package, then bulletin boards are probably a good place to start. Consult Chapter 5: Using Bulletin Boards for more information on bulletin boards.

• If you are looking for access to specialized professional or commercial databases, such as TrademarkScan, then a commercial online service such as CompuServe, Lexis, Medline, or Westlaw will probably be your cup of tea.

For more information on commercial online services, please consult Appendix B: Choice Products.

Then came software

Many people purchase a modem before they get software for it. This is a mistake because the modem they choose may not be compatible with their software. Since software vendors cannot afford to purchase every modem on the market, they do testing either with modems they own or with modems that vendors have donated or loaned to them. Surprisingly, few modem makers make the effort to ensure that their products will be widely supported by loaning out lots of test modems. Take my advice—before purchasing a modem, check with software vendors to see if your intended choice is supported.

Many of the popular programs fall into the following categories:

▽ General-purpose software

This software lets you connect to a variety of bulletin boards or online services. For DOS, packages include Telix, QMODEM Pro, CrossTalk, Procomm Plus, Teleguard, Boyan, QuickLink and Commo; for Windows, DynaComm or Procomm Plus for Windows; for the Macintosh choices include ZTerm, Microphone II, MacIntercomm, White Knight, VersaTerm, or SmartCom II. Use of the BITCOM (PC), or QuickLink II (Mac) software that is often shipped with modems is not recommended. More information on software packages is available in the Software Q&A section later in this chapter and in Appendix B: Choice Products.

▽ Software to connect to a specific online service

Graphical interface software is now available for services such as America Online, CompuServe, or Prodigy, and for bulletin boards such as RoboBoard (PC), FirstClass, NovaLink Pro, hi-BBS, and TeleFinder (Mac). Note that while America Online and Prodigy require use of custom software, CompuServe and graphical BBSes also support nongraphical access. Custom software generally won't work when calling another service, so people usually will also want a general-purpose package in addition to any custom packages. For more information on graphical bulletin board

software, consult Chapter 5: Using Bulletin Boards.

▽ Remote-control software

This software lets you control a Mac or PC remotely. When you are using this software you will see the other machine's screen. Provided that you've entered the correct passwords, you will be able operate the remote computer as if it were your own machine. Farallon's Timbuktu Remote (for the Mac), Co-Session (for the PC), and Carbon Copy (for the PC and Mac) are examples of this kind of software. For more information on remote control software, consult Chapter 22: File Transfer Between Macs, PCs, and UNIX.

▽ Remote local area network software

This software lets you connect your machine to a remote local area network. Apple Remote Access software (ARA) is an example of this. Using the ARA software you can access file servers or printers just as if they were connected to your local machine. For more information on ARA, consult Chapter 22: File Transfer Between Macs, PCs, and UNIX.

▽ Special global network software

While global computer networks can be accessed using general-purpose software, if you would like to connect your computer directly to the network, you will need special software. This special software is covered in Chapter 15: TCP/IP, Chapter 16: UNIX to UNIX Copy, Chapter 18: Introduction to FidoNet, and Chapter 19: PCBoard Networks.

Then came modems

If you do not currently own a modem, you will need to buy one in order to communicate with other computers over the phone lines. The modem encodes digital information into an analog signal using a variety of techniques that are too complicated to get into here.

Commercial versus hobbyist modems

There are two primary markets for modems – the commercial market and the hobbyist market. Modems are designed differently for each market, and so we give separate recommendations for commercial and hobbyist modems in Appendix B: Choice Products.

Commercial-quality modems are designed to provide years of trouble-free service operating 24 hours a day, 7 days a week. Hobbyist modems are designed for casual use but will generally provide years of service to those using them only a few hours a day. Before purchasing a modem, you should decide whether you are looking for a commercial or hobbyist modem.

Modem speeds

How fast a modem do you need? This depends on what services you use and how frequently you use them.

If you are primarily interested in obtaining software and will be calling long distance or using a commercial service to do this, a high-speed modem is probably a good idea. This is because you will be spending a lot of time online and will be billed at a high rate ($6/hour for a night long-distance call, even with a discount plan).

Be aware that your modem can only transfer data as fast as the modem on the other end will support. Today, few of the commercial online services support standards faster than V.32, which can transfer data at 9600 bits per second (bps), commonly also referred to as 9600 "baud". Universities often do not support access at speeds faster than 2400 bps.

If you are interested in electronic mail, computer-mediated conferencing, or news wires, you may or may not need a high-speed modem, depending on your usage level. As your facility increases, you may go from being an occasional user to sending and receiving files. At this point, a switch to a high-speed modem becomes advisable.

If your primary interest is in accessing online libraries, or in chatting interactively, you probably not need a high-speed modem, since most of your sessions will be interactive, and your time online will be limited by your typing speed rather than by the speed of your modem.

The figure below shows how the time to download a 1 Mb file will vary with the speed of your modem. Compared with a 14.4Kbps modem, 300 bits per second is slow indeed!

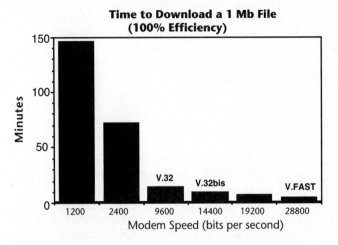

Time to Download a 1 Mb File (100% Efficiency)

Modem standards

Modem standards are approved by a United Nations organization, called the Comité Consultatif Internationale de Télégraphie et Téléphonie (CCITT). CCITT modem standards are prefixed with "V." and a number, as well as potentially the suffix *"bis"* or *"ter." bis* is French for "second item in a series." Hence, the V.42*bis* standard is an extension of V.42. *ter* is French for "third item in a series." The CCITT standards are pronounced "Vee Dot 42" (V.42).

Currently, the fastest international standard is V.32*bis*. These modems operate at speeds of 14,400 bps, often include fax capability, and cost around $500 for the commercial version, or $200 for the hobbyist version. The CCITT has not yet approved a faster standard, called V.FAST, that will reportedly operate at speeds up to 28,000 bps.

If you are an occasional user, then you can get by with a 2400 bps V.42*bis*/fax modem instead, which will set you back $50.

Whatever you decide to buy, avoid modems not compatible with the AT command set originated by Hayes; most telecommunications software will assume AT command set compatibility, so you are just headed for trouble otherwise.

Modem cables

Modem cables connect a computer's serial port to an external modem. If you have an internal modem, you will not need a modem cable. Hardware handshake cables are special cables that improve the performance of external modems operating at 9600 bps or faster, fax modems, or 2400 bps modems implementing compression. Hardware handshaking is explained in the next chapter; all you need to understand now is that if you're buying one of these modems, you need to purchase a hardware handshake cable to go along with it.

It is important to PC users to obtain a "fully connected" serial cable, i.e. one that has all 25 (or 9, as the case may be) pins connected all the way through the cable. For the PC, most modem cables are now constructed this way, although some may not be. Older cables often do not have all lines implemented, and so may not support hardware handshaking.

On the Macintosh, there are three types of modem cables. One is a cable for low-speed modems. Another is a hardware handshake cable for users of high-speed modems. The third is a cable for system operators (called sysops) of a BBS; this cable is not readily available (unlike the other two) but can be purchased from the cable vendors listed at the end of this chapter.

Used modems

If you are interested in a commercial-quality modem at a hobbyist price, you may wish to consider a used modem. Sysops are constantly buying the latest and fastest modems and selling their old modems. This creates an opportunity for you to get a great modem at a reasonable price. Sysops usually sell for 80 percent of the sysop, price which in turn is as little as 60 percent of the suggested retail price. In order to find sysops willing to unload their modems, ask your local bulletin board operator to place an ad for you in the local sysop conference.

Naturally, if you buy a used modem, you will not get a warranty. If this concerns you, you may wish to purchase a refurbished modem direct from the manufacturer. Hayes and US Robotics will sell refurbished modems to users at very reasonable prices (you don't need to be a sysop to purchase them), though there can be a waiting list.

Taking your modem on the road

If you've tried to use a modem in a hotel room, you know that it can be a trying experience. Hilton is the only hotel chain I know of that guarantees guests the ability to use a modem in their room. Many rooms don't have modular plugs, so you've got to disassemble the handset and tap into the wires.

Even if they do have modular plugs, be careful! Some hotel chains put 220V on one of the twisted-pair phone lines to control heating, ventilation, and air conditioning (HVAC). This will fry your modem, and possibly your CPU, if it doesn't zap you first. Bring along a voltmeter, just in case.

Computer Products Plus offers a complete line of equipment for plugging into hotel phone systems. They've even got something that will connect to digital phone systems.

Modem wake-up cables

Once you've hooked into the hotel phone line, you may want to access your office or home computer. Must you leave your computer and modem on all the time you're away, which will prevent voice (non-computer) calls from getting through on that line?

A modem wake-up cable turns your computer on over the telephone, usually by having a modem (which must be left on) detect another modem calling in by turning on the Carrier Detect signal. With a modem wake-up cable, you can leave your machine off and turn it on remotely when needed. If you use a voice/data switch with the wake-up cable, you'll be able to take voice calls on the same line. Be aware that wake-up equipment designed for the Macintosh will usually not work on a PC, and equipment designed for a Macintosh II will not work on a Macintosh Plus.

Making the Cable Connection

When you are purchasing your modem, it is best to get a modem cable at the same time so that a single vendor will be responsible for getting your modem to work. Do not accept a "home-brew" cable from a vendor. Nowadays, professionally manufactured modem cables are readily available at moderate prices.

Despite the widespread use of modems, finding the correct cable for your modem can be a trying experience. If you own a Macintosh 128K or 512K, the old-style Macintosh modem cables are now hard to find; if you own a high-speed modem and want to use it with hardware handshaking, you may also need a special cable. Finally, sysops of Macintosh BBSes, such as those running Hermes, will also need such a cable.

If finding the right cable is difficult and you know how to use a soldering iron, you can make your own. To do this, you'll need a reliable soldering iron; a vise; some heat-shrink tubing; a heat gun; a screwdriver; a wire splicer; and the appropriate DB-25, DB-15, or DIN-8 connectors. You can get all of these from JDR MicroDevices (which does mail order) or Fry's Electronics (which does not). For more information, turn to Appendix D: Cable Compendium.

Note: If you don't know how to use a soldering iron, I don't recommend this. You're likely to produce an unreliable cable, or even possibly injure yourself. Make cables at your own risk!

Cable Vendors

Here are some places that sell modem cables:

Celestin Company has the lowest prices I've seen for a Macintosh hardware handshake cable ($14). They can also make other cables on request. If you can find the diagram for the cable you need, you can fax it to Rogers Specialist, who will make it for you. Cables & Chips offers some exotic cables, such as the hardware handshake cable for the Hermes BBS software, ready-made. If your cable is more standard, Micro Computer Cable is the place to call.

Celestin Company, 1152 Hastings Ave., Port Townsend, WA 98368, (206)385-3767, fax: (206)385-3586, Orders: (800)835-5514, email: celestin@netcom.com (has hardware handshake cables, $14)

MacConnection (Orders: (800)800-3333), has Mac hardware handshake cables. PCConnection (Orders: (800)800-0005) has fully connected modem cables for the PC.

Micro Computer Cable, 16018 Huron River Dr., Romulus, MI 48174; (313)941-6500, fax: (313)941-6574 (no hardware handshake cables)

Cables & Chips, 121 Fulton Street, New York, NY 10038; (800)843-4117 or (212)619-3132 (in NY),fax: (212)619-3982 (has the Hermes hardware handshake cable, no general purpose Mac hardware handshake cable)

Rogers Specialist, 27712 Pinehills Ave., Santa Clarita, CA 91351; (800)366-0579, or (805)251-3085, fax: (805)251-2520 (can make exotic cables if you fax them the diagrams; don't have hardware handshaking cables in stock)

For Macintosh II machines, which can be turned on via the keyboard (ADB) port, you can use the Farallon wake-up cable; for SEs or SE/30s, which are turned on by a switch at the back of the machine, you'll need the PowerKey. As an added bonus, the Farallon cable also does hardware handshaking. It makes the most sense to use the wake-up cable along with remote-control software such as Timbuktu Remote or Carbon Copy Mac because these packages provide password security and allow you to completely control the remote computer.

That still leaves the problem of the dedicated phone line. When your modem is set in auto-answer mode, it will pick up the phone and put a tone on the line, thus preventing voice callers from getting through to your answering machine. What you need is a device that can switch (ideally) between data, fax, and voice, such as an Autoswitch TF 300 Facsimile Switcher. For the PC, Deltronix Enterprises makes a power switch that can be turned on via a touch-tone phone. The switch does not allow the phone line to be used for any other purpose, making it less practical than a wake-up cable.

Software Q&A

What is the difference between freeware and shareware?

Freeware is software which can be used without payment of a fee. Shareware is software which you can use free of charge only during a trial period. If you continue to use the program after this, payment of the shareware fee is required.

What kind of software do you recommend for beginners?

For the Macintosh, I recommend that you purchase either the shareware program ZTerm or a commercial program such as MacIntercomm, MicroPhone II, White Knight, or SmartCom II. The reason I say this is that programs such as ZTerm, MacIntercomm, MicroPhone II, White Knight, or SmartCom II support ZMODEM, as well as VT100 and PC-ANSI emulation, which means that your

downloads will go faster and you won't see weird characters on your screen. The result is a much more pleasant telecommunications experience. If you start with one of these programs from the beginning, you will be more likely to become a fanatic and less likely to give up in disgust.

What free telecommunications software should I get?

I think that you should use a free telecommunications program only until you determine that you are going to be a regular telecommunicator. If you are accessing a UNIX machine on a PC, the best free terminal emulator is PC-Kermit. It offers flawless VT100 emulation, as well as the KERMIT transfer protocol. The latest version also supports TCP/IP.

FreeTerm is the best free terminal program for the Macintosh and so I suppose I must recommend it to you. I am not enthusiastic about it because ZTerm is so much better and costs only $30. Come on, you can afford it! For those looking for the KERMIT protocol, MacKermit is the best solution.

Which shareware telecommuncations software should I get?

Under DOS, if you are looking for something small and fast, I recommend Boyan or Commo. If you need more features, then Telix is the choice. It supports XMODEM, YMODEM, and ZMODEM as well as scripting, and it costs just $39, $12 for a printed manual. For Windows, I recommend Microlink.

On the Macintosh, I recommend ZTerm without reservation. It has the right mix of features (VT100 and PC-ANSI emulation, dialing from a menu, XMODEM, YMODEM, ZMODEM, scripting, and automatic setting of creator and type for .ARC, .GIF, .Z, .ZIP, and .ZOO files) to keep beginners from getting stuck. It's a winner.

What commercial telecommunications software should I purchase?

Under DOS I recommend QMODEM Pro. Although it can seem a bit cumbersome at first, QMODEM Pro packs an enormous number of features into a reasonably priced package. This includes a wide variety of terminal emulations and file-transfer protocols, as well as a QWK-compatible message reader and gateway and fax support. The commercial version of Telix may also be worth a look, expecially since it supports Remote Imaging Protocol (RIP), the emerging bulletin board graphics standard. If you are interested in NAPLPS graphics, you might want to take a look at Troika, which was developed in Russia and is available from Old Colorado Systems. Under Windows, Procomm Plus for Windows is your best choice.

On the Macintosh, Smartcom II is fast and relatively inexpensive ($45 in a sidegrade offer which applies to all competitors), so this is a good choice for general-purpose use. Users looking to connect to UNIX machines in a broad range of situations (terminal emulation, SLIP, Ethernet, VT100, Tektronix emulation) should consider VersaTerm, although since it doesn't offer ZMODEM, it is not the best program for general use. If you are specifically looking to connect to the Internet over a modem, you should consider MacPPP (available via `ftp merit.edu, cd /pub/ppp`), or MacSLIP from Hyde Park Software. Consult Appendix B: Choice Products for listings.

If you require a broad range of transfer protocols (KERMIT, XMODEM, YMODEM, ZMODEM), as well as scripting and an iconic interface, then Microphone II may appeal to you.

If you are an Internet junkie, MacLayers v2.0 allows you to open multiple terminal sessions so that you can send mail, read news, and download a file all at the same time.

What software should I purchase to transfer files between two PCs?

LapLink from Traveling Software is my favorite program for transferring files between PCs over a modem or serial cable.

What software should I purchase to transfer files between two Macs?

If you know absolutely nothing about communications and only want to transfer files with a few associates, you should probably purchase either Timbuktu Remote from Farallon Computing or Apple Remote Access (ARA) from Apple. These two programs work via the Macintosh interface and will therefore get the job done with minimum hassle. However, it should be noted that both of these choices will be less efficient (that is, will take more time for the transfer) than will two Macs doing a ZMODEM transfer using say, ZTerm. For more information on this and other software, please consult Appendix B: Choice Products.

Modem Q&A

What V.32*bis*/V.42*bis*/fax internal modem do you recommend for the PC?

The Intel SatisFaxtion 400E is a V.32*bis*/V.42*bis*/fax modem with a processor and 500K of memory, so it can run in the background while you work on something else. It includes a fax/voice switch, allowing it to coexist on the same phone line as an answering machine (provided the answering machine can be set to pick up **after** the Satisfaxtion board). OCR software is available for the SatisFaxtion board, allowing you to convert faxes to text.

What is a good modem to use with a portable Mac?

The PowerPort Gold modem from Global Village Communications is a portable modem that connects to your ADB port and can send and receive faxes at 9600 bps as well. It operates at 14,400 bps and also does V.42*bis* error correction and compression. Another nice feature is that this modem can wake up your Mac via an incoming phone call.

What V.32*bis*/V.42*bis* external modem do you recommend?

For business or bulletin board use, I recommend the US Robotics Courier V.32*bis*/V.42*bis* or Hayes Ultra modem. These are also the best modems for users wishing to connect to the Internet using the SLIP or PPP protocols, since they perform well in this service. If you are looking to connect with the UUCP-g protocol, a Telebit modem implementing PEP would be more appropriate.

For hobbyist use, I recommend the US Robotics Sportster V.32*bis*/V.42*bis*/fax modem. This modem uses the same Digital Signal Processor technology as USR uses in their high end HST line, but does not support the proprietary HST protocol and costs far less (around $200). Mac owners should purchase the Mac 'N Fax package. The Hayes Optima or Intel 14.4EX are also worth a mention.

A marketing droid claims their company's modem runs at 57,600 bps. How can this be?

Simple. It can't! Many of the laudatory statements made by modem manufacturers about compression are misleading. They say things like "our 2400 bits per second (bps) modem actually runs at 9600 bps with compression." A 2400 bps modem can only communicate at 2400 bps; how could it be faster? What they are trying to say is that because of compression, each bit carries more information.

However, this depends on what you are trying to send. In BBS use, users are most often transferring files that have already been compressed. If you're using MNP-5, transfers could actually be slower because MNP-5 makes precompressed files slightly larger when attempting to compress them and takes longer to transmit them. At least with V.42*bis*, your modem will not be slower in transferring a compressed file, and the V.42 error correction standard on which it depends does provide for improvement in transmission speed by lowering the number of bits needed to transmit a byte from 10 (8 bits plus 1 stop and 1 start bit) to 8.

Even when using V.32*bis* modulation you will only get throughput of 14,400 bps, excluding any compression effect. That's a long way from the 57,600 bps some manufacturers claim. Even with V.42*bis* compression running, it is unlikely that you will need to set your modem to a speed higher than 38,400 bps, and setting your modem to 19,200 bps instead of 38,400 bps may actually make your file transfers go *faster*! This is because at 38,400 bps your software may fill the serial port buffer more quickly than the hardware can empty it, resulting in data loss and retransmissions. In addition, some bulletin boards cannot reliably handle transfers at faster than 19,200 bps, and so you will encounter more errors at 38,400 bps than you will at 19,200 bps.

If you are using a PC, you can improve your chances of reliable communications at speeds above 9600 bps by replacing the Intel 8250 chips on your serial port with 16550AF chips. The 16550AF is pin compatible with the 8250, so a simple swap will do the trick, if the 8250 is in a socket. 16550AF chips are made by National Semiconductor, as well as Texas Instruments, VLSI, and Western Digital. It should be noted that the Western Digital chips are not 100% compatible with the original National Semiconductor design.

For more information

USENET groups

Macintosh archive announcements:
comp.sys.mac.digest

Mailing lists

MS-DOS archive announcements:
`mail listserv@tacom-emhi.army.mil`,
body: `subscribe msdos-ann`

Frequently asked questions (FAQ) lists

comp.sys.mac.comm FAQ:
`ftp rtfm.mit.edu, cd`
`/pub/usenet/comp.sys.mac.comm`

comp.binaries.ibm.pc FAQ:
`ftp oak.oakland.edu, mget`
`/pub/msdos/info/tsfaq*.zip`

FAQ on SIMTEL20 and Garbo archives:
`ftp rtfm.mit.edu, cd`
`/pub/usenet/comp.archives.msdos.d`

Association of Shareware Professionals catalog:
`ftp oak.oakland.edu, mget`
`/pub/msdos/info/asp*.zip`

Chapter 3:
The Tower of Telecombabble

Learning the language of the online aliens

A beginner once wrote to me in a message:

Sometimes I feel like when I logged on, I took a wrong turn and ended up on another planet, where everyone is talking in a language I don't understand.

Why do beginners find telecommunications difficult? Part of the problem lies with the specialized language of computer communications, called telecombabble. In this chapter, we'll help you to decipher the lingo of the aliens from the Online Planet.

Understanding the telephone system

Most of us are used to using ordinary telephones and "voice grade" lines to converse with people down the street or across the globe. Luckily, we do not have to understand how the phone system works in order to place a voice call. Things are somewhat more complicated with data transmission, and so it is useful to give a brief overview of how the system works.

On the way to its destination, your call is routed through the phone company Central Office (or CO for short). The portion of the link from your home to the CO is referred to as the "local loop" and usually consists of copper wire carrying analog voice signals. Analog signals are signals that can take on any values between the maximum and minimum voltages. In contrast, digital signals must either be 1 or 0.

From the Central Office, your call is routed by the switching equipment in the Central Office (and other intermediate locations) to the Central Office in the destination area. The connections between Central Offices are usually digital. From the destination Central

Office, the call travels over another local loop to the destination phone.

In a conventional phone system, once the switching system sets up the route, all traffic for the conversation will travel the same route. This is called "circuit switching."

Modems and the phone system

We have mentioned that connections between Central Offices are usually digital, while the local loop is usually analog. Since computers are digital, this creates a problem: To transmit data over ordinary phone lines, the computer must first translate its data from digital to analog, to be compatible with the local loop.

Carriers and modulation

If you were successful in getting your modem to dial, you probably heard a tone when the bulletin board system picked up the phone. Modems transmit information by varying or "modulating" a basic tone known as the Carrier Frequency. This is the sound you heard when the remote modem picked up the phone. Modulation is what allows modems to send digital data over an analog channel.

Modems use different modulation schemes, depending on their speed, with higher-speed modems using progressively more complex modulation methods in order to squeeze the last bit out of the telephone connection.

Modem speeds are measured in *bits per second* (bps) or *characters per second* (cps). A bit is the smallest unit of computer information, which can be 0 or 1. A byte (also sometimes called an octet) is 8 bits of information. Since the entire alphabet plus other symbols can be represented within a byte, this is also often called a character of information. When transmitted over a modem, often each byte is framed by at least 2 additional bits, requiring 10 bits to transmit a character. These are called the stop and start bits. One kilobyte (Kb or K) is slang for 1024 bytes. Similarly, a megabyte (Mb) is slang for 1,048,576 bytes.

Facsimile

Facsimile machines also use modulation techniques to transmit information, bringing the analog/digital conversion problem to new levels of absurdity. With fax, you take an analog image (a document), convert it to digital (by inserting it into the fax machine), then convert it to analog for transmission over the phone system, where it is promptly converted back to digital (to be received on the other end), and printed out in analog form for viewing. Total: four conversions, and a loss of quality everyone is familiar with.

High-speed connections – ISDN and leased lines

Although most telecommunicators will not have a need for connections at a higher speed than can be achieved using modems over normal phone lines, many businesses and nonprofits do require higher speed connections.

ISDN and leased lines are particularly useful for providing high-speed links to computer networks. Such links are becoming more and more common as global computer networks expand.

One of the differences between using leased lines as links to computer networks and using ordinary phone lines to connect individual computers is the way you add capacity.

When linking two computers over an ordinary phone line without the use of networking protocols, there is no way to allow a third computer to participate in the conversation without purchasing another phone line. This is so because (among other things) networking protocols specify the source and destination for messages transmitted over the connection. Without such information there would be no

way to know who sent the message and who the recipient was.

By specifying the source and destination, networking protocols allow for multiple simultaneous conversations over a single physical connection. This is called "multiplexing."

Since traffic from multiple machines and users can be multiplexed on a single line, it is possible to add capacity by upgrading line speed. For example, a leased line could be upgraded from 14,400 bps to 1.5 Mbps as network traffic levels increase. Leased line bandwidth is primarily limited by the CODEC at the phone company's central office, not by the use of copper wire.

Communications standards

Parallel communications refers to an arrangement whereby many paths (usually eight) are used. Since the multiple paths used by parallel communications cannot be easily handled by a single phone line, serial communication has become the standard for telecommunications.

RS-232

The RS-232 standard is the method by which modems and computers communicate with each other. The standard provides for communication between Data Terminal Equipment (DTE, the computer) and Data Communications Equipment (DCE, the modem). The standard can also be used for communications among computers, as well as between computers and other peripherals such as printers.

While the RS-232 standard defines the use of 25 signals, only a fraction of these are used in practice, and those that are supported may differ between computer and cable vendors. This is part of the reason that you must take care to ensure that the cable you purchase to connect your modem to your computer is the correct one.

High-Speed Connections – ISDN

Why do we need modems to perform digital-to-analog conversions, since once the signal gets to the Central Office, it is often just converted back to digital for transmission between Central Offices? Why not just convert the local loop to digital? Then it would be possible to communicate between computers without any conversions. This is the reasoning behind the Integrated Services Digital Network (ISDN). ISDN replaces analog local loop connections with digital ones, allowing for all digital communications between computers.

To use ISDN, your computer will require an ISDN interface card, instead of a modem. These include a Hayes ISDN card (for the PC), and the Planet ISDN card (for Macintosh). Basic Rate Interface (BRI) ISDN provides two 64 Kbps channels (called "B" channels) that can in some cases be combined to yield 128 Kbps transfer rates, as well as one 16 Kbps channel (called a "D" channel). Be aware that depending on your machine's hardware and chosen card, you may not be able to utilize a 64 Kbps single channel at full speed, let alone two channels at 128 Kbps. For example, on the PC you will need a synchronous card to be able to utilize the Hayes ISDN adapter (which is available at a sysop price of $450) at its full 64 Kbps speed; if you use an asynchronous port, you will be limited to 38.4 Kbps.

ISDN supports both conventional *circuit switching*, as well as *packet switching*. With circuit switching, the same path through the switching network, called a virtual circuit, is used throughout the conversation; with packet switching, individual parcels of information, called packets, may traverse different routes. Packet switching makes more efficient use of system capacity than circuit switching, although the timing of packet arrivals is usually less predictable with packet switching than it is with circuit switching.

With the recent adoption of nationwide ISDN standards (known as National ISDN 1, proposed by Bellcore), ISDN is on the verge of becoming available on long-distance connections. Unfortunately, introduction in some localities has been delayed until late 1996 or later. Where ISDN is offered, it is often a non-tariffed service, allowing the phone company to charge whatever they want for it and to refuse to provide the service (even if they are technically able to provide it) at their option. Even tariffed rates, if they include a per-minute charge, are frequently high enough to scare away the hobbyist, and force businesses to purchase a leased line instead.

ISDN is sometimes jokingly referred to as "I Still Don't Need it," referring to the slow pace of introduction (it was first proposed in 1979). Some vendors (such as Apple, which quietly dropped its ISDN card this year) have given up waiting, but others such as Hayes are more enthusiastic.

However, there is good reason to believe that accelerated acceptance of ISDN would be a boon to global computer networks, bulletin board operators, and perhaps to national productivity in general. For this reason organizations such as the Electronic Frontier Foundation (EFF) have advocated an expanded role for ISDN in a future National Information Infrastructure.

High-Speed Connections – Leased lines

While the average user will only rarely be involved in purchasing a leased line, these lines are frequently used by businesses, government, and educational institutions looking for higher data rates, lower costs, or more reliable connections than can be gotten using ordinary phone lines.

A leased line is a dedicated connection between two locations. Since these connections are semipermanent, there is no need to have them go through the switching system. Leased lines are billed at a fixed fee, which makes them an economical choice for connections between fixed locations that are in use more than a few hours a day.

Even though a leased line is a connection between two locations, connecting via leased line to a global computer network can provide high-speed access to thousands of other sites around the world. This is made possible by the use of packet-switching technology, which divides data streams into portions called "packets," and then routes them between the source and destination within a web of connections. Popular packet-switching technologies include X.25 and Transmission Control Protocol/Internet Protocol (TCP/IP).

The cost of a leased line depends on the distance between the two locations and the speed of the connection. A leased line between two locations using the same Central Office will be much less expensive than a connection stretching across the country. If the cost of a leased line represents a substantial part of the costs of operation for your business, it is recommended that you locate yourself near a Central Office.

Leased lines offer advantages other than just cost savings. They are available at higher speeds than conventional phone connections, which will reach a maximum speed of 28.8 Kbps with the V.FAST standard. Leased lines are available at speeds of 9600, 19,200, 56 Kbps, T1 (1.544 Mbps), and T3 (45 Mbps) speeds. Leased lines can also improve transmission speeds and lower error rates by decreasing noise. As voice signals are sent over phone lines, many factors influence signal quality. These factors produce random bursts of energy (known as burst noise) that interfere with the signal. Much of this noise is introduced by the phone system switching equipment. *Line conditioning* decreases noise by installing filtering devices. Two locations using the same Central Office can bypass the local switching equipment, reducing noise. If the two locations are also on the same telephone exchange, there may be no need to go through transformers, and so the two lines may be directly tied together to create an all-digital connection called a "metallic circuit" or "copper pair." Such links do not need modems, although a *line driver* is required to boost the signal and allow for communication at 19,200 bps at up to 1.2 miles.

A DSU/CSU (which stands for Data Service Unit/Customer Service Unit) is used for leased lines at speeds of 56 Kbps or faster. The DSU/CSU, which runs around $500 at 56 Kbps speeds, and $1,500 for T1, can be driven synchronously using a standard Mac serial port or a PC synch card, which typically uses the same Zilog 8530 SCC chip found on the Mac. A custom cable connects the RS-422 output of the SCC to the DSU/CSU V.35 input jack. The other side of the DSU/CSU connects to the leased line.

The terms "half duplex" and "full duplex" refer to something different in the leased-line context. A half-duplex leased line involves two phone wires, while a full-duplex line (which can run at twice the speed of a half-duplex connection) involves four wires. The important thing to understand is that both half- and full-duplex leased lines can support full-duplex communications. Since they are only marginally more expensive than half-duplex leased lines, full-duplex lines are preferred.

Full versus half duplex

Since phone lines only have a single pair of wires, a modem must be able to both transmit and receive using only a single path. There are two ways to accomplish this. One way involves switching off between sending and receiving so that you are never doing both at once. This is called half-duplex communications. The other way is to send and receive at the same time. This is called full duplex. Full-duplex communication is more complex because you've got to prevent the sending and receiving signals from interfering with each other.

Echoing

In order to provide feedback to the users, when two computers are connected via a full-duplex connection and the user types a character, this character will normally be sent back by the receiving computer and displayed on screen or "echoed." When computers converse over a half-duplex connection, it is not possible to echo the received character, since the transmission only goes one way. Therefore, the sending computer will often echo the character on its own screen. If you connect to a full-duplex computer with your communications program set in half-duplex mode, every character on your screen may show up twice.

Communications settings

If you're a communications beginner, you may have been puzzled by communications settings such as "7-E-1" or "ANSI." This section is designed to explain what these settings mean.

Synchronous versus asynchronous communications

There are two major types of serial communications, synchronous and asynchronous. Synchronous communications refers to an exchange of information that is synchronized, occurring at regular time intervals. In synchronous communications a character is sent every time interval whether there is information to be transmitted or not.

If there is no information to be transmitted, a character signifying "no information" is sent and ignored by the receiving modem. Since synchronous transmission systems transmit on a regular basis, it is relatively easy to know when to look for incoming bits.

In contrast, modem communications is usually asynchronous, that is, when neither machine is sending data to the other, the line is not utilized. This means that communications could resume at any time, and it is possible for one side or the other to look for data at the wrong moment and for bits to be lost.

Framing

An asynchronous communications system where the receiver is out of step with the sender is said to have experienced a framing error. This can occur because of differences in transmission speed between the two systems (*i.e.,* one system is sending at 301 bps, while the other receives at 300 bps), or because of differing stop bit settings. Synchronous communications systems cannot experience framing errors because their characters stop and start at defined times.

Bits per character/stop bits

In order to prevent framing errors, it is necessary to provide a method for regaining synchronization and for distinguishing the beginning of one character from the middle of another character. This task is performed by the use of stop and start bits. Typically, a start bit and a stop bit are used to frame the beginning and ending of each 8-bit character sequence. This means that in synchronous communications, 10 bits of information are normally required in order to transmit one character.

Parity

Today's microcomputers aggregate 8 bits of information into a single character, known as a byte. However, older computer systems did not always use 8-bit bytes when communicating. In order to provide for a primitive form of error checking, IBM mainframes and some UNIX systems instead used 7 bits per byte, with the eighth bit being utilized for error checking.

This system is called parity. Here's how it works. Even parity means that the eighth bit (the parity bit) is always arranged so that the total number of 1 bits in the byte is an even number. Similarly, odd parity means that the parity bit is always arranged so that the total number of 1 bits is an odd number. Mark parity means that the parity bit is always a 1, and space parity means that it is always a 0. The system of parity error detection is primitive because it only protects against errors of a single bit within a byte. If two bits are in error, this method will not work. Since noise on phone lines frequently occurs in bursts, corrupting multiple bits, parity error checking is of limited usefulness in computer communications.

Settings (8-N-1, 7-E-1, etc.)

The combination of bits per character, parity, and stop bits are known as the communications settings. The settings are frequently denoted by three characters separated by dashes. The term "8-N-1" refers to 8 bits per character, no parity, and one stop bit. "7-E-1" refers to 7 bits per character, even parity, and one stop bit. Since one start bit per character is used in all cases, this does not need to be specified.

The 8-N-1 setting applies to virtually all bulletin boards operating on microcomputers, and should be used as the default. The 7-E-1 setting is primarily used for communicating with UNIX computers or IBM mainframes. Options such as "stripping the eighth bit" usually only apply to data sent to the screen, and therefore will not interfere with transfer of binary data.

Software and hardware handshaking

During communication it may be necessary to stop the flow of data. This can be accomplished either in software or in hardware.

If text is being transferred, it is possible to tell the sending computer to pause by using *flow control characters*. This is referred to as software flow control or the XON/XOFF method of handshaking. XOFF ((CTRL)S) is used by the receiver to stop the flow, which does not resume until the receiver sends an XON character ((CTRL)Q).

If binary data is being transferred, this will not work because the XON or XOFF characters could be included as part of the file. This means that another way of pausing must be found. One way is by changing the voltage on one of the lines on the serial port. This is called "hardware handshaking."

For reasons that are discussed later in this chapter, hardware handshaking is recommended for modems operating at 9600 bps or higher, or 2400 bps modems using compression. To enable hardware handshaking, you must have this option turned on within your communications software. You must also ensure that your modem is connected to your computer using a cable that supports hardware handshaking.

Terminal types

If you are using an online service or bulletin board that does not offer its own custom software, then you will need to obtain a general-purpose communications package and set its terminal emulation mode.

Terminal emulation

In the era of mainframes and minicomputers, terminals were used to display information from these large machines. Two very popular standards that emerged from this era were the 3270 standard (for IBM mainframes) and the VT100 standard (for DEC minicomputers). A typical terminal emulation dialog box looks like this (MicroPhone):

```
┌─────────────────── Terminal Settings ───────────────────┐
│ ┌─Terminal ──────────────────────────────────────────┐  │
│ │ Terminal Type: │VT-102/ANSI│      [    Color    ]   │  │
│ │ VT102 Capture:     ☒ on CR        ☐ on Clear        │  │
│ └────────────────────────────────────────────────────┘  │
│ ┌─Formatting ────────────────────────────────────────┐  │
│ │ Font Size:         ◉ 9-Point      ○ 12-Point        │  │
│ │ Columns:           ◉ 80           ○ 132             │  │
│ │ Cursor Shape:      ◉ Block        ○ Underline       │  │
│ └────────────────────────────────────────────────────┘  │
│ ┌─Additional Settings ───────────────────────────────┐  │
│ │ Backspace Key:     ◉ Backspace    ○ Delete          │  │
│ │ ☐ Local Echo       ☐ New Line     ☐ Auto Wraparound │  │
│ └────────────────────────────────────────────────────┘  │
│ Answerback Message:                                      │
│ [                                   ]  ( OK ) [Cancel]   │
└─────────────────────────────────────────────────────────┘
```

Terms you will often see in terminal emulation dialog boxes are "TTY," "VT52," "VT102," "3270" or "ANSI" emulation. TTY stands for teletype and is the simplest form of terminal emulation. Selecting this option will request that your computer function like a teletype, a now-outdated terminal that was created before cathode-ray tube terminals were available. Although setting your program in teletype (TTY) mode does not mean that your computer will send every incoming character to the printer as teletypes did, it does mean that your terminal program will be incapable of positioning the cursor on the screen because teletypes didn't have cathode-ray tubes (CRTs).

The VT100 terminal was the first terminal based on a standard known as ANSI X3.64-1977. However, the two standards, while similar and to some degree interchangable, are not identical. The term "ANSI" or "PC-ANSI" typically refers to extensions to the ANSI standard for the IBM PC (limited graphics characters, color, and video attributes such as blinking).

The VT52 terminal was a precursor of the VT100, and the VT102 is a successor. These terminals are backward compatible, which means that a terminal emulating a VT100 can respond to VT52 commands, and a terminal emulating a VT102 can respond to VT100 commands. The 3270 terminal is used for connecting to IBM mainframes. For emulating the 3270, special-purpose software (and sometimes hardware) is required.

The North American Presentation Level Protocol Syntax (NAPLPS) is a joint ANSI and Canadian Standard Association standard (ANSI X3.110-1983) supporting complex color graphics, animation, and extended character sets. Using the ISO 2022 and 2375 syntax and Dynamic Redefinable Character Set (DRCS) tables, NAPLPS allows for definition of 96 special characters per font, such as mathematical symbols. This is in addition to support for Chinese, Korean, Japanese, Cyrillic, and other language character sets. Since NAPLPS is a vector-based drawing standard, it offers highly compact (frequently under 20K) presentation of complex screens. Although NAPLPS has been adapted for use by

Prodigy, only with the release of Troika from Old Colorado City Communications has it been implemented within a popular general purpose communications program.

RIP is a proprietary graphics protocol from TeleGrafix Communications, Inc. that has been adopted by a number of popular PC products, including QMODEM Pro, Telix, WILDCAT!, Searchlight, PCBoard and Major BBS. RIP allows for complex color graphics, as well as multimedia (including animation, sound and eventually video). Since RIP is a graphical interface construction set (supporting Icons, Menus, and Pointing devices), it does not specify the interface, leaving this up to the creator of the service.

Many communications software packages offer VT100 terminal emulation and support for one or more file-transfer protocols. Today's software also typically offers the ability to transmit at speeds from 300 bps to 19,200 bps or higher with the full range of settings (8-N-1, 7-E-1, etc.) The software may also offer the ability to operate under automated control.

Recognizing icons on the desktop

In the course of your telecommunications adventures, you will be sending and receiving files of various types. For those of you who are Mac users, the figure Mac Telecommunications Iconography covers some of the most popular icons and programs. Most of the time, double-clicking on the icons on the left side of the figure will automatically run the correct program on the right side. Sometimes the desktop needs to be rebuilt or you won't have the program in question. Using the iconography, you can figure out what kind of file you have and how to open it.

Macintosh file structure and MacBinary

Macintosh files differ from MS-DOS files in critical ways. Mac files contain two parts, called the "resource fork" and "data fork." In addition they have other characteristics such as icons and creator and type information. Macintosh file names are also often longer than the 11 characters allowed under MS-DOS. Since most microcomputer protocols were designed for transmission of a single fork along with limited file characteristics such as an 11-character filename and creation date and time, these protocols had to be adapted for use on the Macintosh. Rather than modifying the protocols themselves (which would have left Macintosh owners unable to communicate with other machines), the MacBinary standard was created to allow for transmission of Macintosh files using standard protocols.

MacBinary is layered on top of the file transfer protocol; it operates by converting the file name, data and resource forks, icon information, creator bits, and so on, into a single data stream and transmitting that information first. If the receiving Macintosh is set to "MacBinary on," it interprets those blocks as MacBinary information and reconstructs the file appropriately.

One frequent mistake beginning users make is to receive a MacBinary file with MacBinary turned off, resulting in the MacBinary header being interpreted as normal data. Therefore, the received file will have the MacBinary header on it and will display a generic icon. The Apple File Exchange extension MacBinary AFE is capable of converting Macintosh files to and from MacBinary format and can be used to recover from this mistake. Apple File Exchange is a little-known utility included with the Mac's system software, which is discussed in Chapter 22: File Transfer Between Macs, PCs, and UNIX.

You may also wish to use MacBinary transfer mode to send a text file to another Macintosh. The text file will be received with the creator type and icon that were present on your desktop, rather than a generic icon.

Binary mode

Since .ARC, .ARJ, .GIF, .ZIP, and .ZOO files are usually created on PC compatibles, they will *not* have MacBinary headers. If your communications program is set to receive a MacBinary file and you attempt to download one of these files, your download may be corrupted. This is a frequent problem for users of software that does not implement Smart MacBinary.

In *binary* mode, you will receive the file without attempting to interpret a MacBinary header. This is the mode you would use if you are receiving .ARC, .ARJ, .GIF, .ZIP, or .ZOO files from a PC compatible computer.

If you send a Macintosh file in binary mode, most programs will only send the data fork, without a MacBinary header preceding it. For this reason, you should only send a file with a single fork using binary mode. Examples of this include .ARC, .GIF, and .ZIP files, or Microsoft Word documents saved in MS-DOS format.

Smart MacBinary

Programs such as ZTerm can automatically detect whether an incoming file is being transmitted in MacBinary mode. This is called Smart MacBinary.

ZTerm is also capable of recognizing .GIF, .ARC, and .ZIP files and setting the creator and type fields so that these files can be opened by Giffer, ArcPop, and UnZip, respectively. If you are having problems downloading one of these file types, check to see whether your communications program has MacBinary turned on. You will need to turn it off in order to receive these files.

Transferring text files

While Macintosh text files have a carriage return at the end of a paragraph, and no line feeds, IBM PC text files often use carriage return/line feeds at the end of each line. If your communications software is set to text mode, then data being sent or received will be converted. You will want to use this mode only when sending a text file, because other files sent in text mode will be corrupted. (Most programs send only the data fork of a file in text mode.)

Due to the extra line feeds, an IBM text file opened on a Mac looks like this:

```
This is a file created on an IBM PC and
□saved in text format. When it is opened
□on the Mac there are weird little
□characters on every line.
```

Mac Telecommunications Iconography

Icon | Application to use

Example.GIF

A .GIF file downloaded with
Microphone II or White Knight

Example.GIF

A .GIF file downloaded with
ZTERM

Giffer

GIFConverter

Self Extracting StuffIt.sit
(Does not require application)

StuffIt 1.51 Archive.sit

Deluxe Example.sit

Un-StuffIt Deluxe

Self Extracting Example.SEA
(Does not require application)

Compact Pro Example.CPT

Extractor

examplezip.zip

A .ZIP file downloaded with
ZTERM

examplezip.zip

A .ZIP file after it is decompressed
with UNZIP

UnZip

AppleLink letter

A text file saved within
AppleLink

AppleLink

McSink text file

Generic text file

TeachText

Disintectant.Bin

A file run through
BinHex 5.0 (MacBinary)

BinHex 5.0

CommCloser.Hqx

A file run through BinHex 4.0

BinHex 4.0

McSink, which is available on EXEC-PC, can be used to remove or add linefeeds.

Smart quotes

There are also other ways in which Macintosh text files are different from text files on other computers. The Macintosh contains several characters that are not supported by other computers, such as open and close smart quotes (" and "), apostrophe's and em dashes (—) (selected by typing ⌜OPT⌝– on the keyboard). If you are downloading text files formatted on the IBM PC, you will often want to reformat them to support smart punctuation.

This can be tedious to do manually. Luckily Macify will convert " to the smart quotes " and ", will substitute the smart apostrophe ' for ', and will also handle linefeed and special character removal problems. Macify is available on EXEC-PC.

Dumbing smart quotes

This issue also comes up when you are transmitting smartly punctuated text files to another computer. If you do this, the files will not be interpreted correctly on UNIX or IBM PC machines. Here is an example of a Macintosh text file with smart quotes and apostrophes:

```
In keeping with the book's "hands-on"
philosophy, readers are encouraged to contact
the author via electronic mail with
suggestions on how the book can be improved.
```

Below is what the file will look like if it is transmitted to a UNIX machine. Note that a U has been substituted for the ', an R for ", and an S for ".

```
In keeping with the bookUs Rhands-onS
philosophy, readers are encouraged to contact
the author via electronic mail with
suggestions on how the book can be improved.
```

One answer is to use BBEdit, along with an extension called 827 that converts 8 bit characters to 7 bit ASCII. Another way is to use McSink (BMUG Disk Telecom E1) with an external VCMD, **Straight Quotes**. To do this, select **Load VCMD...** from the **External**

menu of McSink. Then select the **Straight Quotes VCMD**.

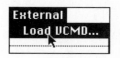

The **Curly Quotes to Straight Quotes** entry will then appear on the **External** menu. This option will convert apostrophes and curly quotes but not em dashes.

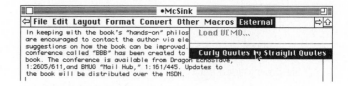

McSink and Vantage also have a million and one other uses and are among the most frequently used desk accessories.

File-transfer protocols

If parity error-checking is so inadequate and the odds of an error are so great, how is computer communications possible? Much effort has been put into developing protocols for catching and correcting errors. Protocols developed for the purpose of transferring files without errors are known as file-transfer protocols.

Early file-transfer protocols such as XMODEM used an error-checking method known as Checksum, in which the receiving computer checked the sum of the incoming characters against a result computed and transmitted by the sending machine.

Later versions of XMODEM, as well as YMODEM, ZMODEM, and other protocols, have used an error-detection technique more foolproof than Checksum known as Cyclic Redundancy Check or CRC. How are errors corrected once they are detected? For each of the protocols mentioned, the offending block is simply re-sent.

Examples of file-transfer protocols include XMODEM, a protocol that transmits 128 bytes of data before waiting for an acknowledgment; XMODEM-1K (sometimes erroneously referred to as YMODEM), which transmits data in 1K chunks; YMODEM, which transmits data in 1K chunks and also allows for transmission of files in batches; KERMIT, a protocol designed for transferring data reliably between unlike computers, including machines operating with 7-byte characters, that can also recover from aborted sessions; and ZMODEM, a protocol which provides for transmission of data in variable increments, depending on line quality, and that boasts many other advanced features such as the ability to recover from aborted sessions.

Which transfer protocol should you use? In most cases, ZMODEM is the best choice, provided that your host supports it. Telix, QMODEM Pro, Procomm Plus for Windows, ZTerm, MacIntercomm, MicroPhone II, and many other packages have fast and reliable ZMODEM implementations. MacKermit and PC-Kermit support the KERMIT protocol, which should be used in situations where ZMODEM cannot be used or is unsuccessful.

Protocols can be classified into several types: ACK/NAK protocols, sliding-windows protocols, and streaming protocols.

ACK/NAK

ACK/NAK protocols send a block of data and then wait for an acknowledgment (ACK), or nonacknowledgment (NAK). If the round-trip time between the sending and receiving systems is long, ACK/NAK protocols become very inefficient. It should be noted that ACK/NAK protocols can be bidirectional, that is, they can be sending and receiving data packets at the same time, while in each direction waiting for an ACK before sending the next block.

∇ XMODEM

XMODEM, the original microcomputer file-transfer protocol, was invented by Ward Christiansen (who was also the first bulletin board operator) in 1978. The original version of XMODEM sent data in 128-byte parcels known as blocks or packets. It also used a one-byte checksum in order to detect errors by computing the checksum on the received bytes and comparing it to the value sent along with the data.

XMODEM waits for acknowledgment from the receiver before sending another block. When communicating over long-distance phone lines or via a packet-switching network, the waiting time for an acknowledgment can be considerable, perhaps as long as one second. These delays will degrade the performance of 1200 bps or faster speed modems. For this reason use of the XMODEM protocol should be avoided whenever possible.

XMODEM has several other notable drawbacks. File sizes are not preserved, which can result in problems with some operating systems. In addition the protocol cannot function over 7-bit communications lines, which means that it cannot be used to communicate with many mainframe and UNIX systems. XMODEM also does not send the filename or creation time/date.

∇ XMODEM-CRC

One of the first modifications to XMODEM was to substitute a 16-bit cyclic redundancy check (CRC) for the checksum method of error detection. At the start of an XMODEM transfer, the receiver sends a byte indicating whether it wants to use the CRC method of error detection (a "C" is sent) or the checksum method of error detection (in which case a NAK or 15H is sent). The CRC method is much more reliable at detecting errors than the checksum, and as a result it has been implemented on the vast majority of systems. Use of CRC error correction does not improve transfer efficiency.

▽ XMODEM-1K

A version of XMODEM utilizing 1K blocks, XMODEM 1K is sometimes (erroneously) called YMODEM. Unlike the "true" YMODEM, XMODEM-1K cannot perform batch transfers, nor does it send the filename or creation time/date. The larger block size means that XMODEM-1K will pause less frequently to wait for acknowledgments on high-quality phone lines. On low-quality lines, the longer blocks will frequently encounter errors, resulting in slower transfer speeds than standard XMODEM.

▽ YMODEM (Batch)

YMODEM is a protocol with 1K blocks and batch transfer features invented by Chuck Forsberg. This is the true YMODEM. YMODEM sends along the filename and creation time/date. Like XMODEM-1K, the 1K block size is a blessing under good line conditions and a curse under bad ones.

▽ KERMIT

A protocol developed at Columbia by Frank DaCruz and others, KERMIT can handle 7-bit communications. On the PC, it is supported by Telix, QMODEM Pro, and PC-Kermit, among others; on the Mac, it is available in Microphone II or MacKermit. In order to allow 8-bit characters to travel over 7-bit communications lines, KERMIT uses two 7-bit bytes to transfer each 8-bit character. This overhead results in the basic KERMIT being the slowest of the file transfer protocols. The basic KERMIT, like XMODEM, sends a single packet and then waits for an acknowledgment.

▽ BIMODEM

Today's V.32*bis*/V.42*bis* modems can transmit at 14.4 Kbps bidirectionally, but the KERMIT, XMODEM, YMODEM, and ZMODEM protocols can only do unidirectional transfers. BIMODEM allows for simultaneous uploading and downloading. This is very useful for global communications networks where machines typically have packets to send in both directions. Assuming equal amounts of information are to be transmitted both ways,

BIMODEM can cut total session time by as much as 50 percent. BIMODEM also includes some nice extensions, such as wildcard capability (requesting *.ZIP).

▽ HSLINK

Another bi-directional protocol that is more popular than BIMODEM, and works very well.

Sliding windows

With ACK/NAK protocols, the sending machine will spend a good deal of time waiting for acknowledgments. Sliding-windows protocols increase the efficiency of transmission by allowing the sender to have several packets simultaneously awaiting acknowledgment.

Sliding windows is therefore like a juggling act, where the maximum number of balls up in the air is known as the window size. Once the protocol has the maximum number of packets in various stages of transmission and acknowledgment, it will not send additional packets until the oldest outstanding "ball" (packet) comes down (is ACK'd). At this point the sliding window moves to the right. In the figure below, this means that block number 7 will not be sent until block number 3 is acknowledged, since the window size is 4 blocks.

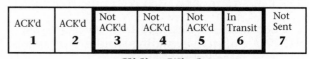

ACK'd	ACK'd	Not ACK'd	Not ACK'd	Not ACK'd	In Transit	Not Sent
1	**2**	**3**	**4**	**5**	**6**	**7**

Sliding Window
(Size = 4)

▽ SEAlink

SEAlink is a sliding-windows version of XMODEM that uses 128-byte blocks and allows for batch transfers. The basic SEAlink implementation uses a window size of 6. As a result, inefficiencies due to long communications delays are decreased. Although popular on the PC, SEAlink is only supported by one Macintosh communications program, Charm, whose menus are in Italian.

∇ SuperKERMIT

SuperKERMIT is a windowing version of KERMIT that is supported by PC-Kermit, and Procomm Plus for DOS and Windows; on the Mac it is supported by QuickLink II, White Knight, and SmartCom. The default window size is 8.

∇ FirstClass Protocol

FirstClass Protocol (FCP) is a proprietary protocol from SoftArc that allows for bidirectional transmission and multithreading. This means that FCP supports doing other things, such as sending messages and chatting in real time, while file transfers are in progress. FCP also supports recovery of aborted transfers.

Streaming protocols

In order to garner maximum efficiency from a file transfer, the window size can be made larger and larger. When the window size reaches the number of blocks in the file, we have a streaming protocol. Streaming protocols do not wait for acknowledgments before sending the next block.

∇ ZMODEM

Developed by Chuck Forsberg, ZMODEM offers many advanced features. These include variable size blocks (which can run from 64 bytes to 8K), a 16- or 32-bit CRC; batch-transfer capabilities; and sending of filenames, dates, and times. ZMODEM supports streaming, meaning that it can send packets continuously, without waiting for acknowledgment or requiring a fixed "window" beyond which it will wait for an acknowledgment. It also includes an ACK/NAK operating mode which is less efficient; as a result, it is desirable to enable streaming if this is part of the configuration. ZMODEM can restart a failed transfer on a subsequent attempt, and allows for automatic startup on the receiver end, which means that you will not need to tell your communications program to receive a file once you have told the sending machine to send it to you. Basic ZMODEM is an 8-bit protocol and therefore may not be usable in

transferring binary data to or from some mainframe or older UNIX systems. ZMODEM is available on many UNIX systems as **sz** (send ZMODEM) and **rz** (receive ZMODEM).

∇ ZMODEM-90

ZMODEM-90 offers several extensions to ZMODEM, such as support for 7-bit transfers, Run Length Encoding (RLE) compression, and "Moby Turbo", which removes XON/XOFF avoidance for marginally improved performance. RLE compression is of value only on redundant data streams. The ZMODEM-90 extensions to ZMODEM are proprietary.

∇ YMODEM-g (Batch)

YMODEM-g refers to the use of the YMODEM protocol without a provision for resending bad blocks. Although errors can be detected in YMODEM-g, they cannot be corrected, so transmission will abort. This protocol is normally used only with modems that provide hardware error correction.

However, this approach is risky because of the possibility of buffer overflows. In this case, YMODEM-g transfers will abort even though the modems performed the data transfer flawlessly.

Modem standards

The first modems were "dumb" devices that required a great deal of work to get them to perform basic functions. With the introduction of the Smartmodem 300, Hayes introduced a modem with its own command set. The Hayes AT Command Set has since become a very widely adopted standard. On the next page are some of the Hayes commands and what they do.

The Hayes Command Set

ATZ
Restores the modem's internal settings to those of the parameter RAM. If your modem is functioning, it should respond with OK. This is a good way of testing the modem connection.

+++ATH
Hangs up during a session. The pause between the escape code (usually +++) and the entry into command mode is known as an "escape sequence," and has been patented by Hayes. The length of pause is set by S12, and the escape character is set by S2. Selecting S2 >127, as most sysops do, disables escapes.

AT&W
Writes the current settings of the modem to the nonvolatile RAM (NRAM), letting you recall these settings using the **ATZ** command. This is one way to avoid entering a complicated modem initialization string. **AT&F** restores the modem's internal settings to the factory defaults, which is useful if your modem is malfunctioning and you wish to set it to a known configuration.

AT&D2
Sets your modem to hang up or disable auto-answer when the DTR signal is negated. This is used with BBSes so they can disconnect the caller. **AT&D0** tells the modem to ignore the DTR signal. This is useful for Mac hardware handshake cables where DTR and RTS are both tied to Handshake out, where you can use either DTR hangup or hardware handshaking, but not both.

ATS0=1
Sets the modem to answer after the first ring. Useful for calling an unattended machine.

ATV0
Sets the modem for numeric result codes. **ATV1** is for verbose result codes.

ATDT
Dials out on a touch-tone phone. This command should be followed by the phone number you wish to dial, such as **ATDT 15108659004.**

ATDP
Dials out on a pulse phone. This command should be followed by the phone number you wish to dial, such as **ATDP 15108659004.**

RTS/CTS Flow Control
How this is enabled depends on the modem. Some use the command **AT&R0** which sets up for standard (CTS/RTS) hardware handshaking. In contrast, **AT&R1** ignores CTS/RTS handshaking: the CTS signal is constantly on, and the modem ignores RTS signals coming from the computer.

ATM0
Turns your modem speaker off. This is useful if you want to instruct your computer to dial out in the middle of the night without waking you up. In contrast, **ATM1** (the default) turns the speaker on until carrier is established.

AT&C1
Sets your modem to assert the Carrier Detect (CD) signal to your computer when it has connected to another modem. In contrast, **AT&C0** tells the modem to always assert Carrier Detect. This is important because when you are running a bulletin board system, it is important to automatically log off callers when they drop the carrier so that someone else doesn't log in on the same line under their account.

ATH0
Hangs up the phone. This only works while the modem is waiting for a command, however; otherwise if the string **ATH0** were to be transmitted to the modem, the session would be terminated. **ATH1** busies out the phone line. For example, this is used when your computer is doing something else (such as processing incoming mail) and will not be available to pick up the phone if it were to ring.

Modulation, error correction, and compression standards

In order for two modems to be able to speak to each other, they must agree on common techniques for communicating. These are called "standards." Modems have standards for modulation, which dictates the basic speed of the connection; for error correction, which corrects for problems caused by noisy phone lines; and for compression, which increases the effective speed of the connection.

The most important concept to understand is the difference between *proprietary* and *open* standards. A proprietary standard is a technique that is the exclusive property of a particular firm. An *open* standard is one that has been agreed upon by a number of vendors.

CCITT standards are open to use by all manufacturers and have attained wide popularity. The global character of CCITT assures that these standards are compatible with all phone systems, although particular modems may or may not be portable from country to country due to differences in power requirements, regulations, and phone jacks.

Microcom of Norwood, Massachusetts, is the developer of the Microcom Network Protocol (MNP) set of standards that are also widely implemented. The MNP standards, (primarily oriented toward error correction and compression) have been widely licensed by modem manufacturers.

Proprietary modulation standards have also been developed by modem vendors such as Hayes (Series V standards), US Robotics (HST standard), and Telebit PEP (Packetized Ensemble Protocol), among others. The major disadvantage of proprietary standards is that in order to communicate using these standards, two modems must be from the same manufacturer.

Proprietary versus open standards

The approval of the V.32 standard by CCITT in 1984 marked the beginning of the end for proprietary modem standards. At the time of its initial release, V.32 was too technically demanding to be implemented inexpensively.

This was because V.32 was a full-duplex 9600 bps standard. This was a difficult technical feat because with both directions operating at high speed, the frequencies of the incoming data could interfere with those of the outgoing data. This problem, called "echo cancellation," drove up the cost of implementing the V.32 protocol.

Rather than implementing echo cancellation vendors developed their own proprietary protocols in order to lower costs. These protocols offered a secondary low-speed channel and therefore were called asymmetrical full duplex, or "pseudo-full duplex." Since switching the direction of high speed transfer took a considerable amount of time (as long as 1 second), these modems were usually unsuited for use in computer networks, and more suited for connecting with online services, where the traffic flow is more nearly uni-directional.

Due to their cost advantages, proprietary modems retained the majority of the market for high-speed modems until 1990 and were particularly popular within the bulletin board and UNIX system operator communities. UNIX system operators gravitated toward Telebit modems, mostly because those modems implemented a special feature designed to speed up UNIX communications known as "protocol spoofing."

However, this feature was not of interest to bulletin board system operators. Since the US Robotics Courier HST modem was considerably easier to set up than the Telebit modem and was offered at discount prices to sysops, US Robotics modems became immensely popular within the bulletin board community. Even today, the odds are good that the bulletin board you connect to will be using a US Robotics modem.

With the development of the Rockwell V.32 chipset, manufacture of V.32 modems was simplified, and the price of these modems had decreased dramatically by 1990. As a result of the price decreases, sales of V.32 modems shot through the roof, and proprietary modems fell off in popularity.

Proprietary Modulation Standards

Standard	Description	Speed
Courier HST 9600	Asymmetrical full duplex	9600 bps
Courier HST 14400	Asymmetrical full duplex	14,400 bps
Courier HST 16800	Asymmetrical full duplex	16,800 bps
Courier HST 19200	Asymmetrical full duplex	19,200 bps
Telebit PEP	Asymmetrical full duplex	19,200 bps
Telebit Turbo PEP	Asymmetrical full duplex	23,000 bps
Hayes Ping-Pong	Asymmetrical full duplex	9600 bps

Open Modulation Standards

Standard	Description	Speed	Duplex	Connection
Bell 103	U.S. standard	300 bps	full	asynchronous
Bell 212A	U.S. standard	1200 bps	full	both
CCITT V.17	Int'l fax standard	14,400 bps	half	synchronous
CCITT V.21	Int'l standard	300 bps	full	asynchronous
CCITT V.22	Int'l standard	1200 bps	full	both
CCITT V.22*bis*	Int'l standard	2400 bps	full	asynchronous
CCITT v.27*ter*	Int'l fax standard	4800 bps	half	synchronous
CCITT v.29	Int'l fax standard	9600 bps	half	synchronous
CCITT V.32	Int'l standard	9600 bps	full	synchronous
CCITT V.32*bis*	Int'l standard	14,400 bps	full	synchronous
CCITT V.FAST	Under development	28,800 bps	full	synchronous

The development and wide acceptance of V.32*bis* was the nail in the coffin for proprietary standards. V.FAST, a 28,800 bps standard under development by CCITT, will probably be the last modulation standard for operation over normal phone lines, since it comes close to the maximum speed attainable.

The table above lists the major CCITT and proprietary modulation standards and their raw speeds, without compression.

Line noise and error correction

Phone lines may contain noise that disrupts the transmission of data. When using a modem, this manifests itself as junk characters appearing on your screen. Since noise often comes in bursts, you will often see several junk characters appear on your screen at a time.

If the noise is coming from your host's end of the connection, garbage characters will appear on your screen. This is relatively harmless unless your computer is set up to automatically take actions based on the incoming characters. Such a setup is known as "scripting." Line noise renders scripting ineffective and even potentially dangerous, since the garbage characters can force your computer to do something you do not want, such as sending or receiving files, or even deleting things off your hard disk.

If the noise is coming from your end of the connection, the host computer will think that you typed the junk characters yourself, and the results may be unpredictable. A visitor to the old BMUG BBS once saw his computer operate as if possessed, eventually downloading a file called "ZEN" without his intervention. However, your encounter with line noise is unlikely to prove as inspirational.

Since line noise is so annoying and potentially dangerous, methods for detecting and correcting errors have been created and built into modems themselves. There are two major standards for error correction: MNP-4 created by Microcom, and the V.42 standard approved by CCITT.

The V.42 standard is actually a method of negotiating between two possible error-correcting standards: Microcom's MNP-4, and Hayes's LAPM. LAPM is the preferred method, so that MNP-4 is used only if one of the modems is not compatible with LAPM. Both MNP-4 and LAPM provide error correction as well as some performance enhancement.

Compression standards

Those of you who have had to compress files before sending, or decompress files after receiving, may understand the convenience of having compression built into a modem.

The major compressions standards are MNP-5, created by Microcom, and V.42*bis*, created by British Telecom and approved by the CCITT. Both MNP-5 and V.42*bis* perform compression *on the fly*, which means that they compress the data in real time, as it is being transmitted.

Since the MNP-5 standard preceded V.42*bis*, it was frequently adopted for use in early V.32 modems. Since V.42*bis* is an extension to V.42, modems implementing V.42*bis* also implement V.42. V.42*bis* error correction provides up to 4:1 compression, and has the added feature of not attempting to compress files that were compressed prior to transmission. MNP-5 offers only 2:1 compression in ideal circumstances, and is usually less than that.

Confusing claims

A good question to ask then is: how does modem compression compare with compression software programs such as StuffIt, PKZIP, and Compact Pro? The answer depends on whether you are online (and watching charges mount) during the compression and decompression process.

If you benchmark the total time it takes to ZIP, ARC or Stuff files, send them, and then decompress them, you will find that it takes longer than to batch transfer the files using the modem's built-in data compression. However, if the files are compressed and decompressed off-line, and phone charges are only incurred during file transfer, then the compression software approach will be less expensive.

If you are primarily transmitting compressed files, you will not see throughputs anywhere near the 38,400 bps and higher claimed by modem marketers. Before you purchase a modem based on such claims, inquire as to the speed of the modem *without* compression. This is likely to be closer to the speed you will experience in practice than throughputs calculated assuming compression.

How modulation, error-correction, and compression layers relate

Within a few seconds (or as long as 45 seconds) of connecting with one another, two modems negotiate methods of modulation, error correction, and compression for the conversation. Then they proceed to transfer data.

Within each layer, modems attempt to negotiate the highest possible standard. If this cannot be accomplished, they *fall back* to the next lowest standard. Fall-back occurs when one of the modems is not capable of communicating via the higher standard. Eventually the two modems find the highest common standard in each layer with which to communicate and begin the conversation.

For example, in the modulation layer, if one modem can communicate via the V.32*bis* standard and the other can only speak V.22*bis*, then the two modems will conduct their conversation with V.22*bis* modulation. Within the error-correction layer, if one modem implements V.42 and the other modem only implements MNP-4, the conversation between the two modems will utilize MNP-4 error correction.

Within the compression layer, if one modem implements V.42*bis* and the other modem implements MNP-5, then the conversation between the two modems will utilize MNP-5 compression. This will happen although technically V.42*bis* does not include a fall-back to MNP-5 as part of the specification; the modem will merely attempt to initiate MNP-5 if V.42*bis* fails. The figure below illustrates how the layers of compression, error correction, and modulation are built on one another.

Compression
V.42*bis* (requires LAPM)
MNP-5
Error Correction
V.42 (LAPM)
MNP-4
Modulation
V.32*bis*
V.32
V.22 *bis*

Fax standards

Fax transmission has its own standards for modulation, compression, and error correction. However, these are usually packaged in a bundle, so that they are easier to understand. For example, Group III, the current most commonly implemented standard for fax, includes the V.29 half-duplex 9600 bps modulation standard, as well as specifications for error correction and compression, which are not part of V.29. Additional modulation standards include V.27*ter*, a 4800 bps fax modulation standard; V.21, a method for negotiation between V.29 and V.27*ter* modulation standards; and V.17, a recent half-duplex 14,400 bps modulation standard for fax transmission.

Understanding high-speed modems

Speed variability – an artifact of compression and error correction

The introduction of error correction and compression in high-speed modems means that

these modems do not operate at a fixed throughput. While carrier rate is fixed (except for fallbacks which can happen at connect or in real-time), effective throughput can vary widely during a single connection, based on the noise on the line and the degree of compression that can be achieved.

For example, if the phone line is very noisy, the modem may have to retransmit several times before data gets through without errors. The user sitting at the terminal will not see any data on his or her screen, and then all of a sudden, a block of characters will come through. This blockiness is an artifact of error correction.

Compression adds to throughput variability. A block of data consisting mostly of text can be effectively compressed, and therefore the modem will be able to send this data using fewer bits. As a result, throughput will be higher than when sending binary data that is not amenable to compression.

The need for modem buffers

Since high-speed modems work at variable effective throughput, the rate at which data enters the modem from the computer may be different from the rate at which it is being sent. As a result, memory is needed within the modem to store incoming characters prior to transmission. This memory is called a *buffer*.

The existence of a buffer allows the computer to drive the modem at close to its maximum possible rate. This is why you will typically set your communications software for rates of 19,200 bps or 38,400 bps with a V.32*bis*/V.42*bis* modem, even though the modem may not be capable of transmitting at those speeds all the time.

When the computer is sending data to the modem faster than the modem can get rid of it, the modem buffer will fill. When the modem's buffer fills up, any further incoming characters will be lost, so a way is needed to tell the computer to stop transmitting data to the modem. This is where hardware handshaking comes in. Hardware handshaking allows the flow to be turned off so that the modem's buffer can empty out again.

UART buffers – the 16550AF chip

On most microcomputers the Central Processing Unit (CPU) does not handle serial communications by itself. Rather, the task of serial communications is handled by a chip known as a Universal Asynchronous Receiver Transmitter, or UART. (An exception is certain NEC 80x6 clone chips that contain their own UARTs).

One of the jobs of the UART is to interrupt the CPU when an incoming character has been assembled. The CPU then acknowledges the interrupt, requests the data from the UART, stores it in memory, and the cycle begins again.

With low-speed modems, many CPU instructions can be executed between UART interrupts. A 300 bps modem can only interrupt the CPU every 33 milliseconds, which is an eternity for a CPU with even an 8 Mhz clock rate. If we assume 4 clock cycles per instruction, this means that a CPU could execute 66,666 instructions between interrupts from a 300 bps modem!

The same 8 Mhz CPU will be able to execute only 1111 instructions between interrupts from a 14,400 bps modem. This might not be enough instructions, particularly if the computer is already in the midst of a critical operation, such as writing to the disk.

The 8250 UART chip found in the original IBM PC contained only enough buffer space to store one byte in addition to the last assembled character. This means that if the CPU could not clear the buffer before another incoming character arrived, then bytes would be lost.

To get around this problem, the 16550AF chip was created. This chip contains 16 bytes of on-chip buffer, enough to ensure that bytes will not be lost except in very extreme circumstances.

If you are using an IBM PC computer with a V.32*bis* modem, then you need a 16550AF chip. Replacing the 16450 or 8250 chips on your serial port board with 16550AFs often presents a problem since many serial port boards now have their UART chips soldered on or surface-mounted. There are also UARTs that are part of the motherboard. You may

therefore have to remove or disable your existing serial ports and search for a board offering two socketed UARTs, but they are out there.

This problem has not occurred on the Macintosh, since the 8530 SCC chip has a 3 byte buffer and is therefore less susceptible to overrun than is the 8250.

Windows 3.0 problems

If you are using Windows 3.0 as well as a high-speed modem, you may find yourself having problems at speeds of 9600 bps or greater. If so, try upgrading to Windows 3.1 (which offers improved communications support), installing a 16550AF UART, or using buffered boards such as the Intel SatisFaxtion board or the ESP serial port board from Hayes.

End-to-end flow control in high-speed modems

In order for flow control to be effective, it must be implemented both in hardware and in software. Both computers must be running software that supports hardware handshaking; the computers must be connected to modems using hardware handshaking cables; and the modems must be set up to recognize the handshaking signals. If any link in this chain is missing, then flow control will fail and lost data may result.

The use of end-to-end flow control allows the "stop flow" signal to propagate from the software layer of one computer to the software layer of another computer. Here's how it works:

Before sending data, the computer (DTE) will sense the voltage on its incoming hardware handshake line, which is known as CTS or in Macintosh lingo, Handshake In (HSKin). If the voltage indicates a "true" condition (if the incoming handshake line is "asserted"), then it will send more data. If the modem (DCE) buffer is full, it will "negate" the CTS signal, and the computer will stop sending.

If the computer's buffer is full, it will "negate" the RTS signal, known in Macintosh lingo as Handshake Out (HSKo). This will tell the modem to stop sending. In order for the modem to prevent its own buffer from overflowing, it will need to stop the other modem from sending. It does this using a low-level flow control mechanism that is part of the V.42 standard.

Under the V.42 protocol, the receiving modem can send a Receiver Not Ready (RNR) frame to the sending modem to tell it to stop. Another mechanism is not to acknowledge the incoming packets. However, this will not work beyond the retransmission time-out period. V.42 is a sliding-windows protocol with a window size of 15 frames and a sequence number modulus default of 128.

After receiving the RNR frame, the sending modem in turn negates its CTS line, signaling to the sending computer that it is not ready to accept data. In response to the negated CTS signal, the sending computer's software stops sending. Thus the "stop flow" signal has propagated back from the receiving computer's software to the sending computer's software.

For more information on Macintosh and IBM PC cable connections, please consult Appendix D: Cable Compendium.

Making the call

In order to connect successfully with another computer or service, you will need to correctly set up your communications software and modem. It may take some iterating to get these settings right. After all, how do you know what the correct settings are for a particular bulletin board unless you've connected with it? One of the things that makes custom software easier to use is that these programs take much of the guesswork out of telecommunicating. They can do this since they only have to connect with one service whose parameters are known ahead of time. Even with general-purpose software though, the pain and confusion of setup should only be a one-time occurrence, since you can usually store frequently used settings and phone numbers in a directory.

Setting up the communications software

Most services advertise the speeds at which they can receive calls. For commercial online services, this usually tops out at 9600 bps; for Internet providers it is often 19,200 bps. For bulletin boards you may wish to set your communications program speed as high as 38,400 bps if you have a V.32*bis*/V.42*bis* modem, or perhaps 57,600 bps if you have V.FAST.

For terminal emulation, ANSI or ANSI-BBS is a good guess if you're dialing a bulletin board; if you're connecting to a UNIX machine, VT100, VT102, or VT220 emulation is a better choice.

For parity and stop bits, choose 8-N-1 unless you are connecting to a UNIX machine or mainframe, for which you should first try 7-E-1. UNIX machines also frequently use 8-N-1. As we discuss in the Troubleshooting section that follows, these choices are not etched in stone. If when you log on, things look weird, you may need to readjust the settings and try again.

Testing your modem

Before attempting to dial, you will need to ensure that your modem is turned on and attached to your computer via a cable connected to your serial port. On the Macintosh, the serial port is the port with the phone icon above it. The other port is the printer port, showing a printer icon.

Initializing the modem

With the advent of high-speed modems, initialization strings have been growing more complex and custom packages now often support dozens of modems.

If your custom software does not explicitly contain an entry for your brand of modem, try "generic Hayes" or a similar setting. If you are using general-purpose software, the first thing you should type to your modem is ATZ. If it is ready to accept commands, it should respond OK. If not, turn it off and on, and try again.

Dialing

If you've gotten an OK, it's time to choose a service or BBS, and use the ATDT command to "tone dial" the phone number.

Modem Result Codes

Modems tell you what is happening by returning either numeric or verbose result codes. It is important to make sure your modem is set up in the right mode for your communications software, for the software will be unable to figure out what the modem is telling it.

Verbose code	Numeric code	What it means
OK	0	Command executed OK
CONNECT	1	Connection established
RING	2	Phone ringing
NO CARRIER	3	Carrier lost or not picked up
ERROR	4	Invalid modem command
CONNECT 1200	5	Connection established at 1200 bps
NO DIALTONE	6	Dialtone not detected
BUSY	7	Busy signal detected
NO ANSWER	8	Other phone doesn't pick up
CONNECT 2400	10	Connection established at 2400 bps
CONNECT 4800	11	Connection established at 4800 bps (non-standard)
CONNECT 9600	12	Connection established at 9600 bps (non-standard)
CONNECT 19200	14	Connection established at 19,200 bps (non-standard)

To find a service, consult the list of commercial services, BBS lists, and Internet providers in Appendix B. Remember to include the full phone number (a 1 for long distance, if applicable, and the area code). Spaces, hyphens, parentheses, and slashes are ignored as part of this command. For example:

```
ATDT 8659004
```

If all has gone well (and you have not turned the modem's speaker off), you will hear the number being dialed, the phone ringing, and then the screech of two modems negotiating a connection. The word CONNECT may appear on your screen, followed by the logon banner of your chosen service.

```
CONNECT 38400
netcom2 login:
```

Troubleshooting

No response

If nothing at all happens, type another (RET); if this fails, try (ESC) a few times. If this doesn't work, try sending a (BREAK). In ZTerm you can do this by selecting **Send Break** from the **Misc** menu; on the PC, type (ALT)B (Prcomm) or (CTRL)end (Telix).

No dial tone

If you do not hear the dial tone or the tones or pulses as the modem dials, then you have a modem without a speaker, your modem is not connected to the phone line, your cable is not working, your telephone line is plugged into the "phone" jack on the modem instead of the "line" or "Telco" jack, or your modem is not plugged in. Check all of these again.

Call waiting

If you have purchased call waiting from your local phone company and someone tries to reach you while you are using your modem, you may be disconnected. In order to maintain a session on a phone line with call waiting, you must add the following onto your dialing string: "*70" for a touch-tone phone or "1170" for a pulse phone. These commands disable call waiting for the duration of your call.

Note that these strings may not be the same in all area codes, and that this method of disabling call waiting is not available in all areas. Those users with call forwarding can also prevent interruption of BBS sessions by forwarding incoming calls on the modem phone line back to itself. This will produce a busy signal on the line. Make sure to reset call forwarding after you are done.

Chock full o' noise

Another of the things that can go wrong is that you can get a very noisy phone connection. In this case, your session may look like this:

```
CONNECT 2400 BMUG 2400 bps
ñW $≠].]êconnected to Akbar & Jeff's Noise Hut,  ALAS....

BMUG Online Jy≤QUØ ËΔíÿßd(SM).  All Wron{}(*gsΔí&%
Deserved.  All private messages on this BBS arJy≤Qÿßde
read by the Exe{utive Director of BMUG,
Steven Jy≤$$≠] ËΔíñW dW Costa, andJy≤YQ$≠]ΔíÿPd the
Chairman of the Board, Gregory  Dow. Every last one of
them!
```

The best thing to do is to hang up, then call from another phone, go through another long distance vendor, or try again later. Most calling areas allow you to use an alternate carrier by dialing their carrier access code (10288 for AT&T, 10222 for MCI, or 10333 for US Sprint) before the number.

Wrong speed

It is possible to connect to your chosen system at the wrong speed. This will look like:

```
CONNECT 2400
x¯x–x‡¯x–ÄxÄÄx,x–¯x,Äx¯xÄ¯x,¯x‡¯x‡¯x–Äx,x¯x–ÄxÄxÄ¯x,¯xÄxx
Äx‡Äx‡Äx,ÄÄ¯ÄxÄx,Äx,¯xÄx–Äx–¯xÄÄx–¯x¯xx‡ÄÄxxÄx–<< x,Äx–
x–¯¯Ä¯Äx‡¯x¯x–<< ¯¯x–,xÄx‡¯Äx–¯Äx–< ,Äx‡ÄÄxx¯x¯¯Ä¯x–ÄÄx,¯
```

Artistic, right? This could happen if you have a 1200 bps modem because the default settings in most programs are for 2400 bps modems. Another way is if you lock the baud rate on the software but not the modem, or vice versa. To fix this, change the data rate to match the number after the word CONNECT.

Wrong duplex setting

If you log on to a computer that is full duplex while emulating a half-duplex terminal, your screen will look like this:

```
What is your FIRST name: bbeerrnnaarrdd
What is your LAST name: aabbboobbaa
Bernard Aboba [Y,n]?
Password: ...........

 9:28:11
21 Nov 91
Welcome to Akbar & Jeff's Full Duplex Emulation Hut!

Bernard, please excuse me while I check your mail...
Press ENTER to continue
```

In order to fix this, set your duplex setting to full. On the other hand, if you log on to a half-duplex computer while your terminal is set to full duplex, your screen will look like this:

```
What is your FIRST name:
What is your LAST name:
Bernard Aboba [Y,n]?
Password: ...........
 9:28:11
21 Nov 91
Welcome to Akbar & Jeff's Half Duplex Emulation Hut!
Bernard, please excuse me while I check your mail...
Press ENTER to continue
```

In order for your typing to show up on the screen, you will need to set your terminal to half-duplex mode. Although the vast majority of computer systems operate in full-duplex mode, some systems such as GEnie are still half duplex.

Wrong settings

If your settings are 8-N-1 (8 bits per character, no parity, and 1 stop bit) and you dial a system which requires settings of 7-E-1, your session will look like this:

```
CONNECT 2400/ARQ
ç
 √↑√↑St:↑Port↑Selector↑≤ç
                          ç
                        "eqıeÛt:↑á
```

This run-on babble with a few intelligible words thrown in is a dead giveaway to improper parity and bits-per-character settings. To fix this, adjust the Data Bits and Parity entries.

Wrong terminal type

If you connect to a computer that is expecting a VT100 terminal and you are in TTY mode, your screen will be filled with strange characters which are VT100 escape sequences that control elements such as cursor positioning, and presentation (color, bolding, and so on). It will look like this:

```
What is your name: bernard aboba
40;37mPassword: ......
H0;30;36m2JJ
                40;36m
H0;30;36m2JJ
 9:28:11
21 Nov 91
Welcome to Akbar & Jeff's VT100 emulation hut!
H0;30;36m2JJ
Bernard, please excuse me while I check your mail...
1;1f7mKPress ENTER to continueK 40;36m
```

To fix the problem, set your terminal emulation to VT100. If you connect to an ANSI

BBS with VT100 emulation, your screen will look like this:

```
CONNECT 14400
CONNECT 14400/ARQ/V32/LAPM/V42BIS
CONNECT 38400 / 02-19-93 (16:59:56)
(Error Correcting Modem Detected)

Windows OnLine
PCBoard (R) v14.5a/100 - Node 5 - PFE9EA574A7B
ZBBBBBBBBBBBBBBBBBBBBBBBBBBBBBBBBBBBBBBBBBBBBBBBBBBBBBBBBBBBBBBBBBBBBBBBBBBBBBBB?
FXXX0121210ZDDDDDDDDDDDDDDDDDDDDDDDDDDDDDDDDDDDDDDDDDDDDDDDDDDDDDD?0121210XXX5
FXXX0121210CDDDDDDDDDDDDDD   Windows OnLine(tm)   DDDDDDDDDDDDDDD40121210XXX5
FXXX0121210J          BOX 1614  Danville, CA 94526-6614          3012(210XXX5
FXXX0121210J       (510) 736-8343 bbs - (510) 736-4376 voice     3012(210XXX5
FXXX0121210J      13 LINES - Including voice support - 7.0 Gigs.  3012(210XXX5
FXXX0121210J    US Robotics - 16,800 bps modem to modem transfers 3012(210XXX5
FXXX0121210J     9,000 Windows 3.x Freeware and Shareware programs 3012(210XXX5
FXXX0121210CDDDDDDDDDDDDDDDDDDDDDDDDDDDDDDDDDDDDDDDDDDDDDDDDDDDDDD40121210XXX5
FXXX0121210J Frank Mahaney    - Publisher of the REVIEW & SYSOP  3012(210XXX5
FXXX0121210J Rich Young       - REVIEW Editor & Operations Mgr.  3012(210XXX5
FXXX0121210J Randy Wong       - Windows Moderator/Comp. News     3012(210XXX5
FXXX0121210J Derek Westfall   - WOL Advertising Director         3012(210XXX5
FXXX0121210J Hugh Hardie      - Windows Tips                     3012(210XXX5
FXXX0121210J Bob Gollihur     - Shareware/Commercial Reviews     3012(210XXX5
FXXX0121210J Ed Hoffman       - Shareware/Commercial Reviews     3012(210XXX5
FXXX0121210J Steve Peschka    - Reviews & Programming & VBasic   3012(210XXX5
FXXX0121210@DDDDDDDDDDDDDDDDDDDDDDDDDDDDDDDDDDDDDDDDDDDDDDDDDDDDDDDDDV0121210XXX5
FXXXXXXXXXXXXXXXXXXXXXXXXXXXXXXXXXXXXXXXXXXXXXXXXXXXXXXXXXXXXXXXXXXXXXXXXXXXXXXXX
@AAAAAAAAAAAAAAAAAAAAAAAAAAAAAAAAAAAAAAAAAAAAAAAAAAAAAAAAAAAAAAAAAAAAAAAAAAAAAAY
DO YOU WISH COLOR (Y or N)...?
```

Instead of like this:

```
CONNECT 14400
CONNECT 14400/ARQ/V32/LAPM/V42BIS
CONNECT 38400 / 02-19-93 (16:55:33)
(Error Correcting Modem Detected)

Windows OnLine
PCBoard (R) v14.5a/100 - Node 5 - PFE9EA574A7B
```

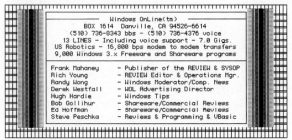

```
Windows OnLine(tm)
BOX 1614  Danville, CA 94526-6614
(510) 736-8343 bbs - (510) 736-4376 voice
13 LINES - Including voice support - 7.0 Gigs.
US Robotics - 16,800 bps modem to modem transfers
9,000 Windows 3.x Freeware and Shareware programs

Frank Mahaney    - Publisher of the REVIEW & SYSOP
Rich Young       - REVIEW Editor & Operations Mgr.
Randy Wong       - Windows Moderator/Comp. News
Derek Westfall   - WOL Advertising Director
Hugh Hardie      - Windows Tips
Bob Gollihur     - Shareware/Commercial Reviews
Ed Hoffman       - Shareware/Commercial Reviews
Steve Peschka    - Reviews & Programming & VBasic
```

```
DO YOU WISH COLOR (Y or N)...?
```

Hardware handshaking

Hardware handshaking problems are one of the most common, and difficult, problems that beginners run into. They are insidious because they often only show up during file transfers, when it is difficult to diagnose the source of the problem.

The problem is most common among recent purchasers of high-speed modems. After picking up a "standard" modem cable at a nearby store, the neophyte brings his or her brand new modem home. Let's say our neophyte is you. Filled with fantasies about attaining transfer rates in the stratosphere, you set your communication program to 57,600 and dial up their favorite BBS to take your new toy "for a spin." Alas, not only does the modem

not perform as advertised, but you find that ZMODEM transfers that used to go through without incident at 2400 bps now abort due to an excessive number of errors. Angry that your new toy doesn't work, you now write a nasty letter to the Sysop, telling him or her to fix the ZMODEM implementation, which is obviously defective.

What's wrong with this picture? The neophyte's problems are not due to the BBS, or their modem, but to his or her own communications settings and modem cable.

Although most PC modem cables support hardware handshaking, garden-variety Macintosh modem cables do not. Therefore if the neophyte was a Mac owner, the "standard" cable he or she purchased probably doesn't support hardware handshaking. Since most computer stores don't stock Macintosh hardware handshake cables, and wouldn't know such a cable if they saw one anyway, the thing to do is to get the cable with your modem. Many mail order outfits now stock them also.

Second, the neophyte's communications program or modem probably isn't set to do hardware handshaking.

Why does this problem arise? With a transfer speed of 57,600 bps the neophyte is forcing the computer to send data to the modem faster than it can receive it. Without hardware handshaking, there is no way for the modem to tell the computer to stop sending. As a result, the modem's internal buffer overflows, and bits are lost. The result is that the packet sent to the other modem contains invalid data, and when it is checked by the file transfer protocol, a "CRC error" occurs. Eventually the file transfer aborts due to too many errors.

Why can't a V.32*bis*/V.42*bis* modem (often advertised as having a maximum transfer speed of 38,400 bps or 57,600 bps) usually send data at this speed? The problem is that the marketing types at the modem vendors have been pulling a fast one. In reality, the V.42*bis* compression that marketing types get so excited about contributes little when users download compressed files, as they do almost all the time. Therefore the neophyte's modem is only operating at its maximum *modulation* speed at best, and probably slower due to line noise. In the case of V.32*bis* modems, the maximum modulation speed is 14,400 bps.

If the file you are transferring is uncompressed, V.42*bis* will compress it on-the-fly, and if the compression is more than 25 percent, the modem might actually be held back by being fed at only 19,200 bps. This is why many "experts" recommend setting the speed to 38,400 bps or even 57,600 bps instead, to ensure that your modem will operate at its maximum possible transfer rate.

In certain circumstances, setting speeds above 38,400 bps may actually LOWER effective transfer rates. This can happen if any of the links in the chain (computer, software, cable, serial port) cannot handle the faster rate, or if the modem is not set up for hardware flow control. The result will be a jump in the error rate, and a decrease in throughput.

Serial port setup problems (for PC users)

I don't know how many times I have gotten calls from friends who have had trouble setting up internal modems or serial ports on the PC. Their problem is almost always an interrupt or address conflict.

If your serial ports do not work correctly, try using software such as MSD from Microsoft to check for conflicts. MSD ships with every copy of Windows 3.x, and is also available on BBSes. It creates a complete report on your setup, including information about memory, installed hardware, interrupts, and port addresses.

No software diagnostic tool can be perfect at diagnosing hardware conflicts however, since by definition these conflicts occur where two or more devices contend for use of a single interrupt or port address, and only one can win. However, these utilities can often disclose a board residing at an unexpected address or interrupt.

If everything works fine under DOS but gives you trouble under Windows, try the Windows control panel. This allows you to set up ports COM1: through COM4:.

Modem troubleshooting Q&A

My modem won't answer when I talk to it. What should I do?

My friend Dave tells me the same thing happens when he talks to his teenage son. However, in this case the cause is probably a bad modem cable. Check the Send light on your modem (it'll have the initials "SD" or "TD" on or near it) as you type in your terminal program. If, when you type, the Send light doesn't go on, the cable is not sending data to your modem. Check to see if your modem cable is plugged in and that you're communicating over the right port. Turn the modem on and off and see if that makes any difference. Change the bps rate on your communications program, in case the modem is listening at a different rate than you're talking to it. Try 300, 1200, and 2400 bps.

At this point, you should try a "known good" cable before concluding that your modem is not working.

How do I get my modem to auto-answer?

You need to put your modem into auto-answer mode in order to instruct it to pick up the phone when it rings. This is useful if someone is trying to call in to be able to send you a file. The command for auto-answer is:

`ATS0=<number of rings>`

Note that it's a zero after the S. The command `ATS0=1` will instruct the modem to pick up after one ring; `ATS0=2` will have it pick up after two rings. If you wish to turn off auto-answer, use `ATS0=0`, which will tell it not to pick up at all.

To send a file after you've established a connection, assuming both sides support ZMODEM, have one side do a ZMODEM send.

Reading the Lights on Your Modem

Very few people take the time to understand the lights on their modems. However, these lights can provide a lot of information about the ongoing status of the communication session. Not all the lights given below will be present on all modems.

```
HS   AA   CD   OH   RD   SD   TR   MR
```

Light   What it means

Light	What it means
AA	Auto Answer. The modem is set up to answer the phone.
ARQ	Automatic Repeat reQuest. If this light is on, error correction is in operation.
CD	Carrier Detect. Modem is connected to another modem. If this light doesn't go off, then your modem is set to always keep Carrier Detect on.
CTS	Clear To Send. The CTS output from the modem is asserted.
DTR	Data Terminal Ready. The DTR input to the modem is asserted.
EC	Error Correction. When this light is on, error-correction protocols are in operation.
FAX	The modem is connected to a fax machine.
HS	High Speed. This means that the modem is ready to communicate at its highest speed.
LAP	The modem is using LAPM error correction.
MNP	The modem is using MNP 1-4 error correction.
OH	Off Hook. On when modem picks up phone to dial.
PEP	Packetized Ensemble Protocol. For Telebit modems only; the modem has connected in PEP mode.
RD	Receive Data. The modem has received bytes from the other modem.
RTS	Ready To Send. The RTS input to the modem is asserted.
SD or TD	Send Data or Transmit Data. The modem is sending data.
SYN	Synchronous mode. On when modem is transmitting synchronously.
TE	Transmission Error. Indicates an MNP or LAPM transmission error.
TR	Data Terminal Ready. On when DTR signal from computer to modem is asserted.
MR	Modem Ready/Test mode. On powerup, or when modem falls back to a lower speed.

The other side should then automatically receive the file. You can send just one file or many, using ZMODEM's batch-transfer feature. If you want to type to each other before initiating the transfer, remember to turn on LOCAL ECHO. Otherwise your typing will show up on the other machine's screen, but not your own.

ZTerm reports 25 percent efficiency with my new high-speed modem, but transfers go at normal speed. Why does this happen?

ZTerm bases the efficiency on the rate reported in the CONNECT <speed> message sent from the modem to the computer. The speed reported in this message is by default the speed at which the computer is talking to

the modem, not the speed that the modems are talking to each other.

The rates can be different if your terminal program is set to the "locked baud rate" option. This is possible because high-speed modems can receive data from the computer at higher rates than they can transmit it to another modem. V.42*bis* or MNP-5 modems compress data so that they can take in more data than they send on a continuous basis without causing a buffer overflow. If they need to stop incoming data from the computer, they can always do that via hardware handshaking.

To fix the problem you need to reset your modem to report the modem-to-modem connection speed instead. The Hayes command AT W2 &W (RETURN) will instruct some modems to report the modem connection speed in the CONNECT <speed> message, rather than the speed at which it connects to the computer. &W saves the current settings to the modem's nonvolatile memory. If you get an error, check your modem manual to make sure the W2 command is supported.

When I try to run my communications program, it says the modem port is already in use by another program. What should I do?

Under Microsoft Windows, this can occur when another application running at the same time has the com port open already. Check on this, and exit from that application. On the Macintosh, this can happen when using a fax modem whose INIT seizes the serial port. If you disable the fax modem INIT, you'll be fine (at least until you try to send a fax!) Another possibility is that you have been using your serial port for another purpose, such as MIDI output or printing, and have forgotten to deactivate the modem port using the Chooser. Try freeing up the port in the Chooser. If that does not work, a previous communications program may have terminated abnormally or may have forgotten to release the port. You can solve this by using the Serial Port Reset program on BMUG Disk Telecom A1.

I have a SUPRA V.32*bis*/V.42*bis* modem and can't use caller ID. What should I do?

With most phone companies that offer Caller ID, you must subscribe to the service to be able to get the information with your modem. If you are a subscriber, typing AT#CID=1 to your modem will activate the caller ID feature. This command is not standardized among manufacturers. Macintosh owners should also be aware that several INITs, including Super Clock v3.9, are known to cause problems under System 7.1. Remove them.

What utilities are available to diagnose hardware conflicts and serial port problems?

Diagnostic packages for the PC include Microsoft Diagnostics (MSD), included with Windows 3.*x*, and QAPlus. On the Macintosh, TattleTale will diagnose your system, and Serial of Champions gives information on the serial ports. See Appendix B: Choice Products for more information on these programs.

What is a GIF, anyway? Every time I try to download one, I can't open it. Why not? Is there a way to see the GIF as I download it? How? Why can't I compress GIF files?

GIF stands for Graphics Interchange Format; it was developed by CompuServe Information Service (CIS). Since the specifications are published and the GIF format can be viewed on an IBM PC, Amiga, Macintosh, or other computer, it is a very useful format for transferring graphics from one machine to another. Under DOS, CSHOW is a popular GIF viewer; WinGIF or the GIF viewer built in to Prcomm Plus (which lets you view GIFs as they are downloaded) is another possibility. On the Macintosh, you can view a GIF (or translate a PICT file to a GIF) using Giffer or GIF Converter, found on BMUG Telecom Disk E1.

GIF files have only data forks and do not contain creator bits or icon information. They are binary files, but since they don't have a resource fork, they won't have a MacBinary header when they are sent to you. As a result, if you download them using the MacBinary setting on your terminal program, your program may interpret the incoming data as text and do auto-translation, such as converting carriage return-linefeed combinations to carriage returns. Bad news – your download will be corrupted. If you are using MicroPhone II, you can fix this by selecting **Protocol Transfer...** from the **Settings** menu and turning MacBinary off.

If you're using ZTerm, you won't have a problem because ZTerm looks at the incoming file extension and automatically sets the creator and file type accordingly. This way, when you double-click on the GIF file, it will open Giffer for you. The program you are currently using is not doing this, which is why you cannot open the GIF files.

On the Mac, the GIFWatcher desk accessory will let you do the same thing. The GIF standard already specifies Lempel-Zev compression, so compression by other programs such as StuffIt will usually not generate any savings.

What is MacBinary? BinHex 4.0? BinHex 5.0?

The Macintosh computer is unique in that its files have two separate parts: a data fork and a resource fork. In addition, Macintosh documents and applications have associated information such as creator types, icons, and so on. In order to transfer all of this in one convenient package, the MacBinary standard was defined. It is a way of taking a Macintosh document or application with two forks, creator info, icon info, and so on, and translating it into a single data stream.

Most Macintosh telecommunications programs now do this conversion on the fly when you upload or download Mac files. This means that if you upload Mac files to a PC BBS, another Mac user will be able to download them just fine. However, if you want to get the Mac file onto a PC BBS by some other means (like through a local area network file server), you will have to manually convert the Mac file to MacBinary format. To do this, you will need a program such as MacBinary AFE or BinHex 5.0.

BinHex 4.0 is another thing entirely. It is used for a different purpose than BinHex 5.0, and will not produce files in MacBinary format. BinHex 4.0 is used to send Macintosh files over networks that allow only 7-bit transfers. This same problem is addressed by the Kermit file-transfer program. In both cases, more bytes must be used to transmit the same information, so file size is increased. Use BinHex 4.0 to convert a file before enclosing it within mail, for example.

Where to go for help – Macintosh

If your setup is functioning, you're probably best off asking your questions online, because there are guaranteed to be many regular communicators there who may have experienced your difficulties themselves. If you haven't even been able to get your modem to work, the BMUG Helpline is probably the place to go next.

Commercial services	America Online, Networking/Communications Forum, or BMUG forum; The WELL, telecommunications forum (go telecom); Electronic Frontier Foundation (go eff)
Macintosh helplines	The BMUG Helpline, (510)540-1742; Apple User Group Helpline, (800)538-9696, extension 500
Macintosh FidoNet conferences (available on MacCircles and Twilight Clone)	BAYNETADMIN for network administrators MACQA or MAC_HELP for questions and answers MACCOMM for Macintosh communications MACNETCOM for networking and telecom MACPOINT for Mac point software like Copernicus, COUNTERPoint, and MacWoof MACSW for Macintosh software MACHW for Macintosh hardware MANSION for Mansion BBS software as well as Copernicus PCMAC for conversion and transfer issues RRH for Second Sight BBS software TABBY for the Tabby FidoNet mailer
USENET conferences	comp.dcom.telecom for telephony; comp.dcom.fax for fax comp.dcom.modems for modems; comp.dcom.isdn for isdn comp.sys.mac.digest (moderated) comp.sys.mac.comm for Macintosh communications
RIME conferences	MAC for general discussion of the Macintosh
ILink conferences	MACINTOSH for general discussion of the Macintosh

Where to go for help – PC

Commercial services

The WELL, telecommunications forum (go telecom);
Electronic Frontier Foundation (go eff)

Helplines

The CompuGuru support line

FidoNet conferences

COMM for communications
HDCONF for hard disks
HST for US Robotics HST modems
LAN for Local Area Networks
OTHERNETS for info on non-FidoNet networks
PCUG for Personal Computer User Groups
PDREVIEW and SHAREWRE for information on shareware
QMODEM for QMODEM support
TECH for technical questions about IBM PC compatibles
TELIX for information on TELIX telecom program
UFGATE for information on send messages between FidoNet and USENET
UNIX for help with UNIX
WINDOWS for help with MS-Windows
ZMODEM for help with ZMODEM

USENET conferences

comp.dcom.telecom for telephony; comp.dcom.fax for fax
comp.dcom.modems for modems; comp.dcom.isdn for isdn
comp.protocols.tcp-ip.ibmpc for IBM PC TCP/IP applications
comp.os.msdos.apps for MS-DOS applications
comp.os.ms-windows.apps for Windows applications
comp.os.os2.apps for OS/2 applications
comp.sys.ibm.pc.misc for general discussion
comp.sys.ibm.pc.digest (moderated)

RIME conferences

BBS CALLER'S DIGEST for information on the *BBS Magazine*
BBS SOFTWARE for discussion of BBS software products
COMMUNICATIONS for modems and telecom software
COMPUTER USER GROUPS for information on user groups
DATAPROTECTION for help with viruses, trojan horses, and so on
EZ READER for support of EZ READER QWK reader
HARDDISK for information on hard drives
IBM for general discussion of the IBM PC
LANTASTIC for support from Artisoft
LOCAL AREA NETWORK for information on LANs
MAJORBBS for help with Major BBS
OMEN TECHNOLOGY for support of Omen Technology Products
ON-LINE for discussion of online services
QMAIL READER for support of Sparkware products
QMODEM for QMODEM support
PROCOMM for support of Procomm and Procomm Plus
TECHNICAL for information on IBM PC hardware
TELIX for discussion of the TELIX communications package
UNIX for discussion of all flavors of UNIX
USROBOTICS for discussion of USR modems
WILDCAT! SUPPORT for help with WILDCAT! BBS
WINDOWS for help with Microsoft Windows

CHAPTER 4: SAFE HEX

You can't be too careful

What is computer security?

Webster's Dictionary defines security as "freedom from worry." Assuming you're not Alfred E. Newman, the operation of a computer might bring forward one or more of the following worries:

• **Data loss.** You might worry that your computer will cease to function of its own volition, leaving you without access to critical files.
• **Theft.** You might worry that someone could gain unauthorized physical access to your computer and steal or damage it.
• **Software pests.** You might worry that your machine might be damaged by malicious software.
• **Cracking.** You might worry that someone might gain access to your machine over a computer network or modem and copy or damage files.
• **Privacy.** You might worry about the release of confidential data.
• **Authentication.** You might worry about someone impersonating you.

This chapter covers breakdowns, theft, and software pests. Since issues of cracking, privacy, and authentication are related to the use of global computer networks, these topics are covered in Chapter 8: Privacy and Security on the Internet.

Data loss

Data loss is the most common security problem. It is also the easiest to protect against.

How often should you back up your system? Whenever you change your files enough to make recovery from the previous backup tedious. How many backups should you keep? I recommend at least three – the most recent backup and two previous backups. At least one of these backups should be archived at a different site, to protect against a natural disaster.

If possible, use widely available backup media. Using an obscure tape format won't do you much good if your backup device fails and you can't find a device to handle the restore. 128 Mb Magneto-Optical or 44 Mb Syquest cartridges combine wide availability and large storage. Devices to read such cartridges have at least a decent chance of being available five years from now.

Maintenance

Computers, like any other appliance, need to be maintained. Floppy drives need to be cleaned and the heads on these drives may need to be aligned. Hard disks can benefit from defragmentation and low-level disk format refresh and monitors can be degaussed.

To keep my hard drives in shape I check the disk directories with routines such as fschk (UNIX), chkdsk (DOS), or Disk First Aid (Macintosh) at least every few days. Remember that under UNIX, you must be in single user mode to safely run fschk.

As part of my weekly maintenance routine, I usually run a disk defragmentation program such as VOPT, and every few weeks, a hard disk refresh program such as Spinrite.

If you are experiencing errors on your floppy disk drives and have no obvious cause for the problem, try cleaning the drive; inexpensive kits are available for this. Also, remember that cigarette smoke is known to cause problems with floppy disks and Syquest cartridges.

Theft

No computer can be more secure than the protections against unauthorized physical access. Machines with SCSI drives can be booted off external drives; workstations can be booted in single user mode; PCs or Macs can be booted off floppy disks. Once booted, intruders can get at critical files. If a machine is important enough to consider securing, it's important enough to lock up. Physical security measures should also extend to backups.

Reasonably priced computer insurance is available from firms such as Safeware, which offers coverage for up to $10,000 for a $120/year premium. Next worry!

Software pests

The threat of malicious software comes from programs known as "bacteria," "worms," "Trojan horses," or "viruses." Bacteria are programs that multiply on a single machine, either by creating multiple copies of files or by repeatedly invoking themselves.

A worm is a program that multiplies itself over a computer network. The most famous example of this was the Internet worm, which reproduced itself over the Internet in November 1988.

A Trojan horse is software with an ulterior motive masquerading as a useful program. These programs may destroy individual data files or reformat your hard disk. One way to protect against a Trojan horse is to transfer a newly acquired program to a locked bootable disk and test it out with your hard disk turned off. Of course, if you have an internal hard drive this is not easily accomplished, nor can Windows or System 7 easily be booted from a single disk.

Viruses are computer programs that spread by attaching copies of themselves to other programs. Programs that have had virus code attached to them are said to be "infected." A virus can attach itself to application software, system files, boot blocks, or (in the case of the Macintosh) even to the invisible desktop file present on a file-storage system. Any executable program is a candidate for harboring a virus. However, viruses can also do damage to data files, even though they do not infect them.

Since there are no useful software packages that operate as viruses (although some have come close!), a virus is something you don't want on your computer, and once it gets there you'll want to be rid of it.

Where do viruses come from? The most common places to pick up viruses are from commonly used computers at desktop publishing shops, university computer centers, or computer stores. If you copy software from one of these machines, or even if you just insert a disk into a machine infected with a virus, you can bring that virus home with you. It is also possible to catch a virus over a network. This is a risk if people are running applications off a server, for example.

Finally, you can catch a virus by transferring infected software from a BBS or commercial online service to your machine. This is one of the less likely ways of becoming infected, since system operators are usually knowledgeable and check files against known viruses.

Occasionally, new viruses do pop up on global computer networks and large bulletin boards. It is hard for system operators to defend against new viruses, since new strains may escape detection by existing antiviral software. For maximum protection, scan a newly downloaded program for viruses, and then execute the program from a floppy disk with the hard drive turned off.

Although viruses are specific to a brand of computer (a Macintosh virus cannot run on a PC and a PC virus cannot be executed on a Mac), today's world of software emulators and computer networks makes it possible for a PC virus to damage data on a Mac and vice versa.

If you have mounted a Macintosh folder on AppleShare as readable and writable, and a PC is set up to access that volume, then a virus running on the PC could damage files on the volume. Similarly, a virus running on a Mac with a mounted Novell server could damage server files.

If your computer is emulating another machine (such as a Mac running the Soft-PC emulation software, a Mac LC with an Apple II emulation card, or a PC or UNIX box running a Macintosh or DOS emulator), then you need to take precautions against viruses on the emulated platform. Emulators are now so good that viruses encounter few incompatibility problems. It's a multiplatform world.

My modem has a virus!

Before you can protect yourself against viruses, you should understand how viruses work, and how they can do damage. Please note that a virally infected program cannot cause any damage merely by being downloaded. It must actually be invoked to be a problem, and for the virus to do damage to hardware such as a computer or peripheral, the device must:

• communicate with the outside world
• have components that can be affected by an inappropriate command

Computers, disk drives, and even printers fit this definition. There is a Mac virus that can damage a PostScript printer by writing inappropriate instructions to the parameter RAM.

Since a modem's parameter RAM can always be reset to the factory settings, modems cannot be permanently damaged this way. However unless register S2>127 (which disables the escape sequence on all modems), it may be possible to cause another modem to hang up by passing an inappropriate sequence of characters.

Hayes has patented their Escape Sequence, which utilizes a required pause to ensure that no character string passing through the modem as a result of ordinary traffic can be interpreted as a command. To avoid paying Hayes for licensing their patent, some manufacturers have adopted an alternative, called the Time Independent Escape Sequence (TIES). Hayes claims that TIES is less reliable than the method taught in their patent, since under TIES a fortuitous string of characters coming across the link can cause the link to go down.

This claim has some merit, but rather than argue it here, it should be pointed out that many sysops disable the escape sequence anway by setting S2>127, and that the Hayes patent has been so well accepted that it is now used in the majority of modems made today.

Corporate precautions

If you are working in a commercial environment, you need to have a corporate policy regarding virus protection and eradication. Some companies try to protect themselves by taking extreme measures such as prohibiting the use of unapproved software. This policy usually doesn't work because it's so extreme that it won't be obeyed.

A more sensible policy is to provide education and support. I recommend that you maintain a library of virus eradication and detection software and dedicate an inexpensive machine of each type to virus disinfection. For Macs this might be a Mac Classic; for PCs it would be a PC XT machine. The machine will boot from a locked floppy with another drive so that people can insert infected floppies for disinfection. The locked boot floppy will prevent the virus protection machine from being infected by partition table or boot sector viruses.

I realize this may seem expensive, but if you are working in a professional environment where time is money, you simply cannot afford the cost of a corporatewide epidemic. If your firm is involved in engineering or software development, you have no other alternative than to act decisively to prevent the damage to your firm's reputation that could result from shipping infected products.

Antiviral software

Antiviral software is of three types: *vaccine* software that detects the operation of a virus, possibly preventing the virus from spreading; *scanning* software that scans a disk for viruses, and *disinfectant* software to disinfect infected volumes once a virus has been detected. Often antiviral software packages are composed of several programs, each specializing in one aspect of virus protection.

In order for a vaccine program to work, it must be operating in the background on your computer. In the PC world, this means that these programs are written as Terminate and Stay Resident (TSR) programs; on the Macintosh they are INITs, software that is loaded on startup. Since these programs are always running in the background and are sensitive to a variety of behaviors that may be exhibited by legitimate software, it is possible for vaccines to disrupt the normal operation of your computer, sometimes severely. This is most often a problem when the computer is to operate unattended, since the vaccine may stop the machine to ask for the OK on a pending file operation. This is why most vaccine packages allow you to adjust their aggressiveness to tolerable levels.

Of course, the vaccine program must always be on guard against being infected itself. One way to do this is for the programs to read- and write-protect themselves. This can interfere with backups, since the backup software will encounter an error when it attempts to read and backup the vaccine program. Therefore you may have to turn off a vaccine in order to do backups.

It is a good idea to run a disinfection program on your hard drive on a regular basis, even if you do not suspect the presence of a virus. On the PC, many users place the disinfection program in their AUTOEXEC.BAT files so that it will run every time the computer is booted. This can be somewhat tedious, particularly if you have a large hard drive, because the program can take several minutes to run and will run every time you boot, whether you are starting up the machine for the first time or have just crashed in a Windows application. With the Norton Antivirus, which I recommend, this is not too bad since the scan takes only a few seconds. I found that utilities such as Pro-Scan took too long and therefore I tended not to use them, which defeats the purpose of having virus-protection software in the first place.

Safe hex on the PC

Viruses infect executable files. On the PC, these include files with the .EXE, .COM, .DRV (driver), .OVL and .OVL?, and .SYS (device driver) extensions. Viruses infecting these files will become active only when the files are run or loaded. Viruses can also infect the boot (floppy and hard drive) and partition table (hard drive only) sectors of a disk. In these cases, the virus will become active as soon as the computer boots up. Boot or partition

sector infections can result from booting or attempting to boot off of an infected disk, or by running software that infects the boot or partition sectors.

If your boot or partition table sectors may have become infected, I recommend that you create a bootable antiviral disk by transferring over a system from a known virus-free computer. Install the virus removal utility on the disk and then write-protect it to ensure that your virus removal disk will not itself become infected. It is a good idea to have antiviral boot disks available in both 5.25-inch and 3.5-inch formats, just in case.

If your virus-protection program signals an infection, boot off your removal disk and then run the virus removal utility to disinfect. In many cases, the removal utility can restore infected files to their previous condition, but in some cases they can't. Since viruses infect executables, you can usually restore your software from the original floppy disks.

It is not this simple if you have a partition or boot sector virus and your software cannot repair the sectors. In that case, you will need to restore them. The boot sector can sometimes be restored by using the SYS command from your write-protected floppy. However, this will not always work, and for it to even have a chance you will need to be booting from the same version of the operating system as is on your hard drive. The Norton Antivirus prepares a rescue disk that can be used to restore boot as well as partition sectors. A partition sector restore is particularly difficult without such rescue software.

If components of DOS or Windows have become infected, it is usually wise to replace them rather than merely disinfecting them. If your COMMAND.COM file has been infected, after disinfecting it replace it with a fresh copy. If the invisible files in MS-DOS have been infected, after disinfecting them you can try to replace them by booting from the write-protected floppy and using the SYS command. If you purchased a copy of the DOS 5 upgrade, a simple way to recover once you have run the disinfection software is to run the upgrade again. This will replace your old system files without your having to reformat. If the upgrade saved your old system files, remember that these are useless since they may have been damaged. If your Windows files have become infected, you will need to reinstall Windows.

It is also a good idea to periodically back up important information about your system onto a floppy, such as the CMOS setup, boot blocks, or file allocation table. Utilities such as Norton Antivirus will do this for you. This way if a virus does slip through and damage your hard disk, you may be able to recover.

Since viruses modify the code of the executable software they infect, one way to detect infection is to make a table of software on a disk, compute an integrity check on each file and then recompute this check to see if it has changed. If so, the file may have become infected.

Where can you get hold of antiviral software? Regular updates to antiviral software are posted in comp.binaries.ibm.pc and are also available from EXEC-PC. The most popular programs are Clean, Virus Shield, and VIRx. There are also commercial packages, such as Norton Antivirus and Microcom's Virex.

I recommend The Norton Antivirus, since it is a complete package with vaccine, scanning, and disinfection components, offers an easy to use interface under Windows and DOS, can rescue boot and partition sectors, and can protect against viruses operating over a network. There are also shareware antivirus utilities such as those from McAfee Associates that are very popular. Please consult Appendix B: Choice Products for more information.

Safe hex on the Macintosh

How can you protect yourself against Mac viruses? One way is to install INITs in your system that will search for suspicious behavior. I am fond of Disinfectant, because it is capable of detecting and eradicating many viruses without impairing the use of your computer. Gatekeeper Aid is a useful companion to Disinfectant because it removes the WDEF virus, which can otherwise prove difficult to get rid of because it is so infectious (WDEF infects disks on insertion). There are also commercial utilities such as Symantec Anti-virus

for Macintosh (SAM) and Virex. Since Disinfectant is on a par with these commercial utilities in detection and is also one of the most effective eradicators, it is a very good choice.

Be aware that several popular antiviral packages, including Disinfectant, will not protect you against infection over the network. For this you need Virus Blockade from Jeff Shulman.

In order to use Disinfectant, you need to both install the Disinfectant INIT to detect virus intrusions and to prepare a disk or disks to use when your computer becomes infected. You should also keep a copy of Disinfectant on your hard disk in order to check downloaded files for viruses before running them.

In order to install Disinfectant, double-click on the Disinfectant icon. Disinfectant will then ask you where you want to store it on your hard drive. After you select a location, it will extract itself onto your hard drive:

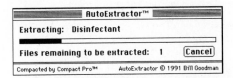

Next, run Disinfectant to install the INIT in your system folder. If you already had an older version of Disinfectant running, you will get the following dialog box:

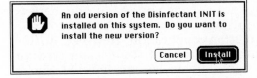

After Disinfectant is done installing the INIT, you will be greeted with a dialog box:

When you reboot, Disinfectant will be running. Should Disinfectant locate any suspicious behavior, it will notify you immediately via a Dialog box so that you can choose to suspend the suspicious activity and investigate further.

Gatekeeper Aid is also on BMUG Utilities 8, and installation is simple. Just decompress the archive from the disk and install Gatekeeper Aid in the System Folder. When you restart, it will load and be set up to run automatically. To check out a file, it saves time to copy the file to a floppy first so Disinfectant will not have to scan an entire hard disk.

Taking the cure

Of course, at some point your computer may become infected anyway, and here a little preparation can go a long way toward easing the pain. If the infection is WDEF, Gatekeeper Aid will alert you with following dialog box:

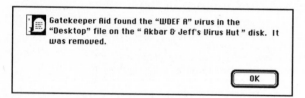

That's the kind of dialog box I like – the problem is already taken care of.

If you have some other virus, you will need to be prepared beforehand. The Disinfectant INIT does not remove viruses – it only detects them. To remove them, you will need to use the Disinfectant application. However, it is possible that the copy of Disinfectant on your hard drive could have become infected. This is why you should keep clean System and Disinfectant floppy disks handy.

Your preparations will vary depending on whether you own a Macintosh with a SuperDrive that can read and write 1.44 Mb diskettes. If you own such a drive, you will be able to fit Disinfectant and a small but functional version of the System and Finder all on one disk. For these purposes it is often easiest to use System 6, booting in Finder mode, since this system will be smaller than System 7 and therefore more likely to fit on a single diskette. In addition, virus eradication with Disinfectant often proceeds more smoothly under the Finder than under Multifinder. Unfortunately, newer Macs will only run with System 7 or 7.1.

After preparing this diskette, you should write-protect (lock) it by moving the tab on the right side of your diskette upward so that the window is open. This will prevent the virus from reinfecting your rescue disk.

If you own an older Macintosh with an 800K floppy drive, you will need to place a clean system and a copy of Disinfectant on separate diskettes and write-protect both of them. You should go with System 6 for this purpose.

When you detect a virus, the first thing you need to do is to shut down the machine and reboot with a clean system on a locked diskette. Even if Gatekeeper Aid has detected and removed the WDEF virus, it is a good idea to **rebuild the desktop** by holding down option-command while rebooting or mounting a diskette. This will ensure that you have a valid Desktop file. Once your system comes up, you will then run Disinfectant, either from the same diskette, or off another locked diskette, in order to disinfect all your volumes.

After you have run Disinfectant, you still need to throw away the system files on all your volumes and reinstall desk accessories and fonts into a clean system.

Although Disinfectant can remove and repair the damage done by many viruses, you may find that some of your applications are irretrievably damaged. If an application that was formerly trouble-free is now crashing, you will need to reinstall that application from the original diskettes. Generally, viruses do not infect data files, although they could conceivably damage these or other files as part of their design.

For more information

USENET groups

| comp.risks | Discussion on computer-related risks |
| comp.virus | Computer virus discussion |

CHAPTER 5:
USING BULLETIN BOARDS

Who you gonna call?

A short history of bulletin boards

The first bulletin board, a joint effort of Randy Seuss and Ward Christensen, went up in Chicago on February 16, 1978, operating on a North Star Horizon 4 Mhz Z-80 CP/M machine with a 5 Mb drive. Written to emulate a cork bulletin board, the system was designed for the posting and reading of messages, with file transfer supported only for system maintenance. Like many other things in the telecommunications world, this "quick hack" caught on and became the paradigm (for better or worse) for virtually every BBS package that has come after it.

According to *Boardwatch Magazine,* there are now at least 100,000 publicly accessible bulletin boards worldwide, with an estimated 10 million users.

What can I do with bulletin boards?

As with Ward Christensen's first system, today's electronic bulletin boards automatically answer phone calls via modem and allow callers to utilize the computer to send and receive messages and files. Some bulletin boards permit more than one person to be connected ("logged on") at a time. This allows for the possibility of real-time games or conversations (called "chats") between two or more users.

While many bulletin boards are general purpose systems, most tend to specialize in one of several ways.

∇ Technical support

These systems are put up by vendors looking to support their particular brand of hardware or software.

∇ Online stores

These systems focus on selling goods or services, often at discount prices.

∇ Special interest

These systems cater to a hobby or professional interest. If done well, these systems can attract callers around the world and become a focal point for discussion on that particular topic. For further information on special interest online resources, please consult Appendix C: Online Resources.

∇ File oriented

These boards specialize in publicly distributable software. They often have gigabytes of storage space and may also mount multiple CD-ROMs. These systems may specialize in software for a particular brand of computer or may cover a wide range of machines. For listings of some of the major file-oriented BBSes, consult Appendix B: Choice Products.

∇ Mail or conference oriented

These systems are usually linked to global computer networks and specialize in offering global electronic mail as well as conferences in which other systems participate.

▽ Chat

This isn't my cup of tea, but for some reason people seem to enjoy typing messages to each other rather than talking at twice the speed over the telephone. More bizarre activities include eating imaginary pizzas online. Personally, virtual Mozarella is something I can do without.

▽ Game playing

I can at least comprehend this type of BBS, even if I don't enjoy it myself. Multiplayer games seem to be a favorite.

How do bulletin boards work?

Bulletin boards can be single line, multi-node or integrated; stand-alone or networked; graphical or textual; audible or silent.

Multi-node versus integrated BBSes

Since microcomputer operating systems were initially single tasking, the first bulletin boards were only capable of answering calls from one or at most two phone lines per machine.

With the advent of multitasking operating systems such as MultiFinder, DESQview, Windows NT, DoubleDOS, and OS/2, it became possible to run multiple copies of the same package on a single CPU. As long as the software is capable of sharing user logs and message bases among tasks, this is workable though by no means elegant. Another way to use single tasking software to handle multiple lines is to use a local area network to allow multiple CPUs to share files located on a central server. Using either approach is said to result in a "multi-node" BBS.

There are also bulletin board packages with their own multitasking built in. These packages allow handling of multiple lines within a single process. The result is much greater efficiency and the ability to handle many lines per CPU. This is the integrated approach.

Stand-alone versus networked

The first bulletin boards operated stand-alone; that is, they did not exchange messages or files with other systems. As a result, only large multiline systems could support active discussion areas.

Starting with FidoNet in 1984, bulletin boards have linked up across the globe. It is now possible for a small system with only a few callers to receive thousands of messages a day from all over the world. For more information on bulletin board networks, please consult Chapter 6: Introduction to Global Networks, Chapter 18: Introduction to FidoNet, and Chapter 19: PCBoard Networks.

Graphical versus textual

Conventional bulletin boards use a text-based interface, which may be partially augmented by the use of ANSI graphics. While allowing for use of color and limited drawing and video attributes, ANSI is an inherently limited graphical medium.

More advanced graphics standards include the North American Presentation Level Protocol Syntax (NAPLPS), the X-Windows protocol (and related protocols such as X-Remote and Alpha-Windows), and the Remote Imaging Protocol (RIP) from TeleGrafix Communications. These graphics standards, while providing the tools to construct user interfaces, do not specify them. This is up to the sysop. RIP is particularly interesting since it supports multimedia.

Packages providing complete user interfaces include FirstClass, NovaLink Pro, TeleFinder, and hiBBS. All use the Macintosh as a server and offer a Macintosh client. FirstClass, NovaTerm, and hi-BBS have also announced support for Windows clients. The FirstClass client supports viewing of multimedia messages including PICTs, sounds, and text, and may in a future release support playback of QuickTime movies.

Audible or silent

Using stored sounds or files transmitted over the modem, bulletin boards are now being heard as well as seen. Sounds can include beeps signifying receipt of mail, voices announcing completion of file transfers, or complex sound or MIDI files. With the adoption of V.FAST modulation and ISDN, real-time playback of MIDI or digitized sound is probably not far off.

Finding bulletin boards

Finding the BBS of your dreams may feel like searching for a needle in a haystack, but there are a number of resources you can consult.

▽ Network lists

BBS networks such as FidoNet maintain listings of participating systems. Since these node lists may be produced by the network software and are critical to the proper functioning of it, they are generally the most complete and up-to-date available.

In order to find a BBS on a particular topic, you can obtain copies of network node lists and search for a particular word in the BBS name, such as "medical," or "collector." For further information on BBS networks, please consult Chapter 6: Introduction to Global Networks, Chapter 18: Introduction to FidoNet, and Chapter 19: PCBoard Networks.

▽ General lists

These are general listings of bulletin board systems, often put together based on input from system operators or BBS users. These lists are generally not as up to date as BBS network listings but will include listings of systems not connected to any network.

▽ Professional lists

These are listings of systems devoted to a profession.

▽ Area code lists

These are listings of systems for a particular area code.

Bulletin boards such as Boardwatch BBS and the Hayes Support BBS and USENET newsgroups such as alt.bbs.lists are good sources to consult if you are looking to obtain any of these lists. *Boardwatch Magazine* also regularly publishes a "List of Lists," giving information on many BBS lists and how to obtain them. The Internet BBS List Archive (`ftp vector.intercon.com, cd /pub/BBS`) is also very good about keeping current versions of various lists, including area code lists.

Logging on to a BBS

After you've found the phone numbers of the system you want to dial, the next step is to log on to the system and obtain an account. As part of this process, there are a few things you need to be aware of.

Manual dialing

Since many bulletin boards have a short life span, a BBS may no longer be operating at the listed number. In many areas, phone numbers are in short supply, so that the local phone company quickly turns over the abandoned BBS number to someone else. The unfortunate recipient then finds his or her phone ringing at all hours of the day and night.

Please do not dial a BBS phone number automatically without first trying the phone number out manually during daytime hours, with the speaker on. If you do find a disconnected system, please report it to the BBS list keeper so that the error can be corrected.

This simple advice will help save innocent people from sleepless nights and may also aid in building bridges to the modemless, who might otherwise view the screeching dialers as a menace to society.

Bulletin Board Lists

Finding the bulletin board of your dreams is not easy, but help is available in the form of regularly updated system lists. Lists of BBSes by area code are posted to the newsgroup alt.bbs.lists.

General lists	List keeper
BBS List archive, many lists	ftp vector.intercon.com, cd /pub/BBS
Boardwatch list of lists	Boardwatch BBS, (303)973-4222
800 #, Hermes, WildCat, PC-Board BBS lists	Hayes BBS, (800)874-2937, (404)446-6336
Computer Shopper BBS List	Computer Shopper BBS, (913)478-3088
THE BBS List	Posted to alt.bbs.lists
	lchang@uoft02.utoledu.edu, AOL: JimJ33
Ameriboards List	Ameriboard, (412)349-6862
US BBS List	available via ftp wuarchive.wustl.edu, get /mirrors/msdos/bbslists/usbbs95.zip
Graphical User Interface BBS list	GUI BBS, (212)876-5885

Network lists	List keeper
Internet BBS list	mail bbs@quartz.rutgers.edu
Internet Public Dialup list	mail info-deli-server@netcom.com, body:SEND PDIAL
NovaLink Pro BBS list	NovaCentral, (714)379-9006
FirstClass BBS list	SoftArc Online, (416)609-2250
TeleFinder BBS list	Narnia-A Telefinder BBS,1:233/11, (217)384-3128
FidoNet nodelist	FidoNet Network Coordinators (see Appendix I)
RIME nodelist	Running Board, (301)229-5623
ILink nodelist	MicroSellar (201)239-1346
WWIV network list	The File Pile BBS, (612)351-0144, login: 0000, password: NETLIST

Professionally oriented lists	List keeper
Stock Market BBSes	Investor's Online Data, (206)285-5359
Medical BBS list	Black Bag BBS (FidoNet 1:150/140), (302)994-3772
Business BBS List	Delight the Customer BBS, (517)797-3740
Legal BBS list	Legal Ease BBS, (509)326-3238
Environmental BBSes	EarthArt BBS, (803)552-4389
Engineering BBS List	The Computer Plumber BBS, (319)337-6723
Ham Radio List	3WINKs BBS, (301)590-9629
Tech Support BBS list	Digicom BBS, (812)479-1310

Area code lists	List keeper
201	dread@micro-c.mcds.com
219, 308, 708, 815	ChicagoLand BBS, (708)403-2826
404	The Oasis, (404)627-2662
408/415/510/707	casey@well.sf.ca.us
805	Missing Link, (805)925-1129

Choosing a password

Immediately after logging on, you will be prompted to enter a password. In choosing your password, please remember:

• Not to use a word in the dictionary or even a variant thereof. Such passwords are vulnerable to dictionary guessing programs.
• Not to use the same password on multiple systems. Sysops, while generally on the up and up, are not all angels. Don't tempt them.
• To change your password regularly.

Validation

When signing on to a bulletin board for the first time you may be asked for information about yourself, including:

• Your name and address
• Work and/or home phone number
• Type of computer or other equipment
• Sex and age

Usually system operators ask these questions in order to verify that you are who you say you are. In theory, this increases user accountability and facilitates cooperation with law enforcement where necessary. Often the logon bulletin provides information on the uses to which this information may be put.

In practice, such questionnaires may fall short of confirming a user's identity. Asking for a user's name and phone number at best allows the operator to determine that a person answering to that name was present at the phone number when the system operator called. For this reason, some sysops now ask for a driver's license as well.

Handles

When logging on to a system for the first time, the software may ask you to specify your handle. A handle is a nickname that a user goes by on a given system. These nicknames may be as innocuous as "Bob," or as suggestive as "The Avenger." The handle may apply to all communications, or only to certain functions such as chatting, messaging, or login listings. On some systems, a user can have more than one handle or can change his or her handle.

Handles are controversial in the online world since they have often been used by misbehaving individuals looking to conceal their identity. As a result entire networks have banned use of handles, and many individuals will not respond to messages coming from handles.

On closer examination, the link between handles and abusive behavior is not clear-cut. Merely allowing handles does not undercut accountability, provided that users are validated. Most problems involving handles have occurred on nonvalidating systems. If used properly, handles provide several benefits:

• User privacy is protected. This is particularly useful for persecuted minorities or those participating in conferences dealing with controversial topics.

• Freer discussion. Users may feel more free to discuss personal issues when the fear of being readily identified is removed.

Use of handles does not in any way constrain the prerogatives of law enforcement. As long as users are validated, law enforcement officials can obtain the real names of handle users suspected of criminal activity (providing they have a proper search warrant or court order).

Privacy

With the passage of the Electronic Communications Privacy Act (ECPA) of 1986, people using electronic communications systems with *the expectation of privacy* may seek legal remedies if their privacy is violated.

Most bulletin boards do not support encryption. Those that do usually support it on the bulletin board (where the message can be read by the sysop prior to encryption) rather than on the user's system (where it may be encrypted prior to transmission to the BBS). As a result, most systems offer little or no guarantees of privacy. To protect themselves from ECPA lawsuits, many sysops now indicate in their logon banners that they do not support private communications as defined under ECPA.

As a result, you should not use bulletin boards to transmit information that you do not wish to become public.

Rules and regulations

At this point in the login process, you may be asked for additional information or informed about any additional rules and regulations.

Additional identification

In addition to general information required of all callers, some systems may require additional information in order to identify callers, obtain increased privileges, or purchase a system membership. This may include:

• Your drivers license (the number or a xerox of the document)
• Credit card number
• Social security number

Caution is advised in answering these questions. At a minimum, systems requesting such information should describe:

• Why the information is needed
• What (if any) restrictions there are on release of the information to third parties
• The history of the system, or references, in order to provide evidence that it is a legitimate and continuing enterprise

Upload/download ratios

In order to ensure that callers contribute something instead of just taking, many sysops implement an upload/download ratio. This means that you must upload one file for every *x* files you download. If the system has a 50:1 ratio, this means you must upload a file for every 50 you download.

Many callers don't like upload/download ratios, and in many cases they encourage callers to upload worthless files in order to get around the limits. A more flexible policy is to count all contributions, including message postings, in the ratio, so that those callers who don't have files to contribute can participate in other ways.

Donations or fees

Most bulletin boards are run as a hobby rather than with the intention of making a profit. Since running a bulletin board is such an expensive hobby, many sysops request a donation to defray expenses before granting full use of the system. Usually you will receive upgraded access privileges within a few days of paying the access fee.

File-transfer tutorial

One of the most popular features of bulletin board software is file transfer. This includes the ability to receive files (downloaded by the user) or send files (uploaded by the user). Some systems support enclosing files within messages to other users; others only support posting of files in public areas, subject to sysop approval.

Downloading (receiving files)

The process by which you transfer software from a bulletin board to your machine (downloading) involves two steps:

• Instructing the bulletin board to transmit the file to you
• Instructing your telecom software to receive the file (not necessary with ZMODEM).

Uploading (sending files)

If you are a shareware author or have a publicly distributable program that isn't available on the bulletin board you're calling, you can contribute this software to the files library. The process by which you send software to a BBS (called uploading) follows these steps:

• Instructing the bulletin board to receive the file from you
• Instructing your telecom software to send the file

What kinds of files would people want to upload and download? If the bulletin board is being used by employees of a company, the files transferred will probably be work-related. These could be anything from complex spreadsheets to word processing documents. In general, any file that you can create on a Macintosh can be transmitted to and from a bulletin board. On hobbyist bulletin boards, two of the most popular things to upload and download are shareware and freeware.

Publicly distributable software

What types of software can be legally transferred using bulletin boards? Software that is publicly distributable, of which there are several subclasses:

∇ Shareware

Software is known as shareware if it requires payment of a fee after a suitable usage period. This fee is not optional! If you use the software, you must pay for it. Shareware authors retain full copyright over their work; there really is no difference between shareware and conventionally distributed software other than the method of distribution.

∇ Crippleware

Since the vast majority of shareware users never pay for the software they use, authors have taken to restricting the capabilities of their publicly distributed products in order to encourage contributions from users. This can be done by requiring a software key to access critical features or by leaving those features out of the publicly distributed product entirely. Such software is known as "demoware" or "crippleware."

∇ Freeware

Publicly distributed software is freeware if no fee is charged for use. This software is still copyrighted; there is just no fee for using it. Since the author retains control over it, he or she has the ability to control how the software is distributed. This may include prohibiting the sale of the software by other persons.

∇ Public Domain

Occasionally, an author places the source or binary code to their software into the public domain. This means that others can use it for

any purpose, such as including parts of the source in a commercial product, without the authors permission. Since placing software into the public domain is an extreme grant of rights, few authors go this far; instead most retain the copyright in order to ensure that their work is not exploited.

Compression formats

Files on bulletin boards and online services are often compressed in order to save hard drive space and time in downloading.

Since compression is so common, one of the first things you should do after becoming an active telecommunicator is to obtain the latest versions of the various compression and decompression utilities.

For further information on compression formats, please consult Chapter 24: Compression Primer.

Uploading a file and how sysops check files

Before uploading a file to a bulletin board, ask yourself:

• **Is the file publicly distributable?** Check the About box and/or documentation to make sure. Sometimes an author may not want his or her program distributed over BBSes, or he or she may want its distribution limited to certain BBSes, even if it is shareware. Please respect the wishes of the author.

• **Is the file already on the BBS?** Check the file listing to make sure it isn't. If it is on the BBS, is your version later than the version on the BBS? If it is, then you can still upload it.

• **Have you included the full documentation?** Most programs are *not* very self-explanatory. Please put the program and documentation together in a single file. If you obtained the file as a single archive, upload it again with no changes or omissions.

Compression Software Guide

In the course of telecommunicating, you will often see files with extensions of .ARC, .ARJ, .CPT, .PIT, .SEA, .SIT, .ZIP and .ZOO. These files have been compressed by various compression programs. When you download these files to your system, you will need to use a decompression program in order to use them. Here is a table of the programs you will need to decompress files with the various extensions. These programs are available on the EXEC-PC BBS.

File extension	Compression decompression	Mac decompression	PC decompression
.ARC	ARC, PKARC (PC)	ArcPop	ARCE
.ARJ	ARJ	UnArjMac	ARJ
.CPT	Compact Pro	Extractor	EXTRACTOR
.DD	Disk Doubler	DD Extractor	
.LZH	LHARC (PC)	MacLHARC	LHARC
.LHA	MacLHA		
.gz	GNU Zip, GNU Unzip	none	GNU Unzip
.HQX	BINHEX 4.0	BINHEX 4.0	BINHEX
.IMAGE	Apple Diskcopy Image format	Apple Diskcopy	
.PAK	PAK	none on Mac	PAK
.PIT	PackIt	UnStuffIt Deluxe	UNPACKIT
.SEA	Compact Pro, StuffIt	self-extracting	
.SHAR	Shar (UNIX)	UnShar	UNSHAR
.SIT	StuffIt, StuffIt Deluxe	StuffIt Lite	UNSIT
.SITD	StuffIt Deluxe	StuffIt Lite	
.TAR	Tar	MacTar	TAR
.ZIP	PKZIP (PC), MacZIP (Mac)	unZip	PKUNZIP
.ZOO	ZOO (PC)	MacBooz	ZOO
.z	pack, unpack (UNIX only)		
.Z	compress (PC, Mac, UNIX)	MacCompress	UNCOMPRESS

• **Have you checked the file for viruses?** If you are not using antiviral software, you are not protecting yourself or the other users on the bulletin board from viruses. Please practice safe hex! If you are not sure that the file is virus-free, please don't upload it. More information on viruses is contained in Chapter 4: Safe Hex.

• **Have you compressed the file using an acceptable compression package?** Most systems accept files only in certain formats. The most commonly accepted formats for the Mac are StuffIt or StuffIt Deluxe, Compactor, Compact Pro, and for the PC, PKZIP, or ARC. Please do not upload files with unacceptable compression methods, as the sysops will just have to uncompress them and compress them with an acceptable program. Sometimes sysops just throw these files out. Also, please do not

upload programs in self-extracting archives, since this increases their size and wastes space on the BBS.

All these rules seem like a lot to ask, but sysops have access to lots of shareware and public-domain software from other sources that is guaranteed to be free of these problems. It is generally simpler for the sysops to compress the files themselves and put them onto the BBS than it is for them to process files that don't obey the rules. Please be kind to your sysop and follow the preceding directions.

Messaging

Message areas on a BBS can be local, regional, or international in scope. Messages posted in local areas stay within the BBS and are not transmitted to other systems. If a conference is described as being part of OneNet, FidoNet, ILink, SmartNet, Intellec, RBBSNet, USENET, or RIME, or you see the term EchoMail or Net News describing a conference, this means that your message will be transmitted to other systems.

Regional conferences are only transmitted within the metropolitan area. Other conferences are transmitted nationwide and possibly worldwide. For example, MAC4SALE is a FidoNet conference currently restricted to Zone 1 (North America). FidoNet conferences such as MACDEV or ECHOMAC are transmitted worldwide.

The local message area is the place to ask questions of sysops, inquire about files, and talk about local events in the area or on the BBS. If your message would have little value to a reader on another system, put it in the local area.

On most networks, there are also regional conferences. For example, on FidoNet in the Bay Area there is a Macintosh conference called BAYMAC; in the New York metropolitan area it is called METROMAC. On USENET, there are Bay Area conferences such as ba.announce. If you are trying to sell or buy some equipment locally, if you are commenting on something going on in the region (spare us the politics, please!), or if you would just like your question to be answered by someone in your region, post it in a regional conference.

Etiquette

When posting messages on bulletin boards or online services there are a few things you should keep in mind:

∇ Don't post in upper case

STATEMENTS IN UPPER CASE are reserved for shouting.

∇ Make your emotional state clear

Electronic messages often give inadequate clues as to the emotional state of the poster. Was a particular message sarcastic, or straightforward? Intended as a joke, or dead

serious? It's sometimes hard to tell. This has spawned the use of symbols known as Emoticons (covered in Chapter 25) that annotate the emotional state of the poster.

A few of the emoticons and acronyms in common use are:

:-) Joke	ROTFL Laughing
;-) Tongue in cheek	IMHO In my humble opinion
:-(Frowning	BRB Be right back

∇ Check your grammar, spelling, and punctuation

Other people will be making judgments about your level of education and intelligence based on your postings. Until they meet you and get the real scoop, why not fool them into thinking you're smarter than you really are?

∇ Keep it short and sweet

Other people are paying to read your messages, so make sure that you're giving them their money's worth. Although most conferencing software has the ability to quote an original message, you should only include the relevant portion that you are responding to, not the whole message.

∇ Words have consequences

Words can do financial and emotional damage. Behind every computer on the network is a person with feelings. Use your time online to inform, communicate, and recreate, not to add more unpleasantness to a world that already has enough.

Also remember that when you post a message to a global conference, anyone could be listening to what you say. Anyone. And there are few limits on what they can do with the information. A statement made on a few seconds thought can be stored in a retrieval system for a lifetime. Therefore it is a good idea to think carefully about whether what you are posting truly represents your point of view, and if so, whether you might be harmed by communicating those thoughts.

▽ Consider your audience

Anything you say in one of the international message areas will be echoed to thousands of people throughout the world, who will look at you as a representative of your system. This puts a very heavy weight of responsibility on your shoulders. If your message is inappropriate (inquiring about a file on your system in the USENET Mac Programmer's message area), confused (asking about where the IBM PC files are on a Macintosh BBS), or unclear on the concept (asking why you can't use your phone line while you're logged on), you will leave a poor impression of your group and its membership throughout the computer-connected world.

If you're not sure that sysops in Japan would like to read your posting, put it in the local message area. Everyone will be happier that way. You may wish to make your message private, but you should realize that on most bulletin board systems, private messages aren't really private, since sysops can and do read them. However, making a message private does help keep the local message area uncluttered and is recommended if your topic is of narrow interest.

Networked message areas

Aside from the local conferences, there are also areas that are connected to global networks such as USENET, FidoNet, RIME, or OneNet. Although the technology of these networks is different, the effect is the same – a message sent from one BBS is relayed to many other systems.

USENET offers many conferences on recreational as well as highly technical subjects, and participants are often highly educated in technical fields such as computer science or electrical engineering. Although they are often bright, they are also very opinionated and can nitpick over obscure points for hundreds of messages on end. On the other hand, they are also likely to know the answer to your question about undocumented Windows calls. For more information on USENET, please consult Chapter 12: USENET.

FidoNet is the world's largest BBS network, with over 22,000 public nodes worldwide and possibly as many private nodes. It's anarchic, feisty, and totally out of control, but I like it anyway. (After all, I'm from Berkeley.)

FidoNet users are also highly opinionated and given to arguing with each other ad nauseam. That's why they pronounce it "Fight-O-Net!" It didn't used to be that way until the more popular FidoNet conferences (like the Macintosh conference, called ECHOMAC) became so large that you could barely keep up with the traffic. Most FidoNet conferences are open to the public and may be carried by any node that chooses to do so.

RIME is the network of bulletin boards running PostLink software. It's not nearly as large as FidoNet, but it is growing rapidly.

OneNet, a relatively new network of FirstClass bulletin boards, is heavily oriented toward the Macintosh.

How to read messages efficiently

Experienced BBSers save time online in several ways. One way is to write a program (called a "script") to log on to the BBS, read messages while capturing to disk, and log off. White Knight, MacIntercomm, and Microphone II are general-purpose communications programs that support scripting. Writing scripts is not difficult since packages such as Microphone can watch you log on and translate your actions into scripts.

Another approach is to keep a downloaded message file on your hard disk and index it with ON Location. ON Location is a fast and easy way to keep track of a million bits of information.

The last way is to use specialized software known as "message readers," "point mailers," or "UUCP software." For more information on this software, please consult the Chapter 16: UNIX to UNIX Copy, Chapter 18: Points, and Chapter 20: Message Readers.

Introduction to message readers and point mailers

Using message readers you log on to your BBS as you would normally and then you download all your new messages in compressed form with an efficient protocol such as ZMODEM. After logging off, you decompress the messages and use special message-reading software to read and reply to them. When you want to send replies, you log on again and this time upload the new messages.

Message readers use several formats for messages. The QWK format is currently supported by WildCat!, PCBoard, Maximus, Remote Access, and TBBS, among others; XRS format is supported by QuickBBS and Remote Access.

Individual BBS packages may also have custom message readers, using their own proprietary packet format. For example, TeleFinder offers an offline mail package called TeleFinder Pro.

More Information on message readers is contained in Chapter 20: Message Readers, and in Appendix B: Choice Products.

Another approach to improving efficiency is to use a FidoNet point mailer such as EZPoint/BinkleyTerm (PC); Copernicus, COUNTERPoint, or MacWoof (Mac); or a UUCP mailer such as Waffle/Helldiver, FSUUCP or UULINK (PC) or UUPC or uConnect (Mac). These programs log you on to the BBS using network protocols, get your messages and requested files, (usually in compressed form), and log off. Copernicus and COUNTERPoint also have various options for selecting and filtering out messages. While doing some statistics on the posting rate of point mail users, I found that these users tend to post three or four times as many messages as nonpoint users. Some would say that this implies their efficiency has increased. More information on point mailers is contained Chapter 18: Point Software.

COUNTERPoint v2.1 supports both the QWK packet format and the FidoNet packet format. As a result, COUTERPoint can be used either as a message reader or a point reader.

Graphical BBS sampler

On the next few pages are screen shots of the graphical interfaces used in FirstClass, TeleFinder, hi-BBS, and NovaTerm. There are also examples of NAPLPS and RIP graphics.

FirstClass server runs on the Macintosh while offering clients for both the Macintosh and Windows. FirstClass allows the system operator to customize icons and background PICTs as well as to add sounds. The added resources reside in a settings file that is unique for each system you will call. MAGIC has taken full advantage of these features to create a very aesthetically pleasing BBS.

The TeleFinder interface is so much like the Finder that at a glance it's almost hard to tell that you're using a BBS at all. As a result, it is very easy for beginners to pick up.

hi-BBS offers an iconic interface for the Macintosh and Windows that centers primarily around mail.

NovaLink Professional v3.0 is a BBS construction set. In NovaView mode, system operators drag and drop function icons into folders in order to create the interface, which users then see when they log on.

The NAPLPS graphics examples come from the Old Colorado Communications system run by Dave "Read my NAPLPS" Hughes. The Roger's Bar and Cursor Cowboy Song examples are actually animations that are remarkably compact (each is less than 5K). The Japanese and Cyrllic text are examples of the multilingual support built into NAPLPS.

RIP is an emerging graphics standard created by TeleGrafix that is supported by BBS software such as WILDCAT!, TBBS, PCBoard, Searchlight, and Major BBS, as well as terminal programs such as QMODEM Pro and TELIX. RIP currently supports transfer of text and images. Graphics can be created in popular formats and converted to RIP, or can be drawn in programs such as RIPdraw or WinRIP. RIP v2.0 will support digital sounds and fonts, including conversion of Adobe Type 1 and TrueType fonts to RIP format. It will also support VGA/full color.

What if you want to try out these systems for yourself? FirstClass, TeleFinder, hi-BBS and NovaTerm clients are available free of charge and are available for download from BBSes or over the Internet.

To view RIP graphics you can purchase one of the commercial programs that supports it, or you can use RIPterm, a free implementation from TeleGrafix. For a listings of shareware NAPLPS terminal programs, consult Appendix B: Choice Products. For a listing of graphical BBSes, consult Appendix G. A complete description of the features of the FirstClass client is included in *The BMUG Online Services Reference*, available from BMUG, Inc., and the MailCom FTP archive. For lists of graphical BBSes, please consult Appendix G: Graphical BBSes.

Bulletin board Q&A

How do sysops spend so much time online? Do you have jobs and family, or are you just bums?

We're ex-bums, actually. In Berkeley, social shame accrues to those who give up being perpetual graduate or undergraduate students and get real jobs. Most sysops I know are gainfully employed. Some even have spouses and children and would appear on the surface to be average citizens like you. They pay their taxes, too.

Someone on our BBS uses the name "Darth Vader." Why?

Sysops and their users have a relationship that is in many aspects similar to that between professionals and their clients. Sysops often find out a considerable amount of information about their callers, and most are responsible about keeping this information in confidence. However, the sysop/user relationship is not a privileged one under the law, and therefore you do not receive the protections in using an online service that you might in consulting a priest or lawyer. Be careful of using the electronic medium as a confessional, since your statements may be permanently recorded.

On many systems you have the right to use a "handle," or a pseudonym, when posting messages. Since unauthorized users have often posted obnoxious messages on global networks using handles, use of pseudonyms is often frowned upon. However, as long as you give the system operator your real name and address, and behave responsibly, there should be no cause for concern.

I called a BBS last week and an elderly woman answered the phone. What's going on?

There are some who say that like a boat, the two best days in a sysop's life are starting the BBS and shutting it down. And like a boat, a neglected BBS doesn't stay in running order for long. Naturally this enormous sink of time and money doesn't go unnoticed by family members. In order to remain married and paying off the mortgage, many system operators decide to give up their systems. I calculated a few years back that the average Bay Area BBS remained in operation less than 18 months.

Unfortunately, phone companies have a nasty habit of immediately turning over the BBS phone number to someone else, before word can get around that the BBS has closed down. The result is a lot of annoying phone calls for the unlucky individual who inherits the phone number.

A similar problem may arise with recycled Internet Protocol (IP) addresses, since Internet BBSes seem to have a fairly short lifespan as well. Internet BBSes are discussed in Chapter 15: Bulletin Boards and the Internet.

I am thinking of converting my BBS over to a graphical interface. What should I be aware of?

Expect a big increase in the login time per user, and the number of postings. Graphical BBSes typically allow users to do other things while downloading, like posting and reading messages, and as a result users will be more active in the message areas. Users will also log on more often, since graphical systems are easier to use. The added postings and activity levels will require more modems and disk space than with a textual BBS. My rule of thumb is to increase both phone lines and disk space by 50 percent.

The FirstClass Interface

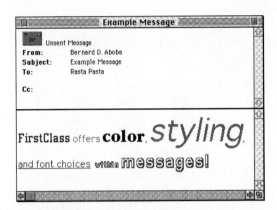

Messaging

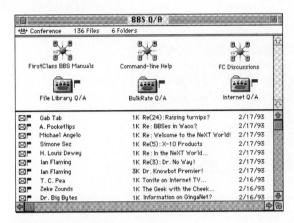

Conferencing

Forms

Résumé

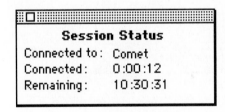

Session status

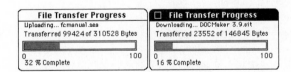

Multiple simultaneous activities

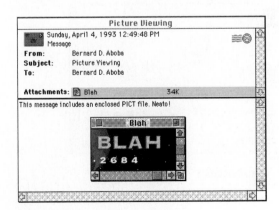

Multi-media file attachments

Do You Believe In MAGIC?
(MAGIC, (416)288-1767)

Logon screen

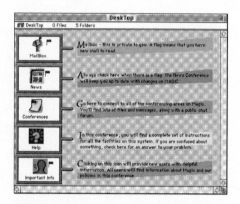

Main menu

Classified ads

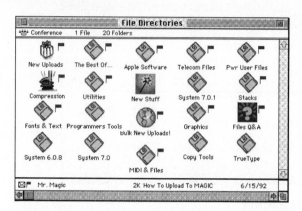

Files areas

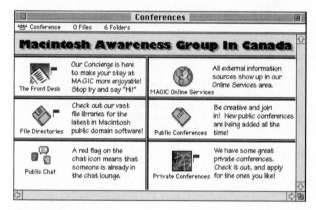

Conference menu

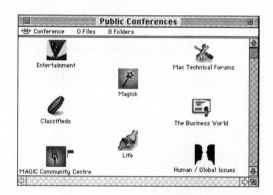

Public conferences

The TeleFinder Interface
(Spider Island BBS, (714)730-5785)

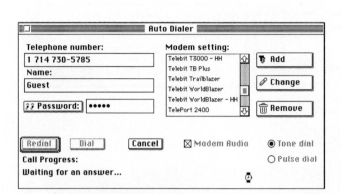

Dialing

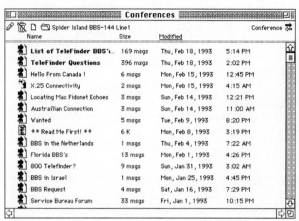

Conferencing

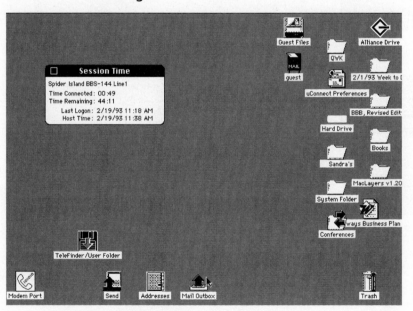

TeleFinder desktop

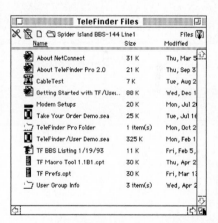

File area

The hi-BBS Interface
(XBR BBS, (514)489-0445)

GUEST Login (password: GUEST)

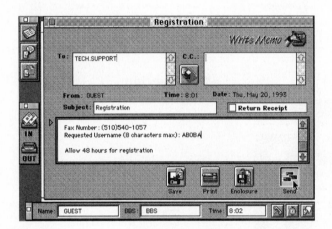

Registration

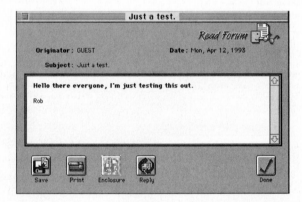

Mail

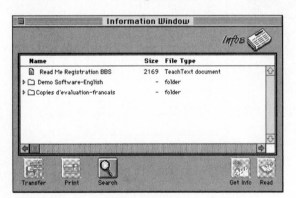

Conferencing

NovaLink Pro – The NovaView Interface

NovaLink Pro v3.0 is a graphical BBS construction set that lets you drag and drop icons to create custom systems. As a result, no NovaLink Pro v3.0 system is alike, but all are composed of the icons given below. Below is an example system built from these tools.

Menu	File Library	Message Forum
Product Library	External	Vote
Send Mail	Read Mail	Send Feedback
Send Document	Send Doc Feedback	List Users
Chat Request	Node Chat	Conference
Jump	Disconnect	Run Script
Display File	File Download	Return
Newscan	Subscribe	Edit Password
Edit Term	Print time	List nodes
Where is user	Send bulletin	Edit batch list
Tree	Messages to me	

The NovaView Interface (con't)
(NovaCentral, (714)379-9006)

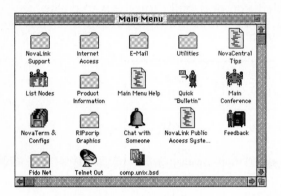

Main menu view

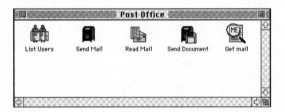

Mail-related icons

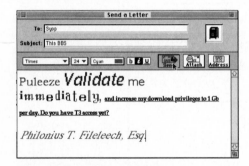

Messaging with color, fonts, and text styles

Folder Views

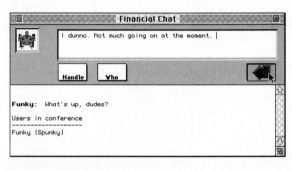

Online chatting

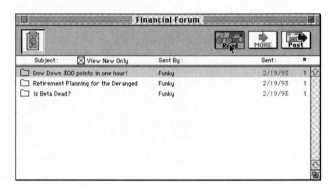

Conferencing

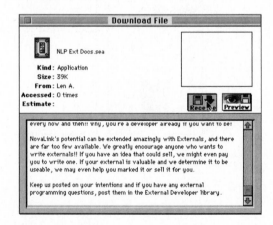

Downloading

NAPLPS Graphics
(Old Colorado Communications, (719)636-2040)

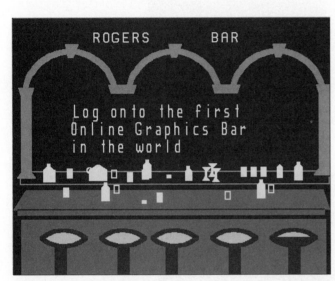

Roger's Bar

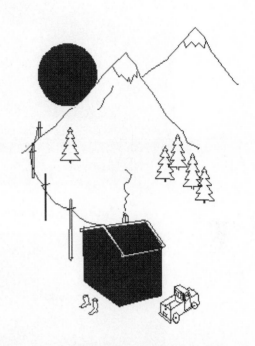

The Cursor Cowboy's Song

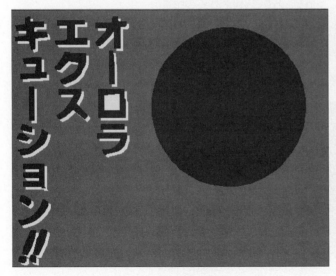

Japanese

Cyrillic

RIP Graphics

Mustang Software HQ! BBS, (805)395-0650

RIPterm by TeleGrafix

Advanced Designs BBS, (708)978-2777

Do you have advice for someone looking to run a BBS as a business?

Yes. Some thoughts:

0. Think twice. Even if you're certain that your BBS will succeed, the reality is that only a fraction of new bulletin boards make money.

1. It's the information, stupid. There are now more than 100,000 publicly accessible bulletin boards. What information can you put online that cannot easily be duplicated? If you couldn't base a publishing or consulting business on this unique advantage, a BBS probably won't fly either.

2. It's the accessibility, stupid. Callers want to be able to dial in and connect reliably, time after time. This means you'll need lots of phone lines and high quality modems, to prevent busy signals and avoid hassles. You'll also need a Univeral Power Supply (UPS), and a spare machine and serial board. Also look for a backup unit, and BBS software that supports rapid backups.

3. It's the user interface, stupid. Make your BBS easy to get around, and more people will want to use it. An interface doesn't have to be graphical to be good, although it certainly helps.

4. It's the billing, stupid. If your software can't handle credit cards, or automate new memberships or renewals, you won't be able to make money. It's that simple. You should also be able to bill by the hour, by usage of particular services, by time of day, or for downloading of particular files.

5. Make the system globally accessible. To build a large user base, callers must be able to reach your system economically. This means making your system accessible via a packet switching network, such as an X.25 network or the Internet.

6. Rely on standards. Demand that your BBS software support established standards. For networking, this means FidoNet, QWK, UUCP, Novell or TCP/IP. For compression it means ARC, PKZIP, StuffIt or Compact Pro. For

terminal emulation it means VT100, ANSI, RIP or NAPLPS.

7. Test for interoperability, don't assume it. Don't trust vendor claims of interoperability. Test before purchasing.

8. Design for growth. Look for BBS software that can be maintained via a script, offers an unlimited user license, and stores messages in a database rather than in individual files. Also go for disk drive interfaces (such as SCSI) that can easily add capacity, and serial boards that support eight or more ports.

9. Don't underestimate the costs. Graphical BBSes without message reader support can double or triple the system load. For such systems, capital investment for equipment, software, modems and phone lines is approximately $10 per user. For RIP, NAPLPS or character-based software, it is $5-7 per user.

10. Purchase software based on maintainability, reliability, scalability and support, not price or platform. An inexpensive BBS is no bargain if it can't be easily maintained, is constantly crashing, can't handle large user bases or isn't well supported. Buy only from vendors who treat customers with respect.

For more information

BBS-related conferences on USENET

alt.bbs	General BBS conferences
alt.bbs.ads	BBS advertisements
alt.bbs.allsysop	Sysop conference
alt.bbs.first-class	FirstClass BBS software
alt.bbs.internet	BBSes on the Internet
alt.bbs.lists	Lists of BBSes
alt.bbs.lists.d	Lists of BBSes
alt.bbs.metal	Metal BBS package
alt.bbs.pcboard	PCBoard BBS software
alt.bbs.pcbuucp	PCBUUCP gateway for PCBoard
alt.bbs.searchlight	Searchlight BBS software
alt.bbs.unixbbs	UNIX BBSes in general
alt.bbs.unixbbs.uniboard	The Uniboard UNIX BBS
alb.bbs.uupcb	The UUPCB gateway for PCBoard
alt.bbs.waffle	Waffle BBS package
comp.bbs.misc	Miscellaneous BBS discussion
comp.bbs.waffle	Another Waffle forum

CIVIC AND COMMUNITY NETWORKING

The new role of the bulletin board

Bulletin boards and global computer networks have made it possible to link users worldwide based on professional interests or affinities.

Technical advances have also brought us community computing systems, bulletin boards focussed on local issues, but big enough to get a sizable fraction of the community online.

Community computing systems differ from traditional bulletin boards in several ways. They are typically designed around the metaphor of a city, rather than the conventional BBS division into message and file areas. This allows areas of the system to be devoted to local governments, K12 programs, small businesses, community activities and entertainment. Community computing systems also offer access to resources such as databases or online libraries, and support public access terminals, which are placed in public libraries, cafes, schools, or even post offices. The resulting diversity of uses and access points encourages public participation.

The key to a successful community computing system is building a wide base of support. Organizers typically recruit participation by local governments, schools, and professional associations. They also adhere to community standards so as to avoid controversy. Few systems allow unrestricted use of `ftp` or `telnet`, since they are "family-oriented" and do not compete with general Internet service providers. Adult material, if present, is segregated in a "red-light district."

For many people, community computing systems are the first bulletin boards they've ever used. This is partly because community computing systems are so much more visible than traditional BBSes, only a fraction of which are listed in any directory. If community computing systems have a "killer application," it is access to social service agencies and professionals such as doctors, lawyers, and accountants. Professional advice, while badly needed, is too expensive for many people, who may wait until it is too late to get help. Community computing systems make it possible for professionals to publicize their practices while serving the public. On the Cleveland Free-Net there is now a waiting list for doctors and lawyers looking to participate.

The Cleveland Free-Net, founded by Dr. Tom Grundner, was the first community computing system, and the prototype for more than a dozen Free-Nets that have followed. The Free-Nets offer accounts at no charge (hence the name "Free-Net") and together comprise the National Public Telecomputing Network (NPTN). Free-Nets are directly connected to the Internet and are typically run as nonprofits, with support coming from a variety of sources, including the business community, local government, and foundations.

However, the Free-Nets are not the only model for community computing. Systems such as NovaLine are run for profit. Cupertino City Net is run as a nonprofit, but charges access fees. Hawaii FYI, Oakland InfoAccess or Santa Monica PEN are run by state or local governments.

Virtually all systems (with the exception of Hawaii FYI, which has a $500,000 annual budget) are run on budgets of $100,000 a year or less, relying heavily on volunteers. While anecdotal evidence is more abundant than hard data, community enthusiasm for these systems is one indication that they are probably doing something right.

On the following pages, we provide a tour of some of the nation's community computing systems.

The Cleveland Free-Net, Cleveland, Ohio

The Cleveland Free-Net is more than an online service; it is the birthplace of the community computing movement and the National Public Telecomputing Network, the computing equivalent of the National Public Broadcasting System.

Founded by Dr. Tom Grundner in 1986, the focus of the Cleveland Free-Net is the delivery of social services. Participation from small businesses is also strong. For information on the history of the Cleveland Free-Net and the NPTN, please consult Chapter 31: Free-Neting, and Chapter 32: How the NPTN Came To Be.

The Cleveland Free-Net's Freeport software is available for $1 to anyone willing to abide by the license terms. The software license requires that the system be operated as a nonprofit and offer free access to all users. It must also be backed by a university, government, or major corporation, and guarantee salary support for necessary staff. Those interested in this software offer should write or call:

T. M. Grundner, Ed.D., President, NPTN, Box 1987, Cleveland, OH 44106; Voice: (216)368-2733; Fax: (216)368-5436; Internet: tmg@nptn.org.

How to get an account

If you try the Cleveland Free-Net and like it, but don't live within a local call of Cleveland, get an account with a packet-switching service. Since your usage will largely consist of sending and reading mail (Free-Net doesn't have much to download), consider one of the less expensive packet-switching services such as PC Pursuit. Fees will be $1 to $1.50 per hour at 2400 bps. For further information on packet switching networks, see Chapter 21: How to Save Money on Your Phone Bill.

To get an account on the Cleveland Free-Net, you have to answer a few questions. About a week later, they'll send you a form to fill out to confirm your information. Three or four weeks after that, they'll send you a letter with your account number and password.

A sample session is shown below:

```
ATDT 12163683888
CONNECT 2400

        Case Western Reserve University
         Information Network Services
        Report problems to:
               nic@po.cwru.edu  or  nic@cwru
        To get help:
               CWRU-TS1> ?

Translating "FNCOM12.CWRU.EDU"...domain server
(129.22.4.1) [OK]
Trying CWNS1.INS.CWRU.EDU (129.22.8.43)... Open
CWRU INS 4.3 BSD (cwns1) (ttype)
```

```
Are you:
        1. A registered user
        2. A visitor
Please enter 1 or 2: 2
Would you like to:
        1. Apply for an account
        2. Explore the system
        3. Exit the system

Please enter 1, 2 or 3: 1
Last login: Tue Apr  2 21:49:19 from psuvm.psu.edu
        <<< FREE-NET ADDRESS TAKER >>>

FOR USERS WHO HAVE HAD ACCOUNTS PREVIOUSLY: User IDs have
been set back to the original password you received in
the mail. If you do not know your original password, log
on as a guest and apply for an account;indicate your ID
number, leave your address, and your original password
will be sent to you via US Mail.

Are you affiliated with CWRU as a student, faculty, or
staff? [y/n] n

Enter your first name: Bernard
Enter your last name: Aboba
Enter your middle initial: D
Enter your address, city, state, and ZIP code. You will
be given two lines for the street address. (the second is
optional)

Street Address: 1442A Walnut St. #62
City: Berkeley
State: CA
Zip Code: 94709
Phone Number: (510)555-1212

This is the information you have given:

NAME
Bernard D Aboba
1442A Walnut St. #58
Berkeley, CA  94709

PHONE NUMBER
(415)549-2684
If this information is correct, type "y": y
mailing this information to the administrator...done.
Thank you.
[Connection to FNCOM12.CWRU.EDU closed by foreign host]
```

Getting on over the Internet

The Free-Net is accessible over the Internet. This is only useful if you already have an Internet account on another system. To get to Free-Net, **telnet** to freenet-in-a.cwru.edu, freenet-in-b.cwru.edu, or freenet-in-c.cwru.edu, and login: **fnguest**.

```
% telnet freenet-in-a.cwru.edu
Trying...
Connected to cwns16.INS.CWRU.Edu.
Escape character is '^]'.
CWRU INS 4.3 BSD (cwns16) (ttyp3)
```

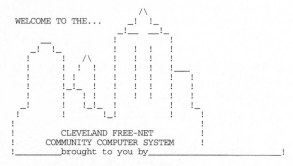

```
             WELCOME TO THE...
```

```
      Case Western Reserve University
      Community Telecomputing Laboratory

Are you:
        1. A registered user
        2. A visitor

Please enter 1 or 2: 1

Enter your user ID (in lower case) at the Login: prompt.
Then enter your password when asked. Note that the
password will not print on the screen as you type it.

Login: ar740
Password:
```

Other Free-Net Systems

Free-Net	Internet address	Phone number
Buffalo Free-Net	telnet freenet.hsc.colorado.edu, login: guest	(716)645-6128
Denver Free-Net	telnet freenet.buffalo.edu, login: guest	(303)270-4865
Heartland Free-Net (Peoria)	telnet heartland.bradley.edu, login: bbguest	(309)674-1100
Lorain County Free-Net	telnet freenet.lorain.oberlin.edu, login: guest	(216)366-9721
Medina County Free-Net		(216)723-6732
National Capital Free-Net	telnet freenet.carleton.ca login: guest	(613)780-3733
Tri-State Online (Cincinnati)	telnet cbos.uc.edu, login: visitor	(513)579-1990
Victoria Free-Net	telnet freenet.victoria.bc.ca login: guest	(604)595-2300
Wellington CityNet	telnet kosmos.wcc.govt.nz login: guest	
Youngstown Free-Net	telnet yfn.ysu.edu, login: visitor	(216)742-3072

Oakland InfoAccess

InfoAccess is an experimental single-line WILDCAT! BBS run by the City of Oakland which focusses on providing information on city services, and the activities of the city council. There is talk of eventually putting the system on the Internet.

Conferences areas include:

```
0) Oakland News
1) Planning Comission
2) Emergency Services
3) City Employees Only
6) CityLine information services
```

File areas include:

```
1) Announcements for Jobs
2) Departmental phone listing
3) City Council Agenda Files
4) Planning Comission
5) Emergency Services
6) Police services
7) Oakland News Bulletin files
```

The system also contains an Oakinfo section with information about city services:

```
InfoAccess Bulletin Menu
  [1]   InfoAccess Menu
 [50]   Library Menu
[100]   City Council/ORA Menu
[150]   City Planning Menu
[200]   Permit Processing Menu
[300]   Emergency Services Menu
[350]   Oakland School Board Meeting Agenda
[400]   Cultural Arts Menu
[425]   Energy Crisis Intervention Program
[450]   Oakland Police Menu
[800]   City Phone Menu
[999]   Special Services

Bulletins updated: ALL
Enter bulletin # [1..999], [R]elist menu, [N]ew, [ENTER]
to quit?
```

Cupertino City Net

Cupertino City Net, which went online in September 1993, began as the idea of Robert Kim, a computer consultant formerly employed by the City of Cupertino. After developing a demonstration system, he showed it to Wally Dean, Cupertino City Council member, who got excited about it and formed a task force including representatives from government, education (K12 and local colleges), and local businesses.

Rather than being funded by local government, the system is primarily funded by memberships, which cost $20/year.

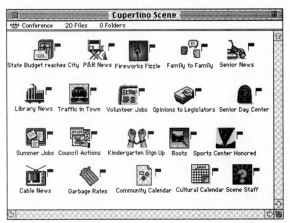

Michigan NovaLine

NovaLine is the world's largest Macintosh BBS, running NovaLink Professional v3.0 with 50 lines. The system runs on a Quadra 950 with 2.4 Gb of hard disk space and AT&T 14.4 Kbps fax modems.

NovaLine is a commercial service emphasizing Michigan, and concentrating on organizations and associations. The system began as an attempt by Dynamic Training Corp. to interlink their clients and provide databases on business issues. In beta testing various systems, clients found a graphical interface much easier to use than either a command line interface or block graphics. It was also clear that their proposed system would need extensive development of external programs. As a result, they chose NovaLink Professional v3.0, which uses a Macintosh as a server.

Services include access to laws relating to small business; federal and state forms, including I9 and W2 forms; online assistance from Human

Resources, Legal, and Marketing personnel; a nationwide employment service; and Night on the Town, a guide to Michigan theatres, limosine services, shows and sporting events. There are also electronic mail boxes for the Governor, Michigan state legislators, congresspeople, and senators. A legislative alert service keeps users informed on upcoming legislation. The system also offers online seminars, classified ads, chatting and 800 number access.

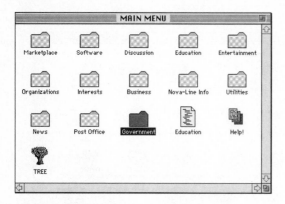

Hawaii FYI

Hawaii FYI is one of the most extensive (and expensive) community computing systems operating today. Funded at $500K per year by the state legislature, the system covers everything from agriculture to activities of state government to access to interactive services such as Hawaii Online. Many of the services are available free of charge, but others are billed and require registration.

Services available include:

* - Secondary Logon required
$ - Registered Fee-Based Service

LEGISLATIVE INFO SERVICES	%ACCESS
ACTION LINE - KHON-TV	%ACTLINE
KSBE ALTERNATIVE ED	%AEP
MILK	%AGMILK
BOARDS AND COMMISSIONS	%BRDCOMM
BUSINESS REGISTRATION	%BREGS
CALENDAR	%CALENDAR
CAPITOL DIRECTORY	%CAPDIR
CHALLENGER CENTER	%CCH
SCHOOL/SCHOLARSHIP INFO	%CKINFO
COLLEGE & CAREER INFO	%CNCINFO
CIVIL DEFENSE	%CVLDEF
DBED BBS	%DBED
STATE DBED ANNUAL RPRT 1989	%DBEDAR
CONSUMER DIAL	%DCCADIAL
DISHING UP LEAD	%DISHLEAD
DLIR INFO SERVICE	%DLIRINFO
COASTAL WATER QUALITY	%DOHWATER
DRIVER'S RENWL TEST Q&A	%DRVTEST
EFFICIENT LIGHTING	%EFFLIGHT
HI. DBED ENERGY DIV.	%ENERDIV
ENERGY INFORMATION SVC	%ENERGY
ENERGY TIPS	%ENERTIPS
FACTS & FIGURES 1990	%FANDF
FISH OF HAWAII	%FISHEDMO
HAWAII'S FISHING LIMITS	%FISHSNL
FYI BULLETIN BOARD	%FYIBBS
FYI CHATLINE SERVICE	%FYICHAT
DBED MONTHLY GAS WATCH REPT	%GASWATCH
GEOTHERMAL ENERGY	%GEOTHRML
GET MORE HAWAII	%GMHPG
NEWS FROM THE GOVERNOR	%GOVNEWS
HEPATITIS B	%HEPB
HHSAA LEAGUES SCHEDULES	%HHSAA
HAWAII INC BBS	%HINCBBS
HOKULE'A INFORMATION SERVICE	%HOKULEA
HAWAII ONLINE	%HOL
SAVING ENERGY & $ AT HOME	%HOMENER
HONOLULU MAG RESTAURANT GUID	%HONMAG
PUBLIC LIBRARY SYSTEM	%HSPLS
HI SOFTWARE SVC CTR BBS	%HSSC
HSTEC PRACTICE TESTS	%HSTEC
*INTERACT!	%INTERACT
LANDLORD-TENANT CODE	%LANTENCD
PRPSD COMM LAUNCH FCLTY	%LAUNCH
DIR OF ST/CNTY/FED OFFS	%LRBDIR
MALUHIA PROJECT	%MALUHIA
HAWAIIAN HOSPITALITY	%OHA
BACKYARD OIL BARRELS	%OILBRL
HAWAIIAN SELF GOV'NANCE	%ONIPAA
PUBLIC HEALTH NURSING	%PHN
$PORTAL	%PORTAL
PVS INFORMATION SERVICE	%PVSINFO
ENERGY RESEARCH	%RER
ON-LINE USER SURVEY	%SATSURV
SEPTIC TANKS	%SEPTANK
STATE ENERGY COORD. RPT.	%SERCAR
STATE ENERGY COORD. RPT. 90	%SERCAR90
FAMILY PLANNING SERVICE	%SEX_INFO
SOLAR TAX CREDITS	%SOLARTAX
STATE PARK INFORMATION	%STEPARKS
SCIENCE TECH.-SOCIETY	%STSBB
SOLAR WATER HEATING/SUNMAP	%SUNMAP
TAX INFORMATION SERVICE	%TAXINFO
TEEN FORUM-KITV4	%TEEN
ENRGY PRJCT SITE GUIDE	%TG
UH CARL SYSTEM	%UHCARL
INSTITUTE FOR PEACE	%UHMPEACE
PEACE EVENTS CALENDAR	%UHSMIPCC
U.S. DEPT OF ENRGY INFO	%USDEPENI
OFFICE OF VETERANS SERVICES	%VETSVC
*YO! KIDS	%YOKIDS
*YO! FYI RAPS	%YORAPS

The U.S. Federal Government Online

Executive Branch

President

`mail president@whitehouse.gov`

Vice President

`mail vice.president@whitehouse.gov`

Press releases and archives

```
mail clinton-info@campaign92.org, subject: receive help
ftp sunsite.unc.edu (152.2.22.81), cd /home3/wais/white-house-papers
ftp maristb.marist.edu, cd /clinton
ftp cpsr.org, cd /cpsr/clinton
```

Federal agencies

Fedworld BBS, (703)321-8020, `telnet fedworld.gov` (192.239.92.201)

Congress

General inquiries

`mail congress@hr.house.gov`

Library of Congress

```
telnet marvel.loc.gov, login: marvel
telnet locis.loc.gov
telnet dra.com
```

The budget

`ftp sunsite.unc.edu, cd /pub/academic/political-science`

House of Representatives Constituent Mail System

The House of Representatives has instituted a pilot constituent electronic mail system. Representatives participating include (all Washington, DC 20515):

Hon. Jay Dickey, 4th Congressional District, Arkansas, Rm. 1338 Longworth House Office Building
Hon. Sam Gejdenson, 2nd Congressional District, Connecticut, Rm. 2416 Rayburn House Office Bldg.
Hon. Newton Gingrich, 6th Congressional District, Georgia, Rm. 2428 Rayburn House Office Bldg.
Hon. George Miller, 7th Congressional District, California, Rm. 2205 Rayburn House Office Building
Hon. Charlie Rose, 7th Congressional District, North Carolina, Rm. 2230 Rayburn House Office Bldg.
Hon. Pete Stark, 13th Congressional District, California, Rm. 239 Cannon House Office Building
Hon. Mel Watt, 12th Congressional District, North Carolina, Rm. 1232 Longworth House Office Bldg.

To obtain the Internet address of your representative, mail a postcard to your representative with your name, email address, and postal address. Electronic mail sent to your representative will be answered by traditional methods: mail sent via the U.S. Postal Service.

Santa Monica PEN

Santa Monica's Public Electronic Network (PEN), which came online in February of 1989, was the first electronic system sponsored by a city government. It is designed primarily as a means to access local government. In addition to mailboxes related to aspects of city government, the system offers conferences on congress, crime, education, environment, homelessness, leisure, national and foreign issues, city planning, science, and youth. There is also access to the public library catalog. The system is accessible both by dialup and via 35 public access terminals, and runs under UNIX on an HP workstation using Caucus conferencing software.

The system is open only to those who live and work in Santa Monica. To login, type **new** in response to the login: prompt to create an account; **hello** if you already have an ID, and **forms** to submit forms to City Hall.

For more information

Information on the National Public Telecomputing Network (NPTN) is available via **ftp ntpn.org**.

To subscribe to the Community and Civic Networks Discussion List on BITNET, **mail LISTSERV@UVMVM.UVM.EDU**, body: **SUBSCRIBE COMMUNET "Firstname Lastname"**

Free-Nets

National Capital Free-Net   Free

National Capital Free-Net (freenet.carleton.ca), David Sutherland, Computing Services, Carleton University, Ottawa, Canada K1S 5B6; (613)788-2600 ext. 3701, (613)780-3733, email: aa001@freenet.carleton.ca

Victoria Free-Net   Free

Victoria Free_net Association (freenet.victoria.bc.ca), c/o Vancouver Island Advanced Technology Centre (VIATC), Suite 203-1110 Government Street, Victoria,

British Columbia Canada V8W 1Y2; (604)385-4302, dialin: (604)595-2300, email: shearman@cue.bc.ca

Wellington CityNet   Free

Richard Naylor, Wellington CityNet (kosmos.wcc.govt.nz), Wellington City Council; P.O. Box 2199, Wellington, New Zealand; +64 4 801 3303, email: rich@tosh.wcc.govt.nz

Denver Free-Net   Free

Denver Free-Net; 4200 E. Ninth Ave., Campus Box c-288, Denver, CO 80210; (303)270-4300, email: drew@freenet.hsc.colorado.edu

Tallahassee Free-Net   Free

Tallahassee Free-Net (freenet.fsu.edu), Hilbert Levitz, Dept. of Computer Science, Florida State University; Tallahassee, FL 32306, (904)644-1796, email: levitz@cs.fsu.edu

Heartland Free-Net   Free

Heartland Free-Net, Lovelace Technology Center; Peoria, IL 61625; (309)674-2544, dialin: (309)674-1100, email: xxadm@heartland.bradley.edu

Buffalo Free-Net   Free

Buffalo Free-Net, (freenet.buffalo.edu), James Finamore, Town of Tonawanda; 1835 Sheridan Dr., Buffalo, NY 14223; (716)877-8800 ext. 451, dialin: (716)645-6128, email: finamore@ubvms.cc.buffalo.edu

Cleveland Free-Net   Free

Supports mail, USENET, and **telnet**, but not **ftp**.

To register, call (216)368-3888, or **telnet freenet-in-a.cwru.edu, freenet-in-b.cwru.edu**, or **freenet-in-c.cwru.edu**, login: **fnguest**.

Lorain County Free-Net   **Free**

Lorain County Free-Net; 32320 Stony Brook Dr., Avon Lake, Ohio 44012, (800)227-7133, ext. 2451, (216)277-2451, dialin: (216)366-9721, email:
aa003@freenet.lorain.oberlin.edu

Medina County Free-Net   **Free**

Medina General Hospital; 1000 E. Washington St., P.O. Box 427, Medina, OH44258-0427; (216)725-1000 Ext. 2550, dialin: (216)723-6732, email: aa001@medina.freenet.edu

Tri-State Online   **Free**

Tri-State Online, (cbos.uc.edu), Cincinnati Bell Directory, Inc.; Room 102-2000, 201 East 4th St., Cincinnati, OH 45201-2301; (513)397-1396, dialin: (513)579-1990, email:
sysadmin@cbos.uc.edu

Youngstown Free-Net   **Free**

Youngstown Free-Net, YSU Computer Center; 410 Wick Ave., Youngstown, OH 44555; (216)742-3075, dialin: (216)742-3072, email:
lou@yfn.ysu.edu

Other systems

Oakland InfoAccess Free

InfoAccess; dialin: (510)238-6561; Oakland Public Library dialin: 238-2253, login: oakland.

Hawaii FYI

Hawaii Information Network Corporation; 201 Merchant Street, Suite 1500, Honolulu, Hawwaii 96813; (808)586-4636, dialin: (808)536-7133.

Community Memory

Berkeley Community Memory Project; 1442A Walnut St. #311, Berkeley, CA 94709; (510)841-1114

Michigan NovaLine

Basic Package	
Setup fee	$4.95
Monthly fee	$4.95
Hourly fee	$3
Nova-Plus package	
Setup fee	$4.95
Monthly fee	$7.95
(includes 3 hours/month)	
Hourly fee	$3
Super-Nova package	
Setup fee	$4.95
Monthly fee	$14.95
(includes 7 hours/month)	
Hourly fee	$3
800 number access	
Setup fee	$4.95
Monthly fee	$4.95
Hourly fee	$11.40

Dynamic Training Corp; Jim Maceri, dialin: (517)351-2546

Santa Monica PEN

Santa Monica Public Electronic Network (PEN); Keith Kurtz, City of Santa Monica, 1685 Main St., P.O. Box 2200, Santa Monica CA 90401; (310)458-8383; dialin: (310)458-8989

Big Sky Telegraph

Big Sky Telegraph; Frank Odasz, Western Montana College, 710 S. Atlantic, Dillon, MT 59725; (406)683-7338, dialin: (406)683-7680, email: franko@bigsky.dillon.mt.us, telnet bigsky.dillon.mt.us [192.231.192.1]

COIN

Columbia ONline Information Network (COIN); Bill Mitchell, University of Missouri - Columbia, Campus Computing, 200 Hinkel Building, Columbia, MO 61211; (314)882-2200, email: ccwam@mizzoui.missouri.edu; dialin: (314)884-7000, telnet bigcat.missouri.edu

Fairbanks Area Computer/Terminal Services (FAC/TS)

FAC/TS includes information on Fairbanks and the interior of Alaska. This includes information on weather, sporting events, entertainment, hunting and trapping and mining.

FAC/TS; P.O. Box 80467, Fairbanks, Alaska 99708; (907)456-5671, dialin: (907)456-4571, (907)456-2123

Cupertino City Net

Wally Dean, (408)252-4505 (City Hall); Robert A. Kim, San Jose, CA; (408)272-4185, dialin: (408)272-3332 (City Connection BBS)

SFNet	$7/month
Deluxe account	$13/month

SFNet; P.O. Box 460693, San Francisco, CA 94146; (415)695-9824, fax: (415)695-9824; San Francisco dialin: (415)824-8747, (415)589-2194; Burlingame: (415)375-8487; Oakland: (510)450-0155; San Leandro: (510)638-8644; Richmond: (510)215-7732; Sausalito: (415)332-3923; San Rafael: (415)454-4983; FidoNet: 1:125/824

SeniorNet

Dr. Mary Furlong, President; #399 Arguello Boulevard, San Francisco, CA 94118; (415) 750-5030

Hawaii SeniorNet Learning Centers

Emeritus College; Honolulu Community College, #874 Dillingham Boulevard, Honolulu, HI 96817; (808) 845-9296

Maui Community College; #310 Kaahumanu Avenue, Kahului, HI 96732; (808) 242-1217

Hawaii SeniorNet Outpost

Kokua SeniorNet Outpost; #237 Queen Emma Square, Honolulu, HI 96813; (808) 528-4839

K-12 systems

CORE

California Online Resources for Education (CORE); Keith Vogt, P.O. Box 3842, 4665 Lampson Ave., Seal Beach, CA 90740; (800)272-8743, email: kvogt@eis.calstate.edu

Virginia PEN

Public Education Network (PEN); Dr. Harold Cothern, P.O. Box 6Q, Richmond, VA 23216; (804)225-2921, email: hcothern@vdoe386.vak12ed.edu

SENDIT

SENDIT; Gleason Sackman, Box 5164, North Dakota State University Computer Center, Fargo, ND 58105; (701)237-8109, email: sackman@sendit.nodak.edu

Ed-Net

Vancouver School Board Multi-Line Education Network; Barry Macdonald, Vancouver Board of Education, dialin: (604)723-8877.

CHAPTER 6: INTRODUCTION TO GLOBAL NETWORKS

FidoNet, USENET, BITNET, RIME: this is how I spend my time...

What is network literacy?

What does it mean to be "network literate?" Literacy is the ability to effectively receive and send information in a designated language. You know you are network literate when your attempts at communication reliably result in the expected response.

Literacy involves both acquiring a set of mechanical skills and an appreciation of cultural norms.

Each of the global networks has its own culture, which evolved from the personality of the founders and the environment in which it originated. Just as behavior appropriate in the United States would be frowned upon in Japan, so too might appropriate behavior on ILink, FidoNet, or RIME meet with disapproval on the Internet or BITNET.

While global computer networks are similar in concept, each network has different traditions and customs, often established early in the network's life by the founders.

The Internet

The Internet began as a research project of the Defense Advanced Research Projects Agency (DARPA) in 1968 and has now grown to become the world's largest computer network.

Purpose

DARPA sponsored the project in order to share resources among the computer groups it was funding. DARPA subsequently shortened its name to the Advanced Research Projects Agency (ARPA), and the ARPA-sponsored network of computers became known as ARPANET.

Hardware and software supported

The original ARPANET was a network of computers connected over leased telephone lines that were communicating with each other using a protocol called Network Communications Protocol, or NCP. With the rise of LANs such as Ethernet and Token Ring, it became clear that no one local area networking technology was going to win, and the future of the ARPANET hinged on its being able to link many different LANs into a single cohesive network. In other words, the ARPANET needed to go from being a single network of computers to becoming a network of networks, or an internet.

This early insight into the importance of portability and extendability has profoundly influenced the development of the Internet Protocols, which now run on dozens of machines and operating systems.

Protocols

Over several years, a new series of protocols was devised for the ARPANET and on January 1, 1983, the ARPANET switched protocols from NCP to Transmission Control Protocol/Internet Protocol, or TCP/IP. The switch from NCP to TCP/IP greatly increased the number of computers that could be connected to the network, which became known as the Internet. In order to take advantage of this greatly increased capacity, the National

Science Foundation (NSF) funded development by Bolt, Beranek and Newman, Inc. (BBN) of a version of the TCP/IP protocol for the version 3.2 release of Berkeley System Distribution (BSD) UNIX, which was written at the University of California, Berkeley.

The inclusion of TCP/IP within BSD UNIX 3.2, and the growing popularity of the Digital Equipment Corporation (DEC) VAX line of machines that ran BSD, quickly spread TCP/IP throughout the nation's universities and research institutions. This began a period of dramatic growth for the Internet that has never let up. As of August 1993, the Internet included more than 2 million hosts.

Transmission Control Protocol/Internet Protocol (TCP/IP) is the primary protocol family used on the Internet, although OSI protocols such as CLNP and TP4 are also used.

Administration

In 1986, the National Science Foundation took over maintenance of the Internet from ARPA and began to reorganize and upgrade it. NSF began funding the creation of dozens of regional networks all over the country. Each of these regional networks typically included several universities. For example, in the Bay Area, Stanford, UC Berkeley, and UC Davis are connected together in a network known as the Bay ARea Research NETwork, or BARRNET. In New England, the regional network is known as NEARNET; in New York, NYSERNET, and so on. At the same time, NSF also funded the creation of a backbone to link these networks together. This backbone, called NSFNet, originally ran at 56 Kbps over leased lines and has subsequently been upgraded to T3 lines running at 45 Mbps, although the network itself is currently running at only 22 Mbps due to router speed limitations.

Services

The Internet offers a dazzling array of services, from electronic mail to remote logins to database access. Increasingly, other networks such as the FidoNet and RIME networks are being connected to the Internet via computers called "gateways." Other networks, such as BITNET, are now running their own protocols

on top of TCP/IP in order to take advantage of the global connectivity of the Internet. This is called "tunneling." More information on the Internet is available in Chapter 7: Introduction to the Internet, Chapter 8: Internet Access, and Chapter 33: How the Internet Came to Be.

UUCP and USENET

In 1978, Mike Lesk created Unix to Unix Copy, or UUCP. UUCP allowed UNIX computers to communicate with each other over phone lines in order to transfer mail and files, and to execute remote commands. UUCP eventually became part of the UNIX operating system, and its ensuing popularity led to a nationwide network of computers, known as UUCP, communicating via this protocol. The electronic mail standard used in communicating over UUCP is known as Request For Comment (RFC) 822.

The User's Network, or USENET, began in 1979, when two students at Duke and the University of North Carolina wrote a program called netnews, whose purpose was to allow people with accounts on UUCP machines to take part in distributed conferences. With electronic mail, an individual could send a message to one other person. Using netnews, a single message would go out to every UUCP-connected computer that was running netnews and subscribed to that conference. According to the January 1993 readership report, more than 70,000 sites now receive net news, resulting in an estimated 2 million readers, and 20,000 messages per day.

Purpose

USENET prohibits advertising, although product information postings are allowable. Conference topics range from discussions of computer-related issues (the comp hierarchy) to social (soc) or recreational (rec) topics.

Many USENET sites are universities and commercial firms, and only carry a restricted set of groups. For example, many commercial firms do not carry social or recreational groups. As with FidoNet, differences over acceptable use policies have spawned creation of alternative networks.

In order to allow discussion of more controversial issues, the alternative (alt) hierarchy was created. New groups often start out in the alt hierarchy, and as they become more popular, are moved into the mainstream USENET hierarchy.

The biz hierarchy was formed in order to allow discussion of commercial topics. As a result, many of the postings in the biz groups would not be allowed elsewhere on USENET.

Hardware and software supported

Since UUCP and USENET were developed for UNIX machines, they have been ported to virtually every machine with a version of UNIX. However, other operating systems are also capable of participating. There are versions of UUCP and news software for the Macintosh, MS-DOS, and Amiga machines, to name a few.

Protocols

Net news is usually transferred from machine to machine using either the UUCP protocol (usually for connections over phone lines), or the Net News Transfer Protocol (NNTP) (for connections over TCP/IP). However, other transfer modes are possible, such as UUCP over TCP/IP or gatewaying followed by transmission over FidoNet protocols. I have even heard of net news being transmitted via KERMIT. The message format is defined in RFC-1036.

Administration

UUCP and USENET have no formal organization yet they are highly organized. There are procedures for adding or deleting UUCP maps or news groups and for posting and archiving Frequently Asked Questions (FAQ) listings.

Services

Unix-to-Unix Copy Protocol, or UUCP, is a protocol by which UNIX machines can communicate over telephone lines. UUCP is more than just a file-transfer protocol; it is a sophisticated protocol that also allows for execution of remote commands, so other services, such as file-transfer or distributed

conferencing applications can be built on top of it.

One such service is called anonymous UUCP. This is used in order to request a file from a remote UNIX system and is the equivalent of FidoNet's File Request.

In 1990, ClariNet began offering access to news wires such as UPI and NewsBytes over USENET. UUCP and USENET messages may only contain 7-bit ASCII data, and as a result binaries are encoded with UUENCODE, BINHEX 4.0, or similar utilities. With programs such as Troika now featuring UUENCODE/DECODE on the fly, NAPLPS graphics may be included within USENET messages. More information on USENET is available in Chapter 12: USENET.

FidoNet

In 1984, Tom Jennings had the idea of allowing bulletin boards to exchange messages with each other. This was accomplished by adding a set of communications protocols (called FidoNet) to his bulletin board software, which was called Fido. FidoNet was an instant hit, and soon hundreds of computers were running the software. As of August 1993, the FidoNet includes 22,000 publicly listed systems worldwide with thousands of additional systems in private use.

Purpose

The public FidoNet is an amateur network administrated by hobbyists on a volunteer basis. Businesses and government agencies are also large users of FidoNet technology, but these users generally use FidoNet software to operate private networks that are neither listed nor available for public access.

Hardware and software supported

Although the vast majority of FidoNet computers connected to it are PC compatibles, FidoNet has also been ported to a wide variety of computers, from the Apple II to UNIX workstations. It is now in use all over the world, including Eastern Europe and Russia.

FidoNet technology is popular in developing countries because it operates over normal phone lines with readily available and inexpensive equipment. With the development of the mailer concept, FidoNet became an easily added addition to most bulletin board packages. As a result the majority of BBS packages now support it. There are also many useful add-ins, such as gateway software, to allow FidoNet systems to communicate via UUCP. FidoNet users are thus able to send mail all over the world.

Protocols

Since FidoNet was an open standard, other vendors were able to create compatible products, called "mailers." Many owners of other bulletin board software wanted to join the FidoNet network but did not want to run the Fido software. Systems Enhancement Associates (SEA) satisfied this need by creating the first "front-end mailer," called SEAdog. SEAdog made it possible to interface many PC-based BBS products to FidoNet by sitting between the BBS and the phone line.

When a call came into the system, SEAdog would answer the phone. If the caller was another FidoNet system, SEAdog would exchange files and messages using the FidoNet protocols. If SEAdog detected a human caller, it would fire up the BBS software instead and the caller would log on to the BBS normally.

The release of SEAdog was the first of a number of FidoNet-compatible products that broadened the market for FidoNet software. Following the release of SEAdog, other mailer products such as BinkleyTerm, Front Door, and D'Bridge were introduced.

Tabby was the first FidoNet mailer product for the Macintosh and established the standards that other Mac mailer products such as Formula 1 have followed. Unlike PC mailer products, with Tabby it is the BBS that senses whether the incoming call is from another FidoNet system or a human. If the call is from another FidoNet system, the BBS calls Tabby. For more information on the creation of Tabby, please see Chapter 39: The History of the EchoMac Network.

In addition to mailer products, several other integrated FidoNet systems were developed. One of these was OPUS, which quickly became the most popular FidoNet software. The Bread Board System, or TBBS, written by Phil Becker, was special because it was the first BBS software for a microcomputer that could handle more than one line at a time. When the TBBS Integrated Mail System (TIMS) was released in 1990, TBBS became the first multiline BBS software with a built-in FidoNet mailer.

While the specifications for FidoNet are publicly available, there are quite a few undocumented features, and there is no formal way to verify compliance. As a result, compatibility problems have been common and are now probably one of the major limitations on the growth of the network.

Administration

The most fundamental design principle of FidoNet is the deep distrust of central authority, and the network has managed to operate smoothly since its central governing body, the International FidoNet Association (IFNA), voted itself out of existence in 1989. Since the software is designed to allow users to split off from the main network and form their own networks if they choose, segments of the network have split off whenever they disagree with FidoNet policies. FidoNet spinoffs include Alternet, Eggnet, and RBBS-Net.

Services

FidoNet originally only allowed transmission of person-to-person mail (NetMail), as well as file transfers. In 1986 Jeff Rush wrote the distributed-conferencing software known as EchoMail, which ran on top of the file-transfer function and was modeled after USENET. EchoMail took off, and soon there were hundreds of EchoMail conferences.

Although FidoNet as a network does not prohibit private mail in EchoMail conferences, almost all regional or international echoes do. This is because the network cannot route messages directly to their destination but instead sends them all over the world, with sysops footing the bill. Even in the case of conferences within a small geographical area, private conference mail is not appropriate, since FidoNet point mailers usually don't support private messages. As a result, any point mail system getting the regional conference can read "private" messages. To prevent these problems, most FidoNet-compatible BBS software either prohibits the creation of private messages within conferences or allows sysops to prevent the export of such messages.

In practice, FidoNet messages may only contain 7-bit ASCII data since control characters such as (CTRL)A are used for message history and routing functions by many mail handlers. However, the protocols do allow for 8-bit file attaches.

More information on FidoNet is available in Chapter 18: Introduction to FidoNet, and Chapter 34: How FidoNet Came to Be.

FidoNet Buzzwords

FREQ
The FidoNet protocols provide methods for sending and receiving files. Sending a file to another system is known as File Attach. Requesting a file from another system is known as File Request, or FREQ.

Mailers
Mailers include BinkleyTerm, Tabby, the FidoNet-compatible mailer for the Macintosh, as well as Formula 1, a Tabby-compatible mailer.

NetMail
Among the services provided by the FidoNet protocols is the ability to send mail from one FidoNet-compatible computer to another. This is known as NetMail.

Gateways
Machines that can speak multiple protocols and can route mail between networks are known as gateways. For example, a FidoNet/UUCP gateway would be capable of communicating in FidoNet protocols and in UUCP protocols.

WWIV networks

At last count, there were thirty-three networks and more than 4000 systems using the WWIV networking software, which debuted in 1988. WWIV compatible networks include WWIVnet (1600 nodes), WWIVLink (618) and IceNET (770 nodes). WWIVLink began in February, 1990. The network coordinator of WWIVnet is Wayne Bell, author of WWIV and WWIVnet. The major advantage of WWIV is that it is one of the easiest networked BBSes to set up.

Purpose

The WWIV networks vary in purpose from hobbyist networks to file distribution networks to networks formed for the purposes of buying and selling hardware and software. Several of the WWIVnet networks allow handles, leaving the decision up to the individual sysop.

Hardware and software supported

The WWIVnet software, which all WWIVnet systems must run, runs exclusively on IBM-PC compatible computers. Most WWIVnet systems also use the WWIV BBS software, although a few use VBBS or other packages. For information on the VBBS interface to WWIVNet, contact Roland De Graph, (616)772-0347. The next version of WWIV will offer FidoNet capability.

Protocols

WWIV mail and conference packets are routed using a shortest path algorithm. Connections among the nodes are included in the CONNECT.0 (in group) and CONNECT.1 through CONNECT.14 (out of group) files. Each node is assigned a four-digit ID number by the group or area coordinator, of which the first two digits are the first and last digits of the system's telephone area code, and the last two digits are chosen by the group or area coordinator. The ID numbers are used to identify systems in netmail conferencing areas, which on WWIVnet are known as "subs."

Administration

The network is split into groups of 50-200 systems, each administered by a group coordinator. Each of the thirteen group coordinators handles the administrative duties such as distributing the nodelist and handing out network ID numbers. Within groups, area coordinators coordinate systems within a given telephone area code. The area coordinators service the local nodes.

WWIVnet systems set up their own links, deciding which subs to carry and when to poll each other. Sysops are not required to carry any subs, and if they want to, they can create their own subs. WWIVnet therefore offers flexibility similar to that offered by FidoNet. The WWIVnet software costs $20 for nonregistered WWIV sysops; it is free for registered sysops. WWIV costs $80, which includes source code; a multi-node version is in development.

Services

WWIVnet maintains FidoNet/WWIVnet gateways, which all have WWIVnet addresses in the 600s. To send mail to WWIVnet from FidoNet, send a message to a gateway system (such as 1:105/25) addressed to:

    n<WWIVNET system #> u<User #>
                or
    n<WWIVnet system #> <User Name>.

For example, to reach User 684 at WWIVnet system 5054, send a message to: **n5054 u684**. WWIVnet members may also be reached over the Internet. To reach User 684 at WWIVnet system 5054 over the Internet, send a message to: **n5054.u684@f25.n105.z1.fidonet.org**.

There are also UUCP gateways with WWIVnet addresses in the 500s. Some of the UUCP gateways are inforail.station.mv.com and dd.ii.UUCP.

WWIVnet does not allow transmission of files, other than small occasional UUENCODE'd files transmitted by Wayne Bell for updating the WWIVnet software. However, other WWIV networks are forming for the purpose of file distribution.

For more information, contact WWIV Software; P.O. Box 720455, McAllen, TX 78504-0455; BBS: (310)798-9993, Support Systems: The Funny Farm, (704)525-1491, or The Dragon Den, (210)631-5841. WWIVnet software is available for download as NETxx.ZIP where xx is the latest version number. In addition, a list of WWIVnet systems is available from any WWIVnet member system by typing **//Net** at the main menu. A list of networks is available from The File Pile BBS (612)351-0144, login: **0000**, password: **NETLIST**.

BITNET

BITNET (which stands for the Because It's Time Network) is a network of IBM mainframes, VAX/VMS machines, UNIX computers and other machines that began in 1981, and now includes more than 3300 systems at 1300 different sites. Some of the BITNET machines are now also on the Internet, allowing for gatewaying of mail between the two networks as well as operation of the BITNET protocols over TCP/IP. One of the primary gateways is the CUNYVM machine, whose domain name is cunyvm.cuny.edu.

Purpose

As a network operated for research and educational purposes, BITNET's Acceptable Use Policy prohibits use of the network for commercial purposes such as advertising or junk mailings.

Hardware and software supported

Originally, BITNET machines connected using leased lines (usually running at 9600 bps) and the Network Job Entry (NJE) protocol for IBM mainframes. Later the NJE protcol was ported to UNIX (UREP) and Vax VMS (Jnet), as well as other machines such as the CDC Cyber.

Protocols

The BITNET II project, begun in 1986 and based on an NSF grant, created the VMNET software that made possible NJE connections over TCP/IP at speeds of 1.5 Mbps (T1) or greater. VMNET communicates on port 175 and now runs on UNIX and Vax VMS architectures in addition to IBM mainframes. The BITNET II architecture was developed in the nick of time, since the growth of the network had begun to create unacceptable delays during 1987 and 1988.

With the deployment of the BITNET II software in 1989, BITNET was reorganized into a backbone architecture with 14 core systems, two for each of seven regions. The core nodes are all located close to NSFNet backbone sites and communicate with each other using TCP/IP. EARN has since also gone to a backbone architecture.

Administration

BITNET is actually a cooperating group of networks. Within the United States, BITNET is run by the Corporation for Research and Educational Networking (CREN), a nonprofit corporation governed by a board of trustees and representatives from the member sites. The European portion of the network is the European Academic and Research Network (EARN), and the Canadian portion is known as NetNorth.

The BITNET Network Information Center (BITNIC) operates at EDUCOM, and the Development and Operations Center (BITDOC) is located at CUNY.

Services

The primary BITNET services are electronic mail, messages (transferred in real time), file transfer, databases (LDBASE), and mailing lists (handled by a program called LISTSERV).

BITNET messages may only contain 7-bit ASCII data, so binaries must be run through UUENCODE/UUDECODE or similar utilities. BITNET files have a maximum size of 300K but may be split in order allow for transmission of larger files. More information on BITNET is available in Chapter 17: Introduction to BITNET.

RIME

In early 1988, Bob Shuck, who was then operating a bulletin board in the Washington,

D.C., area, was looking for a way to link systems in the area running PC Board software. Kip Compton, then in high school, met Bob and decided to develop software to link PC Board systems, which he called PCRelay. At first the network included only ten systems in the Washington area and one system in New York, but it grew rapidly.

Today the RIME network includes more than 1000 systems worldwide and is now based on the next generation of Kip Compton's software, called PostLink. RIME is not the only PostLink-based network, but it is by far the largest. Like most other PCRelay or PostLink networks, most of the systems on RIME still run PCBoard.

Purpose

RIME is a hobbyist network, and as a result there are restrictions on commercial activity.

Hardware and software supported

PostLink is currently available only for PC compatibles. Since the software is written in C++, ports are both possible and likely, particularly to support operation under UNIX.

Although PCRelay was originally written for use with PCBoard systems, the release of Universal Text Interface (UTI) modules for other bulletin board software (including FidoNet capable systems such as OPUS) broadened the software's appeal.

Protocols

In contrast to FidoNet and the Internet, which are both based on publicly documented protocols, RIME is based on a single piece of software (PostLink) whose design remains proprietary. The advanced capabilities of the PostLink software on which RIME is based include a highly scalable design, support for threading, file requests and attaches, return receipts, enclosure of private mail within conferences, automatic network configuration and topology mapping, directory service, time stamping, routing history functions, and more. Users looking to create secure and centrally administered networks would do well to take a serious look at PostLink, particularly since its

C++ design and support for UTIs make it highly portable and compatible with alternative networking technologies (such as TCP/IP).

Administration

RIME is governed by a seven-member steering committee that exerts ultimate authority over the network, controlling the backbone nodes, which are known as NetHubs. Nodes not complying with the dictates of the STEERCOM may face excommunication from the network. The authoritarian culture of RIME carries through to all levels, with individual conference moderators having ultimate authority over users within their conferences, and sysops being forced to rein in misbehaving users under penalty of excommunication. The result is that (surprisingly enough) RIME conferences are generally well behaved.

Services

Many RIME users read their messages using graphical front ends called QWK readers that are available both for the PC and Macintosh. While RIME does not yet have domain and a formal gateway architecture, individual RIME nodes have UUCP connections, via software such as PCBUUCP. PostLink and PCRelay support transfer of both messages and files, as well as enclosure of 8-bit data within messages, making possible conferences for ANSI or NAPLPS graphics.

PostLink and PCRelay both also support sending person-to-person mail within regional and international conferences. Due to the topology of RIME, sending person-to-person mail in an international conference is not wasteful, provided that it is correctly addressed; private messages are filtered and routed directly to their destination. PCRelay based networks also support encryption of messages, although you should be aware that the mail is encrypted on the BBS so that your sysop can still read it.

More information on PostLink is available in Chapter 19: PCBoard Networks, and Chapter 37: How PCRelay (and PostLink) Came to Be.

FrEdMail

In 1984, Al Rogers was working as a teacher in Southern California and had the vision of creating a powerful word processing tool for students that would run on an Apple II. This program, finished in 1985, was called FrEdWriter.

In 1986, Rogers started on a companion program to link together Apple II machines, called FrEdMail for Free Education Mail. Today FrEdMail links together over 200 systems in the U.S., Australia, Puerto Rico, the Virgin Islands, and Ireland. More than 5000 teachers and tens of thousands of students take part in the network.

Purpose

One of the reasons that FrEdMail has been so successful is that it is more than a technology. FrEdMail is an educational program using telecommunications to provide students with an audience for their writing. The FrEdMail Foundation, a nonprofit educational corporation founded to support the FrEdMail network, provides teachers with technical support as well as teaching materials.

Hardware and software supported

FrEdMail runs only on Apple II computers.

Protocols

FrEdMail is based on a proprietary XMODEM-derived protocol.

Administration

The FrEdMail network is administered by the FrEdMail foundation, which creates topology maps, provides technical support, and aids in the continued development of curriculum.

Services

FrEdMail offers standard conferencing and electronic-mail facilities. In addition, based on a grant from the NSF, the FrEdMail Foundation has recently developed a mail gateway to the Internet and a series of moderated USENET conferences called SCHLNet. More information on FrEdMail is available in Chapter 38: How FrEdMail Came to Be, Appendix B: Choice Products, Appendix E: Network Application Forms, and Appendix J: Conference Listings.

Other networks

Fees listed are merely for joining the network, not for additional services such as EchoMail. Typically sysops wanting to pick up conferences pay the bill to call the system carrying the conference. In addition, hubs may require connecting systems to pay a share of their phone bill as well.

Networks using FidoNet technology

▽ RBBS-Net

The RBBS-PC Network (known as RBBS-Net) was founded in 1989 as a way for RBBS-PC systems to exchange messages. It has since grown to over 500 systems. RBBS-Net utilizes FidoNet networking technology, and as a result its administration is similar to FidoNet's, with local "nets" and member "nodes." RBBS-Net systems use Zone 8 to prevent their node numbers from conflicting with established FidoNet zones.

Although RBBS-PC is by far the most popular BBS software used in RBBS-Net, RBBS-Net systems do not need to run RBBS. RBBS-Net has EchoMail and NetMail gateways to FidoNet, giving RBBS-Net systems access to all the FidoNet EchoMail conferences. To reach an RBBS-Net system from FidoNet, send a NetMail message to the local FidoNet/RBBS-Net gateway (such as 1:10/8). Address the message to:

```
<user> @ <RBBS-Net address>
```

For example, to send a message to Akbar Foobar at 8:914/201, send a NetMail message to 1:10/8, addressed to:

```
Akbar Foobar @ 914/201
```

Of course, FidoNet systems can also compile the RBBS nodelist and send mail directly to RBBS-Net systems. In addition, RBBS-Net has Smartnet, Internet, and Alternet gateways.

Rod Bowman, RBBS-Net Network Coordinator, BBS: (714)381-6013, FidoNet 1:10/8, or contact Don Smith, Membership Services, at (419)448-1452. For more info, you can file request RBBS-NET from 1:10/8. A nodelist is updated, distributed, and available weekly from many RBBS systems as RBBSLIST or RBBSLIST.ARC.

▽ Eggnet

Eggnet is a FidoNet technology–based network of over 300 systems. The major difference between Eggnet and FidoNet is that Eggnet fancies itself a democracy. Any changes in policy or leadership require a vote, with a majority carrying the issue. Eggnet offers its own conferences (known as eggomail) and maintains gateways with other networks such as FidoNet.

Steve Kruzich, Eggnet Network Coordinator, BBS: (901)367-0837, FidoNet 1:123/69. For more info, file request EGGPOL2.ZIP from 1:123/17, or contact Hays Turner, FidoNet/Eggnet gateway operator, at (901)324-2024.

▽ Alternet

The Alternet network (not to be confused with the UUNET-sponsored Internet service of the same name) is a FidoNet split-off network centered on the East Coast. Founded to create a network with a higher degree of politeness and chivalry than FidoNet (not hard to do), Alternet has an anachronistic flavor, with network honchos referring to each other as Archdukes, Dukes, Knights, and so on. As with RBBS-Net, Alternet has appropriated its own Zone number so that Alternet and FidoNet nodelists can be compiled together.

Networks using QWK packet technology

▽ Intelec

The Intelec Network includes over 400 systems relaying messages via QNet and PCRelay technology. File conferences are not supported. The network is based on a four-level hub system in which the Net Host BBS is at the root, with regional hubs, hubs, and nodes at successively lower levels of the tree. Systems connect to their hosts, open the appropriate door (either QNet or PCRelay), and transfer messages.

Intelec offers excellent technical support conferences, with Microsoft and vendors of shareware products such as QEDIT and COMMO participating. Discussions display remarkable intelligence and self-restraint.

A short newsletter is distributed every month (*In Basket*), along with a number of supplementary files including a nodelist, conference list, application form, and policy statement. The *In Basket* newsletter is available on many systems as IN-yymm.ZIP, where yy is the year and mm is the month. For example, IN-9204.ZIP is the newsletter for April 1992.

Cliff Watkins, Network Administrator, Intelec, (516)867-4448; alternatively, you can contact one of the regional hubs such as Lobster Buoy (207)941-0805, QWK format or Network XXIII (805)962-0122, PC-Relay Format.

▽ Smartnet

Smartnet, a QWK packet network focused on product support, began with sponsorship from Hayes. The Acceptable Use Policies of Smartnet allow for conferences run by commercial firms (a practice prohibited in most other networks) and firms such as Hayes, QuarterDeck, Practical Peripherals, and Borland retain an official presence on Smartnet. Smartnet allows removal of offensive or even off-topic messages by conference moderators.
Smartnet contains over 250 systems and a wide range of conferences. Smartnet is heavily oriented toward PC users and only a few Macintosh-oriented conferences are available. Smartnet nodes use a variety of QWK packet networking packages, including QNet from Sparkware, RNet by Robert Boksreither, and RoseMail.

Smartnet, Paul Waldinger, BBS (516)536-8723, voice (516)764-5328, or one of the regional hubs such as Toad Hall (415)595-2427.

▽ ILink

The InterLink network (ILink) is descended from the PCBEcho network, which was centered around Memphis, Tennessee, and dissolved in August 1988. With the release of the QNet networking software from Sparkware in September 1988, The Executive Network Information System in Mount Vernon, New York, organized a new network, bringing forty of the old PCBEcho systems with them.

Today the ILink network backbone consists of the network hub and seven national distribution sites located througout North America. ILink also includes nodes in Europe, South Africa, the Middle East, and Asia.

As with FidoNet, ILink does not allow private messsages to be sent within public conferences, and routed mail is not allowed. For sale traffic is restricted to the COMPUTER4SALE conference, and BBS Ads are restricted to the BBS-ADS conference.

Although QMail Deluxe 2 supports ANSI, and QNet technology supports 8-bit data within messages through use of translator software such as VILANSI, ILink restricts the use of ANSI to a single conference, ANSI-ART. A similar policy is likely for NAPLPS graphics. For more information on ILink, please consult Chapter 19: ILink.

Andy Keeves, Executive Network Information System, (914)667-2151, BBS: (914)667-4684. For an application form, download ILDOCxxx.ZIP, and ILAPPxxx.ZIP from MicroSellar BBS, (201)239-1346, or leave a message for Mark Rapp in the ILink conference. Popular ILink BBSes listed in Appendix B include Channel 1, HH Info-Net, Canada Remote Systems, and Aquila BBS.

▽ NorthAmeriNet

NorthAmeriNet, like ILink, was formed in September 1988 after the release of the QNet software from Sparkware, which the network uses exclusively. More than 300 systems participate in the network, most located in Canada. The hub for NorthAmeriNet is CRS, one of the world's largest BBS systems.

Canada Remote Systems, 1331 Crestlawn Dr., Unit D, Mississauga, Ontario, L4W 2P9 Canada, (416)620-1439, (800)465-7562, BBS: (416)798-7730/7731.

Networks using other technology

▽ FirstClass Networks

While the FirstClass server runs only on the Macintosh, both Mac and Windows clients are available. FirstClass allows systems to exchange mail, conferences, and message-routing information (known as "histories"). Since FirstClass messages can include fonts, typestyles and colors, as well as enclosed pictures, sounds, and other files, FirstClass supports these enhancements in the transfer of messages between systems. These advanced features, in addition to the improved ease of use, are the network's primary selling points. Version 2.5 of the FirstClass server will support encryption as well as multi-hop routing of mail.

FirstClass is based on an advanced protocol called FirstClass Protocol (FCP), which supports transfer of files between systems as well as communication between the client software and the BBS (server). Since FCP is an upper layer protocol, it can run on top of AppleTalk, Novell IPX, TCP/IP and X.25, as well as supporting connections over serial lines, LocalTalk, Ethernet, satellites, etc. FCP supports bidirectional file transfers, which in the case of balanced transfers means that uploads and downloads can proceed simultaneously. To establish a link between two systems, sysops fill out a short form asking half a dozen questions about system phone numbers, how they are to link (Appletalk or dialing), and when to call.

Many different gateways are available, including gateways to UUCP/USENET, FidoNet, the Internet, QuickMail, America Online, CompuServe, AppleLink, and fax. Discounts are available for user groups and nonprofits.

The two major FirstClass networks are OneNet, whose central hub is OneNet Boulder, and MacUnion, whose central hub is MacGallery in Wrightsville, Pennsylvania.

OneNet, a FirstClass network founded by Scott Converse of Apple Computer, and which began with five systems as of October 1992, had 191 systems as of June 1993. The network is presently adding more than 15-25 systems a month. Should this growth continue, OneNet will become the largest network of Macintosh-oriented bulletin boards (surpassing the EchoMac Network) some time during 1993. Should the growth continue into 1994, OneNet could become the sixth largest store and forward network, behind FidoNet, UUCP, WWIVNet, BITNET, and RIME.

OneNet currently offers more than a hundred conferences, including conferences relating to the Macintosh and Windows, as well as recreational topics. A list of OneNet BBSes is given in Appendix G, and a listing of OneNet conferences is given in Appendix H.

For further information, a guide to FirstClass client and OneNet is available via `ftp` `netcom1.netcom.com`, `cd` `/pub/mailcom/BMUG_Online_Reference`, `get online.sea.hqx`.

OneNet Los Altos; 4546 El Camino Real # 127, Los Altos, California 94022; (415)948-4775, data: (415)948-1349

SoftArc Inc., 805 Middlefield Rd., Suite 102, Scarborough, Ontario MIV 2T9 Canada, (416)299-4723, fax: (416)754-1856, BBS: (416)609-2250, email: `SoftArc@aol.com`.

▽ InfoLink

InfoLink is the network of NovaLink Pro systems, which form a tree topology with Nova Central, the system operated by Res Nova, at the root. InfoLink supports the transfer of messages with styled text and colors, as well as transmission of images and sounds.

ResNova Software; 5011 Argosy Dr. #13, Huntington Beach, CA 92649; (714)379-9000, fax: (714)379-9014, NovaCentral BBS: (714)379-9006, email: `len.anderson@resnova.com`

Kelly Schwarzhoff compiled the section on other networks.

Summary

Network	Purpose	Protocols/ Specs Available	Adminis- tration	Supported Computers	Services	Size
Internet	General purpose	TCP/IP Yes	Decentralized Management	Widely implemented	Kitchen sink	2,000,000
FidoNet	Hobbyist	FidoNet Yes	Decentralized Anarchy	IBM PC Macintosh	Mail, Conferences, file transfer	22,000
RIME	Hobbyist	PostLink No	Steering Committee	IBM PC (ports possible)	Mail, Conferences, file transfer, directories	1,200
ILINK	Hobbyist	QWK Yes	Governing Council	IBM PC, PCBoard	Mail, Conferences	250
FrEdMail	Education	FrEdMail No	Nonprofit Corporation	Apple II	Mail, Conferences, file transfer	200
BITNET	Research & Education	NJE, TCP/IP Yes	Nonprofit Corporation (CREN)	IBM Mainframe, Vax VMS, UNIX	Mail, Conferences, file transfer	3,500
OneNet	Hobbyist	FCP No	Board of Directors	Macintosh	Mail, Conferences, file transfer	200
SmartNet	Vendor Support	QWK Yes	Sponsoring Vendors	IBM PC, PCBoard	Mail, Conferences	250
InfoLink	Hobbyist	InfoLink, TCP/IP No	Managed by ResNova	Macintosh	Mail, Conferences	5
WWIVnet	Hobbyist	WWIVnet Yes	Networks choose own governance	IBM PC	Mail, Conferences, file transfer	4,000
UUCP	General purpose	UUCP Yes	Decentralized Anarchy	Widely implemented	Mail, Conferences, file transfer, remote commands	15,000

Part II

The Internet

"I sent two men to find out whether there was any king or large city. They explored for three days, and found countless small communities and people, without number, but with no kind of government, so they returned... As for monsters, I have found no trace of them except at the point in the second isle as one enters the Indies, which is inhabited by a people considered in all the isles as most ferocious, who eat human flesh."

– *Letter of Columbus to Luis de Saint Angel announcing his discovery* (1493)

"Thus out of small beginnings greater things have been produced by His hand that made all things of nothing, and gives being to all things that are; and, as one small candle may light a thousand, so the light here kindled hath shone unto many, yea in some sort to our whole nation."

William Bradford, *Of Pilgrim Plantation* (1620-1647)

"It is a great misfortune to be of use to nobody; scarcely less to be of use to everybody."

– Baltasar Gracian, *The Art of Worldly Wisdom* (1647)

CHAPTER 7:
INTRODUCTION TO THE INTERNET

What is the Internet?

Beginning as an ARPA-sponsored research project in 1968, the Internet has grown into the world's largest computer network.

As of August 1993, more than 2 million hosts were connected on 15,000 networks in more than 60 countries, with an estimated 5 to 15 million users. The network is estimated to be doubling in users, networks, and hosts annually.

Many beginners find such figures intimidating. "How can I possibly understand something this large?" they ask. The Internet is so vast, and encompasses so many groups and heterogeneous interests that it is an information ecosystem.

Luckily, just as one does not have to understand the biology of the forest to appreciate its smell after a rain or the soft feel of pine needles underfoot, you do not need to become a full-time student of the Internet in order to appreciate it and use it responsibly.

What can I do with the Internet?

The Internet is more than just a computer network; it is a tool for which new uses are found every day. Asking "What can I do with the Internet?" is like asking "What can I do with a hammer?" Just as a hammer can be used to build anything from a bookshelf to a housing development, how you use the Internet is limited primarily by the law, and your imagination and level of skill. Typical uses of the Internet are as a communications tool, a library, or as a form of entertainment.

▽ Communications tools

The Internet provides tools for one-to-one, one-to-many, or many-to-many communications. The subjects can range from the public to the personal, and from recreation to research. Communications can contain plain text, enclosed files, or multimedia. The context can be "The Real World" or a virtual reality, and it can occur in an online chatting format or by exchange of messages.

The Internet is international and multilingual, with conversations taking place in English, Japanese, French, Spanish, Russian, German, Chinese, and Korean, to name a few languages.

Using the Internet as a communications tool involves learning how to create, address, and send messages in various forms (text, file enclosures, multimedia). This is covered in Chapter 9: Electronic Mail. As part of this process, you will need to learn how to transfer, compress, and convert files, subjects covered in the Tutorial section of this guide.

▽ Libraries

The Internet's online libraries go beyond cataloging of books and serials to offering extensive bibliographic databases as well as online books and journals. Internet sites also archive hundreds of gigabytes of publicly distributable software and data.

The Internet also offers access to resources, which are collections of information on a particular topic, maintained by interested hobbyists or professional groups.

To access resources, you will need to learn how to specify the location of resources and how to use resource catalogs to find what you're looking for. In order to retrieve information, you will need to master specific techniques (mail, file transfer, database search, remote login) for accessing resources.

An Internet resource has a name (such as The Fly Fishing Mailing list), a location (the name of the machine or machines on which it resides, such as fish.edu), allowable access methods (CD-ROM, electronic mail, file transfer, database, remote login), and an associated usage fee (most resources are free).

Just as a novel may be available in the form of a book, a movie, a video, or an audio tape, so too are resources accessible by a variety of methods. As book prices may differ from movie prices, so too may a resource be free in one medium (file transfer) while costing money in another (CD-ROM). For example, a resource about fly fishing may be available as an electronic magazine sent out to a mailing list, a full text database, or a file archive of back issues.

Just as watching *A River Runs Through It* on the big screen is different from reading the book, so too the experience of accessing the fly fishing resource via electronic mail may be different than accessing it interactively with a full-text database, which is in turn different from standing in a stream in your hip boots. Learning to appreciate these differences is part of the task of becoming Internet-literate (and maintaining your grip on reality).

▽ Entertainment

Part of the attraction of the Internet (and for some, the primary attraction!) is that using it can be fun. Recreations include role-playing games, chatting environments, discussion areas on humorous topics, and even Internet Talk Radio and Packet Video Multicasting. More technologically advanced Intertainment will soon be upon us, no doubt, proving that even the most awesome productivity tools can be used to (creatively) waste time.

What's available and what isn't

Although an enormous amount of information is available over the Internet, we have not yet placed even a fraction of the Library of Congress online. Until we do, we'll still need books and librarians, thank you!

Some but by no means all of this information is available free of charge. Much of the free information is contributed by government, academics, hobbyists, researchers, and computer and biotech professionals. That which is posted legally encompasses either information that is not copyrighted, or for which permission for redistribution in electronic form has been obtained.

Copyright law restricts what information can be placed online. You may not post copyrighted material online or resell it in electronic format without permission of the copyright holder. When in doubt, you should assume that material of unknown origin is copyrighted.

Networking technology has evolved more quickly than the social and legal framework for the protection of intellectual property. We do not yet know how to distribute electronic books while protecting the property rights of publishers. As a result, only a few forward-thinking publishers have committed to making their works available over the Internet, even on a paying basis.

Commercial online service providers such as Lexis and Nexis (lexis.meaddata.com), Dialog (dialog.com), Dow Jones (djnr.dowjones.com), Delphi (delphi.com), BIX and CompuServe are now accessible over the Internet. The user interface and services remain the same, although charges may vary.

Of course, obtaining an Internet account does not give you the right to access these services any more than purchasing a car and gasoline gives you the right to free meals at roadside restaurants.

Growth in Internet Hosts and Networks

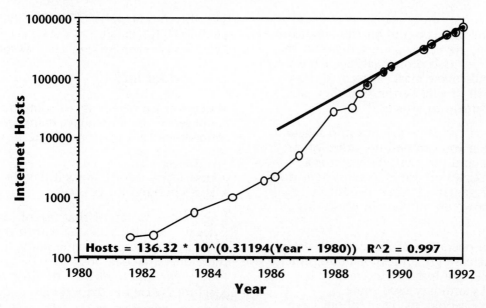

Hosts = 136.32 * 10^(0.31194(Year - 1980))   R^2 = 0.997

Source: RFC 1296, Internet Growth (1981–1991), January 1992, M. Lottor, SRI International

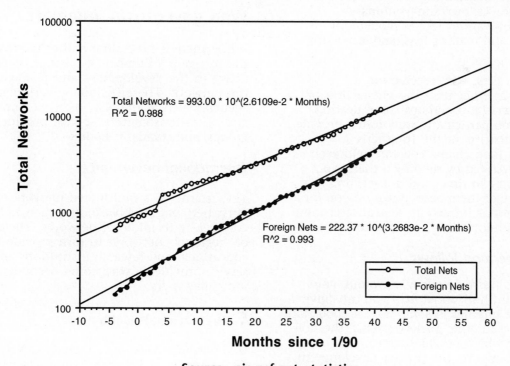

Total Networks = 993.00 * 10^(2.6109e-2 * Months)
R^2 = 0.988

Foreign Nets = 222.37 * 10^(3.2683e-2 * Months)
R^2 = 0.993

Total Nets
Foreign Nets

Source: nis.nsf.net statistics

Ask not what the Internet can do for you...

With the flood of books and articles about the Internet, many newcomers are arriving at the gates dressed in their dinner jackets, expecting to be fed a full-course meal. Instead, all they find is a bunch of wild berries that they are expected to turn into a pie.

The Internet is not an enormous info take-out chain to which you can pull up, order your Info Nuggets, and drive off. Rather, it is a (somewhat fragile) information ecosystem from which future generations can benefit, provided that we do our part in preserving it today.

Although the operation of the network itself is becoming increasingly professionalized, much of what makes the Internet interesting is contributed by ordinary (and some extraordinary) people, many of whom have little or no training in computer science. They contribute by maintaining resources such as software archives, providing summary documents on various topics, moderating conferences and mailing lists, and answering questions.

These volunteers, who receive no compensation other than the satisfaction of helping others (and perhaps some fleeting fame for a job particularly well done), provide the basic nutrients of the Internet's information food chain. You can help keep their souls well-fed by sending a thank-you note from time to time, and not reacting too hastily if one of them bears down on you for a seemingly minor infraction. Repeat after me: This is the Internet. It's supposed to be fun...

Warning: sermon follows

Once you've learned your way around, you might start to think about how you can "give back" to the Internet in some way. A good start is to join the Internet Society (ISOC), the non-profit group which provides a forum for users and which supports the further development of the network. Among other things, ISOC organizes an annual conference (INET), publishes a quarterly magazine, supports the Internet Engineering Task Force (IETF) and

will supervise the distribution of public keys for electronic mail security.

The Internet Society, (703)620-8990, Fax: (703)620-0913, email: `isoc@nri.reston.va.us`, `ftp nri.reston.va.us, cd /isoc`

Is it bad for me?

Whenever they hear about something that is supposed to be enjoyable, many people immediately ask three basic questions:

• Is it legal?
• How many calories does it have?
• Is it cholesterol-free?

I am happy to report that use of the Internet is legal (provided you stay within the rules), and has no calories or cholesterol, although individual attached hosts may be involved in food preparation, such as the Internet Coke Machines (`finger drink@csh.rit.edu`, `finger coke@cs.wisc.edu`) and the Internet Toaster.

Who governs the Internet?

While there is no central authority governing the Internet, a number of organizations are active in the development and management of the network. These include government agencies such as the NSF, network information and operations centers, service providers, user groups, and standards bodies.

Operational governance

The Internet is a multitiered network with "first tier" national backbones such as NSFNet connecting to midlevel networks. The midlevel or "regional" networks in turn provide links to educational and research institutions and local service providers, which offer accounts to individual users.

∇ The national backbones

U.S. national backbones include ESNet (Department of Energy), Milnet (Department of Defense), NSI (NASA), NSFNet (National Science Foundation), and TWB (DARPA). The NSFNet is the largest and most influential of the U.S. national backbones, since it connects the regional midlevel networks that in turn link up to educational and research institutions. While the connectivity provided by NSFNet is very useful, it should be understood that the existence of the Internet itself is not dependent on NSFNet.

The NSFNet backbone (also known as the Interim National Research and Education Network [NREN]) is currently being funded under the High Performance Computing Act signed by President Bush in November 1991. The NSFNet currently operates at an effective 22-Mbps speed with a 45-Mbps capacity, with an upgrade to 155-Mbps in the works.

▽ Mid-level networks

In an effort to stabilize and decentralize the network, the NSF supported the establishment of regional networks, each with their own Network Operations Center (NOC). After an initial period of NSF support, the regionals are to become self-supporting by charging connection fees. This policy of "hardening the regionals" has largely been successful, and today there are more than two dozen regional networks staffed with engineers and technicians.

The midlevel networks generally specialize in providing leased line connections at T1, ISDN or 56-Kbps speeds. For listings of midlevel networks, please consult Appendix B: Choice Products.

▽ Dialup providers

Just as retailers interface with the public, while distributors concentrate on "breaking bulk," a growing number of dial-up providers are now connecting to midlevel networks in order to offer accounts to individuals. Services such as Netcom, World, Holonet, MSEN and Colorado SuperNet are set up to handle a variety of needs. For further information on dial-up providers, please consult Appendix B: Choice Products.

▽ NICs and NOCs

Network Operation Centers (NOCs) and Network Information Centers (NICs) provide support for the operation of the national backbones and midlevel networks.

The recently established InterNIC, discussed later on, serves the Internet community by providing database, registration, and directory services.

Acceptable use policies

Use of government sponsored backbones such as the NSFNet must be consistent with the mission of the sponsoring agencies. The NSFNet Acceptable Use Policy (AUP) was created in order to clarify the acceptable uses of the NSFNet. The AUP distinguishes acceptable from unacceptable traffic based on the purpose of the traffic, rather than the source or destination hosts.

The NSFNet AUP applies **only** to the NSFNet backbone. Within the U.S., the mid-level networks are free to operate by different (and generally less restrictive) acceptable use policies, and outside the US, other countries and regions set policies for the use of their portions of the network. On complex issues such as encryption and privacy, the result can be a complex patchwork of rules within the many jurisdictions.

A modification to the NSF charter passed in 1992 gave the NSF additional flexibility in allowing commercial use of Internet that furthers its development as a research and educationally oriented network. This allowed commercial services such as Dow Jones, Lexis, Nexis, and Dialog to join the network. Allowing these services on the network benefits everyone, since not only do the service providers pay handsomely for the network connection, but universities and government libraries also save on fees they would have to pay to phone companies and commercial packet-switching networks.

As of April, 1994, the NSF will shift from funding the backbone directly to subsidizing access to backbone services by the regionals. As a result, connections to Network Access Points

(NAPs) are due to be provided on an "AUP-free" basis, and the NSFNet AUP will pass into memory.

The myth of "free access"

No Virginia, the Internet is not now and never has been "free." Even if you are not paying for the use of your account, someone else is, although they may not be passing it on to you.

Even if you have paid for your account, you may not have purchased unlimited rights to use it. While many Internet service providers charge a fixed fee for access based on the bandwidth of the connection, in the case of high-speed connections (56 Kbps or faster) this fee may assume that the connection will be in use only a fraction of the time. Just because you've paid for the connection, you may not have purchased the right to fill the bitpipe 24 hours a day, 7 days a week! The Internet is young enough that service contracts are often informal and seldomly explain in detail the assumptions used in calculating the rate structure. As part of the purchase process, have a chat with your service provider about what constitutes reasonable use.

Technical governance

Although the Internet is not centrally controlled, an enormous amount of effort goes into managing its technical development. This work is supervised and encouraged by organizations such as the Internet Society (ISOC), the Internet Architecture Board (IAB), the Intenet Engineering Task Force (IETF), the Internet Research Task Force (IRTF), and the Internet Assigned Numbers Authority (IANA).

The Internet Architecture Board (IAB)

The Internet Architecture Board (IAB) is the committee that is responsible for approving Internet standards. It sponsors two task forces, the IETF (concerned with engineering) and the IRTF (concerned with research issues).

Internet Architecture Board, BBN c/o A. Lyman Chapin, (617)873-3133, Fax: (617)873-4086, email: lyman@bbn.com

The Internet Engineering Task Force (IETF)

There is ongoing work on extending and improving the protocols on which the Internet is based. Internet standards-making takes place in the Internet Engineering Task Force (IETF), which is directed by the Internet Engineering Steering Group (IESG). The standards once developed are reviewed and approved by the IAB.

The IETF authorizes working groups on individual issues. For example, there is a working group on the subject of Uniform Resource Identifiers (URIs).

The IETF receives financial support from a number of sources, including governments and the Internet Society.

Internet Engineering Task Force, (703)620-8990, Fax: (703)620-0913, email: ietf-info@nri.reston.va.us

The Internet Research Task Force (IRTF)

While engineering issues are handled by the IETF, long-term or high-risk research is handled by the IRTF. Like the IETF, the IRTF has a steering committee, the Internet Research Steering Group, and authorizes working groups.

The Internet Assigned Numbers Authority

The Internet Assigned Numbers Authority (IANA) is run by the Information Sciences Institute at the University of Southern California. The IANA assigns numbers for "well-known" TCP and UDP ports, and for options within protocols. For further information, contact iana@isi.edu.

How do I accomplish something on the Internet?

To accomplish things on the Internet, you will need to gain proficiency with available tools. These include basic tools; directories for finding people and resources; meta-tools that add value to the basic tools; filtering and gathering agents; and miscellaneous tools for other functions.

The NSF Acceptable Use Policy

The NSFNet Acceptable Use Policy applies to use of the NSFNet backbone only; connecting networks formulate their own use policies, which are usually more liberal. For questions about this policy, contact the NSF Division of Networking and Communications Research.

General Principle

NSFNet backbone services are provided to support open research and education in and among U.S. research and instructional institutions, plus research arms of for-profit companies when they are engaged in open, scholarly communication and research. Use for other purposes is not acceptable.

Specifically acceptable uses

• Communications with foreign researchers and educators in connection with research or instruction, as long as any network that the foreign user employs for such communication provides reciprocal access to U.S. researchers and educators.

• Communication and exchange for professional development, to maintain currency, or to debate issues in a field or subfield of knowledge.

• Use for disciplinary-society, university-association, government-advisory, or standards activities related to the user's research and instructional activities.

• Use in applying for or administering grants or contracts for research or instruction, but not for other fund-raising or public-relations activities.

• Any other administrative communications or activities in direct support of research and instruction.

• Announcements of new products or services for use in research or instruction but not advertising of any kind.

• Any traffic originating from a network of another member agency of the Federal Networking Council, if the traffic meets the acceptable use policy of that agency.

• Communications incidental to otherwise acceptable use except for illegal or specifically unacceptable use.

Unacceptable uses

• Use for for-profit activities, unless covered by the General Principle or as a specifically acceptable use.

• Extensive use for private or personal business.

Basic tools

∇ File Transfer Protocol (FTP)

Using FTP you can send and receive files. Among other things, this allows you to download software from Internet software archives. Since the FTP program is included with most UNIX implementations, you can access it from a UNIX host or transfer files directly to your microcomputer with appropriate software. For more information on FTP, please consult Chapter 10: File Transfer.

∇ Telnet

`telnet` allows you login remotely to Internet services such as library catalogs; bulletin boards; commercial online services such as Dow Jones, CompuServe, Nexis, or Dialog; or Internet catalogs.

Versions of `telnet` are available for UNIX hosts, as well as on the Macintosh and PC (NCSA Telnet). For more information on `telnet`, please consult Chapter 11: Online Libraries.

∇ USENET

USENET is a distributed conferencing system that is transported mostly over the Internet. With more than 3000 discussion groups, there is an area (or "news group") for almost every taste. You can access USENET via UNIX news readers such as rn, nn, trn, or tin, or directly on your micrcomputer using software such as Trumpet (DOS and Windows), WinVN (Windows), and Newswatcher or Nuntius (Macintosh). For more information on USENET, please consult Chapter 12: USENET.

∇ Electronic mail

Using electronic mail you can send messages and files to users on the Internet as well as on non-Internet networks. Since mail software is included with UNIX, you can access mail from a UNIX host, or via your microcomputer with software such as Eudora for Macintosh and Windows, or nuPOP or POPMAIL for DOS. For more information on electronic mail, please consult Chapter 9: Electronic Mail.

∇ Z39.50

The Z39.50 standard is a protocol for information retrieval. The Wide Area Information Servers (WAIS) project, now a commercial product from WAIS, Inc., first popularized use of Z39.50 on the Internet, and there are now several Z39.50 compatible products and hundreds of publicly accessible databases (called sources). To use them, the user formulates a question in plain English (versions for other languages are also available) and provides a list of selected sources to search.

WAIS then looks for relevant documents, and for the "hits," provides an indication of how closely they conform to the search criteria. You may then select particularly relevant documents and indicate that you want WAIS to "find more documents like this one," in an effort to refine the search.

Major versions of Z39.50 include Z39.50 (88), the version implemented in WAIS, and Z39.50 version 2, which is upwards compatible with Z39.50 (88), and will be the basis of forthcoming implementations.

A great deal of information about the Internet itself is available for retrieval by Z39.50 clients. Since helpful documents are available on virtually every aspect of Internet use, Z39.50 accessible databases can be used as an online help system. Z39.50 clients are available for UNIX, Macintosh, DOS, Windows, and NeXT. For more information on Z39.50, please consult Chapter 14: Information Servers.

Directory services

∇ Finding files

Archie is a catalog of Internet files, cataloging thousands of files in more than 1300 archives. Using Archie you can locate virtually all of the publicly distributable software discussed in this guide. For more information on archie, see Chapter 10: Archie.

▽ Finding people

Knowbot, Ph, Whois, Finger, and the USENET Addresses database are methods for finding someone's electronic mail address. These directories are discussed in Chapter 9: Finding People.

▽ Finding businesses

The Internet Business Pages (IBP) provides a directory of firms doing business over the Internet. IBP is discussed in Chapter 9.

▽ Finding resources

VERONICA, discussed in Chapter 14: Gopher, is a catalog of resources accessible within Gopher. Using VERONICA, you can search thousands of resources.

▽ Finding sites

Hytelnet is a periodically updated catalog of more than 1000 sites accessible via remote login. Sites are cataloged by location, interface, and content, and include online libraries, commercial online services, and bulletin boards. Hytelnet is discussed in Chapter 11: Online Libraries.

Meta-tools

For the beginner, learning to use several Internet tools, each with its own commands and interface, may be somewhat intimidating. In order to ease the burden of having to learn several programs before beginning, Internet meta-tools such as Gopher and World Wide Web were created. These tools allow users to access several tools from a single program. They also add functionality to the basic tools by providing additional facilities such as indexes, bookmarks, and annotations.

▽ Gopher – the Internet as menu

Using Gopher you can perform many Internet functions by selecting items from a menu. Where Gopher does not include built-in support for a function (such as Telnet), it will either gateway the request or invoke another program, which will then return control to Gopher.

Gopher includes support for querying WAIS databases, although certain functions such as relevance feedback are not currently supported. For example, it is possible to use Gopher to access a WAIS index of articles from the UPI newswire. This allows the user to search on "Bosnia" and find all the current articles pertaining to that subject. The database itself resides in a WAIS server, and the query is gatewayed.

Some Gopher clients support bookmarks, which let users create their own menus of frequently used services. For example, your bookmark might include an entry for the alt.fishing news group, an archive of a fishing-related mailing list, and an entry for a database of salmon recipes.

Gopher clients are available under UNIX, as well as DOS, Windows, and Macintosh. For more information, please consult Chapter 14: Gopher.

▽ World Wide Web (W3) – the Internet as Hypertext

World Wide Web, also known as WWW or W3, is a hypertextual front-end to Internet that allows for the linking together of text, files, pictures, sounds, movies, telnet sites, WAIS sources, etc. Since W3 supports annotations, it is possible to create your own personalized web of frequently accessed information.

World Wide Web clients are called browsers. Line mode and X-Window browsers are available for UNIX, and graphical browsers are available for NeXT, Macintosh, and DOS.

The National Center for Supercomputing Applications (NCSA) is developing both servers and browsers for an extended version of W3 called Mosaic. Mosaic supports embedded sounds, movies, and pictures, and already many demonstration hypertexts have been developed.

Traffic levels

In terms of packets, the most popular Internet services are FTP, Telnet, USENET, and electronic mail, in that order. As shown in the top figure on the next page, this "pecking order" is fairly stable over time.

As shown in the bottom figure, W3 is one of the most rapidly growing Internet services. If present trends continue, it will surpass Gopher traffic levels on the NSFNet backbone sometime in 1993, and has already surpassed WAIS.

Filters and agents

The irony of the Information Revolution is that while the amount of information grows, the amount of time in which to assimilate it seems to shrink. How can you keep up with the information available on the Internet without spending an excessive amount of time doing it?

The two major approaches for continuously gathering information automatically are filtering devices and gathering agents. Intelligent agents (also sometimes called "Knowbots") allow for the active gathering of information. In contrast, filtering devices passively pass judgment on material from an incoming data stream, and are simpler to understand and build. An example of a filtering device is the Elm filter tool, discussed in Chapter 9: Mail. This tool operates using simple rules applied to the To:, From: or Subject: headers of mail messages, but there are also more sophisticated filters that can filter based on the body of a message.

If you don't understand why filters are important, you will. Within a year of gaining Internet access, electronic mail shifts from being an enabling technology to a burden. Many of us now receive more than a hundred mail messages a day, way too much to handle without automated assistance.

Other tools

Other Internet tools include Finger, Talk, Internet Relay Chat, and MUDs.

∇ Finger

Finger allows you to find out about other Internet users, but it can also be used to disseminate small amounts of information. Finger clients are available for many operating environments, including UNIX, Macintosh, and Windows. For more information on Finger, consult Chapter 9: Electronic Mail.

∇ Talk

Talk lets you chat person to person with another Internet user. Talk clients are available for many operating evironments, including UNIX, Macintosh, and Windows. For more information on Talk, please consult Chapter 13: Talk.

∇ Internet Relay Chat (IRC)

IRC lets you collaborate in real time with Internet users worldwide. The most common form of collaboration is a real-time conversation, which is provided by standard IRC software. You can access IRC via the `irc` command on a UNIX host, or by `telnet` to a UNIX host running the IRC client software. IRC clients are also available for the Macintosh (IRCle or Homer). IRC is more than just an application; it is also a platform for creating collaborative applications. For example, the HomerPaint application uses IRC in order to provide for collaborative painting. For more information on IRC, please consult Chapter 13: IRC.

∇ MUDs

Multiple User Dungeons (MUDs) are multiuser role-playing games. For more information on MUDs, please consult Chapter 13: MUDs.

∇ Bulletin boards

While some bulletin boards are accessible via telnet sessions, other systems use their own protocols, running on top of TCP/IP. This is known as tunneling.

Traffic on the NSFNet Backbone by Application

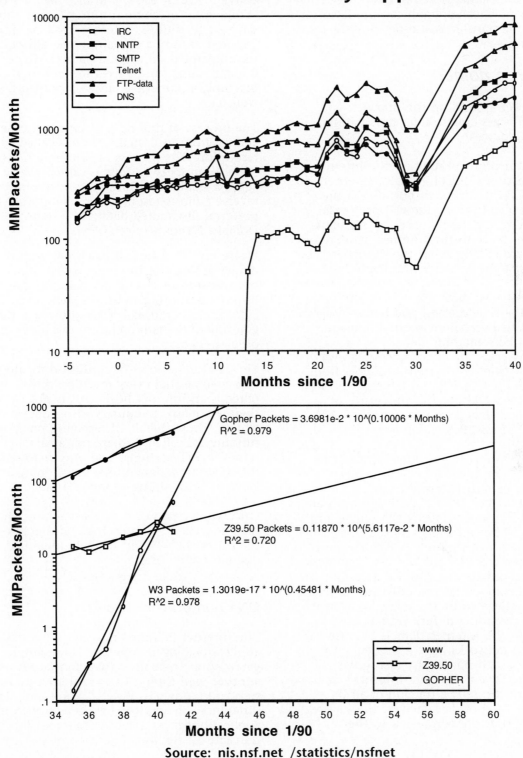

Source: nis.nsf.net /statistics/nsfnet

Graphical BBSes such as FirstClass and NovaLink Professional now run over TCP/IP, providing sophisticated graphical interfaces to messaging, file transfer, real-time chatting and conferencing.

What's in a name?

In order to get around on the Internet, you will need to learn how to refer to machines, users, and resources.

The dominant protocol used on the Internet is the Transmission Control Protocol/Internet Protocol (TCP/IP). Although portions of the Internet are also running the OSI protocols CLNP and TP4, for the purposes of this book, whenever we refer to the Internet, you should assume we are talking about the IP Internet, or the portion of the Internet running TCP/IP.

Internet hosts have both numeric addresses (known as the IP addresses) and names (known as fully qualified domain names). A domain name might be something like haas.berkeley.edu. The domain name grows more specific from left to right as it goes from the top level domain (edu for educational) to a subdomain (berkeley for the University of California, Berkeley) to a machine (haas, the Haas School of Business computer).

The Internet Protocol (IP) address is a 32-bit address that is represented as four octets separated by periods (referred to as a "dotted quad"), such as 192.187.157.2. IP addresses are used by IP to uniquely specify the source and destination addresses of packets sent over the network. Every host running TCP/IP has an IP address, which must be unique. The IP address space is managed by the InterNIC registrar, and it is imperative that you only use addresses assigned or delegated by the registrar, even if you are not intending to link your TCP/IP network with the Internet. This is because disconnected networks have a tendency to "leak" traffic, with potentially disruptive consequences. Even with the Internet's incredible growth, only a fraction of all IP networks assigned or delegated by the InterNIC registrar are connected to the Internet.

Domain names were created purely for the convenience of users, and are not used by IP. While every machine running TCP/IP must have an IP address, Internet hosts are not required to have a domain name, although it is recommended. In most situations where a domain name can be used to refer to a machine, a numeric IP address will work as well.

The process of finding a machine's numeric address from its domain name is called address resolution. The process of finding a machine's name from its IP address is called reverse address resolution. Both address resolution and reverse address resolution are supported by a powerful distributed database system known as Domain Name Service (DNS).

Please note that not all machines with domain names are on the Internet. To facilitate transmission of electronic mail between the Internet and other networks such as UUCP, FidoNet and FrEdMail, DNS allows for the granting of domain names to machines on other networks.

This is often a point of confusion for novices, who assume that every machine with a domain name is an Internet host. This is not the case; there are many computers with domain names which, while capable of receiving mail, are not running TCP/IP and so are not available for telnet or FTP sessions. The only requirement for obtaining a domain name is finding an Internet host willing to forward mail.

Once you've named a user's machine, their mail address is given by the concatenation of their userID, "@", and the fully qualified domain name. Example: aboba@world.std.com. Got it?

DNS and other networks

The Internet is linked to other networks via applications layer gateways. For example, mail gateways are machines that translate from another mail format to the Internet mail standard (known as RFC 822) and back. Due to differences in services between protocols, applications layer gateways may not be able to translate all services. The level of success depends on the protocols involved and the thoroughness of the gateway implementation. For example, FidoNet/UUCP gateways generally translate electronic mail and conferences, allowing FidoNet nodes to send UUCP mail and participate in USENET. Some gateways also translate file sends and requests. For more information on FidoNet/UUCP gateways, please consult Chapter 18: From FidoNet to UUCP and Back.

Although domains were not originally intended to correspond to networks, two store and forward networks, FidoNet and FrEdMail, have domain names, fidonet.org and fred.org. Two other networks, BITNET and UUCP, utilize "pseudo domains," which are not domains at all. Mail destined for these "pseudo domains" is either routed through gateways, or in cases where the receiver has appropriate software installed (such as UREP for BITNET or smail and pathalias for UUCP), sent directly. For more information on DNS, please consult Chapter 15: Bulletin Boards and the Internet.

The yellow pages problem

The only constant on the Internet is change. More machines, users, services, databases, files, and conferences are added every day. This presents users, developers (and authors!) with the challenge of keeping up to date.

How can you keep up with something so large that is changing so rapidly? One part of the problem is to uncover those resources that are of use to you. This is called the resource discovery problem. Another part of the problem is to find those resources once you know which ones you are looking for. This is the resource location problem. Efforts are now under way to provide enhanced directory service, both for user electronic mail addresses ("White Pages"), and for Internet services or resources ("Yellow Pages"). The solution for the Yellow Pages problem involves the use of Uniform Resource Identifiers (URIs).

Resource naming and location

Just as we have the ISBN and Dewey Decimal systems for books, a Uniform Resource Identifier (URI) system is under development

for Internet resources. This includes Uniform Resource Numbers (URNs) and Uniform Resource Locators (URLs).

URNs uniquely identify the publisher as well as the version and format of a particular document, while URLs specify the authoritative source for a document. For example, the authoritative source for updates to the IBM PC TCP/IP Resource Listings is the MailCom anonymous FTP archive on netcom1.netcom.com. The URL for this document is:

```
file://netcom1.netcom.com/pub/mailcom/
IBMTCP/ibmtcp.zip
```

Here, `file` specifies anonymous FTP as the retrieval method. Other types are http [for HyperText Transfer Protocol], news [USENET news group], gopher for a gopher site, and mailto for a mail address. URLs may also specify a port (such as TCP port 80 for http), which we will explain later in this chapter. Examples of URLs are given in the figure which follows.

Resource discovery services

The URN specification has not yet attained standard status. Once it has solidified, resource directories will be put in place that will be searchable by tools such as WAIS, Gopher, and W3. These directories will provide you with the URNs of resources in your field of interest, much as *Books in Print* provides you with the ISBN number of a desired book.

Resource location services

Assuming that you've found the URN for a document, how do you find where the document is kept? This is analogous to trying to locate a bookstore selling a particular book, based on the ISBN number. A service called the URN registrar is under development that solves this problem.

Rather than keeping information on URLs itself, the registrar merely keeps a list of sites that have agreed to translate a particular URN into a URL. To try out a sample URN registrar, **telnet registrar.santjoe.edu 2500** or **mail urn_reg@saintjoe.edu.**

The Domain Name System

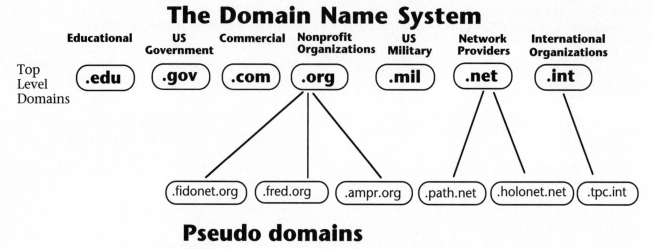

Educational	US Government	Commercial	Nonprofit Organizations	US Military	Network Providers	International Organizations

Top Level Domains

.edu   **.gov**   **.com**   **.org**   **.mil**   **.net**   **.int**

.fidonet.org   .fred.org   .ampr.org   .path.net   .holonet.net   .tpc.int

Pseudo domains

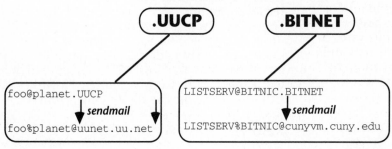

.UUCP   **.BITNET**

```
foo@planet.UUCP
        ↓ sendmail     ↓
foo%planet@uunet.uu.net
```

```
LISTSERV@BITNIC.BITNET
        ↓ sendmail
LISTSERV%BITNIC@cunyvm.cuny.edu
```

TCP/IP Addresses

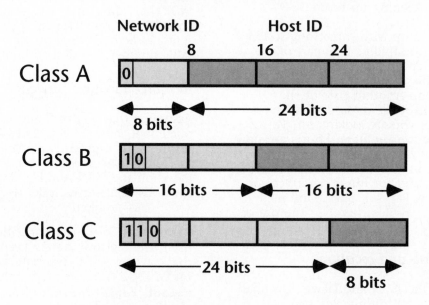

Network ID   Host ID

    8   16   24

Class A   0

← 8 bits → ← 24 bits →

Class B   1 0

← 16 bits → ← 16 bits →

Class C   1 1 0

← 24 bits → ← 8 bits →

Uniform Resource Locators (URLs)

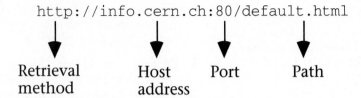

```
http://info.cern.ch:80/default.html
```

Retrieval method   Host address   Port   Path

Examples:

```
news:comp.protocols.tcp-ip.ibmpc
telnet://aboba@world.std.com:23
gopher://world.std.com:70/
mailto:aboba@world.std.com
wais://quake.think.com:210/uumap.src
file://netcom1.netcom.com/pub/mailcom/README
```

The InterNIC

In the spring of 1992, the NSF created the InterNIC in order to support and enhance Registration Services, Directory and Database Services, and Information Services. Among other things, the InterNIC will be developing the catalog of Internet resources. The contract for the InterNIC was awarded to a consortium of Network Solutions, Inc. (NSI) (Registration services), AT&T (Directory services) and General Atomics/CERFnet (Information services).

Registration Services involve keeping track of networks, domains, associations and other Internet entitites, and maintaining the Whois registry. Registration Services also assigns IP network numbers and Autonomous System numbers. The phone number for Registration Services is (703)742-4777. To obtain information by mail, **mail mailserv@rs.internic.net**, body: **help.**

Directory and Database Services includes maintaining lists of file archive sites, Internet services, email address directories and library catalogs. AT&T will also provide directories of email addresses and Internet services via WAIS and Gopher servers, and eventually via X.500. To access the directory of directories, **telnet ds.internic.net**, login: **wais, ftp ds.internic.net**, login: **anonymous,** or

mail mailserv@ds.internic.net, body: **help.** Information is available by calling (908)668-6587, or via **mail admin@ds.internic.net.** To submit information on a resource to the directory of directories, **mail request@ds.internic.net.**

Information Services involves providing information on Internet access, tools, and resources as well as seminars on use of the network. This will eventually include the resource lookup service based on URIs. A referral desk is available at (800)444-4345, (619)455-4600, email: info@internic.net. A variety of mailing lists are also available. To subscribe **mail listserv@is.internic.net,** with the following command in the body:
subscribe <list-name> <your-name>

Example:
subscribe announce Bernard Aboba

Available mailing lists include:

announce	Moderated announcements on InterNIC services
nics	Services for other NICs
net-resources	Moderated list on new Internet resources
net-happenings	Another moderated lists on new, tools, books, resources, etc.

A monthly newsletter called InterNIC Interactive is also available. To subscribe, `mail internic-interactive-request.` Finally, CERFnet provides a central repository of Internet information, available via `ftp is.internic.net`, login: `anonymous`, `get /infosource/INDEX`. The archive is indexed via WAIS as internic-infosource.src, and a Gopher server is available via `telnet is.internic.net`, login: `gopher`. To retrieve information by mail, `mail mailserv@is.internic.net`, body: `help`.

Below is an example of accessing the InterNIC via Gopher. For more information on Gopher, please see Chapter 14: Gopher.

```
% telnet is.internic.net
Trying...
Connected to is.internic.net.
Escape character is '^]'.

SunOS UNIX (is)
login: gopher

Welcome to the InterNIC Information Service Gopher.
Please enter your terminal type

TERM = (vt100)
Press ? for Help, q to Quit, u to go up a menu
Retrieving Directory..-

Internet Gopher Information Client v1.11

InterNIC Information Services InfoSource

  -->  1.  Welcome to the InfoSource/
       2.  InfoSource Update (What's New and Changed).
       3.  InfoSource Table of Contents.
       4.  Provider Lists/
       5.  InterNIC Store/
       6.  About InterNIC Information Services/
       7.  Getting Started on the Internet/
       8.  Internet Information for Everybody/
       9.  Just for NICs/
      10.  NSFNET, NREN, National Information
           Infrastructure Information/
      11.  Beyond InterNIC: Virtual Treasures of the
           Internet/
      12.  Questions or Comments about InfoSource?.
      13.  Searching the InfoSource by Keyword/

Press ? for Help, q to Quit, u to go up a menu
Page: 1/1
```

Protocol layering

Networking is an inherently complex undertaking, yet not everyone interested in using or developing network software is interested in all the details. In order to ease the process of specifying protocols and developing software, network protocols are divided into logically distinct portions known as protocol layers. To simplify communications between the layers, each layer only communicates with layers directly above and below it. Internet Protocol layers include:

• **The application layer.** This layer interacts with the user and includes applications such as Telnet, FTP, Gopher, FSP, W3, WAIS, etc.

• **The transport layer.** This layer handles end-to-end delivery of data (referred to as messages or streams) from the application layer. In the process, data is broken into chunks known as packets or segments and handed off to the Internet layer.

Transport layer protocols include Transmission Control Protocol (TCP) and User Datagram Protocol (UDP). Transmission Control Protocol (TCP) is connection-oriented protocol that reliably delivers segments in sequence. This means that TCP provides error correction and sequencing, and that a connection setup procedure is required before sending data.

In contrast, UDP is a connectionless "best efforts" protocol. This means that each packet is sent individually without a connection needing to be setup beforehand, and that UDP makes no guarantee that packets will arrive error free or in the correct sequence.

• **The Internet layer.** This layer receives packets or segments for delivery from the transport layer and routes them between networks to the destination, as datagrams.

• **The network layer.** This layer receives datagrams for delivery between machines on the same network and accesses the physical hardware in order to transmit them as frames.

• **The physical layer.** This layer provides the physical connections between hosts, allowing signals to propagate.

Data passed up and down the protocol stack is encapsulated and decapsulated. For outgoing data, at each stage of passage from the application layer down to the physical layer, a header is added on. TCP adds a TCP header to data passed to it from the Application layer; IP adds a header to TCP segments passed to it; and the network layer adds another header to IP datagrams that it receives before transmitting it over the physical connection.

Protocol Layering in TCP/IP

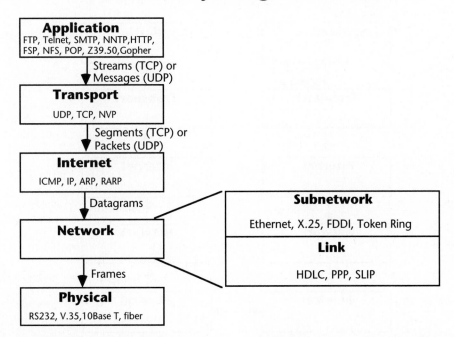

The process of decapsulation begins upon reception, with headers being removed as data travels up the protocol stack from the physical layer to the applications layer of the receiving machine.

Ethernet frames

The Ethernet frames contain 48-bit source and destination addresses as well as a 16-bit protocol type field. A host's Ethernet address is embedded in hardware, and is guaranteed to be unique. The presence of a protocol type field allows more than one protocol to be run on the network simultaneously, i.e., Novell IPX and IP.

IP datagrams

Each Internet Protocol (IP) datagram header contains the source and destination IP addresses, as well as version, length and protocol fields. The source and destination addresses are similar in concept to the sending and return addresses that appear on a letter. The protocol field allows IP to be used with multiple upper level protocols such as UDP and TCP.

The version and length fields give IP a lot of flexibility, since they in principle allow for multiple versions of IP to interoperate, and future additions to the header fields. This flexibility may prove very handy if and when IP is modified.

Ports and sockets

While the Internet Protocol (IP) provides the mechanism for communicating between machines, upper level protocols such as UDP and TCP provide the means by which a process on one machine can communicate with a process on another machine.

Just as an apartment building may have multiple dwellings, a machine may be running more than one application. In order to specify the source and destination applications, identifiers known as port numbers are required. The combination of an Internet address and a port number is known as a socket. A pair of sockets is known as a connection. Since a machine may be running multiple instances of the same application, multiple processes may be using the same socket. However, each connection is unique.

Communications Between Two Processes

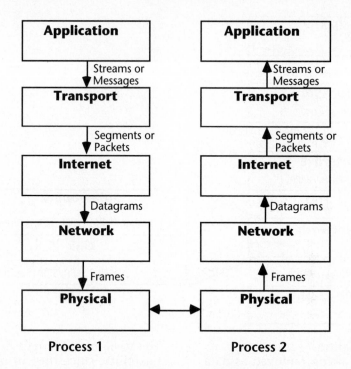

Packet encapsulation and decapsulation

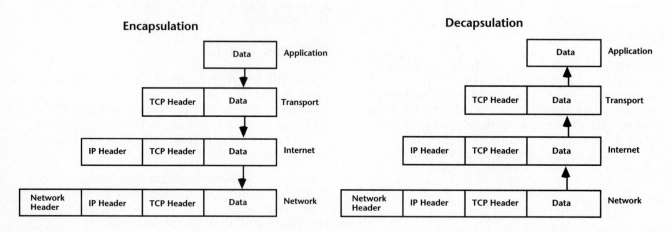

"Well Known" TCP Protocol Ports

Port	Keyword	Description	Reference
5	RJE	Remote Job Entry	RFC 407
7	ECHO	Echo	RFC 862
11	USERS	Currently Active Users	RFC 866
13	DAYTIME	Daytime	RFC 867
15	NETSTAT	Who Is Up or NETSTAT	
17	QUOTE	Quote of the Day	RFC 865
19	CHARGEN	Character Generator	RFC 864
20	FTP-DATA	File Transfer Protocol (data)	RFC 959, 765
21	FTP	File Transfer Protocol (control)	RFC 959, 765
23	TELNET	Terminal Connection	RFC 854, 764
25	SMTP	Simple Mail Transport Protocol	RFC 1047,821, 822, 733
37	TIME	Time Server	RFC 868
39	RLP	Resource Location Protocol	RFC 887
42	NAMESERVER	Host Name Server	IEN 116
43	NICNAME	Who Is	RFC 954
53	DOMAIN	Domain Name Server	RFC 881,882, 883, 920, 921, 973,974
67	BOOTPS	Bootstrap Protocol Server	RFC 951
68	BOOTPC	Bootstrap Protocol Client	RFC 951
69	TFTP	Trivial File Transfer Protocol	RFC 783
70	GOPHER	Gopher Protocol	RFC 1436
79	FINGER	Finger	RFC 742
80	HTTP	HyperText Transfer Protocol	
95	SUPDUP	SUPDUP Protocol	
101	HOSTNAME	NIC Host Name Server	RFC 953
103	X400	X400	RFC 1148,1137,1026,987
104	X400-SND	X400-SND	
109	POP2	Post Office Protocol v2	RFC 1082
110	POP3	Post Office Protocol v3	RFC 1225
111	SUNRPC	Sun Remote Procedure Call	
113	AUTH	Authentication Service	RFC 931
117	UUCP-PATH	UUCP Path Service	
119	NNTP	Network News Transfer Protocol	RFC 977
123	NTP	Network Time Protocol	RFC 1119
127	LOCUS-CON	Locus-con	
143	IMAP2	Interim Mail Access Protocol v2	
144	NEWS	NeWS	
150	SQL-NET	SQL-NET	
156	SQLSRV	SQL Service	
158	PCMAIL-SRV	PCMAIL Server	RFC 1056
161	SNMP	Simple Network Management Protocol	RFC 1157
175	VMNET	VMNET Mail Transfer Protocol	
178	NeXTSTEP	NeXTSTEP Window Server	
191	PROSPERO	Prospero	
210	Z39.50	Z39.50 Information Retrieval Protocol	
513	WHO	WHO	
540	UUCP	Unix to Unix Copy Protocol	
6667	IRC	Internet Relay Chat	RFC 1459

Sockets and Connections

192.187.157.2

Z39.50 Server	NNTP Client
Port 210	Port 4437

TCP	
IP	

140.174.2.71

NNTP Server	Z39.50 Client
Port 119	Port 4522

TCP	
IP	

NNTP client socket:
192.187.157.2 (4437)

Z39.50 server socket:
192.187.157.2 (210)

NNTP server socket:
140.174.2.71 (119)

Z39.50 client socket:
140.174.2.71(4522)

NNTP Connection: 192.187.157.2 (4437) and 140.174.2.71 (119)

Z39.50 Connection: 192.187.157.2 (210) and 140.174.2.71 (4522)

Well-known ports

The source and destination port number is included in both the TCP and UDP headers. Port numbers for server applications are usually pre-assigned so that clients can know how to connect to them. Pre-assigned or "well known port" numbers fall in the range 0-1023, and are assigned by IANA. There are also ports in the range (1024-65535) which are in common use for certain applications, and which IANA has "registered." In contrast, clients typically have their port numbers assigned on the fly.

Note that since IP includes a protocol field, TCP ports are distinct from UDP ports, although protocols using both UDP and TCP typically are assigned the same port number.

The TCP/IP protocol suite

Standardized communication mechanisms exist in every protocol layer. As a result there are applications level protocols, transport protocols, internet protocols, and network protocols.

Network protocols

∇ Ethernet

Ethernet is a local area networking technology which allows multiple hosts to share use of a physical medium (usually coaxial cable or twisted pair) based on the Carrier Sense Multiple Access/Collision Detection (CSMA/CD) technique. Ethernet was developed by Xerox, who have handled assignment of unique addresses for each board or chip sold. Since Ethernet is one of the most common network interfaces used with TCP/IP, beginners often assume that Ethernet and the Internet are synonymous.

∇ SLIP and PPP

Serial Line Internet Protocol (SLIP) and Point to Point Protocol (PPP) are protocols for transmission over a serial line or modem. SLIP is a very simple protocol for framing IP datagrams. As a result, it does not support negotiation of session parameters (such as header compression) and since it has no protocol field, its use is restricted to TCP/IP.

In contrast, PPP is an Internet standard that can also be used with protocols other than TCP/IP, such as Novell or AppleTalk. It supports the negotiation of session parameters (including obtaining the PPP client's IP address). As a result, PPP is easier than SLIP to administer, although SLIP is simpler and has been more widely implemented since it came first.

▽ ARP

The Address Resolution Protocol (ARP), described in RFC 826, is used by a host to determine the physical address of a system on the same network, given its IP address. ARP works by broadcasting an ARP request packet to all systems on the local network. Only the system with the IP address identified in the packet is to respond, with its physical address. The physical addresses, when received, are stored in a table known as the ARP table. ARP only works on LANs that support broadcasting, such as Ethernet.

Hosts looking for a quick and dirty way to set up a single SLIP or PPP connection sometimes use a technique known as Proxy Arp to pretend that the SLIP or PPP connected host is on the local Ethernet. This works by having the Ethernet connected host respond to an ARP query for the remote host with its own Ethernet address. The host then routes incoming datagrams bound for the remote host over the SLIP or PPP link.

▽ RARP

The Reverse Address Resolution Protocol (ARP), described in RFC 903, is used by a host to determine its IP address, given the physical address. This is used at boot time by diskless workstations that have their physical address embedded on the network card but have no disk to store the IP address. RARP requests are also broadcast on the local network, but only the local RARP servers are to reply.

RARP also only works on LANs that support broadcasting, such as Ethernet. It therefore cannot be used by a SLIP link to obtain its IP address; BOOTP is used for this.

Internet Protocols

▽ IP

Internet Protocol (IP) provides for the delivery of datagrams between hosts, including routing between networks.

▽ ICMP

Internet Control Message Protocol (ICMP) uses IP for message delivery, but it is nevertheless considered an Internet level protocol since it provides functions essential to the proper functioning of IP, such as flow control, error messages, packet echoing, and route redirection. Be aware that ICMP can be functioning on a system which has no higher level network services available. Thus, you may be able to `ping` (/etc/ping or /usr/etc/ping in UNIX, various packages on the Mac, DOS, and Windows) a system which will not respond to `telnet` or `ftp`.

Transport protocols

▽ TCP

Transmission Control Protocol (TCP) provides for reliable delivery of data between communicating applications. To the application, TCP provides for transfer of byte streams and end-to-end error detection and correction. In order to differentiate among applications, TCP assigns port numbers to them. Servers receive "well-known port" numbers for clients to know how to set up a connection to them.

▽ UDP

User Datagram Protocol (UDP) provides application-level access to IP. In contrast to TCP, it does not guarantee delivery or sequencing of packets, nor must a connection be established before sending. Application level protocols such as NFS, FSP and TFTP run on top of UDP. Applications built on UDP usually don't ask for passwords or other identification.

Application-level protocols

∇ BOOTP

The BOOTstrap Protocol (BOOTP), described in RFC 951, is used by diskless workstations to obtain their IP address and the name of a file to be executed. It is therefore an alternative to RARP. Unlike RARP, BOOTP requests can be directed to a specific server not on the same physical network. Also, since BOOTP encodes its requests in UDP packets, rather than in network frames, it can be used by SLIP nodes looking to obtain their IP address.

∇ SMTP

SMTP (which stands for Simple Mail Transfer Protocol) is the primary Internet mail delivery protocol. Since most SMTP implementations do not allow mail to be held for pickup, SMTP is mainly used to deliver mail to nodes with dedicated connections. SMTP servers operate on TCP port 25.

∇ POP

Post Office Protocol (POP) is a store and forward protocol that allows for the remote retrieval of mail from a host. This is useful for hosts with intermittent Internet connections since it allows mail to be held for pickup. POP servers are most appropriate for situations where there is a single user per client machine. POP servers operate on TCP port 109 and 110.

∇ IMAP

The Interactive Mail Access Protocol (IMAP) is a client/server protocol that also allows for remote manipulation of mail boxes. Although it is similar in purpose to POP, IMAP supports additional features. These include manipulation of multiple simultaneous mailboxes, support for news as well as mail, storage as well as retrieval of mail, and efficient operation with large mailboxes. As a result, IMAP is preferred by many sites. IMAP2 servers run on port 143.

∇ FTP

File Transfer Protocol (FTP) allows for the transfer of binary or ASCII files between hosts. FTP servers operate on TCP ports 20 and 21.

∇ FSP

FSP is an alternative file transfer protocol running over UDP that was specifically designed for use in anonymous archives. It does not yet have a well-known port allocation.

∇ HTTP

HyperText Transfer Protocol (HTTP) is the stateless protocol used for file transfer within World Wide Web (W3). HTTP servers reside on TCP port 80.

∇ Z39.50

Z39.50 is an information retrieval protocol used by programs such as WAIS and FreeWAIS. Z39.50 servers reside on TCP port 210.

∇ NNTP

Network News Transfer Protocol (NNTP) is the protocol by which USENET news is transferred between Internet nodes. NNTP is a client/server protocol that offers both a "pull" mode in which clients request articles (frequently used by dialup SLIP/PPP users), and a "push" mode in which servers pass on articles. Pull mode NNTP is very CPU intensive, and should not be used for extensive news transfers. NNTP servers operate on TCP port 119.

∇ NFS

Network File Service is a file service protocol that can be used to mount remote volumes on a local machine. Most NFS implementations run over UDP, although versions running over TCP also exist.

∇ TFTP

Trivial File Transfer Protocol (TFTP) is an ACK/NAK file transfer protocol running over UDP that generally lacks authentication facilities and is often used in booting diskless workstations. The lack of authentication facilities can be a security problem if read and write access privileges are not appropriately restricted.

∇ DNS

Domain Name Service (DNS) provides the means by which the name of an Internet host (foo.org) is resolved to an IP address (such as 192.187.157.2). DNS may run over either UDP or TCP, in either case operating on port 53.

The future of the Internet

The Internet is both a vehicle for research on the art and science of networking, and an operational network. As a technology on the leading edge, it is changing rapidly. Here are some of the issues to keep an eye on.

The rise of the Internet BBS

Today there are more than 100,000 public bulletin board systems world wide, offering a vast array of services. As of this writing, only a few dozen of them were accessible via the Internet. Yet it is likely that this trickle will become a flood in the coming years, combining the entrepreneurial spirit and grass-roots support of bulletin boards with the global connectivity of the Internet. It is also likely that entire bulletin board networks will standardize on the Internet as their means of hauling traffic across long distances.

Commercialization

The Internet has enormous potential for increasing the efficiency of business. Examples include Electronic Document Interchange between firms and suppliers; electronic marketplaces and vendor catalogues; electronic employment services; automation of taxation and regulatory processes; multi-media training and learning systems.

Privacy and security

Beyond efficiency improvements, the Internet also has great potential as a medium for carrying out transactions. This will require the ability to keep transactions secure (encryption), and to guarantee that individuals sending messages over the network are who they say they are (authentication). To enable commercial transactions, we will also need means of transmitting funds ("digital cash"), as well as signing ("digital signatures") and dating ("digital timestamping") of contracts.

At the same time, for the Internet to be effective as a communications medium, individuals will need to be assured of privacy and possibly anonymity. Standards for Privacy Enhanced Mail (PEM) have been developed (RFCs 1113, 1114, 1115) and implementations such as RIPEM are available.

For more information on privacy, security, and anonymity issues please turn to Chapter 8: Privacy and Security on the Internet.

Multimedia

The Multipurpose Internet Mail Extensions (MIME), documented in RFC 1341, is a multimedia document standard. With the MIME standard becoming increasingly popular, support is a likely addition to existing Internet applications, and as well as to some BBS software packages.

Multimedia services are also in development. Internet Talk Radio has been in operation for several months now, and IETF meetings are routinely broadcast via Packet Video Multicasting, supported by the Multicast Backbone or MBone. However, it is not clear that current facilities, pricing, and routing schemes can support extensive Packet Video Multicasting.

Mobile connectivity

Already we have seen HP95LX palm top computers on the Internet, and Internet access for mobile computers and Personal Digital Assistants (PDAs) is clearly in our future.

Growth in NSFNet Traffic

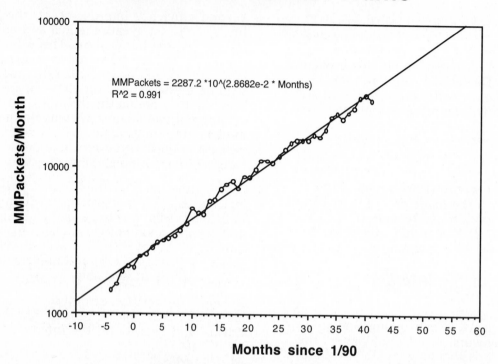

MMPackets = 2287.2 *10^(2.8682e-2 * Months)
R^2 = 0.991

Source: nis.nsf.net /statistics/nsfnet

Fixing potholes on the global data highway

As a work in progress, the Internet is continually under development, and just as a highway under construction is likely to experience traffic jams at times, so too should users expect occasional problems.

Advanced network management tools are now under development that will improve reliability by quickly, remotely, and automatically filling in the potholes on the global data highway.

Conduit to government

The Internet is in the process of becoming a communications vehicle for local, state, and federal governments. Through the deployment of Free-Nets (described in Chapter 32: How The National Public Telecomputing Network Came To Be, and Free-Netting—The Development of Free, Public-Access, Community Computer Systems), dozens of cities in the U.S. and other nations now offer online access to local governments.

At the federal level, many agencies within the executive branch, as well as the House of Representatives and the Senate, now maintain, or are in the process of developing, a presence on the Internet. The effect of such links remains to be seen; creating a means by which millions of people can send mail to their government is not the same as creating a vehicle for responding to so much mail. (Robo-congresspersons, anyone?)

Distance education

Through the funding of the NSF and the participation of many academic institutions, the Internet already offers an impressive list of resources for researchers and educators. Efforts are underway to create more effective tools for distance education, and electronic dissemination of technical information. Such projects include the Mosaic effort described in Chapter 14.

For information on online resources available to educators, see Chapter 26: A Guide to K12Net, Chapter 32: How the National Public Telecommuting Network Came to Be, Chapter 38: How FrEdMail Came To Be, Chapter 11: Online Libraries, Chapter 14: Information Servers, and Appendix C: Online Resources.

Faster, faster!

The number of Internet users is estimated to lie between 5 million and 20 million, based on 2 million hosts and 2.5 to 10 users/site. Should the present explosive growth continue, the Internet will have 100 million users by the late 1990s. This kind of growth rate requires careful capacity planning to avoid bottlenecks.

April 1994 will mark the deployment of a 155 Mbps or faster national backbone known as the Very High Speed BackBone Network Service (vBNS). The vBNS will eventually be upgraded to 622 Mbps speeds later in the 1990s.

CoREN

Although in the medium term the NSF will subsidize the purchase of Internet services by the regional networks, in the long term it is not yet clear whether the regional networks will be purchasing backbone connectivity from commercial providers, or will be constructing their own backbone. On June 1, 1993, BARRNet, CICNet, MIDnet, NEARnet, NorthWestNet, NYSERNet, SURANet, and WestNet announced the formation of the Corporation for Regional and Enterprise Networking (CoREN). Under an agreement with MCI, CoREN retains the option to contract for backbone services with MCI.

The regionals are not the only ones thinking about constructing their own backbone. Community Internet service providers such as San Francisco's Little Garden, Portland's RAIN, and the New England Community Internet have been springing up throughout the U.S. as well as overseas. With over half a dozen such networks now operating or in formation, these community networks (known as ToasterNets) have also been discussing whether to band together to fund construction of a backbone.

Unthinkable futures

The Whole Earth Review recently published an article on Unthinkable Futures, ideas too outlandish to come true. Of course, it is often just these kind of things that come to pass. In the same spirit, I'd like to pass along a few unthinkable Internet futures:

• Beautiful Virtual People (BVPs): People known for their Virtual Personalities, who spend the rest of their lives escaping their moment of net fame. See Info Fugitives.
• Interholics Anonymous: a twelve-step recovery group for MUD, Netrek and IRC users. First step: put down that keyboard!
• Info Fugitives: People falsely accused of crimes on USENET, running away from their "net rep."
• USENET World Wars: Flame wars so widespread that nearly every USENET user is caught up in them.
• SLAUP Suits: Strategic Lawsuits Against USENET Participation. Used by vendors to silence gadflys.
• Virtual Suburbs: placid electronic communities, complete with Virtual Stripmalls and InfoZoning.
• Info Terrorism and Info Muggings: the reason for the creation of Virtual Suburbs. See also Info Fugitives, SLAUP suits, and USENET World Wars.
• Digital Cash Laundering: the ultimate abuse of anonymity servers.
• Virtual Red-lining: banks and other lending institutions refusing to loan money to virtual reality entrepreneurs.
• Personal Info-trainers: Want to improve your Internet navigating skills? Just join The World Info-Gym...
• Use a leather jacket, go to jail laws: the public, sick of Cyberpunk fashion statements, gets tough.
• Packet video multicasting of Geraldo: even thinking about this one gives me a headache.

Got any unthinkable visions for the future of the Internet? Send 'em to `aboba@world.std.com`, subject: `unthinkable`.

Internet Q&A

Is there any software out there to help navigate the Internet?

DOS and Windows users may want to obtain InfoPOP by Clyde W. Grotophorst, `wallyg@fen1.gmu.edu`. This is a listing of important Internet resources. The DOS version of this program operates as a TSR, and the Windows version is available in the form of a Windows Help file. InfoPOP is available via the GMUtant BBS, (703)993-2219, or via `ftp gmuvax2.gmu.edu, cd /library, get ipwin.zip, infpopxx.zip`.

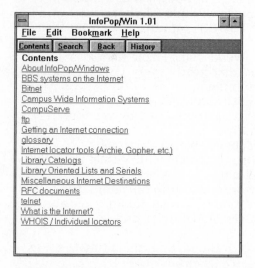

I can send mail to my sister's computer in Kansas, which is an IBM mainframe. Does this mean that the machine is on the Internet?

No! The creation of an extensive gateway system means you are able to send mail to a large number of computer systems that are not on the Internet. The gateway systems handle the translation of mail to and from the RFC 822 format which is the Internet mail standard. This is like having a translator who can speak both Greek and English. If you need to speak with someone who speaks only Greek, you can talk to the translator in English, who will communicate to your target in Greek.
To find out if a system is really on the Internet, you can use `nslookup` or `dig` as outlined in Chapter 9: Debugging.

Why aren't more CD-ROMs available for downloading over the Internet?

Network mounted CD-ROMs are in limited use due to copyright restrictions; there is no technical reason why this can't be done. There are now several shareware and commercial FTP servers for the IBM PC and Macintosh. Mac servers even automatically MacBinary requested files, so that CD-ROMs could be mounted on a Macintosh connected to Internet, and people could download away.

How do I send messages to my French friend who has an account on MiniTel in France?

You can use the American-French MiniTel gateway. However, I've been told by several users that it isn't so great, although I have no experience with it myself. MiniTel is not connected to the Internet via gateways, so you won't be able to send mail there from your Internet account. For information on sending mail to other commercial services, see Chapter 9: Electronic Mail Addressing and Debugging.

I am receiving abusive messages originating from anon.penet.fi. How do I turn this off?

Good luck. anon.penet.fi is a frequently abused anonymous posting service located in Finland. As a first step, I would archive the messages and send them to `help@anon.penet.fi`, requesting that the individual in question have their access to the service revoked.

How can I get information on the future of the Internet?

A good place to start is the Internet Society (ISOC) newsletter or draft documents of the Internet Engineering Task Force (IETF). You can search back issues of the ISOC newsletter or IETF drafts using WAIS. For further information, see Chapter 14: Z39.50.

The future of the NREN is discussed ad-nauseum on the com-priv mailing list. If you think you can stand it, subscribe to this list via `mail com-priv-request@psi.com`.

For more information

RFCs, FYIs and STDs

The Request For Comment (RFC) series, edited by Jon Postel, documents the development of the Internet. Included within the RFCs are the technical standards documents for the Internet, as well as information for new and advanced users, technical papers and proposals, and even some humorous and flippant material. For example, the For Your Information (FYI) series of RFCs are produced to inform and tutor, rather than to document standards.

Since every new version of a standard receives a new RFC number, and many RFCs have now gone out of date, retrieving a list of current standards by RFC number can be time-consuming. To make this easier, current standards are also accessible by STD number. Within the STD numbering scheme, an updated standard retains the same number as the standard it superceded. As a result, the current SMTP standard will always be STD 10, even if RFC 821 is superceded. The first STD document, STD-1, is an index of current standards.

The RFCs as well as a lot of other Internet information, are available via anonymous **ftp** **nic.ddn.mil, ds.internic.net, ftp.nisc.sri.com, nis.nsf.net, nisc.jvnc.net, venera.isi.edu, wuarchive.wustl.edu, src.doc.ic.ac.uk, ftp.concert.net,** or **ftp.sesqui.net.** For those without an Internet account, send an electronic mail message to SERVICE@nic.ddn.mil, or MAILSERV@RS.INTERNIC.NET with a command as the subject. The body of the message is ignored. Information on sending mail to UUCP from FidoNet systems is contained in Chapter 18: From FidoNet to UUCP and Back.

Command and what it does

HELP
Returns help information.

INDEX
Returns an index of available files.

RFC n
Sends you Request For Comment number n.

RFC 822 would get you the Internet electronic mail standard.

WHOIS <last , firstname>
Looks up a person's email address.
Example: **WHOIS Aboba, Bernard**

WHOIS HELP
Returns a help file on **WHOIS**.

SEND <path:filename>
Sends a particular file. Before trying this, you should have requested **INDEX** to find the path to the file. Here's a typical information request message:

```
TO: SERVICE@NIC.DDN.MIL
FROM: Bernard Aboba
SUBJECT: RFC 822
```

This message will get me a copy of Request For Comment 822.

RFC Script

If you often obtain RFCs by email from a UNIX system, you may find the following shell script useful:

rfc: get an internet rfc by email

```
#!/bin/sh
#
if [ $# -ne 1 ]
then
     echo Usage: $0 rfc-to-retrieve
     exit 1
fi
echo RFC $1 | mail service@nic.ddn.mil
```

IETF Drafts

Internet Engineering Task Force (IETF) Draft documents, while current, are available via **mail mail-server@nisc.sri.com,** body: **send internet-drafts/<draft-name>.** For information on obtaining IETF drafts, **mail internet-drafts@nri.reston.va.us.**

USENET groups

Internet access	alt.internet.access.wanted
IRC	alt.irc
Z39.50	alt.wais, comp.infosystems.wais
SLIP	amiga.slip, comp.sys.mac.comm, comp.protocols.tcp-ip.ibmpc
Gopher	alt.gopher, comp.infosystems.gopher
TCP/IP	comp.protocols.tcp-ip, comp.protocols.tcp-ip.ibmpc
FTP	comp.archives

Other groups

Bulletin Board System (BBS) lists	alt.bbs.lists
Internet library lists	comp.internet.library
Public Access UNIX BBS list	alt.bbs
Internet services list	alt.bbs.internet, alt.internet.services
Lists of USENET groups	news.announce.newgroups
UUCP maps	comp.mail.maps, can.uucp.maps
mail	comp.mail,comp.mail.misc
sendmail	comp.mail.sendmail
elm	comp.mail.elm

Multimedia introductions to Internet

Internet tour	ftp nnsc.nsf.net, cd /internet-tour
Internet Cruise	ftp nic.merit.edu
Info-POP/Windows	ftp gmuvax2.gmu.edu, get /library/ipwin.zip GMUtant Online BBS (703)993-2219

Other useful information files

December CMC list	ftp ftp.rpi.edu, cd /pub/communications, get internet.cmc
New User's Questions	ftp nic.merit.edu, get /documents/fyi/fyi_04.txt
Internet Basics	ftp nnsc.nsf.net, get /nsfnet/internet-basics.eric-digest
Surfing the Internet	ftp nysernet.org, get /pub/guides/surfing.2.0.2.txt

CHAPTER 8:
ACCESS TO THE INTERNET

Approaches, Service Providers, Privacy and Security

APPROACHING THE INTERNET

Webster's Dictionary gives as one of the definitions for access "a way of approach." Some of the ways of approaching the Internet include shell accounts, electronic mail access, UUCP links, and TCP/IP connections.

UNIX shell accounts

With this type of account you will have access to almost all Internet services, albeit with the UNIX command-line interface. Since the charges for this type of access are often reasonable ($20-30/month), it is one of the most popular ways to access the Internet.

The important thing to understand about a UNIX shell account is that your computer is not on the Internet. Rather, it is the UNIX host that is on the Internet, while your computer is operating in terminal-emulation mode. To carry out a task, you enter commands on the UNIX host. Since it is the UNIX host that is on the network and completing the task, if you use the FTP protocol to transfer a file, the file will end up on the UNIX host, not on your computer. You will then need to take the extra step of downloading it to your machine.

There are several problems with shell access. For novices, the thought of dealing with the UNIX command line may be somewhat scary. With an ordinary terminal emulator, there is also no way of having more than one application on the screen at a time. Finally, you may find the VT100 versions of popular applications such as USENET Gopher, WAIS, and W3 hard to use.

Help is available. Services such as Holonet offer a menu-based interface that relieve the user of the need to learn UNIX commands. Using a multiwindowing terminal emulator such as MacLayers or UW can allow you to run multiple simultaneous windows on your screen. This would allow you to read USENET, send mail, and FTP a file at the same time.

For those who primarily use only one or two applications, help may be available via Serial Eudora and uqwk. Eudora (discussed in Chapter 9) is a very nice graphical mail application that is available for the Mac and PC and supports retrieving mail over a serial link. uqwk provides a means for using standard message reader software (discussed in Chapter 19) to read mail and USENET. There is also an emerging standard for USENET off-line readers that is more amenable to the addressing and header formats of USENET.

Information on USENET and uqwk is available in Chapter 12: USENET. For an introduction to UNIX, see Appendix F: UNIX Tips and Tricks.

Electronic mail access

Electronic mail can reach the Internet from non-Internet networks and commercial services, and electronic mail connections are readily available and often inexpensive. Using these connections you can send mail, and access mailing lists and mail servers. Mail gateways are even available for interactive services such as FTP and WAIS. With several bulletin boards and commercial services offering graphical interfaces, some pundits have recommended electronic mail as the "easiest" way to access the Internet.

I do not agree. While users with electronic mail accounts may send messages, sign up for mailing lists, and perhaps even request and send files, access to the Internet's interactive services (such as Telnet, IRC, WAIS, Gopher, finger, and W3) is difficult if it can be accomplished at all. Having a database query return in twenty seconds is different from waiting until the next day. Access to interactive conferencing is limited to USENET groups that are gatewayed from a mailing list or BITNET LISTSERV, or mailed to a user from a server machine. Other problems include:

• **Message size limitations.** Gateways may impose restrictions on the maximum size of messages that can pass in or out. While FidoNet protocols impose no maximum on message size, some tosser/scanner configurations have problems with messages larger than 8K. America Online has a maximum message size on incoming mail of 8K (PC) and 27K (Macintosh). Outgoing mail is restricted to 32K on both platforms. BITNET has a maximum message size limitation of 300K.

While the SMTP and UUCP protocols have no maximum message size, some implementations may have problems with messages over 64K, so that larger message should be split into pieces of 64K in order to avoid problems.

• **Reliability problems.** As more and more people have come to depend on electronic mail, they are growing less and less tolerant of problems. Gateways are often the weakest link in a telecommunications network. For example, few FidoNet/UUCP gateways return undeliverable mail (the PIMP gateway for TBBS is an exception); some of the gateways to commercial services have also had reliability problems.

• **Arcane syntax.** Very often gateways require adding special characters to the beginning or end of a mail address, or placing the address on the first line of the message instead of in the TO: field. These procedures, though they might seem simple to the creators of the software, never seem to register with users, who seem to spend the rest of their lives figuring it out.

Again, the PIMP gateway for TBBS has done a good job on this. It integrates with TBBS very cleanly, and allows a response to Internet mail messages using the TBBS standard reply mechanism.

• **Use restrictions.** BBS network gateways are often operated by hobbyists. Since it's their nickel, they make the rules, which need not be consistent or even rational. Some systems refuse to pass "encrypted" traffic, which can include messages encoded by ROT13 or RIPEM or files translated by UUENCODE or BINHEX 4.0. Others bounce "commercial" traffic, which could include replys to for-sale postings on USENET. Finally, some services and bulletin boards may not allow mail accounts to be used for subscribing to mailing lists or accessing mail servers.

For more information on services that can be accessed via electronic mail, see Chapter 10: FTP (section on FTPmail), Chapter 16: Unix-to-Unix Copy, Chapter 9: Mailing Lists and Mail Servers, and Chapter 17: Introduction to BITNET.

UUCP accounts

A UUCP account differs from an electronic mail account in that the user has direct access to the link. As a result, they can remove file-size limitations by their choice of software, and can choose which USENET conferences to receive. Since they are paying their own bill, users can subscribe to mailing lists, use mail servers, send and receive files, or anything else that can be done with such a connection.

UUCP accounts are particularly desirable for users who read many USENET conferences, since messages can be sent in batches and compressed, saving online time. Since UUCP programs with a graphical interface are available (uConnect for Macintosh, and HellDiver for Windows), this method of access can be easy to use, albeit somewhat complex to set up.

Since UUCP links connect machines, not just users, a machine with a UUCP account can serve an entire office. This often makes it a more economical way to connect an entire firm than purchasing individual shell or electronic mail accounts, particularly if the office already has an internal electronic mail system that could be connected to the Internet via a UUCP gateway.

Costs for a UUCP connection are usually on the order of $40 to $75/month, depending on volume. Further information on UUCP is available in Chapter 16: Unix-to-Unix Copy.

Graphical services

A new generation of graphical Internet services is becoming available. These include WorldLink from Intercon and HoloTerm from Information Access Technologies. These custom graphical products address some of the difficulties in setting up TCP/IP connections while affording much of the same ease of use.

TCP/IP connections

Graphical Gopher, Z39.50, USENET, POP, and W3 clients are now available for the Mac and Windows. These require a TCP/IP connection, which allows your machine to communicate with other Internet nodes as a peer. With this type of connection, you will no longer be using terminal emulation to type commands for a host to interpret. When you do a file transfer, the file will come directly to your machine.

TCP/IP connections are particularly desirable for users with a large screen and a high-speed modem, since this gives them the screen real-estate and throughput to run multiple simultaneous graphical applications. You can download a file in one window, read USENET in another window, and have a `telnet` session to Dow Jones in a third window. This is an advance over multiple window programs such as MacLayers or UW in that the applications can be graphical rather than terminal emulation sessions.

TCP/IP connections are of two types: dedicated links and dialup IP links. A dedicated link remains up at all times, while a dialup link is brought up and down as the need requires. Most users opt for the dialup IP account, while BBS sysops or firms typically go for the dedicated link. Connections are available over a modem and ordinary phone line, using the serial protocols known as SLIP and PPP.

Although they offer superior ease-of-use, SLIP or PPP connections generally require you to understand something about TCP/IP. However, the required knowledge is well within reach of the hobbyist or computer professional, so if you're in this category, there's nothing to be afraid of. For further information on TCP/IP, please consult Chapter 15: TCP/IP.

Choosing the access method for you

Since the Internet offers so many "methods of approach," beginners are often confused about how to get started. Some questions to ask before choosing a connection method include:

• **Resource access.** What services do you want? Check Appendix C: Online Resources for a list of resources, and choose a method that supports access to them. Just because you can access a resource by a given method, doesn't mean that it is convenient, however. For example, file transfer is usually more convenient through FTP (via a UNIX shell or TCP/IP connection) than it is using an electronic mail account or a UUCP connection. Similarly, while access to Z39.50 databases by email is supported (waismail), most users find UNIX shell or TCP/IP access to be more satisfactory.

• **Ease of use and installation.** What will it look like, and how easy is it to set up? If you don't have much time, then it is best to go with a shell account or a graphical service such as WorldLink or HoloTerm.

• **Price.** How much will it cost? If you choose a low-cost provider, electronic mail accounts can be the least expensive, but access to services may be restricted. TCP/IP connections are the most expensive, with shell dialup accounts and UUCP accounts somewhere in between.

• **Speed.** How fast is the connection? Is the speed equal for incoming and outgoing traffic? Using a special adapter, cable TV companies are now offering asymmetrical Internet connections for as little as $100/month. An adapter, provided by Hybrid Networks Inc. of Cupertino (408)725-3250, provides up to 10 Mbps for incoming traffic, but requires a dedicated modem connection for outgoing traffic.

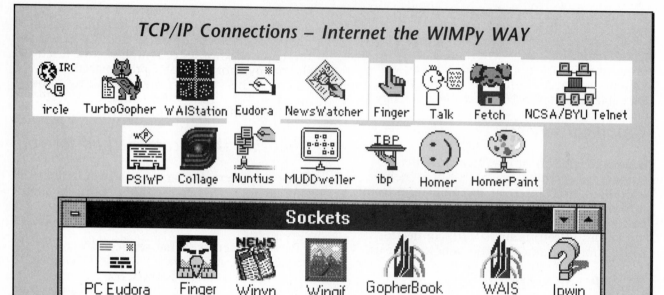

Today you can access Internet the WIMPy way – using a modem and a Windows, Icons, Menus, Pointer (WIMP) interface. For the Macintosh, there is a wealth of publicly distributable Internet software available for download via **ftp sumex-aim.stanford.edu, cd/ info-mac/comm.** Packages include Ircle (Internet Relay Chat), Eudora (mail), Nuntius and NewsWatcher (USENET), MacFinger (finger), MacTalk (talk), Fetch (file transfer), and NCSA/BYU Telnet (**telnet**), MUDDweller (MUDs), Internet Business Pages (IBP, a Yellow Pages for Internet businesses), Collage (a groupware application for sharing screens over Internet), and PSI White Pages (an address lookup facility).

The release of the Windows Sockets specification has simplified the development of TCP/IP software for Windows and resulted in a torrent of new software releases. It also has simplified life for users, who no longer need to worry about conflicts between TCP/IP stacks. As long as users stick with Windows Sockets applications, all that is required are drivers for the hardware, a TCP/IP stack, and a compatible Windows Sockets DLL. The major FTP site for Windows Sockets software is sunsite.unc.edu, cd /pub/micro/pc-stuff/ms-windows/winsock/app. This includes:

pcexxxx.exe	PC Eudora, an SMTP/POP mail client (awesome!)
fingerxx.zip	Finger client
gophbook.zip	Gopher client (Toolbook)
hgopher.zip	Gopher client
wais_wsk.zip	WAIS client
winvnstdxxxx.zip	NNTP newsreader
nt-ftpd.zip	FTP demon for Windows NT
qvtwskxx.zip	WinQVT/Net Telnet/FTP implementation

UUCP and Shell Accounts versus TCP/IP Connections (dialup IP and dedicated line)

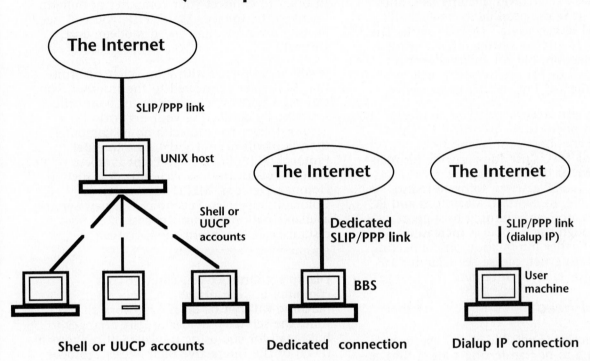

Shell or UUCP accounts   Dedicated connection   Dialup IP connection

Summary of Services Available by Access Method

Access Method	Electronic Mail	USENET	Telnet	FTP	Z39.50
Electronic mail account	X			/	/
UNIX Shell	X	X	X	X	X
UUCP Account	X	X		/	/
TCP/IP Connection	X	X	X	X	X

Key

X = Access to service is available via this method.
/ = Access to service is available, but restrictions may apply.

• **Resource creation.** Can you use it to create your own resources? Service providers such as Holonet and Netcom now allow shell account users to create FTP archives, mailing lists, and mail servers. It is also possible to create mailing lists and mail servers using UUCP accounts. The fullest range of services can be offered using a TCP/IP connection, but for Internet services such as Gopher or FTP archives, this will require a dedicated link, which is expensive.

• **Bulletin board access.** Can you connect your bulletin board to the network? UUCP accounts are the most popular means of accomplishing this, since they provide for mail and news, two of the most popular applications. UUCP gateway software is also widely available. In contrast, Macintosh and PC BBS packages are just beginning to support TCP/IP, although the number is increasing rapidly. For further information on connecting BBSes to the Internet, please see Chapter 15: Bulletin Boards and the Internet.

What do I need?

UNIX shell access is possible at any speed, but if you're going to be transferring a lot of files, a high-speed modem is recommended. Since good VT100-emulation software is available inexpensively, you won't have to spend much on software.

Commercial services offering Internet gateways also typically offer a custom terminal program, so you may not need any other software. They typically either do not support high-speed modems or charge so much for it that it isn't worth it.

For UUCP users transferring a lot of mail and news, a high-speed modem is required. I recommend the Telebit WorldBlazer, since it is a high performance modem commonly used with UUCP. You will also need a high-quality UUCP package, since mediocre packages often yield very poor throughputs. Do not purchase any package that does not support decompression and unbatching of incoming USENET news. Compression and batching of outgoing messages is less important, unless you are expecting a high volume of postings. Recommended packages include uConnect for

the Macintosh, and UULINK, UUPLUS, PIMP (TBBS) and PCBUUCP (PCBoard) for the PC.

In order to connect your computer or bulletin board to the Internet via TCP/IP, you will need an Internet host, high-speed modem, and software.

If you are affiliated with a university or firm that is already connected to the Internet, you can get a network connection for your office machine by contacting your network administrator. To connect a home computer, then you will need a Serial Line Internet Protocol (SLIP) or Point to Point Protocol (PPP) dialup account from service providers such as Holonet, Netcom, MERIT, Speedway or Colorado SuperNet. Speedway is a new service, available nationwide for the cost of a long-distance call; for information, contact support@speedway.net.

Dialup accounts let you connect your computer at your discretion; since your machine will not be on the network all the time, the service provider usually arranges to hold mail for you using the Post Office Protocol (POP) or the Interactive Mail Access Protocol (IMAP).

It is likely that your service provider will take care of much of the hassle for you, but in case your setup doesn't work (more common than service providers would like to admit), please consult the troubleshooting section in Chapter 15: Introduction to TCP/IP.

To get the most out of your SLIP/PPP connection, you will want a V32*bis*/V42*bis* modem. The Telebit WorldBlazer may not have the best performance, but it is popular among service providers and is well supported by software such as MacSLIP, InterSLIP, VersaTerm SLIP, MacPPP, or uConnect.

Costs for dialup TCP/IP connections typically run between $2 and $3/hour, plus a monthly maintenance fee of $20. Dedicated connections run $70/month or more.

TCP/IP Quickstart

Macintosh software

• You will need MacTCP, TCP/IP networking software from Apple. This is available from APDA for around $50 by calling (800)282-2732. Publicly distributable MacTCP software is available via `ftp sumex-aim.stanford.edu, cd /info-mac/comm`. For information on these applications, consult Appendix B: Choice Products.

• To run TCP/IP over a modem, you will also need a SLIP or PPP extension. These include MacSLIP from Hyde Park Software, or VersaTerm SLIP from Synergy Software. Intercon has made InterSLIP available free for private noncommercial use. To obtain it, `ftp ftp.intercon.com, cd /intercon/sales.` PPP extensions include MacPPP, available via `ftp merit.edu, mget /pub/ppp/MacPPP*.*`

• The Guide is an all-in-one package from the California Technology Project that supports mail, news, and Gopher+. The educational price is $45. For information, call (310)985-9631.

PC compatible software

To run TCP/IP on the PC, you will need drivers, a TCP/IP protocol stack, and applications software. To run Windows Sockets compatible applications, you will also need a WINSOCK.DLL for your chosen stack.

• For packet drivers, I recommend the Crywnr drivers. These are available via `ftp boombox.micro.umn.edu, cd /pub/pc/packet-drivers/`.

• A solid TCP/IP stack for DOS (which comes with a WINSOCK.DLL) is available from FTP Software and costs $200. Windows Sockets-compatible stacks and application suites are available from NetManage and Frontier. A shareware Windows-Sockets compatible TCP/IP stack called Windows Trumpet is currently in alpha test.

• A complete suite of DOS TCP/IP applications is available as part of the SLIPDISK distribution. This includes SLIP as well as software for Telnet, FTP, POPMAIL and Gopher, and is available from the University of Minnesota by `ftp boombox.micro.umn.edu, get /pub/slipdial/slipdisk/slipdisk.zip`.

• KA9Q is a very powerful stand-alone TCP/IP implementation that includes routing support as well as support for SLIP and PPP. KA9Q is available via `ftp ucsd.edu, cd /hamradio/packet/tcpip/ka9q`. Sample setups for KA9Q are available via `ftp netcom1.netcom.com, get /pub/mailcom/IBMTCP/ibmtcp.zip`.

• If your host supports PPP, then you can obtain PPP software for the PC via `ftp merit.edu, cd /pub/ppp`. This archive includes a version of NCSA Telnet that supports PPP.

• Many publicly distributable Windows-Sockets applications are available via `ftp sunsite.unc.edu, cd /pub/micro/pc-stuff/ms-windows/winsock/apps`.

Complete listings of TCP/IP software for the PC are available via `ftp netcom1.netcom.com, get /pub/mailcom/IBMTCP/ibmtcp.zip`.

INTERNET SERVICE PROVIDERS

Public-access UNIX systems

There are many public-access UNIX systems not directly connected to the Internet. This means they cannot do `ftp` or `telnet`. However, if you're on a budget, just looking for USENET access, or want to send or receive mail, then these systems could satisfy your needs.

Since most public-access UNIX systems are run by hobbyists, the rates are very reasonable, but don't expect high-quality service. You probably won't get a user manual or be able to call for support, as you can on The WELL.

The NIXPUB list

The NIXPUB list is a weekly list of all public access UNIX systems. Since the list changes very frequently, get the latest version. To get a copy of the NIXPUB list, you can:

1. Download the latest copy from the *NIX Depot BBS, at (215)348-9727.

2. Send the following message via UUCP mail (access via a FidoNet/USENET gateway will do):

```
TO:         archive-server@cs.widener.edu
FROM:       <Your Name>
SUBJECT:    send NIXPUB short

leave this line blank....
```

3. Get weekly updates sent to you by sending the following message via mail:

```
TO:         NIXPUB-list@ls.com
FROM:       <Your Name>
SUBJECT:    Request to subscribe

Please add me to the NIXPUB list...
```

4. Get occasional updates to the list by reading the comp.misc or alt.bbs conferences on USENET. The NIXPUB list is posted periodically to these groups.

Echo, New York City

As a graduate student in NYU's Interactive Telecommunications Program, Stacy Horn paid a visit to The WELL, and it made such an impression that she decided to start a similar service in New York. While working as a telecommunications analyst for Mobil Oil, she founded ECHO with twenty other telecom fanatics in February, 1990.

ECHO has adopted the "you own your words" policy of The WELL, and also shares some of the intelligence and eccentricities, but with a decidedly New York flavor. The system is also 37 percent female, which is very unusual in the online world, where most systems have only 10 percent female members. Many people on ECHO use handles, and people are careful about disclosing personal data in their online biographies (it's New York, what do you want?).

Although the Caucus conferencing software is not particularly intuitive (I flailed around for five minutes before resorting to the pithy and informative Welcome to ECHO quick reference), it is easy to pick up and ultimately more satisfying than The WELL's PicoSpan.

Useful hints

The echo modems sometimes require sending a BREAK, and possibly more than one, in order to connect correctly. In ZTerm, **Send Break** is available under the **Misc** menu; in ProComm, it's (ALT) **B**.

Echo now offers `telnet`, `ftp`, and other Internet services, such as USENET.

Sample commands

The AND NOW? prompt is an invitation to do something. Here are some things you can do:

Command	What it does
`a m`	Sends mail
`a i`	Adds a topic in a conference
`help`	Gets an index of help topics
`hot`	Shows the most active topics in all conferences
`ind`	Shows an index of topics within a conference
`j <conference>`	Goes to a conference
`see <user-id>`	Shows the online biography left by the user.
`sh <topic number>`	Shows the messages within the indicated topic
`o`	Shows who is online now

WorldLink

WorldLink™

WorldLink is a graphical interface Internet service developed by Intercon that connects to the national PSI network. It utilizes a proprietary Intercon protocol, rather than SLIP or PPP, in order to provide interfaces to selected Internet services such as FTP and email. WorldLink allows many things to be done offline. Files can be requested, letters can be written, mail can be read, etc. As of version 1.0, services such as USENET and IRC were promised, but they are not yet available.

While the service is still in its early stages, WorldLink shows some promise of simplifying the process of getting an Internet account and software.

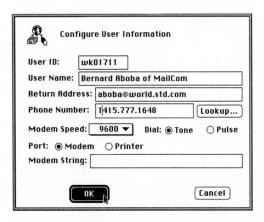

Initial configuration screen

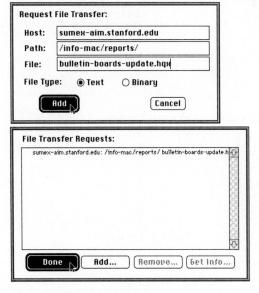

Address Book

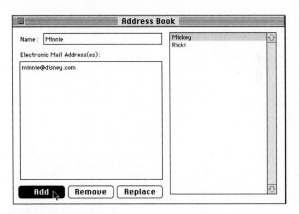

File Transfer Requests

Echo login session

```
ATDT 12129898411
CONNECT 2400
ÜÜ         ÜÜÜÜÜÜÜÜÜÜ          ÜÜÜÜÜ ÜÜ[I sent a break here]ÄÄÄÄÄÄÄÄÄÄÄÄÄÄÄÄ
ÄÄÄÄÄÄÄÄÄÄÄÄÄÄÄÄÄÄÄÄÄÄÄÄÄÄÄÄÄÄÄÄÄÄÄÄÄÄÄÄÄÄÄÄÄÄÄÄÄÄÄÄÄÄÄÄÄÄÄÄÄÄÄÄÄÄÄÄÄÄÄÄÄÄÄÄ
ÄÄÄÄÄÄÄÄÄÄÄÄÄÄÄÄÄÄÄÄÄÄ[I sent a break again]
This is echo.
Enter user name or 'newuser' to register.

login: aboba
Password:

You made it!
Welcome. This is Echo.

Material posted on Echo is the sole property of its author.
Reproduction in any medium without the express permission of
the individual author is strictly prohibited. Echo disclaims all
responsibility for the material posted publicly or privately on
the system.

Copyright (c) 1991  Echo Communications Group, Inc.
***ATTENTION! ---> Echo will be down between 1:00 and 4:00PM on
Tuesday, Sept. 3rd, to install new equipment.

TERM = (vt100-nam) RET
Terminal type is vt100-nam
************************************************

Today's Headline:
"Scott Connor is the Father Of My Daughter", Reveals Crazed Swiss Student.

Caucus (TM) version 2.3/SX. Copyright (C) 1988 Camber-Roth.
Please follow the instructions below to register as a Caucus user.
Type HELP or ? at ANY prompt if you need assistance.

Please enter your full name, in mixed case (capital and small letters):
>Bernard David Aboba, Ph.D.

When your name appears in an alphabetized list, under which word in your
name are you listed?  (For example, 'John Doe' is listed under 'Doe'.)

List me under: (ph.d) aboba
Please enter your telephone number:
>510-555-1212

Please describe yourself briefly in a few lines. When you are
done, type a period (dot) at the beginning of the next line.
>Author, and engineering consultant. Reformed liberal.
>Ex-New Yorker. Ex-Bostonian. Ex-Palo Altoan.
Please wait while Caucus completes your registration...

There's a whole other world in here.
And it all begins in the Central Conference.
Just type 'y' to get in!

Do you wish to join this conference? y

E C H O E
E C H O              Welcome to the Central Conference of Echo!
E C H O       This is where we discuss items of interest to everyone.
E C H O
E C H O              If you need to speak to us over the phone ...
E C H O                 Call: (212) 255-3839 from 9AM - 8PM.
E C H O
E C H O        To see a list of items type 'ind' (for index).
E C H O        To see an item type 'sh' (for show) and the item #.
E C H O E

New    items are: 1-49
No new responses

AND NOW? (? for help)
```

Public conferences on ECHO

Conference Name	Hosts	TO GET THERE
American Mythologies	Marshall Blonsky	j ame
Articles	Stacy Horn	j art
Books	Janet Coleman	j boo
The Central Conference	Stacy Horn	j cen
The Classified Conference	Dave (wraith) Butler	j cla
Community	Iggy	j comm
The Computer Conference	Rob Diamond	j comp
CRIME	Don Delaney/John Keary	j cri
Culture	Miss Outer Boro/Jamie	j cul
Don't Panic!	TBA	j don
Elsewhere	Jeremy Wolff	j els
The Feedback Conference	Stacy/Douglas Horn	j fee
Group	Josiane Caggiano, Phd	j gro
Humor	Danny Lieberman/Steve Sashen	j hum
Inside	Jim Baumbach/Rob Diamond	j ins
The Jewish Conference	David S. Green	j jew
Lambda	Pat O'Hara/Xixax	j lam
The Love Conference	Janet Tingey/Neandergal	j lov
Matrix	Vera In Abstentia	j mat
Media	Xixax	j med
Movies & TV	Erin Clermont/Jonathan Hayes	j mov
The Music Conference	Jim Combs/John Neilson	j mus
The New York Conference	Allen Murdock/KZ	j new
Off Central	Stacy Horn	j off
Panscan	Mark Bloch aka Panman	j pan
Parenting	Dan Swerdlow	j par
Politics	Margaret Segall/Iggy	j pol
PSYCH	Willie Yee, M.D./J. Caggiano, Ph.D.	j psy
Science	Dan Swerdlow/Bruce Schechter	j sci
SF	D. Lieberman/Barbara Krasnoff	j sf
Telecommunications	TBA	j tel
Virtual Reality	Jim Combs	j vir
WAR	Stacy Horn	j war
Wishcraft	Arsinoe and Barbara Lynn	j wis
Working	Janet Coleman/Art Kleiner	j work
Writing	Bruce Schechter/D. Abrahamson	j wri

Private Conferences on ECHO (email host for entry)

Conference Name	Hosts	TO GET THERE
ITP Conference	Jim Combs/Stacy Horn	j itp
MOE (men only)	Dan Swerdlow	j moe
Plain Wrapper	Scott Connor/Joe Rosen	j pla
The Sex Conference	KZ/Alien	j sex
Twelvestep	Anonymous, email to Stacy Horn	j twe
WAC (women only)	Stephania Serena	j wac
WON (women only)	Carmela Federico/Shannon Cain	j won
WIT (women only)	Faith Florer/Stacy Horn	j wit
Zulu	Scott Connor/Jim Baumbach	j zul

The WELL, Sausalito, California

Many public-access UNIX systems are drab places where all you get when you log on is the UNIX prompt. The WELL is a public-access UNIX with soul.

There is a strong respect for privacy and intellectual property on The WELL; you "own your words." People are responsible for what they say, and online postings cannot be republished without permission. This is probably one of the reasons so many prominent people use The WELL. Any conference that is transmitted to the outside world must state so explicitly. There is no link between PicoSpan, The WELL's internal conferencing system, and USENET.

For me, the success of The WELL is proof that people, not hardware or software, make an online service what it is. The WELL has a strong online culture; if a beginner makes a mistake and posts an inappropriate message, he or she is gently (but firmly) informed about the mistake. If an old-hand who should know better is inconsiderate, he or she is likely to get a tongue-lashing to remember.

Another reason that The WELL is so successful is that the place is governed like a kind of town meeting. Users argue things among themselves, and although the administrators have the final say, they are usually responsive to the wishes of the user community. When users requested Internet access, The WELL listened, and it is now linked to BARRNET.

Somehow The WELL manages to achieve this great success despite software that is passable at best. The user base gets along just fine, primarily because they are very computer literate. The WELL user manual is pretty good, but a beginner could sink or swim due to the software's complexity.

The World, Brookline, Massachusetts

Getting on

Barry Shein, founder of World, had been the computing manager for the Boston University Charles River campus before getting into the UNIX contract programming business with Software Tool and Die (STD). When one of the principals left STD, Barry decided to start World. The service began in November 1989, and focused on providing connectivity, rather than a full suite of services such as those offered by CompuServe.

World today provides high-quality Internet access. Two T1 lines go into the offices of Software Tool and Die, providing high-speed links to AlterNet and NEARNET. You can reach virtually all Internet hosts from The World, which was recently approved for routing over NSFNet.

World's modem pool is reliable; I have only rarely encountered a busy signal or an inoperative modem. World offers access to all Internet services, including `ftp` and `telnet`, Internet Relay Chat (irc), Gopher, WAIS, W3, electronic mail, USENET newsgroups, and ClariNet.

I am particularly fond of ClariNet because of its thorough coverage of business and computer-related news. The nn full-screen newsreader is supported, as are rn and GNU emacs.

World views itself as a common carrier; although it will cooperate with law enforcement, it does not censor mail or monitor users. World also has a very liberal policy for information service providers. Setup charges for creating an information service residing on World are minimal. There are no extra fees, only the standard charges for login time (including background processes) and disk space. Access to development tools is available. If you want to set up a business selling oriental rugs over the Internet, you can test the viability of your venture for a few hundred dollars, rather than the thousands of dollars it would cost on most other services.

Conferences on The WELL

Business – Education

Conference Name	TO GET THERE
Apple Library Users Group	g alug
Brainstorming	g brain
Consultants	g consult
Design	g design
Disability	g disability
Energy	g energy91
Homeowners	g home
Kids91	g kids
One Person Business	g one
Telecomm Law	g tcl
Translators	g trans
Work	g work
Electronic Frontier Foundation	g eff

Conference Name	TO GET THERE
Agriculture	g agri
Classifieds	g cla
Consumers	g cons
Desktop Publishing	g desk
Education	g ed
Entrepreneurs	g entre
Investments	g invest
Legal	g legal
Periodical/newsletter	g per
The Future	g fut
Travel	g tra
Computers, Freedom & Privacy	g cfp

Arts – Recreation – Entertainment

Conference Name	TO GET THERE
ArtCom Electronic Net	g acen
Bay Area Tonight**	g bat
Books	g books
Comics	g comics
Flying	g flying
Games	g games
Nightowls*	g owl
MIDI	g midi
Motorcycling	g ride
On Stage	g onstage
Radio	g rad
Science Fiction	g sf
Star Trek	g trek
Theater	g theatre
Zones/Factsheet Five	g f5

Conference Name	TO GET THERE
Audio-Videophilia	g aud
Boating	g wet
CDs	g cd
Cooking	g cook
Fun	g fun
Gardening	g gard
Jokes	g jokes
Movies	g movies
Music	g mus
Pets	g pets
Restaurant	g rest
Sports	g spo
Television	g tv
Weird	g weird

* Open from midnight to 6 AM

** Updated daily

Social – Political – Humanities

Conference Name	TO GET THERE	Conference Name	TO GET THERE
Aging	g gray	AIDS	g aids
Amnesty International	g amnesty	Archives	g arc
Berkeley	g berk	Buddhist	g wonderland
East Coast	g east	Emotional Health****	g private
Environment	g env	Christian	g cross
Couples	g couples	Current Events	g curr
Dreams	g dream	Drugs	g dru
Firearms	g firearms	First Amendment	g first
Frings of Reason	g fringes	Gay	g gay
Gay (Private)#	g gaypriv	Geography	g geo
German	g german	Gulf Crisis	g gulf
Hawaii	g aloha	Health	g heal
History	g hist	Interview	g inter
Italian	g ital	Jewish	g jew
Liberty	g liberty	Mind	g mind
Miscellaneous	g unclear	Men on the WELL **	g mow
Nonprofits	g non	North Bay	g north
Norwest	g nw	Parenting	g par
Peace	g pea	Peninsula	g pen
Poetry	g poetry	Philosophy	g phi
Politics	g pol	Psychology	g psy
Psychotherapy	g therapy	San Francisco	g sanfran
Scam	g scam	Sexuality	g sex
Singles	g singles	Southern	g south
Spirituality	g spirit	Transportation	g transport
True Confessions	g tru	WELL Writers ***	g www
Whole Earth	g we	Women on WELL	g wow
Words	g words	Writers	g wri

* Private conference – mail carolg for entry
** Private conference – mail flash for entry
# Private conference – mail hudu for entry

***Private conference – mail sonia for entry
**** Private conference – mail wooly

Grateful Dead

Conference Name	TO GET THERE	Conference Name	TO GET THERE
Grateful Dead	g gd	Deadplan*	g dp
Deadlit	g deadlit	Feedback	g feedback
GD Hour	g gdh	Tapes	g tapes
Tickets	g tix	Tours	g tours

* Private conference – mail tnf or marye for entry

Computers

Conference Name	TO GET THERE	Conference Name	TO GET THERE
AI/Forth	g ai	Amiga	g amiga
Apple	g app	Atari	g ata
Computer Books	g cbook	Art & Graphics	g gra
Hacking	g hack	HyperCard	g hype
IBM PC	g ibm	LANs	g lan
Laptop	g lap	Macintosh	g mac
Mactech	g mactech	Microtimes	g microx
NeXT	g next	OS/2	g os2
Printers	g print	Programmer's Net	g net
Siggraph	g siggraph	Software Design	g sdc
Software/Programming	g software	Software Support	g ssc
UNIX	g unix	Word Processing	g word

Technical – Communications

Conference Name	TO GET THERE	Conference Name	TO GET THERE
Bioinfo	g bioinfo	Info	g boing
Media	g media	Netweaver	g netweaver
Packet Radio	g packet	Photography	g pho
Radio	g rad	Science	g science
Technical Writers	g tec	Telecommunications	g tele
USENET	g usenet	Video	g vid
Virtual Reality	g vr		

The WELL itself

Conference Name	TO GET THERE	Conference Name	TO GET THERE
Best of the WELL	g best	Deeper	g deeper
Entry	g ent	General	g gentech
Help	g help	Hosts	g hosts
Policy	g policy	Screenzine Digest	g zine
System News	g news	Test	g tests

World is the home of the Online Book Initiative (OBI), which features 100 megabytes of text, including novels by Jane Austin, an online version of *Moby Dick*, the U.S. Constitution, the Koran, and Dickens. If a work is uncopyrighted, of general interest, and in electronic form, it may be appropriate for the OBI.

If you cancel your subscription before you've used up the first hour of connect time, you will not be charged for your time on World. However, you must subscribe to get on the system, and you must formally cancel to avoid being charged. In order to get an account on World, call (617)739-WRLD, and type **new** at the login prompt. You will be asked to choose a login name and password and to provide your credit card number.

You can also reach World through the CompuServe Packet Network (CPN), which now supports V.32/V.42 (no extra charges for high-speed access). However, that will cost you $5.60/hour additional, on top of the regular logon fees. To find the CompuServe number nearest you, dial 1-800-848-4480 by modem, and type **phones** at the CompuServe prompt.

In order to connect to World, respond **WORLD, DOMESTIC** at the Host Name: prompt. It will look like this:

Host Name: **WORLD, DOMESTIC**

You can also connect to World via PC Pursuit. Type **help pc-pursuit** for info on this once you are on World.

Things you can do

World supports Internet Relay Chat (irc), which allows you to talk to several other users on the Internet at a time. To try irc, type **irc** at the prompt. The program has its own online help.

USENET and ClariNet can be accessed via the rn, trn, nn or tin newsreaders. To use nn, type **nn** at the prompt. nn also has its own online help. UNIX mail is available via elm or pine, which many people find preferable to mail. To get into mail, type **elm** or **pine** at the prompt. There is also archie, the Internet global files

catalog. For info on how to use archie, type **archie** at the prompt. World also supports Gopher (**gopher**), World Wide Web (**www**), and WAIS (**swais**).

World also supports the MacLayers terminal emulator, allowing you to open multiple windows at the same time. After you dial in with the MacLayers terminal emulator, turn on MacLayers by typing **layers** at the prompt. This is a very helpful feature. For example, in the screen shot below I have three windows open, running mail, Internet Relay Chat, and nn, the full-screen USENET reader. I have "iconized" the chat and mail windows so they sit at the top of the screen while the nn window is active.

There are a few things you need to know if you want to run MacLayers successfully. You *must* be using 8 bits, no parity, and 1 stop bit for your communications settings. (UNIX-based communications systems usually use 7-E-1.) If you are not using 8-N-1, you will get a rather cryptic error message when you type **layers** at the prompt.

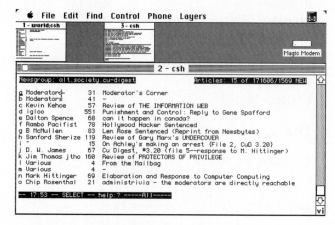

Holonet, Berkeley, California

Services

Holonet is a full-service Internet online service run by Information Access Technology (IAT). The founder of IAT is Arthur Britto, known for developing the popular game Armour Alley.

Holonet's primary claim to fame is its accessibility, customer service, and the full range of Internet services it offers. Holonet is accessible via local call from anywhere in the United States, using PSI's packet-switching network, called PSILink. Other information about IAT can be accessed from the Holonet `Information` menu.

Prior to the release of their Mac and Windows front-end software, Holonet is offering a character-based menu system. On login, the user is presented with a list of the main services (Internet Services, News services, etc.). The user then negotiates through the menus by pressing the first letter of the menu, or `<ESC>` to go back one menu. Most menus offer online help by entering `?`. Once a user feels familiar with the menu system, it is possible to turn on terse mode within the `Personalize` menu.

Things you can do

Holonet offers complete Internet support, including access to `finger`, `whois`, `telnet`, `FTP`, `irc`, `archie`, and `MUD`. Holonet has its own shell for FTP that allows users to scroll through directories at remote sites and download or view any file. Users can also search for files via Archie from within the FTP shell.

USENET conferencing is available, as is access to commercial news services such as USA Today, Newsbytes, and Boardwatch, with FidoNet support planned down the road. Easier-to-use news readers such as nn and tin are available, as are old standards such as rn. For mail, Holonet offers elm. For editors, users can specify vi or pico (a new, easier-to-use editor) from within the `Personalize` menu.

Games such as Hunt (a multiplayer shoot 'em up game) are available from the `Games` menu. Hunt displays a map of the surroundings in ASCII characters. The players then move around and attempt to kill each other with grenades, guns, slime, and other weapons.

IAT is also working on a number of new services that are available from the `Experimental Services` menu. One of these is the World Wide Web (W3), a hypertextual Internet access system. W3 is a massive potpourri of information on everything from weather forecasts (updated several times a day) to Project Gutenberg (a project to make popular books available in electronic form), to a list of C programming commands. W3 also contains links to Z39.50 databases.

Hybrid Networks, Cupertino, California

Hybrid Networks of Cupertino provides Internet connections to cable TV subscribers for $99.95/month. Hybrid Access Service (HAS) connections operate at 10 Mbps for incoming traffic, and modem speeds for outgoing traffic. The service requires a computer with an Ethernet adapter, a high speed modem, and a model 100 Remote Link Adapter that supports DES encryption and costs $1,495. Hybrid will be rolling out the service in the Bay Area in November 1993, then going nationwide. As part of the service, they will be providing Points of Presence (POPs) so people can make a local call for the required outgoing modem connection.

Netcom, San Jose, California

Services

Netcom is a nationwide Internet service provider with a fixed monthly fee, which includes a generous disk allocation (5 Mb). By 1994, Netcom will have points of presence in most major cities. Current points of presence are Alameda, Palo Alto, Pleasanton, San Jose, Santa Cruz, Seattle, Portland, Irvine, Sacramento, San Diego, Atlanta, Los Angeles, Washington, D.C. and Dallas. High-speed V.32*bis*/V.42*bis* access is supported.

Netcom offers access to most applications, including elm, pine, nn, tin, trn, rn, swais, gopher, fsp, www, etc. Most of the USENET newsgroups are available, including ClariNet.

In addition to dialup accounts, Netcom offers SLIP/PPP and UUCP connections for reasonable rates. These services include domain name registration, USENET news feeds, etc. For more information on this, please refer to Appendix B: Choice Products.

Sample Holonet session

```
atdt83-704-1058
CONNECT 2400

Annex Command Line Interpreter   *   Copyright 1991 Xylogics, Inc.
------------ To access Holonet type "holonet" at the service prompt -----------
HoloPacket Class A -- Service name ("?" for help): holonet
Trying...
Connected to holonet.net.

Holonet(SM) Internet Access BBS

Holonet Member Name (Non-members type "guest"): guest

Holonet Guest Services

Please enter your terminal type (? for examples) or <CR> for none: vt100
Note: Prompts ending in a question mark ('?') do not require a <return>.

Holonet Guest Menu
 <D> Holonet Demo (FREE)
 <I> Holonet Information
 <N> Find the closest Holonet Access Number
 <J> Join Holonet (Not Free)
 <S> Talk to System Operator
 ESC Disconnect from Holonet
Your Choice? j
```

This choice leads users through terms and conditions, billing, account naming, passwords, and other aspects of getting on. After it's all done, you will be able to login.

```
Menus do not require a <CR> -- Hit ESCape to leave any menu.
Highlighted menu items indicate sub-menus.

You have mail.

Main Menu
 [G] Games Menu
 [I] Internet Services Menu
 <M> Mail
 [N] News (USA Today, USENET, etc.)
 [P] Personalize Menu
 [X] Experimental Services
 <S> Talk to System Operator
 <H> Holonet Information
 [B] Billing Status
 ESC Logout (normally exits a menu)
Your Choice? i

Internet Menu
 <F> FTP -- File Transfer Protocol
 [I] IRC -- Internet Relay Chat
 [M] MUDs -- Multi-User Dimension/Dungeon/Dialog
 <L> Login -- Internet Terminal Access (Telnet)
 <P> Finger -- Internet User Profile Lister
 <T> Talk to Another Member or to the Internet
 <R> Trace Route to a remote site
 <E> ICMP_ECHO (ping) a remote site
 <W> Whois -- DARPA Internet user name directory service
 <?> Help on the Internet Menu
Your Choice?
```

How to get a Netcom account

To open an account on Netcom, you login as **guest**, with settings of 8-1-N, and VT100 emulation. A sample session is shown below:

```
ATDT 14154240131
CONNECT 2400

netcom login: guest
Last login: Sun Feb 23 21:59:04 from CALNet-pa1.netco
SunOS Release 4.1.1 (SERVER) #3: Sun Jan 5 13:55:30 PST
1992

   Netcom On-line Communication Services

   >>>>
   >>>>     Several T-3000 modems are available at $550.00.
   >>>>
   >>>>
   >>>>     Please use the following email addresses
   >>>>
   >>>>              Account/Billing questions:
accounting
   >>>>         Netnews related questions:    netnews
   >>>>         E-Mail problems/bugs:         netmail
   >>>>         General questions:            support
   >>>>
   >>>>     A network problem was responsible for poor
response
   >>>>     time on the SF POP.  The problem has been
resolved.
   >>>>
You have new mail.

Account Verification
  Account Status :  Active
  Account type   :  System or uucp account

Username: guest
       This disk usage summary is for the last 29 days.
       Your average usage to date is:       0.00 meg
       At this rate your disk charge will be: $   0.00
Welcome to Netcom's Guest Account

The guest account supports the following terminal types:

    [ 1]  vt100  - Most Common
    [ 2]  Sun    - Sunview Window
    [ 3]  sgi    - Silicone Graphics
    [ 4]  hp150  - Typical HP terminal

    Which terminal: 1
```

How to register

```
Netcom Info
Personal Acct
Business Acct
SLIP Accounts
News Feeds
E-Mail System
Netnews
Disk Usage
Service Fees
Billing Info
Modem Pricing
Internet
Access Number
Acct Status
Leave Mail
Emergency
Usage
REGISTRATION
Log off
```

At this point, your display will look like the menu above. To get information about aspects of Netcom, you can move among the topics using the up and down cursor keys on your keyboard. Pressing **<return>** will bring up the topic on your screen. In order to create your account, you will need to select the **Registration** topic and answer the questions that follow.

Old Colorado City Communications

Dave "Read my NAPLPS" Hughes and the Cursor Cowboys are at it again, connecting to the Internet via Colorado SuperNet and to the FidoNet via UFGATE. A bit of the Old West, brought to you by 21st century technology.

Old Colorado City Communications, 2502 West Colorado Ave., #203, Colorado Springs, CO 80904; (719)632-4848, Fax: (719)593-7521, data: (719)632-2658, 632-4111, email: dave@oldcolo.com.

Other services accessible via the Internet

Commercial online services are increasingly making their services available over Internet. Not all of these services support the full suite of protocols (such as FTP, Gopher, or Z39.50) and therefore they are really only "Internet accessible" rather than true Internet systems. Therefore an account on these systems will not give you access to **telnet**, **ftp**, irc, USENET news, or other Internet functions. Among the Internet accessible services are Dow Jones News Retrieval, OCLC, Dialog, Lexis and Nexis, CompuServe, and BIX.

Internet Access Q&A

I really like the idea of graphical Internet access, but can't find a SLIP/PPP provider in my area. What should I do?

Netcom is rapidly expanding across the United States, so if they're not available in your area, they may be soon. They offer SLIP/PPP service at all locations and charge $20/month plus $2/hour.

Speedway now offers SLIP/PPP access anywhere in the U.S. for the price of a long-distance call. This should work out to roughly $6/hour off-peak. For information, contact support@speedway.net.

I really want to join a ToasterNet, but I can't find one near me. What do I do?

Check the MailCom FTP archive for information on ToasterNets, via `ftp netcom1.netcom.com, cd /pub/mailcom/Toaster`.

I live in the middle of nowhere, and can't find an Internet service provider. Who can I turn to?

Delphi is a nationally accessible online service with more than 600 local access numbers. Aside from its own unique services, it offers access to mail, ftp, telnet, IRC, USENET, Gopher, Hytelnet, WAIS, World Wide Web, and more. Since they have a trial offer of five free hours of evening/weekend time, you can see if you like it. For information, call (800)695-4005, or `mail info@delphi.com`. To join by modem, dial (800)365-4636, (RET) `Username: JOINDELPHI, Password: WRD39`. From the Internet, `telnet delpi.com, Username: JOINDELPHI, Password:` WRD39.

How many people are there on the Internet, anyway?

The answer is that we don't really know. Present estimates of five to twenty million users are based on assuming 2.5-10 users on each of the two million systems identified in a census known as the "Domain Walk." There are also at least another one million systems, mostly operating within commercial firms, that lie behind firewalls, and therefore are not counted.

However, one should not conclude that most of these machines or people are active on the network. Recent work by Michael F. Schwartz and John Quarterman, "A Measurement Study of Changes in Service-Level Reachability in the Global Internet," Proceedings of INET 93, indicates that only 35% of sites identified in the Domain Walk were reachable by services such as daytime, netstat, FTP, telnet, SMTP, DNS, finger, Sun portmap, rlogin, rsh, UUCP, klogin, krcmd or kshell.

My suspicion is that the low reachability numbers are the consequence of the large number of microcomputers on the Internet, most of which are not running any server processes.

If I get my Internet connection via a cable provider, will I really get 10 Mbps throughput?

Probably not. While 10 Mbps is the maximum peak transfer rate, effective transfer rates will be much lower. As of this writing only the backbones run at faster than T1 (1.5 Mbps) speeds, and many sites are still connected at 56 Kbps or even 14.4 Kbps. As a result, unless you are accessing resources co-located at the provider's site, you will experience bottlenecks.

Also keep in mind that you will be sharing the 10 Mbps bandwidth with many other users, and that few computers are capable of transferring data over Ethernet at 10 Mbps on a sustained basis.

Still, Internet connections over cable hookups are potentially very attractive, and are worth keeping an eye on.

For more information

The Public Dialup List

Peter Kaminski, kaminski@netcom.com, maintains The Public Dialup Internet Access List, which is posted from time to time to alt.internet.access.wanted. You can get a copy of it by `mail info-deli-server@netcom.com` with `SEND PDIAL` in the body.

You may also be interested in the FAQ from the group alt.bbs.internet, which is available via `ftp` or `mail rtfm.mit.edu.` For more information on retrieving FAQs, see Chapter 12: USENET.

Resources

For a listing of Internet service providers, please consult Appendix B: Choice Products.

PRIVACY AND SECURITY ON THE INTERNET

Innocence lost

As a network originally oriented toward research and education, the Internet is making the transition from a homogenous community of highly educated and technically sophisticated individuals to a heterogeneous user base that reflects the world at large. All kinds of people now use the Internet. This includes many intelligent, sensitive, and friendly individuals, as well as loud-mouths, crackers, bores, pornographers, Don Juans and scam artists. As a result, security issues are increasingly taking center stage.

The release of the Internet worm in November 1988, marked the beginning of this transition. Created by Cornell graduate student Robert Morris, the worm took advantage of security holes to penetrate thousands of Vax and Sun machines running BSD UNIX.

As with the first robbery in a formerly peaceful neighborhood, the release of the Internet worm caused many network administrators to reassess their own vulnerability. The result was an increasing array of security measures, such as construction of network iron curtains known as Firewalls, and restrictions on services with known security problems (such as Finger). Today, thousands of computers in large corporations lie behind barriers erected against network trespassers, and many other sites have restricted access to formerly publicly available services.

The Internet worm incident also led to the creation of the Computer Emergency Response Team (CERT) by DARPA. CERT provides information on network security on a twenty four hour basis. Since CERT's goal is to inform, not prosecute, it has no links with law enforcement.

Finally, the Internet worm incident underscored the importance of continued research efforts on privacy and security. Since the appeal of global computer networks lies largely in their ability to harness the power of cooperating computers, moves toward balkanization are cause for alarm. Rather than being the result of irrational fears, balkanization is the logical response to security threats for which there are no widely accepted solutions. The solution is therefore the development of standards addressing privacy, authentication, security, and billing issues.

Security issues

Some of the issues involved in securing a computer network are:

• **Authentication**, or the ability to determine that someone is who they say they are.
• **Access control**, or the ability to determine who should have access to applications and files.
• **Auditing**, or the ability to monitor user actions.
• **Secure communications**, or the ability to send information without fear of monitoring.

Authentication

Authentication problems can occur in conversations between a user and a computer, or between two computers. A functioning authentication system is a prerequisite for computer security, since if you can't determine the identity of computers or users, other security measures are unlikely to be effective.

Establishing the identity of a machine on the network may require passwording, since some network technologies such as FidoNet or TCP/IP allow the administrator to assign his or her system an arbitrary network address. Note that with PCRelay or PostLink this is not possible, since for the software to operate, the assigned network address must match an encoded key file.

Authentication schemes rely on one of the following techniques (listed in order of increasing intrusiveness and difficulty in forging):

• Passwords, such as personal identification numbers.
• Physical devices, such as a magnetic card.
• Biological techniques, such as voice or finger prints, DNA analysis, etc.

Passwording is by far the most common authentication mechanism, but it is also notoriously weak. Since people have limited memories, passwords must be relatively short, limiting the possible combinations. Passwords may also contain excerpts from dictionary words, further limiting the possibilities. With individuals frequently having multiple accounts, using the same password is often tempting, albeit dangerous.

Since these limitations are part of human nature, even a vigorous education program is likely to meet with only limited success. This has spurred new interest in physical devices such as magnetic cards.

Such cards may contain identification information of arbitrary length, making them much less vulnerable to brute force attack. Assuming they are designed not to be readily copied, such devices can only be used in one place at a time, and if they are lost, they can be invalidated.

While a physical device can be duplicated or stolen, biological identification techniques are in theory more immune to subterfuge. In practice, however, the identification system may itself be accessible by password or physical device.

Access control

Access control facilities present problems due to their complexity and vulnerability to abuse. On operating systems such as UNIX, the superuser has the ability to read, write, and execute all files. Therefore no user can consider him- or herself immune from snooping by the superuser.

UNIX access control facilities are complex enough to elude most novices. Since many public access Internet systems set user files to be world readable by default, many Internet users leave their files on public display, without even realizing it. For more information on UNIX access control facilities, please see Appendix F: UNIX Tips and Tricks.

Since access control mechanisms have so many obvious weaknesses, one solution is to encrypt files so that even if they are accessed inappropriately, they still cannot be used.

Auditing

Auditing is used both for detecting suspicious activity and for investigating incidents after the fact.

Although Internet users may not always be aware of it, their actions are frequently audited. This can be done on their home systems by the system administrator or on remote systems.

For example, many FTP archives now routinely log transactions; LISTSERVs keep records of list subscribers and archive postings; USENET conferences are archived to disk and CD-ROM, and message headers are digested for user directories, etc.

Secure communications

Secure communications is important in the networked environment, since such networks are vulnerable to snooping.

Modem links operate over phone lines stretching over potentially long distances, making them difficult to secure. Local area networks are notoriously vulnerable, since network cards can be put into "promiscuous mode" by monitoring software in order to listen in on network traffic. Even if access to machines is secured, vampire taps can be used to gain access.

Since it is very easy to monitor traffic on a local area network with little chance of detection, all sensitive information, including electronic mail and passwords, should be encrypted before sending it over the network. Such encryption schemes are included within versions of UNIX such as OSF/1 (Kerberos) and SunOS (secure RPC).

Kerberos is an authentication system that uses DES encryption to protect against the snatching of passwords or other sensitive information over the network. It was written for single user workstations and is not appropriate for use on multiuser machines because it stores information in the /tmp directory, which is accessible to everyone.

If your version of UNIX does not already support Kerberos, to install it you will need the source code for your operating system and for each of the applications you want to use it with. The installation is time consuming, and as a result most people will opt for a version of UNIX which has already Kerberos built in.

Basics of encryption technologies

Legal issues

Cryptographic systems such as DES or RSA are classified as munitions under the Export Control Act, and are therefore restricted to those who are citizens or permanent residents of the U.S. or Canada. This is an important constraint since many applications or operating systems (including UNIX, Privacy Enhanced Mail, Lotus Notes, etc.) have cryptographic facilities built in. These facilities must be weakened or removed prior to export. Since cryptographic systems are patentable, infringing implementations may find themselves subject to import controls as well.

Private key cryptography

With a private key cryptosystem, there is only one secret key, used by both sender and recipient. This creates the problem of getting the key from sender to the recipient without compromising it. You can't just encrypt the key, since you'd need to transmit another key for the recipient to use it.

The Digital Encryption Standard (DES) algorithm, created and licensed royalty-free by IBM, was announced by the National Bureau of Standards as an encryption standard in 1975. DES was the first widely used private key encryption system, and implementations of it are now available for many platforms, including the PC and the Macintosh.

DES was originally thought to contain a "trap-door" that would allow it to be easily broken. With twenty years of analysis by the academic community not having yielded the shortcut, it is now thought to be secure against all but those who can afford the computing power to break the code by brute force. Since such computing power typically runs in the millions of dollars, this limits those with the power to decrypt DES to governments or clandestine agencies and organizations.

Public key encryption

Public key cryptosystems solve the key exchange problem by giving each user two keys. One key, the public key, can be given out to anyone. The other key, the private key, is secret. The public and private keys are inverses; that is, a message encrypted by the public key can be decrypted using the private key. Similarly, a message encrypted using the private key can be decrypted using the public key. This eliminates the problem of key exchange, since no private keys are needed prior to sending a message.

The Rivest, Shamir, and Adelman (RSA) algorithm is such a public key system. It is thought to be unbreakable. As a result, it is often used for authentication, with weaker algorithms such as DES being used for encryption. Information on RSA is available by `ftp rsa.com, cd /pub/faq`.

Key escrow technology

Key escrow technology was developed in order to allow law enforcement agencies to easily wiretap and decrypt conversations while still providing some privacy.

Key escrow is a public key technology. The difference is that in addition to being given to the user or embedded into a chip, the private keys are also split into two pieces and given to two civilian government agencies (to be named by the Attorney General) for safe keeping.

If and when intercepted conversations are to be decrypted, a warrant will be given to the two agencies, which will each hand over their portion of the private key.

The Rabin Algorithm, PGP, and RSA

Public Key Partners (PKP) holds the patent rights on the RSA algorithm within the United States and Canada. They claim the patent covers all public key encryption algorithms that make use of the prime factorization of large numbers.

This means that the RSA patent may cover non-RSA algorithms, such as the Rabin algorithm, another public key cryptosystem that was the basis for Rabin Privacy Enhanced Mail (RPEM). To avoid litigation over the RSA patent, RPEM was withdrawn from the market.

Pretty Good Privacy (PGP) is software that uses RSA algorithms without a license and therefore is in violation of the PKP-owned patents. Therefore, PGP may not be imported, used, or sold in the U.S. or Canada, except by licensors of PKP patents, and system operators are advised not to allow this file on their computers. Encryption technology such as PGP is also illegal for export, meaning that it's illegal coming or going!

Digital Signatures

One of the applications of public key cryptosystems is in establishing the authenticity of documents. A document is digitally signed when an individual encrypts a message with his or her private key and sends it to someone. The recipient then decrypts the message with the sender's public key. The document is said to have been signed because a usable document will only be produced when that document was encrypted with the private key, which presumably only the sender knows.

Digital Timestamps

In reality, all a digitally signed document demonstrates is that someone is in possession of your private key.

Digital Timestamping, pioneered at Bellcore, enhances security by adding a timestamp to the signature. This is very useful, since if someone were to steal your key, you would know when it was being used. Also, if you

reported the theft, all uses of the key after a certain time could be invalidated.

Enabling DES key exchange

Public key algorithms can also be used to exchange DES private keys. This is useful when DES is to be used for encryption alongside RSA-based authentication, as in the Internet Privacy Enhanced Mail (PEM) standard.

Two different standards are used for authentication and encryption so as to accommodate the concerns of the law enforcement and national security communities. Since DES is vulnerable to brute force attacks by the well heeled while RSA is not, use of DES encryption allows for surveillance by (presumably authorized) law enforcement or security agencies.

To transmit the DES private key to be used during the conversation, the sender encrypts the DES private key using recipient's RSA public key. The recipient then decrypts the DES private key using their RSA private key, and the conversation can begin.

Finding public keys

How do you find out someone's public key to send them an encrypted message? Some methods for this include:

• Placing the public key in the `.plan` or `.project` files available via **finger**.
• Keeping public keys on a server or in a file.
• Adding your public key to your USENET or mail signature.
• Announcing your public key in a USENET conference. This assumes that those interested in the key are taking note (doubtful) or even reading the conference (even more doubtful).

Privacy

Privacy can be defined as the ability to control the release of information. Since today's computer operating systems typically confer universal read access on the superuser or administrator, encryption is the major avenue for preventing unauthorized releases.

If the information is to be mailed to another person, then encryption is needed to ensure that only the sender and recipient are able to read the message. Authentication is also needed in order to verify the sender's identity. This is the Privacy Enhanced Mail (PEM) problem.

If the information is to be made public, but the identity of the poster is to remain secret, then methods for ensuring anonymity are required. At the same time, some degree of accountability must be maintained.

Privacy enhanced mail

Privacy Enhanced Mail (PEM) is an Internet standard, described in RFCs 1421-1424, that provides for encryption and authentication. PEM utilizes RSA for authentication (licensed from RSA Data Security) and DES for encryption.

The first implementation of PEM, called RIPEM, was written by Mark Riordan (`mrr@scss3.c1.msu.edu`). It is publicly distributable and free for noncommercial use. RIPEM is available by `ftp rsa.com`, login: `anonymous, cd rsaref`, or by `ftp rpub.c1.msu.edu, get /pub/crypt/GETTING_ACCESS`.

The Internet Society will be in charge of granting Policy Certificate Authorities (PCAs) to organizations distributing PEM keys.

Clipper and Capstone

Clipper and Capstone are federal standards for encryption of voice and data. They were both developed by the NSA and are hardware-based key escrow technologies. Capstone differs from Clipper in that it adds several functions, such as support for Digital Signature Standard (DSS) authentication.

Having already been incorporated into AT&T secure phones, Clipper and Capstone are most likely to find application in encrypted telephony and wireless communications, including landline and cellular phones.

Anonymity

With USENET newsgroups now being archived onto CD-ROM and monitored by an increasing array of vendors, recruiters, and software programs, USENET has become a network of record, where statements made in haste may remain on file for decades. In practice, there are few limits on what can be done with archived USENET messages.

The USENET addresses database, kept at `pit-manager.mit.edu`, is a benign example of the possibilities. This machine digests many USENET newsgroups, extracting the message sender's name and mailing address. The database is made available to queries by electronic mail and Z39.50.

Less benign examples can also be imagined. In the future we may see political campaigns in which a candidate's postings to USENET are used in a smear campaign.

Anonymity servers

Anonymity on the Internet is not a new thing, since anyone with a knowledge of inews or rnews can fake headers and post anonymously. Similarly, it is quite simple to spoof the mail posting mechanism. The purpose of anonymity servers is to offer the privilege of anonymous posting to the entire user community.

Anonymity servers may offer degrees of privacy protection ranging from machines that keep no records, therefore offering true anonymity, to machines that keep records for a limited time, allowing for the tracing of postings upon request by a legal authority. Users post messages to the anon servers indicating the recipient or the group they would like to post in, and the anon server then removes any trace of the message sender and posts the message. In the case of anonymous mail conversations, the server usually returns an anonymous ID to the sender that they are to use for the duration of the conversation.

Similar to USENET anon servers, anonymous remailers allow users to send mail anonymously. Remailers have many of the same problems and alleged benefits as anon servers.

Prior to the establishment of the anonymity server at anon.penet.fi, most anonymity servers had served only a limited set of newsgroups, and registered anonymous users. These limitations were imposed in order to avoid disturbing the status quo, and to provide for accountability in posting.

The groups served by previous anonymity servers had generally been limited to those that consented to anonymity, possibly by vote. This avoided requiring existing groups to vote to convert to moderation in order to maintain the status quo. The change in status quo occurs not just because a server allows anonymous postings, since they cannot be distinguished from handles in that regard. Rather, a change occurs when unregistered anonymous postings are allowed, since this may dramatically increase the volume of untraceable (and therefore unaccountable) messages.

On the issue of censorship, as always, moderators are allowed to make choices regarding appropriate messages, including those based on the origin of the posting, whether by anon server, handles or whatever.

The strange case of anon.penet.fi

Since November 1992 an anonymous netnews posting and remailing service has operated on anon.penet.fi. This server differs from previous ones since it allows posting to all newsgroups carried by penet.fi, which receives a full feed, with the exception of local groups.

While in theory one of the benefits of anon servers is to allow for more open posting of controversial statements (to groups like alt.whistleblower), the problems with anon.penet.fi illustrate the difficulty of providing for both anonymity and accountability.

anon.penet.fi currently handles more than 3000 anonymous postings a day, and during some months more than 5 percent of total USENET traffic has been posted anonymously through this site. This has created a tremendous load on the server and its

administrator, Johan Helsingius, making monitoring for abuses nearly impossible.

These abuses have included libelous messages, mail bombs (posting of many messages with malicious intent), and inappropriate and disruptive postings. This illustrates the effects on user behavior of removing accountability, but it is not clear that a solution can be found that will not at least partially diminish the level of privacy protection.

The ARMM race

One of the major issues concerning anon.peneti.fi was whether this server represented a revolutionary change made without user assent, and if so, whether the status quo should be restored, possibly by force.

Without agreement that a USENET group is to be moderated (which comes up when the group is first proposed and discussed), there is no one empowered to disallow anonymous postings. While net news allows cancellation messages, traditionally only the poster of a message has the authority to cancel it. This tradition was strongly reaffirmed after an automated cancellation program called ARMM ran amok.

The ARMM controversy also affirmed that offensive netnews postings are handled by user filtering (such as by kill files) rather than by disciplinary action against posters (other than by heaping of ridicule). Kill files can be set up to filter out anonymous postings, temporarily or permanently if desired. Given the endless squabbles engendered by disciplinary actions (see Chapter 18: Introduction to FidoNet), this makes a lot of sense.

Possible solutions

In order to guard against abuses, anonymity servers probably require some type of record keeping, which may in turn prove a tempting target for law enforcement agencies or courts. Under these constraints, it is doubtful whether anonymity servers will be effective in protecting the identity of witnesses in conferences such as alt.whistleblower. However, there still may be some value for individuals wishing to protect their (legal) postings from surveillance.

To some degree such protection is already afforded by the use of "handles," or accounts shielding the poster's identity. Although handles hardly meet with universal approval, they do provide for accountability as long as the system administrator verifies the identity of the handle user.

The case for childproof digital containers

Pornographers have historically been early adopters of communications technologies, and most recently they have numbered among the early users of multimedia, virtual reality and networking technologies.

Although some argue that such uses of the technology are hardly avoidable, and help fund further development in any case, other observers have raised notes of alarm.

Just as the introduction of new classes of household chemicals dramatically increased the incidence of child poisoning, advocates of child-proof digital containers argue that multimedia and virtual-reality based pornography may dramatically raise the risk of psychological injury to minors to the extent where it may become a public safety issue in the future.

Recent studies appear to demonstrate the ill-effects of exposure to violence on television. This has motivated the development of filtering devices to allow parents to screen out violent shows.

The issue here is similar to that brought up by the ARMM controversy: who is to do the filtering? Opponents of rating schemes argue that it is a form of censorship, and that it will drive up the costs of bringing multimedia productions to market, forcing small firms out of business. They also argue that no single rating system can accomodate the wide variation in community standards.

Advocates for childproof digital containers argue that the development of a rating system and standards for childproofing are needed now, while multimedia standards are still evolving, and before wireless multimedia devices limit the opportunities for parental supervision.

Childproof protocols are relevant for multimedia information which is stored (e.g., tape, disk) or sent over networks (e.g., copper, fiber-optic, wireless). These standards may be exceedingly difficult to modify in the future if they solidify without childproofing.

The technology for childproofing of digital media exists now, and relies on a Digitally Encoded Media Rating (DEMR) which is periodically embedded within the bitstream of digital video and audio information. This mechanism is very effective and is not related to "V-synch." The DEMR is encrypted so that it is tamper-proof, with only the creator of the video having the ability to change it. Only users entering appropriate passwords for adult access can view the video. These passwords would typically be assigned by an adult superuser.

It is also possible to produce devices which are only capable of viewing "G" material. This approach may be safer because there is no possibility of defeating the password protection scheme.

Security Q&A

What is a firewall? Why would I want one?

Many corporations protect their internal networks by using something called a firewall. Firewalls filter packets coming in or going out of an internal network, in order to protect against intruders. Sometimes firewalls are the only machines accessible from the outside world, and in order to allow mail to be routed to the rest of the corporation, firewalls receive the mail and then reroute it as appropriate. As a result, the address sam@hp.com does not actually refer to a user called sam on a machine called hp.com. hp.com is a firewall that readdresses mail to user sam to one of the other computers on the Hewlett-Packard network.

Since a firewall may prevent internal packets from reaching the outside world, users wanting to perform functions such as `telnet` or `ftp` may need to perform these functions from the firewall machine.

The extensive use of firewalls by major sites such as IBM, Hewlett-Packard and Digital Equipment makes it difficult to get an accurate count of machines connected to Internet.

A somewhat less extreme solution is to selectively filter packets based on the TCP or UDP port number. For example, incoming `finger` or `telnet` packets could be thrown away, while incoming or outgoing SMTP connections would be allowed, as would outgoing `telnet` requests. This kind of functionality is provided by almost all commercial routers as well as software such as KarlBridge, available via `ftp 128.146.1.7, cd /pub/kbridge`.

For more information

USENET groups

alt.privacy	General privacy group
alt.security	General computer security
alt.security.pgp	Pretty Good Privacy encryption program
alt.security.ripem	Privacy Enhanced Mail
comp.protocols.kerberos	Discussion of the Kerberos Authentication system
comp.society.privacy	Privacy and security issues
comp.security.misc	Miscellaneous computer security issues
comp.risks	Discussion on computer-related risks
comp.virus	Computer virus discussion

Mailng lists

PEM working group mailing list	`pem-dev-request@tis.com`
Free source code for PEM implementors	`rasref-info-request@rsa.com`
Cypherpunks mailing list	`cypherpunks@toad.com`

Privacy Enhanced Mail (PEM) Working Group

BBN c/o Steven Kent, Chair, (617)873-3988, Fax: (617)873-4086

RSA Data Security

(800)PUBLI-KEY, (415)595-8782, Fax: (415)595-1873, email: `kurt@rsa.com`

Trusted Information Systems

(301)854-6889, Fax: (301)854-5363, email: `pem-info@tis.com`

anonymity servers

For information on anon.penet.fi, `mail help@anon.penet.fi`.

CHAPTER 9: ELECTRONIC MAIL

Software, Directories, Debugging, Mailing Lists and Mail Servers

SOFTWARE

Like most powerful tools, learning to take full advantage of electronic mail can be somewhat mystifying. Yet once mastered, electronic mail will change your life, no question about it. This chapter unlocks the secrets of electronic mail.

Acknowledgments

Without the visionaries at DARPA and the implementors at BBN, SRI, UC Berkeley, and elsewhere, the Internet would not exist. Here's to them!

What can I do with mail?

For many users, electronic mail is their primary online activity. This is because it allows them to communicate much more effectively than is possible using a telephone or typewriter.

Why is that? Electronic mail allows you to communicate with people at remote locations, whether or not they are available when you are. This allows you to communicate with many more people than you could otherwise.

How mail works

The process of sending and delivering an electronic mail message is analogous to sending and delivering an ordinary piece of mail. There are three steps to this:

• Creating the letter (done by you)
• Sorting the mail (done by the post office)
• Delivering the mail (done by the letter carrier)

Creating the letter

With regular mail, after you write or type the letter, you add a stamp, and toss it in the mailbox. In computerese, the program that creates the mail message is known as the Mail User Agent (MUA).

Just as there are no rules about what kind of pen you can use to write a letter, a wide variety of electronic mail software can be used to create the message. The only catch is that just as good penmanship is helpful if you expect anyone to be able to decipher what you write, conforming to mail formatting and addressing standards is critical in the electronic mail world. On the Internet, these standards are described in RFC 822.

Just as with regular mail, you need to put the address of the recipient on the letter, as well as your return address. With electronic mail, you use the sender and recipient's electronic mail address instead of their street address and zip code. These addresses are of the form `user@host.domain`. Example: `aboba@world.std.com`.

As with regular mail, with electronic mail you have the choice of whether you want to send a postcard (which can be read by anyone), or a letter (placed in an opaque envelope). Most electronic mail programs produce messages corresponding to postcards, since they do not provide encryption. However, a new standard called Privacy Enhanced Mail (PEM) provides for the electronic equivalent of an opaque envelope.

Just as it is possible to send a package (object) using mail, with electronic mail you can send a file as well as a letter. You can also use electronic mail to send a message to a list of people. We will cover mailing lists later in this chapter.

Sorting the mail

After the mail has been put into the mailbox, it is brought to the post office and sorted according to the method of delivery. If your message is to be sent airmail, it is routed to a plane headed toward the destination. If it is to be sent ground, then it goes to a mail truck.

Similarly, electronic mail is sorted according to the means of delivery. On UNIX machines, this is frequently done by a program known as sendmail.

Sendmail looks at the address, and at the connections available to the machine, and decides how to send the message. Usually this is with the default delivery mechanism for the machine. Since many machines have only one kind of mail connection (TCP/IP, UUCP, etc.), frequently the default delivery mechanism is also the *only* delivery mechanism.

Just as mail sorters are different from letter carriers, mail-routing programs generally do not deliver the mail themselves. For example, with the exception of mail delivered over the Internet, sendmail merely passes the message off to a transport agent to do the job.

If the message is for a local user, the message is passed to a local mail delivery agent (usually /bin/mail). If it is for a UUCP connection, the message is passed to the UUCP mail delivery agent (usually /usr/bin/uux). If the message should be routed via the Internet, then the message is delivered by sendmail itself, using the Internet mail delivery protocol, the Simple Mail Transfer Protocol (SMTP).

Mail Transport Agents (MTAs)

Just as a letter carrier delivers the mail, electronic mail systems use a Mail Transport Agent (MTA) to get the mail to its destination.

The job of the MTA includes locating the recipient's address (requesting translation of the fully qualified domain name into an IP address), knocking on the door (trying to initiate a mail session), and delivering the mail.

Just as sometimes the recipient's house cannot be found, it is possible that the MTA may not be able to locate the recipient's machine. In this case, the mail needs to be returned with an error message that indicates what went wrong.

The four major protocols used for mail delivery are: the Simple Mail Transport Protocol (SMTP), the Post Office Protocol (POP), the Interactive Mail Access Protocol (IMAP) and Unix-to-Unix Copy (UUCP).

SMTP is a sender-initiated protocol that delivers mail between Internet hosts with dedicated connections. Sender-initiated means that the machine with mail to send contacts the recipient's machine. If after several attempts the recipient's machine cannot be reached, then the message will be returned to sender.

What if the recipient only has a dialup IP connection? In that case they may or not be connected when SMTP attempts delivery. The situation is analagous to the problem that many working people have with UPS parcel deliveries. How are you supposed to be around to sign for the delivery when you're at work?

POP is a store and forward protocol that was created in order to provide for delivery of mail to individuals in such situations. With POP, the dialup IP user obtains an account on a system with a dedicated connection (called the POP server), and then contacts this system with their own machine (the POP client) and transfers mail to the client.

IMAP is a client/server protocol for the remote manipulation of mail boxes. It offers a superset of POP functionality, although the two protocols are not compatible. With IMAP, the client can manipulate multiple mailboxes simultaneously without having to download all waiting messages, since it is possible to first examine subject headers or individual MIME enclosures. IMAP can also be used to read news as well as mail.

UUCP is a store and forward protocol that was developed to allow for communication over phone lines but since has been adapted for use over TCP/IP. Mail for UUCP-connected machines can be delivered at scheduled times, or held for pickup. Since POP and IMAP handle delivery of mail for individuals, while UUCP delivers mail to machines, UUCP is a more convenient delivery mechanism for dialup IP machines that have many users. For more information on UUCP, please consult Chapter 16: Unix-to-Unix Copy.

Putting it all together

In order to send a mail message successfully, your message will need to be created, routed, and delivered.

If you have elected to access the Internet using an electronic mail account, these functions will be handled by your service provider.

If you are accessing Internet using a shell account, your mail user agent will probably be a UNIX program such as mail, elm, or pine; the mail router will probably be sendmail, and the delivery mechanism will probably be SMTP.

For those with UUCP accounts, you will be using an integrated UUCP implementation such as uConnect (Macintosh); FSUUCP, UUPlus, or UULINK (PC); or a user agent such as Mac or PC Eudora, Helldiver (Windows), or various BBS software packages. If your chosen software only offers a user agent, you will also need to select an appropriate transfer application, such as UUPC (Macintosh), FSUUCP (PC), or WAFFLE UUCICO (PC).

If you have arranged a TCP/IP connection, you will be using a mail application running on your machine, such as Eudora or POPmail. The protocol for sending mail will be SMTP, and for receiving mail you will use POP or IMAP.

Mail User Agents (MUAs)

This section offers help on how to use mail user agents such as BSD's mail, System V's mailx, and Eudora. Although it's not the easiest or most powerful program, mail and mailx are reasonable places to start. After getting familiar enough with these programs to read and send messages, I recommend that you switch to Pine. A Pine reference is included in Appendix F: UNIX Tips and Tricks. Since Eudora can work with serial, UUCP, or TCP/IP

connections and offers a graphical interface for the Macintosh and Windows, this is the recommended mail user agent.

The message envelope

Just as ordinary letters need a recipient and return address, so too electronic mail messages require certain information in their "envelopes." Along with providing facilities to enter and edit messages, and handing mail over to the mail router, one of the jobs of the mail application is to fill in the envelope information. The RFC 822 format defines required and optional fields. Here is a description of what they do:

To: This field gives the address of the recipient.

Date: This field gives the date and time of message creation and is supplied by the computer.

From: This field gives the address and name of the sender; it is usually supplied by the computer, possibly from a default preference file.

Subject: This field describes what the message is about.

Mail reply to: If the return address is different from the address of the sender, this field tells where to send the reply. This can be useful if you have a dialup IP account, in which case you will want replies to go to an account on a POP or IMAP server rather than to your computer, which will only be connected intermittently.

Keywords: This optional field allows you to supply keywords to indicate the content of your message.

Cc: This field allows you to send a single message to multiple people. Be aware that when replying to such a message, the replies will go to everyone on the Cc: list.

Bcc: This field (known as "Blind Copy") also allows you to send a single message to multiple people. It is different from Cc: in that the recipients cannot see who else is being copied. When you respond, the reply will not be sent to those on the Bcc: list.

Fcc: This field (known as "Folder Copy") is not part of RFC 822, but it is used by mail programs such as pine. It lets you keep an archive of sent mail messages. This is useful if you send a lot of formal correspondence and need to keep good records.

mail

If you have a UNIX shell account, the chances are good that you've encountered `mail` (BSD) or `mailx` (System V). To use these, just type `mail` or `mailx` at the prompt. You will then be greeted by a list of your waiting messages and the mail prompt, which is an &.

At this point, the most common thing to do is to just type the number of the message you want to read and then press (RET) in order to read the message. Another (RET) will get you the next message, and so forth. There is no way to stop mail once it starts listing a mail message, so look at the size of the message before viewing it. Someone might have sent you a huge file. On the next page are some of the other mail commands.

Example

```
% mail
Mail version SMI 4.0 Wed Oct 23 10:38:28 PDT 1991  Type ?
for help.
"/usr/spool/mail/aboba": 9 messages 1 new
1 bozo@clown.harvar.edu Wed Sep  2 17:22 40/1600  An idea
2 zonker@lobas.com      Sun Sep  6 08:28 44/1824  Re:BBB
&
```

Sending mail

What about sending or replying to mail? Well, you can type r to reply, or when invoking mail, just give the address you want to mail to. You'll be asked for the Subject. Here I send a message to myself:

```
% mail aboba@world.std.com
Subject: Hi there!

This is a message.
EOT
```

At the end of the message, you type (CTRL)D (end of file) to send the message.

Sending a file within mail

You may not enclose binary files within RFC 822 messages. This is because sendmail, the UNIX mail router, uses control characters as commands. Therefore all binary files must first be translated to text. If you are sending a Macintosh file, you will want to use BinHex format. First do a MacBinary upload to your host by using the `rz -b` command; then type: `mcvert -U <file>`. This will leave <file>.hqx on your drive. The command `mcvert <file>.hqx` can be used to convert back to MacBinary.

If you are sending a simple binary file, use uuencode. To send a file to another user, you can use the piping facility of UNIX:

```
uuencode foo.zip foo.zip |mail foo@bar.com
```

If you frequently send files via email, then you may want to make use of the following script:

fsend script: sending a binary file via mail

```
#!/bin/sh
#
if [ $# -ne 2 ]
then
    echo Usage: $0 name-of-file-to-send person-to-send-to
    exit 1
fi
uuencode $1 $1 | mail $2
```

Editing a message

What if you make a mistake and need to edit the message? (Mail doesn't have an editor built in.) Well, then you'll need to know about the commands you can execute inside the mail application. Some of the most useful are:

Command	What it does
~!	Invokes a shell command
~v	Invokes the default editor
~r <filename>	Encloses a file

Important: The escape sequences must be the first characters on a line or mail won't recognize them as commands.

Example

In this example, I send a message to myself enclosing the file edonline:

```
% mail aboba@world.std.com
Subject: Hi there

Here is the edonline file:

~r edonline
"edonline" 45/2216
EOT
```

As with the other messages, the mail message is terminated with a (CTRL)D to end the message.

The .mailrc file

Commands in the .mailrc file are executed before entering the mail session, allowing you to set defaults. For example, you can set your default editor, ignore portions of the mail header, and create nicknames for lists of users whom you send mail to frequently. This last function is performed by the alias command. The format of the command is:

```
alias   <nickname>   <address1>,<address2>
```

Here is an example .mailrc file for System V:

```
set allnet
set ask
set askcc
set hold
set interval=30
set keep
set keepsave
set metoo
set record=/usrs/aboba/mail/.outmail
set EDITOR=/usr/local/bin/pico
set dot
ignore Received Via Message-id Status
ignore Resent-Message-Id In-Reply-to Resent-From
ignore Reset-Date References Sender Sent-by
ignore Apparently-To-Return-Path Telephone
ignore Purpose-In-Life
alias abobas aboba,baboba,jaboba
```

Mail routers

If you are accessing the Internet using a UNIX shell account, you can take advantage of the features provided by mail routing software such as `sendmail`. These include forwarding, mailing lists, and aliases.

Forwarding

If a message is to be delivered locally, sendmail looks at the .forward file in the addressee's home directory for special instructions. The .forward file, which can extend over several lines, has several options.

• Mail can be left in the original spool file as well as forwarded to one or more addresses, either on the local machine or on another machine by putting the forwarding addresses in the .forward file, separated by commas. The spool file is preceded by a \. Example:

```
\aboba, aboba@netcom.com
```

• Mail can be forwarded to a file. The file name is given as a full path, and the file must already exist for sendmail to be able to write to it; it cannot create a new file. Example:

```
/usr/aboba/mailfile
```

• Mail can be piped to a command. Example:

```
| "/usr/aboba/mailscript"
```

The command can be a program or a shell script. If it is a script, the .cshrc or .profile is run first. The command is run within the mail queue spool directory, which you will generally not have privileges to write to, so files should be specified as full paths.

Piping mail to a comand allows you to examine incoming mail messages and take action depending on the message envelope or body. You could, for example, send files about your company based on the subject field or message body. The elm filter program provides a simple language allowing you to construct complex mail handling routines.

The vacation program

The vacation program is used to respond to mail that arrives while you're away. The program, which is invoked by typing **vacation -i**, sends a file named **.vacation.msg** located in your home directory as a reply to incoming mail. To send incoming mail to the vacation program as well as storing it in your spool directory, use the following .forward file:

```
\aboba,| "/usr/local/bin/vacation aboba"
```

To disable vacation, simply remove the .forward file.

Mail Commands

Command	What it does
`cd [directory]`	changes to another directory or home if none is given
`d [message list]`	deletes messages
`e [message list]`	edits messages
`f [message list]`	shows from lines of messages
`h`	prints out active message headers
`m [user list]`	mails to specific users
`n`	goes and type next message
`p [message list]`	prints messages
`pre [message list]`	makes messages go back to system mailbox
`q`	quits, saving unresolved messages in mbox
`r [message list]`	replys to sender (only) of messages
`R [message list]`	replys to sender and all recipients of messages
`s [message list] file`	appends messages to file
`t [message list]`	types messages (same as print)
`top [message list]`	shows top lines of messages
`u [message list]`	undeletes messages
`v [message list]`	edits messages with display editor
`w [message list] file`	appends messages to file, without from line
`x`	quits, do not change system mailbox
`z [-]`	displays next [previous] page of headers
`!`	escapes to shell

Key

A **[message list]** consists of integers, ranges of same, or user names separated by spaces. If omitted, Mail uses the current message.
<message list> is a list of integers or range of integers separated by spaces.
<user list> is a list of names or distribution lists separated by spaces. The distribution names are defined in the .sendrc file.

Escape commands

Command	What it does
`~~`	Quotes a single tilde
`~a,~A`	Autographs (insert 'sign' variable)
`~b users`	Adds users to Bcc list
`~c users`	Adds users to Cc list
`~d`	Reads in dead.letter file
`~e`	Edits the message buffer
`~m messages`	Reads in messages, right-shifted by a tab
`~f messages`	Reads in messages, does not right-shift
`~h`	Prompts for To list, Subject and Cc list
`~p`	Prints the message buffer
`~q,~Q`	Quits, saves letter in $HOME/dead.letter
`~x`	Quits, does not save letter
`~r file`	Reads a file into the message buffer
`~s subject`	Sets subject
`~t users`	Adds users to To list
`~v`	Invokes display editor on message
`~w file`	Writes message onto file
`~.`	End of input
`~?`	Prints this message
`~!command`	Runs a shell command
`~|command`	Pipes the message through the command
`~:command`	Executes regular Mail command

Mail filters

The elm `filter` command can be invoked on incoming mail using the following .forward file:

```
| "(cd /aboba; /usr/local/filter -o /aboba/filter.err)"
```

The `filter` command reads its input from the file `$HOME/.elm/filter-rules.`

Commands to the filter program are if-then-action statements. They are case insensitive and executed in sequence; once an if statement matches the incoming message, the associated action is executed and no further commands are examined. The form of the command is:

```
if (expr and expr) then action
```

Subject, from, or to expressions

```
always
subject = "case insensitive subject"
subject != "case insensitive subject"
to = "case insensitive to field"
to != "case insensitive to field"
from = "case insensitive from field"
from != "case insensitive from field"
(not) <from, subject, to expr>
```

Line count expressions

```
lines = 2
lines > 1
lines < 20
lines <= 30
lines >= 40
lines != 0
```

Actions include:

```
delete
save <save-folder>
savecopy <copy-folder>
execute <command>
forward <address>
leave
```

For more information on filter options and rules, type **man filter**.

filter example

.forward file:

```
| "(cd /home/ie/aboba; /usr/local/bin/filter -o
/home/ie/aboba/filter.err)"
```

/home/ie/aboba/.elm/filter-rules file:

```
if (subject = "typo") then save typofolder
if (subject = "form") then forward form@foo.com
if (subject = "register") then save regfolder
if (from = "bozo") then delete
if (subject = "bozo") then delete
if (from = "President") then forward urgent@foo.com
if (lines >1) then forward aboba@foo.com
```

Eudora

Eudora

Eudora is one of the most popular mail user agents. It is available for both the Macintosh and Windows; can be configured to use a variety of transport agents, including serial connections, UUCP, SMTP, and POP; and supports file attachments, carbon copies, and address books. Best of all, it's free for noncommercial use. For information on how to obtain Eudora, please consult Appendix B: Choice Products.

Configuration for TCP/IP

To use Eudora over TCP/IP, you must obtain a TCP/IP stack separately. For the Mac, this will be MacTCP; for Windows, it should be a Windows Sockets–compliant stack, such as the stack included with NetManage Chameleon. To configure Eudora for TCP/IP, choose **Configure...** from the **File** menu:

This will bring up a dialog box asking for the name of your SMTP and POP servers, as well as other information.

For the POP account, input the address of your account on the POP server. Typically the SMTP server is the machine name of your Internet host; however, since other Internet hosts will also accept mail, you can use another machine name just as well. The return address is usually the same as your POP account, although it doesn't have to be.

Eudora is compatible with the Ph (Phone Book) application discussed in Chapter 9: Finding people. If your organization has a Ph server, insert its address here.

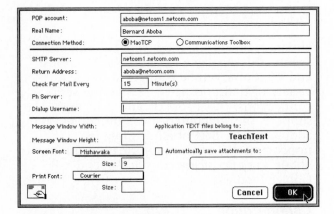

By the way, in case you don't believe that the Windows version of Eudora is virtually identical to the Mac version, here's a screen shot of the same dialog box under Windows. About the only difference in the setups is that under Windows you must add pop3 and port 110 to the SERVICES file kept with your Windows Sockets DLL (see the end of the chapter for the line to enter).

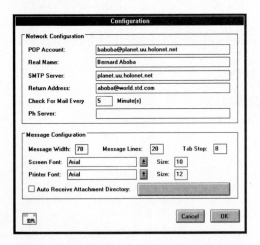

Configuration for UUCP transport

Eudora can also be configured to work with a UUCP transport program. On the Macintosh, compatible programs include uConnect and UUPC.

To instruct Eudora that you will be using UUCP transport and fill in the configuration dialog box with the following entries:

POP Account: `!<Incoming mail path>`

On the Macintosh for a mail file foo in directory telecom, on disk drive Alliance, this would be:

`!Alliance:telecom:foo`

Be aware that Eudora cannot cope with hard drive names that contain spaces. The incoming mail file is expected to be in the standard UNIX mailbox format.

Connection Method: Not important; if you want to mix serial communications or TCP/IP with UUCP, choose the appropriate button.

SMTP Server: `!<UUCP name>!<UUCP host>!<Outgoing mail path>:<user ID>!<starting message number>`

For example, for a system named planet, with UUCP host bozo, with user aboba, on the Macintosh with outgoing spool directory usr within directory spool, on disk drive Alliance, this would be:

`!planet!bozo!Alliance:usr:spool:aboba!7777`

Here the four-digit number begins the naming of the outgoing spool files. For example:

`D.bozo0xxxx` – This is the message file.

`D.planet0xxxx` – This is where the UUCP commands for the UUCP host reside.

`C.bozo0xxxx` – This is the file that stores the UUCP commands for your system.

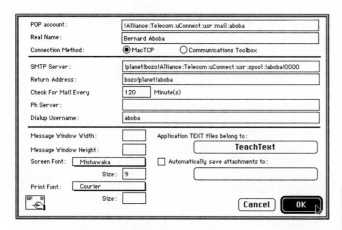

For information on setting up UUCP transport, please consult Chapter 16: Unix-to-Unix Copy.

Configuring Eudora for serial communications

Service providers such as Holonet also support use of Eudora over serial connections. This is convenient because it offers the ease of use of a graphical interface without the hassle of setting up a UUCP or TCP/IP connection. For a copy of the Eudora serial server for UNIX, `ftp sumex-aim.stanford.edu, cd /info-mac/comm`.

General configuration and use

Once you've got the transport-specific elements set up, you will need to configure the other elements of Eudora. Virtually all features of Eudora, including mail checking and file attachments, work with serial, UUCP, and TCP/IP transport mechanisms. However, please note that since Eudora assumes that the transport mechanism is error-free, use in serial line mode without an error-correcting modem can be problematic.

Signatures

Eudora allows you to create a signature file that will appear at the end of every message.

As an example, here is my signature file:

Nicknames

Eudora also allows you to create an address book of nicknames by selecting **Nicknames** from the **File** menu. This brings up a dialog box to create and edit the address book.

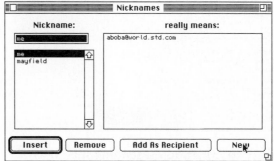

Once you have edited the nicknames, they will appear under the hierarchical menu **New Message To...**

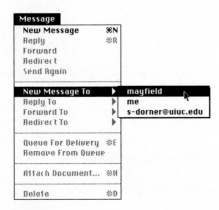

Receiving and sending mail

Checking mail

With Eudora, mail may be picked up at regular intervals, or whenever you choose to look for new messages.

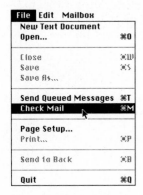

You can check your mail by selecting **Check Mail** under the **File** menu. You will then be presented with a dialog box requesting your password.

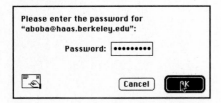

For more information on sending mail over Internet, please consult the remainder of this chapter. Please remember that not all gateways will accept file transmissions. For example, when I attempted to send a file EECP.ARC to

node 1:101/485, the following error message resulted:

```
Date: Sun, 27 Sep 92 13:36:21 EDT
From: Postmaster <Postmaster@zorro9.fidonet.org>
To: akbar@foobar.com
Subject: Rejected Message

The following message was rejected at the gateway.  It
exceeded size limitations and violated rules against file
transmissions and encrypted files. Please do not use this
gateway for any further file transmissions.

>>>To:    sysop@f5555.n101.z1.fidonet.org
>>>Date: Sun, 27 Sep 92 07:18:28 -0700

When I was in Boston over the summer, I noticed your
exquisitely designed modem hut out on route 128. Please
find enclosed my 24 bit color rendering of the hut,
converted with BinHex 4.0.

Akbar Foobar
Internet: akbar@foobar.com

(This file must be converted with BinHex 4.0)
:$'9PBh"I-
63e,Q&bB`!r2cmr2cmr2`%!!!#8b`!!!!"$faS8!23(mIpH+*SCma5
```

Sending mail messages

The Eudora message interface supports Cc: and Bcc:, as well as Reply–To:, and file attachments.

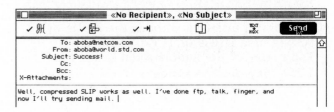

File attachments

Eudora allows you to send and receive files along with your messages. To attach a file, you must first have begun a new message. Do this by selecting **New Message** from the **Message** menu. Binary files will be converted to and from BINHEX, both on the Mac and under Windows. To attach a file to the message, select **Attach Document...** from the **Message** menu.

You will then be asked to select a file to attach. Select a file. At this point your message will look like this.

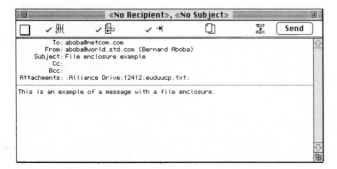

To send the message, just click on the **Send** button. If you are sending a binary file, it will be converted to ASCII text first (this is done with BinHex on both the Mac and Windows). A dialog box will appear to inform you of this.

Receiving files

On receiving an attachment, Eudora will notify you and put up a dialog box for you to select where to store the file. It will then convert the enclosure from ASCII to binary.

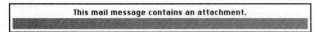

In order to provide an audit trail, Eudora will then leave the rest of the message in your in box, indicating the disposition of the file enclosure:

```
Date: Sat, 1 May 1993 16:50:26 -0800
To: aboba@netcom.com
From: aboba@world.std.com (Bernard Aboba)
X-Sender: aboba@netcom1.netcom.com
Subject: File enclosure
X-Attachments: :Alliance Drive:1336:uConnect Preferences:

This is an example file enclosure.
Bernard Aboba
Author of "Bulletin Boards and Beyond"
Internet: aboba@world.std.com    FidoNet: 1:161/445
MailCom, 5337 College Ave., Suite 326, Oakland, CA 94618
Fax:     (510)540-1057


Attachment converted: 2/1/93 Week to Do:uConnect
Preferences (Type: 'Pref' Creator: 'SkyM')
```

POPmail

POPmail is a Mactinosh MUA developed at the University of Minnesota that requires MacTCP, and supports the POP2, POP3, and IMAP2 protocols. It is available via `ftp sumex-aim.stanford.edu, cd imap`. Since POPmail is one of the few Macintosh MUAs that supports the IMAP2 protocol, it is a good choice for large installations that require the improved scalability that IMAP provides compared to POP.

To set up POPmail, you will need to deal with several of the options on the **Setup** menu, including editing your signature file, and setting your username and server.

To set up your username and server, select **Set Username & Server...** from the **Setup** menu. This will bring up the following dialog box:

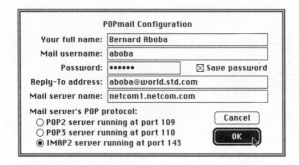

Enter your full name, as well as your username and password on the server machine. It is generally not a good idea to save your password for future sessions, for security reasons. Then enter the address to which replies should be sent (usually the same as your mail address on the server machine), and enter the name of your POP/IMAP server. Finally, select the retrieval protocol.

PC POPmail

PC POPmail is a POP client that runs under DOS and includes its own built in TCP/IP stack. It is available as part of the SLIPDISK distribution from the University of Minnesota. Like Eudora, it can automatically BINHEX 4.0 binary file attachments. Since POPmail requires packet drivers, if you are running over a LAN, you need to install these before running the program. If you want to access POPmail under Windows, remember to install the packet drivers prior to running Windows. To set up PC POPmail, you will want to select the items from the **Setup** menu.

Below is a sample setup for the **Network...** dialog box. Since PC POPmail contains its own built in TCP/IP stack, you will need to enter the gateway and nameserver IP addresses, as well as the IP address of your machine. You will also need to enter the username and domain name of your POP server.

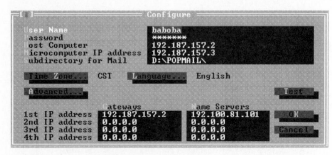

PC POPmail is capable of sending and receiving files via BINHEX 4.0 enclosures.

Hints for setting up POP servers

Setting up a POP server on a UNIX machine is fairly straightforward. However, there are a few "gotchas" to be aware of:

• POP versions include POP2 (which runs on TCP port 109), and POP3 (which runs on TCP port 110). Since Eudora checks for mail on port 110, and other POP3-compatible programs may check for mail on port 109, make sure your machine is listening for connections on both ports. This can be done by adding the following lines to /etc/inetd.conf:

```
pop    stream  tcp  nowait  root  /usr/etc/popper  popper
pop2   stream  tcp  nowait  root  /usr/etc/popper  popper
```

You will also need to add the following lines to /etc/services:

```
pop2          109/tcp            postoffice
pop           110/tcp            postoffice
```

Be aware that if you are running NIS or NetInfo that the configuration may be read from the database instead of from the /etc/services file, so that editing this file will have no effect. Under Windows, you may need to add the following line to your SERVICES file:

```
pop3          110/tcp
```

For more information

POP mailing list	pop-request@ jhunix.hcf.jhu.edu
POP archives	jhunix.hcf.jhu.edu (128.220.2.5)
SMTP	comp.mail.sendmail
UUCP	comp.mail.uucp
UUCP maps	comp.mail.maps
ELM	comp.mail.elm
Mail headers	comp.mail.headers
MIME	comp.mail.mime
Multi-media	comp.mail.multi-media
MUSH	comp.mail.mush

Finding People

You can reach an enormous number of people via mail if you can find the correct mailing addresses. The Knowbot, Finger, Whois, Netfind and the USENET addresses database can help.

The Knowbot

The Knowbot is a front-end for searching other directories, created by Ralph Droms, `rdroms@nri.reston.va.us`. Since it is just a front end, it does not maintain any directories itself.

Accessing Knowbot via telnet

To get to the Knowbot, give the command: **`telnet nri.reston.va.us 185`** or **`telnet sol.bucknell.edu 185`**. Here's what logging on the Knowbot looks like:

```
% telnet nri.reston.va.us 185
Trying 132.151.1.1...
Connected to nri.reston.va.us.
Escape character is '^]'.
Knowbot Information Service (V1.0). Copyright CNRI 1990.
All Rights Reserved.
Try ? or man for help.
>
```

How to use the Knowbot

Once you've gotten to the Knowbot, you'll need to tell it to do something. The Knowbot can understand the following commands:

help, man, ?

These commands will get you information on how to use the Knowbot. Help and ? get you a short help file. Man gets you documentation in the traditional UNIX-manual page format.

query <user name>

This command asks the Knowbot to search its database for someone with the name User Name.

Here's an example:

```
> query Vint Cerf
No matches found for Vint Cerf from service
whois@nic.ddn.mil
Name:         Vinton G. Cerf
Organization: NRI
City:         Reston
State:        VA
Country:      US
E-Mail:       105-0002@mcimail.com
Source:       mcimail
Ident:        105-0002
Last Updated: unknown

No matches found for Vint Cerf from service
ripe@nic.eu.net
```

services

The services command gets you a listing of all the services that the Knowbot has directories for. Here's a sample session:

```
> services
nic
csnet
mcimail
ripe
x500 (be sure to set the org)
finger@a UNIX host
```

Here nic is the Network Information Center, csnet is the Computer Science Network; mcimail is the MCI Mail online service; finger is the UNIX command that finds a user on a given host.

quit or exit

When you want to leave the Knowbot, give it the command **`quit`** or **`exit`**. That should do it!

How to reach the Knowbot via email

For those of you who do not have Internet access, you can also reach the Knowbot by email by sending mail to `kis@nri.reston.va.us` or `kis@sol.bucknell.edu`. In the body of the message include Knowbot commands that will be executed; the results will be mailed back to you.

Here is what the letter will look like:

```
% mail kis@nri.reston.va.us
Subject: Test of Knowbot
query aboba
EOF
```

Here is what the response letter will look like:

```
Message  1:
From kis@NRI.Reston.VA.US Sun Sep 27 18:44:40 1992
Received: by world.std.com (5.57/Sun-OS 4.1.3)
        id AA23719; Sun, 27 Sep 92 18:44:39 -0700
Date: Sun, 27 Sep 92 21:43:55 EDT
X-Mailer: Mail User's Shell (6.5 4/17/89)
From: NRI Directory Services <kis@NRI.Reston.VA.US>
To: aboba@world.std.com
Subject: kis retrieval
Message-Id: <9209272143.aa03794@NRI.Reston.VA.US>
Status: R

Knowbot Information Service (V1.0). Copyright CNRI 1990.
All Rights Reserved.
Try ? or man for help.
Name:        Bernard Aboba
Organization: 1442A Walnut St. #58
City:        Berkeley
State:       CA
Country:     US
Zip:         94709
Phone:       (510) 549-2684
E-Mail:      aboba@WORLD.STD.COM
Source:      whois@nic.ddn.mil
Ident:       BA8
Last Updated: 07-Jan-92.
Unable to connect to csnet@sh.cs.net
No matches found for aboba from service csnet@sh.cs.net
No matches found for aboba from service
mcimail@nri.reston.va.us
```

ufind script – Finding an email address using Knowbot

If you are accessing the Knowbot frequently by email from a non-Internet-connected UNIX machine, you may find the following shell script useful in automating the task. It finds the email address of someone by checking both the Knowbot and usenet address databases (discussed later on).

```
#!/bin/sh
#
if [ $# -ne 1 ]
then
        echo Usage: $0 name-of-person-to-find
        exit 1
fi
echo "\
send usenet-addresses/$1" | mail \
mail-server@pit-manager.mit.edu
echo query $1 | mail kis@nri.reston.va.us
```

Finger

Finger is a command that provides information on a user who is on another system. The information may be provided by the user's employer (in the case of an institutional database such as at Stanford University) or it may be provided by the user, via editing the .plan and .project files in the home directory. In addition to UNIX clients, for those running TCP/IP, clients are available for Macintosh (MacFinger, on sumex-aim.stanford.edu), and Windows (Finger, available from sunsite.unc.edu). There is currently no "finger server" operating over email, so you cannot execute **finger** from a store and forward network. One form of **finger** tells you basic information about an individual, assuming you know the machine to query. The command is of the form:

finger <search string>@host.domain

The <search string> can be a fragment of a name, but it should not contain spaces. Be aware that many UNIX sites limit user IDs to eight characters.

Example

In this example, I search for a user whose name or user ID includes the string "bernard" on the system world.std.com. This might be useful if the person's first name is fairly unique, and I know their system name but not their user ID.

```
% finger bernard@world.std.com
[world.std.com]
world -- The World -- Public Access UNIX -- SUN 4/280
SUNOS 4.0.3
  2:22am  up 22:09,  14 users,  load average: 2.04, 2.22,
2.05

-User-      --Full name--       -What- Idle TTY
-Console Location-
aboba     . Bernard D Aboba            Login Fri 27-Mar-92
11:18PM from netcom.com
ley.
  [1290,1290]  </users/aboba>;  Group: aboba
  Groups: aboba

  aboba has new mail as of Sat 28-Mar-92 12:58AM

Plan: (last modified Mon 9-Mar-92 12:10AM)
Plan: A course of action, measurement, and correction.
Currently, I'm recuperating from the Online User's
Encyclopedia
```

Host finger

Another form of the finger command just uses the host name:

finger @host.domain

This form tells you who is logged in at the time. For example:

```
% finger @140.174.2.71
[140.174.2.71]
Login   Name    Tty Idle Login Time  Office Office Phone
Swps    Tom Jennings slippin *co   1d  Apr 30 12:27
```

Institutional finger

The problem with standard finger is that you need to know which machine the person has an account on. In order to make searching easier, certain universities support an "institutional finger" command of the form:

```
finger <search string>@<domain>
```

When this command is executed, the institutional database is queried, returning the matching machine and user IDs.

Example

```
% finger akbar@mit.edu
[mit.edu]
Student data loaded as of Mar 4, Staff data loaded as of
Mar 3.

Notify the Registrar or Personnel as appropriate to
change your information.

This service is maintained by Distributed Computing and
Network Services. Send Comments regarding this service to
mitdir@mit.edu.

        Use finger help@mit.edu for some instructions.

There was 1 match to your request.

Complete information will be shown only when one
individual matches
your query.  Resubmit your query with more information.
For example, use both firstname and lastname or use the
alias field.

      name: Bmug, Akbar
department: Nuclear Physics, Mascot
      year: G
     alias: A-Bmug
```

Schools with finger

Schools implementing institutional **finger** include:

Domain name	Institution
colorado.edu	University of Colorado
csus.edu	California State University at Sacramento
dartmouth.edu	Dartmouth University
iastate.edu	Iowa State University
mit.edu	Massachusetts Institute of Technology
princeton.edu	Princeton University
sonoma.edu	Sonoma State University
sunysb.edu	State University of New York at Stonybrook
ucsd.edu	University of California at San Diego
uiuc.edu	University of Illinois at Urbana-Champaign
umich.edu	University of Michigan
utdallas.edu	University of Texas at Dallas

Setting your information

Using the **chfn** command, you can change the information that is returned when you are fingered or when you send outgoing mail. Here is how it works:

```
% chfn
Changing finger information for aboba on world.
Default values are printed inside of '[]'.
To accept the default, type <return>.
To have a blank entry, type the word 'none'.

Name [Bernard D Aboba]: Bernard David Aboba
```

You can also change the information in the .plan and .project files. Both files are displayed by the finger command. Finger only displays the first line of the .project file, so this file should be a short description of your latest project. Finger displays the entire .plan file, so in theory it can be as long as you want, although it is recommended that you obey a limit of twenty lines. For finger to make use of these files, they must be readable by others. To do this, set the permissions using chmod:

```
% chmod o+r ~/.plan ~/.project
```

Graphical finger

As mentioned earlier, graphical versions of finger are available for Macintosh (MacFinger) and Windows (finger). MacFinger requires MacTCP, while Windows finger, shown below, requires Windows Sockets.

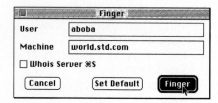

Whois

There are now dozens of whois servers operating on the Internet. Unfortunately they are not yet linked together into a coherent directory system; this is the goal of the whois++ project. As things stand now, you will have to figure out which servers are relevant, which is not an easy task. To query a specific server, use the following syntax:

```
whois -h <server> <search string>
```

How do you know which servers to query? Several educational institutions such as Stanford University now maintain an extensive whois database. Some of the institutions implementing whois are:

Domain name	Institution
csus.edu	California State University at Sacramento
mit.edu	Massachusetts Institute of Technology
ohio-state.edu	Ohio State University
sonoma.edu	Sonoma State University
sunysb.edu	State University of New York at Stonybrook
ucsd.edu	University of California at San Diego
virginia.edu	University of Virginia (use whois.virginia.edu)

A list of whois servers is available via `ftp sipb.mit.edu`, get `/pub/whois/whois-servers.list`

Example

```
% whois -h stanford.edu Gorbachev
                Stanford University Whois Service
 "whois help" for general info      | Problems to
"whois-problem@networking"
 "whois update" for entry update info | Comments to
"help@networking"

Gorbachev, Mikhail (gorby)   (510) 555-1212
   Hoover Institution, Fellow

(returned 1 entry)
```

A more straightforward use of **whois** is when you have someone with a unique last name, such as mine, who is also listed in the nic.ddn.mil whois server, which is the default:

```
% whois aboba
Aboba, Bernard (BA8)          aboba@WORLD.STD.COM
   1442A Walnut St. #62
   Berkeley, CA 94709
   (510) 549-2684

   Record last updated on 07-Jan-92.
```

However, if you are searching for a common name, life can become more complicated:

```
% whois BOZO
BOZO, ALBERT (AB20)                   510-555-1212
BOZO, BERNARD N., JR.  (BBS1)         510-555-1212
BOZO, KEVIN (KB20)  AKBAR@GANDWANA.ORG  510-555-1212
BOZO, MICHAEL (MB17) JEFF@MOOSEHAIR.ORG 510-555-1212
```

In this case, you need to execute another **whois** command using the symbol in parenthesis to get the information:

```
% whois AB20
BOZO, ALBERT (AB20)          [No mailbox]
   BOZO, Inc.
   555 Clown St. #55
   Clownsville, CA 94907
   510-555-1212
Record last updated on 18-Dec-91.
```

LISTSERV whois

While the Internet **whois** is only useful to those with Internet accounts, there is also a LISTSERV version that can be accessed via email. However this command is somewhat different. The LISTSERV version of whois can only be used to find someone who you know is subscribing to a particular LISTSERV. For further information, please consult Chapter 17: BITNET.

Netfind

Netfind is an active search agent developed by Prof. Michael F. Schwartz. To access netfind, **telnet bruno.cs.colorado.edu**, login: **netfind**. Other netfind clients include:

archie.au
ds.internic.net
lincoln.technet.sg
malloco.ing.puc.cl
monolith.cc.ic.ac.uk
mudhoney.micro.umn.edu
redmont.cis.uab.edu

dino.conicit.ve
macs.ee.mcgill.ca
netfind.oc.com
netfind.vslib.cz
nic.nm.kr
nic.uakom.sk

Netfind takes a person's name and a domain, and actively searches for them within the given domain, using a variety of tools. The disadvantage of Netfind is that it can only search sites directly connected to the Internet.

Example

```
Enter person and keys (blank to exit) --> aboba haas
Please select at most 3 of the following domains to
search:
        0. rohmhaas.com (rohm and haas company,
philadelphia, pennsylvania)
        1. br.rohmhaas.com (rohm and haas company,
philadelphia, pennsylvania)
        2. haas.berkeley.edu (university of california,
berkeley)

Enter selection (e.g., 2 0 1) --> 2
( 1) check_name: checking domain haas.berkeley.edu.
Level = 0
MAIL FOR Bernard Aboba IS FORWARDED TO
aboba@world.std.com
NOTE:   this is a domain mail forwarding arrangement to
an outside domain,indicating that "aboba" has probably
moved to another institution.Hence, mail should be
addressed to "aboba@world.std.com".

( 1) check_name: checking host world.std.com.  Level = 0
SYSTEM: haas.berkeley.edu
Login name: aboba        In real life: Bernard Aboba
Directory: /user2/alumni/aboba
Shell: /usr/local/bin/tcsh
Plan:

A course of measurement, action, and correction.

Plans for summer:
1. Finish current software development projects.
2. Chair the Internet track at BBSONE conference in
Colorado Springs.
3. Finish The Online User's Encyclopedia.

SUMMARY:
- The most promising email address for "aboba"
  based on the above search is
  aboba@world.std.com.
```

USENET address database

The machine `pit-manager.mit.edu` maintains a database of addresses of USENET posters. This database contains the names and addresses of thousands of people, many of whom are not listed in other directories. If you think that your intended recipient has been active on USENET, then you might wish to query this database. A script for doing this (as well as simultaneously querying the Knowbot) was given earlier. To use this database, use the command `mail mail-server@` `pit-manager.mit.edu`, body: `send usenet-addresses/<name>`

Example

```
% mail mail-server@pit-manager.mit.edu
Subject: Ignored
send usenet-addresses/aboba
EOT
```

The response to the request looked like this:

```
From daemon@pit-manager.MIT.EDU Sat Mar 28 01:05:30 1992
Received: by world.std.com (5.57/1.33.2)
        id AA03598; Sat, 28 Mar 92 01:05:28 -0800
Received:  by pit-manager.MIT.EDU (5.61/2.1JIK)
        id <AA22838@pit-manager.MIT.EDU>; Sat, 28 Mar 92
04:05:23 -0500
Date: Sat, 28 Mar 92 04:05:23 -0500
From: Mr Background <daemon@pit-manager.MIT.EDU>
Message-Id: <9203280905.AA22838@pit-manager.MIT.EDU>
Subject: Reply from mserv re: send usenet-addresses/aboba
Reply-To: mail-server@pit-manager.mit.edu
X-Problems-To: postmaster@pit-manager.mit.edu
Precedence: bulk
To: aboba@world.std.com
Status: R

aboba@world.std.com (Bernard D Aboba)    (Mar 22 92)
```

You can also access the database via the WAIS source usenet-addresses.src.

SMTP VRFY

Due to security concerns, many machines no longer support finger; instead you might try the SMTP VRFY command. This can be used to verify someone's electronic mail address, by telneting to the SMTP port. The command is of the form:
VRFY <ID>.

Example:

```
% telnet world.std.com 25
Trying...
Connected to world.std.com.
Escape character is '^]'.
220 world.std.com Sendmail 5.65c/Spike-2.0 ready at Thu,
5 Aug 1993 13:29:28 -00
VRFY aboba
250 Bernard D Aboba <aboba>
```

If the individual is using a .forward file to forward mail, the forwarding address will be displayed in response to a **VRFY** command.

Internet Business Pages (IBP)

The Internet Business Pages is a new Internet service created by MSEN. It provides a directory of businesses operating over the Internet. Using the IBP application, you can look up information on a firm or look at the index.

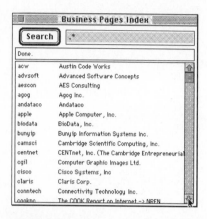

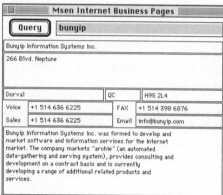

The Macintosh version of IBP is available via `ftp ftp.msen.com, cd directory /pub/ibp`. To obtain information on IBP, `mail ibp-info@msen.com`, subject: `send form`, or `ftp ftp.msen.com, get /pub/ibp/IBPFORM`.

Ph

Ph (which stands for Phone Book), written by Steve Dorner (author of Eudora), is a client/server database. Most often it is used to store names, phone numbers, and email addresses, but it could be used for other information as well, such as restaurants, weather, or area codes.

Ph operates by having the client (Ph) query the server (QI). Queries can be generated by stand-alone clients (available for the Macintosh, UNIX, and NeXT); by Gopher; by Eudora; or by programs such as Synergy Software's VersaTilities.

One of the big problems with electronic mail is that no fuzziness is allowed. Even if there is only one Bernard at foo.com, sending mail to `bernard@foo.com` will not work for sending mail to user ID `aboba`. The Computing Services Office (CSO) at the University of Illinois Urbana-Champaign has created a CSO Nameserver program that solves this problem. It does this by using the directory information in order to find a unique match among the users at the institution. If the name is not unique, then the CSO Nameserver will instead return a list of possibilities.

How do you use Ph?

Since the NeXT Ph client supports the most features, we'll start by exploring that. To use Ph, you must first select a server from the organization of the person you're looking to find. On the NeXT, this is done by selecting from a list of Ph servers that is retrieved from the default server. Since all the Ph servers know about the other ones, it doesn't matter which server you use as your default.

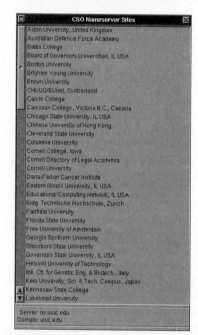

Once you select a Ph server, the NeXT client retrieves a template of the information stored on this server. In order to query the database, you fill out the template, which is matched against the records stored in the database. At least one field marked with a dot must be filled in for the query to be valid.

Wildcard symbols such as * and ? are allowed. However, if you are using a UNIX client you will need to escape these using the \. However, in order to prevent it from being used to generate mailing lists, Ph will not respond to queries resulting in more than twenty hits.

In the next example, I search for people named Aboba on the University of Illinois server. The records meeting the criteria will then be returned in the bottom of the window.

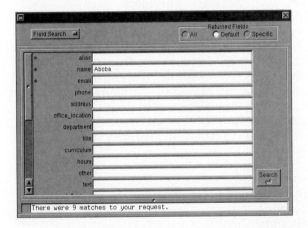

Don't get the idea that all Ph can do is look up names and addresses. Ph Servers have great flexibility and could, in principle, be used to build other things such as résumé databases. Servers are also free to define additional fields, such as "other." For example, on the University of Illinois Ph Server, you can search for a restaurant by specifying name as "restaurant" and the type of restaurant in the other field.

Below, I find a Thai restaurant:

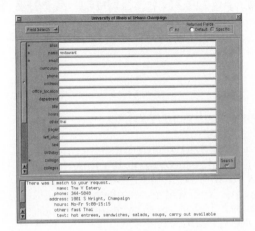

Fields such as "other" are often used to store interesting tidbits like restaurant listings. How do you get at this information if your client does not have a field for "other"? Fields can be entered explicitly into queries, as with the following query to a UNIX Ph client:

```
ph restaurant other=thai text=salad
```

For more information

Whois server source code is available via **ftp sipb.mit.edu, get /pub/whois/whois-servers.source**

For information on netfind, contact netfind@xcaret.com, (800)736-1285, 2060 Broadway, #320, Boulder, CO 80302.

The USENET newsgroup soc.net-people is devoted to finding people. It should only be used as a last resort. To query it, send a message with **subject: <region and country>: <name of person>.**

An updated information file on finding email addresses is maintained by Mark Kantrowitz, mkant@GLINDA.OZ.CS.CMU.EDU, and is posted periodically to the USENET groups soc.college and soc.net-people. It is also available via **ftp a.gp.cs.cmu.edu, cd /afs/cs.cmu.edu/user/mkant/Public/coll ege-email.txt.** You will need to **cd** to this directory directly to get it though, since intermediate directories are protected.

MAIL ADDRESSING AND DEBUGGING

Basics of mail addressing

Now that you've had a basic introduction to how to send and receive mail, it's time to talk about how to address it. Addresses come in several flavors. You will most often see the characters !,@,: and % used in mail addresses. What do they mean?

There are two fundamentally different methods of mail addressing. One technique utilizes the ! symbol and is known as "bang-path addressing." Bang-path addressing, which originated back in the days when most mail was delivered using the UUCP store and forward protocol, specifies the route that a message should take.

The other addressing method is "domain name addressing." Domain name addressing, and the Domain Name Service that supports it, was developed for the Internet and is now the predominant mail-addressing scheme. Domain name addresses do *not* specify routes; rather they are logical groupings of machines that may or may not be in the same vicinity, or even on the same physical network. Since Domain Name Service supports the addition of Mail Exchange (MX) records for non-Internet systems, machines with store and forward connections (such as FrEdMail, UUCP, BITNET, and FidoNet systems) can have domain names.

Domain addressing

A typical fully qualified domain name address is of the form user@host.domain. Example:
`aboba@haas.berkeley.edu`

What does this address signify? Domain addresses are read from left to right. This address specifies a machine in the Educational (.edu) domain, on the UC Berkeley campus, within the Walter A. Haas School of Business.

The .edu domain is one of the generic top-level domains. These include:

.edu	Educational institutions
.gov	U.S. Government agencies
.int	International organizations
.mil	U.S. military
.net	Network providers
.com	Commercial firms
.org	Nonprofit organizations

These top-level domains are in turn subdivided. For example, the educational domain is subdivided into domains for each university, such as .stanford.edu, .berkeley.edu, etc. Within the universities, the subdomain is further divided into domains for each department or machine.

Here are some other examples: applelink.apple.com means that the machine applelink is located within the apple subdomain within the .com domain. portia.stanford.edu is the address of machine portia located at Stanford University, within the .edu domain.

There are also geographic domains, which are denoted by ISO standard country codes, which are given at the end of this chapter. Some of these include:

.ca	Canada
.de	Germany
.fr	France
.jp	Japan
.us	United States

Although domain name addresses were supposed to correspond to logical associations, not to networks, non-Internet networks such as FrEdMail, FidoNet, and packet radio have been given their own domains within the .org domain: fred.org, fidonet.org, and ampr.org.

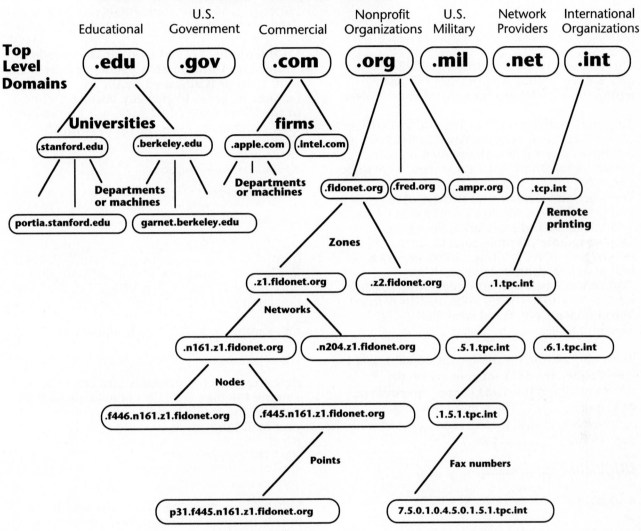

The Domain Name Tree

Within FidoNet, the domain is further subdivided by network, then by node, and finally by point number. For example, my address on FidoNet is:

```
Bernard.Aboba@f222.n125.z1.fidonet.org.
```

This means that I am within node 222 (MacEmma) within network 125 (SF Bay), within zone 1 (North America) of the FidoNet.

Although networks such as BITNET and UUCP do not have their own domains, individual machines may support the pseudo-domain names .BITNET and .UUCP for these networks.

There are also domains created for other purposes. The tpc.int domain was created by Carl Malamud and Marshall T. Rose in order to support remote printing, such as faxing. The software supports printing of text messages, as well as MIME content types such as application/PostScript, and image/tiff. To send a fax to 1(510)555-1212, addressed to Bernard Aboba of MailCom, you'd send mail to `remote.printer.Bernard_Aboba/ MailCom@2.1.2.1.5.5.5.0.1.5.1.tpc.int.` For more information on the tpc.int domain, **mail tpc-faq@town.hall.org**, or get on the tpc.int mailing list via **mail tpc-rp-request @aarnet.edu.au.** The remote printing software is available via **ftp.ics.uci.edu, get /mrose/tpc/rp.tar.Z.**

UUCP-style addressing

A bang-path address looks like this:

```
host1!host2!host3!host4!<user>
```

Before the UUCP mapping project and the development of smart mailers such as smail, it was necessary to give all the details of the routing. However, smart mailers make use of the UUCP maps that are published in `comp.mail.maps` (and compiled by pathalias) in order to create a database that allows them to compute routes. Machines running smart mailers and pathalias therefore do not need to have the path spelled out.

In fact, your host does not even need to be running smail and pathalias for you to take advantage of smart routing. Many sendmail configurations are set up to automatically route mail for the UUCP pseudo-domain to `uunet.uu.net`, which maintains a UUCP map database and is one of the central UUCP sites.

! is the routing symbol used for UUCP-style addressing. Unfortunately, under certain shells (csh, tcsh), it is also used by the history feature. In order to prevent misinterpretation of the !, you must add a backslash (\) before each occurrence. Thus, in the C shell, the address:

```
foobar!planet!aboba
```

would be typed:

```
foobar\!planet\!aboba
```

UUCP mail typically travels over phone lines from one machine to another, via UNIX-to-UNIX Copy. Since the phone calls are often only made at night when phone rates are low, this method of sending mail is slow.

An example of a UUCP-style address is:

```
{hplabs, apple, decwrl}!foobar!bozo
```

Here the {} encloses choices you can make in sending the mail. You do not actually include the {} in the mailing address! So you can send your mail to:

```
hplabs!foobar!bozo OR
apple!foobar!bozo OR
decwrl!foobar!bozo
```

This tells the machine to forward mail to hplabs or apple or decwrl, and whoever gets it will then pass it to machine foobar for delivery to user bozo.

What the @%!

You may also encounter the % symbol within mail addresses. What is the difference between @ and %? The @ symbol has higher priority, and specifies where the mail should be sent first. After it gets there, the % symbol is interpreted by that machine to figure out where to send it next.

Let us look at three addresses:

```
1. bozo@foobar.com
2. bozo%foobar@hplabs.com
3. foobar!bozo@hplabs.com
```

The first address tells your mailer to send mail to user bozo at machine foobar in the commercial domain.

The second address tells your mailer to send mail destined for user bozo at machine foobar via the machine hplabs.com. hplabs will figure out how to route the mail from there. The second form of addressing is useful if the machine foobar does not yet have a Mail Exchange (MX) record, if it is to be reached via the hplabs.com gateway, or if its mail-forwarding machine is not working for some reason. It is up to the machine hplabs.com to figure out how to route the message.

The third address specifies that the message is to be sent first to hplabs.com, and then delivered by the UUCP mailer.

Understanding Domain Name Service

Domain Name Service (DNS), designed by Paul Mockapetris, is one of the fundamental technologies supporting the Internet. DNS is a distributed database service that allows for translation of domain names to IP addresses and provides for the forwarding of mail to non-Internet sites.

The DNS database contains several types of records. If a machine with a fully qualified domain name is on the Internet, then a type A (Address) record is kept, which specifies the machine's IP address. A type PTR record is also kept which allows determination of the domain name from the IP address. A machine on a store and forward network such as a FidoNet or FrEdMail system cannot have a type A record.

However, non-Internet nodes can have a type MX (Mail Exchange) record. This record specifies which Internet host should receive mail for the system. Since it is possible for mail to travel to FidoNet or FrEdMail via gateways, FidoNet and FrEdMail nodes have MX records.

This concept is often very confusing for beginners, who wonder "since foobar.fidonet.org has a domain name, how come I can't **telnet** to it?" The answer is that the **telnet** service is only supported by machines with IP addresses.

How does DNS work?

Domain Name Service is provided by hosts known as name servers. These machines agree to answer queries about a portion of the domain name space within their Zone of Authority.

For example, zeus.ieee.org is the primary name server for the fidonet.org domain. If this machine is unavailable, then a secondary name server will be queried. The secondary name server for the fidonet.org domain is lll-winken.llnl.gov. These machines maintain the MX records for the fidonet.org domain that specify how mail is routed to the individual FidoNet nodes. If an MX record is unavailable, or the name resolver is not operating correctly, an "unknown host" error message will result. For further information on how to set up mail forwarding between BBS networks and the Internet, please consult Chapter 15: Bulletin Boards and the Internet.

At the risk of beating this topic into the ground, here are several possible addresses and what will happen to mail sent each way:

```
Bernard.Aboba@balooga.fidonet.org
Bernard.Aboba%balooga.fidonet.org@apple.com
apple!balooga!Bernard.Aboba
Bernard.Aboba@f222.n125.z1.fidonet.org
```

The first address tells the mailer to send mail to user Bernard.Aboba at the machine balooga.fidonet.org. For mail sent this way to arrive successfully, the machine from which it is sent has to either know how to send mail to balooga.fidonet.org itself (such as via a sendmail.cf file created for this purpose) or be capable of using Domain Name Service to query the name servers for the FidoNet domain. If none of these things is true, the message will be bounced.

The second address tells the mailer to send the message to machine apple.com; then apple.com will forward mail for

"Bernard.Aboba%balooga.fidonet.org" from there. In this case, it is apple.com that needs to route mail to balooga.fidonet.org, not the home machine. After receiving the mail, the machine apple.com then converts the % syntax to "Bernard.Aboba@balooga.fidonet.org" and processes it from there.

The third address tells the mailer to send the message to machine apple, which it must be able to reach through the UUCP maps database or UUCP setup files. When apple gets it, it will forward it to balooga. If balooga is neither a UUCP link nor has a UUCP map entry, the mail will bounce. Therefore, method three is the most specific method for routing mail because it alone specifies exactly which route the mail should follow.

The fourth address will actually be routed differently than the first address, even if they specify the same machine. This is because the routing will be specified by the FidoNet name servers. In the case of FidoNet node 1:125/222, mail will be routed through the FidoNet/UUCP gateway for Fidonet network 125, rather than through apple. From there it will be sent to 1:125/222 by FidoNet Netmail. Contrast this with what happens to mail addressed to balooga.fidonet.org, which is routed to apple.com and then sent by UUCP to balooga.

Interpreting a return address

The easiest way to find a person's address is to have them send mail to you. You then interpret the mail they send in order to get their return address. Here's how to do it:

```
From  kumr!taunivm.tau.ac.il!BGUVM.BITNET!BLATZ
From: BLATZ%BGUVM@taunivm.tau.ac.il (Simon Blatz)
To:   Ari Davidow <ari.davidow@f444.n161.z1.fidonet.org>,
Date: Mon, 18 Nov 91 08:13:42 IST

             The San Francisco - Moscow Teleport

                        Simon Blatz
```

In the previous message, the first FROM: is the path that the message traveled; the second line is the domain-style return address. The TO: field is the address to which the message was sent, which should be you. There may also be a REPLY-TO: address.

In order to send a return message, you should first try the reply address, then the domain address. If that doesn't work, you can use the path. Here's an example of a return message posting:

```
To: BLATZ%BGUVM@taunivm.tau.ac.il
From: Ari Davidow
Subject: Got your message

I got your message, and am returning it using the address
on the second line (domain-style addressing).
```

Troubleshooting

Despite your best efforts, sometimes mail is returned as undeliverable, with error messages attached. This is referred to as "bounced mail." The bounced mail message contains all the information you need to figure out what went wrong, if you can interpret it.

Most mail is returned because of a typographical error. Remember that domain name addresses cannot tolerate errors in puctuation. An extra space, period or comma will most likely cause the message to be returned. If this happens to you, fix the punctuation problem and try again.

Another frequent problem is that of an unreachable host. This typically generates error messages such as "bad system name," or "unknown host." This problem can result from the system being down, or lack of an MX record or UUCP map entry.

How do you figure out what went wrong? Tools for mail debugging include nslookup and dig, as well as WAIS databases such as domain-organizations.src, uumap.src, bitearn-nodelist.src, and fidonet-nodelist.src.

Use of the nslookup and dig programs requires a shell account or TCP/IP connection, whereas WAIS databases can be queried using these methods as well as electronic mail and UUCP.

Nslookup

Nslookup stands for "Name Service Lookup." This service provides information about the records on file with DNS. This allows you to ascertain whether a particular site has a TCP/IP address (A record), alias name (CNAME record) or a Mail Exchange record (MX record) on file. This helps in tracking down problems.

Anatomy of a bounced mail message

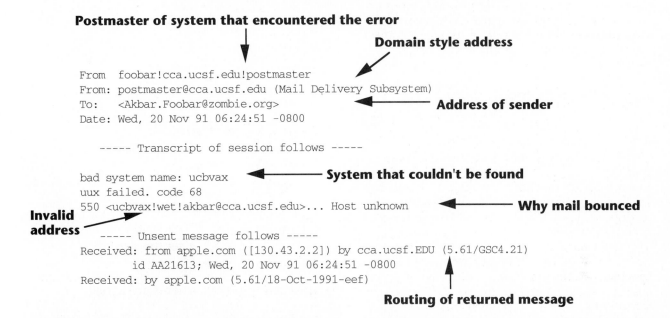

Postmaster of system that encountered the error

Domain style address

```
From    foobar!cca.ucsf.edu!postmaster
From: postmaster@cca.ucsf.edu (Mail Delivery Subsystem)
To:   <Akbar.Foobar@zombie.org>
Date: Wed, 20 Nov 91 06:24:51 -0800

     ----- Transcript of session follows -----

bad system name: ucbvax
uux failed. code 68
550 <ucbvax!wet!akbar@cca.ucsf.edu>... Host unknown
     ----- Unsent message follows -----
Received: from apple.com ([130.43.2.2]) by cca.ucsf.EDU (5.61/GSC4.21)
        id AA21613; Wed, 20 Nov 91 06:24:51 -0800
Received: by apple.com (5.61/18-Oct-1991-eef)
```

Address of sender

System that couldn't be found

Why mail bounced

Invalid address

Routing of returned message

Debugging mail addresses with Z39.50

If nslookup doesn't show a mail record for your intended site, all is not lost. It is possible that you may have mispelled the domain name, or the site may be a BITNET or FidoNet node, or have a registered UUCP-map entry.

Using Z39.50, Gopher, or World Wide Web, you can search for your intended host. Databases of BITNET, FidoNet, UUCP, and Domain Organizations are all searchable via Z39.50. Here are some of the relevant databases:

WAIS-compatible Database	What it includes
bitearn.nodes	BITNET nodes database
domain-organizations.src	Domain name database
domain-contacts.src	People in charge of domains
fidonet-nodelist.src	FidoNet nodelist databaseuk-
name-registration-service.src	Name register for United
Kingdomusenet-addresses.src	Directory of USENET users
uumap.src	UUCP maps database

For more information on searching these databases using Z39.50, Gopher, and World Wide Web, please consult Chapter 14.

For example, what if I attempt to `telnet` to machine foo.org, and get an error message? Using Nslookup, I can determine if foo.org is on the Internet or just has an MX record. If mail bounces from foo.org, Nslookup lets me figure out how mail is supposed to reach foo.org.

Debugging with nslookup

`nslookup` can be used either in command line mode or interactively. If called from the command line with a host name, `nslookup` resolves the TCP/IP address of the host by looking up the machine's A record. If called without an argument, `nslookup` can also recall records of types MX (mail), NS (name service), A (TCP/IP address), SOA (Start of Authority), or ANY (all records).

Nslookup commands

Command	What it does
`set type=MX`	Searches for mail records
`set type=A`	Searches for TCP/IP addresses
`set type=ANY`	Searches for all types of information
`set debug`	Sets debug mode on, prints more info on search
`set nodebug`	Turns debug mode off

Example 1

Mail to `balooga.fidonet.org` has been bouncing, while mail for `f4447.n161.z1.fidonet.org` has been going through, even though these two names both refer to the same system. The following nslookup session shows that no MX record exists for balooga.fidonet.org, while there is a record for f4447.n161.z1.fidonet.org. The query also discloses that the name servers for f4447.n161.z1.fidonet.org are zeus.ieee.org (primary top level), polaris.llnl.gov (secondary), and lll-winken.llnl.gov.

```
% nslookup
Default Server: world.std.com
Address: 192.74.137.5
> set type=ANY
> balooga.fidonet.org
Server: world.std.com
Address: 192.74.137.5

*** world.std.com can't find bmug.fidonet.org: Non-
existent domain
> f4447.n161.z1.fidonet.org
Server: world.std.com
Address: 192.74.137.5

Non-authoritative answer:
f4447.n161.z1.fidonet.org          preference = 10,
mail exchanger = lll-winken.llnl.gov
Authoritative answers can be found from:
lll-winken.llnl.gov     inet address = 128.115.14.1
ZEUS.IEEE.ORG  inet address = 140.98.1.1
POLARIS.LLNL.GOV       inet address = 128.115.14.19
```

Example 2

I am told that Foo Systems is on the Internet as foo.org. However, when I give the command `telnet foo.org`, I get the message:

`foo.org: Unknown host`

How can I find out what is going on?

By default nslookup looks up the TCP/IP address of the named node. Do a `set type=MX` to get the mail record instead. In this example, I determine that foo.org does not have a TCP/IP address (A) record but does have a mail (MX) record. Although it is possible that foo.org may have an unregistered TCP/IP address, this is unlikely since the A record and MX record would probably have been processed at the same time. Therefore my conclusion is that foo.org does not have an IP address.

```
% nslookup
Default Server: world.std.com
Address: 192.74.137.5
> foo.org
Server: world.std.com
Address: 192.74.137.5

*** No address information is available for foo.org
> set type=MX
> foo.org
Server: world.std.com
Address: 192.74.137.5
foo.org preference = 10, mail exchanger = holonet.net
holonet.net  inet address = 157.151.0.1
```

Debugging with dig

dig performs a similar function to Nslookup, but via a command line interface rather than interactively. The form of the dig command is:

```
dig <options> @<server> <name of system> <record>
```

Dig options include:

-x   Returns the domain name of a machine, given the IP address.

Examples

dig -x 157.151.0.1

Returns the domain name of the machine with TCP/IP address 157.151.0.1. In order for this query to be successful, the machine in question must have registered an "in-addr.arpa" domain name for reverse-name resolution. Most sites do, but some may not.

```
% dig -x 157.151.0.1

; <<>> DiG 2.0 <<>> -x
;; ->>HEADER<<- opcode: QUERY , status: NOERROR, id: 6
;; flags: qr rd ra ; Ques: 1, Ans: 1, Auth: 2, Addit: 2
;; QUESTIONS:
;;      1.0.151.157.in-addr.arpa, type = ANY, class = IN

;; ANSWERS:
1.0.151.157.in-addr.arpa.  35012   PTR      holonet.net.

;; AUTHORITY RECORDS:
151.157.IN-ADDR.ARPA.   31270   NS
NOMAD.HOLONET.NET.
151.157.IN-ADDR.ARPA.   31270   NS      ORAC.HOLONET.NET.

;; ADDITIONAL RECORDS:
NOMAD.HOLONET.NET.   172083   A      157.151.0.2
ORAC.HOLONET.NET.    172083   A      157.151.0.1

;; Sent 1 pkts, answer found in time: 10 msec
;; FROM: world to SERVER: default -- 127.0.0.1
;; WHEN: Thu Jan 21 13:31:51 1993
;; MSG SIZE sent: 42  rcvd: 169
```

dig foo.org any

Returns all records associated with the machine foo.org.

```
% dig foo.org any

; <<>> DiG 2.0 <<>> foo.org any
;; ->>HEADER<<- opcode: QUERY , status: NOERROR, id: 6
;; flags: qr rd ra ; Ques: 1, Ans: 3, Auth: 2, Addit: 3
;; QUESTIONS:
;;      foo.org, type = ANY, class = IN
```

```
;; ANSWERS:
foo.org.       172111  NS      NOMAD.HOLONET.NET.
foo.org.       172111  NS      ORAC.HOLONET.NET.
foo.org.       85815   MX      10 holonet.net.

;; AUTHORITY RECORDS:
FOO.org.       172111  NS      NOMAD.HOLONET.NET.
FOO.org.       172111  NS      ORAC.HOLONET.NET.

;; ADDITIONAL RECORDS:
NOMAD.HOLONET.NET.     172111  A      157.151.0.2
ORAC.HOLONET.NET.      172111  A      157.151.0.1
holonet.net.   85815   A      157.151.0.1

;; Sent 1 pkts, answer found in time: 0 msec
;; FROM: world to SERVER: default -- 127.0.0.1
;; WHEN: Thu Jan 21 13:31:23 1993
;; MSG SIZE  sent: 26  rcvd: 187
```

dig foo.org mx

Returns only MX (mail) records associated with foo.org.

Electronic Mail Q&A

How to I get updated information on Internet mail connections?

The Internetwork Mail Guide, maintained by Scott Yanoff, is updated and is available by anonymous **ftp csd4.csd.uwm.edu [128.89.7.4], get /pub/internetwork-mail-guide.**

What's the easiest way to find out my friend's Internet address?

The easiest way is to call him or her on the phone and ask for their Internet address. Alternatively, you can have your friend send you a letter.

When I send mail to f444.n161.z1.fidonet.org, it bounces. What gives?

This was the FidoNet address of the old BMUG ZBBS. Alas, poor ZBBS, I knew it well... The ZBBS was put to sleep on September 15, 1992, and has not risen again. The ZBBS node number (161/444) was removed from the Nodelist the next week and therefore cannot be reached by mail from any network. The Berkeley Mail Hub (f445.n161.z1.fidonet.org) is now also down due to hardware problems.

I'm trying to send mail to a site in Europe but the mail keeps bouncing. What should I do?

Check the A and MX records of the site with nslookup or dig. If it doesn't have them, try UUCP addressing. Using Gopher or Z39.50, you can search for the UUCP map entry of the site; the database is uumap.src. This will tell you if the site has registered its UUCP map. If you find the site, this means that it should be reachable from any site running smail and pathalias. If there is no UUCP-map entry, then you will have to manually route it, and the easiest way to figure out the route is to have your recipient send you mail and then use the return address.

How do I know if an organization has a domain name?

Try searching the Z39.50 database domain-organizations.src. This will allow you to find the domain name you're looking for if you don't have the exact name of the site. A database of domain contacts is also available, as domain-contacts.src.

I received a message which indicated that the sender "could not be authenticated." What does this mean?

It means that the message may be forged. Most SMTP implementations now check the fully qualified domain name of the sender against its IP address. If they do not match, then the recommended remedy is to indicate on the message that the sender's identity could not be verified.

I would like to send mail to a user on Prodigy. How do I do it?

To send mail to a Prodigy user, send mail to foo@prodigy.com, where "foo" is the userID. Be aware that the recipient must be using the Mail Manager software and should have registered to receive Internet Mail. Prodigy users can get information on Internet mail via the **JUMP INTERNET** command.

My mail host runs IMAP2 protocol instead of POP. What clients can I use?

POPmail II for the Macintosh or PC Pine for DOS support the IMAP2 protocol (port 143). For the Mac, the MailStrom and MacMS clients are also available via **ftp sumex-aim.stanford.edu, cd /imap/clients.** The UNIX IMAP2 server is in the /imap/server directory.

I am trying to send a letter to someone on the Internet, but the mail transfer does not go through. What should I do?

Try running **mail** in debugging mode, with the **-v** option. This will show you the conversation with sendmail as the mail is being sent. **mailx** doesn't have an equivalent debugging mode. Here's an example of mail's debugging output:

```
%m %33 %~> /usr/ucb/mail -v aboba@planet.uu.holonet.net
Subject: Test of mail with debugging option
This is a test of the mail debugging option.
EOT
%m %34 %~> aboba@planet.uu.holonet.net... Connecting to
planet.uu.holonet.net (.

220 holonet.net Sendmail 5.57/Ultrix3.0-C ready at Mon, 8
Mar 93 07:0
>>> HELO netcom2.netcom.com
250 holonet.net Hello netcom2.netcom.com, pleased to meet
you
>>> MAIL From:<aboba@netcom.com>
250 <aboba@netcom.com>... Sender ok
>>> RCPT To:<aboba@planet.uu.holonet.net>
250 <aboba@planet.uu.holonet.net>... Recipient ok
>>> DATA
354 Enter mail, end with "." on a line by itself
>>> .
250 Ok
>>> QUIT
221 holonet.net closing connection
aboba@planet.uu.holonet.net... Sent
```

I want to send a file to someone in BinHex form. How do I do it?

Here is a shell script that will handle this for you, after you download the file to your UNIX host with **rz -b**.

```
#!/bin/sh
if [ $# -ne 2 ]
then
      echo Usage: $0 filename email-address
      exit 1
fi
if [ ! -f "$1" ]
then
      echo $1 : no such file
      exit 1
elif [ ! -r "$1" ]
then
      echo file not readable
      exit 1
elif [ ! -s "$1" ]
then
      echo file of zero length
      exit 1
fi
echo "OK, I'll be busy, so please be patient."
MAC_LINE_LIMIT=960
export MAC_LINE_LIMIT
if mcvert -U $1
then
      for file in *hqx
      do
           /usr/ucb/Mail -s $file $2 < $file
      done
      ls *hqx
      echo "Cleanup time\! answer me carefully\!"
      rm -i *hqx
fi
```

The Simple Mail Transport Protocol

SMTP, which uses TCP protocol port 25, is called the Simple Mail Transport Protocol for a reason. It is, in fact, pretty simple, using readable text for data and commands. Here is a list of commands and what they do:

SMTP Commands

Command	What it does
`EXPN <recipient>`	Same as VRFY in sendmail implementation
`HELO <hostname>`	Introduction command. Tell Sendmail your hostname
`MAIL FROM: <sender>`	Specifies who the sender is
`RCPT TO: <recipient>`	Specifies the recipient; can be used many times
`DATA`	Following text is the message, ends with a single dot
`RSET`	Resets the system
`NOOP`	Does nothing
`HELP`	Gives a short help message
`QUIT`	Exits SMTP
`VRFY <recipient>`	Verifies account or forwarding address of recipient

Mail addressing compendium

This section shows how to address electronic mail to many different sites.

To and from commercial online services

Service	To service	From service to Internet
America Online	`<ID>@aol.com`	`<ID>@host.domain`
AppleLink	`<ID>@applelink.apple.com`	`<ID>@host.domain@INTERNET#`
AT&T Mail	`<ID>@attmail.com`	`internet!host.domain!user`
CONNECT	`<ID>@DCJCON.DAS.NET`	`<ID>@host.domain@DasNet;` `To: DasNet on first line`
BIX	`<ID>@dcibix.das.net`	`<ID>@host.domain`
CompuServe	`<ID>@compuserve.com`	`>INTERNET:<ID>@host.domain` `ID=<number>.<number>`
Delphi	`<ID>@delphi.com`	`<ID>@host.domain`
GEnie	`<ID>@genie.geis.com`	`<ID>@host.domain@INET#`
Holonet	`<ID>@holonet.net`	`<ID>@host.domain`
MCIMAIL	`<First_Last>@mcimail.com OR` `<ID number>@mcimail.com`	`<ID>@host.domain`
Netcom	`<ID>@netcom.com`	`<ID>@host.domain`
Portal	`<ID>@cup.portal.com`	`<ID>@host.domain`
Prodigy	`<ID>@prodigy.com`	`<ID>@host.domain`
SprintMail	`/PN=First.Last/O=<ORG>/` `ADMD=TELEMAIL/C=US/@sprint.com`	`<ID>@host.domain`
WELL	`<ID>@well.sf.ca.us`	`<ID>@host.domain`
World	`<ID>@world.std.com`	`<ID>@host.domain`

Examples

America Online	`mailcom@aol.com`	`aboba@world.std.com`
AppleLink	`UG0001@applelink.apple.com`	`aboba@world.std.com`
BIX	`bmug@dcibix.das.net`	`aboba@world.std.com`
CONNECT	`bmug@DCJCON.DAS.NET`	`aboba@world.std.com`
CompuServe	`70009.1484@compuserve.com`	`>INTERNET:aboba@world.std.com`
Delphi	`aboba@delphi.com`	`aboba@world.std.com`
Holonet	`aboba@holonet.net`	`aboba@world.std.com`
Netcom	`gorby@netcom.com`	`gorby@netcom.com`
Portal	`John_Doe@cup.portal.com`	`aboba@world.std.com`
WELL	`dipper@well.sf.ca.us`	`aboba@world.std.com`

From Internet to network

Network	**To Network**
Berkeley	`<user ID>@<node>.berkeley.edu`
Internet	`<user ID>@<domain>`
BITNET	`<user ID>@<node>.bitnet or`
	`<user ID>%<node>@cunyvm.cuny.edu`
UUCP	`uunet.uu.net!<host>! <user ID>`

Examples

Berkeley	`drmicro@garnet.berkeley.edu`
Internet	`info-mac@sumex-aim.stanford.edu`
BITNET	`LISTSERV@BITNIC.BITNET or`
	`LISTERV%BITNIC@cunyvm.cuny.edu`
UUCP	`ucbvax!apple!bmug!Elmer.Fudd`

From network to FidoNet

Network	**From Network to FidoNet**
Berkeley	`<First.Last>@p<point>.f<node>.n<net>.z<zone>.fidonet.org`
Internet	`<First.Last>@p<point>.f<node>.n<net>.z<zone>.fidonet.org`
BITNET	`<First.Last>%p<point>. f<node>.n<net>.z<zone>.fidonet.org`
UUCP	`<UUCP host>!<Fido Gateway UUCPname>!<network>!<node>!<First.Last>`

Examples
(user name = Bernard Aboba, FidoNet address = `1:125/222`)

Berkeley	`Bernard.Aboba@f222.n125.z1.fidonet.org`
Internet	`Bernard.Aboba@f222.n125.z1.fidonet.org`
BITNET	`Bernard.Aboba%f222.n125.z1.fidonet.org`
UUCP	`apple!bmug!125!222!Bernard.Aboba`

From network to TCP/IP packet radio

Network	**From Network to packet radio**
Berkeley	`<ID>@<node>.ampr.org`
Internet	`<ID>@<node>.ampr.org`
BITNET	`<ID>@<node>.ampr.org`
UUCP	`uunet!<node>.ampr.org!<ID>`

Examples
(user name = Bernard Aboba, Packet radio node = sanjose)

Berkeley	aboba@sanjose.ampr.org
Internet	aboba@sanjose.ampr.org
BITNET	aboba@sanjose.ampr.org
UUCP	uunet!sanjose.ampr.org!aboba

From network to Planet BMUG

(User name = Bernard D. Aboba, domain name = bmug.org)

Outside Network	From Outside Network to Planet BMUG
ACSNet (Australia)	Bernard_D._Aboba%bmug.org@munnari.oz
DEC ENET	DECWRL::"Bernard_D._Aboba@bmug.org"
JANET (UK)	Bernard_D._Aboba%bmug.org@uk.ac.ucl.cs
JUNET (Japan)	Bernard_D._Aboba@bmug.org

From network to FrEdMail

Network	From network to FrEdMail
Internet	<ID>@<node>.<domain>.fred.org
BITNET	<ID>@<node>.<domain>.fred.org
UUCP	uunet!<FrEdMail gate>!<host>!<USER ID>

FrEdMail domains (mail exchanger in parthenthesis) = .cerf.fred.org (nic.cerf.net), .uiuc.fred.org (uxc.cso.uiuc.edu), .upr.fred.org (upr2.clu.net), .mich.fred.org (merit.edu), and .llnj.fred.org (acme.fred.org).

Examples
(user name = Bronko Nagorsky, USERID = BNAGORSK (first letter of first name, plus up to seven letters of last name), example system = sdcoe, gateway = cerf)

Internet	BNAGORSK@sdcoe.cerf.fred.org
BITNET	BNAGORSK@sdcoe.cerf.fred.org
UUCP	uunet!ocnside!sdcoe!BNAGORSK

From FrEdMail to Network

Network	From FrEdMail to network
CompuServe	<host>!<host>!<FrEdmail gate>!<USER-ID>@COMPUSERVE.COM
Internet	<host>!<host>!<FrEdmail gate>!<ID>@<HOST>.<DOMAIN>
BITNET	<host>!<host>!<FrEdmail gate>!<ID>@<HOST>.bitnet
UUCP	<host>!<host>!<FrEdmail gate>!UUNET!<HOST>!<ID>

FrEdMail gateways = sdcoe (San Diego), uiuced (Champaign, Illinois), orillas (Puerto Rico), chpchat (Michigan), lawrenc (New Jersey). Nodes may need to route through several hosts to reach a gateway; each FrEdMail system contains a network map that shows routes to the gateways.

Examples

(sending systems: ESCUSD in California, FLOMO in Missouri, BLUEJAY in Michigan):

CompuServe	`ocnside!sdcoe!71545.371@COMPUSERVE.COM`
Internet	`stlouis!uiuced!aboba@world.std.com`
BITNET	`chpchat!!funky@cunyvm.bitnet`
UUCP	`ocsnside!sdcoe!uunet!apple!bmug!Bernard.Aboba`

Remote printing

(example: fax recipient Akbar Foobar of Slimola Systems at 1(510)555-1212). Note spaces replaced by underscores. Some countries, area codes or exchanges may not be reachable, and payment may be required.

Fax machine	`remote.printer.Akbar_Foobar/Slimola@2.1.2.1.5.5.5.0.1.5.1.tpc.int`

To nations via UUCP

UUCP bang-path routing is only needed if the machine in question does not have a fully qualified domain name *and* is not listed in the UUCP maps. Mail to systems with fully qualified domain names will be routed using MX records; those with UUCP map entries can use uunet.uu.net as a gateway, as follows: **`<host>!<user ID>@uunet.uu.net`**.

In the case where both a domain name and UUCP map entry are absent, the following UUCP gateway information may come in handy:

Country	From Internet to country
Argentina	`uunet!atina!<host>!<user>` (gateway = atina.ar)
Austria	`uunet!tuvie!<host>!<user>` (gateway = tuvie.at)
Belgium	`uunet!prib2!<host>!<user>`
China	`user%beijing@ira.uka.de`
Denmark	`uunet!diku!<host>!<user>`
Finland	`uunet!mcsun!tut!<host>!<user>`
France	`uunet!inria!<host>!<user>`
Germany	`uunet!unido!<host>!<user>` **or**
	`uunet!unido!uka!<host>!<user>` (XLINK)
Great Britain	`uunet!ukc!<host>!<user>`
Iceland	`uunet!mcsun!hafro!<host>!<user>`
Italy	`uunet!mcsun!i2unix!<host>!<user>`
India	`uunet!shakti!<host>!<user>`
Indonesia	`uunet!indogtw!<host<!user>`
Japan	`uunet!kddlab!<host>!<user>`
Korea	`user%domain@relay.cs.net`
	`uunet!halla!<host>!<user>` (SDN)
Malaysia	`uunet!mimos!<host>!<user>`
Netherlands	`uunet!mcsun!<host>!<user>`
	`uunet!hp4n!<host>!<user>` (NLnet)
Spain	`uunet!mcsun!goya!<host>!<user>`
Sweden	`uunet!mcsun!enea!<host>!<user>`
Switzerland	`uunet!mcsun!cernvax!<host>!<user>`

From nations to UUCP

Country	From Internet to country
Argentina	atina!uunet!<host>!<user>
Austria	tuvie!uunet!<host>!<user>
Belgium	prlb2!uunet!<host>!<user>
China	beijing!ira!<host>!<user>
Denmark	diku!uunet!<host>!<user>
Finland	tut!mcsun!uunet!<host>!<user>
France	inria!uunet!<host>!<user>
Germany	unido!uunet!<host>!<user> or
	uka!unido!uunet!<host>!<user> (XLINK)
Great Britain	ukc!uunet!<host>!<user>
Iceland	hafro!mcsun!uunet!<host>!<user>
Italy	i2unix!mcsun!uunet!<host>!<user>
India	shakti!uunet!<host>!<user>
Indonesia	indogtw!uunet!<host<!user>
Japan	kddlab!uunet!<host>!<user>
Korea	user%domain@relay.cs.net
	halla!uunet!<host>!<user> (SDN)
Malaysia	mimos!uunet!<host>!<user>
Netherlands	mcsun!uunet!<host>!<user>
	hp4n!uunet!<host>!<user> (NLnet)
Spain	goya!mcsun!uunet!<host>!<user>
Sweden	enea!mcsun!uunet!<host>!<user>
Switzerland	cernvax!mcsun!uunet!<host>!<user>

International connectivity

August, 1993

Copyright © 1993 Lawrence H. Landweber and the Internet Society. Unlimited permission to copy or use is hereby granted subject to inclusion of this copyright notice.

In the following, BITNET is used generically to refer to BITNET plus similar networks around the world (e.g., EARN, NETNORTH, GULFNET, etc.).

This version of the Connectivity Tables (PostScript, ditroff, text forms) maps in PostScript, and earlier versions are available by anonymous **ftp ftp.cs.wisc.edu, cd connectivity_table.**

Key

Number of entities with international network connectivity = 127. The two-letter codes are the country codes from the ISO 3166 standard.

The two-letter codes are used in domain name addressing, so using this list you can figure out what country your mail is coming from. Please note that Russia and other states of the former Soviet Union are not listed here; many of them still use the .su domain, for Soviet Union.

BITNET
Col. 2 (entities with international BITNET links)
b: minimal, one to five domestic BITNET sites, 19 entities
B: widespread, more than five domestic BITNET sites, 32 entities

IP Internet
Col. 3 (entities with international IP Internet links)
I: = operational, accesible from entire IP Internet, 57 entities
i: = operational, not accesible via the NSFNet backbone, 2 entities

UUCP
Col. 4 (entities with domestic UUCP sites that are connected to the Global Multiprotocol Open Internet)

u: minimal, one to five domestic UUCP sites, 53 entities

U: widespread, more than five domestic UUCP sites, 64 entities

FidoNet
Col. 5 (entities with domestic FidoNet sites that are connected to the Global Multiprotocol Open Internet)

f: minimal, one to five domestic FidoNet sites, 25 entities

F: widespread, more than five domestic FidoNet sites, 59 entities

FrEdMail (Added by B.A.)
Col. 6 (entities with domestic FrEdMail sites that are connected to the Global Multiprotocol Open Internet)

r: minimal, one to five domestic FrEdMail sites, 2 entities

R: widespread, more than five domestic FrEdMail sites, 1 entity

OSI
Col. 7 (entities with international X.400 links to domestic sites that are connected to the Global Multiprotocol Open Internet)

o: minimal, one to five domestic X.400 sites, 8 entities

O: widespread, more than five domestic X.400 sites, 23 entities

Email connections to Albania, Algeria, Angola, Gambia, Malawi, Mongolia, Morocco, Qatar, St. Lucia, and Vietnam have been reported but have not been verified or are not yet stable and hence are not included in the table or in the above totals.

# Code		Country
------	AF	Afghanistan (Democratic Republic of)
------	AL	Albania (Republic of)
------	DZ	Algeria (People's Democratic Republic of)
------	AS	American Samoa
------	AD	Andorra (Principality of)
------	AO	Angola (People's Republic of)
------	AI	Anguilla
-I----	AQ	Antarctica
------	AG	Antigua and Barbuda
BIUF--	AR	Argentina (Argentine Republic)
--u---	AM	Armenia
---f--	AW	Aruba
-IUFro	AU	Australia
BIUF-o	AT	Austria (Republic of)

# Code		Country
--U---	AZ	Azerbaijan
------	BS	Bahamas (Commonwealth of the)
b-----	BH	Bahrain (State of)
------	BD	Bangladesh (People's Republic of)
--u---	BB	Barbados
--UF--	BY	Belarus
BIUF-O	BE	Belgium (Kingdom of)
------	BZ	Belize
------	BJ	Benin (People's Republic of)
--uf--	BM	Bermuda
------	BT	Bhutan (Kingdom of)
--U---	BO	Bolivia (Republic of)
------	BA	Bosnia-Hercegovina
--uf--	BW	Botswana (Republic of)
------	BV	Bouvet Island
BIUF-O	BR	Brazil (Federative Republic of)
------	IO	British Indian Ocean Territory
------	BN	Brunei Darussalam
biUF--	BG	Bulgaria (Republic of)
--u---	BF	Burkina Faso (formerly Upper Volta)
------	BI	Burundi (Republic of)
------	KH	Cambodia
--u---	CM	Cameroon (Republic of)
BIUF-O	CA	Canada
------	CV	Cape Verde (Republic of)
------	KY	Cayman Islands
------	CF	Central African Republic
------	TD	Chad (Republic of)
BIUF--	CL	Chile (Republic of)
--u--O	CN	China (People's Republic of)
------	CX	Christmas Island (Indian Ocean)
------	CC	Cocos (Keeling) Islands
B-u---	CO	Colombia (Republic of)
------	KM	Comoros (Islamic Federal Republic of the)
--u---	CG	Congo (Republic of the)
------	CK	Cook Islands
bIuf--	CR	Costa Rica (Republic of)
--uf--	CI	Cote d'Ivoire (Republic of)
-Iuf-o	HR	Croatia
--U---	CU	Cuba (Republic of)
bI----	CY	Cyprus (Republic of)
BIUF--	CZ	Czech Republic
BIUF-O	DK	Denmark (Kingdom of)
------	DJ	Djibouti (Republic of)
------	DM	Dominica (Commonwealth of)
--Uf--	DO	Dominican Republic
------	TP	East Timor
bIu---	EC	Ecuador (Republic of)
b-U---	EG	Egypt (Arab Republic of)
------	SV	El Salvador (Republic of)
------	GQ	Equatorial Guinea (Republic of)
-IUF--	EE	Estonia (Republic of)
---f--	ET	Ethiopia (People's Democratic Republic of)
------	FK	Falkland Islands (Malvinas)
------	FO	Faroe Islands
-Iu---	FJ	Fiji (Republic of)
BIUF-O	FI	Finland (Republic of)
BIUF-O	FR	France (French Republic)
--u---	GF	French Guiana
--u---	PF	French Polynesia
------	TF	French Southern Territories
------	GA	Gabon (Gabonese Republic)
------	GM	Gambia (Republic of the)
--UF--	GE	Georgia (Republic of)
BIUF-O	DE	Germany (Federal Republic of)
---F--	GH	Ghana (Republic of)
------	GI	Gibraltar
BIUF-O	GR	Greece (Hellenic Republic)
-I-f--	GL	Greenland
--u---	GD	Grenada
b-uf--	GP	Guadeloupe (French Department of)
---F--	GU	Guam
--u---	GT	Guatemala (Republic of)
------	GN	Guinea (Republic of)
------	GW	Guinea-Bissau (Republic of)
------	GY	Guyana (Republic of)
------	HT	Haiti (Republic of)
------	HM	Heard and McDonald Islands
------	HN	Honduras (Republic of)
BI-F--	HK	Hong Kong (Hisiangkang, Xianggang)
BIUF-o	HU	Hungary (Republic of)
-IUF-o	IS	Iceland (Republic of)

# Code		Country
bIUf-O	IN	India (Republic of)
--u---	ID	Indonesia (Republic of)
b-----	IR	Iran (Islamic Republic of)
------	IQ	Iraq (Republic of)
BIUFrO	IE	Ireland
BIUF--	IL	Israel (State of)
BIUF-O	IT	Italy (Italian Republic)
--u---	JM	Jamaica
BIUF--	JP	Japan
------	JO	Jordan (Hashemite Kingdom of)
--Uf--	KZ	Kazakhstan
---f--	KE	Kenya (Republic of)
--u---	KI	Kiribati (Republic of)
------	KP	Korea (Democratic People's Republic of)
BIUF-O	KR	Korea (Republic of)
-I----	KW	Kuwait (State of)
--U---	KG	Kyrgyzstan
------	LA	Lao People's Democratic Republic
-IUF--	LV	Latvia (Republic of)
------	LB	Lebanon (Lebanese Republic)
--u---	LS	Lesotho (Kingdom of)
------	LR	Liberia (Republic of)
------	LY	Libyan Arab Jamahiriya
---f--	LI	Liechtenstein (Principality of)
--UF-o	LT	Lithuania
bIUF-o	LU	Luxembourg (Grand Duchy of)
---F--	MO	Macau (Ao-me'n)
------	??	Macedonia (Former Yugoslav Republic of)
------	MG	Madagascar (Democratic Republic of)
--u---	MW	Malawi (Republic of)
bIUF--	MY	Malaysia
------	MV	Maldives (Republic of)
--u---	ML	Mali (Republic of)
--u---	MT	Malta (Republic of)
------	MH	Marshall Islands (Republic of the)
------	MQ	Martinique (French Department of)
------	MR	Mauritania (Islamic Republic of)
--uf--	MU	Mauritius
BIUf--	MX	Mexico (United Mexican States)
------	FM	Micronesia (Federated States of)
--UF--	MD	Moldova (Republic of)
------	MC	Monaco (Principality of)
------	MN	Mongolia (Mongolian People's Republic)
------	MS	Montserrat
------	MA	Morocco (Kingdom of)
--u---	MZ	Mozambique (People's Republic of)
------	MM	Myanmar (Union of)
--u---	NA	Namibia (Republic of)
------	NR	Nauru (Republic of)
------	NP	Nepal (Kingdom of)
BIUF-O	NL	Netherlands (Kingdom of the)
------	AN	Netherlands Antilles
------	NT	Neutral Zone (between Saudi Arabia and Iraq)
--U---	NC	New Caledonia
-IUF-o	NZ	New Zealand
--u---	NI	Nicaragua (Republic of)
--u---	NE	Niger (Republic of the)
------	NG	Nigeria (Federal Republic of)
------	NU	Niue
------	NF	Norfolk Island
------	MP	Northern Mariana Islands (Commonwealth of)
BIUF-O	NO	Norway (Kingdom of)
------	OM	Oman (Sultanate of)
--U---	PK	Pakistan (Islamic Republic of)
------	PW	Palau (Republic of)
b-uF--	PA	Panama (Republic of)
--u---	PG	Papua New Guinea
--u---	PY	Paraguay (Republic of)
--Uf--	PE	Peru (Republic of)
--uF--	PH	Philippines (Republic of the)
------	PN	Pitcairn
BIUF--	PL	Poland (Republic of)
bIUF-O	PT	Portugal (Portuguese Republic)
bIUF--	PR	Puerto Rico
------	QA	Qatar (State of)
--u---	RE	Re'union (French Department of)
BI-f--	RO	Romania
BiUF--	RU	Russian Federation
------	RW	Rwanda (Rwandese Republic)
------	SH	Saint Helena
------	KN	Saint Kitts and Nevis
--u---	LC	Saint Lucia

# Code		Country
------	PM	Saint Pierre and Miquelon (French Dept.)
------	VC	Saint Vincent and the Grenadines
--u---	WS	Samoa (Independent State of)
------	SM	San Marino (Republic of)
------	ST	Sao Tome and Principe (Democratic Republic)
B-----	SA	Saudi Arabia (Kingdom of)
--Uf--	SN	Senegal (Republic of)
--u---	SC	Seychelles (Republic of)
------	SL	Sierra Leone (Republic of)
bIuF--	SG	Singapore (Republic of)
bIUF--	SK	Slovakia
-IUF-O	SI	Slovenia
--u---	SB	Solomon Islands
------	SO	Somalia (Somali Democratic Republic)
-IUF-O	ZA	South Africa (Republic of)
BIUF-O	ES	Spain (Kingdom of)
--U---	LK	Sri Lanka (Democratic Socialist Republic of)
------	SD	Sudan (Democratic Republic of the)
--u---	SR	Suriname (Republic of)
------	SJ	Svalbard and Jan Mayen Islands
--u---	SZ	Swaziland (Kingdom of)
BIUF-o	SE	Sweden (Kingdom of)
BIUF-O	CH	Switzerland (Swiss Confederation)
------	SY	Syria (Syrian Arab Republic)
BIuF--	TW	Taiwan, Province of China
--uf--	TJ	Tajikistan
---f--	TZ	Tanzania (United Republic of)
-IUF--	TH	Thailand (Kingdom of)
--u---	TG	Togo (Togolese Republic)
------	TK	Tokelau
--u---	TO	Tonga (Kingdom of)
--u---	TT	Trinidad and Tobago (Republic of)
bIUF-o	TN	Tunisia
BI-F--	TR	Turkey (Republic of)
--U---	TM	Turkmenistan
------	TC	Turks and Caicos Islands
--u---	TV	Tuvalu
---f--	UG	Uganda (Republic of)
-iUF--	UA	Ukraine
------	AE	United Arab Emirates
bIUF-O	GB	United Kingdom (United Kingdom of Great Britain and Northern Ireland)
BIUFRO	US	United States (United States of America)
------	UM	United States Minor Outlying Islands
--UF--	UY	Uruguay (Eastern Republic of)
--UF--	UZ	Uzbekistan
--u---	VU	Vanuatu (Republic of, formerly New Hebrides)
------	VA	Vatican City State (Holy See)
-IU---	VE	Venezuela (Republic of)
------	VN	Vietnam (Socialist Republic of)
------	VG	Virgin Islands (British)
---f--	VI	Virgin Islands (U.S.)
------	WF	Wallis and Futuna Islands
------	EH	Western Sahara
------	YE	Yemen (Republic of)
---f--	YU	Yugoslavia (Socialist Federal Republic of)
------	ZR	Zaire (Republic of)
--uf--	ZM	Zambia (Republic of)
--uf--	ZW	Zimbabwe (Republic of)

Please send corrections, information, and/or comments to:

Larry Landweber
Computer Sciences Dept.
University of Wisconsin - Madison
1210 W. Dayton St.
Madison, WI 53706
lhl@cs.wisc.edu
FAX 1-608-265-2635

MAILING LISTS AND MAIL SERVERS

What are mailing lists and mail servers?

Mailing lists use electronic mail to create a form of distributed conferencing. A mail message sent to a mailing list will be redistributed to all the members of the list, rather than just being sent to a single mail box. The message is said to have been "exploded" or "reflected."

Mailing List Managers (MLMs) are programs which automate the handling of subscription requests, and provide additional functionality such as searching and filtering or directory services. The BITNET LISTSERV program is an example of an MLM.

Mail servers use electronic mail to respond to commands contained within the message envelope or body. The most frequently provided service is to retrieve a requested file for the user, but mail servers can also provide many other services, including gatewaying of services that are normally only available to Internet users, such as Z39.50 queries.

Although many MLMs and mail servers now operate on UNIX machines, these facilities are not specific to any network, operating system, or transport mechanism. In this chapter I will show you how to create a mailing list on a Macintosh using uConnect. The PCBUUCP gateway package for PCBoard and the PIMP gateway for TBBS also offer mailing list capabilities.

What are the advantages of mailing lists and mail servers?

Any machine that can receive electronic mail can subscribe to a mailing list or access a mail server; no additional software is required. In contrast, to receive USENET, or to request a file via UUCP or FTP, additional software is needed that may or may not be available for a particular machine, operating system, or bulletin board package. Even if software is

available, it may not have been installed on the machine on which the user has an account.

Assuming that the administrators of the receiving machines give their users permission to subscribe to mailing lists or access mail servers (which they may not), mailing lists and mail servers can include users on any network that can receive mail in RFC 822 format. These include commercial services such as MCI Mail, CompuServe, AOL, Prodigy, and GEnie, as well as machines on the Internet, BITNET, UUCP, FidoNet, FrEdMail, OneNet, and WWIVNet networks. As a result, mailing lists are the most widely connected distributed conferencing medium, and mail servers are a convenient way of extending the benefits of the Internet to users on non-Internet networks.

Other advantages of mailing lists

Aside from connectivity issues, mailing lists offer other advantages over distributed conferencing systems such as USENET.

In order to create a conference within the USENET core, it is necessary to go through the newgroup creation process discussed in Chapter 12: USENET. Although USENET newsgroups may be moderated or unmoderated, and may set their own rules on issues such as anonymous postings, the newsgroup creation process can be contentious.

Forsaking USENET core distribution has its limitations as well. Many groups are created within the alternative hierarchies such as the alt hierarchy. Although the alt news group creation process is considerably easier than for core USENET groups, alt conferences may not be moderated. In addition, alt conferences are carried by only a fraction of the sites that carry USENET core conferences.

Creating the conference on another network such as FidoNet, RIME, or ILink also has limitations. FidoNet's Echomail conferencing mechanism does not support moderation (although the Groupmail conferencing mechanism can be made to do so), although gatewaying is supported. RIME or ILink conferences may not be gatewayed, which restricts access to a small subset of potentially interested users.

The most profound difference between mailing lists and distributed conferences such as netnews is that mailing lists are private, while netnews is an inherently public medium. While distribution of a conference cannot be controlled, distribution of a mailing list can be. Mailing lists have a wide range of moderation options, do not have to go through an approval process, and are accessible by all sites that can receive email.

News software supports conversion of mailing lists into newsgroups and newsgroups may be gatewayed to lists. However, this should not be done without the permission of the mailing list administrator or newsgroup moderator, since this changes the nature of conference or list.

What kinds of mailing lists are there?

Several types of mailing lists are available. These include:

• **Unmoderated mailing lists.** In unmoderated mailing lists, messages sent to the mailing list are automatically "exploded" to all the people on the list.

• **Moderated mailing lists.** In a moderated mailing list, contributors send their messages to the list moderator who chooses which messages to retransmit to the list.

• **Electronic journals.** An electronic journal goes one step beyond the moderated mailing list by requiring more formal submissions. Journals usually focus on an academic discipline and may include use of referees.

Other issues

Other issues in the design of a mailing list are:

• **Digestification.** The messages can be sent out individually, or collected for a period of time and then sent out as a single file. Some mailing list programs give the reader the choice of digested or individual postings.

• **Distribution restrictions.** While most mailing lists are open to anyone who wants to join and is willing to obey the rules, restricted distribution mailing lists subject users to an approval process prior to granting access. Users may restrict users by profession (a mailing list for surgeons only, for example), or other criteria. These lists may have varying degrees of moderation.

• **Searchability.** Mailing list messages can be archived for later retrieval. Messages can be queried by subjects, author, or full text. Readers can request a regular listing of subject lines only, and then can request messages later if they so choose.

• **Bounced mail.** If users lose their account, or their machines goes down, mail from the mailing list can bounce back. In the worst case, this can end up going back out to the mailing list; at best, the mailing list program will automatically remove the user from the list.

• **Headers.** Although there currently is no standard for mailing-list headers, a movement is afoot to include more information in the headers of messages coming from Mailing List Managers. As a result, headers coming from some MLMs now identify the MLM, and include fields for the owner of the list, the person to contact in case of errors, and the address to which automated commands should be directed.

Disadvantages of mailing lists

In addition to their advantages, mailing lists also have some major weaknesses when compared with distributed conferencing mechanisms.

▽ Mailing lists are inefficient

While mailing lists distribute messages to individuals, distributed conferencing systems distribute messages to sites. If there are many more individuals than sites (usually the case), mailing lists are very inefficient, since each machine stores multiple copies of the same message. With distributed conferencing systems, a message is at worst stored once on each machine, and at best (when using USENET with an NNTP server to retrieve messages), only once for a group of machines.

Mailing lists send out messages whether you are reading them or not. Very often people will get on mailing lists and then forget they asked for them. The sysop is left receiving (and paying for!) messages that nobody reads. Turning off the flow may be non-trivial since a given MLM may only accept unsubscribe messages from the original subscriber.

▽ Mail programs were not designed for distributed conferencing.

USENET news readers were designed with many-to-many communications in mind. As a result, they have built-in features to decrease noise (such as distribution limitation, reply by mail, deletion of postings, etc.). Mailing list participants instead participate with mail programs that were designed for one-to-one communications. As a result, the default response is usually to reply to the mailing list rather than to the individual (although many mail programs do ask if the CC: list should be copied). There is no way to limit distribution to a local area or region, or to delete the message after posting (assuming that the list is unmoderated). The result is increased noise.

These weaknesses have led many systems to prohibit mailing list subscriptions. So as not to make the arguments against mailing lists more convincing, you should:

• Post a message on your system asking if someone is already getting a particular mailing list before asking for it yourself. This allows the sysop to create a local mail exploder for the list, requiring the message to be transmitted only once over the network. On some systems,

mailing lists also can be gatewayed into a conference area where it can be read by all.

• Make sure to turn off your mailing lists when you go away for vacation or stop using a system.

• Don't subscribe to more mailing lists than you have time to read. Just because a list might be fun "when I have some spare time" is not sufficient justification for someone to pay for you to receive hundreds of messages that you will never read.

Subscribing to a mailing list

Mail relating to administrative functions of the mailing list is generally sent to a different address than mail for the list itself. Although there is no standard for this, if the list is called `frat@planet.com`, then administrative requests typically go to either `frat-request@planet.com` or to `listserv@planet.com`, depending on the MLM being used.

The list of lists

Before subscribing to a mailing list, you'll have to know what mailing lists to subscribe to. There is now a Z39.50-compatible database of Internet mailing lists, called mailing-lists.src. To find out what lists to subscribe to, search this database with Z39.50, Gopher, or World Wide Web. Alternatively, you can retrieve the list via `ftp ftp.nisc.sri.com, cd /netinfo/interest-groups`.

Creating a mailing list under UNIX

Mailing List Manager (MLM) software provides a number of useful functions, including digestification, sophisticated headers, and automated handling of subscription requests. Popular packages running under UNIX include the LISTSERV program (not the same as the BITNET program of the same name), TULP, and the Majordomo server.

If you are planning a list for a large number of people, it is highly desirable to use an MLM rather than using the UNIX built-in mailing list facilities. A description of these facilities follows.

Mailing lists for outgoing mail

Using your .mailrc file and the `alias` command, you can set up an outgoing mailing list on your account. Addressing mail to the alias will cause the message to be sent to all the people on the list. Here is an example of a .mailrc file with the alias mailist:

```
alias mailist info@foo.org aboba philonious
```

Here there are three users on the mailist list, two on the local machine, and one on another machine (`info@foo.org`).

Mailing lists for incoming mail

However, adding an alias to the .mailrc file does not cause incoming mail addressed to the alias to be automatically "exploded" to the list. In order to have incoming mail sent to all the members of a list, you will need to modify the aliases file used by sendmail. This requires root permission.

sendmail stores its list of aliases in the /etc/sendmail/aliases (or sometimes the/etc/aliases or /usr/lib/aliases) file. These aliases are different from those that you put in your own .mailrc file because they apply to mail that is received rather than just to mail that is being sent. The sendmail aliases are also different because they are global; anybody can use them. The format of the aliases file is:

```
<alias name>: <address1>,<address 2>...
```

For example, on my machine I have:

```
#set up mail file for fraternity
frat: sam@bongo.edu, fred@gonzo.edu, gordo@snipper.com
frat-request: bozo@clown.harvard.edu
alias sharks: :include:/usr/list/sharks
owner-frat: bozo@clown.harvard.edu
Postmaster: aboba
bernard: aboba
decode: "|/usr/bin/uudecode"
```

This file sets up a mailing list for a fraternity. Assuming that the home machine is planet.com, mail sent to `frat@planet.com` would be "exploded" to the three people on the list. The owner-frat list tells sendmail whom to send error messages to if there is a problem with the frat list. The frat-request list tells sendmail to forward administrative mail for the frat list to `bozo@clown.harvard.edu`.

This aliases file also specifies that mail addressed to `Postmaster` or `bernard` should be sent to user `aboba`. Just as with the .forward file, the aliases file may also pipe mail for a particular name to a program. This is what the decode alias does. The list of users on the sharks list is kept in /usr/list/sharks.

In order to use the aliases file after you have modified it, you must first compile it via the command **newaliases**, or **sendmail -bi**. Since modifying the aliases file requires root permissions, you will not be able to make these modifications yourself with an ordinary user account. However many service providers provide these services for a fee.

Advantages of mail servers

Many people are interested in accessing Internet services but cannot afford the expense of getting an account with an Internet service provider. By making their requests through mail servers, these users can access the benefits of the Internet without the expense.

Of course, there is no free lunch, since someone else (the mail server host) is footing the bill. Given the current rate of growth of global networks, you should think it over carefully before operating a mail server. The volume of requests may eventually consume a substantial fraction of your machine's CPU time, or disk space, with no benefits (other than good will) accruing to you or your organization.

A better solution may be to let an Internet service provider such as Holonet or Netcom run the mail server. Netcom allows registered users to install and run mail servers free of charge, but the users must install and maintain the server themselves; Holonet handles the installation but charges a small fee.

Currently file transfer is the primary service gatewayed by mail servers, although Z39.50, Gopher, and W3 requests can also be handled via mail. For information on waismail, put the command **mail waismail@quake.think.com**, **HELP** in the body of the message. For information on W3 mail requests, put the command `mail LISTSERV@info.cern.ch`, `HELP` in the body of the message.

Disadvantages of mail servers

Mail servers have their own problems. While the goal of mail servers is to provide services for users on non-Internet networks, very often the gateways between those networks and Internet operate over modems. As a result, it is easy to overload the gateway.

If every tenth user on a 3000-user system requests a 250K file once a week, the result would be 75 Mb/week of traffic. Since BBS network gateways systems may only have 40 Mb of free disk space, a glitch in the gateway system could result in a huge backlog, hard drive overflow, and possible lost requests. If several systems shared the same gateway, saturation of the gateway link is a virtual certainty.

For this reason, many bulletin boards do not allow users to access mail servers. Please consult your system administrator before accessing such a service.

Creating a mail server under UNIX

You can turn an ordinary account into a mail-server without requiring root permission; with root permission it is possible in addition to give the server an arbitrary name, such as `fishing@foo.edu`.

To do this, use the piping feature of sendmail. As discussed earlier, before delivering mail to your mailbox, sendmail looks at the .forward file in your home directory to see if you have specified an alternative to local delivery such as:

1. Putting the message into a file. Example: `/Net/rhino/Users/amm/.maillog`

2. Forwarding mail to another address. Example: `netrhino@rhino.com`

3. Piping mail to a program or shell script. Example: `| "/aboba/bin/mailscript"`

Note: When using this option, the chosen program runs in the mail queue spool directory as if executed by the mail recipient. Therefore, file references should be written out.

The program to which the message is piped can process it any way it pleases. It can be written in c, shell script, a text processing language such as perl, or a mixture of all three. Perl-based mail servers (such as Squirrel Mail Server) have the advantage of being both extendable and easily portable. For listings of mailing list and mail server software, consult the end of this chapter.

Setting up mailing lists with uConnect

What if you want to set up a mailing list but don't have a shell account? uConnect lets you create both outgoing mailing lists (where one message gets sent to many people) and mail "exploders" where incoming mail gets redirected to a list. These features are known as System aliases and System mailing lists.

In describing how these features work, I'll assume that you've already got uConnect configured. Information on how to configure the program is included in Chapter 16: Unix-to-Unix Copy.

What we're going to do

In this section, we will assume that your host has the domain name fun.com. You are looking to create mailing lists for your two favorite hobbies, fly fishing and contra-dancing. To add themselves to the mailing list, you'll tell people to send mail to `fishing-request@fun.com` or `dancing-request@fun.com`. To send a message to the group, you'd address it to `fishing@fun.com`, or `dancing@fun.com`.

Creating aliases

In order to maintain the mailing lists, you will want to have mail for `fishing-request` or `dancing-request` be forwarded to whomever is maintaining these mailing lists. This is done via the `alias` feature.

Setting up aliases this way allows the people maintaining the mailing lists to receive mail about list additions or subtractions at the address of their choosing. To do this, select **System Aliases...** from the **Configuration** menu under the **File** menu.

This will bring up a dialog box:

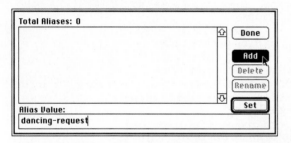

Click on the **Add** button, and then type in the alias. Once you have done this, you can then select the alias name and type in the real address that it corresponds to. This need not be an address on your machine.

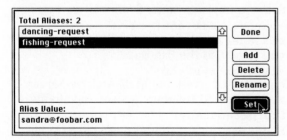

Setting up the lists

The next thing to do is to set up the mail exploder itself. To do this, select **System Mailing Lists...** from the **Configuration** menu under the **File** menu.

This will bring up a dialog box. To create a mailing list, click on **New.**

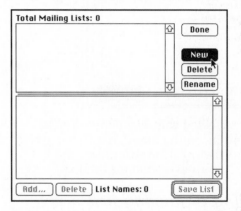

You are then prompted for the list name.

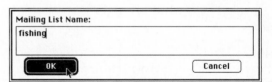

Once you've created the list, you can then add names to it by clicking on the **Add...** button.

This will bring up another dialog box to enter the address.

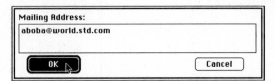

Once you're done, you can save the list by clicking the **Save List** button.

Mailing lists created this way apply to both outgoing and incoming mail. That is, when you send mail to the list from uConnect, the message will go to everyone on the list.

A sampling of mailing lists

Apple II BBSes:
a2-bbs-request@pro-cynosure.cts.com
Adoption:
adoption-request@think.com
Argentina:
argentina-request@ois.db.toronto.edu
Bagpipes:
pipes-reqest@sunapee.dartmouth.edu
Ballroom dancing:
ballroom-request@athena.mit.edu
Catalunyan culture and language:
catalunya-request@cs.rice.edu
CD-ROM electronic publishing:
`mail Mail-Server@knex.via.mind.org,
SUBSCRIBE CDPub <First> <Last name>`
Chemical engineering:
trayms@cc.curtin.edu.au
Christian computer graphics:
GodlyGraphics-request@acs.harding.edu
Hungarian electronic resources:
`mail gtoth@phoenix.princeton.edu,`
subject: **HIX**, body: **HELP all**

Horseback riding:
equestrians-request@world.std.com
International trade:
info-request@tradent.wimsey.bc.ca
Internet commercialization:
com-priv-request@psi.com
Jewish law:
avi_feldblum@att.com
Job opportunities:
employ-request@oti.disa.mil
Latin American research:
lasnet-reqeust@emx.utexas.edu
Fiction magazine:
intertxt@network.ucsd.edu
MIDI music:
`mail netjam-request@xcf.berkeley.edu,`
subject: **request for info**
Ernest Hemingway:
dgross@polyslo.calpoly.edu
UNIX security:
security-request@cpd.com
Supra Fax modems:
`mail subscribe.xamiga.linet.org, body:
#supra username@domain;`
BBS Sysops:
sysops-request%dasys1@uunet.uu.net
TCP/IP over packet radio:
tcp-group-request@ucsd.edu
United We Stand America:
`mail subscribe@xamiga.linet.org, body:
#united username@domain;`
Weight lifting:
weights-request@fa.disney.com
Employment for young scientists:
ysn-adm@zoyd.ee.washington.edu

For more information

"Publicly Accessible Mailing Lists," posted regularly to news.answers; available via `ftp pit-manager.mit.edu, cd /pub/usenet/news.answers/mail/mailing-lists`. To add to the list, `mail arielle@taronga.com`.
"A Summary of Available Mail Archive Server Software," posted to news.answers; available via `ftp pit-manager.mit.edu, get /pub/usenet/news.answers/mail/archive-servers`

Mailing list managers mailing list:
Brent@GreatCircle.com

CHAPTER 10: FILE TRANSFER

FTP, FSP and Archie

WHAT IS FTP?

FTP stands for "File Transfer Protocol." An Anonymous FTP archive is one which lets you login without a userID. However, the use of the term *anonymous* is something of a misnomer, since FTP asks you to give your Internet address as your password before connecting you to the remote computer.

Acknowledgments

Thanks to the folks who maintain all the marvelous FTP archives.

Starting with FTP

To start out, you need to type:

ftp <host address>

where <host address> is the address of the machine you're trying to get to. If you're trying to **ftp** to sumex-aim.stanford.edu (a popular **ftp** site), you type:

ftp sumex-aim.stanford.edu

The **ftp** program will then come back with something like:

Name (<host address>:<your local id>):

Here <your local id> is your account name on your Internet machine. Respond with:
anonymous

It will then type something like:

Password (<host address>:anonymous):

To which you will reply with your Internet address, such as: **aboba@world.std.com**.

FTP Commands

Here is a partial list of FTP commands supported by my machine; your machine may be somewhat different. To get a list of commands that your FTP supports, type **?** or help at the FTP prompt. Here are the commands that are typically used:

Command	What it does
ascii	Sets ASCII transfer mode
binary	Sets binary transfer mode
cd	Changes directory
cd bozo	Changes to directory bozo
cdup	Goes up a directory level
cdup	Goes up a directory level
close	Closes a connection
dir	Directory listing
get	Downloads a file
get bozo.hqx	Downloads bozo.hqx
ls	Directory listing
ls -1R	Recursive directory listing
mget <list>	Downloads a list of files
mget maclay*	Downloads all files starting with maclay
mput <list>	Uploads a list of files
mput lay foo	Uploads files lay and foo
open	Opens a connection
pwd	Lists current directory

A kinda big problem

OK, Mr. Big Shot. So you've just FTP'd to lotsafiles.podunk.edu. You've navigated your way through the directory structure to find the files. The question is, what do those files do? Most FTP archives don't include file descriptions. This is because the files are usually described in newsgroups. The messages in the newsgroups tell what the programs do, and then just refer people to the appropriate anonymous FTP site to get to them.

A further problem is that it is often hard to find the latest version of a program, or to discover what a given piece of software does before transferring it. It is customary for an FTP archive to include an index file showing what is available, but not all sites do this. The `whatis` command in Archie is designed to access a database of file descriptions. The database is by no means complete, but it is growing all the time. For more information on Archie `whatis`, refer to the section on Archie.

A not-so-big problem

You've just transferred your file, and it has an extension on it that you've never seen before. You peek at the file, and it's all gobbledygook. Have you just wasted your time? Probably not. Below are some typical extensions and which programs you need to run to be able to use them.

A nasty little bug

In theory, using the above extensions, you should be able to download the archive and then unarchive it on your computer. However, in real life it isn't so simple. Many files on the Internet are compressed with UNIX compress and have the .Z extension.

Unfortunately, MacCompress and most PC versions of uncompress will not successfully decompress archives over about 500K. The solution is to uncompress them and repack them with zip.

How to download files to your computer

Now that you've got the stuff on your Internet machine, how do you get it to your system? A good way to do this is to use PC-Kermit or MacKermit on your end, and Kermit on your host's end. How do you get a copy of MacKermit? MacKermit is available via `ftp sumex-aim.stanford.edu, cd /info-mac/comm`.

If you're ready for something really slick, you can get the file from the remote machine, and download it to your computer all in one command by typing:

```
ftp> get sample.zip "|sz -b -"
```

Under SunOS 4.1.1, you can also redirect standard input from a file to FTP:

```
% ftp -n ftp.site < foo &
```

Where foo contains FTP commands:

```
user anonymous <you>@<yourhost>
binary
get /pub/file.Z
```

How to get a list of anonymous FTP sites

A list of anonymous FTP sites can be obtained via `ftp pilot.njin.net, cd /pub/ftp-list`. In order to encourage use of Archie, this list has been discontinued, but it is still of general interest. The sample session shows you how to transfer this list to your machine. Major anonymous FTP sites are shown on the next page. Major repositories of Macintosh files are indicated in boldface.

Extension	Mac Decoder	PC Decoder
.arc	ArcPop	ARC
.hqx	BinHex 4.0, StuffIt LITE or Deluxe	
.shar	sh	UNSHAR
.tar	MacTar	TAR
.uu	uulite	UUDECODE
.Z	MacCompress	UNCOMPRESS
.zip	UnZIP	PKUNZIP
.zoo	MacBooz	ZOO

File extensions and the programs to unarchive them

Internet Address	What the machine holds
anise.acc.com	Berkeley utils ported to A/UX, Motorola DSP 56000 repository
ftp.apple.com	**tech-notes, worm papers**
aramis.rutgers.edu	idea, RFCs
argus.stanford.edu	netinfo
arisia.xerox.com	sunfixes, mac, LispUsers, tcp/ip, Portable Common Lisp
bbn.com	uumap
brownvm.brown.edu	mac
cc.sfu.ca	msdos, mac
cs.orst.edu	Xlisp, smalltalk, TOPS Terminal,NeXT
cs.toronto.edu	AIList, sun-Spots, many other mailing list archives, CA domain reg. forms, RFCs, NETINFO, DOMAIN,IETF, INET-DRAFTS, Current C News,dvix, logging `ftpd`, Jove, sunOS SLIP et al, S/SL, TeX, UofT BIND, X applications
dartvax.dartmouth.edu	Macintosh stuff in /pub/mac
doc.cso.uiuc.edu	msdos (pcsig), mac
f.ms.uky.edu	mac, msdos, unix-pc
grape.ecs.clarkson.edu	Opus BBS, msdos, graphics, lots
indri.primate.wisc.edu	macintosh TransSkel TransDisplay TransEdit
jpl-mil.jpl.nasa.gov	TeX, mac, GNU, X11R2, X11R3
mac.archive.umich.edu	**mac archives**
nic.ddn.mil	netinfo, RFCs, IEN, IETF
nisca.ircc.ohio-state.edu	alt.fax
nnsc.nsf.net	Network Info, Internet Resource Guide
noc.byu.edu	byu-telnet (login:**guest,** password:**anonymous**)
oak.oakland.edu	**Mirrors simtel20**
oswego.oswego.edu	GNU, mac, kermit
pilot.njin.net	Original distribution point of `ftp`-list
ssyx.ucsc.edu	mac-hyperunix, some unix
sumex-aim.stanford.edu	**mac archives, Mycin (sun4), imap**
tank.uchicago.edu	mac
uunet.uu.net	usenet archives, much more
uxa.cso.uiuc.edu	mac, msdos (pcsig)
watsun.cc.columbia.edu	kermit
wsmr-simtel20.army.mil	**msdos, unix, cpm, mac (tenex)**
wuarchive.wustl.edu	**Mirrors simtel20**

NeXT FTP sites

The major FTP sites for NeXT users are:

sonata.cc.purdue.edu	/pub/next
cs.orst.edu (Oregon State)	/pub/next
etlport.etl.go.jp (Japan)	/pub/NeXT
pellns.alleg.edu	/pub (academic apps)
otter.stanford.edu	(mathematica)
src.doc.ic.ac.uk (UK)	(mirror of nova/sonata)

More FTP commands

Command	What it does
ascii	Sets ASCII transfer type
bell	Beeps when command completed
binary	Sets binary transfer type
bye	Terminates ftp session and exits
cd	Changes remote working directory
cdup	Changes remote working directory to parent directory
close	Terminates ftp session
cr	Toggles carriage return stripping on ASCII gets
dir	Lists contents of remote directory
disconnect	Terminates ftp session
get	Receives file
help	Prints local help information
image	Sets binary transfer type
lcd	Changes local working directory
ls	Lists contents of remote directory
mdir	Lists contents of multiple remote directories
mls	Lists contents of multiple remote directories
mode	Sets file transfer mode
open	Connects to remote ftp
prompt	Forces interactive prompting on multiple commands
put	Sends one file
pwd	Prints working directory on remote machine
quit	Terminates ftp session and exits
recv	Receives file
remotehelp	Gets help from remote server
runique	Toggles store unique for local files
send	Sends one file
status	Shows current status
tenex	Sets tenex mode (for tenex machines like simtel only)
verbose	Toggles verbose mode
?	Prints local help

A typical session

Here's the transcript of a session where I **ftp pilot.njin.net** to get a copy of the latest list of FTP sites. My typing is in boldface.

```
[2] % ftp pilot.njin.net
Connected to pilot.njin.net.
220 pilot.njin.net FTP server (SunOS 4.0) ready.
Name (pilot.njin.net:aboba): anonymous
Password (pilot.njin.net:anonymous):aboba@world.std.com
331 Guest login ok, send ident as password.
230 Guest login ok, access restrictions apply.
ftp> dir
200 PORT command successful.
150 ASCII data connection for /bin/ls (128.32.136.6,2204) (0 bytes).
total 2
dr-xr-sr-x 2 0  0    512 Apr 24 1990 bin
dr-xr-sr-x 8 22 1    512 Dec 18 15:24 pub
226 ASCII Transfer complete.
127 bytes received in 0.01 seconds (12 Kbytes/s)
ftp> cd pub
250 CWD command okay, requested file action completed.
ftp> dir
200 PORT command successful.
150 ASCII data connection for /bin/ls (128.32.136.6,2205) (0 bytes).
total 590
-rw-r--r-- 1 22  1    353631 Apr 10 1990 AmigaDNet.zoo
dr-xr-sr-x 2 22  1    512 Oct 3 1989 ISETL
drwxr-sr-x 2 30644 18023   512 Dec 18 15:24 TCF
drwxr-sr-x 2 22  1    512 Feb 20 1990 damail
drwxr-sr-x 5 30750 21060    512 Aug 6 23:54 ftp-list
drwxr-sr-x 2 22  1    512 Sep 4 15:04 ncsa.22c
-r--r--r-- 1 22  1    214737 Aug 10 1989 sVsendmail.tar.Z
drwxrwsrwt 2 22  1    1024 Jan 11 14:07 scratch
226 ASCII Transfer complete.
525 bytes received in 1.5 seconds (0.34 Kbytes/s)
ftp> cd ftp-list
250 CWD command okay, requested file action completed.
ftp> dir
200 PORT command successful.
150 ASCII data connection for /bin/ls (128.32.136.6,2207) (0 bytes).
total 334
-rw-r--r-- 1 30750 21060   861 Mar 24 1990 0README
-rw-r--r-- 1 30750 21060   334 Jan 16 1990 bydomain
-rw-r--r-- 1 30750 21060   23832 Jul 9 1990 bydomain.vms
-rw-r--r-- 1 30750 21060   3364 Jun 1 1990 formlist.perl
-rw-r--r-- 1 30750 21060   141622 Jan 13 07:01 ftp.list
-rw-r--r-- 1 30750 21060   7701 Aug 18 23:01 ftphelp
-rw-r--r-- 1 30750 21060   33890 Aug 21 15:23 ftpserv.tar.uu
-rw-r--r-- 1 30750 21060   411 Jan 14 1990 getfile
-rw-r--r-- 1 30750 21060   18569 Apr 27 1990 getinfo
-rw-r--r-- 1 30750 21060   2855 Aug 21 15:46 help
226 ASCII Transfer complete.
1027 bytes received in 4.1 seconds (0.25 Kbytes/s)
ftp> get ftphelp
200 PORT command successful.
150 ASCII data connection for ftphelp (128.32.136.6,2209) (7701 bytes).
226 ASCII Transfer complete.
local: ftphelp remote: ftphelp
7897 bytes received in 1.1 seconds (7.2 Kbytes/s)
ftp> get ftp.list
200 PORT command successful.
150 ASCII data connection for ftp.list (128.32.136.6,2210) (141622 bytes).
226 ASCII Transfer complete.
local: ftp.list remote: ftp.list
143590 bytes received in 8.5 seconds (16 Kbytes/s)
ftp> quit
221 Goodbye.
```

A really big problem

There are signs that the current system of FTP servers is beginning to break down in the face of the tremendous growth in Internet traffic. It is now common to find major archives such as wsmr-simtel20-army.mil, wuarchive.wustl.edu, or sumex-aim.stanford.edu at their caller limit, unable to take further FTP connections. If a site indicates that it cannot accept more callers, try at a different time of day, such as early morning.

This situation will probably only get worse, since many archives are funded by universities with limited budgets. The appearance of commercial FTP archives is probably inevitable.

Fetch

Fetch

Fetch, written by Jim Matthews of Dartmouth, is a graphical FTP implementation that requires MacTCP. When you run Fetch, you are greeted with the following dialog box:

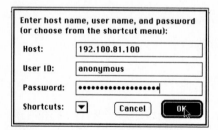

The location of the host you wish to connect to can be entered by domain name or IP address. In this case, I have requested connection to Internet node 192.100.81.100.

Many sites on the Internet have a file section open to the public. This section can be accessed by running FTP with the User ID set to anonymous and the user's Internet address as the password. After clicking on the **OK** button, Fetch will connect the user to the selected host, displaying the directory hierarchy of the machine.

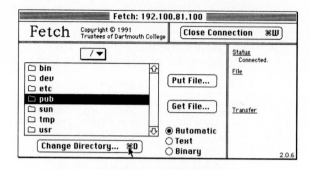

By clicking on folders, you can open them and browse for interesting files. Usually the pub directory is where the public files are kept; other directories may require passwords for access. In this case, I have navigated down into the /pub directory to transfer a file.

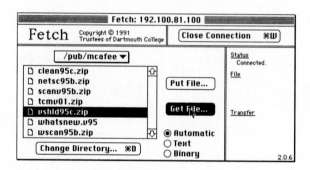

After selecting **vshld95c.zip**, I click on the **Get File...** button to bring up a save dialog box.

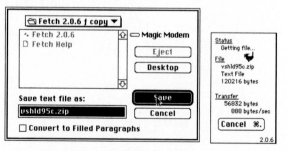

After clicking on **Save**, the file transfer status is displayed in the Status area.

FTPd

FTPd

FTPd is a shareware FTP server for the Mac, written by Peter Lewis. It works by mounting System 7 shared volumes over FTP. To set up, you need to enable file sharing, select folders to share, and mount them. In the example below, I mount the folder called Internet Software for FTP. Once mounted, the folder will change the icon to that of a shared folder.

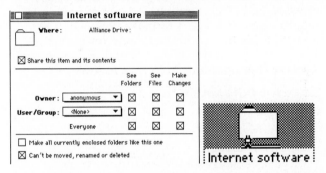

To make the shared folder accessible, you need to run the FTPd application, as well as to set up preferences and privileges by selecting **Preferences** and **Privileges** from the **File** menu. This will bring up these two dialog boxes:

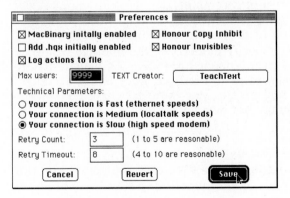

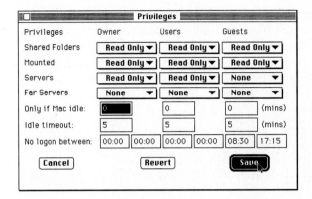

Once this is done, the folder is available for FTP:

```
% ftp mailcom.com
Connected to mailcom.com.
220 Peter's Macintosh FTP daemon v1.0.9 awaits your
command.
Name (mailcom.com:aboba): anonymous
331 Guest log in, send Email address (user@host) as
password.
Password:
230-Welcome to the Bulletin Boards and Beyond FTP
archive. This archive is experimental and may vanish
without a trace at any time. However, while you're here
and we're here, enjoy!
230 Anonymous login to 1 volumes.
ftp> ls
200 PORT command successful.
150 ASCII transfer started.
Internet software
226 Transfer complete.
19 bytes received in 0.32 seconds (0.057 Kbytes/s)
ftp> cd "Internet software"
250 Change directory successful.
ftp> ls
200 PORT command successful.
150 ASCII transfer started.
Chat 1.0.0
Collagev1.0B9
```

FTP by email

Limitations of FTPmail

If you don't have an account on an Internet host, you can still obtain files via FTPmail. This has the following limitations:

• Limits on the size of mail messages. Gateways frequently have message size limitations. For example, some FidoNet tosser/scanners cannot handle messages larger than 8K. If a properly functioning message splitter is not installed, parts of your file request may be lost.

• Bandwidth limits on your email connection. If at some point the file needs to be transmitted via modem, this will create a severe bottleneck. Assuming that the file is transmitted via V.32*bis*/V.42*bis* at 1800 characters/second (as high a transfer rate as you're likely to see), a 1 Mb file would clog the link for more almost 10 minutes. If only 150 people out of the many millions of Internet users attempted the same thing on a given day, the link would be saturated.

The results of your FTPmail commands will not come back to you interactively, but they will be processed in batch, so if you make a mistake, you will have to transmit another batch request. It can take a while to get things right.

Using FTPmail

To use FTPmail, send a message to ftpmail@decwrl.dec.com, and within the text of the message, include one of the following command words, each on separate lines. Keep in mind that if you're sending the message from a system that automatically wordwraps (such as TBBS), you will need to put a space on each line before the command word.

reply <MAILADDR>
set reply addr, since headers are usually wrong

connect [HOST [USER [PASS]]]
default to gatekeeper.dec.com, anonymous

ascii
files grabbed are printable ASCII
binary
files grabbed are compressed or tar or both

chdir PLACE
"get" and "ls" commands are relative to PLACE (only one CHDIR per ftpmail session)

compress
compress binaries using Lempel-Ziv encoding

compact
compress binaries using Huffman encoding

uuencode
binary files will be mailed in uuencode format

btoa
binary files will be mailed in btoa format

ls (or **dir**) PLACE
short (long) directory listing

get FILE
get a file and have it mailed to you

quit
terminate a script

Anonymous FTPmail

FTPmail works by executing the text of your message as FTP commands. After any help requests you may want to make, you will include your FTP commands, one on each line. The overall structure of an FTPmail message (assuming anonymous FTP) is as follows:

```
REPLY<yourname@yourhost.domain
CONNECT<ftphost.domain, anonymous,
yourname@yourhost.domain>
UUENCODE
CHDIR<directory}
GET<file}
<other FTPmail commands>
QUIT
```

Example:

```
REPLY aboba@world.std.com
CONNECT ftp.uu.net, anonymous, aboba@world.std.com
UUENCODE
CHDIR /info
GET anon-ftp-list.Z
QUIT
```

This list of commands will result in your receiving a uuencoded message containing a listing of files in the pub directory. If you didn't specify **UUENCODE**, the message would have been encoded anyway, but via the BTOA (binary to ascii) method. Since BTOA decoders are rare on the Mac (StuffIt Deluxe has one), this may not be a good idea.

Example

In addition to the **FTPLIST** command, you can get a list of anonymous **ftp** sites by sending a message to bitftp@pucc.princeton.edu, containing the following sequence of FTPmail commands:

```
FTP pilot.njin.net UUENCODE
USER ANONYMOUS
CD pub/ftp-list
DIR
GET ftp.list
QUIT
```

This will result in your receiving a uuencoded message containing the file `ftp.list`. uuencode is a program that converts 8-bit binary data into 7-bit files. You can undo this by using the Macintosh program uudecode.

Creating your own anonymous FTP archives

Internet service providers such as Netcom and World now offer users the ability to create their own anonymous FTP archives.

On Netcom, the user's anonymous FTP archive is located within the ~ftp/pub directory. For example, my directory is ~ftp/pub/mailcom. To make files available for downloading, all you have to do is copy them into this directory and set the permissions appropriately. For more information on UNIX permissions, please consult Appendix F: UNIX Tips and Tricks.

In the following example, I change directories to ~ftp/pub/mailcom and then check the file permissions. In order to be readable by anonymous users, directories must have both read and executable permission for "others"; files must have read permission.

It is wise not to allow others write permission on directories or files. Since you are being billed for used disk space, you do not want your area to be used as a temporary storage area by another user.

Example

```
% cd ~ftp/pub/mailcom
% ls -lg
total 127
drwxr-xr-x  2 aboba users0    512 Apr 18 13:36 BBB_Updates/
drwxr-xr-x  2 aboba users0    512 Apr 18 13:32
BMUG_Online_Reference/
drwxr-xr-x  2 aboba users0    512 Apr 27 12:56 IBMTCP/
-rw-r--r--  1 aboba users0   2851 Apr 18 14:07 README
drwxr-xr-x  2 aboba users0    512 Apr 18 13:54 UC_Extension/
-rw-r--r--  1 aboba users0 110930 Apr 18 13:26 super.cpt.hqx
% cd BBB_Updates
% ls -lg
total 840
-rw-r--r--  1 aboba users0 201944 Apr 14 22:45 BBB1.ZIP
-rw-r--r--  1 aboba users0 473820 Apr 18 13:34 bbb1.cpt.hqx
-rw-r--r--  1 aboba users0 147856 Apr 14 22:33 bbb2.cpt.hqx
```

FTP Q&A

What are the best archives for Macintosh files on the Internet?

Currently, ftp.apple.com, wuarchive.wustl.edu, mac.archive.umich.edu and sumex-aim.stanford.edu are the most popular Macintosh archives.

What are the best archives for PC files on the Internet?

wsmr-simtel20.army.mil and its mirrored archives (such as wuarchive.wustl.edu and oak.oakland.edu) are the most popular archives for PC-compatible software. A popular archive for Windows files is ftp.cica.indiana.edu.

What is the best way to establish an FTP server on a PC?

If you are running DOS, try KA9Q, the TCP/IP implementation by Phil Karn. If you are running Windows NT, then you might try the NT FTP server available on rhino.microsoft.com or sunsite.unc.edu. You might also consider inexpensive UNIX clones running on PC-compatibles, such as BSD/386, Coherent, Linux, or NetBSD. For more information, see Chapter 15: TCP/IP.

For more information

USENET groups relating to FTP

Group	What it is about
comp.archives	Discussion of new archives
comp.archives.admin	Discussion of administration of FTP archives

FSP

Acknowledgments

FSP was created by Wen-King Su (wen-king@cs.caltech.edu), and is now maintained by Phil Richards (pgr@sst.icl.co.uk) and Pete Bevin (pete@sst.icl.co.uk). Hats off!

What is FSP?

FSP (which stands for "File Slurping Protocol") is a robust file transfer protocol designed specifically for use by anonymous archives. Although it is not yet in wide use, FSP's advantages over FTP are considerable, so that it is likely to grow in popularity. In contrast to FTP:

• FSP supports ACK/NAK transfers over UDP. This makes it slower than FTP, which runs over TCP, but it also results in lower loading of the server.

• FSP does not support passwording, since it is designed for use in anonymous archives.

• A variety of client interfaces are available. These include X tools as well as FTP-like clients and implementations offering a variety of file manipulation and directory navigation commands (resembling standard UNIX commands), designed for execution from the UNIX shell.

• FSP supports continuation of aborted transfers, and is less susceptible to line noise. This makes it ideal for long file transfers over SLIP or PPP (such as downloading of Linux or NetBSD binaries).

• FSP does not yet have a "well known" port allocation. You will therefore need to download the FSP server list in order to know how to connect to the various archives.

FSP commands

Here is a partial list of FSP commands supported by the FTP-like client written by Phil Richards (pgr@sst.icl.co.uk).

Command	What it does
open <host> <port>	Outputs files to the screen
port <number>	Sets port number
cat <filelist>	Outputs files to the screen
cd <dir>	Changes directory
get <filelist>	Downloads files
grab <filelist>	Moves files
put <filelist>	Uploads files
rm <filelist>	Deletes files
pwd	Shows host, directory, port
rmdir <dir>	Removes a directory
mkdir <dir>	Makes a directory
tar <tarfile> <filelist>	Downloads files into a tar archive. The -r option does it recursively.
quit	Leaves FSP

An example FSP session

```
% fsp ftp.germany.eu.net 2001
source: can't open `~/.fsprc'
fsp> cd /pub/network/inet/fsp
-- directory `/pub/network/inet/fsp':
        owner:  no                      delete: no
        add:    no
        mkdir:  no                      read:   yes
fsp> ls
INFO                        fspcli-1.2.tar.gz
fsptool-1.3.tar.gz          awayd11.tar.gz
fspcli.readme               pcfsp102.zip
fsp.271.tar.gz              fspclient.0.0-h+.tar.z
vmsawayd11.zip              fspadmin1.1.tar.gz
fspsh113.tar.gz
fsp> get fspcli.readme
fsp> quit
```

Sample FSP server sites

Domain name	Port
erratic.bradley.edu	21
fsp.luth.se	6969
ftp.Germany.EU.net	2001
mosaic.cs.caltech.edu	21
muser.brad.ac.uk	6996
taxus.uib.no	9000
vlsi37.coe.northeastern.edu	2121
wuarchive.wustl.edu	21

For more information

USENET groups

alt.comp.fsp   General FSP discussion

FSP FAQ

```
fsp taxus.uib.no 9000, get
/fspdist/FAQ
```

Lists of FSP sites

`ftp` (or fsp on port 2001)
`ftp.germany.eu.net` (192.76.144.75),
`get /pub/lists/fsp-servers.`

FSP software

UNIX client and server

```
ftp ftp.germany.eu.net, mget
/pub/network/inet/fsp.*
```

```
ftp ftp.germany.eu.net, mget
/pub/network/inet/fspadmin*.*
```

```
fsp taxus.uib.no 9000, get
/fspdist/fsp.*
```

FTP-like client

```
ftp ftp.germany.eu.net, mget
/pub/network/inet/fsclient*.*
```

UNIX perl clients

```
ftp ftp.germany.eu.net, mget
/pub/network/inet/fscli-*.tar.Z
```

```
ftp ftp.germany.eu.net, mget
/pub/network/inet/fspsh*.*
```

```
fsp taxus.uib.no 9000, get
/fspdist/fscli-*.*
```

UNIX shell client

```
fsp taxus.uib.no 9000, get
/fspdist/fspsh*.*
```

X client

```
ftp wuarchive.wustl.edu, mget
/pub/fsptool*.tar.Z
```

```
ftp ftp.germany.edu.net mget
/pub/network/inet/fsp/fsptool*.*
```

```
fsp taxus.uib.no 9000, get
/fspdist/fsptool*.*
```

MS-DOS client

```
ftp ftp.germany.edu.net mget
/pub/network/inet/fsp/pcfsp*.zip
```

OS/2 client

```
ftp ftp.germany.edu.net mget
/pub/network/inet/fsp/fsp*.zip
```

Finding Files with Archie

Acknowledgments

Archie was created by the Archie Group at McGill, Bill Heelan (`wheelan@cs.mcgill.ca`), Peter Deutsch (`peterd@cc.mcgill.ca`), and Alan Emtage (`bajan@cs.mcgill.ca`). It's a neat idea. Give the guys a hand!

The directory of directories

An enormous amount of useful information is available over the Internet if you know where to look for it. If you don't, finding what you want can be very time-consuming. Archie is a regularly updated catalog of more than 1300 **ftp** sites. Every night it does an anonymous **ftp** to 1/30 of the sites and does a recursive directory listing. Over the course of a month, each of the sites in the database is updated. This means that a given directory is not guaranteed to be up to date on any given day, but it will not be more than a month out of date. Also, since Archie does not cover every **ftp** site, it is conceivable that it could miss your file. If there's a site you want added to the database, you should send mail to `archie-admin@cs.mcgill.ca`.

Archie also offers a catalog of file descriptions, via the **whatis** command. This catalog is imperfect, since the entries are by title, not by holding.

Access to Archie

Archie clients are available for the Macintosh, DOS, and NeXT, as well as for UNIX. Archie is also accessible via electronic mail, and Z39.50 search.

The UNIX client software, Archie, is run from a command line interface and connects with one of the Archie servers. Archie servers are now available at the nodes in the next column.

Node	Location
archie.ans.net	New York
archie.rutgers.edu	New Jersey
archie.sura.net	Maryland
archie.unl.edu	Nebraska
archie.funet.fi	Finland
archie.au	Australia
archie.nz	New Zealand
archie.doc.ic.ac.uk	United Kingdom
cs.huji.ac.il	Middle East
archie.ncu.edu.tw	Far East

Command-line access

If archie is installed on your home machine, you can run searches from the command-line. To run the command-line Archie client, type:

```
archie -s <string to search for> > outfile &
```

The & is added in order to allow the process to run in the background, since Archie can take a while. Outfile is the file to store the output in. Just typing **archie** without anything else will get you information.

Telnet access

In order to run Archie interactively, **telnet** to one of the Archie server sites, and `login`: **archie**. Here's what this will look like:

```
%world telnet  archie.rutgers.edu
Trying...
Connected to dorm.Rutgers.EDU.
Escape character is '^]'.
SunOS UNIX (dorm.rutgers.edu) (ttyq8)

login: archie
```

```
ARCHIE: Rutgers University Archive Server [November 20
1992]

Australian      users: archie.au
European        users: archie.funet.fi
United Kingdom  users: archie.doc.ic.ac.uk
Middle East     users: cs.huji.ac.il
Far East        users: archie.ncu.edu.tw
```

How to use Archie

At the `archie>` prompt, you can type a command or **help** if you want instructions. Below are examples of the Archie commands and what they will produce.

about, bugs, email, plans

Each of these commands will get you a short explanation message. **about** gives information about Archie; **bugs** gives a list of known problems; **email** describes how you can access Archie by Internet mail; **plans** provides information on future plans for Archie.

mailto <mail-address>

You may decide that you would like to have the result of an Archie search mailed to you for your records. This could be useful, for example, if you are logged on via a dumb terminal. To do this, use the **mailto** command to set the address to mail results to.

mail

While the **mailto** command merely sets the mail address, it does not request that the results of a particular command be mailed to you. This is what **mail** does. After you have gotten the results for a command that you would like to mail, type **mail** and Archie will set about mailing the results to you. The request will be handled in the background, so you can just go on to the next command.

list

This command lists the machines covered by the Archie database. Here is an example of it:

```
archie> list
682 sites are stored in the database

a.cs.uiuc.edu          128.174.252.1  20:25 10 Jul 1991
ab20.larc.nasa.gov     128.155.23.64  05:01 27 Jun 1991
accuvax.nwu.edu        129.105.49.1   05:09 27 Jun 1991
*
*
*
xylogics.com           132.245.1.95   05:46 26 Jun 1991
yallara.cs.rmit.oz.au  131.170.24.42  05:47 26 Jun 1991
zaphod.ncsa.uiuc.edu   141.142.20.50  06:00 26 Jun 1991
zariski.harvard.edu    128.103.28.10  06:09 26 Jun 1991
zeus.cs.umu.se         130.239.1.101  06:11 26 Jun 1991
```

help

This command gets you a help file.

prog

prog searches the Archie database for a file. The simplest way to search with **prog** is to give it a substring within the name of the program you're looking for. Here's a session where I was looking for a program called "ppp":

```
archie> prog ppp
# matches / % database searched: 513 / 99%
Host munnari.oz.au (128.250.1.21)
Last updated 05:09 15 Jul 1991
Location: /ietf
  FILE  rw-r--r--  1158 Jun 13 1990 ppp-charter.txt
*
*
*
Host ucdavis.ucdavis.edu (128.120.2.1)
Last updated 05:04 23 Jun 1991
 Location: /dist/ppp
  FILE  r--r--r--  149698 May 16 1990 netppp.tar.Z

Host ucdavis.ucdavis.edu (128.120.2.1)
Last updated 05:04 23 Jun 1991
Location: /dist/ppp
  FILE  r--r--r--  91319 May 16 1990 pppsrc.tar.Z

Host ucdavis.ucdavis.edu (128.120.2.1)
Last updated 05:04 23 Jun 1991

 Location: /pub
  FILE  rw-r--r--  24643 Mar 26 09:44 dialppp.zip
```

More complex uses of prog

Archie has several possible search modes, which are set by giving it the command **set search <mode>**. The search modes are **sub**, **subcase**, **exact**, and **regex**.

In search mode "sub" you search for substrings and ignore case; this is the most common search mode. In mode "subcase" you also look for substrings but searches are case sensitive. In mode "exact" Archie looks for a file name identical to what you requested including case, not a name containing the string you specify.

"regex" is the most complicated mode. This searches for files specified by what is known as "regular expressions." Regular expressions are a means for directing searches that are used by UNIX programs such as ed, sed, grep, and awk. While full discussion of regular expressions would take several pages, a few hints are given on the next page.

^ is used to specify the beginning of a word. For example ^ppp will match ppp.tar.Z but not gloppp.Z.

$ matches the end of a word. For example $ppp will match floppp but not nopppy.Z.
. is used to match any character except for a carriage return. Therefore ^p.p would match pnp, ppp, or pop but not pp.

[] matches any characters in the brackets. For example, [0-9] matches any number; [a-zA-Z] matches any upper- or lower-case character.

[^] matches any character *except* those in the brackets. For example, [^0-9] matches any nonnumeric character.

+ will match one or more copies of the expressions before the *. Therefore, [0-9]+ will match 1023 but not the null string.

* will match zero or more copies of the expressions before the *. Therefore, [0-9]+\.[0-9]* will match 123 and 2.123 but not .123.

If you want to match a character used for special purposes like *,.,^ or +, you need to put a backslash (\) before them, as in *.

site

This command lists the files at a given site. Here is an example:

```
archie> site uunet.uu.net
 drwxrwxr-x   512 Jun 4 1990 Census
 drwxrwxr-x   512 Jan 8 09:36 ClariNet
 drwxrwxr-x   512 Feb 8 15:14 NCSA_Telnet
 drwxrwxr-x   512 May 23 05:00 NeWS

 *
 *
 *
```

whatis <search string>

While the rest of the Archie commands help you find a given file, the **whatis** command is designed to tell you what the file does. It works by printing out all the lines of the database (approximately 3000 entries are in it so far) that contain the string. The **whatis** Archie command has the potential to be immensely useful, if people would only mail in

descriptions. If you want to add a description, mail it to **archie-admin@cs.mcgill.ca**.

Other set commands

Before executing your search, you may also want to set various parameters of your session. Commands include:

set autologout <minutes>
Maximum idle time before forced logout.

set maxhits <number>
The maximum number of hits for Archie to return.

set pager or **unset pager**
Display results one page at a time or let it scroll

set term <terminal>
Set the terminal type, such as VT100.

set status or **unset status**
Show progress of search or not.

How to leave Archie

To leave Archie, type **bye**, **exit** or **quit**. You'll be left back at your home machine.

How to use Archie via email

You do not have to have an account on an Internet host to use Archie. It is possible for you to send batch commands to Archie via electronic mail, have them execute, and then have the results sent back to you.

Of course, the results of your request may be truncated by mail systems along the way if they are too long. For example, some FidoNet mail processors cannot handle mail larger than 8K. A given BBS or online service may also have a message size limitation. As a result, email access to Archie (or FTP for that matter) may be problematic for users with email access.

To access the Archie mail server, send a message to **archie@cs.mcgill.ca**. The subject and text of the message are interpreted as commands, each command on a separate line. Archie will interpret your requests, execute them, and mail the results back to you.

Example

Here is a transcript of a session involving multiple **whatis** queries:

```
% telnet archie.unl.edu
Trying 129.93.1.14...
Connected to archie1.unl.edu.
Escape character is '^]'.

SunOS UNIX (archie1)

login: archie
Last login: Sat Mar 28 12:00:32 from dn87pg25kip7.Pri
SunOS Release 4.1.1 (ARCHIE) #3: Mon Nov 25 10:43:05 CST 1991

#########################################################################
```

```
       Welcome to the ARCHIE server at the University of Nebraska - Lincoln

       Please report problems to archie-admin@unl.edu.  We encourage
    people to use client software to connect rather than actually logging in.
    Client software is available on ftp.unl.edu in the /pub/archie directory.

    If you need further instructions, type help at the unl-archie> prompt.

#########################################################################

unl-archie> whatis nntp

nntp                    Network News Transfer Protocol

unl-archie> whatis binhex

comb-binhex             Combine binhex files which have been split into
                        pieces back into one file
xbin                    Convert files from binhex format to what
                        "macput" expects (Mac)

unl-archie> whatis btoa

btoa                    Binary/ascii packer with repair features

unl-archie> whatis stuffit

sit                     produce StuffIt archives for downloading to the
                        MacIntosh
unl-archie> whatis zip
unzip                   Unbundles ZIP files
unzip_gs                UnZip for Unix

unl-archie> quit
Connection closed by foreign host.
```

Here are the commands:

path <path>

This command lets you specify the routing by which the results should be returned to you. Since Archie can figure out your mail address from the incoming mail header, you shouldn't need to use this unless you have trouble.

prog <regular expression>

This command searches for a filename that meetsthe criteria given by the regular expression. The Archie mail server has only the regular expression mode right now.

site <site name>|<IP address>

This command gets you a list of all the files at a given site, which can be specified either by its name or its IP address.

compress

This command requests that your response be compressed by the UNIX compress program and then run through UUENCODE. This will result in a smaller file coming back, so there's less chance it will be eaten by mail processors with size limitations.

To read the output on the Mac, you will need to utilize UULITE and then MacCompress (BMUG Disk Telecom D1).

whatis <searchstring>

whatis also works via email.

quit

This tells Archie to stop looking for more commands. Be nice, put it in at the end.

Archie clients

Archie

Versions of the Archie client are available for the Mac, NeXT and DOS. For listings, please consult Appendix B: Choice Products. Below is an example screen from the MacArchie client:

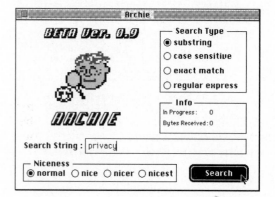

Accessing Archie via Z39.50 and Gopher

Archie may also be searched via Gopher and Z39.50. The WAIS-compatible Archie source file is `archie-orst.src`; you may also want to check the source for the uunet and wuarchive archives: uunet.src and wuarchive.src. See Chapter 14 for more information on Gopher and Z39.50.

For more information

The authors of Archie may be reached by mail to `archie-l@cs.mcgill.ca`. For information, `ftp quiche.cs.mcgill.ca, cd archie/doc, as whatis.archie, and archie.man.txt`.

CHAPTER 11:
ONLINE LIBRARIES

When is a library not a library?

What do I need?

To access online libraries, you need to round up the usual suspects – a modem, a cable, a terminal program, and a computer. You should also locate the system nearest you. In order to conform to the terms of the license agreements on their bibliographic databases, many university libraries now restrict access to faculty, students, or staff. Therefore, do not be surprised if many of the things you want to do require a password, or payment of extra fees. Listed systems with (7-E-1) after their name should be accessed using 7 bits, even parity, 1 stop bit.

Acknowledgments

Without the University of California, there would be no MELVYL or GLADIS. Without the state legislature, there would be no University of California. Let's hope they don't change their mind!

Basics of telnet and tn3270

Most Online Public Access Catalogs (OPACs) are accessible via **telnet** and **tn3270**. Telnet clients are available for many machines, including the Macintosh, DOS, and Windows; a DOS **telnet** server is also available.

Most versions of UNIX also now come with built-in **telnet** and **tn3270** support. For UNIX, the commands take the following form:

```
telnet <machine name> <port number> or
tn3270 <machine name> <port number>
```

Here <machine name> can be either the fully qualified domain name of the machine, or the IP address. Using the UNIX **telnet** command, you can have only one connection open at a time, and must close a connection before opening a new one. In contrast, Macintosh, DOS, or Windows **telnet** clients such as NCSA Telnet (Macintosh) or KA9Q (DOS) allow multiple simultaneous connections.

The port number is optional and defaults to the **telnet** port of 23 if it is left out. The port number is mainly used for debugging purposes, such as to see if SMTP, NNTP or POP servers are functioning on their assigned ports. For example, to check whether a pop server I've installed is listening on port 110, I can issue the following command:

```
telnet localhost 110
```

Similarly, to check on the NNTP server on port 119 or the SMTP server on port 25, I can issue these commands:

```
telnet localhost 119
telnet localhost 25
```

Here localhost (or the IP address 127.0.0.1) stands for the machine that I am on.

The 3270 terminal was designed for use with IBM mainframes. It operates in block-transfer mode and has a special keyboard with special function (PF) keys. For those mainframe applications that require connecting machines to emulate the 3270, the **tn3270** is used instead of **telnet**. Note that even when using the **tn3270** command, you will still have the problem of emulating the 3270 keyboard, possibly on a system (such as one with the standard Macintosh keyboard) without any function keys at all. **telnet** commands include:

close
Closes the connection

display set echo
Toggles local echoing. Default is off; typing **set**

`echo` once turns it on. Use this command if what you type doesn't show up on the screen.

set escape <char>

The escape character is the character that lets you end a `telnet` session. The default is (CTRL)]. This command is used to change it to another character. This is required if you are going to be telnet'ing through a chain of sites. Otherwise, escaping out of one session will end all of them. Also make sure your escape character doesn't conflict with a program use.

open <name>

Opens a connection to the named machine

quit

Quits `telnet`

(CTRL)Z

Suspends `telnet` (To return, type `%telnet`)

?

Gets help listing

Braving the telnet jungle with Hytelnet

Hytelnet, first created by Peter Scott, is a Michelin Guide for `telnet`, listing information and directions to thousands of interesting `telnet` sites worldwide. Versions of Hytelnet are available for UNIX, Macintosh, and DOS. The DOS version of Hytelnet runs as a TSR. Both DOS and UNIX versions are available via `ftp access.usask.ca`.

With the Macintosh version of Hytelnet (which requires both MacTCP and HyperCard), you must first configure the stack by clicking on **Configure**. The configuration card lets you enter the paths to the `telnet` and `tn3270` applications, as well as the config.tel files for those applications. Locations of `telnet` and `tn3270` applications are given at the end of this chapter. To log in to a site, first navigate to the card of the site you're interested in, then click on **Go for it!**. This launches NCSA Telnet.

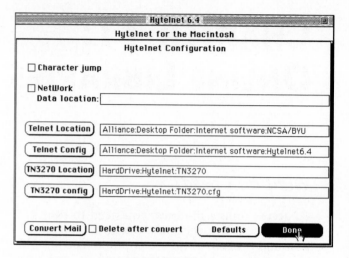

Within Hytelnet, sites are listed by catalog name as well as by interface.

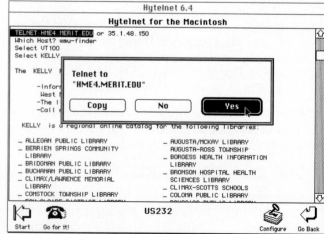

Hytelnet UNIX client

It is also possible to access a UNIX client version of Hytelnet via `telnet access.usask.ca`, `login: hytelnet`. Hytelnet navigation comands include:

⬇	Select next
⬆	Select previous
–>	Jump to next
<–	Previous topic
hjkl	vi cursor key functions
+	page down
–	page up
?	help
m	main menu
q	Quit Hytelnet

Below is a typical session:

```
%telnet access.usask.ca
Ultrix UNIX (access.usask.ca)

login: hytelnet
Last login: Mon May 10 22:48:57 from Alice-Thurman.te
ULTRIX V4.3 (Rev. 44) System #12: Tue May  4 13:56:42 CST
1993

        Welcome to Access, running Ultrix 4.3
        Mail problem reports to root.

                Welcome to HYTELNET
                   version 6.4.x

        What is HYTELNET?          <WHATIS>
        Library catalogs           <SITES1>
        Other resources            <SITES2>
        Help files for catalogs    <OP000>
        Catalog interfaces         <SYS000>
        Internet Glossary          <GLOSSARY>
        Telnet tips                <TELNET>
        Telnet/TN3270 escape keys  <ESCAPE.KEY>
        Key-stroke commands        <HELP>

...............................................
Up/Down arrows MOVE  Left/Right arrows SELECT    ? for
m  returns here      q  quits  help              HELP
                                                 anytime

...............................................
        HYTELNET 6.4 was written by Peter Scott
        E-mail address: aa375@freenet.carleton.ca
```

The Library of Congress

The Library of Congress is available via `telnet dra.com`, `telnet locis.loc.gov`, or via a Gopher operating at marvel.loc.gov. The Library Of Congress Information System (LOCIS), available via `telnet locis.loc.gov` (140.147.254.3), includes more than fifteen million Library of Congress catalog records, as well more than ten million other entries. Information accessible via LOCIS includes the Library of Congress Catalog, databases of

federal legislation, copyright information, organizations, and foreign law, as well as a catalog of braille and audio publications.

On the NeXT there is also a graphical interface to the Library of Congress catalog. The LC application allows you to query the catalog as well as to order books through various online bookstores.

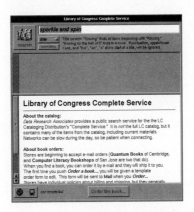

Below is a sample LOCIS session in which I locate the Electronic Communications Privacy Act of 1986.

```
% telnet locis.loc.gov
 L O C I S :  LIBRARY OF CONGRESS INFORMATION SYSTEM

    To make a choice: type a number, then press ENTER

1   Library of Congress Catalog     4   Braille and Audio
2   Federal Legislation             5   Organizations
3   Copyright Information           6   Foreign Law
*     *     *     *     *     *     *     *     *     *
7   Searching Hours and Basics
8   Documentation and Classes
9   Library of Congress General Information
12   Comments and Logoff

      Choice:
2
            FEDERAL LEGISLATION

These files track and describe legislation (bills and
resolutions) introduced in the US Congress, from 1973
(93rd Congress) to the current Congress (the
current Congress is the 103rd).  Each file covers a
separate Congress.

CHOICE
FILE

1    Congress, 1981-82    (97th)                  CG97
2    Congress, 1983-84    (98th)                  CG98
3    Congress, 1985-86    (99th)                  CG99
4    Congress, 1987-88    (100th)                 C100
5    Congress, 1989-90    (101st)                 C101
6    Congress, 1991-92    (102nd)                 C102
7    Current Congress, 1993-  (103rd)             C103
8    Search all Congresses from 1981-->current
9    Search all Congresses on LOCIS 1973-->current
     Earlier Congresses: press ENTER
12   Return to LOCIS MENU screen.
```

(session continued on next page)

```
Choice:
3

WEDNESDAY, 05/12/93  04:46 P.M.
***CG99- THE LEGISLATIVE INFORMATION FILE FOR THE 99TH
CONGRESS, which was updated on 10/30/89 and contains
16,370 records,is now available for your search.

CONTENTS:  CG99 summarizes and tracks legislation
introduced during the 99th Congress.  Status of bills is
updated within 48 hours of action.

   TO START   RETRIEVE to find:
EXAMPLES:
SEARCH: member name  ------------->   retrieve rep kemp
                                      retrieve sen kennedy
         bill number  ------------->   retrieve h.r. 1
         subject keywords  --------->   retrieve day care

FOR HELP:  Type the word HELP and press the ENTER key.

   READY FOR NEW COMMAND:
ELECTRONIC COMMUNICATIONS PRIVACY ACT

To DISPLAY, see EXAMPLES at bottom.
FILE: CG99

LAST COMMAND:  RETR ELECTRONIC COMMUNICATIONS PRIVACY ACT

SEARCH RESULTS:

SET#    ITEMS    WITH THE WORDS OR TERMS
----    -----    -----------------------
 1        5      ELECTRONIC COMMUNICATIONS PRIVACY ACT

---EXAMPLES: display (DISPLAYs the set created by
RETRIEVE)
 help display     (gives more info about DISPLAY command)
    OTHER
COMMANDS: help browse  retrieve  select  combine  limit
history  end

READY:
DISPLAY ALL

ITEMS 1-3 OF 5              SET 1: BRIEF DISPLAY
FILE: CG99
                        (ASCENDING ORDER)
1. H.R.3378: SPON=Rep Kastenmeier, (Cosp=38); OTLI=A bill
to amend title 18,United States Code, with respect to the
interception of certain communications, other forms of
surveillance, and for other purposes.
2. H.R.4952: SPON=Rep Kastenmeier, (Cosp=35); Public Law:
99-508(10/21/86); OTLI=A bill to amend title 18, United
States Code, with respect to the interception of certain
communications, other forms of surveillance,and for other
purposes.

3. H.R.5664: SPON=Rep Wright; OTLI=A bill to strengthen
Federal efforts to encourage foreign cooperation in
eradicating illicit drug crops and in halting
international drug traffic, to improve enforcement of
Federal drug laws and enhance interdiction of illicit
drug shipments, to provide strong Federal leadership in
establishing effective drug abuse prevention and
education programs, to expand Federal support for drug
abuse treatment and rehabilitation efforts, and for other
purposes.

NEXT PAGE:          press transmit or enter key
SKIP AHEAD/BACK:    type any item# in set
Example--> 25
FULL DISPLAY:       type DISPLAY ITEM plus an item#
Example--> display item 2
READY
```

Arizona State University

The Arizona State University OPAC offers access to databases such as the UnCover periodicals database and the ERIC educational database. Access to UnCover is offered through an arrangement with the Colorado Alliance for Research Libraries (CARL), which is an outstanding online library in its own right. ASU also offers access to Arizona statistics as well as the Grolier's Encyclopedia, and materials from their own collection.

To reach the ASU OPAC, `telnet car.lib.asu.edu`. You will need to select your terminal emulation and then you will be directed to the main menu:

```
The ASU Libraries Online Catalog offers the following:

1.  ASU LIBRARIES CATALOG (books, journal titles, other
cataloged materials)

2.  OTHER ASU LIBRARIES SPECIALIZED COLLECTIONS AND
DATABASES (AZ & SW, Maps, Solar Energy, Song Index...)

3.  JOURNAL INDEXES, ERIC, & UNCOVER (Article Access)
NOTE: SEE LIBRARY NEWS (#8) FOR JOURNAL CANCELLATIONS

4.  ENCYCLOPEDIA (Grolier's Academic American, c. 1992)

5.  INFORMATION DATABASES (AZ Statistics, Child Care...)

6.  ARIZONA LIBRARIES

7.  OTHER LIBRARY CATALOGS (including Gov. Publications,
1976- )

8.  LIBRARY NEWS, HOURS, AND INFORMATION
(*** Includes proposed journal cancellations ***)

Enter the NUMBER of your choice, and press <RETURN> 3
```

Here is the journals section:

```
1. ASU Libraries   2. Specialized   3. Journals/ERIC
4. Encyclopedia    5. Info Databases 6. AZ Libraries
7. Other Libraries 8. Library News

          JOURNAL INDEXES AND UNCOVER

3.  JOURNAL INDEXES

30.  Applied Science and Technology Index, late 1983-
31.  Business Periodicals Index, mid 1982-
32.  Education Index, late 1983-
36.  Uncover -- Article Access (all subjects), 9/1988-
37.  ERIC (Education Documents/Journals) 1966-
38.  ERIC Thesaurus
39.  ERIC RIE
40.  ERIC CIJE
41.  IAC Expanded Academic Index
```

Several of these databases, such as the Business periodicals index, require an account number for access.

Chapter 11: Online Libraries

The Washington & Lee Law Library

The Washington & Lee Law Library offers gateways to Archie, Hytelnet, various Gophers and about 2500 libraries. It is therefore just about the easiest way to get to everything. To try it out, `telnet liberty.uc.wlu.edu`, `login: lawlib`.

Here's just a bit of what you'll see when you get there:

```
1    ->    changes/notes/new features
2    ->    leave a message for system operator
3    -> to Archie
4    -> to Files (local)
5    -> to Gopher (W&L)
6    -> to Gopher High-Level Menus (search & link to
            about 160,000 entries)
7    -> to Gophers (newly added to W&L's Gopher)
8    -> to Hytelnet
9    -> to Indexes/Databases
10   -> to Legal Sources
11   -> to Libraries (U.S.)
12   -> to Netfind
13   -> to Usenet Newsreaders
14   -> to WAIS Databases (local menu)
15   -> to WAIS Databases (SWAIS and Gopher menus)
16   -> to WWW (WorldWideWeb)
17   EDIN: Economic Development Information Network,
            Pennslyvania
18   Lehigh University, Campus Information
19   Lund University Electronic Library (Gopher)
20   MarketBase: Online Catalog of Goods and Services

1-2714 Search Move Next Last eXit Color Email
Restrict set       Arrange by name
&&& escapes interactive connections (Use if no exit
instructions)
```

OCLC

The Online Computer Library Center (OCLC) is among the nation's foremost electronic libraries. Databases include the Reader's Guide to Periodical Literature, the PsycFIRST database from the American Psychological Association, the Newspaper Abstracts and Periodical Abstracts databases from UMI, the MiniGeoRef database from the American Geological Institute, and more. To reach OCLC, you must first obtain an account. You may then access the service via `telnet epic.prod.oclc.org`.

For information on getting an account, contact OCLC, 6565 Frantz Road, Dublin, OH 43017-3395, (800)848-5878

Dialog

The Dialog online service is also accessible over the Internet, via `telnet dialog.com`. As with OCLC, you must have an account before using it. Since DIALOG offers access to an incredible number of databases (over 400 at last count), and is complex enough to deserve its own book, we won't go into detail here. For information on obtaining an account, contact DIALOG Information Services, 3460 Hillview Avenue, Palo Alto, CA 94304, (800)334-2564.

Getting onto MELVYL and GLADIS

If you are in the Bay Area, perhaps the best place to start is MELVYL, the online library of the University of California. The dialin numbers for MELVYL are:

(510)642-7400   for 1200 bps
(510)642-6092   for 2400 bps
(510)643-9600   for 9600/14400 bps

At the "Request" prompt, type `annex`(RET).

When "connecting" appears, press (RET)(RET). Then type `telnet gladis`(RET) or `telnet melvyl`(RET).

Once in MELVYL, enter `?` at the `Terminal?` prompt to find the code for your computer. Type `VT100` if your software offers VT100 emulation.

Exploring MELVYL

Through MELVYL you can access many databases, including online catalogs, periodicals databases, and other library systems. With the periodical databases you can search for articles by title, subject, author, or key words.

Magazines indexed online include computer-industry trade journals, scholarly and medical periodicals, and several major newspapers such as the *New York Times* and the *Los Angeles Times*. These capabilities are available only to students, faculty, and staff of the University of California, but if you have access it's really neat.

Modem login example

```
Request:   ANNEX
Press the "Return" key 1-2 times until you get the annex (arrow) prompt.
Annex1 port07==>  TELNET MELVYL
When finished with the MELVYL system, log off and you will be returned to the annex prompt.
Annex1 port07==>  HANGUP
```

Internet login example

```
% telnet melvyl.berkeley.edu
Trying 31.1.0.11...
Connected to melvyl.berkeley.edu.
Escape character is '^]'.

DLA LINE 138 (TELNET) 17:22:48 09/12/92   (MELVYL.UCOP.EDU)
Please Enter Your Terminal Type Code or Type ? for a List of Codes.

TERMINAL? VT100

Press RETURN for the MELVYL System ->

              Welcome to the University of California's

                    MELVYL* LIBRARY SYSTEM

----------------------- =>> SYSTEM NEWS <<= --------------------------
       The MELVYL MEDLINE database will be unavailable Sunday morning,
     September 13, from midnight to 10 a.m.  Type SHOW DLA2 NEWS for details.
----------------------------------------------------------------------

(c)1984. *Registered trademark of The Regents of the University of California.
======================================================================
OPTIONS:  Choose an option, or type any command to enter the CATALOG database.

   HELP        - For help in getting started.

   [return]    - Press RETURN to choose a database for searching.

   START <db>  - Type START <database name> to begin searching in a database.
```

MELVYL Databases

Within MELVYL, you first choose which database to search. These include databases of periodicals and books, as well as online services such as MEDLINE. As long as you remain within MELVYL, the same commands will work within any database. A listing of MELVYL databases is given below; to choose a database, just type its name, for example **COMP** for the computer periodicals database or **MED** for MEDLINE. A listing of other databases you can reach from MELVYL is given at the end of this chapter.

Melvyl Catalog databases

TEN	Ten-Year MELVYL Catalog—materials published from 1982–1992
CAT	Full MELVYL Catalog—UC libraries and the California State Library
PE	Periodical Titles—California Academic Libraries List of Serials

Article databases
(UC users only; password may be required)

MAGS	Magazine & Journal—1000 magazines and journals
NEWS	Newspaper Articles—five major U.S. newspapers
CC	Current Contents—6500 scholarly journals
CCT	Current Contents—tables of contents of 6500 scholarly journals
MED	MELVYL MEDLINE—4000 medical and life-sciences journals
COMP	Computer Articles—200 computer-related magazines and journals

Command overview

Within MELVYL, the FIND command is first used to select catalog entries. The selection can then be further narrowed, displayed, or saved. The major commands are:

FIND	Selects entries
AND, OR, and **NOT**	Further narrows selection
DISPLAY	Displays the selection
SAVE SET	Saves the selected entries

Find commands

The Find command syntax is:

FIND <index> <query>

Where <index> is one of of the following:

Index	What it does
SU	Searches by subject word
XS	Exacts subject word at the beginning of the subject heading
KW	Keyword
AU	Author
TW	Title word
XT	Exacts title word at the beginning of the title
JO	Journal title word
XJ	Exacts journal word at the beginning of the Journal name
SF	Subfile (limits search to a particular database)

The query is a series of words separated by the connectives AND, OR, and NOT.

Subfiles

ABD	Area business database
AI	Academic index
CD	Computer database
HI	Health periodicals index
LRI	Legal resources index
LIB	Library journals
MI	Magazine index
MC	Management contents
NNI	National newspaper index
NW	Newswires
TI	Trade and industry index

Example

`FIND SU TCP OR IP`	Finds subject entries with TCP or IP
`FIND SU TCP AND NOT IP`	Finds subject entries with TCP but not IP
`FIND KW INTERNET OR MATRIX`	Finds keyword entry with Internet or Matrix
`FIND AU NIXON,R AND AGNEW,S`	Finds entry with authors Nixon and Agnew
`FIND AU NIXON,R AND NOT SF NW`	Finds entry with author Nixon, but not in the subfile Newswires.

AND, OR, and NOT

Connectives can also be used to further narrow a search. For example:

```
FIND AU ABOBA, B
AND KW BULLETIN BOARDS
```

This initially selects entries by author B Aboba, and then narrows the list to those that include the keyword bulletin boards.

Display

The `DISPLAY` command outputs the selection to the screen. The syntax is:
`DISPLAY <entry list><display options><print options>`
Where <entry list> is a range of items, such as:

`ALL`	Displays all entries
n_1 n_2 n_3	Displays entries n_1, n_2, and n_3
n_1 - n_2	Displays entries n_1-n_2
`BY n`	Displays every n-th entry

Where <display option> is:

`ABS`	Shows abstracts within articles
`LONG`	Shows the long version of the entry
`SHORT`	Shows the short version of the entry
`AU`	Shows author entry
`TI`	Shows title entry
`SU`	Shows subject entry

Where <print option> is:

`CONT`	Displays continuously, without page breaks
`PAGESIZE n`	Displays with n lines between page breaks

Example

`DISPLAY ALL SHORT ABS CONT`	Continuously displays short entries, including abstracts
`DISPLAY 1-10 LONG`	Displays page by page in long firm entries 1–10
`DISPLAY BY 5 PAGESIZE 20`	Display every 5th entry, 20 lines/page

Author search example

```
Search request: FIND AU BERNARD ABOBA
Search result:  3 citations in the Computer Articles database

Type HELP for other display options.

1. Aboba, Bernard.
      All Mac functions accessed via modem with Timbuktu-Remote. (evaluation)
      MacWEEK v3, n17 (April 25, 1989):102 (2 pages).
      Pub Type:  Evaluation.

2. Aboba, Bernard.
      Screen recorder: a boon for visual presentation. (evaluation)
      MacWEEK v3, n17 (April 25, 1989):103 (2 pages).
      Pub Type:  Evaluation.

3. Aboba, Bernard.
      An EtherPort in the storm. (Hardware Review) (EtherPort SE) (evaluation)
      Macworld v5, n5 (May, 1988):174 (3 pages).
      Pub Type:  Evaluation.
```

Other libraries on the Internet

Some of the other popular online libraries include:

System	Institution	Phone
Colorado Alliance of Res. Libraries	Colorado Library System	(303)863-1350
LUMINA (7-E-1)	University of Minnesota	(612)626-6009
MELVYL and GLADIS (7-E-1)	University of California Catalog	(510)642-6092
Online Legal Periodicals and Citations	Texas State Law Library, Austin	(512)463-1371
UT Library Online Catalog	University of Texas at Austin	(512)471-9420
Public Library Catalog	Montgomery County, MD	(301)217-3906
FEDLINK	Federal Library Info Network	(202)707-9656
HOLLIS	Harvard Online Catalog	(617)495-9500
National Agricultural Library	U.S. Dept. of Agriculture	(301)344-8510

Internet address	Library
dra.com, locis.loc.gov	Library of Congress catalog
gladis.berkeley.edu	University of California book catalog
pac.carl.org	Colorado Association of Research Libraries
hub.nnsc.nsf.net	Simple Wide Area Information Server, login as "wais",TERM = "vt100"
192.58.246.4	Cleveland Public Library
nike.cair.du.edu	University of Colorado
uicvm.uic.edu	University of Illinois Chicago library
luis.wustl.edu	Washington Universities Main Libraries
128.175.13.6	University of Delaware
lib.dartmouth.edu	Dartmouth Library
garcon.cso.uiuc.edu	University of Illinois, Urbana Champagne
kuhub.cc.ukans.edu	University of Kansas
infotrac.rpi.edu	Rennsaleer Polytechnic Institute
utaus.cc.utexas.edu	University of Texas, login as auscat
irishmvs.cc.nd.edu	University of Notre Dame Library
lumina.lib.umn.edu	University of Minnesota Library
janus.uoregon.edu	University of Oregon Library
aim.umd.edu	Maryland Access Info
umcat.umd.edu	Maryland libraries
bootes.unm.edu	University of New Mexico, login: STUDENT1
bull.utulsa.edu	University of Tulsa, login: LIAS, TU
cts.merit.edu	University of Michigan
nls.adp.wisc.edu	University of Wisconsin
lib.cc.purdue.edu	Purdue University (use tn3270)
liberty.uc.wlu.edu	Washington & Lee Law Library

DATABASES OUTSIDE THE MELVYL SYSTEM (Accessible from Melvyl)

ASIA	Asian and Pacific studies—UC Davis
ERIC	Education article & report citations (database on Stanford system)
HAPI	Hispanic American Periodicals Index (database on ORION system)
LEGISLATE	Daily U.S. Congressional and regulatory information
NASA	Space and earth sciences—NASA Online Data & Information Service
OCEAN	Oceanography—OCEAN Information Center
RUTGERS	Reference materials and campus information—Rutgers University
WEATHER	Weather forecasts and information—University of Michigan

LIBRARY CATALOGS OUTSIDE THE MELVYL SYSTEM – CALIFORNIA

COAST	California State University, Long Beach (VT100 only)
GLADIS	UC Berkeley
HAYSTAC	California State University, Hayward (VT100 only)
NRLF	Northern Regional Library Facility (for Microterm ACT5A, Tandem, Televideo, WYSE, and VT100)
ORION	UC Los Angeles (account required)
POLYCAT	California Polytechnic State University, San Luis Obispo (VT100 only)
SFSU	San Francisco State University Investigator system (VT100 only)
STANFORD	Stanford University
UCSFCAT	UC San Francisco (VT100 only)

LIBRARY CATALOGS OUTSIDE CALIFORNIA

ASU	Arizona State University
BOSTON	Boston University
CAMBRIDGE	Cambridge University, England
CARL	Colorado Alliance of Research Libraries
CFN	Cleveland Free-Net
CMU	Carnegie Mellon University
DARTMOUTH	Dartmouth College
DRA	Digital Research Associates—Library of Congress (VT100 only)
EPIC	OCLC, Inc. (account required)
HARVARD	Harvard University HOLLIS Library System (VT100 only)
LIBROS	University of New Mexico General Library
MICHIGAN	University of Michigan MIRLYN Library System (VT100 only)
MONT	Monterrey Institute of Technology (ITESM), Mexico (VT100 only)
OXFORD	Oxford University, England
PRINCETON	Princeton University
PSU	Pennsylvania State University
RLIN	Research Libraries Group (account required)
RPI	Rensselaer Polytechnic University
UDEL	University of Delaware
UMD	University of Maryland
UNM	University of New Mexico
UTENN	University of Tennessee
VATECH	Virginia Tech
YALE	Yale University ORBIS Library System (VT100 only)

Dow Jones News Retrieval

Dow Jones News Retrieval is now accessible over the Internet by giving the command `telnet djnr.dowjones.com`. Although you cannot perform any Internet functions using the service, with the new off-peak fixed rates many people will find DJNR irresistible, since it offers an incredible variety of business and economic information.

Useful Dow Jones commands

(Not included in Tier 1, 2, or 3 Off-peak fixed pricing)

`//FYI`	Online help and tutorial
`//SYMBOL`	Lets you look up the ticker symbol of a particular firm
`//QUICK <symbol>`	Provides a summary of all the information available on a particular company, including news, financial statements, statistical comparisons and investor reports. Obtain the stock symbol before giving this command. Not all information available via **//QUICK** is included within the Tier 1,2, or 3 fixed pricing scheme.
`//DB`	Dun & Bradstreet Reports
`//INVEST`	Analyst reports on particular companies
`//MMS`	Economic, currency, debt, and stock market trends
`//OAG`	Official Airline Guide
`//STORE`	Online shopping

Tier 1: New & Quotes ($25/month)

`//CQ` and `//CQE`	Current stock market quotes
`//HQ`	Daily stock market data, up to one year old as well as monthly summaries back to 1979
`//FUTURES`	Futures and Index quotes
`//DJA`	Dow Jones Average
`//DJNEWS`	Dow Jones News

Tier 2: Forecasts & Analyses ($25/month)

`//FUNDS`	Mutual Funds performance reports
`//WATCH`	Corporate ownership data
`//WSW`	Wall Street Week transcripts
`//MG`	Media General Financial services
`//EPS`	Zachs Corporate Earnings Estimator
`//SP`	Standard and Poor's Profiles and Earnings Estimates
`//INNOVEST`	Innovest Technical Analysis Reports
`//BUSINESS`	News Retrieval's Business and Finance report
`//RELEASE`	Press Release Wires

Tier 3: General Interest ($12.95/month)

`//ENCYC`	Online Encyclopedia
`//CAREER`	Career Management advice
`//SCHOOL`	College Selection Service
`//SPORTS`	Sports News
`//BOOKS`	Book reviews
`//MOVIES`	Movie reviews

Online literature

The Online Public Access Catalogs (OPACs) are primarily catalogs and periodical search services. However, more and more books are also ending up online. If you still read, maybe you'd like to have a look at them. Since the Great Literature CD-ROM is available for $35 and includes the text of many great books (and some not so great ones), you'd probably be better off getting the CD if you want more than a few of the classics. For information, contact Bureau Development, Inc., 141 New Road, Parsippany, NJ 07054

Project Gutenberg

The objective of Project Gutenberg is to make noncopyrighted works of value available in electronic form. This includes novels such as *Moby Dick,* the collected works of Shakespeare, Jane Austin, etc. The work of Project Gutenberg is therefore parallel to Barry Shein's Online Book Initiative, housed on world.std.com.

There is now a BITNET LISTSERV on Project Gutenberg. To subscribe, send email to `LISTSERV@UIUCVME.BITNET` and on the first line of the text, put: `SUB GUTNBERG <Name>`. Here `<Name>` is your legal name, such as `Bernard Aboba`, not your user ID.

Online Book Initiative

The Online Book Initiative (OBI) was started by Barry Shein, Chief Sysop of The World.

Texts in the Online Book Initiative archives are available via anonymous `ftp` from world.std.com in directory /obi/. Some of the works available include works by A. E. Houseman, Charles Dickens, Sir Arthur Conan Doyle, Emily Bronte, Ezra Pound, the Founding Fathers, George Bush, Henry David Thoreau, Jane Austen, Katherine Mansfield, Kipling, Lewis Carroll, Martin Luther King, Melville, Phillip Agee, Tennyson, Wilfred Owen, William Blake, William Butler Yeats, John Milton, Aesop, Joseph Conrad, and J. W. Barrie.

For more information

More and more libraries are coming online all the time. These include public, university, and national libraries (such as the Library of Congress). Many university libraries are now also accessible via the Internet.

Library Guides

Due to the rapid pace of change, online library lists go out of date rapidly. If you have access to USENET, you can get the latest list of Internet libraries by reading the USENET group `comp.internet.library`. A list of libraries is also included in the Internet Resource Guide, available by anonymous FTP to `nnsc.nsf.net`.

If you do not have an Internet account but can reach the Internet via email, you can get the latest list of libraries by sending mail to `LISTSERV@UNMVM.BITNET`. On the first line put **GET Internet LIBRARY**.

Several guides to Internet libraries are available via `ftp ftp.unt.edu, cd /pub/library`. These include Billy Barron's guide to OPACs (library.*), Dana Noonan's guide (metlib2.txt), and Deidre Stanton's guide to Australian and New Zeland OPACs.

Periodicals listings

The Association of Research Libraries maintains a directory of electronically distributed periodicals. To obtain this directory, send mail to `LISTSERV@OTTAWA.BITNET`. On the first line put **GET ejournl1 directory**, and on the second line put **GET ejournal2 directory**.

CHAPTER 12: USENET

What is network news?

Network news is a huge distributed conferencing system that as of August 1993, involved an estimated 100,000 sites, 4,000 newsgroups, and over 2 million users.

Network news offers something for everyone. If you are a technical or business professional, net news offers many moderated and unmoderated conferences on specific topics, peopled by individuals with a very high level of expertise. If you are a hobbyist, net news also offers discussion groups for hobbies such as cooking and fishing.

Although the terms network news and USENET are often used synonmously, the term USENET actually refers to a specific set of newsgroups (sometimes referred to as *core* hierarchies) that are administered based on agreed-upon rules. These include procedures for creation and removal of newsgroups, and rules against commercial use outside of product announcements.

Network news has grown so large that it is virtually impossible to read even a substantial fraction of it. Therefore describing it is like describing *War and Peace* after skimming it for five minutes.

In a regularly reposted message on the newsgroup news.announce.newusers called "What is USENET?," Professor Gene Spafford (spaf@cs.purdue.EDU) approached defining USENET by discussing what it is not. In rebuttal, Edward Vielmetti posted "What is USENET? NOT" (which also has become a classic, being reposted on news.answers), which argued that USENET was changing so quickly that it was difficult to characterize, that

it was many of the things that Professor Spafford said it wasn't or might soon become.

USENET versus other hierarchies

USENET hierarchies include:

comp: Groups relating to computers.

news: Groups relating to USENET itself, such as group creation, news server administration, etc.

rec: Recreation-related groups.

sci: Science-related groups.

soc: Societally oriented groups, such as those relating to politics or a particular ethnic group.

talk: Blabbing, potentially on controversial topics.

misc: Miscellaneous groups; anything not fitting in the other categories.

There are also other hierarchies outside of USENET. These hierarchies are free to create their own rules and procedures. These include:

alt: This hierarchy is for discussion of controversial topics. Since USENET conference creation rules do not apply within the alt hierarchy, it is also frequently used to start new groups.

amiga: This hierarchy is for discussion of the Amiga computer by Commodore Business Machines.

biz: This hierarchy is for commercial discussions, which are not permitted on USENET. This might include posting of marketing materials or price lists.

bionet: This hierarchy is for biological and biochemical research. Postings in some of these groups may be searchable via Z39.50

using electronic mail (see Chapter 14 for details).

bit: This hierarchy is for LISTSERV lists gatewayed from BITNET. As a result, BITNET rules apply to postings.

gnu: Discussion of Free Software Foundation products such as gcc compiler, GNU Emacs, etc.

hepnet: Hierarchy for the High Energy Physics Network.

ieee: Institute of Electronic and Electrical Engineers hierarchy.

k12: K12Net hierarchy. See Chapter 26 for more information.

opinions: Hierarchy for posting of court decisions, including those of the U.S. Supreme Court.

pubnet: Hierarchy shared by public access Internet services such as World and Netcom.

vmsnet: Hierarchy for discussion of DEC's VMS operating system.

Finally, there are institutional, local, regional and national hierarchies: Examples include:

ucb: University of California, Berkeley hierarchy.

sco: Hierarchy for conferences relating to the Santa Cruz Operation.

ba: Bay Area regional hierarchy.

ca: California regional hierarchy.

chile: Chilean hierarchy.

de: German hierarchy.

fj: Japanese hierarchy.

relcom: Russian hierarchy.

Where to start

In order to orient the uninitiated, a number of conferences have been developed catering to the new user. On starting to read net news, you should subscribe to these conferences.

news.announce.newusers contains periodic postings of interest to new users. These include a series of tutorials that have now become classics, including "What is USENET?" and "What is USENET – NOT." Lists of USENET and alt hierarchy conferences are periodically

posted to this conference, so it's a good place to start if you want to figure out where to go next.

Lists of active newsgroups and alternative newsgroup hierarchies are also posted to news.announce.newgroups, which is also where the Call For Votes, Results, and Request For Discussion notices are posted. These relate to the creation of new groups, discussed later.

news.announce.conferences is where international symposia are announced; this group is not for announcement of new newsgroups. news.lists also contains lots of useful information, including lists of USENET and alt groups.

Just the FAQs, ma'am

A comprehensive system has been developed for posting and archiving Frequently Asked Questions (FAQ) listings. FAQ listings were developed in order to avoid discussing the same topics over and over again.

One of the first rules of good citizenship is to read a newgroup's FAQ listing before posting. FAQ listings are typically posted to the newgroup on a regular basis (often monthly or bi-weekly), as well as to the .answers newsgroup for the relevant hierarchy, such as alt.answers, comp.answers, sci.answers, misc.answers, soc.answers, or rec.answers. FAQs in USENET hierarchy groups are also posted on news.answers.

If you can't find the relevant FAQ file in one of these groups, FAQs are also available via `ftp rtfm.mit.edu, cd /pub/usenet-by-group/<conference-name>`, or via `mail mail-server@rtfm.mit.edu,` body: `help.`

The moderator of news.answers and the maintainer of the FAQ system is Jonathan Kamens, who deserves our thanks. Before sending mail to the FAQ maintainer requesting a copy of the FAQ, please make an effort to obtain the FAQ file by one of these methods. If you aren't willing to take your time to do this, don't be surprised if the FAQ maintainer refuses to take their time to mail you the FAQ file.

Access to network news

There are many ways to read net news. These include using a newsreader on a UNIX host, getting a news feed, using a message reader, or obtaining net news on CD-ROM.

▽ UNIX newsreaders

This is the most common way to read network news. UNIX news readers include tin, nn, trn, and rn. Although rn is the most common reader, it is line-oriented and fiendishly difficult to use. Many systems now also offer full-screen readers such as nn and tin. For beginners, the forthcoming release of pine with news reading capability is recommended.

▽ Message readers

Message readers allow users to download message packets and view them offline. Popular packet formats on other networks include the QWK standard, first created for PCBoard systems and used on systems on PCRelay/PostLink, QNet, and FidoNet networks.

UQWK is a QWK packer for UNIX that is available via `ftp ftp.gte.com, cd /pub/uqwk`. The program both packs up mail and news in QWK format, and accepts reply (REP) packets from the user. However, the original QWK standard has not caught on with network news readers since it was not created to handle the long header fields of news messages. The long awaited QWK II standard, recently released, addresses this issue.

A new net news packet standard has also been developed. Both packers and readers are now available for several platforms, and more are on the way. For more information, consult alt.usenet.offline-reader.

You may ask "How is using a message reader different from receiving mail and news via UUCP?" The advantages of a message reader over receiving messages using UUCP include:

• Ease of setup for users. Users do not need to understand anything about UUCP, nor do they need a UUCP implementation to download message packets and read them.

• Ease of administration. Message packers create packets on the fly, and use compression methods such as ZIP. In contrast, news servers create packets whether users request them or not, and use the less efficient UNIX compress, or in the case of NNTP, no compression at all. The result is that system administrators can save many megabytes of disk space by using message readers instead.

• Cost savings. Since message packers use ZIP compression technology and ZMODEM transfer protocols, files are transferred more efficiently than by using the UUCP protocol and UNIX compress. Since ZMODEM transfers speeds can be up to 50 percent faster than UUCP, and ZIP compression 20 percent more effective than UNIX compress, total savings can be large.

These benefits can acrue regardless of packet format. For more information on USENET message packers and readers, see the "For more information" section at the end of this chapter.

▽ UUCP

UUCP access to USENET offers some of the same advantages as message readers, such as support for batch downloading and compression. However, UUCP software is more complex to set up and as a result is not as popular with beginners. USENET implementations for microcomputers include uConnect (Macintosh), and FSUUCP, UULINK, UUPlus, and Waffle/HellDiver for the PC.

▽ BBSes

BBSes offer the ability to import USENET conferences into the message base. If you have a BBS in your area that carries USENET, this may be an attractive alternative.

If you connect to a FidoNet system that carries conferences gatewayed from USENET and supports points, you can also read USENET via point software such as MacWoof or EZPoint. For more information on Points, please turn to Chapter 18: Point Software.

However, be aware that such systems often carry a restricted number of groups and may not support features such as moderated newsgroups, keyword searches, expiration dates, message cancellation, or kill files.

▽ CD-ROM

If your questions typically refer to material more than two weeks old, you also may consider subscribing to Net News CD, which delivers you a CD of virtually all of USENET every two weeks or so.

▽ NNTP newsreaders

Graphical newsreaders operating over TCP/IP are now available for the Macintosh and Windows. On the Macintosh, these include Nuntius and NewsWatcher; under Windows, publicly distributable graphical readers include WinVN and Windows Trumpet.

▽ Cable and satellite feeds

News feeds are now available by satellite from firms such as PageSat (pagesat@pagesat.com) and proposed services such as VODEM and cable company feeds are also in the works. These services typically only support read-only access, but most sites receive much more than they post in any case. For information on VODEM, contact jbrown@speedway.net.

Basic features of the network news message format

The network news message format, defined in RFC 1036, was designed as an extension of the mail message format of RFC 822. Since the news message format defines the capabilities of the system, it is worthwhile to briefly discuss some of the header fields:

Approved: For moderated newsgroups. Indicates that the message has been approved for posting, and by whom.

Date: The date the message was created.

Expires: Indicates the date after which the message should be expired.

Followup-To: indicates which article this message is a reply to.

From: Indicates who posted the message.

Keywords: Indicates keywords describing the message, which may be searched.

Lines: The message line count.

Message-ID: A unique identifier that includes the year and date as well as the poster's site. The message ID allows news servers to detect and eliminate duplicate messages.

Newsgroups: Indicates the groups to which the message is to be posted. There can be more than one; this is called cross-posting.

NNTP-Posting-Host: Indicates the host posting the message via NNTP. This may not be the same as the machine of the poster.

Organization: The organization of the poster.

Path: This field indicates the machines to which the message has travelled. This field is used in order to prevent a message being sent to the same machine twice.

Subject: Indicates what the message is about.

Supersedes: This field is used for periodic postings that are to supercede earlier versions of the same posting.

Xref: Refers to the article number within the other groups to which a message is posted.

Below is a message header taken from the moderated newsgroup news.announce.newusers.

```
Xref: netcom.com news.lists:1690 news.announce.newusers:568
news.answers:7288
Path:
netcom.com!csus.edu!wupost!howland.reston.ans.net!gatech!ent
erpoop.mit.edu!senator-bedfellow.mit.edu!athena.mit.edu!jik
From: jik@athena.mit.edu (Jonathan I. Kamens)
Newsgroups: news.lists,news.announce.newusers,news.answers
Subject: List of Periodic Informational Postings, Part 2/5
Supersedes: <periodic-postings2_731400219@athena.mit.edu>
Followup-To: poster
Date: 5 Apr 1993 05:52:59 GMT
Organization: Massachusetts Institute of Technology
Lines: 1428
Approved: news-answers-request@MIT.Edu
Expires: 19 May 1993 05:52:47 GMT
Message-ID: <periodic-postings2_733989167@athena.mit.edu>
References: <periodic-postings_733989167@athena.mit.edu>
NNTP-Posting-Host: pit-manager.mit.edu
```

Language support

Alternative character sets used on USENET include Japanese, Vietnamese, Korean, Chinese and Russian, to name a few. For information on Chinese newsreaders, see the FAQ for alt.chinese.text, also posted in news.answers. RFC 1459 discusses Vietnamese character sets. RFC 1468 discusses Japanese character sets.

Network news traditions

Network news has strong traditions that beginners often find baffling. These include signatures, distributions and rot13.

Signatures

Network news users often append material to the end of their messages, such as information on how to reach them. This can be helpful in case the message header does not provide a usable electronic mail address. The appended material is known as the signature, and it is kept within a file known as the signature file.

Since signatures are appended to most messages, they comprise a not insignificant fraction of the total traffic volume. In order to keep costs down, users are expected to keep signatures to a minimum. Information such as your email address, U.S. mail address, and fax number is sufficient. If you have something particularly witty to say, you might append a one-line phrase, but anything more is likely to engender complaints from the net police.

Flaming

Murphy's Second Law of Distributed Conferencing is:

Your chances of getting the answer to a question are proportional to the probability of being called an idiot for asking.

Network news has an elaborate tradition that is often difficult for beginners or "newbies" to grasp. Rule-breakers are kept in line by tirades known as "flames." Other punishments are also available: those heedless of strong traditions against advertising and censorship, may eventually earn a conference in the alt.fan hierarchy devoted to making fun of them.

Flame wars also often center on philosophical arguments with no clear means of resolution, such as a debate between advocates of Intel and Motorola processors. The tradition of flaming is so strong that there are even

conferences wholly devoted to flaming, such as alt.flame. If you enjoy being insulted, post a question in this conference and see what happens.

Offensive material

Many conferences in the USENET or alternative hierarchies contain potentially objectionable material. This includes everything from offensive jokes to material of an adult nature or newsgroups inappropriate for access by children. Educators and parents may therefore struggle with reconciling the educational value of network news with the presence of such material.

It should also be understood that community standards differ both within the U.S. and in other countries. Material which may not be cause for concern in New York City may be illegal in other parts of the world.

One of the fundamental principles of net news is the absence of censorship. Just as with security, the responsibility for what appears on a machine rests with the administrator of that machine, *not* with other administrators or the network itself.

If you find yourself in a group that allows anonymous postings, or handles, or anything else you find offensive, you can:

• Set your newsreader to ignore offensive postings.
• Read such postings, but refuse to reply to them.
• Read or create your own moderated groups where such postings are not allowed.

If you administer a site on which you wish to restrict access to material you find offensive, you can:

• Find a conferencing medium more geared toward K12 education, such as FrEdMail, or software more amenable to central control, security, and authentication, such as PCRelay and PostLink.
• Refuse to import offensive conferences.
• Restrict access to certain groups.

Anatomy of a Flame

Inane subject heading

```
Joanne Foobar: >>>What has USENET done to my brain? Tue, 3 Aug 93 05:16
In article <CC7nK0.G9x@foo.com> stan@foo.com (Stan Foobar) writes:
>In article <ZD4mM0.G7z@foo.com> joanne@foo.com (Joanne Foobar) writes:
>>In article <XP5nI0.G5w@foo.com> john@foo.com (John Foobar) writes:
>>>In article <DE7yJ0.G3p@foo.com> stan@foo.com (Stan Foobar) writes:
```

Cascade of replies

Wasteful quoting of previous inane messages

```
>>>>Your supercilious drivel does not belong in a newsgroup.
>>>>What kind of idiot are you?
>>>>-Stan
```

Gratuitous insult (required)

Annoyed retort

```
>>>First class. Should I create a mailing list for it, then?
>>>-John
```

Inane reply

```
>>No! There is already a mailing list for drivel: com-priv@psi.com.
>>-Joanne
```

```
>Why are you continuing this idiotic conversation?
>Are you some kind of trouble maker?
>-Stan
```

Countering gratuitous insult

```
Oh! Not a cascade!
Are you some kind of parrot?
-Joanne
```

Inane reply to inane reply to inane reply

• Mail postings from unmoderated conferences to referees prior to reposting on the system, effectively converting an unmoderated conference into a moderated one for the site in question. However, if you do this, you may not pass on the altered group to other sites.

rot13

One method for screening objectionable material is to encipher it, therefore requiring an individual to willfully make an effort to read it.

Rot13 is a weak cipher that involves replacing characters in a message with characters 13 positions ahead in a cyclic rotation. It is used within core groups such as rec.humor; since the alt hierarchy was designed to carry controversial material, it is not used there. If you encounter a rot13 message, you can use your newsreader to decipher it.

Distributions, local and regional conferences

It is useful to limit the distribution of a post if you are selling an item such as a car, which cannot be easily transported over long distances, or are looking for a job in the local area. In both cases there is no need for readers halfway around the world to see your message, since it will be of no use to them.

One way of limiting distribution is to place your message into a local conference. For example, there are groups local to a particular Internet service. There are also regional groups such as ba.forsale. If there is no local conference for your topic, you can post your message in a global conference, but limit distribution to your local area. For example, to sell a NeXT cube, you could post to comp.sys.next.marketplace, yet limit the distribution to the Bay Area or your local university.

To limit distribution to a local group outside your area, post the message from a machine in that area. Don't try to post a job opening for distribution only within Japan from a Chicago area Internet service provider. This won't work unless the Chicago service provider had a link to Japan, since all news servers to which it fed the message would reject it as not applying to them, and therefore the message would not propagate.

For information on distributions, see the posting Known Geographic Distributions, posted in news.lists. A list of distributions is also given at the end of this chapter.

The .newsrc file

The .newsrc file is used by UNIX newreaders in order to keep track of the groups you have subscribed to, and the messages you have read. A typical .newsrc file might look like:

```
alt.flame: 1-5531
alt.noodle:
comp.protocols.ppp! 1-47
news.lists!
```

Here the ! means that you are unsubscribed; the numbers indicate the message you have read, and : indicates you have subscribed. The above .newsrc indicates that you are an avid reader of alt.flame, subscribe to alt.noodle, but haven't read anything in the group (no doubt because there is no traffic), subscribed to comp.protocols.ppp, but only read up to message 47 before unsubscribing, and unsubscribed to news.lists.

The newsreader gotcha

One of the most annoying things about UNIX newsreaders is that they usually default to asking you whether you want to subscribe to each group when you first start reading news. With more than 3000 newsgroups, this is ludicrous.

How do you turn this off? Most newsreaders create the .newsrc file when started, with each group having a : after groups (for subscribe). They then replace the : with a ! for each group you unsubscribe to. You can short circuit this process by quiting the newreader shortly after startup, and editing the .newsrc file yourself.

Better yet, you can use the shell script below to unsubscribe to all groups before editing:

unsubscribe shell script

```
#!/bin/sh
#
sed -e s/:/!/ $HOME/.newsrc >$HOME/.newsrc.new
rm $HOME/.newsrc; mv $HOME/.newsrc.new .newrc
```

After you've set up your .newsrc file, the next step is to tell your newsreader not to prompt for new groups. How this is done will depend on your reader, but it is usually handled either from within the initialization file, or as a command-line option.

tin

tin is a full screen hierarchical newsreader, which can be used to read news from a remote NNTP server. Command-line options include:

-f <file>	Instead of the .newsrc use <file> for the list of groups.
-M <address>	mail unread news to an address. Be careful with this one!
-q	Don't ask for new newsgroups.
-r <NNTP serv>	read news from server set in NNTPSERVER environment variable, or /etc/nntpserver.
-w	Post and quit option.
-Z	Exit with unread news status. Exit code = 0 for no news, 1 for error, 2 for unread news.

When tin starts up, it creates the .tin directory, and the setup files within it, such as tinrc and attributes. In order to get your .newsrc file created without having to answer a zillion questions, type **q** after the program starts up.

```
% tin
tin118 1.1 PL8 (c) Copyright 1991-92 Iain Lea.
Reading news active file...
Subscribe to new group relcom.rferl (y/n/q) [n]: q
Reading attributes file...
Reading newsgroups file...
Creating .newsrc...
```

You will then be placed in the group overview mode; type **Q** to exit tin. Run the shell script to turn all groups off, and edit the file to subscribe to selected groups. Use the **-q** option in order not to be prompted for new groups.

Environmental variables read by Tin include:

ORGANIZATION	Sets the Organization field when posting. Can also be specified in the file $HOME/.tin/organization
REPLYTO	Have replies go to another address. Can also be specified in the $HOME/.tin/replyto file.
TINRC	This variable contains command-line options that should be invoked on entering tin. For example, you can do a **setenv TINRC -q** to never see new newsgroups.

Tin reads signature files from $HOME/.Sig or $HOME/.signature. The kill file is located in $HOME/.tin/kill.

Since Tin is a hierarchical newsreader, to read an article, you must first select a group, then a thread, then an article within it. This is what the group selection menu looks like:

```
Group Selection (1)                    h=help

1   40  netcom.internet  Internet access at Netcom


<n>=set current to n, TAB=next unread, /=search pattern,
c)atchup, g)oto, j=line down, k=line up, h)elp, m)ove,
q)uit, r=toggle all/unread, s)ubscribe, S)ub pattern,
u)nsubscribe, U)nsub pattern, y)ank in/out

        *** End of Groups ***
```

Group manipulation commands include:

<n>	set current group to n
TAB	next unread
/	search pattern
c	catchup
g	goto group
j	line down
k	line up
h	help
q	quit
r	toggle unread

Note that the Subscribe and Unsubcribe pattern options only apply to groups already selected in the .newrc file. Once you've unsubscribed to a group and changed the .newrc file, you can't subscribe to it using the pattern selection mechanism.

Thread manipulation commands include:

<n>	set current thread to n
TAB	next unread thread
/	search pattern
CTRL K	Kill/select
a	author search
c	catchup
j	line down
k	line up
K	mark thread read
l	list thread
m	mail
q	quit
r	toggle unread
s	save
w	post

Tin article reading commands include:

a	Search forward for author
A	Search backward for author
C	Mark articles in group as read and move to next group
d	Rot-13 decoding toggle
D	Cancel posting. Only applies to articles you posted.
f	Followup posting with quoting
F	Followup posting without quoting
h	Help screen
k	Mark thread read and advance to next thread.
m	mail article to someone
M	configure options
n	next article
N	next unread article
p	previous article
P	previous unread article
Q	quit
r	reply by mail with quoting
R	reply by mail without quoting
s	save article
t	exit to group level
w	post article
z	mark as unread
/	forward search
?	backward search
|	pipe article to command

nn

nn is a popular full screen newsreader, much easier to use than rn.

Command line options include:

-a0   marks all articles as unread.

-s<string> Searches for articles matching subject <string>.

-X   Includes unsubscribed as well as subscribed groups. Can be combined with the search option.

The init file

When you first start up nn, it creates the .nn directory, as well as .newsrc file, and reads from the .nn/init file. Useful options are:

new-group-action 0
Ignores new newsgroups

new-group-action 1
Inserts new newsgroups at start of .newsrc

new-group-action 2
Inserts new newsgroups at end of .newsrc

new-group-action 4
Asks if you want to add each group (default)

sequence
Lists groups to be shown, in order of appearance. If you don't want to see a group, put a ! in front of it. For example !alt says not to subscribe to alt groups, comp.protocols says to show all comp.protocols groups.

stop <int>
Shows <int> lines of a message before prompting to continue.

In the next column is a listing of nn commands.

Command	What it does
A	advance to next article or group
a-z	select article
B	go back one article or group
C	cancel an article
D	decrypt rot13 article
(SPACE BAR)	next screen
(RET)	same as (SPACE BAR) , but don't mark
/	regular expression search
.	repeat regular expression search
F	follow up
H	show complete digest
I	mark article
G	goto group or open folder

Command	What it does
=	go back to menu
?	online help
J	change marking of menu articles
K	Kill file setup
M	mail article
N	next group
P	previous group
R	reply to article by mail
S	save article with full header
-	select range of articles
*	select all articles with current subject
!	shell command prefix
(TAB)	skip lines starting with same char as last line
~	unselect all articles
U	unsubscribe or subscribe to group (toggle)
V	version information
Y	show overview of groups
:q!	quit nn without updating .newsrc
:X	quit nn, mark current group as read
:!<shell command>	execute command
:bug	send a bug report
:cd <dir>	change directory
:compile	compile & reload kill file
:decode	decode uuencoded article(s)
:man	read online manual
:mkdir <dir>	create directory
:post	post new article
:pwd	print current directory
:rmail	read incoming mail
:show groups	show subscriptions, etc.
:show kill	how kill file entries
:sort <mode>	sort menu by subject, age, or arrival
:unread (N)	mark last N articles of current group as unread
:unshar	unshar article(s)

NNTP newsreaders

While most people still use traditional newsreaders, graphical newsreaders operating over TCP/IP are remarkably powerful and easy to use. These include NewsGrazer (NeXT), Newswatcher, InterNews, and Nuntius (Macintosh), and WinVN and Windows Trumpet (Windows). All of these programs require a TCP/IP stack. For the Macintosh this will be MacTCP; for Windows, it will be a

Windows Sockets–compliant stack, such as Trumpet Winsock.

TCP/IP newsreaders utilize the Network News Transfer Protocol (NNTP) to transfer news, although there are some (such as uConnect) that can also use UUCP over TCP/IP. All these programs support NNTP v1.0; version 2.0 of NNTP, which will support authentication and compression, is due out shortly and will be backwards compatible.

Newswatcher

NewsWatcher

Newswatcher provides a graphical, threaded interface to net news. Since you can see all the groups that your host subscribes to, you can easily move between them without having to continually subscribe or unsubscribe.

Starting up

When entering NewsWatcher, the software requests the list of newsgroups from the news server specified in the user's .newsrc file. It also requests the full group list.

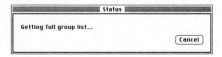

Reading news groups

After the list of groups has been retrieved, it will be displayed in a window, along with a list of new groups.

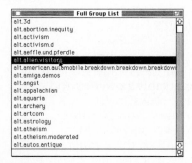

In order to read a given group, double-click on it. The articles in the group will then be retrieved from the Net News Transfer Protocol (NNTP) server.

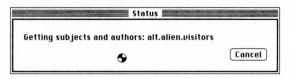

After the articles have been retrieved, the group window will then open up, showing all the threads in the group.

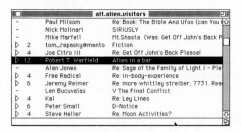

To look at the messages within a thread, select a thread by clicking on it.

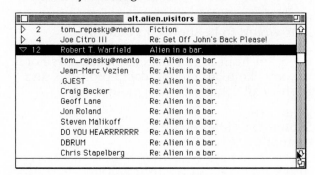

Setup

Before using Newswatcher, you will need to select **Personal Information...** from the **Prefs** menu, which will bring up a dialog box.

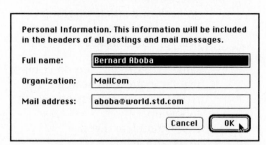

Newswatcher will need information on your remote host in order to write to and read from your .newsrc file. This can be set by selecting **Remote Host Information...** from the **Prefs** menu.

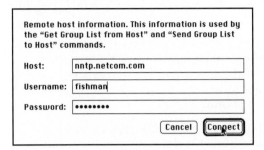

You will also need to give information about the server by selecting **Server Information...** from the **Prefs** menu.

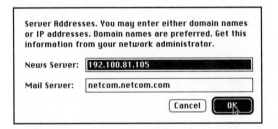

At the end of every message, Newswatcher will append a signature file. This can be set up via the **Signature...** entry on the **Prefs** menu.

Here is the signature dialog box:

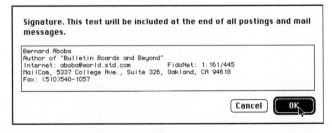

It is also possible to set other preferences via the **Other Options...** selection from the **Prefs** menu.

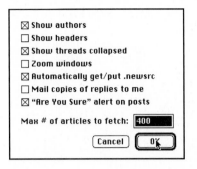

Nuntius

Nuntius is another Macintosh NNTP reader, that takes a hierarchical approach to reading news. For example, here is the path to comp.sys.mac.comm:

When you open up a conference, Nuntius threads it by subject. You can then select a subject:

When you double click on the subject, it opens into a window, with messages shown in outline form.

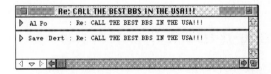

As with System 7, clicking on the triangle allows you to see the individual messages in the thread.

InterNews

InterNews is a highly recommended Macintosh NNTP newsreader from Dartmouth that is free for educational use, and $25 for commercial use. It can be obtained via **ftp ftp.dartmouth.edu, cd /pub/mac**. InterNews threads messages by subject, separates out the headers, and allows you to create icons representing collections of newsgroups. It is therefore the most appropriate newsreader for use by beginners.

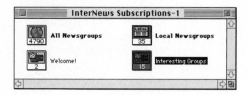

WinVN

WinVN is a Windows-sockets compatible NNTP newsreader. To set it up, you must edit the WINVN.INI file before you begin. This includes setting the NNTP server name, the username, the mail address, and the organization. Below is an example setup file:

```
[winvn]
UseSocket=1
NNTPHost=planet.uu.holonet.net
CommString=COM1:9600,e,8
DoList=1
NetUnSubscribedColor=0,60,200
GroupSeenColor=0,0,200
FontSize=0
FontFace=
FontBold=0
NewWndGroup=1
NewWndArticle=0
ThumbTrack=0
SaveArtAppend=1
UserName=Bernard Aboba
MailAddress=aboba@world.std.com
Organization=MailCom
NNTPPort=119
ArticleFixedFont=1
ArticleFontFace=Helv
ArticleFontSize=18
PrintFontFace=0
PrintFontSize=40
AskComm=0
```

Creating a USENET newsgroup

Rules have been devised for creating groups within the USENET newsgroup hierarchy. The steps are:

1. **Request For Discussion.** A Request For Discussion (RFD) is posted to

news.announce.newgroup and in groups or mailing lists relevant to the topic. All the details of the conference need not be worked out prior to the RFD announcement, since this is one of the reasons for the discussion period.

Actual discussion of the RFD takes places in news.groups. The goal of the discussion period is to come to agreement on aspects of the proposal, such as whether the group is needed at all, and if so, whether it should be moderated (and who will moderate) and what the group should be called.

2. **Call For Votes.** After discussion has crystallized and it is decided that the group is needed, a Call For Votes (CFV) announcement is issued in news.announce.newgroups.

The CFV announcement should include instructions on how to vote. A fair chance must be given to yes or no proponents; often this is done by establishing mail servers for yes and no votes, both on the same machine. CFV announcements are repeated during the voting period to remind people of the ongoing vote.

3. **Voting.** Voting periods last 21 to 30 days, after which time votes are tallied and a list of voters and how they voted is posted to news.announce.newgroups for verification. Winning groups must have at least 100 more yes than no votes and at least a 66 percent favorable response. Groups that are voted down must wait at least six months to be voted on again.

During the process, the moderator of news.announce.newgroups will post a periodic message on the status of the various proposals, as well as listings of the newly created groups. The results of the votes are also posted to this group. Of course, just because a group is created doesn't mean that sites will subscribe to it, although the chances of that happening for core groups is high.

Creating an alt newsgroup

The above rules do not apply to the alternative or local newsgroup hierarchies. Creating an alt group is considerably simpler, which is why many new groups are begun in this hierarchy. This is not always a wise decision, since alt groups are distributed less widely than core USENET groups. If it is intended that a group eventually become a core USENET group, it may make more sense to start the group there. Once a group has been started in the alt hierarchy, it may not be easy to get people to switch to the equivalent core group if and when it is created.

The recommended procedure for creating an alt group is:

• First choose a group name.
• Post a proposal for the group, including the proposed name and charter in `alt.config`.
• Listen to advice on whether the group is needed, and what it should be named.
• Since there is no formal vote for creation of alt groups, if reaction is generally favorable, you can post a "newgroup" control message, or you can get a news administrator to post one for you. In order to convince other administrators of the group's legitimacy so that they will honor it, the control message should include an explanation and be posted from a normal account, as opposed to a "handle".

While some newsgroup administrators will automatically create the group, others will examine the newgroup control message and the discussion in alt.config and make a decision on a case-by-case basis. If the group appears especially stupid, some administrators may even post a "rmgroup" message in response to the "newgroup" message in order to prevent the group from being created. Many stupid alt groups are now being created, such as alt.adjective.noun.verb.verb.verb, generalizing from previous groups such as alt.swedish.chef.bork.bork.bork, alt.french.captain.borg.borg.borg, and alt.supreme.court.bork.bork.bork.

Network news Q&A

I noticed a news group called alt.enya.puke.puke.puke. Is this legitimate?

No. This group was never proposed in alt.config. Unfortunately, since many Internet sites now process group creation messages automatically, such groups may take a while to be killed, if ever.

Where can I get source code for UNIX mail utilities? Archivers? Net news software?

Try `ftp ftp.uunet.net`.

What are the alt.fan groups about?

Having an alt.fan group named after you is used as a form of punishment on USENET. Rabid flamers inhabit these groups, berating the person for whom the group is named, calling everything they say "stupid," referring to their personal or physical inadequacies, etc. Hell hath no fury like an alt.fan.

What are all these kibo newsgroups?

Kibo is the Virtual Personality of James Parry, who created the alt.religion.kibology newsgroup as a joke. The alt.politics.kibo, alt.imploding.kibo, and alt.exploding.kibo newgroups followed. By use of an indexing program, Mr. Parry is able to make Kibo appear omniscient by responding to references to Kibo in any of thousands of newsgroups.

For more information

Informational postings

news.answers

A Guide to Buying and Selling on USENET
Mailing Lists Available in USENET
Netnews/LISTSERV Gateway Policy
List of Periodic Information Postings
USENET University FAQ
Known Geographic Distributions
Known University Distributions
Creating A New "alt" Group—Guidelines
Publicly Accessible Mailing lists
alt.usenet.offline-reader FAQ
nn Frequently Asked Questions

Answers to Frequently Asked Questions

FAQs	news.answers, comp.answers, rec.answers, soc.answers, sci.answers, alt.answers, misc.answers
FAQ Archive	`ftp rtfm.mit.edu`, `get /pub/usenet-by-group/<group_name>/`

Help with network news

USENET Q&A	news.announce.newusers
Maps of USENET	news.lists.ps-maps
USENET questions	news.newusers.questions
UUCP	comp.mail.uucp
Group lists	news.lists
FAQs	news.answers
Net news software	news.software.readers
	news.software.nn
USENET policy	news.admin.policy
Administration	news.admin.technical
Message readers	alt.usenet.offline-reader

Sources for network news software

tin	`ftp.uu.net,  cs.orst.edu`
nn	`ftp.uu.net,  cd /news/nn`
	`samba.acs.unc.edu,`
	`/pub/news`
Newsgrazer	`cs.orst.edu`
rn	`ftp.uu.net,  cd  /news/rn`
trn	`ftp.uu.net,  cd  /news`
xrn	`ftp.uu.net,  cd`
	`/packages/X/contrib`
INN	`ftp.uu.net`

Geographic distributions

Geographic distributions available on USENET:

5col: Pioneer Valley/Massachusetts/USA
aa: Ann Arbor/MI/USA
ab: Alberta/CAN
akron: Akron/OH/USA
amiga: Amiga Programmers/Germany*/Germany
atl: Atlanta/GA/USA
atl: Atlantic Provinces/NS, New Brunswick*, Prince
Edward Island*, Newfoundland*/CAN
aus: Australia
austin: Austin/TX/USA
az: Arizona/USA
ba: San Francisco Bay Area/CA/USA
bc: British Columbia/CAN
belwue: Baden-Wuerttemberg/Germany/Europe*
bergen: Bergen County/NJ/USA
bnet: Belgium*
ca: California/USA
can: Canada
capdist: Capital
District/Albany*,Schenectady*,Troy*/NY/USA
ch: Switzerland
chi: Chicago/IL/USA
chico: Chico/CA/USA
chile: Chile
cle: Cleveland/OH/USA
cmh: Columbus/OH/USA
co: Colorado/USA
cov: Coventry/MIDLANDS/UK
dc: Washington D.C./USA
det: Detroit/MI/USA
dfw: Dallas-Ft Worth/TX/USA
dsm: Des Moines/IA/USA
ed: Edinburgh/SCOT/UK
edm: Edmonton/AB/CAN
es: Spain/EUNET
fj: Japan
fl: Florida/USA
ga: Georgia/USA
hfx: Halifax/NS/CAN
houston: Houston/TX/USA

hsv: Huntsville/Alabama*/USA
ia: Iowa/USA
ie: Ireland
il: Illinois/USA
il: Israel
in: Indiana/USA
iowacity: Iowa City/IA/USA
ka: Karlsruhe/BELWUE/Germany*/Europe*
kc: Kansas City/Kansas City metro*/USA
kingston: Kingston/ONT/CAN
ks: Kansas/USA
kw: Kitchener-Waterloo/ONT/CAN
ky: Kentucky/USA
la: Los Angeles county/CA/USA
lon: The London UK area/England*/UK
lou: Louisiana/USA
md: Maryland/USA
mhk: Manhattan/KS/USA
mi: Michigan/USA
miami: Miami/FL/USA
midlands: Midlands/UK
milw: Milwaukee/WI/USA
mlb: Melbourne/BREVARD/FL/USA
mn: Minnesota/USA
mo: Missouri/USA
mtl: Montreal/QC/CAN
na: North America/Mexico*,CAN,USA
nc: North Carolina/USA
ne: New England/Connecticut*,Massachusetts*,Maine*,New
Hampshire*,Rhode Island*,Vermont*/USA
neworleans: New Orleans/LOU/USA
nj: New Jersey/USA
nlnet: Netherlands
no: Norway
ns: Nova Scotia/CAN
ny: New York/USA
nyc: New York City/NY/USA
nz: New Zealand
oau: Orlando/FL/USA
oc: Orange County/CA/USA
oh: Ohio/USA
ok: Oklahoma/USA
ont: Ontario/CAN
or: Oregon/USA
ott: Ottawa/ONT/CAN
pa: Pennsylvania/USA
pdx: Portland/OR/USA
pgh: Pittsburgh/PA/USA
phl: Philadelphia/PA/USA
pnw: Pacific North West/Idaho*,OR,WA/USA
qc: Quebec/CAN
relcom: Relcom/Russia*/SU
rg: Rio Grande Valley/New Mexico*/USA
sac: Sacramento/CA/USA
sarasota: Sarasota/FL/USA
sba: Santa Barbara/CA/USA
sbay: South Bay Region/San Francisco Bay
Area/California/US
sbay: Santa Clara and Santa Cruz Counties/CA/USA
scot: Scotland/UK
scruz: Santa Cruz county/CA/US
sdnet: San Diego county/CA/USA
sea: Seattle/WA/USA
seattle: Seattle/WA/USA
sfnet: Finland
stgt: Stuttgart/Baden-Wuerttemberg/Germany/Europe
stl: St. Louis/MO/USA
su: Soviet Union
tba: Tampa Bay Area/FL/USA
tdw: Tidewater/VA/USA
tn: Tennessee/USA
tor: Toronto/ONT/CAN
triangle: Research Triangle Park area/NC/USA
tx: Texas/USA
uk: United Kingdom
usa: United States of America
utah: Utah/USA
va: Virginia/USA
vic: Victoria/BC/CAN
wa: Washington/USA
wgtn: Wellington/NZ
wi: Wisconsin/USA
wny: Western NY(Rochester,Buffalo)/NY/USA
sa: south africa

CHAPTER 13: REAL-TIME CONVERSATION

Talk, IRC, and MUDs

WHAT IS TALK?

Talk is a program for conversing in real time with one other person logged onto another Internet site. With Internet Relay Chat (irc) several people talk to each other. Talk is therefore like a person-to-person telephone call, while irc is like a conference call. With MUDs, several people interact with each other, but within a virtual reality.

Using talk

To talk to someone, use the command:

```
talk <their address>
```

For example, to chat with foo@bar.net, type:

```
talk foo@bar.net
```

If the other person is logged on, your screen will be cleared, with a dotted line appearing in the middle:

```
[Connection established]
```

```
---------------------------------------------------
```

With talk, what you type goes above the dotted line, and the response goes below it. This is somewhat more convenient than some chat programs where messages and responses are mixed together, making it difficult to see who said what.

The other person must be logged on for the talk request to succeed. If they are not online,

your screen will briefly divide as if a talk session were about to commence, but then you will get the message:

```
[Your party is not logged on]
```

```
---------------------------------------------------
```

When someone wishes to talk to you, you will receive the following message on your screen:

```
Message from Talk_Daemon@world at 14:31 ...
talk: connection requested by foo@bar.net.
talk: respond with:  ntalk foo@bar.net
```

If you want to talk to them, respond with:

```
talk <their address>
```

For example, in this case I would type:

```
talk foo@bar.net
```

Once I do this, my screen will clear, and the dotted line will appear, along with the `Connection established` message.

Be aware that talk facilities may vary between operating systems. For example, HP/UX doesn't include talk as part of the basic OS, and sometimes the appropriate command is named **ntalk**.

How to leave talk

To get out of talk, just press the Esc key on your keyboard, or alternatively type (CTRL)D or (CTRL) C. This will interrupt the session and return you to the prompt.

Example session

Here is a talk session in progress. Note that what I type is given in boldface, and the response is in normal type.

```
OKOK. You can send me mail here if you need me. I'll be
checking in during
the day...
----------------------------------------------------------

OK.  I'm going to ask him about the GUI interface. Bye...

-oo-
```

MacTalk

MacTalk is a Macintosh implementation of talk that requires MacTCP. By selecting **Talk...** from the **File** menu, you can initiate a conversation. In the following example, I attempt to converse with aboba@world.std.com.

After clicking on **Talk**, MacTalk attempts to initiate the conversation by querying the remote machine, which informs the remote user that someone has requested a conversation with them. The status of the talk request is presented within a window that can be brought up by selecting **Status** from the **File** menu.

Internet Talk Radio

Internet Talk Radio (ITR), the creation of Carl Malamud, is a weekly recorded interview program. Sponsored by firms such as Sun Microsystems and O'Reilly & Associates, ITR concentrates on scientific or technical issues. These include a "Geek of the Week" interview with Internet technical figures.

To listen to ITR, you can receive the tranmission live or can retrieve the programs from an FTP archive. Be aware that the ITR files are enormous, often over 20 Mb, and sound quality was erratic on some of the earlier programs.

Since session transcripts would take up a fraction of the space, there are those who argue that Internet Talk Radio is a collosal waste of network bandwidth. While the .au format used in the FTP archive is not directly playable by many Macintosh or PC sound programs, information on conversion utilities is available from the FTP archives, mailing lists and USENET groups given below.

For more information

ITR information

USENET	`alt.internet.talk-radio`
For information	**mail info@radio.com**
For site listings	**mail sites@radio.com**
W3 URL	`http://www.ncsa.uiuc.edu/` `radio/radio.html`

ITR archives

```
ftp ftp.nau.edu, cd /talk-radio
ftp cse.ogi.edu, cd /pub/talk-radio
ftp ftp.uoregon.edu, cd /pub/internet-
talk-radio
```

INTERNET RELAY CHAT

What is IRC?

Imagine a worldwide version of CB radio, with people from all over the world discussing a myriad of topics in more than a dozen different languages. Internet Relay Chat (IRC) is a client/server application that allows people from all over the world to chat in real time as on a party line. In IRC, the clients pass messages to the servers, which communicate with each other.

IRC also has other applications. The clients passing messages to each other may be controlled by humans, or by computers, communicating in a higher-level protocol. The potential applications for IRC-based collaboration are many; the first example was HomerPaint, a collaborative painting program.

Acknowledgments

To Jarkko Oikarinen of Finland (`jto@tolsun.oulu.fi`), the author of IRC.

Accessing IRC

IRC servers include:

csd.bu.edu
nic.funet.fi
ucsu.colorado.edu
coombs.anu.edu.au
badger.ugcs.caltech.edu
poly.polytechnique.fr
sunsystem2.informatik.tu-muenchen.de

IRC is organized into channels that each have a particular topic or theme. Although the language spoken in most channels is English, IRC is widely used all over the world, and so there are also channels for conversation in other languages. IRC commands begin with a /, and are case insensitive. To get into IRC, just type **irc** at the prompt.

IRC commands

/help <topic>

This command gives help on various topics of IRC. The topic NEWUSER gives a paragraph introduction to the program. Other help topics include:

```
!          ADMIN    ALIAS      ASSIGN    AWAY      BASICS
BIND       BYE      CD         CHANNEL   CLEAR     COMMANDS
COMMENT    CONNECT  CTCP       DATE      DIE ECHO
ENCRYPT    EXEC     EXIT       FLUSH     HELP      HISTORY
IF         IGNORE   INFO       INTRO     INVITE    IRCII
JOIN       KICK     KILL       LASTLOG   LEAVE     LINKS
LIST       LOAD     LUSERS     MAIL      MODE      MOTD
MSG        NAMES    NEWUSER    NEWUSER~  NICK      NOTE
NOTICE     NOTIFY   ON         OPER      PART      QUERY
QUIT       QUOTE    REDIRECT   REHASH    REPORT    SAVE
SERVER     SET      SIGNOFF    SLEEP     SQUIT     STATS
SUMMON     TIME     TOPIC      TRACE     TYPE      USERS
VERSION    WAIT     WALL       WALLOPS   WHILE     WHO
WHOIS      WHOWAS   WINDOW
```

/LIST [-MIN n] [-MAX n]

This command lists the channels that are open, and the number of people on the channel. Since this can be a long list, you may wish to use the **-MIN** option to limit the list to only those channels that have a certain number of users present. For example **/LIST -MIN 5** only lists those channels with five or more participants.

/NAMES [-MIN n] [-MAX n]

This command shows the nicknames of the users on every channel. Since hundreds of channels can be open, it is a good idea to restrict the list with the **-MIN** option.

/CHANNEL or /JOIN <Channel Name>

If you see a channel that interests you in the listing, you can join it with this command. For example, **/JOIN #Macintosh** will put you into the Macintosh channel of irc. If a channel has a # at the beginning of the name, it means that you can join several of these channels at once.

/INVITE <Nickname> [<channel>]

This command invites someone to converse on a channel, which by default is your current channel.

/LEAVE <Channel>

This command disconnects you from a channel.

/NICK <Nickname>

This command sets your nickname (limited to nine characters) for the session. For example **/NICK BOZOBRAIN** will set your nickname to BOZOBRAIN. If your chosen nickname conflicts with someone else's, it will not be accepted. If you use IRC regularly, you may want to include the statement
set IRCNICK=<nickname> in your .login file.

/NOTIFY [-] <Nickname>

This command tells you whenever someone enters IRC. **/NOTIFY BOZOBRAIN** will tell you when BOZOBRAIN enters IRC; **/NOTIFY -**

BOZOBRAIN will remove BOZOBRAIN from the notify list.

/WHOIS <nickname>

This command shows the real identity of the person using the nickname. **/WHOIS *** shows who is on the channel. Use **/SET AUTO-WHOWAS ON** in order to automatically execute a /whowas command if someone is not logged on.

/WHOWAS <nickname>

This command shows you who last used a particular nickname.

/WHO <channel name>

This command shows who is on a channel. **/WHO *** lists users in the current channel.

/SIGNOFF or /QUIT

This command gets you out of IRC.

Message oriented commands

/MSG <nickname> <message>

This command sends a private message. Note that only this message will be private; to start a private conversation, use **/QUERY** instead.

/QUERY <nickname>

This command initiates a private conversation. This is better than using **/MSG**, since once the conversation is started, everything you type will go to your conversant, without having to give a **/MSG** command for each line. Typing **/QUERY** will end the conversation.

/AWAY <message>

This command sends a message to anyone who tries to contact you via **/MSG** or **/WHOIS**, telling them you're not at your terminal.

/IGNORE <nickname> | user@domain <types to ignore>

This command prevents messages from <nickname> or from user@domain from coming to you. Types of messages you can ignore:

Message types	What will be ignored
ALL	All messages
INVITES	Invitations to chat
MSG	Private messages
NONE	Don't ignore anything
NOTICE	Notices
PUBLIC	All public conversation (use carefully, negates most of the usefulness of IRC!)

/DCC <action> <nickname> <filename>

DCC allows you to send and receive files over IRC. Actions include:

SEND	Sends file <filename> to user <nickname>
GET	Accepts file <filename> for transfer from user <nickname> who has executed a SEND command
CLOSE	Rejects an attempted transfer
LIST	Shows the status of DCC transfers

/DCC SEND BOZOBRAIN FOO sends file FOO to BOZOBRAIN.

/DCC GET FOOSENDER FOO receives the file from the user who sent file FOO.

/HELP DCC displays the help file on DCC.

Example

In this session I run IRC, list the available channels, take a nickname, join the Macintosh conference, and send a message to someone who was reading *MacWeek* (drats!).

```
% irc
*** Connecting to port 6667 of server world.std.com
*** Welcome to the Internet Relay Network, aboba
*** Your host is world.std.com, running version 2.7.1d
*** If you have not already done so, please read the new
user information with
+/HELP NEWUSER
*** This server was created Fri Jan 31 1992 at 16:17:46
EST
*** There are 567 users on 156 servers
*** 50 users have connection to the twilight zone
*** There are 137 channels.
*** I have 4 clients and 2 servers
MOTD - world.std.com Message of the Day -
MOTD - Be careful out there...
MOTD -
MOTD - ->Spike
* End of /MOTD command.
```

```
/list
```

```
*** Channel    Users  Topic
*** #OCEAN      2
*** #MrYuk      1
*** #clueline   2
*** #Soap       1
*** #Macintosh  2
*** #Maine      5
*** #RxHere     1
*** #Sweden     1
*** #viet       2
*** #taiwan     3
*** #ham-radio  1
*** #deutsch    2
*** #amiga      3
*** #asians     3
*** #Tandy      1
*** #christian  5
*** #AppleIIgs  8
*** #golf       12
```

```
/channel Macintosh
*** aboba has joined channel #Macintosh
```

```
/nick DTPME
*** aboba is now known as DTPME
```

```
/who #Macintosh
```

```
Channel     Nickname  S   User@Host (Name)
#Macintosh  DTPME     H   aboba@world.std.com (Bernard D
Aboba)
#Macintosh  TheWizard G   dmm@worf.harvard.edu (David
Meleedy)
#Macintosh  QuickTime H   someone@129.180.5.147
(somewhere)
```

```
/msg TheWizard Know anything about how Word 5.0 handles
fonts?
```

```
-> *TheWizard* Know anything about how Word 5.0 handles
fonts?
```

```
*** TheWizard is away: reading MacWeek
```

Ircle

ircle 1.0

Ircle is a Macintosh terminal emulator for Internet Relay Chat. It requires MacTCP.

When you first fire up Ircle, if you haven't created a preferences file, you will be prompted with the following dialog box:

Choose a nickname and a server from the list given at the beginning of the article (it doesn't matter which one, so choose the one closest to you). Also give your mail address and real name. If you want to change your preferences later, choose **Preferences...** from the **File** menu.

Other commands can be chosen from the **Commands** menu. Selecting one of these commands will not bring up a dialog box; it merely causes the command to be inserted in the command window. In the window below, I had to type in the `-MIN 5` modifier myself before hitting return to send the command. The results of the command are displayed in the terminal window.

```
bozobrain talking to (nobody)   csd.bu.edu   10:56:42
/list -MIN 5
```

Homer

Homer   HomerPaint

Homer is a less traditional implementation of IRC that cooperates with other applications such as HomerPaint to allow for using IRC as a collaborative environment.

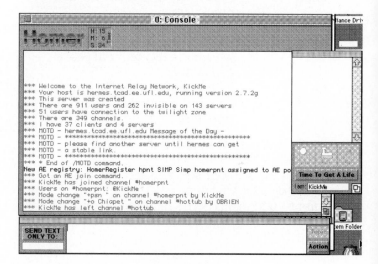

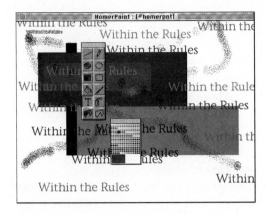

For more information

IRC mailing lists and conferences

alt.irc
Discussion on IRC, all versions

alt.irc.ircii
Focuses on IRC II

operlist-request@eff.org
Mailing list for IRC operators, discusses IRC servers

LISTSERV@grasp1.univ-lyon1.fr
European IRC operators

irchat-request@cc.tut.fi
Mailing list for European users of IRC

d12p+@andrew.cmu.edu
IRC II mailing list (low traffic)

ircd-three-request@eff.org
IRC 3.0 mailing list

Archives of the operlist mailing list are available via **ftp cs.bu.edu, cd /irc/operlist**. The Frequently Asked Questions (FAQ) file for alt.irc is available as /irc/support/alt-irc-faq from the same machine.

IRC information

A useful primer on IRC II has been provided by Nicolas Pioch, pioch@poly.polytechnique.fr, pioch@grasp1.univ-lyon1.fr. It is available via **ftp cs.bu.edu, cd /irc/support/IRCprimer.txt.Z**, as well as **ftp adagio.fy.chalmers.se, cd /pub/irc/docs/IRCprimer.txt.Z** (Europe).

Software sources

IRC Software

IRC server software is available via **ftp cs.bu.edu, cd /irc/servers**. IRC client software is also available via **ftp cs.bu.edu, cd directory /irc/clients**. Ircle is in /irc/clients/macintosh; MS–DOS clients are in /irc/clients/ms-dos. A VMS client is available in /irc/clients/vms.

Playing in the MUDs

Kelly Schwarzhoff

What is MUD?

Multiple User Dungeons (MUDs) are virtual environments in which people can interact. There are hundreds of MUDs ranging from casual social MUDs to adventure MUDs. MUDs are maintained by MUD wizards who have spent thousands of hours maintaining the MUDs.

If you hate spending $100 on a board game that never changes, MUDs are for you. New MUD environments are constantly being created and enhanced. Best of all, you will not pay anything above your standard access fees to play in the MUDs.

Be aware that MUDs are potentially addictive and have ruined more than a few lives. If you don't know when to stop, then you shouldn't start with MUDs.

Kinds of MUDs

Types of MUDs include TinyMUDs, LPMUDs, and MOOs. TinyMUDs are more socially oriented games where people gather in groups and discuss and joke about various subjects. LPMUDs (whose name comes from the initals of the primary author, Lars Penjl) resemble Role-Playing Games (RPGs). Players have quests to attain. MUD Object Oriented (MOO) is an extendible MUD built on an object-oriented language. There are also variations within the categories.

Accessing MUD

You can reach a MUD by `telnet` to a MUD server. The Belgariad is a good MUD to start with. To connect to the Belgariad, type `telnet csa.bu.edu` (128.197.10.202) `4201` from the UNIX shell.

Keep in mind that when connecting to a MUD, you must specify both the address (such as `csa.bu.edu` for the Belgariad) and the port (`4201` for the Belgariad) that you wish to connect to.

Rules of the game

Each of the types of MUDs offers dozens of commands. To get a list of commands, type `help` or `commands` at the prompt. To get an explanation of a command, type `help <command>`. For example, if you want to know what the inventory command does, type `help inventory`. Most MUDs work on a grid system. To move east, you type `east`; to move west, you type `west`, etc.

A useful command is `say`. If a room contains another character, you can talk to him or her by typing, `say <comment>`.

MUDs are administered by wizards. Most MUDs either display the wizards when you connect or you can get a list of Wizards by typing `help wizards`. Wizards are excellent sources of information in case you get confused.

Roles you can play

While some MUDs are set in the Middle Ages, other MUDs are set in different time periods. For example, Space Madness (accessible by typing `telnet moebius.math.okstate.edu 6250`) is a futuristic space adventure. Everyone has different preferences, and the best way to find a MUD you like is to explore them.

For the fanatic

Experienced MUD users can become a Wizard. On many MUDs, Wizards can add and change the existing MUD by using a language similar to C. For example, Wizards in LPMUDs use a language called LP-C. LambdaMOO MUDS use an object-oriented programming language.

It is also possible to create your own MUD. The MUD FAQ describes the various MUDs available. Before you decide to create a MUD though, make sure to ask the system administrator for permission!

Role-Playing Games (RPGs) within MUDs are becoming increasingly popular. The characters gather in a virtual room and one of the players serves as the Gamemaster (game administrator). The Gamemaster describes the make-believe scenario that is taking place and players tell the Gamemaster how they will react.

A graphical MUD, called BSXMUD, is currently available on robin.lysator.liu.se on port 7475. It requires uses of special client software, which is currently only available for the PC. It is available via `ftp lysator.liu.se, cd /pub/lpmud/bsx`. You will need to download both MSCLIENT and the FOSSIL driver X00V124.ZIP. Be aware that the program requires EGA graphics and that it is very difficult to read the text in MSCLIENT.

MUDDweller

MUDDweller is a Macintosh interface to MUDD that requires MacTCP. To set it up, you will need to choose a MUDD server. To enter the server to connect to, choose **TCP/IP Address** under the **Configure** menu.

Since MUDDweller does not handle name resolution, you will have to enter the TCP/IP address of your designated server. To connect to the Belgariad, try the settings given in the next column.

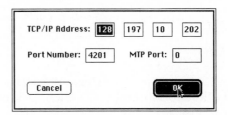

Once you've entered this information, you will be able to connect to the server by choosing **Open Connection** from the **Configure** menu.

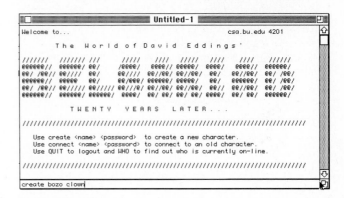

MUD Q&A

Do MUD players have real lives to go along with their virtual ones?

Many MUDers only use the MUDs once in a while, and to them it's just another thing to do, like playing tennis or going to watch a movie. However, there are some MUDers who spend their entire day playing MUDs. In many MUDs you can tell how long people have been on with the `who` command. Be aware that those that have been on for a long time may not be playing with a full deck.

I've heard that there are Gophers within MUDs. Is this true?

Yes. The MOO-Gopher allows for the inclusion of Gophers within MUD environments. To try out a MOO-Gopher, `telnet jayshouse.ccs.neu.edu 1709`.

Examples

The Belgariad

In this session I **telnet** to the Belgariad MUD. I then specify my character and password, then set my character's description and sex. I then lock my character, and go off to explore the Belgariad.

```
% telnet csa.bu.edu 4201
Trying 128.197.10.202...
Connected to csa.bu.edu.
Escape character is '^]'.
Welcome to....
```

```
                   Running PennMUSH 1.50
         Located at csa.bu.edu 4201 (128.197.10.202 4201)
Based on the Belgariad and the Malloreon, by David Eddings.

Use create <name> <password> to create a character.
Use connect <name> <password> to connect to your existing character.
Use connect Guest Guest to connect to the guest character.
Use QUIT to logout.
Use the WHO command to find out who is online currently.

------------------------------------------------------------------------

create Bozsnoz <secret>
------------------------------------------------------------------------

Congratulations on your newly created character. The Realm of the
BELGARIAD  welcomes you! For more information about this game, type 'news'. To find out more about commands, type 'help'.

The code here changes quite often. Please make sure to read news regularly.
The help system is quite extensive; please read this and consult the manual
before asking an administrative assistant ("royalty") or wizard for help.

------------------------------------------------------------------------

*****************************************************************
NEW CODE: read news patchlevel 1. |*| ATTENTION: No further brothels will be built. There will be a wizmeeting soon,
probably Monday night, open to the public, to discuss this and other matters. Your cooperation is expected.

*****************************************************************
Last connect was from world.std.com on Thu Jul  9 13:29:45 1992.
Common Room(#2296RHAJ)
There are numerous cots and blankets arranged in rows in this room. Although the
accommodations are spartan, they are clean and cheap. The floor is covered in
blue carpet, and rather faded, plain tapestries hang on the walls, keeping out
some of the chill of the cold Rivan winters. This is the common room of the Silver
Wolf Inn, where weary travelers can get a night's rest for only a few coins. The
only exit is the door to the east, leading out into the hallway.
Contents:
Combat Setter
New Players' Guide
Obvious exits:
Hallway <H>
New Players' Guide says, "Hello, Bozsnoz. Look at me for some help."

@sex me = male
Bozsnoz - Set.
@desc me = A 6 foot tall, bald man with green eyes.
Bozsnoz - Set.
@lock me = me
Locked.
```

(session continued on the next page)

```
WHO
Player Name          On For   Idle   Doing
Alyssa               00:04    19s
Bozsnoz              00:04    0s
Balgor               00:05    1m     IC -- Cherek Army! INJAJIAFA
Eledin               00:07    5s     It's back! I'll never doubt Pol again.
Demcal               00:08    4m     Oppose the Triumvirate! Apply NOW!
Varana               00:11    18s    Be all you can earn! Be a Tolnedran!
Damian               00:11    2s     Coding...no problems, really.
Polgara              00:12    1m
Henrik               00:13    7s
Jonick               00:14    4s     OOC: QUITE BUSY! !page_ok
Young_Wolf           00:15    18s    BOTSPOT OOC. Page_OK
There are 11 players connected.
look
Common Room(#2296RHAJ)
There are numerous cots and blankets arranged in rows in this room. Although the
accommodations are spartan, they are clean and cheap. The floor is covered in
blue carpet, and rather faded, plain tapestries hang on the walls, keeping out
some of the chill of the cold Rivan winters. This is the common room of the Silver
Wolf Inn, where weary travelers can get a night's rest for only a few coins. The
only exit is the door to the east, leading out into the hallway.
Contents:
Combat Setter
New Players' Guide
Obvious exits:
Hallway <H>
H
You open the door and go out of the room.
Guest Hallway
This is a long hallway, with many doors on either side. The floor is covered with
blue and red wall-to-wall carpeting. There are torches every several yards, ra
diating a cheerful light. A set of stairs lead down into the main room of Riva's
Silver Wolf Inn. One door to the west opens into a large common sleeping room;
behind the rest of the doors are numerous private rooms.
Contents:
Provan
Obvious exits:
Jethric  Kheris  Pixel  Stairs <S>  Common Room
stars
stairs
```
[And so on...]

Marches of Anton

The following is a sample session from an LPMUD (Marches of Antan, `chema.ucsd.edu` `(132.239.68.1) 3000`):

```
You are in a lush field of wildflowers. Dense vegetation borders the
field on three sides, and slightly higher ground can be seen to the west.
Butterflies and hummingbirds flit about the verdant field, and the rays
of the afternoon sun grace this pastoral scene with golden light. No
sign of human intrusion or waste mars this beautiful meadow; it looks
as if you are the first to come upon this tranquil vista.
    There are two obvious exits: west and east.
A colorful butterfly.
> look colorful butterfly
This butterfly flutters tantalizingly just out of reach. Occasionally
it makes an attempt to fly down to one of the flowers, but one of the
other butterflies always intercepts it, and sends it flying away. The
butterfly hovers in the air, miserably, or so it seems to you.
> w
The field of flowers gives way to somewhat higher ground on which a
thorny field of thistles and brambles has overgrown a narrow path which
leads west to a small structure.
    There are two obvious exits: west and east.
A Giant Dragonfly.
> The dragonfly darts at you!
The dragonfly darts at you!
The dragonfly darts at you!
> kill Dragonfly
You missed Dragonfly.
> Dragonfly nicked Azathon.
The dragonfly emits a loud buzzing sound.
You scratched Dragonfly.
Dragonfly grazed Azathon.
You nicked Dragonfly.
```
[And so on...]

For more information

Technical papers

Technical papers relating to mud are available via `ftp parftp.xerox.com, cd /pub/MOO/papers`.

USENET Groups

Several USENET newsgroups are dedicated to MUDing:

Conference	Purpose
rec.games.mud.admin	Administration issues
rec.games.mud.announce	Announcement of new MUDs
rec.games.mud.diku	Discussion of DikuMUDs
rec.games.mud.lp	Discussion of LPMUDs
rec.games.mud.misc	Miscellaneous MUD subjects
rec.games.mud.tiny	Discussion of TinyMUDs

A MUD Frequently Asked Questions file (known as a FAQ) is available via `ftp ftp.math.okstate.edu, cd pub/muds/misc/mud-faq directory`. It is also posted in all the `rec.games.mud` newsgroups periodically, or can be gotten from jds@math.okstate.edu as a last resort.

A list of MUDs is available via `ftp caisr2.caisr.cwru.edu cd /pub/mud`, in the `rec.games.mud.announce`, `rec.games.mud.misc`, and `alt.mud` newsgroups, or by email from scg@mentor.cc.purdue.edu.

Resources

While `telnet` works fine for connecting to MUDs, there are a number of MUD client programs that add features such as automatically logging your character on, or triggering actions in response to certain actions, such as saying hello whenever a new player enters the room. Client packages include:

Mac MUDDweller. MUDDweller contains an ordinary terminal emulation mode, but when it connects to MUDs it supports additional features. These include command history, a session log, and MTP (a file transfer protocols used in many MUDs). MUDDweller is available by FTP from rudolf.ethz.ch in the /pub/mud directory.

TinyTalk. A replacement for `telnet` during MUD sessions, Tinytalk has a number of features, such as macro support and command history. Tinytalk is available by FTP from piggy.ucsb.edu in the /pub/mud/clients directory.

A more complete list of clients is available in the MUD FAQ.

Interesting MUDs

MUDs

Ivory Tower
`telnet marvin.macc.wisc.edu 2000`

Nightmare
`telnet jericho.connected.com 6000`

The Round Table
`telnet ac.wfunet.wfu.edu 2222`

MOOs

Xerox Parc lambdaMOO
`telnet lambda.parc.xerox.com 8888`

MagicMOO
`telnet dougal.aston.ac.uk 7777`

Post Modern Culture MOO
`telnet dewey.lib.ncsu.edu 7777`

TinyMUCKs

Halcyon
`telnet hobbes.cs.mcgill.ca 1256`

Chapter 14:
Information Servers

Z39.50, Gopher, and World Wide Web

Z39.50 and WAIS

Wide Area Information Servers (WAIS) is a client/server database supporting document retrieval via the Z39.50 protocol. The father of WAIS, and now president of WAIS, Inc., is Brewster Kahle. Brewster developed the WAIS project while he was an employee of Thinking Machines, the parallel supercomputer firm. Along with Dow Jones, Apple, and Peat Marwick, the initial WAIS development efforts produced public-domain client and server prototypes.

Since its development, WAIS has spread like wildfire throughout the Internet. There are currently more than 400 publicly accessible databases, with the number doubling every year.

WAIS, Inc., was founded in 1992 in order to spearhead the commercialization of WAIS. The WAIS, Inc., product line focusses mainly on UNIX-based server products as well as consulting and support. The term WAIS is now a trademark of WAIS, Inc., and therefore is only used in this book to refer to specific products from WAIS, Inc. We will use the term "WAIS-compatible" or Z39.50 to refer to products from other vendors.

Despite the name, WAIS-compatible databases operate both over wide area networks such as the Internet, and on local area networks. Queries may also be submitted via electronic mail.

Servers implementing Z39.50 index documents in a wide variety of formats, and can be used to provide access to spreadsheets, databases, pictures, movies, and sounds as well as text.

Z39.50 clients are available for the Macintosh, NeXT, DOS, and Windows environments.

The Clearinghouse for Networked Information Discovery and Retrieval (CNIDR) FreeWAIS project has taken responsibility for the continued development of publicly distributable clients and servers. Despite the use of the name FreeWAIS, the CNIDR code is copyrighted, and therefore may not be used commercially.

Both the WAIS, Inc., and CNIDR implementations of Z39.50 are moving toward compliance with the full Z39.50-1992 specification; the latest server versions from both organizations support boolean queries.

Many WAIS-compatible databases are used to provide information about global networks. These include indexes of Domain Organizations, UUCP sites, and BITNET and FidoNet nodes; a database of electronic mail addresses of USENET participants; and databases of Internet documentation, FAQ files, and USENET newsgroups. These databases form an "online help system" that provides instant solutions to user problems, and after becoming familiar with them, many users wonder how they got along without Z39.50.

During my own Internet sessions, I frequently leave the WAIS application running in order to be able to run queries as the need arises. Many organizations in the public and private sector have recognized the value of Z39.50. WAIS is also being used by EPA and DOE, the Library of Congress, Rice University, and Perot Data Systems.

Relevance feedback

WAIS includes relevance feedback; when you ask a question, you get back matching documents as well as an estimate of their relevance to your query. The relevance computation is based on the frequency with which the keyword phrases are used, the proximity of keywords to each other, use of the words in the document title versus text, etc.

Based on the initial search results, it is possible to focus the search further, by selecting the most relevant documents as examples and telling WAIS to "find more documents like these."

Queries may be rerun on a regular basis, making it possible to keep up to date on important subjects.

Access methods

WAIS may be accessed via electronic mail (waismail), via `telnet` to a site running the UNIX client (swais), or via a TCP/IP connection from a machine running a client for DOS, Windows, Macintosh, or NeXT.

swais

swais is a WAIS client for UNIX. If your machine has a TCP/IP connection, you can also access WAIS via client software for your platform, or alternatively you can `telnet` to a machine running swais, via `telnet` `quake.think.com` or `nnsc.nsf.net`, `login:` `wais`. Information on WAIS is available via `ftp think.com`.

swais Commands

swais commands include:

swais command	What it does
j, down arrow, ^N	Moves down one source
k, up arrow, ^P	Moves up one source
J, ^V, ^D	Moves down one screen
K, <esc> v, ^U	Moves up one screen

swais command	What it does
###	Positions to source number ##
m	Mails current item to an address
|	Pipes current item into a UNIX command
/sss	Searches for source sss
<space>, <period>	Selects current source
=	Deselects all sources
v, <comma>	Views current source info
<ret>	Performs search
s	Specifies new sources
w	Selects new keywords
X, -	Removes current source permanently
o	Sets and shows swais options
h, ?	Shows help display
H	Displays program history
q	Leaves WAIS
R	Shows relevant documents
S	Saves current item to a file
v	Views current item information
r	Makes current item a relevant document
u	Adds document to list of sources

Example

```
% telnet quake.think.com
Trying 192.31.181.1...
Connected to quake.think.com.
Escape character is '^]'.

SunOS UNIX (quake)

login: wais
Welcome to swais.
Please type user identifier (i.e user@host): aboba@world.std.com
TERM = (vt100)
Starting swais (this may take a little while)...
```

When swais starts up, you will see the following screen:

```
SWAIS                         Source Selection              Sources: 431
 #          Server                    Source                  Cost
001:   [        archie.au]  aarnet-resource-guide            Free
002:   [    munin.ub2.lu.se] academic_email_conf             Free
003:   [wraith.cs.uow.edu.au] acronyms                       Free
004:   [     archive.orst.edu] aeronautics                   Free
005:   [ bloat.media.mit.edu] Aesop-Fables                   Free
006:   [ ftp.cs.colorado.edu] aftp-cs-colorado-edu           Free
007:   [nostromo.oes.orst.ed] agricultural-market-news       Free
008:   [     archive.orst.edu] alt.drugs                     Free
009:   [      wais.oit.unc.edu] alt.gopher                   Free
010:   [sun-wais.oit.unc.edu] alt.sys.sun                    Free
011:   [     wais.oit.unc.edu] alt.wais                      Free
012:   [alfred.ccs.carleton.] amiga-slip                     Free
013:   [      munin.ub2.lu.se] amiga_fish_contents           Free
014:   [    coombs.anu.edu.au] ANU-Aboriginal-Studies    $0.00/minute
015:   [    coombs.anu.edu.au] ANU-Asian-Computing       $0.00/minute
016:   [    coombs.anu.edu.au] ANU-Asian-Religions       $0.00/minute
017:   [    coombs.anu.edu.au] ANU-CAUT-Projects         $0.00/minute
018:   [    coombs.anu.edu.au] ANU-French-Databanks      $0.00/minute

Keywords:

<space> selects, w for keywords, arrows move, <return> searches, q quits, or ?
```

The right corner of the screen gives the total number of sources (431 in this case). To submit a query, select the sources by manipulating the cursor, and then input the keywords to search on. WAIS will then return a list of documents that contained your keywords.

Example 1

In this example, I search the Bible for references to Job. To select the Bible, I have to find it in the list of sources (the database list at the end of this article should help you in this), select it by typing **<space>**, and then input the keyword by typing **w**.

```
SWAIS                         Source Selection              Sources: 431
 #          Server                    Source                  Cost
037:   [      ericir.syr.edu] AskERIC-Helpsheets             Free
038:   [      ericir.syr.edu] AskERIC-Infoguides             Free
039:   [      ericir.syr.edu] AskERIC-Minisearches           Free
040:   [      ericir.syr.edu] AskERIC-Questions              Free
041:   [ndadsb.gsfc.nasa.gov] astropersons                   Free
042:   [          archie.au] au-directory-of-servers         Free
043:   [     doppler.ncsc.org] AVS_TXT_FILES                 Free
044:   [ndadsb.gsfc.nasa.gov] BGRASS-L                       Free
045:   [       snekkar.ens.fr] bib-dmi-ens-fr                Free
046:   [wais-server.ens-lyon] bib-ens-lyon                   Free
047:   [     junon.matups.fr] bib-math-orsay-fr              Free
048: * [ cmns-moon.think.com] bible                          Free
049:   [       zenon.inria.fr] bibs-zenon-inria-fr           Free
050:   [           bio.vu.nl] biology-compounds              Free
051:   [         net.bio.net] biology-journal-contents        Free
052:   [       wais.funet.fi] bionic-ai-researchers          Free
053:   [       wais.funet.fi] bionic-algorithms              Free
054:   [       wais.funet.fi] bionic-arabidopsis             Free

Keywords: job

Enter keywords with spaces between them; <return> to search; ^C to cancel
```

The maximum number of references (40) were found:

```
SWAIS                          Search Results                   Items: 40
  #     Score   Source                      Title                   Lines
001:   [1000] (cmns-moon.think)  Job: Chapter 42  42:1 Then Job answered     61
002:   [ 960] (cmns-moon.think)  Job: Chapter 1   1:1 There was a man in t   78
003:   [ 837] (cmns-moon.think)  Job: Chapter 35  35:1 Elihu spake moreov    37
004:   [ 837] (cmns-moon.think)  Job: Chapter 26  26:3 How hast thou coun    35
005:   [ 756] (cmns-moon.think)  Job: Chapter 37  37:1 At this also my he    66
006:   [ 756] (cmns-moon.think)  Job: Chapter 32  32:1 So these three men    65
007:   [ 756] (cmns-moon.think)  Job: Chapter 2   2:1 Again there was a da   54
008:   [ 735] (cmns-moon.think)  Job: Chapter 34  34:1 Furthermore Elihu     98
009:   [ 735] (cmns-moon.think)  Job: Chapter 33  33:1 Wherefore, Job, I     87
010:   [ 715] (cmns-moon.think)  Job: Chapter 31  31:1 I made a covenant     81
011:   [ 715] (cmns-moon.think)  Job: Chapter 25  25:3 Is there any numbe    12
012:   [ 715] (cmns-moon.think)  Job: Chapter 23  23:1 Then Job answered     45
013:   [ 715] (cmns-moon.think)  Job: Chapter 17  17:1 My breath is corru    46
014:   [ 715] (cmns-moon.think)  Job: Chapter 7   7:4 When I lie down, I s   46
015:   [ 715] (cmns-moon.think)  Ezekiel: Chapter 14  14:1 Then came cert    81
016:   [ 694] (cmns-moon.think)  Job: Chapter 27  27:3 All the while my b    56
017:   [ 694] (cmns-moon.think)  Job: Chapter 18  18:1 Then answered Bild    61
018:   [ 694] (cmns-moon.think)  Job: Chapter 16  16:1 Then Job answered     59

<space> selects, arrows move, w for keywords, s for sources, ? for help
```

The references can be examined individually by using the cursor keys and typing (SPACE) to select them. To mark a document as relevant, position the cursor, and then type **r**. You can then rerun the keyword search. Below is the result of selecting returned result 001 as relevant. Notice that verses containing both *Job* and *answered* increase in relevance as a result.

```
SWAIS                          Search Results                   Items: 40
  #     Score   Source                      Title                   Lines
001:   [1000] (cmns-moon.think)  Job: Chapter 23  23:1 Then Job answered     45
002:   [ 289] (cmns-moon.think)  Job: Chapter 9   9:1 Then Job answered an   86
003:   [ 285] (cmns-moon.think)  Jeremiah: Chapter 52  52:1 Zedekiah was    131
004:   [ 260] (cmns-moon.think)  Job: Chapter 35  35:1 Elihu spake moreov    37
005:   [ 258] (cmns-moon.think)  Job: Chapter 29  29:1 Moreover Job conti    62
006:   [ 256] (cmns-moon.think)  Job: Chapter 33  33:1 Wherefore, Job, I     87
007:   [ 256] (cmns-moon.think)  Job: Chapter 6   6:1 But Job answered and   70
008:   [ 251] (cmns-moon.think)  Job: Chapter 32  32:1 So these three men    65
009:   [ 240] (cmns-moon.think)  Job: Chapter 34  34:1 Furthermore Elihu     98
010:   [ 240] (cmns-moon.think)  Job: Chapter 11  11:1 Then answered Zoph    44
011:   [ 238] (cmns-moon.think)  Job: Chapter 19  19:1 Then Job answered     75
012:   [ 235] (cmns-moon.think)  Job: Chapter 16  16:1 Then Job answered     59
013:   [ 228] (cmns-moon.think)  Job: Chapter 15  15:1 Then answered Elip    82
014:   [ 228] (cmns-moon.think)  Job: Chapter 12  12:1 And Job answered a    69
015:   [ 227] (cmns-moon.think)  Job: Chapter 22  22:7 Thou hast not give    65
016:   [ 227] (cmns-moon.think)  Job: Chapter 8   8:1 Then answered Bildad   50
017:   [ 216] (cmns-moon.think)  Job: Chapter 31  31:1 I made a covenant     81
018:   [ 209] (cmns-moon.think)  Job: Chapter 1   1:1 There was a man in t   78

<space> selects, arrows move, w for keywords, s for sources, ? for help
```

Example 2

In this example, I use swais to find an electronic mail address, using the usenet-addresses database. This is a database of people who post on USENET. This database can also be queried by electronic mail. For information on how to do this, consult Chapter 9: Finding People.

```
SWAIS                          Source Selection              Sources: 431
 #              Server                        Source              Cost
397:    [    next2.oit.unc.edu]  unix.FAQ                         Free
398:    [    wais.fct.unl.pt]    unl-di-reports                   Free
399:    [    sol.acs.unt.edu]    UNTComputerDoc                   Free
400:    [    sunsite.unc.edu]    US-Budget-1993                   Free
401:    [    quake.think.com]    US-Gov-Programs                  Free
402:    [pegun.law.columbia.e]   us-judges                        Free
403:    [   gopher.stolaf.edu]   US-State-Department-Travel-Advi  Free
404:    [     spk41.usace.mil]   usace-spk-phonebook              Free
405:    [   es-cit.esusda.gov]   usda-rrdb                        Free
406:    [        nic.sura.net]   usdacris                         Free
407: *  [        wais.cic.net]   usenet-addresses                 Free
408:    [ cmns-moon.think.com]   usenet-cookbook                  Free
409:    [ pit-manager.mit.edu]   usenet                           Free
410:    [ ridgisd.er.usgs.gov]   USGS_Earth_Science_Data_Directo  Free
411:    [ oac.hsc.uth.tmc.edu]   ut-research-expertise            Free
412:    [        wais.cic.net]   utsun.s.u-tokyo.ac.jp            Free
413:    [        wais.cic.net]   uumap                            Free
414:    [        wais.cic.net]   uunet                            Free

Keywords: aboba

Enter keywords with spaces between them; <return> to search; ^C to cancel
```

Here is the result of the search:

```
SWAIS                          Search Results                Items:  3
 #    Score    Source                 Title                     Lines
001:  [1000]   (usenet-addresse)  aboba@world.std                   1
002:  [1000]   (usenet-addresse)  aboba@world.std                   1
003:  [ 333]   (usenet-addresse)  aboba@netcom.com     (Sep 21 92)
```

WAIS found two addresses: one at world.std.com and one at netcom.com.

waismail

waismail is an electronic mail interface to WAIS. Since there are at least two different versions of waismail (one running at `quake.think.com` and another at `net.bio.net`), if you are using a waismail server other than these two machines, there is no way to know ahead of time what commands it will accept.

However, both machines work by sending the message to `waismail@host.domain` and by enclosing the commands within the body of the message. The subject field is ignored. Both servers also respond to the command `help` with a help file.

quake.think.com waismail

Of the two servers, the one at `quake.think.com` is the most general, allowing the user to query all public Z39.50 sources.

To search a single source, use:

search <source-name> <keywords>

The `<source-name>` field is a source-name, but without a .src extension. For example:

search uumap planet

This will search the UUCP maps database for a machine called `planet`. This would be useful if I was planning on giving my machine this name and wanted to see if it was taken. For a listing of Z39.50 sources, see the end of this chapter.

If more than one source is to be searched, the multiple sources are separated by spaces and enclosed in quotes. For example:

```
From: aboba@world.std.com
To: waismail@quake.think.com
Subject: waismail search example

search "uumap domain-organizations" planet
```

This will search both the `uumap` and `domain-organization` sources for a machine named `planet`. If the query refers to an unknown database, then waismail will return a list of searchable databases. Here is the response to the previous search request:

```
Date: Sun, 2 May 93 21:07:33 PDT
From: WAISmail@quake.think.com
To: aboba@world.std.com (Bernard Aboba)
Subject: Your WAIS Request:  Waismail example 1

Searching: uumap domain-organizations

Keywords: planet

Result # 1 Score:1000 lines:  0 bytes:    183 Date:    0
Type: TEXT
Headline: #N    planet
DocID: 7717 7900
/u3/wais/mirror/uumap/u.gbr.6:/u3/wais/wais-
documents/uumap@wais.cic.net:210%TEXT

Result # 2 Score:1000 lines:  0 bytes:     71 Date:    0
Type: TEXT
Headline: %D planet.co.nz
DocID: 2350548 2350619
/u3/wais/mirror/netfind/RFOnly:/u3/wais/wais-
documents/domain-organizations@wais.cic.
net:210%TEXT
```

The response gives a list of documents, identified by DocIDs. To retrieve one of the listed documents, send another message, containing the following command:

retrieve <DOCID> or
DOCID: <DOCID>

The <DOCID> field must be reproduced exactly as in the reply message, including all punctuation and spaces. You must also leave a blank line after a DOCID command. For example:

```
From: aboba@world.std.com
To: waismail@quake.think.com
Subject: waismail search example

DocID: 7717 7900
/u3/wais/mirror/uumap/u.gbr.6:/u3/wais/wais-
documents/uumap@wais.cic.net:210%TEXT
```

To use relevance feedback based on one of the returned documents, use the following command:

like <DOCID>

net.bio.net waismail

The `net.bio.net` waismail software was written by Kenton Hoover. It allows you to search and retrieve documents in one pass and does not require use of DOCIDs; however, it only covers Bioscience sources. Sources are specified by the **source** command; the maximum number of document hits returned is specified by the **depth** command, and the query keywords are listed on a separate line. For more information, send the **help** command. Example:

```
From: aboba@world.std.com
To: waismail@net.bio.net
Subject: waismail search example

source uumap
depth 5
planet
```

WAIS over TCP/IP

WAIStation

Z39.50 clients are available for Macintosh (WAIStation), NeXT (WAIStation), and Windows (WWAIS) machines running TCP/IP. For more information on obtaining clients, please consult the end of this chapter. This section goes over the use of the Macintosh client, called WAIStation; operation of other graphical clients is similar.

When you first fire up WAIStation, you will be greeted with two windows, one a window of sources, the other a window of questions. If you are just starting to use WAIStation, both windows will be empty. Luckily, the WAIStation distribution comes with sources, including the source Directory-of-servers, which is a common place to begin the search. To add sources to your source window, select **Open Source...** from the **Source** menu. You can then select one of the sources in the Source Directory that is included in the WAIStation distribution.

How do we know which sources to examine? One of the sources included with every client is the Directory-of-servers database, which is a directory of publicly accessible Z39.50 servers. If you don't have any servers to start with, the best way to begin is to first query the Directory-of-servers database.

Before doing this though, you have to pose a question. To open the question window, select **New Question** from the **Question** menu. In the question window, you can then enter your question, and select the sources you wish to query for the answer.

In the example below, I query the Directory-of-servers to find out which servers have information about Fluid Mechanics:

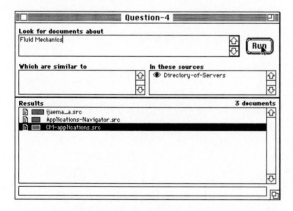

The search discloses a database called CM-applications. By double-clicking on this database, you can save it to your hard disk, after which you can use it as a source to search on.

The next step in my search is to query the CM-applications database on the same subject, Fluid Mechanics. CM-applications is a database of applications for the Connection Machine, a massively parallel supercomputer built by Thinking Machines of Cambridge, Massachusetts. The results of the search come back in the Results list box:

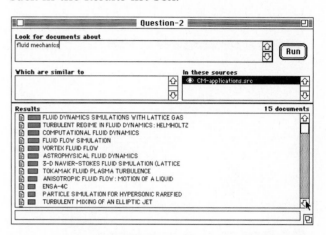

One of the nice things about WAIS is that once you have performed the initial search, you can then focus or redirect the search by instructing WAIS to look for articles more like some of the ones it had previously found. In the next screen shot, I search for more information on turbulent mixing, shocks, or detonations.

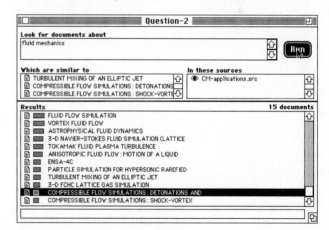

HyperWais and WWAIS

Z39.50 has also been implemented within HyperCard (Macintosh) and Toolbook (Windows). Both implementations require TCP/IP. HyperWAIS requires MacTCP; WWAIS requires a Windows Sockets compatible TCP/IP stack.

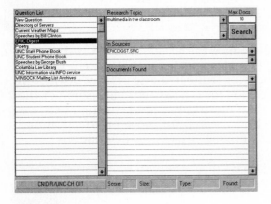

HyperWAIS

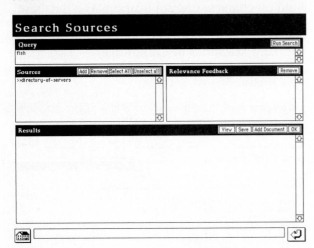

WWAIS

DowQuest

DowQuest is a service of Dow Jones News Retrieval (DJNR) that is based on WAIS technology. Using DowQuest you can search news stories for particular keywords. Just as with WAIS, if you find a relevant document, you can use this to improve your search. From anywhere on DJNR, you can reach DowQuest via the `//dowquest` command. In the sample session that follows, note that when I employ relevance feedback, different documents are returned.

```
% telnet djnr.dowjones.com
Trying 143.131.190.15...
Connected to djnr.dowjones.com.
```

```
Escape character is '^]'.
WHAT SERVICE PLEASE????
ENTER PASSWORD
     @@@@@@@@@@@@

   DOW JONES NEWS/RETRIEVAL COPYRIGHT (C) 1993
   DOW JONES & COMPANY, INC. ALL RIGHTS RESERVED
BOSNIAN SERB LEADER ACCEPTS
PEACE PLAN BUT U.S. SKEPTICAL;
BRITAIN REFUSES TO APPROVE
USE OF FORCE, SEE //NEWS.
ENTER QUERY
  //dowquest
                    DOWQUEST
     Copyright (C) 1993 Dow Jones & Company, Inc.

DowQuest searches articles from more than 350 sources of
current business information, including The Wall Street
Journal, Barron's, Business Week,Fortune and Forbes.  All
articles are copyrighted by their publisher.

TO VIEW INSTRUCTIONS or copyright notices, press
(Return).For additional information, type HELP at any
point while using DowQuest.

TO BEGIN A SEARCH: Enter several words that are relevant
to the subject you are interested in and press (Return).

ENTER QUERY:
  superoxide dismutase
DOWQUEST                        STARTER LIST
HEADLINE PAGE 1 OF 4

  1 Corrections
    NEW YORK TIMES: PAGE A-2 , 04/02/93  (92 words)

  2 Biotechnology PatentWatch: U.S. Patents: Bio-
Technology . BIOTECHNOLOGY NEWSWATCH, 04/05/93  (93
words)

  3 Bio-Tech Genl -2: Studies Infant Lung Treatment >BTGC
    DOW JONES NEWS SERVICE , 02/24/93  (186 words)

  4 PatentWatch: Process for preparing active
extracellular .BIOTECHNOLOGY NEWSWATCH, 09/21/92  (192
words)

TO IMPROVE A SEARCH: Type SEARCH and the numbers of up to
three articles that are examples of your subject.
TO VIEW AN ARTICLE:  Enter article number and press
(Return).
Enter BEST and article number to see "best" section.
TO PRINT ARTICLES:   Type PRINT and the article numbers.

PRESS (RETURN) FOR MORE HEADLINES. TYPE HELP FOR MORE
INFORMATION.

  SEARCH 3
DOWQUEST                        SECOND SEARCH
HEADLINE PAGE 1 OF 4

  1 Bio-Tech Genl -2: Studies Infant Lung Treatment >BTGC
    DOW JONES NEWS SERVICE , 02/24/93  (186 words)

  2 Bio-Tech Genl Patent-2-: Gene Linked To Lou . . .
    DOW JONES NEWS SERVICE , 03/23/93  (274 words)

  3 Biotechnology PatentWatch: U.S. Patents: Bio-
Technology . . .
    BIOTECHNOLOGY NEWSWATCH, 04/05/93  (93 words)

  4 Bio-Tech Genl's Biolon -2:Pdt For Use In Ophthalmic .
DOW JONES NEWS SERVICE , 03/25/93  (141 words)

TO IMPROVE A SEARCH: Type SEARCH and the numbers of up to
three articles that are examples of your subject.
TO VIEW AN ARTICLE:  Enter article number and press
(Return).
Enter BEST and article number to see "best" section.
TO PRINT ARTICLES:   Type PRINT and the article numbers.

PRESS (RETURN) FOR MORE HEADLINES. TYPE HELP FOR MORE
INFORMATION.
```

For more information

Z39.50 USENET groups

Group	What it's for
alt.wais	General discussion
comp.infosystems.wais	Primary Z39.50 group

WAIS mailing lists

`wais-discussion@think.com`
To subscribe: `wais-discussion-request@think.com`
A digested, moderated general discussion list.

`wais-interest@think.com`
To subscribe: `wais-interest-request@think.com`
Moderated list of announcements of new software releases.

`wais-talk@think.com`
To subscribe: `wais-talk-request@think.com`
Unmoderated discussion of WAIS development.

`Z3950IW`
To subscribe:
`LISTSERV@nervm.nerdc.ufl.edu`
Developer-oriented list on Z39.50 implementation.

`ZIP`
To subscribe: `zip-request@kudzu.concert.net`
List on the FreeWAIS implementation of Z39.50-92.

`SIG-WAIS`
To subscribe: `sig-wais-info@cnidr.org`
Announcements of meetings and presentations of interest to the Z39.50 community.

WAIS Bibliography

Available via `ftp think.com, get /wais/bibliography.txt`

Z39.50 directory of servers

`ftp think.com, get /wais/wais-sources.tar.Z`

GOPHER

What is Gopher?

Gopher is client/server tool for distributed document search and retrieval. In addition to supporting Z39.50 queries, Gopher also supports access to FTP archives, USENET news, Archie, Ph servers, `telnet`, and more.

Gopher server software is free for use by universities and other educational institutions. However, the server software may not be used commercially without a license from the University of Minnesota.

Accessing Gopher

Gopher may be accessed via `telnet` to sites running UNIX client software or over TCP/IP using Gopher clients for DOS, Windows, or Macintosh. Gopher client sites available for `telnet` include:

Site	Login
consultant.micro.umn.edu (134.84.132.4)	gopher
panda.uiowa.edu (128.255.63.234)	gopher
gdunix.gd.chalmers.se (129.16.221.40)(SWEDEN)	gopher
gopher.uiuc.edu (128.174.33.160)	gopher
gopher.unt.edu (129.120.1.42)	gopher
tolten.puc.cl (146.155.1.16) (CHILE)	gopher
info.anu.edu.au (150.203.84.20) (Australia)	info

Once you log in, Gopher will present you with a screen like the following:

```
Internet Gopher Information Client v1.00beta

Root gopher server: gopher.micro.umn.edu

-->  1.  Information About Gopher/
     2.  Computer Information/
     3.  Discussion Groups/
     4.  Fun & Games/
     5.  Internet file server (ftp) sites/
     6.  Libraries/
     7.  News/
     8.  Other Gopher and Information Servers/
     9.  Phone Books/
    10.  Search lots of places at the U of M <?>
    11.  University of Minnesota Campus Information/
```

Gopher is organized as a menu tree. By using the cursor and other navigation keys, you can navigate the branches of the tree.

Using Gopher you can:

• Search the Archie database (under Internet file server, menu 5 from the U.M. Gopher)
• Telnet to Online Libraries (menu 6, Libraries)
• Access other Gophers worldwide (menu 8, Other Servers from the U.M. Gopher)
• Find out about Humor, Music & Recipes (menu 4, Fun & Games from the U.M. Gopher)
• Access Online Books (menu 6, Libraries from the U.M. Gopher)
• Access Z39.50 databases (menu 8, Other Servers from the U.M. Gopher)

UNIX Gopher client commands

Here are the UNIX Gopher client commands:

Gopher command	What it does
RET `<Right>`	Views current item
0-9	Moves to a line #
k C-p ⬆	Moves pointer up
j C-n ⬇	Moves pointer down
u `<Left>`	Goes up a level
m	Goes to first screen
n	Next search item
q	Exits Gopher
s	Saves item to file
D	Download file
>	Goes to next page
<	Goes to previous page
=	Displays information about current item.
O	Changes options
/	Searches for item
?	Help screen

Bookmark commands

a	Adds item to list
A	Adds directory/search to list
d	Deletes item from list
v	Views list

Each menu item in Gopher can be identified by its extension:

/	Item is a directory
.	Item is a text file
<?>	Item is a search index
<CSO>	Item is a phone book
<TEL>	Item is a `telnet` session
<)	Item is a sound (looks like a speaker)

Bookmarks

Bookmarks are a useful way of keeping a list of frequently used items close at hand. Selecting an item and then typing **a** will allow you to add the item to your bookmark list.

```
+-------------------------------------------+
|                                           |
|  Name for this bookmark?  Connectivity List |
|                                           |
|           [Cancel ^G] [Accept - Enter]    |
|                                           |
+-------------------------------------------+
```

Typing **v** will then let you view your list of bookmarks:

```
Internet Gopher Information Client v1.11

            Bookmarks

-->  1.  Connectivity List.
```

Transferring files

Once you have selected an item, you can transfer it to your computer by typing **D** for download. This will get you the following dialog box:

```
+-----------------------------------+
|  1. Zmodem                        |
|  2. Ymodem                        |
|  3. Xmodem-1K                     |
|  4. Xmodem-CRC                    |
|  5. Kermit                        |
|  6. Text                          |
|                                   |
|  Choose a download method:        |
|                                   |
|   [Cancel ^G]  [Choose 1-6]       |
|                                   |
+-----------------------------------+
```

Mailing files

Using the default Gopher pager you can mail or save files. The default Gopher pager displays the following at the bottom of a page:

```
-- Hit SPACEBAR for more --
```

Hitting (SPACE) shows the next page. Typing **q** results in the following:

```
Press <RETURN> to continue, <m> to mail, <s> to save:
```

Typing (RET) goes back to the previous item. Typing **m** brings up the following dialog box:

```
+-------------------------------------------+
|                                           |
|  Mail current document to:  aboba@world.std.com |
|                                           |
|          [Cancel ^G] [Accept - Enter]     |
|                                           |
+-------------------------------------------+
```

You will only see the <s> entry if you have an account on the Gopher machine, since Gopher cannot save files to your account on your home machine. If you try an unauthorized save, you'll get the following error message:

```
+--------------Gopher Error--------------+
|                                        |
|  Sorry, can't save files in securemode |
|                                        |
|           [Cancel - ^G] [OK - Enter]   |
|                                        |
+----------------------------------------+
```

VERONICA

With so many Internet resources, no menu system can offer both comprehensive coverage and ease of use. VERONICA (which stands for Very Easy Rodent-Oriented Netwide Index to Computerized Archives) indexes thousands of resources in Gopherspace, letting you search Gopherspace by keyword.

To reach VERONICA from the University of Minnesota Gopher, select menu entry **9**, **Other Gopher and Information Servers** and then **2**, **Search Gopherspace Using VERONICA**. Then select **2** again for **Search by keyword**.

Here is what the search screen looks like:

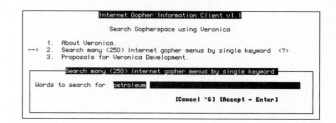

A Roadmap of the University of Minnesota Gopher

Top Level

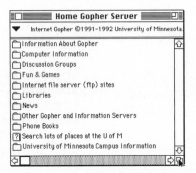

Main Menu

Second Level

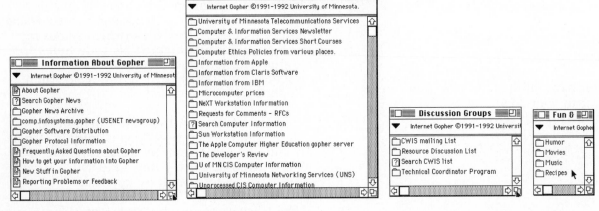

Gopher Information   Computer Information   Discussion Groups   Fun

Roadmap to University of Minnesota Gopher (cont'd)

Second Level

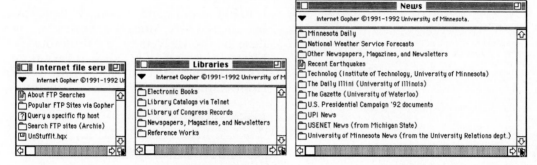

File servers   **Libraries**   **News**

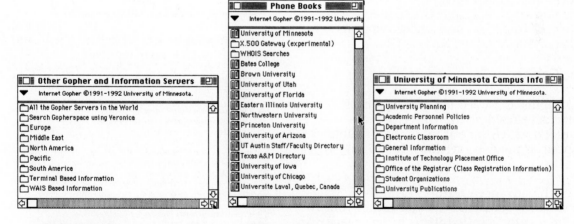

Other Info   **Phone Books**   **University of**
(includes Z39.50 and   **Minnesota**
VERONICA)

VERONICA understands boolean queries, which means that your query can contain the operators AND, NOT, OR, (, and). Once the relevant gopherspace resources are located, they appear on a menu:

```
Internet Gopher Information Client v1.1

Search many (250) Internet gopher menus by single
keyword : petroleum

-->  1. Crude oil and petroleum products overview (table A).
     2. Crude oil and petroleum products overview (table B).
     3. EIA-Petroleum-Supply-Monthly.src <?>
     4. Canadian Occidental Petroleum Ltd..
     5. EIA-Petroleum-Supply-Monthly.src <?>
     6. Wildlife management and petroleum dev.
     7. The influence of varying domestic petroleum income on
           the Norwegi.
     8. Northeast Petroleum - Forest Resources Cooperative
           Symposium, 1st.
     9. Northeast Petroleum - Forest Resources Cooperative: A
           successful .
    10. Impacts of the petroleum sector on Norwegian forestry
           and forest .
    11. Petroleum Supply Monthly - from the Energy Information
           Agency <?>
    12. EIA-Petroleum-Supply-Monthly.src <?>
    13. BP sells interest in Australian mine.
    14. EIA-Petroleum-Supply-Monthly.src <?>
    15. EIA-Petroleum-Supply-Monthly.src <?>
```

Graphical Gophers

The VT100 version of Gopher available via **telnet** is pretty bare bones, but not so for the graphical user interface versions, which offer advanced features. These include TurboGopher, which runs on the Macintosh and requires MacTCP; and GopherBook, which is based on ToolBook, runs under Windows, and requires a Windows Sockets DLL.

TurboGopher

TurboGopher is an accelerated version of Gopher developed at the University of Minnesota, which runs at more than double the speed of previous versions. It's so easy to use that it's addictive.

One of the advanced features of TurboGopher is bookmarks. Bookmarks let you gather your most frequently accessed items in one place, creating your own customized menu.

I highly recommend making VERONICA a bookmark entry, since it is buried two levels deep in the University of Minnesota hierarchy. Using VERONICA is easy from TurboGopher. First navigate to the **Search Gopherspace using VERONICA** menu.

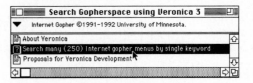

Double-clicking on this entry will bring up the keyword search dialog box.

After clicking on **OK**, VERONICA will find all the relevant Gopher databases.

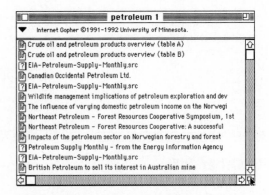

Double-click on individual entries to access the databases.

Downloading files

To download with TurboGopher, first navigate to the file you're looking to download:

Double-click on it. This will bring up the save dialog box:

Select a location for the file, and click on the **Save** button. The file will then be downloaded to your disk:

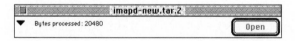

HGopher and GopherBook

HGopher is a Windows Sockets-compatible version of Gopher available from sunsite.unc.edu which support Bookmarks. Since it is based on Windows Sockets, it can be run alongside other Windows Sockets software such as PC Eudora, WinVN, Windows Mosaic, Finger, Windows Trumpet, WWAIS, or Win QVT/Net. This is what it looks like when it's running:

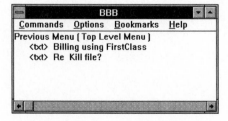

To set up the home Gopher, the temporary directory and the available viewers, select **Gopher Setup...** under the **Options** menu. If for some reason you need to overide your TCP/IP stack's DNS implementation, (not likely), select **Network Setup...** from the **Options** menu.

GopherBook is a version of Gopher based on ToolBook, which runs stand-alone and also suports Bookmarks. The Bookmark window is shown below:

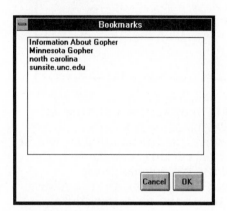

Gopher Servers

Gopher Server

Gopher server applications (available for UNIX, DOS, and the Macintosh) let you make information available to other Gopher users worldwide.

To set up Gopher Server, which runs on the Macintosh, you first need to run the Gopher Server application. When you do, it will put up the following dialog box:

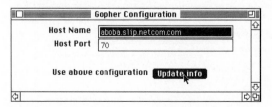

Leave the Gopher Server application running in the background. You do not need to configure it further in order to have it publish material. The configuration is done via a HyperCard stack called Gopher's Helper, which comes with the server and must reside in the same folder.

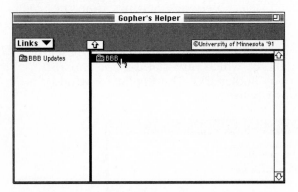

Using the Gopher's Helper stack, you will navigate around your hard drive in the left panel. The right panel corresponds to the name under which the left-hand folder will be published. Double-clicking on a name in the right panel allows you to change the nickname. Here I have published the folder BBB Updates under the nickname BBB. Creating nicknames has the effect of creating a Gopher Alias file in the same directory as your Gopher Server.

How can other people access your Gopher Server once you've created it? Unless you notify the Gopher people by sending mail to gopher@boombox.micro.umn.edu, your Gopher will not be visible to the world. However, you can still reach it by selecting **Another Gopher...** under the **File** menu in TurboGopher.

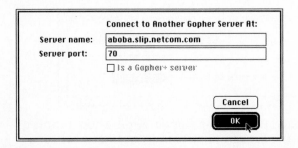

Enter the address and port of your Gopher Server, and the next thing you know, you'll be presented with a TurboGopher view of your server.

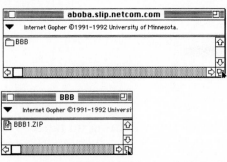

Since it is not obvious what the files in these directories are, it usually makes sense to put a "READ.ME" file within each directory that people can browse.

Indexing net news

The Gopher on World indexes the ClariNet UPI news feed using WAIS, and makes it available for subscriber use only. Here is the top level menu for The World's Gopher:

```
           Internet Gopher Information Client v1.1

              Root gopher server: world.std.com

        1.   Information About The World Public Access UNIX/
-->     2.   The World's ClariNews UPI Index/
        3.   OBI The Online Book Initiative/
        4.   Internet and USENET Phone Books/
        5.   Shops on The World/
        6.   Book Sellers/
        7.   Bulletin Boards via the Internet/
        8.   FTP/
        9.   Government Information/
        10.  Internet Information and Resources/
        11.  Libraries/
        12.  Mailing List Archives/
        13.  Membership and Professional Associations/
        14.  News and Weather/
        15.  Other Gopher and Information Servers/
        16.  Periodicals, Magazines, and Journals/
        17.  University of Minnesota Gopher Server/

Press ? for Help, q to Quit, u to go up a menu  Page: 1/1
```

To search the UPI news feed, select item **2** and press ⟨RET⟩.

You will then be asked to provide search keywords:

```
             Internet Gopher Information Client v1.1

                  The World's ClariNews UPI Index

  -->  1.  Information About The ClariNews UPI index.
       2.  Search ClariNews UPI Index <?>


     +-----------------Search ClariNews UPI  Index--------+
     |                                                    |
     | Words to search for    bosnia                      |
     |                                                    |
     |    [Cancel ^G] [Accept - Enter]                    |
     |                                                    |
     +----------------------------------------------------+
  Move to item number: 2
```

The search then returns a list of news stories.

```
             Internet Gopher Information Client v1.1

               Search ClariNews UPI Index: bosnia

  -->  1.  U.N. leader, Security Council to meet urgently on Bosnia    ..4/news/.
       2.  Clinton nears decision on Bosnia   /UPI-data/1993/May/May  1/news/.
       3.  Security Council meets in urgent session on Bosnia   ../May  4/local/.
       4.  Security Council meets in urgent session on Bosnia   ..y/May 4/news/.
       5.  Clinton nears Bosnia decision   /UPI-data/1993/May/May  1/news/.
       6.  Bosnia wants U.S. air strikes against Serbs    ..1993/May/May 4/news/.
       7.  Austrian charity becomes Bosnia's biggest aid program   ..ay 2/news/.
       8.  Clinton favors 'military steps' in Bosnia    ..a/1993/May/May 1/news/.
       9.  U.N. prepares to implement peace plan in Bosnia-Herzegovina    ..ews/.
      10.  Karadzic says Bosnian Serbs not demanding more territory    ..1/news/.
      11.  Bosnian-Serb parliament rejects peace plan, sets referendum    ..ews/.
      12.  Bosnian Serbs discuss peace plan   /UPI-data/1993/May/May  5/news/.
      13.  Bosnian Serbs accept peace plan   /UPI-data/1993/May/May  2/news/.
      14.  Bosnian Serbs consider conditions for accepting peace plan    ..news/.
      15.  U.S.-Russian Kremlin meeting focuses on Yugoslav conflict    ../news/.
      16.  What Newspapers Are Saying   /UPI-data/1993/May/May  5/news/.
      17.  UPI NEWS AT A GLANCE [May 5 6 am PDT]    ..-data/1993/May/May 5/news/.
      18.  UNHCR says 'ethnic cleansing' increasing    ..ta/1993/May/May 4/news/.

  Press ? for Help, q to Quit, u to go up a menu
  Page: 1/5
```

For more information

Gopher mailing lists

gopher-news-request@boombox.micro.umn.edu

Gopher conferences

alt.gopher   Discussion on gopher
comp.infosystems.gopher   More discussions on gopher

WORLD WIDE WEB

What is World Wide Web?

World Wide Web (W3) is system for creating and browsing distributed hypertexts. W3 hypertexts link machines around the globe, and they contain links to files and newsgroups, as well as to `telnet`, Gopher, Archie, and Z39.50 servers.

Many Internet services provide access to a textual client, which can be accessed by typing `www`. To point the client to a specific hypertext, rather than using the generic home page, use the WWW_HOME environmental variable. For example:

```
%setenv WWW_HOME=/ie/home/aboba/default.html
```

Graphical W3 clients are available for Macintosh, NeXT, and X11, and full-screen and line-mode browsers are available for UNIX. W3 can also be accessed via `telnet` to the following sites:

```
telnet  eies2.njit.edu  (128.235.1.43)
telnet  fatty.law.cornell.edu
(132.236.108.5) (Cornell Law Library)
telnet  info.cern.ch  (128.141.201.74)
telnet  ukanaix.cc.ukans.edu
telnet  sun.uakom.cs
telnet  info.funet.fi  (128.214.6.100)
telnet  vms.huji.ac.il  (128.139.4.3)
```
(Hebrew University of Jerusalem English/Hebrew Hypertext),login: `www`

Finally, W3 (and by extension, Z39.50 and Gopher) can also be accessed via mail. For more information on this, add the command `mail listserv@info.cern.ch`, `help` in the body of the message.

How does W3 work?

Within W3, there are documents and links. Within a document, there can be links to other documents, parts of a document, files, telnet sites, newsgroups, etc. The links can be local or to machines on the other side of the world.

It is also possible to search an index document on a remote server by keyword. The result is returned as a document that consists of links to the results of the search. It is the keyword-search facility that allows for the gatewaying of Z39.50 and Archie queries. In the case of Z39.50, the resulting document consists of links to documents returned by the Z39.50 server as "relevant" to the query; in the case of Archie, the resulting document consists of links to the found files.

The hypertextual format of W3 is also natural for representing network news, which is organized as a hierarchy. Within a group, messages are threaded by topic, and they also refer to each other.

Since the W3 scheme is so general and supports so many protocols, it is the most flexible of the Internet meta-tools. However, the extra complexity also makes W3 clients harder to implement, which has slowed the system's wide dissemination. Until the launching of the NCSA Mosaic effort, W3 had primarily been developed by volunteers, since the original team's first priority was supporting High Energy Physics research at CERN.

In an effort to move W3 forward, the NSF has funded the NCSA Mosaic effort. Mosaic is an extended version of W3 that supports extensions such as support for formatted text with fonts, as well as embedded images, sound, and video, and text and voice annotation. The potential of such a global multi-media hypertext system is so incredible that it has only barely been explored.

Mosaic clients as well as external viewers for PostScript, JPEG, sounds, and MPEG movies are now available for X (xmosaic), Windows and Macintosh (MacMosaic). There are also Mac as well as UNIX servers. Clients may also support machine-specific formats. For example, in addition to standard formats, MacMosaic also supports QuickTime and display of PICTs.

Chapter 14: World Wide Web

The Cornell Law Library Web

The Cornell Law Library offers an experimental W3 server that contains some legal materials such as the U.S. Constitution and recent U.S. Supreme Court decisions. Here is a sample session:

```
planet:1# telnet fatty.law.cornell.edu
Trying 132.236.108.5...
Connected to fatty.law.cornell.edu.

Escape character is '^]'.

SunOS UNIX (fatty)

login: www
Last login: Wed Apr  7 17:49:32 from cunyvm.cuny.edu
SunOS Release 4.1.2 (NEWSLIP) #1: Thu Sep 3 13:07:29 EDT 1992

!!
ppid is 4310
telnet is in.telnetd
action is /usr/local/etc/wwwdriver.all


This WWW service is provided by the Legal Information
Institute, Cornell Law School, Ithaca, NY.

It provides a line-mode browser for using the World Wide Web
software. Better, X-Windows-based browsers are available if
you are running a workstation or PC which is capable of using
X-Windows. We have so far tested the software with
OpenWindows, X11, and DESQview/X. Clients exist for NeXT and
OSF/Motif machines as well.

You can get information on WWW and WWW browsers by telnet from
info.cern.ch. The document address for this material is

http://fatty.law.cornell.edu.:80/usr2/wwwtext/lii.table.html

For further information:
tom@law.mail.cornell.edu

Press the return key to continue....

                    LEGAL INFORMATION INSTITUTE -- WWW DOCUMENTS


                            U.S. LEGAL MATERIALS

An experimental product of the Legal Information Institute, Cornell Law School.
There is no guarantee, implied or otherwise, that the data here is either
accurate or complete. This is an experimental version only.

  U.S. CONSTITUTION[1]

  RECENT DECISIONS OF THE U.S. SUPREME COURT[2]

  U.S. ADMINISTRATIVE PROCEDURE ACT (INCLUDING FREEDOM OF INFORMATION ACT AND
  PRIVACY ACT)[3]

  U.S. COPYRIGHT ACT[4]

  U.S. PATENT ACT[5]

  U.S. LANHAM ACT (TRADEMARKS)[6]

1-10, <RETURN> for more, Quit, or Help:
```

Introduction to Mosaic

Mosaic is an enhanced version of World Wide Web, supporting hypertext dcouments with embedded graphics, sounds and movies. Mosaic also features support for a smorgasbord of protocols (WAIS, Gopher, FTP, Archie, Finger, Mail, and USENET to name a few). These enhanced capbilities make Mosaic the most capable Internet navigation tool developed to date, and a promising multimedia development tool.

Running XMosaic

To run the X version of Mosaic, you will need an implementation of X for your machine, such as MacX (Macintosh), or versions from NCD or NetManage (PC). In a reversal of the normal terminology, the X implementation for your microcomputer is called the Server, while the application running on the host is called the client.

The first step in running Mosaic is to install the X client (xmosaic) on your host machine. This may be as simple as transferring over the xmosaic binaries, since ftp.ncsa.uiuc.edu offers compiled versions of Mosaic for SPARC, DEC (MIPS and Alpha architectures) and RS6000.

Once you've got the client running, start up your X implementation, as well as a telnet application. Using telnet, login to your host, and tell X where to display:

```
% setenv DISPLAY <IP address>:0
```
Example:

```
% setenv DISPLAY 192.187.157.2:0
```

At this point, you can then run the xmosaic client in the background.

```
% xmosaic &
```

Soon after this, your X server may notify you that an application is trying to connect, and ask if you want to accept the connection.

Alternatively, your X implementation may support the use of remote commands. You can accomplish this with MacX by selecting **New Command...** from the **Remote** menu. The following command window will then appear:

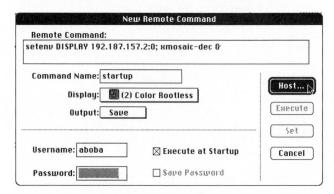

Fill in the name and text of the remote command, as well as your username and password. When you are done, click on the **Host...** button in order to tell MacX which host the command is to be sent to. After you have filled this out, click on the **Execute** button in order to send the command.

The Xmosaic client may take as long as five minutes to start up, and may produce a long list of error messages on the UNIX host system, which may include problems with fonts that may not be available on your X server. Don't worry about the messages; in my experience they are seldom fatal.

How do I create my own W3 server?

Adding to the W3 system is as easy as creating a link between an existing document and a resource on your system. Since you can run an anonymous FTP server on the Macintosh (FTPd, see Chapter 10: File Transfer) or PC (KA9Q, see Chapter 15: TCP/IP), if this is all you want to do, you do not need to set up a full-fledged W3 server.

However, if you want to create your own W3 or Mosaic documents, you will need to run a full-fledged W3 server. To do this you can run the NCSA's UNIX HTTPd server, which runs on port 80 and is available from NCSA via **ftp.ncsa.uiuc.edu, cd/Mosaic/ncsa_httpd**. An easy to use Macintosh HTTP server written by Chuck

Shotton (called MacHTTP) is available via **ftp sumex-aim.stanford.edu, cd /info-mac/comm**. MacHHTTP supports HTML v0.9 as well as AppleScript. NCSA has also promised a Macintosh Mosaic server.

Understanding HTML

W3 documents are authored using the HyperText Markup Language (HTML), a subset of SGML. HTML commands, called tags, are embedded within ASCII text, and are reminiscent of typesetting languages such as nroff or TeX, although HTML is somewhat simpler. As with those languages, HTML does its own word wrapping, unless you turn it off.

Most HTML commands require two tags, one for the beginning, and one for the end of the command. The text to be operated on resides in between. Tags are surrounded by angle brackets, with ending tags such as </h1> sporting a /, while beginning tags do not.

Converting to HTML

Utilities are available to convert documents created in FrameMaker or Rich Text Format (RTF) to HTML for use with Mosaic.

Daniel Connolly (connolly@convex.com) has written a package to convert from FrameMaker to HTML. The package is available via **ftp info.cern.ch, cd /pub/WWW/src**.

Chris Hector (cjh@cray.com) has written an RTF to HTML translator (called rtftohtml). It converts text and styles; pictures are saved separately and cross-referenced in the text. This makes it easy to use a batch conversion utility such as Hijaak to convert the pictures to a Mosaic-supported format such as GIF or JPG.

For more information

Information on Mosaic is available via **ftp ftp.ncsa.uiuc.edu, cd /Mosaic/mosaic-papers**.

To retrieve a paper by J.J. Berners-Lee, et al entitled "World Wide Web: The Information Universe," **ftp info-cern.ch, get /pub/www/doc/ENRAP_9202.ps**

CERN maintains a LISTSERV that handles mailing list subscriptions, as well as allowing people to query WWW by email. Mail for the LISTSERV is sent to listserv@info.cern.ch. If you would like to talk to a person, **mail www-request@info.cern.ch**.

Contact: Tim Berners-Lee, WorldWideWeb project, CERN, 1211 Geneva 23, Switzerland, +41 22 767 3755, Fax: +41 22 767 7155, email: timbl@info.cern.ch

Mosaic contact: Marc Andreessen, Software Development Group, National Center for Supercomputing Applications, 605 E. Springfield, Champaign, IL 61820, marca@ncsa.uiuc.edu, mosaic@ncsa.uiuc.edu

W3 LISTSERV commands

HELP
Gets help file

HELP <list>
Gets help about various topics

ADD <address> <list>
Subscribes to a mailing list at the given address. If <address> is omitted, then the address in the FROM line of the message is used.

DELETE <address><list>
Unsubscribes to the list

SEND <document>
Requests a WWW document. <document> must be a complete URL, such as: http://www.vuw.ac.nz:80/overseas/www-faq.html.

W3 mailing lists

Announcements about WWW: www-announce@info.cern.ch

Mailing list for developers: www-talk@info.cern.ch

USENET news groups

comp.infosystems.www   General WWW discussion

The Mosaic Interface

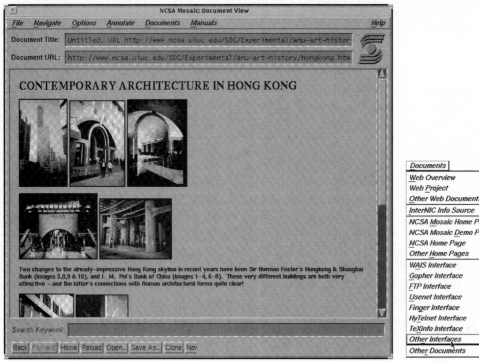

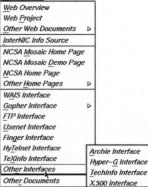

XMosaic

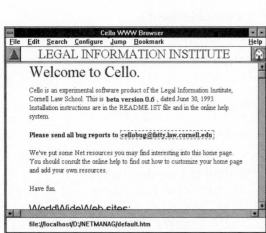

Windows Cello Client

MacMosaic

HTML Command	Purpose	Example
`<title>`	Document title	`<title>The Online User's Encyclopedia</title>`
`<h1>`	First level header	`<h1>This is a first level header</h1>`
`<h2>`	Second level header	`<h2>This is a second level header.</h2>`
`<i>`	Italics	`<i>This is a sentence in italics.</i>`
`<b>`	Bold	`<b>This is a sentence in bold.</b>`
`<p>`	End of paragraph	This is a sentence that goes on and on. And this is the end of a paragraph. `<p>`
`<code>`	Monospace font (will be word wrapped)	`<code>This is a sentence in a monospaced font.</code>`
`<img`	Embedded image (text aligned with the top of the image, bottom is default)	`<img align=top src="plant.gif">`
`<dl>`, `</dl>`	Glossary beginning/ending	`<dl>`
`<dt>`	Word titles	`<dt>Z39.50`

`<dd>`	Glossary descriptions	`<dd>An ANSI protocol used in WAIS.`
		`<dt>ZMODEM`
		`<dd>A file transfer protocol developed by Chuck Forsberg.`
		`</dl>`

`<ul>`, `</ul>`	Bulleted list beginning/ending	`<ul>`

`<li>`	List item	`<li> A phone line.`
		`<li> BBS software.`
		`<li> A modem.`
		`</ul>`

`<ol>`, `</ol>`	Numbered list beginning/ending	`<ol>`

`<li>`	List item	`<li> A phone line.`
		`<li> BBS software.`
		`<li> A modem.`
		`</ol>`

`<pre>`	Preformatted text (no word wrapping, mono-spaced font)	`<pre>`
		`01234567890123456789012345678901234567890`
		`|-------------|------------------------|`
		`| This table   |                        |`
		`| will stay    |                        |`
		`| formatted    |                        |`
		`|-------------|------------------------|`
		`</pre>`

`&lt`	Escape sequence for <	This is a sentence with lots of &lt &lt symbols. `<p>`
`&gt`	Escape sequence for >	This is a sentence with lots of &gt &gt symbols. `<p>`
`&amp`	Escape sequence for &	This is a sentence about A &amp P. `<p>`
`<a`	Local Hypertext link	`<a href="/pub/mailcom/bbb1.html">BBB Update 1</a>`
	Global Hypertext link	`<a href="http://internaut.com/pub/bbb1.html"> BBB Update 1 in HTML form</a>`
	Link to a Gopher	`<a href="gopher://marvel.loc.gov/"> Library of Congress Gopher </a>`
	Link to a file	`<a href="file://internaut.com/pub/bbb1.sea.hqx"> BBB Update in Word format </a>`
	Link to a newsgroup	`<a href="news:comp.protocols.tcp-ip.ibmpc"> comp.protocols.tcp-ip.ibmpc newsgroup </a>`
	Link from an image to a hypertext	`<a href="http://internaut.com/pub/bbb1.html"> <img src="bernard-picture.gif"></a>`
	Link to a mail address	`<a href="mailto:aboba@world.std.com"> </a>`

HTML example

```
<TITLE><I>The Online User's Encyclopedia</I></TITLE>

<h1>What do I get?</h1>

<I>The Online User's Encyclopedia</I> is an 832 page guide to the online world.
This document outlines some of the features and benefits of the guide.<p>
<h2>Sample topics</h2>
<ol>
<li> <a href="http:chapt4.html">A guide to Safe Hex</a>
<li> <a href="http:chapt5.html">A guide to BBSes and Civic Networks.</a>
<li> <a href="http:chapt7.html">A guide to TCP/IP for the Mac and Windows.</a>
</ol><p>
<h2>Additional benefits</h2>
<ul>
<li> <a href="http:updates.html">Electronic updates.</a>
<li> <a href="http:lists.html">Access to the MailCom FTP archive.</a>
<li> <a href="http:disc.html">Discounts on products and services.</a>
</ul>
<p>
For further information on <I>The Online User's Encyclopedia</I>, please contact:
<b><a href="mailto:aboba@world.std.com">aboba@world.std.com</a></b><p>
<a href="http:clicme.html"><img align=top src="bernard.gif"></a>
```

Example viewed by the Cello Windows W3 client

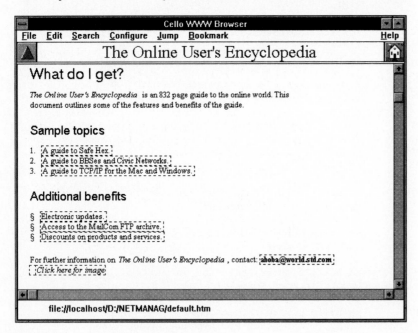

CHAPTER 15: TCP/IP

Copyright © 1993, MailCom, all rights reserved. Reprinted by permission.

INTRODUCTION TO **TCP/IP**

The Internet has grown so large partly because TCP/IP is compatible with so many networking technologies, computers, and operating systems. Most UNIX versions have TCP/IP built in, but TCP/IP is also available for minicomputers, supercomputers, IBM mainframes, and Vax VMS machines, as well as the Macintosh, PC, and Amiga. TCP/IP has been run successfully on virtually every conceivable physical connection, including Ethernet, Token Ring, LocalTalk, X.25, modems, serial cables, packet radio, or satellite links. It can run over a 2400-bps modem or 622 Mbps ATM links (though not as efficiently as we might like).

Since Internet hosts connect via so many networking technologies, various connection mechanisms are needed to stitch the disparate parts together. These include repeaters, bridges, routers, applications gateways and firewalls.

Repeaters, bridges, routers, gateways, and firewalls

In the figure on the next page, we diagram the behavior of repeaters, bridges, routers, applications layer gateways, and firewalls within the application (A), transport (T), internet (I), network (N), and physical (P) layers.

The function of a repeater is to seamlessly link two networks into one logical network by copying frames between them. Repeaters are typically implemented in hardware and do not modify the network frames in any way.

A bridge connects segments of the same network and filters traffic between them based on Ethernet or IP addresses. This is useful if the network is heavily loaded, since bridges can isolate the heavily loaded section, preventing it from degrading performance on the rest of the network. Since bridges must decide when to pass along frames from one side of the bridge to the other, they must understand the network topology. Since bridges connect segments of the same network, segments on each side of the bridge must have the same IP network ID. For example:

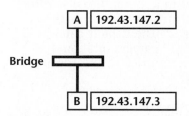

The function of the router is to interconnect networks to build an internetwork. Routers receive datagrams on one physical connection and retransmit them on another physical connection. For example, a router could be used to connect an Ethernet network to a Token Ring network or a network operating over serial lines. A given datagram may pass through a dozen routers to reach its destination. Since a router is on more than one network, it also has multiple TCP/IP addresses, one for each network to which it is connected.

For example, the router shown below has both the TCP/IP address 192.43.147.2 and 192.108.136.6.

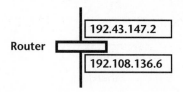

Repeaters, Bridges, Routers, Firewalls, Gateways

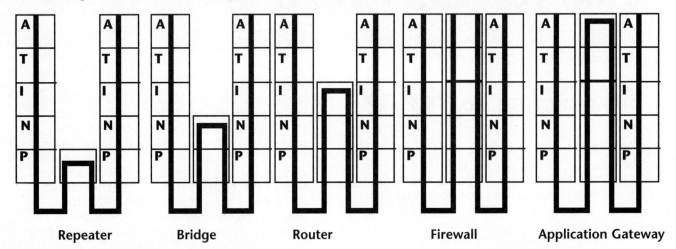

| Repeater | Bridge | Router | Firewall | Application Gateway |

When referring to TCP/IP, the term "gateway" is also used to refer to a router, usually in the context of phrases such as "default gateway," or "routing gateways." The default gateway is the router to which IP datagrams should be sent when the other entries in the routing table do not apply.

By receiving frames on one medium and sending them on another, routers stitch the disparate networking technologies of the Internet into an enormous patchwork quilt. In the diagram shown below, LocalTalk, Ethernet, and X.25 networks are connected by routers. Just as someone could translate between English and Chinese by first translating English to French, and then French to Chinese, LocalTalk hosts can communicate with X.25 hosts by sending packets through the LocalTalk/Ethernet and Ethernet/X.25 routers.

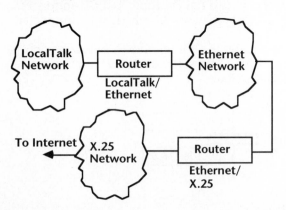

The function of an applications layer gateway is to translate between protocols, such as in gatewaying electronic mail between FidoNet and UUCP, or making NFS volumes mountable over AppleShare.

The function of a firewall is to protect an internal network from intrusion by outsiders, yet to provide a minimal level of connectivity. In the figure above, the firewall processes packets up to the application layer but prevents the routing of datagrams between the outside world and the internal network. The term firewall is also sometimes used to refer to routers configured to pass only certain datagrams between the networks it connects.

Routers and addressing

We have discussed how each datagram contains the IP address of both the sender and the destination system.

In order to allow efficient retrieval of the network information, 32-bit Internet addresses are separated into a network ID and a host ID. The network ID portion of the TCP/IP address identifies the network that the host is connected to, while the host ID portion uniquely identifies a host within a network. Since individual networks can have a few or many hosts, the Internet provides for several address classes. These include Class A (7 bits of network ID and 24 bits of host ID), Class B (14 bits of network ID and 16 bits of host ID) and

Class C addresses (21 bits of network ID and 8 bits of host ID). There are also class D addresses (used for multicasting), and class E (reserved), but these are for special purposes.

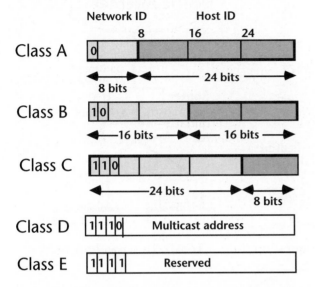

Since the first bit of a class A address must be a zero, and network IDs 0 and 127 are reserved for special purposes, a class A network address must be in the range of 1 to 126. 127 is reserved for the loopback address, which refers to the local host. Since the first two bits of a Class B address are 10, the first octet of these addresses runs from 128 to 191. Since Class C addresses start with 110, the first octet of Class C address runs from 192 to 223.

Since Class A addresses use the first octet as the network ID, class B use the first two octets, and Class C addresses use the first three octets, you can tell a system's IP address class and network ID, just by glancing at the first octet of the address:

Address	Class	NetID	HostID
10.28.3.4	A	10	28.3.4
140.174.2.71	B	140.174	2.71
192.187.157.2	C	192.187.157	2

By making it easy to separate the network ID from the host ID, the TCP/IP addressing scheme makes for efficient routing. From origination until the datagram reaches its destination network and host, routing decisions are based solely on the destination network.

How routing works

For the Internet layer to carry out the task of routing datagrams, it needs to know how to direct them.

For networks with a single route to the Internet, these directions are very simple. Let us assume that you lived in a small town with only one highway, a Main Street, and no airport. If you were appointed the official Traffic Director, what would you do when people came to you for directions? If someone came to you asking for directions to a place in town, you'd point them toward Main Street. If they asked for directions to any place else, you'd point them toward the highway.

Each of the basic cases on the next page is like that small town in that there is a small local network (Main Street), and a single highway leading out of town (the SLIP/PPP link to the Internet). As a result, datagrams for the local network go out over the Ethernet and datagrams for any place else go out over the SLIP/PPP link.

For the case of the single computer with a SLIP/PPP link, things are even simpler. This is like a small town with only one building and a single road heading out of town. If someone comes in and asks how to get somewhere, and they're not looking for your place, you just point them towards the road!

Since we're dealing with computers, these concepts have to be expressed somewhat more formally, but if you can understand the problem of directing traffic in a small town, you've grasped all you need to know about TCP/IP routing to put a single machine (or a small group of machines) on the Internet.

In the figures on the next page, the Internet service provider's equipment is not shown on the diagrams. However, it should be understood that there is another router on the provider side of the link.

For each of these "small town" cases, the routing instructions are simple enough that they can be entered manually and left alone. This is known as static routing, and is the only type of routing that most SLIP/PPP users or BBS sysops will ever need to know about.

Internet Connection Options

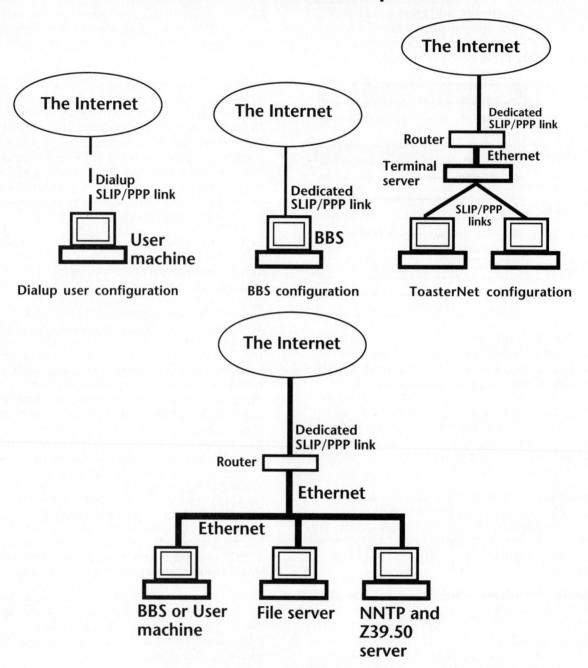

Dialup user configuration

BBS configuration

ToasterNet configuration

Connected network configuration

For each of these "small town" cases, the routing instructions are simple enough that they can be entered manually and left alone. This is known as static routing, and is the only type of routing that most SLIP/PPP users or BBS sysops will ever need to know about.

The other type of routing, dynamic routing, is only needed in more complex situations, such as when there is more than one route to the Internet, or when the network is in a state of flux and manual modifications to the routing table would become tedious.

Example

Let's look at an example of routing in the most complex of our "small town" cases. In the case below, we have two Class C networks, one a local Ethernet (192.32.162), and the other a SLIP/PPP network (192.108.136). The networks are linked by a router, sometimes also called a gateway router or gateway. Note that the router has two network addresses, one for each network it is on: one on 192.32.162, and the other on 192.108.136. This is critical, since it signifies to systems on these networks that the router is on the same physical network. Note also that there must be another router on the other side of the SLIP/PPP link.

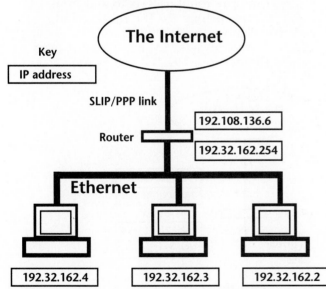

The router shown above does not have to do very much. If a packet comes in over the SLIP/PPP interface with an address of

192.32.162.x, it is retransmitted over the Ethernet interface. Similarly, if a packet comes in over the Ethernet interface with a network address other than 192.32.162, it is transmitted over the SLIP/PPP interface, which is said to be the default route.

How are the routing instructions just described translated into a form that the computer can understand? This is done through use of a routing table. The routing table contains entries for host-specific routes (individual buildings), routes to individual networks (Main Street), and default routes (the highway out of town). In our case, the routing table for the router will look like:

Network or Host	Router	Hop Count
192.32.162	192.32.162.254	1
Default gateway	192.104.136.6	1

The address in the first column gives the network address, and the second column gives the interface to which traffic for that network should be directed. The third column is the hop count, or the number of routers that must be crossed to get to the destination network. In the case that there are multiple routes available, the hop count is used to calculate the shortest path to a destination network. In order to indicate a slow speed connection, hop count numbers are often inflated. Since there is only one route to the Internet in this example, the hop count is set to 1 and is irelevant. Note that in some implementations the address 0.0.0.0 signifies the default gateway, which is 192.104.136.6.

TCP/IP implementations that support routing (MacTCP currently does not) do so via a command that adds and deletes entries from the routing table. KA9Q (PC) and NetMac (Macintosh) support the route command; NetManage Chameleon supports construction of a routing table using the Windows interface, which is somewhat easier.

Subnet addressing

The TCP/IP protocol was designed prior to the microcomputer revolution, and as a result, it was not imagined that there would be many networks with large numbers of hosts. For example, class A provides for 126 networks of 16,516,350 hosts each; class B provides for 14,282 networks of 64,770 hosts each, and class C provides for 2,097,150 networks of 254 hosts each.

For networks at large sites such as universities or corporations, a single class B address is more attractive than using many class C addresses. A single class B address makes for simplified routing tables and avoids propagating to the outside world detailed information about internal network structure. However, putting so many hosts on a single network is not practical, since this would result in traffic overload.

The solution is to allocate a portion of the host ID to a subnet ID, thus subdividing the class B address space into multiple networks with a smaller number of hosts on each. This subnetting is for internal use only and is not transmitted to the outside world, which continues to view the site as a single class B network with a single routing table entry.

The division of a network into subnets is accomplished by use of a bitmask that is ANDed with the IP address to produce a network address that includes a subnet portion. For example, for a class B network that uses the third octet of the IP address for subnetting, the subnet mask would be 255.255.255.0.

The procedure for applying the subnet mask is illustrated on the next page. The procedure is typically less complicated in practice than it is in theory, since subnet bit masks almost always have contiguous ones and zeros.

The use of bitmasks also solves the problem of testing an address against the routing table. Whether subnetting is used or not, each routing table entry has a bitmask associated with it. The Internet layer performs an AND operation of the bitmask and the destination IP address, and then compares it to the entry in the routing table. If the entries match, the Internet layer sends the datagram to the router listed for that entry; if not, it tries the next table entry. Without subnetting, the bitmask for a Class A network is 255.0.0.0; for a Class B

address it is 255.255.0.0, and for a Class C address it is 255.255.255.0.

Please note that the subnet ID portion of an address can never be all 0s or 1s, and that all portions of a subnet must be connected on the same physical network. This can at times impose severe restrictions on allowable address assignments.

Network setup with subnet masks

The figure on the next page illustrates two alternative setups, including TCP/IP addresses and subnet masks for each.

The setup given below is typical of a user looking to put his or her microcomputer on the Internet. The SLIP/PPP link between the stand-alone system and the Internet service provider's router is denoted by a dotted line, signifying a dialup IP connection. Since the systems in this example have class C addresses, the subnet mask of 255.255.255.0 implies no subnetting.

In this example, the SLIP/PPP interface on the router has the network address 192.32.162, the same as the stand-alone host. This is not an accident—in fact it is a requirement since routers can only route packets to and from networks they belong to. The router in this example also has the TCP/IP address 192.108.136.6, in order to signify that it takes part in the network 192.108.136 as well.

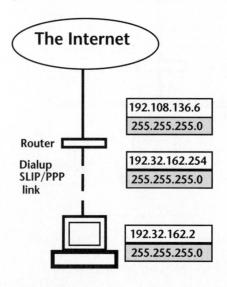

The second example is for a large bulletin board that has separated the functions of BBS, file server, and USENET news/Z39.50 server, placing each function on separate machines, linked together by Ethernet. Here the BBS network has a class B address and a subnet mask of 255.255.255.0. This divides the Class B two-octet hostID into 256 subnets of 254 systems each. As with subnet IDs, host IDs can also never be all 0s or all 1s.

This local area network is linked to the Internet by a high-speed dedicated SLIP or PPP link (denoted by a thick straight line). Here routers are required both on the BBS side of the dedicated SLIP/PPP link, as well as on the provider side.

Just as with the previous example, the routers have addresses on each of the networks to which they connect. Since the local Ethernet network ID is 192.32.162, the router must also have an address on this network, namely 192.32.162.254. The router also has an address of 192.108.136.6 for the SLIP/PPP interface. Please note that there is also another router on the provider's side of the link that is not shown in the figure.

Subnet do's and dont's

Remember that all machines on the same physical network must have the same subnet address, and that the combination subnet/network ID must be unique. Also, subnetIDs cannot consist of all 0s or all 1s.

Exercise: Why are the following configurations illegal?

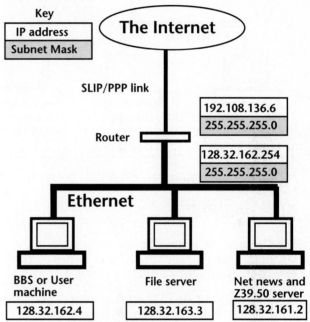

Illegal configuration 1

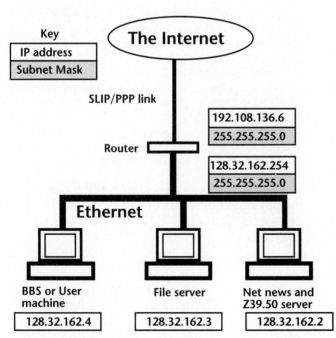

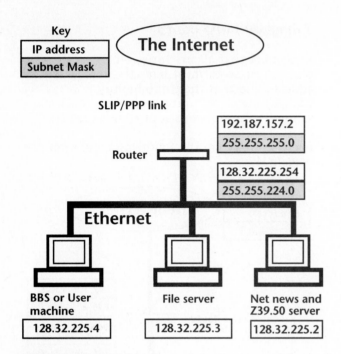

Key
IP address
Subnet Mask

The Internet

SLIP/PPP link

192.187.157.2
255.255.255.0

Router

128.32.225.254
255.255.224.0

Ethernet

BBS or User machine
128.32.225.4

File server
128.32.225.3

Net news and Z39.50 server
128.32.225.2

Illegal configuration 2

SLIP and PPP

For the user or system operator looking to connect a single machine or a network to the Internet, there are several options:

• **A dialup SLIP or PPP connection.** This connection is intermittent; it is typically brought up at scheduled times or based on demand. For example, it can be brought up when there are outgoing network packets and brought down after a period of inactivity. Not all applications are amenable to such as link. Since X Windows generates constant traffic, the link must always be up, even when the application is idle.

Note that it is generally the user's system that initiates the dialup IP session; most service providers will not initiate a dialup IP connection on their end if there are packets for the user's machine. This implies that while dialup IP connections may work well for users, they are not generally satisfactory for BBS sysops looking to accommodate incoming `telnet` or `ftp` sessions. Note also that since the system will not always be available for SMTP mail delivery, a means must be

developed (IMAP, POP or UUCP) for picking up mail from a forwarding site.

Dialup IP service is available from Netcom, Holonet, MERIT, and Colorado SuperNet for $2-3/hour plus a monthly maintenance fee. For Netcom's $20 monthly maintenance fee you also get a free unlimited use of a UNIX shell account.

• **A dedicated SLIP or PPP link.** This kind of link is always available. It allows the BBS to receive mail via the SMTP protocol and to handle incoming `telnet` or `ftp` sessions. The dedicated link can also be used to connect to a terminal server, which can offer support SLIP or PPP dialin users at reasonable cost. For low-speed connections, the link to the service provider can be handled by a modem; for higher speeds, ISDN connections or leased lines are required.

Dedicated SLIP and PPP connections are rapidly declining in price. For example, for a 14.4 Kbps dedicated link, The Little Garden (TLG) ToasterNet charges a $250 installation fee, plus a loan of a high-speed modem, and $70/month plus phone charges.

• **A dedicated link handled by a router.** Systems with heavy network traffic will probably want a dedicated router, rather than trying to force a server or the BBS system to perform this function. This is because routing packets at high speed is a CPU-intensive task that will degrade performance of machines that are interacting with users. For similar reasons, it is also a good idea to separate the BBS system from file and database servers, and machines that process incoming net news.

Higher speed dedicated connections vary in price depending on your location, but for T1 level service, fees of $800-5000/month are typical.

VJ compression

Serial Line IP (SLIP) is a simple framing protocol for transmitting Internet Protocol (IP) packets over a serial line. It does not route or error correct IP packets. Since it does so little, SLIP is relatively easy to implement. The more sophisticated Point-to-Point Protocol (PPP) supports error correction as well as multiple protocols.

Both SLIP and PPP offer a feature known alternatively as "Van Jacobson compression," or "header compression," named after Van Jacobson, a top-notch TCP/IP researcher working at Lawrence Berkeley Labs. Versions of SLIP incorporating Van Jacobson compression are referred to as "Compressed SLIP" or CSLIP. Header compression has an important effect on the "feel" of `telnet` sessions.

Here's why. At the slow speeds typical of keyboard entry, without header compression each letter is sent as a separate packet with a 40-byte TCP/IP header, plus 2 bytes added by SLIP. When using modem links, the result of adding 42 bytes of overhead for each character can be an uncomfortable keyboard feel for the typist. This will result when the packet roundtrip time gets much above 200 ms, which is the average time between key depressions of a 60-word-per-minute typist.

What can we do? Well, most of the 40-byte TCP/IP header contains information that changes infrequently throughout the transmissions of a given connection or session, such as the source and destination IP address and Port number. As a result, the header can be assumed to stay nearly constant, with changes transmitted only as necessary. This innovation, introduced by Van Jacobson (and therefore known as "VJ compression"), can shave the 40-byte header to as little as 5 bytes. That is often enough to produce a better keyboard "feel." However, be aware that if you are using GUI software, you may not be able to "feel" the difference between a compressed and noncompressed session, since much of the time you will be using the mouse, not the keyboard. Also keep in mind that VJ compression only applies to TCP/IP headers, *not* to the data portion of the packet.

Another factor influencing SLIP/PPP performance is the "ping latency" of the modem. This refers to the modem's internal buffering scheme. The best modems give standard ping response times of 163 msec over a 14,400 bps connection; poorer choices can yield ping times of 230 msec or higher.

Setting up SLIP/PPP

Before attempting to connect to your SLIP connection, your host should provide you with setup information. This should include:

• The domain name and IP address of the remote host.
• The domain name and IP address of your machine.
• The domain name and TCP/IP address of the nearest Domain Name Server.
• The subnet mask.
• The domain name and TCP/IP address of the default gateway, as well as addresses of secondary gateways.
• The domain name and TCP/IP address of an NNTP server.
• Sample configuration files, such as the sendmail.cf file, the /etc/hosts listing, etc.
• Whether the host is using header compression.
• Whether your TCP/IP address will be assigned statically, dynamically, or from the server.

Do not attempt to connect before you have this information, since it will just waste your time and money and may cause problems for the network. In particular, do not attempt to initiate a connection using a "made up" TCP/IP address, since this may conflict with an existing address. This is probably the quickest way to get people *very* angry at you.

Static addressing means that your TCP/IP address will always be the same. This makes it easy to configure your setup files. Dynamic addressing means that the host will send you a message containing your TCP/IP address when you log on. This can be problematic if your software doesn't support grabbing the address and inserting it into the setup files. If not, then you have to edit your setup files every time you log on. Yuck! Products that can handle dynamic addressing include MacSLIP and Chameleon.

You can retrieve your address (and other parameters of the connection) from the server using the configuration retrieval features of PPP, or if you are using SLIP, via the Bootstrap Protocol (BOOTP).

Personal SLIP/PPP Account Vital Information
DO NOT LOSE THIS PAGE!

My SLIP/PPP account name is:
(case sensitive!)

_____

My access phone number is:

_____

My subnet mask is:

_____

Example: 255.255.255.0

My chosen protocol is: (choose one)

_____ SLIP _____ CSLIP _____ PPP

I am obtaining my TCP/IP address:

_____ statically _____ dynamically _____ from the server

My primary domain name server is:

_____

Example: 192.181.100.105

My fully qualified domain name is:

_____

Example: aboba.slip.netcom.com

My SMTP server is:

_____

Example: netcom1.netcom.com

My NNTP server is:

_____

Example: nntp.netcom.com

My SLIP/PPP account password is:
(case sensitive!)

_____

My TCP/IP address is:

_____

Example: 192.187.157.2

My default gateway is:

_____

Example: 192.187.157.254
Note: the default gateway must be
on the same network as you are!

My Maximum Transfer Unit (MTU) is:

_____

Example: 1006 for SLIP, 576 to avoid
fragmentation

My secondary domain name server is:

_____

Example: 192.181.100.101

My POP server account is:

_____

Example: aboba@netcom1.netcom.com

My POP server password is:

_____

My Ph server is:

_____

Troubleshooting

If your logon sequence appears to be working but you cannot reach any remote sites, this section may help. In order to troubleshoot a SLIP or PPP connection, you will need to become familar with tools such as ping, traceroute, and netstat.

Ping tests the functioning of the network layer by generating an ICMP echo request. If the interface is functioning and the targeted host is up, then the echo request datagram should be received and an ICMP echo reply should be transmitted back to the local host.

Traceroute tests the functioning of the internet layer by simulating the route traveled by a datagram targeted to a specified destination address. If routing tables are set up correctly for routing of packets both to and from the local host, then traceroute should show the datagram reaching its destination.

Netstat provides information on sockets and routing tables, as well as statistics on the functioning of individual interfaces.

To compress or not to compress

If the send and receive lights on your modem briefly flicker and then after that only the send light goes on, you may have a problem with header compression. When compressed SLIP/PPP is used, the first outgoing TCP/IP packet is not compressed, but subsequent packets are compressed. This means that if the host is not using compression, or if for some reason its compression software is incompatible with yours, the first packet will arrive fine, but subsequent packets will be lost. One way to check this out is to ask your host to turn off compression and see if the problem goes away.

Ping

Ping, which is available in almost every TCP/IP implementation, both probes connectivity and provides a measure of propagation time.

A successful ping does *not* indicate that header compression is working correctly. This is because ping uses the ICMP echo facility, not TCP packets. Since ICMP packets are not

affected by header compression, it is possible to execute a successful ping on a SLIP/PPP link where the local and remote hosts disagree on the form of compression to be used. This is where a TCP testing facility such as that provided by MacTCP Watcher comes in handy.

For PC users, ping is supported within KA9Q as well as within various Windows TCP/IP packages. On the Macintosh, ping is supported by MacTCP Watcher as well as a program called MPing. MPing was created by Apple Computer, and is available via `ftp ftp.apple.com, get /dts/mac/netcomm/mactcp-1-1-examples.hqx`. Since it is quite buggy (it will not run on a Quadra, for example), I recommend using MacTCP Watcher instead.

MacTCP Watcher

MacTCP Watcher

MacTCP Watcher by Peter Lewis, available via `ftp sumex-aim.stanford.edu, cd /info-mac/comm` is a very nice diagnostic program for TCP/IP. It includes ping, and also tests TCP, UDP, and Domain Name Service. About the only thing that the program lacks is traceroute.

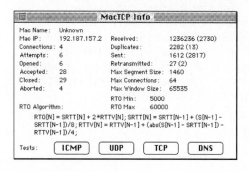

Example

After recently bringing up a SLIP connection, I found that I was unable to `telnet` or `ftp` to sites such as sumex-aim.stanford.edu. To diagnose the problem, I ran ping to determine if the connection was functioning. This demonstrated connectivity with two of the computers on the service provider's local area network. Attempts to ping more distant sites were unsuccessful; only the send light flickered on the modem, but no response was received.

Since the modem (physical layer) and SLIP link (network layer) appeared to be functioning, the next step was to test the internet layer using `traceroute`. This provided a clue to what was going on, as we'll discuss a bit later.

Netstat

Netstat

Versions of Netstat are available for the Macintosh, Windows, DOS, and UNIX. This utility provides diagnostics on sockets, interfaces, and the routing tables. The information provided is different for each implementation. For the Macintosh, there is a version of Netstat included with the MacSLIP package from Hyde Park Software. In order to obtain statistics, run Netstat, and then select **Open Trace** from the **File** menu.

Netstat will then keep statistics on packets from that point on. Unlike the UNIX version, Macintosh Netstat does not keep statistics on collisions, so you cannot use it to see if your local area network is saturated.

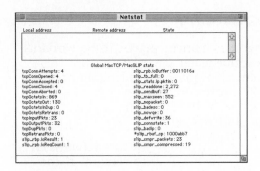

Example

Below are examples of the various netstat options under UNIX.

The **-a** option lists all sockets, including servers. Example:

```
% netstat -a
Active Internet connections (including servers)
Proto Recv-Q Send-Q Local       Foreign     (state)
tcp      0      0    *.printer    *.*        LISTEN
tcp      0      0    *.smtp       *.*        LISTEN
tcp      0      0    *.z3950      *.*        LISTEN
tcp      0      0    *.ns         *.*        LISTEN
tcp      0      0    *.gopher     *.*        LISTEN
tcp      0      0    *.http       *.*        LISTEN
                        .
                        .
                        .
udp      0      0    *.time       *.*
udp      0      0    *.daytime    *.*
udp      0      0    *.chargen    *.*
udp      0      0    *.echo       *.*
udp      0      0    *.ntalk      *.*
udp      0      0    *.talk       *.*
udp      0      0    *.biff       *.*
udp      0      0    *.tftp       *.*
udp      0      0    *.sunrpc     *.*
udp      0      0    *.syslog     *.*
```

The **-nr** option outputs the routing table.

```
% netstat -nr
Routing tables
Destination      Gateway          Flags  Refs   Use
Interface
127.0.0.1        127.0.0.1        UH     0      8921   lo0
192.187.157.2    127.0.0.1        UH     3      10442  lo0
default          192.187.157.254  UG     0      28324  ppp0
192.187.157      192.187.157.2    U      4      30947  en0
```

The **-i** option shows the state of all network interfaces. Example:

```
% netstat -i
Name  Mtu  Network      Address        Ipkts Ierrs Opkts Oerrs Coll
en0   1500 192.187.157  192.187.157.2    18     0    18    0    0
lo0   1536 loopback     localhost      50304    0  50304   0    0
ppp0* 1500 192.187.157  192.187.157.2  28793   241 28212   0    0
ppp1* 1500 none         none             0      0     0    0    0
en0   1500 none         none            18      0    18    0    0
```

Looking at the ratio of Coll/Opkts gives you an idea of whether your network is saturated or not. Collision rates over two percent indicate a possible problem.

Traceroute

Traceroute is a program that simulates the route that a packet travels between your system and a distant Internet node. This is useful for figuring out why a packet didn't get to the right destination. Versions of traceroute exist for UNIX and the PC (KA9Q's hop check command). Unfortunately, I do not know of any Macintosh implementation of traceroute; if you can't find one, try executing traceroute on a machine other than your local host.

Example

Back to the case of the missing datagrams. After successfully pinging the remote host, I decided to try a traceroute from machine world.std.com to my remote host, 192.100.81.110. Here's what the traceroute looked like:

```
% traceroute 192.100.81.110
traceroute to 192.100.81.110 (192.100.81.110), 30 hops max, 40
byte packets
 1  Boston.MA.ALTER.NET (192.74.137.200)  4 ms  3 ms  3 ms
 2  Portland.OR.ALTER.NET (137.39.29.2)  112 ms  110 ms  111 ms
 3  San-Jose2.CA.ALTER.NET (137.39.8.1)  159 ms  137 ms  143 ms
 4  San-Jose1.CA.ALTER.NET (137.39.45.1)  145 ms  133 ms  216 ms
 5  Palo-Alto.CA.ALTER.NET (137.39.46.2)  136 ms  133 ms  148 ms
 6  SU5.BARRNET.NET (192.31.50.1)  138 ms  167 ms  133 ms
 7  SU-C1.BARRNET.NET (131.119.251.101)  135 ms  133 ms  148 ms
 8  SCU1.BARRNET.NET (131.119.49.2)  142 ms  143 ms  136 ms
 9  NETCOM.BARRNET.NET (131.119.108.2)  148 ms  143 ms  148 ms
10  CALNet-sj5.netcom.com (192.100.81.110)  181 ms  *  141 ms
```

This traceroute indicates that node 192.100.81.110 is up and reachable from the rest of the Internet. Evidently, it was possible to route packets from the outside world to 192.100.81.110, but not from the local host to the outside world. What was going on?

In order for you to be able to communicate with sites outside your service provider's local area network, those sites must be able to figure out how to route packets to your node. This means that your network ID must be "advertised" to the core gateways, those routers that know how to reach all networks.

With the Internet expanding at an incredible pace, backbone service providers are swamped with requests. It therefore can take several weeks for routing tables to change to allow a

site to become known to the outside world. How can you tell if your network ID has been advertised? A traceroute to 192.187.134.3 gave:

```
% traceroute 192.187.134.3
traceroute to 192.187.134.3 (192.187.134.3),
30 hops max, 40 byte packets
 1  Boston.MA.ALTER.NET (192.74.137.200)3 ms  3 ms  3 ms
 2  Washington.DC.ALTER.NET (137.39.12.1)16 ms  14 ms  35 ms
 3  College-Park.MD.ALTER.NET (137.39.28.2)16 ms  15 ms  15 ms
 4  College_Park.MD.NSS.NSF.NET (192.41.177.254)19 ms 22 ms 17 ms
 5  College_Park.MD.NSS.NSF.NET (192.41.177.254)16 ms !N 22 ms
!N 19 ms !N
```

College–Park.MD.NSS.NSF.NET is a core gateway, and the !N is an error message meaning "network unreachable." This indicates that router College–Park.MD.NSS.NSF.NET could not find network 192.187.134 in its routing tables. Had this been a !H, it would have meant "host unreachable." In this case the problem would have been with an individual link.

Arp

The **arp** command can be used to get information about the arp table, as well as to set up proxy arp. The **-a** option dumps the arp table, while the **-s** option allows for a host to perform proxy arp, that is, to respond to ARP requests for another host with its own Ethernet address. In the example below, pub stands for "publish," which means that your host will respond to arp requests for the other host. Example:

```
%arp -s <other host address> <your ethernet address>  pub
```

Internet Q&A

I am using class B addresses of 128.162.32.2 and 128.162.192.3 and a subnet mask of 255.255.192.0 and nothing is working. What's wrong?

Remember when I said that the subnet ID portion of an address cannot be all 0s or all 1s? In this case you are reserving 2 bits for subnet ID and 14 bits for host ID. In order for the 2 bits of subnet ID to not be all 0s or 1s, the allowable address space is 128.162.64.1 to 128.162.191.254.

TCP/IP ON THE PC

Why do I care?

The IBM PC offers a wide range of TCP/IP applications and development kits for DOS, Windows, and Windows NT. These include a number of very capable and easy to use commercial packages for Windows, as well as a cornucopia of publicly distributable software for DOS and Windows. Using this software, PC owners can now put their machines on the Internet as well as build their own internets.

In this section I will discuss the hardware and software needed to put an IBM-PC compatible on the Internet using SLIP or PPP. I will also discuss the use of publicly distributable packages such as KA9Q to build complex network configurations.

Components of a TCP/IP solution

Running TCP/IP software on IBM-PC compatibles involves choosing hardware and software to implement each layer of the TCP/IP protocol stack. While the IBM PC offers unparalleled flexibility, the incredible range of choices can also be very confusing. The hardware and software required to get applications running on the PC is shown below.

Applications Layer	Applications
Transport Layer	Windows Sockets & TCP/IP Stack
Internet Layer	
Network Layer	Shims, Drivers & Multiplexers
Physical Layer	Network Card or Modem

Mission possible

The task of the PC user of TCP/IP (should you choose to accept it) is to ensure that all of these layers are compatible with each other. The easiest way to do this is to decide on what software you want to run first. Many applications now come with a version of Windows Sockets and a TCP/IP stack. If you purchase a network card that is recommended by your software vendor, you'll be home free, since these cards will probably come with driver software that is compatible with your TCP/IP stack.

The situation is somewhat more complex if you already have a network card with a driver that is not supported by your chosen application, or if you want to simultaneously run applications requiring different TCP/IP stacks. In this case you'll need to understand packet multiplexors, drivers, and shims. We'll discuss those later on.

Physical layer

Every host must have hardware to support a network connection. This includes:

- Ethernet cards
- Token Ring cards
- AppleTalk cards
- Serial Ports

If you are using Ethernet, remember that if you are using BNC connectors, connecting even two machines requires use of tees and terminators, and that if you break the continuity on the network, you not only disconnect the machine you are working on, but all the other machines as well. Other Ethernet wiring schemes such as twisted pair are not so fickle.

You should also be aware that other network cards (such as Arcnet) will also work, provided that they can support appropriate drivers or NetBIOS.

Network layer

Since there are many different network adapters, writing software that accesses network adapters directly would be a tremendous amount of work and would require constant revisions to the code.

Instead, drivers are used that mask the differences between network adapters, allowing TCP/IP stacks to access adapters for a particular network technology with a common interface. Drivers are network-level software and do not provide any higher-level services.

Drivers

There are three major driver specifications for the PC:

- **Network Driver Interface Standard (NDIS)** [specified by 3Com and Microsoft]
- **Open Datalink Interface (ODI)** [specification by Novell]
- **Packet drivers** [specification by FTP Software]

The Packet Driver specification is freely available (`ftp vax.ftp.com, get packet-d.ascii`). Since the programming interface provided by packet drivers is different for each networking technology, a TCP/IP stack written for an Ethernet packet driver cannot use an AppleTalk packet driver. Packet driver interfaces include Class 1 (Ethernet), Class 3 (802.5 Token Ring), and Class 6 (SLIP). However, it is possible to write packet drivers that mimic one network technology (such as Ethernet, Class 1) while providing support for another technology (such as SLIP [Class 6], Token Ring [Class 3], or Arcnet). This is attractive since most publicly distributable software only supports the Class 1 or Class 6 interfaces.

The largest and best known collection of packet drivers is maintained by Crynwr Software (`nelson@crynwr.com`). This collection was formerly called the Clarkson Drivers. For 3COM drivers, try `ftp ftp.3com.com`, or for technical information, `mail info@3com.com`. For marketing and product information, `mail leads@hq.3mail.3com.com`.

Microsoft and 3Com also developed their own freely available driver specification, called NDIS. NDIS is used by Lan Manager, Windows For Workgroups (WFW), and Windows NT. LAN Manager uses NDIS 2.0, Windows NT uses 3.0, and WFW supports 2.0 and will support 3.0.

Novell also developed its own driver specification, called ODI. Unlike the other two driver specifications, developers looking to develop drivers for ODI must pay a fee to Novell. The ODI specification, while freely available, is proprietary in that Novell does not consider input from other vendors. However, unlike packet drivers, ODI drivers are independent of network technology.

Another important difference between NDIS, ODI and packet drivers is support for multiple protocols. While NDIS and ODI support the simultaneous use of multiple protocols, packet drivers do not. This difference is important when we discuss shims.

Your network card probably came with one or more NDIS, ODI, or packet drivers. TCP/IP stacks have been written for each of these driver interfaces, so the driver is not as important as whether your chosen TCP/IP stack is compatible with it.

Shims

If your card came with an NDIS or ODI driver but your chosen application requires a packet driver, you will need to install a shim. A shim is software that runs on top of one set of drivers to emulate another set. Shims are available to run packet drivers over ODI or NDIS, in order to run software expecting a packet driver over NDIS or ODI instead. There is also a shim for running ODI over Packet Drivers.

Shims are also useful if you are looking to simultaneously support programs requiring different driver interfaces. For example, you may be running software requiring an NDIS driver alongside software requiring a packet driver interface. You must use shims in this case because you cannot have packet drivers for two different interfaces running at the same time.

Shims include DIS_PKT, which provides a packet-driver interface over NDIS; ODIPKT, a packet driver over ODI; and PDETHER, an ODI interface over packet drivers. However, there is no NDIS-over-packet-driver shim. The reason for this has to do with multiple protocol support of NDIS that is lacking in packet drivers.

NDIS drivers were written to work with multiple protocols. Support of multiple protocols is possible when using network frames that contain a protocol field (such as Ethernet or PPP), thus allowing the driver to demultiplex incoming frames by protocol.

For example, NDIS Ethernet drivers can be used with NETBEUI as well as IP. I don't know of NDIS PPP drivers supporting multiple protocols, but it's possible. Packet drivers on the other hand, were written only to be used with a single protocol at a time, usually IP.

Since NDIS drivers can run multiple protocols, they examine all incoming frames, and pass them on to the appropriate protocols. Packet drivers, on the other hand, examine only incoming frames for a specific protocol which is usually IP. This means they can only support one protocol at a time.

Packet multiplexing

NDIS and ODI drivers are capable of supporting multiple protocols simultaneously, provided that your protocol implementation is compatible with them.

However, supporting multiple protocol stacks of the same type is much trickier. For example, an IP datagram does not indicate which stack the datagram is for; it only contains information on the IP address and port of the source and destination. Sending the datagram to all stacks and letting them respond will not work, since a datagram meant for one stack's open port will generate an ICMP error message on the other stack where the port is not open. Some datagrams (such as an ARP broadcast) need to be interpretted by all stacks. What is done in that case? Of course, there is also the problem of port conflicts if multiple stacks attempt to open the same port.

PKTMUX is a clever program that solves this problem for TCP/IP stacks using packet drivers. By tracking outgoing datagrams from each TCP/IP stack, PKTMUX builds a table of connections, indicating which socket pairs belong to which stacks. This allows it to route incoming datagrams to the correct stack.

If it is uncertain which stack to send a datagram to, PKTMUX will send it to all of them, but will only allow resulting outgoing ICMP error messages if all the stacks complain. Otherwise, PKTMUX will assume that the packet was correctly received by one of the stacks.

Since even PKTMUX will not be able to help in cases of port conflicts, do not attempt to run two versions of the same application with PKTMUX. Since the whole point of PKTMUX is to be able to simultaneously run different applications, this isn't much of a constraint.

All this cleverness does come at a cost. Applications running with a packet multiplexer can see as much as a 40 percent degradation in performance.

Even with this performance penalty, however, chances are that you'll find PKTMUX to be a godsend, since so many publicly distributable DOS TCP/IP applications (such as KA9Q, NCSA Telnet, PC Gopher III, and Win QVT/Net, etc.) come with their own built-in TCP/IP stacks and could not be run in tandem otherwise.

It is also possible to combine the use of shims and PKTMUX. This is necessary if you want to run Novell IPX applications simultaneously with multiple TCP/IP stacks.

Note that PKTMUX (or any multiplexer, for that matter) is not needed to allow multiple applications to access the same stack.

SLIP drivers

Packet drivers for SLIP or PPP can be implemented either directly (Class 6), or by simulating the Ethernet packet driver interface (Class 1). Ethernet simulation works by enclosing IP datagrams coming in on the SLIP or PPP link in fake Ethernet frames, and stripping off the frame headers on outgoing packets. This is frequently used in practice, since almost every TCP/IP application supports the Class 1 interface, while many do not support the Class 6 interface.

The major publicly distributable SLIP/PPP packet drivers are:

CSLIPPER.EXE	Compressed SLIP driver by Peter Tattam (Class 1, 6)
SLIPPER.EXE	Uncompressed SLIP driver by Peter Tattam (Class 1, 6)
ETHERSL.COM	Crynwr uncompressed SLIP driver, using Ethernet simulation (Class 1)
ETHERPPP.EXE	PPP driver, using Ethernet simulation (Class 1)
UMSLIP.COM	Uncompressed SLIP driver from University of Minnesota (Class 1, 6)

The SLIPPER and CSLIPPER drivers are recommended since they are fast, support PKTMUX, and operate trouble-free with many applications. CSLIPPER should be used when possible, since it supports compressed SLIP. As of this writing, I hadn't tried ETHERPPP, so I can't give a verdict on it.

Running packet drivers under Windows

As if figuring out drivers, shims and multiplexers wasn't enough, there are additional complications that arise when running DOS TCP/IP applications with Windows.

The first thing you need to understand is that packet drivers and PKTMUX (if used) are loaded *before* running Windows.

For DOS applications with their own built-in TCP/IP stacks (such as KA9Q, PC-Gopher III, and NCSA Telnet, etc.), you will also need to run WINPKT.COM when running the applications under Windows. In enhanced mode, Windows 3.x runs DOS sessions as "virtual machines." WINPKT.COM provides a "virtual packet driver interface" for each "virtual machine," looking at the incoming packets and switching to the correct virtual machine before delivering them. This dramatically reduces your chances of crashing Windows.

Finally, applications such as WinQVT/Net also require PKTINT, which allows them to access packet drivers from protected mode.

TCP/IP Stacks

The TCP/IP protocol stack runs on top of the driver software and uses it to access your hardware. If you are running a TCP/IP protocol stack that requires drivers that aren't available for your hardware, you're in trouble, unless a shim or the Crynwr drivers can save you. Check into this before purchasing!

A number of TCP/IP protocol stacks are now available, including FTP's PC/TCP, Distinct TCP, Frontier, NetManage (NEWT), and a Windows Sockets version of the Trumpet TCP/IP stack (shareware, in beta). For more information, see Appendix B: Choice Products.

Windows Sockets

Just as forcing TCP/IP stack implementors to support every network adapter directly makes little sense, so too have applications developers grown tired of supporting multiple TCP/IP stacks, each with their own applications programming interface.

The Windows Sockets specification was created to solve this problem. Originating at a Birds of a Feather session at Fall Interop '91, the idea behind Windows Sockets is to define an Application Binary Interface (ABI) for both Windows and Windows NT, to allow use of any conforming TCP/IP protocol implementation.

Windows Sockets is implemented as a DLL, and provides a Berkeley-sockets–style interface to TCP/IP. WINSOCK.DLL provides 16-bit support, and WSOCK32.DLL provides 32-bit support. Each TCP/IP implementation requires its own version of a Windows Sockets DLL. Trumpet Winsock, currently in beta test, will be the first publicly distributable Windows Sockets-compatible TCP/IP stack. All other Windows Sockets-compatible stacks are commercial.

Microsoft has indicated that Windows Sockets will be supported by Windows, Windows For Workgroups, Wind32s, and Windows NT. It will also support protocols other than TCP/IP in the future. Under Windows NT, Microsoft will provide Windows Sockets support over TCP/IP and IPX/SPX. DEC will be implementing DECNet. Windows NT will include mechanisms for multiple protocol support in Windows Sockets, both 32-bit and 16-bit.

All major TCP/IP vendors have pledged support for Windows Sockets. FTP Software, Distinct, Frontier, Wollongong, and NetManage are now shipping Windows Sockets TCP/IP stacks, and Microsoft is offering Windows Sockets TCP/IP stacks for Windows For Workgroups and Windows NT. Other vendors supporting Windows Sockets include 3Com, Beame & Whiteside, IBM, JSB Corporation, LAN Design, Microdyne, Network Research, Novell, Sun Microsystems, and Ungermann Bass.

Pointers to further information on Windows Sockets are given at the end of this section.

Applications

The release of the Windows Sockets specification has been a boon to Windows TCP/IP development activity. Recent releases include TCP/IP applications suites running under Windows, my favorite of which is Netmanage Chameleon, which includes a Windows Sockets DLL and support for SLIP, CSLIP, and PPP. Chameleon also offers NFS as an add-on; however, be aware that the NFS features only work within Windows and not within virtual DOS sessions.

There are also a number of publicly distributable Windows Sockets applications, such as PC Eudora (POP/SMTP), WinVN (NNTP), HGopher (Gopher), Cello (W3), Finger (finger), and Windows Trumpet (NNTP). For information on Windows Sockets applications, consult the newsgroups alt.winsock or comp.protocols.tcp-ip.ibmpc.

It should be noted that IBM's OS/2 TCP/IP package has gotten very good reviews. Please see the newsgroup comp.os.os2.networking for details.

SLIP and PPP for the PC

To connect your PC to the Internet using a modem, you will need to use either Serial Line Internet Protocol (SLIP) or Point-to-Point Protocol (PPP).

For DOS TCP/IP implementations, I recommend KA9Q. This supports SLIP/CSLIP/PPP, Ethernet, asynchronous and synchronous cards, and Packet Radio. It also multitasks and has no problems with reassembly of fragmented packets. Unfortunately, KA9Q cannot be used as a TCP/IP protocol stack to run other applications. Therefore, if you need an application beyond those that KA9Q supports (Telnet client/server, FTP client/server, SMTP client/server, Gopher server, NNTP server, lp daemon), you will need to look elsewhere.

The best alternative for DOS users is the SLIPDISK distribution from the University of Minnesota. This can be made to work with the CSLIPPER packet driver, and therefore will support SLIP/CSLIP. The SLIPDISK distribution comes with a dialing application (PHONE), as well as several compatible applications, including DOS versions of `telnet`, gopher, popmail, and `ftp`. For PPP support in DOS, there is a special version of NCSA Telnet for PPP, available via `ftp merit.edu, cd /pub/ppp`, as well as a PPP packet driver called EtherPPP, available at the same location.

For Windows, it is simplest to stick with Windows Sockets applications, while purchasing a TCP/IP stack which supports SLIP.

Configuring SLIPDISK

SLIPDIAL is part of the SLIPDISK package for the PC, available via `ftp boombox.micro.umn.edu`. To get this running, you will need to choose a method for dialing out. To do this, you can use the PHONE application; however, this was intended to load the UMSLIP driver rather than CSLIPPER. As a result, it may be simpler to use a DOS terminal emulator with a scripting language, such as Telix, or QMODEM. Use this program to dial out and log you in to the SLIP host, at which point you'll quit the program and load CSLIPPER. Be aware that you may need to disable DTR on the modem so that the program will not hang up on exit.

KA9Q

KA9Q is a DOS-based TCP/IP implementation that can route. It handles LocalTalk, X.25, Ethernet, and up to four serial lines running SLIP/PPP, all at the same time. It's an amazing piece of software, and free for noncommercial use to boot. Please contact Phil Karn for commercial licenses. I have tried the latest version of KA9Q (January 1993), but found that it locked up, so I am now back to using v2.1. KA9Q is usually run from a startup script, such as my script STARTNOS.BAT:

```
\nos\drivers\8003pkdr
\nos\net -d \nos
```

Here I first load the packet drivers for my 8003 Ethernet card, then run KA9Q (NET.EXE). The KA9Q package then reads commands from a configuration file, called AUTOEXEC.NOS.

Configuring KA9Q with CSLIP and PPP

The KA9Q configuration files on the next two pages are for use with a single CSLIP or PPP interface.

Configuring KA9Q as a router

The KA9Q configuration in the next figure uses two interfaces, one a CSLIP interface to an Annex terminal server (sl0), the other to an Ethernet interface (lan) with another machine (a NeXT) attached. Note the use of hardware handshake (c), Van Jacobson compression (v) and the VJSLIP designation on the serial line, as well as the strange interrupt settings (Interrupt 5, port is COM3). One of the nice things about KA9Q is that it is flexible enough to deal with such situations.

Chameleon

Chameleon is a Windows-based TCP/IP package that uses NDIS drivers. In addition to the standard FTP, Telnet, Finger, SLIP, Mail, Net News, etc., it offers advanced features including BOOTP client, BIND, SNMP, and static routing.

In order to help with debugging, Chameleon offers ping, as well as the NEWT program, which offers information on the status of ARP tables, interfaces, routing tables, sockets, and gateways/DNS, as well as provides statistics on IP, ICMP, UDP, and TCP. About the only thing that is missing is traceroute.

To get your network card to be recognized, you will have to invoke the NETBIND.EXE application early in your AUTOEXEC.BAT file. You will also need to edit the PROTMAN.INI file to load an NDIS driver for your hardware. I got lost here, but NetManage's tech support guided me through it. It is possible to run Chameleon alongside packet-driver using software such as KA9Q or FTP's PC/TCP. However, you will have to watch out for conflicting TCP/IP stacks. Chameleon's stack runs as a DLL, so it is unloaded when you leave Windows; however, if you also load another stack as a TSR, you will have to unload it before running Chameleon.

In order to set up SLIP under Chameleon, you need to create a scripting file to call out. The scripting language is in the familiar expect-send-expect format. Chameleon is capable of handling static, dynamic, and server addressing. Below, the DEFAULT script uses dynamic addressing (-i parameter) and the SLIP0 script uses static addressing. The $u variable stands for the user name, and $p is for password; both are input in a dialog box.

```
[DEFAULT]
SCRIPT=ogin: $u$r word: $p$r -n $6$c$r -i
TYPE=SLIP

[SLIP0]
SCRIPT=ogin: $u$r word: $p$r
TYPE=SLIP
```

CSLIP configuration file for KA9Q

```
# Set the host name
#
hostname aboba.slip.netcom.com
ip address [192.187.134.3]
#
# Configure COM3 on Interrupt 5, at 38400 bps with
# RTS/CTS (c) and Van Jacobson Compression (v) and MTU = 1008
#
attach asy 0x3e8 5 vjslip sl0 8092 1008 38400 cv
ifconfig sl0 netmask 255.255.255.252
#
route add default sl0
# route all packets over sl0 by default (sl0 is the route to
# the Internet)
#
# Time To Live is the maximum number of hops a packet can take
# before it is thrown away. This command prevents an inadvertent
# infinite loop from occuring with packets in the network.
#
ip ttl 400
#
#-------------------------------------------------
#
# The Maximum Segment Size is the largest single transmission that
# you care to receive. An mss of 216 will force folks to send you
# packets of 256 characters or less (counting the overhead).
#
tcp mss 1048
#
#-------------------------------------------------
#
# The Window parameter establishes the maximum number of bytes that
# may be outstanding before your system expects an ack. If window is
# twice as big as mss, for example, there will be two active packets
# on the channel at any given time. Large values of window provide
# improved throughput on full-duplex links, but are a problem on the
# air. Keep mss <= window <= 2*mss if you're on the air.
#
#
tcp window 6888
#
#-------------------------------------------------
#
# This entry will open net.log in the \spool directory and will
# record the server activity of your system. If you don't want a log,
# comment out this line; if you do, make sure you have a \spool
# directory!
#
log \spool\net.log
#
#-------------------------------------------------
#
# Each of the servers (services you will provide) must be turned
# on before they will be active. The following entries turn all
# of them on. To turn any function off use the command 'stop' after
# NET gets fired up, or just comment out the line here.
#
start ftp
start echo
start discard
#start telnet
start smtp
#
isat on
#
domain addserver 192.100.81.101
domain addserver 192.100.81.105
smtp gateway 140.174.7.1
#
#
# Just for yucks, lets try calling the other end.
comm sl0 atdt14082411528
# THE END
```

PPP configuration file for KA9Q using a dialer

```
# Set the host name
#
hostname aboba.slip.netcom.com
ip address [192.187.134.3]
#
# Configure COM3 on Interrupt 5, at 38400 bps with
# RTS/CTS (c) and Van Jacobson Compression (v) and MTU = 1008
#
attach asy 0x3e8 5 ppp pp0 1024 256 38400
ifconfig pp0 netmask 255.255.255.252
dialer pp0 dialer.ppp
ppp pp0 trace 2
ppp pp0 quick
ppp pp0 lcp open
ppp pp0 ipcp open
#
route add default pp0
# route all packets over pp0 by default (pp0 is the route to
# the Internet)
#
#
ip ttl 400
#
#------------------------------------------------
#
tcp mss 1048
#
#------------------------------------------------
#
#
#
tcp window 6888
#
#------------------------------------------------
#
#
log \spool\net.log
#
#------------------------------------------------
#
# Each of the servers (services you will provide) must be turned
# on before they will be active. The following entries turn all
# of them on. To turn any function off use the command 'stop' after
# NET gets fired up, or just comment out the line here.
#
start ftp
start echo
start discard
#start telnet
start smtp
#
isat on
#
domain addserver 192.100.81.101
domain addserver 192.100.81.105
domain suffix netcom.com
domain cache clean on
smtp gateway 140.174.7.1
#
#
# THE END
```

dialer.ppp file:

```
control down
wait 1000
control up
wait 1000
wait 2000
send "at\r"
wait 3000 "OK"
send "atdt8659004\r"
wait 60000 "login: "
send "<userID>\r"
wait 5000 "word:"
wait 1000
send "<password>\r"
```

CSLIP and Ethernet routing configuration file for KA9Q (Proxy ARP version)

```
# Set the host name
#
hostname gate.slip.holonet.net
#
# Configure COM3 on Interrupt 5, at 38400 bps with
# RTS/CTS (c) and Van Jacobson Compression (v)
#
attach asy 0x3e8 5 vjslip sl0 8092 576 38400 cv
ifconfig sl0 ipaddress [157.151.0.253] netmask 255.255.255.0
#
# Packet driver at 0x60; probably an Ethernet card of some kind.
#
attach packet 0x60 lan 2 1500
ifconfig lan ipaddress [157.151.64.1] netmask 255.255.255.0
#
#   Set Routing Tables
#
route add default sl0
# The local Ethernet has a Class C network address so
# route all IP addresses beginning with 157.151.64 to it.
route add 157.151.64/24 lan
#
#   Use Proxy ARP
arp publish 157.151.64.1 ether 00:00:c0:33:f3:13
arp publish 157.151.64.254 ether 00:00:c0:33:f3:13
#
#   For PC AT
isat on
#
# Add Domain Name Servers
domain addserver 157.151.0.2
domain addserver 157.151.0.1
smtp gateway 157.151.0.2
#
# Time To Live is the maximum number of hops a packet can take
# before it is thrown away. This command prevents an inadvertent
# infinite loop from occuring with packets in the network.
#
ip ttl 400
#
# The Maximum Segment Size is the largest single transmission that
# you care to receive. An mss of 216 will force folks to send you
# packets of 256 characters or less (counting the overhead).
#
tcp mss 576
#
# The Window parameter establishes the maximum number of bytes
# that may be outstanding before your system expects an ack.
# If window is twice as big as mss, for example, there will be two
# active packets on the channel at any given time. Large values of
# window provide improved throughput on full-duplex links, but are a
# problem on the air. Keep  mss <= window <= 2*mss if you're on the air.
#
tcp window 6888
#
# This entry will open net.log in the \spool directory and will
# record the server activity of your system. If you don't want a log,
# comment out this line; if you do, make sure you have a \spool
# directory!
#
log \spool\net.log
#
# Each of the servers (services you will provide) must be turned
# on before they will be active. The following entries turn all
# of them on. To turn any function off use the command 'stop' after
# NET gets fired up, or just comment out the line here.
#
start ftp
start echo
start discard
#start telnet
start smtp
#
#   Display Name and IP Address
#
hostname
ip address
#
# Just for yucks, lets try calling the other end.
comm sl0 atdt7041063
# THE END
```

Diagnosing problems with your setup

Frequently used UNIX diagnostic utilities include `ifconfig` (checks the configuration of the network interfaces), `ping` (tests IP layer connectivity), `traceroute` (simulates the route that a packet takes between two sites), `netstat` (routing table information), `tcpdump` (protocol analyzer), and `arp` (IP to Ethernet address mappings).

KA9Q includes `ifconfig`, `ping`, and `traceroute` functions. In KA9Q `hop check` is equivalent to `traceroute`. The Trumpet TCP/IP stack also has a `hopchk2` command that is a `traceroute` equivalent.

The DNPAP tools (check the MailCom IBMTCP directory for listings) include Ethernet packet catchers, networking monitors, and a network host profiler.

Netmanage Chameleon comes with its own set of tools and so is relatively self-contained.

PC TCP/IP Q&A

How do I run both a Novell application and a TCP/IP application requiring a packet driver on the same machine?

You have two choices in doing this. You can interface to your network hardware either with packet drivers or with Novell ODI drivers. If you go with ODI drivers, you can use ODIPKT to run your packet driver applications over ODI; if you choose packet drivers, you can use PDETHER to run the ODI applications over packet drivers.

How do I get DESQview X to run over the network?

V1.0 of DESQview X did not include a TCP/IP protocol stack. Surprise! The FTP software stack or the Novell LanWorkPlace stack was needed. They've corrected the situation in subsequent revisions. Contact QuarterDeck for assistance.

What publicly distributable TCP/IP stacks are there that I can use to develop my own applications?

In writing an application, you can use device drivers provided by particular vendors, or you can opt for an Application Binary Interface (ABI) that supports multiple TCP/IP protocol stacks, such as Winsock. Since all major TCP/IP vendors will be implementing Windows sockets, Winsock-compliant applications are definitely the wave of the future. For information on the current schedule for Winsock implementations of the major vendors, `ftp sunsite.unc.edu`, `get /pub/micro/pc-stuff/ms-windows/winsock/vendors`. The Trumpet Winsock is the first publicly distributable Windows Sockets-compatible TCP/IP stack. There is presently no Winsock interface for DOS, although several firms have been talking about producing one.

Device drivers are included with PC-NFS and Beame & Whiteside's BW-TCP. Free examples of ABIs are the WATTCP API, the NCSA API (public domain), the Trumpet ABI from Peter Tattum, and the NuPOP ABI.

How do I get information on Winsock?

Information and files relating to Winsock are available via `ftp sunsite.unc.edu, cd /pub/micro/pc-stuff/ms-windows/winsock`. To retrieve files via email, `mail ftpmail@sunsite.unc.edu`, or `ftp@decwrl.dec.com`, body: `help`.

A FAQ on Windows Sockets is available via `ftp sunsite.unc.edu, cd /pub/micro/pc-stuff/ms-windows/winsock/FAQ`. The FAQ is also available on rhino.microsoft.com.

A listing of vendors supporting Windows Sockets is available via `ftp sunsite.unc.edu, cd /pub/micro/pc-stuff/ms-windows/winsock/vendors`.

My service provider says that my TCP/IP implementation has a problem with fragmentation. What does that mean?

While IP can support datagrams as large as 65,535 bytes, different physical media may require smaller datagrams. For example, Ethernet can only handle datagrams of around 1500 bytes. If an IP implementation receives a datagram that is too large to be transmitted over a given media, the datagram will need to be split into fragments and reassembled later.

Although support for fragmentation and reassembly is a requirement of host TCP/IP compatibility, a few TCP/IP implementations do not remember the old admonishment, If you take it apart, remember to put it back together! The problem seems to crop up most frequently with DOS-based shareware and freeware products, KA9Q excepted.

If your implementation has such a problem, there is not much you can do, other than complain to the developer and try a new TCP/IP stack.

IP Fragmentation

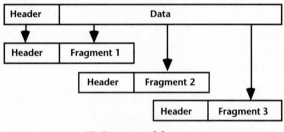

IP Reassembly

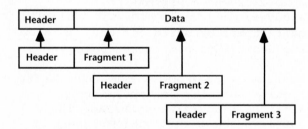

I would like to put my HP95LX palmtop on the Internet. Is this possible?

Yes! A special slimmed-down version of KA9Q is available that will run on the larger version of the HP95LX. It is available via `ftp ucsd.edu, get /hamradio/packet/tcpip/ka9q/ noshp95.zip`.

Where can I get information on setting up PPP on the PC?

As of yet, I have not had much luck with PC implementations of PPP, including KA9Q and NetManage Chameleon. Since I have no problems with SLIP or CSLIP on either package, I'd recommend sticking with these for now. One thing that might change my mind is EtherPPP, a recently released PPP packet driver. After I've toyed with this, I'll put down my observations in the MailCom FTP archive, `ftp netcom1.netcom.com, get /pub/mailcom/IBMTCP/ibmtcp.zip`.

Where can I get information on setting up PPP under UNIX?

The comp.protocols.ppp FAQ is the best place to start. It is posted to the group as well as to news.answers periodically. It can also be retrieved by FTP or mail from rtfm.mit.edu, as described in Chapter 12: USENET.

For more information

Appendix B: Choice Products includes listings of Windows Sockets compatible applications, and TCP/IP implementation vendors.

Sample setup files, answers to frequently asked questions, and more complete listing of DOS and Windows TCP/IP applications are available from the MailCom FTP archive via `ftp netcom1.netcom.com, get /pub/mailcom/IBMTCP/ibmtcp.zip`.

USENET newsgroups covering TCP/IP for the PC include comp.protocols.tcp-ip.ibmpc and alt.winsock.

A review of TCP/IP implementations, including SLIP/PPP and driver support, is available via `ftp ftp.cac.psu.edu, cd /pub/dos/info/tcpip.packages`.

TCP/IP ON THE MACINTOSH

MacTCP SLIP setup

MacTCP comes with AdminTCP and MacTCP control panels that both allow you to configure a host. Once you've got the configuration set, in order to lock the configuration, remove the AdminTCP control panel. This insures that properly configured machines stay that way.

In order to put up a SLIP link, you will need to run MacTCP alongside a SLIP extension such as MacSLIP, InterSLIP or VersaTerm SLIP. Once you install the SLIP extension, when you bring up the MacTCP control panel, you will see the SLIP icons alongside the icons for the other network drivers, such as LocalTalk and EtherTalk. Select the appropriate driver, and if you are using SLIP, enter your assigned IP address, if you have been given one by your host. Click on **More...** to bring up the MacTCP configuration dialog.

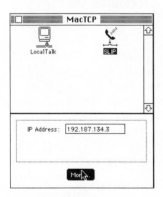

MacSLIP setup

If you were given a fixed IP address from your host (also known as a "static address") then you should select **Manually** for the method to **Obtain Address**. If you were not given a fixed

IP address, and your host will assign you an IP address each time you call in, you will have to adjust your MacSLIP login script to use the given address, which we will discuss later. Select **Dynamically** for the method to **Obtain Address**.

With dynamic assignment, your host sends you a text message with your assigned IP address for that session after you have logged in to the server. In order for MacTCP to be informed about the assigned address, you will need to do some scripting.

For your host, use of dynamic assignment has some advantages. If your host has 16 phone lines, then only 16 IP addresses can be in use for SLIP/PPP connected hosts at the same time. If these addresses can be assigned dynamically whenever hosts connect, then only 16 IP addresses will be needed, even though there might be hundreds of SLIP/PPP accounts.

Dynamic assignment also imposes some limitations. Since the host will only assign one address dynamically, not a suite of addresses, dynamic assignment cannot connect an entire network to the host, since *all* network nodes would need to receive IP addresses dynamically, not just one. To connect a network, use the **Server** or **Manual** modes.

Also, dynamic addresses tend to slow down the first contact with the network (startup can take 1-2 minutes), and they depend on all systems on the network using fully qualified domain name addressing; if not it is possible that files will go to your previously used address. You will also need a static address in order to register your site.

Note that MacTCP v2.0 can only handle a single interface and therefore cannot route. This is reflected in the choice of driver that you made when you first opened the MacTCP control panel. You can choose SLIP, PPP, EtherTalk or LocalTalk, but not more than one at the same time. To do this you will need something else such as a dedicated router; software such as NetMac, a Mac port of KA9Q; a PC running PCROUTE or KA9Q; or a UNIX machine.

If your host muttered something about "getting the address from the server," then you need to select **Server** for the method to **Obtain Address**. In this case, MacTCP will use RARP or BOOTP to obtain the address, and the IP address of your node will be cleared.

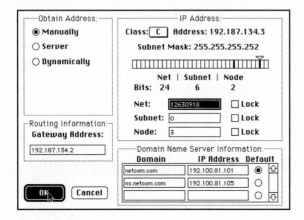

Setup for PPP

To set up MacPPP, you will need to select the PPP extension within the MacTCP control panel. Since your IP address will be assigned by the host, you do not have to fill it in.

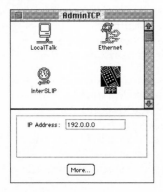

MacPPP Setup

Click on **More...** to bring up the MacTCP configuration dialog. Select **Server** from the **Obtain Address** field, and set the address class and subnet mask appropriately. You will also

need to enter the gateway address and primary and secondary domain name servers.

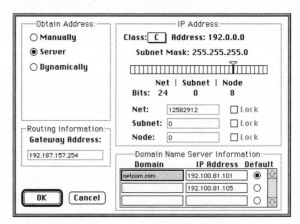

Domain name server

Your host will provide you with the domain name and IP address of a primary and secondary domain name server. Insert these addresses into the appropriate fields, and choose the primary server as the default.

Subnet mask and gateways

The most important part of the MacTCP configuration is the choice of a gateway address and subnet mask. This is somewhat tricky, because SLIP/PPP was added to MacTCP as an afterthought, rather than being designed into it from the beginning. As a result, MacTCP sometimes needs to be tricked into acting correctly with gateways.

The gateway node is the system on your network through which traffic must pass to get to the rest of the Internet. MacTCP only has room for a single gateway node; therefore this system is also the default route. The gateway node is on two networks: yours and another network. Gateways have *two* TCP/IP addresses, one for each network connection.

In the case of SLIP/PPP configuration, your SLIP/PPP host is your gateway since all traffic bound for the outside world must first pass through the host. Therefore MacTCP should not really have to ask you what the gateway address is; the gateway must be the remote host.

However, since MacTCP was not created with SLIP/PPP in mind, it is not that intelligent. In fact, it can be downright stupid. Unless the gateway IP address is on the same network as your node, MacTCP will not be able to figure out where to send packets, even though there is only one choice – the SLIP/PPP interface!

What if you find that the network portion of the IP address for your gateway does not match the network address of your node? Since the gateway's IP address was assigned by your host, you can't change it, and your host probably doesn't want to go through the bother of changing it, anyway. Luckily, you don't need to. In order to get MacTCP to function correctly if your gateway is not on your network, **you must enter a bogus gateway address!**

In the gateway field, you must enter a gateway address on the same network as your system, with an arbitrary (and nonzero) value for the network node. In the example, I chose 192.187.134.2, even though this address had already been assigned to another node.

Jeepers creepers! Didn't I just warn you about making up IP addresses for testing purposes? What about the poor individual whose IP address I inserted as the gateway address? Won't he or she be getting my packets?

The answer is no. The gateway address is used for routing purposes only, in order to make a decision whether to send a packet out via the SLIP interface. Using this bogus gateway address will convince MacTCP that all packets are to be routed via the SLIP interface.

MacPPP

MacPPP is a free implementation of PPP for the Macintosh, available via `ftp merit.edu`, `cd /pub/ppp`. According to my tests, MacPPP is 10-15% slower than MacSLIP, giving transfer rates of only 1300 cps, but it is easier to set up.

The first thing you need to do in installing MacPPP is to install the PPP extension and Config PPP control panels, and reboot your machine.

PPP Extension   **PPP Control panel**

The next thing to do is to configure MacPPP itself. Bring up the Config PPP control panel. Select the port that your modem is on, as well as the baud rate and phone type. If your modem and cable support hardware handshake, select this entry. You will also need to set your modem's parameter RAM appropriately for this. For your first login, it is best to select Terminal Window. This will allow you to debug the login script.

Next, click on the **Configure Server** button. This will bring up the PPP server dialog box. MacPPP allows you to connect to multiple PPP hosts. Name your host, and type in the phone number and modem initialization string. Then click on the **Connect Script...** button in order to create your login script.

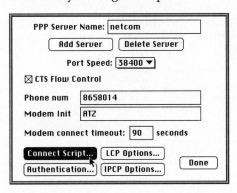

This is where you type in the script entries that will log you on to the PPP host. Replace Sfoo with your PPP account name, and goo with your password.

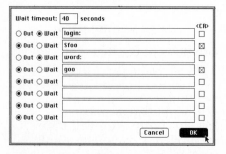

When you are done, click on **OK**.

Next, click on **IPCP Options** in the Configure Server dialog box. This will bring up another configuration window. Here I indicate that the connection will be setup for Van Jacobson compression. Note that since your TCP/IP address will be retrieved from the server, there is no need to enter it here.

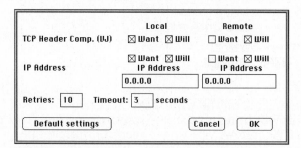

When you are done, click on **OK** again. The final dialog box is brought up by clicking on the **LCP Options** button in the Configure Server dialog box. This is where you will input things like your Authentication ID, Maximum Receivable Unit, etc. My host was not using Authentication, so this field is left blank.

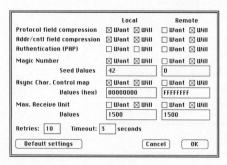

Once again, when you are done, click **OK**.

Now that you've got MacPPP set up, how do you get it to dial? MacPPP will dial automatically when you bring up a MacTCP application such as NCSA Telnet. As soon as you enter the application, a dialog box will pop up.

You will hear the modem connect, and then MacPPP will appraise you of the various stages of the protocol negotiation. When the connection is complete, the Open PPP button will be grayed out, and the Close PPP button will be enabled. Also, the state will change to PPP Up.

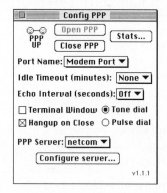

What if something goes wrong? In order to check the login script, you can select **Terminal Window**. After the connection is complete, this will cause a window to pop up showing you the progress of the session.

In the case below, we can see that my script must have been OK, since I received a message from the host indicating my IP address.

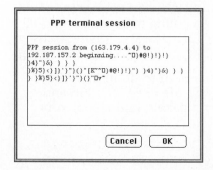

At any time during your session, you can check the statistics on your connection by clicking on the **Stats...** button in the Config PPP window. This produces output roughly comparable to that of netstat under UNIX. Here is what the Statistics dialog box looks like:

In octets:	2735	LCP Opts	Local	Remote
Out octets:	1198	PFC	☒	☒
In packets:	34	ACFC	☒	☒
Out packets:	39	PAP	☐	☐
CRC errors:	0	Magic	0000002A	E0BE773E
Header errors:	0	ACCM	00000000	00000000
Hdw overruns:	0	MRU	1500	1500
Sfw overruns:	0	IPCP Opts		
Framing errs:	0	VJ Comp	☒	☒
Out of buffers:	0		Slots 16	Slots 16
			C-id ☒	C-id ☐
[Update] [OK]		IP addr	Local 192.187.157.2	Remote 163.179.4.4

Creating login scripts for MacSLIP

SLIP Extension

MacSLIP from Hyde Park Software is the most efficient SLIP implementation on the Mac, giving transfer rates in excess of 1500 cps with V.32*bis*/V.42*bis* modems. Since this software costs only $50, I recommend it.

In order to connect with MacSLIP you need to create a written script that logs you in. You also need to put in the appropriate modem initialization string rather than having it given to you. Constructing this script is most of the work in getting the software set up.

MacSLIP is very flexible. The MacSLIP scripting language can handle virtually every SLIP situation, including dynamic address assignment, or complex login sequences over a port selector or router. The technical support for MacSLIP is excellent. Hyde Park Software (the developers) were instrumental in tracking down the source of my initial problems with the package, which turned out to be on my SLIP host's end of things.

The first step in configuring MacSLIP is to select the version of SLIP you want to use. If your host supports compressed SLIP, then you

will want to choose the **Always** option. If not, then select **Never**. **Automatic** means that MacSLIP will try to figure out whether the host is using compressed or uncompressed SLIP.

The MTU entry refers to the Maximum Transfer Unit size in bytes, which is the maximum TCP/IP packet size that will be used by the host. It is desirable to coordinate the MTU size with your host; otherwise the host may have to split up packets that would be inefficient.

The MacSLIP dialog box also allows you to choose a log file as well as a scripting file. Several sample scripts are provided for the package; in my case, I copied the example script to the file **Netcom.scr** and then edited it.

Finally, it is useful to use CTS flow control so that you can get maximum modem efficiency. You will need a hardware handshake cable in order to support this.

Once you have configured the MacSLIP dialog, you will need to edit the parameters in the scripting file. Within the script file, these parameters have been denoted by $ symbols such as $user, $password, $initstring, and $phone. These variables refer to your login id, password, modem initialization string, and host phone number, respectively. Selecting **Parameters...** in the menu will bring up a list box, allowing you to fill in the values for your host. Parameters such as passwords can be hidden so that they cannot be easily accessed.

It should be noted that **the initialization string must set the modem for hardware**

handshaking if this has been selected in the MacSLIP dialog box.

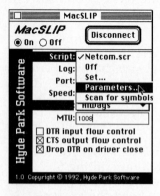

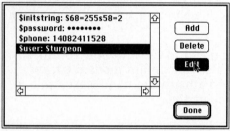

Once you have gotten your script set up and have edited your parameters, you can select **Connect...** on the MacSLIP dialog, and MacSLIP will attempt to log you in. A Script Status dialog box will then come up, informing you of the status of the session in progress.

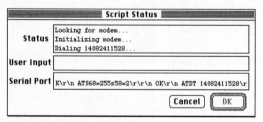

Once you have been successfully logged in, the Script Status dialog will vanish and you will be left with the default button saying **Disconnect** instead of **Connect**.

In order to provide information on the progress of the session, the log file SLIP.LOG (previously selected in the MacSLIP dialog) gives a log of the connection. Here's what it looks like for a successful connect:

```
Log Opened at 09/02/92 15:08:32
message "Netcom logon script starting..."
message "Looking for modem..."
label findmodem
flush
send "AT\r"
read "AT\r\r\n"
read "OK\r\n"
matched "OK"
break
message "Initializing modem..."
label initmodem
flush
send "ATS68=255s58=2\r"
read "ATS68=255s58=2\r\r\n"
read "OK\r\n"
matched "OK"
break
message "Dialing 14082411528..."
flush
send "ATDT 14082411528\r"
read "ATDT 14082411528\r\r\n"
read "CONNECT 9600\r\n"
read "\r\n"
read "\r\n"
read "NETCOM On-line Communication Services, Inc.\r\n"
read "\r\n"
read "\r\n"
read "\r\n"
read "netcom login: "
matched "login:"
break
label login
message "Logging in as Saboba..."
label user
flush
send "Sfoor"
read "Sfoo\r\n"
read "Password: "
matched "Password:"
break
message "Sending password..."
flush
send "********\r"
read "\r\n"
read "SL/IP session from (192.100.81.110) to
192.187.134.3 beginning...."
matched "beginning..."
goto setslip
message "Enabling SLIP mode on server..."
flush
message "Script complete"
flush
return 1
Script ending with status 1
Log Close at 09/02/92 15:09:04
```

If you are having problems with MacSLIP scripts, you can find some examples via `ftp` **boombox.micro.umn.edu, cd /pub/macslip-scripts.**

InterSLIP

InterSLIP   InterSLIP Control

InterSLIP is a SLIP extension that InterCon has generously made free for private non-commercial use. It can be obtained via `ftp ftp.intercon.com, cd /intercon/sales`.

The software is a self-extracting archive of a Disk Image file, so you will need Apple's Disk Copy in order to copy the image onto a floppy so that you can install it. Once you do this, the disk should look like this:

Double click on the **Installer Script** icon to install InterSLIP. This will install the InterSLIP extension as well as the InterSLIP Control control panel. It will also install InterSLIP Setup in your Apple menu.

After this is done, reboot your machine, and bring up the AdminTCP or MacTCP control panel. Select InterSLIP, and then click on the **More...** button in order to complete your setup.

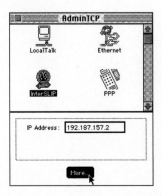

Select Manually as the method of obtaining your address, and fill in the gateway and Domain Name Server addresses.

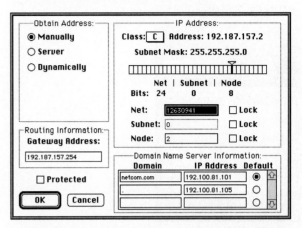

Now you are ready to select **InterSLIP Setup** from the Apple menu. Select **New...** from the **File** menu in order to configure InterSLIP for the host, and name the new configuration:

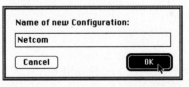

Next, input the proper setup parameters for this host. Note that the IP and Nameserver addresses entered in this dialog box must agree with those entered in your MacTCP configuration.

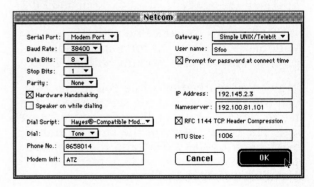

Once you have configured InterSLIP, the configuration should show up in the InterSLIP Setup window. To dial the host, click on the **Connect** button.

PPP on the NeXT

A version of PPP is available for the NeXT. NeXT PPP v0.2 supports Van Jacobson header compression, and is available from `ftp merit.edu, get /pub/ppp/next-ppp0.2.tar.Z`.

Since NeXT PPP v0.2 will not compile under NeXTSTEP v3.0, users are advised to use the binaries that come with the distribution to get it set up.

I've been using NeXTPPP for a few months now and am quite enamored of it, although it is obviously not for everyone (a friend spent two full days trying to get it installed without success, and he still gets on me for recommending it to him).

If you need help with setup, send me NeXTmail (`aboba@world.std.com`), and I'll send you a copy of my scripts. A few hints: NeXTPPP seems to work fine with a WorldBlazer modem, but for some reason, seems to have trouble working with a T2500.

To give you motivation while you're mucking with this, take a look at the screen shots from all the NeXT TCP/IP applications on the next page. The combination of the large monitor, the stability of NeXTSTEP, and the graphical applications makes the NeXT a pretty incredible Internet workstation.

NeXT applications include FTP+, Gopher, WAIStation (Z39.50), Library of Congress, Weather, NewsGrazer (USENET), Archie (files lookup), and World Wide Web. These applications are available from the archives at `cs.orst.edu`, or `sonata.cc.purdue.edu`.

NeXT TCP/IP Applications

NewsGrazer

Gopher

Library of Congress

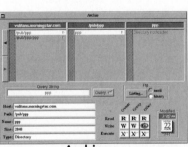

Archie

Weather

Gazeteer

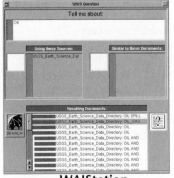

WAIStation

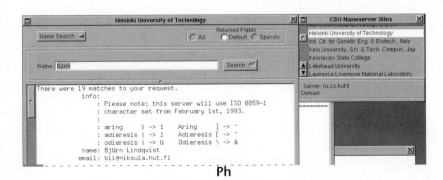

Ph

BULLETIN BOARDS AND THE INTERNET

Why do I care?

In Webster's dictionary, *interaction* is defined as "mutual or reciprocal action or influence." This recognizes that true interactive technologies allow both sides to control what transpires. Taken to the logical extreme, the ideal interactive service is one in which viewers cannot be distinguished from broadcasters.

The convergence of bulletin board and Internet technology has the potential to create an interactive medium of extraordinary diversity. The Internet, through its global accessibility, makes it possible to reach large audiences. Bulletin boards, through their ease of use, make it possible for ordinary people to create their own programming.

The Internet and the BBS: strange bedfellows

Given the current exponential growth in users, hosts, and networks, the Internet faces substantial challenges in the years ahead. Current strains on the Internet's Information Ecosystem include:

• **Overloading of FTP archives.** Several major FTP archives are now so heavily loaded that either access is very difficult (wuarchive.wustl.edu) or transfers have been restricted to non-business hours (sumex-aim.stanford.edu). With traffic doubling every year, the universities maintaining large general software archives have found it difficult to justify pouring more and more resources into a money-losing activity with only tenuous links to their academic mission.

• **Low service reachability.** According to recent research by Michael F. Schwartz and John S. Quarterman, "A Measurement Study of Changes in Service-Level Reachability in the Global Internet," INET '93, only 35 percent of sites identified in the domain walk database are reachable via common services such as telnet or ftp. This indicates that the majority of additions to the network are consumers of services, rather than providers.

• **IP address space depletion and explosive growth in routing tables.** While one of these problems can be temporarily lessened by worsening the other, it is not easy to develop long-term solutions for both.

While bulletin boards will not solve the Internet's problems (nor vice versa), the convergence of the Internet and bulletin board technology may offer at least marginal relief in several arenas:

• **Creation of commercial FTP archives.** Many bulletin boards now offer file archives equal of superior to their Internet counterparts. Commercial FTP archives supported by bulletin boards may buttress the FTP archive system, although whether they will be able to participate effectively in the Archie system remains to be seen.

• **Increased service reachability.** BBSes are generally more secure than conventional UNIX systems, and so are less likely to require firewalls.

• **Conservation of IP address space.** The new crop of graphical BBSes offers economy, ease of use and administration as well as multimedia support. This may allow many users to access the Internet at low cost. Since BBSes typically have an order of magnitude more users per system than is the case for the typical Internet host, bringing BBSes on the Internet may help conserve IP address space. This may prove particularly valuable in bringing the K12 educational community online without exacerbating the address depletion problem.

• **Increasing interconnections with BBS Networks.** Internet BBSes can provide a mechanism for gatewaying messages between BBS networks and the Internet, and may lower the costs of transporting BBS network traffic. BBS networks such as FidoNet, RIME, and WWIVnet are popular in areas of the world that have few if any Internet hosts.

• **Development of low-cost IP solutions.** The BBS world, with its focus on low-cost solutions, is likely to foster development of low cost Internet service providers, as well as TCP/IP compatible hardware and software.

Types of Internet BBSes

Several models for Internet based bulletin boards now exist. These include:

• **The UNIX BBS.** This type of bulletin board runs UNIX, along with a BBS package such as Waffle, TEAMate, CocoNet, Magpie, Citadel, or XBBS. Since most versions of UNIX include TCP/IP, it is relatively simple to attach such a system to the Internet, as well as to integrate Internet applications such as mail, Gopher, WAIS, Archie, etc. This system can also easily run server processes such as FTP, Gopher, etc.

• **The client/server graphical BBS.** This BBS runs a client/server protocol to provide a graphical interface. Such protocols, which are layered on top of TCP/IP, typically support file transfer, messaging, and real-time chatting, as well as multiple simultaneous operations. Since these systems typically run under an operating without preemptive multitasking, it is generally not possible to run TCP/IP server processes on the same machine as the BBS.

• **The telnet accessible BBS.** This is a traditional BBS attached to the Internet via a terminal server or TCP/IP FOSSIL driver. Such a system typically only allows telnet into the system, but does not support other functions such as outgoing telnet, or FTP client/server. Another difficulty with such a configuration is that without a gateway, each node of the BBS will require its own TCP/IP address, which can be confusing to users.

• **The gateway attached BBS.** This is a BBS that uses a supplementary gateway system to provide for incoming and outgoing telnet, FTP client/server, and other services. The gateway system can be running MacOS, UNIX, Novell, or even DOS (KA9Q). This configuration is used with a BBS that does not support preemptive multitasking, in order to off-load the TCP/IP networking tasks to the gateway system. The gateway may also act as a rotary, handing off incoming telnet sessions to the first available BBS node.

Bulletin boards versus resources

Running an Internet BBS is not for everybody. For many people, it makes more sense to establish an Internet resource than to operate an Internet BBS.

Internet service providers such as Netcom and Holonet now offer the ability to create your own mailing lists, mail servers, and FTP archives at very low cost. The tools for making use of these services are described in Chapter 9: Mailing Lists and Mail Servers and Chapter 10: FTP archives. For many hobbyists, this is an attractive alternative to running an Internet BBS, or even putting up a resource on their own.

If you want to run a large service, offer multiple servers, or manage several resource collections of the same type, you may choose to put up your own resource. Making a resource available to the public via FTP, Gopher, W3 or mail can easily be accomplished using a Mac or PC and a dedicated SLIP/PPP connection. KA9Q can act as both an FTP and Gopher server, while the Mac can be a server for FTP (FTPd), Mosaic (MacHTTP), and Gopher, as well as offering mailing lists (uConnect). Gopher and FTP servers for the Mac are available via `ftp sumex-aim.stanford.edu, cd /info-mac/comm`; an HHTP server is available via `ftp mac.archive.umich.edu`.

Billing

One of the most important issues in setting up a commercial online service is billing. Before putting up an Internet BBS service, it is worthwhile to think about whether you want to manage billing yourself or enlist the assistance of a service provider.

Giving these tasks over to someone else allows you to concentrate on other things. This may prove particularly attractive for those services that bill by the hour; bulletin board software packages are generally not very strong in the accounting and billing area.

Internet online services such as Holonet and Pathways now offer Internet connections for bulletin board services and can maintain the network connection as well as handling billing.

Costs

Just how expensive is it to create an Internet BBS? A great deal depends on your location and the size of the system you want to put online.

For those of you who live in an area with a ToasterNet, a dedicated 14.4-Kbps TCP/IP connection may be available for as little as $70/month. This does not include phone charges or installation fees. For information on fees for commercial providers, consult Appendix B: Choice Products.

For higher-speed connections, you will also need to pay the cost of a leased line between your location and the service provider. The cost of this will depend on the distance beween your system, the phone company's central office, and your provider. Additional costs include those for Ethernet cards, ISDN adapters, routers, etc.

If all this sounds like it can amount to a considerable sum, you're right. However, running *any* type of BBS is an expensive proposition, and adding the expense of an Internet connection to this may make good business sense in many circumstances.

Accessing Internet BBSes

While accessing an Internet BBS in text mode can be easy as using telnet, connecting to BBSes with a graphical interface is considerably more complicated.

How you will access your chosen BBS depends to a large extent on the type of computer you have, how the BBS is set up, and what protocols the interface requires. The BBS may be accessible via modem, by dialin via a port selector, by connection over the Internet, or by some combination of these.

The system may offer a custom graphical interface, support for graphical protocols such as NAPLPS or RIP, or support for PC-ANSI or VT100 emulation.

In connecting to the BBS, the user needs to choose the type of computer they will be using (Mac or PC), the means of connection (simple modem connection, scripted modem connection, or TCP/IP) and the protocols for accessing the service (graphical clients, RIP/NAPLPS, or VT100). Some combinations of these choices may not be available.

For example, if the Windows graphical client software does not support Windows Sockets, then it will not be possible to access the BBS from a Windows interface using TCP/IP. Similarly, if a Macintosh graphical client does not support the Communications Toolbox, then logins over TCP/IP will not be possible.

If a client is to be able to log in to a system using a port-selector (or any other connection scheme requiring a complex set of dialing instructions), then the client will need to support scripting. On the Macintosh platform, this is handled by the Calypso or CCL Communications Toolbox tools (available by `ftp sumex-aim.stanford.edu, cd /info-mac/comm`). Since Windows does not offer an equivalent, graphical Windows clients need to build in scripting facilities.

If a graphical client cannot be used, the user will have to find alternatives. One of these might be to access the service via `telnet` from a UNIX host or SLIP/PPP connection. This can provide a VT100 or PC-ANSI interface to the service, which may be acceptable. However, no Macintosh software currently supports RIP and the Tam Tam NAPLPS software does not support MacTCP or Comm Toolbox.

ToasterNets: Low Cost IP Connectivity for the Masses

Just as food cooperatives pioneered the sale of organic foods in the 1960s, Internet Cooperatives (known as ToasterNets) are bringing low-cost Internet connections to local communities.

ToasterNets work by purchasing Internet connectivity at T1 speeds, and reselling slower-speed connections to members. Typical charges for a resellable T1 connection are $2000/month. The first ToasterNet, The Little Garden (TLG), was founded in San Francisco by John Gilmore and John Romkey. Tim Pozar, author of the UFGATE FidoNet/UUCP gateway, was one of the first customers, and Tom Jennings (tomj@wps.com), founder of FidoNet, followed, and now manages TLG. ToasterNets have also sprung up in other regions of the country, such as the New England (NECI) the Pacific Northwest (RAIN), and Santa Cruz.

ToasterNets typically charge members upfront for the equipment and labor needed to set up the connection. This includes a pro-rata share of a router and terminal server, as well as the cost of an additional modem and phone line. Part of this fee (for example, the fee for the modem) may be refundable. They also typically bill members for a share of the high-speed Internet connection, based on bandwidth. Typical maintenance fees are in the range of $70-100/month for a dedicated connection. Typical equipment for setting up a ToasterNet includes:

• **Terminal servers.** These are relatively maintenance free, and frequently offer support for both SLIP and PPP. Recommended models include the Livingston PortMaster. Costs of $150-200 per line are typical.

• **PC-based routers.** These routers are typically quite a bit less expensive than top-of-the-line routers from Cisco, as well as more expandable. Typical costs are $2600 for the bare chasis, and $1000 for add-in Ethernet, Synchronous, or Asynchronous cards.

• **Bridges.** The Combinet Everywhere 150 bridge supports ISDN and Ethernet connections and goes for $900. It supports 128 Kbps throughput as well as data compression. A Combinet Everywhere 200 or 400 bridge is required at the main site. These run $1690 to $2190. You will also need ISDN Network Termination devices (NT1s) and Terminal Adapter units (TAs) on each end. Together an NT1 and TA run approximately $500. Combinet can be contacted at (408)522-9020.

• **Leased lines and CSU/DSUs.** ToasterNets typically purchase a T1 connection since it is usually only marginally more expensive than a 56 Kbps leased line while offering much greater connectivity. Typical T1 costs are $1000 for installation, plus $1500 for a CSU/DSU. 56 Kbps CSU/DSUs typically run around $500. Typical monthly service charges for T1 are $168 per end plus $21/mile between central offices. 56 Kbps lines typically run $56 per end plus $10/mile between central offices. In order to minimize charges, it is desirable to locate the router near (or at) the Central Office.

• **Low cost UNIX clone servers.** In order to provide NNTP, POP, Z39.50, HTTP, and Gopher service, an 80x86 machine running an inexpensive UNIX clone is typically employed. Alternatives include BSDI, NetBSD or Linux. BSDI is a reasonably priced commercial product based on the Berkeley NET/2 tape that supports synchronous cards as well as multiport serial cards. NetBSD is a freeware BSD implementation also based on the Net/2 tape, but which lacks the driver support of BSDI. Linux is a freeware implemetion which has more of a System V flavor.

For more information on ToasterNets, consult the MailCom Internet archive via ftp netcom1.netcom.com, cd /pub/mailcom/Toaster.

You should also consider how you will transfer files over a TCP/IP connection. If the BBS software does not support ZMODEM or YMODEM over TCP/IP, then you may be forced to use protocols such as KERMIT or XMODEM, which will be slow. In this case, the you may wish to use FTP instead, if the BBS supports this.

Mapping the possibilities

On the next page, I've mapped out some of the options for connecting to Internet BBSes. The table is a matrix, showing the options for a combination of BBS setup and user platform.

The columns of the matrix represent the BBS setup. These include a Modems column, for a server that will be taking calls over a modem. The Port Selector column is for systems that must be accessed via a port selector, or by a complex dialing scheme (such as connection over an X.25 network). The Internet column shows the requirements for systems that will be accessed over the Internet. The rows show the options for users of the Macintosh, Windows, and DOS operating systems. Where table entries show numbered alternatives, the alternatives are listed in order from the most desirable option (in my opinion) to the least desirable.

Macintosh

In accessing BBSes, the Communications Toolbox comes in handy in a variety of circumstances. These include situations where network connections are required, such as when the BBS is accessible via an X.25 network or the Internet. Comm Toolbox support is also useful when a complex dialing sequence is needed. This might be required when a system is accessed through a port-selector or a packet-switching service such as PC-Pursuit. Using the Comm Toolbox, you can combine scripting with network access.

Calypso

Calypso is a Comm Toolbox tool that supports scripting of connections using the Apple CCL scripting language.

Calypso requires an underlying connection tool in order to work. This might include a serial tool (for modem connections), the MacPad tool (for X.25 connections), or a Telnet tool (for connections made over the Internet).

To set up a Calypso connection, you will need to choose Calypso as the connection method and then select an underlying connection mechanism, such as the Serial Tool, MacPad, or a Telnet tool. You will also need to select the CCL script to run in order to connect. This is how the pieces fit together:

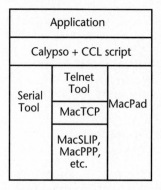

The first thing you need to do to set up Calypso is to obtain the software and install it. Then you will need to select **Communications Toolbox** as the mode for using your client software and to select the Calypso tool. The configuration dialog box will then pop up.

Access Strategies for Internet BBSes

Client	Server		
	Direct Modem Dialin	*Port Selector Dialin*	*TCP/IP access*
Macintosh	1. Modem GUI client (FC or NLP) 2. Client supporting NAPLPS, PC ANSI, or VT100 + transfer protocols (TamTam, ZTerm, MPII or MacIntercomm)	1. Scripting GUI client (Calypso + CCL script) (FC or NLP) 2. Scripting client supporting PC ANSI, or VT100 + ZMODEM, YMODEM and KERMIT (MP II or MacIntercomm)	1. Communications Toolbox GUI client (FC or NLP) 2. Server TCP/IP daemons (FTP, NNTP, etc. + Mac TCP/IP GUI clients 3. Client supporting comm toolbox + NAPLPS, PC ANSI, or VT100 + ZMODEM, KERMIT and YMODEM (MP II or MacIntercomm)
Windows	1. Windows GUI client (FC) 2. Client+server supporting PC ANSI, or VT100 + transfer protocols (ProComm Plus for Windows)	1. Scripting Windows GUI client 2. Scripting client+ server supporting PC ANSI, or VT100 + YMODEM, ZMODEM, and KERMIT (ProComm Plus for Windows)	1. Windows Sockets– compliant GUI client 2. Server TCP/IP daemons + Windows TCP/IP GUI clients 3. Int 14h TCP/IP driver + server telnetd support + PC ANSI, or VT100 + ZMODEM, KERMIT and YMODEM (WinQVT/Net)
DOS	1. DOS GUI client 2. Client+server supporting NAPLPS, RIP, PC ANSI, or VT100 + transfer protocols (Troika, RIPterm, QMODEM Pro, TELIX)	1. Scripting DOS GUI client 2. Scripting client+ server support for RIP, PC ANSI, or VT100 + ZMODEM, YMODEM, and KERMIT (QMODEM Pro, TELIX)	1. DOS GUI client with built-in stack 2. Server TCP/IP daemons + DOS TCP/IP clients 3. Server telnetd support + Int 14h TCP/IP driver + RIP, PC ANSI, or VT100 + KERMIT ZMODEM, and YMODEM (QMODEM Pro)

Calypso requires that you choose a Connection Tool. This is done by selecting one of the choices from the **Connection Tool** list:

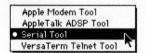

If you are dialing out via modem, choose the serial tool; if you are logging in via a port selector over the Internet, you will use a Telnet tool; for an X.25 connection, you will use the MacPad tool. Once you make the selection, you encounter another dialog box in order to set up your chosen tool for Calypso.

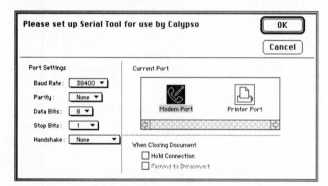

Before choosing a Telnet tool, it is a good idea to contact the BBS system operator for recommendations, since your chosen BBS may require a particular Telnet tool or settings to function. Below is the setup for the VersaTerm Telnet Tool:

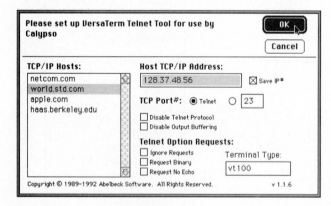

The TGE TCP tool setup is shown in the next column.

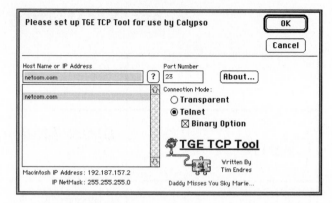

Note: the TGE TCP Tool, which is available via `ftp sumex-aim.stanford.edu, cd /info-mac/comm`, requires a license for commercial use.

FirstClass client setup

FirstClass client supports the Comm Toolbox, though future versions may not require telnet tools for logins over the Internet. To get FirstClass client to run over the Internet, select **Communications Toolbox** as your chosen method of connection.

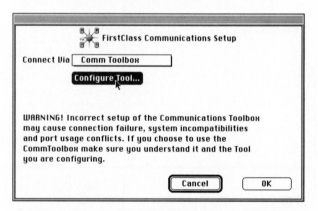

Choose an appropriate Telnet tool, such as the VersaTerm telnet tool or TCPack telnet tool. Please note that the TGE TCP Tool is not compatible with FirstClass client.

You will then need to configure your chosen telnet tool. If required, enter the system's IP address and domain name:

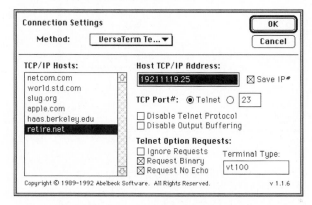

Note that **Request No Echo** must be checked. The other settings (including the port number) may differ based on the server setup. For example, the **Request Binary** setting is often checked by systems looking to have both command-line and graphical logins on the standard telnet port 23. This should be all you need to do, other than installing MacTCP and if needed, an appropriate SLIP or PPP extension.

NovaTerm client setup

NovaTerm supports direct TCP/IP or X.25 logins without requiring purchase of additional comm toolbox tools, although use of Comm Toolbox is also supported.

To setup NovaTerm for use under TCP/IP or X.25, you must have loaded the appropriate protocol stack and drivers (for TCP/IP this is MacTCP and a SLIP/PPP extension) and connected to the network; otherwise the **TCP/IP** or **X.25** menu option under **Connection Type:** will be grayed out. In the case shown below, I have selected **TCP/IP**:

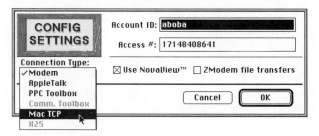

The dialog box will now change to reflect your protocol selection; fill in your host's address, and click on **OK**.

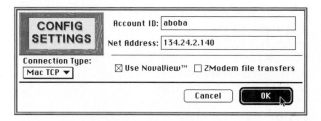

NAPLPS and RIP

Currently, no Macintosh communications program supports Remote Image Protocol (RIP), the BBS-oriented multimedia protocol which is no relation to TCP/IP's Routing Information Protocol, also known as RIP. If the system you are trying to connect with supports NAPLPS, then you will need to use a NAPLPS-emulation program called Tam Tam, from Communications Infographiques Mac Gregor Inc., P.O. Box 125, Station E, Montreal, Quebec H2T 3A5, Canada. While Tam Tam supports scripting and TELETEL, VT100, TTY, and NAPLPS emulation, it does not support Comm Toolbox and therefore cannot be used for communications over the Internet. A screenshot of Tam Tam is shown here:

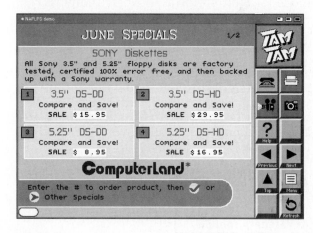

VT100

If the BBS supports only VT100, then one alternative is to access it by dialing in to an Internet host with a normal program and using `telnet` to transfer to the BBS. Files can then be downloaded using a standard protocol such as ZMODEM, or YMODEM. If either of these protocols proves problematic, KERMIT can be used as a last resort.

What if you have an Internet link available and want to make the connection to the BBS using TCP/IP? In this case you will need a Comm Toolbox compatible terminal program, such as Microphone II, VersaTerm, MacIntercomm or Termy.

Termy

Termy

If you can't afford a commercial Comm Toolbox–compatible terminal program, you might try Termy, a freeware program by Tim Endres. Termy is compatible with the TGE TCP tool (also by Tim Endres), so that you will be able to `telnet` to your chosen BBS over the Internet. By installing the appropriate Communications Toolbox file transfer tools (such as KERMIT, XMODEM, and YMODEM), you will be able to download files using these protocols over TCP/IP. Be aware that you will need to set up the TGE TCP tool in binary mode for 8-bit protocols to work! Termy, as well as the KERMIT and YMODEM Communications Toolbox tools, is available via `ftp sumex-aim.stanford.edu`, `cd /info-mac/comm`.

Prior to using Termy you should first install your Comm Toolbox tools, such as the TGE TCP tool, KERMIT and YMODEM transfer tools, etc. You will then need to select your preferred transfer tool.

After selecting your preferred transfer method, you will need to complete one of the dialog boxes for KERMIT, XMODEM, or YMODEM.

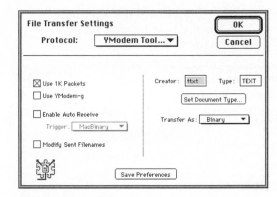

YMODEM Tool

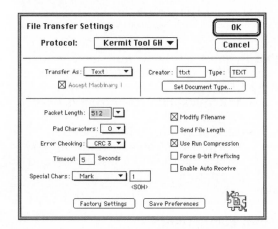

Kermit Tool

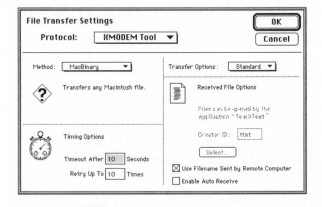

XMODEM Tool

Once you have selected and configured the desired tool, all you need to do is to select **Receive File...** from the **Terminal** menu to begin the download.

Windows

If your BBS offers a Windows client, then you can use this to dial in directly via modem. Unless you can find a scripting GUI client for Windows, if the BBS is behind a port selector or only reachable by some other method of scripted login, you may be out of luck.

Similarly, unless the client supports Windows Sockets, you will not be able to get a graphical interface logging in directly over the Internet. However, you will be able to log in to an Internet host and `telnet` to the BBS. Assuming that the BBS supports protocols such as ZMODEM or YMODEM, you will be able to download from the system using a Windows terminal emulator such as Procomm Plus for Windows. This will support PC-ANSI and VT-100 sessions. Currently there are no RIP or NAPLPS clients under Windows.

If ZMODEM and YMODEM are not available on the BBS, then you might want to try FTP to retrieve files. You can use programs such as NetManage Chameleon to connect over the network to do the FTP, or you can dial into an Internet host and retrieve the file from there. If FTP is not supported, you may be stuck with a 7-bit protocol such as KERMIT, which should work under virtually any circumstances.

DOS

If your chosen BBS software has a graphical DOS client, you should try this first. However, unless the DOS client has scripting capability, you will not be able to reach the server if a complex login sequence is required.

Since there are DOS versions of NAPLPS (Troika) and RIP (Telix and QMODEM Pro), this mode of connection can be handled by modem connection. Since these programs support switching between text mode and graphical mode, it is possible to control the dialing process. In addition, Telix and QMODEM Pro support full-featured scripting languages. This means that access to systems behind a port selector are no problem.

Network connections are a somewhat different story. Int 14h redirection is a method for redirecting output meant for the serial port out via a TCP/IP socket. This is supported by QMODEM Pro, for example, but I don't know if it will work with other programs.

If NAPLPS or RIP access is not possible, then PC-ANSI or VT100 mode will have to do. Programs such as Win QVT/Net can handle telnet and FTP as well as VT100 support, so this is one possible choice. Note that I have not tried downloading over `telnet`, so I have no idea how well this works. Of course, you can also dial in to an Internet host and `telnet` to the BBS, in which case most standard terminal emulators such as Telix, Procomm, etc., will work. If ZMODEM and YMODEM are not available, or do not work, then you can try FTP. This can be done using KA9Q over the network, or you can dial in to an Internet host and retrieve the file from there. If FTP is not supported, you may be stuck with KERMIT, which will work under virtually any circumstances.

Strategies for connecting Internet BBSes

There are quite a few ways to connect a BBS to the Internet. These include terminal servers, UNIX BBSes, DOS BBSes with TCP/IP FOSSIL drivers or TCP/IP compatible BBSes.

Terminal servers

In principle, any BBS can be made available for `telnet` access by connecting it to a terminal server. Systems such as Spacemet (spacemet.phast.umass.edu, 128.119.50.48) and Oklahoma University (oubbs.telecom.uoknor.edu, `129.15.3.15`), have used this approach. Oklahoma University uses a Datability VCP1000 terminal server connected to a router, CSU/DSU, and leased line. The system runs TBBS.

Spacemet uses an 8-port Emulex P2500 terminal server connected to the local UMass Ethernet on one end, and a PC with an 8-port Digiboard on the other. The system runs the Maximus BBS package under DESQview. A program called WAITCHAR runs and when it determines that a signal has arrived, calls up the BBS.

Terminal server products include those from Annex, Datability, Emulex, and Livingston. For more information on terminal server products, see Appendix B: Choice Products.

It is also possible to use a UNIX workstation as a terminal server. This is what Community News Service (CNS) of Colorado Springs does.

UNIX BBSes

One obvious attraction of UNIX BBSes is that most versions of UNIX come with TCP/IP built in. Assuming that the BBS software supports import and export of RFC 822 (mail) and RFC 1036 (USENET) message formats and can execute external commands or shell scripts, you will be able to customize it to provide virtually any Internet service.

Hardware

If you can afford it, I would recommend going with a Sun workstation running SunOS. Most publicly distributable software will compile more easily under SunOS than under other platforms, so this can save you a lot of time. You are also likely to have good success with DEC Ultrix.

Be aware that Solaris v2.1 (shipping with the newer Sun workstations) is different enough from SunOS that many programs written for SunOS will not compile under Solaris v2.1 without modification. Compatibility with software may also present a problem for other System V derivatives such as HP/UX.

If you cannot afford a workstation, the next best alternative may be BSDI, a port of the BSD UNIX to the Intel architecture, described on the next page. BSDI is compatible with a number of UNIX BBSes, including Waffle, Citadel and XBBS. Several midlevel regional networks now use 486 machines running BSDI as NNTP/FTP/SMTP servers, with good results.

Whatever machine you purchase, it is recommended that you get an internal CD-ROM drive to go with it. UNIX distributions are now so large that some versions (Solaris, NeXTSTEP) are only available on CD-ROM. Even if you have the option of purchasing UNIX on floppy disks, loading it from CD-ROM will save a lot of time and will eliminate the possibility of damaging one of the many disks.

When purchasing a UNIX machine, also remember to get enough memory and a large enough hard drive. Running hard drives off a SCSI interface is recommended, since this lets you add more external drives as needed; IDE controllers typically only allow two drives, which can be very limiting. A BBS might start with a 1.2 Gb drive, and 20 Mb of RAM.

If purchasing a 486, make sure to get a machine that is adequately cooled and that has a Pentium upgrade option. At the higher speeds (50 and 66 Mz), the 486 can get very hot, and this can result in erratic behavior. People report that attaching large heat sinks to their 486 chips helps.

Budget UNIX alternatives

Aside from UNIX versions such as Dell System VR4 (available for $1295 in a complete package which includes SLIP), Solaris v2.1, and System VR4.2, there are now several inexpensive and highly capable UNIX alternatives out there. These include:

∇ BSD/386

**BSD386 v1.0 binary license $495
Additional binary licenses $200
Source code license $1045
Upgrade program $195/year**

BSD/386 is a commercial port of the Berkeley System Distribution (BSD) NET/2 tape to the

Intel architecture, with relatively few bugs and lots of driver support. It is in my opinion the finest inexpensive UNIX-like operating system on the market. It is available on CD-ROM, and comes with a very complete selection of utilities, including X11R5, NFS, SLIP and synchronous PPP. Driver support is good; this includes sync cards, Adaptec SCSI cards, CD-ROM drivers and soon, Digiboard multiport cards.

Binaries are available for $495, with additional licenses available for an extra $200. The upgrade program is $195/year, and a source code license is $1045. These prices are very reasonable, considering that BSD/386 is very complete. Features due in future releases include support for Novell IPX, SCO binaries, and Digiboards. For information on BSDI, see the comp.unix.bsd newsgroup.

Berkeley Software Design, Inc.; 7759 Delmonico Drive, Colorado Springs, CO 80919; (719)593-9445, fax: (719)598-4238, email: kolstad@bsdi.com.

∇ 386BSD and NetBSD

386BSD, originally described in *Dr. Dobb's Journal* in 1991, is a freeware port of the Net/2 tape to the Intel architecture. Development has now split into two camps: 386BSD and NetBSD. The 386BSD team is lead by Bill and Lynne Jolitz and is oriented toward adding cutting-edge technology to BSD. The NetBSD team is more focussed on popularizing the platform by concentrating on bug-fixes and application ports.

Binaries and source code for both 386BSD and NetBSD are available via `ftp agate.berkeley.edu, cd /pub/386BSD, cd /pub/NetBSD`. Both 386BSD and NetBSD include TCP/IP support (with SLIP), floating point, Taylor UUCP, SCSI support, a full spate of BSD utilities, and passwording. Both 386BSD and NetBSD are based on the NET/2 tape from UC Berkeley, and with the encryption utilities separated out, both are legal for export. Users of NetBSD report that recent releases are quite stable, although driver support is limited but improving. Certain multi-port cards are now supported, as are IDE, ESDI, and SCSI drives,

although asynch and ISDN cards were not, at last look. For more information on 386BSD and NetBSD, check out the comp.os.386bsd.* newsgroups described at the end of this section.

∇ Linux

Linux is a UNIX alternative that does not depend on any UNIX Systems Laboratories or BSD code. Linux resembles System V more than BSD, and as a result, less software is available for it than for 386BSD and NetBSD, since many BSD programs will not compile under Linux. Linux now supports TCP/IP as well as X-windows and even offers several FidoNet mailers (NIXMAIL, and a UNIX port of BinkleyTerm). For information on Linux, check out the comp.os.linux newsgroup, as well as the Linux mailing list, `linux-activists-requests@niksula.hut.fi`. For more information, `finger torvalds@kruuna.helsinki.fi`.

∇ COHERENT

COHERENT is a commercial product from the Mark Williams Company. It is not a complete UNIX implementation and does not currently offer TCP/IP or X-Windows support, although this is rumored to be coming in version 5.0. Version 4.0 does support UUCP and USENET and running standard Intel UNIX binaries, large model C compilations and more than 230 UNIX commands.

COHERENT v4.0 requires only 14 Mb of disk space, sells for $99.95, comes with complete documentation, and is supported by several BBS packages, including CocoNet. It resides in its own partition, but can access a DOS partition. Support is available by phone and BBS. For more information on COHERENT, check out the comp.os.coherent newsgroup.

UNIX BBS software

The UNIX BBS software market is not as large as for MS-DOS or Macintosh, although there are still several capable packages available. Popular inexpensive packages include Uniboard (covered in the group alt.bbs.unixbbs.uniboard), and Waffle (covered in alt.bbs.waffle). General discussion of UNIX BBS packages takes place in alt.bbs.unixbbs. For further information on UNIX BBS software, please consult Appendix B: Choice Products.

Putting a NovaLink Pro v3.0 server on the Internet

NovaLink Pro v3.0 supports Telnet logins directly without requiring a Comm Toolbox Telnet tool, although Comm Toolbox is also supported. As a result, setting up NovaLink Pro for Telnet sessions is very simple.

Before configuring a NovaLink Pro v3.0 server for Internet use, you must first set up MacTCP, and select the appropriate interface, such as EtherNet, AppleTalk, SLIP, or PPP. For those connecting a BBS to the Internet over a modem, PPP is a desirable choice because MacPPP (available free via `ftp merit.edu, cd /ppp`) will automatically dial out and connect when it detects TCP/IP traffic. This means that when the BBS boots, it will automatically come back on the network if NLP v3.0 is set as the startup application. This feature is particularly desirable if your systems runs with crash detection/reboot.

Once you have MacTCP configured, run NovaLink Pro server, and select **Configure Nodes...** from the **Server** menu.

This will bring up the Configure Node Settings Dialog box. To add a TCP/IP node, select TCP/IP from the **Add Node Type** list. Other choices include AppleTalk, Comm Toolbox, Local, and Serial.

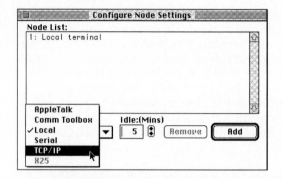

Once you've selected TCP/IP, click on the **Add** button. A TCP/IP node will be added to the list, and you're done!

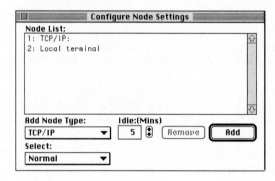

TCP/IP FOSSIL drivers

BBS packages such as Searchlight, Fido, OPUS, Maximus, Remote Access, Waffle, and WILDCAT! utilize FOSSIL communications drivers. TCP/IP FOSSIL drivers are now available from Murkworks and TASP that allows these packages to be directly connected to the Internet without terminal servers.

Murkworks tools include a `telnet` driver running over Novell LanWorkPlace for DOS. With this approach, each node has its own IP address; with multi-node packages such as PCBoard /M, a single system can handle up to ten `telnet` connections.

For large systems, Murkworks provides a Telnet Daemon NLM that supports FOSSIL over SPX. With the NLM, users `telnet` to the Novell server and are redirected to an open node automatically. In the LanWorkPlace for DOS approach, users cannot automatically be redirected to an open node if their chosen

BBS node has maxed out on `telnet` connections.

Using these telnet tools, ANSI support, QMAIL, and ZMODEM downloads will work as they would with a normal modem session, provided that the user establishes a binary `telnet` session. However, if the user is running a 7 bit `telnet` session from a PC or a dumb terminal, then `ftp` support will be needed.

Murkworks is also working on adding FTP server support. This is likely to be popular with some of the large systems that have file libraries competitive with Internet FTP archives. For more information on Murkworks products, please contact `bkc@murkworks.com`.

TAPCIS has also developed FOSSIL interfaces to TCP/IP and X.25. TASP installs as a TSR requiring 76K of RAM, and handles FOSSIL Int 14h calls, behaving as though it were a modem. The software supports comm ports, Ethernet cards, or multiport boards. For information, contact: Daniel J. Karnes, NMS & Systems Engineering; TASP Development Group, Silverado, CA 92676-0233, (909)245-2286, email: `djk@tasp.tasp.net`.

Adding BBS networks to The Matrix

The initial step toward integrating a BBS network with the Internet is usually to obtain domain name service and set up a system of mail gateways. The next step is to connect the backbone nodes using TCP/IP. This has the advantage of allowing for higher-speed transmission, and possibly for lower costs as well, depending on the level of traffic.

BITNET and USENET have already made the transition to TCP/IP, and it is likely that other store and forward networks will follow. On the Macintosh, the Communications Toolbox has made such transitions easier by allowing developers to build in compatibility with multiple connection types. On the PC, things may be as simple as redirecting I/O from FOSSIL communications drivers to a TCP/IP stack. This technique is called "INT 14h redirection."

What if you are running a store and forward BBS network and would like to provide your nodes with a fully qualified domain name so that they can receive and send mail? What is involved in providing Domain Name Service for your network?

Myths about Domain Name Service

First, let's dispense with a few myths about DNS:

• Acquiring a domain name for a BBS network does not require the network to have systems on the Internet. Name service can be handled entirely by service providers and Internet hosts can gateway mail and news to your network.

• No central authority mandates a naming scheme for your network, such as the somewhat unwieldy FidoNet naming scheme (i.e. `p2.f445.n161.z1.fidonet.org`). However, for reasons that will be described, hierarchical naming schemes are generally chosen because they are easy to maintain.

• Acquiring a domain name is not expensive. Services such as Holonet offer DNS at very reasonable rates. If a willing Internet host can be found, an entire BBS network can acquire name service for free. If correctly set up, this will continue to operate with little additional effort.

• DNS and routing are unrelated issues. A network need not be able to handle multihop routing in order to acquire a domain name. For those networks that cannot route, systems will need to contact their regional Internet host directly to pick up mail. For networks that can forward one hop, mail hub systems can be set up that poll the regional Internet host and then distribute mail to local systems.

• DNS and conference gatewaying are unrelated issues. To acquire a domain name, a BBS network need not gateway conferences to USENET; it need only be able to generate mail messages in RFC 822 format.

• Acquiring a domain name does not bring a BBS network under "government control."

DNS is provided by individual Internet hosts, not by the NSF or any other government agency. Although mail traveling over the NSFNet backbone is subject to the Appropriate Use Policy, alternative connections are possible.

The truth about DNS

What DNS *does* do is make it easier for users of a BBS network to receive and send mail from the Internet. If set up correctly, this requires little or no special effort on the part of the individual BBS network nodes.

There are two major strategies for providing domain name service to BBS networks. One strategy, adopted by FidoNet, (`fidonet.org`) is to have the gateway software reside on a series of gateway BBSes. In the case of FidoNet/UUCP gateways, this software provides support for UUCP communications (mail and news), as well as routing within the FidoNet network. Currently, the most popular FidoNet/UUCP gateway products are UFGATE (coauthored by Tim Pozar), FredGate, and PIMP. For more information on these products, please consult Appendix B: Choice Products.

Another strategy is to install the gateway software on the Internet host. This is the approach taken by the FrEdMail network (`fred.org`).

While this approach eliminates the need for the BBSes to purchase gateway software (since the Internet host communicates with them using their intranetwork protocol), it increases the amount of work required of the Internet host. This makes it harder to recruit hosts, and as a result this approach was considered and rejected by UFGATE coauthor Tim Pozar when he was planning the FidoNet/UUCP gateway system.

Network address to domain name mapping

Whichever method is chosen, the first step in providing domain name service for a BBS network is to decide how to map BBS network addresses to fully qualified domain names. We discuss the choices made by the FidoNet and FrEdMail networks below.

FidoNet addressing scheme

One way to handle the name mapping problem would have been to give each FidoNet node a unique name: boombox.com, fishfiends.org, etc. However, this would require installing and keeping track of the name of every node in the FidoNet Nodelist. Since the nodes in the nodelist change on a weekly basis, this would require a lot of work.

Instead, the FidoNet node number (such as 1:161/5555) is used to construct a hierarchical domain name such as:

`f5555.n161.z1.fidonet.org`
While such an addressing scheme may seem clumsy to some, it in no way restricts the ability of an individual node to add a second MX record giving them a shorter domain name; the scheme merely gives all FidoNet nodes a default domain name without unduly burdening the FidoNet hostmaster.

For example, node 1:161/5555 could be addressed both as `f5555.n161.z1.fidonet.org`, or as `boombox.fidonet.org, or boombox.com.`

The `f5555.n161.z1.fidonet.org` address is supported for all FidoNet nodes by default. The second addressing type (`boombox.fidonet.org`) is for FidoNet/UUCP gateways, and would be registered once 1:161/5555 installs its gateway, registers the UUCP host name `boombox` in the UUCP maps, and informs the FidoNet hostmaster about the gateway. The hostmaster will then create a Mail eXchange (MX) for `boombox.fidonet.org.`

The third address, boombox.com would not be handled by the FidoNet hostmaster (since it is not part of the `fidonet.org` domain) but could be installed by an Internet service provider. Charges for this go as low as $25 (Holonet).

FrEdMail Addressing Scheme

With FrEdMail, systems each have a unique node name, i.e., `bonita`. This node name is mapped to a domain name address of the following form:

`<node>.<region>.fred.org`

Here `<region>` is the name of an Internet regional network, such as `cerf` for CERFnet. By way of example, the node `bonita` within the CERFnet region would have the address `bonita.cerf.fred.org`.

DNS and sendmail

While a full description of DNS and sendmail could easily take up an entire volume, their application to BBS networks is fairly simple.

FidoNet

In the case of FidoNet, MX records are created on a network basis, and stored on the zone hostmaster, indicating the machines for which mail to a specific FidoNet network should be sent. For example, the MX record for network 161 in zone 1 is:

`*.n161.z1.fidonet.org IN MX 10 111-winken.llnl.gov`

This indicates that all mail for network 161 in zone 1 is to be delivered to the Internet machine `111-winken.llnl.gov`. The number 10 refers to priority of the record, with lower numbers indicating that this host should be tried first. Since there is only one record in this case, the number chosen does not matter.

It is then the responsibility of `111-winken.llnl.gov` to pass the mail along to the FidoNet/UUCP gateway for network 161.

This is accomplished by sendmail (or an equivalent) which (assuming fidogate as the FidoNet/UUCP gateway) translates:

`<node>.n161.z1.fidonet.org`

to:

`fidogate!1!161!<node number>`

sendmail then queues the mail for delivery via UUCP. Note that from the Internet host's

point of view, the FidoNet/UUCP gateway is just another UUCP host; no gateway software resides on the Internet host.

FrEdMail

The FrEdMail addressing scheme (`bonita.cerf.fred.org`) requires an MX record for each gateway. For example, the MX record for handling delivery of mail by the cerf gateway is:

`*.cerf.fred.org IN MX 0 nic.cerf.net`

As a result, all mail for the cerf gateway will be delivered to machine `nic.cerf.net`.

Including the gateway name within the domain name has the disadvantage of requiring hosts to change their name whenever gateways change. A better solution might have been to divide the network into regions, such as `bonita.pacific.fred.org`. This would allow mail routing to remain transparent to the user; a change from CERFNet to BARRnet as the gateway, for example, could be accomplished without users even being aware of the change.

FrEdMail systems connect directly with their Internet gateway hosts, which set them up as UUCP links. The outgoing UUCP packets are never sent over UUCP; instead, a process initiated by `cron` converts the packets to the FrEdMail format and stores them in the account of the calling BBS. It is also possible for the Internet host to modify their sendmail.cf file and install a new mailer called fmailer, which will take the outgoing packets and store them in the BBS directory without having to run a cron process. Either way, when the BBS calls in, a nonabortable .profile script runs and initiates a file transfer using XMODEM, YMODEM, or ZMODEM.

In order to route mail for the FrEdMail BBSes via UUCP, there are two approaches: one uses aliases, and the other requires modifications to the sendmail.cf file. Either way, mail for

`<ID>@<node>.cerf.fred.org`

is instead sent to: `<node>!<ID>`

For example, mail to

`bnagorsk@bonita.cerf.org`

is sent to: `bonita!bnagorsk`

Since the Internet host must set up UUCP accounts for each FrEdMail node in their region, this involves quite a bit of work for the Internet host. Since FrEdMail is small, and since it is composed of schools with a long-term commitment to telecommunications, the system works fine. However, in a network with many nodes and high turnover (such as FidoNet), this method would quickly become very tedious for the Internet hosts to administer. However, it would be possible to modify the system so that the Internet hosts then passed mail on to a series of mail hubs, which then routed mail within the FrEdMail network. This would dramatically lessen the number of connections maintained on each Internet host. However, for ease of maintenance it would also require another hierarchy in the network address (i.e., `bonita.sdhub.cerf.fred.org`), and would require modification of the sendmail.cf file on the host so as to route the mail to the mail hub systems.

For more information on the FrEdMail gateway system, **ftp nic.cerf.net, cd /pub/fredmail.** For further information on the FidoNet/UUCP gateway system, please consult Chapter 18: From FidoNet to UUCP and Back.

Pseudo domains

Although BITNET and UUCP are not domains, many machines nevertheless support sending of mail to nodes on these networks using "pseudo domain" addresses such as planet.UUCP or BITNIC.BITNET.

Mail routers such as sendmail support pseudo domains by rewriting addresses for the bogus domains to route through known gateways. For example, the address `foo@planet.UUCP` is rewritten as `foo%planet@uunet.uu.net`, where `uunet.uu.net` acts as the Internet/UUCP gateway. Similarly, mail for `LISTSERV@BITNIC.BITNET` is rewritten as `LISTSERV%BITNIC@cunyvm.cuny.edu`. The

important thing to understand is that this may or may not be supported on a given host. Providing for mail connectivity for a new store and forward network using pseudo domains is unworkable, since this would require convincing many system administrators to modify their configuration files, which is unlikely. Instead, administrators of store and forward networks should set up domain name service by one of the methods previously described.

For more information

Internet BBSes

alt.bbs.internet
Information on Internet BBSes, including a regularly posted list of systems.

Network Operation Center (NOC) administration

comp.network.noctools.announce
comp.network.noctools.bugs
comp.network.noctools.d
comp.network.noctools.submissions
comp.network.noctools.tools
comp.network.noctools.wanted

386BSD and NETBSD Newgroups

comp.os.386bsd.announce
386BSD announcements (moderated). To post an announcement, **mail 386bsd-announce@agate.berkeley.edu**

comp.os.386bsd.apps
386BSD applications.

comp.os.386bsd.bugs
Bugs and fixes.

comp.os.386bsd.development
386BSD development.

comp.os.386bsd.misc
386BSD related material not covered elsewhere.

comp.os.386bsd.questions
386BSD Q&A.

Part III

Store and Forward Network Guide

"Laws and institutions must go hand in hand with the progress of the human mind."

– Thomas Jefferson, letter to Samuel Kercheval, July 12, 1816

"Do not be bullied out of your common sense by the specialist; two to one, he is a pedant."

– Oliver Wendell Holmes, Sr., *Over the Teacups* (1891)

CHAPTER 16: UNIX TO UNIX COPY

Not for UNIX machines only

What is UUCP?

Unix to Unix Copy, or UUCP, is a protocol that started with UNIX, and is widely used with UNIX, but is also implemented on VMS, Amiga, MS–DOS, Macintosh OS, and other operating systems. UUCP communications most often occurs over dialup telephone connections, although it can also occur over dedicated lines along with protocols such as TCP/IP. UUCP is more than just a file transfer protocol; it also allows for execution of remote commands. Using UUCP, you can:

• Send a file to another system
• Request a file from a system
• Receive and send electronic mail
• Receive and send network news
• Execute remote commands, and receive the results

Note that sending and receiving files and executing remote commands is likely to work only over one hop, not many, unless you happen to be lucky enough to be using a path through machines all with the same version of UUCP and an agreement to pass files. Also, the commands that you can execute remotely with UUCP are almost always limited to a very small set.

UUCP requests are queued for execution until the sending and receiving systems connect. How often this occurs depends on whether the systems are set up to connect whenever there is something to be delivered ("demand calling"), or whether they will wait until a scheduled time ("polling"), which is often in the evening, when phone rates are lower.

Why do I care?

When people say that their system is "on the Internet," very often they mean that their machine can communicate with Internet hosts via UUCP. This is highly misleading, since UUCP connections offer only a small subset of the functionality of a true Internet connection. With UUCP you basically have only mail, news and possibly file transfer. You do not have access to the plethora of real Internet services such as remote login, interactive file transfer, finger, gopher, WAIS, WWW, IRC, etc. For information on TCP/IP networking, please consult Chapter 15: TCP/IP.

UUCP is economical and widely implemented. UUCP connections may be available from a nearby site for the cost of a phone call, or can be purchased from commercial providers, at rates starting at $30/month. Using UUCP you can schedule sessions to occur late at night when phone rates are lower, and news can be batched and compressed in order to save on phone charges.

If you are not yet ready to consider a TCP/IP connection for your workstation, microcomputer or BBS, yet you anticipate moderate to heavy levels of traffic, then a UUCP connection may be for you.

Steps to getting a UUCP connection

In order to set up your UUCP connection, you will need:

• A telephone line
• A modem, a computer, and a cable
• A host with which to exchange mail and/or network news
• A UUCP implementation

If you are going to be doing extensive UUCP communications, I recommend that you purchase a Telebit modem, since it supports spoofing of the UUCP-g protocol, which greatly improves performance.

UUCP implementations for personal computers are listed in Appendix B: Choice Products. These include stand-alone implementations as well as gateway packages.

The easiest way to get a mail and news feed is to sign up with one of the commercial providers listed in Appendix B: Choice Products (see entries under Chapter 8). If you are looking for a free feed, your search can be quite difficult, since many universities and firms have stopped adding additional links. The brute force way to go about it is to get hold of the UUCP maps for your area and call sites until you find one that will give you a feed. Several Internet sites are map servers, which means that you can send them email to request the UUCP maps for your area. One of the map servers is ieee.org. **mail map-request@ieee.org**, with a subject of **help** or **list** will get you information on how to use the map server. Here's what the message will look like:

```
TO: map-request@ieee.org
SUBJECT: help

The message text can be anything.
```

Maps are also available via **ftp ftp.uu.net, cd /uumap/,** or can be retrieved by mail using FTPmail (see Chapter 10: FTP for information). Finally, the WAIS-compatible source uumap.src is an index of all the sites in the UUCP map databases. Searching this source will tell you if a site has a UUCP map entry; however, it is not much help in finding a UUCP site near you. The uumap.src source can be searched by mail using waismail (consult Chapter 14: Z39.50). If you have an Internet account, and you don't have a WAIS client installed on your system, you can **telnet quake.think.com**, login: **wais**, and use the swais client, which offers a VT100 interface.

UUCP map entries and Domain Name Service

Every UUCP system must have a name. In order to uniquely identify your site, you should choose a UUCP name that is not in use by another system. You can ensure that this is the case by searching the WAIS database uumap.src.

Just choosing a name doesn't tell other systems how to reach you. To do this, you need to submit a UUCP map entry and obtain Domain Name Service. A UUCP map entry will allow systems known as "smart mailers" to compute how to route mail to your system without having a full "bang-path" style address.

Map entries are mailed to the local map administrator, who in turn posts them to the newsgroup comp.mail.maps. Maps in comp.mail.maps are compiled by a program called pathalias, which creates a database that is used by smail to compute the route. A UUCP map entry form is included in Appendix E: Network Application Forms.

While posting a UUCP map entry will allow sites running pathalias and smail to reach you via UUCP, submitting a UUCP map entry does not provide a fully qualified domain name. There is no registered UUCP domain, because domains are not generally intended to represent networks (although they sometimes do, such as in the use of the fidonet.org, fred.org, and ampr.org domains).

Unless you obtain domain name service, your system will not have a domain name, but may be addressable from systems set up to support the UUCP "pseudo-domain." Using this addressing method, a system with the UUCP name of planet would be addressed as planet.UUCP. It should be understood that this addressing scheme is only valid on a system by system basis, and therefore is not recommended.

In order to provide Domain Name Service (DNS) for your system (and allow your system to be called hubub.com) you will need to register a DNS name, and then establish a Mail eXchange (MX) record for your system. Many commercial providers (such as Holonet) offer such a service for a nominal fee. More information on MX records is available in Chapter 15: Bulletin Boards and the Internet.

Variants of UUCP

There are many different versions of UUCP, and the differences among the versions are the cause of more than a small amount of confusion. Commonly encountered versions of UUCP include Basic Network Utilities (BNU), also known as HoneyDanBer UUCP, which is the UUCP shipped with System V and Sun OS release 4; The Berkeley System Distribution (BSD) 4.3 UUCP, which is based on the Version 2 UUCP created by AT&T back in 1987 and is shipped with NeXTSTEP. There is also Taylor UUCP, which is capable of using both BNU and BSD configuration files as well as its own configuration format. Taylor UUCP is offered under a GNU copyleft and is shipped with BSD/386 and NetBSD. Taylor UUCP has most recently been modified in order to support a variant of ZMODEM and in a forthcoming version will support file-size limitations.

If your system has an L.sys file in the /etc/uucp directory, then you probably have a BSD v4.3 or Version 2 UUCP. If you have a file named sys, then you have Taylor UUCP. If you have a file called Systems, you probably have BNU.

Finally, there are versions of UUCP for microcomputers. These include Waffle, UUPC, UULINK, UUPlus, FSUUCP, UFGATE and MKS UUCP for MS-DOS, and UUPC and uConnect on the Macintosh.

Components of a UUCP implementation

UUCP implementations are composed of several programs, including uucico, uucp, uux, uusend, uuq, uusnap, uulog, uuclean, uuto, uupick and uuname. All of these commands must be typed in lower case on a UNIX system, and some may not be available on a particular implementation.

uucico

The purpose of uucico (which stands for Unix-to-Unix Copy In, Copy Out) is to establish the connection between systems and to carry out file transfers. This is the program that must be called when a UUCP host receives a call from a remote system; it is also the application that carries out the polling of the remote system.

uucico offers command-line options for its execution, including:

`-g <grade letter>`	Priority option
`-r<mode>`	The role. <mode> = 1 for master (outgoing calls), 0 for slave (incoming)
`-x<debug #>`	Debugging option Debugging levels go from 1 (lowest) to 9 (highest)
`-s<site>`	Site to call

Chat scripts

In order to poll, uucico executes a script, which on Version 2 or BSD-derived UUCP implementations is contained in the L.sys file. The script is written in an expect-send-expect-send format, with spaces between each send and expect entry; a carriage return is implied after each send entry.

The purpose of the script is to log on to the host system in order to execute the remote system's uucico program.

For hosts running bulletin board software, the uucico program is frequently called up via a door; for UNIX systems, uucico is set as the caller's login shell.

uucp

The uucp command is used to transfer files between one system and another. In command-line implementations, it is invoked very much like a standard UNIX copy command:

```
uucp foo bozo\!~/foo
```

Here ~ is shorthand for /usr/spool/uucppublic, the directory that handles a large proportion of UUCP business, and the \ is an escape character used to prevent confusion with the history command in the C shell.

The `uucp` command can also be used with the following options:

-m   Send a return receipt when the file arrives at its destination

-r   Queue the request

Be aware that for the requested file transfer to go through:

• You must have permission to access the relevant files or directories. You cannot send a file that you do not have permission to read, nor can you request that a file be written into a directory for which you do not have read permission.

• UUCP must be set up to allow the transfer of the relevant files. This is a separate issue from UNIX permissions; you may have read access to a file that UUCP may not be set up to allow you to transmit or request. The /usr/spool/uucppublic directory is usually open to reading and writing by everyone, as well as being enabled for remote UUCP access. Therefore it is a good choice for a directory in which to retrieve or send a file via UUCP.

uux

`uux` is used to request remote execution of a command. In order to prevent security problems, most systems only allow for execution of a very restricted set of commands, such as `rmail`, `rnews`, `ruusend`, `uusend`, `finger`, `lpr`, and `who`. Many systems do not even allow execution of `uusend`, `lpr`, `who`, or `finger`. Those systems that do support file sends or requests usually severely restrict the directories available to these commands for security reasons. Here is an example of a `uux` command:

```
uux "bozo\!who >/aboba/foo"
```

If your request cannot be handled, you will receive a mail message back like this:

```
Date: Sat, 23 Jan 93 18:20:12 -1000
From: bozo!nuucp
Content-Type: text
Content-Length: 105
Apparently-To: planet!root

remote execution [uucp job planetA03g2 (1/23-15:31:51)]
          who
execution permission denied to planet!root
```

uusend

uusend lets you forward a file through multiple hops. Example:

```
uusend foo bozo\!planet\!~/foo
```

uuq

uuq lets you manipulate pending UUCP jobs. It only lists outgoing jobs. It shows you the machines the jobs are going to, what the commands are, how much space the jobs take, when the jobs were queued, and the sequence number of the job. Options include:

-d <job number>   Deletes specified job.

-l   Prints long version.

-s <system>   Restricts output to host <system>

Example:

```
planet:10# uuq
bozo: 1 job
POLL

holonet: 1 job
POLL

uunet: 1 job
0000
planet:12#
```

uusnap

uusnap provides a snapshot of the current status of UUCP. It tells you how many command, data and executable files are queued. It doesn't distinguish between outgoing and incoming files. Example:

```
planet:9# uusnap
uunet   1 Cmd --- --- LOGIN FAILED  Retry time reached Count: 3
holonet 1 Cmd --- --- LOGIN FAILED  Retry time 7 mins
bozo    1 Cmd --- --- LOGIN FAILED  Retry time reached
```

uulog

uulog displays the log entries since the log file was last deleted, and it tells you what ran at what time, who ran it, what happened when it ran, etc. Options:

-s<system>   Restricts output to one system

-u<user>   Restricts output to user who queued the job

uuclean

uuclean cleans out the spool directory. Options include:

`-o<number>`   Deletes file more than <number> days old.

`-n<number>`   Deletes file more than <number> hours old.

Often uuclean is executed regularly by a cron entry. Make sure that the deletion interval is larger than the frequency at which the uuclean job runs or you will lose jobs!

uuname

The **uuname** command lists the hosts that have correct entries in the script file (L.sys or equivalent). This includes your system. To only list the UUCP name for your system, try **uuname -l.**

uuto

uuto is a System V command for sending a file to a remote system and placing it within the public directory there. The syntax is:

`uuto <file> <uucp address>`

Example:

`uuto /aboba/junk.txt foobar!bozo`

uupick

uupick is a System V command for retrieving files sent by a remote system via uupick. uupick checks your subdirectory within the public directory, and then queries whether you want to retrieve each file it finds. Typing **m** to a request moves the file; **d** deletes it; **q** quits, and ***** lists the available commands.

Technical details

While the beginner will not have to know the technical details of how UUCP works, these details can become important to the system administrator who is trying to debug a UUCP connection or improve its efficiency.

Protocol variants

UUCP negotiates one of several transfer protocols on startup. UUCP transfer protocols include:

∇ UUCP-g

UUCP-g is the original UUCP transfer protocol and is present in all versions. It has gotten a bad reputation because poor implementations of it often transmit data in 64-byte chunks, half the size of even the early version of XMODEM. The protocol does provide for packets sizes of up to 4096 bytes and window sizes of 7. UUCP-g requires an 8-bit connection.

In order to improve transfer speed with UUCP-g, a technique known as "protocol spoofing" is used. Protocol spoofing works by fooling the sending modem into believing that it has received an immediate acknowledgment. As a result, the sending modem quickly sends another block of data. When the real acknowledgments arrive from the receiving system, the modem throws them away. The result is that UUCP's error-detection and correction protocols are turned off. In order to prevent errors in transmission, hardware error correction is needed. Since Telebit's Trailblazer modem was the first to implement this technique, Telebit modems are very common in the UNIX world.

∇ UUCP-f

UUCP-f originated in BSD UUCP. This is a 7-bit protocol that uses checksums on the entire file instead of by packet, and does not offer flow control. UUCP-f should only be used over error-corrected connections such as X.25 networks, or when linking error-correcting modems. UUCP-f is efficient for transfer of text but very inefficient for use in 8-bit situations, such as transmission of compressed USENET news. If receiving USENET, consider asking your feed to turn off compression, particularly if a V.42*bis* connection is possible.

∇ UUCP-h

UUCP-h is a version of UUCP that is optimized for HST modems. It is similar to t protocol.

▽ UUCP-t

UUCP-t is an 8-bit protocol that originated in BSD UUCP and includes no error checking or flow control. It was originated for use in situations such as transmission of UUCP over TCP/IP. Maximum block size is 1024 bytes.

▽ UUCP-e

UUCP-e is similar to UUCP-t (though incompatible), but it originates in HoneyDanBer UUCP or BNU.

▽ UUCP-G

UUCP-G is an improved version of g protocol for System VR4, which can accept alternate window and packet sizes.

▽ UUCP-x

A BNU protocol developed for use with X.25 networks.

▽ UUCP-z

Included with some versions of Taylor UUCP, UUCP-z uses a ZMODEM variant for transfers. Transfer rates between two UUCP-z systems can reach 1300 cps (based on a 14.4 Kbps connection), whereas a typical UUCP-g transfer rate is 700-900 cps.

The protocol negotiation process

When the remote uucico is fired up, the two implementations negotiate the parameters for the session, including the protocol, file limits if any, grade of files to be transferred, debugging level, and ability to restart aborted transfers. To negotiate the protocol type, the called system outputs a list of protocols that it supports, and the calling system selects from the list. If the protocol is UUCP-g, additional handshaking occurs.

At this point, the conversation can begin. The calling system starts out in Master mode, while the called system starts out as the Slave. The Master starts by sending files to the Slave. The Slave can refuse the incoming files if the send

is unauthorized or the call has occurred at an inappropriate time.

When the Master is finished sending files, the Master offers to close the connection; if the Slave has nothing to send, the session ends. If not, the Slave and Master switch roles. The former Slave then begins to send files as the Master. When it is done, it offers to close the session; if there is nothing more to send, the session ends, otherwise the two machines switch roles again. The continuous role-switching ability built into UUCICO allows the transmission of files that were queued while the connection was in progress.

UUCP file naming

Outgoing UUCP jobs are composed of three files: a command file, a data file, and an executable command file. The command file tells uucico how to send the other two files to the remote site. After the files are sent the command file is deleted. Incoming UUCP jobs only have two files: a data file and an executable file. The executable file tells uucico what to do with the data file.

As a result, you should always have as many data files as you have executable files. If uusnap discloses a mismatch, then something has gone wrong. Possible solutions include cleaning out the spool directory.

Example

After queuing a mail message to `bozo\!planet\!aboba`, three files were created: a job control file in the /usr/spool/uucp/C. directory; a data file in the /usr/spool/uucp/D.planet directory, and an executable command file in the /usr/spool/uucp/D.`planetX` directory.

The job control file was named C.bozoA03h4. The A refers to the processing grade, which runs from A–Z, then a–z, with A being first. The processing grade is useful because **uucico** can be invoked with the **-g <grade>** option to send only jobs with **<grade>** or higher. This allows you to send mail only during the day when connecting to a given site, letting news come through at night when rates are less expensive. 03h4 was the job ID that showed up in the **uuq** command. Here is what was in the file:

```
planet:105# cat C.bozoA03h4
S D.planetB03h2 D.planetS03h2 agent - D.planetB03h2 0666
S D.planetX03h0 X.planetA03h3 agent - D.planetX03h0 0666
```

Here S refers to a file send; R would imply a file request, and X would be an execution request. D.planetB03h2 is the file name on our system; D.planetS03h2 is the name on the destination system. **agent** is the sender of the file. - refers to the options included in the execution of the command that generated the file; D.planetB03h2 is once again the file name on our system. 0666 are the file permissions on our system. The data file will contain the mail message, was named D.planetB03h2, and looked like this:

```
planet:32# cat D.planetB03h2
From root  Sun Jan 24 01:33:56 1993 remote from
planet.uu.holonet.net
Received: by planet.planet.uu.holonet.net (NX5.67c/NeXT-
3.0)
        id AA00869; Sun, 24 Jan 93 01:33:56 -1000
Date: Sun, 24 Jan 1993 01:33:24 -1000 (GMT-100
From: Operator <planet.uu.holonet.net!root>
Subject: Test of UUCP
To: bozo!foo!bar!aboba
Message-Id: <Pine.3.05.9301240124.A865-7100000@planet>
Mime-Version: 1.0
Content-Type: TEXT/PLAIN; charset=US-ASCII

This is a test of UUCP. Let's see what the D.* and X.*
files look like!
```

The executable commands file was named D.planetX03h0. In this case, the X stands for eXecutable command file; the 03h0 is referred to in the job control file. The file looked like this:

```
planet:36# cat D.planetX03h0
U agent planet
R agent
F D.planetS03h2
I D.planetS03h2
C rmail foo!bar!aboba
```

Here the U line gives the sender of the file and the system name; the R line gives the return address, which might be different from the sender in a multihop transfer. The F line gives the name of the file to transfer; the I line identifies the file to be routed to standard input; and the C line gives the command that is to be executed on the remote system. An O line, if present, would identify the file for standard output.

UUCP on personal computers

There are now many options for using UUCP on personal computers. These include both stand-alone programs and BBS gateways.

Stand-alone programs (such as uConnect, FSUUCP, and UULINK) usually offer complete interfaces to UUCP and USENET. They transfer mail, files and news and provide programs to read and create messages, thus combining the Mail User Agent (MUA) and the Mail Transport Agent (MTA). Stand-alone products usually are designed for a single user.

In contrast, BBS gateway products are designed to operate with a bulletin board environment. As a result, they are usually specific to a given BBS system or message format. Since the BBS provides message reading and sending facilities, these capabilities do not need to be included with the gateway. In addition, BBS gateways are usually written to handle multiple users, each with their own user IDs, signature files, and so on.

Note that while stand-alone products often can be used to construct a gateway with the addition of an import/export routine, the reverse is not the case—gateways do not usually include a Mail User Agent for reading and replying to mail and news.

UUCP on the Macintosh

Versions of UUCP for the Macintosh include UUPC (freeware) and uConnect (a commercial product).

UUPC

UUPC by Dave Platt, Gary Morris, Drew Derbyshire, Sak Wathanasin and others is a freeware UUCP implementation for the Macintosh. It supports f and g protocols, scheduling, System 7 as well as System 6.0.x, high speed modems, and incoming as well as outgoing calls. UUPC is compatible with Toadnews (a compression and batching utility), rnMac (a news reader), and Eudora (a mail reader). UUPC, Toadnews, and rnMac are all available via **ftp sumex-aim.stanford.edu,**

cd /info-mac/comm. Below is a typical installation within a UUCP folder on a drive called Alliance. UUPC uses Config, home, mail, spool and tmp directories, which are pointed to by the UUPC settings file. Note also the ToadNews and rnMac folders, and various Eudora files, such as UUCP Eudora Settings, In.toc, Out.toc, Eudora Nicknames, In, Out, Trash, and Eudora Long.

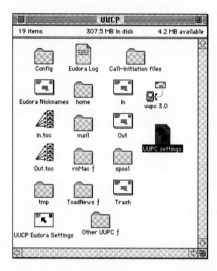

The Config folder is particularly important, since it contains the Systems and Schedule files. In the UUPC distribution samples of these files are included as Sample Schedule file, and Sample Systems file; remember to change the name to Schedule and Systems when you are finished editing them. Schedule is a file which lists when UUPC should be run; Systems contains the login sequence for each site.

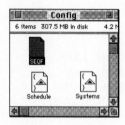

After arranging the files into folders, edit the UUPC settings file with ResEdit.

Double-click on each of the string resources, and fill in the appropriate settings for your setup. Sample values for the resources are given at the send of this section.

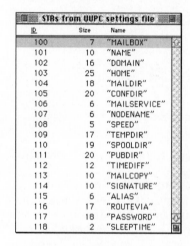

A typical string resource will look like this:

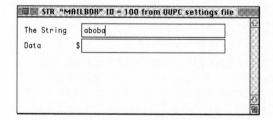

Here is my setup:

```
MAILBOX       aboba
NAME          Bernard Aboba
DOMAIN        planet.uu.holonet.net
HOME          Alliance:uucp:home:aboba
MAILDIR       Alliance:uucp:mail
CONFDIR       Alliance:uucp:config
MAILSERVICE   holonet
NODENAME      planet
SPEED         19200
TEMPDIR       Alliance:uucp:tmp
SPOOLDIR      Alliance:uucp:spool
PUBDIR        Alliance:uucp:public
TIMEDIFF      -0800 (PST)
MAILCOPY      mail.sent
SIGNATURE     signature
ALIAS         alias
ROUTEVIA      holonet
PASSWORD      myword
SLEEPTIME     5
```

Once you're done setting up UUPC, it is time to move on to other cooperating applications such as Eudora. Setup of Eudora with UUCP is discussed in Chapter 9: Electronic Mail Software, but below is a sample configuration running with UUPC:

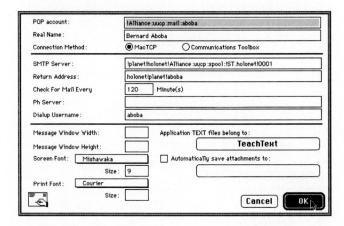

After you've got the other applications set up, it's time to try getting UUCP to handle inbound and outbound traffic. In the next column is an example of an inbound session.

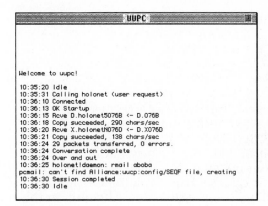

An outbound session would look something like this:

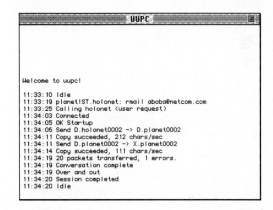

Example Systems file

```
INCOMING Any a HAYES!&M4&B1B0 19200 - g7
#
# Permit anonymous-UUCP access... any system
# is allowed to connect.
#
ANONYMOUS Never
#
# connect to host via Port a (modem as shown)
# or b (printer port).
#
holonet Any a DIR 19200 - g "" \rATZ\
    OK ATQ0E1M0V1\
    OK ATDT7041063 CONNECT help): holonet\
    ): mylogin assword: mypassword none: uucp
```

Example Schedule file

```
0 9,10,11,12 * * * holonet
```

uConnect

uConnect

uConnect (formerly called uAccess) is a complete Macintosh implementation of UUCP/USENET. In addition to supporting UUCP mail and USENET news, uConnect allows you to set up your own mail "exploders" and aliases. It can also handle multiple UUCP hosts, scheduling, compression, and batching. In this section I discuss how to set up UUCP using uConnect.

Preferences

uConnect requires setting an impressive array of preferences. To get to the array of preference choices, select `Configure` and `Preferences...` from the `File` menu.

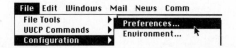

Selecting `Header Styles...` will bring up a dialog box of Header Styles. Here I just select a `custom header` rather than letting uConnect figure it out.

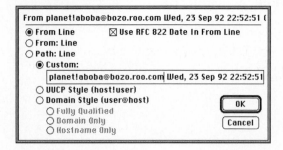

Selecting `Mail & News...` will also bring up a dialog box.

The signature file is a file with information about yourself, such as your address, email address, and fax number. You can append it to the end of your mail and news messages if you choose. So as to not create too much extra traffic, please keep your signature file to a few lines. One other item to note is that the Default Reply-To need not be the address from which you are sending mail; it could be another account somewhere else, as it is in this case.

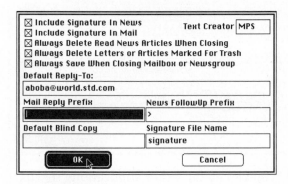

Environment

To set up your UUCP and domain name and that of your host, you need to select `Configuration` and `Environment...` from the `File` menu.

If you do not have domain name service, you should enter `UUCP` for the domain. Please also enter the UUCP name of your host, NOT its fully qualified domain name. Please also remember that your host's UUCP name must also be used when defining the connection. (Don't worry, I'll bang you over the head again about this one.)

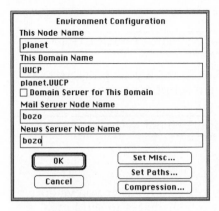

User Identification

To start off, you should identify yourself by selecting **Configuration** and **User Identification...** from the **File** menu.

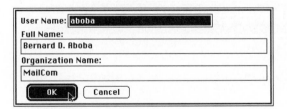

This will bring up the following dialog box:

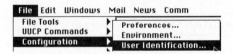

Setting up the mail server

To configure the Mail Server, select **Configuration** and **Mail Server...** from the **File** menu.

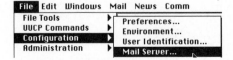

This will bring up the settings file for the Mail Server. I recommend using the Apple Modem to make the connection, since I tried the Serial

Tool and it didn't work. Please note that the correct setting for the Modem Tool is **No Dialing**. This is not because the Modem Tool doesn't dial; it does. The button just tells uConnect that *it* shouldn't dial. **No Dialing** would also be selected with other tools such as the Telnet Tool. The **Easy Login** button lets you specify the login name and password. This will work fine if when you dial up you get the UNIX login: prompt. If you need to log in through a port selector, you will need to select **Custom Login** here, and **Edit...,** and then input a few more expected strings and replies.

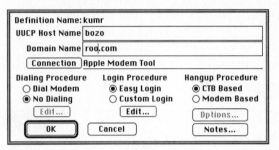

Please note: By default when you enter the rest of the domain address (roo.com in this case) into the domain name field, uConnect will add this string onto the definition name, making it bozo.roo.com. Beware! Since the UUCP name is bozo, uConnect will look for the name bozo when looking to see if it has mail for this site. If you have let uConnect use the fully qualified domain name bozo.roo.com as the definition, it will not be able to find the outgoing mail.

To fix this problem, you must select **Configuration** and **All Servers...** from the **File** menu.

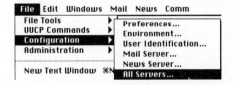

This will bring up a dialog box that will let you rename the offending server by clicking the **Rename...** button.

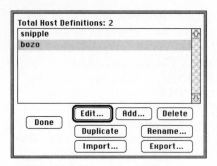

Setting up the connection

On the Modem Tool, you can select the type of modem you are using, and the speed, handshaking, phone number, and so on. I recommend just using CTS handshaking, unless your modem is set up to ignore DTR. If not, it will hang up whenever the handshake line goes down.

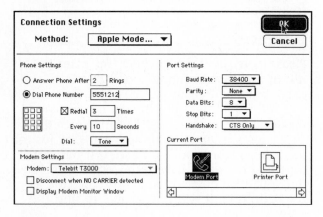

Making your first call

If you've done all this, then you're ready to send your first message. Select **Compose Letter…** from the **Mail** menu.

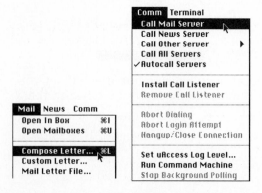

You can ask uConnect to poll the mail server at any time, or if you have **Autocall Servers** selected on the **Comm** menu, then uConnect will call out to deliver mail right after you post a letter:

☐ MASTER: Calling 'bozo' DIRECT CTBHUP

A windoid will then track your progress through the login script:

☐ UUSTART_PASSWD Got the password prompt.

Loop-back test

The first thing to try to do after you've gotten the connection established is to send mail to yourself. Try calling your host to deliver the letter to yourself, and then try calling back in five minutes or so. You should find that you have a letter waiting. When uConnect processes the incoming mail, it will put the following message in a windoid:

☐ New information has been delivered.

You can then select Open Inbox from the **Mail** menu to open your mail:

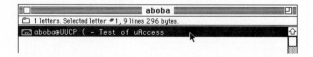

Double-clicking on the letter will open it up:

```
From planet!bozo.roo.com!planet!aboba Wed Sep 23 22:49:19 1992 remote from
bozo
Received: by planet.com (uC-1.5v4); Wed, 23 Sep 92 23:18:26 GMT
Received: by bozo.roo.com (/\==/\ Smai13.1.25.1 #25.3)
    id <nOmXmEQ-0002ACC@bozo.roo.com>, Wed, 23 Sep 92 22:59 PDT
Received: by planet.com (uC-1.5v4), Wed 23 Sep 92 23:06:53 GMT
From: aboba@planet.com (Bernard D. Aboba)
To: bozo!planet!aboba
Subject: Test of uConnect
Date: Wed, 23 Sep 92 23:06:53 GMT
Organization: MailCom
Reply-To: aboba@planet.com
Message-ID: <01050136.eda8dd@planet.com>
X-Mailer: uConnect - Macintosh Release: 1.5v4

This is a test message

------------------------------------------------------------
Bernard Aboba
Internet: aboba@world.std.com
```

As you can see, this letter appears to be correctly (albeit strangely) routed, by the bang-path planet!bozo.roo.com!planet!aboba.

Mailing lists

uConnect is also capable of setting up mailing lists. For more information on how to do this, please consult Chapter 9: Mailing Lists and Mail Servers.

Gateway feature

uConnect includes a gateway facility that allows it to be interfaced to bulletin board software with the addition of an import/export routine. When the gateway option is turned on, uConnect will send out packets left in its outgoing directory and will not process packets arriving in the inbound directory.

Mac UUCP gateways

Today any Macintosh BBS package that is compatible with Tabby can also support UUCP through use of John Sinteur's importers. The importers were designed to work with UUPC, but can be made to work with uConnect as well. Since Tabby-compatible BBSes already have import/export routines to move messages into and out of the BBS message base into a form appropriate for FidoNet, all the importers have to do is to translate between the UUCP packet format and the FidoNet format. The flow of control is shown in the figure in the next column. UUCP Your BBS is available from systems on the OneNet Member Network.

UUCP on the PC

There are now many options for using UUCP on the PC. These include stand-alone programs, UUCP/USENET BBS software, and BBS gateways. Stand-alone programs include UULINK and FSUUCP. Since these packages are complete and come with their own documentation, they are the best choice for individuals looking to get a UUCP connection.

Waffle, which is available for both DOS and UNIX, is a BBS package designed for USENET/UUCP, and so it is a good choice for those wanting to get a system running quickly.

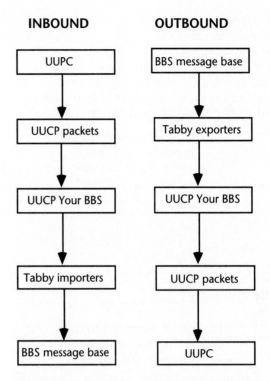

Flow of Control for "UUCP Your BBS"

UUCP gateways exist for many PC BBS packages, including PCBoard (uuPCB and PCBUUCP), Major BBS (Major Gateway/Internet), TBBS (PIMP), and FidoNet (UFGATE and FREDGATE) systems.

UFGATE is appropriate for users of *.MSG-style FidoNet BBSes such as OPUS or Fido. Users of BBS programs with monolithic message bases (such as QuickBBS, Remote Access, and Maximus) will want to use FREDGATE instead. FREDGATE is more general than UFGATE because it exports and imports to *.PKT files that can be tossed or sent by any BBS that supports FidoNet.

For more information on stand-alone and BBS gateway products, please consult Appendix B: Choice Products.

FSUUCP

FSUUCP operates as a stand-alone UUCP package, as well as the transport mechanism for import/export utilities such as the PIMP TBBS/UUCP gateway. The philosophy of FSUUCP is to be as close as possible to the

UNIX implementation. This makes the package easy to set up for sysops already familiar with UNIX UUCP, and gives users the option of accessing a wealth of existing books and articles. FSUUCP is available via **ftp toys.fubarsys.com** (129.65.100.239). Files included in the FSUUCP distribution are:

UUCICO.EXE	Communications module
UUXQT.EXE	Processes files from UUCICO. Can queue multihop jobs and uncompress and unbatch incoming files
UUSNAP.EXE	UUCP snapshot program. Tells how many files are waiting for each host
UUQ.EXE	UUCP queue control
BATCHER.EXE	Batches up news
EXPIRE.EXE	Expires messages
MAIL.EXE	Mail program
POSTNEWS.EXE	News posting program
READNEWS.EXE	News reading program
UULOG.EXE	Displays the log file

Since FSUUCP is a suite of cooperating programs, the pieces can be used together or integrated with other parts using a batch script. The script typically invokes the UUCICO program, then follows with a call to UUXQT to process the incoming packets.

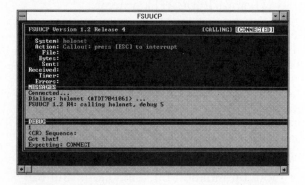

Waffle and Helldiver

Waffle is a BBS package that offers complete UUCP/USENET support. In the DOS version this includes an implementation of UUCICO. Since Waffle is modular, you can use the entire package to read and post news and mail, or you can just use Waffle as a transport mechanism for another package.

Fredgate, the USENET/FidoNet gateway, relies on Waffle's UUCICO in order to transport packets that it then translates to and from the FidoNet *.PKT format. This allows you to read news and mail from a FidoNet BBS interface. You can also use Waffle along with a Windows front-end called Helldiver. Since Helldiver and Waffle both run $30 shareware, the combination gives you a graphical interface to mail and news for $60. Not bad. Waffle and Helldiver are available via **ftp csn.org, cd /pub/dos/waffle.**

To get the Waffle-Helldiver combination working, you've first got to install Helldiver and Waffle. To install Waffle, use the -D parameter to PKZIP to uncompress the Waffle distribution:

```
PKUNZIP -D WAF165.ZIP
```

Since you'll be running the combination under Windows, you will also need to create a program group folder for the combination, and install the individual programs in it. Here I've placed Helldiver and an icon for Waffle within the same folder:

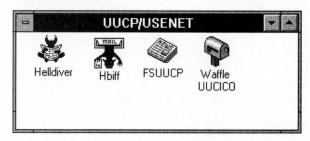

The Waffle UUCICO icon actually represents a DOS batch script called UUSHELL.BAT:

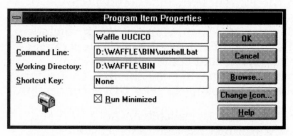

UUSHELL.BAT is extremely simple. All it does is execute UUCICO (told to poll my default host, Holonet), and then run UUXQT to process the incoming packets.

FSUUCP Setup Files

UUCP.BAT

```
set FSUUCP=D:\FSUUCP
set TZ=PDT
set USER=ABOBA
uucico -r1 -x5 -s%1
uuxqt -s%1
mail
```

FSUUCP.CFG

```
#
# Lines beginning with "#" are comments
# Blank lines are ignored
# Format:
# option          value
#
# This file must be modified to meet your specific system configuration

# System Information
sysname         planet.uu.holonet.net
logname         planet
user            aboba
handle          aboba
smarthost       holonet

# Directory Information
home            d:\fsuucp\home
spool           d:\fsuucp\spool
libdir          d:\fsuucp\lib
pubdir          d:\fsuucp\spool\uucp\public
news            d:\fsuucp\news
logfile         d:\fsuucp\spool\uucp\logfile
#ramdisk

# Modem & Calling Information
iinit           AT S0=1
# for MNP modems, you may try: AT &F M1 \N3\V1\Q3\J0\C1 S7=90
oinit           AT Z
# NOTE: port is now the com port, ie. 2 = COM2
port            2
# for MNP modems, use 90 seconds
timeout         45
retry           10

# Feature Information
editor          visual
organization    FSUUCP 1.2 Release 4 System
attribution     In article %i, %f said:
```

```
@ECHO OFF
UUCICO -r1  -sholonet
UUXQT
BATCH
```

While I run this script manually by clicking on the Waffle icon, you could also have the script executed at predetermined time using a Windows version of Cron, WinCron.

Next, set up Waffle by editing the SCRIPTS, DIALERS, and SYSTEMS files in the UUCP directory. Examples of these configuration files are given at the end of this section.

You will also need to add a statement to your AUTOEXEC.BAT file setting the WAFFLE environmental variable to point to the location of the Waffle STATIC configuration file, as follows:

SET WAFFLE=D:\WAFFLE\SYSTEMS\STATIC

Finally, you will need to run the Waffle BBS and log in as NEW to create user names for the people that will be using Helldiver. Waffle's multi-user support means that you can create as many users as you want.

Assuming everything has been set up, when you double-click on the Helldiver icon under Windows, you will get a Waffle login window:

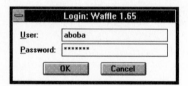

After logging in, you will then see the Helldiver main window:

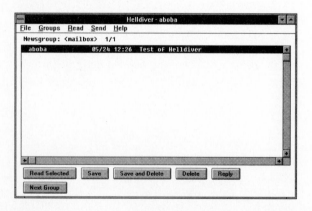

At this point, the first thing to do is to edit your signature file by selecting **Edit Signature** from the **Send** menu:

Once you are finished, you can save the signature file by selecting **Save** from the **File** menu. You can also edit your newgroup subscriptions by selecting **Subscriptions...** from the **Groups** menu:

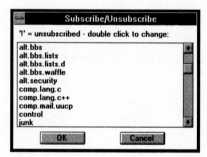

To check your mailbox, select **Go to Mailbox...** from the **Groups** menu. If you have any mail, it will be shown to you. Double-clicking on a message will let you read it.

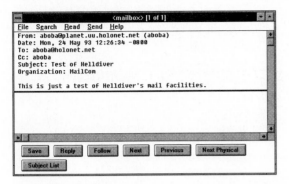

If you would like to send mail, select **Mail** from the **Send** menu. This will bring up a mail envelope window:

After finishing editing the message, select **Exit and Send** from the **File** menu. This will bring up a send dialog box.

If you click on **Yes**, the message will be queued for delivery by Waffle.

BBS gateways

Commercial BBS gateways for specific BBS software packages include PCBUUCP (PCBOARD), PIMP (TBBS), and Major Gateway/Internet (Major BBS). Publicly distributable general FidoNet/UUCP gateway packages include UFGATE (OPUS and Fido), and Fredgate (other FidoNet BBSes). Publicly distributable gateways are available via `ftp zeus.ieee.org, cd /pub/fidonet/ufgate`, or `ftp m.ehd.hwc.ca, cd /pub/msdos/fido`. Programs in these directories include ufg_103.arc, the UFGATE

distribution file, and fred*.zip or .arj, the Fredgate distribution.

BBS gateway products typically contain utilities for the following functions:

• **UUCICO**. This program transfers files via the UUCP protocol, dialing out when asked to poll, and taking over communications when a host dials in.

• **Import**. This routine takes received UUCP packets and tosses them into the BBS message base. Import routines typically call uncompress and may use unbatch utilities.

• **Export**. This routine takes BBS messages bound for UUCP or USENET and exports them in the form of UUCP packets. Export routines typically call the compression and batching utilities.

• **Compress**. This utility compresses outgoing packets in UNIX compress format.

• **Uncompress**. This utility implements UNIX uncompress, decompressing incoming packets.

• **Batching**. This utility combines several outgoing messages into a single file, saving transfer time.

• **Unbatching**. This utility takes incoming messages in a single file and separates them into individual messages. Some packages may toss messages directly from the batched incoming packets and therefore may not need this utility.

Not all gateways support compression and batching, but these features are desirable since they usually result in higher effective transfer rates (with the exception of UUCP-f connections, where compression is not useful). Compression and batching are most important for inbound news, since most properly functioning BBS gateways do not export many news articles.

Waffle Setup Files

WAFFLE\UUCP\SYSTEMS

holonet Any   g WB19200 toHolo 7041061 username password

WAFFLE\UUCP\DIALERS

WB19200 Default 19200 "" ATZ OK ATQ0E1M0V1 OK ATDT\T
CONNECT \m\c

WAFFLE\UUCP\SCRIPTS

toHolo "" \r help): holonet): \L word: \P none: uucp

WAFFLE\SYSTEM\STATIC

```
; /waffle/system/static -- Main WAFFLE configuration file
; We have only included parameters that you are most
; likely to change. A full list is available in the
; STATIC.DOC file.After your system is running and
; stable, you might delete the comments from this file.
:(It will load much faster).
; - - - - - - - - - HARDWARE PARAMETERS - - - - - - -
; The COM port to be used by Waffle. Can be 1, 2, 3,
:or 4.

device: 2

; Default modem speed. The modem init string will be set
:at this rate, so it should be the fastest speed your
:modem supports.

speed: 19200

; Initialization string for your modem. This depends a
: lot on make and model. String below is for a Hayes
: 2400:

initialize: AT H0 M1 S0=1 V1 E1 X4

; - - - - - - - - - SYSTEM PARAMETERS - - - - - - - -
-

; Nodename. If you are in a domain, this should be set to
: your domain; otherwise, you can use UUCP as your
: domain.

node: planet.uu.holonet.net

; Nodename aliases (you can list more than one.) If you
: have a domain, list your .UUCP address here.

alias: planet.UUCP

; The name of your system as it appears in the UUCP maps,
: or as it appears to your UUCP neighbors.

uucpname: planet

; Your organization. This should be some short
: description of your system or company. Try to include a
: geographic area if possible.

organ: MailCom

; Timezone. First: the TZ name, second: number of hours
: west of GMT, third: daylight savings time, if
: applicable.

timezone: PST 8 PDT

; Number of lines in the general-purpose buffer. Note
: that a high number will use lots of memory (256 * 80
: bytes is about 20K).

buflines: 256
```

```
; The command to allow new users onto your system. If you
; don't want new users, comment this line out.

new: new

; Where to send mail when it's not to your neighbors, or
: if it's domain addressed. You can also make this a
: bangpath. See docs.

smarthost: holonet

; Usenet backbone. This is only used in the case of
: moderated groups,so you don't have to chnage it.
: Generally not the same as smarthost.

backbone: ucbvax.berkeley.edu

; Forum configuration files. These must be present in
: your /waffle/system directory with the same names.

forums: local usenet

; - - - - - - - - - MESSAGE HEADERS - - - - - - - - -

; When sending MAIL, headers which are requested from
; the user. For news, see the 'local' or 'usenet' files.

ask: Subject

; Headers which are not listed when reading message,
: except when the VERBOSE command is used.

ignore: Path Message-ID References In-Reply-To Sender

; These are the headers which may be altered by the user.
: If you run a public system be careful about which are
: listed here.

alter: Subject Keywords Summary Distribution Reply-To
Organization

; - - - - - - - - - PROMPTS - - - - - - - - -

; People generally change the prompts to give their
; system a more individual look.

prompt: %B%|%T (?=help!) -> %

; Prompts that appear in the SCAN command.
; The first characters are highlighted in VT100 mode.

scan:           [^RET^] %[-%], ^Q^)uit: %
scan_end:       ^P^ost, ^L^ist, [%[-%]] ^Q^uit: %

; Prompts that appear in the NEW command.
; "Qs" stands for Quickscan, a historical remnant.

newscan:        ^Qs>^ %
newscan_end     ^Qs>^ Post here? %

error:          Monkey + Typewriter = %i.%|
boardname:      %B

; The prompt that users see when they dial up.
; For a more Unixy appearance, set to something like
"%|login: %"

login:          %|Login or NEW: %

; - - - - - - - - - ACCESS RESTRICTIONS - - - - - - -
- -

mail_ok     : 1
NetMail_ok  : 2
journal_ok  : 4
poof_ok     : 1
plan_ok     : 1
chat_ok     : 0
ch_level    : 6
ch_name     : 8

; These are the directory paths used by the FILES
section. See FILES.DOC
; if you want to split the section across multiple
```

```
: drives.

disks      : D: D:\FILES

; For BBS only - uncomment these two lines if you want
: ranks displayed on local messages
;
; ch_rank: 5
; comment: Level %L: %R

; For BBS only - uncomment this line if you want cookies;
: it is the minimum access required to add cookies.
;
; cookie_ok  : 1

; - - - - - - - - - LIMITS BY ACCESS LEVEL - - - - - -
; Number of calls that users are allowed in
; one day, listed for access 0 through 9:

calls:     2  2  2  3  3  3  4  4  5  99

; Number of posts that users are allowed in one
; call, listed for access 0 through 9:

posts:     0  3  3  3  3  4  4  5  6  99

; Number of mail messages that users are allowed
; to send in one call, listed for access 0 through 9:

mails:     3  5  5  8  8  8  8  8  9  99

; Upload:Download (UL:DL) ratio for callers by access.
; For example, 20 means 1K uploaded for every 20K
downloaded.

ratios:    20  20  20  20  20  20  20  20  20  20

; Minutes permitted each day (even over multiple calls)
; listed for access 0 through 9:

times:     45  70  70  90  90  90  90  90  90  90

; - - - - - - - - - - DIRECTORIES - - - - - - - - - -

; The 'root' location of your FILES transfer section.
; Comment out if you don't want a FILES section.

;files: C:\FILES

; The UUCP spool directory. Subdirectories will be
: created as needed. This should be on a disk with enough
: free space to hold your traffic.

spool: D:\WAFFLE\SPOOL

; Temporary directory. This isn't used much, so there is
: very limited advantage to putting it on a ram disk.

temporary: D:\WAFFLE\TEMP

; User directories. One directory will be created for
: each active user on your system (either with mail or
: personal files.)

user: D:\WAFFLE\USER

; Waffle directory. Beneath this should be ADMIN, BIN,
: EXTERN, HELP, INFO, MENUS, SYSTEM, TEXT, UUCP and WORDS
: subdirectories.

waffle: D:\WAFFLE
```

Gateway Integration issues

In creating a BBS gateway you will typically need to integrate these utilities using scripts. The major choices to be made are:

• Will your host call you, or will you call your host, or both?
• If your host calls you, how will you drop into the UUCICO program?
• How will you handle moderated conferences, mailing lists, or LISTSERVs?
• Will you allow file attaches or requests?
• Will you allow execution of remote commands?
• Will you gateway conferences or mail to or from USENET?
• Will you immediately send any pending mail or news, or wait until scheduled polling periods?

▽ To call or be called

If you will be calling your host, you need to set up events for the times at which you want to poll. This is done by calling a batch script in response to an external event. Most networkable BBSes have an event scheduling facility that substitutes for the UNIX cron capability.

▽ Dropping to UUCICO

More complex is the issue of having your host call you. This implies that you need a means for exiting your BBS software and calling up the UUCICO communications program. If your BBS software has a door facility, you can give the calling host access to the door and call up UUCICO this way. If not, you will need to figure out how to have the BBS exit with an errorlevel, and then trap the errorlevel with a batch script and execute UUCICO.

A complication arises when the BBS is running an external mailer, such as BinkleyTerm. BinkleyTerm and other mailers now include facilities for exiting to the UUCICO program via a *gateway string* sent to the mailer. This causes the mailer to exit with a predefined errorlevel that can be trapped by a batch script, causing UUCICO to be run. On the calling UUCP system's side, this reflects itself in the need for increased waiting times in order to allow the mailer program to be unloaded and the UUCICO program to be called up.

▽ Moderated conferences, mailing lists, LISTSERVs

Only a few gateways (such as Merlin Systems' PCB-UUCP) support moderated conferences, and offer Mailing List Managers (MLMs). These features are very desirable since they make life easier for the system oeprator.

Moderated conferences are conferences where mail is sent to the conference moderator, not to the group. For gateways that do not support moderation, the only solution is to make the conference read-only on the BBS. This is awkward because it inevitably results in users asking "Why can't I post in this conference?" On a large system, the added support load from these kinds of questions can cost more than the entire gateway package.

Gatewaying mailing lists to conference areas is also desirable because mailing lists are one of the most frequently requested features for users wanting UUCP access. Without this feature, many users on the same BBS can request individual subscriptions to a mailing list, wasting large amounts of UUCP connection time and disk space. Of course, one alternative is not to allow users to subscribe to mailing lists, but telling people they can't use UUCP for the single-most requested BBS feature won't garner many happy users. It is also nice to be able to create your own mailing list, although few gateways support this.

▽ File attaches or requests

The ability to send and receive files is a frequently requested feature, albeit an expensive one. This is because a large BBS system can end up transferring tens of megabytes of files a day if each user sends a decent-size file infrequently.

Many gateways support file sends and receives, but frequently this feature is turned off to save the sysop money. One way to get around this problem is to enable the feature only after payment of an extra fee, which may depend on usage.

▽ Remote command execution

UUCP is not merely a protocol for exchange of mail and news, although this is all that most gateways support. UUCP also provides for remote execution of commands, and if your gateway allows this, you need to think carefully about what remote commands you will allow. For example, I do not recommend allowing remote execution of DELETE or FORMAT commands!

▽ Gatewaying conferences and mail

A true gateway package is capable of routing mail or news from one network to another. For example, you can translate a USENET conference into FidoNet EchoMail format and send it to other FidoNet nodes, or vice versa. Similarly, you could allow UUCP mail to be sent to other systems through yours. Before implementing passthrough, make sure this is allowed under the licensing agreement for your software, as well as the agreement with your service provider.

Gatewaying mail and news is not merely a technical decision—it affects other users on both of the gatewayed networks. Gatewaying newsgroups is risky because duplicate checking facilities are often disabled by gateway message translators. This means that if the FidoNet EchoMail message you gateway to USENET should somehow find its way back to FidoNet, FidoNet dupe checkers may not be able to kill it. The result could be a torrent of abuse from other system operators. The possibility of network disruption is quite real; BBS gateways have on occasion spewed hundreds of duplicate messages into USENET.
Fear of duplicates has lead networks such as ILINK and RIME to prohibit conference gateways.

Gatewaying mail also requires careful consideration. Establishing a fully functional gateway between the Internet and a BBS network is a group project involving the administrators of the BBS network, Domain Name Servers, and Internet hosts. Individual sysops should not attempt to establish such gateways on their own.

A single gateway, or even a series of uncoordinated gateways, will not ensure reachability for all nodes in the BBS network. After all, most BBS networks are now international. What will happen when your node receives mail bound for Brazil? Are you willing to cover the costs of delivering the mail? If not, are you willing to answer complaints from sysops who have routed mail through you, only to see it thrown away?

The solution is to establish a cooperating group of gateways, allowing mail to be routed to gateway nodes close to the destination. This is covered in Chapter 15: Bulletin Boards and the Internet.

∇ Crash mail versus polling

Users sending mail often are interested in having the message delivered as quickly as possible. Ideally, this means having the BBS poll the host immediately after the caller logs off. For this to work, the BBS must be able to exit with an errorlevel when mail is sent; the gateway then checks for outgoing mail and news.

Many BBSes either cannot generate such an errorlevel, cannot cooperate with a gateway running on a separate machine, or cannot continue to operate while running an external program. In this case, you will need to set up polling times when the gateway will call the host.

UFGATE

UFGATE is a series of programs that are linked together with batch scripts to gateway mail and conferences between the FidoNet and UUCP/USENET networks. It supports compression and batching as well as mail and news, but it does not support queuing or execution of remote commands. Since UFGATE assumes that you are running BBS software that stores messages as individual files in the FidoNet *.MSG format, it is most appropriate for use with the Fido and OPUS bulletin board software.

What you need to make UFGATE work

Most of the work in setting up UFGATE comes from obtaining all the software you'll need. Components included with the UFGATE distribution include:

• MAILIN—imports UUCP mail into FidoNet *.MSG format
• MAILOUT—exports FidoNet *.MSG mail to UUCP format
• NEWSIN—imports USENET conference messages into FidoNet EchoMail format
• NEWSOUT—exports FidoNet EchoMail messages into USENET format
• UUSLAVE—UFGATE's version of UUCICO
• CUB—handles compression, decompression, batching, and unbatching of news
• FLSUPD—handles file transfers

The flow of control is:

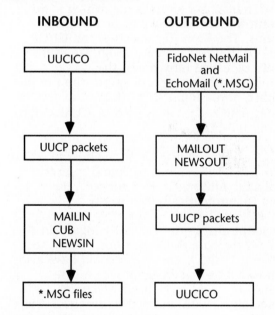

Flow of Control for UFGATE

Ancillary software that is often used alongside UFGATE is:

• BNU or X00.SYS—FOSSIL communications driver programs, available over the FidoNet SDS
• EECP—allows posting of UUCP mail within conferences and placing of address within the TO: field

- USRCHEK—checks the last user to an OPUS BBS to see if it was the host system
- SPLIT—breaks up incoming UUCP/USENET messages over 8K
- SQUISH—FidoNet mail tosser/scanner
- AT—sends specified command to a modem on a given port
- DTR—raises or lowers DTR on a given serial port
- AREAFIX—handles automatic updating of conferences

Setup files

Most of the setup information for UFGATE is contained in the UFGATE.CTL file. My experience is that few sysops have problems with UFGATE.CTL, since the options are well explained in the docs and a sample file is provided.

UFGATE utilitizes an L.sys file, which is similar in form to that used by BSD or Version 2 systems. The L.sys file specifies the UUCP name of the host system (bong), when it should by called (any time), the communications port and speed, the phone number, and a login script in send-expect format. The L.sys file is used by UUSLAVE in polling the host.

In this example, I also allow the host to dial in. In this case a way must be found to execute UUSLAVE. Although OPUS supports doors, I chose to automatically exit to the USRSRCH.BAT batch script after every login. The script checks the currently logged in user to see if they are the UUCP host, and if so, invokes UUCICO. This script could have also been called up as a door, in which case UUSLAVE would have been executed immediately, without needing to check the host ID.

The script UUCP.BAT handles the polling of the host. It is executed in response to a scheduled external event in the late evening. The first few lines of the script handle import and export of FidoNet mail. It is important that this occur prior to import/export of UUCP/USENET, since UFGATE modifies messages in place.

That is, the *.MSG files are themselves translated to RFC822 format. If FidoNet scanning is done after news export, then downstream FidoNet nodes will see FidoNet messages with RFC822 headers, and signatures, which they may dislike intensely. Since I have made this mistake myself, and have the arrows in my back to prove it, take my advice and do your FidoNet scanning first!

The order of scanning and news export is not an issue for gateways that do not modify exported message areas, which is more desirable.

The middle of the batch script packs up outbound news and mail, then asks UUSLAVE to poll the host (bong). After the polling session is complete, inbound mail is processed; inbound news is uncompressed, unbatched, and tossed; inbound files are processed; and the BBS is restarted.

The most complex capability to provide is the ability to immediately send any UUCP mail or news messages left by the users. This is accomplished by the RUNOPUS.BAT file within which the BBS operates.

This batch script is the core of most networked BBSes. It is structured as a classic event loop, where the BBS generates the events, and the batch script responds to them and then loops back to handle the next event.

I will focus only on the events related to interfacing the gateway software. These include Errorlevel 53, the UUCP polling event; and Errorlevel 50, user logoff; and Errorlevel 7, the new mail event.

Errorlevel 53 is generated late at night and is the occasion on which we call the UUCP.BAT file. Following the nightly UUCP poll, the RIME network poll is also executed.

Errorlevel 50 is generated whenever a user logs off. The RUNOPUS.BAT script checks whether the exiting user was the UUCP host; if so, it unpacks the inbound mail and news. This event is not really necessary, since these statements could have been included within the USRSRCH.BAT script instead.

Errorlevel 7 is the event that allows for immediate sending of UUCP mail. To respond to this event, FidoNet mail that is too large is split so that it will not crash the export routine, and then mail is tossed and packed. Next, outbound mail and news is packed up, and if there is mail and news to deliver, then the host (bong) is polled.

Sample setup files for UFGATE are given at the end of this chapter.

UFGATE limitations

Since UFGATE imports and exports messages into the *.MSG format (using the newsin, mailin, newsout, and mailout programs), it is only a good choice for systems that use *.MSG files for their internal message base, such as Fido or OPUS. Most BBSes today use other message base formats, so FredGate's import and export utilities (which use the *.PKT files instead) are more general. To go from your BBS internal message format to *.PKT and back, you will need a FidoNet mail tosser/packer, which is available for most packages.

If you are merely importing USENET messages into FidoNet, be aware that UFGATE does not support moderated conferences; such conferences should be marked as READ-ONLY. Also be aware that USENET messages often contain enclosed files; if your message tosser has a message size limit, you will need to run a message splitter. Such a splitter is run in the setup files given at the end of the chapter.

Fredgate

Fredgate is a package written by Michael Butler, imb@asstdc.oz.au, that can be used to construct FidoNet/UUCP gateways for any FidoNet-compatible BBS. Programs included in the Fredgate distribution include:

• FREDTOSS—Uncompresses and unbatches USENET news packets, and calls FRED–UF to translate them. Also, calls MAIL-UF to translate UUCP mail to FidoNet packets.
• FRED-UF—translates USENET news packets to FidoNet *.PKT packets.
• MAIL-UF—translates UUCP mail to FidoNet *.PKT packets.

• SCAN-FU—Scans for FidoNet NetMail (in *.MSG format) addressed to UUCP or Fredmail, and outputs it to FidoNet *.PKT format for translation by FRED-FU.
• FREDSCAN—Takes as input uncompressed FidoNet *.PKT files, and creates outgoing USENET news files, calling FRED-FU and COMPRESS to translate and compress them as needed.
• FRED-FU—translates FidoNet *.PKT files to batched USENET news packets.

Most of Fredgate's setup information is contained in the CONFIG.FIL file. Sample Fredgate setup files are available to users of the Holonet UUCP service, or via **mail holofido@holonet.mailer.net.**

Integration issues

Fredgate works with (and only with) Waffle's UUCICO. It must be integrated with the BBS software in a method similar to UFGATE. For example, when the UUCP host calls in, opening a door, UUCICO must be called and inbound mail must be processed:

```
REM UUCP host has called in, opening the
REM UUCP door
UUCICO -r0 -x4
REM Process incoming UUCP and USENET
FREDTOSS -c config.fil -h apple -d Delete
REM Toss FTSC packets with SQUISH
SQUISH IN SQUASH -SREST
```

For a poll, outbound mail and news must be processed, and then UUCICO is called to perform the poll:

```
REM Scan for outgoing UUCP mail
SCAN-FU -c config.fil -d delete
REM Scan for outgoing FidoNet mail
SQUISH OUT SQUASH -SREST
REM Translate outgoing USENET news
FREDSCAN -c config.fil -a 1:161/445.0 -h apple -d delete
REM Call UUCICO to perform the poll
UUCICO -s apple -x4 -t90
```

After the poll is executed, the inbound routines must be called again. The flow of control is shown in the figure on the next page.

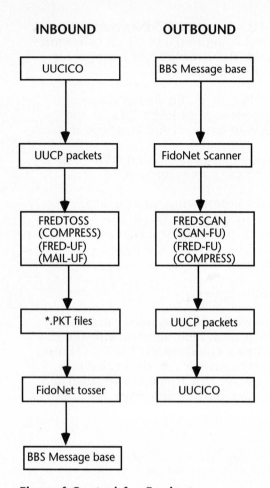

INBOUND	OUTBOUND
UUCICO	BBS Message base
UUCP packets	FidoNet Scanner
FREDTOSS (COMPRESS) (FRED-UF) (MAIL-UF)	FREDSCAN (SCAN-FU) (FRED-FU) (COMPRESS)
*.PKT files	UUCP packets
FidoNet tosser	UUCICO
BBS Message base	

Flow of Control for Fredgate

Gotchas

Relying on FidoNet tosser/scanner software as Fredgate does has its limitations. Although FidoNet Technical Standards specify no limits on message size, tosser/scanners typically impose limits anywhere from 8K to 64K. Since USENET and UUCP mail messages can be much larger, incoming messages must be split. Typically, this is done by having Fredgate toss big messages into a special directory, then calling a program such as SPLIT to split the messages.

Fredgate, Michael Butler, Assorted C Software, P.O. Box 595, Kensington, N.S.W., Australia 2033, email: ibm@asstdc.oz.au, 3:712/515@fidonet

BSD UUCP

While BSD 4.3 UUCP is shipped with implementations such as NeXSTEP, other implementations such as BSD/386 and NetBSD come with Taylor UUCP instead. However, BSD control files are also of use on these systems, since Taylor UUCP can make use of existing BSD style control files. This section contains hints on how to set up BSD UUCP.

The setup described here does not enable other people to dial in to your machine; it only handles dial out. Therefore there is no getty on any of the serial ports. The MailCom FTP archive (**ftp netcom1.netcom.com, get /pub/mailcom/BBB_Updates/bbb2.cpt.hqx**) provides two sample sendmail configuration files, one for a UUCP connection that will appear to be inside the host's domain, i.e., foo.uu.planet.com, and another for a machine connected via both UUCP and TCP/IP that has a separate domain assigned to it. These two sendmail configurations should cover many situations.

File setup and ownership

The UUCP setup files reside in the directory /etc/uucp. Here is a short summary of what they are and what they do:

UUCPNAME	Gives the UUCP name of your machine. Required.
L.sys	Dialing scripts for hosts. You must edit this file.
L-devices	Describes the devices on your machine. You usually will need to edit this file.
L.cmds	Lists commands that your machine can execute on request from remote systems. Since it is possible to introduce security problems by adding commands to the list, additions should be made with caution. You may even wish to delete commands in the NeXT-supplied file, such as who or finger.
L.aliases	Lets you use multiple names for a host. You usually won't need to use this capability.

USERFILE Specifies what files can be accessed by remote hosts and local users. Since setting up this file incorrectly can cause security problems, beginners should not edit this file.

In order for the UUCP program to be able to use these files, they need to be owned by the user uucp of the daemon group. In the process of editing the files, you may change their ownership. When you are done editing files in the /etc/uucp directory, check the ownership with the `ls -lg` command. As you can see in the following example, the file L.sys is owned by root of the wheel group, instead of uucp of the daemon group:

```
planet:15# ls -lg
total 25
-rw-------  1 uucp daemon  2372 Jan 12 20:31 L-devices
-rw-r--r--  1 uucp daemon   300 Dec 29 07:12 L-dialcodes
-rw-r--r--  1 uucp daemon   250 Dec 29 07:13 L.aliases
-rw-r--r--  1 uucp daemon   911 Dec 29 07:13 L.cmds
-rw-------  1 uucp daemon   713 Dec 31 22:11 L.holo
-rw-------  1 uucp daemon   359 Dec 25 03:46 L.nogood
-rw-------  1 uucp daemon   644 Dec 31 22:49 L.oldholo
-rw-------  1 root wheel    721 Jan 23 12:27 L.sys
-rw-------  1 uucp daemon   333 Dec 29 07:14 USERFILE
drwxr-xr-x  3 uucp daemon  1024 Jul 21  1992 UUAIDS/
-rw-------  1 uucp daemon     7 Dec 25 04:33 UUCPNAME
-rwxr-xr-x  1 uucp daemon 11631 Dec 29 17:48 uucp.day.sh*
```

Let's change it back using chown and check to see that everything is OK:

```
planet:14# chown uucp.daemon *
planet:15# ls -lg
total 25
-rw-------  1 uucp  daemon 2372 Jan 12 20:31 L-devices
-rw-r--r--  1 uucp  daemon  300 Dec 29 07:12 L-dialcodes
-rw-r--r--  1 uucp  daemon  250 Dec 29 07:13 L.aliases
-rw-r--r--  1 uucp  daemon  911 Dec 29 07:13 L.cmds
-rw-------  1 uucp  daemon  713 Dec 31 22:11 L.holo
-rw-------  1 uucp  daemon  359 Dec 25 03:46 L.nogood
-rw-------  1 uucp  daemon  644 Dec 31 22:49 L.oldholo
-rw-------  1 uucp  daemon  721 Jan 23 12:27 L.sys
-rw-------  1 uucp  daemon  333 Dec 29 07:14 USERFILE
drwxr-xr-x  3 uucp  daemon 1024 Jul 21  1992 UUAIDS/
-rw-------  1 uucp  daemon    7 Dec 25 04:33 UUCPNAME
-rwxr-xr-x  1 uucp  daemon11631 Dec 29 17:48 uucp.day.sh*
```

Setting your UUCP name

The first thing to do when setting up UUCP is to choose a UUCP name. The /etc/UUCPNAME file contains the UUCP name of your system. Under NeXT UUCP, this name must be the same for all sites you call.

In the examples that follow, I have chosen the UUCP name planet. Therefore my /etc/UUCPNAME file looks like:

```
planet:16# cat /etc/uucp/UUCPNAME
planet
```

To check that your UUCP name has been entered correctly, you can ask the system to tell you its UUCP name:

```
planet:26# uuname -l
planet
```

The L.sys file

The L.sys file contains the dialing scripts for your UUCP conections. The first line for each entry gives the UUCP name of the machine to which we are connecting; the times at which we can connect (ANY means any time of day); how you will dial (DIR means direct; you will tell UUCP how to dial the modem), the speed (19,200 bps here), and the device to use. Here cua stands for Port A (without hardware handshake), and cufa stands for Port A (with hardware handshake).

The device and speed indicated in the L.sys file must have a corresponding entry in the L-devices file, as we will see. The following L.sys is set up to work with a Telebit WorldBlazer modem operating with UUCP protocol spoofing and hardware handshake.

L.sys

```
# L-sys: Please read UUAIDS/L-sys.samples for some
# discussions on how to
# use this file as well as the documentation that can be
# found in the
# Digital Librarian on uucp.
#
uunet Any TCP uucp uunet.uu.net\
  ogin:--ogin: Uuucp
#
bozo Any DIR 19200 cufa\
  ABORT BUSY\
  "" ATZ\
  OK ATQ0E1M0V1\
  OK ATDT14156666666\
  ogin: Utest\
  assword: blahblah\n\c
#
holonet Any DIR 19200 cufa\
  ABORT BUSY\
  "" ATZ\
  OK ATQ0E1M0V1\
  OK ATDT7041061\
  CONNECT~75 ""\
  help):~75 holonet\
  ):~35 test\
  Password:~15 blahblah\
  none:~35 uucp\r
```

Try to avoid blank lines in the L.sys file; a bug in UUCP can give you unpredictable results if you don't. To make sure that all the L.sys entries have been recognized, try the uuname command without any arguments.

This should give you a list of all systems:

```
planet:26# uuname
kumr
holonet
lanet
```

Please also remember that the example L.sys file was written for a modem that had had its parameter RAM configured beforehand. The **ATZ** command restores settings to those stored in the parameter RAM. Please consult Appendix D: Cable Compendium for information on modem configuration.

L-devices file

The /etc/uucp/L-devices file describes the serial port devices available on your system. In this example, we are using direct dialing on port A, so the entry that matters is the 9600 speed entry for cua (Call Unit A, or Port A, no hardware handshake), and the 19,200 speed entry for device cufa (Call Unit A, or Port A, with hardware handshake).

/etc/uucp/L-devices

```
# L-devices:
# Consult UUAIDS/L-devices.samples for more examples and
# discussion as
# well as UUAIDS/L.sys.samples
#
#
# If you do not plan to dial into your cube, then you can
# use the following
# settings.  You may delete those lines which have
# baudrates that your modem
# does not support.
#
# Note: For those modems that you may wish to use that
# uucp knows how to
# manipulate properly, you may use the ACU (automatic
# call unit) settings.
# Please read UUAIDS/L-devices.samples for a discussion
# on which modems are
# supported.
#
ACU ttya unused 300  direct
ACU ttya unused 1200 direct
ACU ttya unused 2400 direct
ACU ttya unused 9600 direct
ACU ttya unused 19200 direct
ACU ttyb unused 300  direct
ACU ttyb unused 1200 direct
ACU ttyb unused 2400 direct
ACU ttyb unused 9600 direct
#
#
# Note: For those off beat modems that uucp does not know
# how to
# manipulate directly. This means that a dialing script
# in L.sys will
# take care of the chore of dialing.
#
DIR ttya unused 300  direct
DIR ttya unused 1200 direct
DIR ttya unused 2400 direct
DIR ttya unused 9600 direct
DIR ttya unused 19200 direct
DIR ttyb unused 300  direct
DIR ttyb unused 1200 direct
DIR ttyb unused 2400 direct
DIR ttyb unused 9600 direct
#
#
# For those who want to be able to dialin to their cubes
# as well as dialout,
# please consult the Digital Libraries for the wiring
# diagram for proper modem
# cable.  You may use the following settings provided
# that you have this special
# modem cable. Note that most modem cables which have a
# 25 pin D connector on
# one end and a 8 pin Mini-Din connector on the other DO
# NOT have the Carrier
# Detect line (pin 8 on the 25 pin D connect) connected
# to Clear To Send line
# (pin 2 on the 8 pin Mini-Din connector). This prevents
# the modem from being
# able to tell your Cube if the modem is busy or not.
# Therefore, for the
# following settings, you must insure you have this
# special modem cable.
#
# For those modems that uucp knows about:
#
ACU cua unused 300  direct
ACU cua unused 1200 direct
ACU cua unused 2400 direct
ACU cua unused 9600 direct
ACU cua unused 19200 direct
#
# For those unusual modems which have dialing scripts in
# L.sys which know how
# to dial them.
#
DIR cua unused 300  direct
DIR cua unused 1200 direct
DIR cua unused 2400 direct
DIR cua unused 9600 direct
DIR cufa unused 19200 direct

DIR cua unused 19200 TelebitTone
```

Polling intervals: /etc/crontab.local

In order to tell UUCP when to call out, you will need to edit the entries in the file /etc/crontab.local. cron is an application that can execute tasks at regular intervals.

The first five entries in the crontab file are the minute (0-59), hour (0-23), day of the month (1-31), month (1-12), and day of the week (0-6, with 0=Sunday). A * in a field means that any value is acceptable.

The next entry is the user to run the command under; here it's uucp. The final entry is the command to run.

In the following example, every hour from 4:03 to 20:03 PM, I am going to poll holonet; at 6:03 and 20:03 I am going to poll kumr. These polls will occur every day of the week, every month of the year. The first five entries can be given as a comma-delimited list; a range (1-3).

```
3 4-20 * * *   uucp  /usr/lib/uucp/uucico -r1 -sholonet
3 6,20 * * *   uucp  /usr/lib/uucp/uucico -r1 -sbozo
```

Sendmail: the final frontier

So far we've told UUCP how to get messages in and out of your system. The final element is to instruct sendmail how to use the UUCP connection correctly.

To help you in setting up sendmail, two sample sendmail setup files were included within the second update to the first edition of *Bulletin Boards and Beyond*. One of the files is for a machine with a UUCP connection but no TCP/IP connection. The other is for a machine with a TCP/IP connection. They are available via `ftp netcom1.netcom.com, cd /pub/mailcom/BBB_Updates/bbb2.sea.hqx` or `bbb2.zip`.

Please note the following modifications that need to be made to the standard NeXT sendmail.cf file for a lone UUCP connection:

1. At the beginning of the sendmail.cf file, you will need to decide on your naming convention. Assuming that your domain name is of the form <UUCP host>.<provider domain>, you will use the uncommented version of the following:

```
# Use this for simple uucp hosts without a domain (i.e.
# planet)
#D$w
# If you want the gateway machine to appear to be INSIDE
# the domain, (such as planet.uu.foo.net) use:
#
D$m
```

If you are working with a provider that sets its domain names this way, change the `uu.holonet.net` entry to the entry appropriate for your provider. Otherwise, comment out this entry and use the other one instead.

2. Set the `DR` and `CR` fields to the name of your primary UUCP site (which in this case was holonet).

3. Note the `DMuucp` line. This is required to tell sendmail to use the UUCP mailer.

4. If you want sendmail to send out the mail immediately instead of waiting until the scheduled polling times, remove the `-r` entry in the line:

```
A-uux - -r $h!rmail ($u)
```

UUMon

A graphical UUCP monitor is available for NeXT, called uumon. This makes it easier to manually poll hosts, and watch the result of the session, so I recommend installing it before working with UUCP. uumon is shareware written by Thomas Baker and is available via `ftp sonata.cc.purdue.edu, cd /pub/next/submissions, get uuMon.tar.Z`. Below is a screen shot of uumon in action.

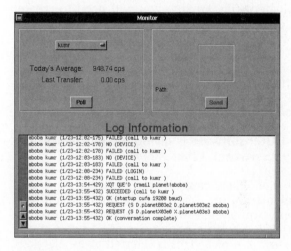

UUCP Q&A

I would like to run UUCP over TCP/IP. How do I do this?

Several microcomputer packages such as uConnect support this. UNIX versions of UUCP offer varying levels of support. Taylor UUCP supports both the UUCP-t protocol (which suspends error correction over a TCP connection), as well as TCP/IP callouts. HoneyDanBer UUCP also offers support for assignment of preferred protocols to given hosts and can be made to support UUCP dialout over TCP/IP via the TLI facility. BSD v4.3 UUCP versions do not support protocol assignment but do support TCP/IP callout via the device TCP. The L.sys entry will look like this:

```
poo Any TCP uucp poo.foo.com\
login: roo word: moo
```

If you are using a version of UUCP that doesn't support protocol assignment or dialout over TCP/IP, things are more complicated. You will have to get UUCP to log in to your own machine and then run a script that will telnet to the site you are looking to connect with. The L.sys entry will perform the initial log in to your own machine; at this point a script set as the login shell will take over.

To enable the login, put a getty on a pseudo-terminal such as ttyp0 by modifying /etc/ttys. You will also need an entry in the L-devices or equivalent file. Finally, you will need to create the direct dialing script in the L.sys file or equivalent to log in. After all this is done, you will negotiate an error-correcting protocol over a reliable connection, which is somewhat inefficient. You should also enable the UUCP TCP port in the /etc/services and /etc/inetd.conf files.

My UUCP software is giving me efficiencies of only 25 percent. What should I do?

The most likely cause is your UUCP implementation. Many UUCP implementations support only the lowest common denominator of UUCP-g, with a packet size of 64 bytes and a window size of 3. This is referred to as UUCP-g (3,64). The performance penalty paid by not supporting larger window sizes can be high. If you are in this situation, using a Telebit modem, which implements protocol spoofing, can increase transfer rates considerably.

You may also be able to improve throughput by adjusting your USENET news setup. You will pay a performance penalty if your setup does not support batching since there is a time interval involved in setup for each file transmission. If you are connecting with UUCP-g, compression is also helpful, even if you already have a V.42*bis* modem, since even use of UNIX 12-bit compress will speed transfers over a V.42*bis* connection. If you are negotiating a UUCP-f connection, compression will not help you, since 8-bit data will be "quoted" for transmission over the 7-bit data

path. The result is that the file is considerably expanded. A better idea in this case is to avoid compression and take advantage of a V.42*bis* connection.

Another possible reason for low throughput is disk fragmentation. If your system stores messages as single files, the disk may become fragmented so that transfers cannot proceed at full speed. Things can be particularly slow if you are storing more than 255 messages in a single DOS directory. Decrease your message expiration times, or run a disk optimizer and see if this helps. Further suggestions: Make sure you are set up for hardware handshaking. If you are running on a Macintosh, Serial Of Champions can provide more information on serial transfer efficiency.

UUCP does not offer support for bi-directional protocols, so if you can receive your mail and news using a gateway and a protocol which does support bi-directional transfers (such as recent versions of BinkleyTerm) you can speed things up considerably.

For more information

For discussion of UUCP, check out the comp.mail.uucp newsgroup. Information and help with UUCP gateway software is available by `ftp zeus.ieee.org, cd /fidonet, get uu2fido.txt` and `uucphelp.txt`. For lists of FidoNet/UUCP gateway systems, `cd /fidonet/fidomaps, get gateways.1st` and `fidouucp.1st`. For copies of the UFGATE and WAFFLE software, `cd /fidonet/ufgate`. For further information, contact hostmaster@fidonet.fidonet.org. The UFGATE conference on FidoNet is the place to go for help with FidoNet/UUCP gateway software.

UUCP archives

FSUUCP and UUPC, MUSH, and SMAIL utilities are available via `ftp oak.oakland.edu, cd /pub/msdos/uucp`.

Waffle and its utilities are available via `ftp oak.oakland.edu, cd /pub/msdos/waffle`.

UFGATE files

L.SYS – SYSTEM SETUP FILE

```
#  L.sys table for uuslave
#
bong Any,1 com2 9600 15105551212 in: gong\r\c word: plong\r\c

#
#
```

USRSRCH.BAT - Batch file to startup UUSLAVE on host callin

```
echo off
rem          keep a short log of all users
             type mailchek.dat >>uc.log
rem          startup uuslave if it is bong calling
             usrchek mailchek.dat bong nop
rem          errorlevel of 60 indicates that last caller was bong
             IF ERRORLEVEL 60 goto uus
             goto mch
:uus
             cd \uf
rem          start up UUSLAVE to handle inbound UUCP call
             uuslave -b2 -c -x1
             d:
             cd \opus
             goto exit
rem          otherwise check the user's mail
:mch
             yms_ms
:exit
rem          end-of-batchfile
```

UUCP.BAT - File to poll UUCP host nightly

```
rem          Run FidoNet outbound and inbound first, so that outbound Fido
rem          EchoMail doesn't go out with UUCP headers.
             d:
             cd\squish
             opusfix d:\opus\echotoss.log d:\qmail\areas.bbs
             bop-date /ad:\qmail\areas.bbs /fd:\opus\echotoss.log /dd:\msg\email
             squish in squash -srest
             squish out squash -srest
             d:
rem          USENET PROCESSING
             cd \uf
rem          process outbound USENET stuff
             newsout
rem          process outbound UUCP mail
             mailout
rem          go onhook
             AT COM2: Z
             DTR COM2: ON
rem          poll host
             uuslave -b2  -c -x4 -sbong
:unpack
rem          put phone off hook
             DTR ON
             AT COM2: H1
             AT COM2: M0
rem          toss inbound UUCP mail
             mailin
rem          decompress and unbatch any inbound files
             cub -d -u -B
rem          toss inbound news
             newsin
rem          process any inbound files
             flsupd d:\uf\files\mac -lusenet.log
rem          put phone back on hook
             AT COM2: Z
             DTR COM2: ON
rem          restart OPUS
             runopus
```

RUNOPUS.BAT - Central Batch Script for operation of OPUS/UFGATE/RIME BBS

```
echo Off
Rem Begin the Event Loop
:Loop
          cls
          d:
          CD \Opus
          AT COM2: Z
          DTR COM2: OFF
REM       Run OPUS, using the control file OPUS.CTL
          Opus opus
:chklevel
Rem ********************************************************************
Rem *                                                                  *
Rem *                  Explanation Of RUNOPUS Batch File               *
Rem *                                                                  *
Rem *    ErrorLevel |   Meaning                                        *
Rem *               |                                                  *
Rem *         255   | MicroSoft "C" Internal Stack Overflow Exit.      *
Rem *               |                                                  *
Rem *          60   | User apple logged off (inbound USENET mail)      *
Rem *               |                                                  *
Rem *          54   | Remote sysop drop to DOS                         *
Rem *               |                                                  *
Rem *          53   | Poll of UUCP and RIME networks                   *
Rem *               |                                                  *
Rem *          50   | Opus user logoff                                 *
Rem *               |                                                  *
Rem *          23   | Hard drive maintenance event (1st Sunday of mo)  *
Rem *               |                                                  *
Rem *          20   | Premail                                          *
Rem *               |                                                  *
Rem *          15   | System usage report event                       *
Rem *               |                                                  *
Rem *          10   | Postmail cleanup, renumbering, arcing.           *
Rem *               |                                                  *
Rem *           7   | EchoMail inbound or user message entered.        *
Rem *               |                                                  *
Rem *           3   | Serious Error - Missing USER file, FOSSIL driver *
Rem *               | not Loaded, etc.                                 *
Rem *               |                                                  *
Rem *           2   | Opus Internal Error. Ok to re-cycle.             *
Rem *               |                                                  *
Rem *           1   | Opus Exit - Control-C at Console, or user        *
Rem ********************************************************************
REM       Handle the system events
REM       On Microsoft Error, go back into the event loop and run the BBS
          If ERRORLEVEL 255 goto Loop
rem       Drop to DOS through doorway for remote sysoping
          If ERRORLEVEL 54 goto remsys
rem       UUCP Network polling event
          If errorlevel 53 goto poluucp
rem       User log off event - process mail created by user, if any
          If errorlevel 50 goto enduser
rem       Hard disk maintenance event (run Spinrite, VOPT, CHKDSK, etc.)
          if errorlevel 23 goto disrep
rem       Premail event (scan conferences, etc.)
          if errorlevel 20 premail
rem       Weekly system usage report
          if errorlevel 15 report
rem       Postmail event (Expire messages, toss mail, etc.)
          If ERRORLEVEL 10 postmail
rem       Incoming EchoMail event, so call the tosser/scanner
          If ERRORLEVEL 7 goto squish
rem       Something has gone wrong, so handle the error
          If ERRORLEVEL 3 goto Error
rem       OPUS internal error, so go back into event loop
          If ERRORLEVEL 2 goto Loop
rem       User has requested exit, so drop to DOS
          If ERRORLEVEL 1 goto End
Rem       Go back into the event loop
          goto loop
:disrep
Rem       We got here to run the weekly hard disk maintenance event
Rem       Which is contained in the batch file hardm.bat
          call hardm
Rem       After we're done, go back into Event Loop
          goto loop
:remsys
Rem       We got here because the sysop wanted to drop to DOS remotely
Echo      Running DOS Outside
Rem       Call Doorway software
          call door
```

```
Rem          Door way has ended, so rerun OPUS
             opus opus -o
Rem          Check the error level
             goto chklevel
:poluucp
Rem          poll UUCP host
             call uucp
echo         UUCP poll executed >>uucpol.log
Rem          poll RIME host
             call sendmail
echo         RIME poll executed >>rimpol.log
rem          scan for incoming RIME and UUCP mail
             cd\squish
opusfix d:\opus\echotoss.log d:\qmail\areas.bbs
bop-date /ad:\qmail\areas.bbs /fd:\opus\echotoss.log /dd:\msg\email
             squish in squash -srest
             squish out squash -srest
             goto loop
:Error
Echo
Echo         Serious Error - Opus Halted.
             Goto End
:squish
Rem          scan mail
             d:
             cd \opus
             DTR COM2: ON
             AT COM2: H1
             AT COM2: M0
Rem          Allow users to send UUCP mail in the UUCP conference, with Internet
Rem          address in the TO: field.
             eecp id d:\msg\uucp UUNET to uucp
             eecp m d:\msg\uucp
             cd\qmail
Rem          Allow outgoing and incoming UUCP messages larger than 8K.
             split d:\msg\uucp
             split d:\msg\bad_msgs
             split d:\msg\email
             cd\squish
Rem          Apply OPUS bug fix for Squish
             opusfix d:\opus\echotoss.log d:\qmail\areas.bbs
Rem          OPUS Date conversion for Squish
bop-date /ad:\qmail\areas.bbs /fd:\opus\echotoss.log /dd:\msg\email
             squish in squash -srest
             squish out squash -srest
REM          Handle outgoing UUCP and USENET
:fidcp
             cd \uf
REM          Put errant UUCP files in their proper place
             copy *.x bong
             del *.x
             copy *.d bong
             del *.d
             mailout
             newsout
REM          If outgoing mail exists, send it
             IF EXIST \uf\bong\*.DAT GOTO uuit
             goto checkit
:uuit
             AT COM2: Z
             DTR COM2: OFF
Rem          Run UUSLAVE outbound
             uuslave -b2 -c -x1
Rem If there is incoming mail, convert and toss it
             IF EXIST \uf\bong\*.D GOTO TOSSIT
             IF EXIST \uf\bong\*.X GOTO TOSSIT
             goto checkit
:tossit
             DTR COM2: ON
             AT COM2: H1
             AT COM2: M0
rem          decompress and unbatch incoming
             cub -d -u -B
rem          import mail
             mailin
rem          import news
             newsin
:checkit
             cd \opus
rem          notify users of incoming mail
             yms update
:enduser
rem Enduser has logged off. Check if it was bong.
             DTR COM2: ON
```

```
           AT COM2: H1
           AT COM2: M0
rem        check if user was bong
           usrchek mailchek.dat bong nop
           If ERRORLEVEL 60 goto unpack
           GOTO SKIP
rem        handle inbound usenet stuff
:unpack
           cd \uf
:mailin
           mailin
rem        decompress and unbatch any inbound files
           cub -d -u -B
rem        process any inbound news
           newsin
           flsupd \uf\file\mac -lusenet.log
           cd \opus
Rem        handle AREAFIX requests
           areafix ec
Rem        notify users of incoming mail
           yms update
:skip
           erase mailchek.dat
           erase echotoss.log
           del \uf\usenet.log
           goto loop
:End
```

BSD UUCP files

/etc/ttys

```
#
# name      getty                       type        status          comments
#
# If you do not want to start the window server by default, you can
# uncomment the first entry and comment out the second.
#
# console   "/usr/etc/getty std.9600"   NeXT                on secure
console     /usr/lib/NextStep/loginwindow      NeXT             on secure window=/usr/lib/NextStep/WindowServer
onoption="/usr/etc/getty std.19200"
#ttya       "/usr/etc/getty knj.9600"   vt100               on secure
ttya        "/usr/etc/getty std.19200"          unknown         off secure
ttyb        "/usr/etc/getty std.9600"   unknown     off secure
ttyfa       "/usr/etc/getty std.19200"          unknown         off secure
ttyfb       "/usr/etc/getty std.9600"   unknown     off secure
ttyda       "/usr/etc/getty D9600"              unknown         off
ttydb       "/usr/etc/getty D9600"              unknown         off
ttydfa      "/usr/etc/getty D9600"              unknown         off
ttydfb      "/usr/etc/getty D9600"              unknown         off
ttyp0       none                        network
ttyp1       none                        network
ttyp2       none                        network
```

/etc/gettyttab

Added line:

```
g|std.19200|19200-baud:\
        :sp#19200:
```

/etc/crontab.local

```
3 4-20 * * *    uucp    /usr/lib/uucp/uucico -r1 -sholonet
3 6,20 * * *    uucp    /usr/lib/uucp/uucico -r1 -sbozo
```

CHAPTER 17:
INTRODUCTION TO BITNET

The "Because It's Time" Network

What is BITNET?

BITNET is a worldwide collection of networks communicating via the Network Job Entry (NJE) protocols. BITNET, which stands for "Because It's Time," began in 1981 as a link between IBM mainframes at the City University of New York (CUNY) and Yale University, sponsored by CUNY's Vice Chancellor, Ira Fuchs, and the director of the Yale Computing Center, Greydon Freeman. The BITNET charter is to "connect the world's scholars," and the network is oriented toward education and research.

BITNET grew rapidly, with six systems connected after the first year, and twenty after two years. In 1984, OUNET was started up in order to connect eight universities in Ontario; this later became NetNorth, the Canadian network, and was connected to BITNET via a link to Cornell in 1985. In 1984, IBM funded the development of a European network called EARN. This initially included sixty nodes and connected to BITNET via a leased line from Rome, Italy, to CUNY in New York. As of March 5, 1993, there were ten BITNET networks spanning fifty three countries, with 3303 machines connected at 1300 sites. Of these sites, 1068 had registered Internet domain names.

BITNET was originally implemented as a store and forward network using the Remote Spooling Communications Subsystem (RSCS) software on IBM mainframes, communicating over low-speed leased lines (mostly at 9600 bps). Since then, the NJE protocols have been ported to a variety of architectures, including VAX VMS, UNIX, CDC Cyber, Sperry, and Prime.

In order to address projected bottlenecks and ensure the continued evolution of BITNET technology, the National Science Foundation funded development of the BITNET II protocols, starting in 1986. Among the goals of BITNET II were to allow communication via NJE over TCP/IP, as well as to allow development of interactive services. The later goal was not realized.

The deployment of the VMNET software, which started in 1988, came just in the nick of time, since during 1987 and 1988 BITNET experienced growing pains. With the development of VMNET, many BITNET nodes now communicate using NJE over TCP/IP via high-speed leased lines.

With universities turning away from mainframes and embracing the Internet, BITNET membership peaked in 1991, and is now slowly shrinking.

The topology of BITNET

BITNET began as a tree topology, with CUNYVM at the root. This topology does not scale well, since a large part of the traffic must pass through the root. Tree networks are also vulnerable to disruption by network outages, especially if the tree is too deep.

These concerns were addressed in 1989, along with the development of the BITNET II protocols. BITNET was reorganized into seven regions, each with two core nodes located near NSFNet backbone sites. The fourteen core BITNET nodes now form a complete network, with each core node connected to every other core node. Since there are many alternate paths between core nodes, disruption due to isolated outages is minimized.

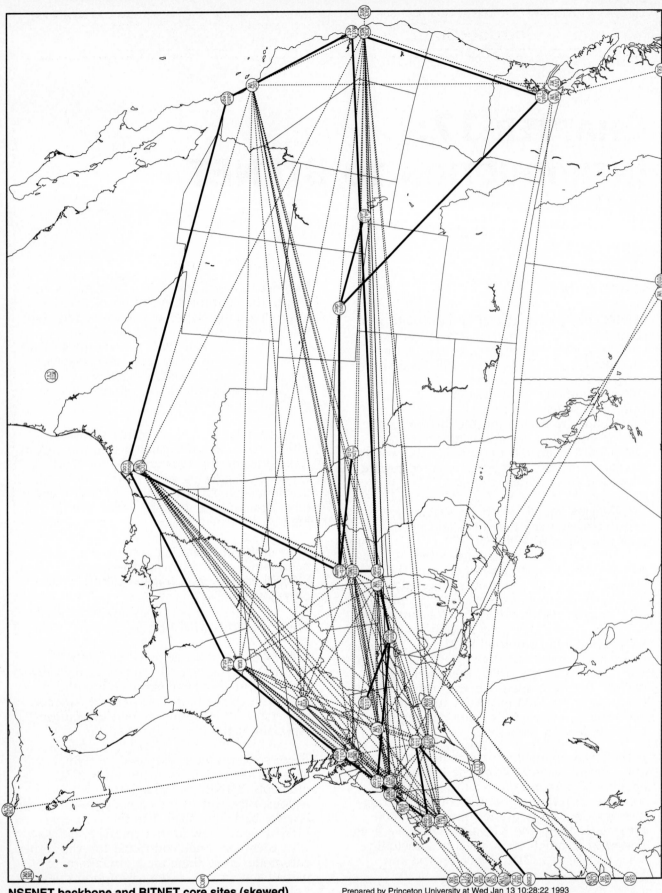

NSFNET backbone and BITNET core sites (skewed)
mixed-case named circles are CNSS nodes

Prepared by Princeton University at Wed Jan 13 10:28:22 1993
netmap-1.5 program by Brian Reid, map data from World Data Bank II
Lambert Conformal Projection [44˚N,33˚N], Map center: [40˚N, 96˚ 30´W]
Image resolution 300/in., stroke limit 1 pixels

The BITNET Core

Region and Machine	Domain name
Region 1	
MITVMA - MIT	MITVMA.MIT.EDU
YALEVM - Yale	YaleVM.CIS.Yale.Edu
Region	
CUNYVM2 - CUNY	CUNYVM.CUNY.EDU
CORNELLC - Cornell	cornellc.cit.cornell.edu
Region	
PUNFSV2 - Princeton	
PSUVM - Penn State	psuvm.psu.edu
Region	
UMDD2 - University of Maryland	
VTBIT - Virginia Polytech	
Region	
UGA - University of Georgia	uga.cc.uga.edu
UICVM - University of Illinois, Chicago	uicvm.uic.edu
Region	
RICEVM1 - Rice	ricevm1.rice.edu
UIUCVMD - University of Illinois at Urbana-Champaign	vmd.cso.uiuc.edu
Region	
UCBCMSA - University of California, Berkeley	cmsa.berkeley.edu
USCVM - University of Southern California	vm.usc.edu

Who runs BITNET?

BITNET is a collection of autonomous networks, each with its own form of governance. Within the United States, BITNET is run by the Corporation for Research and Educational Networking (CREN), a nonprofit corporation.

BITNET Networks

ANSP (South America)
BITNET (USA and Mexico)
CAREN (Japan, Korea, Taiwan)
EARN (Europe)
ECUANET (Ecuador)
GULFNET (Saudi Arabia)
HARNET (Hong Kong)
NetNorth (Canada)
RUNCOL (Columbia)
SCARNET (South America)

Rules and regulations

Since BITNET was established for purposes of education and research, there are restrictions on commercial activity. The CREN Acceptable Use Policy (AUP) prohibits:

• Disruption of network services or individual nodes
• Interfering with the work of other BITNET users
• Use of the network for commercial purposes such as marketing, bandwidth reselling, or business transactions between commercial organizations
• Advertising. Users may discuss product advantages and disadvantages, and vendors may respond to questions.
• Breaking the law using BITNET
• Chain letters or broadcasting of messages

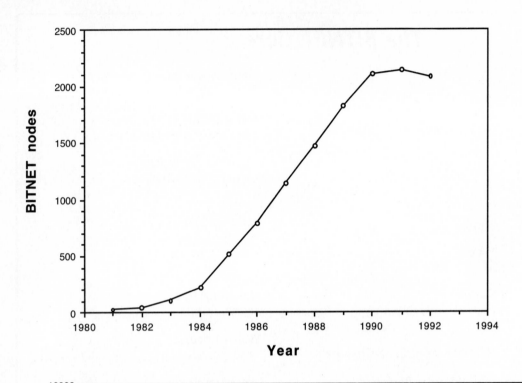

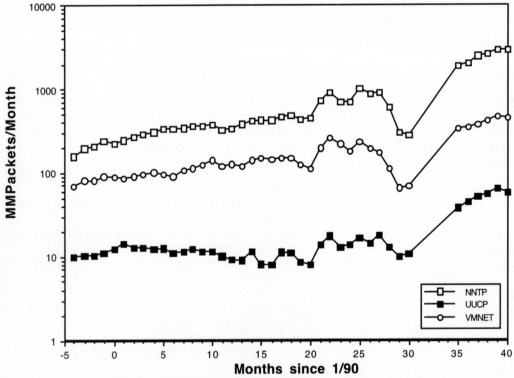

NSFNet Backbone Traffic in millions of packets/month for VMNET (BITNET II), NNTP and UUCP

Chapter 17: Introduction to BITNET

BITNET services

BITNET services include electronic mail and messaging facilities, a mail server facility known as LISTSERV, the RELAY chatting service, a database service known as LDBASE, user directories, and file transfer.

Electronic mail

Users accessing the BITNET network from BITNET machines use the following addressing scheme, reminiscent of the original ARPANET addressing syntax:

```
<USER> AT <NODE> or <USER>@<NODE>
```

For example:

```
BERNARD AT CUNYVM or BERNARD@CUNYVM
```

Messages

The BITNET Message facility allows for interactive communications over the network. On VM/CMS BITNET systems, you can send a message like this:

```
TELL NICOLE AT YALEVM Wanna meet for lunch?
```

On VAX VMS systems, the equivalent command would be:

```
SEND NICOLE@YALEVM "Wanna meet for
```

You can send a longer message just by entering the **SEND** command without a message; you'll then be prompted for input, and whatever you type will be sent until you leave a line blank:

```
SEND NICOLE@YALEVM
```

You cannot send messages to a BITNET node from another network.

Mail gateways

The large majority of people reading this guide will be accessing BITNET from other networks, such as the Internet or FidoNet. Assuming that their machines support the .BITNET pseudo-domain, users on non-BITNET networks may address mail to BITNET sites as follows:

```
<USER>@<NODE>.BITNET
```

Example:

```
BERNARD@YALEVM.BITNET
```

Be aware that since there is no .BITNET domain, mail to the .BITNET pseudo-domain is actually routed through BITNET/Internet gateways. If your host bounces mail to .BITNET addresses, try the following alternative addressing scheme:

```
BERNARD%YALEVM@cunyvm.cuny.edu
```

Since 1000 of the more than 3300 BITNET nodes have an Internet domain address, these nodes can also be addressed using their fully qualified domain name.

LISTSERVs

A LISTSERV is a mailing LIST SERVice. Although it is similar to a mailing list the LISTSERV software runs on BITNET machines and the commands are different from those for UNIX-based mailing lists. LISTSERV mailing lists exist on almost every conceivable topic.

How can you subscribe to a LISTSERV? Before you can send or receive mail with LISTSERV, you need to know which LISTSERV to subscribe to. You can get a listing of LISTSERV lists and groups by anonymous **ftp lilac.berkeley.edu, cd netinfo**. WAIS, Gopher, and World Wide Web also provide databases of LISTSERV lists. For more information see Chapter 14.

LISTSERV mailing list commands

For administrative requests to a LISTSERV, such as subscribing or unsubscribing to a list, and finding out about LISTSERVs, you send mail to `LISTSERV@<NODE>.BITNET` with commands in the body of the message. You will then receive a message back from the LISTSERV relating the disposition of your request.

To subscribe to a mailing list, the command is **SUB <list>**.

Here is an example message:

```
world% mail LISTSERV@UHUPVM1.BITNET
Subject: anything goes here
SUB PACS-L Bernard Aboba
```

This command puts me on the PACS-L list, and I will remain on the list until I indicate otherwise. Other useful commands include **SET <list> NOMAIL** command, which turns off a list when you go away on vacation (**SET <list> MAIL** turns it on again), and the **UNSUB <list>** command, used to unsubscribe.

Once your subscriptions are set up, you will no longer interact with the LISTSERV program, but instead will send mail to the mailing lists you have subscribed to. This is important to remember, since messages sent to LISTSERV will never reach your intended group, and control messages sent to the group will be sent to everyone on the list, getting them angry.

LISTSERV gateways

The bit.* newsgroups on USENET are gatewayed from BITNET LISTSERV lists. Since reading these groups via USENET requires only one copy of a message to be kept for each news server (as opposed to a copy for every subscriber), please check to see whether your desired list is available via USENET before subscribing to a LISTSERV.

If multiple people at your site are interested in the same LISTSERV list, it is more efficient to have your system administrator subscribe to the list via a "mail exploder" mail address that will relay the incoming messages to local readers, instead of having the readers subscribe individually. Having your system administrator subscribe means that only one copy of each message needs to be brought in over the network. A list of gatewayed groups is included in Appendix J: Conference Lists.

LISTSERV Mailing list commands

Command	What it does
Lists Global /<string>	Gets a listing of LISTSERV groups containing <string>
Lists Global	Gets a listing of LISTSERV groups available on the server
HELP	A brief help listing
Info <topic>	Gets information on a topic. If topic is omitted, gets a list of help topics
Query <list>	Finds out options for a given list
Query *	Options for all subscribed lists on a server
RELEASE	Gives site contact
REGister <your_name>	Associates your name with your email address (Allows you to omit <your_name> on subscription requests)
REV <list>	Shows subscribers to the list
SET <list> NOMAIL	Temporarily suspends a subscription
SET <list> MAIL	Reactivates a subscription
SUBscribe <list> <your_name>	Subscribes to a particular group
UNSUBscribe <list>	Unsubscribes to a particular group
SHOW LINKs <node list>	Shows network links of nodes in <node list>
SHOW PATHs <start node> <node list>	Shows routing path from start node to nodes in <node list>
SHOW NETwork	Network statistics
SIGNOFF <list>	Unsubscribes from a particular group
SIGNOFF *	Unsubscribes from all groups on a given server
SIGNOFF * (NETWIDE	Unsubscribes from all lists on the network

LISTSERV file transfer commands

You can also request files from a LISTSERV. LISTSERV lists sometimes have associated files, and in order to find out what files are available, you submit the command **IND <list>** to the list. For example:

```
world% mail MIZZOU1.missouri.edu
Subject: anything
IND MUNUG-L
```

This will get us a listing of the available files for the Missouri NeXT User Group mailing list. Once we have the list, we can then choose a file to transfer.

File transfer commands include **GET** and **SENDME**, which are synonymous. The response to **GET** or **SENDME** commands consists of two mail messages. One message contains the disposition of the job (completed or stopped with an error, resources consumed, etc.), and the other consists of the file.

File transfer

To send a file to another user on BITNET from an IBM mainframe, use the

```
SENDFILE <filename> <ext> <mode> <username> AT <system>
```

Example:

```
SENDFILE MYFILE MYTYPE A NICOLE AT
```

On VAX VMS systems the command is:

```
SEND/FILE <filename>.<extension>
```

Example:

```
SEND/FILE MYFILE.MYTYPE
```

It is not possible to access the file send or receive facility directly from non-BITNET networks. However, it is possible to send and receive files from users on BITNET by enclosing them within mail messages.

LISTSERV database commands

Many of the LISTSERV lists are archived, and can be searched as a database. To find out what databases are available, send the **DATA LIST** command to LISTSERV. For example:

```
world% mail MIZZOU1.missouri.edu
Subject: anything
DATA LIST
```

In order to perform a search of the database, send the following commands within the message:

```
//
//database search dd=rules
//rules dd *
search <key> in <list>
index
/*
```

For example:

```
world% mail MIZZOU1.missouri.edu
Subject: anything
//
//database search dd=rules
//rules dd *
search DSP in MUNUNG-L
index
/*
```

To then retrieve the selected messages (based on the returned index):

```
world% mail MIZZOU1.missouri.edu
Subject: anything
//
//database search dd=rules
//rules dd *
search DSP in MUNUNG-L
print all of 3567 4476
/*
```

For more information

Help

HELP-NET list

```
mail LISTSERV@TEMPLEVM.BITNET
SUB HELP-NET
```

NETMONTH Magazine (the monthly BITNET guide)

```
mail NMONTHED@UNTVM1.BITNET
SUBSCRIBE NETMONTH your_name
```

Example:

```
SUBSCRIBE NETMONTH John Smith
```

LISTSERV file transfer commands

`GET <file list>`	Requests a given file
`GET INFO FILELIST`	Gets a listing of all help files on the LISTSERV
`GET REFCARD`	Gets a summary of LISTSERV commands
`GET TOOLS FILELIST`	Gets a listing of LISTSERV tools
`GET <file><type>`	Retrieves a file
`INDex <list>`	Gets the file list associated with the group
`SENDME <file list>`	Requests a given file

LISTSERV database commands

`DATAbase List`	Gets a listing of databases on the server
`UDD`	Search user directory database

BITNET Databases (on MIZZOU1.missouri.edu)

ACTIV-L	Archives of "Activists Mailing List"
AFAM-L	Archives of "African-American Research"
AMLIT-L	Archives of "American Literature Discussion Group"
ASHE-L	Archives of "Association for the Study of Higher Education Discussion"
BITEARN	Information on all BITNET nodes
CLONE-L	Archives of "Discussion of PC Clone computers at MU"
CREWRT-L	Archives of "Creative Writing in Education for Teachers and Students"
CSACM-L	Archives of "Mizzou Student ACM Chapter Discussion"
CSGRAD-L	Archives of "MU Computer Science Graduate Student Distribution"
ENGLMU-L	Archives of "ENGLMU-L"
FAMILY-L	Archives of "Academic Family Medicine Discussion"
FEMREL-L	Archives of "Open discussion of women, religion, and feminist theology"
HOTEL-L	Archives of "Hotel and Restaurant Educators Discussion"
HRD-L	Archives of "Human Resource Development Group List"
MMNUG-L	Archives of "Mid-Missouri Network Users Group"
MMUSER-L	Archives of "Multi-Media Users Group"
MODOWN-L	Archives of "MOREnet Outage Announcements"
MOPOLY-L	Archives of "Discussion of Missouri political issues"
MOUSER-L	Archives of "MOREnet User's Discussion List"
MUINFO-L	Archives of "INFORMU Editors Discussion Group"
MUNUG-L	Archives of "Missouri University NeXT User's Group"
OXYGEN-L	Archives of "Oxygen Free Radical Biology and Medicine Discussion Group"
PEERS	Information on all the LISTSERV servers in the network
PSRT-L	Archives of "Political Science Research and Teaching List"
SCR-L	Archives of "Study of Cognitive Rehabilitation"
WIOLE-L	Archives of "Writing Intensive Online Learning Environments"

LISTSERVs with help information

You can also get more information on LISTSERVs and BITNET by sending mail to the following addresses. The subject can be anything, with the commands placed in the body of the message:

Address	Command	What it does
LISTSERV@pucc.princeton.edu	GET BITNET CNTRYCNT	Gets distribution of BITNET sites
LISTSERV@pucc.princeton.edu	GET BITNET SITES	Gets BITNET node list
LISTSERV@pucc.princeton.edu	GET BIT2PLAN PROPOSAL	Gets BITNET regionalization plan
LISTSERV@BITNIC.BITNET	GET BITNET OVERVIEW	Gets you an overview of BITNET
LISTSERV@BITNIC.BITNET	GET BITNET CHARTER	Gets you the BITNET charter
LISTSERV@BITNIC.BITNET	GET MAIL MANNERS	Mail etiquette on BITNET
LISTSERV@BITNIC.BITNET	GET CREN NET_USE	CREN Acceptable Use Policy
LISTSERV@BITNIC.BITNET	GET INFOREP LISTINGS	BITNET site representative list
LISTSERV@BITNIC.BITNET	GET BITNODE FILELIST	Gets a list of files about BITNET
LISTSERV@BITNIC.BITNET	GET BITNET USERHELP	Gets you a help file
LISTSERV@BITNIC.BITNET	GET BITNET SERVERS	Gets you a list of file servers
LISTSERV@BITNIC.BITNET	GET LIST GROUPS	Gets you a list of groups
LISTSERV@NDSUVM1.BITNET	GET LISTSERV LISTS	Gets you a list of lists
LISTSERV@BITNIC.BITNET	INDEX NETINFO	Gets you the Index of network info
LISTSERV@BITNIC.BITNET	GET JOINING BITNET	Information on joining BITNET
LISTSERV@UHUPVM1.BITNET	GET KOVACS PRV2N1	How to manage a LISTSERV
LISTSERV@MIZZOU1.missouri.edu	GET LISTFAQ MEMO	Frequently asked LISTSERV questions
LISTSERV@MIZZOU1.missouri.edu	GET LISTSERV MEMO	Guide to LISTSERV
LISTSERV@MIZZOU1.missouri.edu	GET LISTFILE MEMO	Guide to file servers
LISTSERV@MIZZOU1.missouri.edu	GET LISTDIST MEMO	Guide to distribution feature
LISTSERV@MIZZOU1.missouri.edu	GET LISTDB MEMO	Guide to database functions
LISTSERV@MIZZOU1.missouri.edu	GET LISTUDD MEMO	Guide to BITNET user directories
LISTSERV@MIZZOU1.missouri.edu	INFO FILELIST	List of BITNET information files
LISTSERV@MIZZOU1.missouri.edu	INFO REFCARD	Gets you a BITNET reference card
LISTSERV@MIZZOU1.missouri.edu	INFO DATABASE	Gets you info on LISTSERV database
LISTSERV@MIZZOU1.missouri.edu	LIST GLOBAL	Gets you a list of LISTSERV lists
LISTSERV@auvm.american.edu	GET NETGATE GATELIST	Listing of BITNET/USENET gateways

FTP archives

A directory of LISTSERVs is available via `ftp lilac.berkeley.edu, login: anonymous, cd netinfo`. The following files are available via `ftp auvm.american.edu`:

File	What it's about
WHATIS.BIT	What is BITNET?
BITNET.SERVERS	BITNET servers
BITNET.USERHELP	BITNET help file

BITNET Conferences on USENET

To gateway a conference from BITNET to USENET, send mail to: news-admin@auvm.american.edu. For a listing of gateway sites, send mail to: listserv@auvm.american.edu, with **GET NETGATE GATELIST** in the body.

User directory servers

Server		Institution	Access methods
COMSERVE	@ RPIECS	Rensselaer Polytechnic Institute	MAIL or MESSAGE
DIRECTORY	@ UCDASVM1	University of Calgary	MAIL
DIRECTORY	@ UNCAMULT	University of Calgary	MAIL
FINGER	@ CUVMA	Columbia University	MESSAGE
FINGER	@ DRAKE	Drake University	MESSAGE
FINGER	@ NDSUVM	North Dakota State University	MESSAGE
FINGER	@ SPCVXA	Saint Peter's College	MESSAGE
IDSERVER	@ PSUVM	Pennsylvania State University	MESSAGE
INFO	@ IRUCCIBM	Cork University	MAIL
INFO	@ RITVAXD	Rochester Institute of Technology	MESSAGE
LOOKUP	@ RITVM	Rochester Institute of Technology	MESSAGE
PHSERVE	@ UIUCVMD	University of Illinois	MAIL or MESSAGE
NAMESERV	@ BRANDEIS	Brandeis University	MESSAGE
NAMESERV	@ DREW	Drew University	MAIL or MESSAGE
NAMESERV	@ UNCAMULT	University of Calgary	MAIL
QNAMES	@ BANUFS11	University of Antwerp	MESSAGE
UTSERVER	@ UTKVM1	University of Tennessee	MESSAGE
VMNAMES	@ UREGINA1	University of Regina	MESSAGE
VMNAMES	@ WEIZMANN	Weizmann Institute of Science	MESSAGE
WHOIS	@ ALBNYVM1	State University of New York	MAIL or MESSAGE
WHOIS	@ UKCC	University of Kentucky	MAIL or MESSAGE

NAMESERV commands (NAMESERV@DREW.BITNET)

HELP	Get help file
REGISTER <your_name> <keywords>	Register in the directory
SEARCH/FIELD <keyword>	Search directory
SEARCH/NAME <name>	Search directory

WHOIS commands (WHOIS@ukcc.uky.edu)

HELP	Get help file
FIND <name>	Find a user
FIND <name> AT <node>	Find a user at a site
QUERY LOCATIONS	Get location list
GUESS <last name>	Approximate find

ASTRA database sites

Sites	Help files	What they are
ASTRADB@ICNUCEVM.BITNET	GET META DOCUMENT	List of databases and descriptions
	GET ASTRAIMM DOCUMENT	Installation and maintenance
	GET ASTRAFS DOCUMENT	System specifications
ASTRASQL@ICNUCEVM.BITNET	HELP	General help document
ASTRADB@IFIBDP.BITNET	HELP	General help document
ASTRADB@IFIIDG.BITNET	HELP	General help document
ASTRADB@IRMKANT.BITNET	HELP	General help document

BITNET Journals

Send subscription to	Command	What it's about
IRMUFFO@VTVM1.BITNET	SUB AIR	Planning research
LISTSERV@DSORUS1I.BITNET	SUB AMALGAM \<your_name\>	Mercury poisoning and dentistry
MCCABE@MTUS5.BITNET	SUB ATHENE	Amateur fiction. Specify ASCII or PostScript
LISTSERV@UBVM.BITNET	SUB BIOSPH-L \<your_name\>	Environmental newsletter
WHITE@DUVM.BITNET	SUB DRAGONZINE	Science fiction fantasy newsletter
LISTSERV@UWAVM.BITNET	SUB DISTED \<your_name\>	Distance education
EJOURNAL@ALBNYVMS.BITNET	SUB EJOURNAL	Computer-mediated conferencing and electronic text

Sample LISTSERVs

Send subscription to	Command	What it's about
LISTSERV@INDCMS.IUPUI.EDU	SUB RUSSIA	Russian Conference
LISTSERV@UKCC.UKY.EDU	SUB GARDENS	Gardens and Gardening
LISTSERV@INDYCMS.BITNET	SUB EC	European Community
LISTSERV@UBVM.BITNET	SUB EUEARN-L	Computers in Eastern Europe
LISTSERV@UHUPVM1.BITNET	SUB AASNET-L	African American Student Network
LISTSERV@UCDCVDLS.BITNET	SUB AAVLD-L	American Association of Vet Lab Diagnosticians
LISTSERV@CMUVM.BITNET	SUB ABSLST-L	Association of Black Sociologists
LISTSERV@WUVMD.BITNET	SUB ACSOFT-L	Academic Software Development
LISTSERV@MIZZOU1.missouri.edu	SUB AESRG-L	Applied Expert Systems Research Group List
LISTSERV@MIZZOU1.missouri.edu	SUB AESRG-L	Applied Expert Systems Research Group List
LISTSERV@WMVM1.BITNET	SUB AFRICANA	Information Technology and Africa
LISTSERV@UGA.BITNET	SUB AGRIC-L	Agriculture discussion
LISTSERV@DGOGWDG1.BITNET	SUB AHC-L	Association for History and Computing
LISTSERV@GWUVM.BITNET	SUB AHL	American Health Line News Service
LISTSERV@GREARN.BITNET	SUB AIRCRAFT	The Aircraft Discussion List
LISTSERV@CUNYVM.BITNET	SUB AIRLINE	The Airline List
LISTSERV@UCSBVM.BITNET	SUB ALBION-L	British and Irish History
LISTSERV@YORKVM1.BITNET	SUB ALF-L	Academic Librarian's Forum
LISTSERV@PSUVM.BITNET	SUB AMINT-L	Academy of Management International
LISTSERV@MIZZOU1.missouri.edu	SUB AMLIT-L	American Literature Discussion Group
LISTSERV@AUVM.BITNET	SUB AMUSIC-D	ALLMUSIC Digest
LISTSERV@USCVM.BITNET	SUB AMWEST-H	History of the American West (moderated)
LISTSERV@VTVM2.BITNET	SUB APASD-L	APA Research Psychology Network
LISTSERV@JPNSUT00.BITNET	SUB APNET-L	Asia Pacific Network
LISTSERV@YORKVM1.BITNET	SUB ARTCRIT	Art Criticism Discussion Forum
LISTSERV@TTUVM1.BITNET	SUB ASEH-L	American Society of Environmental Health
LISTSERV@ICNUCEVM.BITNET	SUB ASTRA-UG	ASTRA Newsletter
LISTSERV@ICNUCEVM.BITNET	SUB ASTRA-OG	Bug reports
LISTSERV@INDYCMS.BITNET	SUB AUTORACE	Autoracing discussion
LISTSERV@BRUFPB.BITNET	SUB AVIATION	General Aviation List
LISTSERV@UA1VM.BITNET	SUB BEER-L	Homebrew Digest List
LISTSERV@VTVM1.BITNET	SUB BEVPUB-L	Blacksburg Electronic Village
LISTSERV@UKCC.BITNET	SUB BGRASS-L	Bluegrass music
LISTSERV@ARIZVM1.BITNET	SUB BIRDCNTR	Bird Watching

Send subscription to	Command	What it's about
LISTSERV@HEARN.BITNET	SUB BIOMCH-L	Biomechanics and Movement Science listserver
LISTSERV@UBVM.BITNET	SUB BIOSPH-L	Biosphere, ecology, Discussion List
LISTSERV@UMDD.BITNET	SUB BIOTECH	Biotechnology Discussion List
LISTSERV@TCSVM.BITNET	SUB BITNET-2	Discussion of BITNET II
LISTSERV@UMAB.BITNET	SUB BITUSE-L	Bitnet User's Group
LISTSERV@UAFSYSB.BITNET	SUB BLIND-L	Computer Use by and for the Blind
LISTSERV@PUCC.BITNET	SUB BRFC-L	BITNET RFC Discussion List
LISTSERV@UGA.BITNET	SUB BRINE-L	Brine Shrimp Discussion List
LISTSERV@USCVM.BITNET	SUB BRS-L	BRS/Search Full Text Retrieval Software Disc+
LISTSERV@TAMVM1.BITNET	SUB BUCKS-L	Gigabucks Discussion List
LISTSERV@ULKYVM.BITNET	SUB BUDDHA-L	Buddhist Studies Forum
LISTSERV@INDYCMS.BITNET	SUB C-L	Discussion of C Programming
LISTSERV@WVNVM.BITNET	SUB CANCER-L	WVNET Cancer Discussion List
LISTSERV@UVVM.BITNET	SUB CANEWS	CA*net Newsletter
LISTSERV@YORKVM1.BITNET	SUB CARECON	Caribbean Economy
LISTSERV@UA1VM.BITNET	SUB CANDLE-L	Candle Products Discussion List
LISTSERV@UHCCVM.BITNET	SUB CARL-L	CARL User's Information List
LISTSERV@SAUPM00.BITNET	SUB CARS-L	Discussion forum about cars
LISTSERV@SUVM.BITNET	SUB CBDS-L	Circuit Board Design System (CBDS) Interest Group
LISTSERV@UCCVMA.BITNET	SUB CDROM-L	CD-ROM
LISTSERV@IRLEARN.BITNET	SUB CELTIC-L	CELTIC-L - The Celtic Culture List
LISTSERV@NIHLIST.BITNET	SUB CFS-L	Chronic Fatigue Syndrome discussion CFIDS/ME
LISTSERV@NIHLIST.BITNET	SUB CFS-NEWS	Chronic Fatigue Syndrome Newsletter CFIDS/ME
LISTSERV@GREARN.BITNET	SUB CHESS-L	The Chess Discussion List
LISTSERV@UBVM.BITNET	SUB CHPOEM-L	Chinese Poem Exchange and Discussion List
LISTSERV@IUBVM.BITNET	SUB CJUST-L	Criminal Justice Discussion List
LISTSERV@RPITSVM.BITNET	SUB CMC	Computer Mediated Communication
LISTSERV@UNCCVM.BITNET	SUB CNIDR-L	Networked Information Discovery and Retrieval
LISTSERV@INDYCMS.BITNET	SUB COHERENT	Coherent operating system
LISTSERV@UNLVM.BITNET	SUB COMICW-L	COMIC Writers Workshop
LISTSERV@UALTAVM.BITNET	SUB COMLAW-L	Computers and Legal Education
LISTSERV@UVMVM.BITNET	SUB COMMUNET	Community Networking
LISTSERV@WUVMD.BITNET	SUB COMPMED	Comparative Medicine List
LISTSERV@AUVM.BITNET	SUB COMSOC-L	Computers and Society ARPA Digest
LISTSERV@UOTTAWA.BITNET	SUB CONTENTS	Religious Studies Publications Journal
LISTSERV@UOTTAWA.BITNET	SUB CONTEX-L	Ancient Texts Discussion Group List.
LISTSERV@MIZZOU1.BITNET	SUB CREWRT-L	Creative Writing in Education for Teachers
LISTSERV@JPNTUVM0 .BITNET	SUB CRYPTO-L	Forum on Cryptology and Related Mathematics
LISTSERV@IUBVM.BITNET	SUB CSNPROJ	Community Service Project Discussion List
LISTSERV@UMAB.BITNET	SUB DBLIST	Databases for Dentistry
LISTSERV@UHCCVM.BITNET	SUB DEMING-L	The W. Edwards Deming Forum
LISTSERV@IRLEARN.BITNET	SUB DIABETES	International Research Project on Diabetes
LISTSERV@EMUVM1.BITNET	SUB DIAL-IPX	Dial in Access to IPX Network
LISTSERV@UBVM.BITNET	SUB DIET	Support and Discussion of Weight Loss
LISTSERV@UAFSYSB.BITNET	SUB DIRECT-L	MacroMind Director for the Macintosh
LISTSERV@UTXVM.BITNET	SUB DISASTER	Disaster Plans and Recovery Resources
LISTSERV@RPITSVM.BITNET	SUB DIST-HAM	Info-Hams redistribution
LISTSERV@RPITSVM.BITNET	SUB DIST-MDM	INFO-MODEMS Mailing List
LISTSERV@RPITSVM.BITNET	SUB DIST-MIC	Info-Micro Mailing List
LISTSERV@UWAVM.BITNET	SUB DISTED	Online Journal of Distance Ed. and Communications
LISTSERV@NCSUVM.BITNET	SUB E-EUROPE	Eastern Europe Business Network
LISTSERV@AEARN.BITNET	SUB EARLYM-L	Early Music List

Chapter 17: Introduction to BITNET

Send subscription to	Command	What it's about
LISTSERV@VTVM2.BITNET	SUB EAT-L	FoodLore/Recipe Exchange
LISTSERV@RPITSVM.BITNET	SUB EJCREC	Electronic Journal of Communication
LISTSERV@TAUNIVM.BITNET	SUB ENERGY-L	Energy List
LISTSERV@BUACCA.BITNET	SUB EPP-L	Albert Einstein Papers Project and Discussion
LISTSERV@UNBVM1.BITNET	SUB EPPD-L	Engineering and Public Policy Discussion List
LISTSERV@UIUCVMD.BITNET	SUB EUDORA	Eudora mailing list
LISTSERV@BROWNVM.BITNET	SUB EUDPC-L	Eudora on the PC List
LISTSERV@UBVM.BITNET	SUB EUEARN-L	Discussion of Eastern Europe Telecom
LISTSERV@ITESMVF1.BITNET	SUB FILM-L	Film making and reviews list
LISTSERV@UMAB.BITNET	SUB FLYFISH	Fly Fishing Digest
LISTSERV@CMUVM.BITNET	SUB FOODWINE	Discussion List for Food and Wine
LISTSERV@UNMVMA.BITNET	SUB FORENSIC	Forensic Med. Antho. Death Invest.
LISTSERV@UNCVM1.BITNET	SUB FSDNURSE	Federal Service Doctoral Nurses List
LISTSERV@BITNIC.BITNET	SUB FUTURE-L	(Peered) The Future of BITNET
LISTSERV@FINHUTC.BITNET	SUB GEOGRAPH	Geography
LISTSERV@PTEARN.BITNET	SUB GEOLOGY	Geology Discussion List
LISTSERV@UBVM.BITNET	SUB GIS-L	Geographic Information Systems Discussion
LISTSERV@UBVM.BITNET	SUB GOLF-L	The Golf Discussion List
LISTSERV@HUEARN.BITNET	SUB HBONE-L	Hungarian IP Backbone
LISTSERV@UMINN1.BITNET	SUB HEBREW-L	(Peered) HEBREW-L Jewish & Near Eastern Studies
LISTSERV@UCSBVM.BITNET	SUB HESSE-L	The Works of Hermann Hesse
LISTSERV@MSU.BITNET	SUB HYPERCRD	Hypercard Discussion List
LISTSERV@UMAB.BITNET	SUB HYPERMED	Biomedical Hypermedia Instructional Design
LISTSERV@PUCC.BITNET	SUB INFO-AUX	LISTSERV list for A/UX discussion and software
LISTSERV@MAINE.BITNET	SUB INNOPAC	III Online Public Access Catalog Discussion
LISTSERV@UMDD.BITNET	SUB INNS-L	International Neural Network Society
LISTSERV@ICNUCEVM.BITNET	SUB INTERNET	ARPA-Internet News
LISTSERV@IRLEARN.BITNET	SUB IRTRAD-L	Irish Traditional Music List
LISTSERV@ULKYVM.BITNET	SUB ISLAM-L	History of Islam
LISTSERV@JPNKNU01.BITNET	SUB J-FOOD-L	Japanese food & culture discussion list
LISTSERV@TEMPLEVM.BITNET	SUB JAZZ-L	Jazz Lovers' List
LISTSERV@NDSUVM1.BITNET	SUB KIDCAFE	KIDCAFE Youth Dialog
LISTSERV@NDSUVM1.BITNET	SUB KIDFORUM	KIDFORUM KIDLink Coordination
LISTSERV@NDSUVM1.BITNET	SUB KIDLEADR	KIDLEADR KIDLink Coordination
LISTSERV@NDSUVM1.BITNET	SUB KIDLINK	KIDLINK Project List
LISTSERV@NDSUVM1.BITNET	SUB KIDPLAN	KIDPLAN KIDLink Planning
LISTSERV@NDSUVM1.BITNET	SUB KIDPLAN2	KIDPLAN2 Kidlink Work Group
LISTSERV@NDSUVM1.BITNET	SUB KIDPROJ	Special KIDLink Projects
LISTSERV@NDSUVM1.BITNET	SUB KIDS-ACT	KIDS-ACT What can I do now?
LISTSERV@ASUACAD.BITNET	SUB KIDZMAIL	KIDZMAIL: Kids exploring issues
LISTSERV@TRITU.BITNET	SUB KIMYA-L	Kimya ve Kimya Muhendisligi Grubu
LISTSERV@NDSUVM1.BITNET	SUB KINDEX	KINDEX - KidLink Subject Summaries
LISTSERV@NDSUVM1.BITNET	SUB KINDEXW	Weekly KidLink Subject Summaries
LISTSERV@ULKYVM.BITNET	SUB KINST-L	Hand Microsurgery Research Network
LISTSERV@VCCSCENT.BITNET	SUB KLARINET	Klarinet - Clarinettist's Network
LISTSERV@NCSUVM.BITNET	SUB KUDZU-L	WAIS Initiative for North Carolina
LISTSERV@KENTVM.BITNET	SUB K12NAV-L	Internet navigation course for K12 educators
LISTSERV@KENTVM.BITNET	SUB K12NAV-N	Internet navigation course for K12 educators
LISTSERV@NIHLIST.BITNET	SUB LANMAN-L	Microsoft LAN Manager discussion list
LISTSERV@AUVM.BITNET	SUB LAWSCH-L	Law School Discussion List
LISTSERV@MARIST.BITNET	SUB MBA-L	MBA Student curriculum discussion
LISTSERV@TTUVM1.BITNET	SUB MBU-L	Megabyte University (Computers & Writing)

Send subscription to	Command	What it's about
LISTSERV@UTARLVM1.BITNET	SUB MECH-L	Mechanical Engineering Discussion List
LISTSERV@UKANVM.BITNET	SUB MEDIEV-L	Medieval History
LISTSERV@POLYVM.BITNET	SUB MEDIMAGE	Medical Imaging Discussion List
LISTSERV@UBVM.BITNET	SUB MEDLIB-L	Medical Libraries Discussion List
LISTSERV@NDSUVM1.BITNET	SUB MEDNETS	MEDNETS Medical Telecom Networks
LISTSERV@TAUNIVM.BITNET	SUB MEH2O-L	Middle East Water List
LISTSERV@UABDPO.BITNET	SUB MEMSNET	Mineral Economics and Mgmt Society
LISTSERV@UBVM.BITNET	SUB NETTRAIN	Internet/BITNET Network Trainers
LISTSERV@RPITSVM.BITNET	SUB NEWBOOKS	New Books in Communication
LISTSERV@MITVMA.BITNET	SUB NIHONGO	Japanese Language Discussion List
LISTSERV@DB0TUI11.BITNET	SUB NUTEPI	Nutritional epidemiology
LISTSERV@TAMVM1.BITNET	SUB ODP-L	Ocean Drilling Program Open Discussion List
LISTSERV@UHUPVM1.BITNET	SUB PACS-L	Public-Access Computer Systems Forum
LISTSERV@UHUPVM1.BITNET	SUB PACS-P	Public-Access Computer Systems Publications
LISTSERV@BITNIC.BITNET	SUB PAROUTE	Pathalias Routing Mailing List
LISTSERV@UBVM.BITNET	SUB PERDIR-L	Personnel Directors, Associates, Managers
LISTSERV@UCSFVM.BITNET	SUB PRIE-L	Packet Radio Internet Extension List
LISTSERV@OSUVM1.BITNET	SUB PROCUR-B	Commerce Business Daily - Procure
LISTSERV@UTARLVM1 .BITNET	SUB RE-FORUM	Real Estate Forum
LISTSERV@ASUACAD.BITNET	SUB RUSSIAN	Russian Language Issues
LISTSERV@UBVM.BITNET	SUB RUSTEX-L	Russian TeX and Cyrillic text processing list
LISTSERV@MARIST.BITNET	SUB SASUG	Marist SAS Users Group
LISTSERV@BINGVMB.BITNET	SUB SEISM-L	Seismological Data Distribution
LISTSERV@BINGVMB.BITNET	SUB SEISMD-L	Seismological Discussion
LISTSERV@UNMVMA.BITNET	SUB SIGTEL-L	SIG/Tel (Special Interest Group/Telecom)
LISTSERV@NMSUVM1.BITNET	SUB SIMEDU-L	Simulation Applications in Business/Education
LISTSERV@UNMVMA.BITNET	SUB SM-LADB	Latin America Data Base
LISTSERV@RICEVM1.BITNET	SUB SUNSPOTS	(Peered) Sun Microsystems hardware and software
LISTSERV@UBVM.BITNET	SUB SUNSPOTS	(Peered) Sun Spots Discussion
LISTSERV@UKCC.BITNET	SUB SUPERIBM	Super Computing Issues Forum
LISTSERV@BROWNVM.BITNET	SUB TCL-DGST	THINK Class Library Digest List
LISTSERV@UAFSYSB.BITNET	SUB TOOLB-L	Asymetrix Toolbook product discussions
LISTSERV@UICVM.BITNET	SUB WIN3-L	Microsoft Windows Version 3 Forum
LISTSERV@NERVM.BITNET	SUB Z3950IW	Z39.50 Implementors Workshop
LISTSERV@BRUFPB.BITNET	SUB 21ST-C-L	Forum about the 21st century discussions

Chapter 18:
Introduction to FidoNet

Meaning in madness

Introduction

FidoNet began as a network of bulletin board hobbyists, and now connects more than 22,000 systems worldwide, with the number growing at over 40 percent a year. Since FidoNet software is inexpensive and readily available, and the FidoNet protocols are more efficient than UUCP, in many countries FidoNet has become the primary mechanism for transporting electronic mail and conferences.

This chapter attempts to make FidoNet concepts clear to the lay user. It is not reasonable to expect a beginner, or even an intermediate telecommunicator, to grasp most of the material in this chapter on the first pass. Understanding FidoNet is like learning a new language: If you aren't fluent, it's hard to know what anyone's talking about. However, if you persevere, one day you will understand all the babble you've heard about FidoNet.

A large part of the obscurity arises from the way FidoNet developed. FidoNet sysops have long been wary of having their amateur network exploited by commercial interests. To protect FidoNet's freedom, the weekly Nodelist is not made available through normal distribution channels. This creates a kind of chicken and egg problem – how do I find the FidoNet BBS nearest me? Get a copy of the Nodelist. How can I get a copy of the Nodelist if I don't have the number of a FidoNet BBS?

In order to help get you started on FidoNet, I have listed the phone numbers and locations of the North American Filebone nodes in Appendix I. These systems carry the weekly Nodelist, in addition to file areas relating to dozens of interests. The list of Filebone nodes is regularly updated in the FILEBONE.NA file, also available from the Filebone nodes. Since the Nodelist also has all the phone numbers of the help nodes in it, it is also a good resource for assistance.

Acknowledgments

A word of thanks is due to Tom Jennings, who started the whole mess back in 1984. If he'd known what was going to happen, he might not have done it, but that's probably the reason that we don't have 20-20 hindsight. Thanks to Tom, thousands of grown men and women are now wasting weeks of their time yelling at their computer screens and removing large sums of money from their bank accounts in order to buy bigger hard disks and faster CPUs. Here's to you, Tom!

FidoNet administration and control

Checks and balances

A deep distrust of central authority lies behind the design of the FidoNet network. Just as the framers of the Constitution sought to keep any one branch of government from becoming too powerful, so FidoNet's design keeps any single individual or group of individuals from controlling the network.

FidoNet is a protocol, not a piece of software. The specifications for the FidoNet, called the FidoNet Technical Standards documents, are publicly available.

As a result, FidoNet-compatible software is available from a number of vendors. You do not have to purchase your software from any particular vendor in order to run a FidoNet-compatible system.

A number of networks use the FidoNet protocols. The largest of these is called FidoNet. FidoNet was formerly governed by an organization called the International FidoNet Association (IFNA). IFNA, a 501.c.3 nonprofit, started out as a mechanism to support FidoNet but grew increasingly unpopular and was dissolved by its board of directors in 1989. There are also several alternative networks, such as RBBSNet, AlterNet, and EggNet, that also adhere to the FidoNet protocols but have their own administration separate from FidoNet.

In fact, you don't have to be a member of *any* network to use FidoNet-compatible software! For example, several government agencies use FidoNet-compatible software in order to link their branch offices. For security reasons, they do not wish to belong to any network. It is estimated that more than half of all the FidoNet-compatible software worldwide is used to construct private networks.

The open nature of the FidoNet protocols provides another check on the behavior of the FidoNet network administrators: Should the administrators impose policies that are too strict or fees that are too high, users may leave FidoNet to join one of the alternative networks, or create their own.

Network administration

Power within each of the large FidoNet-compatible networks is decentralized, with local entities being given a large amount of control. In the paragraphs that follow, I will refer to FidoNet, but it should be understood that the discussion will also apply to other FidoNet-compatible networks such as RBBSNet, AlterNet, and EggNet.

A zone is a large part of the FidoNet, usually referring to a continent or a substantial portion of the globe. Zone 1 is North America.

Each zone is broken down into regions, which are usually states or groups of states. For

example, Region 10 consists of California and Nevada.

Regions are further broken down into networks, usually covering a metropolitan area. For example, Network 125 covers San Francisco and all points north to Eureka, California. Originally, regions and networks were at equal levels in the hierarchy; the "nets within regions" concept originated in 1988.

There are usually many networks within a zone. Larger networks are further broken down into hubs. Hubs are usually local calling areas or regions within which a toll-free call can be placed. The hubs service the individual BBSes of the network, which are known as nodes.

Finally, points are FidoNet-compatible programs used by individuals to receive echoes and files only from a particular node, called the "Boss" node.

The major difference between points and nodes is that points do not appear in the Nodelist. The only way to reach them is to send mail to the Boss node, which passes it on to the points. Most users aren't points.

The functionality of point software varies. The only thing that all point software is *required* to do is to be able to call its Boss node. Point software is not required to be able to receive calls, and few point implementations can handle this.

Each node is assigned a number within its particular network, and in turn, each network is assigned a number. The combination of the zone, network, and node numbers constitutes a FidoNet address.

FidoNet addresses are of the form:

```
<zone>:<network>/<node>
```

Example: 1:125/222

Point addresses are of the form:

```
<zone>:<network>/<node>.<point>
```

Example: 1:125/222.2

FidoNet services

FidoNet services include electronic mail (NetMail), distributed conferencing (EchoMail and GroupMail), file send and receive (File Attach and Request), and distributed files conferences (File Distribution Networks).

As with other networks, within FidoNet the structure and administration of network services is separate from the structure and administration of the network itself. This point is often difficult for beginners to grasp, since some of the same people administer both the network and individual services.

The independence between network services and the network itself is illustrated by differences in the delivery of individual services. While FidoNet nodes are capable of routing person-to-person mail through other systems, these messages (known as NetMail) are almost always sent directly from the sender to the receiver. NetMail routing, if any, is handled on a local network by local network basis. Similarly, File Requests or Attaches are almost never routed.

On the other hand, the EchoMail and GroupMail distributed conferencing services are routed, as is the Gofer distributed file request service.

EchoMail administration

EchoMail is a distributed conferencing service with many conferences, only a fraction of which are widely distributed over the network of Regional Echo Coordinators, known as the backbone. It is called the backbone because a large number of conferences travel over it (more than 500) at high speed (16.8Kbps) in compressed form. Currently the backbone uses US Robotics high-speed modems.

To qualify for backbone distribution, conferences must satisfy several criteria, including a minimum traffic level. Newly created conferences frequently are distributed off the backbone, then are moved to backbone distribution if they catch on. Putting a conference on the backbone tends to make it more widely available, and may lower the cost of distribution.

Each zone has coordinators for EchoMail, known as the Zone EchoMail Coordinator. Within the zone, each region has a Regional Echo Coordinator, or REC, whose job is to be part of the backbone. The REC agrees to receive all conferences requested by the Network Echo Coordinators within the region. Since this is usually a large volume of material, it is imperative that the REC have a high-speed modem, a fast computer with a large hard drive, and lots of extra time.

Each network also has a coordinator for EchoMail, called the Network Echo Coordinator, or NEC. The NEC distributes requested conferences to the local hubs, which pass them on to individual BBSes, called nodes. Just as hubs pass on echoes to nodes, the nodes can pass them on to points.

The FidoNet EchoMail distribution system just described is therefore much like a natural gas distribution system in that a big pipe is used to haul the gas long distances, but as the pipeline reaches the city, it splits off into a series of smaller and smaller pipes to distribute the gas.

Mail hour

All FidoNet systems in a zone are required to be able to receive mail during a period that begins simultaneously throughout the zone. This hour of activity is known as Zone Mail Hour (ZMH). ZMH ensures that all FidoNet systems in the zone will be synchronized when they attempt to send and receive mail. FidoNet systems may encourage mail transmission by adding additional mail hours, but they must always be able to send and receive mail during the ZMH.

Most point users are interested in using their computer for other purposes. They do not want to be required to have their point software set up to receive calls at a particular time, and so points are not required to take part in Mail Hour.

Continuous mail systems are able to receive mail around the clock, not just during Mail Hour or other reserved periods.

The Nodelist

Every week, each zone compiles a list of its bulletin boards. The zone lists are then merged into one large list called the Nodelist. The Nodelist is a directory of FidoNet systems, used by every system to deliver messages and files to each other. As of July 1993, over 22,000 systems were listed in the Nodelist, which is the largest, most accurate list of bulletin boards ever compiled. The number of systems in the Nodelist is growing at over 40 percent per year.

The Nodelist entry for each system includes information on the system such as its FidoNet address, phone number (which may be unpublished), maximum modem speed, and ability to receive mail continuously.

The Nodediff

It would not make sense for each FidoNet system to receive a complete copy of the Nodelist every week, because only a fraction of the information changes on a weekly basis. Instead, only the difference between last week's and this week's Nodelist is transmitted. This is called the Nodediff. Software called a "Nodelist compiler" takes the information from the Nodediff and last week's Nodelist and creates the new Nodelist every week.

The FidoNews

FidoNet also has a weekly electronic newspaper, called the FidoNews, which is currently edited by a two-person team, Sylvia Maxwell and Donald Tees, with help from Tim Pozar, co-author of UFGATE.

Submissions to the FidoNews are handled electronically, with articles being mailed to the FidoNews system, which processes and lays out the weekly FidoNews automatically. The FidoNews is used to keep members informed about changes in network policy, new releases of software, or other issues of concern to the network. FidoNews is available via `ftp`

`ftp.ieee.org, cd ~ftp/pub/fidonet/fidonews`, or within the newsgroup comp.org.fidonet.

FidoNet services

NetMail

NetMail is the exchange of messages between one FidoNet system and a single other FidoNet system. For example, via NetMail you can send an electronic mail message to a given user at another FidoNet system. The first few versions of the FidoNet software only implemented NetMail.

EchoMail

If you wanted to form a discussion group on a particular topic, say hard disk drives, NetMail wouldn't be very useful because your message could only go to a specific person, not the entire group. To use NetMail, you'd have to know the address of every member in the group, and it's not usually possible to predict the address of new members.

EchoMail is a "fully distributed redundant database" that gets around the limitations of NetMail by allowing a message to be placed in a public conference and to be sent to many FidoNet nodes at once.

How does EchoMail work? EchoMail processors create files containing messages that are sent via the File Attach feature of the FidoNet protocols. This file is called a "SCAN." When unpacked by the receiver, the messages are unpacked and placed into the respective message areas. This is called a "TOSS."

In order to correctly route the message and diagnose problems, an EchoMail message contains several hidden fields that describe which systems have already received ("SEEN-BY") the message; the route the message has travelled to date ("PATH"), and information on the conference the message is in ("AREA"). In addition, there are several visible fields, which include information such as the originating system ("Origin Line") and the programs that have already processed the message ("Tag Line" or "Tear line").

Usually included in the "Origin Line" is information on the location, phone number, and FidoNet address of the sending node.

EchoMail conference topics

Each EchoMail conference has an assigned topic, such as Macintosh Desktop Publishing (MACDTP). Within each conference, a moderator is assigned to help keep users on the subject.

There are now more than 600 different conferences on FidoNet, and the number is growing every day. If you would like to discuss a topic likely to interest 100 other people, it is probably an acceptable topic for an EchoMail conference on FidoNet.

Rules of etiquette

With the invention of EchoMail, it soon became clear that many of the conventions surrounding NetMail no longer applied. For example, in NetMail, it is clear who your audience is: the specific person you are sending the message to. With NetMail it is also clear who is paying for your message to be sent: the sysop of the sending system.

With EchoMail, almost anyone could read your message, possibly in distant parts of the globe. In addition, sysops all over the world must pay to retransmit your message. These two factors dramatically change the rules that the EchoMail message poster must follow.

While the rules for each conference are slightly different, there are several overall principles that have evolved over the years that you need to pay attention to.

∇ Inappropriate postings

Inappropriate postings are of two types. One is a message that does not relate to the topic of the conference in which it is posted. The second is a message of only local interest that has been posted nationally or globally.

Inappropriate messages in nationwide EchoMail conferences include:

- Job listings, except in employment conferences
- BBS ads, except in conferences for that purpose
- For sale ads, except in conferences for that purpose
- Questions or other material relating to the local system
- Private mail
- Complaints about other inappropriate postings
- Messages soliciting funds or advocating illegal behavior
- Messages libeling a person

∇ Duplicate postings

Please do not post messages to multiple conferences. This has the result of increasing total network traffic without increasing the amount of information being transmitted.

∇ Commercial use

FidoNet is a hobbyist network. Bills are paid by sysops and contributing users. For this reason, advertisements and other commercial traffic is prohibited, except in conferences specifically reserved for those purposes, such as For Sale conferences. Anyone with a commercial interest in a particular company or product should identify himself or herself as such. Detailed questions about the operation of particular products are best dealt with in Product Support conferences supported by the vendor, if they exist.

∇ Opinions versus facts

Please distinguish facts, which are objectively verifiable, from opinions, which are conclusions based on those facts. Use of phrases such as "in my opinion" help distinguish the two clearly in the reader's mind. Be prepared to supply facts and to explain the reasoning behind your opinions if asked to do so.

∇ Handling of complaints

Conferences are usually administered by NetMail. This means that the moderator will contact you about an inappropriate posting by NetMail, and if you wish to contest that ruling, you should reply via NetMail. Please do not contest a moderator's ruling by posting within the conference, and do not respond to an inappropriate posting with a posting of your own within the conference. Finally, please do not send NetMail to an inappropriate poster. That is the job of the moderator.

∇ Pseudonyms or handles

The policy on handles varies by conference. In Macintosh-related conferences, all users are required to use their real names.

∇ Inappropriate moderation

Moderators are supposed to gently guide the readership of their conference, not terrorize them. Unfortunately, if a moderator steps out of line, under FidoNet rules removal is very difficult. Instead, the usual procedure is to create another conference on the same subject and drop the old one. This is very confusing to the users (why are there three Macintosh For Sale conferences? What is the difference between them?) and wastes sysop time. But that's the way it is.

The FidoNet.NA file

The FIDONET.NA file is a list of all the conferences distributed over the FidoNet backbone, which is distributed to the Echo Coordinators (by a program called TICK) to inform them about what echoes are available. A separate, more detailed description called the "EchoList" (ELIST) is also maintained.

The EchoList

Every month, the EchoList Administrator of FidoNet publishes a list of discussion topics available on the FidoNet backbone. The list includes the name of the conference, the moderator, and a brief description of the subject matter. I've reprinted a version of the list in Appendix J.

File Requests and Attaches

FidoNet systems can exchange files as well as messages. This is called "File Request" or FREQ (if a system asks for a file) and "File Attach" (if a system sends a file). Like NetMail, File Requests and Attaches only occur between two individual systems.

Gofer

Tosser/scanners do not route file requests. GOFER, written by Bill Auclair, 1:141/545, is a program that allows for multihop file requests via file attach or NetMail. Assuming that the nodes along the designated path are local calls from each other, Gofer allows users to make file requests free of long-distance phone charges. A Gofer routed File Request is known as a Distributed File Request," or DFREQ.

In order to support selection of the files to request, GOFER is run in door mode, allowing users to browse and choose files on available systems.

JVARCSERV

JVARCSERV is the FidoNet equivalent of Archie. System operators submit compiled versions of their file listings to a central site running the JVARCSERV program, which responds to search requests sent via NetMail over the FidoNet network. JVARCSERV does not respond correctly to requests gated to FidoNet from other networks. The process for submitting a JVARCSERV file listing is to:

• Compile file listings using the JVFC file list compiler, which accepts listings in files.bbs or PCBoard formats. The compiler can be file requested from node 2605/620 as JVFC.

• Submit listings to the central server by NetMail, file attach, or (in the case of Macintosh listings) using a TICK file conference. Shokwave Rider, 1:2605/620, handles Macintosh JVARCSERV submissions either by NetMail or by submission to the MAC-ARCH TICK conference.

Anatomy of an EchoMail Message

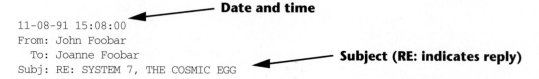

Date and time

```
11-08-91 15:08:00
From: John Foobar
  To: Joanne Foobar
Subj: RE: SYSTEM 7, THE COSMIC EGG
```

Subject (RE: indicates reply)

```
 JF> Boy oh boy oh boy! System 7 is so great I can hardly stand it!
```

Quoting previous message

```
PLEASE PLEASE PLEASE not another System 7 message. I can't run System 7, because
I'm still using a Lisa with a Profile hard drive. Hearing about System 7, publish
and subscribe, and all those goodies, makes me ill!

John
```

Product tag line (MacWoof)

Guiltware trial date (payment overdue!)

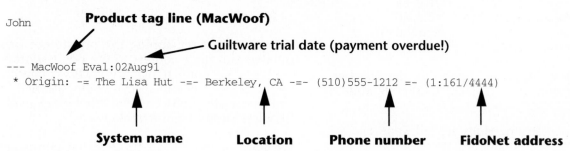

```
--- MacWoof Eval:02Aug91
 * Origin: -= The Lisa Hut -=- Berkeley, CA -=- (510)555-1212 =- (1:161/4444)
```

System name　　　**Location**　　　**Phone number**　　　**FidoNet address**

• Update the listing on a regular basis, using a file list compiler and the JVFC program. The compiled update can then be automatically sent using robot file attach software or the HATCH program.

JVARCSERV commands

HELP	Gets a helpfile listing
REGINFO	Information on how to add your node's file listings to the server
PROG <string>	Searches for <string> in filename listings
WHAT <string>	Searches for <string> in description listings
LISTNODES	Shows nodes covered by server
LISTMAGIC <node>	Shows Magic name files available on a FidoNet node
LISTSECTIONS <node>	Shows file sections on a FidoNet node

File Distribution Networks

Just as EchoMail was a generalization of NetMail, File Distribution Networks (FDNs) are generalizations of File Request/Attach. Using software such as TICK, it is possible to send a file to many systems at once, establishing a "conference" consisting of a common file library. This capability is very useful in promulgating new releases of important shareware such as FidoNet network utilities.

There are currently File Distribution Networks (FDNs) for the Macintosh (MSDN), Windows (WinNet), and the PC (SDS, for FidoNet-related software only, PDN for programming related material, and SDN for general PC stuff). In order to allow access to several FDNs with a single phone call, a backbone has been created that is called the "FileBone." A list of all the FileBone conferences is published monthly as FILEBONE.NA and is available from all FileBone sites. The list keeper is Kevin Snively, 1:116/29. Filebone Technical Coordinator is John Souvestre, 1:396/1.

The FDNs currently carried by the Filebone are:

ADANet	Programmers Net
Amiga Net	RA File Net
ANSIClub	Remote Access
CADNet	RoboBoard
Clipper Net	SkyNet
DeskTop Pub Net	Southern CA
GSDS (Genealogy)	Scouting
GeoWorks Net	SEA
Ham Net	SoundNet
IDC Net	Spitfire
IMail	TAG Net
LanNet	UtilNet
MSDN (Macintosh)	Wildcat!
Novell Net	WinNet
	Windows NT

The Three Star Systems supporting the first tier of the Filebone are: 1:13/13, 1:138/148, and 1:396/1.

The current Filebone Hubs are (all Zone 1):

13/13:	138/148:	396/1:
12/12	105/72	104/821
100/375	114/150	106/1555
116/29	124/7009	123/19
120/364	153/150	147/7
133/677	326/110	170/610
232/16	347/116	231/120
271/296	2410/116	280/2
278/707		282/114
278/709		289/13
2220/200		351/200
2613/210		387/255
		3629/201

Private networks (points)

Since the FidoNet protocols were not originally designed with point systems in mind, several kluges have been necessary in order to allow FidoNet to function smoothly with points.

According to the FidoNet Technical Standards, FidoNet addresses consist of a 2-byte field for the network number and another 2-byte field for the node number. These is no space reserved for the point number. However, in order for points not to conflict with existing nodes in the Nodelist, they must be assigned a unique address. How is this accomplished?

Points are assigned a private network number that is not in use by any other network within a particular zone. The assignment is made by the zone coordinator. The private network number is unique to all points on a particular Boss node. For purposes of interaction with the Boss system, the point assumes a FidoNet address of the folowing form:

```
<zone>:<private network number>/<point number>
```

For example, the address of point number 2 on 1:161/445, which was assigned the private network number 30541, is:

```
1:30541/2
```

The process of remapping the private network number and node address to the point address is known as "point remapping." This is handled by the boss node and special "point-aware" mail processing software. Not all FidoNet mail handlers support point remapping.

We have previously mentioned that points are not listed in the Nodelist. Since all points must be capable of receiving mail through their Boss nodes, all that is needed to send mail to a point is the address of the Boss. Therefore, private networks and their points do not need to be included in the Nodelist in order to deliver mail.

Since points are not listed in the Nodelist, special care must be taken to avoid confusing nonBoss FidoNet nodes. A point's private network/node number is never included in the "SEENBY" or "PATH" listings that accompany a message as it travels within the network.

A better solution, known as 4D addressing, allows points to be addressed without private network numbers. 4D is supported by Frontdoor, Intermail, and BinkleyTerm 2.56 (which also supports private networks).

FidoNet for sysops

Anatomy of a FidoNet system

Every FidoNet system needs to perform certain tasks, and it is worthwhile to go over what these are. It should be pointed out that several of these tasks are optional, and that in some implementations, multiple tasks are combined into a single program. Nevertheless, the vast majority of FidoNet systems conform to the following task breakdown:

Scheduler

In FidoNet, events are scheduled to occur at specific times. For example, mail goes out during Zone Mail Hour, mail processing occurs at 1 AM Pacific Standard Time, and so on. In effect, the FidoNet scheduler acts as the event generator in an event loop, which should be familiar to graphical user interface programmers. The difference is that the events are mostly internally generated, rather than externally generated. The other programs in the FidoNet implementation can be thought of as responses to the various events, being executed whenever their event arises.

Message Editor

This program allows users to view incoming messages and reply to them. Eight-bit characters (ASCII 128-255) and low-order nonprinting codes (2–31) are prohibited within FidoNet messages, with the exception of the Soft Carriage Return (8Dh). This means that binary files may not be enclosed within messages but should be sent via File Attach.

Scanner

This program collects outgoing mail, deciding which messages have already been sent and which ones still need to go out. FidoNet standards do not define the form in which a message is stored. They do, however, define how those messages should look when they are transmitted to other systems. Therefore, if a FidoNet implementation does not store the messages in FidoNet Standard format (referred to as *.MSG format), the scanner must make the conversion. Scanners either place the messages in *.MSG files for packing, or (if the scanner and packer are integrated) place them in outbound packets.

Router

Most FidoNet implementations support static routing of messages. In lieu of sending a message directly to its intended destination, the router may substitute another path based on instructions in the configuration file. Note that for routing to succeed, all nodes along the intended path must agree to forward messages. Since most nodes turn off routing, special arrangements are typically needed. Most often, the routing function is integrated into the packer.

Packer

This program takes messages already in FidoNet *.MSG format and puts them together into a packet. The packet usually has a filename extension of .PKT.

The packer is often integrated into the scanner for increased efficiency. Integrated scanner/packers (such as TMail for TBBS) handle scanning of new message and basic packing in a single pass.

Compressor

This (optional) program compresses the outgoing packet. The program most often used for this purpose is ARC, by Systems Enhancement Associates. This is the only approved format and must be version 5 or lower. However, other archivers such as PKZIP are also used and are agreed upon on a link-by-link basis.

Nodes also regularly send mail without pre-arrangement in whatever archive format they prefer. If the receiving system is not set up to handle the archiving format, manual intervention will be required.

The compressor and packer may also be combined.

Mailer

This program responds to the request of the scheduler for an outgoing mail delivery, or it picks up the phone on an incoming call. For outgoing mail, the Mailer transmits the packets (in compressed form, if the system chooses to do this) to the recipient system. For incoming mail, the Mailer receives incoming packets in compressed or uncompressed form.

Decompressor

This program looks at incoming mail and uncompresses those packets that have arrived in compressed form. Sometimes, a routine is used which looks at the incoming packet and decides that of several decompression routines is appropriate. In that way, it is possible to handle multiple compression formats.

Unpacker

This program takes the uncompressed packets and breaks them up into individual messages.

Mail Tosser

This program tosses incoming messages into the appropriate message areas. If the BBS uses the *.MSG message format, then the messages are tossed into individual directories; otherwise they are translated and added to the message base. Very often, the unpacker and tosser are combined for the sake of efficiency. For example, TMail for TBBS takes messages directly from packets and puts them in the message base in a single pass.

Mix and Match

The modular structure of FidoNet software means that you can mix and match components. If you don't like the tosser that came with your system, you can replace it with another one; the same goes for the mailer, and other parts of the system. As long as your final implementation performs all of the tasks correctly, there's no problem.

As a final example, the next figure shows how TBBS, OPUS, and Copernicus II fit within the hierarchy described here.

A day in the life of a message

"One day, you post a message. That night, in the wee small hours of morning, the mail handler runs, crashes, and dumps your message in the bit bucket. Your message has lived a day." – Chuck Meyer

EchoMail was created in order to allow users of many different FidoNet systems to participate in distributed conferencing on various subjects of interest. In order to explain how EchoMail works, we will be following a message from its birth all the way to its inclusion in the message base of another FidoNet-compatible bulletin board.

Messages are created by users and stored within the message base of a particular bulletin board. The first step on the road to global distribution is for the message to be converted from the local BBS format to the FidoNet message format. This format is known as the *.MSG format, because messages are often numbered 1.MSG, 2.MSG, and so on. Each FidoNet message contains a hidden field at the bottom called the "SEENBY" field. This field is used to indicate whether a particular node has already seen a particular message. If it has, then there is no reason to send it to that system again. This helps prevent duplicate messages from propagating throughout the network.

Most FidoNet software looks at a file called AREAS.BBS (or on OPUS, ECHO.CTL) to see to which systems a particular message should be distributed to. It then compares those systems to the SEENBYs for the message and eliminates any systems that have already gotten the message. The *.MSG files are then lumped together into a FidoNet packet, with each packet containing messages for a particular destination. The packets are placed in the outbound directory, awaiting transmission at a future time. Using EchoMail technology, a given message may end up in a number of different packets, depending on how many systems are listed to receive it in the AREAS.BBS file.

Function	TBBS	OPUS	COPERNICUS II
Scheduler	TIMS	OPUS	SCHEDULER
Message Editor	TBBS or TMM	OPUS	COPERNICUS II
Scanner	TIMS and Net Mail Utilities (NMUs)	OPUS or SQUISH	COPERNICUS II
Router	TIMS and NMUs	SQUISH	COPERNICUS II
Packer	TIMS and NMUs	OMMM or SQUISH	SEND
Compressor	NMUs	ARC or w/SQUISH any method	ARCMAIL COMPRESS
Mailer	TIMS	OPUS	CALL
Decompressor	Any method (w/ SPAZ)	Any method (w/ SPAZ or SQUISH)	ARCMAIL EXTRACT
Unpacker	TIMS	OPUS or SQUISH	DELIVER
Dupe killing	NMUs	OPUS or SQUISH	DELIVER
Tosser	TIMS	OPUS or SQUISH	SCRIBE
Message maintenance	MFSQZ	O_RENUM	SCRIBE

At an appointed time, usually late at night, the FidoNet mailer calls out, or the destination system calls in. At that time the packet is transmitted to the destination. The destination unpacks the messages into *.MSG files and then sorts them by the destination echo conference. After unpacking, it will compare the SEENBYs in the *.MSG files against its own AREAS.BBS file in order to determine where to send the message. The destination BBS may read the *.MSG files directly (OPUS and Fido work this way), or convert the files to its own internal message format (TBBS, QuickBBS, Maximus, and Remote Access do it this way).

Conferencing technologies

There are two major conferencing technologies available to FidoNet systems: EchoMail and GroupMail. Of these, EchoMail is by far the more common. However, GroupMail does have important advantages that the sysop should be aware of.

In EchoMail technology, a system makes a copy of an outgoing EchoMail message for every system it is connected to. In GroupMail technology, the message is copied and stored only once. In cases where a node is processing mail for hundreds of systems (such as in the case of a point network), this can be a crucial advantage.

There are also topological differences between the two concepts. In EchoMail technology, any nonlooping topology is technically workable. This does not mean that any old topology is desirable—just that it will work. Here are some examples of topologies that are workable under EchoMail:

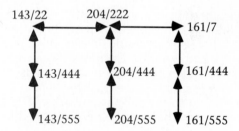

Topology A: Backbone

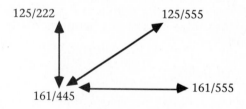

Topology B: Star

In Topology A, network hubs form a backbone for transmitting conferences between networks. In this case, the hubs are 143/22, 204/222, and 161/7. Within each network, nodes relay conferences to each other. By restricting internetwork links, this topology makes it less likely that a looping topology will be created by accident, as could happen, for example, by node 204/555 establishing a link with node 161/555.

However, it should be noted that in Topology A, it can take as long as 6 hops for a message generated by 143/555 to reach 161/555.

In Topology B, all nodes call a central system (161/445) to pick up their mail, and they do not establish links with each other. Therefore loops cannot occur, and messages can reach other nodes in a maximum of 2 hops. The problem with this topology is that it is more expensive and does not scale well. While it works fine for three connections, if 161/445 were to try to serve all 100 nodes in a conference, the phone bills would skyrocket because all nodes would have to call 161/445, even if it were located across the country. For this reason, Topology A is generally preferred, provided that the links within networks do not get too long, so as to cause excessive delays.

In GroupMail technology, only Topology B, the Star, is allowable. As mentioned previously, this topology can result in very high phone bills if carried out on a national scale. To mitigate this, GroupMail technology is sometimes combined with EchoMail technology to produce a network with stars in each region, the stars being connected by a national backbone.

The greatest advantage of GroupMail is that the load scales with the number of conferences, not the number of points. This is a big advantage for systems handling many points.

Control fields

FidoNet EchoMail messages contain several fields used for control purposes. As a user, you do not need to be concerned about these fields. However, as a sysop you will probably need to know about them sooner or later.

The AREA: field

The AREA: field is put on the first line of the message and specifies which conference the message is in. For example, AREA: ECHOMAC would specify a message in the ECHOMAC conference. The AREA: field is used by the message tosser in order to separate incoming EchoMail into the correct message areas.

FidoNet bulletin boards typically keep a list of all the EchoMail conferences in a file called AREAS.BBS or ECHO.CTL. If a tosser finds a message from an area not specified in the AREAS.BBS or ECHO.CTL file, it will toss the message into a default bin, such as the NetMail area, or a directory called BAD_MSGS. EchoMail conference names specified in the AREAS.BBS file should match those in the AREA: field *exactly*; some tossers may even be case-sensitive.

The tear line

A tear line put after the message text consists of three dashes, followed by product-identification information. Example "--- RIMEGATE v0.01". The tear line identifies the product or products that processed the message so as to allow the software to be identified if there is a problem. Tear lines are limited to 35 characters, including the three dashes.

The tear line should always come *before* the Origin line. If you see a message with a tear line *after* the Origin line, this is usually indicative of a problem. Since the presence of an Origin line indicates that the message has already been processed for export, further processing is pointless, and can in some circumstances lead to duplicates.

The Origin Line

This line, which is preceded by a *, comes after the tear line and identifies the system originating the message. An origin line might be:

    * ORIGIN: Fish fiends Hub (1:161/5555)

Some software is sensitive to misbehaving Origin lines. In general, the Origin line should be no longer than 79 characters and should not contain special characters such as a *.

The SEENBY list

The SEENBY list comes after the Origin line and is used to identify those systems to whom the message has already been routed. Nodes in the SEENBY list are sorted in ascending order. For example, a SEENBY list might be:

```
SEEN-BY: 125/222 125/555 161/445 161/555 203/34
```

The SEENBY list is used to prevent the generation of duplicates and may not be stripped by message processors. Before sending an EchoMail message to a system, the SEENBY list will be examined to see if the system has already received the message. If so, then the message is not sent.

However, the SEENBY mechanism is not foolproof. Duplicates can be generated by any looping topology involving more than three systems. To understand why, let's look at two examples.

Topology 1

The topology below, although improper, will not generate duplicates. This is because when node 125/222 receives a message, it will forward it to 125/555 and 161/444, including each node in the SEENBY list. Before node 161/444 attempts to forward the message to 125/555, it will notice that the message has already been sent to 125/555 and will not send it. Therefore a looping topology with only three nodes in the loop will not generate duplicates.

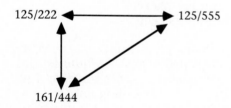

Topology 2

The following topology is improper and will generate duplicates. This is because node 161/444 will not know that node 161/555 is already receiving messages via 125/555; the SEENBYs of the messages it receives only show nodes 125/222 and 125/555 as having received the message. Therefore, any time there is a looping topology where a node is more than one hop away from another node, duplicates will be generated.

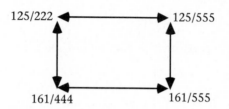

Exercise

Which of these topologies generate duplicates? Why or why not?

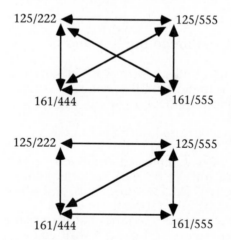

The PATH list

The PATH list was added as an "invisible field" in 1989 for debugging purposes. While the PATH keyword is preceded by a (CTRL) A in order to keep it invisible to users, the information is available to the system operator for diagnostic purposes. Prior to this, to track down a problem, echo moderators often had to request the echo control files of all nodes in a conference. Since many sysops didn't respond to such requests, "dupe loops" were hard to uncover.

The PATH list is needed because while the SEENBY list tells which nodes a message has been sent to, it does not specify which path the message has travelled. For example, in Topology 2, node 1:161/555 would be experiencing duplicate messages. A look at the PATH list for one of the pair in a duplicated message might look like:

PATH: 125/222 161/444 161/555

The other message in the pair would look like:

PATH: 125/222 125/555 161/555

From this pair of PATH lists, we would be able to reconstruct the topology of the network and realize that we need to break one of the links to 161/555.

Under Policy 1, EchoMail stars, Backbone nodes, or EchoMail hubs must implement the PATH list.

Naming of outbound packets and files

In diagnosing problems with FidoNet systems, it is useful to understand the naming conventions for outbound packets and files.

Naming uncompressed outbound packets

The names of uncompressed outbound packets are not standardized, since this information is not transmitted. Thus SEAdog, Opus, and other systems use different formats. The Opus, TBBS/TIMS and BinkleyTerm format is to name uncompressed outbound packets with eight digits, followed by a file extension. The eight digits are the hexidecimal encoding of the destination net/node number. For example, file 01040023.OUT is destined for node 0104/0023 or 260/35. Note that zone numbers are not encoded in the packet name.

The filename extensions on outbound packets denote the schedule for delivering the packet:

.OUT	Normal packet; delivered during mail delivery periods
.HUT	Packet is on Hold for pickup by the destination node
.CUT	Destination system can receive Continuous Mail
.DUT	Destination system cannot receive Continuous Mail

The outbound packets are bundles of outbound FidoNet *.MSG formatted messages.

Naming compressed packets

The naming of compressed packets is standardized, since this information is transmitted to other systems. Usually compression is used in order to minimize packet disk space and transmission time. Since compressed packets must be distinguished from uncompressed ones, they cannot have the same naming scheme. Compressed packets names are given by eight digits and a file extension. Here the eight digits are the difference between the destination net/node address and the source net/node address, in hexadecimal. Therefore, if my node were 1:161/445 and if I were sending mail to node 1:161/444, the packet would be named 00000001.MO1.

The filename extensions on compressed packets usually denote the day on which the packet was created and the packet number, x:

.MOx	Monday packet
.TUx	Tuesday packet
.WEx	Wednesday packet
.THx	Thursday packet
.FRx	Friday packet
.SAx	Saturday packet
.SUx	Sunday packet

Therefore 00000001.MO1 would be the first Monday packet; 00000001.SU7 would be the seventh Sunday packet for that node, and so on. Since there is no scheduling encoded in the compressed packet name, compressed packets are sent via the file attach mechanism discussed later. Be aware that some systems do not use this scheme; early versions of oMMM created only .MOx files. Also, a later version of ARCmail arbitrarily introduced an "enhanced" naming convention, allowing x to be any letter of the alphabet. Most software (other than ARCmail) will choke on such names.

What archiving mechanism is used? All Fido systems must be able to create and expand ARC version 5 archives; however, other formats can be used by arrangement between the sender and the receiver. For example, if node 1:161/445 wants to send .ZIP packets to node 1:161/444 and informs the other node of this, it's OK.

This is made easier by the existence of packer/tossers such as SQUISH (for PC) that can handle multiple formats. On the Macintosh, Zip Extract is a Tabby add-on that can decompress ZIPmail archives.

How are the packets named inside the archive file? If each packet were named with an eight digit destination net/node number and a file extension denoting scheduling, the chances are that the names would overlap.

Instead, the packets are denoted by the extension .PKT and are given an eight digit number to uniquely identify them.

Naming file attach lists

Since the names of File Attach lists are not transmitted to other systems, there is no standard for this. For OPUS and BinkleyTerm, as with outbound packets, lists of outbound files are given by eight digits, followed by a file extension. The eight digits are the hexidecimal encoding of the destination net/node number, as discussed previously.

The filename extensions are different:

.FLO	Normal File Attach
.HLO	Files are on Hold for pickup by the destination node
.CLO	Destination system can receive Continuous Mail
.DLO	Destination system cannot receive Continuous Mail

Note that the File Attach packet does not include the files themselves, but merely a list of files, with full path names. The File Attach list is an ordinary text file with the name of each file given on a separate line. The file paths are preceded by the following characters which specify the processing to occur after the file is successfully sent:

#	Truncate file to zero-length after sending (for compressed files)
^	Delete file after sending

The File Attach mechanism is not just used to send files; it is also used to send compressed packets. For example, if the file 01040023.FLO were a Normal File Attach going to node 260/35 from node 260/34, it might look like this:

```
#C:\OPUS\OUTBOUND\00000001.SU7
^C:\FILE\GRAPHICS\BOZO.GIF
C:\FILE\INFO\INFO.DOC
```

Here the file 00000001.SU7 is an outgoing compressed packet that is to be truncated to zero length after sending; the file BOZO.GIF is a file that is to be deleted after sending; the file INFO.DOC should be sent but left as is.

Naming file request lists

File Request files are given by eight digits, followed by a .REQ extension. The eight digits are the hexidecimal encoding of the destination net/node number, as discussed previously. The file contains a list of those files on the destination system that are to be requested. Ordinarily, a system will honor file requests only when they are receiving a call; you cannot hold a file request file for pickup.

More about the Nodelist

The FidoNet Nodelist is a listing of all publicly accessible FidoNet systems. In order to be on the Nodelist, you must be willing to disclose the phone number of your system to your Network Coordinator.

This does not necessarily mean that your system's number has to be included in the Nodelist; nodes can request to be unlisted. In this case, mail will be routed to the Network Coordinator, who will either deliver mail to the unlisted node (therefore the need for a phone number), or have the unlisted node pick it up.

The FidoNet Nodelist is the most complete and up-to-date bulletin board list in existence. It is remarkable that it has worked as well as it has, since there are now more than 20,000 systems listed, on six continents. As of March 1993, the Nodelist was more than 1.8 Mb in size and was doubling roughly every two years. Since many FidoNet systems operate with hard drives as small as 40 Mb, the size of the Nodelist files is beginning to become a problem. In six years, one can foresee an 8 Mb Nodelist file that could take a long time to process.

Therefore some kind of distributed Nodelist service is probably inevitable. One possibility is to allow each zone to maintain its own Nodelist, with mail for other zones being routed through Zone Gateways, which would be included in all lists. Mail would be picked up from the Zone Gateways by the Regional Coordinators, which would in turn pass it to the Network Coordinators, which would deliver mail or hold it for pickup by the individual nodes. However, for this to work, a billing system would need to be devised to handle cost sharing. The SQUISH mail tosser/packer for the PC includes a billing option that is a step toward such a system.

Getting hold of the Nodelist

Before you can compile the Nodelist, you need to get a copy of it. The Network Coordinators (NCs) are in charge of the distribution of the Nodelist.

Unfortunately, you will usually not be able to obtain the Nodelist just by dialing the number of your local NC. Many of the NC systems are mail-only, which means that they will not allow human callers to log in. If you attempt to access these systems, they will tell you that they are processing mail and that you should call back later.

Of course, if you have a working FidoNet system, you could just file request the NODELIST (usually as NODELIST, NODELIST.ZIP or NODELIST.ARC) from the

NC, and be done with it. But how do you perform a file request without a Nodelist?

The answer is to use point software (such as MacWoof) that does not require a working Nodelist in order to perform a file request or send messages. You can use such software to obtain the Nodelist by file request, or you can request a FidoNet node assignment from the Network Coordinator.

Compiling the Nodelist

Once you've gotten a copy of the Nodelist, you need to uncompress it and compile it. Nodelists are sent under the name NODELIST.Axx, or NODELIST.Zxx, where xx is the last two digits of the day of the year, corresponding to the Friday on which the Nodelist was produced. The A stands for ARC compression, while Z is for ZIP. For example, if the Nodelist were produced on Friday, January 2, and compressed with ARC, it would be named NODELIST.A02. The next week's nodelist would be named NODELIST.A09, and so on.

You will then run an extraction program such as ARCE or PKXARC (for ARC) or PKUNZIP (for ZIP archives) to uncompress the Nodelist. It will then uncompress to NODELIST.xxx, where xxx is the full three-digit date of the year. Therefore NODELIST.Z02 would uncompress to NODELIST.002.

Next you will compile the Nodelist. Compilation produces several files that are used by your BBS software. Since each BBS uses a different set of files in a different format, there is no standard format for the compiled Nodelist files. You will therefore need to obtain a Nodelist compiler that supports your brand of BBS software.

If you are using a PC, I recommend the XLAXNODE or SYSNL compilers. XLAXNODE requires payment of a $25 fee for automatic operation (if you don't pay the fee, you can still run it manually); it is one of the faster compilers and can support the Version 6, Version 7, and SEADog formats. SYSNL doesn't offer as many features as XLAXNODE, but it is very fast, and free.

If you are using XLAXNODE, you will compile the Nodelist using the **XLAXNODE** command. Here is what it looks like:

```
D:\OPUS>XLAXNODE
XlaxNode Version 2.54 Copyright 1991 Scott
Samet (1:135/990)
Scan: XLAXNODE.CTL
Done: XLAXNODE.CTL
Control File scan time: 0.03 min.
Control File Uses OK; 353K Remains for Buffers
and Sort
```

XLAXNODE will find the latest NODELIST (the one with the highest xxx digits) and will compile it, using the commands stored in the file XLAXNODE.CTL. Below is a typical XLAXNODE.CTL file. Here the PUBLIST statement specifies the nodelists to compile; the VERSION7 statement tells XLAXNODE how to do the compilation; the DIAL statement specifies the local area code; the COST statement specifies the amount to deduct for mail to area codes outside the zero specified areas; and the PASSWORD statement passwords connections between with the specified nodes.

```
node 1:161/445
maxbaud 19200
PUBLIST NODELIST NODEDIFF
VERSION7 INTERLIST
ROUTE
fidotxt
noroute
nocomments
addr 1/1  IFNA NEWS
nodelist
DIAL
    1-510-          /
END
COST 2 3
    1-510-849- 0
    849- 0
    1-908-727-7514 0
END
PASSWORD 1:125/1071 <secret>
PASSWORD 1:125/1322 <secret2>
PASSWORD 1:161/400 <secret3>
PASSWORD 1:125/2 <secret4>
```

If you are using a Macintosh, you will need to obtain AutoNodes, which is a complete Nodelist compilation package for Tabby. It works unattended, and can unARC incoming NODEDIFF or NODELIST files, update the Nodelist, and compile the Tabby nodes file.

Compiling the Nodediff

Every week you will receive a difference file, named NODEDIFF.Axx. As before, the xx

stands for the last two digits of the date. When uncompressed, this file will look like NODEDIFF.xxx. The NODEDIFF file is the difference file that needs to be applied to the previous week's NODELIST to bring it up to date.

If you are running on a PC, you will need to run the XLAXDIFF program to update the NODELIST. You will then compile the NODELIST again, using XLAXNODE.

On a Mac, AutoNodes can handle the entire process for you.

Nodelist compilation options

The NODELIST.BBS file that is used by the BBS software contains information that is different for each system, such as a field for the COST of calling a node. Since it would not be practical to create and distribute Nodelist files that were different for every node, customized fields are added to the NODELIST.BBS file by the compilation process, which takes as input a NODELIST.xxx file that is the same for all nodes on the network.

The Nodelist compilation process has other uses as well. Through proper use of Nodelist compilation options, you can secure your system against improper access, change phone numbers of nodes, and handle billing.

Passwording

If you are holding mail for pickup, what is to prevent a hacker from firing up a FidoNet system under your recipient's node number and stealing mail? Similarly, what is to prevent the hacker from sending packets under another system's address? Passwording, that's what.

A single password is used in a session between two nodes, regardless of who is calling whom. Therefore, if I am node 1:161/444 and my password for a session with 1:161/445 is FOOBAR, then I need to insert FOOBAR as the password under node 1:161/445; 1:161/445 also needs to insert FOOBAR as the password entry under node 1:161/444. If these passwords don't match, the session will fail.

Phone numbers

Nodelists are mailed out weekly, but often it may take several weeks for a requested change to appear. What if a system changes phone numbers and the new number has not yet appeared in the Nodelist? You can specify the new phone number through the XLAXNODE.CTL file.

Do NOT attempt to change the phone number within the Nodelist itself. To prevent tampering, the Nodelist file contains a built–in checking mechanism that will detect any modifications and abort the compilation process.

Costing

Through the Nodelist compilation process, you can specify the costs that are billed to users sending NetMail to other nodes. The cost tables can be as extensive as you want. Of course, the BBS software must support these cost tables, debiting users for NetMail usage, and crediting payments.

Zone elimination

For security reasons, you may choose to only compile the portions of the Nodelist that deal with your zone. This will prevent other nodes from routing mail to other continents through your node.

Alternative networks

FidoNet is only one of many networks based on FidoNet technology. Alternative networks each create their own weekly Nodelists, which can be compiled every week along with the FidoNet Nodelist. In order to prevent conflicts among Nodelists, the alternative networks have been assigned their own Zones. For example RBBSNet is Zone 8. These Zones should not conflict with preexisting Zone numbers, although sometimes that happens.

For example, the MacList is a list of Macintosh-oriented BBSes that use Zone 6. While this zone number was available at the time that the MacList was created, it is now taken. Therefore, you will be unable to compile both the MacList and the FidoNet Zone 6

information at the same time. How do you create and maintain your own private Nodelist? NODELIST.BBS files can be created or modified with an ordinary text editor and then sent to all systems on your private network.

Routing

Routing is generally integrated into mail processing software for the sake of efficiency. Routing of EchoMail or NetMail is set up through a routing configuration file. File attaches, file requests, and update requests cannot be routed.

Although BBSes handle routing differently, a good example of the options available in routing is provided by the commands supported by SQUISH, currently one of the most popular FidoNet message processors. SQUISH organizes a set of related routing commands into a group called a "SCHEDULE," which is given a name. All commands within the named SCHEDULE are executed at the same time by executing the command:

```
SQUISH [parameters] -s<schedule name>
```

In SQUISH, the routing commands are specified in the ROUTE.CFG file. Within the route commands, <list> is a list of FidoNet nodes, separated by spaces. An acceptable list is:

```
1:125/555 1:161/444 1:2605/611 2:243/100
```

The keywords ALL, HOSTS, OURNET, and OTHERS may also be used in place of a list. These keywords refer to all nodes in FidoNet, all FidoNet hosts, all nodes in the local network, and all nodes NOT in the local network.

SQUISH Verbs

SCHED `<schedname>` `<list>`
Starts a schedule of routing commands, names it <schedname>; <list> is the list of nodes to which it applies.

ROUTE `<priority><node><list>`
Routes traffic to the <list> via <node>

SEND `<priority><list>`
Specifies which nodes may be called, and what their priorities are

POLL `<priority><list>`
Calls the listed nodes for mail pickup

CHANGE `<old pri><new pri><list>`
Changes the routing for the nodes in <list> from the old priority <old pri> to a new priority <new pri>

Priority designations

HOLD
Hold for pickup

CRASH
Send immediately

Examples

CHANGE HOLD CRASH 1:161/444
Change the HOLD designation to CRASH on packets for node 1:161/444.

ROUTE HOLD 1:2605/611 2:243/100
Route packets for 2:243/100 through node 1:2605/611, but hold the packets for pickup by 1:2605/611.

ROUTE CRASH 1:2605/611 2:243/100
Route packets for 2:243/100 through node 1:2605/611, but send them immediately.

POLL CRASH 1:125/125
Call node 1:125/125, and send all mail to this node immediately.

Example routing schedule:

```
SCHED REST ALL
  SEND HOLD 1:all
  CHANGE HOLD CRASH 1:161/444
  ROUTE HOLD 1:2605/611 2:243/100
  ROUTE HOLD 1:109/70 1:109/421
  ROUTE HOLD 1:125/41 8:914/201

SCHED POLL ALL
  ROUTE CRASH 1:2605/611 2:243/100
  ROUTE CRASH 1:109/70 1:109/421
  CHANGE HOLD CRASH 1:125/125
  POLL CRASH 1:125/125
  CHANGE HOLD CRASH 1:125/555
  POLL CRASH 1:125/555
  CHANGE HOLD CRASH 1:2605/611
  POLL CRASH 1:2605/611
  CHANGE HOLD CRASH 1:161/7
  ROUTE CRASH 1:125/41 8:914/201
  POLL CRASH 1:161/7
```

Exercise

What does the command **ROUTE CRASH 1:125/41 8:914/201** do? Try looking up 1:125/41 in the FidoNet nodelist and 8:914/201 in the RBBSNet nodelist. Why is this statement necessary?

The batch script

The batch script lies at the heart of a FidoNet system. It operates as an event loop, running the BBS software, processing the events that it generates, and looping back. What follows is the outline of a batch script for TBBS. It is kept very simple and easy to follow by the use of the CALL statement introduced in DOS 4.0. This statement calls another batch script as a subroutine; the script executes and then returns. The use of the CALL statement is encouraged, since it encourages modularity.

```
:loop
c:
cd \tbbs
mltbbs /F /U /R /O:TIMS,SYSOM,TDBSOM
if errorlevel 25 goto mail_window
if errorlevel 15 goto hardm
if errorlevel 1 goto remote_host
if errorlevel 0 goto shut
:mail_window
call mw
goto loop
:hardm
call hard
goto loop
:shut
echo I've been asked to shut down.
goto exit
:remote_host
mlhostecho Hang-up to restart TBBS
:exit
```

Here the errorlevels were generated by TBBS, and with the exception of built-in errorlevels such as 0 and 1, they can be preprogrammed by the sysop.

Errorlevel 25 is the mail event, which was programmed to occur at 2:30 PM and 5:30 AM every day. When this event occurs, the batch file MW.BAT is called. MW.BAT processes inbound and outbound mail and imports any received files into the file directory.

Errorlevel 15 is the hard disk maintenance event, which is scheduled to occur on Sundays at 7:30 AM. As can be seen in the batch script, the subroutine HARD.BAT is called in response to this event. Errorlevel 1 corresponds to a remote shutdown command executed by a sysop in the sysop menu; the response to this event is to run the TBBS remote host program, called mlhost. When the sysop logs off, mlhost automatically reboots the system, which reruns the batch script. Errorlevel 0 is a requested shutdown and is the only event that can exit the batch script. All other events are processed and then loop back to run TBBS.

Polytickle nonsense

Policy 1

Policy 1 (more formally known as General EchoMail Policy 1.0), proposed on October 2, 1990, describes the distribution policy for FidoNet EchoMail within Zone 1 (North America). Policy 1 defines the duties of the EchoMail coordinators, EchoMail moderators, Regional Coordinators, and other FidoNet honchos. It also describes EchoMail technical requirements, moderator election and removal policy, and lots of other useful stuff. Very few people seem to have read Policy 1, so misinformation is rampant (such as the claim that there is no way to dismiss an EchoMail moderator; in fact, this is clearly spelled out in Policy 1). Policy 1 should be required reading for every FidoNet sysop.

Policy 4

FidoNet was designed so that it could not easily be controlled by a central authority, and the network itself has always had a strong anarchist contingent. On the other hand, the network does have some structure to it, and it is useful to have a document to describe that structure.

Policy 4 (more formally known as Draft FidoNet Policy Document version 4.06) was an attempt to document, and to some extent create, a structure to govern FidoNet. It was released on May 5, 1989, and promptly ignited a firestorm of criticism.

Policy 4 created a top-down governing structure for FidoNet, with network, regional, zone, and international coordinators. The International Coordinator was given the power to replace the Zone Coordinators, who could appoint the Regional Coordinators, who could appoint the Network Coordinators. At the same time the International Coordinator was to be selected by the Zone Coordinators, who in turn were to be selected by the Regional Coordinators. The process by which these elections and appointments were to take place was never specified.

Some worried that this structure was inherently undemocratic; some worried that it was too vague to define who was in charge of whom and could lead to endless infighting; some thought that the whole idea of a policy document for an anarchic network was a mistake. The argument over Policy 4 gave birth to EGGNet, a network based on FidoNet technology but that is governed democratically. Policy 4 was never ratified and remains a draft to this day. It is available from FidoNews BBS, 1:1/1, (415)863-2739 as POLICY4.ARC.

Creating an echo

There is no procedure for creating a nonbackbone echo. All you need is one other sysop to agree to carry the echo, and you're in business. However, it probably is a good idea to find out if there's already a conference on that topic. The next step might be to put an article in FidoNews, asking if anyone else is interested in your proposed conference. Sysops interested in receiving it will then write you back, and you can add them to your list.

Backbone echoes

A conference may be added to or deleted from the backbone only by request of the recognized conference moderator. A conference must be listed with the Echolist coordinator before it can be carried on the backbone. To be carried on the backbone, a conference should first demonstrate that it can sustain traffic of at least 30 to 50 messages per week. It is also recommended, although not required, that the conference first be transmitted off the backbone for a period of at least six months. While backbone distribution makes a conference more available, it does not necessarily make it any better; you need to establish a track history of providing useful information before requesting allocation of backbone resources.

EchoMail fees

Under Policy 1, system operators may not profit from the distribution of EchoMail. However, they may recover their costs.

Censorship

Under Policy 1 system operators may not censor messages passing through their nodes.

Moderator duties

The duties of a conference moderator are to post the conference rules at least once a month; to keep the conference on topic and watch out for illegal activities; to maintain the Echolist listing.

Moderator elections

In FidoNet, electing a moderator is like getting married in a country where divorce is very difficult. There is a means for electing a moderator, but under Policy 1, the only way to get rid of a moderator is by a 75 percent vote of Network and Zone Echo Coordinators. This procedure is so arduous that in practice moderators can serve as long as they like and elections are called only when they resign.

To fill an open moderator slot, someone who isn't running volunteers to coordinate the election. Then a deadline period passes during which candidates submit their names. Sometimes the candidates submit statements along with their nominations, and these are gathered and transmitted over the network. A deadline for voting is then set, and sysops are allowed to cast ballots by NetMail to the

election commissioner, who counts the votes and announces the winner after the deadline has passed.

Instead of getting rid of a moderator, the practice on the EchoMac network is to create another conference on the same topic, but with a different name. Nodes on the old conference are then canvassed and asked to switch over to the new conferences. If the moderator is sufficiently disliked, then most of the nodes switch over and the moderator is left alone, raging to an audience of one.

Killing an echo

Although a dying conference will be removed from the backbone when its traffic falls below a certain threshold, there is no procedure for killing outright. It may therefore limp along with only an occasional message, leaving connected sysops to wonder whether it is really dead or whether something is wrong with their setup.

FidoNet Domains

A router (sometimes also called a gateway) is a piece of software that connects two networks, allowing messages to pass between them. FidoNet technology supports routing of messages between the half a dozen networks now based on the FidoNet protocols. These networks include RBBSNet, AlterNet, EggNet, MacList, and FidoNet. Multiple networks have the potential to create problems since if these networks were to assign conflicting node numbers, it would become impossible for one system to compile all of the node lists, preventing the networks from communicating with each other. In order to prevent this, the networks are allocated zone numbers, and given authority to allocate network and node numbers within those zones. For example, Zone 8 is RBBSNet.

Systems serving as routers between the networks compile nodelists from multiple networks, and since the zone allocations prevent node number conflicts, they are able to route traffic between networks.

A somewhat simpler system is now under consideration. This involves adding a domain component to the FidoNet address. The new address format would be:

```
<zone>:<network>/<node>.<point>@<domain>
```

For example, under this system a node address would be `1:161/445.2@FIDONET`.

Note that although FidoNet domain support has been available for several years, it has never been widely adopted. FidoNet domains are generally used to operate in multiple FidoNet networks and maintain separate nodelist files for the mailer. Despite the common use of the word "domain," FidoNet domains have no relationship to the Internet's Domain Name Service, and FidoNet domain addresses are not fully qualified domain names.

Gateways

Beginning in the late 1980s, gateways began to be developed between the major computer networks.

With the implementation of Domain Name Service (DNS, described in RFC 1035), it became possible for non-Internet networks to have domain names, through the use of Mail eXchange (MX) records. This has lead to the creation of domains for store and forward networks such as FidoNet (fidonet.org) and FrEdMail (fred.org).

Gateways versus multihomed hosts

Since the FidoNet architecture is so open, it is relatively easy to connect FidoNet systems to other networks. For example, software exists to allow FidoNet systems to communicate with UUCP systems, QNet networks, and RIME.

Is every system that is connected to two or more networks a gateway? The answer is no. Gateways offer *both* the ability to speak two protocols, *as well as the ability to route packets between networks*. A true gateway does not just link a single node to another node. It links two or more networks. A node that can speak two protocols but cannot route is called a "multihomed host."

More and more vendors are advertising their products as gateways without implementing gateway functionality. Remember, if you can only reach a single node on the other network, it's not a gateway, it's just a multihomed host.

UFGATE, the FidoNet/UUCP software, is a true gateway, allowing any node on FidoNet to reach any node on UUCP, and vice versa. In 1986, Tim Pozar, Gary Paxinos, and John Galvin began work on UFGATE, which translated both electronic mail and distributed conferences between the FidoNet and UUCP or USENET. With the release of UFGATE in 1988, it became possible for FidoNet nodes all over the world to communicate with USENET, UUCP, and Internet systems. For more information on UFGATE, see Chapter 35: The Story of the UFGATE.

The FrEdMail/Internet link is another true gateway. In 1990 FrEdMail became connected to Internet via the gateway node known as SDCOE. The development of the FrEdMail/Internet link was funded by the National Science Foundation, and as a result, FrEdMail was authorized to use the NSFNet as its backbone to route packets nationwide. As with FidoNet, FrEdMail was assigned a domain (fred.org) within the Domain Name System (DNS), and Domain Name Servers were set up to route mail from Internet to FrEdMail.

Although individual RIME nodes connect to UUCP, there is no gateway between RIME and UUCP, and as a result RIME has not been assigned a domain.

With the release of Universal Text Interface (UTI) software for PCRelay and PostLink, it is possible for these packages to translate to and from the FidoNet *.MSG format. This allows FidoNet and PCRelay or PostLink systems to exchange messages. However, additional software would be needed to allow general routing of messages between the networks, so the UTI only provides multihomed host, rather than gateway, capability.

Homebrew multihomed hosts

How would we transmit messages between FidoNet and a QNet network, for example? To build a functioning multihomed host, we need to find software to fulfill every function, *but we do not need to change every function in order to transfer messages between two disparate networks.* In the figure Elements of a Gateway, only the functions in bold need to be replaced in order to link two networks.

Outgoing mail

To send outgoing mail, the Outgoing Translator, which translates between the internal message format and the external format, needs to be modified to produce messages acceptable for export to the new network. Similarly, a new packer must be used to pack up those messages into a format for export. Since different networks often use different compression schemes (USENET uses compress, while FidoNet uses ARC), a different compressor is often required. Since the networks operate using different protocols, the mailer must be replaced. However, once the message is transmitted to the other system, it will be received within that system's native format so that the receiving system can process it normally.

Incoming mail

For incoming mail, the system must be modified to decompress packets packed in the alien format, unpack the messages, kill any duplicates, translate the messages to the native BBS format, and put them into the right message sections.

Cheating

Some of these steps can be dispensed with in a "quick and dirty" implementation. For example, you can dispense with compression and perhaps even packing. This will increase transmission times, sometimes dramatically, but the downside is that this technique can be used in a "quick hack." Similarly, the dupe-killing step can be dispensed with if your standards for topology are rigid enough. If you translate formats before tossing, you may be able to invoke an existing tosser, which saves you from writing one yourself. This leaves us with outgoing and incoming translators.

Example 1

In the case of linking between QWK and FidoNet systems, a translator exists on the PC to translate FidoNet *.PKT files into QWK packets and back. The software is available from:

Geoffrey Sy, 51 Wyatt Walk, Toronto, Ontario, CA, M5A 3T3; BBS: (416)287-9002 (HST), (416)286-8734 (HST/2400).

The program includes two programs: MSG2REP, which packs *.MSG files into a QWK REP packet, and QWK2MSG, which takes messages from the QWK REP format and imports them into the FidoNet system.

Example 2

Through use of the FidoNet/UUCP gateway software such as PCBUUCP, PIMP, UFGATE or Fredgate, PostLink (RIME), and a FidoNet implementation such as OPUS or BinkleyTerm, a mail hub can exchange mail between networks such as FidoNet, RIME, and UUCP.

A diagram of the relationship between the networks, a mail hub and the main BBS system is given below. Here the hub passes messages between a PostLink network such as RIME and FidoNet, and between FidoNet and UUCP. Note that in the figure the hub does not gateway between RIME and UUCP, and that the BBS implements the FidoNet and UUCP protocols.

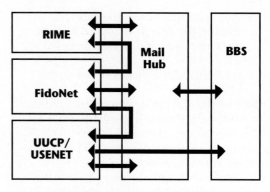

How a gateway works (contributed by William Sommers)

Elements of a Gateway

Elements left alone	Elements replaced for outgoing mail	Elements replaced for incoming mail
Scheduler Message Editor Scanner		
	Outgoing translator **Packer** **Compressor** **Mailer**	
		Decompressor **Unpacker** **Dupe killer** **Incoming translator**
Tosser Message Maintenance		

FidoNet Q&A

How do I get information on FidoNet?

Information on FidoNet is accessible via Internet in several forms. zeus.ieee.org maintains an archive of FidoNet-related material available for anonymous `ftp`. Included in this archive are files from the FidoNet Software Distribution System, in directory /pub/fidonet/sds. FidoNet/UUCP gateway files are available in directory /pub/fidonet/ufgate. Issues of Fidonews are available in /pub/fidonet/fidonews.

Tim Pozar has recently made the FidoNet nodelist available for search using Z39.50 or Gopher. The source file is fidonet-nodelist.src.

How do I get help with a FidoNet product?

In addition to the national echo coordinator, there are nodes that have agreed to serve as national help centers for various BBS products, such as Remote Access, OPUS, Fido, TBBS, and so on. These nodes are purely volunteers and are generally not paid by the developers. Although Macintosh products such as Copernicus or Tabby do not have national help node entries in the Nodelist, they do have support echoes.

How can I get a Nodelist entry?

In order to join FidoNet, you must first demonstrate that your system is working by sending NetMail to the local network coordinator requesting a node assignment. Usually, your geographical location will determine which network you are in; you are left to select an unused node number within that network. Check the Nodelist and find a number that has not been assigned. Suggest this to your network coordinator; he or she will most likely OK it. Once you get the approval, you're off to the races. For more information on getting a Nodelist entry, File Request POLICY4.ARC from one of the Regional Echo Coordinators.

How can I get a copy of the Nodelist?

Your local network coordinator probably keeps this available for File Request under the Magic Name NODELIST, NODELIST.ZIP, or NODELIST.ARC. If not, send him or her a message asking how to get it. If you're really desperate, you can File Request the Nodelist from one of the FileBone sites listed in Appendix I, FidoNet Organization and Help Nodes.

How can I get a copy of the FidoNet Technical Standards?

To get the latest versions of the FidoNet Technical Standards, call the FidoNet Technical Standards BBS, which is listed in the weekly FidoNet Nodelist. The phone numbers of this system as well as the other FidoNet help nodes are given in Appendix I, FidoNet Organization and Help Nodes.

To whom do I send my UUCP map entry if I'm setting up a FidoNet/UUCP gateway?

Mail the UUCP map entry to `hostmaster@fidonet.fidonet.org`.

I advertised my car for sale in EchoMac. Someone said I was being "excessively annoying." What did he mean?

The original golden rule of FidoNet was:

Thou shalt not annoy and though shalt not be easily annoyed.

"Excessively annoying" is a FidoNet term that means annoyance beyond the level that a tolerant person would accept. You were posting a message that was "off topic," that is, it was unrelated to the Macintosh within the EchoMac conference. Not only that, but you were trying to carry out a commercial transaction in a conference that does not allow that.

How can I get a copy of OPUS?

OPUS is a FidoNet-compatible bulletin board package that runs on IBM compatibles. There is no version of OPUS for the Macintosh. The best way to get a copy of OPUS (or other PD or shareware FidoNet BBSes such as Maximus or Remote Access) is to call one of the nodes on the Filebone. If the software isn't available for downloading, send mail to the FidoNet help node for the software you're looking for, asking how you can obtain it.

Most PC based bulletin boards and FidoNet utilities are too complicated to set up without help from other sysops. These include BBS packages such as OPUS, Maximus, TBBS, and Remote Access, or FidoNet mailers such as

BinkleyTerm and Front Door. A possible exception is Fido, which is much simpler than most, with a single 150K .EXE file performing all functions. Install is via text files, with Fido creating directories and doing other setup aspects for you.

Echoes and Feeds Q&A

How do I find out what echoes are available on FidoNet?

The national echo coordinator of FidoNet maintains a list called the Echolist, which contains all conferences distributed over the FidoNet backbone. This list can be gotten by File Requesting ELIST from the National Echo Coordinator or individual Network Echo Coordinators. It is also on reserve at several EchoMac systems on a regular basis. For a list of nonbackbone Macintosh conferences, request MACECHOS.ARC from Ralph Merritt at 1:2605/611.

How do I get a feed for an echo?

When PC Pursuit changed their pricing structure in 1989, the FidoNet backbone had to revert to using traditional long-distance carriers along with high-speed USR modems. The result was that a new method for paying for EchoMail distribution had to be developed. Typically, each node pays an EchoMail fee to their network coordinator, who pays money to the regional echo coordinator, who gets a huge phone bill and writes checks to AT&T, US Sprint, MCI, and so on.

In order to get a feed for a backbone echo, you must contact your network echo coordinator. The network echo coordinators are listed in the weekly Nodelist, as is the national echo coordinator.

How can I get a copy of the FidoNews if I'm not a sysop?

FidoNews is now accessible in the `comp.org.fidonet` conference on USENET. The Internet address of the FidoNews editors is `fidonews@fidonews.fidonet.org`.

How do I set up BinkleyTerm?

Information on BinkleyTerm setup is available in this chapter under Point Software.

I want to run FidoNet on the Macintosh, but I hear that Tabby was discontinued in November, 1993. What do I do?

Tabby was the only complete FidoNet implementation for the Macintosh prior to being discontinued. This meant that to run FidoNet you had to purchase Tabby, even if you replaced portions of Tabby (such as the mailer) with alternatives such as Formula 1.

This is no longer case, with the release of Aeolus from Delphic Software. Aeolus is a Tabby-compliant FidoNet mailer tosser/scanner for the Macintosh that requires Formula 1 and ZipExtract. Extended features include:

- Up to 999 areas, with 999 nodes each 999 Entries in the routing table
- 999 Outgoing nodes per event
- 999 events
- Built in echo management via AreaMan SmartPack for reduction in message disk space Support for points

For information, contact Mike Marshburn, Delphic Software, PUMA BBS, 1:207/204.

What is MacKennel?

MacKennel is a new FidoNet mailer for the Macintosh from Craig Vaughan, author of MacWoof. It works with a variety of BBS software products, including NovaLink Professional. It comes in three versions.

Version 1, which costs $75, offers:
- Manual or automatic session operation
- Seamless integration with NovaLink Pro and other BBSes
- Unlimited echo support
- ARC and ZIP mail packet processing
- Support for 4D and pointnet style addressing
- WAZOO and FTS-0001 sessions

Version 2, which goes for $150, adds:
- Frontend operation on BBSes that accept ADSP/PPC logins.
- Stand alone operation

- Scheduling
- Distribution of echoes to a single node
- NetMail routing

Version 3, which goes for $250, adds:
- An integrated nodelist processor
- Zone support siwth direct and host routing
- Point support

MacKennel requires the Communications Toolbox, System 6.0.5 or greater, and a minimum of 2 Mb RAM.

MacKennel is available from ResNova Software; 16458 Bolsa Chica St., Unit 193, Hungtington Beach, CA 92649; (714)379-9000.

For more information

Nodelist

The FidoNet Nodelist is available for download from one of the FileBone nodes, listed in Appendix I: FidoNet Organization and Help Nodes. Note: the Nodelist is large (at last count, over 20,000 systems were listed in the Nodelist), and will take a long time to print. Try browsing it on screen instead.

Echo List

Available as FILEBONE.NA from the echo list coordinator (given in the Nodelist). FidoNet Node 1:1/201, EchoList Coordinator, Toms River, NJ; (908)506-0472

FileBone List

Available as FILEBONE.NA from the FileBone Coordinator, FidoNet Node 1:396/1, New Orleans, LA (504)889-2019

FidoNet software archives

FidoNet BBS utilities are available via `ftp` `oak.oakland.edu, cd /pub/msdos/fido`.

FOSSIL drivers are available via `ftp` `oak.oakland.edu, cd /pub/msdos/fossil`.

FidoNet Technical Standards

FidoNet technical standards documents are available from the FidoNet Technical Standards BBS, given in the Nodelist:

Document	Description	Author
FTS-LIST	Description of FTSC standards	
FTSCLIST	List of all FTSC documents	
FTSCPROD	List of FTSC product codes	
FTS-0001	Basic FidoNet Technical Standard	R Bush
FTS-0001	A basic FidoNet technical standard	R Bush
FTS-0007	SEAlink protocol extension	P Becker
FTS-0008	Bark file request protocol extension	
FSC-0007	RFC-822–style packet proposal	R Heller
FSC-0022	Application for FTSC product code	
FSC-0034	Gateways to and from FidoNet	R Bush
FSC-0038	Proposed domain gating protocol	J Nutt
FSC-0039	A type-2 packet-extension proposal	M Howard
FSC-0040	Proposed modem-handling extension	M Shiels
FSC-0041	MSGID / REPLY: A proposal (v002)	J Nutt
FSC-0042	A modified gateway agreement	S Furber
FSC-0043	Some hints on recognizing control lines in FidoNet message text	R Bush
FSC-0044	Improved duplicate detection	J Decker
FSC-0045	Proposed new packet header	T Henderson
FSC-0049	Passing domain names in FTS-0006 sessions	B Hartman
FSC-0050	Character set identifier for message editors	T Sundblom
FSC-0051	A system-independent way of transferring special characters	T Gradin
FSC-0052	A proposal for making the PATH zone aware	G van der Land
FSC-0053	Specifications for the ^aFLAGS field	J Homrighausen

FidoNet Node 1:1/20, FidoNet Technical Standards BBS; (604)589-8561; Internet: Available by anonymous `ftp zeus.ieee.org` [140.98.1.1], `cd pub/fidonet/ftsc`.

Introduction to EchoMac

What is this EchoMac thing anyway? anyway? *anyway? anyway?*

In current usage, the term "EchoMac" refers both to a series of conferences and services provided by FidoNet-compatible computers and also to an individual conference carried on the FidoNet backbone. In order not to cause confusion, I will use the term "EchoMac Network" when referring to the former, and "ECHOMAC" when talking about the latter.

While all of the computers on the EchoMac Network are FidoNet-compatible, not all the computers are part of the FidoNet network or Macintoshes. Many of the nodes on the EchoMac Network are part of alternative networks, such as Alternet or RBBSNet, and quite a few of the systems run on PC compatibles.

EchoMac Network services include EchoMail conferences on various Macintosh topics; a distribution system for newly released publicly distributable Macintosh software, called the Macintosh Software Distribution Network (MSDN); a list of Macintosh-related conferences (MacBone); and a list of Macintosh-oriented bulletin boards, called the MacList.

Among the conferences carried on the EchoMac Network are ECHOMAC, the general Macintosh conference; TABBY, the conference for users of the Tabby FidoNet mailer for the Macintosh; FIRSTCLASS, a conference for FirstClass sysops; MACCOMM, the conference on communications; MACHELP, the conference for questions and answers; and MAC4SALE, a conference for buyers and sellers of Macintosh hardware and software. For user group members, there is MUGADMIN, which discusses various aspects

of running a Macintosh User Group. The EchoMac Network also offers support conferences for users of point software such as Copernicus, COUNTERPoint, and MacWoof, and bulletin board software such as Mansion, Hermes, FirstClass, NovaLink Pro, Second Sight, and WWIV. A full list of conferences is provided at the end of this section.

How to access EchoMac Network services

Many of the services on the EchoMac Network can be accessed by simply logging on to an EchoMac Network BBS near you. A list of sites is included in Appendix H: Network BBSes.

By logging on to an EchoMac Network BBS, you will be able to read messages in the EchoMac Network conferences, although every BBS will not carry all of them. You will also be able to download files, some of which may be distributed as part of the Macintosh Software Distribution System (MSDN), which is now transported over the FileBone.

The FidoNet Nodelist is available for downloading from many of the FileBone nodes. An alternative to the Nodelist is the FidoNet Regional Coordinators. For a listing of FileBone nodes, as well as the FidoNet Regional Coordinators and Help Nodes, please consult Appendix I: FidoNet Organization and Help Nodes.

Macintosh conferences on FidoNet

Nonbackbone conferences

Conference	Subject
ALTERMAC	Alternet General Mac-Oriented Conference
AMUG	Arizona Mac User Group Conference
AMUGNEWS	AMUG Applelink/Product Announcements
BAYMAC	Bay Area Macintosh Conference
BAYNETADMIN	Network Administrators' Conference
BBB	Support for Bulletin Boards and Beyond
CPOINT	COUNTERPoint Support Echo
FIRSTCLASS	Support for the FirstClass BBS software
MAC_ADS	Macintosh Advertisements/For Sale
MAC_HELP	Macintosh Help for Beginners
MACDTP	Macintosh Desktop Publishing
MACFILES	Macintosh Files available for FREQ (sysop access only)
MACFREQS	Macintosh Files available for FREQ
MACLIST	MACLIST Nodelist Updates/Administration
MACNOV	Macintosh Novice Programming
MACPB	Macintosh PowerBook Conference
MACPOINT	Macintosh Point Software
MACQA	Macintosh Questions and Answers
MACSYS7	System 7 Echo
MACUK	Macintosh United Kingdom - U.S. Conference
MACVIRUS	Macintosh Virus Prevention
METROMAC	NY/NJ Metropolitan Macintosh Conference
MSDNSYSOP	Macintosh Software Distribution Network Conference
MUGADMIN	Macintosh User Group Administration
NJMUG	New Jersey Macintosh User's Group Echo
NOVALINK	NovaLink Pro Support Conference
PCMAC	PC/Macintosh conversion and transfer issues
PUBADD	Public Address
PUBADDTEST	Public Address Beta Testers
RRH	Second Sight BBS Support
SIMCITY	Discussions of the SimCity Game
TABBY	Tabby (Macintosh mailer) Support
TBBSMAC	Macintosh sysops running TBBS
WIRETAP_SUP	Wiretap Telecom Program Support
WWIVMAC	World War IV BBS Support

Backbone conferences

ECHOMAC	National General Macintosh Conference
HERMES_SYSOPS	Hermes Sysop Conference
MAC_GAMES	Macintosh Games and Entertainment
MAC_TELEFINDER	TeleFinder Conference
MAC4SALE	Macintosh Hardware and Software For Sale
MACCOMM	Macintosh Communications
MACDEV	Macintosh Developers
MACFSALE	Macintosh For Sale Echo
MACHW	Macintosh Hardware
MACHYPE	Macintosh HyperCard-Related Topics
MACSYSOP	Macintosh Sysop-Only Conference
MACSW	Macintosh Software
MACWOOF	MacWoof Point Mailer
MANSION	Mansion BBS Support
SYSTEM7	System 7.0 Conference

File services

MSDN

The Macintosh Software Distribution Network (MSDN) is one of the file conferences carried over the FileBone. File areas include programming, telecommunications, demos, and several others. MSDN distributes shareware files of interest to Macintosh sysops and users, making them available for File Request to any and all comers. Several message areas are also part of MSDN.

The MSDN is divided into files areas. These include:

MSDNSYSOP   **MSDN Sysops**
The sysop-only conference on the Macintosh Software Distribution Network (MSDN), as well as the support echo for MacTick.

MSDNADMIN   **MSDN Coordinators**
The administrative conference for MSDN coordinators. This conference is mandatory for those people and closed to everyone else.

MDNADMIN   **Administration and information**
This is for distribution of MSDN policy documents, application forms, and other administrivia.

MDNDEMO   **Demonstration software**
A home for "crippleware."

MDNGAMER   **Games**
For games, educational or otherwise.

MDNEDUC   **Educational**
For educational software.

MDNINFO   **General information**
Information on computer and communications subjects.

MDNOTHER   **Other files**
For software that doesn't fit in one of the other categories.

MDNPCMAC   **Macintosh related PC files**
These are files that are for the PC, but they are Mac related. Examples are PC programs that decompress Macintosh formats like Compactor; software to convert Mac formats to PC formats, and so on.

MDNPROG   **Macintosh programming**
Source code and programmer utilities.

MDNTELE   **Telecommunications**
Telecommunications software.

MDNUTIL   **Utility programs**
Utilities, such as disk or conversion utilities or Finder enhancements.

Author submissions

Authors wishing to have their software distributed over MSDN should fill out an author registration form and mail it with their software to the appropriate MSDN area administrator (called a "hatcher"). Files can be sent on a disk (uncompressed and 800K floppies) or via FidoNet mail. As part of the form, the author includes a password that will then be required for future updates, which should be sent to the same hatcher as the original submission. Since only a single hatcher and the author will have the password, this ensures against "hacked" versions masquerading as updates. A list of hatchers is available from Duncan McNutt, 2:243/100.

For more information on MSDN

Duncan McNutt, Am Bier 9, D-6000 Frankfurt 50, Germany; BBS: 049-6101-41471, email: 2:243/100.

Nonpublic areas

The MacList pseudonodelist is distributed through this area. If you want a copy of the MacList, you can File Request (FREQ) it from 1:2605/611, among other nodes.

FileBone

The FileBone is the equivalent of the FidoNet backbone for files, a network of computers with large hard disks that store many hundreds of megabytes of files on several topics. These include the PDN, or Programmer's Distribution Network (files for programmers); Winnet, the network of Windows files; and the MSDN.

MACFREQS

Point software also comes in handy in making use of the MACFREQS conference. MACFREQS is not part of the MSDN; it is a conventional EchoMail conference listing newly uploaded files from BBSes around the nation. Using point software such as COUNTERPoint, you can request the desired files from the posting nodes.

A typical message on MACFREQS looks like this:

```
From: Maria Langer
To: All Mac Sysops Msg #66, 13-Mar-91 05:08am
Subject: New files on the Electronic Pen

-=-=-=-=-=-=-=-=-=-=-=-=-=-=-=-=-=-=-=-=-=-=-=-=-
 New files available for File Request from
 The Electronic Pen BBS - (2605/157)
 Bps rates supported: 300/1200/2400/9600 - Sysop: Maria
Langer
-=-=-=-=-=-=-=-=-=-=-=-=-=-=-=-=-=-=-=-=-=-=-=-=-

 FREQ name: ApplesToOranges.cpt Size: 12K
 ApplesToOranges is a Desk Accessory that converts the
 units of a number from one type to another, such as
 inches to centimeters or gallons to liters.

 FREQ name: Can't Touch This.cpt Size: 13K
 Sound of MC Hammer saying "Can't touch this!"

 FREQ name: Swatch 1.1.cpt Size: 18K
 Swatch v1.1 shows the heap of all running applications.
 Colors distinguish relocatable, non-relocatable, and free
 memory (patterns for B&W). Magnifying glass allows
 blowing up a heap image. Swatch helps you track
 down heap problems. By Joe Holt. Freeware.

 FREQ name: Tax Forms.cpt Size: 17K
 Excel Tax Forms v1.0. Federal Income Tax forms 1040 &
 Schedule A; Excel spreadsheets for calculating both
 standard & itemized deductions and calculating the tax
 due for any filing status & income level. Created with
 Excel 1.5 by Donald P. Levine (should run with any
 version of Excel). Docs included. Freeware.

-=-=-=-=-=-=-=-=-=-=-=-=-=-=-=-=-=-=-=-=-=-=-=-=-
 File Requests are honored 24 hours a day except during
 ZMH. For a full list of available files, FREQ "FILES.CPT"
 or "FILES.TXT". For uploads within the past 30 Days, FREQ
 "NEWFILES.TXT".
-=-=-=-=-=-=-=-=-=-=-=-=-=-=-=-=-=-=-=-=-=-=-=-=-
-- informant 1.00
--- Tabby 2.2
 * Origin: The Electronic Pen 201-767-6337 (50:5201/316)
(1:2605/157)
```

If you are using point software it is possible for you to respond to this message by File Requesting one of the files listed from the posting node. Of course, you will need to do this during the times specified in the message. In this particular case, the system supports 9600 bps access, so a File Request could be done at high speed.

COUNTERPoint, Copernicus II, or MacWoof support File Requests from BBSes other than the Boss.

However, be aware that large unapproved File Requests will probably result in the sysop imposing File Request limitations or even disabling File Request capability. When in doubt, ask permission first.

Magic Names

Magic Names are names you can use to request certain files on a FidoNet-compatible bulletin board using your point software. The files aren't actually stored under these names, but when you ask for them, the BBS is smart enough to know what you're talking about. Some or all of these names may require passwords for access.

Standard magic names are names that most systems should respond to. Network coordinator standard names are the magic names that network coordinator nodes should respond to. Mac standard names are names that all regional MSDN hubs should respond to. Nonstandard names are names that a given system may or may not respond to. Here is a list of Magic Names and what requesting them will provide:

Standard names

ABOUT
Information about the system you're calling.

FILES
A listing of all files available on that system.

NEWFILES
A listing of all newly uploaded files.

Network coordinator standard names

NODEDIFF
The difference file that updates the previous week's Nodelist to this week's.

NODELIST
The complete FidoNet nodelist, updated weekly and usually compressed with ARC.

Mac standard names

MACLIST
A listing of Macintosh-oriented BBSes on the FidoNet, updated weekly. Very useful.

Nonstandard names

ARCHFILES
A list of Pete Johnson's shareware utilities for Red Ryder Host.

ELIST.NAM
A listing of all the conferences on the FidoNet backbone.

ELIST.CPT
A listing of all the conferences on the FidoNet backbone, compressed with Compact Pro.

INFORMANT.SIT
Shareware EchoMail message posting utility.

TIDE.SIT
Free RRHost file area editor.

Nodes and the Magic Names they support

Almost any FidoNet node (see the Nodelist for phone numbers)

FILES, ABOUT

Tiger's Den, Phoenix, AZ 1:114/27, 6:6008/1, (602)992-9879 (HST, V.42bis)

FILES, NEWFILES, Nodelist, NODEDIFF, MACLIST, ELIST.NAM, ELIST.CPT

EchoMac Q&A

What will participating in the EchoMac Network cost me?

To participate in the EchoMac Network, you will need to find a local BBS near you that carries the conferences and you will need to pay the membership fee, if any, which usually runs between $25 and $60/year. If you want to be a point node (highly recommended), you can use EZPoint, MacWoof, Copernicus II, COUNTERPoint, and in a future version, Alice. This will set you back another $60. Not counting phone bills, the startup cost of getting on to the EchoMac Network should be under $200.

What can I do with it?

Using the EchoMac Network, you can download the latest Macintosh shareware, solve problems you have with your Macintosh, or talk to other Mac users about developments affecting them; in general, anything a user group can do can probably be done over the EchoMac Network.

What BBS software is available for the Macintosh? Does it work with FidoNet?

If price is your primary consideration, Hermes or Second Sight should be your choice. If you'd like your callers to be able to utilize a front end with a Mac interface, then you should consider TeleFinder, NovaLink Pro, or FirstClass. Hermes, Second Sight, FirstClass, NovaLink Pro, and TeleFinder are Tabby compatible. This allows them to use Tabby (discontinued in November, 1993) as well as other Tabby-compatible mailers such as F1. If your BBS runs a FidoNet compatible mailer, you can communicate all over the world, and receive conferences on almost any imaginable topic.

When released, Public Address will reportedly have its own built-in FidoNet mailer. Information on where to purchase FidoNet mailers is available in Appendix B: Choice Products.

How do I find the EchoMac BBS nearest to me?

The MacList is a good source for this information. Unfortunately, not all Macintosh-oriented BBSes have registered in MacList. A comprehensive list of Macintosh BBSes connected to the EchoMac Network is given in Appendix H.

Where should I post a message about my great new BBS?

Messages about new BBSes are allowed in the MACSYSOP conference. MACSYSOP, as well as almost all the other nonbackbone conferences, are carried by node 1:2605/611 ("The Right Choice BBS") in New Jersey.

File distribution Q&A

How do I download the files in the MACFREQS area of the BBS?

Copernicus or MacWoof allow you to call only the Boss node. Therefore, you will not be able to do a File Request to systems posting new file listings in the MACFREQS conference without changing the settings for your Boss. However, Mike Lininger's COUNTERPoint lets you get around this. To get phone numbers of systems posting in MACFREQS, you can either check their *tag lines* (the last few lines stuck on the end of their messages) or look them up in the weekly MacList. A copy of a recent MacList is included on BMUG Disk Telecom A1. Using these phone numbers, you can either File Request the files using COUNTERPoint or call up the BBSes and download directly, if they will allow you to do this as a nonmember.

Detailed conference descriptions

ALTERMAC
General Macintosh conference on Alternet

ALTERMAC is the general Macintosh conference carried by the Alternet network. Alternet is an offshoot of FidoNet that claims to enforce stricter etiquette rules than its older and larger cousin. Perhaps the stricter etiquette rules scared away most ECHOMACers, who are a loud and raucous bunch, because this conference hardly has any traffic.

AMUG and AMUGNEWS
The Arizona Macintosh Users Group conference

AMUGNEWS is for product announcements and material from AppleLink. The AMUG conference is for AMUG members.

BAYMAC
The Bay Area Macintosh conference

BAYMAC is one of the more successful conferences on FidoNet. It was started by the author, Raines Cohen, and Vern Keenan in 1987, and has had only one recorded flaming incident in all that time, a modern record. Maybe it's because we're all so mellow here in the Bay Area. I dunno.

CPOINT
COUNTERPoint conference

This one is for users of the COUNTERPoint point system.

ECHOMAC
General Macintosh conference

This one is too big already. If any of the other conferences fit your topic, put your message there instead. If you've got a question, put it in MACHELP or MACQA.

FIRSTCLASS
FirstClass BBS software support

This conference is for questions and answers about the FirstClass server and client software from SoftArc.

FPGROUP
Freedom and privacy conference

If you have a concern relating to constitutional freedoms or privacy issues in the electronic communications domain, this is the place to discuss it. Current topics include encryption techniques; junk fax, telemarketing, and email; credit reports; direct mail; the Electronic Communications Privacy Act of 1986; Operation Sun Devil; search and seizure law; the California Penal Code, and so on.

HERMES_SYSOPS
Hermes sysop conference

This is a conference for users of the Hermes bulletin board software.

HULKMSGS
Networked wrestling games

This is conference for users playing networked wrestling games.

MAC_ADS
For sale advertisements for Mac hardware and software

The MAC_ADS conference is an alternative to the MACFSALE conference carried on the backbone. Post here if you're looking to buy Mac hardware or software. However, it's not such a great place to offer things for sale – prices offered are frequently lower than what you can get otherwise.

MAC_HELP
Help with Macintosh problems

The MAC_HELP conference is the place to ask for assistance with a Macintosh problem that is not System 7 related (the SYSTEM7 or MACSYS7 conferences should be used for this), or related to specific hardware or software discussed in other conferences.

MACCOMM
Macintosh communications

This conference is for discussion of Macintosh telecommunications, including modems and software such as White Knight, MicroPhone II, and ZTerm.

MACDEV
Macintosh developers

This conference is for Macintosh developers. Virtually everyone in the echo is working in C, Pascal, or assembler. If you're a novice developer, you should post in MacNov instead. If you're working with HyperCard XCMDs or HyperTalk, try MACHYPE.

MACDTP
Macintosh desktop publishing

The conference to discuss large screens, color graphics cards, desktop publishing software, and so on.

MACFREQS
New uploads from around the country

This conference describes newly uploaded files around the U.S. that can be gotten via File Request. However, the binaries are not transmitted as part of the conference; you have to call long distance to File Request them.

MACFILES
New uploads of interest to sysops

This conference is similar to MACFREQS but is available only to sysops.

MAC4SALE
Macintosh hardware and software for sale

This conference is the backbone equivalent of MAC_ADS.

MAC_GAMES
Macintosh games

Check out this one if you're stumped about how to proceed in an adventure game and need hints.

MACHW
Macintosh hardware

This conference is about Macintosh hardware, such as CPUs, hard disks, floppy drives, printers, scanners, monitors, and so on.

MACHYPE
HyperCard

This is the conference for those interested in HyperCard, from novices to developers.

MACNETADMIN
The Macintosh network administrators' conference

If you administer an AppleTalk network at the office, this one is for you.

MACNETCOM
Networking and communications

The nonbackbone alternative to Maccomm, this conference talks about communications software as well as aspects of networking on the Macintosh.

MACNOV
Novice developers

The nonbackbone alternative to MACDEV. Primarily for developer wannabe's who are just getting started.

MACPB
PowerBook conference

This is a conference about PowerBooks, including software and hardware for the PowerBook.

MACPOINT
Macintosh point mailer conference

This is a general conference about point mailers. However, if you have a specific question about a mailer, you should post it in an official support conference such as CPOINT (COUNTERPoint), MANSION (for Copernicus II), MACWOOF (for MacWoof).

MACSW
Macintosh software

If it's a Macintosh application, talk about it here, as long as it isn't discussed in any of the other conferences.

MACSYSOP
Macintosh sysop's conference

If it relates to bulletin board software, system administration, or networkwide services such as the MACLIST, it probably belongs here.

MAC_TELEFINDER
TeleFinder Support conference

If it relates to the TeleFinder Host or User software, then it belongs here.

MACUK
United Kingdom Macintosh conference

I'm not sure why this conference is shipped over to the States. It's mostly filled with local comments from London bulletin boards. I suppose it serves us right – we've been forcing the British to read the drivel in ECHOMAC for years!

MACVIRUS
Macintosh viruses

What to do if your Mac is acting strangely and you think it may have caught something.

MACWOOF
MacWoof point mailer

Where to go to discuss MacWoof, the shareware point mailer by Craig Vaughan.

MANSION
Support conference for Mansion BBS and Copernicus

This conference is where you go if you want to discuss Mansion, the Macintosh BBS package, or Copernicus, the point mailer for the Mac. Michael Pester, the author of Mansion and Copernicus, runs this conference.

METROMAC
NY/NJ metropolitan area Macintosh conference

If you live in New York or New Jersey, put local messages about the Macintosh here.

MSDNSYSOP
Macintosh Software Distribution Network conference

The conference for support of the Macintosh Software Distribution Network and associated software such as MacTick.

MUGADMIN
Macintosh user group administrator's conference

The conference supporting Macintosh User Group administrators. This conference promotes general cooperation between Macintosh user group leaders worldwide, including exchange of newsletters and articles, help with financial matters, recommended speakers, and other aspects of user group administration.

NJMUG
New Jersey Mac Users Group conference

This is a conference for members of the New Jersey Mac Users Group.

NOVALINK
NovaLink Pro bulletin board software support conference

The conference for support of the NovaLink Pro bulletin board software.

PCMAC
PC-Macintosh file transfer and conversion

What if you've got a .PCX file you want to convert to PixelPaint format? How do you do it? This is the conference to read.

PUBADD and PUBADDTEST
Public Address

Public Address is a long-awaited AppleTalk- and FidoNet-compatible Macintosh BBS that will

have source code available. If you're interested in finding out what Public Address can do, read this conference. PUBADDTEST is for beta testers of Public Address.

RRH
Red Ryder Host conference

Red Ryder Host is now renamed Second Sight, but the conference name remains the same. Second Sight is the Macintosh BBS software supported by the FreeSoft Company, publishers of White Knight, formerly Red Ryder.

SIMCITY
Discussion of the Sim City game

If you're addicted to Sim City, this is the place to go to get help with the game.

SYSTEM7
Discussion of Macintosh System 7

If you're running System 7 or would like to be, this is the conference for you.

TABBY
TABBY support conference

This is the support conference for Tabby, the Macintosh FidoNet external mailer written by Michael Connick. If you need to find out how to get Tabby to work with your Macintosh BBS, this is the place.

WIRETAP_SUP
Wiretap support

This is the support conference for Wiretap, the telecom program.

WWIVMAC
World War IV BBS support

This is the support conference for WWIV, the Macintosh version of the PC-based BBS that was ported to the Macintosh by Terry Teague.

POINT SOFTWARE

What's the point?

Until a few years ago, the only way to connect to FidoNet was to run or use a FidoNet bulletin board system. Since all nodes listed in the FidoNet Nodelist must be available to receive network mail during the Zone Mail Hour, this was not convenient for people who used their machine for other purposes and did not want to leave their computer on overnight.

How could these people connect to FidoNet yet be able to receive and send mail without having to satisfy the Zone Mail Hour requirement? Points were created to solve this problem.

Point systems fully implement the FidoNet protocols, but they are not listed in the Nodelist. They receive and send all their mail through another FidoNet node, called the Boss system. Since points interact with the network primarily through the Boss system, other nodes can send mail to the point through the Boss, rather than having to reach the point system directly. This allows the point system to skip the Zone Mail Hour requirement.

Points also help alleviate some of the pressure on the network created by its rapid growth. With more than 20,000 systems listed, the Nodelist is getting rather large (1.8 Mb at last look), and at some point may push up against MS-DOS memory limitations. The point concept helps restrain Nodelist growth by allowing thousands of nodes to connect to the network without a Nodelist entry.

Even though points don't have a Nodelist entry, they do have a FidoNet address. How are point addresses assigned? FidoNet is a decentralized network where a good deal of authority is delegated from zone coordinators to regional coordinators to network coordinators. For example, node number

assignments are usually made by network coordinators and then forwarded to the Nodelist coordinator. This decentralization is very important, because a centralized network could not hope to keep up with the growth that FidoNet is experiencing.

In the case of points, the sysop is assigned a network number within which he or she has complete authority to assign point node numbers. For example, if I am assigned network number 30541, I then have complete authority to assign point numbers from 1 up to 65535 (the node number is 16 bits long). As a result, the address of point node 2 would be 30541/2.

What's so great about points?

Point software is economical because it automates downloading of files and messages, decreasing your time online. In addition, the messages are transmitted in compressed form, often in the late evening or early morning when telephone rates are lower.

While these benefits are also offered by message readers, points add some additional capabilities, such as NetMail and File Requests/Attaches. With a Nodelist providing phone numbers of the systems you want to call, point users are also able to File Request from or File Attach to any FidoNet system worldwide.

The additional functionality comes at the cost of added complexity, and as a result points are less popular than QWK message readers. This is particularly true on the PC where even simplified point implementations such as EZPoint require integration with a full FidoNet implementation such as BinkleyTerm. This isn't as intimidating as it looks at first glance, though; later in this chapter, we provide sample setup files.

Points are most popular on the Macintosh, where the release of the new generation of point packages such as Copernicus II, MacWoof, and COUNTERPoint has made them much easier to setup and use.

The impact of point software

The best way to understand the impact of points is to examine the traffic in the ECHOMAC conference, to see the percentage of total traffic created by points since the release of Copernicus I (the first Macintosh point software) in 1989.

As of January 1992, over 60 percent of all messages posted in the ECHOMAC conference originated from point mailers – either Copernicus, COUNTERPoint, or MacWoof. Similarly, the volume of network traffic has gone off the charts. The ECHOMAC conference is now passing over 1000 messages a week.

Setting up point software

You will need to get a network and node number assigned by a FidoNet sysop before you can use your point on that system. Each network/node number assignment comes with a password that uniquely identifies your system. This prevents other users from masquerading as you and reading your mail.

There may also be passwords required in order to do a Magic Name request of the file listings ("FILES"). You may also be given a password for the AREAFIX message board manager. Each of these passwords can be different. Make sure to ask your sysop for all the passwords when you get your network/node number assignment.

Most sysops do not charge for assigning a network and node number, although they do usually require that you become a member of their BBS for some nominal fee. You should be aware that many of the larger bulletin boards may have limits on the total number of points they can handle due to bugs in their AREAFIX or mailer software.

How do you find the BBS nearest you that supports points? Consult Appendix I: FidoNet

Organization and Help Nodes and Appendix H: Network BBSes to find a system near you.

When you get your network/node number assignment, write it down on the next page so you won't forget it. Since you will not be able to easily change your AREAFIX password, write that down too. Explanations for the rest of the entries on the form follow.

Magic Names

Magic Names are names you can use to request certain files from your Boss BBS. The files aren't actually stored under these names, but when you ask for them, the BBS is smart enough to know what you're talking about. On many systems, Magic Names include FILES (for the FILES.ZIP listing), USERS (for the USERS.ZIP listing), and ABOUT (for the latest listing of BBS hours of operation).

If you have purchased point software, you will be able to request files from any node on the FidoNet network. First you will have to find the Nodelist nodes to call and fill in the phone numbers and network/node information in your point. You can then request files by magic name. A Magic Name is a special File Request set up for certain files that you'll want quick access to.

For example, MACLIST is the Magic Name for a list of Mac-oriented BBSes on FidoNet that is updated weekly. NODELIST is the name for the current FidoNet Nodelist in compressed form.

Magic Names may also have passwords, which you will need to give when you request the file. On many BBSes, FILES, which is a Magic Name for a current list of all files on the BBS, requires a password. Ask your host for the list of Magic Names and Passwords when you receive your point address. For more information on Magic Names, consult the section Introduction to EchoMac.

Chapter 18: Point Software

Other information

The "private network number" is a number assigned to your BBS by the International FidoNet Network Coordinator, who at the time of this publication is George Peace. This number identifies all point nodes from that BBS so that if something goes wrong with them, the problem can be traced.

Your domain address provides a means for people to send you mail, provided that they have accounts on computers linked to the Internet either directly or via gateways. Computers linked to the Internet via gateways include commercial services such as AOL, CompuServe, GEnie, Prodigy, MCI Mail, AppleLink, and Connect.

Zones are areas of the FidoNet, which divide the continents and subnetworks such as RBBSNet and AlterNet.

AREAFIX

On many BBSes, you send NetMail to a "Magic User Name" to change your message areas. On most systems, this Magic User Name is AREAFIX. You'll also need the AREAFIX password, which is placed in the subject field of the message when you are requesting that conferences be added or deleted.

AREAFIX is a program that runs on your Boss system to handle your message area requests. On most systems, it runs once a day, late at night. AREAFIX processes your requests to delete and add message areas. The new areas will take effect at the next mail processing period. When you start off, your Boss BBS does not know which message areas you want, so it does not package them for you. Therefore, don't be surprised if you don't get any messages when you dial in with Copernicus, COUNTERPoint, or MacWoof. First you need to send an AREAFIX message requesting the conferences you'd like to receive.

When you first get your network/node number assignment, your point mailer will not be set up to receive *any* message areas at all. You can have your point mailer call the Boss from here to kingdom come, and nothing will happen. To

actually start receiving conferences, you need to use of the AREAFIX utility that runs on your Boss BBS.

Use AREAFIX by addressing a NetMail message to AREAFIX, with your AREAFIX password (assigned when you got your point network/node number) in the subject field. Also put any command line options into the subject field. Note: In order to send a message to AREAFIX with Copernicus, you need to add the name AREAFIX into the Copernicus address book! Make sure to do this, or you'll be wondering how to get Copernicus to send a message.

Turning on message areas

To turn on a message area, send a NetMail message to AREAFIX, with your password as the subject. Then in the body of the message, put the names of the echoes you want to receive. Note that you cannot do this from within the BBS if you are logged on as a normal user, because your point's network/node number will not be identified. You must do it from within your point software.

```
TO: AREAFIX
FROM: John Foobar
SUBJECT: <Password>

MacPoint
Mansion
BAYMAC
---
```

AREAFIX will then send you a message notifying you that your request has succeeded or failed. The message will look like this:

```
TO: John Foobar
FROM: AREAFIX on 1:161/444
SUBJECT: Re: Node change requests

Additions/Deletions
AREA: STATUS:
------------------------- ----------------------
-------
MACPOINT ..................... Added area.
MANSION ...................... Added area.
BAYMAC ....................... Added area.
Active areas on 1:161/444
MACPOINT
MANSION
BAYMAC
MACNETADMIN

Total found: 4
Note, a '*' indicates you're the feed on the echo.
--- AREAFIX v1.20
```

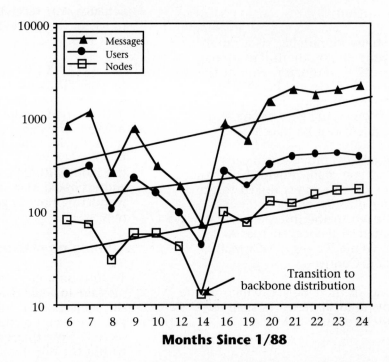

Messages/month, users, and nodes within the ECHOMAC conference. ECHOMAC has experienced steady growth since the release of Copernicus.

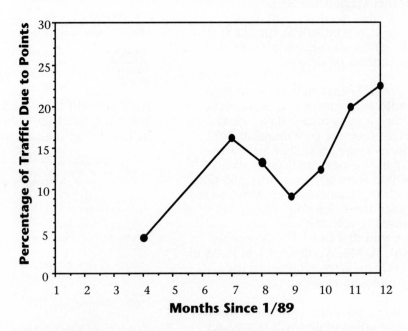

The percentage of traffic in ECHOMAC posted by users of point software is increasing.

Personal BBS Vital Statistics
DO NOT LOSE THIS PAGE!

My FILES "Magic Name" password is:

_____

Other "Magic Names" and their passwords are:

Magic Name   **Password**

_____   _____

_____   _____

_____   _____

I am part of Zone _____, in the continent of _____
(Zone 1 is North America, Zone 2 is Europe)

My private network number is: _____
                                        (Example: 30541)

My assigned point number is: _____

My FidoNet address is:

Zone:_____Network:_____/Node:_____.Point #_____
(Example: 1:161/5555.2)

In order to modify my message areas, I send mail to:_____
                                               (not case-sensitive)

with a password of: _____
                              (not case-sensitive)

My session password is: _____
                                  (not case-sensitive)

My domain address is:

_____._____@p_____.f<node>.n<etwork>.z<zone>.fidonet.org
First name Last name   Point #

(Example: Bernard.Aboba@p2.f5555.n161.z1.fidonet.org)

Turning off message areas

To remove an area, just put a minus sign (-) before the area. The message would look like this:

```
TO: AREAFIX
FROM: John Foobar
SUBJECT: <Password>

-MACNETADMIN
---
```

AREAFIX will then reply to your message:

```
TO: John Foobar
FROM: AREAFIX on 1:161/445
SUBJECT: Re: Node change requests

Additions/Deletions
AREA: STATUS:
------------------------------ ----------------------
-------
-MACNETADMIN.................. Deleted.
Active areas on 1:161/444
MACPOINT
MANSION
BAYMAC

Total found: 3
Note, a '*' indicates you're the feed on the echo.
--- AREAFIX v1.20
```

Other AREAFIX commands

-R   Rescan

This requests that the BBS scan through its messages to make sure you've gotten all your mail.

-Q   Query request

This requests a list of all message areas available on the BBS.

How to use these commands

Include the command line switches on the subject line, as follows:

```
TO: AREAFIX
FROM: John Foobar
SUBJECT: <Password> -Q

Here is a line of filler text, which is necessary for
some reason.
---
```

You need to put at least one line in your message for AREAFIX to work. Another "creature feature."

AREAFIX will reply to your message with a conference list:

```
TO: John Foobar
FROM: AREAFIX on 1:161/444
SUBJECT: Query request on 1:161/444

Areas available to 1:161/444 to 1:30541/2

* BAYMAC
* MACPOINT
* MANSION
UFGATE
MEADOW
MACDEV
Total found: 20
Note: a '*' indicates you're already active for the
echo.
--- AREAFIX v1.20
```

Point mail etiquette

Here are some important tips on how to stay on the good side of your sysop:

∇ Don't request conferences you won't read

If you request conferences via AREAFIX and are no longer interested in them, please send an AREAFIX message deleting these conferences. If you don't do this, tons of EchoMail will pile up on your sysop's hard disk. This often happens when people go away for vacation. When you get back, you'll have 1 Mb or more of mail waiting. Sysops have been known to delete point mail packets that get too large. Be forewarned.

∇ Stick to low-volume conferences

Do not request high-volume conferences unless you intend to read them. ECHOMAC is now up to 1000 messages a week; that's almost 1 Mb weekly. If you only log in occasionally, you are not going to want to spend an hour and a half at 2400 bps downloading the week's messages. Just tossing the messages into the right areas could take half an hour. Stick to low-volume, high-information-content conferences. These include conferences such as MACCOMM, MAC4SALE, MACHELP, or SYSTEM7. Post a message asking for conference recommendations before you do an AREAFIX request.

∇ Subscribe to a conference for your point software

I recommend that point users subscribe to the support conference for their software. Conference names include MANSION for Copernicus users, MACPOINT for COUNTERPoint users, and MACWOOF for MacWoof users.

∇ Keep your tag line clean

Keep your tag line free of remarks that could be construed as racist, obscene, or politically incorrect. If you live in Berkeley, this would include a tag line advocating use of styrofoam containers or the abolition of rent control. Point mail nodes with offensive tag lines are subject to immediate disconnection!

∇ Choose your polling time carefully

Set Copernicus, EZPoint, MacWoof, or COUNTERPoint to dial in at a time when the Boss BBS is lightly used.

Macintosh point software

Tabby-compatible mailers

Tabby was the first FidoNet-compatible mailer for the Macintosh, and set the standards for Macintosh mailers. It was written for use with Macintosh BBSes such as FirstClass, Second Sight (formerly Red Ryder Host), Mansion, Hermes, NovaLink Pro, WWIV, and others. As a full FidoNet mailer, it is capable of processing the Nodelist and its weekly updates, sending and receiving FidoNet NetMail and conferences, answering as well as dialing, and other features that are not included with point mail systems such as Copernicus, MacWoof, or COUNTERPoint. If you are thinking of running your own BBS, or if you are envisioning heavy-duty point use, you will probably want to buy a Tabby-compatible mailer instead of Copernicus and use that alongside COUNTERPoint. Tabby-compatible mailers, which include Tabby (discontinued in November 1993) and F1, are supported in the TABBY conference on Alternet.

Copernicus

Copernicus was the first Macintosh point mail system. It does everything, from establishing the FidoNet connection to creating the interface that lets you read and respond to your mail. I have found it to be quite reliable, although there are aspects of the user interface that I would quibble with. Copernicus II is available at a reasonable price ($59.95) and is well-supported by Michael Connick and Michael Pester via the Mansion conference.

COUNTERPoint

COUNTERPoint is a replacement for the Mail Reader application in Copernicus, so it does not include a FidoNet mailer application. As of version 2.1, it can also function as a QWK message reader. COUNTERPoint is compatible with both Copernicus and Copernicus II, as well as Tabby. Many people prefer COUNTERPoint's user interface to that of Copernicus. COUNTERPoint is supported in the MacPoint conference.

MacWoof

MacWoof is an integrated point system by Craig Vaughan. MacWoof was written as a single application, rather than as a series of programs that cooperate, which is how Copernicus and COUNTERPoint do it. This means that MacWoof is easier to install and maintain than Copernicus or COUNTERPoint. Craig is the author of one of the earliest BBS packages, as well as a co-author of the Language Systems Fortran compiler. Since he has put an enormous amount of work into MacWoof, it's a rapidly maturing and very well supported product.

MacWoof is available in two versions, the demoware version and the release version. While the demoware version is fine for figuring out what MacWoof can do, if you do not pay the shareware fee within 30 days, many sysops will not allow you to continue to use it to connect to their system since you would be stealing from Craig. If you are happy with MacWoof, you should purchase the release version by sending in your shareware fee to Craig. The release version of MacWoof includes a manual and support from Craig via the MacWoof conference.

Installing MacWoof

The trickiest part of installing MacWoof is installing the Comm Toolbox. If you are using System 6.0.5–6.0.8, you need to get ahold of the Comm Toolbox installer disk. This is available from bulletin boards such as MacCircles, MacEmma, and Twilight Clone. You need to use the installer to install the Comm Toolbox into your system, and then you need to place the Serial Tool into the Communications Folder in your System Folder.

If you've got System 7, things are slightly different. Since the Comm Toolbox is built into System 7, you will not need to use an installer to install it. However, the tools themselves are not included in the System 7 Personal Upgrade Kit, so you will need to obtain those through APDA. With System 7, drag the Serial Tool into the System Folder and click OK when it asks you if you want to put it into Extensions. Once the Communications Toolbox is installed, you're ready to double-click on the MacWoof application and get it running.

When "The Woofer" starts up, select **New Msg File** from the **File** menu.

Doing this will get you a dialog box asking what to name your message file. You can name it whatever you'd like, but I suggest something descriptive like "MacEmma BBS Msgs," so that you can distinguish message files created for different systems, in case you point off more than one (not recommended, but some people like to live dangerously).

MacWoof will then ask you some simple questions. First, it brings up a dialog box called Point Info. Fill in your name where it says to do so; the Origin: entry is for a "tag line" that will be placed at the end of each message you send. Think of something witty, but not obscene or offensive. Your domain is FidoNet, and if you're in North America, your Zone is 1. The Zone for Europe is 2. When you arrange to become a point with your sysop, you will be assigned a point net and point node number.

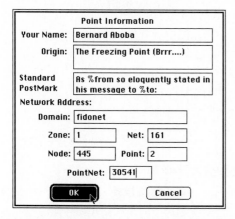

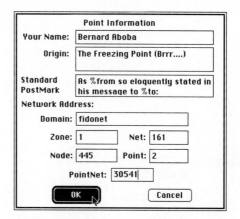

The Boss Net and Node numbers can be found in your Boss' FidoNet address. For example, for 1:161/445, the network number is 161, the node number is 445, and the Point Net number is 30541. If you want to modify these entries after you are done, you can do so by selecting **Point Info** from the hierarchical **File** menu.

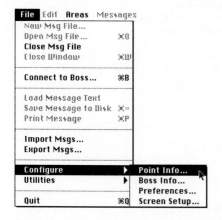

MacWoof will then ask you some simple questions. First, it brings up a dialog box called Point Information.

The next thing MacWoof will ask for is the Boss Information.

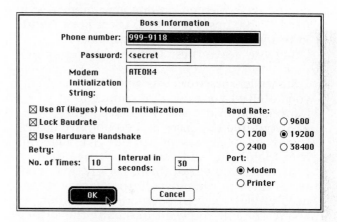

Select your modem speed and enter the phone number. If you don't have the phone number of the system you want to connect to, you can get it from the MacList. When setting the bps rate, make sure the rate is the lower figure when comparing your modem's speed and the speed of your Boss system. If you want to modify the settings later, select **Configure** and **Boss Info...** from the **File** menu.

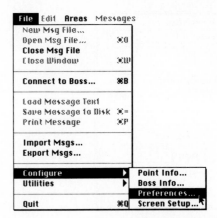

If your Boss system sports a high-speed modem and you have one as well, for maximum transfer speed you should use a hardware handshake cable and operate your modem at a fixed 19,200 bps. To do this, select **Lock Baud Rate** and **Use Hardware Handshake**. Otherwise, leave these two checkboxes alone.

Your session password was given to you when you received your network connection information from your sysop. Keep this password in a safe place and do not give it out to anyone. Many sysops will not give them out over the phone, and you can't change them easily once you've got them. Luckily, MacWoof stores them in the program, so you may never need to look for your password again. After you're done, if you want to modify the entries in this dialog box, you can select **Boss Info...** from the **File** menu. Congratulations! You've just installed MacWoof!

User Preferences

If you want to change your User Preferences later, select **Preferences...** from the **File** menu.

The settings that follow work just fine. If you would like to have MacWoof open the Subjects window on startup, or if you wish to display the routing information, which is "hidden" at the bottom of each EchoMail message, you can change that here. Click **OK** when you're done.

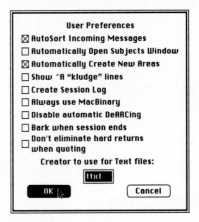

Testing it out

The first thing you want to do after you get MacWoof installed is test it to see if it can call out. You do this by selecting **Connect to Boss** from the **File** menu.

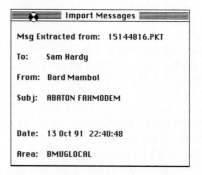

MacWoof will then put up several windows showing you the progress of your session. Since you haven't requested any message areas yet, don't expect much to happen.

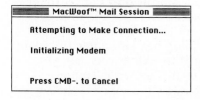

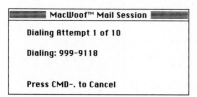

However, once you've requested message areas by sending a NetMail message to AREAFIX, you'll begin to get messages. The AREAFIX request will take effect two mail events after you send your AREAFIX message.

You will know it has succeeded when MacWoof begins to send you packets and toss messages, as shown here.

MacWoof will automatically add message areas to your message files as the new messages come in. When this happens, you will see some new entries in your **Areas** menu.

Requesting files with MacWoof

To request files from your Host BBS, you need to select **File Requests...** from the **File Transfer** menu.

This will bring up the following dialog box:

Type in the name of the file you want to request, as well as its password, and click on the **Add** button to add this file to the list. If you don't know which file you want, you should request FILES, which is usually a list of all the files on the Boss system. On many Boss systems this file is passworded.

File Requesting from other nodes

In browsing the MACFREQS conference, you will often see files that you would like to download. Fortunately, MacWoof has the capability of allowing you to call nodes other than your Boss, so you can do a File Request. However, you must be very careful when doing this or you can screw up the EchoMac Network!

Remember that MacWoof can handle only one Boss system at a time. This means it cannot separate File Requests and messages meant for one system from those meant from another. If you switch Bosses while there are outgoing mail packets or File Requests pending, these may be routed to your newly selected system instead of the old one. Therefore, you must complete all pending message uploads, File Attaches, or File Requests with your Boss before selecting another Boss. If you do not, you will end up sending messages to, or requesting files from, the wrong system.

Please also keep in mind that each sysop has different rules about File Requests. Some sysops allow File Requests only at certain hours of the day, or from "known" users. Others may password individual files or their entire library. File Request is a privilege, not a right! The most polite thing to do is to request permission before making repeated File Requests, and if you are going to be File Requesting on a regular basis, then you should probably make a donation to the sysop to defray costs.

If you want to request a file from another host, you need to use MacWoof's **Boss Info...** and **Point Info...** menu selections to change the information about your Boss. Replace your old information with the information on the new system you wish to call. However, you should leave your point network and node number

the same, so that the sysop of the new host can trace the origin of the call.

Tips for System 7

I have tested Copernicus II and COUNTERPoint v2.1 under System 7 and they both work without problems. When installing Copernicus under System 7, you must specify operation under MultiFinder. Upgrades to COUNTERPoint are free. You can upgrade your version by sending a stamped, self-addressed envelope to Mike Lininger.

MacWoof also works under System 7. However, it must be set up slightly differently. The Comm Toolbox is part of System 7, so you won't need to install this. However, the Toolbox tools are not part of the System 7 distribution, so you will need to obtain them from another source. MacWoof requires the Serial Tool. To install this tool, drag it to your System Folder; a dialog box will come up asking if you want to put it in Extensions. Say yes. That's all there is to it! The Serial Tool is available from BBSes, such as MacCircles.

Sending UUCP mail with MacWoof

To send UUCP mail within MacWoof, first select **NetMail** from within the **Areas** menu.

You will then be greeted with the following message window:

Type in the subject of your message and your name. To send the message through the gateway, address it to UUCP. Type in the address of the nearest FidoNet/UUCP gateway system in the net and node fields. If you don't know the nearest gateway, you can look up gateway nodes in Appendix I: FidoNet Organization and Help Nodes.

PC point software

EZPoint

Ezpoint

One of the easiest PC point systems to set up is EZPoint. EZPoint functions as a message reader, tosser, and packer/unpacker, so the only additional software you need is a FidoNet mailer such as BinkleyTerm or FrontDoor.

EZ does it

Before running EZPoint for the first time, you need to add the following line to your AUTOEXEC.BAT file:

```
SET BBS=D:\EZPOINT
```

This command tells EZPoint where to find its files. In this case, I have created the EZPOINT directory on drive D:. You will also need to create a directory for the message areas. EZPoint stores messages for each echo in a separate file.

Finally, you need to create directories for your chosen mailer, such as BinkleyTerm. These directories will include directories for inbound and outbound mail.

To start EZPoint, change drives, go into the EZPOINT directory, and invoke EZPoint:

```
D:
CD \EZPOINT
EZPOINT
```

When invoked for the first time, EZPoint will display the configuration menu. Enter the information corresponding to your setup. If you want to change any of the settings, type the letter corresponding to the configuration

parameter (**E** for Editor, and so on). EZPoint will then ask you to input the parameter again. The Editor (**E**) entry lets you choose your favorite message editor. The Writefile (**W**) entry specifies the file to which you want to save messages using the **W** command in EZPoint. The More (**M**) entry lets you decide whether to pause after every screen. Beautify (**B**) turns color on or off.

If after you're done you later want to change one or more of these parameters, you can bring up the configuration menu again via the EZPoint **x** command.

The setup for a point node follows. Note that the inbound and outbound directories must correspond to those used by your mailer. The Message Base directory entry is the directory in which EZPoint will store your messages, one file per conference area. You are free to use a utility other than PKARC/PKXARC as the packer/unpacker, although if you do, you must notify the systems you connect with so that they will be prepared to generate and unpack packets in this format.

```
      Node <N>: 1:30541/2
     Point <N>: 1:161/445.2
     Sysop <S>: Bernard Aboba
    System <S>: Bernard's Point
 Signature <S>: Wherever you go, there you are
    Editor <E>: esp
   Inbound <P>: d:\binkley\file\email
  Outbound <P>: d:\binkley\outbound
  MsgBases <P>: d:\binkley\msgs
    Packer <A>: PKARC -a
  Unpacker <A>: PKXARC
 Writefile <W>: d:\binkley\message.sav
   Trigger <T>: 100
      More <M>: On
 ClrScreen <C>: On
   HotKeys <H>: On
     Decor <D>: Mono
  Beautify <B>

Change what parameter:
```

EZPoint can also be configured as a regular FidoNet node. In the following figure, the changes are in the Node (**N**) setup and in the System and Signature (**S**) entries.

```
       Node <N>: 1:161/445
    Route-to <N>: 1:125/125
      Sysop <S>: Bernard Aboba
     System <S>: Mail Hub
  Signature <S>: apple!hub (510)555-1212
     Editor <E>: esp
    Inbound <P>: d:\binkley\file\email
   Outbound <P>: d:\binkley\outbound
   MsgBases <P>: d:\binkley\msgs
     Packer <A>: PKARC -a
   Unpacker <A>: PKXARC
  Writefile <W>: d:\binkley\message.sav
    Trigger <T>: 100
       More <M>: On
  ClrScreen <C>: On
    HotKeys <H>: On
      Decor <D>: Mono
   Beautify <B>
```

Once you have finished configuring EZPoint, the program is ready to use. EZPoint commands include the following:

```
           Message Command Help

A)rea change            P)revious message
B)ody text change       R)eply
C)hange attributes      V)ersion of EZPoint
D)estination change     W)rite message
E)nter a message        X)change options
G)oodbye                Z)ap area options
H)uh? display again     -) backward thread
I)nquire (search)       +) forward thread
J)ump to DOS            =) read continuous
K)ill a message         !) mark message
L)ist messages          @) recall message
M)ove (forward a message) ?) help screen (this)
N)ext message           C/R) next/previous
O)rigin change          #) specific message
```

Area change lets you view another message section. Body text change, Change attributes, and Destination change affect the body, attributes, and destination of a message, respectively. Inquire lets you search for messages with a keyword in the message envelope.

You may have noticed that we have not talked about creating message areas for your incoming echoes. You do not need to do this with EZPoint, since it creates message areas on the fly within the message base directory. Here is what the message area menu looks like:

```
0> MAIL: MSG [3] 1 - 3: a
Message Area (Enter for list):

----- Message Areas -----
 0> MAIL        1> SYSTEM7    2> TUB       3> TBBS
 4> CDROM       5> NORCAL     6> APPLE     7> MACSYSOP
 8> ECHOMAC     9> MACFSALE  10> MACHW    11> MACSW
12> MACWOOF    13> UNIX      14> PROSOFT  15> MEADOW
16> MACGAMES   17> MACDEV    18> MANSION  19> HERMESSYSOP
20> MACHYPE    21> MACCOMM
Message Area:
```

BinkleyTerm setup

Since BinkleyTerm, the popular FidoNet mailer, is deserving of its own book, we cannot cover all the configuration options. However, sample BINKLEY.CFG setup files are provided for the point and node configurations.

For more information

For information on where to obtain FidoNet utilities such as EZPoint, BinkleyTerm, and XLAXNODE, please consult Appendix B: Choice Products.

EZPoint Messaging system

```
#2 <SYSTEM7> 14 Mar 93 17:39:20
From: Akbar Foobar
To:   ALL
Subj: My car has exploded! 03-14-1993


My car exploded today while on my way to work. I believe the problem had something
to do with an incompatibility of my PowerBook 165c, which I was using to play games while
driving. The newspaper blamed it on the gasoline truck that I hit, but I think it is a System
7.0 bug, since the explosion occurred a few instants after I got a system bomb that asked if I
wanted to restart. I clicked OK, and then, boom! I never indicated that I wanted to restart
that way!

And while I'm on the subject, I would like to put in a few words for that
More?
```

BinkleyTerm Status Screen

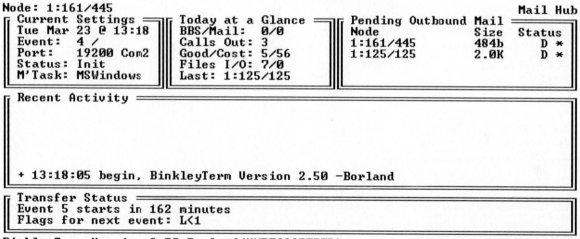

```
Node: 1:161/445                                                    Mail Hub
┌ Current Settings ═┐┌ Today at a Glance ═┐┌ Pending Outbound Mail ═┐
│ Tue Mar 23 @ 13:18 ││ BBS/Mail:  0/0     ││ Node          Size   Status │
│ Event:  4 /        ││ Calls Out: 3       ││ 1:161/445     484b     D *   │
│ Port:   19200 Com2 ││ Good/Cost: 5/56    ││ 1:125/125     2.0K     D *   │
│ Status: Init       ││ Files I/O: 7/0     ││                             │
│ M'Task: MSWindows  ││ Last: 1:125/125    ││                             │
└────────────────────┘└────────────────────┘└─────────────────────────────┘
┌ Recent Activity ═══════════════════════════════════════════════════════┐
│                                                                         │
│                                                                         │
│                                                                         │
│ + 13:18:05 begin, BinkleyTerm Version 2.50 -Borland                     │
└─────────────────────────────────────────────────────────────────────────┘
┌ Transfer Status ═══════════════════════════════════════════════════════┐
│ Event 5 starts in 162 minutes                                           │
│ Flags for next event: L<1                                               │
└─────────────────────────────────────────────────────────────────────────┘
BinkleyTerm Version 2.50-Borland<UNREGISTERED>          Press Alt-F10 For Help
```

BINKLEY.CFG file for point 1:161/445.2

```
;-----------------------------------------------------------------------
; BINKLEY.CFG - Configuration File for BinkleyTerm 2.50
; -----------------------------------------------------------------------
; This configuration file is for a point system, 1:161/445.2
; -----------------------------------------------------------------------
;
; Comm Port
Port      2
; Baud rate
Baud      19200
Carrier   80
; Dialing prefix
Prefix |ATDT
StatusLog    d:\binkley\binkley.log
Downloads    d:\binkley\downloads\
CaptureFile  d:\binkley\session.log
LogLevel 5
Gong
; Adjust baud rate
AutoBaud
; System name
System    Bernard's Point
Sysop     Bernard Aboba
Address   1:161/445.2                    ; Default address
PrivateNet 30541
Boss      161/445
BossPhone 5551212
BossPwd   <secret>
; NetMail goes here
NetMail   d:\binkley\msgs\email\
; Incoming packets go here
NetFile   d:\binkley\file\email\
; Outbound packets go here
Hold      d:\binkley\outbound\
; Nodelist goes here
Nodelist  d:\binkley\
; Version7 nodelist
Version7
; Go into unattended (mailer) mode
Unattended
BoxType 2
; List of files available for File Request
Okfile    d:\binkley\okfile.lst
; Maximum 2 file requests per session
MaxReq    2
; Maximum bytes of downloading per session
MaxBytes  400000
; Maximum time per session
MaxTime   30
Timeout 20
Banner You have connected to the Foobar zone, good luck...
BBSNote Thank you.  Now loading BBS.  Please wait...
DoingMail Sorry, we're not available right now.  Processing mail only.
EnterBBS Please press your Escape key to enter the BBS, or wait a few moments.
; ExtrnMail 140 Gimme UUCP
; ExtrnMail 150 Gimme WidgetLink
; MailNote  Now loading UUCP...please wait...
; BBS Exit
; BBS Spawn
; BBS Batch
; AfterMail    Unpack.Bat
; CleanUp      Scrub.Bat
; Packer       Pack.Bat
; NoWaZOO
;
Janusbaud 2400
JanusOK /Arq/V32
                                    JanusOK /V32
```

BINKLEY.CFG file for node 1:161/445

```
; ------------------------------------------------------------------------
; BINKLEY.CFG - Configuration File for BinkleyTerm 2.50
; ------------------------------------------------------------------------
;
; Comm Port
Port      2
; Baud rate
Baud      19200
Carrier   80
; Dialing prefix
Prefix |ATDT
StatusLog     d:\binkley\binkley.log
Downloads     d:\binkley\downloads\
CaptureFile   d:\binkley\session.log
LogLevel 5
Gong
; Adjust baud rate
AutoBaud
; System name
System    Bernard's FidoNet System
; Sysop name
Sysop     Bernard Aboba
; Node address
Address   1:161/445.0
; NetMail goes here
NetMail   d:\binkley\msgs\email\
; Incoming packets go here
NetFile   d:\binkley\file\email\
; Outbound packets go here
Hold      d:\binkley\outbound\
; Nodelist goes here
Nodelist  d:\binkley\
; Version7 nodelist
Version7
; Go into unattended (mailer) mode
Unattended
BoxType 2
; List of requestable files
Okfile    D:\binkley\okfile.lst
; Maximum requests per session
MaxReq    2
MaxBytes  400000
MaxTime   30
ReqTemplate d:\binkley\sample.tpl
Timeout 20
Banner You have connected to the BMUG zone, good luck...
BBSNote Thank you.  Now loading BBS.  Please wait...
DoingMail Sorry, we're not available right now.  Processing mail only.
EnterBBS Please press your Escape key to enter the BBS, or wait a few moments.
; ExtrnMail 140 Gimme UUCP
; ExtrnMail 150 Gimme WidgetLink
; MailNote  Now loading UUCP...please wait...
; BBS Exit
; BBS Spawn
; BBS Batch
; AfterMail   Unpack.Bat
; CleanUp     Scrub.Bat
; Packer      Pack.Bat
; NoWaZOO
;
Janusbaud 2400
JanusOK /Arq/V32
JanusOK /V32
```

FROM FIDONET TO UUCP AND BACK

Why should I read this section?

This chapter is designed to teach users of FidoNet systems who do not run their own FidoNet/UUCP gateways how to send mail back and forth to UUCP systems using the gateway machines for their networks.

I will start by showing how to get your message from your local FidoNet node to a FidoNet/UUCP gateway and describing what a FidoNet/UUCP gateway is. Once you've figured out how to get your message out of FidoNet, you'll need to learn how to get it where you want it to go.

This section is dedicated to Tim Pozar, John Gilmore, and Garry Paxinos. Without them, there wouldn't be a UFGATE.

What do I need?

You're gonna need some patience to get through this one. Most people can't figure out FidoNet/UUCP gateways on the first try. The procedure for sending mail through the gateway is not intuitive.

Information and help with FidoNet/UUCP gateways is available by `ftp zeus.ieee.org`, `cd /fidonet`, `get uu2fido.txt`, `uucphelp.txt`. For the latest lists of FidoNet/UUCP gateway systems, `cd /fidonet/fidomaps`, `get gateways.lst`, `fidouucp.lst`. For copies of the UFGATE and WAFFLE software, `cd /fidonet/ufgate`. The UFGATE conference on FidoNet is the place to go for help with FidoNet/UUCP gateway software.

Introduction

Connecting one network to another network is something of a miraculous process, because not only do you connect one computer to another (unlike) computer, allowing them to talk to one another, but suddenly any machine on one network can talk to any machine on another network. For the price of one link, you can get hundreds and even thousands of connections going.

Of course, there is a price you'll have to pay for UUCP access. It's not much: A fee of $50 to your local sysop and $0.30 per message will probably cover it.

Sending messages from FidoNet to the Internet

To make use of the FidoNet/UUCP gateways, if you are on the FidoNet, you need to send a message to the gateway node. A gateway is a machine that speaks more than one protocol so that it can be on two different networks at the same time. The gateway receives messages via one protocol in one format and retransmits them in another format, using another protocol.

UFGATE, and Fredgate are UUCP/FidoNet gateways. That means that they can receive messages via the FidoNet protocol in FidoNet message format and retransmit them in RFC822 format, using the UUCP protocol. They can also receive UUCP messages and retransmit them as FidoNet NetMail, as well as translate from FidoNet EchoMail format to USENET news format and back.

Unless your system is running specialized gateway software such as PCBUUCP (PCBoard), Major/Internet Gateway (Major BBS) or PIMP (TBBS), in order to have FidoNet NetMail sent out via the gateway, you need to send NetMail to a gateway node. If your sysop is running a program called EECP, it is also possible for you to put mail into an EchoMail section and have it automatically sent to the gateway node. EECP is available on the FidoNet SDS (See Appendix I for listings of FileBone nodes).

If you go the NetMail route, send a message addressed to UUCP, with the UUCP address on the first line of the message, addressed to the gateway node. An example is:

```
TO:   UUCP
FROM: Bernard Aboba
SUBJECT: Test
Net/Node: 1:161/445

TO:  well!ari
Hi there, Ari!  How 'ya doing?

-----
```

How do you figure out which gateway node to send the message to? Appendix I lists the gateways for various FidoNet networks. If for some reason you can't find the appropriate gateway there, try sending a message to the FidoNet node from the Internet. From the header of the message received on the FidoNet system you will be able to determine the gateway node's address. You can then address outgoing mail to the gateway.

One problem with this form of gateway addressing is that replies will not automatically be sent correctly just by entering a reply in your BBS software. You will have to enter the reply address on the first line of the message, which is somewhat confusing.

If you go the "blessed echo conference" route with EECP, the address is placed directly into the TO: field of the message. This will only work if the address is 36 characters or fewer, since that is all that FidoNet standards will support. In this case, the message looks like this:

```
TO:  well!ari
FROM: Bernard Aboba
SUBJECT: Test

Hi there, Ari!  How 'ya doing?

-----
```

When EECP gets this message, it takes the UUCP address out of the TO: field, substitutes

UUCP for it, and puts the address on the first line so it looks just like the previous message. Since setup of EECP involves configuring the gateway address, it is automatically inserted and you will not have to worry about figuring it out.

More sophisticated gateways such as PIMP (written as a TBBS option module) simplify replying to UUCP messages by allowing use of the TBBS reply function. In processing the message, PIMP takes care of addressing.

Intra-FidoNet routing

It is possible to have mail routed within FidoNet once it gets to a gateway node. Many gateway nodes will not route mail because of the expense, so you need to check on this before you do it. Here's how to route mail within FidoNet from node 1:161/445 to 1:125/222:

```
apple!foobar!1!125!222
```

The syntax for routing mail within FidoNet is:

```
<host>!<gateway>!<zone>!<network>!<node>
```

Pickup and delivery

Mail that travels from the Internet to FidoNet and vice versa is passed through FidoNet/UUCP gateways on the way to the destination. Those gateways pass mail on to systems within their network. Default gateways have also been established for those networks that do not have their own FidoNet/UUCP gateways.

The system is occasionally abused. For example, one user on the East Coast requested that a large file be forwarded to his FidoNet system. Since there is no FidoNet/UUCP gateway within his network, the task of delivering the huge file fell to the default gateway operator who resided in Arizona. Needless to say, the operator was not thrilled with the idea of making a long-distance call to deliver the file. Should this kind of behavior spread, it is likely that FidoNet/UUCP gateways across the country will hold mail for pickup rather than delivering it.

If you expect to receive mail from the
Internet on a regular basis, you may want to
inquire as to whether your sysop will allow his
or her FidoNet/UUCP gateway to pick up mail.
If you make such a request, be prepared to pay
the resulting phone bills.

Since gateway nodes deliver mail on their own
nickel, they may place restrictions on the
content or size of messages passing through
their systems. Since they are doing you a favor
by acting as a gateway, there is no one to
whom you can complain. Restrictions may
include:

• Prohibitions on commercial traffic.
• Limitations on message size. While FidoNet
has no theoretical message size limit, some
tosser/scanners may have difficulty with
messages over 64K, and others have problems
with messages larger than 8K.
• Prohibitions on encryption. Most gateways
object to routing of encyrpted mail through
their systems. The definition of encyrption is
up to the gateway operator, but may include
prohibitions against passing files translated by
UUENCODE or BINHEX, or messages processed
by ROT13.

Sending messages from the Internet to FidoNet

Messages sent from the Internet to FidoNet
are addressed as :

`<First.Last>@p<point>.f<node>.n<network>.z<zone>.fidonet.org`

For example, to send mail to 1: 161/445.2, you
would address it to:

`Bernard.Aboba@p2.f445.n161.z1.fidonet.org`

CHAPTER 19: PCBOARD NETWORKS

PCRELAY AND POSTLINK

PCRelay and PostLink are store and forward networking programs written by Kip Compton that are used on more than a dozen different networks. PostLink is a successor to PCRelay that is a separate product. While some former PCRelay networks such as RIME have switched to PostLink, other networks continue to stick with PCRelay.

Both PostLink and PCRelay are based on a tree topology with backbone machines called "Net Hub(s)" at the root. Use of a shallow tree topology allows a conference message to take only one or two days to be transmitted across the country. In contrast, nonbackbone FidoNet EchoMail messages can take up to a week. The hierarchical topology also simplifies routing, thus eliminating any "node tables."

PostLink and PCRelay also provide advanced network services. Nodes generate routing packets, and the Net Hubs dynamically adjust routing tables so that a node can disconnect from one location and reconnect at another without disruption. Since the PostLink/PCRelay design does not require that each node maintain a list of all nodes, only Net Hubs have complete knowledge of network topology. At other levels of the tree, local hubs, regional hubs, and super-regional hubs only know how to route to the branches below them. All messages that cannot be routed by a hub based on its knowledge of the tree branches below it are routed to the next level hub. The tree topology also ensures that duplicate messages cannot be generated internally. Since this does not protect against duplicates transmitted to the network via gateways, strict rules usually govern gateway

connections involving PostLink or PCRelay networks.

PostLink was created in order to allow for much larger networks than could be handled by PCRelay. PostLink is also portable, being written in C++. In the future this will allow it to run under UNIX and other operating systems such as Windows NT. For more information on the design of PostLink, please see Chapter 37: How PCRelay (and PostLink) Came to Be.

Features of PCRelay

Special features of the PCRelay software include: routed mail, public key encryption, and reader-only mailboxes. In a PCRelay network, unlike FidoNet, it is possible to send person-to-person mail within a conference area. This should be done by routing the mail directly to your chosen recipient so other users won't have to read it. This works with PCRelay because hubs can separate routed mail from conference mail and send it *only* to the destination node, rather than echoing it to dozens of systems. In contrast, FidoNet software doesn't do an echo-to-network-mail conversion for private messages. Since private unrouted PCRelay mail will be relayed to many systems, you should only use private mail along with routing.

Creating a mailbox

Before you can send or receive person-to-person mail, you must establish a mailbox. Establishing a mailbox will also enter your name in the global directory listing kept by a Net Hub.

In order to request a mailbox, you can send a message to PCRELAY within any conference.

The message should have the word ADD on the first line. It will look like this:

```
TO:          PCRELAY
SUBJECT:     Gimme my mailbox!
FROM:        John Foobar

ADD

PCRELAY:FOOB -> #1/2 RelayNet (tm)
4.10       The Mailbox Hut = 510-555-1212
```

To delete a mailbox, send a message to PCRELAY within any conference, but the message should have the word DELETE on the first line. It will look like this:

```
TO:          PCRELAY
SUBJECT:     Gimme my mailbox!
FROM:        John Foobar

DELETE

PCRELAY:FOOB -> #1/2 RelayNet (tm)
4.10       The Mailbox Hut = 510-555-1212
```

Routing mail

Once you have a mailbox, you can send and receive person-to-person (routed) mail. First determine the address of the node to send the mail to. Once you've found your recipient and the node they're reading from, you can send routed mail in a conference that you and your recipient agree on. Make sure it's a conference your node carries!

When you send routed mail, you must put the destination node on the first line of the message text. If you are using TBBS, you must also leave a blank line after that (by typing Space and then Return) in order to make sure that TBBS does not wordwrap something onto the address line.

Here's an example of routed mail sent to the node CHANNEL, which is located in Boston:

```
TO:          Joanne Foobar
SUBJECT:     Hello there
FROM:        John Foobar

->CHANNEL

Nice to talk to you!

PCRELAY:FOOB -> #1/2 RelayNet (tm)
4.10       The Routing Hut = 510-555-1212
```

Here the arrow (->) consists of a dash followed by a greater-than sign.

Return receipt requested

PCRelay also allows you to request a receipt with routed mail. To use this, put a * after the system name you want to send the message to. Your message will look like this:

```
TO:          Joanne Foobar
SUBJECT:     Hello there
FROM:        John Foobar

->CHANNEL*

Let me know if you get this!

PCRELAY:FOOB -> #1/2 RelayNet (tm)
4.10       The Routing Hut = 510-555-1212
```

Encryption

Although PCRelay networks do not offer private mail as defined under the Electronic Communications Privacy Act of 1986, they do allow for encryption of messages. This is another major difference from FidoNet, which prohibits encryption of messages within conferences. The encryption feature provides a measure of protection against spying by hubs. However, the feature does not protect the users from the sysop.

PCRelay encryption is a public key system. To request a key, send a message TO: PCRELAY, with the word **KEY** on the first line. Here's what it looks like:

```
TO:          PCRELAY
SUBJECT:     Gimme my key!
FROM:        John Foobar

KEY

PCRELAY:FOOB -> #1/2 RelayNet (tm)
4.10       The Encryption Hut = 510-555-1212
```

After a day or so, you will receive a return message specifying your public and private keys. The public key is the number you give out so people can send messages to you. The private key is what you use to decrypt those messages. Note: Since the sysop can read the messages specifying your public and private keys, your private messages are not really protected. The message you will receive specifying your keys will look like this:

```
TO:          John Foobar
SUBJECT:     KEY
FROM:        PCRELAY

PUBLIC KEY: 45444
PRIVATE KEY: 762839
```

For example, your friend's public key is 45444. In order to send her an encyrpted message she must decode with her private key and insert two tildes (~~) on the first line next to her public key. Here's what it looks like:

```
TO:        Joanne Foobar
SUBJECT:   Are we encrypted yet?
FROM:      John Foobar

~~45444

Joanne -
Are you free for dinner on Wednesday night? My Boss has
invited us to his home for a dinner of grilled antelope.
Leave your antlers at home!

PCRELAY:FOOB -> #1/2 RelayNet (tm)
4.10    The Encryption Hut = 510-555-1212
```

Features of PostLink

PostLink offers multicasting, or the ability to send a routed message to several nodes at once. With PostLink you do not have to create a mailbox before sending person-to-person mail; routed messages are automatically encrypted.

PostLink supports being able to refer to nodes either by their IDCODE or by their site number. The IDCODE is a twelve character string (which may contain numbers) that uniquely identifies a node. The site number is also unique and is purely numeric. Both the IDCODE and site number are found on the tag lines added to the end of each message by PostLink. The site number is found next to the # symbol on the tag line containing the string "PostLink(tm)". The name just prior to the site number is the IDCODE. For example, in the message below, the IDCODE originating node is CLOWN and the site number is 69.

```
TO:        Joanne Foobar
SUBJECT:   Clowns jubilee approaching
FROM:      John Foobar

Wanted to remind you of the clown's jubilee on May 15.

* The PostLink Hut, Berkeley, CA (510)555-1212 14.4
* PostLink(tm) v1.03 CLOWN (#69) : RelayNet(tm)
```

To send a message to someone who might be on one of several nodes, use the –> characters, as with PCRelay. The routing information should be on the first line of the message. What if –> is used to quote previous messages? PostLink generally can't get confused by this because programs that quote messages generally put a (SPACE) after the –> characters; PCRelay works the Johne way. Since PostLink

supports multicasting, you can include multiple site names instead of just one. Here is an example of a multicasted message:

```
TO:        Joanne Foobar
SUBJECT:   My souffle has fallen!
FROM:      John Foobar

->CHANNEL RUNNINGA RUNNINGB
The souffle which I have been baking for the last 2 hours
collapsed a minute ago. I am crushed.

* The PostLink Hut, Berkeley, CA (510)555-1212 14.4
* PostLink(tm) v1.03 FOOB (#69) : RelayNet(tm)
```

Return receipts are supported by placing the characters <– at the end of the routing list. This will get you return receipts from all nodes that the message is routed to. Sorry, you cannot get just one return receipt; the <– symbol must be placed at the end of the routing list. Here is an example of a message requesting a receipt:

```
TO:        Joanne Foobar
SUBJECT:   Please respond!
FROM:      John Foobar

->CHANNEL RUNNINGA RUNNINGB <-
I have been trying to email you for over a week. Are you
on vacation? Inquiring minds want to know!

* The PostLink Hut, Berkeley, CA (510)855-1212 14.4
* PostLink(tm) v1.03 FOOB (#69) : RelayNet(tm)
```

RIME

RIME is the largest PostLink network, with over 1000 nodes. It is governed by a five-member steering committee (STEERCOM), which has absolute authority over the network. The Steering Committee is led by Bonnie Anthony, sysop of the Net Hub system.

Every RIME node must carry several conferences, including COMMON and RIMENEWS. Carrying the COMMON conference ensures that if you leave a message for a RIME user there, they will get it. COMMON messages are not to exceed ten lines, and after the users have found each other, they are to continue the conversation somewhere else. RIMENEWS is for information on RIME. All nodes also regularly receive a conference list, updated network rules, and listings of nodes and hubs. RIME claims ownership of messages posted in their conferences and forbids gatewaying to other networks, including the use of points. Disobeying the STEERCOM can get you or your system suspended from the network.

A sampling of RIME Conferences

Conference	What it's about
Common	Area carried by all RIME boards. Used to contact other users. Messages limited to 10 lines.
Technical	Conference centering on PC clone hardware
Communications	General conference about modems and communications
Medical	General health issues, for the nonmedical person
Legal	General legal issues, for the nonlawyer
Macintosh	General Macintosh discussion
Uplink	General discussion, to get to know people. No controversial stuff.
Music	All kinds of music, from heavy metal to Mozart
Broadcast Professionals	People in radio or TV broadcasting
Financial	Investments
Roots	Geneology
Vacation	Where to go, what to see. Get recommendations from people who've been there.
Military	People in the armed services
Disabled	Conference for people with disabilities.
Job Bank	For hire and job wanted ads
Pets	Advice on all kinds of pets, from gerbils to pot-bellied pigs
Cuisine	Cooking and food
Newusers	Help for new users of BBSes and the RIME network
Parents	Ask other parents how they stay sane
Senior Citizens	For those over 55
Scuba	For people interested in diving
Engineering	For engineers
Ecology	For environmentalists
Boating	For those interested in boating
Phones	Telephone-industry issues
Fire/EMS	Fire and emergency medical services personnel
Police	For police people
Weather	Scientific aspects of weather
Running	For joggers and runners
Weight Management	Weight loss
Japan Conference	Aspects of Japanese culture and life
Musicians	For performing musicians
German & Yiddish	Practice your German and Yiddish
Wirewrap	Electronics-oriented conference
Rimenews	Required conference (read-only) conferencing the RIME network
French Language	For those who want to speak French
Spanish Language	For those who want to speak Spanish
Occupational Health and Safety	Issues related to job safety
Bible Studies	For those interested in discussing the Bible
BBS Caller's Digest	For discussion about the magazine
ModemNews	Magazine about modems and communications
Medieval	For members of the Society for Creative Anachronism and similar organizations
Cancer Recovery	For those recovering from the disease
Aquarium	For those who like fish as pets
Europe/USSR	Issues of European integration, Eastern Europe, and so on

ILINK

What is ILink?

The InterLink network was formed out of the remnants of the PCBEcho network, after the network disbanded with the release of QNet in September 1988. After it was discovered that InterLink was a trademark registered to Bank of America and IBM, the network name was changed to ILink, which has since been registered as a service mark. As of February 1993, more than 250 systems belonged to ILink.

Goals of ILink

ILink is an exclusive international network that carefully reviews systems applying for membership. The goal of the network is to provide a high signal/noise ratio conferencing system for users. The network currently supports WILDCAT! and PCBoard systems, but support for other BBSes and computers is under consideration. ILink is a message-only network and does not carry files.

ILink now offers more than 200 conferences. The emphasis is on professionally oriented forums, such as those for computer professionals, as well as conferences for support of commercial and shareware products, although there are also recreational and social areas. ILink encourages support conferences, which include Mustang, Novell, Quarterdeck, PCBoard, Robocomm, QMAIL and QNet, Hayes, PKWARE, US Robotics, and AT&T.

In order to start a conference on ILink, the conference is first proposed in the ILINK-INFO conference. If reaction is favorable, the conference will be started.

Network organization

ILink is an international network that includes nodes in Saudi Arabia, Luxembourg, Scotland, Canada, Slovenia, England, South Africa, Northern Ireland, Switzerland, the Netherlands, France, Germany, Belgium, Sweden, Denmark, Finland, Norway, and Taiwan.

ILink is organized as a four-level tree network, with National Hosts at the top level, National Distribution Site (NDS) mail hubs at the next level, Strategic Mail Distribution Sites below them, and member systems at the bottom.

The national hosts (EXECNET in the U.S.) are responsible for coordinating mail distribution within a country. The national hosts link up with EXECNET on a nightly basis, and the NDS systems then connect with their national hosts at least once a day, usually from 2 AM to 7 AM. The NDS systems are required to carry at least four days' worth of messages on all ILink conferences.

Strategic Mail Distribution Sites receive their mail from the NDS systems and redistribute it to the member systems. In order to guarantee receipt of all the previous day's messages, they often call shortly after the National Hub/NDS exchange period. The maximum number of nodes connected to a mail hub is fifteen in order to lessen the damage from a hub going down.

Systems dial out under control of a scriptable communications program such as Robocomm and exchange PKZIP compressed packets using protocols such as ZMODEM. QNet or TNet are used to extract outgoing .REP packets from the message base and toss incoming mail packets into the message base. On the host side, the network is interfaced as a DOOR program that is entered by the calling system, often requiring an additional password.

Cost reimbursement

Under ILink rules, a mail hub (NDS system) may charge up to $52/year to connected nodes to defray long-distance costs. Not all NDS systems charge this much, but they may not charge more.

Sysops with subscription BBSes may not charge callers extra for access to ILink; sysops with free systems may not charge for ILink access at all.

Gatewaying

ILink does not permit gatewaying of conferences to other networks. In spite of this, since many ILink systems carry conferences from other networks (including FidoNet, USENET, and RIME), accidental cross-linking of conferences has become a problem. To eliminate cross-posted messages, messages are checked for proper ILink net tags, which are not present in accidentally gatewayed messages. Messages without tags can then be removed by the NDS systems. For this to work, system operators must format tags correctly so that their messages will not be eaten by tag checkers.

The future of ILink

In order to continue to move mail efficiently as the load grows, ILink is considering the use of 56 Kbps or T1 leased lines as well as technologies such as satellite or Internet links.

Rules and regulations

ILink has been noted for the relative civility of its online discussions. In order to maintain quality, there are behavioral standards for users and sysops in addition to a well-defined administrative structure.

User rules

ILink has the following rules for users:

• On ILink, "you own your words." This means that users are responsible for what they say

and that their words are not to be used without permission.

• Activities may not violate U.S. law.

• No private messages are allowed in ILink areas, nor does ILink carry routed mail (unlike RIME).

• Profanity and flames are strongly discouraged.

• Encryption is not allowed, nor is use of UUENCODE. Graphics character sets such as RIP, ANSI, or NAPLPS are only allowed in conferences for that purpose.

• Substantial quoting of previous messages is discouraged, both because it is wasteful and because of possible copyright violation.

First-time rule breakers may be informally warned by the conference moderator. If the behavior continues for five days, an official warning may be issued. Disregarding formal warnings will result in suspension from the conference for a period of thirty days to six months. Further noncooperation will result in removal of access to the conference. Should the user be expelled from three conferences, all network privileges will be revoked for six months, preventing the user from accessing any conferences.

Sysop responsibilities

ILink member systems agree to:

• Operate seven days a week, twenty four hours a day, with the exception of system maintenance periods. U.S. systems must transfer mail packets at least four times a week, international systems at least twice a week.

• Run the latest versions of their BBS software and mail door.

• Take at least fifteen conferences, not including administrative conferences. Administrative conferences include the ILINK conference for administrators, sysops, and moderators; the NETNEWS conference for announcements; the NETUSERS conference for user complaints and concerns; and the

ILINK-INFO conference for information on ILink. All conferences should be designated with standard names. Member systems are also expected to subscribe to the administrative conference of their NDS node, if one exists.

• Keep an eye on their users. ILink sysops are expected to take responsibility for educating their users in ILink procedures and to respond to concerns of network administrators.

• Correctly format their taglines, which should look like this:

```
* QNet 2.0: ILink: Akbar's Mail Hub Berzerkeley, CA
```

Administrator responsibilities

ILink is a hobbyist network, and administrators serve on a volunteer basis. This includes the National System Administrators, who have national responsibility for the operation of the network and authority over network officers. Administrative functions are not necessarily coincident with mail-system responsibilities, so that the National System Administrator is not necessarily the sysop of the National Host system.

Administrative positions include:

• **Forum Administrator.** This person maintains the conference listings, creates and removes conferences, and appoints conference moderators.

• **Standards Administrator.** The network bouncer. Enforces the rules and removes misbehaving systems when necessary.

• **Admissions Administrator.** Coordinates the admissions juries, informs admitted and rejected systems, and evaluates systems during the trial period.

• **Records Administrator.** Distributes conference listings and prepares the monthly node list and annual membership statistics.

• **Vendor Relations Administrator.** Handles concerns of commercial and shareware vendors and solicits contributions to network upkeep. Recruits additional vendors.

• **Public Relations Administrator.** Promotes ILink and responds to user complaints and suggestions.

• **Legal Administrator.** An attorney who provides part-time legal advice to the network.

• **Planning Administrator.** Handles long-range strategic issues as well as contingency plans for network outages.

Conference moderators are not part of the network administrative structure but nevertheless play a very important role. Moderators are responsible for preparing the conference description for the monthly Forum listings as well as for maintaining their conference in conformance with network rules.

Grievance procedures

ILink has a formal grievance procedure. This involves mediation by the National Distribution Site sysop (unless they are involved), followed by formal arbitration if this is unsuccessful. The arbitration procedure allows individuals to respond to and rebut the charges.

How to join ILink

ILink looks for systems with involved, active sysops who take responsibility for their system and users. Applications are reviewed by a jury of five who log on to candidate systems anonymously. The jury members perform a screen capture of bulletins, message areas, and file areas and then report their evaluations.

The goal is to determine the system's vitality and the level of sysop participation. The jury looks for:

• Active, involved sysops. If there is a sysop team, this is OK, as long as there is a defined chain of authority so that someone is taking responsibility for the system.

• Systems with an active, involved user base. The jury checks the message base as an indicator of the level of activity on the system.

• Systems operating at least six months, with sysops who have mastered the intricacies of network mail systems. ILink is not a training ground for sysops.

• Public participation by the sysop in the message areas. If the sysop answers queries privately, this won't help the chances of admission, since the jury won't have any evidence of participation. Active sysops are important, since if there is a problem with a user, ILink network administrators want to ensure prompt sysop response.

Things ILink tries to avoid are:

• Systems that allow aliases in unrestricted conference areas. ILink defines an alias as an obvious fictitious name, such as "FISH FIENDS." An exception is made for conferences that accept aliases, such as the RECOVERY conference.

• Systems involved in illegal activities. BBSes with even a hint of illegal activity will be disqualified.

Rejected systems must wait at least four months before reapplying and may not apply more than twice in a twelve month period.

After systems are admitted, they enter a six month trial period, during which they can be dismissed for misbehavior without an appeals process.

For more information

ILink regularly updates information on the network. These files are available for download by new callers on the following systems:

Software Society	(908)777-7380
MicroSellar	(201)239-1346
BCS BBS	(213)962-9202

The files are:

ILAPPxx.ZIP	ILink application form generator, for PCBoard, Wildcat!, and Remote Access systems
ILDOCxx.ZIP	General information on ILink and requirements for joining
ILCONFxx.ZIP	ILink conference list
ILNKmmdd.zip	ILink node list

To join ILink, download and fill out the ILink application form and then upload it as a comment to sysop on the system specified in the ILAPP document. Although the eventual goal is to get application processing times down to three weeks, sysops have waited as long as four months for a response.

A sampling of ILink Conferences

Conference	What it's about
ADM_MEET1	ILink Administrators forum. Off-limits to others.
AI	Artificial Intelligence
AMIGA	AMIGA user's conference
ANSI-ART	Conference for ANSI pictures, which are not allowed in other conferences
ASTRONOMY	Astronomical conference
ATHLETICS	Exercise and fitness
AUDIO	High-end audio conference
AUTORACING	Car racing
AVIATION	Flying planes
BBS-ADS	Advertisements for BBSes
BBS-POLICY	How to run a BBS
BOOKMARK	Books and reading
CAREERS	Jobs and employment. Includes local, state, and national listings.
CARS&DRIVING	Automobiles
CD-ROMS	CD-ROM (data) conference. Audio CDs discussed in AUDIO.
CHESS	Discussion and games in progress
CHITCHAT	Personal discussions considered off-topic on other conferences
COCONUTS	Conference for ILink moderators and sysops. Off-limits to users.
COLLECTORS	People who collect stuff, and what they collect
COMEDY	Tasteful and nonracist jokes
COMPUTER4SALE	Buy and sell computer equipment
CONSPIRACYJFK	Conference for conspiracy theories
CONSULTING	Consultants conference
CONSUMERISSUES	Problems and policies with vendors
COUNTRYMUSIC	Discussion of country music
DOS_USENET	Discussion of BBS USENET gateways
DOWNUNDER	Conference for New Zealand and Australia
DUTCH	Conference for the Netherlands. In Dutch.
ECOLOGY	Environmental conference
ECONOMICS	Discussion of economic policy and choices
EEC	European Economic Community
ELECTRONICS	Consumer electronics
EMERGENCY	Policy, fire fighters, emergency room workers, etc.
ESPANOL	For Spanish speakers, mostly in Spanish
EUROCHAT	Chitchat for European systems
FANTASY&SF	Science fiction
FEMINISM	Women's conference
FRANCE	For French speakers, mostly in French
GARAGESALE	An online garage sale
GERMAN	For German speakers, mostly in German
GREEK	Discussion of Greece. In English.
HAMRADIO	Radio enthusiasts, including packet radio
HANDICAP	Computer use by the handicapped
HANDICRAFTS	Arts and Crafts
HEALTH	Medical issues and medical care
HISTORY	World history
HOMEGARDEN	Discussion for green thumbs and wanna-bes
ILINK	ILink administrative conference
ILINK-INFO	Information on ILINK, for new users or discussion on new conferences
INVESTOR	Investing and personal finance

JAZZ	Jazz music
LEGAL	Legal issues. Discussion for lawyers and nonlawyers.
MACINTOSH	Macintosh users
MEDIA	Discussion of movies and television
MEDICAL	Discussion of medicine, including computer use
MID_EAST	Discussion of the Middle East
MIDI	Discussion of MIDI music
MODERATORS	ILink moderator's conference
MOZART	Classical music conference
NETADMIN	ILink network administrator's conference
NETUSERS	Q&A with the moderators
NEWSLETTER	Conference for ILink newsletter volunteers. Off-limits to users.
OUTDOORS	Discussion of the great outdoors
PARENTS	Got kids? This one's for you.
PETS	Cats, dogs, snakes, etc.
PHILOSOPHY	Why are we here? Who are us, anyway?
PHOTOSIG	Taking pictures
POLICE	For discussion of law enforcement, justice system, etc.
PR-WIRE	Press releases
PSYCHOLOGY	Human behavior. What a mystery...
QUALITY	Quality control. How to make it happen.
REAL_ESTATE	Discussion about buying and selling. No properties for sale.
RECOVERY	Twelve step programs
ROCKNROLL	Popular music area
ROLEPLAY	Ongoing games between users
SATELLITE	Satellite TV discussion
SAUDI	Conference with Saudi Arabia
SCANDINAVIA	Conference with Norway, Denmark, Sweden, and Finland
SCI-TECH	Science and technology
SMALLBUSINESS	Discussions about small business
SOAPOPERA	As the world turns...
SPACE	Space shuttle and NASA
SPORTS	Spectator sports
STARTREK	Both original series and "New Generation"
TELECOM	Modems and BBSes
TELECOMMUTE	Stay home and work by modem instead
TRANSATLANTIC	Discussions across the Atlantic
TRAVEL	Travel advice
UNIX	System V, BSD, COHERENT, LINUX, 386BSD
VEGETARIANS	Veggies.
VIDEO	VCRs, Camcorders, etc.
WEIGHTCONTROL	Dieting and weight loss
WINE&BEER	Zymurgy and wine making
WOMEN	Women's issues
WRITERS	Are you a writer? Try this one.

CHAPTER 20:
USING MESSAGE READERS

What do I need?

In order to make use of message reader software, you will need to join a bulletin board that supports it. Many PC-based BBSes (such as Not Even Odd in Queens, New York, and Channel 1 in Boston) support the QWK format, and QWK support is supported by the QSO option module for TBBS. In addition, Internet online services such as HoloNet now support QWK, and a new USENET message reader format. The XRS format is supported by BBS software such as Remote Access.

Currently, Macintosh message reader software supports the XRS format (Alice) as well as the QWK format (Freddie and Freddie). For Windows, WinQWK supports the QWK format.

Acknowledgments

Hats off to Sparky Herring who created the QWK format. A word of thanks is also due to the author of Alice, Michael Keller; the author of WinQWK, Doug Crocker; and the author of Freddie, Kem Tekinay.

ZMODEM, UnZip, Alice, or Freddie

The preceding heading is not an excerpt from an X-rated movie but rather the three-step process that you'll need to go through to use message reader software.

Message readers are used to read packets prepared in a special format. Before sending them to you, your BBS will compress them, often using a PC format such as PKZIP. It will then send the packet via a communications protocol such as ZMODEM. Although ZIP packets are the de-facto standard, QWK message packers can use other compression methods instead, and typically allow you to

select the compression method as part of the configuration process.

In order for you to read the packets, you must first receive them. For this, you can utilize any telecommunications program. In order to decompress the packets, you will need decompression software. On the Macintosh, this software is UnZip; on the PC it is PKUNZIP. Finally, in order to read the packets you will need message reader software such as Alice (XRS), Freddie (QWK), or WinQWK (QWK). The process is shown in the figure on the next page.

Points versus message readers

We have just described the (rather complicated) process that you need to go through in order to use a message reader. In contrast, point software such as MacWoof (Mac) or Copernicus/COUNTERPoint (Mac) will automatically download the FidoNet packet, decompress it, and let you view it. Why, then, should you use a message reader instead of a point mailer?

The reason is that many sysops find point mailers very difficult to support on their end. Under the conventional FidoNet mail processing method known as EchoMail, a message is packed up and compressed for each system to which it is transmitted. If a system has 500 points carrying an echo, this means that not only will the message take up 500 times the disk space, but it will also take 500 times as long to prepare the packets. If a BBS takes one minute to prepare a packet for each point, it will be down for more than eight hours servicing 500 points!

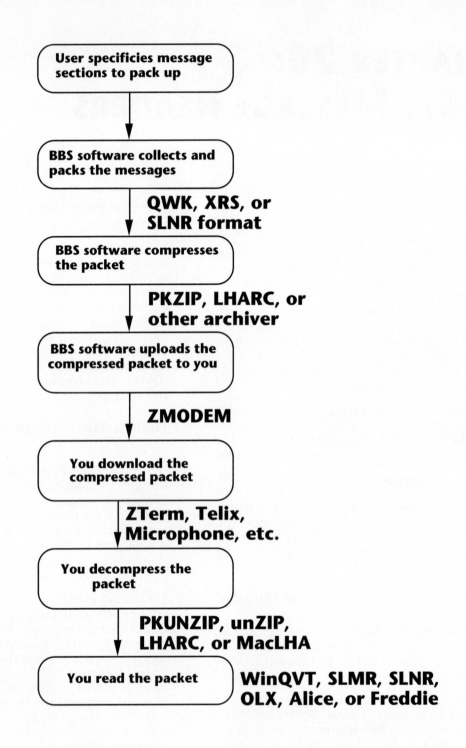

Tabby supports a better way of distributing messages, known as GroupMail. GroupMail archives each message only once, so that a system with 500 points will not expend more disk space or CPU time than a system supporting 10 points. However, sysops not running Tabby often find GroupMail very difficult to integrate into their BBS operation. Even if your chosen system runs GroupMail, point mailers also have other problems. Most FidoNet mailers do not currently support restrictions on access, such as time or download limits for points. This makes equitable distribution of resources difficult.

Finally, BBS utilities such as AREAFIX often have difficulty supporting a large number of points because they cannot handle multiple AREAS.BBS files gracefully.

In contrast, QWK packets are created and compressed only on request, and are deleted after being sent. They therefore occupy only temporary drive space, and if a user goes away on vacation, no packets pile up on the sysop's hard drive.

The other nice thing about QWK technology is that it operates within the BBS validation and security system; the caller logs in, and therefore all caller constraints remain in force during the session. In contrast, a point session does not involve the BBS at all, and the only security mechanisms are those supported by the FidoNet mailer (usually not much).

These advantages have made message readers much more popular among system operators than point mailers.

Message readers for the Macintosh

Alice

Alice is a message reader that supports either the XRS or QWK packet formats. Systems supporting XRS include Remote Access and QuickBBS; many systems support the QWK format, including PCBoard, TBBS, Maximus, and WildCat. The QWK format is rapidly becoming a standard because the specifications are publicly available. Channel 1 BBS, described in Part I: Quickstart, supports the QWK format, as does Not Even Odd in Queens, New York. HoloNet, the Internet online service described in Chapter 8: Internet Access, also supports the QWK format.

If Alice lived here, you'd be home by now

Alice is fairly easy to set up. When you double-click on the application for the first time, you will be greeted by a blank window entitled BBS Systems. It will look something like this:

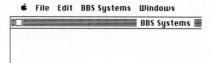

In order to set yourself up for using Alice with your favorite BBS, you will need to use the **Add New Box** command under the **BBS Systems** menu.

Alice will then ask you what kind of packets you wish to import:

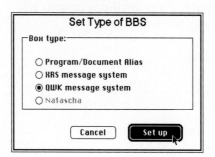

After this you will get you the following dialog box:

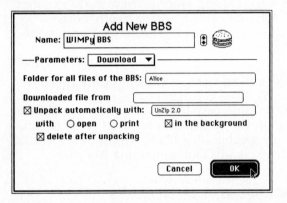

Fill in the name of the BBS and select its icon. You will then have to specify the parameters for uploading and downloading. For downloading, many BBSes are now using PKZIP v2.04 or higher, so it is a good idea to use UnZip v2.0, which can handle these archives, rather than v1.02, which is included with Alice. Make sure that the path to "Download files from the BBS" corresponds to the default downloading directory of your communications program. Otherwise, Alice won't be able to find the incoming packets! When in doubt, just put Alice in the same directory as your communications program, and everything should be fine.

Don't forget to also fill in the parameters for uploading. With the release of MacZip v1.0, the Macintosh can now create ZIP packets. Here is an example of the dialog box with the upload parameters filled in:

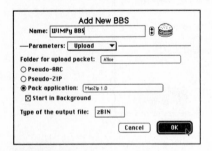

After you've filled out this dialog box, the icon for the BBS will appear in the **BBS Systems** window, like so:

We're not done yet. You must also set the **Global Parameters**, which is also available from the **BBS Systems** menu.

The dialog box displayed after selecting this menu choice looks like:

"Show 'Faces'" refers to a file of icons that give you a rough idea of what various people on the EchoMac Network look like. The concept of face files was first introduced with the COUNTERPoint point interface. Alice will read the face file bundled with COUNTERPoint.

Reading and replying with Alice

Assuming that you've set up the paths correctly, you should be able to open a downloaded packet by just double-clicking on the BBS icon. If not, you will have to manually run UnZip v2.0 on the packet.

Once Alice has found and unpacked the incoming packets, it will open up a window of the sections you've selected:

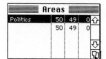

In addition, Alice will open up a message window:

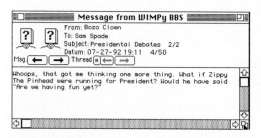

To reply to a message, select **Answer** from the **Message** menu.

This will bring up the Answer window:

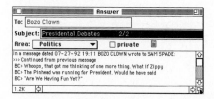

Remember that replying to messages does not put them onto your chosen BBS! The messages only end up on your host when you next call in and exchange mail packets.

The procedure for uploading packets is similar to that for downloading, except in reverse. Alice will create the outgoing packets and you will compress them and then upload them to your chosen BBS. MacZip v2.0 is recommended for compression.

Using Freddie

Freddie

Freddie is a QWK reader for the Macintosh written by Kemal Tekinay. To use Freddie, first download a QWK packet. Specify the ZIP compression method if you have a choice, and download the packet with ZMODEM if possible. ZIP compression and ZMODEM transmission will produce the smallest possible phone bill (unless you can use ARJ compression on the BBS end, and unARJ on the Mac end). Once you download the packet, use UnZip to decompress the packet and then use Freddie to examine it.

Message Readers for the PC

Using WinQWK

winqwk

WinQWK is an outstanding QMail (QWK) reader for Windows. It is available from EXEC-PC as well as on WinNet (part of the FidoNet Filebone).

Since WinQWK is only a message reader, not a telecommunications program, it assumes you have already downloaded a QWK packet from your BBS. To do this, run the QMAIL door on your favorite BBS, select conferences to archive, and request that QMAIL create a packet for downloading.

Use a telecommunications program with ZMODEM so that the file transfer will go as quickly and smoothly as possible.

Once you've got the QWK packet downloaded, fire up WinQWK to look at the packet. Since it will call PKUNZIP, PKXARC, or another appropriate decompression program to uncompress the packet, you should have these on your hard drive and in your DOS PATH statement. In order to select the packet, choose **Open** from the **File** menu. The following dialog box results:

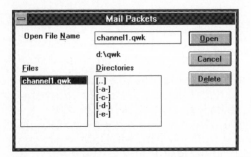

WinQWK will now unpack the packet, calling PKUNZIP in full-screen mode. After this is done, and assuming that the packet decompression is successful, you will be greeted with a dialog box of Message Areas:

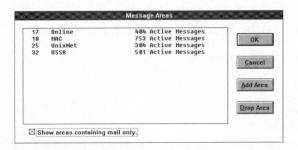

Next, choose an area to look at. In this example, I chose to browse the USSR echo. The typical message window shown below has a number of functions:

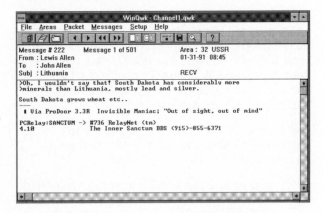

The little magnifying glass represents the Search function. Here's what the Search dialog box looks like:

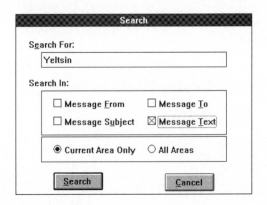

This is a very powerful feature because it can search both the message envelope (the TO:, FROM:, and SUBJECT: fields) and the message text. It puts all the messages that include the search string into a search area and then lets you browse them. In this example, I searched for the occurrence of the string Yeltsin in the text. Here's the result of the search:

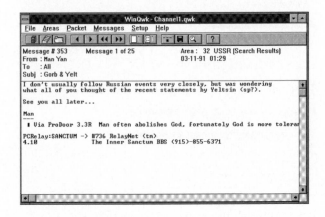

You can also get a list of subjects, if you'd like to browse the messages that way. Here's what the subject listing looks like:

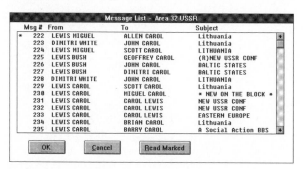

OLX

Online Express (OLX) is an MS-DOS QWK message reader that is bundled with QMODEM Pro. Integrating a telecommunications program and a message reader streamlines the process of downloading and reading a packet. With QMODEM Pro, you can go right from a scripted download of a QWK packet into the OLX reader, and OLX can be set to automatically decompress incoming packets.

The first step of the process is to write a script which will log you on to the BBS, call up the message reading door, download a QWK packet, and log off. This is easy to do with QMODEM Pro, since it can watch your keystrokes and create a script from them automatically.

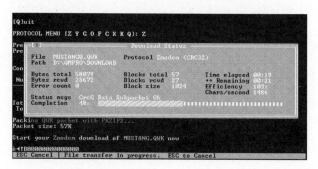

The next step is to enter OLX and select the incoming packet for examination:

At this point the packet will be decompressed:

```
PKUNZIP <R> FAST! Extract Utility Version 2.04c 12-28-92
Cpro. 1989-1992 PKWARE Inc. All Rights Reserved.
Shareware version
PKUNZIP Reg. U.S. Pat. and Tm. Off.

  80386 CPU detected.
  EMS version 4.00 detected.
  XMS version 2.00 detected.
  DPMI version 0.90 detected.

Searching ZIP: D:/QMPRO/DOWNLOAD/MUSTANG.QWK
  Inflating: SESSION.TXT
  Inflating: MESSAGES.DAT
```

If you are having problems decompressing packets, try setting OLX to call PKUNZIP, rather than trying to decompress the packets itself. This will avoid problems if and when a new version of PKZIP is released.

When the decompression is finished, you will be prompted to select the conference to read:

You can then read individual messages, or go to another conference.

When it comes time to reply, OLX supports the addition of tag lines on the end of messages, which are often humorous in nature:

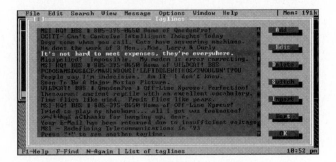

For more information

Information on the QWK format

FIDOQ110.ZIP (Fido to QWK translator)
QWKLAY13.ZIP (QWK layout info)
QWKSPC12.ZIP (QWK specifications)

EXEC-PC; P.O. Box 57, Elm Grove, WI 53122; voice: (414)789-4200, data: (414)789-4210

Message reader archives

Offline reader software is available via ftp oak.oakland.edu, cd /pub/msdos/ offlinemail

Part IV

Tutorial

"These libraries...perhaps have contributed in some degree to the stand so generally made throughout the colonies in defense of their privileges."

–*The Autobiography of Benjamin Franklin,*
Part V: Principles and Morals

"Liberty cannot be preserved without a general knowledge among the people, who have a right... and a desire to know; but besides this, they have a right, an indisputable, unalienable, indefeasible, divine right to that most dreaded and envied kind of knowledge, I mean of the character and conduct of their rulers."

– John Adams, *A Dissertation on the Cannon and Feudal Law,* 1765

Chapter 21:
How to Save Money on Your Phone Bill

Without being indicted

What do I need to know?

Today there are a bewildering array of options available for saving money on your phone bill – so many options that many people throw up their hands in confusion and don't bother to use any of them.

The alternatives really aren't that complicated, though. They fall into two categories: phone discount services and packet-switching networks.

Packet-switching networks

Packet-switching networks allow you to contact a distant site via a local call. The Internet is one such network; if you have an account on any Internet machine, you can remotely login to another machine via the **telnet** command.

There are also X.25 packet-switching networks, such as Tymnet. Through these networks you can connect to commercial services such as America Online, Portal, and Delphi. Finally, commercial online services such as CompuServe have their own packet-switching networks that can be used to access their services, as well as those of services such as The WELL and EXEC-PC.

From time to time, services spring up that rent time on packet switching services in order to provide cut-rate access to bulletin boards. These are generally of two types: out-dial services and services for specific BBSes. With an out-dial service, you use the packet-switching service as a substitute long-distance carrier, connecting to it locally and then teleporting to your destination city or a location close to it (called an out-dial port). You then pay for a phone call between the out-dial port and your chosen BBS. This is economical only if your chosen BBS is close to the out-dial port. The most popular out-dial service is PC-Pursuit, and therefore BBSes within a toll-free call of an outdial port are called "PC-Pursuitable" or just "Pursuitable." Out-dial services generally operate at 2400 bps.

In most cases users handle the complexity of PC-Pursuit logins by writing scripts. If your chosen program does not script, you may find PC-Pursuit tedious to use.

The other type of packet-switching service only allows calls to selected BBSes, with the packet-switching service routing your call all the way to the destination. If your service can be reached this way, this is preferable to an outdial service. Both CompuServe and Global Access currently offer 9600 bps (V.32) access this way.

If you are considering a packet-switching service, you should ask yourself whether you are primarily interested in activities that can be automated, such as downloading or batch receipt of messages, or activities that cannot, such as playing games or chatting. If you are primarily interested in automated activities, keep in mind that packet services may charge extra for characters transmitted above a certain amount. Efficient automated communications will generally exceed this allocation, forcing extra fees.

Those extra fees are often substantial enough that communicators using scripting, QWK mailers, or point mailers may prefer purchase of a V.32*bis* modem and use of a long-distance discount program, as opposed to use of a 2400 or 9600 bps modem and a packet-switching service.

Phone discount plans

If a packet-switching network is not available to reach your destination, or if it does not operate at your chosen speed (only CRIS, CompuServe and Global Access support V.32, and they can only be used to access a select number of services), you should consider a phone discount plan. In order to select the plan that is right for you, use your previous month's phone bill as a baseline against which to compare the fees of the discount plan. When you examine the bill, ask yourself:

• Are calls clustered within a particular area code? If so, you may wish to consider a long-distance discount service such as Reach Out America (see "Long-distance services" below). If calls are clustered within an area code, or to a particular exchange, the discount plan offered by your Regional Bell Operating Company (RBOC) may be appropriate.

• Are calls primarily evening (5 PM–11 PM Sunday–Friday), night (11 PM–8 AM Monday–Friday, all day Saturday, and Sunday from midnight to 5 PM), or day (8 AM–5 PM)? If you have a lot of day calls, consider whether you can move the traffic to other times by using store and forward software to send voice, fax, or data when rates are lower. I have found that simply being aware of when the billing rates change can help me schedule calls more effectively.

• What is the division of your calls between voice and data? If mostly data, does your modem run at 9600 bps or slower? If so, you are eligible to use a packet-switching service. Services supporting 9600 bps (V.32) include CompuServe Packet Network (CPN) and Global Access.

The bottom line

Figuring out which savings plan is right for you, and deciphering the bill after you choose one, is a daunting task. Most people just pick a plan

based on word of mouth and pay the bill when it arrives, with no idea whether their choice was the right one or not. It is rare for anyone to go through all the alternatives, calculating the estimated bills under the various plans in order to figure out the optimum. Some rules of thumb that I have used are:

• If you are a communications beginner, your monthly phone bill for modem calls is under $20/month, and you have a 2400 bps modem or slower, you will not benefit from any of the discount plans, unless you are also generating more than $10/month in calls to a particular area code or exchange. In this case, you should look into a long-distance or local discount plan. Use of packet-switching services would entail purchase of a scripting communications program, which will effectively negate any savings you might get, if you include the price of the software.

• If you are a communications intermediate with a monthly modem phone bill of $50/month or more, you probably have favorite BBSes or services. You may wish to consider long-distance and local discount services, as well as upgrading your modem to V.32*bis*/V.42*bis* and changing your calling habits. If your favorite BBS is accessible by high-speed packet-switching networks such as Global Access, then you should sign up for this, since Global Access only charges $4/hour nonprime, and long-distance discount plans run $6/hour at best. If Global Access does not support your chosen BBS, then you should look into a long-distance discount plan. Be aware that packet-switching networks typically support V.32, not V.32*bis*.

These strategies are generally preferred to accessing 2400 bps packet-switching services, because high-speed modems have come down in price dramatically in the last year, tipping the balance in their favor. In contrast, PC Pursuit requires complex dialing commands, and while it is inexpensive ($1/hour for usage within your basic allocation), you will often have trouble getting through to your desired city.

For those oriented toward messaging, I recommend using store and forward software such as UUCP, message readers, or FidoNet points, which will allow you to automate your logons and shift calls to evening and night hours.

• If you are an intermediate or advanced communicator with a monthly bill of $100/month or more, you should definitely purchase a V.32*bis*/V.42*bis* modem. You should also consider automated message reading, UUCP, or point systems.

In-state calling (within California)

Telephone service   811-7600
Full weekday rates   8 AM–5 PM, M–F
Evening rates   5 PM–11 PM, M–F
(30% off full weekday rates)
Night/weekend rates   11 PM–8 AM, M–F,
Saturday and Sunday all day, and holidays
(60% off full weekday rates). Holidays include
January 1, President's Day (third Monday in
February), July 4, Labor Day, Thanksgiving
Day, and Christmas Day.

Although the vast majority of readers have a phone, it is worthwhile to go over the options for basic phone service, because the various savings plans will build on that. In California, there are three types of residential phone service: Flat-Rate Service, Measured-Rate Service, and Universal Lifeline Telephone Service. Under Flat-Rate Service, you may make an unlimited number of local calls of any duration. Under Measured-Rate Service, you get a $3 calling allowance to Zones 1, 2, and 3, which are mapped out in your telephone book. Under Universal Lifeline Telephone Service (which you are only eligible for if your household gross income is less than $14,300 for a family of one or two and you have only one phone) you pay 50 percent of the Measured-Rate Service with an allowance of 60 local calls, or 50 percent of Flat-Rate Service with unlimited local calls. California readers will probably want to purchase the Flat-Rate Service.

Although you might take it for granted, the conditions and rates of your basic phone service change frequently, and they differ between states. For example, some states bill local calls by duration for residential customers,

which can result in dramatically increased charges for telecommunicators.

Pacific Bell Call Bonus   811-7600

Pacific Bell offers a variety of bonus calling plans that apply to calls made within a metropolitan area. All call-bonus plans have a setup fee of $5.

Wide-Area Plan
$6.75/month, allowance of
$8.50/month

The Wide-Area Plan has the widest coverage but only applies during specific hours. Under the plan, you may make calls to the 415, 510, 707, and 408 area codes (the 408 area code excludes Monterey). You must call within discount hours, which are 12 PM to 2 PM and 9 PM to 8 AM Monday–Friday, and all day Saturday and Sunday.

Circle Plan $4.75/month

The Circle Plan gives a 30 percent discount on all calls made within a 40-mile radius.

Community Plan
$7.45/month, and allowance of
$14.90/month
$14.90/month, and allowance of
$29.80/month
$22.35/month, and allowance of
$44.70/month

The Community Plan is the most specific of the call bonus programs. With the Community Plan, you pay a monthly rate, and you get an allowance that is double the monthly fee. This applies only to specific prefixes within a community; although charges vary, a single plan is $7.45/month, with an allowance of $14.90; a double plan is $14.90/month with an allowance of $29.80, and triple is $22.35/month with an allowance of $44.70. If you exceed your allowance, you get a 30 percent discount against the remaining calls.

Long-distance services

Each major long-distance carrier now offers long-distance discount plans. You do not have to choose the long-distance plan from your existing carrier, although if you don't, you'll have to add special access codes to your dialing string. Since some telecommunications programs cannot handle very long dialing strings, try breaking the dialing command into two parts, or go with a program such as ZTerm which allows long dialing strings.

Reach Out America   (800)222-0300

To be eligible for Reach Out America, you do not need to be a subscriber to AT&T long-distance service. However, if you are not, you will need to add the access code for AT&T to your dialing string so that the special rates will apply. Each Reach Out America plan has a $5 order-processing fee.

The night/weekend time period includes all day Saturday, Sunday until 5 PM, and Sunday through Friday 10 PM–8 AM. Evening discount applies from 5 PM–10 PM Sunday–Friday. Daytime discount is 8 AM–5 PM Monday–Friday.

Half-Hour Plan
$4.00/month for 30 minutes during night/weekend
$0.12/minute additional night/weekend
20 percent discount on calls made during the evening

The Half-Hour Plan is designed for callers who make 30 to 60 minutes of night/weekend calls a month.

Basic Plan
$7.15/month for first hour
$0.11/minute additional night/weekend
5% discount on international and in-state calls

The Basic Plan is similar to the Bonus Plan but does not include discounts on evening calls between 5 PM and 10 PM. AT&T Calling Card and Call Ma Card calls can be included in the plan for an additional $2/month.

Evening Plan
$7.80/month for first night/weekend hour
$0.11/minute additional night/weekend minutes
20% discount on calls made during the evening
5% discount on international and in-state calls

This plan is for callers who make an hour or more of night/weekend calls and also place evening calls. AT&T Calling Card and Call Ma Card calls can be included in the plan for an additional $2/month.

24-Hour Plan
$8.70/month for first hour night/weekend
$0.11/minute additional night/weekend minutes
25% discount on evening calls
10% discount on day calls
5% discount on international and in-state calls

This plan is designed for callers who make an hour or more of night/weekend calls but also place day and evening calls. AT&T Calling Card and Call Ma Card calls can be included in the plan for an additional $2/month.

AT&T Select Saver
$1.90/month
$0.12/minute for night/weekend and evening calls
$0.20/minute for daytime calls
5% discount to other area codes

Select Saver is only available for out-of-state calls to a specific area code; connection requires payment of a $5 order-processing fee.

For comparison purposes, normal daytime rates are $0.25/minute, and normal night/weekend rates are $0.16/minute.

Anyhour Plan
$12.00/month for one hour any time
$0.12/minute for night/weekend and evening calls
$0.20/minute for daytime calls
5% discount on international and in-state calls

This plan is designed for customers who make two or more hours of calls, with one-third of them during the day, or make one hour of day calls.

Sprint Callers Plus
(800)877-4646 (general info)
(800)366-7587 (Callers Plus info)

The Callers Plus program is like a Frequent-Flyer program. Every time you make a long-distance call, you accumulate bonus points that can be exchanged for long-distance credits, travel, or merchandise. You accumulate 10 points for each net dollar of long-distance calls (net dollars exclude taxes). Minimum points needed to redeem is 5000 points. If you redeem 5000 points, you will get a credit for thirty minutes of free calling or a $4.07 credit. At the dollar value of the credit, this translates to a discount of less than 1percent.

Callers Plus service is automatically provided to all Sprint customers who average more than $20/month on long distance.

MCI Prime Time Plan   (800)444-4444
$7.50/first hour, $0.1083/minute additional

The Prime Time Plan applies to out-of-state calls only. Hours are Monday–Friday 5 PM–8 AM, all day Saturday, Sunday until 5 PM, and 11 PM Sunday night until 8 AM Monday morning.

Prime Time Plan members also get a 10 percent discount on out-of-state calls made outside of the Prime Time Plan hours.

MCI Prime Time Combined (800)444-4444
$8.75/first hour, $0.1083/minute additional

The Prime Time Combined Plan covers calls in and out of state. Other than a higher first-hour fee, the charges and conditions are the same as for the Prime Time Plan.

Prime Time Combined members also get a 10 percent discount on in- or out-of-state calls made outside of the plan hours.

MCI Daytime Plan   (800)444-4444
$12/first hour, $0.20/minute additional

Hours for the Daytime Plan are Monday–Friday 9 AM–5 PM.

MCI SuperSaver Plan   (800)444-4444
$5/first hour, $0.083/minute additional

Hours for the SuperSaver Plan are midnight Friday till midnight Saturday. There is a maximum of five hours/month on this plan.

MCI Friends and   (800)444-4444
Family Plan

This plan has no monthly fees. To use it, you list the numbers you call most often; if they have MCI, you get a 20 percent discount on calls any time of day. This plan can be used in addition to other plans, such as Prime Time or Prime Time Combined.

Packet-switching services

Global Dialup Services (GDS)
$39/installation + $39/month
WorldLink (Mac), PSILink (PC) $29/month
(2400 bps), $39/month (9600 bps)
WorldLink Lite (Mac) $19/month (2400 bps), $29/month (9600 bps)
PSILink Lite (PC) $19/month (2400 bps), $29/month (9600 bps)

Global Dialup Services (GDS) is a service of PSI that allows you to connect to the Internet by a local call from many major cities. If you are running an Internet BBS, this allows callers to use your service without needing another Internet account to `telnet` from. PSI also offers Internet access via a variety of methods, including a Macintosh interface service created in association with Intercon, called WorldLink. The PC version is called PSILink.

PSI, 11800 Sunrise Valley Drive, Suite 1100, Reston, VA 22091; (703)620-6651, fax:(703)620-4586, email: `info@psi.com`.

CompuServe Packet Network

CompuServe Packet Network (CPN) is one of the most expensive packet-switching services, but in terms of the quality of connection and the ease of use, it is one of the best.

CPN does not offer outdial services, so you cannot use it to call a system that has not signed up with them. The WELL is accessible via CPN, but CompuServe refused to disclose what other services are available, since they consider that privileged information.

In order to access CPN, you need to call your local CompuServe access number, which you can get by calling (800)848-8990 and navigating their voicemail system. Once you call your local access number and it asks you for the host name, you can type WELL and get to The WELL. Information on access rates for The WELL is available when you sign up as a new user. Rates vary, depending on what service you are trying to call, so it is best to contact your destination service first. As to how you choose a destination service, since they consider that proprietary information, is beyond me.

CompuServe Information Service, Inc., 5000 Arlington Centre Boulevard, Columbus, OH 43220; (800)848-8990. Access number (510)482-0190; (510)434-1580 for 9600 bps V.32/MNP-4.

PC Pursuit
$30 signup fee
Normal membership
$30/month minimum for 30 hours nonprime time
Family membership
$50/month minimum for 60 hours nonprime time
Extra hours
$3/hour nonprime, $10.50/hour prime time
$5 password change fee

The charges for PC Pursuit are $30/month for 30 hours of nonprime-time use (6 PM–7 AM weekdays, 24 hours on Saturday, Sunday and holidays). If you use more than 30 hours per month, the fees go way up. In effect, PC Pursuit punishes volume users, rather than giving them preferential rates. This "volume undiscount" caused a great many PC Pursuit users to switch to other services. In order to sign up for PC Pursuit, dial your local TymNet access number and type c pursuit at the @ prompt.

PC Pursuit, (800)835-3638, BBS: (800)877-2006; Customer Service: (800)336-0437. Nonprime time is 6 PM–7 AM local time Monday–Thursday, 6 PM Friday–7 AM Monday, and all day New Year's Day, July 4th, Labor Day, Thanksgiving, and Christmas Day. Prime time

hours are 7 AM–6 PM local time, Monday–Friday.

CRIS
Normal user membership
$20/month minimum for 10 hours any time
Additional hours:
$3.50/hr for daytime, $2/hr off-peak
BBS provider fee signon: $50

CRIS is a new breed of packet switching service. It allows high-speed access (up to 14.4 Kbps) to a selection of BBS services for $2/hr off-peak.

CRC, 406 North Jackson, Bay City, Michigan 48708, (517)895-0500, (800)745-CRIS, fax: (517)895-0529, email: jim@cris.com

Global Access
$20 signup fee + $10/month maintenance
$4/hour nonprime, $15.50/hour prime time

Global Access, G-A Technologies, Inc., P.O. Box 31474, Charlotte, NC 28231, (704)334-DATA, (800)377-DATA for phone number near you. To log in to the BBS, type:

```
CONNECT 9600
@D
TELENET
816 60002.72
TERMINAL=D1
@C GLOBAL
GLOBAL CONNECTED
                        Welcome to Global Access!
            Outdials Avail:  45 Cities (as of 6-
Aug-92)
Please Login: guest
Connected...
Loading BBS .... Please Wait ......
RemoteAccess 1.11/Professional
Please enter your full name:
```

For more information

Information and software relating to PC Pursuit is available via ftp oak.oakland.edu, cd /pub/msdos/pcpursuit.

CHAPTER 22:
FILE TRANSFER BETWEEN MACS, PCs AND UNIX

And other strange mating rituals of computerdom

Why should I read this section?

The microcomputer revolution did not bring all the benefits it promised, at least partially because of the proliferation of incompatible hardware and software. If you've ever tried to transfer a file between a Mac, a PC, and a UNIX machine, you've probably encountered a few problems. This chapter provides solutions.

What do I need?

Nothing right now. By the end of this chapter, you'll probably have a good idea of what additional hardware or software to purchase.

Acknowledgments

Without Steve Jobs, there might not be a Mac.

Introduction

In transferring files between two computers, the first step is to get the file from one machine to another. The second step is to convert the file into a format that the receiving machine can understand. This chapter talks about file transfer; the next one covers file conversion.

There are several ways to get files from one machine to another. If the machines are close together, a serial or parallel cable will do. If the machines are connected by local or wide area networks, files can be exchanged that way. If they are located within walking distance, sneaker-net or disk exchange might be appropriate. Finally, for machines separated by long distances, transmission by modem is attractive.

Mac to PC

Disk Exchange

~ AccessPC

Disk exchange is one of the easiest ways to transfer files between machines that are close together. To ensure that all IBM, Macintosh, and UNIX machines in your firm can exchange diskettes, you will need to equip all machines with drives that can read 3.5-inch 1.44 Mb diskettes.

Macintosh computers equipped with 3.5-inch SuperDrives (also known as Floppy Drive High Density or FDHD) can read and write IBM 3.5-inch diskettes using Apple File Exchange (AFE). They can also mount diskettes on the desktop using software such as DOS Mounter from Dayna, AccessPC from Insignia, and PC Exchange from Apple. Owners of 1.44 Mb drives on the PC can use Mac-In-DOS from Pacific Micro to read and write Macintosh diskettes. Not only are these solutions reasonably priced, but they also require no additional hardware, provided your machine has the right kind of drive. All Macs produced since September 1988 have shipped with SuperDrives.

Users should be aware that most transfer programs will only transfer a Mac file's data fork. This means that to transfer files from the Mac to the PC, they should be saved either in a PC format (available in many packages) or as text. Alternatively you may use BinHex 5.0 or MacBinary AFE to combine the resource and data forks and other relevant information into a single data stream. Transferring PC files to the Mac is less complex since the PC files have only a single fork.

If your Mac doesn't have a SuperDrive, consider selling it to purchase one that does. It's that much of a convenience if you transfer files often. Plus, selling your Mac and buying a new one is often less expensive than upgrading.

If you insist on keeping the old clunker, there are several add-on products that will allow you to read 5.25-inch and 3.5-inch PC disks on a Macintosh. Apple offers a NuBus card and 5.25-inch drive for the Mac II that will allow you to read IBM PC 360K diskettes. This drive does not allow you to mount PC diskettes at the Finder level, despite costing several hundred dollars. It also cannot read 1.2 Mb diskettes, the most common PC disk format. Dayna offers a similar drive that can read 1.2 Mb diskettes and does mount the disks on the desktop.

Syquest cartridge exchange

DOSTransfer

Using a PLI Syquest drive and the DOSTransfer software, you can format and write a Syquest cartridge on the PC and then read the entire cartridge on the Macintosh. This is a very fast way to transfer 44 or 88 Mb of files.

DOSTransfer operates as a control panel device, and all you have to do to make it work is install it in your system folder. In order to transfer files, insert a DOS formatted Syquest cartridge and bring up DOSTransfer.

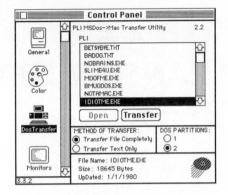

Software emulation

SoftPC

As IBM PC software developers pay even less attention to the PC's ROM BIOS than Mac developers do to the Apple Developer's Guidelines, full PC compatibility can be guaranteed only by fairly strict adherence to PC hardware standards. For example, as the vast majority of PC telecommunications programs bypass the ROM BIOS serial routines to address the PC's serial chips directly, those chips must generally be present and in the proper locations for such software to function. In order to save money, Macintosh MS-DOS cards have often attempted to use Macintosh hardware such as the Mac serial ports or disk drives instead of including appropriate PC hardware. The result is incompatibility with some PC software.

A better solution is to purchase a software emulator such as SoftPC. When I first encountered SoftPC, I was flabbergasted. It's more compatible with DOS software than Windows 3.0! The SoftPC/AT add-on, which runs 50 percent faster, is also available and does EMS as well as 80287 emulation. With the SoftPC/AT addon, I have yet to find a PC program that can't be run under SoftPC/AT. Since SoftPC sells for under $250 mail order, this is a very viable option if you have a 68020 or 68030 machine. If your Mac has a SuperDrive, you can even insert an IBM 1.44 Mb formatted disk and have SoftPC boot off it! If you have a CD-ROM drive, you can also mount IBM CDs and browse them using the appropriate PC software. SoftPC even runs in the background under Multifinder or System 7.

Insignia, maker of SoftPC, has recently introduced a Windows version of SoftPC. Although I haven't seen it, the odds are that this software is more compatible with Windows v3.1 than with OS/2 v2.0. Insignia also offers AccessPC, a utility that allows you to mount PC disks on the desktop. This works well with SoftPC, allowing you to mount a SoftPC-emulated PC hard drive on your Macintosh desktop and transfer files to and from it.

Apple File Exchange

Apple File Exchange

Although Apple File Exchange is shipped with every Macintosh, the Installer does not install the software onto your hard drive, so you will have to look for it on your system software disks. For example, on the System 7 disks, AFE is located on the Install 2 disk.

AFE works with Macs equipped with 1.44 Mb SuperDrives. All Macs shipped after September 1988 have had these drives as standard equipment. Older machines can be upgraded to the newer drives by bringing your machine to an Apple Dealer.

One of the critical things to understand about AFE is that it does not mount PC formatted diskettes on your desktop; it only transfers (and with the appropriate modules, coverts) files. If you insert a PC-formatted diskette without AFE running, you will get the "This is not a Macintosh Disk" dialog box. If you want to be able to mount PC-formatted diskettes, then you need to purchase a utility such as AccessPC, or the Apple DOS mounting utility, called PC Exchange. For more information on these and other file transfer products, please consult Appendix B: Choice Products.

Transferring files with AFE

Since you cannot insert PC disks until AFE is running, you will need to start up the software first and then insert your PC disk.

When you do, you will be greeted with a screen something like this:

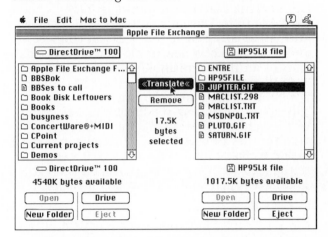

In order to transfer a file from the PC diskette to the Macintosh, select one of the PC files from the right-hand list and click on the **Translate** button. This will bring up the following dialog box and move the file onto your Mac hard disk.

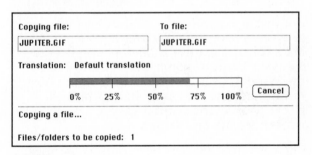

Translation

Using AFE this way will only move a PC-formatted file onto your Macintosh. It will not give the file a format that can be read by a Macintosh program. You will need to purchase extra software to do this. If you find AFE tolerable, you may wish to purchase translators that will work with AFE. Alternatively, you can purchase stand-alone translators. For more information on file format translation, please refer to Chapter 23: File Conversion.

Cable and modem transfer

If your PC does not have a 3.5-inch drive, or if your Macintosh does not have a SuperDrive, then you will need to find another way to accomplish the transfer. A practical solution is the LapLink Mac III Connectivity Pack, available from Traveling Software. This comes with an amazing cable that lets you connect the serial port of a new or old Mac to the serial port of an IBM-compatible machine. LapLink Mac III transfers files at over 100 Kbps. Since it's built for file transfer, it can copy directories, including subdirectories, selections of files, and so on. LapLink Mac will also transfer files to portable PCs that may not have a slot available for a network card. It's very automated so that you can start a transfer, go and have lunch, and when you come back, it will be done.

Since LapLink Mac works over a modem, it is a solution for machines located far away from each other. Since it also uses very efficient file-transfer protocols and can transfer many files and directories at once, it is a good choice to take on the road with your PowerBook.

Modem transfers – MicroPhone II

Another reasonable way to transfer files between a Mac and a PC over a modem (or two Macs for that matter) is Microphone II from Software Ventures. Both the Macintosh and the Windows versions come with a mini-host script that functions as an instant bulletin board system. The script is easy to set up and worked for me on the first shot.

MicroPhone's file transfer protocols are rock solid, so the odds are very high that this will work. If you don't have Microphone on the PC side, I recommend using Telix, since its ZMODEM protocol implementation is solid.

Screen control – Mac to PC

Farallon has recently introduced a version of Timbuktu that lets you contol a PC over the network using a Macintosh. However, Timbuktu Remote does not yet offer this feature. A future release of Microcom's software, Carbon Copy Mac, will reportedly allow you to dial into a PC running Carbon Copy PC and control it remotely from the Mac. Of course, you'll need a copy of Carbon Copy Mac and Carbon Copy PC.

PC to Mac Disk Exchange

Software from PLI (MacToDOS), Insignia (MacDisk), Pacific Micro (Mac-In-DOS),REEVEsoft (MacSEE), and Acute Systems (MAC-ETTE) is available to read and write Macintosh disks from the PC. MacSEE and MAC-ETTE are shareware; see Appendix B for listings.

Mac to Mac

Modem transfers – ARA

Perhaps the simplest way to transfer a file between two Macintoshes is by using Apple's Remote Access (ARA). Although ARA is no longer bundled free with each PowerBook, you may purchase a copy from an Apple dealer for $200.

When you call another Macintosh that has ARA set up to answer the phone, your Mac can mount folders set up for file sharing on the remote machine. Your Mac can also become part of the remote system's AppleTalk network, provided that the remote machine grants you the privilege to do this. To copy files between machines all you do is click and drag.

In order to use ARA, both the remote system and the calling system need to be set up. Use the ARA installer to put the software onto your computer; don't just copy the material into your system folder. To set up the remote system, you need to run the Remote Access application that the ARA installer will move onto your hard disk. It will bring up a dialog box that looks like this:

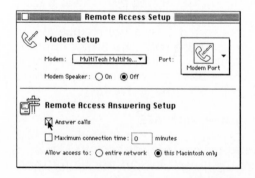

Choose the port to connect your modem to, and select your modem type from the list. For security purposes you will need to decide if you will allow the caller to get access only to your Macintosh or to the rest of the network, such as printers or shared folders on other machines. Think this over carefully. Also make sure to check the box that says "Answer calls" so that the remote system will pick up the phone. You will also need to choose the settings on the calling system.

One of the nice things about ARA is that you can set up the remote file sharing system as an alias under System 7. Instead of an actual hard disk icon on your desktop you will have the alias icon. When you double-click on the alias for Java, a remote server, a password dialog box will appear:

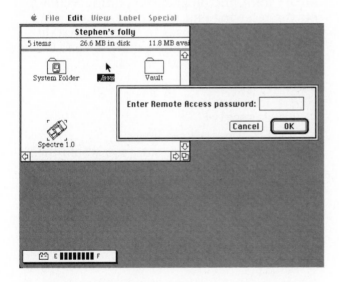

Assuming that you've entered the password correctly, ARA will initiate a connection to the remote machine. You don't even have to tell it to dial!

Once you're connected, you'll be provided with a standard AppleShare dialog box. This

provides a nice extra layer of security, allowing you to give various groups of users access to different folders on the server.

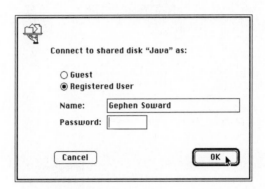

Once ARA has checked your password, the remote shared volume will be mounted on your desktop.

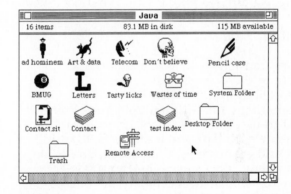

Caveats

Although ARA is marvelously easy to use, it is much faster to save a document directly to an ARA-mounted volume than it is to do a Finder copy. ARA can take twice as long to transfer a file via a Finder copy as by a direct save.

Timbuktu Remote

Timbkutu Remote lets you remotely control the screen of another Macintosh. It installs as a desk accessory and is easy to use.

Here's a screen shot of how I set it up to answer the phone:

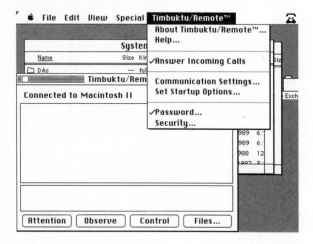

Mac or PC to UNIX

8 bit vs. 7 bit

When transferring Mac files to a UNIX machine there are several considerations you should keep in mind. One is that if you are transferring a file with multiple forks, you will need to use BinHex 4.0 first in order to combine both data and resource forks as well as icon and creator-type information, and so on, into a single data stream. BinHex 4.0 is therefore similar to MacBinary in concept, except that it also converts 8-bit data to 7-bit data.

Why are files often stored in 7-bit form on UNIX machines? Since FTP offers a binary transfer mode, files in FTP archives could just as well be stored in MacBinary format. Many UNIX machines now have no problems with 8-bit data transfers, and many support ZMODEM transfers. Perhaps the only good reason for storing files in 7-bit format is to allow for compatibility with FTPmail or other services that allow transfers of files within mail messages, since several networks do not allow 8-bit messages. For this reason, single-fork files (such as .GIF files) are often converted to 7-bit using a program called UUENCODE.

Several versions of UUENCODE/UUDECODE are available for the PC. On the Macintosh, StuffIt Deluxe can handle

UUENCODE/UUDECODE, as can UUTool and UULite. See Appendix B for listings.

Kermit

MacKermit

The KERMIT protocol is a foolproof way to transfer files back and forth to UNIX machines, since it can convert an 8-bit data stream to 7-bits before transmission, and therefore will work over 7- or 8-bit connections. When you transfer a file with the KERMIT protocol, you should understand that the file will arrive on the receiving machine in binary form; the program supporting KERMIT on the receiving end will convert the incoming 7-bit data back to 8 bits to recreate the file. To start up Kermit under UNIX, type:

```
% kermit
C-Kermit, 4F(095) 31 Aug 89, VAX/Ultrix
Type ? for help
C-Kermit>receive
Q.,,. VVV
```

On the Macintosh or PC side, you would then use Kermit to send the file to the UNIX system. In order to send a file from the UNIX machine to your machine, you would type the following and then select **Receive file…** from the **File** menu in MacKermit, or type **receive** in PC Kermit.

```
% kermit
C-Kermit, 4F(095) 31 Aug 89, VAX/Ultrix
Type ? for help
C-Kermit>send rs6000
Escape back to your local Kermit and give a
RECEIVE command...
```

Disk Exchange

Many UNIX machines, such as the Sun SPARC series, are capable of reading DOS formatted 3.5-inch disks. For UNIX-compatible machines running on PC-compatible hardware, this capability may be quite sophisticated and may include the ability to run DOS software (VP/ix) or execute DOS commands (Xenix or SCO UNIX). For these systems it is often simplest to use your SuperDrive to read and write DOS-formatted diskettes.

tar format

If you are transferring many files in several directories, all at the same time, it is often convenient to use the UNIX tar facility to archive the files before transferring them. MacTar is a program for dearchiving or creating UNIX tar archives; versions are also available for PC.

LAN transfers

If both the UNIX system and the PC or Mac are on a local area network, then you have several options for transferring the file. If the LAN supports TCP/IP, you can use a program such as NCSA-Telnet on the Mac or PC to download the file using Files Transfer Protocol (FTP).

Another possibility is to transfer the file by mounting an NFS volume on the UNIX machine and copying the Mac or PC file onto it. NFS software for the Mac includes InterCon's NFS/share and Cayman's NFS product; for the PC, Sun's PC NFS is recommended.

For further information on UNIX communications, please consult *UNIX Communications* by Anderson, Costales, and Henderson, Howard SAMS, 1991 (listed in Appendix A: Communications Bibliography).

Specifications Q&A

How do I get the specifications for MacBinary? For BinHex 4.0? For ZMODEM?

For the details on ZMODEM, we recommend that you contact the author, Chuck Forsberg. Be aware that you will have to pay for the specifications of the latest release of ZMODEM, ZMODEM-90, or Moby Turbo. Information on ZMODEM/YMODEM/YAM is available from Telegodzilla, the Omen Technology BBS that Chuck runs in Portland, Oregon. Telegodzilla can be reached at (503)621-3746.

As for the MacBinary and MacBinary II specifications, as well as BinHex 4.0 specs, these are available on CompuServe.

How do I get the specifications for KERMIT?

Details on Kermit, including source code, are available via `ftp cunixc.cc.columbia.edu` or `cuvmb.cc.columbia.edu` on the Internet. Alternatively, you can write to Kermit Distribution, Columbia University Center for Computing Activities, 612 West 115th Street, New York, NY 10025.

File transfer Q&A

How can I transfer a file from a VAX machine?

Other than local area network software, your best bet is to use Kermit. You can get a copy of Kermit for your VAX (whether it runs VMS or BSD) from Columbia. Mac or PC Kermit will allow you to communicate with VAX Kermit to transfer files.

I want to network a Mac to an IBM machine. How do I do this?

If your installation is 80 percent Macintosh and 20 percent PCs, you might consider PC AppleShare or TOPS. PC AppleShare is now available from Farallon Computing, and TOPS is available from Sun. However, you should be aware that both TOPS and PC AppleShare are RAM hogs, which can make it difficult to run standards such as Lotus 1-2-3 or Windows 3.0. For this reason they are not beloved by network administrators in the corporate world. However, you might want to live with it, since both the software and AppleTalk cards are relatively inexpensive.

If your workplace is 80 percent PCs and 20 percent Macs, PC AppleShare doesn't make much sense. In this case, you're probably going to go with something like Novell Macintosh, LAN Manager for Macintosh, or a Mac implementation of NFS. Be aware that all these alternatives will require Ethernet cards on the Macs and the PCs.

What kind of 5.25-inch IBM drive do you recommend for the Mac?

The DaynaFile is the best 5.25-inch IBM drive for the Mac, because it will read 1.2 Mb as well as 360K diskettes and will mount them on the desktop (DOS mounter is included). However, it might be worthwhile to have the PC disks written in 1.44 Mb 3.5-inch format instead, so that if your Mac has a SuperDrive, you can read them directly. I recommend use of AccessPC from Insignia in this situation, so that the 3.5-inch IBM disks will mount on the desktop. Pacific Micro has a product Mac-In-DOS, which will allow you to read, write, and format Mac diskettes on a PC.

For more information

FidoNet conferences

PCMAC	Mac-PC compatibility issues

USENET groups

comp.unix.msdos	DOS software running under UNIX
comp.protocols.kermit	The KERMIT protocol
comp.protocols.misc	Miscellaneous file transfer protocols
comp.protocols.nfs	The Network File System protocol

When we send files, we often have to hang up the modems and call over the phone to get it working. Is there some way to transmit both voice and data at the same time?

Using ARA, you could transfer a voice file along with your data, but this would slow the data transfer to a crawl. If you use ZTerm to do the transfer, it will occur at maximum speed, and it should just work. No more phone calls!

CHAPTER 23:
FILE CONVERSION

And other bedside miracles

Introduction

Getting the file from here to there is only half the battle. You've got to be able to read it, too! If you're handed a diskette with some files on it, how do you get them into your favorite application?

The first problem is if you don't even know what kind of file you have. Luckily, you can tell a lot about the file by the file extension. Before you can convert the file, you need to look it up in the table at the end of this chapter to figure out what you have and the kind of conversion you are trying to do.

The most common types of conversions are:

> **Cross-platform conversions, same application**
> **Word processing to word processing**
> **Spreadsheet to spreadsheet**
> **Raster graphics to raster graphics**
> **Vector graphics to vector graphics**
> **Vector graphics to raster graphics**

We will discuss each of these conversions in turn.

Cross-platform compatibility

Remember those applications with versions on the PC and Macintosh? Surely such applications must be capable of transferring files between the Mac and PC versions, right? Guess again, greenhorn!

As it turns out, several popular cross-platform packages do not really offer full cross-platform compatibility, only application interface compatibility. This is not enough to allow for productive multiplatform use.

Although WordPerfect's conversion facilities are very good (usually converting embedded graphics without difficulty), if you have embedded graphics you will find conversions between Mac Word 5.0 and Word for Windows 2.0 to be shaky at best. PICT images frequently do not carry over correctly and will require retouching. The stylesheets carry over with the text, but you must have the same fonts installed on both platforms in order for the documents to look the same, and even then, TrueType metrics are not identical across platforms.

Importing Windows Word 2.0 files into Macintosh Word 5.1 is a lot easier than converting in the other direction, since Word for Windows 2.0 seems to choke on Macintosh format files. Since Mac Word 5.1 supports export to Windows Word 2.0 format, I suggest doing it that way.

There are also problems in transferring between the Macintosh and the PC version of PageMaker. PC PageMaker cannot convert many files from Mac PageMaker 4.0. However, files imported from Mac PageMaker 3.2 usually convert over just fine, so if you can go backwards, you will be able to do the conversion.

Users of Ventura Publisher for the Macintosh and the PC report that the two packages use different hyphenation algorithms so that files imported from one to the other do not hyphenate or paginate the same way, resulting in hours of lost effort.

In summary, do not rely on vendor claims of cross-platform compatibility. Go through conversion of a typical document on your own before purchasing, to see how much work is involved.

Word processing and spreadsheets

Word processing to word processing

The best group of word processor translators is something called PC MacLink, from DataViz. They will handle virtually all word processing formats, but generally they will not handle embedded graphics.

I have sometimes attempted to export from Mac Word 5.1 using the RTF facility. Be aware that Word 5.1 has extended RTF to support things like the equation editor by inserting binary objects into RTF; other word processing formats won't know how to interpret these objects and won't be able to convert them. In converting between MS-Word 5.1 and WriteNow on the NeXT, I also had problems with stylesheets not carrying over. You should use RTF only if a direct conversion is not available.

Font to font

For a truly compatible word processing conversion, you will need the same fonts on both machines. If you are using Adobe fonts on one platform, the same fonts are now available for use on the Mac, PC, or NeXT platforms. If you are using TrueType fonts, TrueType Converter by Chris Reed will bring over many Macintosh TrueType fonts to the Windows environment. Be aware that there is no guarantee that TrueType fonts will paginate the same way under Windows as they did on the Macintosh, due to differences in the underlying graphics model.

Spreadsheet to spreadsheet

If you need to run 1-2-3 macros on the Macintosh, get Lotus 1-2-3 for Macintosh. Microsoft Excel v4.0 for Windows or Mac can read and write Excel 3.0, Excel 2.1, SYLK, Text, CSV, WKS, WK1, WK3, DIF, DBF 2, DBF 3, and DBF 4 formats. It can also read and execute Lotus 1-2-3 macros. If you are going from Lotus 1-2-3 to Excel 4.0, and you own Excel, you will not need to purchase a converter. Be aware that if you are translating from Excel to Lotus, there are many functions in Excel that are not

in Lotus so that the conversion may have problems.

Raster graphics to raster graphics

In the hierarchy of conversion nightmares, the easiest problems to solve are those that involve converting between two bitmap formats. Collage Complete (PC), Picture This (Mac), or GraphicConverter (Mac) can handle most of these, and if they can't, you can always convert to GIF and go from there. GIF is also useful for cross-platform conversions. If you can convert a Macintosh bitmap into GIF format and transfer the GIF to the PC, you will then be able to use the Hijaak software to convert the GIF to a great many PC bitmap graphics formats.

If you need to convert to or from UNIX raster formats, you will want to get hold of Image Alchemy or deBabelizer.

Trouble with TIFFs

The TIFF standard requires implementations to be able to read files written in either Motorola or Intel byte ordering. Most Mac TIFF implementations followed the standard, but PC implementations often did not, implementing only Intel byte ordering. You may also have trouble because of the addition of LZW compression to the TIFF 5.0 standard; readers who can only handle uncompressed TIFF 4.0 files will choke on compressed TIFF 5.0 files. TIFF 6.0 will support JPEG compression.

If you have a TIFF file in Motorola byte ordering and need to save it with Intel byte ordering to be able to use it on the PC, I recommend the DataViz translators.

JPEG formats

JPEG compression algorithms offer very good compression ratios with only slight loss in image quality. As a result JPEG compressed formats are rapidly becoming the standard.

On the Macintosh you can convert between GIF and JPG format using Imagery. On the PC, you can use JPEG v2.0.

PICT to BMP

Collage Complete or deBabelizer can convert PICT files to BMP files.

BMP to PCX

Paint Shop Pro can handle this one, as can many other utilities (see Appendix B: Choice Products for listings).

PICT to PCX

This can be handled by GraphicConverter, Picture This, deBabelizer or Collage Complete.

Vector graphics to vector graphics

Vector to vector format conversions are still a problem area. Picture This still cannot convert Micrographx Designer or Corel Draw files to or from PICT, nor can it export to the Computer Graphics Metafile (CGM) format. Luckily, Hijaak can convert PICT files to CGM, GEM, or DXF formats, which in turn can be imported by many PC vector drawing programs.

Converting to DXF format should be a last resort because the .DXF file format does not support features such as fill patterns and text styling. Therefore you will lose a good deal of your graphics along the way and will need to rework the file.

If you are starting out with a Claris CAD file, or don't have a PC, you may have to pay through the nose to convert files. Claris Graphics Translator will do the conversion between Claris CAD or MacDraw II and IGES and DXF formats, but for the hefty price of $299.

Vector graphics to raster graphics

Conversion of vector graphics to raster form is usually straightforward. Hijaak can handle many of these conversions, as can GraphicConverter and Picture This to a more limited extent.

What's my format?

Raster graphics formats

Extension	Software
.BBM	Electronic Arts Deluxe Paint
.BIT	Monochrome bitmap (PC, raster)
.BMP	Bitmap format for Windows or OS/2. Can be read by Windows Paintbrush.
.CUT	Format for Media Cybernetics Dr. Halo PC graphics program
.CMU	CMU Window Manager Dump files (UNIX)
.DIB	IBM/Microsoft OS/2 Bitmap format
.FAX	One of dozens of incompatible FAX formats
.FSV	USENET Face Saver
.GIF	Graphics Interchange Format file, a graphics file format developed by CompuServe, portable between many different types of computers
.IFF	Amiga Interchange Format
.IMG	Digital Research GEM Paint
.JIFF	Format utilizing JPEG compression (JFIF)
.JPG	File compressed using JPEG/JFIF format
.LBM	Electronic Arts Deluxe Paint
.MAC	Claris MacPaint file (usually used on PC-based BBSes, raster)
.MGR	Window Manager Dump files (UNIX)
.MSP	Microsoft Paint Format
.PCL	HP-Laserjet "print file" format
.PCX, .PCC, or .DCX	PC Paintbrush format
.PGM	PBMPLUS gray-scale format
.PM4	PageMaker PC
.PNT	MacPaint file (raster)
.PPM	PBMPLUS color format
.PZI	Application Techniques Pizazz Plus
.RAS	Sun Raster
.RLE	Run-length encoded (raster)
.SC?	RIX Softworks ColorRIX Format
.TGA	Truevision TARGA (raster)
.TIF or .TIFF	Tagged Image File format (raster) in one of several modes: monochrome, gray scale, color with enclosed palette, RGB color, or fax
.XBM	Xwindows Bitmap
.XDO	Xerox Doodle Brush files

.Extension	Software
.XWD	Xwindows Window Dump file
.WIN	Truevision TARGA Format
.WPG	WordPerfect graphics format

Vector graphics formats

.AI	Adobe Illustrator
.CDR	Corel DRAW (vector)
.CGM	Color Graphics Metafile format (vector)
.DRW	Same extension used by MacDraw and Micrographx Draw, but different formats! (both vector, though)
.DXF	Graphics format used by AutoCAD (vector)
.EPS or .EPSF	Encapsulated PostScript. Used by Adobe Illustrator and Aldus Freehand.
.GEM	GEM Draw (vector). Used by Ventura Publisher.
.HPGL	HP plotter output file (vector)
.PIC	Graphics format used by Lotus 1-2-3 (vector) and Paul Mace Pictor and Grasp
.PS	PostScript file. A popular way of distributing documents that can be printed by anyone with access to a PostScript printer, regardless of computer type. On the Macintosh, these files can be created by selecting "PostScript ® file" as the destination when printing. Can be sent to a PostScript printer by a utility such as SendPS.
.WMF	Windows Metafile Format

Other formats

.ARC	ARC archive (see Chapter 24: Compression Primer)
.BIN	MacBinary format. When you download this file, it will appear on your disk with its original name. MacBinary is discussed in Chapter 3: The Tower of Telecombabble.
.CPT	Compact Pro archive (see Chapter 24: Compression Primer)
.CSV	Comma-separated values
.DBF	dBASE format
.DCA	IBM Interchange format (see RFT)

Extension	Software
.DD	Disk Doubler archive (see Chapter 24: Compression Primer)
.DOC	Microsoft Word file (either DOS or Windows)
.DOX	MultiMate 4.0
.gz	GNU zip
.HQX	File run through BINHEX 4.0 Program. BINHEX 4.0 is discussed in Chapter 3: The Tower of Telecombabble.
.LHA	LHARC archive (see Chapter 24: Compression Primer)
.LZW	LHARC archive (see Chapter 24: Compression Primer)
.PIT	PackIt archive (see Chapter 24: Compression Primer)
.RTF	Rich Text Format
.RFT	IBM interchange format
.SHAR	UNIX shar archive
.SIT	StuffIt Archive (see Chapter 24: Compression Primer)
.SYL	Microsoft SYLK format (spreadsheet)
.TAB or .TSV	Tab separated values
.TAR	UNIX Tar archive (see Chapter 24: Compression Primer)
.TXT	Text file; can be read by TeachText, McSink, or another text file-reading utility
.UU	Program run through UUENCODE.
.W42	WordPerfect version 4.2
.W50	WordPerfect version 5.0
.W51	WordPerfect version 5.1
.WKx	Lotus 1-2-3 file format where x = 1, 2, or 3.
.WP	OfficeWriter (sometimes also WordPerfect)
.WPG	WordPerfect file
.WRI	Windows write
.WRK	Symphony (spreadsheet)
.WRT	MacWrite file
.WRD	Microsoft word file
.WS	WordStar format
.XCL	Excel spreadsheet format
.XLS	Excel version 2
.XY	XYWrite III
.z	Pack archive (see Chapter 24: Compression Primer)
.Z	Compress archive (see Chapter 24: Compression Primer)
.ZIP	PKZIP archive (see Chapter 24: Compression Primer)
.ZOO	ZOO archive (see Chapter 24: Compression Primer)

File conversion Q&A

I am trying to export from Mac Word v5.1 to Word for Windows 2.0, but it keeps crashing. What should I do?

Embedded graphics are often lost in converting between word processing formats. Word's conversion utilities are buggy, particularly when attempting to convert large files with embedded graphics. One trick that works for me is to split the file into small pieces, each with only a few pictures. I then export each of the pieces to Word for Windows format and put them back together on the PC.

Don't even think about trying to import the Mac document in its original format using Word for Windows. I have never seen the Word for Windows import facility work correctly on Mac Word files. However, Mac Word 5.1 can successfully import Word for Windows 2.0 documents, sometimes even large ones.

How can I find out more about the JPEG format?

Contact the X3 Secretariat, Computer and Business Equipment Manufacturers Institute, 311 First Street NW, Suite 500, Washington, DC 20001-2178.

I am trying to convert Windows BMP screen shots to Macintosh PICT format. How should I do this?

Windows BMP files are not compressed, and so they take up a great deal more room than other formats such as PCX or GIF. For this reason using BMP format is not recommended. Take your screen shots in PCX format instead, and if you need to transfer them, you can embed them in a Word for Windows 2.0 document and then import the file into Mac Word.

What is Apple's Easy Open?

Easy Open is a System 7 extension descended from XTND technology that will be included in a future system software release. Distributed by vendors such as DataViz, rather than by Apple itself, the goal of Easy Open is to make file conversion transparent. For example, instead of seeing a "The document...could not be opened" message, the user will be offered translation options.

How can I move files from Windows format to Mac Format?

The closest things we have to standard Windows formats are BMP and PCX for Graphics and Windows Write for word processing.

The best software for translating word processing documents is made by DataViz, called MacLink Plus/PC. The best graphics translator for the PC is called Collage Complete. Collage Complete will convert many PC formats to many other formats, including GIF or PICT format. Wherever possible, I recommend converting from PCX rather than from BMP since most converters seem to have an easier time with this. If you create a PICT file on the PC, remember to change the type and creator bits so that the file can be properly recognized.

Problem: If your PC file is something like Micrographx Designer, you will have converted from a vector file to a bitmap in the process. Not so good. What you really need is a program that will convert from Designer to PICT directly.

How can I move files from the Mac to Windows?

I recommend moving the file to the PC first, then using a converter such as Collage Complete. I have been able to successfully convert PICT and GIF files to various PC formats using this method. For further information on how to move the file from the Mac to the PC, consult Chapter 22: File Transfer Between Macs, PCs, and UNIX.

I need to work on a presentation with someone who has a PC. How can I do this?

Microsoft PowerPoint claims to be capable of translating files produced on the Macintosh so that they can be opened by the Windows version of the program. I haven't tried this so I can't tell you if it really works or not (see comments on compatibility of Mac Word and Win-Word earlier).

How can I convert files from an Apple II word processor to the Macintosh?

You can use Apple File Exchange to transfer the file from a disk written under ProDOS to the Macintosh. Your next step will be to convert the file to a Macintosh word processor format.

If your file is in AppleWorks format, then it can be read by translators in Microsoft Works, ClarisWorks, and MacWrite II. Microsoft's translator comes in the form of an AFE module called WORKS-WORKS TRANSLATOR. Unfortunately, it has a serious bug: It will truncate the output file after 20K. For this reason you may find it easier to use MacLink Plus, which can translate AppleWorks file format to virtually any other Macintosh word processing format.

If you are using AppleWriter, you can just import the document into another word processor since AppleWriter saves its files in ASCII format. However you will then have to redo the formatting.

How do I convert from PostScript to another format?

TechPool Software's Transverter Pro has a built-in Postscript interpreter that allows it to handle conversions between PostScript, Adobe Illustrator, PICT, CGM and WMF.

I used Hijaak on the PC to convert a file to PICT format, but now MacDraw can't open it. Why not?

FileTyper 1.0.1

Hijaak (or any other PC-based converter) does not give the file the creator and type information needed to associate it with an application. You will need to enter this information manually, using utilities such as FileTyper. Using FileTyper, you can set the Type, Creator, and Finder Flags.

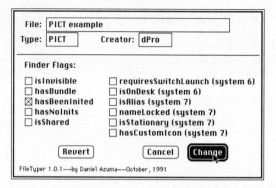

Here is a listing of the types and creators for various applications:

File	Type	Creator
Excel Binary	XLS4	XCEL
Excel Text	TEXT	XCEL
GifConverter GIF	GIFf	Gcon
Lotus 1-2-3	LWKS	L123
Lotus text	TEXT	L123
MacPaint	PNTG	MPNT
MacWrite	WORD	MACA
MSWord Binary	WDBN	MSWD
MSWord Text	TEXT	MSWD
PICT (MacDraw)	PICT	dPro
Teachtext	ttro	ttxt
Teachtext text	TEXT	ttxt
unZIP	pzip	pzip

How can I convert files from Apple II Paintworks™ to the Macintosh?

deBabelizer will read Paintworks™ files and can convert them to many formats, including PICT.

For more information

FidoNet Echoes

PCMAC — Transfer and conversion issues

USENET groups

comp.graphics — Discussion of computer graphics

CHAPTER 24: COMPRESSION PRIMER

Or how to .SIT without choking on a .PIT

What do I need?

Most of the shareware or public domain software described here is available on the Internet archives sumex-aim.stanford.edu or oak.oakland.edu or on EXEC-PC (414)789-4352.

Acknowledgments

There are a lot of great compression products by a lot of developers. However, three authors come to mind: Phil Katz, author of PKARC and PKZIP; Bill Goodman, author of Compact Pro; and Ray Lau, author of StuffIt. These products have garnered the most support in the Mac and PC communities. Here's to you!

Introduction

Compression and decompression is one of the most confusing topics in telecommunications. There are more than a dozen different compression formats in common use today, with corresponding decompression utilities. Many of these compression programs have changed their algorithms during their history, or have only released partial specifications, and as a result decompression programs are often hard pressed to keep up.

In order to write this article, I located the different compression and decompression programs and tried compressing and decompressing to see what worked best. There are no doubt some programs or versions that I have overlooked; if so, please send me a note, and I'll try to get things updated for the next edition.

If keeping up with compression utilities is so time-consuming, why do people use them?

The answer is the savings they provide, in time and money. When telecommunicating, you have to pay the online service fee, in addition to any fees to the phone company. As a result, people have a keen interest in minimizing the amount of time spent online. Today's MNP-5 and V.42*bis* modems provide compression on the fly, but the compression is not as good as what you can get by compressing files beforehand. Compressing files prior to transferring them saves downloading time and also guarantees that you get all the files related to a program in one package – the documentation, order forms, data files, program, and so on.

People also use compression programs to save hard drive space. There are now programs such as Stacker (IBM or Mac) that utilize compression as part of the operating system, doubling the size of your hard drive. Although I use Stacker on my PC, I often wish I didn't, since many programs are incompatible with it. Unfortunately, once you start with one of these programs it is hard to stop, since you now have more data on your hard drive than you could fit on it if you switched back.

The most popular formats for the Macintosh are Compact Pro (.CPT), and StuffIt (.SIT). You will also occasionally see files compressed with PackIt (.PIT). On the PC side, most BBSes have their files compressed with PKZIP (.ZIP) or an ARC variant (.ARC). You will also see files compressed with PAK (.PAK), ZOO (.ZOO), ARJ (.ARJ), and LHARC (.LZH). On UNIX machines you will see files compressed with compress (.Z), gzip (.gz or .z) or tar (.tar). There are also specialized compression formats for graphics, such as .JIF and .GIF (all machines).

Before uploading a file, please be considerate enough to consider the recipient's preferred compression format. Sysops generally prefer the most efficient format so they will be able to put as many files as possible on the BBS. For example, while Disk Doubler is popular and easy to use (it operates from a Finder menu), it also does not compress files as well as Compact Pro or StuffIt. As a result, few BBSes permit Disk Doubler uploads.

When do I have to pay a shareware fee for compression programs?

On the Macintosh, shareware fees are only required if you use the compression program, not the decompression program. For example, StuffIt LITE requires a shareware fee, but UnStuffIt Deluxe, UNSTUFF, and UnStuffIt DA do not; Compact Pro requires a shareware fee, but Extractor does not. PackIt required a fee, while UnPackIt did not. However, there are exceptions. MacCompress and MacLHA, both of which can create archives as well as decompress, are free. Extractors for PC files, such as MacBooz, UnZip, and ArcPop are also free.

On the PC side, LHARC, ARJ, GZIP and compress are free for noncommercial use, while ARC, PKZIP, PAK, ZOO, and others are shareware.

Macintosh compression formats

What are the differences between StuffIt, StuffIt Deluxe, StuffIt Classic, StuffIt LITE, StuffIt Expander, UnStuffIt, UnStuffIt DA, UNSTUFF, and UnStuffIt Deluxe?

For years, StuffIt was the almost universally accepted Mac compression program. The last shareware version was StuffIt LITE. StuffIt Expander is the freeware expander that can extract files from StuffIt LITE or StuffIt Deluxe archives. StuffIt Classic, also known as StuffIt 1.6, can only unstuff archives created by StuffIt Deluxe 2.0 or earlier. Therefore you should upgrade to StuffIt LITE, since this can handle StuffIt Deluxe 3.0 archives. The commercial version of StuffIt is called StuffIt Deluxe and is now in version 3.0. Since the compression format changed between version

3.0 and version 2.0, if you attempt to unstuff v3.0 files with an earlier version of the software, you will get an error message.

Files created in StuffIt format are given the .SIT extension. Files created in StuffIt Deluxe format are sometimes given the .SDX extension, and sometimes .SIT. Aladdin Systems, publisher of StuffIt Deluxe, prefers that you use .SIT, because StuffIt Deluxe archives can be decompressed by the free program StuffIt Expander, which can also expand Compact Pro and PackIt archives. Therefore, anyone can decompress a StuffIt Deluxe v3.0 archive. Extractor, the companion decompression program to Compact Pro, can also only decompress StuffIt v1.5.1 files. The SITtoCPT utility will convert StuffIt v1.5.1 files to compactor format. This is useful because Compact Pro archives are usually smaller and decompress more quickly.

Aladdin has released a shareware version of StuffIt Deluxe v3.0, called StuffIt LITE. Why they called it StuffIt LITE, and not just StuffIt v3.0, I don't know. With StuffIt LITE, you can compress files in the new StuffIt Deluxe v3.0 format, or in StuffIt v1.5.1 format. With the release of UNSTUFF, the StuffIt decompressor for the PC, IBM compatibles can now decompress archives created by StuffIt 1.5.1 through StuffIt Deluxe 3.0.3. Be aware that other PC StuffIt extractors such as UNSIT version 2.3 can only decompress StuffIt 1.5.1 archives.

UnStuffIt was the free desk accessory that would decompress StuffIt v1.5.1 archives from the Apple menu. UnStuffIt Deluxe is also free and will not only decompress StuffIt archives, but will also decompress StuffIt Deluxe v2.0. However, it won't work with StuffIt Deluxe v3.0 archives, so forget about it and just use StuffIt Expander. You can also forget about UnStuffIt DA, since it only works with older archives. If you're willing to pay the shareware fee, you should get StuffIt LITE instead of StuffIt version 1.5.1.

StuffIt Deluxe v3.0 will also decompress .ARC and .ZIP files created on the PC. StuffIt LITE does not have this feature, as well as others like scripting, HyperCard XCMD's, and lots of other neat stuff.

What does .PIT mean? .CPT?

.PIT is the extension given to files created with PackIt, which is not used much anymore. They can be decompressed using UnStuffIt, StuffIt, StuffIt Classic, or StuffIt Deluxe, in addition to PackIt and UnPackIt. If you need to decompress a .PIT file on a PC, use unPACKIT. Be aware that it will not decompress encrypted files created by PackIt III. .CPT is the extension given to files created by Compact Pro. These files can be decompressed on the PC with PC Extractor. They can also be decompressed on the Mac by Extractor, which is free. Compact Pro is fast and highly efficient, and a lot of intermediate or advanced users like it for that reason. However, the user interface could use improvement, and we find that beginners are confused by it. Compact Pro will also decompress files compressed by StuffIt v1.5.1 or by PackIt III.

Which compression utility should I use if I only use a Macintosh?

Both Compact Pro and StuffIt LITE or StuffIt Deluxe are good programs. If you can afford the $70 for StuffIt Deluxe, I recommend it because it can also decompress .ZIP and .ARC files, and because it supports AppleEvents and scripting. StuffIt Deluxe is also slightly faster and creates slightly smaller archives than Compact Pro.

I just downloaded a ZIP file and when I double-click on it, it won't unZIP. Why not?

ZTerm is smart enough to set the file type and creator bits correctly when downloading non-Macbinary files like ARC, ZIP, and GIF files. If you use other telecommunications programs on the Macintosh, you'll have to do it yourself, using FileTyper. If double-clicking opened unZip v1.0 and it couldn't handle the archive, try unZip v2.0 since this now can decompress archives from versions of PKZIP up to 1.93.

What is MacCompress?

MacCompress is a program that can compress or uncompress UNIX .Z archives. It can also compress files in a special "MacCompress mode" that is not compatible with UNIX compress.

When using MacCompress to compress files for decompression under DOS or UNIX, make sure that your DOS or UNIX compress program and MacCompress are using the same type of compression. For example, if you use 16-bit compression in MacCompress, you'll need to use 16-bit decompression in UNIX or DOS uncompress.

MacCompress is convenient because it can compress entire folders. When it is run on applications, or data files with resource forks, it compresses the data fork only and leaves the resource fork alone. It also includes file names, creator bits, and other Macintosh-specific information in the file so that it can later be decompressed without problem.Unfortunately, MacCompress does not use the MacBinary standard to perform this operation; this means that if you transfer the file to a UNIX system, and then use uncompress on it, you will not be able to transfer it back to the Mac and then bring it back to the original form with BinHex 5.0.

Like the UNIX version of compress, MacCompress replaces the files it compresses with the .Z archives when asked to compress, and similarly deletes the .Z archives when decompressing.

Since UNIX compress and uncompress also have DOS versions, compress is a universal compression utility. This is helpful if you find this chapter mind-boggling and are trying to simplify your life. LHARC and GZIP are also a universal compression utilities, with both compression and expansion available on the Mac, PC, and UNIX.

However, users of MacCompress should be aware that the program has troubles decompressing files over 500K in size. This is very inconvenient, because compressed PostScript files are usually larger than this. With UNIX versions of PKZIP now available, I have often found it necessary to uncompress the file and then ZIP it before downloading. Since the ZIP format is more efficient than compress, this will save on downloading time. While UNSTUFF allows you to decompress StuffIt Deluxe archives on the PC, the UNIX equivalent, unsit, can decompress only StuffIt

1.5.1 archives. This means that StuffIt is not yet a universal compression utility.

PC compression formats

There are quite a few compression programs for the IBM PC. An .ARC archive can be created on an IBM PC by the program ARC, or by PKARC. StuffIt Deluxe v3.0 will decompress ARC files created by ARC v6.2 or earlier, or by PKARC v3.6 or earlier. On the Mac, ArcPop will also decompress ARC v6.2 archives or PKARC v3.6 archives. I do not recommend using of MacARC v0.03 because it will not decompress ARC archives later than v5.1, or PKARC archives.

Systems Enhancement Associates (SEA) has recently released a commercial version of ARC, called ARC+Plus 7.12. This program can create archives that cannot be decompressed by ARC v6.2, PKXARC, StuffIt Deluxe, or ArcPop. Therefore, there is no Macintosh program on the market that will decompress all .ARC files. ARC+Plus 7.12 is not common enough for this to be a problem.

If you wish to create .ARC archives on the Macintosh, you must use ArcMac v1.3 or later. However this program is quite slow and is idiosyncratic in its operation (it uses an MS–DOS interface called the Martian Operating System).

StuffIt Deluxe v3.0 opens .ARC files. If you cannot get it to work, first make sure you have version 3.0; that you are using Expert Menus; and that you have installed the software with the installer disk, and not just copied pieces of it from a friend. It's only $70 (mail order), so go and get your own copy and don't come complaining to us!

The .ZIP format, created by PKZIP, is another PC compression format. On the Mac, MacZip or ZipIt can create PKZIP archives. The Macintosh decompression program to use is UnZip 2.0. It will unzip archives created by PKZIP v1.93. StuffIt Deluxe v3.0 will only handle archives from PKZIP v1.1. I do not recommend using ZipPop because it does not handle PKZIP v1.1 or later archives, and UnZip v2.0 is free. If you stick to UnZip v2.0 you'll be safe.

What is ZOO? LHArc? PAK?

These are all PC compression programs. Of these, the Mac program that will uncompress ZOO files is called MacBooz; the Mac program to uncompress LHARC files is called MacLHARC or MacLHA. There is no program to decompress .PAK files on the Macintosh at the moment.

What does the extension .LZH mean? .PAK? .ZOO? .ARJ? .gz?

.LZH is the extension given to files created by LHARC on the PC. Mac LHARC 0.41 can decompress archives created by PC LHArc 1.13c; MacLHA 2.0 can decompress archives made by PC LHA 2.0. Mac LHARC can also create .LZH files that can be decompressed on the PC, provided they are created in the normal (non-MacBinary) mode.

.ZOO is the extension given to files created by ZOO on the PC. MacBooz can decompress these files on a Macintosh.

.ARJ is the extension given to files created by ARJ on the PC. unArjMac can decompress these files on the Mac.

.gz is the extension for GNU Zip (known as GZIP under DOS), which has versions for Mac, UNIX, and PC.

UNIX compression formats

I downloaded a large file in .Z format, but when I tried to uncompress it, the software blew up. What should I do?

MacCompress and versions of PC uncompress have problems uncompressing large files, often resulting in crashes. In order to avoid problems, I suggest you use UNIX uncompress on the archive, and then recompress it with another compression utility such as ZIP, now available for UNIX. Since neither UnZIP for Mac nor PKUNZIP have problems with file size (other than lack of disk space), your problems will vanish. You can use the zipress shell script to automate the process.

Zipress script
Convert a file from .Z format to .zip

```
#!/bin/sh
#
if test $# -ne 1
then
        echo Usage: $0 file-to-zip
        exit 1
fi
uncompress $1.Z
zip -m $1.zip $1
```

For information on where you can get the UNIX version of ZIP, check Appendix B.

MacCompress often cannot uncompress files compressed in 16-bit mode under UNIX. Several PC uncompress utilities can only uncompress 14-bit files. If you are unsure whether your uncompress utility can handle 16-bit compression, you can specify 14-bit mode by using the following UNIX command:

```
compress -b 14 <filename>
```

Will compression speed file transfers if you are already using V.42bis?

Yes. Below are test results with various compression methods done over a V.42*bis* connection on a ZMODEM download. The tests show that even 12-bit UNIX compression results in very substantial incremental savings over V.42*bis* compression on the fly. These timings do not count the time to compress the file; it is assumed that this is done offline.

Compression method	File Size	Time to download, secs	Time savings
none	123265	65	0
Compress, 12 bits	68245	43	34%
Compress, 14 bits	61323	38	41%
Compress, 16 bits	58403	36	44%
ZIP	47859	29	55%
ARC	67692	43	34%

Which compression utility should I use if I want to compress files on a PC and have them decompressed on a Mac or UNIX?

Use PKZIP. On the Mac you can decompress .ZIP files created by PKZIP v1.93 with UnZip v2.0, or from v1.1 or earlier with StuffIt Deluxe v3.0. Under UNIX, you can use unzip. Alternatives are LHARC or GZIP on the PC. If you compress with LHA v2.13 on the PC, you can decompress them with MacLHa v2.0 on the Macintosh, or lharc under UNIX. You can also compress them with GZIP on the PC, and you can decompress them with GNU Zip on the Macintosh or GNU unzip under UNIX. Another alternative is to use the PC version of Compress, along with MacCompress and UNIX uncompress.

Which compression utility should I use if I need to compress files on a PC, Mac, or UNIX and have them decompressed on any machine?

You can use ZipIt or MacZip and unZip (Mac), PKZIP and PKUNZIP (PC), or zip and unzip (UNIX). You may also use lharc (UNIX) with MacLHA and PC LHA, or compress and MacCompress. Use MacCompress in UNIX mode on the Macintosh and the compress and uncompress utilities on the PC or UNIX. Free versions of compress and uncompress are available for the PC, in addition to commercial versions that are available as part of the MKS Toolkit from Mortice Kern Systems. Compress and uncompress are usually included with UNIX.

There is also a StuffIt 1.5–compatible stuffer for UNIX (sit), as well as a decompressor (unsit). On the PC, there is a decompressor (unsit). If you use StuffIt Deluxe or StuffIt LITE in v1.5 mode, you will be able to create archives on the Mac and decompress them under UNIX or on the PC. Being able to decompress Mac files on the PC or UNIX only makes sense if they are produced in a universal format such as ASCII text or .GIF. These files can be viewed on any machine.

Finally, there is GNU Zip, which is available for Mac, PC, and UNIX.

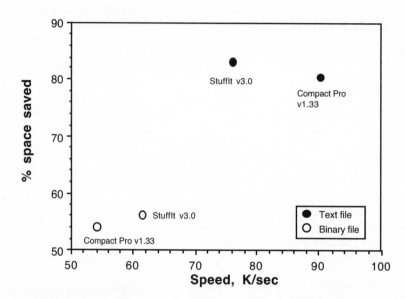

Percentage saved versus speed, Macintosh compression programs, text file document (Naval numerics library source code), and binary application (FrameMaker). Tests done on Mac Centris 610, 8 Mb, 80 Mb drive, System 7. Speeds based on an average of compression and decompression times. Versions are StuffIt Lite v3.0 and Compact Pro 1.33.

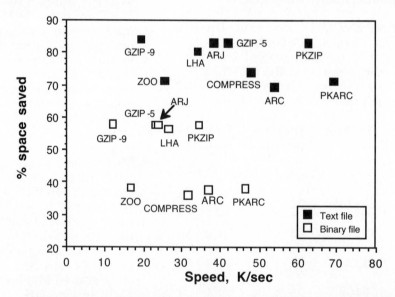

Percentage saved versus speed, PC compression programs, text file (Naval numerics library source code), and binary application (FrameMaker). Tests done on IBM PC clone 386/25 MHz with cache, 8 Mb RAM, DOS 5.0. Speeds based on an average of compression and decompression times. Versions are GZIP 1.2.1, PKZIP 2.04g, ARC 6.2, PKARC 3.5, LHA 2.55, ARJ 2.39f, COMPRESS 4.30d, and ZOO 3.1.

Compression Programs for Mac and PC

Extension	PC creator	PC extractor	Mac creator	Mac extractor
.ARC	ARC v6.2 ARCA	ARCE v6.2	ArcMac v1.3	MacARC (for ARC v5.1 or earlier)
	PKARC v3.61	PKXARC v3.61	(earlier)	ArcPop v1.3b StuffIt Deluxe v3.0 (for ARC v6.2 or
.ARJ	ARJ v2.41	ARJ v2.41		unArjMac v2.21
.CPT		ExtractorPC v1.0	Compact Pro	Extractor
.LZH	LHARC v1.13c LHA v2.55	LHARC v1.13c LHA v2.55	LHARC v1.13c MacLHa v2.0	LHarc v0.41 MacLHa v2.0
.gz	GNU zip v1.2.1	GNU zip v1.2.1	gzip	gzip
.HA	HA v0.98	HA v0.98		
.HPK	HPACK v7.8	HPACK v7.8		
.HQX		xbin v2.3	BinHex v4.0	BinHex v4.0
.PAK	PAK v2.51	PAK v2.51		
.PIT		UNPIT	PackIt III	PackIt III UnPackIt UnStuffIt Deluxe StuffIt Deluxe
.SIT		UNSTUFF	StuffIt v1.5.1 StuffIt Deluxe v3.0 StuffIt LITE	UnStuffIt UnStuffIt Deluxe StuffIt LITE UnStuffIt DA (StuffIt v1.5.1) Extractor Compact Pro
.SDX			StuffIt Deluxe v3.0 StuffIt LITE	UnStuffIt Deluxe StuffIt LITE StuffIt Deluxe v3.0 StuffIt Deluxe
.SQZ	Squeeze v1.083	Squeeze v1.083		
.TAR	tar	tar	MacTar v2.0	MacTar v2.0
.UU	uuencode	uudecode	uutool v2.02	StuffIt Deluxe uulite v1.2
.Z	compress v4.3	uncompress	MacCompress v3.2 (UNIX mode) MacCompress v3.2 (Mac mode)	MacCompress v3.2 (UNIX mode) MacCompress v3.2 (Mac mode)
.ZIP	PKZIP v2.04 Info-Zip Zip v1.9	PKUNZIP v2.04 Info-Zip Unzip v5.0	MacZip v1.0 (PKZIP v1.1)	UnZip 2.0 StuffIt Deluxe v2.1 (PKZIP v1.1)
.ZOO	ZOO v2.10	BOOZ v2.10		MacBooz v2.1

Compression Programs for UNIX and Amiga

Extension	UNIX creator	UNIX extractor	Amiga
.ARC	arc v5.21	arc v5.21	Arc v0.23
.ARJ		unarj v2.30	
.CPT			
.gz	GNU zip	GNU unzip	
.HQX		mcvert	
.HPK	hpack v7.8	hpack v7.8	
.LZH	lharc v1.02	lharc v1.02	lharc
.PAK			
.PIT		unpit	
.SIT	sit	unsit	
.SDX			
.TAR	tar	tar	tarsplit
.UU	uuencode	uudecode	uudecode
.z	pack	unpack	
.Z	compress	uncompress	compress
.ZIP	zip v1.9	unzip v5.1	PKAZIP
.ZOO	zoo v2.1	zoo v2.1	Amigazoo

For more information

USENET groups

comp.compression   Main compression forum
alt.comp.compression   Alternative compression group
comp.compression.research   Research on compression

FAQs

comp.compression FAQ   rtfm.mit.edu:/pub/usenet/news.answers/compression-faq
Compression guide   ftp.cso.uiuc.edu:/doc/pcnet

CHAPTER 25: EMOTICONS AND OTHER JARGON

Cutting through the technobabble

You don't understand? Look at 'em sideways!

Basic emoticons

@#*&^$	You know what this means
<-	Referring to self
:-)	Smile, implies a joke
;-)	Winky; a flirtatious and/or sarcastic remark ("Don't hit me for what I just said")
:-(	Frowning; did not like that last statement or is upset or depressed about something
:-I	Indifferent; better than frowning but not quite as good as a happy emoticon
:-P	Tongue-in-cheek remark
:->	Biting sarcastic remark; worse than a :-)
O :-)	Angel
}:->	Devilish remark
>;->	Winky and devil combined. A very lewd remark.

Abbreviations

AFK	Away from keyboard
BAK	Back at keyboard
BFD	Big *'n deal
BRB	Be right back
BTW	By the way
FBN	Fly by night
GMTA	Great minds think alike
GTTBRAIBRB	Gone to the bathroom and I'll be right back
IMHO	In my humble opinion
IMNSHO	In my not so humble opinion
J/K	Just kidding
LOL	Laughing out loud
NIFOK	Naked in front of keyboard

OTF	On the floor (laughing)
ROTFL	Rolling on the floor laughing
TTFN	Ta ta for now
TTYL	Talk to you later
WYSIAYG	What you see is all you get

Laughter

:-)	ha ha
I-)	hee hee
I-D	ho ho
:->	hey hey
I-P	yuk

Advanced

2B I ^ 2B	Hamlet
:-8	Talking out of both sides of your mouth
:-) :-) :-)	Loud gaffaw
(:-...	Heart breaking message
@>->-	A rose
I-O	Yawning/snoring
I-I	Asleep
:'-(	Crying
:'-)	So happy, s/he is crying
:-D	Laughing
:-o	Shouting
:-O	SHOUTING!
:-I	hmm
X-(	Just died
:-X	Lips are sealed
:-9	Licking his/her lips
:-c	Bummed out
:-C	Really bummed

Grooming and appearance

{:-)	Hair parted in the middle
}:-)	Above in an updraft
&:-)	Curly hair
@:-)	Wavy hair
{:-)	Wears a toupee
}:-(	Toupee in an updraft
:-}	Beard
:-()	Mustache
:-#|	Bushy mustache
:-{}	Wears lipstick
:-#	Braces
:-B	Buck teeth
:-$	Mouth wired shut
:-x	"My lips are sealed"
:-p	Sticking its tongue out (at you!)
:~i	Smoking
:~j	Smoking and smiling
:-?	Pipe smoker
:/i	No smoking
:=)	Two noses
:^)	Broken nose
:-~)	Runny nose
`:-)	Shaved off one eyebrow
:-X	Bow tie
@:I	Turban
?-)	Black eye
8-)	Glasses
%-)	Broken glasses
g-)	Pince-nez glasses
B-)	Horn-rims
8:-)	Glasses on forehead
B:-)	Sunglasses on forehead
%-)	Staring at a green screen for fifteen hours straight
K:P	Little kid with a propeller beenie

What's my line?

<<<<(:-)	Hat salesman
(:->-<	Thief – stick 'em up!
<):-)	Fireman
:-[	Vampire
B-)	Batman
{`	Alfred Hitchcock
:-E	Bucktoothed vampire
:-F	Bucktoothed vampire with one tooth missing
:-%	Banker
[:]	Robot
E-:-)	Ham-radio operator
(:I	Egghead
{o-)	Cyclops
=:-)	Hosehead
-:-)	Punk rocker
-:-(	(Real punk rockers don't smile)
+:-)	Priest
*<:-)	Santa Claus
=I:-)=	Uncle Sam
7:)	Reagan
<:I	Dunce
(-:	Left-handed
:*)	Drunk
8-)	Swimmer
O-)	Scuba diver
:-/	Skeptical
C=:-)	Chef
@=	Pronuclear war
(8-o	Mr. Bill
*:o)	Bozo the Clown!
P-)	Pirate
	Invisible Man

Off the wall

:-I	"Have an ordinary day"
:-q	Touching tongue to nose
:-#	Censored
:-7	Wry statement
:-*	Just ate something sour
:-)~	Drooling

Off the wall (cont'd)

:-`	Chewing tobacco
(:–IK–	Formal message
II*(	Handshake offered
II–)	Handshake received
<&&>	Rubber chickens
><><	Argyle socks
(I==I)	Message on four wheels
:-@	Screaming
:-&	Tongue-tied
<:>==	Turkey
:-}	Handlebar mustache in an updraft
3:]	Pet smiley
3:[	Mean Pet smiley
d8=	Your pet beaver is wearing goggles and a hard hat
[:-)	Wearing a walkman
:-:	Mutant smiley
.-)	One eye
,-)	Ditto...but winking
C=}>;*{))	Mega-Smilie: a drunk, devilish chef with a toupee in an updraft with a mustache and a double chin
	The Invisible Smilie

More strange emoticons

:^)	Pointy nose (righty)
:-e	Disappointed
:-<	Real sad smiley
:-v	Talking-head smiley
}:^#})	Mega-smiley: updrafted bushy-mustached pointy-nosed smiley with a double chin
:-8(	Condescending stare
;-)	Wink
>:-<	Mad

Midgets

:)	Midget happy emoticon
:) -	Also happy
:<	Midget frown
:>	Midget smile
:]	Gleep: a friendly midget emoticon who will gladly be your friend
=)	Top hat
:@ -	Shouting
:D -	Laughter
:(-	Sad
:[-	Real Downer
:O -	Yelling
:C -	Bummer
:,(-	Crying
[] -	Hugs and...
:* -	Kisses
II -	Asleep
I^o	Snoring

Theatricals

:-) :-(	Theatrical comments
8-I	Suspense
O–+	Female
<–O	Male
I-O	Birth
8-#	Death

USENET interpretations

~~:-(	net.flame
O I-)	net.religion
8 :-I	net.unix-wizards
X-(	net.suicide
E-:-I	net.ham-radio
>:-I	net.startrek
3:o[	net.pets

CHAPTER 26:
A GUIDE TO K12NET

Rob Reilly and the K12Net Council

Copyright © 1992 K12Net, all rights reserved. Reprinted by permission.

What is K12Net?

K12Net is a decentralized network of electronic bulletin board systems (BBSes) extending throughout North America, Australia, Europe, and Asia, including the states of the former Soviet Union, which was created to serve students in the Kindergarten through 12th grades. K12Net nodes share curriculum-related conferences or "echo forums," making them available to students and educators at no cost and usually by a local phone call. We currently have 150+ FidoNet nodes. The weekly K12Net traffic is about 70K to 90K, which is roughly 800 to 1100 messages.

K12Net provides millions of teachers, students and parents in metropolitan and rural areas throughout our planet with the ability to meet and talk with each other to discuss educational issues, exchange information, and share resources on a global scale.

Unlike other school-oriented networks, K12Net's explosive growth since its founding in September 1990 can be attibuted to several factors that make it unique:

1. K12Net provides students, teachers, and community members with access to *free* international telecommunications capabilities with an educational orientation via a local call. This frees up classroom, student, and home budgets for other things.

2. It is relatively easy and inexpensive to set up a K12Net BBS. The only equipment required is an MS–DOS or Macintosh computer, a modem, and a phone line, which may already be available. System software is very low cost, if not free, and technical operation skills are developed in-house. When trained, students can act as system operators.

3. It is decentralized. Each participating BBS is locally owned, controlled, and operated. It can be oriented to serve the needs of the local school and is an excellent vehicle for developing community relations.

4. It is a superb vehicle for providing students, teachers, and parents with a gentle introduction to telecommunications as a classroom tool to promote literacy, a global perspective, and competency in 21st-century information technologies.

What can K12Net do for you and/or your classroom?

K12Net is a window to the world. It allows you to transcend rural isolation and community colloquialism by freely, conveniently, and inexpensively conversing with people in Canada, Hawaii, Sweden, or Australia. You will develop friendships, explore other cultures, gather insight, and exchange opinions with other people all over the world. You will become a bona fide member of the "global village."

K12Net provides a vehicle for wide-area collaborative classroom projects using telecommunications. Use K12Net to jointly gather data and draw conclusions about the distribution of acid rain across North America. Publish a classroom-based electronic newsletter for immediate international distribution. Compare fast-food prices in a multitude of different currencies throughout the world and develop theories as to the economic reasons for their variations.

K12Net lets you rub elbows with other professional educators throughout the world. Find out how educators in the next school district, state, or nation are using technologies, materials, and methodologies to improve education. Discover why the "movers and shakers" in the educational world meet here to gather and explore new ideas and concepts.

K12Net is a great equalizer. Online discussions transcend social stigmas based on age, learning disabilities, or other handicaps that might otherwise tend to limit dialogue. No one needs to know that you may be 12 years old or in a wheelchair or have dyslexia. All anyone else will see is your words...

K12Net is an information-gathering facility. The online world is particularly well suited for asking "Say, does anyone know..." questions to large groups of people.

K12Net FidoNet conferences

Public conferences

K12_ART_ED	Arts and Crafts Education (excluding music)
K12_BUS_ED	Business Education
K12_COMP_LIT	Computer Education: technical assistance and exchange for computer educators and students
K12_HLTH_PE	Healthy and Physical Education
K12_LIF_SKIL	Life Skills: home economics, career skills, legal issues, safety education
K12_LANG_ART	Language Arts Education: reading, writing, literature, grammar, composition, and so on
K12_MATH_ED	Mathematics Education
K12_MUSIC_ED	Music and Performing Arts Education
K12_SCI_ED	Science Education
K12_SOC_STUD	Social Studies Education: history, civics, social sciences, and so on
K12_SPEC_ED	Compensatory education: learning disabled, and so on
K12_TAG	Talented and Gifted Education: challenges specific to educating intellectually and/or artistically gifted students
K12_TECH_ED	Technology Education: robotics and engineering, industrial and manufacturing technologies, drafting, design, CAD/CAM, and Vocational Education

Ancillary conferences

K12_NEWS	K12Net NEWS (all should read): a place for announcements at the network level. Should be READ ONLY.
K12_ELE_CHAT	Elementary School Chat: All-purpose chat echo. Grades K–6.
K12_JR_CHAT	Middle School Chat: All-purpose chat echo. Grades 7 and 8.
K12_SR_CHAT	Senior High School Chat: All-purpose chat echo. Grades 9–12.

Foreign-language conferences

K12_FRANCAIS	French-only discussion for level-1 students
K12_SPAN_ENG	Spanish-English practice echo. Native Spanish speakers are urged to correspond in English and native English speakers are urged to write in Spanish providing exciting, interactive practice for beginning- and intermediate-level students.
K12_GERM_ENG	Same format as K12_SPAN_ENG but for German language

Restricted-access conferences

K12.SYSOP

K12.SYSOP: **This is for sysops ONLY.** For discussion of network operation, coordinating echo installation and distribution, technical problems with system software and hardware, and so on. This is solely for people directly involved with system operation. Do NOT allow nonsysops in here! Direct all other conversation to K12.TCH_CHAT.

K12.TCH_CHAT

TEACHER CHAT: **For K-12 professional educators ONLY.** This is an all-purpose CHAT echo with emphasis on the design and evolution of K12Net. Access should be provided through "flags" or security levels in individual user accounts.

K12.PROJECTS

TELECOMMUNICATIONS PROJECTS: **for ALL professional educators.** For the discussion of various curriculum-driven, classroom projects, advertising for "partners" for specific projects, and so on. Suggest user account level access. Note that K12.CH0 is for administration of project currently in progress.

Channel conferences

Channel conferences are used for special projects. These could be things like writing a class book. In order to get a channel assigned to you, you need to send a message to the Channel Coordinator, Andy Vanduyne, 1:260/375. Note: you must carry all of the previously mentioned conferences in order to be eligible to carry channel conferences.

Library and node listings

To get hold of the K12Net library listing, file request K12FILES.ZIP from FidoNet node 1:321/218. A listing of K12Net nodes (which you'll need in order to find the nearest site to connect with) is available for file request as K12NODE.ZIP.

For more information

For more information on K12Net, you can also contact any of the following K12Net Council of Coordinators (board of directors) for further information. If you would like information on K12Net echoes, contact the K12Net curriculum coordinator Gleason Sackmann. An information packet (which contains much of the same information presented here) is also available via `ftp ftp.uu.net as /doc/k12net.tar.Z` or by UUCP as `uunet!~/doc/k12net.tar.Z`. Once you've got

the file, you'll need to use Compress (or MacCompress) to uncompress it and then tar or (MacTar) to dearchive it.

K12Net Council of Coordinators

Gordon Benedict, Calgary, Alb, Canada 1:134/49, `benedict@ucnet.ucalgary.ca`

Jack Crawford, Stanley, NY USA 1:260/620 `jack@k12net.org`

John Feltham, T'ville, QLD, Australia 3:640/706 `jfeltham@sol.deakin.oz.au`

Janet Murray, Portland, OR USA 1:105/23 `jmurray@psg.com`

Rob Reilly, Lanesboro, MA USA 1:321/218 `rreilly@athena.mit.edu`

Gleason Sackmann, Bottineau, ND USA 1:288/5 `sackman@plains.nodak.edu`

Mort Sternheim, Amherst, MA USA 1:321/109 `sternheim@phast.umass.edu`

Helen Sternheim, Amherst, MA USA 1:321/110 `hsternheim@phast.umass.edu`

Andy Vanduyne, Norwood, NY USA 1:2608/75

Louis Van Geel, Mortsel (Antwerp), Belgium 2:295/3

USENET newsgroups corresponding to K12Net Fido echoes

FidoNet Echo	Usenet newsgroup
K12_TCH_CHAT	k12.chat.teacher
K12_ELE_CHAT	k12.chat.elementary
K12_JR_CHAT	k12.chat.junior
K12_SR_CHAT	k12.chat.senior
K12_ART_ED	k12.ed.art
K12_BUS_ED	k12.ed.business
K12_COMP_LIT	k12.ed.comp.literacy
K12_HLTH_PE	k12.ed.health-pe
K12_LIF_SKIL	k12.ed.life-skills
K12_MATH_ED	k12.ed.math
K12_MUSIC_ED	k12.ed.music
K12_SCI_ED	k12.ed.science
K12_SOC_STUD	k12.ed.soc-studies
K12_SPEC_ED	k12.ed.special
K12_TAG	k12.ed.tag
K12_TECH_ED	k12.ed.tech
K12_LANG_ART	k12.lang.art
K12_GERM_ENG	k12.lang.deutsch-eng
K12_SPAN_ENG	k12.lang.esp-eng
K12_FRANCAIS	k12.lang.francais

Sites carrying K12Net

bellcore.bellcore.com	Bell Communication Research
bbn.com	Bolt, Beranek and Newman
bonnie.concordia.ca	Concordia University
decwrl.dec.com	Digital Equipment Corp.
dove.hist.gov	US National Institute of Standards & Technology
csus.edu	California State University at Sacramento
europa.asd.contel.com	Contel Federal Systems
fernwood.mkp.ca.us	Anterior Technologies
gateway.sequent.com	Sequent Computer
infonode.ingr.com	InteGraph Corporation
jhereg.osa.com	Open System Architects
lll-winken.llnl.gov	Lawrence Livermore National Labs
news.tcs.com	Teknekron Communication System
piccolo.cit.cornell.edu	Cornell University
pmafire.inel.gov	Idaho National Engineering Lab
spool.mu.edu	Marquette University
vuse.vanderbilt.edu	Vanderbilt University
world.std.com	Software Tool & Die
sendit.nodak.edu	North Dakota Higher Education Computer Network
m2xenix.psg.com	Pacific Software Group
uunet.uu.net	UUNET Technologies

CHAPTER 27:
HOME CONTROL

Open the refrigerator door, Hal.

Copyright © 1992, MailCom. All rights reserved. Reprinted by permission.

What do I need?

If your primary interest is home control, you will need to purchase some X-10 appliance modules (which can receive events), and at least one controller or security module that can send events.

If you purchase the X-10 compatible CP290 computer interface module, software for your Macintosh is included with the interface. The software can control up to 16 devices, turning them on or off at preselected times. Since the CP290 has its own processor and memory, once it is programmed, it does not have to continue to be attached to your computer for it to work. A CP290, a few appliance modules , and one of the home-security bundles will suffice to put together a reasonable home-security system.

If your primary interest is industrial control, then the Radiant system is more appropriate. Radiant's Common Sense Node (which supports eight programmable digital inputs/outputs, four analog inputs, and four power relay outputs) comes with Macintosh software.

The return of the Refrigerator SIG

Back in 1984, Steve Jobs introduced a computer so simple there would be no need for user groups. "There are no user groups for refrigerators, are there?" he was reported to have said. Seven years and hundreds of thousands of user group memberships later, the user group movement shows no signs of abating.

In 1987, a group on the ECHOMAC conference got a good laugh out of imagining what would have happened had Steve Jobs decided to

design a refrigerator instead of the Mac. They concluded that there would now be refrigerator user groups taking calls from starving users trying to figure out how to recover food from their computerized iceboxes. The group nicknamed itself "The Refrigerator SIG."

It was only a matter of time before the other shoe dropped. The era of the smart lamp, thermostat, and sprinkler is already here. Can the smart refrigerator be far behind? This article talks about the current home-control standard, X-10. It also talks about future standards, such as Radiant, CEBus, and LON, which will usher in the era of the Smart Refrigerator. You mark my words!

The history of home control

X-10 Home Controls, Inc., has been in the home-control business since 1978. Even so, their devices have not been manufactured inexpensively or distributed widely until the last few years.

X-10–based products transmit their signals primarily over home electrical wiring; because the transmission scheme is fairly primitive, it is only possible to transmit at 60 bits per second. At this rate, transmission of complex commands is very difficult. As a result, the X-10 protocols are designed to allow only very simple commands, like: all units off, all lights on, on, off, dim, and bright. The last four commands are to be directed to a specific unit, identified with a house code, which runs from A to P, and a number, which runs from 1 to 16. Altogether, 256 devices can be on the bus.

In contrast, future home-control technologies such as Radiant, LON, and CEBus will transmit at much higher rates. Radiant is based on

AppleTalk protocols running over twisted-pair wiring, and therefore runs at 230.4 Kbps. The most recently adopted version of the power line specification for CEBus tops out at around 10,000 bps, which is enough to transmit data from many types of sensors and possibly even voice or graphics. CEBus over other media, such as infrared and twisted pair, also transmit at similar rates.

Rather than just allowing for sending of simple commands like on or off, CEBus and Radiant implement an OSI protocol stack with seven layers. In the case of Radiant, the protocol stack is AppleTalk, with HyperCard XCMDs to send messages to the control devices. The LONTalk specification, produced by EcheLON, also is implemented according to the OSI model. This means that fairly complex client/server communications can occur over Radiant, CEBus, or LON.

A major difference between Radiant, CEBus, and LON is the degree of implementation in hardware. Since Radiant is based on AppleTalk, other than a Zilog 8530 chip used to implement the physical layer, the rest of the protocol stack is implemented in software. This means that Radiant devices are relatively simple to design and inexpensive to produce. Also, since all Macintosh computers come with AppleTalk built in, every Macintosh ever made is capable of communicating with Radiant devices without the need to purchase special interface hardware.

With LON, all the layers but the application layer are implemented in hardware. This means that LON is likely to be quite fast. However, it is doubtful that control systems really need speeds much above the 230.4 Kbps available with Radiant's AppleTalk-based system. In addition, since no computers come with LON built in, special interface hardware is needed to connect the computer to the LON network.

With CEBus, it is not yet clear how many levels of the protocol stack will be hardware based. Although CEBus looked like the early favorite, they have spent the last year ironing out compatibility problems in the power line standard between the proposed spec and the X-10 protocols. As a result, they have had to throw out chip designs that had gone all the

way to manufacture. Overall, they are no further along than they were a year ago, while LON has been rolling along, shipping hardware and developer's kits.

Looking back over the history of the computer industry, industry-standards committees have a sad history when pitted against single-minded developers. My guess is that EcheLON has the edge at this point.

Radiant, a recent San Francisco–based startup, is a clear underdog in the battle against CEBus and LON. However their technology is simpler, less expensive, and easier to develop for. Anyone with access to a Macintosh, Think C, and AppleTalk documentation can become a Radiant developer. Meanwhile LON is charging big bucks for their development kits.

Media, media on the wall

Home-control standards like X-10, Radiant, CEBus, and LON are all mini local area networks. As such they need a medium over which to transmit their signals. Since home control needs to be inexpensive and easy to use for people to use it, it wouldn't make sense to require expensive cabling.

For this reason home-control networks most often utilize common media like the electrical wiring in the house, twisted-pair phone wire, or infrared or radio-wave propagation. Before you set out to do a home-control project, however, you should be aware that these media have certain limitations.

For example, very often the electrical wiring in a house is not continuous. That is, X-10 signals sent from a wall outlet in one part of the house may not be able to reach outlets in another part of the house. This can happen if your home is wired so that those outlets are on different circuits, which is very common.

Twisted-pair phone wire will only work in an office where one of the pairs is not being utilized and is therefore available for an AppleTalk network. Similarly, radio waves or infrared communications is not foolproof either; you may find that you will need to vary the direction at which you point your remote control device, or you need to actuate the device repeatedly before the signal is picked up correctly.

X-10 products, particularly simpler ones such as the appliance modules, are well made and durable. Others, such as Window Sensors, need to be maintained so that they do not fire accidentally. However, none of the modules were designed for industrial use or for constant abuse from children. More complex modules such as burglar alarms need to be maintained and checked regularly so that they will continue to function reliably.

For these reasons it is not advisable to operate potentially hazardous appliances such as an electric oven or a coffee maker using home-control equipment. If a malfunction could be catastrophic, you need to retain responsibility for vigilance yourself, not delegate it to a computer.

How the X-10 system works

Those who have ever programmed a Mac, scripted in HyperCard, or know something about object-oriented programming can relate to the fundamental concept of the X-10 Home Control System, events.

How are the events transmitted? The X-10 system operates over two media: the electrical wiring in your home, and via the airwaves.

The X-10 system is built around individual modules that can send and receive events. What are these events? Well, the X-10 system is not very sophisticated, so the events are on, off, dim, bright, all units off, and all lights on. That's it!

Doesn't sound very powerful does it? Well, there you would be wrong, because depending on the device, it can interpret the events any way it chooses. Therefore, while a lamp could turn itself on when it receives an on event, a siren could put out an ear-numbing screech.

However, you would be right in concluding that the X-10 system is not sophisticated enough to control devices such as stereos, TVs, microwave ovens, or other appliances that need to be sent instructions much more complex than on, off, or dim to be told what to do. It also cannot send numerical data, such as

temperature, humidity, and so on, from one sensor to another.

These shortcomings are addressed by the competing standards for the next generation in home control, Radiant, CEBUS, and LON. However, those standards have not yet produced inexpensive, mass-marketed products, and X-10 has. Today for $100 you can purchase a powerful X-10 burglar alarm, or a complete appliance- or thermostat-control system that is controlled by your computer.

X-10 modules typically plug into an electrical outlet and use the wiring of your home to transmit and receive events. They do this by sending signals at the zero crossing of the 60 Hz power line. Several modules can also send and receive messages over the airwaves. For example, the Home Security System Base Receiver can receive commands from a remote control unit to turn the home-security system on or off.

There are several classes of X-10 modules. One of these is the sensor module, which includes things like motion sensors and window/door sensors. These sensors send an on event when they are triggered, but they cannot receive events. Also in this class are timer modules, which send events depending on time of day, and sun downer modules, which send them depending on the received light.

Another class is the appliance module. These are things like the lamp module or the general appliance module. These modules plug into your electrical outlet, and then you plug your appliance into them. These modules can only receive events, and when they do, they turn the appliances plugged into them on or off. There are also wall modules that you can build into the wall. Also in the appliance module class is the thermostat module. Since your thermostat cannot plug into this module, the module is placed underneath your thermostat and generates (or stops generating) heat. This convinces the thermostat to turn on or off.

In yet another class are the gateway modules. These modules are used to gateway X-10 commands between the electrical system (which the appliance modules are connected to) and other media such as the telephone system (the telephone responder module) or the airwaves (remote control modules). This means you can turn your lights on or off by phone or via remote control from outside the house. Getting interested?

Each X-10 device capable of receiving events has an address that is assigned by turning two dials on the module. Setting these dials is like setting the SCSI ID on some hard drives, except that addresses do not necessarily have to be unique. This is because most modules only read from the wiring but do not write information to it, so there is no possibility of contention for media access. You give modules the same address if you want the attached appliances to respond identically to a command. Once you've plugged the appliance modules into outlets, plugged the appliances into the modules, and given the modules unique addresses, you're ready to use the CP290 software.

X-10 software

Macintosh version

For a $49.95 product, the CP290 software is pretty neat. You can design a layout of your home and then place icons representing your home appliances on the layout. You can even design your own icons if you want. Here's an example layout with appliance icons:

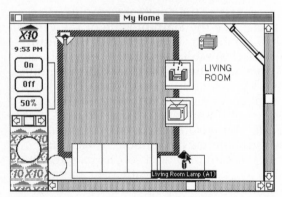

Double-clicking on the living room lamp icon lets you edit the events for that appliance. With a lamp, you can send an on, off, or dim command. In the screen shot below, I'm having a dim event occur every day of the week at 10:39 PM. The living room lamp should go down to around 50 percent power at

that time, based on the setting of the scroll bar.

When you're done editing the event log you can ask the software to plot out when the events are scheduled to occur:

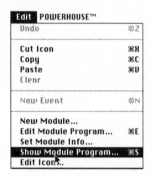

This display is the result:

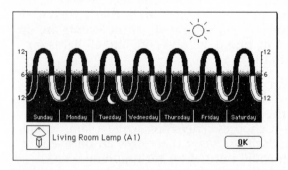

Finally, when all the editing is done, you you can save the schedule to your CP290 unit.

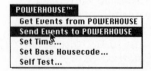

MS–DOS software

On the PC, several DOS-based X-10 utility packages are available. X10Utils is among the most useful of these. It consists of a series of executable modules with a command line interface. It therefore can be interfaced in complex ways to other software such as BBS software or voicemail packages like BigMouth.

With BBS software, the X-10 commands can be executed on demand via Doors, or as events occurring at regular times of the day. Since the BigMouth voicemail package has a feature that allows for the execution of commands based on touch-tone input, a script called from BigMouth could also be used alongside X10UTILS to create an integrated voicemail/X-10 system.

The X10UTILS include X10DIR (which sends a single X-10 command to a selected module); X10DNLD (which executes a series of X-10 commands placed in a file), X10EVENT (which downloads a single X-10 Event to the CP290), X10MON (which monitors events as they occur), X10UPLD (which uploads the event file from the CP290), and X10TIME (which uploads or downloads the time to the CP290).

Ideas for using X-10

The X-10 system is designed so that each module has its own processor and memory. This means that the modules do not require a computer to operate. For example, the home-security systems are completely self-sufficient and can be used just like appliances.

Nevertheless, if you have a computer, you can do some neat things. The CP290 interface kit allows your Macintosh to send events to any X-10 device that operates over electric wiring. Since the CP290 contains its own nonvolatile memory, it can store events to be sent at particular times during the week.

You could program the CP290 to turn on your coffee machine at 8:00 AM on weekdays, and automatically turn it off at 9:30 AM, in case you forgot to do so yourself. You could wake up by having your TV or stereo go on.

I once lived in a house that did not have adequate heating. I had to purchase two space heaters and an electric blanket. Since the house wiring was limited, I couldn't have two heaters on at the same time. Also, in order to keep my electric bill down, I didn't want to leave the heaters and electric blanket on all night.

Given these constraints, my desire was to make sure that both my bedroom and bathroom were warm when I got up in the morning. I also liked the idea of crawling into a warm bed.

To accomplish this, I programmed the CP290 to turn the two heaters on and off at 15-minute intervals from 5 AM to 6 AM during the weekdays, when I usually got up. Only one heater was on at a time. Both heaters went off at 8 AM, when I would usually leave for work. On weekends, the heaters went on and off from 8 AM to 9 AM.

On weekdays, the heaters went back on and off from 6 PM to 7 PM. That way, when I got home around 7 PM, the house would be warm. The electric blanket went on around 9 PM and went off around 11 PM.

As strange as this program might sound, it worked well for me for almost two years, until I moved to an apartment with a functioning heating system.

More advanced ideas

Although X-10 is not designed to allow transmission of measurements, such as temperatures, light levels, or humidities over the network, you can compensate for these failings by purchasing additional hardware. For example, if you were to purchase a Radiant Common Sense module, you could then take measurements of parameters such as temperature, humidity, and so on, and then (using a HyperCard XCMD) send X-10 events to appliances in response to the measurements. For example, if it was after midnight and the temperature was over thirty two degrees, you could send an X-10 command to the thermostat module to turn down the heat. However, as sunrise approached, you could let the thermostat setting return to normal. The way this works is the thermostat module is mounted just below the actual thermostat. It contains a small heating element to fool the thermostat. X-10 modules are also capable of turning relays on and off, and closing draperies, among other things.

So even though your thermostat cannot respond to temperature information directly, it can nevertheless be controlled via X-10. The Radiant Common Sense module can take in eight channels of A/D and D/A and drive relays. Equivalent cards are also available for the PC for less than $200.

The forthcoming release of AppleScript brings to mind some interesting possibilities. The CP290 does not allow you to monitor events sent over electric wiring. To do this, you need the TW523 Two-Way Power Line Interface. With the TW523, you can have your Mac intercept X-10 events sent over electrical wiring and send other events to respond to these. Unfortunately, there is not an equivalent to the TW523 for events sent over the airwaves like those sent by the window and motion sensors.

With AppleEvent-aware CP290 software, and other applications that can interpret AppleEvents, much more powerful X-10 applications would be possible. While X-10 currently offers a telephone responder, it is not possible to use the responder and an answering machine on the same line. With AppleEvents it would be possible to have a voicemail system such as the TFLX send events to your appliances, depending on which key you pressed on your touch tone-phone. This would allow you to call in and turn things on and off without having to use up an extra phone line, like the telephone responder module does.

X-10 scripts (doing a little DOS)

Since the concepts behind X-10, Radiant, CEBus, and EcheLON are inherently object oriented, in order to take full advantage of all this, you've got to have a meta-language capable of handling and creating events. Since we don't have AppleScript yet, I'll have to illustrate this point with examples from DOS

batch scripts to give you an idea of what you'll soon be able to do.

Under DOS, voicemail systems such as BigMouth can shell out to a batch file or program of your choice if a certain series of touch tones is received. BBS software such as OPUS can generate events (ERRORLEVELS in DOS) that DOS batch scripts can trap and respond to. Since lots of DOS programs can operate from the command line, it is easy to respond to these events by sending X-10 events or faxes, transmitting messages over the phone, calling out by modem, and so on.

To give you an idea of how this works on the PC, I've written a batch script. This script makes use of the OPUS BBS software to generate events at various error levels at preselected times of the day. Other software like BigMouth could also be used; however in this case you'd need to generate your own events based, for example, on the time of day. In the case of FidoNet-compatible BBS software such as OPUS, event times and error levels are set within the software. The batch script then responds to these events by doing various things. X10DIR is a program to send an X-10 event to a particular module; STALL is a program that waits a specified amount of time (in seconds), and CCOMSEND is a program that will send a fax. Here is the script:

```
:LOOP
OPUS BBS -O
IF ERRORLEVEL 50 GOTO HEATERON
IF ERRORLEVEL 40 GOTO HEATEROFF
IF ERRORLEVEL 30 GOTO LIGHTSON
IF ERRORLEVEL 25 GOTO BREAKIN
IF ERRORLEVEL 20 GOTO DINNER
IF ERRORLEVEL 10 GOTO LUNCH
GOTO LOOP
:HEATERON
REM Turn on the space heater
X10DIR A2 ON
GOTO LOOP
:HEATEROFF
REM Turn off the space heater
X10DIR A2 OFF
GOTO LOOP
:LIGHTSON
X10DIR A1 ON
GOTO LOOP
:BREAKIN
REM Turn on all the lights
X10DIR A2 ON
X10DIR A3 ON
REM Send a FAX via the
REM Complete Communicator board
CCOMSEND BREAKIN.TXT 555-1212 /x
REM GO INTO LOOP TURNING LIGHTS ON AND
OFF
```

(script continued on next page)

```
:FLASH
X10DIR A2 ON
X10DIR A3 ON
STALL 1
X10DIR A2 OFF
X10DIR A3 OFF
GOTO LOOP
:DINNER
REM TURN OFF TV IN CHILDREN'S ROOM
X10DIR A5 OFF
GOTO LOOP
:LUNCH
REM REMIND ME BY FLASHING MY DESK LAMP
X10DIR A6 ON
STALL 1
X10DIR A6 OFF
STALL 1
X10DIR A6 ON
GOTO LOOP
```

While writing such a script is easy for DOS, it is much more difficult to do on the Macintosh without AppleScript. While it is theoretically possible to do all of this under HyperCard, in practice few manufacturers of fax hardware, for example, support control of their hardware by XCMDs. There are also no XCMDs for control of X-10 devices although these are not hard to write.

However, when we get AppleEvent-aware applications that can listen for home-control events and send appropriate AppleEvents to other applications to send faxes, dial out, and so on, we will have the basic tools to make all of this work.

Hooking it all to your phone

Talking Technology, Inc., offers the BigMouth (single-line) and PowerLine (two-line) voicemail board. These cards are easily programmed using the software that comes with the board, or alternatively, the developer's toolkit or SpeakEasy interpreted development language.

To give you an idea of how powerful BigMouth is, it was possible to develop a fax-back system (a system that will allow a caller to input the phone number of his or her fax machine and receive a fax on it after hanging up) with only fifteen lines of DOS batch script.

Here's how the system works:

1. BigMouth is executed within an "event loop" by the batch script RUNBIG.BAT.

RUNBIG.BAT listing

```
REM             Load the Complete Communicator
REM         Background code
REM
CCBACK /N
REM             Go into the BigMouth directory
REM
CD \BIGMOUTH
REM
REM             Begin the event loop
:LOOP
REM
REM             Enter BigMouth and wait for
REM         incoming calls
BIGMOUTH W
REM
REM             Extract phone number entered from
REM         the BigMouth Log
REM
AWK -f FAX.AWK BIGMOUTH.LOG >FAX.BAT
REM
REM             Save the log to another file, and
REM         then delete it
REM
COPY BIGM.LOG + BIGMOUTH.LOG BIGM.LOG
DEL BIGMOUTH.LOG
REM
REM             Execute the batch script prepared
REM         by awk
REM
CALL FAX
REM             Handle more events
REM
GOTO LOOP
```

2. BigMouth is programmed to exit to DOS after playing a message telling the caller what to do and recording the phone number entered as touch tones in its logfile, BIGMOUTH.LOG. The entry in BIGMOUTH.LOG looks like:

```
10:41:17PM 2-25    25 UPDATE1 8499026*
```

Here UPDATE1 refers to the particular document selected by the caller. This was selected (again by touch-tone input) before a phone number was requested.

3. The utility awk is used to extract the phone number (the last field) and output the batch script FAX.BAT, which is then executed. Here is the awk program to do this:

FAX.AWK listing

```
/UPDATE1 /{print "CCOMSEND UPDATE1.DOC",$5}
/UPDATE2 /{print "CCOMSEND UPDATE2.DOC",$5}
/UPDATE3 /{print "CCOMSEND UPDATE3.DOC",$5}
/UPDATE4 /{print "CCOMSEND UPDATE4.DOC",$5}
```

Here the stuff between the slashes is the stuff that awk is to look for. Once it finds it, it is to execute the command after the slashes. This is printing out a line in the batch script telling CCOM (the Complete Communicator board) to queue up a fax for the phone number entered in the BIGMOUTH.LOG file. Since the phone number is the fifth field in the log entry (as separated by spaces, commas, and so on), it is output as $5.

The total amount of programming here is less than twenty five lines of code in awk and DOS batch script. The result, however, is a fax-back system that is the equal of systems costing over $1000 for a total hardware cost of under $400.

The thing to keep in mind is that this particular approach could work just as well for controlling your home. For example, instead of executing CCOMSEND (the CCOM fax spooling routine), we could have executed X10DIR in order to turn a particular light, heater, or applicance on or off.

Automated gardening

Ever gone away on vacation and had difficulty finding someone to take care of your plants? Not interested in installing a sprinkler system? Recent advances have made automated drip irrigation systems a reality. Wade Manufacturing, which has been making irrigation equipment for more than fifty years, now offers drip irrigation equipment for the gardening enthusiast, known as ACU-DRIP. Drip irrigation systems deliver water directly to the plant roots, rather than sprinkling it on the surface and letting it filter through the soil. This has several advantages:

• Evaporation is lessened, decreasing water consumption by as much as 70%.
• Weed growth is stunted, since water is delivered only to the roots of desired plants.
• Fertilizer can be delivered at the same time.

Since drip irrigation uses much less water, it may be possible to run the system from an elevated water tank, rather than a garden faucet. I have found that Alhambra 2.5 gallon water containers can be hooked up to ACU-DRIP equipment by use of a Clam Shell Hose Repair unit from Rain Bird. For this to work, you need to minimize pressure drop in the lines, which implies short tubing runs. You

may also need to install a timer-controlled valve to turn the flow on and off. I do not know of an X-10 controlled valve that does this. However, the Radiant Common Sense CNX module supports sensors for temperature, soil moisture, wind speed and direction, as well as barometers, rain gauges, and light level sensors. It also can control water valves and DC motors.

A few more hints for designing drip irrigation systems:

• Test the system above ground first. Once you've buried the irigation system, it's very hard to know if it's working or not. Test it above ground first, checking to make sure that the drippers are delivering the correct amount of water.

• Be careful of leaks. As anyone who has worked with piping knows, it can be quite a chore to get every joint and connection water tight. This is critical, because if you have a leak, the benefits of drip irrigation can go down the drain.

• Use the right size tubing. Use small tubing sizes (0.25 inch or less) only for offshoots of the main line, which should be 0.5 inches or greater. If you try to use long lengths of small tubing, you may find that you will be unable to deliver enough water, due to excess pressure drop.

For more information

Voicemail archive

```
ftp oak.oakland.edu, cd
/pub/msdos/voicemail/
```

Weather archive

```
ftp oak.oakland.edu, cd
/pub/msdos/weather/
```

X-10 archive

```
ftp oak.oakland.edu,
cd /pub/msdos/x-10/
```

Part V

Memories and Visions

The Founding of the Philadelphia Public Library
From *The Autobiography of Benjamin Franklin*

"At the time I established myself in Pennsylvania, there was not a good bookseller's shop in any of the colonies to the southward of Boston. In New York and Philadelphia the printers were indeed stationers; they sold only paper, etc., almanacs, ballads, and a few common school-books. Those who loved reading were obliged to send for their books from England; the members of the Junto had each a few. We had left the alehouse, where we first met, and hired a room to hold our club in. I proposed that we should all of us bring our books to that room, where they would not only be ready to consult in our conferences, but become a common benefit, each of us being at liberty to borrow such as he wish'd to read at home. This was accordingly done, and for some time contented us.

"Finding the advantage of this little collection, I proposed to render the benefit from books more common, by commencing a public subscription library. I drew a sketch of the plan and rules that would be necessary, and got a skillful conveyancer, Mr. Charles Brockden, to put the whole in form of articles of agreement to be subscribed, by which each subscriber engaged to pay a certain sum down for the first purchase of books, and an annual contribution for increasing them. So few were the readers at that time in Philadelphia, and the majority of us so poor, that I was not able, with great industry, to find more than fifty persons, mostly young tradesmen, willing to pay down for this purpose forty shillings each, and ten shillings per annum. On this little fund we began. The books were imported; the library was opened one day in the week for lending to the subscribers, on their promissory notes to pay double the value if not duly returned. The institution soon manifested its utility, was imitated by other towns, and in other provinces. The libraries were augmented by donations; reading became fashionable; and our people, having no public amusements to divert their attention from study, became better acquainted with books, and in a few years were observed by strangers to be better instructed and more intelligent than people of the same rank generally are in other countries."

The Autobiography of Benjamin Franklin, Part VIII: Continuation of the Account

CHAPTER 28: FREE AS AIR, FREE AS WATER, FREE AS KNOWLEDGE

Bruce Sterling

Copyright © 1992 Bruce Sterling. All rights reserved. Reprinted by permission.

The commodification of information

You wouldn't guess it sometimes to hear some people talk, but we don't live in a technocratic information society. We live in a highly advanced capitalist society. People talk about the power and glory of specialized knowledge and technical expertise. Knowledge is power – but if so, why aren't knowledgeable people in power? It's true there's a Library OF Congress. But how many librarians are there IN Congress?

The nature of our society strongly affects the nature of our technology. It doesn't absolutely determine it; a lot of our technology is sheer accident, serendipity, the way the cards happened to fall, who got the lucky breaks, and, of course, the occasional eruption of genius, which tends to be positively unpredictable. But as a society we don't develop technologies to their ultimate ends. Only engineers are interested in that kind of technical sweetness, and engineers generally have their paychecks signed by CEOs and stockholders. We don't pursue ultimate technologies. Our technologies are actually designed and produced to optimize the financial return on investment. There's a big difference.

Of course there are many elements of our lives that exist outside the money economy. There's a lot going on in our lives that's not-for-profit that can't be denominated in dollars. "The best things in life are free," the old saying goes. Nice old saying. Gets a little older-sounding

every day. Sounds about as old and mossy as the wedding vow "for richer or poorer," which in a modern environment is pretty likely to be for-richer-or-poorer modulo our prenuptial agreement. Commercialization. Commodification, a favorite buzzword of mine. It's a very powerful phenomenon. It seems to me to be getting more powerful year by year.

Academia, libraries, cultural institutions are under protracted commercial siege. This is "MacNeil-Lehrer News Hour," brought to you by publicly supported television and, incidentally, AT&T. Welcome students to Large Northeastern University, brought to you by Pepsi-Cola, official drink of Large Northeastern. Ye shall know the truth, and the truth shall make ye employable. Hi, I'm the head of the microbiology department here at Large Northeastern. I'm also on the board of directors of TransGenic Corporation. The Chancellor says it's OK because a cut of the patent money goes to Large Northeastern.

Welcome to the Library of Congress. Jolt Cola is the official drink of the Library of Congress. This is our distributed electronic data network, brought to you by Prodigy Services, a joint venture of IBM and Sears. You'll notice the banner of bright-red ads that spools by your eyeballs while you're trying to access the electronic full-text of William Wordsworth. Try to pay no attention to that. Incidentally, there's a Hypertext link here where you can order our Wordsworth T-shirt and have it billed to your credit card. Did I mention that the Library of Congress is now also a bank? Hey, data is data! Digits are digits! Every pixel in cyberspace is a potential sales opportunity. Be sure to visit our library coffee-bar, too. You can rent videos here if you want. We do souvenir umbrellas, ashtrays, earrings, fridge magnets, the works. We librarians are doing what we can to survive this economically difficult period. After all, the library is a regrettably old-fashioned institution that has not been honed into fighting trim by exposure to healthy market competition. Until now, that is!

The heresies of Benjamin Franklin

The American library system was invented in a different cultural climate. This is how it happened. You're Benjamin Franklin, a printer by trade and your average universal genius, and it's the Year of Our Lord 1731. You have this freewheeling debating club called the Junto, and you decide you're going to pool your books and charge everybody a very small fee to join in and read them. There's about fifty of you. You're not big people, in the Junto. You're not aristocrats or well-born people or even philanthropists. You're mostly apprentices and young people who work with their hands. If you were rich, you wouldn't be so anxious to pool your information in the first place. So you put all your leather-bound books into the old Philadelphia clubhouse, and you charge people forty shillings to join and ten shillings dues per annum.

Now forget 1731. It's the 1990's. Forget the leather-bound books. You start swapping floppy disks and using a bulletin board system. Public spirited? A benefit to society? Democratic institution, knowledge is power, power to the people? Maybe... or maybe you're an idealistic nut, Mr. Franklin. Not only that, but you're menacing our commercial interests! What about our trade secrets, Mr. Franklin? Our trademarks, copyrights, and patents. Our intellectual property rights. Our look-and-feel. Our patented algorithms. Our national security clearances. Our export licenses. Our FBI surveillance policy. Don't copy that floppy, Mr. Franklin! And you're telling me you want us to pay taxes to support your suspicious activities? Hey, if there's a real need here, the market will meet it, Mr. Franklin. I really think this "library" idea of

yours is something better left to the private sector, Mr. Franklin. No author could possibly want his books read for free, sir. Are you trying to starve the creative artist?

Let's get real, Mr. Franklin. You know what's real, Mr. Franklin? Money is real. You seem to be under the misapprehension that information should be free and that enabling people to learn and follow their own interests will benefit society as a whole. Well, we no longer believe in society as a whole. We believe in the economy as a whole – a black hole! Why should you be able to think things, and even learn things, without paying somebody for that privilege? Let's get to brass tacks, the bottom line. Money. Money is reality. You see this printed dollar bill? It's far more real than topsoil or oxygen or the ozone layer or sunlight. You may say that what we call reality is just a piece of paper, with some symbols on it, but that's sacrilege! This is the Almighty Dollar. Most of the dollars we worship are actually stored in cyberspace. Dollars are just digital ones and zeros in a network of computers, but that doesn't mean they're only virtual reality and basically one big fantasy. No, dollars are utterly and entirely real, far more real than anything as vague as the public interest. If you're not a commodity, you don't exist!

Can you believe that Melville Dewey once said, "free as air, free as water, free as knowledge?" Free as knowledge? Let's get real, this is the modern world – air and water no longer come cheap! Hey, you want breathable air, you better pay your air conditioner's power-bill, pal. Free as water? Man, if you've got sense you buy the bottled variety or pay for an ionic filter on your tap. And free as knowledge? Well, we don't know what "knowledge" is, but we can get you plenty of data, and as soon as we can figure out how to download it straight into student skulls, we can put all the teachers into the breadline and librarians as well.

There's a basic problem with showing Mr. Franklin the door. The problem is that Mr. Franklin was right, and Mr. Franklin is still right. Information is not something you can successfully peddle like Coca-Cola. If it were a genuine commodity, then information would cost nothing when you had a glut of it.

God knows we've got enough data! We're drowning in data. Nevertheless we're only gonna make more. Money just does not map the world of information at all well. How much is the Bible worth? You can get a Bible in any hotel room. They're worthless as commodities but not valueless to mankind. Money and value are not identical.

The struggle for attention

What's information really about? It seems to me that there's something direly wrong with the Information Economy. It's not about data, it's about attention. In a few years you may be able to carry the Library of Congress in your hip pocket. So? You're never gonna read the Library of Congress. You'll die long before you access one tenth of one percent of it. What's important – increasingly important – is the process by which you figure out what to look at. This is the beginning of the real and true economics of information – not who owns the books, who prints the books, who has the holdings. The crux today is access, not holdings. And not even access itself but the signposts that tell you what to access – what to pay attention to. In the Information Economy everything is plentiful – except attention.

That's why the spin doctor is the creature who increasingly rules the information universe. Spin doctors rule our attention. Never mind that man behind the curtain. No, no! Look at my hand! I can make a candidate disappear. Watch me pull a president out of a hat. Look! I can make these homeless people disappear in a haze of media noise. Nothing up my sleeve. Presto! The facts don't matter if he can successfully direct our attention. Spin doctors are like evil antilibrarians; they're the Dark Side of the Force.

Librarians used to be book-pullers. Book-pullers. I kind of like the humble, workaday sound of that. I like it kind of better than I like the sound of "information retrieval expert," though that's clearly where librarians are headed. Might be the right way to head. That's where the power seems to be. Though I wonder exactly what will be retrieved and

what will be allowed to quietly mummify in the deepest, darkest deserts of the dustiest hard disks.

I like libraries and librarians. I owe my career to libraries and librarians. I respect Mr. Franklin. I hate seeing books turned into a commodity and seeing access to books turned into a commodity. I do like bookstores, too, and of course, I earn my living by them, but I worry about them more and more. I don't like chainstores, and I don't like chain distributors. We already have twelve human beings in the U.S. who buy all the science fiction books for the twelve major American distributors. They're the information filters and the attention filters, and their criterion is the bottom line, and the bottom line is bogus and a fraud. I don't like megapublishers either. Modern publishing is owned by far too few people. They're the people who own the means of production, and worse yet, they own far too much of the means of attention. They determine what we get to pay attention to.

Of course, there are other ways, other methods, of delimiting people's attention besides merely commercial ones. Like aesthetic and cultural means of limiting attention. Librarians used to be very big on that kind of public-spirited filtering. Conceivably, librarians could get that way again with another turn of the cultural wheel. Librarians could become very correct. Holdings must be thinned, and even in electronic media the good old delete key is never far from hand. Try reading what librarians used to say a hundred years ago. Your ancestral librarians were really upset about popular novels. They carried on about novels in a tone of voice that would sound very familiar to Dan Quayle's. Here's a gentleman named Dr. Isaac Ray in the 1870s. I quote him: "The specific doctrine I would inculcate is, that the excessive indulgence in novel-reading, which is a characteristic of our times, is chargeable with many of the mental irregularities that prevail upon us to a degree unknown at any former period."

Here's the superintendent of education for the State of Michigan in 1869. "The state swarms with peddlers of the sensational novels of all ages, tales of piracy, murders, and love intrigues – the yellow-covered literature of the world." Librarian James Angell in 1904: "I think it must be confessed that a great deal of the fiction which is deluging the market is the veriest trash, or worse than trash. Much of it is positively bad in its influence. It awakens morbid passions. It deals in the most exaggerated representations of life. It is vicious in style."

These worthies are talking about the authors who corrupt the values of youth, authors who write about crime and low life, authors who drive people nuts, authors who themselves are degraded and untrustworthy and quite possibly insane. I think I know who they are talking about. Basically, they're talking about me.

Here's the President of the United States speaking at a library in 1890. "The boy who greedily devours the vicious tales of imaginary daring and blood-curdling adventure, which in these days are too far accessible, will have his brain filled with notions of life and standards of manliness which, if they do not make him a menace to peace and good order, will certainly not make him a useful member of society." Grover Cleveland hit the nail on the head. I feel very strongly, I feel instinctively, I feel passionately that I am one of those nails. Not only did I start out in libraries as that greedy devouring boy, but thanks to mind-warping science fictional yellow-covered literature, I have become a menace to Grover Cleveland's idea of peace and good order.

Far too accessible, eh, Mr. President? Too much access. By all means let's not provide our electronic networks with too much access. That might get dangerous. The networks might rot people's minds and corrupt their family values. They might create bad taste. Do you think this electrical networking thing is a new social problem? Think again. Listen to prominent literateur James Russell Lowell speaking in 1885. "We diligently inform ourselves, and cover the continent with speaking wires.... [W]e are getting buried alive under this avalanche of earthly impertinences ....[W]e ...are willing to become mere sponges saturated from the stagnant goosepond of village gossip."

The stagnant goosepond of the global village. Marshall McLuhan's stagnant goosepond. Who are the geese in the stagnant pond? Whoever

they are, I'm one of them. You'll find me with the pulp magazines and the bloodcurdling comics and the yellow-covered works of imaginary daring. In the future you'll find me or my successors in the electronic pulps. In the electronic zines, in the fanzines, in the digital genres, the digital underground. In whatever medium it is that really bugs Grover Cleveland. He can't make up his mind whether I'm the scum from the gutter or the "cultural elite" – but in either case he doesn't like me.

He doesn't like cyberpunks. That's probably not news to you. But he's not going to like cyberpunk librarians either. Don't deceive yourselves on that score.

Weird ideas are tolerable as long as they remain weird ideas. Once they start actually challenging the world, there's smoke in the air and blood on the floor. Cybernetic librarians are marching toward blood on the floor. It's cultural struggle, political struggle, legal struggle. Extending the public right-to-know into cyberspace will be a mighty battle. It's an old war, a war librarians are used to, and I honor them for the free-expression battles they have won in the past. But the terrain of cyberspace is new terrain. I think that ground will have to be won all over again, megabyte by megabyte.

Bruce Sterling is the author of several books, including the recently published (and highly recommended) book entitled *The Hacker Crackdown, Law and Disorder on the Electronic Frontier* from Bantam Hardcover.

CHAPTER 29:
THOUGHTS ON THE GREAT VOYAGE

The Great Network Experiment

Today, more than two hundred years after the voyage of Columbus, we stand on a different shore, about to embark on another voyage.

Should present trends continue, the Great Network Experiment begun by ARPA may connect more than one hundred million people by the year 2000. This technology has come so far, so fast, that merely following its progress leaves us breathless.

On the eve of this great voyage, it is unsettling to reflect on how little we know about the vast uncharted Cyberspace continent. Despite our considerable experience, we really have no more of a glimpse of the new world than Columbus had, peering toward the horizon before setting sail. It is therefore hard to deny a certain feeling of apprehension, as befits the start of any experiment of undetermined outcome.

The forces that pull us all

Before setting sail, let us reflect on the forces that propel us on this voyage.

First is the sense that we have no choice: that we must ride this wave, or be swept up in its turbulent eddies.

Second is the idea that this technology brings with it a tremendous potential for profit, and that taking full advantage of it might boost the economy.

Third is the notion of participating in another ennobling experiment.

Fear, greed, pride. The telecommunications revolution has harnessed three of the great motivators. The fourth, lust, is also in no short supply, but needs no explanation here.

Yet these factors do not fully explain the grassroots networking movement. In a fit of temporary insanity, tens of thousands of people have set up electronic bulletin boards for themselves, or for their schools and businesses. On the Internet, the number of archives, databases, mailing lists, gophers and newsgroups is growing at an explosive rate.

These electronic fruit stands have not been spawned merely for the novelty of it, nor generally in the pursuit of profit. While some settlers are enticed by rumors that the streets are paved with gold, others are driven by a dream. For some, it is a dream of freedom: the students at Tiananmen Square, sending out faxes to the world as the tanks bore down on them. For others it is a dream of refuge: outcasts looking for a place among friends. For still others, networks offer opportunities for self-education: electronic libraries and schools, and access to millions of other users as instructors. Let us reflect for a moment on how many of us might not be where we are today without the help of a few good friends, books, or teachers. The grassroots networking movement isn't driven by fear, greed, pride, or lust. It's about access to information, education, community, and ultimately, power.

Building electronic books

The printing press brought books to an audience beyond the clergy, making possible an educated citizenry, and ultimately, the

Reformation and the American Revolution. The electronic book promises a similar impact.

The destiny of the electronic book is to move education out of the classroom. Today's world requires highly specialized skills; at the same time we are told that an individual will over a lifetime have multiple careers. This implies an intense need for retraining, which is not currently being met.

You can't address these kind of needs merely by extending the paper metaphor into the electronic realm. Since electronic books are usually priced higher than the paper versions, and are less widely available, why not get the paper version if the two offer similar capabilities?

Effective training requires clear goals, practice, measurement, and followup. Most importantly, it also requires interaction among the students. The electronic book will not meet its potential until it contributes to all phases of the education process, and develops a communications component.

NCSA's Mosaic is an important step along this road. Offering color, fonts, text with embedded sounds, pictures and movies, hypertext links, and built-in support for a smorgasbord of protocols, Mosaic is the most sophisticated Internet access tool developed to date, as well as a promising online authoring tool. Yet while Mosaic is a start, many capabilities still remain to be added.

Yet creating exceptional electronic books remains backbreaking work, which is why we do not have very many of them. The ultimate goal is to create an effective means of leveraging experience, but without overburdening the experts. The importance of creating authoring tools that are attractive to experts cannot be overemphasized.

When the Prodigy System first came online, it advertised the presence of various celebrities. Entranced by the idea of writing a letter to a famous syndicated columnist, I signed up for the service. While my first few letters did get a response, the mail volume quickly reached a level where most of the celebrities had to bow out.

We also need better authoring tools in order to decrease development costs, and standardized viewing platforms in order to increase accessibility. The competition to develop authoring tools and viewing platforms lies at the heart of the battle for the soul of the electronic book.

The final hurdle for the electronic book will be linking them to global networks. For entertainment titles, we can envisage a multimedia rental store; in fact, many of today's video stores stock game titles already. It is similarly easy to imagine university bookstores stocking electronic textbooks, or conventional bookstores stocking combined book/software products.

What is more difficult is to imagine how copyrighted materials will be handled on computer networks. Since these networks have not yet developed a system for protecting intellectual property, few publishers have consented to placing their books online. Today's online libraries concentrate on catalog listings; the books themselves are generally unavailable. If global networks are to become an effective distribution medium for electronic books, a way must be found to compensate copyright holders, while allowing users to browse online without thrashing through a thicket of copyright and licensing restrictions. The alternative is electronic Potemkin libraries: grand facades with empty shelves.

Building community networks

Since we are a long way from settling the Electronic Frontier, it is not clear whether we are building the electronic equivalent of Paris, or Woodstock.

Invite one hundred million guests for dinner, and your spouse will ask some pointed questions, such as How will we feed them? Where will they sleep?

Where indeed?

This thing we call telecommunications, that to many of us seems so natural, is actually a learned facility encompassing many skills. This guide started as a fifty page primer, and ended up at its present size based on suggestions of readers like yourself. Even now, it remains a work in progress.

There are those who argue that better software is the solution, and to some extent this is true. However since communications technology is inherently complex, it is very difficult to completely hide what goes on "under the hood." As a result, some understanding of the technology is a practical requirement.

We are talking about bringing this understanding to one hundred million people by the year 2000. It's hard to imagine how this can be done without some kind of grassroots education program, some kind of "training wheels." Community computing systems offer a solution.

Community computing systems are highly visible community resources provided for modest or no cost, and supported by local government, nonprofits, educational institutions and businesses.

There are those that argue that "free" community networks are too constricting. This argument is hard to refute; after all, we would not depend on public libraries for all our books. However, just as libraries do not exist solely to lend books, community computing systems do not exist purely to deliver services.

Community networks also have the mission of promoting telecommunications literacy itself, much as public libraries promote reading. From this perspective, the most important goal is achieving a wide level of participation. It is to be expected that people will "graduate" from community computing services to Internet service providers, bulletin boards and online services, but that is as it should be.

Since telecommunications infrastructure is so expensive, finding the money for community networks is difficult. Yet I would not go too far in dismissing the impracticality of the Free-Nets. The Free-Net idea is wonderfully impractical, in much the same way that public libraries and National Public Radio are. Yet they seem to have a powerful appeal that goes beyond the logic of money, and already more than half a dozen Free-Nets have opened. If

that ideal can be harnessed and combined with some bottom-line logic, we will have something very special.

On government participation

While the government has had a critical role in funding the research that spawned the telecommunications revolution, it has had a difficult time fully utilizing networking technology in its own operations.

Government adoption of networking technology is one of the more important steps that it can take in furthering the development of the industry. Some of the benefits are:

• **Cost savings.** Although cost savings are easier to project than to realize, there is clearly a role for networking technology in enabling downsizing within government.

• **Better understanding of the technology.** Until legislators and government employees use this technology on a daily basis, there is little hope of their developing sufficient understanding to permit sensible regulation.

• **Development of the market.** Given the government's awesome purchasing power, adoption of networking technology is likely to result in enhanced demand for improvements in hardware and software.

• **Enhanced communication with citizens.** The pressures for government participation as an online information provider are already becoming almost overwhelming. The recent publication of electronic mail addresses for the President and Vice President brought forth a torrent of electronic mail from correspondents who were clearly expecting something more than a written thank-you note in return. To have any hope of satisfying such expectations, goverment must go far beyond merely supporting electronic messaging as a mode of correspondence. It must commit to automating the work of the agencies themselves.

While government has much it can do, one thing it should not be involved in is operating conferencing systems. Inevitably, there are people who use electronic forums inappropriately. They must be restrained, if only because if they are not, everyone else will leave. Saddled with first amendment restrictions, government run conferencing systems have had a very difficult time reigning in abusive behavior.

The allure of asymmetrical channels

One of the attractions of global networks is that providing information is only marginally more difficult than consuming it.

While the vision of an inherently democratic medium may sound good to visionaries and telecommunications activists, it may not be nearly as attractive to government agencies, media conglomerates, or even consumers.

The problem is that we cannot deploy truly interactive media on a wide scale without improving the responsiveness of our institutions. Most government agencies are not currently prepared to handle a large volume of incoming traffic. Media conglomerates are very good at producing high design value material for high-bandwidth channels. They are not as well equipped for receiving high-bandwidth input from the viewing audience, although there are exceptions (America's Favorite Home Videos). There would therefore seem to be good grounds for a marriage between traditional information providers and asymmetrical data channels.

Evidence for such a marriage is already widespread. For example, some cable television firms now offer an asymmetric data channel coming into the home at 10 Mbps, with a phone line and modem for outgoing data. This could be used to connect to the Internet, or to broadcast recent Securities and Exchange Commision filings, the full text of legislation, or real estate, employment, and other listings.

Since cable technology is both faster and more economical than ISDN in many applications, it is likely to gain at least a fair degree of acceptance. The danger is that this economy will be bought at the expense of diversity in content. Unless we allow consumers to become providers, there is no way to offer real diversity no matter how many cable channels we have.

However, asymmetrical channels do not necessarily imply undemocratic media. Consumer usage patterns are also highly assymetrical, with most users of global networks and bulletin boards downloading much more than they upload. As long as consumers are allowed to become providers (possibly by use of other media such as ISDN), and the differences in bandwidth between outgoing and incoming traffic remains within typical usage patterns, many users may be satisfied. This is what allows firms to transmit Network News or FidoNet EchoMail by satellite, and why even a hundred fold increase in traffic could easily be accomodated by a 10 Mbps inbound cable channel, provided that the channel is not overloaded.

Where angels fear to tread

Technological revolutions begin with prominent promises, and hidden perils. In the early days, proponents are lauded as visionaries, and naysayers are derided as cranks. Yet naysayers have their purposes; it is only when the perils appear and are recognized that the real work of finding a place for a technology begins. As with any other technology, the information revolution has its problems: CyberScams, loss of privacy, the commodification of information. With the rapid growth of networks, only recently have we had the "critical mass" needed to explore the problems and develop solutions.

To date, the Cyberspace community has been remarkably homogeneous, but as the population of the Cyberspace continent swells, it will no doubt come to more closely reflect society at large. While leveraging the voice of the ordinary citizen, Cyberspace has also served as a megaphone to malcontents and a haven to hucksters.

CyberSmog has transformed more than one thriving Cyberspace neighborhood into a battlefield or ghost town. While many Cyberspace settlers are drawn to the medium by visions of A Shining City, bringing people online does not change human nature.

The saying that "all is fair in love and war," was never more true than in Cyberspace. We have had Cyberspace Don Juans, and men masquerading as women. The threat to the viability of the medium should not be underestimated: in the virtual world, trust is as precious as oxygen.

As likely as not, our current preoccupations will carry over into the online medium. A glance at the ten most popular USENET newsgroups reveals that the most popular topics are learning to use the network, online shopping, employment, humor and sexuality. Plus ça change...

The Top 10 USENET Newgroups

Group	Percent of sites receiving	Percent of people reading
news.announce.newusers	91%	12.9%
misc.forsale	83%	11.4%
misc.jobs.offered	85%	11.2%
news.answers	87%	9.9%
alt.sex	67%	8.3%
rec.humor.funny	82%	7.4%
rec.arts.erotica	73%	7.0%
news.groups	90%	6.2%
rec.humor	81%	6.1%
news.announce.newgroups	90%	5.8%

Source: Reid, Brian, "Top 40 Newsgroups in Order by Popularity," March 1993, posted to news.lists and news.groups.

While agents and filters may offer some solutions to the noise problem, they are not a panacea. The reality is that few of us relish interacting with them. All of us have had unpleasant interactions with voicemail systems or automated resume sorters, and for myself, I hardly relish my interactions with even the best of these systems.

The reality is that agents and filters are often substitutes for real accessibility. For example, it is hard to argue that corporate hiring processes have grown less discriminatory due to use of resume sorters. In fact, it is possible that accessibility will decrease; more than one voicemail system I've encountered doesn't even let you dial for information.

Part of the problem is that agents are often complex, insecure, or expensive. Getting one working is so difficult that many of these devices limp along in a semi-broken state, spewing out rudeness with impressive efficiency. It is hard to imagine any kind of "electronic community" peopled by agents.

Nevertheless, with cable operators offering 10 Mbps links into the home, filters are rapidly moving from an interesting idea to a practical necessity. We will probably eventually see as many filters on cable hookups as there are now on water taps.

The information economy

One of the undesirable side effects of The Discovery was that the Spanish became obsessed with gold. What the Spaniards failed to realize was that by flooding their economy with gold, they merely increased the money supply without providing more goods and services for the money to purchase. The result was inflation.

Similar dangers await those who become obsessed with the information economy. The purpose of an information infrastructure is to strengthen our existing manufacturing and service industries, not to replace them. Information for its own sake is like a freeze-dried meal without water. It is only valuable if you have the other ingredients of a healthy economy.

The bulletin board of the future

Although I have access to graphical Internet applications on multiple platforms, several UNIX shell accounts, and various accounts on commercial services, I spend most of my time online using bulletin boards. I suspect this will still be true five years from now, although the systems themselves will no doubt be different.

Bulletin board technology is in the midst of a transition, like so many other aspects of telecommunications. Yet this does not imply that bulletin boards are in any danger of extinction. Judging by recent surveys and the growth in the FidoNet nodelist, the number of publicly accessible systems is growing by more than 40 percent per year.

The August 1993 issue of *Boardwatch* estimated that there are more than 100,000 publicly accessible bulletin boards worldwide, used by more than thirteen million people. This figure gives only a partial picture of the usage of bulletin boards, since it does not include systems within private networks. In contrast, the same issue estimated that five million people are currently using commercial services.

Those predicting the demise of the bulletin board forget that BBSes, now more than fifteen years old, have already been through several technology transitions. These include the transition from CP/M to IBM PC technology beginning in 1981, and the transition to store and forward networking that began with FidoNet in 1984.

BBS technology is more adaptable than it is given credit for. With several TCP/IP-compatible BBS packages already on the market and the imminent release of FOSSIL drivers for TCP/IP, there will soon be no shortage of TCP/IP-compatible BBS products.

There are good reasons why BBS networks may find the Internet attractive. One is that traffic levels of BBS networks are outgrowing dialup modem links. Sometime in the next few years, they will need to switch to another technology for backbone transport, whether it be ISDN, satellite links, cable TV hookups, or dedicated lines.

At the rates charged by ToasterNet providers such as The Little Garden ($70/month), BBS network hubs will find that dedicated Internet connections are economically competitive with satellite links. This is because hubs typically have substantial outgoing as well as incoming traffic, and therefore are not well adapted to satellite technology.

The second trend is internationalization. The percentage of non-U.S. systems is increasing on virtually every BBS network. Transporting BBS network backbone traffic over the Internet can provide very substantial savings over leased lines or phone calls. Depending on the size of the country, satellite links may also be

attractive, particularly for nations with outmoded telephone networks.

The Internet is also likely to prove attractive for many sysops. Packet-switching services based on X.25 have been "promising" for years, but so far have been unable to provide affordable high-speed access.

In comparison, Internet access is available from many providers for as little as $20/month. Most of these services support high-speed modems, typically at no extra charge. Given the explosive growth of the Internet, Internet BBSes will soon have a large pool of potential customers.

In addition to traditional BBS setups, TCP/IP based systems offer two new configurations: the BBS as packet switch and the userless BBS.

The advent of Internet service providers known as ToasterNets has pioneered the BBS as packet-switch. With ToasterNets there are no file areas, no menus; in fact, there is no bulletin board at all. The primary purpose of the service provider is to route packets.

This approach has major advantages to system operators. Providers operating as packet switches closely resemble phone system switches that have common carrier status. The sysop as chaperone, private investigator, computer consultant, and therapist is replaced by the sysop as connectivity technician.

With the rise of client/server technologies such as Mailing List Managers, WAIS, W3, and Gopher, we are also seeing systems that respond to queries from around the world, but which do not maintain a user list. This is the userless BBS.

This approach also has advantages for sysops; rather than focussing on account maintenance (which takes up the majority of sysop time), the operator can focus on providing services.

CHAPTER 30:
THE POLITICS OF THE ELECTRONIC COMMUNICATIONS PRIVACY ACT

Copyright © 1990 Bernard Aboba. All rights reserved. Reprinted by permission.

The Electronic Communications Privacy Act (ECPA) of 1986 was a landmark piece of legislation that is likely to affect online services and hobbyist bulletin boards for many years to come. Since the ECPA is a complex and often arcane piece of legislation, it is very hard to understand without looking at the history of how it came to be. In understanding the politics of ECPA, this chapter relies heavily on the transcripts of the House Judiciary Committee Hearings on H.R. 3378, which eventually became the Electronic Communications Privacy Act.

During the hearings on ECPA in 1985-86, only one member of the online service industry, The Source (subsequently acquired by CompuServe) submitted an opinion. Though endorsing the bill, the assessment hinted at possible long-term costs imposed by the lack of preemption of state standards.[1] However, this one-page assessment hardly made an impression on the hearings compared with the impressive lineup of spokespeople from the ACLU, cellular communications firms, Regional Bell Operating Companies (RBOCs), broadcasting groups, credit and banking firms, and computer and telecommunications industry associations, all lined up in support of the bill.

Only the U.S. Department of Justice, manufacturers of scanning equipment, and amateur radio associations expressed strong reservations about the bill. However, since the

passage of ECPA, the long-term costs of the legislation and its effects on commercial and hobbyist conferencing systems have become apparent. Ironically, none of these effects were anticipated at the hearings.

The Politics of ECPA

The ECPA was supported by the cellular phone, telephone, packet-switching, paging, and broadcasting industries; private firms owning large communications networks; miscellaneous computer and communications trade associations; the ACLU and Consumer's Union; and credit bureaus. Law enforcement. agencies were supportive but skeptical. The only vigorous opposition came from amateur radio associations and manufacturers of scanning equipment, which, while protesting loudly, saw few of their recommended modifications enacted into law.

Also playing a role were sponsoring legislators, such as Senator Patrick Leahy of Vermont, and Charles Mathias of Maryland, as well as Representatives Robert Kastenmeier and Carlos Moorhead. Senator Leahy, in his opening remarks at the hearings on the bill, set the stage for the legislation:

"At this moment phones are ringing, and when they are answered, the message that comes out is a stream of sounds denoting ones and zeros.... What is remarkable is the fact that none of these transmissions are protected from illegal wiretaps, because our primary law, passed back in 1968, failed to cover data communications, of which computer-to-computer transmissions are a good example."

---

[1] Hearings of the Committee on the Judiciary, House of Representatives, H.R. 3378, Electronic Communications Privacy Act, 99th Congress, No. 50, 1986, pp. 409.

Outline of ECPA[2]

Broadened Protection of Communications

The ECPA amended the Omnibus Crime Control and Safe Streets Act of 1968 (which covered wire tapping of common carriers) to prohibit monitoring of all electronic communications systems not designed to be accessible by the public. This includes voice, data, and video on nonpublic systems, and applies to communications regardless of the mode of transmission.

Search and Seizure

To obtain access to communications such as electronic mail, the government is required to obtain a warrant on probable cause. Law enforcement must also obtain a court order based on reasonable suspicion before obtaining toll records of telephone calls or gaining access to records of an electronic communications system that concern specific communications.

Criminal Penalties

Criminal penalties can result from unauthorized access to computers if messages are obtained or altered. Felony charges can be brought if the violation was commited maliciously or for commercial gain, in which case the act is punishable by up to one year imprisonment and a $250,000 fine. In other cases, a term of imprisonment of six months and a maximum fine of $5,000 is applicable.

Civil Penalties

Civil damages may be pursued for violation of the rights contained in the act.

Disclosure

Electronic communications systems operators may not disclose electronic messages without authorization except in special circumstances.

---

[2] Public Law 99-508, 99th Congress, The Electronic Communications Privacy Act of 1986.

"When Congress enacted that law, Title III of the Omnibus Crime Control and Safe Streets Act of 1968, it had in mind a particular kind of communication – voice – and a particular way of transmitting that communication – via a common carrier analog telephone network. Congress chose to cover only the "aural acquisition" of the contents of a common carrier wire communication. The Supreme Court has interpreted that language to mean that to be covered by Title III, a communication must be capable of being overheard. The statue simply fails to cover the unauthorized interception of data transmissions."[3] Senator Leahy also had more practical reasons for supporting the bill. The rapidly growing U.S. cellular communications industry had become alarmed by the ease with which cellular communications could be monitored. Television sets built during the period 1966 to 1982 were capable of picking up cellular conversations on UHF channels 80-83.[4] This was possible because cellular communications used the same frequency modulation techniques utilized in transmitting television sound. In addition, scanning equipment, for several hundred dollars, was capable of receiving cellular communications in the 800-Mhz band.[5] During 1985, several incidents threatened to make the vulnerability of cellular communications into front-page news. For example, private conversations of state legislators in Austin were intercepted and made available in the public press, with embarrassing consequences.[6]

This ease of reception threatened the viability of the cellular industry. In response, according to Richard Colgan of the Association of North American Radio Clubs, "cellular firms resorted to pervasive misrepresentation of the actual

interception vulnerability of cellular."[7] In fairness to the cellular industry, cellular communications does provide certain inherent protections against interception. For example, since each half of the conversation is transmitted on different frequencies, usually it is only possible to listen in on one side of a conversation. In addition, while it is easy to pick up *some* conversation, it is difficult to pick up a *particular* conversation of interest. Also, the frequencies will shift during passage from one cell to another. However, given the relatively large cell size, frequencies are likely to be stable over the average life of a call. In his remarks, Senator Leahy stated that the ECPA was needed to help the cellular industry get off the ground, and that the American people and American business wanted the ECPA.[8] A more emotional defense was made by John Stanton, Executive Vice President of McCaw Communications, who stated: "The inhibition of the growth of cellular technology and paging technology, forced by the lack of privacy, is unfair."[9]

Law enforcement interests and businesses were also in favor of the bill. In 1986, the nation was just becoming aware of the threat posed by computer crime and the need for laws allowing prosecution of perpetrators. The ECPA was therefore viewed by elements of law enforcement and business as a vehicle for criminalizing the act of breaking into computers. Businesses such as GTE Telenet, EDS, and Chase Manhattan thus supported the ECPA as a computer crime bill. Telephone companies such as AT&T even attempted to tack on additional computer crime provisions covering breaking into their switching equipment.

In retrospect, the preoccupation with computer crime distorted evaluations of the ECPA. Computer crime was more effectively addressed by state penal code revisions such as California Penal Code §502 – Computer Crime,

---

[3] (Hearings, H.R. 3378, Committee on the Judiciary, 99th Congress, No. 50, pg. 2)

[4] Association of North American Radio Clubs, Supplemental Statement to the Hearings on H.R. 3378.

[5] Hearings, pg. 92-95.

[6] Ibid.

[7] Hearings, pg. 334.

[8] Hearings, pg. 2

[9] Hearings, pg. 92.

and §499c – Trade Secrets. The purpose of ECPA was to ensure privacy rather than to define the criminal uses of computers.

The cellular industry had no such illusions. Mr. Philip Quigley, CEO of pacTel Mobil Co. described the economic benefits of ECPA by noting that without legislation, "defending the right [to privacy] could take years of litigation." "Individuals can use scanning devices today... [it is our intent] to merely excise out... the capability that exists today to zone in on the channels and the frequencies that are associated with cellular telephony."[10] Without the ECPA, the industry would have faced the need to incorporate expensive encryption technology into their systems. For example, John Stanton of McCaw Communications testified that "Encryption devices make it difficult to roam from system to system," generated scratchy sound, and required 30 percent more investment for the base unit, and 100 percent for the phone.[11] The Association of North American Radio Club's Richard Colgan estimated high grade commercial encryption as costing $40 for the encryption chip (quantity one), plus associated circuitry. [12] In either case, the net cost for several million subscribers was estimated in the tens if not hundreds of millions of dollars.

Industry associations such as ADAPSO pointed out the trade benefits of the legislation, since Asia had not developed privacy protection, although Europe had done so.[13] McCaw's John Stanton commented that if the U.S. passed the ECPA, then it would enjoy superior communications privacy to that available in Europe.[14]

Representatives of the nation's amateur radio enthusiasts were among the staunchest opponents of the bill. Richard Colgan represented their position. "While we have no animosity towards cellular, we cannot sit idly by while they use their influence to make dubious changes in public policy, largely to benefit their bottom lines..."[15] In response to the concerns of amateur radio enthusiasts, and scanner manufacturers, the interception standard was changed from "willful" to "intentional," so as to allow for "inadvertent" interceptions.

Manufacturers of scanning equipment were vigorously opposed to ECPA since the use of their devices was restricted by the act. Richard Brown of Regency Electronics, a manufacturer of radio band scanners, argued cellular radio licensees have never had any expectation of privacy, that cellular operators, not the public, should bear the burden of securing cellular communications, and that protecting specific radio frequencies was imprudent.[16]

This last point deserves elaboration. Under ECPA, monitoring of cordless phone frequencies is not prohibited, although it is hard to argue that the average individual's "expectation of privacy" is any different for a cordless phone than it would be for a cellular phone. In fact, an educated individual might even expect *less* privacy for a cellular call, argued Richard Colgan, because the range of cellular communications is so much larger than for cordless phones, thus making interception easier.[17]

The most careful analyst of the ECPA was the U.S. Department of Justice, as represented by James Knapp, deputy assistant attorney general of the criminal division. Knapp concurred with the Amateur Radio enthusiasts that cellular and cordless phone technology, as well as tone and voice pagers, were easily intercepted and therefore could not presume

---

[10] Hearings, pp. 26-29.

[11] Hearings, pp. 92-95.

[12] Hearings, pp. 333.

[13] Hearings, pp. 74-77.

[14] Hearings, pp. 92-95.

---

[15] Hearings, pp. 147-171.

[16] Hearings, pp. 373-385.

[17] Hearings, pp. 147-171.

an "expectation of privacy."[18] Knapp also expressed skepticism about the wisdom of criminalizing hobbyist behavior.[19] Knapp was however in favor of extending coverage to electronic mail. Finally, he argued for extension of the crimes for which wire tapping could be authorized, beyond those enumerated in Title III. This suggested modification to the act was subsequently incorporated.[20]

In contrast to the detailed arguments submitted by the parties discussed here, the one-page letter submitted by The Source had a minor impact at best, suggesting that the ECPA, by not preempting state statutes, could expose the online service industry to an entangling web of federal and state statutes.[21]

Analysis of the economic effects of ECPA

The parts of ECPA that have ramifications for online services and hobbyist bulletin boards mostly have to do with access to stored messages. Although access to services is often offered via a packet-switching network, or could even be achieved via use of cellular modems or other radio transmissions, worries about the privacy of such access are not likely to be major concerns of customers.

An important aspect of ECPA is the presence of both criminal and civil penalties. This provides an important incentive for aggrieved parties to pursue litigation through contingency-fee arrangements. The implications of this for the online service business are serious. For example, the fee for sending an EasyPlex message on CompuServe is on the order of a few dollars, depending on the time spent in composing the message. For that fee, Compuserve takes on the

responsibility of not disclosing the message, which could conceivably be worth millions to the sender and intended recipient.

Of course, this burden is not theirs alone. Operators of corporate communications systems (who were big supporters of ECPA) are also likely targets. Indeed, several ECPA suits against employers and municipalities have recently been filed. The potential for litigation also exists for hobbyist systems such as computer bulletin boards.

Government regulations fit into two categories: economic regulation and social regulation. In the economic category are price controls on crude oil, and tarriffs. Equal opportunity legislation is a regulation of the social type. The cost of a social regulation can be broken down into two parts. One is the cost of complying with the regulation, either by modification of business practices or payment of imposed penalties; another is the cost of resolving ambiguities in the legislation through establishment of case law. In the case of ECPA, reflection discloses that the establishment of precedent is likely to be more expensive than compliance. For a service to modify sysop access privileges, and to introduce encryption of private mail and passwords, would probably entail an expenditure on the order of a few million dollars for software development and testing. In contrast, were only 0.01 percent of CompuServe's subscribers to file an ECPA lawsuit, given 500,000 subscribers and average legal fees and penalties per case of $100,000, the bill would come to over $10 million.

Due to its concentration on cellular industry concerns, the ECPA concentrates more on ensuring privacy for users than on limiting the responsibilities of providers. Due to differences between messages in transit and stored messages, cellular firms end up forcing the costs of privacy onto hobbyists and outsiders, while providers of online services are forced to bear those costs themselves. In view of the potentially horrendous litigation burdens, there is a strong incentive to limit the ability of system administrators to read or disclose private mail.

The key to complying with the act is the notion of "expectations of privacy." This

---

[18] Hearings, pp. 223-224.

[19] Hearings, pp. 227.

[20] Public Law 99-508, 99th Congress, The Electronic Communications Privacy Act of 1986.

[21] Hearings, pp. 409.

notion governs both the legal aspects of ECPA and determinants of end-user satisfaction. Under the ECPA, privacy is only enforced for systems in which users were lead to "expect privacy." Thus, a sysop has two alternatives: to explicitly address those expectations via an education campaign, or to play a game similar to the one played by the cellular industry by denying that privacy is a significant issue.

One of the concerns voiced by the cellular industry in backing ECPA was that its budding industry could ill afford the cost of solidifying the right to privacy via litigation or adoption of encryption technology. Yet that is precisely the course that the ECPA has forced on the online service industry. Nor were the concerns of a budding industry entirely genuine. Within the next two years, the revenues of cellular communication firms will exceed those of all the participants in the information services industry.

Bibliography

1. Electronic Communications Privacy Act of 1986, Public Law 99-508, 99th Congress, 2nd session.

2. Hearings of the Committee on the Judiciary, House of Representatives, H.R. 3378, Electronic Communications Privacy Act, 99th Congress, No. 50, 1986.

3. California Penal Code, Section 502, Computer Crime; 502.7, Obtaining telephone or telegraph services by fraud; 499c, Trade Secrets.

4. Wallace, Jonathan, and Lance Rose, SYSLAW, 2nd edition, PC Information Group, Winona, MN, 1992.

Firms Submitting Opinions on H.R. 3378

Phone Companies

Southwestern Bell
AT&T
Ameritech
Pacific Telesis
Bell South
Northwestern Bell
United States
Telephone Assoc.

Radio Hobbyists

Association of North
American Radio Clubs
American Radio Relay
League
Natl. Assoc. of Business
& Educational Radio

Cellular Communications

PacTel Mobile
McCaw Communications
Motorola
Centel Corp.

Packet Switching

GTE Telenet

Misc. Associations

Electronic Mail Assoc.
ADAPSO
National Assoc. of Man.
Assoc. of American
Railroads
IEEE

Paging

Telocator Network

Computers and Electronics

Tandy

Law Enforcement

U.S. Dept. of Justice

Online Services

The Source

Citizen's Groups

ACLU
Consumer's Union

Scanner Man.

Dynascan
Regency Electronics
Uniden

Firms with Private Networks

Chase Manhattan
EDS

Credit Bureaus

American Credit Services

Broadcasters

National Assoc. of Broadcasters
Radio-TV News Directors Assoc.
Satellite TV Industry Assoc.
CBS

Source: Hearings, Committee on the Judiciary, House of Representatives, H.R. 3378, ECPA, 99th Congress, No. 50, 1986.

Chapter 31: Free-Neting – The Development of Free, Public-Access, Community Computer Systems

T. M. Grundner, Ed.D., National Public Telecomputing Network

Copyright © 1991 T. M. Grundner. All rights reserved. Reprinted by permission.

The future is here

For the past twenty years, futurists have been making a common prediction. Someday, we are told, everyone will be able to use computers to send electronic mail across town or around the world, access medical and legal information, find out what's going on at their children's schools, complain to the mayor about the potholes, access the local public library card catalog, and so forth, all without ever leaving the comfort of home.

For some that vision has become reality via one or more of the many commercial videotex companies that now exist. But the high cost of those commercial services have, in general, prevented most average citizens from using them.

For the past five years researchers at Case Western Reserve University in Cleveland, Ohio, have been working on the development of extremely cost-efficient methods of delivering community-based computerized information and communications services. Their work has resulted in a system that is so inexpensive to operate that it can be provided by virtually any community as a free public service.

This chapter will touch on two aspects of their work. The first is the development of the Cleveland Free-Net™, a prototype community computer system that currently averages about 2000 logins a day and provides over 125 information and communications services to the Cleveland area. The second is the development of the National Public Telecomputing Network, a nonprofit organization devoted to disseminating this technology to other cities and linking them together into a common network.

Because of space limitations, the following will only briefly outline these developments. Those wishing more information may contact the author at addresses shown at the end of the article.

The Cleveland Free-Net

The Cleveland Free-Net is a free, open-access, community computer system operated by Case Western Reserve University. Established in July 1986, the central Free-Net computer has been programmed to allow anyone with a home, office, or school computer and a device called a modem to call in, 24 hours a day, and access a wide range of electronic services and features. These services range from free world-wide electronic mail to information in areas such as health, education, technology, government, arts, recreation, and the law.

The key to the economics of operating a Free-Net is the fact that the system is literally run by the community itself. Every feature that appears on the system is there because of individuals or organizations in the community who contribute their time, effort, and expertise to bring it online and operate it. On the Cleveland Free-Net, for example, there are over 250 sysops (system operators) who are doctors, lawyers, educators, community group representatives, hobbyists, and so on, each operating their own area and, thereby, contributing to the electronic whole. This is in contrast to the commercial systems that have very high personnel and information-acquisition costs and must pass those costs on to the consumer.

The first version of the Free-Net attracted over 7000 registered users and averaged between 500 and 600 calls a day on ten incoming phone lines. In August 1989 Free-Net II opened and currently averages over 2000 logins a day on forty eight telephone lines. At the moment the Free-Net has a user base of about 10,000 people, which is expected to grow eventually to at least 15,000 to 20,000 registered users in the Cleveland area. Eighty-six percent of Free-Net users are over the age of twenty (average age 35.5 years), with a very deep middle-class socio-economic penetration.

Inherent in the project from the beginning was the idea that, if we were successful, we would make every attempt to disseminate this technology to other cities. As a result, in September 1989 the National Public Telecomputing Network was born.

The National Public Telecomputing Network (NPTN)

The concept behind NPTN is not new. You are probably familiar with National Public Radio and Public Broadcasting on television. To understand NPTN, simply substitute community computer systems for radio or television stations, and you have the core of what the organization hopes to accomplish.

NPTN is a nonprofit corporation that is funded completely by voluntary membership dues from the users of its community computer systems, corporate and foundation grants and donations, and other fund-raising activities.

One of its main objectives is to establish as many community computer systems as possible throughout the country. To that end the necessary software is being made available to qualified parties, on a license basis, for $1 a year. Each Free-Net system is an affiliate of NPTN, which provides intersystem electronic mail-handling and other services. In addition, NPTN provides Cybercasting services whereby a wide variety of quality news and information features are delivered to the affiliates via NPTN feed – a concept very similar to that of any radio or television broadcasting network. A five-city network of NPTN community computers currently exists, with more expected to come online later this year.

Services

The list of services available on any given Free-Net is limited only by the resources of the community in which it operates. The Cleveland system, for example, has sixteen "buildings," which cover areas such as: government, the arts, science and technology, education, medicine, recreation, libraries, community affairs, business and industry, and law. It even has a "Teleport," which will transfer people to other area computer systems such as the Cleveland Public Library and other major libraries throughout northeast Ohio, and a "post office" to provide free electronic mail.

NPTN network services include such features as national and international electronic mail via the Internet; the dissemination of U.S. Supreme Court opinions within minutes of their release; and the "Congressional Memory Project," which provides summaries of House and Senate bills and how our congressional representatives voted on them. Hopefully NPTN will soon be providing a networkwide electronic news service.

The greening of a medium

Toward the end of the last century the public library as we know it today did not exist. Eventually, however, literacy became high enough (and the cost of books cheap enough) that the free public library became feasible. People in cities and towns all over the country got together to make free public access to the printed word a reality. The result was a legacy from which virtually everyone reading this document has, at one point or another, benefited.

We believe we have reached a point in this century where computer "literacy" has gotten high enough (and the cost of the equipment low enough) that a demand for free, public access, computerized information systems has developed.

The Cleveland Free-Net proved it could be done. NPTN is currently about the business of establishing these systems in cities throughout the country. And the futuristic dream of universal information and communication services for the community – all of the community – is not that far from becoming a reality.

For more information about the Cleveland Free-Net or NPTN, please contact: T. M. Grundner, Ed.D., President, NPTN, Box 1987, Cleveland, OH 44106; Voice: (216)247-5800; Fax: (216)247-3328; Internet: tmg@nptn.org.

Chapter 32:
How the National Public Telecomputing Network Came to Be

T. M. Grundner, Ed.D., as told to Bernard Aboba

Copyright © 1992 T. M. Grundner. All rights reserved.

How the Free-Net began

It all began in 1984 when I was working in a school of medicine as a quality-control specialist, overseeing their educational program. I am a doctor of education by training, and at the time I was an assistant professor in the department of family medicine at Case Western Reserve University.

We had residents and medical students, and our training sites were far apart, so I came upon the idea of setting up a department BBS on an Apple II+ with a 300 baud modem. This was to be for departmental use only, but within a week the number got out and lay people started calling in; they would ask questions of the physicians, who would answer them. Being a medical educator, I looked at that, and thought "We've got lay people crashing our system to get access to medical information. What would happen if I created a system that encouraged people to do this?"

So in 1985 I sat down and wrote a bulletin board program from scratch. I called it "St. Silicon's Hospital and Information Dispensary." It was set up as an electronic hospital and medical information system, but it operated like a real hospital, so people would understand how it worked. When they logged on, it asked "Have you been a patient at St. Silicon before?" If not, they would go to the

admitting desk and we would get information on them.

The heart of the system was the clinic. People could go in, ask medically related questions, and get answers in twenty four hours from a board-certified physician. Within a few weeks we were getting 300 calls a week. It was saturated from the early morning until 1 AM.

Clearly, we were looking at a new medium for medical information dispensing. It wasn't radio, it wasn't television, it wasn't print. I wrote an article for the *New England Journal of Medicine* on it, and it got a lot of attention. AT&T saw the article and donated one of its 3B2 400 minicomputers to us. They said "Take this work, develop and expand it with this, and keep in touch."

The 3B2 400 was a true UNIX multiuser machine. I looked at that and the Apple II, and tried to figure out what to do next. The Apple II was an electronic hospital, and I wondered "what would happen if I created an electronic city, part of which would be an electronic hospital?" We would have a post office, a government house, and a library in addition to the hospital. That was the beginning of Free-Net 1, the first version of the Cleveland Free-Net.

The sections of Free-Net 1 were run primarily by volunteer doctors and lawyers and politicians and hobbyists, each operating a piece of the system to give us a coherent whole. We ran Free-Net 1 for four years, until 1989. Then Case Western Reserve University got interested in it, took over the system, and developed the software for it, what we now refer to as Free-Net 2. The system currently averages around 10,000 logins a day, with 40,000 registered users and 250 to 275 special-interest areas operated by the community itself.

One of the interesting things about Free-Nets is that the enthusiasm doesn't need to be manufactured; all you need is to give it a vehicle to let it come out. One of the big questions that people asked when we started was, "If you put up the community computing system, will you get doctors and lawyers to participate as volunteers?" In point of fact, we have waiting lists of physicians wanting to become a part of this thing.

What has also been amazing is that the Free-Net draws as many users out of blue-collar neighborhoods as out of the upscale neighborhoods. We put terminals in libraries to make it more accessible, but modems aren't that big an obstacle. Many of our Free-Net users are logging on with Commodore 64s that they dragged out of the closet seven or eight years after they bought them. People are putting $30 and $50 modems on those old machines, and they've got access to a whole world of information. At first it surprised me, but then it made perfect sense.

I grew up in a blue-collar family; my dad was a factory worker. Every two weeks there would be someone coming by to sell encyclopedias. They knew that blue-collar families wanted their kids to do better, to give them advantages they never had. That hasn't changed. We've still got blue-collar families that want their kids to be part of the information age. With the way the technology is going now, for $250 you can hook up.

The National Public Telecomputing Network

After CWRU took control of the Cleveland Free-Net, we decided that it would be a waste if there were only one system like this. So we created a nonprofit organization called the National Public Telecomputing Network in order to disseminate the technology.

The easiest way to understand NPTN is to think about Public Broadcasting or National Public Radio. NPTN tries to do three things:

1. It tries to organize communities to bring Free-Nets online.

2. It helps with technical and financial support to get them up and running.

3. It helps the Free-Nets after they're running, by providing Cybercasting services to meld them together to form a common organization and network. This is similar in concept to network radio or television.

If you own a radio station, you have your own local hosts or DJs, but you also might take a feed from Mutual Radio. NPTN works the same way. A Free-Net would utilize local resources for most of what it does, and also take high-quality feeds from NPTN. The Cybercasting services would range from Supreme Court Decisions (we're one of twelve sites for that) to Educational feeds (we have an educational program called Academy One).

NPTN is growing rapidly. We will have sixteen systems online by the end of 1992. Twelve are in the U.S. and four are overseas, which includes a Wellington, New Zealand, site called Wellington City Net; an Ottawa, Canada, site called National Capital Free-Net; and two systems hooking up in Germany, in Erlengen and Bayrauth. On November 13, 1992, the minister of education for Finland will announce the Finland Free-Net, running out of Helsinki, as a national K-12 system. We've also got a system coming up in Vancouver. It's close, but there is no specific date. We also have twenty other systems in various stages of development. The shortest time from conception to getting online has been three months; at this rate we'll have systems in many of the major U.S. cities by 1994.

The idea was never to create CompuServe North, but to introduce telecomputing to the average person. Now in terms of engineering, you could have one central system, but we wanted to create pockets of development so people could learn how to use the technology within the context of their own community. The systems respond to the information needs of the community. So the system in Cincinnati is different from the one in Cleveland, which is different from Peoria.

For example, Cincinnati Free-Net is quite business-oriented; it's operated by Cincinnati Bell Telephone, which has contacts in the business community. On the other hand, Cleveland Free-Net is owned and operated by the university, so our strength is medical and social services.

One of the threads that runs through all the systems is education. Academy One is a huge K-12 program, involving 230 K-12 Schools across the U.S. It uses the Free-Nets for access, and in addition to NPTN, it provides special resources for the K-12 community.

For example, once a month we hold an online event. One month we simulated space shuttle launches, where each school played a role in the mission and they were tied together with community computing. We had a virtual Olympics where schools from Cleveland to Estonia ran athletic events and reported their best swimming times or longest jumps. We then sent out ribbons for first, second, and third places. There are a variety of other programs. We have online news services and electronic books.

On the National Research and Education Network (NREN)

Community computing is a way of giving access to the benefits of NREN without eating up bandwidth. The network people do not want 230 million people with network access, but if you do it via community computing, you can give sensible access without blowing the whole thing apart.

The way it's being done now doesn't make sense. There's a balkanization, with librarians, K-12 people, medical-information people, and government all wanting their own network. It can't be done financially, and it doesn't make sense functionally. Take a K-12 or college

network. Say you have a bunch of schools on Internet and they do all this neat stuff, they can telnet and do email. What happens the day after graduation? The kid comes back and says, "I want to use my account," and you have to say, "Sorry, you're not a student anymore." It's like having mandatory drivers education in a world without automobiles.

The National Science Foundation still doesn't understand community computing. Its policy toward funding networking and education is based on a National Institutes of Health (NIH) model. If you get an NIH grant for a cure for cancer, there are thousands of hospitals to utilize your discovery. But what if I got an NSF grant and discovered a way to use modems in education that would jump kids reading levels two grades in a year? What would I do with it? There's no delivery mechanism. Yet they insist on using the same process as if there were one.

That is why we are not affiliated with the NSF K-12 program. The NSF has not developed a vehicle for supporting the grass roots, because people are always talking about physical bandwidth, but that's not the issue. What we're lacking is something with enough conceptual bandwidth. The concept of community computing has got that: a road map to the future that includes everybody and makes sense.

One of the things we will be working on in the new year is federal legislation. The way we think it should be done is to have an equivalent of the Corporation for Public Broadcasting. It would be a free-standing nonprofit corporation and receive its core funding from Congress, but it would not be a branch of government. We call it the Corporation for Public Cybercasting. The point of CPC would be to support community computing systems by developing Cybercasting services. CPC would also have the goal of bringing populations of underrepresented peoples, like minorities, women, handicapped, seniors, and K-12, into the information age. The bill would stipulate that any network funded in whole or in part by the federal government would have to connect to community computer systems.

On teledemocracy

Government can do a lot for NPTN, but we can also do a lot for government. Right now, within twenty minutes of a Supreme Court decision, we have full text. We just finished Campaign '92, where we covered the full text of press releases from the candidates. So when people went into the voting booths, they could look at what the candidates actually said, as opposed to what the news media said they said.

The position papers of the winners stay online, the losers are deleted. So if you want to know what Governor Clinton said about anything, it will be publicly online as long as he's in office. If you want to know what Governor Voinovich said in 1990 about development in Northeastern Ohio, you can look it up and hold the politicians accountable. We have a similar thing with the House and Senate. Every week we take two or three bills and we show what the bill was about and how our delegation voted, and it goes into a permanent database. This year a lot of people were rummaging through those bills to see how their senators and congresspeople voted.

TV can't do this, radio can't do it, newspapers could but they don't. Computers remember, TV sets don't.

This medium has tremendous power to improve the quality of government. We are now wrapping up a project for the Office of Technology Assessment, OTA. The Senate wanted OTA to get information on how people felt about government information services. We ran an OTA teleforum on NPTN, so if you posted something in Cleveland, your posting would appear in Youngstown and Fargo. People saw this and took it very seriously. Congress really wants to know what we think. Fine!

It was the kind of thing Perot talked about, with electronic town halls. I see enormous potential for raw dissemination of information from the federal government. There are information sources like Census data that should be available to everyone. The government purchases a zillion reports a year, so people should be able to find out what's

online and how to get it by having indexes on community computing systems.

Another area that we can improve is communications between people and their representatives. There are no technological reasons why I shouldn't be able to send mail to anyone on capitol hill, or to the Department of Education or Department of Commerce, to throw in my two cents' worth. That connection point needs to be made, and it can and should be made using this medium.

In all of our organizing committees we strongly suggest that you have representatives from a broad community, especially city government. This is what builds the community commitment to Free-Nets, it's what makes it work. On some of our systems the chamber of commerce has been helpful; they see it as a viable part of the infrastructure of their communities. Among the biggest users of our systems are small and medium-size businesses. If you're in Cleveland and are TRW or BP America you've got email, but small businesses doesn't have it, and they use it to link to suppliers and customers. So you develop business infrastructure; you get bills of materials and purchase orders sent back and forth.

On the appropriate use of computers

Community computing is not about rummaging about the Internet to your heart's content. It's about controlled access to electronic mail and telnet to library resources. There is no FTP capability, so you don't have to worry about kids downloading porn. The objective is to give the people who paid for these networks the chance to benefit.

Over time, we've come to better understand the medium. We used to Cybercast the full text of books, but we don't do that anymore because reading books off a screen is not useful. Instead, we do campaign '92 and electronic versions of various newspapers and news services.

Many of our Cybercasting services are read-only, so we can control the quality of the material, but there are also open discussion sections. NPTN is the only one who can post to congressional memory, but along with the campaign papers, next to them, was a conference in which everyone could post, and there were interesting discussions.

To create a system everyone can accept, you have to set up some standards, in terms of what language can be used. We try to adhere to FCC-type standards. Last fall, we had a situation where people were posting files with highly inappropriate language in the subject lines. There were a lot of people getting upset, like the K-12 educators. So we had a big debate, and the university looked at it and said, "The Free-Net is a version of the Quadrangle, where anyone can give a speech and use any kind of language."

I disagreed. My argument was that it was much more like the campus radio station, where there are things you can't put out, and the First Amendment won't change that.

Our solution was to develop a red-light district in the electronic city. You send a little form that says you're over eighteen, so you can go into a certain area. But the rest of the system stays clean. The red-light districts are local and conform to community standards; this allows us to enforce FCC standards on what goes out over the network.

On the mission of NPTN

When I started out, I thought it would develop this way almost from the beginning. What I didn't appreciate was how much it would cost me personally and professionally. Had I known what it would cost me financially and in terms of my family life, I probably wouldn't have done it. But once it seizes you, it's hard to give up and walk away from. The road has been long and difficult. People have put up barriers to stop NPTN, to try to steal it, to demolish it. My own family has suffered. It's not something I recommend to anybody.

But it's something that seizes you. The sensible thing is to forget you ever started it and go on to something else. Until this point I've been an employee of CWRU. As of next week I will be a full-time employee of NPTN, which adds a whole new dimension to fund-raising. Either this will work or I'll be an unemployed 47-year-old with no hope of getting back into the job market.

My devotion to NPTN has put me into a choice position: either I give up the security of a monthly paycheck, which could last until my retirement, and let NPTN die, or I give it all up to keep the dream alive. We've tried the "better mousetrap" approach, asking people, "Isn't this so great that you want to support it?" and we found that the answer was "No."

Trying to get funding for community computing is a hellacious process. We go to corporate donation services. They look on the list of things they fund: things like soup kitchens, or shelters for battered women. Community computing isn't on the list. Even with all the demonstrated efficacy, we need to have the pump primed.

Fundraising for a national network from sources like RBOCs, foundations, or major corporations is even worse, which is why we need the government to help with some of the core funding. It's easier to convince someone to support a Free-Net in the local area, where their investment will be visible and they'll get tangible benefits. The problem is when the company is in Virginia and they're being asked to invest in a national network, the core of which is in Cleveland. That's tough. We can get support for the leaves, but how to get support for the roots? That is the question.

We are now in a grow or die situation. I have to build a core structure to meet the kinds of demands we have from our local Free-Nets, to support them and refine the concepts of Cybercasting. In other words, I've got to find core funding for the organization.

Relying on the private sector won't build a National Network. We are going to need legislation, and to get that we are going to have to get this higher in the national consciousness. I am hopeful because the vice president understands the technology, which was better than the Bush campaign. You couldn't get files of position papers out of them in electronic form. It was like pulling teeth. With the Clinton campaign, they were calling us.

On marketing myopia

In 1985, we were tapping the early adopters with St. Silicon. Back then it was hobbyists. Now it is computer literate people, people who use computers in the workplace. With a modem and simple software, it's not much of an extension to get them online.

The problem is with other groups. For example, aside from SeniorNet, nobody is going after services for senior citizens. More senior citizens are computer literate today because of the workplace. They're healthier, with more disposable income, and more mentally intact. Why aren't we finding out what their information needs are and how we can meet them? Because industry figures they're sitting in rocking chairs.

SeniorNet does a terrific job of developing computer literacy among seniors, particularly among some of the older seniors who weren't in the workplace when the micro revolution started. The problem is that their system runs partly on commercial services, and so it does not matter how well off the participants are, they'll have one eye on the clock no matter what. We have thought of having SeniorNet provide literacy, and then plug them into a community computer system.

This kind of broadening of the audience is critical. Ask a Videotext executive where they're going to get their customers three to five years from now? Competition is increasing and how many times can you divide that pie before there's nothing left? What I have been saying is that they need a way to increase market penetration or they will be dead in five years. But although there is a self-interest for Videotext in sponsoring community computing, they just don't get it.

CHAPTER 33:
HOW THE INTERNET CAME TO BE

Vinton Cerf, as told to Bernard Aboba

Copyright © 1993 Vinton Cerf. All rights reserved. May be reproduced in any medium for noncommercial purposes.

The birth of the ARPANET

My involvement began when I was at UCLA doing graduate work from 1967 to 1972. There were several people at UCLA at the time studying under Jerry Estrin, and among them was Stephen Crocker. Stephen was an old high-school friend, and when he found out that I wanted to do graduate work in computer science, he invited me to interview at UCLA.

When I started graduate school, I was originally looking at multiprocessor hardware and software. Then a Request For Proposal came in from the Defense Advanced Research Projects Agency, DARPA. The proposal was about packet switching, and it went along with the packet-switching network that DARPA was building.

Several UCLA faculty were interested in the RFP. Leonard Kleinrock had come to UCLA from MIT, and he brought with him his interest in that kind of communications environment. His thesis was titled *Communication Networks: Stochastic Flow and Delay*, and he was one of the earliest queuing theorists to examine what packet-switch networking might be like. As a result, the UCLA people proposed to DARPA to organize and run a Network Measurement Center for the ARPANET project.

This is how I wound up working at the Network Measurement Center on the implementation of a set of tools for observing the behavior of the fledgling ARPANET. The team included Stephen Crocker; Jon Postel, who has been the RFC editor from the beginning; Robert Braden, who was working

at the UCLA computer center; Michael Wingfield, who built the first interface to the Internet for the Xerox Data System Sigma 7 computer, which had originally been the Scientific Data Systems (SDS) Sigma 7; and David Crocker, who became one of the central figures in electronic mail standards for the ARPANET and the Internet. Mike Wingfield built the BBN 1822 interface for the Sigma 7, running at 400 Kbps, which was pretty fast at the time.

Around Labor Day in 1969, BBN delivered an Interface Message Processor (IMP) to UCLA that was based on a Honeywell DDP 516, and when they turned it on, it just started running. It was hooked by 50 Kbps circuits to two other sites (SRI and UCSB) in the four-node network: UCLA, Stanford Research Institute (SRI), UC Santa Barbara (UCSB), and the University of Utah in Salt Lake City.

We used that network as our first target for studies of network congestion. It was shortly after that I met the person who had done a great deal of the architecture: Robert Kahn, who was at BBN, having gone there from MIT. Bob came out to UCLA to kick the tires of the system in the long haul environment, and we struck up a very productive collaboration. He would ask for software to do something, I would program it overnight, and we would do the tests.

One of the many interesting things about the ARPANET packet switches is that they were heavily instrumented in software, and additional programs could be installed remotely from BBN for targeted data sampling. Just as you use trigger signals with oscilloscopes, the

IMPs could trigger collection of data if you got into a certain state. You could mark packets and when they went through an IMP that was programmed appropriately, the data would go to the Network Measurement Center.

There were many times when we would crash the network trying to stress it, where it exhibited behavior that Bob Kahn had expected, but that others didn't think could happen. One such behavior was reassembly lock-up. Unless you were careful about how you allocated memory, you could have a bunch of partially assembled messages but no room left to reassemble them, in which case it locked up. People didn't believe it could happen statistically, but it did. There were a bunch of cases like that.

My interest in networking was strongly influenced by my time at the Network Measurement Center at UCLA.

Meanwhile, Larry Roberts had gone from Lincoln Labs to DARPA, where he was in charge of the Information Processing Techniques Office. He was concerned that after building this network, we could do something with it. So out of UCLA came an initiative to design protocols for hosts, which Steve Crocker led.

In April 1969, Steve issued the very first Request For Comment. He observed that we were just graduate students at the time and so had no authority. So we had to find a way to document what we were doing without acting like we were imposing anything on anyone. He came up with the RFC methodology to say, "Please comment on this, and tell us what you think."

Initially, progress was sluggish in getting the protocols designed and built and deployed. By 1971 there were about nineteen nodes in the initially planned ARPANET, with thirty different university sites that ARPA was funding. Things went slowly because there was an incredible array of machines that needed interface hardware and network software. We had Tenex systems at BBN running on DEC-10s, but there were also PDP8s, PDP-11s, IBM 360s, Multics, Honeywell... you name it. So you had to implement the protocols on each of these different architectures.

In late 1971, Larry Roberts at DARPA decided that people needed serious motivation to get things going. In October 1972 there was to be an International Conference on Computer Communications, so Larry asked Bob Kahn at BBN to organize a public demonstration of the ARPANET.

It took Bob about a year to get everybody far enough along to demonstrate a bunch of applications on the ARPANET. The idea was that we would install a packet switch and a Terminal Interface Processor or TIP in the basement of the Washington Hilton Hotel, and actually let the public come in and use the ARPANET, running applications all over the U.S.

A set of people who are legendary in networking history were involved in getting that demonstration set up. Bob Metcalfe was responsible for the documentation; Ken Pogran who, with David Clark and Noel Chiappa, was instrumental in developing an early ring-based local area network and gateway, which became Proteon products, narrated the slide show; Crocker and Postel were there. Jack Haverty, who later became chief network architect of Oracle and was an MIT undergraduate, was there with a holster full of tools. Frank Heart who led the BBN project; David Walden; Alex McKenzie; Severo Ornstein; and others from BBN who had developed the IMP and TIP.

The demo was a roaring success, much to the surprise of the people at AT&T who were skeptical about whether it would work. At that conference a collection of people convened: Donald Davies from the UK, National Physical Laboratory, who had been doing work on packet switching concurrent with DARPA; Remi Despres who was involved with the French Reseau Communication par Paquet (RCP) and later Transpac, their commercial X.25 network; Larry Roberts and Barry Wessler, both of whom later joined and led BBN's Telenet; Gesualdo LeMoli, an Italian network researcher; Kjell Samuelson from the Swedish Royal Institute; John Wedlake from British Telecom; Peter Kirstein from University College London; Louis Pouzin who led the Cyclades/Cigale packet network research program at the Institute Recherche d'Informatique et d'Automatique (IRIA, now INRIA, in France). Roger Scantlebury from NPL with Donald Davies may also have been in attendance. Alex McKenzie from BBN almost certainly was there.

I'm sure I have left out some and possibly misremembered others. There were a lot of other people, at least thirty, all of whom had come to this conference because of a serious academic or business interest in networking.

At the conference we formed the International Network Working Group or INWG. Stephen Crocker, who by now was at DARPA after leaving UCLA, didn't think he had time to organize the INWG, so he proposed that I do it.

I organized and chaired INWG for the first four years, at which time it was affiliated with the International Federation of Information Processing (IFIP). Alex Curran, who was president of BNR, Inc., a research laboratory of Bell Northern Research in Palo Alto, California, was the U.S. representative to IFIP Technical Committee 6. He shepherded the transformation of the INWG into the first working group of 6, working group 6.1 (IFIP WG 6.1).

In November 1972, I took up an assistant professorship post in computer science and electrical engineering at Stanford. I was one of the first Stanford acquisitions who had an interest in computer networking. Shortly after I got to Stanford, Bob Kahn told me about a project he had going with SRI International, BBN, and Collins Radio, a packet radio project. This was to get a mobile networking environment going. There was also work on a packet satellite system, which was a consequence of work that had been done at the University of Hawaii, based on the ALOHA-Net, done by Norman Abramson, Frank Kuo, and Richard Binder. It was one of the first uses of multiaccess channels. Bob Metcalfe used that idea in designing Ethernet before founding 3COM to commercialize it.

The birth of the Internet

Bob Kahn described the packet radio and satellite systems, and the internet problem, which was to get host computers to communicate across multiple packet networks without knowing the network technology underneath. As a way of informally exploring this problem, I ran a series of seminars at Stanford attended by students and visitors. The students included Carl Sunshine, who is now at Aerospace Corporation running a laboratory and specializing in the area of protocol proof of correctness; Richard Karp, who wrote the first TCP code and is now president of ISDN technologies in Palo Alto. There was Judy Estrin, a founder of Bridge Communications, which merged with 3COM, and is now an officer at Network Computing Devices (NCD), which makes X display terminals. Yogen Dalal, who edited the December 1974 first TCP specification, did his thesis work with this group, and went on to work at PARC where he was one of the key designers of the Xerox Protocols. Jim Mathis, who was involved in the software of the small-scale LSI-11 implementations of the Internet protocols, went on to SRI International and then to Apple where he did MacTCP. Darryl Rubin went on to become one of the vice presidents of Microsoft. Ron Crane handled hardware in my Stanford lab and went on to key positions at Apple. John Shoch went on to become assistant to the president of Xerox and later ran their System Development Division. Bob Metcalfe attended some of the seminars as well. Gerard Lelann was visiting from IRIA and the Cyclades/Cigale project, and has gone on to do work in distributed computing. We had Dag Belsnes from University of Oslo who did work on the correctness of protocol design; Kuninobu Tanno (from Tohoku University); and Jim Warren, who went on to found the West Coast Computer Faire. Thinking about computer networking problems has had a powerful influence on careers; many of these people have gone on to make major contributions.

The very earliest work on the TCP protocols was done at three places. The initial design work was done in my lab at Stanford. The first draft came out in the fall of 1973 for review by

INWG at a meeting at University of Sussex (September 1973). A paper by Bob Kahn and me appeared in May 1974 in IEEE Transactions on Communications and the first specification of the TCP protocol was published as an Internet Experiment Note in December 1974. We began doing concurrent implementations at Stanford, BBN, and University College London. So effort at developing the Internet protocols was international from the beginning. In July 1975, the ARPANET was transferred by DARPA to the Defense Communications Agency (now the Defense Information Systems Agency) as an operational network.

About this time, military security concerns became more critical and this brought Steve Kent from BBN and Ray McFarland from DoD more deeply into the picture, along with Steve Walker, then at DARPA.

At BBN there were two other people: William Plummer and Ray Tomlinson. It was Ray who discovered that our first design lacked and needed a three-way handshake in order to distinguish the start of a new TCP connection from old random duplicate packets that showed up later from an earlier exchange. At University College London, the person in charge was Peter Kirstein. Peter had a lot of graduate and undergraduate students working in the area, using a PDP-9 machine to do the early work. They were at the far end of a satellite link to England.

Even at the beginning of this work we were faced with using satellite communications technology as well as ARPANET and packet radio. We went through four iterations of the TCP suite, the last of which came out in 1978.

The earliest demonstration of the triple network Internet was in July 1977. We had several people involved. In order to link a mobile packet radio in the Bay Area, Jim Mathis was driving a van on the San Francisco Bayshore Freeway with a packet radio system running on an LSI-11. This was connected to a gateway developed by Virginia Strazisar at BBN. Ginny was monitoring the gateway and had artificially adjusted the routing in the system. It went over the Atlantic via a point-to-point satellite link to Norway and down to

London, by land line, and then back through the Atlantic Packet Satellite network (SATNET) through a Single Channel Per Carrier (SCPC) system, which had ground stations in Etam, West Virginia, Goonhilly Downs England, and Tanum, Sweden. The German and Italian sites of SATNET hadn't been hooked in yet. Ginny was responsible for gateways from packet radio to ARPANET, and from ARPANET to SATNET. Traffic passed from the mobile unit on the Packet Radio network across the ARPANET over an internal point-to-point satellite link to University College London, and then back through the SATNET into the ARPANET again, and then across the ARPANET to the USC Information Sciences Institute to one of their DEC KA-10 (ISIC) machines. So what we were simulating was someone in a mobile battlefield environment going across a continental network, then across an intercontinental satellite network, and then back into a wireline network to a major computing resource in national headquarters. Since the Defense Department was paying for this, we were looking for demonstrations that would translate to militarily interesting scenarios. So the packets were traveling 94,000 miles round trip, as opposed to what would have been an 800-mile round trip directly on the ARPANET. We didn't lose a bit!

After that exciting demonstration, we worked very hard on finalizing the protocols. In the original design we didn't distinguish between TCP and IP; there was just TCP. In the mid-1970s, experiments were being conducted to encode voice through a packet switch, but in order to do that we had to compress the voice severely from 64 Kbps to 1800 bps. If you really worked hard to deliver every packet, to keep the voice playing out without a break, you had to put lots and lots of buffering in the system to allow sequenced reassembly after retransmissions, and you got a very unresponsive system. So Danny Cohen at ISI, who was doing a lot of work on packet voice, argued that we should find a way to deliver packets without requiring reliability. He argued it wasn't useful to retransmit a voice packet end to end. It was worse to suffer a delay of retransmission.

That line of reasoning led to separation of TCP, which guaranteed reliable delivery, from IP. So the User Datagram Protocol (UDP) was created as the user-accessible way of using IP. And that's how the voice protocols work today, via UDP.

Late in 1978 or so, the operational military started to get interested in Internet technology. In 1979 we deployed packet radio systems at Fort Bragg, and they were used in field exercises. The satellite systems were further extended to include ground stations in Italy and Germany. Internet work continued in building more implementations of TCP/IP for systems that weren't covered. While still at DARPA, I formed an Internet Configuration Control Board chaired by David Clark from MIT to assist DARPA in the planning and execution of the evolution of the TCP/IP protocol suite. This group included many of the leading researchers who contributed to the TCP/IP development and was later transformed by my successor at DARPA, Barry Leiner, into the Internet Activities Board (and is now the Internet Architecture Board of the Internet Society). In 1980, it was decided that TCP/IP would be the preferred military protocols.

In 1982 it was decided that all the systems on the ARPANET would convert over from NCP to TCP/IP. A clever enforcement mechanism was used to encourage this. We used a Link Level Protocol on the ARPANET; NCP packets used one set of one channel numbers and TCP/IP packets used another set. So it was possible to have the ARPANET turn off NCP by rejecting packets sent on those specific channel numbers. This was used to convince people that we were serious in moving from NCP to TCP/IP. In the middle of 1982, we turned off the ability of the network to transmit NCP for one day. This caused a lot of hubbub unless you happened to be running TCP/IP. It wasn't completely convincing that we were serious, so toward the middle of fall we turned off NCP for two days; then on January 1, 1983, it was turned off permanently. The guy who handled a good deal of the logistics for this was Dan Lynch; he was computer center director of USC ISI at the time. He undertook the onerous task of scheduling, planning, and testing to get people up and running on TCP/IP. As many people know, Lynch went on to found INTEROP, which has become the premier

trade show for presenting Internet technology.

In the same period there was also an intense effort to get implementations to work correctly. Jon Postel engaged in a series of Bake Offs, where implementers would shoot kamikaze packets at each other. Recently, FTP Software has reinstituted Bake Offs to ensure interoperability among modern vendor products.

This takes us up to 1983. 1983 to 1985 was a consolidation period. Internet protocols were being more widely implemented. In 1981, 3COM had come out with UNET, which was a UNIX TCP/IP product running on Ethernet. The significant growth in Internet products didn't come until 1985 or so, where we started seeing UNIX and local area networks joining up. DARPA had invested time and energy to get BBN to build a UNIX implementation of TCP/IP and wanted that ported into the Berkeley UNIX release in v4.2. Once that happened, vendors such as Sun started using BSD as the base of commercial products.

The Internet takes off

By the mid-1980s there was a significant market for Internet-based products. In the 1990s we started to see commercial services showing up, a direct consequence of the NSFNet initiative, which started in 1986 as a 56 Kbps network based on LSI-11s with software developed by David Mills, who was at the University of Delaware. Mills called his NSFNet nodes "Fuzzballs."

The NSFNet, which was originally designed to hook supercomputers together, was quickly outstripped by demand and was overhauled for T1. IBM, Merit, and MCI did this, with IBM developing the router software. Len Bozack was the Stanford student who started Cisco Systems. His first client: Hewlett-Packard. Meanwhile Proteon had gotten started, and a number of other routing vendors had emerged. Despite having built the first gateways (now called routers), BBN didn't believe there was a market for routers, so they didn't go into competition with Wellfleet, ACC, Bridge, 3COM, Cisco, and others.

The exponential growth of the Internet began in 1986 with the NSFNet. When the NCP to TCP transition occurred in 1983 there were only a couple of hundred computers on the network. As of January 1993 there are over 1.3 million computers in the system. There were only a handful of networks back in 1983; now there are over 10,000.

In 1988 I made a conscious decision to pursue connection of the Internet to commercial electronic mail carriers. It wasn't clear that this would be acceptable from the standpoint of federal policy, but I thought that it was important to begin exploring the question. By 1990, an experimental mail relay was running at the Corporation for National Research Initiatives (CNRI) linking MCI Mail with the Internet. In the intervening two years, most commercial email carriers in the U.S. are linked to Internet and many others around the world are following suit.

In this same time period, commercial Internet service providers emerged from the collection of intermediate-level networks inspired and sponsored by the National Science Foundation as part of its NSFNet initiatives. Performance Systems International (PSI) was one of the first, spinning off from NYSERNet. UUNET Technologies formed Alternet; Advanced Network and Systems (ANS) was formed by IBM, MERIT, and MCI (with its ANS CO+RE commercial subsidiary); CERFNet was initiated by General Atomics which also runs the San Diego Supercomputer Center; JVNCNet became GES, Inc., offering commercial services; Sprint formed Sprintlink; Infonet offered Infolan service; the Swedish PTT offered SWIPNET, and comparable services were offered in the UK and Finland. The Commercial Internet eXchange was organized by commercial Internet service providers as a traffic transfer point for unrestricted service.

In 1990 a conscious effort was made to link in commercial and nonprofit information service providers, and this has also turned out to be useful. Among others, Dow Jones, Telebase, Dialog, CARL, the National Library of Medicine, and RLIN are now online.

The last few years have seen internationalization of the system and commercialization, new constituencies well outside of computer science and electrical engineering, regulatory concerns, and security concerns from businesses and out of a concern for our dependence on this as infrastructure. There are questions of pricing and privacy; all of these things are having a significant impact on the technology evolution plan, and with many different stakeholders there are many divergent views of the right way to deal with various problems. These views have to be heard and compromises worked out.

The recent rash of books about the Internet is indicative of the emerging recognition of this system as a very critical international infrastructure, and not just for the research and education community.

I was astonished to see the CCITT bring up an Internet node; the U.N. has just brought up a node, un.org; IEEE and ACM are bringing their systems up. We are well beyond critical mass now. The 1990s will continue this exponential growth phase. The other scary thing is that we are beginning to see experimentation with packet voice and packet video. I fully anticipate that an Internet TV guide will show up in the next couple of years.

I think this kind of phenomenon is going to exacerbate the need for understanding the economics of these systems and how to deal with charging for use of resources. I hesitate to speculate; currently where charges are made they are a fixed price based on the size of the access pipe. It is possible that the continuous transmission requirements of sound and video will require different charging because you are not getting statistical sharing during continuous broadcasting. In the case of multicasting, one packet is multiplied many times. Things like this weren't contemplated when the flat-rate charging algorithms were developed, so the service providers may have to reexamine their charging policies.

Concurrent with the exponential explosion in Internet use has come the recognition that there is a real community out there. The community now needs to recognize that it exists, that it has a diversity of interests, and that it has responsibilities to those who are dependent on the continued health of the network. The Internet Society was founded in

January 1992. With assistance from the Federal Networking Council, the Internet Society supports the IETF and IAB and educates the broad community by holding conferences and workshops, by proselytizing, and by making information available.

I had certain technical ambitions when this project started, but they were all oriented toward highly flexible, dynamic communication for military application, insensitive to differences in technology below the level of the routers. I have been extremely pleased with the robustness of the system and its ability to adapt to new communications technology.

One of the main goals of the project was "IP on everything." Whether it is frame relay, ATM, or ISDN, it should always be possible to bring an Internet Protocol up on top of it. We've always been able to get IP to run, so the Internet has satisfied my design criteria. But I didn't have a clue that we would end up with anything like the scale of what we have now, let alone the scale that it's likely to reach by the end of the decade.

On scaling

The somewhat embarrassing thing is that the network address space is under pressure now. The original design of 1973 and 1974 contemplated a total of 256 networks. There was only one LAN at PARC, and all the other networks were regional or nationwide networks. We didn't think there would be more than 256 research networks involved. When it became clear there would be a lot of local area networks, we invented the concept of Class A, B, and C addresses. In Class C there were several million network IDs. But the problem that was not foreseen was that the routing protocols and Internet topology were not well suited for handling an extremely large number of network IDs. So people preferred to use Class B and subnetting instead. We have a rather sparsely allocated address space in the current Internet design, with Class B allocated to excess and Class A and C allocated only lightly.

The lesson is that there is a complex interaction between routing protocols, topology, and scaling, and that determines what Internet routing structure will be necessary for the next ten to twenty years.

When I was chairman of the Internet Activities Board and went to the IETF and IAB to characterize the problem, it was clear that the solution had to be incrementally deployable. You can deploy something in parallel, but then how do the new and old interwork? We are seeing proposals of varying kinds to deal with the problem. Some kind of backward compatibility is highly desirable until you can't assign 32-bit address space. Translating gateways have the defect that when you're halfway through, half the community is transitioned and half isn't, and all the traffic between the two has to go through the translating gateway and it's hard to have enough resources to do this.

It's still a little early to tell how well the alternatives will satisfy the requirements. We are also dealing not only with the scaling problem, but also with the need not to foreclose important new features, such as concepts of flows, the ability to handle multicasting, and concepts of accounting.

I think that as a community we sense varying degrees of pressure for a workable set of solutions. The people who will be most instrumental in this transition will be the vendors of routing equipment and host software, and the offerers of Internet services. It's the people who offer Internet services who have the greatest stake in assuring that Internet operation continues without loss of connectivity, since the value of their service is a function of how many places you can communicate with. The deployability of alternative solutions will determine which is the most attractive. So the transition process is very important.

On use by other networks

The Domain Name System (DNS) has been a key to the scaling of the Internet, allowing it to include non-Internet email systems and solving the problem of name-to-address mapping in a smooth scalable way. Paul

Mockapetris deserves enormous credit for the elegant design of the DNS, on which we are still very dependent. Its primary goal was to solve the problems with the host.txt files and to get rid of centralized management. Support for Mail eXchange (MX) was added after the fact, in a second phase.

Once you get a sufficient degree of connectivity, it becomes more advantageous to link to this highly connected thing and tunnel through it rather than to build a system in parallel. So BITNET, FidoNet, AppleTalk, SNA, Novell IPX, and DECNet tunneling are a consequence of the enormous connectivity of the Internet.

The Internet has become a test bed for development of other protocols. Since there was no lower level OSI infrastructure available, Marshall Rose proposed that the Internet could be used to try out X.400 and X.500. In RFC 1006, he proposed that we emulate TP0 on top of TCP, and so there was a conscious decision to help higher-level OSI protocols to be deployed in live environments before the lower-level protocols were available.

It seems likely that the Internet will continue to be the environment of choice for the deployment of new protocols and for the linking of diverse systems in the academic, government, and business sectors for the remainder of this decade and well into the next.

CHAPTER 34: HOW FIDONET CAME TO BE

Tom Jennings, Ken Kaplan, and Ben Baker

Copyright © 1984, 1985 Tom Jennings, Ken Kaplan, and Ben Baker. Reprinted by permission.

FidoNet's purpose

FidoNet's purpose is very simple: It is a hobby; a noncommercial network of computer hobbyists ("hackers" in the older, original meaning) who want to play with, and find uses for, packet-switching networks. It is not a commercial venture in any way. FidoNet is totally supported by its users and sysops, and in many ways is similar to ham radio in that other than a few "stiff" rules, sysops run their system in any way they please, for any reason they want.

When FidoNet was first tested, there were two nodes: Myself here at Fido #1 in San Francisco and John Madill at Fido #2 in Baltimore. John and I did all of the testing and development for the first iteration of FidoNet. Its purpose: to see if it could be done, merely for the fun of it, like ham radio. It quickly became useful; instead of trying to call each others' boards to leave messages or making expensive voice phone calls, FidoNet messages became more or less routine.

This was version 7 of Fido, sometime in June 1984 or so; it did not have routing, File Attach, retry control, error handling, cost accounting, log files, or any of the niceties added since. A packet was made, a call placed, the packet transferred, and that was it. This was adequate for a month or two, when there were less than twenty nodes.

In August of 1984, the number of nodes was approaching thirty; the net was becoming clogged, believe it or not. FidoNet wasn't too smart about making calls then. With thirty

systems, coordination became difficult. Instead of a simple voice phone call to the (very few!) sysops to straighten out problems like modems not answering, wrong numbers, clock problems, and so on, it took days to get the slightest problem repaired. There were by then six nodes in St. Louis, and Fido #1 was making separate phone calls for each, when obviously one could be made. Enter the beginnings of routing.

The "original" FidoNet was very simple and friendly. You told me at Fido #1 that you had a FidoNet node ready, I put you in the list, with your phone number, and people called up and downloaded the list. Done!

Well... at first, "everyone knew each other"; We were in more or less constant contact. However, when the node numbers got into the twenties, there were people bringing up Fido nodes whom none of us knew. This was good, but it meant we were not in close contact anymore.

The Net started to deteriorate. Every single week, without fail, there was at least one wrong number, usually two. To impress on you the seriousness of wrong numbers in the node list, imagine you are a poor old lady, who every single night is getting phone calls every two minutes at 4 AM. No one says anything, then they hang up. This actually happened. I would sit up and watch when there was mail that didn't go out for a week or two, and I'd pick up the phone after dialing and was left in the embarrasing position of having to explain bulletin boards to an extremely tired, annoyed person.

There were also cases where the new node wasn't really up yet, and the number given was a home phone to be used temporarily, but I'd forget that and include it in the list anyway. Or the new node wasn't really up yet, and we'd all make calls to it and it would not answer. Or worse, the modem would answer but the software wasn't running, and we'd get charged for the call.

This obviously could not go on. We had to have some way to make sure that at least the phone numbers were correct! I started a new policy: Before giving out a node number and putting it in the list, I had to receive a FidoNet message from the new node, directly. This verified that at least the new Fido was halfway running. At the time, Fido had a provision whereby Fido #1 could set the node number remotely. I'd send a message back and presto, a new node was up.

Well, this didn't work properly either. At the same time, the Fido software was changing so rapidly to accomodate all the changes (literally a version a day for a few weeks there) that I was losing new node requests, getting wrong numbers caused by illegible handwriting, and all sorts of other problems. Out of laziness I would still assign nodes "word of mouth" and get in the same trouble as before.

The people in St. Louis (Tony Clark, Ben Baker, Ken Kaplan, Jon Wichman, and Mike Mellinger) had their local Fidos going strong and understood what FidoNet did, how it worked, and what it was about. They volunteered to take over the node list, handle new node requests, and leave me with the software. They tightened up on the FidoNet message requirement, and in a few months had the "error rate" (wrong numbers, and so on) down to practically zero, where it is today.

Though I did the programming, Ken Kaplan, Ben Baker, and the crowd in St. Louis did much of the design and most of the testing of routing, forwarding, and local nets. They still remain the experts on the intricacies of routing and help sysops set up local nets.

Please keep in mind that the entire process, from 2 nodes to over 50, took only three months! Fifty nodes is more than it sounds; at

that level, it becomes a large-scale project. FidoNet went from about 50 nodes in September 1984 or so to 160+ in January/February 1985. As of August 1993, FidoNet has over 22,000 nodes worldwide.

The original FidoNet was organized very simply. Each FidoNet system (each node) had a number that served like a phone number, uniquely identifying it. The Nodelist, generated by the folks in St. Louis, contained information on all known FidoNet systems. Every system on FidoNet had a current copy of the Nodelist, which serves as the directory of systems.

FidoNet had been growing steadily since it started by accident in May 1984 or so. The Nodelist continued to get out of hand. It is impossible to overemphasize the amount of work involved in keeping the Nodelist accurate. Basically, the guys in St. Louis were keeping track of hundreds of FidoNet systems in Boston, Los Angeles, London, Stockholm, and Sweden, and publishing the results weekly. There has never been such a comprehensive and accurate list of bulletin board systems generated.

We talked for many months as to how we could possibly find a solution to the many problems. We were at the point where if a solution was not found in a few months (by August 1985 or so), FidoNet would collapse due to the sheer weight of its Nodelist.

The newsletter, *FidoNews,* was, and still is, an integral part of the process of FidoNet. *FidoNews* is the only thing that unites all FidoNet sysops consistently. Please keep up to date on it and stock it for your users if you have the disk space. And contribute if you can!

There were many constraints on the kinds of things we could do. We had no money, so it had to be done for zero cost. Centralization was out, so obviously localization was in, but just how to do it was a total unknown. We thought of going back to having people in different areas handle new node requests in their area, but that always generated confusion as to whom a person should go to, how to avoid having someone requesting a node number from different people simultaneously, and so on.

The old method of routing was very different than the current method, and much more complex. Instead of Fido automatically routing to hosts, each sysop had to specify (via the ROUTE.BBS file) how all routing was done in the system. The was done originally by hand, and later by John Warren's Nodelist program.

Then of course there was the problem that no matter what we did, it would not be done overnight. (Ha ha.) It would take many weeks at the least, possibly months, so that whatever we did had to be compatible with the old method as well.

We went through probably hundreds of ideas in the next few months, some possibly useful, some insane. Eventually the insanity boiled down to a pretty workable system. We chatted by FidoNet and by voice telephone. Eventually, we settled on the two-part number scheme, like the phone company does with area codes and exchanges. It accommodated backward compatibility (you can keep your present node number) and the new "area code" (net number) could be added into an existing field that had been set to zero. (This is why everyone was originally part of Net #1).

When a fortunate set of circumstances brought Ezra Shapiro and me to St. Louis to speak to the McDonnell Douglas Recreation Computer Club, we planned ahead for a national FidoNet sysops' meeting that weekend. Ken and Sally Kaplan were kind enough to tolerate having all of us in their living room.

The meeting lasted ten continuous hours; it was the most productive meeting I (and most others) had attended. When we were done, we basically had the whole thing laid out in every detail.

We stuck with the area code idea (now known as net and region numbers) and worked out how to break things up into regions and nets. It was just one of those rare but fortunate events. During the morning, things went "normally," but in the afternoon solutions fell

into place one by one, so that by late afternoon we had the entire picture laid out in black and white. Two or three months of brainstorming just flowed smoothly into place in one afternoon.

What we had done was exactly what we have now, though we changed the name of "Admin" to "Region" and added the "alternate" node and net numbers. (We still seem to be stuck with that terrible and inaccurate word "Manager." Any ideas?) I previously had a buggy test hack running using area codes, and the week after the meeting it was made to conform to what we had talked about that Saturday.

When Fido version 10C was done, it accomplished more or less everything we wanted, but it sure did take a long time. 10C was probably the single-largest change ever made to Fido/FidoNet, and the most thoroughly tested version. At 10M, there are *still* bugs left from that early version, in spite of the testing.

Once the testing got serious, and it looked like we had a shippable version, St. Louis froze the node list and started slicing it into pieces to give to the soon-to-be Net and Region Managers. (That word again!) This caused a tremendous amount of trouble for would-be sysops; not only was it difficult enough to figure out how to get a node number, but once they did, they were told node numbers weren't being given out just yet. Explaining why was even harder, since this wasn't written yet. It was a typical case of those who already knew being informed constantly of updates but those in the dark having a hard time keeping up. Things were published fairly regularly (am I remembering "conveniently" or "accurately" on this part?).

Eventually, Fido 10C was released and seemed to work fairly well, ignoring all the small-scale disasters due to bugs, and so on. We couldn't just swap over to the new area code business until very close to 100 percent of all Fidos were using the new version. This was (for me) an excruciating period, basically a "hurry up and wait" situation. There had not been a Nodelist release for a month or two, and for all practical purposes it looked like FidoNet had halted...

Finally, on June 12, we all swapped over to the new system; that afternoon, sysops were to set their net number (it had been "1" for backward compatibility), copy in the new Nodelist issued just for this occasion, and go. I assumed the result was going to be perpetual chaos, bringing about the collapse of FidoNet. Almost the exact opposite was true; things went very smoothly (yes, there were problems, but not when you consider that FidoNet consisted of microcomputers owned by almost 300 people who had never even talked to each other).

Within a month or so, just about every Fido had swapped over to the area code, or net/node, architecture. With a few exceptions, things went very smoothly. No one was more surprised than pessimistic me. As of August 1985, there wasn't a single system still using the old node number method.

This is all well and good as far as the software goes, but it made a mess for new sysops. For we sysops who have been around for a while, there was no great problem, since we saw the changes happen one by one. However, new sysops frequently came out of the blue armed with a diskette full of code and attempted to set up a FidoNet node.

Actually, I don't understand how anyone does it. The information needed is not recorded in any place that a nonsysop could find. On top of that, most of it is now totally wrong! If you follow the original instructions, it said "call Fido #1...." Of course, now it tells you to find your region manager. Region manager??? Well, a list of region managers was published in *FidoNews,* but unless you read *FidoNews,* how does anyone ever find out? I'll probably never know.

Anyway, the original reason for all the changes was to *decentralize* FidoNet. It just wasn't possible for Ken Kaplan to keep accurate, up-to-date information on every Fido in the U.S. and Europe. The decentralization has been more or less a total success. The number of problems introduced

were negligible compared to the problems solved, and even most new problems are by this time solved.

It is interesting to note that with the thousands of systems there are today, the national FidoNet hour is less crowded than it was when there were only fifty nodes. Please, keep in mind that no one has done anything like this before; we are all winging it, and learning (hopefully) as we go.

FidoNet today is a network quickly approaching the levels of complexity of commercial networks, and it has many more capabilities than many "mini" networks, such as USENET, which has no routing or hosts. Only the Internet has some of the features of FidoNet. The southern California local network is three levels deep, with hosts in Orange, Los Angeles, Ventura, San Bernardino, and San Diego counties.

Please be patient with problems. None of us is paid to do this, and it is more and more work as time goes on. Somehow it all seems to get done.

CHAPTER 35:
THE STORY OF UFGATE

Tim Pozar, as told to Bernard Aboba

Catching the UNIX bug

Around 1986, I started learning about UNIX on The WELL. I got a book by Rebecca Thomas and figured out how UNIX worked, and then I discovered USENET. At that point, I said "there must be a way of getting this without having to pay The WELL!" I met John Gilmore in 1986 or '87 through Hugh Daniels, who was a sysop on The WELL. John had downloaded a UUCICO clone called UUSLAVE, and he gave me an account on Hoptoad, in San Francisco, in the Haight, which was his machine, so I didn't have to use The WELL anymore to read USENET. John gave me the UUSLAVE that he beefed up, which was originally written for Berkeley UNIX, and said, "Do an MS-DOS port of this." So I started on the MS-DOS port. There was an Amiga port as well, and later there was even a Mac port. I started working on a program called Fido-UUCP that would convert Fido messages into UUCP messages.

Then I got a message from someone on FidoNet saying "John Galvin is also working on gateway stuff." He was further along in most of the areas, so we incorporated my stuff into his program. Another guy by the name of Gary Paxinos started working on the later ports on UUSLAVE, and also did MAILOUT, MAILIST, and MAILFORWARD. So Gary, John, and I worked together. We got a lot of help and code from each other.

We started in 1986 and worked on it for a few months; we had it in beta for almost a year, then released it as beta in late 1987. It went out in final form in early 1988 and went through three revisions very quickly. The first one was to fix a major bug, 1.01; then it went to 1.02 and 1.03, where it is today.

When we finally got the UUSLAVE going, I went down to SRI, to the people at the Network Information Center (NIC), and proposed to them to connect this network called FidoNet, running on MS-DOS, to the Internet. They got excited by that, saying "Wow, people can send mail from their PCs now!" So they helped me establish the domain IFNA.ORG.

You should understand why I picked IFNA.ORG rather than FIDONET.NET. FIDONET.NET was too vague because it just described a protocol, not a Nodelist. The Nodelist was critical for routing of messages. We couldn't route messages to systems implementing FidoNet protocols if we didn't know how to reach them! IFNA.ORG was defined by the IFNA Nodelist, which made it possible to do routing. That is why today the domain FIDONET.ORG applies only to systems in the "St. Louis Nodelist," not Alternet, RBBS-Net, EGGNET, or others. When IFNA fell into disfavor, we made it FIDONET.ORG.

I first proposed to the NIC people that we use the f445.n161.z1.fidonet.org addressing scheme that we have today, mapping the FidoNet Nodelist hierarchy of nodes, nets, and zones onto Internet domains. However, they didn't like it; they wanted a flat namespace, such as foo.org, instead. In hindsight, it's good that we didn't go that way. It would have been difficult to route mail with a flat namespace like that.

The next thing we had to figure out was how to set up the MX records to route mail. We needed the MX records because we decided to have many gateway systems instead of just one, and we needed to be able to figure out which gateway to send the mail to. Luckily, Lee Damon came along and defined how the early routing worked once we had the addressing ready. To handle the routing, Lee developed an extremely complex sendmail file; the guy who is doing it now is Burt Juda.

For sites that don't have their own forwarders, the mail goes to ieee.org; there, Burt has sendmail rewrite the address to smail, then smail builds out the UUCP bang path; then it goes back to sendmail, and at that point sendmail starts up an SMTP session and sends it to its first Internet address. All mail goes out SMTP, because ieee.org doesn't have UUCP connections. One of the most frequent SMTP connections to ieee.org is UUNET, which forwards mail by UUCP to the next site. The changeover from Lee to Burt resulted in a turbulent few months until things settled down. In order to guarantee that all mail would be deliverable, we had to have a default gateway that routed all mail not handled elsewhere. David Dodell was extremely kind to agree to be the default, which he is to this day.

When everything had settled down and people first started seeing FidoNet addresses on USENET, some people freaked out. About half really liked it, and the rest thought, "Oh, no! It'll ruin the USENET!" Those people didn't realize how much the Internet benefitted from being connected to FidoNet. As it turned out, for several years, mail to Third World countries and Eastern Europe was routed through FidoNet. FidoNet was the first network in Poland, and FidoNet BBSes have been sprouting up in Russia as well. FidoNet was inexpensive and reliable, so it became very popular in the Third World and in developing countries that couldn't afford TCP/IP.

Over the last year, I've been working on building The Little Garden, a low-cost Internet service provider in San Francisco, specializing in 14.4 Kbps SLIP and PPP connections. This was the first ToasterNet, and is now linked to other ToasterNets in Santa Cruz and Portland.

At home I've got a dedicated link between The Little Garden and my UNIX system via Point to Point Protocol (PPP). I'm also running KA9Q, a software TCP/IP router based on IBM PC–compatible hardware that runs on top of the Crynwr packet drivers under DOS. For a while, I was also running Fido in another DESQview window, but I've shut down the Fido system now. When it was running I could receive the FidoNet Nodelist, then FTP it down to my Macintosh, which runs MacTCP. Mine was probably the first FidoNet system connected directly to the Internet!

CHAPTER 36:
HOW QMAIL CAME TO BE

Mark "Sparky" Herring, as told to Bernard Aboba

The birth of PCBEcho

My first logon to a bulletin board system was in March, 1979. It was a Forum-80 system, and ran on a TRS-80, two drives, 160K of total disk space. My programs now take up more room than that system could hold.

My interest in telecommunications started from that day forward; I was always a modem junkie. At the time I was nineteen and a freelance consultant based in Memphis doing work for Radio Shack customers. My expertise turned out to be telecommunications and database management.

I started getting involved in the local group of BBSes. We were running Fido off a system called Radio Free Memphis, along with a friend named Jim Key. Jim was really into telecommunications; over the years he ran a number of boards: Fido, DBBS, and finally PCBoard. Jim was starting to get a little discouraged with PCBoard because he misssed the echoes that Fido had and no one had yet written echoing software for PCBoard. I remember talking to Jim in February 1987 and telling him to "send me the PCBoard message format, and maybe I can figure out how to write my own echo software."

The first system we echoed with was "Unusual Situations" run by Jim Pottkotter. We were moving mail between two systems internally, which was the first time that was ever done on PCBoard. Adding the third system, "Sleepy Hollow" out of Los Angeles was a tough nut. This was the beginning of PCBEcho.

As we started to grow we got all kinds of systems involved. We got Ed Hopper's BBS, EXEC-Net, LANs BBS, Far-West. Most of these are around today. We eventually had more than fifty systems hooked up to PCBEcho.

The birth of QMAIL

In 1985, while on vacation in the Smoky Mountains, I had thought about what would happen to our hobby if measured service came in. Under measured service you are charged by the minute, there is no such thing as a local call. Under measured service, people wouldn't be able to call their local BBS and stay on for an hour. They couldn't afford it. I decided that the solution was an offline mail reader.

The idea behind this was that instead of reading one message at a time, you quickly gather up all the messages, download them, and hang up the phone. You then read them at your leisure. If you create any replies, you call up the bulletin board later and upload your replies.

In September 1987 a friend of mine named Dan Mascheck moved from Memphis to a little town outside of Houston called Wharton, Texas. Dan missed his connections in Memphis, but the long distance phone bills were eating him alive. I told Dan I would come up with something to add to PCBEcho so he could get his messages and hang up.

I wrote the basic QMAIL format in thirty minutes for Dan I never thought I was writing this for the world; I wrote it for a friend who needed it. It was based on the PCBoard message format because Jim Key ran PCBoard.

I wrote QMAIL as an external program for PCBoard, called a Door. In addition to handling messages, QMAIL Door was designed to pack up file listings and system bulletins as well, so callers wouldn't miss anything important.

There was also a message reader to go with it, which was shareware. As I was writing it, sysops kept telling me they wanted to buy a copy of it. Their systems were getting choked, people were staying online for an hour at a time, and the phones were always busy. Word got around about QMAIL and by the time I released it on April 15, 1988, I had thirty two orders and thought I might be lucky if I sold 50 copies of the door and a couple of copies of the reader. I've been working with QMAIL doors and readers since then.

The QMAIL reader was originally a shareware product, but after we had sold eighty doors in the summer of 1988, and we only had fifteen readers registered, I decided to change strategy. I decided that when someone registered the shareware reader, we would send them a copy of QMAIL Deluxe, an advanced version of the reader, and that's what started the readers taking off.

I never thought I'd make a living off this, but now we have 1650 copies of QMAIL Door out there, and we have 15,000 copies of the reader registered.

It was the right place at the right time with the right idea, but being nicknamed Sparky didn't hurt at all, because people remember the name. The nickname was given to me by a Radio Shack center manager in 1979. I didn't like the name, but I couldn't get rid of it, so I called my company Sparkware. Some people think I'm Radar's friend off "M*A*S*H*", or I have something to do with ham radio, but it was given to me. He named me Sparky because I was a nineteen year-old doing serious computer work, which was unusual.

QNet

With PCBEcho there were two kinds of systems: a hub system and a node system. A hub received calls and the nodes initiated calls. However, there was only one system that had the hub software, which was Jim Key, so it was a star-cluster network. Everyone else had node software so you had to go through him.

PCBEcho quickly reached its limits, and so I began work on QNet after the release of QMAIL Door. QNet was not upwardly compatible with PCBEcho; it was a completely different product, and most of the PCBecho systems converted over.

QNet was the beginning of the networks we have today: ILINK, Smartnet, NorthAmeriNet, UNINet, Intellec. It was released in June, 1988. My guess is that QNet and its derivatives might be in use on 4000 to 5000 systems worldwide.

Why was QNet designed? As a loss leader for QMAIL door. A system doesn't need a door if they don't have a lot of traffic. Once they join a network their traffic goes up and they need to buy a mail door. So QNet has stimulated the demand for QMAIL doors and readers.

QNet is a spanning-tree network, with a single root, the QNet Master Hub, which does a fair amount of work. However, it is more flexible than PCBEcho because there are many regional hubs, which can receive calls and forward mail on to the high-level hubs. As with PCBEcho, the nodes initiate the calls but do not receive them.

One of the issues in any network is how to prevent duplicates. With QNet this is done inside the QMAIL door. I calculate a CRC of the message before it's inserted, so if there's a duplicate CRC, I erase the message. The lookup table is as big as the PCBoard message base.

QNet was written as a message echoing program; it does not support file transfers now, although I am looking at supporting file request from node to hub. I do not want to support node-to-node file request because this would mean routing file requests, and it doesn't seem fair for an intermediate system to have to pay to have a file routed through them. There have been three major releases of QNet over five years.

The future of QMAIL

QMAIL is an open standard, and as a result there are clones of both the door and the reader. I had thought of the idea of protecting the standard, but you can't copyright a format. In addition the QMAIL format was based on other work, so I figured the best way to protect my work was to have the best product.

A lot of people complain about the QMAIL standard, but I wrote it for a friend, I had no idea it would become so popular. To give you an idea of how different things were back then, when I created QMAIL, PCBoard could only handle nine conferences and now there are systems with 5000. At the time the PCBoard manual said, "If you need more than nine conferences, you don't know how to run a BBS!" People still rib them about that.

I am working on a QMAIL II standard now, and when I'm ready I'll have it out there, probably sometime this year. I want to include multimedia extensions and things like that. The QMAIL II standard will also be public.

The future of the bulletin board

I think the future of BBSing is the client/server approach rather than the dumb terminal. We've taken ANSI as far as we can.

Whose server and whose client is going to make it? This is going to be a war that is going to be fought for a couple of years. In the next five years we'll probably see a client/server standard emerge that will be for files, messages, everything. Graphical front ends will also be important; our front end will run under Windows eventually.

Chapter 37:
How PCRelay (and PostLink) Came to Be

Kip Compton, as told to Bernard Aboba

Copyright © 1993 Kip Compton. All rights reserved.

The birth of PCRelay

I wrote the first version of PCRelay in 1987, during spring break of my sophomore year in high school. I had been running a BBS, mostly for the students at the high school I attended, since my freshman year. I used PCBoard to run my bulletin board, and networking was a new phenomena at that time in the PCBoard world.

A friend of mine, Bob Shuck, decided to start a network called Capitol Uplink. Bob founded the network with about ten people, of which I was one. Bob was also a member of the PCBEcho network, a network run out of Tennessee using PCBEcho networking software, written by Mark "Sparky" Herring. These were the days before Qmail and Qnet.

PCBEcho was, unfortunately, not available to all of us, because the PCBEcho network wanted to have only one BBS in each city on their network. Each BBS called directly into the central hub. They promised to eventually update their software to allow a treelike structure, but in the meantime, Capitol Uplink used software called PCBMail... the plan was to all join PCBEcho and drop PCBMail once the PCBEcho software had been improved to handle more sites.

Unfortunately, that never happened. We were stuck using PCBMail, which had its share of bugs, including the requirement that you repack your message bases after each mail run.

(Repacking the message bases in those days took a long time, and the entire system had to be down while repacking.)

During this time, I had been taking AP Computer Science in school, and in the spring, I was required to write a "Mastery Program," which was supposed to give us an inkling of what it was like to write a program of reasonable size. We were supposed to work on our program for about four weeks, and I decided that rather than write some sort of toy program that would never be used again, I would write something useful, namely a replacement for the terrible PCBMail software, which we could use on Capitol Uplink.

So, working mostly over my week-long spring break, I wrote PCBRelay 1.0 in Turbo Pascal. The program seemed to work very well, and had a number of features that PCBMail did not have (including a "dynamic hub" that allowed mail to be dynamically updated – PCBMail only updated the mail once a day), and it had none of the bugs that PCBMail had. Of course, being the first version, it had its own share of bugs... I passed it out to the others on Capitol Uplink (at that time still about ten people), and we all stopped using PCBMail.

I did get an "A" on my project, and several of the people on Capitol Uplink pointed out that I should really sell my program to people, since it was certainly better than PCBMail, which was being sold. So I began to sell my program, and to constantly update it, both with ideas that I had and, more important, with ideas that my customers had. With its new software, Capitol Uplink began to interest people outside of the Washington, D.C., area, and it grew to what is now RIME.

PCRelay uses a spanning tree topology, where nodes call hubs, which pass mail to regional hubs, which in turn pass mail on to the NetHub. Done this way, you don't have to have a nodelist, you only have to know how to reach the node above you. You also don't have to worry about dupe loops in a tree, although you do have to worry about salability, especially at the upper levels of the tree.

Early on, I decided that I would allow anyone to purchase my software, and that I wouldn't get involved in network administration. So you could start your own network and use PCRelay; there are now more than a dozen public PCRelay based networks, of which RIME is the largest, with over 1000 nodes.

There are also private networks. Network policies differ; RIME charges a yearly network fee, some others don't, but that's up to them. I keep in close touch with RIME because they're the largest network, and are therefore generally on the cutting edge of any problems. My BBS is only on one network, a small alpha testing network that I use to test new code. I suppose that my policy of making my software available to anyone who wanted to start a network was deeply effected by the unavailability of PCBEcho to our network; if PCBEcho had been available for all of us to use, I would not have had to write PCRelay in the first place.

I kept working on PCRelay throughout high school and stayed with it when I came to MIT in 1989 to go to college. I'm currently a student in the electrical engineering and computer science department there. When I'm done, I'm thinking of going to grad school in computer science. I'm interested in networking primarily, especially some higher-end applications of networks including real-time audio and video.

As my abilities have grown and as people have had ideas, I kept improving PCRelay, and it has developed some advanced features. One that

people said was impossible to implement was reference numbers. Say you leave me message number 100, and it ends up on your system as message 353, and someone replies to it. How do you link the threads correctly and have one system refer to the message as number 100, while the other one refers to it as 353? The fact that many networking programs do not support this feature has led to the widespread use of "quoting" in messages, which dramatically increases the size of messages.

PCRelay and PostLink also support routed mail, encrypted mail, and return receipts. The latest version of PCRelay is 4.10. It was written mostly in Turbo Pascal with some assembler and C. I am also the author of MegaMail, a QWK and MegaMail packet reader; there's a free MegaMail door that uses the same Universal Text Interfaces (UTIs) as PCRelay.

With 1000 nodes on RIME we were at the point where we were testing the limits of PCRelay. The idea that 1000 people would be using PCRelay, let alone 1000 on a single network, was not in my mind when I designed it. It became clear to me that there were better ways to do things, and that's where PostLink comes in. I started PostLink in 1991, although I had been working on many of the things included in PostLink before then. PostLink is much more sophisticated than PCRelay, both in the flexibility it provides and in the ability to handle more mail and sites on a single network. PostLink was designed to be able to handle networks consisting of 10,000 or more nodes. It is designed for more conferences, more users, more of everything.

PostLink was written in C++ rather than Pascal primarily for portability. Bonnie Anthony is the coordinator of the RIME network. As Bonnie has been networking PCs together to support more and more phone lines coming into her hub, it has become clear that it might be easier to have the software running on larger machines. The mail tossing is not computationally intensive, it's I/O intensive. The only thing that involves a computation is the compression of messages, and many modems now have compression built in, so you don't even necessarily have to do that. So there's a mismatch with the LAN architecture – on a LAN, you have a lot of CPU power but your I/O is slowed by the LAN. On a larger multitasking computer, you have less CPU power but faster I/O since you do not have to go across the LAN.

One thing that people like about PCRelay is the performance. Most networks using PCRelay elect to have a relatively shallow tree, so mail travels rapidly from site to site. To have a shallow tree you need big hubs, and it's easier to do that with big machines. Another reason to make it portable was to allow PostLink to run on other computers, such as the Macintosh, and other operating systems, such as Windows NT.

PostLink is a packet-oriented system with a very brief header for destination and source addresses, so you can pass data through routers. All packets have this universal header, which allows new packet types to be introduced without revamping all of the software on a particular network. (This is similar to the idea behind Internet packet headers.) This is different from PCRelay, where everything is treated individually (for example, a file object is different from a mail object). PostLink has true multicasting so you can have multiple destination sites. We're planning on having a third-party API, so people can write applications using PostLink as a network service layer. PostLink is a connectionless protocol; it does not guarantee delivery, which is similar to the UDP (User Datagram Protocol) system available on the Internet. Of course, since PostLink cannot guarantee that a particular path is "live" at any given moment, programming with PostLink will be a bit different than programming with UDP. PostLink attaches an audit stamp each time a packet travels through a system. This audit stamp contains both where the packet was and when it was there. Thus, it is possible to figure out where a packet has been and when it was there when it is received. In the future, I expect to be able to do extensive performance analysis of networks using these audit stamps. Of course, these audit trails also provide an effective security mechanism as well, helping to prevent forged packets.

One of PCRelay's weaknesses is that it doesn't have its own built-in communications; you have to script the transfers using Robocomm, or Telix, or some other communications program. PostLink comes with XMODEM, YMODEM, and ZMODEM built in, as well as supporting external protocol drivers such as DSZ by Chuck Forsberg or HSLink by Sam Smith. HSLink is bidirectional; with the advent of a widely available symmetric modulation scheme for modems (namely V.32 and V.32*bis*), bidirectional transfers are a big win for the regional hubs, especially with file sends. PostLink also has its own built-in scripting language with an automatic learning mode. You log in manually the first time, then that's it; PostLink can automatically do your mail runs for you from that point on. PostLink also uses UTIs, so it runs with all systems that can do PCRelay.

When I started out I had no idea it would get this large, I thought it would just be for the ten of us. By now, with 200,000 users accessing RIME alone, there is no particular audience in mind. There is going to be some kind of global information network, and there has to be lower-end ways of getting on to it (the "rural roads" of the network community if you like). This is the grand purpose of PostLink, if there is one. FidoNet is the one to do it now, but it was developed a few years ago and it's healthy to have competition.

The future of PostLink

With the new PostLink API, programs make a function call, they receive a blob of data, and they register channels that are like TCP/IP sockets. This makes it possible to write PostLink applications, and it lets me evolve the packet structure without interrupting what other people are doing with it.

The equivalent of point software is very possible with PostLink, since the nodes don't have to be available all the time; only the hubs do. There is no nodelist. The information you need is very distributed. The feasibility of pointlike software was certainly taken into consideration when PostLink was designed.

We have thought of making PostLink run in "real time." (In other words have continuous links between some sites on the network.) It is something we should be able to do now , which we couldn't do before with PCRelay. You could have some sort of backbone, instead of a Nethub at the root of the tree. The nodes on the backbone could be connected continuously, say over the Internet. ISDN may come at some point. Five years ago they said it was supposed to be here by now, but it isn't. ISDN would be wonderful for BBSing; 128 Kbps is orders of magnitude faster than even the fastest modems today, and it is unlikely that even extravagant modems operating over analog phone lines will be able to achieve the performance possible with relatively simple modems operating on ISDN lines.

We have thought of satellite transmission. It is fairly cheap to get a channel on a satellite and have people get one-meter dishes and put them out in their yard. The satellite provides a reasonable bandwidth (56 Kbps), but in only one direction. Sites would still need to make phone calls to transmit messages but could receive all of their messages over the satellite link, eliminating the bulk of the long-distance time.

We have also thought of nontree topologies, allowing nodes to call each other directly, rather than having mail go up the tree and then down again. This is CrashMail, which is great because of speed, but it requires a front end (or that the authors of the BBS software conform to some standard at login time), because you can't store enough information to call an arbitrary computer and log on without having some sort of standard.

Some bridge to USENET or Internet is likely in the future. But we want to have PostLink stable before we move to UNIX. I will also be doing ports to other PC operating systems. Windows has taken off—in version 3.1 the communications drivers are very usable; they support up to 56 Kbps. OS/2 is out and there are a reasonable number of sysops experimenting with it, and it does do communications better than DOS. And of course there is Windows NT, which looks really exciting, as it itself is quite portable.

CHAPTER 38: HOW FREDMAIL CAME TO BE

Al Rogers, "Mr. FrEd," as told to Bernard Aboba

Copyright © 1993 Al Rogers, All rights reserved.

The birth of FrEdMail

The seed for FrEdMail was planted in the summer of 1984 while I was working at the San Diego County Office of Education as Computer Coordinator. Having been a classroom teacher for twenty years, I was critically interested in how educational software was being developed. Teachers were just beginning to use computers in the schools, but educational software wasn't that well developed. The issue was, how do you effectively use this tool in education?

Since I was especially interested in effective methods of teaching writing, it was obvious early on that computers had a role to play in this area. The first major educational word processor for Apple II was Bank Street Writer, and it was not a very good word processor. Not only was it awkward to use, but it didn't begin to address any of the issues of blending a good word processing program with a good writing program. FrEdWriter was an early attempt to begin designing tools that could support a good writing program. Because it was free, many schools were able to begin designing writing programs without having to worry about software budget limitations. FrEdWriter also introduced the concept of Prompted Writing and enabled teachers to begin focusing on the development of effective writing instruction. FrEdWriter was the first in a suite of tools I began working on to support effective writing instruction in the schools.

Now, an important thing in writing is the issue of audience. A good writing teacher tries to find an audience beyond the teacher. It was then that the whole idea of telecommunications came into play, and we began to explore that, to find good audiences for student writing.

We started with a program called ASCII Express on the Apple II to connect school A to school B. This was a hassle, because teacher A had to coordinate with teacher B so the two machines would be available at the same time. So we began looking at an asynchronous approach, which is when we started playing with bulletin boards.

In 1985, I read an tiny article in *InfoWorld* on FidoNet, and we bought one of Tom Jennings's early FidoNet programs to evaluate. But for a school environment, it was too complex, and also at that time the schools didn't have IBMs, they had Apple IIs. So I started looking into an Apple II–based system.

FrEdMail is not the only networking tool for the Apple II. But it is the only tool written by teachers for teachers, and it doesn't require special technical skills. It almost installs itself, and it makes no assumptions about knowledge. It doesn't say things like "create this directory," or "create this path." It's designed for teachers with no special technical skill. Our sysops are English teachers, science teachers, even some first-grade teachers. Furthermore, we began to develop the online environment on FrEdMail to appeal to the culture of the classroom and to enable teachers to conduct a variety of online learning projects with their students when access to a phone line was at a premium.

I set up the first FrEdMail system in 1985. We had five systems in San Diego, operated by teachers, housed at different schools. The idea was to find out if this was going to be an effective way to get students to buy into writing and a cooperative learning experience.

At the end of the first year, I asked the question, "Do we go forward with this or should we junk it?" And the answer from everyone was, "This is powerful, we need to go forward." So we did.

We grew very slowly at first, getting new systems involved based on personal contacts. I made a tour of the East Coast in 1986 and contacted people in various school district regions whom I had met at conferences. In the fall of 1986 we set up systems in Philadelphia, Connecticut, Rhode Island, New York, and Puerto Rico. We started out with 1200 baud modems and were calling coast to coast. We never really promoted ourselves, but through conferences and personal contacts, word got around. Today our network has over 200 systems nationwide.

Eventually, we had to deal with the issue of routing. I use Appleworks to maintain a master database of all our systems. Every week or two I mail out an up-to-date path list that sysops install to provide up-to-date message routing instructions. This enables FrEdMail users to use a standard Internet domain name address of the format user@system. Although the FrEdMail network uses bang-path addressing, like on UUCP, the custom path.list at each site is able to translate any domain address into the proper bang bath address. So it performs the same function as pathalias in UUCP.

As the network continued to grow and expand, I did it as a sideline up until 1990. Finally in 1990, I decided I had to get out of it altogether, or get it funded. So in November 1990, I resigned from the county office, and I set up the FrEdMail Foundation.

In the Fall of 1990, CERFNet in Southern California received a grant from the National Science Foundation to work with the FrEdMail Foundation to build a gateway between FrEdMail and Internet. CERFnet provided many critical resources for us, including a part-time UNIX programmer for two years. Today we have nine gateways into the Internet, operating between a FrEdMail host running on an Apple IIe or IIgs and a university or network Internet host operating UNIX.

Today, we have more than 200 systems on the FrEdMail network. We also have a powerful 486 UNIX machine at CERFnet managing our network traffic among our nine gateway regions.

Part of the reason we were so successful is that our focus has not been only on networking, but always on "what do we do with the kids?"

We learned that having the tool was useless, without an appropriate task. So early on we began dealing with this issue, and finding ways to build online collaborative learning projects, so that it wasn't just chit-chat but a real tool in the hands of a teacher to deliver a standard curriculum. Teachers who use FrEdMail find it's not an add-on to the curriculum; rather, they find it's the standard way they do things.

From the standpoint of the technology, FrEdMail occupies two niches: one niche addresses the lack of infrastructure, the lack of technical expertise, and the lack of money. We can deliver a FrEdMail bulletin board for a few hundred dollars, as opposed to a system that requires a local network and 56 Kbps line or something like that. Of course, you can't bring in as many people, but where the district superintendent of schools hasn't touched his first keyboard, there's no other way.

The other niche is in showing teachers how to use telecommunications constructively. We're looking for ways to provide a variety of services to teachers out on the Internet. We're currently in the process of setting up thirty-five USENET conferences to educators, along the lines of ClariNet. We're providing a moderated service, which will provide noise control and avoid many of the problems associated with the USENET subculture.

With the growth of Internet in K-12 schools, many other educators have been learning the same lessons we have. But we've been doing it a long time, and we have a collection of expertise that we're trying to share about how to make it work within the curriculum. We've never really promoted ourselves, but we're getting ready to do this now.

On curriculum

We found out a long time ago that pen pals don't work, and so we've gone several steps beyond that idea. Of course, there's a lot of one-on-one correspondence that grows out of FrEdMail, and we believe it's a great by-product of a good project, but we don't try to build a curriculum out of personal student correspondence and pen pals.

There are many different scenarios that we've pursued in our learning projects. An example that we're doing on November 6 is NewsDay. On that day thirty-five classes will post ten articles each on our NewsDay newswire service. Students will have spent two weeks acting as reporters for their local area, state, and nation. Each class will pick the ten best news articles for posting. For the two or three days following NewsDay, the students at each site will download articles, read, select, and edit them. They then assemble and publish their own newspaper, which they then mail to all the participating sites. So an enormous amount of reading and writing is done for this project, but within a framework that really gets the kids motivated.

Another project we're doing is Tele-Field trips. We're collecting from teachers a list of places their classes will visit during the school year. Every three or four weeks we publish a database of these excursion destinations. If a teacher sees a destination that applies to his or her curriculum, the students will write questions for the other class to answer. When students visit an excursion destination armed with questions posed by their peers, they will be more likely to keep their eyes open to come back and report than they would be if they were just doing it for a teacher.

Another project we'll do three times this year is Geogame. Each participating class must research and answer eight questions about their local geography and then send it to us. We collect the responses, scramble the cities, and mail the list to all participating classes. The kids have to match the descriptions with the cities. For our first Geogame we had over fifty cities, and within that were schools in Puerto Rico, South Africa, Finland, and the Virgin Islands.

On censorship and control

Every one of our systems is operated closely in conjunction with a school environment. Most of them are operated in a school building, some are operated at home, or at colleges of education. We are very clearly a traditional school building and classroom enterprise. We don't publish the phone number and addresses of any students, and we try to watch that sort of thing.

We don't have flaming on our network, although we sometimes have spirited discussion. There are virtually no instances of obscenity, because of the identity with the school environment. There are no youngsters online whom we don't know. In the four or five cases in the past six years where we've had to speak to a youngster, in three of those instances, the teacher caught the problem before anyone else did.

Because the system that the students are on is operated by someone they know, there's a degree of accountability. There are different levels of access, where students can only post local messages, before they can be given network access. So it's a nice laboratory for children to learn network etiquette, to learn to be polite. When new users log in our disclaimer states our rules, which includes that users must be polite, we won't allow profanity, and the sysop is the sole determiner of what is obscene.

This is in contrast with the culture of Internet and USENET. The culture of USENET is anarchy, which is not deemed a "safe" environment for most members of the K-12 educational establishment. FrEdMail is a membership consortium, which involves an annual fee and requires standards of participation that all our sysops agree to. As professional educators, we agree on that, because the local school board is looking over our shoulder. So we have not had to deal with pornography or abuse.

On the technology of FrEdMail

The Internet is our major backbone now. The gateway software was finished in 1991, and we're working the bugs out of it now. We currently have nine gateways, and we're putting up four more. We're getting a lot of inquiries, and a lot of systems are looking at this gateway approach.

We have Domain Name Service for FrEdMail, (fred.org), and have developed a four-level hierarchy, with MX records maintained on nic.cerf.net. Each of our nine gateways represents a region, each of which can serve a large number of nodes down line. Most of our gateways are located at universities that serve as partners and mentors to the FrEdMail users in their location. The gateway hosts determine the region name:
`jedson@monark.ualr.fred.org` is served by the University of Arkansas, Little Rock; `rrivera@orillas.upr.fred.org` is served by the University of Puerto Rico. My machine bonita gets its mail from CERFnet, so my FrEdMail address is `arogers@bonita.cerf.fred.org`.

Our goal now is to get as many gateways set up as we can. We want to create a network that cannot be decapitated, so that if I drop off the face of the map, they'll still be able to continue service to their users.

I should also add that running a gateway is a great way for a university to get into a partnership with a school district. To the university it looks like a user account, but when you login there is a script that mediates the communications with the Apple and uses XMODEM to exchange messages. The scripts for the gateway are available via **ftp nic.cerf.net, cd /pub/FrEdMail**.

On Internet and NREN

We're using Internet mainly as a backbone for our existing network. One of the questions we are answering is: How can Internet be more usefully used? The problem is that a lot of people are bringing teachers to the Internet and dumping them off. But what's there to do?

Everyone mentions NASA SpaceLink, the Weather maps, libraries, and other "places." But few people get real specific about how to incorporate these resources into the curriculum. I have a concern that there isn't much on the Internet that meets the needs of the majority of K-12 educators, who don't have the skills, who only get on occasionally, and who may never learn the system if they only get on infrequently.

Yet clearly Internet represents the future mainstream for education. I think it will be very influential. But it will take some new software tools; and it must go beyond the UNIX interface. There must be more attention given to the culture and logistics of the classroom, to coordinate and organize student activities.

We're trying to help with that by giving teachers tools beyond the standard newsreader tools, so they can find and join or build a community of interest without being overwhelmed. There's a heavy load of student logistics and classroom logistics out there, and a lot of teachers are facing them on an individual basis, but we're looking at what we can do to help it in software development geared specifically to solve classroom logistic problems, and problems associated with creating and coordinating a student project online.

FrEdMail exploits the network as a communications tool, not a data retrieval tool. We don't archive large quantities of data. And we haven't even begun to address FTP, Telnet, and other things, which is another whole ball of wax. We just focus on teacher-to-teacher, classroom-to-classroom communications. Consequently, store and forward networks fit into that quite nicely.

On telecommunications and society

FrEdMail started out as an experiment, and there is no way that I'd have predicted that I'd be spending my life doing this on a full-time basis. I knew that telecommunications as a medium was extremely powerful. I had that feeling in my guts. This has been forcefully articulated in Alvin Tofler's book, *PowerShift,* which has become FrEdMail's manifesto.

Toffler talks a lot about telecommunications and the restructuring of our society.

In our culture, telecommunications is becoming extremely important. The NREN will become the primary transportation infrastructure in the information age... the electronic equivalent of the industrial era railroads. Although we have many youngsters who have access to this technology through their parents' wealth or foresight, the large majority of our society is totally oblivious to the changes taking place around us.

I understood this when for the fifteenth time, my mother said to me, "What is it you do for a living?" Our society doesn't have a metaphor for telecommunications; the best we have as a symbol is the modem. As I look at the challenges facing us to develop a telecommunications mindset, I am reminded of the frog in the kettle. If you put a frog in a kettle of cold water, and slowly heat it, it will adjust its body temperature until it boils to death without being aware. Our society is shutting its eyes to the importance of this technology; the average school superintendent doesn't have a clue to the importance of these new technologies.

The public school system is the only one in the position to educate students about telecommunications. So I want as many schools as possible to begin building a metaphor for what this computer-mediated communications is all about. And until we can build a cultural metaphor as we have for the telephone, we will be in danger of having an extremely stratified economic structure, with enormous inequities, and we'll be like that frog in the kettle.

It took about eighty years for the telephone to become commonly used; the telephone was invented in 1876 and didn't become widely used until after World War II. But we don't have eighty years with this technology. We have to bring our communities up to speed so they'll say, "Yes, it's important to spend $10K on routers and a 56 Kbps line to get our schools hooked up to Internet."

On literacy

Marshall McLuhan says you always implement a new technology in the metaphor of an old technology. One of the things I like about telecom is that it is text based, and I covet that for our school-based environment. I dread the day when we're hooked up with fiber optics and full-motion video, because we've already lost so much of our ability to work with text. And those who lose the ability to communicate in a text-based medium will have lost a lot, because real information will always be couched in a text-based form.

Telecommunications is the last frontier of written literacy in this country. When you look at the growth of electronic mail through CompuServe, MCIMail, as well as the Internet, there are people who would not think of putting pencil to paper who correspond with dozens of people via electronic mail. There are those who say, "Why should I have to write? I've got television to give me information, and I've got a telephone to talk to people." But people who learn telecommunications can read and write.

So I'm not looking forward to the fiber-optic NREN, but I won't be a Luddite and throw my shoes at the wheel.

For more information

The FrEdMail/Internet gateway software is available via `ftp nic.cerf.net, cd /pub/fredmail, get freduucp.tar.Z, fredux.tar.Z`, and there is a $250 technical support fee. For information, contact `greggb@pro-fred.cerf.fred.org`.

Information on the SCHLNet USENET conferences is available from `fred@acme.fred.org`.

The FrEdMail Foundation, P.O. Box 243, Bonita, CA 91908, (619)475-4852, email: `arogers@bonita.cerf.fred.org`.

Chapter 39:
The History of the EchoMac Network

Told by Tim Pozar, Leo Laporte, Vernon Keenan, Michael Connick, Bernard Aboba, and Richard Bollar

Tim Pozar

At the time I became a sysop in the early 80s, I was living in Fresno, running a program called BYE on a CP/M machine. They had an I/O control byte in CP/M where you could reroute standard in and standard out. So BYE would answer the phone, set that I/O control byte, monitor Carrier Detect, and then restart. It wasn't a BBS really; it was more of a remote-control program.

When I moved to San Francisco, I brought that machine to work at radio station KLOK-FM as my word processor, and that's where I met Leo. He had started at KLOK-AM, and when they aquired KGO-FM, he moved up to San Francisco to work on the FM side. KGO-FM became KLOK-FM after KLOK bought it.

At the end of 1984, Leo and I were working together at KLOK when he saw an article on Fido in *InfoWorld,* which he pointed out to me. It had Tom Jennings's phone number in it, so I called Tom's BBS and downloaded the Fido software. We had just got a bunch of Eagle Computers, and Eagle had gone bankrupt. We started the KLOK BBS at that point; it was something for callers and also a way for me to access my desktop machine.

I first communicated with Tom via email, but I finally met him in person in early 1985. He had a Northern California meeting of FidoNet sysops, extremely informal, at The Oasis in Menlo Park. We met at The Oasis because it was the old Homebrew Computer Club hangout. I was one of the first people there, and there was this guy

with a T-shirt of a dog eating a disk, the symbol of FidoNet. That was Tom. A bunch of other people showed up at that point, around twenty people. Ever since then, I have stayed in touch with him, and Tom is working with me now at the radio station.

Harry Chesley was running a Macintosh-oriented FidoNet BBS at that time, I believe. Then Leo went out and bought a clone, and I came over and installed Fido for him. Leo also went out and bought a Mac, and he would upload Mac programs to his BBS.

Leo Laporte

The story of MacQueue began when my favorite BBS, Harry Chesley's BBS in San Francisco, shut down. Harry was the author of PackIt, the shareware compression software, and later HyperBBS. I loved Harry's BBS, but then he lost his Mac. To show you how creative he was, in order to inform people about the crash, he hooked his modem up to an HP calculator! You'd get a message saying "Sorry, there isn't much on here, we're running off an HP calculator." I was very frustrated when Harry's BBS went down, so that's how I got started.

I had met Tim Pozar when he was the chief engineer at KLOK-FM, where I worked. KLOK was sold and became KKSF, and then I went to work at KNBR. Tim knew Tom Jennings, who was the father of Fido, and that's how I found out about FidoNet.

Tim Pozar had set up a BBS for KKSF, and I played around setting one up for KNBR. I got the Fido software from Tim, and I had a PC that I didn't know what to do with. In fact I tried to sell it and no one wanted it. So I figured, "I might as well do this with it." There wasn't, in the fall of 1985, any good Macintosh BBS software, or BBSes, for that matter.

The problem was that everybody who wanted to do a Macintosh BBS wanted to do it on the Mac, but the software was terrible. Mac people weren't willing to get a PC-based BBS going. They thought there was something morally inferior about it. No one had taken advantage of the power of FidoNet.

Fido's big strength wasn't BBSing, but networking. I applied for a node and got it, and set up MacQueue in October 1985. I don't even remember having to spend much energy publicizing it. It took off almost immediately, so it obviously filled a need. I put on it everything I had or knew about the Mac. It turned out – and it's probably always the case – that the bulk of people started to download stuff. Ten to twenty percent were interested in messages.

I met Steve Maller at a users' group meeting in San Francisco, and Steve became my assistant sysop. This was early in Steve's career, when he was a trainer, teaching people how to use software. I needed someone to be around when I wasn't. Unfortunately, the software we were using to run the BBS remotely was buggy; if you hit Backspace, it would hang. So the idea of having a remote sysop didn't work well; the sysoping had to be done by me eventually.

I didn't have to make any effort to get great people on the BBS. There was nothing else comparable to MacQueue. We got about 55,000 calls over three years, probably a few thousand logins. We got callers from Japan, Finland, all over. There was a guy who logged in every few weeks from Japan, and the line quality was always terrible. Even local people had terrible line problems. I would sit and watch them fend off all the garbage on their screen. It was fun; I had the BBS networked with TOPS to my Mac so I could transfer files.

When you run a BBS, it's like being an elected official: You have a constituency, you have an audience, and you want to do stuff for them, so it makes sense to write software. As a sysop, you only serve because the callers let you; it only thrives as long as they let you be their sysop.

That's why I created QDial and MacArc. In those days, there were a million and one things that needed to be done. Those were obvious things, and they were written in response to need. There was no demon dialer for the Mac. It is currently illegal to do this, and it might have even been illegal then. After ten dials there is a recording that comes on and says stop. But it was the only way to get into MacQueue, it was so busy.

In 1986, I was finishing QDial when the Challenger went down. So the program had that association for me. MacArc was the same thing. I think this is one area where there is still a huge need. Both the Mac and the PC compression programs use the same algorithms. Running a BBS on the PC, it becomes clear that there has to be a way for them to work together. But not many people were doing both, then. It was obvious there had to be a way of unpacking PC ARCed files. The big problem was that the byte orders were reversed.

At the time, ARC was the standard for the PC and PackIt was the Mac standard. I don't even think that Harry thought PackIt was the solution. I got the source code for ARC from System Enhancement Associates. SEA was funny about copyrights, and they were giving Phil Katz a hard time, so I said "I don't want to face this problem," and stopped development with unARCing. The PC world was changing rapidly because Phil Katz's program was so much better, and I didn't want to have to continually update the code, so eventually I gave up that effort.

But now it's stabilizing; it would be a good time for a program that could do both. It's amazing that with all the commercial software companies writing bridge and translation software, no one has done it. The best Mac commercial compression products aren't even as good as the best PC shareware products. The Mac has just not kept up in that area.

One of the reasons that MacQueue was successful was that it was laissez-faire. I didn't validate people, the donations were voluntary, and I didn't get mad at people who just downloaded. That kind of stuff offended me about most

BBSes. I didn't like enforcing any rules. The spirit was important: "Here it is, it's online, do whatever you want." There was a time limit, of course. I did ask for money, but the way I did it was that I'd give you access to a special section with a few extra pieces of software. I got maybe a few checks a month. The only real expense was the phone bill. I eventually bought a few new hard drives. It wasn't very expensive to run, and I probably broke even.

I'm not sure exactly when I first met Vern. I knew of him; there weren't that many Mac BBSes, and there were very few on FidoNet, only a dozen. I was aware of EchoMail when it was written, and it was Vern who came up with the idea of a Macintosh conference on it. There was no structure to the echoes then, no backbone. Vern and I didn't use the backbone for a long time, because we didn't think there was a need for it; it would just slow things down.

ECHOMAC was just Vern and me for a while. It got going pretty soon after MacQueue did. I was very anarchistic, and I didn't like the idea of a backbone and a list of nodes, but we had to do it because we had tremendous duplication problems. I think the source of the problem was not having a backbone. We couldn't keep track of who was sending what to whom.

We set up our own network. Hosts talk to hosts, and no one else talks to hosts. In theory that should have worked well, but eventually we got on the backbone, and duplicates were unmanageable. There was also a lot of screaming.

MacQueue and ECHOMAC had a certain spirit. At the time, CompuServe was being heavy-handed; they've learned since that this wasn't a good policy. I thought there needed to be a grass roots, populist conference that was not subject to censorship or the whims of sysops. I still believe that that is the real essence of FidoNet. To be out of the mainstream, not under the same commercial pressures, the fascistic tendencies of big companies. With H&R Block running a service, it's going to be corporate in mentality, but when you have a bunch of hackers with beat-up PCs, it's going to be different. The stuff that is happening on Prodigy now is exactly the kind of stuff I was afraid of, and that ECHOMAC was started to prevent.

CompuServe has 500,000 users, but at the time I was very much against them. The quality of traffic was secondary to the fact that it was there. There were always a lot of individualists on ECHOMAC, and that made it hard to control. There were some people who couldn't deal with that chaos. There was some guy back East who was always offering to take it over and whip it back into shape. ECHOMAC was like a flower, it had its own rhythm. The people who love it are very individualistic and will never submit to authority.

My problem was always that I didn't like getting involved in these big hierarchies and organizations. I preferred a populist approach, but it couldn't go on forever. The reason I took it down was that I just couldn't provide access. I had given copies of MacQueue to a lot of people. Vern set up MacTribune as a Q clone, and there was Chuck Farnham's BatCave BBS in San Jose and Bernard Aboba's MailCom in Palo Alto, BMUG's in Berkeley, John Lamb's Now and Zen in Sacramento. I wasn't willing to get faster PCs and more lines, because you were talking big money then. I didn't have the resources to expand. When BMUG made the commitment to Fido and multiline, MacQueue wasn't needed anymore.

In 1988, I took it down because other BBSes were serving the need better than I was. I feel pretty good and satisfied about how it happened. It lived about the right length of time, until other people could take up the slack. I don't feel like I'm responsible for it, but it's kind of neat to be the father of all this. It's one of those things that you're just there for at the beginning, and it takes on a life of its own. It took the EchoMail program, the Fido software, to get it going, so a lot of people had responsibility.

Vernon Keenan

In 1984 I was messing around with bulletin boards on a DEC Rainbow and working at Northwestern Memorial Hospital in Chicago in the Spine Unit. I found out about FidoNet by browsing CompuServe forums, and also hunting around Chicago-area bulletin board systems. It was your basic "computer hacker gets bored on weekend and dials modems" thing.

So I started FidoNet node number 444 on the Chicago net. I ran the system on an IBM PC/XT with a 30 Mb drive. I tried adding RLL drives, but never had too much success. In fact, the same original hard drive has been running Macintosh Tribune since 1985, six years now. US Robotics was right in my backyard in Skokie, so I got a modem through their modem deal and actually went to the modem factory once to get my modem fixed. Bob Elliot was the coordinator for the Chicago network at that time. I've always been good at learning new systems, but it was a challenge.

I called my system Spine Fido. It resided at the hospital, and it was Mac-oriented. Then I started up another node at my house in Evanston, called ConsultNet, and got the two of them talking. That was the first EchoMac Network. I got the ECHOMAC conference set up between my house and Spine Fido.

My assistant sysop in Chicago was someone by the name of Mike Borsetti. He was Italian, and his family lived in Italy, so he wanted to get the Italian connection going. As a result, we had more Italian users than you would normally expect. We even had some email going back and forth in Italian. I've had a lot of calls from overseas, primarily from Oceania and Europe, from Australia, the Netherlands, Japan, Britain, and, of course, Italy, over the years.

At that point I started searching for other Mac-oriented systems in the Nodelist, and I found a node called MacQueue. Any node with Mac in the name, I called. When I first called Leo Laporte, he was in the middle of a broadcast on KNBR, so it was somewhat awkward. Leo had a more popular, more complete Mac system in the Bay Area, and that really got ECHOMAC going.

The primary focus was Mac product information and rumors. It was like Mac the Knife before *MacWEEK*. At that time, there was nothing besides the monthlies, no news source like *MacWEEK*, so we tried to be an alternative to CompuServe. Leo was also into programming, and he loved to answer those kinds of questions. It was great; it was fun.

In August 1986 I moved to the Bay Area to work for Genentech, and I said to myself, "No way am I going to run a bulletin board," but four months later I had Macintosh Tribune going. Around that time we switched from Fido to OPUS, when everyone else did. There were features in OPUS that Tom didn't include until Fido version 12.

The growth of the conference was tremendous. By 1986, we had dozens of nodes, fifty or sixty – people just started picking it up. It kept growing, and growing, and growing. We also had a big Bay Area focus. People around the world liked to read it because it used to be concentrated. Back then we had more advanced users than we have today.

It was always exciting. It actually helped get me into the computer industry, too. Right now, I am a writer and an analyst. Henry Norr got to know me through sysoping, and I've been a contributing editor for *MacWEEK* now for four years. I continue to specialize in networking and telecommunications products.

In 1986 to 1987, we had a meeting with Tim Pozar, Harry Chesley, Leo Laporte, and few other people in the Software for Less consulting shop and we talked about creating a client/server approach to BBSes. We were always frustrated by the ASCII interfaces of ECHOMAC, and we were looking to develop a Finder-like interface, like AppleLink, with folders and areas you could double-click on. We were envisioning something like AOL is today, but we never programmed it.

In 1989, my interest started to wane, so Bill Sommers became the sysop for the Tribune and has been ever since. I dropped it for two reasons: My life got busier; and you go through periods where you get enthusiastic, and then you realize how much time it is taking up in your life.

This year I moved to Santa Cruz, and so I shut down Macintosh Tribune. It will be back with a different number.

Michael Connick

I have been a computer consultant for the last twenty-five years in the area of communications. At one point I worked for the Navy on some of the early ARPANET software. That was my introduction to wide-area networking.

I should also mention that a lot of FidoNet was inspired by USENET and the Internet. The whole idea of EchoMail, first written by Jeff Rush from Texas, who soon after lost interest in FidoNet and went off to other things, was inspired by USENET. He came up with the idea of adding the AREA line, piggybacking on the NetMail interface so nobody had to make any extensions to the protocols to make EchoMail work. EchoMail differs from NetMail in the special lines in the message that distinguish it, such as the AREA line and the SEENBY line that traces which systems have already seen the message.

I first got involved with the Mac in August 1984, and was the very first customer for Consulair C in September 1984. I worked on Mouse Exchange, which was the first Macintosh bulletin board software, for a couple of years, and got out of Macintosh software development for a while. Then I got the idea for a next-generation Macintosh BBS, like what TeleFinder is today – a BBS running a special program that would make it transparent to the fact that you were using a modem at all. It would look like the Finder. Doing that required reliable protocols between the BBS and the terminal program.

As soon as I started thinking about communications protocols, I started thinking of industry standards like X.25 and HDLC. My specialization is miltary software, UNIX internals, and communications. Once I started down that line, I thought, "Wouldn't it be great if BBSes could talk to each other?" I started with the idea of creating a proprietary protocol that would draw on the industry standards. I had heard about FidoNet systems here and there because I'd always been interested in BBSes. So I started to investigate FidoNet and found this incredible amateur network. So instead of coming up with this Macintosh BBS program with a proprietary protocol, what I decided to do was to get Macintoshes hooked into FidoNet. In fact, there were already Macintosh FidoNet conferences in 1987, but they could only be accessed by PC BBSes. So at that point I dropped the idea of writing a BBS and started on Tabby, with the idea that it would work with all BBSes. The first implementation of Tabby was for Mouse Exchange.

When I first looked at the FidoNet protocols, I was horrified. It was very primitive. I thought of using the Comm Toolbox to make FidoNet work over AppleTalk or EtherTalk, but FidoNet is not a robust protocol, not an industrial-strength protocol. I don't think anyone would be that interested in carrying it over a packet-switched network, especially since there are gateway links between USENET, FidoNet, and the Internet.

FidoNet had one big thing going for it, though, which was popularity. Implementing FidoNet was extremely difficult, because in 1987 it was undocumented. I had to reverse-engineer it. I got the FidoNet Standards Committee documentation and wrote an implementation that followed those specs, and discovered that I couldn't talk to any other mailer! There were big gaps in the documentation. The only way I got it to work was by trial and error. I wrote many specialized pieces of software to monitor the communications line and figure out what was happening. It was a monumental task, which resulted in my first successful session in May 1987.

In May 1987, my Mouse Exchange had its first successful session with another FidoNet node. When I asked for info on the FidoNet protocols from the authors of existing programs, I found they were all incredibly friendly and helpful and very supportive, even though they were all IBM PC people. People like Thom Henderson, author of SEAdog, which is a commercial package, were extremely patient and answered lots of questions. In fact, Thom licensed SEAlink to me for $1. Tom Jennings, creator of FidoNet, was very supportive, and very patient with lots of questions.

A FidoNet system is not just a communications package. There are all these other pieces of software: EchoMail processors, Nodelist handlers and compilers, archivers. It had to be written so that it was easy to use. So it was a full year after my first telecommunications session that I had a package that was complete and usable by anyone but me, could handle EchoMail and NetMail and compile the Nodelist, and so on. Overall, it was much more difficult than I had thought it would be.

When I first started working with Tabby, I made different versions that would work with each package. The authors were very cooperative. Scott Watson gave me internal docs and source code for his formats so Tabby would work with Red Ryder Host; Michael Pester did the same. But after a while there were more and more Mac BBSes, so I couldn't add any new features to Tabby because I was maintaining so many versions.

Also, Tabby had reached a critical mass where there were enough Tabby people that they could act as a lobby for me with BBS authors. So, at one point I made a standard interface mechanism between Tabby and *all* BBSes, so that they had to follow *my* rules instead of me following theirs. When I established the mechanism and promised I would never change it, new BBSes could immediately be compatible with Tabby. That was the generic import and export standard, the way that Tabby stores EchoMail and gets it to and from the Macintosh BBS programs. I also provided all of the authors with information on how to tell whether they were being called by a FidoNet system or by a human being, and then tell Tabby why it was being called.

One thing that is different about Tabby is that on a PC system, the mailer answers the telephone. With Tabby, a BBS answers the phone. That was a strong feeling on my part. On PC systems, when you call up, you don't get a BBS, you get a mailer program that sits there and looks at whether you're a FidoNet system or not. After it determines you're a person, you're talking to Binkley or FrontDoor, and it tells you to wait while the BBS program is loading. I found this annoying as a user. The users are second class! They are inconvenienced to allow for the networking software. In Tabby, I wanted the BBS to answer the phone and be ready to deal with a caller right away. So I had to come up with a way for BBSes to distinguish between humans and FidoNet, and if it was a FidoNet system, to launch a Tabby program and write out a file in a certain format, telling me the bps rate on the port the connection was made on.

Tabby can be launched for one of three reasons. First, a running BBS determines that a Fido has called. This is called Crash Mail. Tabby looks for the file CONNECT.BBS and if it finds it, it knows that a BBS was running and that a FidoNet system called. Tabby gets the port and bps rate

from this file. Second, Tabby can also be started as a result of a normal event, such as Zone Mail Hour, the one-hour period when all FidoNet systems must be running their mail software, or (third) it can be another scheduled time for it to run.

Tabby did continuous mail from the beginning. I felt that that was vital. Otherwise, you'd be limited to prearranged mail slots. Scott Watson, Michael Pester, and Terry Teague supported this from day one. When Hermes first came out, Frank Price made the program Tabby compatible, but didn't want to support Crash Mail. He had valid technical reasons, but as soon as Hermes people got Tabby and realized they didn't have continuous mail, they started clamoring for it, and Frank buckled, as has everyone else who came at it that way. Since then, all Macintosh BBSes have within a short time been made Tabby compatible.

I'm a believer in standards. I went through some trouble to make sure that the Tabby standard would be easy to follow so that authors could make their programs Tabby compatible. I've also been a fanatic about following all of Apple's rules. When MultiFinder first came out, there was a bug in the launch trap and I had to do a little dancing around, but when System 7.0 came out, Tabby ran perfectly without me changing a line of code. When Apple tells you to follow all the rules they lay down, if you do, you'll benefit, and if you don't, you'll suffer; they're right! I was very concerned with System 7, because it was such a major rearchitecture, but I didn't have to change a line.

I wanted Tabby to run on small machines. For a FidoNet mailer, you need EchoMail, NetMail, interfaces to BBSes, and to process the Nodelist. If Tabby were a monolithic program, it would require a large Mac. There are people running Tabby on a Mac 512Ke; each program requires very little resources or memory.

Tabby has had a totally unforeseen impact. Something I learned in my career in software was that if you come up with a good product, people will use it in ways you don't foresee. And eventually, your users know more about your product than you do! I have an EchoMail conference called TABBY, and 98 percent of the questions are answered by other Tabby users. Many times I don't know the answer to the questions, but my users do! They're using every kind of Macintosh and modem imaginable, and they know lots of things about hardware combinations that I could never duplicate.

When I wrote Tabby, I took a different architectural approach: I wrote it as a series of cooperative programs. It was the precursor to the idea of IAC, AppleEvents, and so on. I also invented my own mechanism for communication between programs, which is just based on files. What I call an Event is the execution of a series of Tabby programs. The file called Launch.Next lists the programs to be run at a particular time for a particular reason. It takes the program's name off the list, then gets the next name and launches it. I had no idea that people would take advantage of this ability and make wonderful utilities. People started writing all kinds of "Tabby-compatible" programs through the Tabby Events programs using Launch.Next, pulling their program names off the list. So people have written all kinds of powerful extensions to Tabby. But I never foresaw that I was developing a generalized mechanism for extensions.

Of course, I quickly published standards on how Launch.Next worked, and published code on how to do it, since there had been some misunderstandings. There are at least sixty Tabby utilities now that use that mechanism! Now there's a Pascal version, so anyone who wants to write a Tabby program already has the code. In fact, I've written a couple of utilities that took advantage of this, being a copycat to my own users.

With Tabby out, and stable, I got back to the idea of a BBS where the end-user had a natural Mac interface. I always felt that when a Mac user got on a traditional PC BBS, it was command-based, and you lost the advantages of the Mac way of doing things. So I wanted a BBS program to allow the end user to have the Mac interface, but also to provide a very efficient management of the communications line. I felt it was criminal, having run BBSes since the early 1980s, to make someone sit there and read messages, at the speed they can read, tying up the phone line. So I wanted users to be able to read the messages at their leisure, on their own systems, after the telephone communication had been broken, so that someone else could get on the BBS.

It dawned on me that the FidoNet community already had that in the idea of points, which is a piggybacking onto the FidoNet protocol that allows for compression, which increases the bandwidth. Why not take that protocol, which stuffs data into the modem as fast as it can take it, and apply that to the management of user sessions on the BBS? The two big advantages are that the end users cut their phone bill, and the BBS can support a lot more users. A traditional BBS can support forty calls a day with a single line, because the calls are grouped together in the early morning and evening. The average connection is quite long – half an hour, three-quarters of an hour. A point system can be automated to call in the middle of the night, when you're sleeping. The information is compressed, and the modem runs at close to the theoretical maximum speed, so the connection is measured in minutes. That way, a BBS handling points can take hundreds of calls a day. This concern for phone bills is also reflected in Tabby itself. If Tabby tries a system three times in a row and the session aborts three times, it will mark the system as undialable. I've tried to protect sysops from catastrophic phone bills.

It was very easy to take the Tabby engine and strip it down and turn it into a point engine, but what I didn't have the time to do was to write the end-user interface. In the beginning, I wanted to put together a point engine that would work with a HyperCard interface, so that people could do their own interface. I'd provide a common access mechanism, the mailer portion, and you'd do everything else.

The more I looked into it, the more impractical the HyperCard interface looked. At about that time, Michael Pester had hit a development plateau with Mansion and said he had some free time. He was the first (and only!) person to offer to cooperate with me on point software. He wrote what ended up being called Copernicus. Copernicus is now just coming out in version II, which has a very nice user interface. Some people didn't like the style of the Copernicus I interface, so Mike Leninger wrote COUNTERPoint, which was a different interface, while still making use of my mailer engine. So it allowed people the choice, which is what this whole business is about. The most important thing is that people do things the way they like. I should also mention that there is now a shareware point system, MacWoof, which is the first one that is integrated and not based on Tabby. Craig Vaughan wrote his very own FidoNet communications module.

For point systems to work well, there have to be some changes on the BBS side as well. The traditional way in FidoNet is that the EchoMail conference is a giant tree, with the moderator at the root and branches at every node. What happens on a typical FidoNet system is that you make a copy for each system you feed. That's OK, but if you're handling a hundred echoes, with five systems each, you've got a huge number of duplicate messages, which eats up a lot of disk space. When you've got 200 points, 500 points, the amount of disk space is huge. So you can't have a large number of points unless you get around this problem.

Under GroupMail, a new technology invented by Thom Henderson, only one copy of a message is kept, no matter how many systems you feed it to. GroupMail also saves processing time as well. I came up with a subset of GroupMail, which I call PointMail. I borrowed Thom's technology – he was very helpful in explaining how it worked, what the gotcha's were. On our system, we process 800 to 1000 EchoMail messages a day. Some of the biggest systems process several thousand messages a day. You'd need a Macintosh IIfx to handle it all. On those kinds of systems, GroupMail is essential.

So Thom Henderson has been very helpful to me. Through Thom, I got involved in Alternet. Many of the founders of Alternet were in New Jersey. For a while, there was a political war in FidoNet, just as in any large anarchy. There is no central governing body in FidoNet; no official committee with lots of power. There are informal organizations and rules, but it is held together by the honor system and common interests. Any time you get a few thousand people together with strong opinions (which sysops are), you get into cases of misunderstanding. At various times, people have decried FidoNet's inefficiencies and tried to organize things and get lots of rules, which caused mass rebellion.

As a reaction to that, Alternet was founded. Its main premise was that all this stuff should be fun, and that people should treat each other with respect. "Being polite," while at the same time having a good time, making light of the

concept of the organization to run a network. So the titles of the people who have different duties are titles of nobility. The head of Alternet is the "Archduke." People poke fun at the people who are responsible for running the network.

For a while, many of the Tabby sysops were joining Alternet because I was in it. I had info on it in the Tabby docs, and people said, "I think I should join that too." I didn't care; I've never really cared which network people belong to. There's EchoNet, a large network, but there are also hundreds I don't know about. There are gaming networks, and others where people with special interests focus all their network traffic on a single topic. There are also private FidoNet networks that are used by commercial businesses and government. FidoNet is strictly amateur and cannot be used for commercial purposes, which is why people who are commercial need to form their own networks.

In the early days of Tabby, I was approached by the State Department to transfer information from consulates all over the world. They felt that one of the easiest ways to do that was through the FidoNet protocol. The U.S. Postal Service has a large FidoNet network, as does the Forest Service. Some commercial businesses have machines call each other through PBXs. There are lots of commercial users of the FidoNet protocol. But the vast majority are the amateur sysops.

FidoNet continues to evolve. I'm working on the next implementation of Tabby, which will include ZedZap. When I first started working on Tabby, ZedZap didn't exist, so I started working on FTS-0001, and I added SEAlink. Though ZedZap started to catch fire, I ignored it. I've come under unbelievable pressure for that. ZedZap offers higher performance, although there are arguments that SEAlink is pretty close in that department. ZedZap can pick up and restart a session and not have to start over. So, 14.5 minutes into a 60-minute session, if the line drops, I can restart without having to lose all that time. ZedZap will recognize that the session has been aborted and pick up where it left off.

One thing about FidoNet is that it's unpredictable; you never know what's coming next. I'm not a file person, I'm interested in using BBSes to communicate rather than exchange programs, although most people probably use it for downloading. Our own BBS has almost no files, but it does have a wide variety of EchoMail areas. We have echoes on writing, cooking, film, and lots of other nontechnical subjects.

There is a continued explosive growth in FidoNet. People have always greatly underestimated FidoNet's growth. It's a wonderful community; I've come to know so many people electronically all over the world. At Macworld Expo, I met people I had known for years whom I had never seen.

There are a lot of people on FidoNet in Russia, Eastern Europe, and all over the world. The possibility for exchange is enormous. There are no Tabbys in Russia, but there are Tabbys in Europe, Africa, Japan, and all over Asia. There are tremendous numbers of Tabby systems in Canada, but I don't know why it's so popular there. Canada is just barely second to the U.S., with 300 systems.

One of the things I tell sysops is that when they run Tabby, their BBS changes, and it will never be the same. You go from having local users to having tens of thousands of users all over the world. Someone in Japan or Africa can communicate just as well with your users as someone down the block. The sheer volume of information is staggering. How many echoes are there? Six hundred? And those are just the well-published ones. There are probably thousands of conferences!

One of the great boons to that kind of global communication is the Internet gateway system. I am always sending messages back and forth from Bell Labs to my home system or my consulting firm through the Internet gateway, which in this area is run by Rutgers. If people want to get data from FidoNet to their packet-switched network, they should go through the gateways.

Bernard Aboba

I first found out about MacQueue from BMUG. It was early 1987, and I was the sysop of the Stanford Macintosh Users' Group bulletin board in Palo Alto. I replaced Steve Deering, who decided to devote more time to his Ph.D. dissertation. I was looking for a new BBS setup

because at the time we were running Mouse Exchange on a Lisa with a 10 Mb Profile drive under MacWorks. It was crashing all the time, and I would have to reformat the hard drive every week. I didn't like that much.

I called BMUG for a recommendation and Steve Costa at BMUG gave me the phone number of MacQueue, which had gotten BMUG's award for the best BBS several times in a row. I got on MacQueue, and I was amazed at what I saw. Not only did they have more information on Macintosh programming than I'd ever seen in one place, they had something called EchoMail, which allowed you to talk to people all over the country.

I decided that we should get rid of the Lisa and buy an IBM PC to run Fido instead. When I proposed that to the Board of Directors at SMUG, they almost had a heart attack! They didn't like that it was a PC, and they didn't like the idea of a BBS making phone calls on its own. Even when I got a local community college to offer to donate the system, they still weren't interested. They decided to buy a Macintosh Plus and a 300 Mb hard drive instead, which cost a ton of money. We would run Red Ryder Host and have the best collection of files around. The only problem was that our disk library wasn't nearly as good as BMUG's.

So we decided that we would invite all the Bay Area sysops to a conference at Stanford, which we called a Pow-wow. We would talk about bulletin boards and communications, and trade files with each other. That way we would get files to fill our new hard drive. I called Tom Jennings and asked him to speak, and he told me about Tim Pozar, who was writing a FidoNet/UUCP gateway that Tom was excited about. From Tim, I also heard about DASNet, which was offering to connect online services to each other and to the Internet. Erik Fair came down from U.C. Berkeley to talk about USENET, and we had Mary Eisenhart of *MicroTimes*, and Phil Sih of Portal.

At the conference, Vern Keenan of MacTribune was very persuasive about why BMUG and other sysops should give up running their BBSes on the Mac and join the FidoNet revolution. He was like Johnny Fidoseed, loaning a PC-based OPUS BBS to sysops around the Bay Area to copy and going over the setup with them. I copied Vern's

BBS and set up MailCom in Palo Alto; Chuck Farnham put one up in San Jose called BatCave, and BMUG also put up an OPUS in Berkeley. Pat O'Connor, who was running MacCircles under Red Ryder Host, also went to FidoNet, but used TBBS. All of these used Leo's file library, which Vern brought with him to the conference.

We were very excited by Tim's UFGATE gateway as well, because that meant that once we were on FidoNet, we could also send UUCP mail and receive USENET conferences. I had been a system administrator of a Vax UNIX system at Stanford, and with my time there coming to an end, I wanted to be able to read comp.sys.mac and other conferences.

At the same time, Vern suggested that we undertake a publicity campaign to get user groups on FidoNet. I uploaded information on FidoNet to GEnie, to CompuServe (where they took it off), and on AppleLink for the User Group Connection. Raines and I wrote an article for Just Add Water on User Groups and FidoNet, and he also started MUGADMIN, the echo for user groups.

BMUG's PD-ROM also came out of the Pow-wow. We got so many files from all the sysops that we filled the 300 Mb drive that SMUG had bought. At this point, we had so many files that not only did we have enough for the BBS, we also had enough to cut a CD-ROM. I had a friend named Steve Freedman who was one of the pioneers in optical media, who was working on an electronic anatomy text book, and is now at Microsoft. So I got excited about putting out a CD-ROM of publicly distributable software, and I proposed that to the SMUG Board of Directors. I even found a hardware vendor who was interested in bundling it with their CD-ROM drives.

The SMUG directors didn't like the idea. They were afraid that doing a CD would jeopardize their disk sales. At the time, they were charging $4 per disk, and the disks were only 400K, so it was a good way to make money. Several of the people who ran SMUG had MBAs, and I was just an engineering graduate student who didn't know anything about business, so I didn't know how to argue. Still, I knew they were wrong, and sure enough, within two years SMUG was virtually out of business. I was able to stick to my guns against business types after that.

One afternoon, I read a note on the BMUG BBS looking for a volunteer to run the BMUG telecom special interest group. I thought to myself: Why not? I started coming up to Berkeley to do the SIG and got to know Raines Cohen and Phil Reese of BMUG better, and tried to convince them to do a CD. Although there were big arguments about it, BMUG decided to invest in both a new PC-based BBS and doing a CD. Those were the biggest financial decisions BMUG had made up to that point.

That was how I got involved in the PD-ROM – not only collecting files from SMUG's 300 Mb hard drive for it, but also downloading files from the Sumex archives at Stanford. There was period when Stephen Howard and Raines stayed up for a week doing the CD, and I stayed up an entire night downloading files for it. There was one section I worked on in particular, which was a collection of archives from USENET, FidoNet, and ECHOMAC. It was the first collection of its type on CD, and it was really useful to browse.

However, it wasn't all fun. With the rapid expansion of ECHOMAC, things were getting out of control, new users were getting on and dumping garbage in the Echo, and there were a lot of duplicate messages. So I volunteered to be moderator in January 1988, and I tried to figure out the routing. Boy, it was a mess! The echo was half on the backbone and half not; there were dupes and broken connections because of that.

This was around the time that MacQueue started to have problems. I convinced Raines that BMUG needed to step in and take the place of Leo to stabilize the EchoMac Network, and he agreed. A Compaq PC was donated to BMUG, and I cloned MailCom and UFGATE onto that. That was how the BMUG Mail Hub was born, and how BMUG BBS got connected to USENET.

It took nearly six months to make the transition from MacQueue as the hub of the EchoMac Network to a more traditional backbone distribution system. Several of the hub nodes would not break their connections and were spewing dupes into the network at a furious rate. I finally had to strong-arm people to break links and set up proper routing. Everyone on ECHOMAC was complaining about things, and it took nearly six months to fix, but by July 1988,

ECHOMAC had become a true backbone conference, distributed by NECs.

At that point, I decided to step aside as moderator. There were two big problems – topology and inappropriate messages – and while I had concentrated exclusively on topology, the garbage-message problem had gotten out of control. People seemed to want someone who would be more of a strong-arm than a technician, so I decided to step aside in January 1989. Richard Bollar volunteered to take my place, although I stayed on as moderator of MACHYPE and MACDEV.

In September 1988, I was elected to the Board of Directors of BMUG, and for the next two years I worked on the financial aspects of BMUG and did very little sysoping. With the Mac market becoming increasingly business-oriented, user groups were facing a lot of pressure, and BMUG had to go from being a volunteer organization to being a professionally managed one. It was a big transition, which BMUG went through successfully.

In September 1990, I got back to sysoping again after Raines Cohen got a job at *MacWEEK* and Phil Reese left for Los Angeles. There were also a bunch of other changes for me at that time; I moved to Berkeley and quit my job as an engineering consultant to go into business.

In January 1991, I met a representative of a small company called SoftArc, at MacWorld Expo. They had a new BBS called FirstClass, which was entirely graphical, and they gave me a copy of the client software to try out. I called the SoftArc Online system in Canada and was impressed. After that, I recommended that BMUG convert to FirstClass.

With the release of FirstClass v2.0 in the summer of 1992, the conversion began and on September 16, 1992, the BMUG BBS went back to running on a Macintosh again. Things were rocky at the beginning, but the users are very excited about the new system. It's easy to use, and they're using it two or three times as frequently as they did before; the load is way up. It's these advances that keep me as excited about sysoping now as I was years ago.

Richard Bollar

I was given a modem with my original Mac when I got it in 1984. At the time I was in school and living in Washington, D.C. At first, the only Macintosh bulletin board I knew of was Terry Monk's system, called Monks Boa. It was an interesting group of people, which included Paul Heller, who a little bit after that started up a files board called Twilight Clone as an auxiliary.

After regularly spending my daily allotment on both Twilight Clone and Terry Monk's system, I decided to start my own BBS in October 1986. It was a little system that was just for messages, and eventually I found out about FidoNet, which gives people a really inexpensive way to talk about things. Michael Connick had written a Macintosh FidoNet mailer called Tabby, and since Red Ryder Host didn't support Tabby and Mansion did, I switched to Mansion and started receiving echoes.

At the time there were only three Macintosh echoes: ECHOMAC, MACDEV and MACHYPE, all moderated by Bernard Aboba. When Bernard decided to step down as ECHOMAC moderator, I decided to volunteer.

This was a rocky time for the network, since Macintosh Tribune and MacQueue, which had been the major hubs, started having problems and as a result, the East and West Coasts got separated. Intermittently, we would see a large batch of messages from the West, and then nothing. The problem was not fixed until June 1989, when BMUG replaced MacQueue as the West Coast Hub, MacTrib came back online, and ECHOMAC made the transition to a backbone conference.

It wasn't easy at first. I had only been in FidoNet for about six months and hadn't had experience as a moderator before in FidoNet. But I'm a manager in my real job, and so a lot of it is common sense. What is our point? Our point is to talk about Macs, not to blast people, to try to stay on topic and keep the cost down for the people who pay the bills, the sysops. My moderator messages were designed to keep people talking about Macs, to kill the off-topic messages, and douse the flame wars.

When it came down to what a moderator was supposed to do, I found that fairly tedious, especially toward the end. What I found most frustrating is that sysops weren't giving people access to the network. I would send a message to a user saying, "Your conversation is not interesting to everyone. Why not do it over NetMail?" But they didn't have access to that. I have a problem with this because you can access NetMail by routing it to the Regional Echo Coordinator. I have free access to NetMail on my board because I feel so strongly about it.

When I lived in Atlanta I had thirty-five NetMail messages a month, and they were only a minute each, or $3.50/month to give everyone access. As far as I'm concerned, that saves me money by not having off-topic messages and the flame wars they generate. Also, I want to encourage the idea of people sending UUCP mail via NetMail and the FidoNet/UUCP gateways.

Why did I step down as ECHOMAC moderator? A couple of things happened. I changed jobs and moved to Atlanta and became more busy. It was very important for me to read every message. Nobody reads every message anymore, it's inconceivable; the traffic in ECHOMAC is now more than 1000 messages a week. But I had to do it just so people would know that I was reading it. I would have a couple of hundred messages to go through and it became a chore. Reading ECHOMAC casually continues to be fun.

I also started to feel I wasn't making any progress on some of the things that are important. The moderator doesn't have a whole lot of control over the conference. If they're starting flame wars I can ask the hub to cut them off, but in general you don't have that much power, which I found frustrating. There were some people who didn't care. ECHOMAC was their public chat area, because they knew that a friend somewhere else had access. And after a while that began to wear on me.

There was the time I went nuts. I hadn't been checking the echo for several weeks and had to go through thousands of messages, and there was so much junk in the conference that I got mad and posted a message blasting fifty-five people. I was having a very bad day when I read that the next day. I got a lot of NetMail over that one.

All you had to do was to keep it to "interesting Mac stuff." But everyone got off on blasting Scott Watson or Norm Goodger over his origin line "Jesus is the reason for the season." If you sat and watched, people were testing what they could get away with. In 1990 I decided that I couldn't get myself to do it anymore, but somehow I got elected again: I was nominated, and I got the most votes. Then I did it until the next year, when I put my foot down and said, "If nominated I won't run, and if elected I won't serve." Liz Clayton was elected, and she has been serving since then.

After I left office, I took a long break and didn't read EchoMac for six months. Now I sort of scan it, look at the headers and who is writing. Now I can do that, which I couldn't do before. It was great fun, and I'm glad I did it.

As a result of getting involved I learned a lot about FidoNet, more than I ever thought I would know. In real life, I'm an accountant for Marriot Hotels, so I travel a lot. I would read EchoMac while I was travelling around, which was 80 percent of the time. I would sit and download the stuff to my point.

I wish I had a picture of me in a post office in India, taking the phone apart, trying to plug my PC laptop in using alligator clips and a Telebit modem. The Telebit worked, and I got more EchoMail than I cared to deal with.

I use PCs and Macs both. My laptop is a Compaq 386, because at the time I got it, Apple didn't have laptops. I'm pretty much in both worlds; my bulletin board runs on the PC and I have a IIci that I do all my fun stuff on.

I switched from Mansion to Remote Access in 1991, using Front Door as a mailer. The reason I switched to a PC was that it was cheaper; it could run two lines without a performance problem, and I also wanted to get more involved in the administrative part of FidoNet, which Tabby wasn't designed to do.

I became a part of the EchoMail Coordinator structure in Atlanta where I was distributing echoes for a hub. I could distribute to eight nodes three or four megabytes of mail in a few minutes. I now have a two-line system running.

The only thing that would get me to switch back to the Macintosh would be FirstClass. It is easier to use, and I'm in favor of it.

One of the things that has been unique about my system is the Swizzle Echo. This is patterned after a watering hole, where people come to shoot the breeze. I created the conference because I have moved frequently over the years and want to keep in touch with my old friends as I travel. I've got a couple of boards in Washington, a couple in Atlanta, and now some in San Francisco where I moved in 1992. So I hear from a lot of the same faces as in 1986, although I keep moving.

People have commented on how everyone in the Swizzle Echo seems to know each other, even though they are located all across the country. Wherever I have been, I have parties where I invite everyone over to see the Swizzle board, so everyone does know each other. This is one of the things that make it fun – eventually everyone who reads the conference does know me. I post my travel stories in the conference, although I'm a few years behind by now.

Bill Sommers carries Swizzle in San Francisco now, and we are good friends. It is funny how we met. Bill had a caller who logged on with the name Fish Fiends, who was announcing Bay Area Aquarium Society events on ECHOMAC, a global conference, and wouldn't stop. So I sent Bill some NetMail about it, and we got to know each other. We also had in common an interest in Kate Bush's music, and he ended up taking Swizzle Stick.

Part VI

Appendices

APPENDIX A:
COMMUNICATIONS BIBLIOGRAPHY

Other books besides this one

Why should I read this section?

I know that after reading this book you may be tired, and not interested in reading another one. But for some, reading one book just makes you more hungry for information. If you fall into that category, this section is for you.

A lot of books have come out on telecommunications in the last year. Most fall into the category of rarely used references. As an acknowledged telecommunications addict, I buy virtually all of them. Here are my opinions:

Books for the beginner

The Media Lab, Stewart Brand, Penguin Books, New York, NY, 1988

A Gee-Whiz look at one of the nation's top media research laboratories and its flamboyant director, Nicholas Negroponte. For the beginner, this book is likely to be great fun, and a mind opener.

EcoLinking, Don Rittner, Peachpit Press, Inc., Berkeley, CA, 1992

I am crazy about this book. It's physically beautiful (a great cover and wonderful layout, with lots of neat drawings and pictures), well organized, short, and reasonably priced. Although it is oriented toward environmentalists, it has a good overview of global networks, online services, and bulletin boards.

The Hacker Crackdown, Bruce Sterling, Bantam Books, New York, NY, 1992

The complete story of the 1990 hacker crackdown, much of which had not previously been told. Bruce Sterling brings to this book his considerable talents as an author and a techno-historian; this book is hard to put down.

Future Developments in Communications, Second Edition, James Martin, Prentice-Hall, Englewood Cliffs, NJ, 1977

In telecommunications, a thirteen-year-old book is archaic. What is most interesting about this one is how accurate the author's vision of the future was. I'm looking forward to the third edition.

Computers and Communications, Dr. Koji Kobayashi, The MIT Press, Cambridge, MA, 1988

An overview of computers and communications for the businessperson/novice, written by the CEO of NEC. Presents a vision of the coming merging of computers and communications that is literate and persuasive. A must-read for everyone in the communications business.

Signal, The Whole Earth Catalog of Information, Kevin Kelley, Harmony Books, New York, NY, 1988

This book covers a lot of different subjects, with telecommunications occupying only a small part of it. Still, it's creatively done, and there's lots of oddball stuff in there that you'd never know about unless you had Signal. For example, did you know that there is now a coffee-table book of full color photographs of tattoos? Now there's a conversation piece!

The Complete Handbook of Personal Computer Communications, Alfred Glossbrenner, St. Martin's Press, New York, NY, 1990

It seems that over half of all books and articles on communications consist of discussions of what the various online services offer. Forget them; this, and other books by Alfred Glossbrenner, are the ones to get. While this book doesn't attempt to offer comprehensive coverage of the hobbyist arena of BBSes and wide area networks, it does cover the major services such as CompuServe, Delphi, Dow Jones, Huttonline, Investor's Express, NewsNet, MCI Mail, etc. It also discusses how to send a telex or a fax.

Introduction to PC Communications, Phil Becker, with Mike Robertson, Mark Chambers, Phil James, and Alan C. Elliot, Que Corp., Carmel, IN, 1992

This book is both a well-written introduction to communications and a solid technical reference for the advanced programmer. Although it's heavily oriented towards the IBM-PC, there is a great deal of general material that will be of value to anyone. If I could take only three communications books with me to an island, this would be one of them.

Dvorak's Guide to PC Telecommunications, Second Edition, John Dvorak and Nick Anis, Osborne/McGraw Hill, Berkeley, CA, 1992

The second edition of this book has a lower price ($39.95 versus $49.95) and a nicer layout, but the coverage is similar to that of the first edition. Aside from the usual beginner material, this book contains quite a bit of unique material, such as chapters on Minitel and videotex services, international telecommunications, advanced operating environments (OS/2, DESQview, Windows, UNIX), Amiga communications, ISDN, and wireless communications. However, the book does manage to omit some basics: there is no mention of how to get a modem to auto-answer! (Type `ATS0=1`).

Desktop Communications, David A. Honig and Kenton Hoover, John Wiley & Sons, New York, NY, 1990

Although the subtitle of this book says it is for IBM-PC, PS/2, and compatible machines, much of the book applies to any computer. This is one of the best beginning books around, thoroughly covering the basics of RS-232, cables, modems, LANs, protocols, and mail systems. If only they would publish a Macintosh version!

Zen and the Art of the Internet, Brendan Kehoe, Prentice-Hall, New York, NY, 1992

This is a short anthology of information on the Internet taken from various online archives. It is not very different from the draft of the book that is available online in PostScript form via `ftp ftp.sura.net, get pub/nic/zen-1.0.ps`. Compared with *The Internet Companion*, this book is a more technical introduction.

Approaching Home Automation, Bill Berner and Craig Elliot, Approaching, Inc., Chicago, IL, 1993

If you liked the chapter on Home Control, this is the place to go next. A thoroughly readable guide to X-10 technology from both the PC and Mac perspectives.

The Internet Companion, Tracy LaQuey with Jeanne C. Ryer, Addison-Wesley Publishing Co., Reading, MA, 1992

This easy-to-read book packs an amazing amount of information into a very small space. In only 200 pages it takes you from an introduction to Internet to a list of resources. There are lots of books double the size of this that say half as much and cost three times the price. This one's only $12.95. A perfect Christmas gift.

The Mac Shareware Emporium, Bernard J. David and Maria Langer, Brady Books/Prentice-Hall, New York, NY, 1992

The best of the crop of shareware books that came out in 1992. More than just a catalog, this book describes the applications in depth, includes two diskettes, and is the only such book that provides detailed information on all the ways of obtaining shareware, including BBSes and user groups, as well as commercial online services (although it probably should have listed some Internet sites as well). Maria Langer knows what she's talking about because she has been involved in the distribution of Macintosh software on FidoNet, selecting programs, and ensuring that they are available nationwide at a low cost. The book includes a list of BBSes where you can get the programs that aren't included on the diskettes. Good work, Maria!

Telecommunications and society

The Invisible Weapon. Telecommunications and International Politics (1851-1945), Daniel R. Headrick, Oxford University Press, Inc., 1991

If information is power, then telecommunications and politics must be inextricably linked. This book examines the relationship.

The Electronic Commonwealth: the Impact of New Media Technologies on Democratic Politics, Jeffrey B. Abramson, Basic Books, New York, NY, 1988

Electronic Democracy or Demagogracy? This books examines the role that new media is likely to have on the political process.

Contemporary Issues in American Distance Education, Moore, M.G., et al., Pergamon Press, New York, NY, 1990

This book offers a variety of perspectives on distance education.

Integrating Telecommunications into Education, Roberts, N., et al., Prentice Hall, Englewood Cliffs, NJ, 1990

Goes beyond gee whiz to the task of integrating telecommunications into the curriculum.

Forecasting the telephone: a retrospective technology assessment, Ithiel de Sola Pool, ABLEX Pub., Norwood, NJ, 1983

The retrospective school of policy analysis argues that the best way to gain a perspective on the future is to understand the past. This book describes early uses of the telephone.

The printing press as an agent of change, Elizabeth L. Eisenstein, Cambridge University Press, New York, NY, 1979

This book is a look back at the impact of the printing press on early-modern Europe.

Books for the intermediate

UNIX Communications, Second Edition, Bart Anderson, Bryan Costales, and Harry Henderson, The Waite Group, Howard W. Sams, Indianapolis, IN, 1991

Thorough yet readable coverage of mail, elm, mush, mh, USENET, rn, nn, UUCP, cu, and FTP. This book is well written, well illustrated, well organized, and well worth the price. If you are a user and can only afford one reference on UNIX communications, this is the one to have.

The Internet Resource Guide, Bolt Beranek and Newman, Cambridge, MA, 1991

This guide was put together by BBN at the behest of the NSF. You can get a computer-readable copy either by anonymous `ftp nnsc.nsf.net` or on BMUG Disk: Telecom F1.

User Service Internet Resource Guide, Third Edition, NorthWestNet Academic Computing Consortium, Inc., Bellevue, WA, 1992

The NUSIRG guide is the best publicly distributable Internet Guide, containing particularly thorough sections on resources for K–12 education and supercomputing. It's available in PostScript form via `ftp ftphost.nwnet.net` in the NUSIRG directory or on BMUG Disk: Telecom F1. If you download it via `ftp`, remember to uncompress it and then recompress it with zip before downloading; the file is so large that MacCompress will choke on it otherwise. Hard copies are available for $20 from NorthWestNet, NUSIRG Orders; 15400 S.E. 30th Pl., Suite 202, Bellevue, WA 98007.

The Whole Internet Catalog, Ed Kroll, O'Reilly & Associates, Sebastopol, CA, 1992

Attractively illustrated, well written and thorough, this book is written from the UNIX perspective and is appropriate for the technical user. It provides particularly good coverage of Netnews, Gopher, WAIS, and World Wide Web. Recommended.

Internetworking with TCP/IP, Second Edition, Douglas Comer, Prentice-Hall, Englewood Cliffs, NJ, 1988

The standard text on TCP/IP. The second edition is a two-volume set, with the first volume being a description of the algorithms, and the second being a description of applications programming interfaces. If you're on a budget, try picking up the much less expensive first edition, which is very similar to book one in the two-volume set, but is just half the price. This book provides an excellent balance between theory and practice. Well written, too. The first volume should be accessible to both intermediate and advanced users who are unfamiliar with TCP/IP.

TCP/IP Network Administration, Craig Hunt, O'Reilly & Associates, Sebastopol, CA, 1992

This book is a gem, bridging the gap between theory and practice. It includes material on establishing domain-name service, configuring routing tables, setting up sendmail, troubleshooting TCP/IP connections, and setting up your machine as a server for FTP. There is probably more practical information in this book than all the other TCP/IP books combined.

Practical Internetworking with TCP/IP and UNIX, Smoot Carl-Mitchell and John S. Quarterman, Addison-Wesley Publishing Co., Reading, MA, 1993

This book is a guide to setting up and debugging TCP/IP networks running on UNIX machines. It includes both an introduction to the TCP/IP protocol, and practical networking information, such as a guide to routing protocols, DNS and sendmail, remote line printer access, and debugging tools. This book complements O'Reilly's offering on the subject, rather than competing with it. Recommended.

DNS and BIND, Paul Albitz and Cricket Liu, O'Reilly & Associates, Sebastopol, CA, 1992

A badly needed book describing the workings of the Domain Name System and BIND software. A must for network administrators, particularly those looking to set up gateways to BBS networks.

The Matrix, John S. Quarterman, Digital Press, New Bedford, MA, 1990

This book is written by a computer scientist in an encyclopedic style, so it may not be the best book for a novice. However, many hobbyists and computer professionals will find it irresistible. Have you ever wondered what INDONET is? What a LISTSERV is? This book answers common questions about how the Internet works. It is also scrupulously accurate.

The Matrix contains thorough and accurate descriptions of BITNET, ARPANET, and FidoNet technology, and gateway links. Although its encyclopedic style makes it more of a reference than a good read, I've found it to be a valuable resource.

Managing UUCP and USENET, Tenth Edition, Tim O'Reilly and Grace Todino, O'Reilly & Associates, Newton, MA, 1992

This handbook is the best reference on maintaining UUCP or USENET connections. A patient and thorough trip through the steps of establishing connections, testing the links, maintaining security, installing Netnews, and administering UUCP. Be aware that this book does not cover Taylor UUCP, an increasingly popular version included with 386BSD.

Using UUCP and USENET, Tim O'Reilly and Grace Todino, O'Reilly & Associates, Newton, MA, 1992

This handbook is oriented towards UUCP and USENET users. It includes an overview of UUCP and the USENET network and discusses accessing remote file systems; using UUCP; reading news, and determining the status of a file transfer.

The C Programmer's Guide to Serial Communications, Joe Campbell, Howard W. Sams, Indianapolis, IN, 1987

This book is a classic. Written by a former English major turned communications programmer, this book takes you from the basics of ASCII to writing machine-independent code (independent between CP/M and DOS, at least) for XMODEM. It flows well, covers the subject with breadth and depth, and is highly educational. If you already know C and like to get into the nitty-gritty, you'll love this book.

!%@:: A Directory of Electronic Mail Addressing and Networks, Second Edition, Donnalyn Frey and Rick Adams, O'Reilly & Associates, Sebastopol, CA, 1991

With its list of organizations and their Internet addresses, country codes, and other lists, this book offers reference material that is not available elsewhere. However, it appears to have been laid out by database software and as a result is heavy on maps and brief information on the networks, but weak on discussion about what all the information means and how you can use it. This book needs a larger introduction to help beginners over some of the humps.

Users' Directory of Computer Networks, Tracy LaQuey, Digital Press, Bedford, MA, 1990

This book is, as the title indicates, a directory of computer networks. Lots of maps, directories, and other listings. It's overpriced, but the Internet addicts out there will probably snap it up anyway.

UNIX Papers for UNIX Developers and Power Users, Edited by Mitchell Waite, Howard W. Sams, Indianapolis, IN, 1987

This book covers a grab bag of topics, including an introduction to USENET from a user's point of view and a discussion of the various UNIX mailers, including Berkeley Mail, AT&T Mail, MH, etc. There is a chapter on UNIX shells, basics of AWK, C++ under UNIX, writing UNIX device drivers, Remote File System (RFS), using Ethernet with UNIX, the microcomputer version of UNIX, and future UNIX directions. A good book for a sysop who is operating or contemplating the operation of a UNIX BBS, although it is now somewhat out of date.

DOS Meets UNIX, Dale Dougherty and Tim O'Reilly, O'Reilly & Associates, Newton, MA, 1988

If you want to run a UNIX BBS while still running DOS software such as BinkleyTerm, or if you want to network a PC BBS with a UNIX file server, this is the book for you. It has sections on PC-Interface and PC-NFS, dual operating environments (Merge and VP/ix), disk partitioning, and hardware issues involved in running DOS under UNIX.

Lex & Yacc, Tony Mason and Doug Brown, O'Reilly & Associates, Sebastopol, CA, 1990

Lex and Yacc are tools for constructing lexical analyzers and parsers. They generate C code that you can then compile. Originally developed for UNIX, they are now available for a variety of operating environments, including MS-DOS and the

Macintosh. Tools such as Lex and Yacc are useful, for example, for writing software that will parse mail messages into a stack, allowing you to search the messages at your leisure. This is probably the best book on these tools.

Syslaw, Second Edition, Lance Rose, Esq., and Jonathan Wallace, Esq., LOL Productions, PC Information Group, Inc., Winona, MN, 1992

This book goes beyond a dry rendition of the law relating to the operation of bulletin board systems by offering a lawyer's perspective on how to run a system. With the frequency of litigation skyrocketing, if you run a bulletin board, you probably can't afford not to purchase this book.

The AWK Programming Language, Alfred V. Aho, Brian W. Kernighan, and Peter J. Weinberger, Addison-Wesley Publishing Co., Reading, MA, 1988

AWK is one of the neatest programs ever written. It allows you to do an incredible variety of text processing tasks in the blink of an eye. With the recent release of GNU AWK for the PC, every PC BBS can use AWK to analyze caller logs, create user directories of echo conferences, analyze network topologies, etc. This book explains the ins and outs of AWK. After reading it, you will be writing AWK scripts that will amaze you.

Programming perl, Larry Wall and Randal L. Schwartz, O'Reilly & Associates, Sebastopol, CA, 1990

Perl is the successor to AWK and is now available for virtually every flavor of UNIX. It can be used to build anything from password checkers (which reject easily cracked passwords submitted by users) to mail servers.

UNIX Shell Programming, Stephen G. Kochan and Patrick H. Wood, Hayden Books, Indianapolis, IN, 1985

Concentrates on the Bourne Shell but includes sections on the C Shell and Korn Shell. Thorough and easy to read. Useful for sysops running BBSes on UNIX machines.

UNIX Networking, Edited by Stephen G. Kochan and Patrick H. Wood, Hayden Books, Indianapolis, IN, 1989

If you need to network UNIX machines to other UNIX machines or to OS/2, this is the book for you. Includes sections on UUCP, TCP/IP, Network File System (NFS) and Remote Procedure Call (RPC), Streams, Remote File System (RFS), OS/2 to UNIX networking, X Window System, and NeWS.

Mastering Serial Communications, Peter W. Gofton, Sybex, San Francisco, CA 1986

This book is heavily oriented toward IBM-PC's but fails to get into the nitty-gritty of protocols. Get the *C Programmer's Guide to Serial Communications* instead.

Digital Cellular Radio, George Calhoun, Artech House, Norwood, MA, 1988

If you've ever thought of investing in a cellular communications company, this book will scare you out of it. It discusses the history of mobile radios, and the incredible waste of resources that has gone into building an outmoded analog cellular system that will soon have to be replaced by digital cellular. Goes on to discuss the fundamentals of digital cellular technology. Fun reading for the telecommunications fanatic.

Advanced MS-DOS Batch File Programming, Dan Gookin, Windcrest Books, Blue Ridge Summit, PA, 1989

If you're running a FidoNet BBS on a PC, you're going to need to become a DOS batch script expert. This book will teach you nearly everything you need to know.

DOS PowerTools, Second Edition, Paul Somerson, Bantam Books, New York, NY, 1990

When you get into writing DOS batch scripts for FidoNet systems, you'll discover that you can't do everything you need to do because the DOS batch file language is missing quite a few capabilities. This book (and the software that comes with it) will fill in most of those gaps, allowing you, for example, to run a disk optimizer on the third Friday of every month.

This book also includes sections explaining different DOS versions, disk organization, use of DEBUG and EDLIN, ANSI drivers, hints for writing DOS batch scripts, and DOS environment usage. At $39.95, this book is expensive but well worth it. A must-have for sysops running BBSes on PCs.

Get *** CONNECTED to Packet Radio, Jim Grubbs, K9EI, Sky Publishing, Springfield, IL, 1986

A guide to the equipment, software, and licenses you'll need to get started as a packet radio operator. However, much of the equipment referred to in this book appears to be out of date, and the book looks somewhat amateurish, being printed in a monospaced font.

Your Gateway to Packet Radio, Stan Horzepa, WA1LOU, America Radio Relay League, Newington, CT, 1989

The introductory book on packet radio. Includes discussion of some of the newer Macintosh and PC hardware and software for packet radio, and an extensive glossary.

Books for professionals

Internet System Handbook, Edited by Daniel C. Lynch and Marshall T. Rose, Addison-Wesley Publishing Co., Reading, MA, 1993

This book is a technical introduction to the Internet, written by solid authorities. Although it is a bit on the pricey side ($59), it offers a lot of material that you won't be able to find elsewhere. Highly recommended.

Practical UNIX Security, Simson Garfinkel and Gene Spafford, O'Reilly & Associates, Sebastopol, CA, 1991

If you are a UNIX systems administrator, you must purchase this book. Quite readable and at times even entertaining.

NeXTSTEP Network and System Administration, NeXT Computer, Inc., Addison-Wesley Publishing Co., Reading, MA 1992

This book covers NeXTSTEP v3.0 and centers largely on NetInfo. Unfortunately, it does not talk much about use of UUCP, SLIP, or PPP on the NeXT, although it does provide good coverage of sendmail. As a result, you will probably need this book to get your NeXT up on the net.

Data Communications, Computer Networks and OSI, Fred Halsall, Addison-Wesley Publishing Co., Workingham, England, 1988

Written more for the engineer than the computer scientist, this book describes networking from an OSI vantage point.

Computer Networks, Andrew S. Tannenbaum, Prentice-Hall, Englewood Cliffs, NJ, 1988

The standard text on networking, for an introductory course. Covers an incredible amount of ground. You won't be able to write code after reading this, but you'll understand more about how things work.

MacWorld Networking Handbook, Dave Kosiur, Ph.D., and Nancy E. H. Jones, IDG Books, San Mateo, CA, 1992

The most complete source of information on Macintosh networking, written for those already inducted into the Macintosh networking cult. This book fills a need and is attractively designed and reasonably priced. However, I cannot recommend it for beginners since many of the acronyms used are not defined in the glossary, and the book launches into a discussion of AppleTalk protocols without having presented enough introductory material first.

Kermit, Frank da Cruz, Digital Press, Bedford, MA, 1987

If you need to get files onto a UNIX machine or an IBM mainframe, you probably could benefit from this book. Starts with the basics of communications; discusses RS-232, ASCII, and cables; and then moves on to a user manual for the Kermit program. Detailed explanations of the Kermit protocols as well as example code are included.

An Introduction to TCP/IP, John Davidson, Springer-Verlag, New York, NY, 1988

A brief overview of TCP/IP for the computer-literate nonspecialist. Strangely, this book covers some things that *Internetworking with TCP/IP* does not go into, such as details of the Ethernet and 802.3 datalink layers. Written from the Ungermann-Bass perspective.

Campus Networking Strategies, Edited by Caroline Arms, Digital Press, Bedford, MA, 1988

This book discusses the history and achievements of the campus networks that developed during the 1980s. Administrators of large academic or business networks will learn much from the experience gained by those who built these mammoth networks.

Periodicals

Adye, T., Berners-Lee, T., Brobecker, S., Camacho, A.;"Online communications in the DELPHI experiment," *Computer Physics Communications,* 57(1-3), pp. 466-471

Alexander, A.W., and J.S. Alexander, "Intellectual property rights and the sacred engine: scholarly publishing in the electronic age," *Advances in Library Resource Sharing* 1(1990), pp. 176-192

Allen, Brian, "The do-it-yourself computer fair: planning, pitfalls, and payoff," *Small Computers in Libraries* 8(6), pp. 6

Balas, Janet L., "OPACS and much more," *Computers in Libraries,* 13(1), pp. 28

Beals, D.E.,"Computer mediated communication among beginning teachers," *T.H.E. Journal,* 18(9), pp. 74-77

Berners-Lee, T.J., "Electronic publishing and visions of hypertext," *Physics World,* 5(6)

Berners-Lee, T.J., Cailliau, R., Groff, J.F., Pollermann, B., "World-Wide Web: the information universe," *Electronic networking: research applications and policy,* 2(1), pp. 52-58

Berners-Lee, T.J., Cailliau, R., Groff, J.F.,"The world-wide web," *Computer networks and ISDN systems,* Nov. 1992, vol. 25, nos. 4-5, pp. 454-459

Blasko, Larry, "Electronic books turn new page in publishing," *San Jose Mercury News,* June 28, 1992, pp. 9F

Brunell, M., "Profile: NORDUnet," *ConneXions: The Interoperability Report,"* 4(11), pp. 18-23

Burgard, Michael, "Bulletin Boards for business," *UNIX World,* 8(8), pp. 95

Carlitz, Robert D., "Common knowledge: networks for kindergarten through college," *EDUCOM Review* 26(2), pp. 25-28

Casselman, Grace, "Mounties to lay charges following BBS raid," *Computing Canada,* 17(25), pp. 24

Chappell, D., "Components of OSI: a taxonomy of the players," *ConneXions: The Interoperability Report,* 3(12), pp. 2-10

Cisler, Steve, "Guides and democratizing information," *Database,* 14(1), pp. 81-83

Cisler, Steve, "Mastering Internetworking," *Database,* 15(6), pp. 89

Cisler, Steve, "An essay on the openness of networks, electronic free speech, and the security of computers," *Online Access,* 14(6), pp. 101-103

Cisler, Steve, "Future Visions," *Online Access,* 15(6), pp. 90-92

Cisler, Steve, "Apple Library of Tommorrow conference report," *Database,* 14(3), pp. 96-97

Cisler, Steve,"The library community and the National Research and Education Network," *Wilson Library Bulletin,* 64(10), pp. 51

Cisler, Steve, "NREN Update: More Meetings and New Tools," *Database*, April 1991, pp. 96-98

Collis, B.A., "The evaluation of electronic books, educational and training," *Technology International*, 28(4), pp. 355-363

Corbin, R.A., "The development of the National Research and Education Network," *Information Technology and Libraries*, 10(3), pp. 212-220

Crowcroft, J., "UK Internet protocol connectivity activities," *ConneXions: The Interoperability Report*, 5(6), pp. 20-23

Danca, Richard A., "Fed buyers get on-line GSA schedule service," *Federal Computer Week*, 6(12), pp. 4

Denning, P., "The Internet Worm," *American Scientist*, March-April 1989, pp. 126-128

Deutsch, P., Emtage, A., and Heelan, B., "Archie: an Internet electronic directory service," *ConneXions: The Interoperability Report*, 6(2), pp. 2-9

Divia, R., Berners-Lee, T.J., "A timeless way of interfacing," *AIP Conference Proceedings*, 1990, no. 209, pp. 231-232

Endoso, Joyce, "Army expands BBS to offer computer contract info," *Government Computer News*, 11(10), pp. 61

"Executives in MBA program use BBS to communicate," *T.H.E. Journal*, 19(9), pp. 48

"Fast takes on pornographic bulletin boards," *Computer Weekly*, December 3, 1992, pp. 17

Finnegan, G.A.,"Wiring information to a college campus: a port for every pillow," *Online Access*, 14(2), pp. 37-40

Gardner, W., "The electronic archive: scientific publishing for the 1990s," *Psychological Science*, 1(1990), pp. 333-341

Geffert, Bryn, "Community networks in libraries: a case study of the Freenet P.A.T.H.," *Public Libraries*, March/April 1993, pp. 91-99

Goldstein, S., and C. Michau, "Convergence of European and North American research and academic networking," *ConneXions: The Interoperability Report*, 5(4), pp. 20-27

Goode, J., and M. Johnson, "Putting out the flames: the etiquette and law of email," *Online Access*, 15(6), pp. 61-65

Harnad, S., "Scholarly skywriting and the prepublication continuum of scientific inquiry," *Psychological Science* 1(1990), pp. 342-344

"How Seagate, Seiko Instruments use BBS for business," *Communications News*, 29(8), pp. 24

Hudspeth, DeLayne, "The electronic bulletin board: appropriate technology," *Educational Technology*, 30(7), pp. 40

Hunter, B., "Linking for learning: computer and communications network support for nationwide innovation in education," *Journal of Science Education and Technology* 1(1)

Jennings, D., et al., "Computer networking for scientists," *Science*, February 28, 1986, pp. 943-950

Kahle, B., Medlar, A., "An information system for corporate users: Wide Area Information Servers," *ConneXions: The Interoperability Report*, 5(11), pp. 2-9

Kanin, B., "Information policy and the Internet," *Government Publications Review*, 18(5), pp. 451-472

Kalin, S.W., and R. Tennant, "Byond OPACs: the wealth of information resources on the Internet," *Database* 14(4), pp. 28-33

Kinnaman, Daniel E., "Move over public television - here comes the National Public Telecomputing Network," *Technology & Learning* 12(3), pp. 14

Lowry, C.B., "Converging information technologies: how will libraries adapt," *CAUSE/EFFECT*, 13(3), pp. 35-42

Lucier, R.E., "Knowledge management: refining roles in scientific communication," *EDUCOM Review* 25(1990), pp. 21-27

Machovec, George S., "The NPTN and the Cleveland Free-Net community computer system," *Online Libraries and Microcomputers*, 8(11), pp. 1-4

Maciuszko, Kathlen L., "A quiet revolution: community online systems," *Online Access*, November 1990, pp. 24-32

Malamud, Carl, "Free-Nets are a sound corporate investment," *Communications Week*, February 24, 1992, pp. 17

Mogul, J., "Subnetting: A Brief Guide," *ConneXions: The Interoperability Report*, 3(1), pp. 2-9

Moore, M.G., and M.M. Thompson, "The effects of distance learning: a summary of the literature," Penn State University

Neavill, G.B., "Electronic publishing, libraries, and the survival of information," *Library Resources and Technical Services,* January/March 1984, pp. 76-89

Quatermann, J.S., "Etiquette and ethics," *ConneXions: The Interoperability Report,* 3(4), pp. 12-16

Oakerson, A., "With feathers: effects of copyright and ownership on scholarly publishing," *College and Research Libraries*, September 1991, pp. 425-438

Phillips, G.M., G.M. Santoro, and S.A. Kuehn, "The use of Computer-Mediated Communication in training students in group problem-solving and decision-making techniques," *American Journal of Distance Education*, 2(1), pp. 38-51

Piternick, A.B., "Electronic serials: realistic or unrealistic solution to the journal crisis?" *The Serials Librarian*, 21(2-3), pp. 15-31

Raeder, A.W., Andrews, K.L., "Searching library catalogs on the Internet: a survey," *Database Searcher*, September 1990, pp. 16-31

Ronfeldt, David, "Cyberocracy, cyberspace, and cyberology: political effects of the information revolution," P-7745, The Rand Corporation, Santa Monica, CA; rand.org:/pub/Reports

Ross, Steven M., et al., "Helping at-risk children through distance tutoring: Memphis ACOT," *T.H.E. Journal,* 16(6), pp. 68

Schwartz, Karen D., "Military scraps paper memos for UNIX bulletin board," *Government Computer News*, 11(20), pp. 54

Shapiro, N., Anderson, R., "Toward an ethics and etiquette for electronic mail," R-3283-NSF/RC, The Rand Corporation, Santa Monica, CA; rand.org:/pub/Reports

Seiler, L.H., "The concept of the book in the age of the digital electronic medium," *Library Software Review*, 11(1), pp. 19-29

Silva, Marcos, "Internet and public libraries," *ABQ/Quebec Library Association*, Sept.-Dec. 1992, pp. 11-13

Simpson, Charlie, "BBS buyers binge: electronic forum for buyers and sellers of equipment established," *Midrange Systems,* 6(10), pp. 3

Spafford, Eugene H., "The Internet Worm: crisis and aftermath," *Communications of the ACM*, June 1989, pp. 678-687

St. George, A., "A voice for K12 networking," *Research and Education Networking* 3(1), pp. 10-12

Stockman, B., "Current status on networking in Europe," *ConneXions: The Interoperability Report*, 5(7), pp. 10-14

Strangelove, Michael, "Free-Nets: community computing systems and the rise of the electronic citizen," *Online Access*, 8(1), pp. 46-47

Swaine, Michael, "Three days of the ponderer," *Dr. Dobbs Journal*, 18(6), pp. 137

Swayze, Kevin, "City of Waterloo sees huge potential for its BBS," *Computing Canada*, 18(24), pp. 57

"The Internet Gopher: a distributed information service," *ConneXions: The Interoperability Report*, 5(11), pp. 23

Tomer, C., "Information technology standards for libraries," *Journal of the American Society for Information Science*, 43(8):566-570, Sept. 1992

Van Gelder, Lindsy, "The Strange Case of the Electronic Lover," *Ms.*, October 1985, pp. 94

Watkins, Beverly T., "University hopes campuswide network will help give it a competitive edge," *Chronicle of Higher Education*, 38(34), pp. A18

Watkins, Beverly T., "Free-Net helps Case Western fulfill its community-service mission," *Chronicle of Higher Education*, 38(34), pp. A21

Obtaining RFCs

Internet Request For Comment (RFC) documents are available by FTP or email from the following sources:

`ftp nic.ddn.mil`, login: **anonymous**, password: **guest**, get `rfc/rfcnnnn.txt` (where nnnn is the number),

`ftp nis.nsf.net`, login: **anonymous**, password: **guest**, get `RFC/rfcnnnn.TXT-1` (where nnnn is the number). Email: `mail nis-info@nis.nsf.net`, in body: **SEND RFCnnnn.TXT-1**.

FYI #	Title	Date	RFC # (if any)
16	Connecting to the Internet: What Connecting Institutions Should Anticipate	8/92	1359
15	Privacy and Accuracy Issues in Network Information Center Databases	8/92	1355
14	Technical Overview of Directory Services Using the X.500 Protocol	3/92	1309
13	Executive Introduction to Directory Services Using the X.500 Protocol	3/92	1308
12	Building a Network Information Services Infrastructure	2/92	1302
11	A Catalog of Available X.500 Implementations	1/92	1292
10	There's Gold in them thar Networks! or Searching for Treasure in all the Wrong Places	12/91	1290
9	Who's who in the Internet: Biographies of IAB, IESG,and IRSG members	5/92	1336
8	Site Security Handbook	7/91	1244
7	Answers to commonly asked "experienced Internet user" questions.	2/91	1207
6	FYI on the X Window System	1/91	1198
5	Choosing a name for your computer	8/90	1178
4	Answers to commonly asked "new internet user" questions	5/92	1325
3	Where to start: A bibliography of internetworking information	8/90	1175
2	Tools for monitoring and debugging TCP/IP internets and interconnected devices	4/90	1147
1	Introduction to the FYI notes	3/90	1150

For more information

An Internet bibliography has been compiled by the librarian of the University of North Carolina Chapel Hill Institute for Academic Technology. It is available via `ftp gandalf.iat.unc.edu` [192.154.79.4], login: **anonymous**, get `/guides/irg-14.txt`. Alternatively, it is available via `ftp sunsite.unc.edu` [152.2.22.81], login: **anonymous**, get `/pub/UNC-info-/AIT/irg-14.txt`. Finally, it is available on the Sunsite gopher, `telnet sunsite.unc.edu`, login: **gopher**, UNC-CH Information and Facilities menu.

APPENDIX B:
CHOICE PRODUCTS

The envelope please...

Glossary of terms

Recommendation

Means that I currently use, or have used, this product on a regular basis, and that I was, or am, happy with it. Of course, your experience may be different; and if so, send me mail at `aboba@world.std.com`, `subject:` `suggestions` to express your opinion.

Suggestion

Means that I checked this product out only briefly, or have heard or read good things about it from people I trust, and therefore, you should take the suggestion with a grain of salt. Again, if your experience is different, please let me know.

Downright Speculation

Means that neither I nor anyone I trust has tried this product and therefore it's a shot in the dark. However, it is a product that meets an important need and so is worth knowing about. Caveat emptor!

Chapter 1 – Overview

This portion includes reviews of user groups and CD-ROM products.

User Groups

Recommendation
BMUG   **$45/year**

The BMUG newsletter is the *Reader's Digest* of the Mac world, offering reprints of the best articles from other user groups, magazines, and newsletters. BMUG has SIGs that meet at least once a month, and a weekly main meeting in Berkeley where vendors present their stuff to a notoriously ill-mannered peanut gallery, with a raffle at the end.

BMUG also meets once a month in San Francisco and the South Bay, and offers a Helpline and BBS for members.

BMUG; 1442A Walnut St. #62, Berkeley, CA 94709-1496; (510)549-2684, BBS: (510)849-2684, fax: (510)849-9026

Downright Speculation
WUGNET

WUGNET (Windows User Group NETwork) publishes a bimonthly journal on Windows, and offers individual, corporate, and group memberships.

Windows User Group Network (WUGNET); P.O. Box 1967, Media, PA 19063; (215)565-1861, fax: (215)565-7106, email: `76457.2064@compuserve.com`

Organizations for the online community

The electronic communications medium is evolving from the preserve of educated middle-class citizens in developed countries to a global crossroads. This is happening ahead of the development of rules to govern the community we are so rapidly creating. To a certain extent the electronic frontier resembles the Wild West, with sheriffs, gunslingers, preachers, and ordinary citizens struggling to mold the frontier community. Luckily there are also nonpartisan organizations exploring the long-term issues.

Computer Professionals for Social Responsibility

CPSR is a California 501.c.3 nonprofit organization that is concerned with the social issues of computing in general, including use of computers in defense applications, workplace automation, and the impact of computers on privacy and freedom.

CPSR; P.O. Box 717, Palo Alto, CA 94302, email: cpsr@csli.stanford.edu, (415)322-3778, fax: (415)322-3709. To subscribe to the mailing list on work and computers, type `mail listserv@sunnyside.com`. When the mail program starts, type the following command in the body of the message: `help`. For the mailing list on intellectual property, type `mail int-prop-request@jf.eng.sun.com`.

Free Software Foundation

The Free Software Foundation is a loosely associated group of people led by Richard Stallman who believe that access to excellent software should be free and are willing to contribute to that goal by writing it. The Free Software Foundation puts out a series of tools under the GNU label (which stands for GNU is Not UNIX). These include GNU Emacs, GNU C, GNU UUCP, and GNU AWK (GAWK), to name a few. GNU Software is distributed under a CopyLeft agreement.

The Free Software Foundation; email: gnu@prep.ai.mit.edu.

League for Programming Freedom

The League for Programming Freedom, also led by Richard Stallman, focuses on the legal and social issues surrounding access to software, such as "look and feel," copyrights, and software patents.

League for Programming Freedom; 1 Kendall Square #143, P.O. Box 9171, Cambridge, MA 02139; email: league@prep.ai.mit.edu.

Internet Society

The Internet Society is a nonprofit organization for those interested in the present and future of the Internet global computer network. The society provides assistance and support to groups and organizations involved in the use, operation, and evolution of the Internet. The society also produces a regular newsletter and holds an annual meeting.

The Internet Society; 1895 Preston White Dr., Suite 100, Reston, VA 22091; (703)648-9888, fax: (703)620-0913, email: isoc@isoc.org; for information, `ftp nri.reston.va.us, cd /isoc`.

National Public Telecomputing Network (NPTN)

The NPTN encourages the deployment of free public access bulletin boards (called Free-Nets), in an effort to encourage the development of a National Public Telecomputing Network along the lines of National Public Radio. The first Free-Net, Cleveland Free-Net, was established as a partnership between Case Western Reserve University and the city of Cleveland and has become a valuable tool for increasing the effectiveness of local government, small businesses, and ordinary citizens. As of early 1993, there are 15 Free-Nets, with the number due to double in 1994. NPTN offers a number of projects and programs to its affiliates, including a Teledemocracy Project and a catalog of Cybercasting services.

By creating the Free-Net model and placing Free-Net terminals in public libraries, the NPTN has put forward a vision of how a National Research and Education Network could be extended to the general public.

T. M. Grundner, Ed.D, President, NPTN; Box 1987, Cleveland, OH 44106, email: info@ntpn.org, (216)247-5800, fax: (216)247-3328.

The Electronic Bar Association Law MUG

The Electronic Bar Association Law MUG was the first law oriented BBS and is a source of information for lawyers interested in using computers in their practices.

Law MUG, c/o Barry Lowe; 505 N. Lasalle St. #575, Chicago, Illinois 60610; BBS: (312)661-1740, FidoNet 1:115/661, LawNet 7:70/6

Electronic Frontier Foundation

students	**$20/year**
nonstudents	**$40/year**

The Electronic Frontier Foundation (EFF) was founded by Mitchell Kapor and John Barlow in July 1990 in response to a wave of arrests conducted by the Secret Service as part of Operation Sun Devil. Since then the EFF has undertaken a range of programs and activities, including a landmark suit (which they won) against the Secret Service for the unlawful search and seizure of computers, BBS systems, books and manuscripts at Steve Jackson Games in Austin, Texas. The EFF has also taken an active role in the hearings on the future of the National Research and Education Network (NREN). The EFF's focus in the policy arena is on access to ISDN service.

Information on the Electronic Frontier Foundation, as well as issues of the *EFFector Online* newsletter, is available via `ftp ftp.eff.org, cd /pub/EFF`. Questions on FTP access to EFF can be sent to `ftphelp@eff.org`. The EFF operates a forum on The WELL (`go eff`) and CompuServe (`go EFFSIG`), as well as USENET newsgroups (comp.org.eff.talk and comp.org.eff.news). To receive comp.org.eff.talk, `mail eff-talk-request@eff.org`. To add yourself to the EFF mailing list, `mail eff-request@eff.org`. To submit a posting to the moderated group, `mail eff@eff.org`. Membership is $20/year for students and $40/year for nonstudents.

The Electronic Frontier Foundation, Inc.; 1001 G St., NW, Suite 950 East, Washington, DC 20001; (202)347-5400, fax: (202)393-5500, email: `eff@eff.org`

Center for Civic Networking

Center for Civic Networking; 91 Baldwin St., Charlestown, MA 02129; (617)241-5064, email: `mfidelman@world.std.com`

Telecommunications Policy Roundtable

The Telecommunications Policy Roundtable was founded in order to address policy issues extending beyond the EFF agenda. These include issues relating to cable television, and problems of horizontal and vertical integration in new information markets. Principle organizers of the coalition include Jeff Chester of the Center for Media Education, Marc Rotenberg of Computer Professionals for Social Responsibility, and Prue Adler from the Association of Research Libraries (ARL).

Jeff Chester, Center for Media Education; P.O. Box 330039, Washington, D.C. 20033; (202)628-2620, email: `cme@digex.net`

CD-ROM

CD–ROM software for the PC is available via `ftp oak.oakland.edu, cd /pub/msdos/cdrom`.

Code of Federal Regulations

EPA (All 15 volumess)	**$695**
Federal Register	**$1950**

Counterpoint Publishing specializes in CD-ROMs of federal regulations. The Code of Federal Regulations is published annually for each of 50 agencies. In between publications, the Federal Register lists all new and proposed regulations, on a daily basis, including hearings.

Counterpoint offers annual Federal Regulations CDs for each of the 50 agencies. For those who can't get enough of this kind of thing, the EPA CD (40 CFR) represents more than 15 volumes of written material.

Federal Register CD subscribers receive a weekly CD of the Federal Register.

Counterpoint Publishing; 84 Sherman St., P.O. Box 927, Cambridge, MA 02140; (800)998-4515, fax: (617)547-9064

County and City $745

This CD is very useful for firms looking to relocate. It offers demographic and economic statistics on cities and counties across the nation.

Slater Hall Information Products; 1301 Pennsylvania Ave. NW, Suite 507, Washington, DC 20004; (202)393-2666, fax: (202)638-2248

Disclosure Corporate Snapshot $995

This database is a complete source of financial information on publicly traded U.S. corporations. It includes two years' worth of balance sheets and income statements; a five-year summary of sales, net income, and earnings per share; holdings of institutions and corporate officers; text of the annual reports, including footnotes; and listings of subsidiaries. This CD can be searched by many criteria, including SIC code, ticker symbol, or corporate name. Updates are available annually. For PC or Macintosh.

Bureau of Electronic Publishing; 141 New Rd., Parsippany, NJ 07054; (800)828-4766, technical support: (201)808-2700

National Trade $360

This CD, put out annually by the U.S. Department of Commerce, is designed to aid U.S. firms looking to export. It includes statistics on U.S. and foreign economies, background information on tariff and trade regulations, market research, and more than 100,000 other documents.

U.S. Department of Commerce; (202)482-1986

PhoneDisc
QuickRef+	**$69**
PhoneDisc Residential	**$99**
Quarterly update	**$299**
PhoneDisc Business	**$99**
Quarterly update	**$299**
PhoneDisk Reverse	**$349**
Quarterly update	**$950**

The QuickRef+ CD includes phone numbers for 100,000 businesses, associations, and organizations. The Reverse CD is a listing of 80 million U.S. residential + 9.5 million businesses. It can be searched by name, phone number, street, business, zip code, state, or city. For IBM PC only.

Digital Directory Assistance; 5161 River Rd., Building 6, Bethesda, MD 20816; (301)657-8548, fax: (301)652-7810

Bureau of Electronic Publishing; 141 New Rd., Parsippany, NJ 07054; (800)828-4766, technical support: (201)808-2700

National Directory $69

A listing of 120,000 U.S. businesses, with addresses, and telephone, fax, and telex numbers. For Macintosh.

Bureau of Electronic Publishing; 141 New Rd., Parsippany, NJ 07054; (800)828-4766, technical support: (201)808-2700

Thomas Register $1495

The Thomas Registers are the bible for manu-facturing and equipment suppliers. This CD is published annually.

Thomas Publishing Co.; 510 Penn Plaza, New York, NY 10001; (212)290-7291, fax: (212)290-7307

Zip++	**$995**
Quarterly updates	**$295**

The Zip++ CD gives the addresses and zip codes (with 4-digit extensions) of over 90 million people and businesses in the U.S.

Arc Tangent Inc.; 4200 Parliament, Suite 600, Lanham, MD 20706; (800)368-5806, fax: (301)731-0360

Libraries and education CDs

Library of Congress
database $1260

Contains more than 4 million bibliographic records for books, maps, music, serials, visual materials, and computer files cataloged by the Library of Congress from 1968 on. LAN license included.

Library of Congress, Customer Services Section, Cataloging Distribution Service; Washington, DC 20541-5017; (800)255-3666, (212)707-6100, fax: (202)707-1334

ERIC database $650

Bibliographic database covering published literature in education from 1966 on. Available for Macintosh and PC.

ERIC Clearinghouse on Information Resources; Syracuse University School of Education, 030 Huntington Hall, Syracuse, NY, 13244-2340, (315)443-3640, email: ERIC@SUVM.ACS.SYR.EDU

CBIS Federal; 7420 Fullertin Rd., Suite 110, Springfield, VA 22153-2852; (703)440-1440, (800)443-ERIC, fax: (703)440-1408

Dialog Information Services; 3460 Hillview Ave., Palo Alto, CA 94303; (800)334-2564, (415)858-3785, fax: (415)858-7069

U.S. Census 1990

The 1990 U.S. Census is available on CD-ROM, as is the TIGER map database, covering the entire U.S. This material is also available online via CompuServe and Dialog.

Customer Services; Census Bureau, Washington, DC 20233; (301)763-2074, BBS: (301)763-1580

Center for Electronic Data Analysis, University of Tennessee; 316 Stokley Management Center, Department of Marketing, Logistics, and Transportation, Knoxville, TN 37996; (615)974-5311

USENET on CD

Net News CD
Annual fee   **$349.95**
Instead of spending hours using ill-behaved news readers, why not access USENET on CD-ROM? The Net News CD subscription brings you a CD of virtually all of USENET every two weeks. Readers are available for Mac and UNIX.

Sterling Software; 1404 Fort Crook Rd. S, Bellevue, NE 68005; (800)643-NEWS, (402)291-8300, (402)291-2108, fax: (402)291-4362, email: cdnews@sterling.com

Consumer CDs

Great Literature Personal Library
$99

Although you can obtain several of the works on this CD-ROM over the Internet, if you want more than a few of them, you can probably obtain them more quickly and cheaply by purchasing this CD-ROM. The Personal Library includes the full text of 943 books, including 70 works by Shakespeare; Dante's *Divine Comedy; Aesop's Fables;* and works by Byron, Bacon, Lewis Caroll, Cervantes, Confucius, Dickens, Homer, Moliere, Plato, Plutarch, Poe, Sophocles, Thoreau, Virgil, Voltaire, Whitman, and Wordsworth. Available for PC or Mac.

Bureau of Electronic Publishing; 141 New Rd., Parsippany, NJ 07054; (800)828-4766, technical support: (201)808-2700

Phoenix-CD   **$69**

A complete library of more than 655 Mb of files for the IBM-PC, all compressed with PKZIP and checked for viruses.

Bureau of Electronic Publishing; 141 New Rd., Parsippany, NJ 07054; (800)828-4766, technical support: (201)808-2700

MegaCD-ROMs

SDN Plus   **$19**

The SDN Plus CD includes 600 Mb of software with more than 7200 files from the FidoNet Shareware Distribution Network (SDN). This CD includes *Boardwatch* Magazine Online Edition, FidoNet *FidoNews*, the WinNet, DESQview, Doors, and FidoNet software distributions. A must for any FidoNet sysop looking to set up a BBS.

MegaCD-ROM1   **$19**
MegaCD-ROM2   **$19**

The MegaCD-ROMs are collections of publicly distributable IBM software, checked for viruses. The MegaCD-ROM1 was pressed as of 1/92; the MegaCD-ROM2 disk has 65% newer or different files than the MegaCD-ROM1 disk.

Profit Press; 2956 N. Campbell Ave., Tucson, AZ 85719; (800)843-7990, (602)577-9696, fax: (602)577-9624

Walnut Creek CD-ROMs

Walnut Creek CD-ROM offers inexpensive and regularly updated CDs of the most popular Internet software archives. In a fraction of the time and cost it would take to download these files from Internet, you can have them all at your fingertips. Nice work!

Simtel20 CD   **$24.95**

Simtel20 is the Internet's largest archive of MS-DOS software. The Simtel20 CD offers a snapshot of the entire Simtel20 archive, over 640 Mb of software, with an index that describes each file. In ISO 9660 format.

Info-Mac CD-ROM   **$39.95**

Sumex-aim Info-Mac is the Internet's largest archive of Macintosh software. This CD includes more than 4000 programs from that archive, in Mac format. Since the Sumex-aim archives are maintained by experts and regularly updated, this is one of the best, if not the best, CD of publicly distributed Macintosh software.

X11R5 and GNU   **$39.95**

The source code for X11R5, comp.sources.x archives, GNU sources, and sparc binaries. In ISO 9660 format.

Source Code CD   **$39.95**

USENET source archives, the UNIX-C archive from Simtel20, lots of MS–DOS source code—600 Mb in all. In ISO 9660 format.

CICA Windows CD   **$24.95**

140 Mb of Windows software from the CICA Windows archive at Indiana University. In ISO 9660 format.

AB20 Amiga CD   **$24.95**

130 Mb of software from the ab20.larc.nasa.gov Amiga archives, just before it went offline. Includes comp.sources.Amiga and comp.binaries.Amiga. Not compatible with CDTV. In ISO 9660 format.

OS/2 CD   **$24.95**

150 Mb of OS/2 software from the novell.com and hobbes.nmsu.edu archives. In ISO 9660 format.

Project Gutenberg CD   **$24.95**

Several thousand literary works in plain ASCII.

Bibliotech CD   **$39.95**

Another CD of literary works.

GIFS Galore CD   **$24.95**

More than 6000 color images with viewers for MS-DOS, Windows, Mac, Amiga, Atari-ST, NeXT, Sparc, DECStation, and X11. In ISO 9660 format.

Walnut Creek CD-ROM; 1547 Palos Verdes, Suite 260, Walnut Creek, CA 94596; (800)786-9907, (510)947-5996, fax: (510)674-0821, email: `rab@cdrom.com`. Current version of the catalog is available via `ftp cdrom.com, cd /pub/catalog`. Shipping and handling is $5/order for U.S./Canada, $10 for overseas, and $15 for express airmail.

Coyote Data CD-ROMs

Simtel20 CD

This SIMTEL20 CD is updated quaterly, and offers keyword and category search capabilities.

Coyote Data, Ltd.; 1142 North Main, Rochester, MI 48307, (800)451-7093, (303)656-8265, fax: (313)651-4071, email: `71756.444@compuserve.com`.

InfoMagic CD-ROMs

InfoMagic offers CD-ROMs oriented toward UNIX and the Internet.

UNIX CD   **$50**

This CD-ROM includes 386BSD v0.1 with patches, LINUX, X-Windows ports for both, GNU software, and DOS utilities for compress and tar. In ISO-9660 format with Rockridge extensions.

Internet CD   **$50**

This CD-ROM includes RFC's, IEN's, NetInfo documentation, the BSD NET/2 tape, and documentation on WinSock, packet drivers, GNU and X source code, and UNIX Internet software. It also includes RF's in HyperText for Windows.

InfoMagic, Inc.; `Joel@InfoMagic.com`

CD-ROM catalogs

CD-ROM Handbook

The most complete free catalog of CD-ROM I've seen, covering products from more than 150 vendors. Includes CD-ROMs for libraries, business, science, education, and recreation. 189 pages.

EBSCO Subscription Services; P.O. Box 325, Topsfield, MA 01983; (508)887-6667, fax: (508)887-3923

Dialog Database Catalog

A catalog of databases available on the Dialog online service, many of which are now on CD-ROM via Dialog ONDISC.

Dialog Information Services; 3460 Hillview Ave., Palo Alto, CA 94303; (800)334-2564, (415)858-3785, fax: (415)858-7069

Directory of CD-ROM Databases

A catalog of CD-ROMs related to international business, social sciences, health sciences, health and safety, and food and agriculture.

SilverPlatter Information, Inc.; 100 River Ridge Dr., Norwood, MA 02062-5026; (617)769-2599, (800)343-0064, fax: (617)769-8763

Educational Resource Guide

Oriented toward educators; a catalog of teaching tools in many media: videos, films, videodiscs, software, and CD-ROMs.

Modern; 5000 Park St. N., St. Petersburg, FL 33709; (800)243-6877, fax: (813)546-9323

Chapter 2 – Modems, Cables and Software

Software archives

Information and software on Macintosh communications is available via `ftp sumex-aim.stanford.edu, cd /info-mac/comm.`

Information and software relating to the shareware version of Telix is available via `ftp oak.oakland.edu, cd /pub/msdos/telix.`

Information and software relating to the shareware version of QMODEM is available via `ftp oak.oakland.edu, cd /pub/msdos/qmodem.`

Information and software relating to Prodigy is available via `ftp oak.oakland.edu, cd /pub/msdos/prodigy.`

Laptop stuff

Downright Speculation
Laptop Catalog   **$2**

A catalog of useful equipment for laptop owners.

The Complete Portable, Inc.; 505 Shawn Lane, Prospect Heights, IL 60070; (800)328-4827 ext. 3317, (612)944-8404, fax: (708)577-6551

Downright Speculation
Hotel kits

Computer Products Plus, Inc.; 16351 Gophard St., Huntington Beach, CA 92647; (714)847-1799, fax: (714)848-6850

Wake-up equipment

Downright speculation
Remote switch   **$69**

This remote switch will work with any machine, has a 1500-watt rating, and can turn a computer on or off from a touchtone phone.

Deltronix Enterprises; 26861 Trabuco #E161C, Mission Viejo, CA 92691; (714)380-8969 ext. 2, BBS: (714)837-9677 ($10 savings for online order)

Downright Speculation
Computer Sentinel   **$169**

Computer Sentinel monitors your computer and automatically reboots a BBS if it locks up.

Access Solutions Corporation; 18 Ivy Lane, Cherry Hill, NJ 08002; (609)667-7628, BBS: (609)667-5652

Suggestion
**Farallon remote
wakeup cable**   **$31**

Farallon doesn't sell standard cables; however, the remote wakeup cable also doubles as a hardware handshake cable, which is a real asset if your machine can be woken up via ADB).

The Mac Zone; (800)248-0800.

Farallon Computing; 2470 Mariner Square Loop, Alameda, CA 94501; (510)814-5100 (main office), (510)814-5000 (customer service), fax: (510)814-5020

Downright Speculation
PowerKey   **$64**
PowerKey Remote   **$32**

PowerKey Remote lets you wake up a Macintosh SE, SE/30, or other machine that can't be turned on via ADB. PowerKey allows you to turn your peripherals on from a Mac II keyboard and turn them off with Shutdown.

MacConnection; (800)334-4444

General electronics

ORA Electronics; 9410 Owensmouth Ave., Dept. 44, P.O. Box 4029, Chatsworth, CA 91313; (818)772-4433, fax: (818)718-8626

JDR MicroDevices; 1238 South Bascom Ave., San Jose, CA 95128; (408)280-7144, fax: (408)947-8234

Fry's Electronics; 340 Portage Ave., Palo Alto, CA; (415)496-6000, fax: (415)496-6044

Fry's Electronics; 1177 Kern Ave., Sunnyvale, CA; (408)733-1770, fax: (408)725-6800

Fax modems – sending and receiving

Suggestion
US Robotics Sportster Mac 'N Fax
V.32*bis*/V.42*bis*/Fax   **$199**

The recent price reductions by US Robotics make the Sportster Mac 'N Fax modem the hobbyist modem against which all others will be compared. This modem lacks features of the Courier line, such as support for the proprietary HST protocol. Still, the modems have been performing well, and customers report few problems.

US Robotics; 8100 N. McCormick Blvd., Skokie, IL 60076-2999; (708)933-5501, fax: (708)982-0823, BBS: (708)982-5092

PC fax software

Suggestion
PaperWorks v1.0   **$249.95**

PaperWorks lets you control your PC by faxing specially coded forms. PaperWorks scans received faxes and performs a data-store, -distribute, or -retrieve function in response to commands entered on the special forms. Supported functions include recall of documents by fax and storage of incoming faxes for subsequent distribution to multiple locations. Supports the Intel Satisfaxtion board, the Complete Fax and Complete Communicator boards from Complete PC, and the CEI proFax from Singapore Technologies.

Xerox; (800)432-9329

Downright Speculation
FaxMaster   **$149**

This package includes character recognition software that will convert a fax to ASCII format, Microsoft Excel format, or Rich Text Format. Since received faxes are often huge files, it includes a feature called SuperCompression that lets you squeeze them down by a ratio of 30 to 1. Faxmaster requires 4 Mb disk space to install.

Caere Corp; 100 Cooper Court, Los Gatos, CA 95030; (408)395-7000, (800)535-7226, fax: (408)354-2743

PC fax modems

Suggestion
ZyXEL U-1496E   **$300**

The U-1496E is an external V.32*bis*/V.42*bis*/FAX modem that supports 14.4 Kbps Fax (Group 3), Caller ID, fall-back/fall-forward rate negotiation, automatic call-back, and a five-year warranty. Versions are available with Macintosh, DOS, or Windows fax software.

ZyXEL USA; 4920 E. LaPalma Ave., Anaheim, CA 92807; (714)693-0808, fax: (714)693-0705, BBS: (714)693-0762

Suggestion
Intel SatisFaxtion 400e   **$499**

The Satisfaxtion board is an internal V.32*bis*/V.42*bis*/fax modem for the PC that includes its own processor and memory, so that it won't slow down your machine. It supports CAS and is compatible with a large number of fax applications, such as PaperWorks and Faxmaster.

Intel Corp.; CO3-11, 5200 N.E. Elam Young Pkwy., Hillsboro, OR 97124-6497; (800)538-3373, (503)696-8080

Fax machines – receiving

Suggestion
Fax Busters

We don't want to poop anyone's party, but a fax machine still can't be beat for receiving faxes. The fax machine at the BMUG office has behaved like a champ, despite enduring amazing amounts of abuse.

They've never been sorry they didn't get a fax modem instead.

If you're going to be buying a fax machine, you might consider getting a discontinued model and saving a few bucks. Fax Busters specializes in buying discontinued models and bringing them to you at low prices.

Fax Busters, U.S. Communications Corp.; 19 Driscoll Dr., Framingham, MA 01701; (508)877-3622

Fax/voice switch

Downright Speculation
Autoswitch TF 300
Facsimile Switcher   **$119.95**

If you have a fax modem and an answering machine and you don't want to get another phone line, this is the thing. The Autoswitch can detect an incoming Fax, or else transfer the call to your answering machine, which you plug into the Autoswitch.

Command Communications; 10800 E. Bethany Dr., Aurora, CO 80014; (303)750-6434, fax: (303)750-6437

Modems for use with UUCP

Recommendation
Telebit WorldBlazer   **$635**

The WorldBlazer is a V.32*bis*/V.42*bis*/*Fax* modem from Telebit that also supports MNP 5 and Turbo PEP. It also supports *protocol spoofing*, which dramatically boosts the speed of UUCP communications. This is the modem you want for communicating via UUCP at the fastest possible speed. I don't know why other modem makers don't support protocol spoofing on their V.32*bis*/V.42*bis* modems. Do you?

Telebit; 1315 Chesapeake Terrace, Sunnyvale, CA 94089; (800)835-3248, fax: (408)734-3333

UUNET Technologies, Inc.; 3110 Fairview Park Dr., Suite 570, Falls Church, VA 22042; (703)204-8000, fax: (703)204-8001, email: info@uunet.uu.net

AnDATAco; 940 Enchanted Way, Suite 104, Simi Valley, CA 93065; (805)523-9191, fax: (805)581-6079

Modems – bulletin board/sysop use (non-UUCP)

Recommendation
Dual Standard
HST/V.32bis/V.42bis/16.8K $500

The Mercedes Benz of modems. No US Robotics Modem has ever failed while in service in "The BMUG Zone," the Bermuda Triangle of the computer world. If you can afford one, buy it, and don't ever worry about modems again. If you can't, go for one of the lower-speed models, pick up a refurbished one from USR, or buy a used one from a local sysop.

A combination of sysop discounts, V.32*bis* (faster than ordinary V.32 by half), V.42*bis* error correction, compatibility with most BBSes, and a new 16.8K proprietary HST mode makes the Dual Standard HST/V.32*bis*/V.42*bis* /16.8K the ultimate modem.

US Robotics, 8100 N. McCormick Blvd., Skokie, IL 60076; (800)237-5330, (800)342-5877, (708)982-5010, fax: (708)982-5235

Portable modems

Suggestion
WorldPort 2496   **$379**

Another battery-powered pocket-size wonder. It supports V.42*bis*, has a power-saver mode, and multiple file/fax sending. Comes with menu-driven software.

US Robotics, 8100 N. McCormick Blvd., Skokie, IL 60076; (800)342-5877, (708)982-5010, fax: (708)982-5235

ISDN adapters

Suggestion
ISDN Adapter (Sysop price) $495

This adapter supports the National ISDN 1 standard, and can handle up to 38.4 Kbps in asynchronous mode, or 64 Kbps in synchronous mode.

Hayes Microcomputer Products, Inc., ISDN Technologies; 501 Second St., Suite 300, San Francisco, CA 94107; (415)974-5544, fax: (415)543-5810, BBS: (800)874-2937

Windows communications drivers

Downright Speculation
HiCom/9 $99

The HiCom/9 serial port driver for Window 3.1 provides support for multiport boards such as the DigiBoard and Comtrol cards.

Cherry Hill Software; 300 East Greentree Road, Suite 217, Marlton, NJ 08053; (609)983-1414, fax: (609)983-4188

Downright Speculation
Windows Communication Device Driver
                                              $59

This driver supports up to nine communication ports on various interrupts.

QuaTech, Inc.; 662 Wolf Ledges Parkway, Akron, OH 44311; (800)553-1170, (216)434-3154, fax: (216)434-1409

Personal communicators

This entry in choice products is ridiculous because most of these products haven't even shipped yet. Still, because we know you want one of these *so* badly, we've included this info so you can pester the firms involved and hope to be the first in line when the products do come out.

Downright Speculation
AT&T/EO communicator
EO 440 $1999
EO 880 $2999

These products are based on the AT&T Hobbit processor and the Go operating system, and include support for General Magic's Telescript. It supports pagers, voice mail, fax, and electronic mail. The EO 440 weighs 2.2 pounds and includes 4 Mb RAM and 8 Mb ROM, where the mail, fax, and networking software resides; a PCMIA slot; a microphone; room for an optional V.32*bis* modem and a 20 Mb hard disk. Cellular communications is also optional. The AT&T communicators are tablet-size units, much too large to carry around in your pocket.

AT&T Microelectronics, Personal Communications Systems Division; 4994 Patrick Henry Dr., Santa Clara, CA 94954; (800)372-2447, ext. 848, fax: (215)778-4106

EO, Inc.; 800A East Middlefield Rd., Mountain View, CA 94043; (415)903-8100, fax: (415)903-8190

Recommendation
HP100LX $745/$595

I've been using the HP95LX (now available in a 1 Mb version) for almost two years now, and I love it. The HP100LX is an improved version, with an 80 column screen instead of 40 columns. This is a real PC that runs every DOS application that will fit on it. Considering that it comes with cc:Mail Mobile, Lotus 1-2-3 v2.4, a calendar, a memo writer, a phone book, a calculator, a filer/setup program, and a stripped-down communications program, the price is very reasonable.

There are optional packages that allow you to communicate between the HP100LX and your home PC or Macintosh; add a radio communications capability; add additional RAM; and communicate via a modem. There is even a version of KA9Q that allows you to put the HP100 on the Internet via SLIP! I'm just waiting for the first complete BBS package for it, myself.

Hewlett-Packard Co.; 3000 Hanover St., Palo Alto, CA 94304; (800)443-1254, Dept. 785, (415)857-1501

Motorola Paging and Wireless Data Group; 1500 N.W. 22nd Ave., Boynton Beach, FL 33426; (407)364-2000

Newton

Although the Newton has gotten a lot of bad press, it is still the harbinger of things to come. When Apple adds CD-ROM capability, access to Apple Online Services, and vendors develop new software for it, it is likely that sales will surge. In particular, Newton will support General Magic's Telescript, which will add a new dimension to the online experience. The Newton is the only personal communicator with a prayer of getting me to give up my HP95LX.

Apple Computer, Inc.; 20525 Mariani Ave., Cupertino, CA 95014; (408)996-1010

Mac network fax software

Suggestion
FAXstfNET $495

This software lets Macs on an AppleTalk network have common access to a fax modem. It supports 14,400 bps send/receive modems, background send/receive, scheduled transmission, and broadcast.

STF Technologies, Inc.; P.O. Box 81, Concordia, MO 64020; (816)463-2021; fax: (816)463-7958

Modems – portable

Suggestion
Global Village PowerPort Gold

This is the V.32*bis*/V.42*bis* modem for the PowerBook.

Global Village Communications; 685 East Middlefield Rd., Building B, Mountain View, CA 94043; (415)390-8200, fax: (415)390-8200

Cables

Suggestion
Celestin Company
Hardware Handshaking Cable   **$14**

Celestin Company has the lowest prices we've seen for a Macintosh hardware handshake cable. They also make other cables on request.

Celestin Company; 1152 Hastings Ave., Port Townsend, WA 98368, (206)385-3767, fax: (206)385-3586, orders: (800)835-5514, email: celestin@netcom.com

NuBus Serial Port Boards – Macintosh

Recommendation
Hurdler Serial Boards
2 port	**$299**
4 port	**$379**

These are the NuBus serial port boards to get if you're on a budget. They only go up to 38,400 bps, but that's fast enough for BBS use. Software is also provided for accessing the ports via HyperCard, the Comm Toolbox, the Control Panel, or FKEYS. These are the most popular boards for use with FirstClass.

Creative Solutions; 4701 Randolph Rd., Suite 12, Rockville, MD 20852; (301)984-0262, (800)367-8465, fax: (301)770-1675

Downright Speculation
DigiCHANNEL Nu/Xi
4 port	**$995**
8 port	**$1295**

If you're intending to run eight or more serial ports under A/UX, you'll find that the field thins out quickly. The DigiCHANNEL Nu/Xi is pricey, but it's got its own 68000 on the board running at 12 MHz, along with 256K of RAM, and 128K of ROM. The DigiCHANNEL has four DMA channels and can run in asynchronous as well as synchronous mode. This board also runs under Mac OS.

DigiBoard; 6400 Flying Cloud Drive, Eden Prairie, MN 55344; (612)943-9020, fax: (612)943-5343, BBS: (612)943-0812

Downright Speculation
AXiON serial switch   **$159**

The AXiON serial switch lets you connect three serial devices to one of the Mac's serial ports and switch among them via a control panel device. Don't change cables again!

AXiON; 1150 Kifer Rd., Sunnyvale, CA 94086; (408)522-1900, fax: (408)522-1908

Communications software – Macintosh

Recommendation
ZTerm v0.90
Shareware   **$30**
(BMUG Disk: Telecom A1)

ZTerm is Mac software like it used to be – simple, and as fast as a bat out of hell. For novice users looking for a reasonably priced telecommunications program, ZTerm simply cannot be beat. It's hard to select the wrong options or make a mistake; and menus are sensibly arranged and don't proliferate like a bad dream.

David P. Alverson; 5635 Cross Creek Court, Mason, OH 45040

BMUG; 1442A Walnut St. #62, Berkeley, CA 94709-1496; (510)549-2684, BBS: (510)849-2684, fax: (510)849-9026

Suggestion

Smartcom II   **$100**
Sidegrade   **$45**

Although I don't use it, I got quite a few letters recommending that I leave Smartcom II out of the first edition. However, its proponents claim that Smartcom II is fast, inexpensive, and user-friendly.

Hayes Microcomputer Products, Inc.; 5835 Peachtree Corners East, Norcross, GA 30092; (404)840-9200, Fax: (404)441-1238, BBS: (800)874-2937, (404)446-6336

Recommendation

MacIntercomm v1.1   **$129**

If you are plagued by aborted transfers, then MacIntercomm will cure what ails you. It is optimized to run in the background, and nothing (except rebooting) will slow it down, not even formatting a floppy. The ANSI emulation in MacIntercomm is also the best available, enabling blinking and full 16-color ANSI. Although I miss certain ZTerm features such as Smart MacBinary and correct typing of .GIF, .ZIP, and .ARC downloads, and the VT100 emulation has some quirks, the solidity and speed of file transfers in this product has me addicted.

New World Computing; 20301 Ventura Blvd., Suite 200, Woodland Hills, CA 91364, (818)999-0606 ext. 218, fax: (818)593-3455, Support: (818)999-0607, email: shannon@inter.com

Suggestion

MacKermit   **Free**
(BMUG Disk: Telecom D1)

MacKermit is a full implementation of Kermit for the Macintosh, including server mode and VT100 emulation.

Bill Catchings, Frank da Cruz, Bill Schilit, Matthias Aebi, Paul Placeway; Columbia University; email: Info-Kermit@cunixc.cc.columbia.edu.

Suggestion

MicroPhone Pro   **$295**
Microphone II v4.0   **$195**

Using MicroPhone is like driving one of those James Bond cars, the kind that can fly, glide over the water, and act as a submarine if need be. It now supports XCMDs, Icons, custom dialog boxes, XMODEM, YMODEM, ZMODEM, and KERMIT, as well as Apple Events. In order to support development of further Internet capabilities, Software Ventures has split the MicroPhone product line into a high-end package,

called Microphone Pro, and a low-end package, called Microphone II. The Pro package includes Internet capabilities, while the Microphone II line does not.

Software Ventures; 2907 Claremont Ave., Berkeley, CA 94705; (510)644-3232, (800)336-6478 (inside CA), (800)336-6477 (outside CA), fax: (510)848-0885

Communications software – PC

Suggestion

QMODEM Pro   **$99**

Qmodem Pro offers an amazing array of features. It fully supports the mouse via pull-down menus and resizable windows. It includes an offline mail reader called OLX which allows for viewing multiple QWK packets and conferences; supports faxing of text or PCX files with any Class 2 fax modem; offers gateways to MCI Mail and CompuServe; supports 125 modems; emulates TTY, ANSI, WYSE 50, VT 102, 220, 302, and TVI 925 terminals; supports XMODEM YMODEM KERMIT CompuServe B, and ZMODEM protocols; and includes a scripting language. But can it brew coffee?

Mustang Software, Inc.; P.O. Box 2264, Bakersfield, CA 93303; (805)395-0223, fax: (805)395-0713, BBS: (805)395-0650. GEnie: Mustang RoundTable; CompuServe GO PCVENA; America Online: MUSTANG, email: jim.harrer@mustang.com

Recommendation

TELIX v3.21   **$41**
Manual   **$15**

TELIX is inexpensive and has the features that most beginners want. It supports TTY, ANSI, VT102, VT52, AVATAR, and ANSI emulation; CIS Quick B, KERMIT, Modem 7, SEAlink Telink, XMODEM, YMODEM, and ZMODEM protocols; the SALT scripting language; DOS shells; and much more. The commercial version is due out soon, and will support RIP.

deltaComm Development; P.O. Box 1185, Cary, NC 27512-1185; (919)460-4556, (800)859-8000, fax: (919)460-4531, BBS: (919)481-9399

Recommendation
PC Kermit   **Free**

It is amazing how many of the leading PC
communications packages still cannot perform
passable VT100 emulation. PC-Kermit is free and it
works. The latest version includes TCP/IP support,
which makes it possible to download a file over the
Internet.

EXEC-PC; P.O. Box 57, Elm Grove, WI 53122;
(414)789-4200, BBS: (414)789-4210

Suggestion
DynaComm Asynch v3.1   **$249**

DynaComm offers a scripting language; GIF and
REGIS viewers, ZMODEM supports, TCP/IP, and
solid VT100 to VT340 emulation. The dialing
directory comes with numbers for many BBSes. If
you are looking for a full-featured package, this may
be the one for you.

FutureSoft, Inc.; 12012 Wick Chester Lane, Suite
600, Houston, TX 77079-9842; (713)496-9400, fax:
(713)496-1090

Recommendation
Procomm Plus for Windows   **$149**

Procomm Plus for Windows is the package that most
users will want to purchase. It allows you to view
GIF files as you download them, it's is compatible
with the Aspect scripting language of DOS Procomm,
and it offers VT100 emulation and ZMODEM.

Datastorm Technologies; P.O. Box 1471, Columbia,
MO 65205; (800)326-4999, (314)443-3282, fax:
(314)875-0595

Suggestion
WinQVT   **Free**

WinQVT can emulate a VT220, VT100, or VT52
terminal, and can upload or download via the
KERMIT, XMODEM, YMODEM, and ZMODEM
protocols. Scripting is not supported. The network
version of the software is also quite something,
supporting graphical Internet access over TCP/IP.

QPC Software; P.O. Box 226, Penfield, NY 14526

EXEC-PC; P.O. Box 57, Elm Grove, WI 53122;
(414)789-4200, BBS: (414)789-4210

Downright Speculation
UW/PC v1.02   **Free**

UW/PC is the IBM-PC–compatible version of the UW
multiwindowing terminal emulator first developed
for the Macintosh by John Bruner. UW/PC can
emulate an ADM31 or VT52 terminal but does not
support ANSI emulation or file transfer. UW/PC
utilizes John Bruner's UW server code running on
the UNIX side, so you first will need to install the
UNIX back end of UW under UNIX in order to use it.

UW/PC: Rhys Weathersley; 5 Horizon Dr., Jamboree
Heights QLD 4074, Australia; email:
`rhys@batserver.cs.uq.oz.au`

UW UNIX server: John Bruner; Lawrence Livermore
National Laboratory, P.O. Box 5503, L-276,
Livermore, CA 94550; email: `jdb@mordor.s1.gov`

Available via `ftp world.std.com, get`
`/sources/pc/comm/uw.`

Remote control

Recommendation
Carbon Copy Plus PC   **$119**
Carbon Copy for Windows   **$79**
(limited-time offer)

I've used this one under an incredible number of
circumstances, and it has always pulled through.
Carbon Copy is simply the most bulletproof of all
the PC remote-control programs.

MicroCom; 500 River Ridge Dr., Norwood, MA
02062-5028; (617)551-1000, (800)822-8224, fax:
(617)551-1021, international fax: (617)551-1007

Downright Speculation
Screenlink Twinpack   **$99**
Network version (unlimited zones) **$299**

ScreenLink was formerly the Macintosh version of
Carbon Copy. This is a better value than Timbuktu
Remote, because you get two copies of the software
in each package, and because it works over both
AppleTalk and remote serial hookups. It's like
getting two copies each of Timbuktu and Timbuktu
Remote in every box; for large installations the
savings can add up to serious money.

Datawatch Corporation; Triangle Software Division,
P.O. Box 51489, Durham, NC 27717; (919)490-1277,
ext. 610, fax: (919)490-6672, BBS: (919)419-1602

Online services

101 Online
Basic Service	**$9.95/month**
Advanced services	**$10–75/hour**

101 Online is based on French Minitel technology. The advantage of this is that you can hook into the services of the French Minitel system, making it an attractive way to do business in France. The disadvantage is that the service requires a Minitel terminal, it cannot be used via your personal computer, it is very slow, and it can be incredibly expensive. The service is billed through Pacific Bell, and although the monthly fee is only $9.95, advanced services (which comprise most of what is available) cost extra. Charges for advanced services are not given on menu selections; therefore, you don't see the charge rate for the service until after you've made the menu selection. No Internet gateway is available.

101 Online; 200 California St., Sixth Floor, San Francisco, CA 94111; (800)310-1101

AT&T Mail
Maintenance	**$3/month**
Per message	**$0.50**
(1K or less)	
1001–2000k bytes	**$0.80**
2001–3000k bytes	**$0.05/1K**

AT&T Mail is a message-oriented service that charges by the message, not by the hour. However, their rates are higher than MCI Mail's.

AT&T Mail; (800)624-5672

America Online
Maintenance (includes 5 hrs)	**$9.95/month**
Additional hours	**$3.50/hour**

AOL is moderately priced and offers a graphical user interface on both the Mac and the PC (Geoworks and Windows). Among the more interesting services are Mercury Center (San Jose Mercury) and Chicago Online, which focus on the Peninsula and Chicago, respectively. There is now an Internet gateway, (aol.com) allowing you to send and receive mail from all over the world. However, the gateway is unreliable and the message size limitations are so severe as to preclude use of the gateway for anything other than mail. The PC version of AOL can only handle incoming messages up to 8K; the Macintosh and Apple II versions can handle up to 27K. Incoming messages are limited to 32K.

America Online; 8619 Westwood Center Dr., Vienna, VA 22182; (703)448-8700, (800)827-6364 ext. 5181 (signup)

American PeopleLink
Prime	**$17.95/hour**
Nonprime (1200)	**$5.95/hour**
Nonprime (2400)	**$9.95/hour**
Nonprime (9600)	**$18/hour**

American PeopleLink has outstanding Amiga forums and software libraries. There is no Internet gateway.

American PeopleLink; 165 N. Canal St., Suite 950, Chicago, IL 60606; (800)524-0100

BIX
Monthly	**$13**
Daytime hourly	**$9**
Off-peak hourly	**$3**
(via Tymnet)	
BIXnavigator	**$9.95**

BIX is a favorite among software and hardware engineers, and is therefore a very good place to get technical information. BIX offers a Windows terminal emulator called BIXNavigator, and an Internet link is now available.

Delphi Internet Services, Inc.; 1030 Massachusetts Ave., Cambridge, MA 02138; (617)491-3342, (800)695-4775: To join BIX, call (800)695-4882, login: **bix**, Name? **bix.byte**

BRS: After Dark
Signon	**$75**
Monthly Minimum	**$12**
Hourly (off-peak)	**$10–25**

BRS is a bibliographic online service offering access to more than eighteen major business databases, including Disclosure and ABI/Inform. No Internet gateway is available.

BRS Information Technologies; 8000 Westpark Dr., McLean, VA 22102; (703)442-3870

CompuServe
Startup	**$39.95**
Alternative Plan rates:	
Maintenance	**$2.50/month**
1200/2400 bps	**$12.50/hour**
9600 bps	**$22.50/hour**
Basic Services Plan:	
Maintenance:	**$8.95/month**
Extended services:	
1200/2400 bps	**$8/hour**
9600 bps	**$16/hour**

Although it is definitely overpriced, CompuServe offers a tremendous number of services. There are more vendor support forums on CIS than on any other service. Through IQUEST you can search trademark and other databases. In the financial arena, CIS services include online brokerages such as Quick & Reilly and Max Ule, and access to corporate information via Standard & Poor's Disclosure, Value Line, and Institutional Brokers' Estimate System. CompuServe's Information Manager software, available for both the Macintosh and Windows, allows access to a fraction of services via a graphical user interface; the remaining services are accessed via a terminal emulation window. Two rates structures are available. The Basic Services Plan offers unlimited usage of a limited number of Basic Services for $8.95/month, with other services costing extra. The Alternative Plan offers a lower monthly maintenance rate, with all services being billed on an hourly basis at higher rates.

CompuServe, Inc.; 5000 Arlington Centre Blvd., P.O. Box 20212, Columbus, OH 43220: (800)848-8199, Customer service: (800)848-8990

Recommendation
Delphi

Monthly fee	
(includes first hr)	**$5.95/month**
Hourly	**$6**
20/20 plan	**$20/month**
Internet access	**$3/month**

Delphi began as the Kussmaul online encyclopedia, but has since grown into a general-purpose online service. While other commercial services talk about the Internet, but only offer gateways, Delphi is a genuine Internet service, offering FTP, Telnet, Gopher, Archie, WWW, WAIS, and more. Delphi acquired BIX from McGraw Hill last year. A graphical navigator program called Messenger-Lite is available now, with a full graphical interface in development.

Delphi Internet Services, Inc.; 1030 Massachusetts Ave., Cambridge, MA 02138; (617)491-3342, (800)695-4005. Direct dial access: (617)576-0862, (RETURN)(RETURN) Username: **your_ID** Password: **your_password**

Dow Jones News Retrieval

Startup fee	**$29.95**
Renewal (annual)	**$18**
Prime	**$12.60– $129.60/hr(!)**
Off-peak rates (8:01 PM to 6 AM):	
Tier 1 – New & Quotes	**$25/month**
Tier 2 – Forecasts & Analyses	**$25/month**
Tier 3 – General Interest	**$12.95/month**
Tiers 1 & 2	**$45/month**
Tiers 1 & 3	**$35/month**
Tiers 2 & 3	**$35/month**
Tiers 1, 2, & 3	**$49.95/month**

Dow Jones is now accessible over the Internet and now also offers a fixed monthly rate for off-peak use, which is good news since it's one of the most useful business online services around. To access DJNR over Internet type **telnet djnr.dowjones.com**. When it asks What Service? type **djnr**

Dow Jones; (609)520-4649, ext. 165, fax: (609)520-4775

GEnie

Maintenance (includes 4 hrs)	**$8.95/month**
Prime	**$9.50/hour**
Nonprime (300/1200/2400)	**$3/hour**
high speed	**$9.50/hour**

GEnie is a general-purpose online service that at one time was the least expensive online service. As a result it attracted a large number of support forums. They also offer gateways to other services such as Dow Jones News Retrieval. Prime time is 8 AM to 6 PM.

GE Information Services; 401 N. Washington St., Rockville, MD 20850; (800)638-9636

Recommendation
MCI Mail

Startup fee	**$35/year**
Message fee	**$0.50**
(500 bytes or less)	
(501 to 1K bytes)	**$0.60**
1K up to 10K	**$0.10/1K**
Over 10K	**$0.05/1K**

MCI Mail was at one time the most popular mail service because it does not charge by the hour, only by the message. Even today, MCI is a reasonable alternative for users who want to subscribe to mailing lists, since you are not charged for receiving messages, only sending them. MCI has a gateway to Dow Jones News Retrieval. The service also now supports KERMIT, ZMODEM, and 9600 bps access. Discounts are available for heavy users via a $10/month "preferred pricing" plan.

MCI Mail; 1111 19th St. NW, Washington, DC 20036; (800)444-6245

Downright Speculation
Microsoft Download Service

Technical notes are available from download from the Microsoft Download Service, reachable at (206)936-MSDL. Microsoft also maintains a CompuServe forum (GO MICROSOFT). Finally, Microsoft also offers recorded or fax answers to commonly asked questions via their FastTips line, at (206)635-7245.

Microsoft Corp.; One Microsoft Way, Redmond, WA 98052-6399; (800)443-4672, fax: (206)883-8101

Prodigy

Startup fee	**$49.95**
(with modem)	
Monthly fee	**$14.95**
(no hourly fee, includes 30 messages)	

Prodigy is the McDonald's of online services: It has served the most customers, but it's not exactly filet mignon. Prodigy supports a wide array of consumer-oriented services; however, file transfer was not supported until recently. There is now a charge for email ($0.25) beyond the 30 messages offered within the basic package. The addition of this charge resulted in a highly publicized controversy. Prodigy uses the same interface on the PC and the Mac, which means that the Mac version does not support the Macintosh interface. An Internet gateway is reportedly in the works.

Prodigy; 445 Hamilton Ave., White Plains, NY 10601; (800)776-3449, fax: (914)993-3531

Recommendation
The WELL, Sausalito, CA

Maintenance	**$15/month**
Hourly fee	**$2**

Many public access UNIX systems are drab places, where all you get when you log in is the UNIX prompt. The WELL is a public access UNIX with soul. The WELL is the only online service I know of where I learn something every time I log on. It is particularly recommended for those interested in telecommunications; this is where the experts hang out to chew the fat. The WELL is accessible over Internet as `well.sf.ca.us`.

The WELL; 27 Gate Five Rd., Sausalito, CA 94965; (415)332-4335, fax: (415)332-4927; to register, call (415)332-6106 (2400 bps) and type NEWUSER at the `login:` prompt.

Telecommunications publications

Recommendation
Boardwatch $36/year

Far and away the best publication covering the bulletin board scene. One problem though – there is so much useful information packed in every issue that you'll never want to throw the magazine away. Since Boardwatch doesn't publish an annual index, lately I've found myself frantically paging through old issues to find something I vaguely remember reading about. How about a Boardwatch CD, indexed full text?

Boardwatch; 8500 W. Bowles Ave., Suite 210, Littleton, CO 80123; (303)973-6038 (voice), fax: (303)973-3731, (303)973-4222 (Boardwatch BBS, FidoNet 1:104/555)

Suggestion
Whole Earth Review $20/year

Although Whole Earth Review is a tad too hip for me, covering everything from organic gardening to feminist poetry, it is also has a futuristic slant. The articles on telecommunications are thought-provoking and well researched. Recent topics include articles on electronic democracy, the National Research and Education Network (NREN), and electronic media and the Bill of Rights.

Whole Earth Review; P.O. Box 38, Sausalito, CA 94966-9932; (415)332-1716

Recommendation
Matrix News $30/year

Matrix News offers indepth coverage of the present and future of the Internet, as well as statistical analysis of trends. John Quarterman, author of *The Matrix*, serves as editor; the managing editor is Smoot Carl-Mitchel. This newsletter is not currently available on newsstands.

Matrix News, Matrix Information and Directory Services, Inc. (MIDS); 1120 South Capitol of Texas Highway, Building 2, Suite 300, Austin, TX 78746; (512)329-1087, fax: (512)327-1274, email: mids@tic.com

Recommendation
Wired $20/year

Don't be deceived by the terminally hip layout of this magazine. Wired writing is frequently sceptical, irreverent, and on target. It takes a global view, covering everything from cable installations in India to TechnoPork in Europe. If you only can afford one publication about the online world, this is it.

Wired; 544 Second St., San Francisco, CA 941707-1427, (415)904-0660, fax: (415)904-0669. Subscriptions: (800)SO-WIRED, email: subscriptions@wired.com

Suggestion
InterTek   **$3/issue**

InterTek presents opposing viewpoints on the *social* aspects of the ongoing telecommunications revolution. Quite a few well-known authors grace the pages of this magazine, which hopefully will become a permanent fixture.

InterTek, Steve Steinberg; 325 Ellwood Beach #3, Goleta, CA 93117

NewsWires

Recommendation
ClariNet

Full ClariNews	**$28/month**
Daily Newsbytes	**$10/month**
All products	**$35/month**

Campuswide site licenses:	
<5000 enrollment	**$175/month**
5000–20,000K enrollment	**$350/month**
20,000K+ enrollment	**$580/month**

ClariNet is an incredibly useful collection of news services that provides a daily diet of business and technology information that is vastly superior to anything you can get through TV, radio, and newspapers. With ClariNet and a graphical news reader such as uAccess, Copernicus II, COUNTERPoint, or WinQWK, it is tempting to give up reading newspapers altogether.

Prices quoted above (except for campus site licenses) are for up to 2 users. Call ClariNet for details of the volume-discount program. ClariNet's primary distributors are Anterior, UUNET, and PSI.

ClariNet Communications Corp; 4880 Stevens Creek, Suite 206, San Jose, CA 95129; (800)873-6387, fax: (408)296-1668, email: info@ClariNet.com

Downright Speculation
InfoMat   **$25/quarterly**

Over 100K of news on computers, software, and telecommunications.

Distributed on a weekly basis by Computer Shopper and USA Press BBS (913)478-9239

Recommendation
Newsbytes   **$15-80/month**
Interface software   **$35**

Newsbytes covers PCs, UNIX, business, Apple, trends, telecom, and legal issues. It can be picked up via FidoNet or a script. Interface software is available for TBBS, Major BBS, PCBoard, Coconet, WILDCAT! or RBBS. Pricing varies according to BBS size. It is distributed by AIS, (612)785-7855.

Newsbytes; 406 West Olive St., Stillwater, Minnesota 55082; (612)430-1100, fax: (612)430-0441, BBS: (612)753-5286

Downright Speculation
NYSE Quotes   **$25/month**

Distributed Monday through Friday by Boardwatch BBS; (303)973-4222

Downright Speculation
USA Today   **$25/month**
TDBS Interface   **$100**

This offers news stories on a variety of subjects, in more depth than *USA Today.*

Distributed Monday through Friday by Boardwatch BBS, (303)973-4222

Online magazines

Suggestion
Eeeek Bits   **Free**

A weekly view of the online world from a lighter perspective.

Eeeek Publishing Co., P.O. Box 331, Manhattan Beach, CA 90266, BBS: (310)371-3734

Downright Speculation
BIX Bulletin Board eXchange
Quarterly   **$49**

Byte Information eXchange; 70 Main St.,
Peterborough, NH, 03458; (603)924-9281

Recommendation
Boardwatch Magazine   **$25/month**

An electronic version of *Boardwatch* magazine.

Distributed by Boardwatch BBS; (303)973-4222

Downright Speculation
Online Digital Music Review
6 issues   **$25**

Distributed once a month during the summer, twice
a month the rest of the year by USA Press BBS;
(913)478-9239

Downright Speculation
Video Online
6 issues   **$25**

Distributed once a month during the summer, twice
a month the rest of the year by USA Press BBS;
(913)478-9239

Downright Speculation
Business Sense
6 issues   **$25**

Distributed free by USA Press BBS if you get Video
Online and Online Digital Music Review; (913)478-
9239

Chapter 3 – Diagnostic Software

MSD v2.00   **Free w/Windows**

MicroSoft Diagnotics (MSD) is an undocumented
diagnostic package that comes with Windows 3.0. It
will tell you lots of things about your memory,
video, network, OS, Mouse, adapter, disk drive, LPT
and COM ports, IRQ status, TSR programs, and
device drivers. To access it, just type MSD; it is
installed in the default Windows directory.

Microsoft Corporation; One Microsoft Way,
Redmond, WA 98052-6399; (800)443-4672, fax:
(206)883-8101

QAPlus   **$159.95**

QAPlus diagnoses hardware and LAN-configuration
problems on the PC. There is also a version for
Windows and for support professionals.

Diagsoft, Inc.; 5615 Scotts Valley Dr., Suite 140,
Scotts Valley, CA 95066; (800)DIAGSOFT, (408)438-
8247, fax: (408)438-7113

TattleTale   **Free**

John Macino's TattleTale will tell you about your
Mac's hardware configuration, installed drivers, etc.

John Mancino, Decision Maker's Software, Inc.; 1910
Joslyn Place, Boulder, CO 80304; fax: (303)449-6207,
email: 70337.2143@compuserve.com,
JGCMan@aol.com, D0391@applelink.com

Serial of Champions   **Free**

Mark Throckmorton's Serial of Champions for the
Macintosh will tell you how much time your
computer spent waiting for responses from the
remote machine, how much time the modem spent
waiting for your Mac, and what fraction of the time
you spent sending or receiving. This is helpful in
figuring out the cause of slow transfers. This utility
is exclusively available over ZiffNet/Mac.

Mark Throckmorton; 2120 Ardenne Drive, Ann
Arbor, MI 48105; (313)662-7902, email:
72220.1611@compuserve.com

Chapter 4 – Antivirus Protection and Insurance

Insurance

Recommendation
Safeware
$0 to $2000 coverage   **$49**
$5000 to $10,000   **$120**

Don't rely on homeowner's or renter's coverage to
replace your computer in the event of theft or a
natural disaster; many of those policies will not
cover these things.

Safeware; 2929 N. High St., P.O. Box 02211,
Columbus, OH 43202-2211; (800)848-3469

Security organizations

The Forum of Incident Response Teams (FIRST)

FIRST is an association of computer security response teams.

FIRST, National Computer Systems Laboratory, National Institute of Standards and Technology; A-216 Technology, Gaithersburg, MD 20899; (301)975-3359, email: `csrc@nist.gov`

Internet Computer Emergency Response Team (CERT)

CERT was created by DARPA after the Internet worm incident exposed the need for an organized response to security problems. Operators of Internet systems that have had been broken into should contact CERT; CERT maintains a 24-hour hotline.

CERT, Software Engineering Institute; Carnegie Mellon University; 5000 Forbes Ave., Pittsburgh, PA 15213; (412)268-7090, fax: (412)268-6989, email: `cert@cert.org`; documents and software available via `ftp ftp.cert.org`. For information on viruses `cd /pub/virus-l/docs`.

Mac antivirus software

Recommendation
Disinfectant v3.2   Free
(BMUG Disk: Utilities 8)

Disinfectant is both an INIT that detects virus activity and an application that disinfects your machine. Unless you work on a networked machine, in which case you will want to use Virus Blockade as well, Disinfectant and GateKeeper's Aid are all the virus protection you will need (see below). The latest version now protects against the MBDF A virus.

John Norstad, Academic Computing and Network Services, Northwestern University; email: `j-norstad@nwu.edu`

Recommendation
GateKeeper's Aid v1.2.7   Free
(BMUG Disk: Utilities 8)

GateKeeper's Aid detects and eliminates viruses such as WDEF and MBDF A. Just insert it in your system folder and forget about it. It is compatible with, and complements, Disinfectant.

Suggestion
VirusBlockade II v2.0

This is the software to get if you want to protect against viruses transmitted over the network.

Shulman Software Co.; 364 1/2 Patterson Dr., Suite 300, Morgantown, WV 26505-3202; (304)598-2090, email: `KILROY@applelink.apple.com`; `76136.667@compuserve.com`

PC antivirus software

McAffee Associates

McAffee virus scanning utilities are available via `ftp oak.oakland.edu, cd /pub/msdos/virus`

VIRUSCAN v8.9v97   Shareware, $25
VALIDATE v0.4

SCAN scans volumes for viruses in partition tables and boot sectors, in memory, and in executable files. It does this by searching for virus code patterns or by comparing against tables compiled by VALIDATE, which is included with VIRUSCAN and VHIELD, as well as Clean-Up. It can also create recovery disks to be able to restore partition tables or boot sectors. It performs a self check to protect against modification.

VSHIELD v5.1v97   Shareware, $25
VSHIELD1 v0.2
CHKSHLD v1

VSHIELD is a TSR that looks for viruses in memory, partition tables, boot sectors, system files, and itself; it also scans for viruses before programs are executed. Both VSHIELD and VSHIELD1 rely on codes compiled by VIRUSCAN. CHKSHLD sees if VSHIELD or VSHIELD1 has been loaded. VALIDATE computes Cyclic Redundancy Checks (CRCs) on files to see if the file has been modified.

Clean-Up 8.9V97   Shareware, $35

Clean-Up searches for and removes viruses identified by VIRUSCAN from boot sectors and parition tables or executable files. It protects itself against modification by using VALIDATE. It should be stored on a write-protected bootable floppy.

McAfee Associates; 2710 Walsh Ave., Suite 200, Santa Clara, CA 95051;(408)988-3832, fax: (408)970-

9727. Available via `ftp mcafee.com` (192.187.128.1), or by calling their BBS: (408)988-4004

Integrity Master v1.43

Integrity Master is a shareware file integrity system.

Available via `ftp oak.oakland.edu, get /pub/msdos/virus/i-m143.zip`.

ThunderByte

ThunderByte is a very fast shareware virus scanner.

Available via `ftp oak.oakland.edu, get /pub/msdos/virus/tbav602.zip`.

VIRx v2.8   Free

VIRx is a freeware virus-detection-only version of VPCScan, which is part of Microcom's commercial Virex software. Since VIRx can only detect viruses, not repair them, you will need to use it along with other software for full protection. VIRx is updated approximately every six weeks.

Available via `ftp oak.oakland.edu, get /pub/msdos/virus/virx28.zip`.

Virex $99.95

Microcom, Virex Information; P.O. Box 51489, Durham, NC 27717; (919)490-1277

Recommendation
The Norton Anti-virus v2.0 for DOS/Windows

Symantec Corp.; 10201 Torre Ave., Cupertino, CA 95014-2132; (408)253-9600, BBS: (408)973-9598 (300/2400), (408)973-9834 (9600), virus faxline: (310)575-5018, help with faxline: (310)477-2707

Chapter 5 – Bulletin Boards

BBS software archives

Publicly distributable BBS software for the PC is available via `ftp oak.oakland.edu, cd /pub/msdos/bbs`.

PCBOARD files are available via `ftp oak.oakland.edu, cd /pub/msdos/pcboard`

RBBS-PC files are available via `ftp oak.oakland.edu, cd /pub/msdos/rbbs-pc`.

NAPLPS files are available via `ftp oak.oakland.edu, cd /pub/msdos/naplps`.

NAPLPS graphics

Downright Speculation
Troika v1.0 $150

TeleDraw is the first general-purpose communications program to support NAPLPS graphics and the DRCS character set tables. It offers XMODEM and ZMODEM, as well as dialing directories. UUENCODE and UUDECODE are built to allow binary enclosures.

Old Colorado City Communications; 2502 W. Colorado Ave., Suite 203, Colorado Springs, CO 80904; (719)636-2040, fax: (719)593-7521, BBS: (719)632-2656, email: dave@oldcolo.com

Downright Speculation
Personality Plus $25

Personality Plus is the shareware NAPLPS terminal emulator put out by MicroStar. Since it does not offer file-transfer protocols, it is not appropriate for general use.

MicroStar Software Ltd.; 100-34 Colonade Rd. N., Nepean, Ontario Canada K2E-7J6; (613)727-5696, fax: (613) 727-9491, BBS: (613)727-5272

Downright Speculation
Turmodem $35

Turmodem is the terminal emulation program for the TurBoard BBS. It can handle external protocols such as ZMODEM, as well as TTY, ANSI, and NAPLPS modes.

Shawn Rhoads, Software@Work; P.O. Box 566491, Atlanta, GA 31156; (404)395-6525, fax: (404)395-6326, BBS: (404)395-6327

TurBoard: TeleMedia; P.O. Box 566491, Atlanta, GA 31156; (404)395-6525, BBS: (404)395-6327, (404)395-6326

Downright Speculation
WinRIP $49

WinRIP offers drawing facilities as well as an icon
editor. It can also convert Windows icons to RIP
format, and can convert Windows Metafiles to RIP.

Ken Waddon; Axis Point BBS, 17 Agricola Place,
Enfield, EN1 1DW, England; 44-81-292-3093, BBS:
44-81-292-0677, FidoNet: 2:254/43.

Other graphics

Downright Speculation
RIPTerm

RIP is a proprietary graphics protocol that competes
with NAPLPS and is supported by Telix, QMODEM
Pro, WILDCAT!, PCBOARD, and Major BBS, among
other packages.

TeleGrafix Communications, Inc.; 16458 Bolsa Chica
#15, Huntington Beach, CA 92649; (714)379-2131;
fax: (714)379-2132; BBS: (305)473-2000, Demo
Systems: ArenaBBS: (714)840-3520; Nova Central:
(714)379-9006; RIP Demo Midwest: (708)978-2777

Downright Speculation
GIF2NAP

GIF2NAP by Shawn Rhoads converts color GIF files
to NAPLPS graphics.

Shawn Rhoads, PC Atlanta BBS, (404)395-6327,
FidoNet 1:133/904.

Macintosh Bulletin Boards

Planet BMUG, Berkeley, CA—(510)849-2684

Now running the FirstClass graphical interface
software and sporting a new name, the bulletin
board of the Berkeley Macintosh User Group
remains one of the most popular hangouts for Mac
users. With more than 4500 users, it's very likely
that someone else on the system has had the same
problem as you, and messaging focuses on
troubleshooting and "how do I do this?" BMUG
membership ($45/year) is required to gain access to
the BBS.

Despite the new name, Planet BMUG offers many of
the same services as the old PC-based BBS, namely
access to UUCP mail, as well as FidoNet and
USENET Macintosh conferences. Planet BMUG is

also a hub of the OneNet Member Network. For
more information on Planet BMUG, consult *The
BMUG Online Services Reference* from BMUG, Inc.

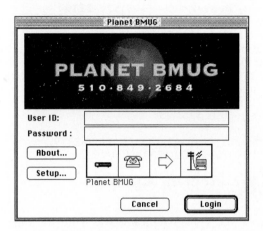

BMUG Boston, Boston, MA—(617)721-5840

Run by the former BCS-Mac Sysops, BMUG Boston is
a FirstClass BBS running on eleven phone lines, a
1.2 Gb drive from Fujitsu, and V.32*bis*/V.42*bis*
modems. Many message sections are shared with
the Planet BMUG system in Berkeley. Full access to
BMUG Boston is restricted to BMUG members. For
more information on BMUG Boston, consult *The
BMUG Online Services Reference*.

OneNet, Los Altos, CA—(415)948-1349

Run by Apple employee Scott Converse, this system
is the global hub of the rapidly expanding OneNet
Member Network, a network of FirstClass BBSes.
OneNet was the first large FirstClass BBS and is still
one of the best, getting more uploads on some days
than CompuServe or America Online. If you are a
FirstClass sysop looking to hook up to the OneNet
Member Network, this is the system to call for

information. Donations to OneNet are requested but not required.

MacCircles, Denver, CO—(303)526-2219

MacCircles is dedicated to "The Art of Conversation," as well as all things Macintosh. Sysop Pat O'Connor, long the Grand Dame of Bay Area Sysops, moved to Denver in February 1992, and the Bay Area has been missing her ever since. MacCircles runs on three phone lines, and membership costs $25/year.

MacCircles BBS, Genesee, CO; (303)526-2219, FidoNet 1:104/326, 300/1200/2400/9600 bps

Atlanta Mac User Group, Atlanta, GA—(404)727-2684

The Atlanta Mac Users Group BBS was named as one of the top 100 BBSes in the United States by *Boardwatch* Magazine in 1992. It now runs FirstClass with six lines and offers an outstanding library of files. Nonmembers can log on for 30 minutes a day and read email, but downloading is restricted to members. AMUG membership costs $30/year.

Twilight Clone, Rockville, MD—(301)946-8677

With 19 lines running on a PC under TBBS, Twilight Clone is the second-largest Macintosh BBS in the United States, and one of the central electronic gathering place for Mac users in the Washington D.C. area. The Clone carries 60 conferences on the FidoNet and USENET networks, as well as offering point access to 1000 FidoNet and USENET conferences on its mail hub, which is run as a separate machine. The Clone also offers online databases such as the King James Bible, the CIA World Fact Book, and the U.S. Postal Zip Code directory. The system has more than 780 Mb of storage. Clone membership is $60/year for up to 2 hours/day, $90 for 4 hours/day.

Heller Information Services, Inc.; P.O. Box 6669, Silver Spring, MD 20916; (301)946-8600, fax: (301)946-3269; BBS: (301)946-8677, FidoNet 1:109/716, email: clone.info@his.com

MAGIC—(416)288-1767

With a spectacular user interface built with custom icons and background PICTs, this system gets my vote as the best-looking BBS anywhere. MAGIC offers a huge file library with tens of thousands of files; access to USENET conferences, including ClariNet news wires; OneNet Member conferences; various special interest groups; and a complete set of help files.

Suggestion
AMUG BBS

AMUG membership	**$30**
BBS membership	**$25**

AMUG BBS runs on TeleFinder, with the AMUG CD-ROM mounted online. It also runs Tabby, so it's connected to FidoNet, a pretty good combination.

AMUG; P.O. Box 10593, Scottsdale, AZ 85271; (602)892-5454, info: (602)892-2402

AMUG BBS; 718 E. Campbell Ave., Gilbert, AZ 85234; guests: (602)495-1713; registered users: (602)437-9622 (Hayes Ultra), (602)926-4026 (USR HST/DS 9600)

Downright Speculation
MacTel

Judging from the volume of mail in the MacUK echo, these systems must handle immense traffic. No other system in Europe comes close.

MacTel Metro, London, UK, 44-81-543-8019, FidoNet: 2:253/202, 9600 bps; MacTel HQ, Nottingham UK, 44-602-455497, FidoNet: 2:253/200, 9600 bps; MacTel Web, Ipswich, UK, 44-473-610139, FidoNet: 2:253/201 or 2:253/208

PC bulletin boards

Boardwatch BBS—(303)973-4222

The electronic home of *Boardwatch* Magazine, the premiere magazine of the online world. This is a good first stop because Boardwatch BBS has lots of lists of other bulletin boards, as well as an online database of magazine issues since January 1988. It also offers online newspapers, such as USA Today, Online Digital Music Review, Newsbytes, Jeffrey Lantz's Business Sense, EEEK Bits, and over 5000 closing stock quotes. Fees on Boardwatch BBS are $60/year, which includes a subscription to the printed magazine. New callers get 30 minutes to try out the system.

Boardwatch Magazine; 8500 W. Bowles Ave., Suite 210, Littleton, CO 80123; (303)973-6038, fax: (303)973-3731, FidoNet 1:104/555

Aquila BBS—(708)820-8344

Aquila is Chicago's largest BBS, with more than 6 Gb of files, as well as conferences from the FidoNet, ILink, RIME, USENET, and Prognet (for programmers) networks. It offers USA Today and Boardwatch magazine. Membership with 2 Mb of downloading per day, 2 hours of online time, and Internet access is $60/year; with 3 Mb downloading it's $75/year.

Aquila BBS; 4430 E. New York St. #201, Aurora, IL 60504; (708)898-5488, fax: (708)820-8813, email: kevin.behrens@aquila.com

Canada Remote Systems—(Missisauga, Ontario – (416)213-6002

Canada Remote Systems has some very impressive numbers. There are 200 phone lines (83 of which are high speed), 21 Gb of files (plus 5 Gb of CD-ROM), and 5000 conferences. CRS offers USENET, RIME, and ILink conferences, all accessible via QWK readers, as well as a Fax gateway. Stock market, Canadian Press, Newsbytes, Microbytes, and UPI news wires are also available. The annual membership fee is $99.95 for U.S. members. CRS supports IBM, Macintosh, Apple II, C64/C128, Amiga, Atari, NeXT, and CP/M computers.

Canada Remote Systems; 1331 Crestlawn Dr., Mississauga, Ontario, L4W 2P9; (416)620-1439, tech support: (416)620-1571

Exec-PC, Elm Grove, WI—(414)789-4360

Exec-PC is today the world's largest BBS, with more than 250 lines installed. It has the most complete IBM PC-compatible file library that I've ever seen and more high-speed lines to access them. If you work with PC compatibles, a subscription to EXEC-PC is probably the smartest investment you can make. Think of the $60/year fee as insurance against being stuck without an important utility.

In the last year, sysop Bob Mahoney has broadened the scope of the Macintosh file library. EXEC-PC now offers Apple system software, as well as a collection of Macintosh files that is just behind systems like Twilight Clone, OneNet, or MacCircles. For cross-platform software such as compression programs, and file transfer and conversion software, EXEC-PC cannot be beat.

EXEC-PC; P.O. Box 57, Elm Grove, WI 53122; (414)789-4200, fax: (414)789-1946, BBS: (414)789-4210

FedWorld, Washington, DC—(703)321-8020

FedWorld, a system run by the U.S. Department of Commerce, offers access to more than 50 federal agencies, including the Library of Congress, the Government Printing Office, the Internal Revenue Service, the National Science Foundation, the National Institute of Standards and Technology (NIST), and the Departments of Defense, Agriculture, Justice, Labor, Treasury, Energy, and Commerce.

FedWorld runs on a 50 MHz 486 PC with four lines. Settings are 1200/2400/9600, 8-N-1.

Channel 1, Boston, MA—(617)354-5776

Channel 1 is the largest bulletin board in New England. Running on PCBoard, it offers access to RIME, ILink, and USENET conferences, as well as a very large file library. Channel 1 has an excellent PC file collection as well as a substantial Macintosh file area, but it really excels in messaging. Channel 1 has more conference areas on more networks than any system I've seen.

The neat thing about having all these message areas is the ease with which you can access them. Channel 1 supports the QWK message format, which you can read via Alice or Freddie on the Macintosh or WinQWK under Windows. From the Conference menu you can have Channel 1 compress a file of messages to you with PKZIP and then transmit them to you via ZMODEM. The combination of variety, compression, and fast transfer rates makes Channel 1 one of the best message-oriented boards. Membership fees vary based on the length of membership and the type of access desired (USENET privileges are extra) but start at $85/year for regular membership.

Channel 1; P.O. Box 338, Cambridge, MA 02238

PC OHIO, Cleveland, OH—(216)381-3320

PC-OHIO is a PCBoard–based BBS operating on more than 30 phone lines with 15 Gb of storage space. The system carries over 1000 conferences on RIME, FidoNet, Smartnet, and UNINET. Other network connections include Biznet, Chucklenet, Friendsnet,RFnet, Racenet, Sportsnet, Petnet, and Intellec. QWK packet messaging is supported. Membership fee for 6 months with 1 hour/day and a 2 Mb maximum for downloading is $30; 12 months with 1 hour/day and 2 Mb maximum is $48; 2 hours/day and 4 Mb is $72. Registration is accepted by fax at (216)291-3307.

Windows Online, Danville, CA—(510)736-8343

Windows Online specializes in files for Windows 3.0, including programming information. Running 13 lines with USR Dual Standard V.32*bis*/V.42*bis* modems, Windows Online offers 5 Gb of storage, 750 Mb of which is for Windows. They also publish a weekly electronic magazine for Windows users, called *WinOnLine Review*. Windows Online is a member of the ILink, RIME (Relaynet), Smartnet, and Intellec networks. Since the staff of Windows Online takes care of the file library themselves, they don't have to rely on uploads.

Memberships cost:

1 year Mail Membership (limited to 100K/day)	**$39**
6 months Full Membership (300 files, 1.25 Mb/day)	**$49**
1 year Full Membership (700 files, 2.00 Mb/day)	**$89**
1 year SUPER Membership (2000 files, 5 Mb/day)	**$199**

Frank Mahaney, Windows Online; Box 1614, Danville, CA 94526-6614; (510)736-4376

HH Info-Net BBS, New Hartford, CT—(203)738-0342

HH Info-Net claims to have the best Windows file collection around. A member of the ILinK, FIDO,

Smartnet, NANet, and UNiNet networks, HH Info-Net offers both a large file library as well as mounted CD-ROMs of popular Internet archives such as the Simtel 20 (DOS) and CICA (Windows) archives. Fax and QWK mail doors are available. Regular membership is $90/year and includes 90 minutes of online time and 2.5 Mb of downloading per day. Premium membership is $140 and includes 150 minutes and up to 4 Mb of downloading per day.

ExecutiveNetwork, New York, NY—(914)667-4066

ExecutiveNetwork is the home of the ILinK network, a network of PCBoard systems. The system offers access to many ILinK conferences via QMAIL, as well as tens of thousands of files.

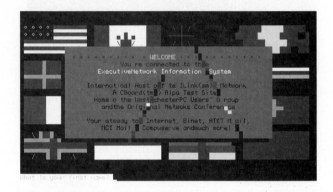

Macintosh BBS software

Recommendation
FirstClass v2.5

100 Telecom user pack	**$395**
250 Telecom user pack	**$595**
500 Telecom user pack	**$995**
1000 Telecom user pack	**$1595**
Multiport Server upgrade	**$895**
Command Line Option	**$295**

Although there are still many outstanding bugs, FirstClass has come a long way in the last year, and has now established itself as the leading Mac BBS product. FirstClass is based on a client/server architecture. The client is entirely graphical and freely distributable; it supports logins over AppleTalk, TCP/IP, or serial lines (without remote AppleTalk drivers). One particularly noteworthy client feature is the ability to carry on multiple activities simultaneously: A user can download while using the message forums and chatting online, all at the same time. The server supports multiple lines using its own built-in multitasking.

Despite the iconic user interface, the software is highly efficient, rivaling character-based systems in terms of responsiveness. A Mac IIfx can handle 17 simultaneous V.32*bis* callers plus AppleTalk users without noticeable slowdowns.

The server software supports mounting of CD-ROMs, access to individual conferences by privilege, and the ability to enclose files within messages. Systems may sport custom icons, background PICTs, sounds, custom forms, and other enhancements. Upgrades to FirstClass are free; technical support is available by phone and online (via AOL, FidoNet, OneNet, and SoftArc Online BBS). There is no annual support payment.

FirstClass supports customization via custom icons and background PICTs that reside in the client software. Forms and database development kits are available that allow linking of FirstClass to external databases and the creation of fully graphical add-in applications.

FirstClass also comes with a built-in gateway for linking FirstClass systems; the gateway can transmit messages with styled text, fonts, color, and file enclosures. Text, PICT, and sound files may be viewed using the client software. The FirstClass Protocol (FCP) is bidirectional, allowing callers to upload and download at the same time.

FirstClass supports arbitrary links between systems, allowing system operators to form private networks if they choose. Operators do not have to link up with SoftArc Online or networks such as MacUnion or OneNet, although they may choose to do so. A forthcoming release will support duplicate control as well as multihop routing of messages among FirstClass systems as well as to external networks.

Recent releases of the server software offer support for multiple volumes and dramatic decreases in garbage-collection times.

With the addition of compatible Communications Toolbox `telnet` tools, FirstClass can be accessed over the Internet with a graphical interface; a technical note that describes this is available. UUCP, Internet (SMTP, NNTP, UUCP, and POP3), fax, and FidoNet gateways are available, along with gateways to Microsoft Mail, QuickMail, AppleLink, CompuServe, Novell MHS, and Pagers. There is also a Scriptmaker gateway that allows you to "roll your own."

SoftArc offers a Windows version of the client software. Educational and nonprofit discounts are available.

SoftArc, Inc.; 805 Middlefield Rd., Suite 102, Scarborough, Ontario, Canada MIV 2T9; (416)299-4723, fax: (416)754-1856

Suggestion
NovaLink Professional v3.05

3 sessions + 20 clients (serial only)	**$200**
3 additional sessions + AppleTalk	**$400**
Additional sessions (AppleTalk or serial)	**$50**
Modem NovaTerm 2.1	
50 packages	**$60**
100 packages	**$120**
200 packages	**$200**
unlimited	**$299**
AppleTalk NovaTerm AT 2.1	
per package	**$20**

NovaLink Pro is a graphical BBS construction set that allows sysops to create systems with graphical or text-based interfaces. Construction of external applications with limited graphics is supported via a development kit. While NovaLink supports the addition of custom icons, icons for individual conferences cannot be customized, and background PICTs are not supported.

In v3.0, the software operates in one of three modes: NovaView, an iconic interface; a NovaLink Pro v2.1 compatible mode; and VT100 mode. NovaView interfaces can be developed by dragging icons from a palette into the Menu Design folder. Construction of NovaLink Pro v2.1 interfaces uses a development tool called Mondrian. Regardless of the mode chosen, there is also a scripting language called NovaScript, that supports subroutines that let sysops automate aspects of their operation.

NovaLink Pro v3.0 supports multithreading, which lets you do more than one thing on the system simultaneously, provided that the multithreading protocol is selected. A FidoNet gateway is available.

NovaLink Pro v3.0 can handle TCP/IP, AppleTalk, and serial line sessions simultaneously and includes a built-in network called InfoLink. New features include support for moderated file conferences, bidirectional file transfers, and styled text in messages. InfoLink operates using a tree structure, with NovaCentral serving as the root, and now includes hubs on the East Coast and in Europe.

TCP/IP support is available as an add-on for NovaLink Pro 3.0, including support for `telnet` (client/server), SMTP mail (incoming and outgoing), and NNTP news transfers. ZMODEM is supported for file transfers over TCP/IP.

ResNova has announced its intention to develop a Windows version of NovaTerm, as well as to support future versions of Remote Image Protocol (RIP).

ResNova Software; 5011 Argosy Dr. #13, Huntington Beach, CA 92649; (714)379-9000, fax: (714)379-9014, NovaCentral BBS: (714)379-9006, email: len.anderson@resnova.com

Downright Speculation
hi-BBS v2.0
Two-line version $369

hi-BBS is a graphical BBS package that supports mail, forums, and live chatting; XTND translators for viewing documents online; file attachments; playback of sounds; multiple downloads; AppleEvents; CD-ROM; X.25 and ISDN; automatic invoicing of subscribers; and Macintosh and Windows clients. To log in to the XBR system, use **GUEST** for user and password, and then press `RET` for subject.

XBR Communications; 5253 Decarie Blvd., Suite 550, Montreal, QB Canada H3W 3C3; (514)489-1001, fax: (514)489-4966, email: xbr@applelink.apple.com, BBS: (514)489-0445

Suggestion
Second Sight (Formerly Red Ryder Host)
v2.1 $135

Second Sight is the grand old man of Macintosh BBSes. There are more third-party utilities that work with Second Sight than any other Mac BBS. BMUG ran Second Sight until 1987, when it switched to TBBS; conversion was not that hard, because with its custom menus, Second Sight is a lot like TBBS. It can handle 255 message sections, and unlimited file transfer libraries. However, Second Sight does not handle the large number of lines that FirstClass can. If you're going to run Second Sight, you should also get the utilities written by Pete Johnson.

The Freesoft Company; 105 McKinley Rd., Beaver Falls, PA 15010; (412)846-2700 M–F 9 AM – 5 PM EST, fax: (412)847-4436

Pete Johnson, Apple Computer, Inc.; 20525 Mariani Ave., Cupertino, CA 95014; (408)996-1010

Suggestion
Public Address

Public Address is a modular, multiuser, comand-line driven Mac BBS package that includes source code. More than just another "Mac BBS hope," Public

Address has generated a lot of excitement because it offers built-in support for FidoNet, as well as AppleTalk logins. Joe BBS says check it out! Available via `ftp minerva.cis.yale.edu, cd /pub/owenc`. For information, send mail to goberfield@aol.com.

Downright Speculation
MUBBS v1.13   Free

MultiUser BBS for Macintosh (MUBBS) is a publicly distributable multiline Macintosh BBS. It is free, and like Public Address, has an architecture that makes it easy to add external modules. MUBBS is available on the Space Sciences BBS; (805)259-6407, (818)998-2076, or from Palmdale, (805)268-8815

MUBBS maintains a LISTSERV. To join the mailing list, send mail to the following addresses:

To put yourself on the list:
mubbs!request@quake.sylmar.ca.us
To remove yourself from the list:
mubbs!cancel@quake.sylmar.ca.us
To send something to the whole echo:
mubbs!submit@quake.sylmar.ca.us
To reach a real human:
ssbbs!nateh@quake.sylmar.ca.us

N. Hawthorne; AOL: "N Hawthorne"

Downright Speculation
Taniwha BBS   Free

The Taniwha BBS package utilizes many of the capabilities of the Comm Toolbox and is customizable by those familiar with C programming. Written to work with the Taniwha multiport serial card. Includes source code.

BMUG; 1442A Walnut St. #62, Berkeley, CA 94709-1496; (510)549-BMUG, fax: (510)849-9026

Suggestion
TeleFinder v3.1
User group price:

100 users + BBS-In-A-Box	**$199**
Unlimited users	**$425**
AppleTalk support	**$149.95**
TeleFinder/user	**Free**
TeleFinder Pro user	**$79.95**

TeleFinder lets users interact with a bulletin board using a Macintosh desktop metaphor. Unique features such as support of AppleEvents and export of billing information make Telefinder easy to maintain. New additions to v3.1 include real-time chatting, preview of compressed PICT and JPEG pictures, and formatted text within messages. TeleFinder supports multiport cards and up to

32,000 users. These features make TeleFinder the ideal BBS for companies (such as desktop publishing service bureaus) that are looking to get a system online with minimal hassle. As with other graphical BBSes, sysops switching to TeleFinder from a command-line BBS should expect dramatic increases in usage.

The standard TeleFinder client package is freely distributable. A deluxe version of the client is also available, called TeleFinder Pro. This includes off-line reader capability, mini-host, standard terminal emulations (TTY, VT52, VT100, ANSI), and support for UserLand Frontier. Both versions can display PICTs and bitmap files.

User groups can purchase TeleFinder as part of a bundle with the BBS-In-A-Box CD-ROM put out by Arizona Mac Users Group (AMUG) for an extremely attractive $199 price. When purchased with the BBS-In-A-Box CD, TeleFinder provides a great combination of ease of use and access to a huge current file library. However, the Finder interface does not work as well for messaging, although TeleFinder is Tabby compatible via TF/Link. FidoNet and UUCP gateways are on the way.

Spider Island Software; 4790 Irvine Blvd., Suite 105-347, Irvine, CA 92720; (714)669-9260; fax: (714)669-1383; BBS: (714)730-5785; America Online: SpiderIsla; email: 73457,2756@compuserve.com

Downright Speculation
TF/Link   **$25**
UUCP Your BBS

TF/Link links TeleFinder to Tabby; UUCP your BBS links any Tabby compatible BBS to UUCP.

J. W. Sinteur; Strawinskypad 82, 2324 DB Leiden, The Netherlands, email: sinteur@fourc.nl

Downright Speculation
WWIV   **$30/shareware**

WWIV offers a lot of things, including support for Tabby, ZMODEM, voting, and external applications. It's also pretty reliable.

Terry Teague; 530 W. Dana St., Mountain View, CA 94041; email: 76354.324@compuserve.com

BMUG; 1442A Walnut St. #62, Berkeley, CA 94709-1496; (510)549-BMUG, fax: (510)849-9026

Suggestion
BBS-In-A-Box   **$99**

The Arizona Macintosh User Group (AMUG) has scored a coup on this one. BBS-In-A-Box includes

over 7000 Mac files in compressed format, with directories for Second Sight and TeleFinder. The CD also includes material licensed from Apple, such as the Macintosh Technical Notes, Just Add Water (the User Group Manual), sample User Group Bylaws and Articles of Incorporation, Apple II Tech Notes, a User Group Directory stack, Windoid stacks, System 6.0.5/6.0.7, HyperCard, LaserWriter training, and several other items.

Michael Bean; 718 E. Campbell Ave., Gilbert, AZ 85234; (602)892-5454, FidoNet 1:114/56 (Michael Bean), GEnie: Michael Bean, AppleLink: UG0116, BBS: (602)495-1713

PC BBS software

FOSSIL drivers

Recommendation
TCP/IP FOSSIL drivers

Brad Clements of MurkWorks has developed a FOSSIL communications driver for TCP/IP. FOSSIL is supported by a wide variety of PC-compatible multi-node packages.

MurkWorks; P.O. Box 631, Potsdam, NY 13676; (315)265-4717, fax: (315)268-9812, email: bkc@murkworks.com

Downright Speculation
DGFOSSIL   **$149**

DGFOSSIL is a multi-port FOSSIL driver that supports use of DigiBoards with up to 32 ports on multi-node BBS packages.

Software America; P.O. Box 690895, Tulsa OK 74128-0895; (918)234-0707, fax: (918)234-0777

Multi-node software

The following BBS packages can handle multiple lines but only via use of multiple CPUs or multitaskers such as DESQview:

Recommendation
WILDCAT! v3.55	
Single line	**$129**
Multiline (1-10 lines)	**$249**
Multiline (1-250 lines)	**$499**
WILDCAT! (IM)	**$799**
wcPRO! Utilities	**$99**
wcMHS Gateway	**$299**
wcUUCP Gateway	**$299**

Long a favorite for single-line applications, with WILDCAT! v3.55 is now one of the most powerful BBS packages, as well as one of the easiest to set up. Despite a number of powerful features, it offers a simple menu structure. WILDCAT! supports doors; Novell LANs; links to networks such as QWK (TNet), FidoNet (WildMail!), UUCP, and RIME (UTI available); QWK packets using the TomCat Door. Gateways are also available to MCI Mail, CompuServe, Novell MHS, and fax. WILDCAT! comes with the WCONVERT utility to convert from PCBoard, GAP, and other packages; and the WSFILE utility, which can be used to install CD-ROMs.

There are also a variety of third-party utilities available for WILDCAT!, including the CATSCAN utility, which automatically scans uploads for viruses; LIVECAT, a utility that manages doors; WCFF!, which processes FidoNet File (Tick) echoes; WMINFO!, which does statistical analysis of EchoMail; BobCat, a call-back verifier; and the DATAVIEW utility, which allows for viewing of .ZIP, .ARC, and .LHZ files.

A new version of the software, called WILDCAT! (IM), requires the DigiChannel "i" or "e" cards, and supports up to eight lines on an 80386 machine. This requires DESQview 386, as well as 8 Mb RAM. DOORWAY is included with WILDCAT! IM, which allows for the running of remote applications from a doorway.

Mustang Software, Inc.; P.O. Box 2264, Bakersfield, CA 93303; (800)999-9619, (805)395-0223, fax: (805)395-0713, BBS: (805)395-0650

WildMail!, WMINFO!, and WCFF!, Online Computer Resources; 2036 Columbus Parkway #405, Benicia, CA 94510; (707)552-1122, BBS: (707)552-0602 (ten lines), FidoNet 1:161/123

Tnet and Tomcat, Technique Computer Systems; 110-1841 Oak Bay Ave., Victoria, British Columbia, Canada V8R 1C4; (604)598-2141, BBS: (604)598-1546

BobCat and LIVECAT, Live Systems; 3800 Old Cheney Rd., Suite 101, Lincoln, NE 68516; (800)869-0366, BBS: (402)421-2434

Suggestion
Maximus

Maximus was written to work with SQUISH, the premiere FidoNet mail tosser/packer. Both Maximus and SQUISH are now available both for DOS and OS/2, as is BinkleyTerm, one of the most popular mailers. Maximus supports QWK packers, points, and configurable menus, as well as a monolithic message base.

EXEC-PC; P.O. Box 57, Elm Grove, WI 53122; (414)789-4200, BBS: (414)789-4210

Suggestion
Remote Access v2.02

Remote Access is a QuickBBS clone that is compatible with multitaskers such as DESQview and DoubleDOS. It supports up to 200 message areas, as well as FidoNet mailers such as BinkleyTerm or FrontDoor.

wantree development; 108 West 3rd St., Bonner Springs, KS 66012, (913)441-1336, (800)648-9800, fax: (913)441-0442, BBS: (913)441-0595

Suggestion
PCBoard v15.0

Single line (no doors)	**$120**
Single line with doors	**$170**
Multiline with doors	
3 lines	**$240**
6 lines	**$350**
9 lines	**$460**
99 lines	**$970**
Annual support	**$60**

PCBoard is considered by many to be the world's leading bulletin board software. Since it does not have a scheduler or multitasking kernel built in, it operates with one CPU per phone line. However, this does not limit the number of phone lines that can be supported, because PCBoard is completely network compliant, working on any system supporting NETBIOS. This includes Novell, LANtastic, 3Com, Network OS, and other networking software.

Although it means that large PCBoard systems use a lot of hardware, the lack of internal multitasking means that the interfacing of doors and standard DOS software is very easy. As a result, thousands of applications can work with PCBoard. Among these are FidoNet, USENET, QNet, InterMail, and PostLink networking software, QWK support; external protocols, etc.

QNet, a QWK Packet–based conferencing system, is available and is being used by networks such as Intellec, NorthAmeriNet, and Smartnet.

Since PostLink was developed for PCBoard (all other BBS software interfaces to the network via conversion programs called Universal Text Interface—UTI—modules), PCBoard is probably the way to go if you intend to join PostLink-based networks such as RIME.

New features in v15.0 include support for RIP, real-time chatting, file enclosures within messages, and a new PCBoard Programming Language (PPL).

Clark Development Company, Inc.; 3950 South 700 East, Suite 303, Murray, UT 84107; Information: (801)261-1686, fax: (801)261-8987, orders: (800)356-1686, data: (801)261-8976

Downright Speculation
Searchlight v3.0

Single line	**$99**
3 lines	**$179**
10 lines	**$299**
unlimited lines	**$399**

Searchlight supports QWK, FidoNet and PostLink networking; DigiBoards; CD-ROMs, built-in virus checking, up to 15 external protocols, and RIP as well as LANs, Windows, and OS/2 operation. There are no limits to the number of conferences and messages, and up to 10 nodes can be multitasked on a single PC using DESQview.

Searchlight; P.O. Box 640, Stony Brook, NY 11790; (516)751-2966, (800)780-LITE, BBS: (516)689-2566

Downright Speculation
Synchronet

2 nodes	**$99**
4 nodes	**$149**
16 nodes	**$199**
250 nodes	**$399**

Synchronet supports FidoNet, QWK, and PostLink networking, multiport serial boards, online chat, RIP, CD-ROMs, incoming fax, and external transfer protocols, at a very reasonable price.

Digital Dynamics; P.O. Box 501, Yorba Linda, CA 92686; (714)529-6328, fax: (714)529-9721, BBS: (714)529-9525, (714)529-5313

PC BBS software – integrated

Recommendation
TBBS v2.2

2 lines	**$295**
16 lines	**$895**
32 lines	**$1495**
64 lines	**$1995**
TDBS v1.2	
2 lines	**$395**
16 lines	**$995**
32 lines	**$1795**
64 lines	**$2395**
TIMS v1.1	**$149**

SYSOM	**$100**
QSO v1.0 (QWK module)	**$100**
Interchange v1.0	**$149**
UltraChat	**$195**

TBBS v2.2 with TIMS is the only MS-DOS multiple-line BBS capable of handling continuous FidoNet mail. Recent TBBS 2.2 improvements include ZMODEM, UNIX-style conferencing, internationalization, and support for a QWK packet add-in called QSO. Although it's expensive, it may not have the most features, and it may not be the easiest to set up, TBBS is very efficient. The SYSOM option module is essential; if you are looking to set up FidoNet, don't even think of purchasing TBBS without the TIMS option module and newly revamped net mail utilities.

TBBS is extremely flexible, letting you create your own menu system. It is reliable, documentation is good, and support is excellent. It also integrates well with FidoNet, having recently released new and improved net mail utilities.

With the TIMS integrated mailer, TBBS can receive FidoNet mail continuously on multiple lines without shutting down. Support is not available for RIME networking, but Jack Rickard has recently developed a UUCP option module called PIMP.

Other recently introduced option modules include QSO, a QWK message packer; and Interchange, a dial-out package that lets you link a TBBS system to other services. Third-party applications are available for a host of functions, including Billing (TBill), NAPLPS Graphics (SNAP), Games, and more.

Since TBBS lets you run as many as 64 lines on a single PC, it is one of the least expensive alternatives for setting up a large system. However, as of v2.2, it can't operate in protected mode or support extended memory (it does support EMS, though). Source code is not available. A chatting module called UltraChat supports linking of multiple TBBS systems for real-time conferencing, and offers user-selectable interfaces. LAN support is in the works; look for MHS gateways and the ability to look like an async server to a LAN (using NACS/NASI protocol) for LAN-based logons. TBBS supports running of dBASE III+ programs in multiuser mode via the TDBS database, and many third-party applications are now available, including games. eSoft supports TBBS via phone and modem, as well as via a newsletter called *Possibilities*.

eSoft, Inc.; 15200 E. Girard Ave., Suite 3000, Aurora, CO 80014; voice: (303)699-6565, fax: (303)699-6872, BBS: (303)699-0153, email: alan.bryant@esoft.com.

Tbill, GO-2, SNAP, Wild Side, Video Poker, Chain Links; GW Associates; P.O. Box 6606, Holliston, MA 01746; (508)429-6227, fax: (508)429-3859, BBS: (508)429-8385

Downright Speculation
Oracomm Plus

2 lines	$390
9 lines	$490
16 lines	$590

Oracomm offers a nice mix of ease of use and powerful networking capabilities. Since it is descended from the Dial Your Match package, it remains very popular as a dating and chatting system. However it is also popular as a plug-and-play business solution where the power (and complexity) of TBBS or Major BBS would be overkill. Oracomm Plus has a well-designed proprietary mail exchange system (OraNet) as well as FidoNet support and database capability.

A unique feature of Oracomm Plus is the ability to interface with the PCW Weather Station, so that weather data can be collected and transmitted between multiple sites. Oracomm Plus also supports *text branching,* which allows for construction of online tests and adventure games. Multiline chatting and EMS memory are also supported. Since Oracomm Plus allows for linking of messages, it can support ANSI graphics screens of greater complexity than any other package. Oracomm Plus allows for all system configuration parameters to be changed remotely at any time and includes provision for additional remote sysop passwording. However, DOS commands cannot be executed in remote sysop mode.

Files descriptions are located within a database in Oracomm Plus. This makes it very easy to find a desired file. A text database feature allows searching on arbitrary fields. The message system is relatively easy to use, although more powerful features such as full text search on the message base are not available. There is no third-party program for Oracomm Plus. Support is available by voice and bulletin board, and I found the staff enthusiastic and knowledgeable.

Surf Computer Services, Inc.; 1103 East Cliff Rd. Burnsville, Minnesota 55337; (612)894-5580, fax: (612)895-9136, BBS: (612)894-5879.

Downright Speculation
DLX $795/16 lines

DLX distinguishes itself by being one of the easiest DOS multiline BBSes to set up. It is a favorite for chatting and online-dating services, and can handle

up to 32 lines. However, it does not support network mail or add-on databases.
DLX info: (818)894-4150

Downright Speculation
Falken v6.65

2 lines	$99
4 lines	$249
8 lines	$399
16 lines	$549
24 lines	$629
32 lines	$699

Falken is a new breed of BBS that supports integrated multitasking without use of LANs or DESQview, as well as doors written for DOS. It also supports Fido and QWK mail, mailing lists, RIP, multi-line chat, CD_ROMs, and several multiport cards, including DigiBoards. Falken systems can also link up and chat with each other. Numerous Falken doors are available from Bill Bell at Two Minute Warning.

Info*Share; P.O. Box 1501, Woodbridge, VA 22193; (703)791-2910, BBS: (703)803-8000

Two Minute Warning; P.O. Box 1252, Columbia, MD 21044; BBS: (410)964-6400.

Suggestion
The Major BBS v6.1

8 lines	$508
14 lines	$757
20 lines	$1006
(up to 256 sessions supported)	
Source Code	$385
FidoNet NetMail	$99
Major Gateway/Internet	$199

Major BBS is written in C and offers source code access. This has been a boon to sysops and third-party developers who have created their own add-ons and customizations to Major BBS. It also has become a major technological advantage, since with the advent of protected-mode compilers, Major BBS can now operate in protected mode with a large linear address space, resulting in high efficiency. The product can handle up to 256 sessions in the current release.

With third-party development proceeding at a breakneck pace (more than 25 add-ons were available at last count) and with the Major BBS being available in five different editions (Standard Edition, Configurable Menus (MenuMan), Online Mall, File Libraries, and Entertainment), a Major BBS sysop has a very wide latitude in choosing how to configure the system.

It is possible to link together two Major BBS systems by phone to create wide-area chat networks. Major BBS also offers a Novell LAN support option, which is critical for many businesses. This means that you can log on to Major BBS via IPX Direct circuits. Support is available for FidoNet, PostLink, QWK packet, and UUCP networking. However, Major BBS must shut down to receive FidoNet mail, unlike TBBS.

There are now quite a few areas (such as online gaming, global chatting, LAN support) in which Major BBS has carved out a clear advantage. Support is excellent; Galacticomm supports Major BBS via phone, modem, and a newsletter entitled *The Major News*. New features in v6.1 include support for calling out to another machine, RIP and multilingual support, and DLL add-ons.

Galacticomm, Inc.; 4101 S.W. 47th Ave., Suite 101, Fort Lauderdale, FL 33314; (305)583-5990, fax: (305)583-7846, demo system: (305)583-7808, Example Systems: (805)736-5674 (FidoNet Option), (714)996-6666 (MedCom Info Systems), (305)321-2410 (The GRID, showcase for third-party products), (305)370-9376 (Superdemocracy Foundation BBS)

Mjrmail (QWK packet program for Major BBS); Farwest BBS, P.O. Box 1296, Station E, Victoria, British Columbia, Canada V8W 2W3; (604)381-6462, BBS: (604)381-3934

Downright Speculation
RoboBOARD/FX

RoboBoard is a graphical user interface BBS with a custom terminal program that runs under DOS. It supports up to 256 colors on SVGA.

Hamilton TeleGraphics Inc.; P.O. Box 633, Aylmer Quebec, Canada J9H 6L1; (819)682-6670, fax: (819)685-0994, BBS: (819)682-7771

Duke Graphics; 4130 LaJolla Village Drive, Suite 107-169, LaJolla, CA 92037-1480; BBS: (619)793-8360, (619)793-8361

RoboBOARD Europe; Wilhelm Busch Strasse 4, 55126 Mainz, Germany; BBS/Fax: +49-6131-474483

Downright Speculation
SAGELINK v3.1

SAGELINK is a door that runs under SearchLight. It offers hypertext capabilities via a custom terminal program It supports bookmarks, searching, cross references, an integrated compiler, compression, and a free document reader.

SageNet BBS: (304)724-5227

UNIX BBS Software

Downright Speculation
CocoNet

2 users	$395
4 users	$695
8 users	$995
16 users	$1295
32 users	$1595
64 users	$1895
Unlimited	$2195

CocoNet delivers outstanding ease of use to system administrators who are willing to live with its proprietary orientation. In order to maintain a consistent user interface, all additions to the CocoNet BBS must be programmed via CocoTalk, the developer's package. The problem is that CocoTalk doesn't support scrolling windows, which means you cannot simply add a UNIX command or shell script to a menu. Also, the custom terminal program that comes with CocoNet, CAP, cannot handle scripting. This means that CAP cannot be used to login over port selectors or PC Pursuit, which is a serious disadvantage.

Included in the price is a site license to the custom terminal emulator, CAP. Currently, CAP versions are only available for the PC, but Mac OS and NeXT versions are due. If you can live with CocoNet's limitations, you will be rewarded with one of the finest BBS user interfaces available today.

CocoNut Computing, Inc.; 7946 Ivanhoe Ave., Suite 303, La Jolla, CA 92037; voice: (619)456-2002, fax: (619)456-1905, BBS: (619)456-0815,7-E-1, 1200/2400 bps; email: whofan@well.sf.ca.us

Suggestion
Waffle (available for A/UX)
Source code $120

If you already have A/UX and don't have much money left over, then Waffle is the way to go. For $120, Waffle will provide you with integrated USENET conferencing and UUCP mail internal forums, interfaces with the UNIX mailer, and B or C news. Access may be controlled by group; external protocols such as DSZ or RZ/SZ are supported; an internal or external file system may be utilized; terminals in the termcap database are recognized; external programs may be linked to the menu structure; and internal mailing lists and quoting are supported.

A listing of Waffle sites is available by sending email to: waffle-site-list-request@mcb.com. Additions, changes, or deletions from the list can be sent to: waffle@mcb.com.

Thomas E. Dell; P.O. Box 4436, Mountain View, CA 94040; (408)245-SPAM, (Demo System, 300/1200/2400), email: dell@apple.com

Downright Speculation
XBBS v7.95

This bulletin board implementation is very popular. XBBS may be integrated with USENET and UUCP mail by purchasing of conferencing software such as AKCS.

Sanford Zelkovitz; (714)821-9670, XBBS support BBS: (714)821-9671

Suggestion
AKCS

80386 version	$399
SunOS 4.1 version	$999
MIPS Magnum	$999
MIPS 32/3360	$1499
DEC 5000	$3000
(source code required)	
Nonprofit prices:	
80386 version	$299
SunOS 4.1 version	$499
MIPS Magnum	$499
MIPS 32/3360	$999

The conferencing system currently favored by Big Sky Telecom, and several other BBSes running under the XENIX or SCO UNIX operating systems. Also available for other UNIX flavors, such as SunOS 4.1 and MIPS RISCos. Similar to PicoSpan, but more flexible. Can handle file enclosures, import and export from UNIX mail and news, custom menu interfaces, execution of UNIX shell commands, extensive privilege settings. Supported by a SYSADMIN conference available from the MCS.

Karl Denninger, Macro Computer Solutions, Inc.; 415 South E. Garfield, Mundelein, IL 60060; (312) 296-9058, fax: (708)808-1190, BBS: (312)248-0900

Downright Speculation
Magpie $200

Magpie has a unique architecture in which message and files sections are intertwined within an outline form. It is now being used by NYCENET, a Board of Education BBS in New York at (718)461-8650.

Steve Manes; 648 Broadway, Suite 300, New York, NY 10012; (212)533-1692, BBS: (212)420-0527, login: **bbs**; email: manes@magpie.nycenet.edu

Downright Speculation
Caucus

Caucus has established itself with a solid user base in the minicomputer community. It is priced like a mainframe or minicomputer software package and offers high-quality technical support. However, if you are on a low budget, Caucus is probably not for you. This is the conferencing system now in use at the Walter Haas School of Business at the University of California at Berkeley.

Camber-Roth; 1223 People's Ave., Troy, NY 12180; (518)273-0983, fax: (518)276-6380

Downright Speculation
QTACH2

4 lines	$500
8 lines	$750
12 lines	$850
16/20/24 lines	$100/4 users
Developer's Package	$50
On-Cmd dBASE III+	$800
Email Option	$45

If you are ready for something completely different, you might be interested in QTACH2, which runs under the QNX operating system. QNX is Not Quite UNIX, but it is now POSIX compatible, and so a large fraction of UNIX code compiles and runs under it. QTACH2 is written as a client-server application and is therefore much more memory efficient than typical UNIX BBSes. Since QTACH2 runs under a multitasking operating system, it can handle multiple continuous mail sessions as well as process mail continuously. There are rumors of a UUCP implementation for QNX and QTACH2. QTACH2 is currently in beta testing and as a result is continually in the process of change.

Sector Technologies; 1851 Hawthorne, Jameson, PA 18929-1333; (215)491-0929, fax: (215)491-0919

Downright Speculation
TEAMate

10 lines	$2495
20 lines	$3995
UNIX Editor	$395
Annual support	15%
Nonprofit prices:	
Free for software, 15% of standard list for	
annual support	

Through its integrated outlining system, TEAMate provides organization to online information in a way that no other BBS can match. Outlines may be modified so as to support online collaboration; and user read and write privileges may be assigned by the sysop. TEAMate allows any UNIX command or application to be integrated into the menu structure.

Remote maintenance and system backup can be performed while the BBS is online. TEAMate is not a complete BBS system; online chatting, database, and other modules are not included and must be provided from other sources. File transfer is supported via file enclosures. TEAMate supports outlining; file enclosure; keyword search of message envelopes, including search by date range; a custom terminal program (only available for IBM-PC); carbon copy mail; the XMODEM protocol; and facilities for data import and export. A UUCP mail interface is optional. Publicly distributable graphical clients are available for Windows v3.1, Macintosh, and Motif.

Requires 10 MHz 286 machine with 4 Mb RAM (10 users), 20 MHz 386 machine with 6 Mb RAM (20 users); SCO XENIX or Interactive UNIX operating system. MS-DOS single-line version also available.

MMB Development Corporation; 904 Manhattan Avenue, Manhattan Beach, CA 90266, (800)832-6022, (310)318-1322, fax: (310)318-2162, BBS: (310)318-5302

Downright Speculation
ZMAX/Xchange

8 lines	**$995**
unlimited (396)	**$1495**
16 lines	**$1495**
unlimited	**$2495**
(SPARC, NCR, AViiOn)	
Annual support	**$100**

ZMAX/Xchange utilizes pop-up and pull-down menus requiring use of a VT100 emulator. Other UNIX software and commands may be integrated into the BBS menus. An animated brochure is available, running under MS–DOS.

Available for 386 UNIX versions such as SCO UNIX, SCO XENIX, AT&T UNIX, Interactive UNIX, and Everex ESIX. Also available for AT&T 3B2, Sun SPARCStation, Data General AViiOn, NCR TOWER.

Z/Max Computer Solutions, Inc.; 8287 Loop Rd., Raddisson Woods Office Park, Baldwinsville, NY 13027; (315)635-1882, fax: (315)635-1908, BBS: (315)635-1950, (315)635-1947, Login: **zmax** Password: **xchange**

Downright Speculation
UNIBOARD

UNIBOARD is a Remote Access look-alike for UNIX. It offers interfaces to USENET and UUCP, can create custom menus, and comes with system administration tools.

Riccardo Pizzi; Rimini, Italy; data: 39-541-27135 (HST/PEP/V.32), email: **pizzi@nervous.com, uunet!nervous!pizzi**. To download a crippleware version that can be enabled by a software key, **ftp nic.funet.fi, mget /pub/unix/386ix/svr4/comm./UBBS103*** (binary mode).

Chapter 8 – Internet Access

These providers offer dialup accounts to individuals, including shell accounts, UUCP accounts, and SLIP/PPP accounts.

Dialup access by country

Argentina

ARNET

UNDP Project ARG-86-026, Ministerio de Ralaciones Exteriores y Culto; Reconquista 1088 1er. Piso - Informatica, (1003) Capital Federal, Buenos Aires, Argentina; +(541)313-8082, fax: +(541)814-4824, email: pete@atina.ar

Australia

AARNet

AARNet, the Australian Academic and Research Network; GPO Box 1142, Canberra ACT 2601, Australia; +61 6 249 3385, email: G.Huston@aarnet.edu.au

Connect

Connect; 29 Fitzgibbon Crewcent, Caufield, Victoria 3161, Australia; +61 3 5282239, fax: +61 3 5285887, email: connect@connect.com.au

Bolivia

UnBol

Prof. Clifford Paravicini, Facultad de Ingenieria Electronica, Univ. Mayor de San Andres, La Paz, Bolivia, email: clifford@unbol.bo

Bulgaria

BGnet

Daniel Kalchev, c/o Digital Systems; Neofit Bozveli 6, Varna - 9000, Bulgaria; voice/fax: +359 52 234540, email: postmaster@bulgaria.eu.net

Canada

ARnet

Alberta Research Network, Director of Information Systems, Alberta Research Council; Box 8330, Station F, Edmonton, Alberta, Canada, T6H 5X2; +1 (403)450-5188, fax: +1 (403)461-2651, email: neilson@titan.arc.ab.ca

BCnet

BCnet Headquarters; Room 419 - 6356 Agricultural Rd., University of British Columbia, Vancouver, B.C., Canada V6T 1W5; + 1 (604)822-3932, fax: +1 (604)822-5116, email: Mike_Patterson@mtsg.ubc.ca

CA*net

CA*net Information Centre, Computing Services, Universtiy of Toronto; 4 Bancroft Ave., Rm. 116, Toronto, Ontario, Canada M5S 1A1; + (416)978-5058, fax: +1 (416)978-6620, email: info@CAnet.ca

MBnet

Director, Computing Services, University of Manitoba, 603 Engineering Building, Winnipeg, Manitoba, Canada R3T 2N2; +1 (204)474-8230, fax: +1 (204)275-5420, email: miller@ccm.umanitoba.ca

NBnet

Director, Computing Services, University of New Brunswick; Fredericton, New Brunswick, Canada E3B 5A3: +1 (506)453-4573, fax: +1 (506)453-3590, email: DGM@unb.ca

NLnet

Newfoundland and Labrador Network, Director Computing and Communications, Memorial University of Newfoundland; St. John's, Newfoundland, Canada A1C 5S7: +1 (709)737-8329, fax: +1 (709)737-4569, email: wilf@kean.ucs.mun.ca

NSTN

Nova Scotia Technology Network, General Manager; NSTN Inc., 900 Windmill Rd., Suite 107, Dartmouth, Nova Scotia, Canada B3B 1P7; +1 (902)468-6786, fax: +1 (902)468-3679, email: martinea@hawk.nstn.ns.ca

ONet

ONet Computing Services, University of Toronto; 4 Bancroft Ave., Rm. 116, Toronto, Ontario, Canada M5S 1A1, +1 (416)978-5058, fax: +1 (416)978-6620, email: eugene@vm.utcs.utoronto.ca

Prince Edward Island Network

University of Prince Edward Island, Computer Services; 550 University Avenue, Charlottetown, P.E.I., Canada C1AZ 4P3; +1 (902)566-0450, fax: +1 (902)5660-0958, email: hancock@upei.ca

RISQ

Reseau Interordinateurs Scientifique Quebecois, Centre de Recherche Informatique de Montreal; 744, Jean-Brillant, Suite 500, Montreal, Quebec, Canada H3T 1P1; +1 (514)340-5700, fax: +1 (514)340-5777, email: turcotte@crim.ca

SASKnet

Computing Services; 56 Physics, University of Saskatchewan, Saskatoon, Saskatchewan, Canada S7N 0W0; +1 (306)966-4860, fax: +1 (306)966-4938, email: jonesdc@admin.usask.ca

UUNET Canada

1 Yonge St., Suite 1801, Toronto, Ontario, Canada M5E 1W7; +1 (416)368-6621, fax: +1 (416)369-0515, email: info@uunet.ca

Czechoslovakia

CESNET

Czech Educational and Scientific Network, Milan Sterba, Milan.Sterba@vse.cs, Ivo Smejkal, ivo@vse.cs, Jiri Orsag, ors@vscht.cs

CSEARN

Jan Gruntorad, tkjg@csearn.bitnet

SANET

Bobovsky, bobovsky@csearn.bitnet, Karol Fabian, Karol.Fabian@uakom.cs, Vladimir Kassa, kassa@iaccs.cs

Appendix B: Choice Products

Denmark

DEnet

Danish Network for Research and Education, UNI-C, The Danish Computing Centre for Research and Education; Building 305, DTH, DK-2800 Lyngby, Denmark; +45 45 03 83 55, fax: +45 45 93 02 20, email: Jan.P.Sorenson@uni-c.dk

Dominican Republic

REDID

Asesor Cientifico Union Latina; APTD0 2972, Santo Domingo, Republica Dominicana; +1 (809)689-4973, +1 (809)535-6614, fax: +1 (809)535-6646

Estonia

BALTBONE

Ants Work, Deputy Director, Institute of Cybernetics, Estonian Academy of Sciences; Akadeemie tee 21, EE 0108 Tallinn, Estonia; +007 0142 525622, fax: +007 0142 527901, email: ants@ioc.ee

Europe

EUNET

email: glenn@eu.net

Finland

DataNet

Seppo Noppari, Telecom Finland; P.O. Box 228, Rautatienkatu 10, 33101 Tampere, Finland; 358 31 243 2242, fax: 358 31 243 2211, email: seppo.noppari@tele.fi

FUNET

Finnish University and Research Network; P.O. Box 40, SF-02101 Espoo, Finland; +358 0 457 2711, fax: +358 0 457 2302, email: sadeniemi@funet.fi

France

EARN-France

Dominique Dumas; 950 rue de Saint Priest, 34184 Montpellier Cedex 4, France; +33 67 14 14 14, fax: +33 67 52 57 63, email: bruch@frmop11.bitnet

Fnet

FNET Association; 11 rue Carnot, 94270 Le Kemlin-Bicetre, France; +33 1 45 21 02 04, fax: +33 1 46 58 94 20, email: contact@fnet.fr

Germany

DFN

DFN-Verein e. V., Geschaeftsstelle; Pariser Strasse 44, D-1000 Berlin 15, Germany, +49 30 88 42 99 22, fax: +49 30 88 42 99 70, email: dfn-verein@dfn.dbp.de

Greece

ARIADNE

ARIADNE, NRCPS Demokritos; 153 10 Athens, Greece; +31 1 6513392, +30 1 6536351, fax: +30 1 6532910, +3- 1 6532175, email: postamster@isosun.ariadne-t.gr

Hungary

HUNGARNET

Geza Turchanyi, h2064tur@ella.hu

EARN Hungary

Laszlo Csaba, ib006csa@huearn.bitnet, Laszlo Zombory, H340zom@ella.hu

Ireland

HEANET

HEANET, Higher Education Authority; Fitzwilliam Square, Dublin, Ireland; +353 1 761545, fax: +353 1 610492, email: jhayden@vax1.tcd.ie

Israel

ILAN

Israeli Academic Network Information Center, Computer Center, Tel Aviv University; Ramat Aviv, Israel; +972 3 6408309, email: hank@vm.tau.ac.il

Italy

GARR

Gruppo Armonizzazione delle Reti per la Ricerca, Ufficio del Ministro per l'Universita e la Ricerca

Scientifica e Tecnologica, Lungotevere Thaon di Revel; 76, I--00196 Roma, Italy; +39 6 390095

IUnet

Alessandro Bernie, DIST, Universita di Genova; Via Opera Pia, 11A, 16145 Genova, Italy; +39 10 353-2747, fax: +39 10 353-2948, email: ab@dist.unige.it

Japan

WIDE

Prof. Jun Murai, KEIO University; 5322 Endo, Fujisawa, 252, Japan; +81 466 47 5111 ext. 3330, email: jun@wide.ad.jp

Latvia

Baltnet

Guntis Barzdins, email: gbardzdin@cs.lu.riga.lv, Ugis Berzins, ugis@fidogate.riga.lv, sergei Rotanov@rotanov@lumii.lat.su

Lithuania

Institute for Mathematics, Vilnius, Laimutis Telksnys, telksnys@mamii.lt.su

Mexico

ITESM

Ing Hugo E. Garcia Torres, Director, Depto. de Telecomunicaciones y Redes, ITESM Campus Monterrey; E. Garza Sada #2501, Monterrey, N.L., C.P. 64849, Mexico; +52 83 582 000 ext. 4130, fax: +52 83 588 931, email: hugo@mtecv1.mty.itesm.mx

Norway

UNINETT

UNINETT secretariat, SINTEF Delab; N-7034 Trondheim, Norway; +47 7 592980, fax: +47 7 532586, email: sekr@uninett.no

Poland

NASK

Daniel J. Bern, bern@plwrtu11.bitnet, Andrzej Zienkiewicz, osk03@plearn.bitnet

EARN Poland

Tomasz Hofmokl, fd150@plearn.bitnet

Romania

Florin Paunescu, florin@imag.fr, Paul Dan Cristea, pdcristea@pi-bucuresti.thdarmstadt.de

Russia

Relcom

Demos; 6 Ovchinnikovskaya nab., 113035 Moscow, Russia; +7 (095)231-2129, +7 (095)231-6395, fax: +7 (095)233-5016, email: postmaster@hq.demos.su, info@hq.demos.su

South Africa

UNINET

Foundation for Research Development; P.O. Box 2600, Pretoria 0001, South Africa; +27 12 841-3542, +27 12 841-2597, fax: +27 12 804-2679, email: uninet@frd.ac.za

Spain

RedIRIS

Secretaria RedIRIS, Fundesco, Alcala 61, 28014 Madrid, Spain; +34 1 435-1214, fax: +34 1 578-1773, email: secretaria@rediris.es

Sweden

NORDUNET

c/o SICS, P.O. Box 1263, S-164 28 Kista, Sweden; +46 8 752-1563, fax: +46 8 751-7230, email: NORDUNET@sics.se

SUNET

SUNET, UMDAC; S-901 87 Umea, Sweden; +46 90 16 56 45, fax: +46 90 16 67 62, email: ber@sunet.se

SWIPNet

14.4K charges	
Install	**40,000 SEK**
Monthly	**3800 SEK**

64K charges	
Install	**50,000 SEK**
Monthly	**10,000 SEK**

SwipNet is a subsidiary of Tele2 AB, owned 60% by the Swedish conglomerate Kinnnevik and 40% by Cable & Wireless. They offer both 14.4K and 64K service. Prices include a Cisco router and the access line to the nearest SWIPnet Pop. Commercial firms must also pay an international transfer charge. At current exchange rates, $1 = 5.75 SEK.

SwipNet; P.O. Box 6048, S-164 06 KISTA, Sweden; 46 8 924040, fax: 46 8 963695, email: `wallner@swip.net`. Contact: Olle Wallner

TIPnet

TIPnet, MegaCom AB, Kjell Simenstad; 121 80 Johanneshov, Stockholm, Sweden; +46 8 780-5616, fax: +46 8 686-0213

Switzerland

SWITCH

SWITCH Head Office; Limmatquai 138, CH-8001 Zurich, Switzerland; +41 1 256-5454, fax: +41 1 261-8133, email: `postmaster@switch.ch`

Taiwan

TANet

Computer Center, Ministry of Education; 12th Floor, No. 106, Sec. 2, Hoping E. Rd., Taipei, Taiwan; +886 2 7377010, fax: +886 2 7377043, email: `nisc@twnmoe10.edu.tw`

United Kingdom

CONNECT

UK PC Users Group; P.O. Box 360, Harrow HA1 4Lq, England; 44 081 863-6646, fax: 44 0 81 863-6095, email: `info@ibmpcug.co.uk`

Demon

Demon System, Ltd.; 42 Hendon Lane, London N3 ITT, England; +44 81 349-0063, email: `internet@demon.co.uk`

JANET

Joint Academic Network, JANET Liaison Desk, c/o Rutherford Appleton Laboratory, Chilton Didcot; GB-Oxon OX11 OQX, United Kingdom; +44 235-5517, email: `JANET-LIAISON-DESK@jnt.ac.uk`

PIPEX

Unipalm, Ltd.; 216 The Science Park, Cambridge, CB4 4WA, United Kingdom; +44 223 424616, fax: +44 223 426868, email: `pipex@unipalm.ca.uk`

UKnet

UKnet Support Group, Computing Laboratory, University of Kent; Canterbury, Kent CT2 7NF, United Kingdom; `postmaster@uknet.ac.uk`

National service providers

Advanced Network and Services, Inc. (ANS)

ANS; 2901 Hubbard St., ITI Building, G-1, Ann Arbor, MI 48105; (313)663-7610, fax: (313)663-2927, email: `info@ans.net`

Suggestion
Hybrid Access System

IN Channel service	**$99/month**
Model 100 adapter	**$1495**

Hybrid Networks provides Internet access using cable TV channels. Their asymmetric link, running at 10 Mbps for incoming traffic, and 14.4 Kbps (modem) for outgoing traffic, requires a Remote Link Adapter (RLA), which is available in Ethernet versions (model 100) or S-bus (model 200). Service is available in the Bay Area now, and will eventually be rolled out nationwide.

Hybrid Networks, Inc.; 20863 Stevens Creek Blvd., Suite 300, Cupertino, CA 95014-2116; (408)725-3250, fax: (408)725-2439, email: `css@hybrid.com`

Downright Speculation
Performance Systems International, Inc.
Mail flat fee

Quarterly fee	**$75**
USENET and Mail flat fee	
Quarterly fee	**$225**
Setup fee	**$75**

UUPSI offers flat-fee USENET news and mail service, with no connect charges.

Performance Systems International, Inc.; 11800 Sunrise Valley Dr., Suite 1100, Reston, VA 22091; (800)82P-SI82, (703)620-6651, fax: (703)620-2430, email: `all-info@psi.com` for a list of mailboxes to get info at, such as `scs-info@psi.com` (standard connection service), `uupsi-info@psi.com` (UUCP service), etc.

Recommendation
Information Access Technologies (IAT)
HoloNet

HoloDNS	**$25**
56 kbps SLIP monthly	**$1000**
19.2 kbps SLIP monthly	**$750**
9600 bps SLIP monthly	**$500**

IAT offers nationwide access to the widest range of services of any Internet provider. These include UUCP, SLIP, PPP, and dial-in accounts; dedicated lines, ISDN connections, and leased line services; USENET feeds via NNTP, UUCP, and QWK packet methods; and a variety of services for BBS operators looking to put their systems on the Internet, including Domain Name Service, and gateways for various BBS products. The HoloMailer service lets people set up their own mail servers. HoloNet also provides UUCP service for QuickMail, Microsoft Mail, and Novell MHS. A graphical interface to Internet is in the works. The IAT service, called HoloNet, is a menu-based system that does not offer access to the UNIX shell.

IAT; 46 Shattuck Square, Suite 11, Berkeley, CA 94704, (510)704-0160, fax: (510)704-8019, dialin: (510)704-1058, email: info@holonet.net

Sprint Communications Co., Government Systems Division

SprintNet offers some of the best deals around on resellable T1 links for ToasterNets.

SprintLink; 13221 Woodland Park Road, Herndon, VA 22071; (703)904-2167, fax: (703)904-2680

Downright Speculation
Alternet

T1 monthly	**$2000**
56 kbps monthly	**$1000**
19.2 kbps monthly	**$750**
9600 bps monthly	**$500**
9600 bps SLIP	**$500**

Typical monthly local loop:

T1	**$750**
56 kbps	**$500**
19.2 kbps	**$130**
9600 bps	**$130**
9600 bps SLIP	**$130**

Typical startup fees:

T1	**$5000**
56 kbps	**$2000**
19.2 kbps	**$3000**
9600 bps	**$1500**
9600 SLIP	**$1500**

Initial hardware:

T1	**$1000**
56 kbps	**$500**
19.2 kbps	**$500**
9600 bps	**$500**
9600 bps SLIP	**$250**
(no router)	

Be aware that the costs given above do not include additional hardware you may need. Service at 56 kbps or faster requires a dedicated router at your location. The local loop costs are for connection to the nearest U.S. Sprint Point of Presence (POP) and are therefore typical costs only; your mileage may vary. The startup fees include one-time costs such as a startup fee from UUNET and the installation cost for the line to the POP. UUNET also sells Telebit modems at some of the lowest prices around.

UUNET Technologies, Inc.; 3110 Fairview Park Dr., Suite 570, Falls Church, VA 22042; (703)204-8000, fax: (703)204-8001, email: info@uunet.uu.net

Recommendation
Netcom Online Communications Services, Inc.

Dialup Account	
Signup fee	**$15**
(unlimited use, autobilled)	**$20/month**
USENET/UUCP service	
(unlimited)	**$45/month**
Personal SLIP	
Signup fee	**$50**
Maintenance fee	**$20/month**
Hourly fee	**$2**
Dedicated port SLIP	
Installation fee	**$650**
Monthly fee	**$160**
SLIP leased line (9600)	
Installation fee	**$650**
Monthly fee	**$180**
SLIP leased line (19,200)	
Installation fee	**$650**
Monthly fee	**$250**
SLIP leased line (38,400)	
Installation fee	**$650**
Monthly fee	**$275**

Netcom is a nationwide Internet service provider. Personal SLIP/PPP access is available at all access points. Netcom also allows users to create their own anonymous FTP server directories and mail servers, without additional charges.

Netcom Online Communications Services; 4000 Moorpark Ave., Suite 209, San Jose, CA 95117;(408)554-UNIX, fax: (408)241-9145, email: info@netcom.com; dialin access: Alameda: (510)865-9004; San Jose: (408)241-9760; Palo Alto: (415)328-

9940; Pleasanton: (510)426-6610, Santa Cruz: (408)459-9851, Irvine: (714)708-380, Washington, D.C.: (703)255-5951, Atlanta: (404)303-9765, Dallas: (214)753-0045, Los Angeles: (310)842-8835, Sacramento: (916) 965-1371, San Diego: (619) 234-0524, Seattle: (206)547-5992

Pathways

Signup fee	$25
Maintenance	$8/month
Hourly rate	$3

Pathways; (415)346-4188, (800)758-4777, email: info@path.net

U.S. dialup providers

California

a2i
Dialup accounts

Standard dialup	$20/month
3 months paid in advance	$15/month
6 months paid in advance	$12/month

UUCP service

Standard feed	$35/month
Low volume	$20/month

a2i offers Internet access as well as news and mail feeds via UUCP. Accounts include 5 Mb of disk allocation. a2i serves area code 408.

a2i Communications; 1211 Park Ave. #202, San Jose, CA 95126-2924; (408)293-8078, dial-in: (408)293-9010, login: **guest**, email: info@rahul.net

Downright Speculation
Anterior Technology
USENET service

Setup fee	$50
Monthly maintenance	$30
Hourly, incoming calls	$1.95

Anterior offers all of the conferences on USENET, including the ClariNet news services. Anterior also gateways between wireless data networks such as Mobitex and the Internet via their Radiomail service.

Geoff Goodfellow, Anterior Technology; 2600 Campus Drive, San Mateo, CA 94403; (415)286-7800, fax: (415)286-7801, email: info@fernwood.mpk.ca.us, info@radiomail.net

Suggestion
CRL

Dialup Account

(unlimited use, autobilled)	$17.50/month
(unlimited use)	$19.50/month
USENET/UUCP service	
(unlimited)	$45/month
Dedicated SLIP/PPP	
(unlimited)	$150/month

CRL is a Bay Area Internet service provider offering SLIP/PPP, UUCP, and dialup accounts. CRL offers 800 service as well as Bay Area-wide service.

CRL; Box 326, Larkspur, CA 94977; (415)381-2800, fax: (415)381-9578, dialup access: (415)389-UNIX, email: support@crl.com, info@crl.com

Cyberspace Station

Account Setup fee	$10
1 hour/day access	$20/month
6 month prepayment fee	$15/month

204 N. El Camino Real, Suite E626, Encinitas, CA 92024; (619)944-9498, ext. 626, dial-in: (619)634-1376, help@cyber.net

Portal Communications Corporation

Signup fee	$19.95
Monthly fee	$19.95/month

Portal; 20863 Stevens Creek Blvd., Suite 200, Cupertino, CA 95014; (408)973-9111, fax: (408)725-1580, email: CS@cup.portal.com, info@portal.com

The WELL

Maintenance	$15/month
Hourly fee	$2
CPN access	$4/hour

Supports Picospan conferencing, mail, USENET, ftp, telnet, and other Internet services.
To register, call (415)332-6106 (2400 bps), login: NEWUSER.

The WELL; 27 Gate 5 Rd., Sausalito, CA 94965; (415)332-4335, fax: (415)332-1669, email: info@well.sf.ca.us

Colorado

Community News Service

Setup fee	$35
Monthly minimum (10 hrs)	$20
Extra hours	$2/hour
Disk space	$2.5/Mb per month

CNS offers full access to Internet via the UNIX shell, as well as ClariNet newsgroups. CNS offers a 25% discount for educators and educational institutions.

Community News Service; 1155 Kelly Johnson Blvd., Suite 400, Colorado Springs, CO 80920; (719)592-1240, fax: (719)592-1201, dial-in: (719)570-1700, email: klaus@cscns.com

Colorado SuperNet (Colorado)

Domain Name Service	**$20**
Setup Fee (all accounts)	**$20**
UUCP, SLIP, dialup	**$2/hour**

In addition to serving businesses and educational institutions, Colorado SuperNet also offers UNIX dialup accounts with access to mail, newsgroups, telnet, ftp, WAIS, Gopher, W3 and other services;. They also offer UUCP accounts, and SLIP/PPP access.

Colorado SuperNet; P.O. Box 39, Golden, CO; (303)273-3471, fax: (303)273-3475, email: Kharmon@csn.org

Old Colorado City Communications

Monthly fee	**$25**

Old Colorado City Communications; 2502 W. Colorado Ave., Suite 203, Colorado Springs, CO 80904; (719)632-4848, fax: (719)593-7521, data: (719)632-2658, 632-4111, login: **newuser**, email: dave@oldcolo.com

Indiana

Gator Communications

Gator offers mail and news feeds and maintains the regional UUCP mapping database.

Gator Communications; P.O. Box 151, South Bend, IN 46624-0151; (219)232-3900, dial-in: (219)289-0777, (317)251-7391, email: larry@gator.rn.com

Massachusetts

World

Maintenance	**$5/month**
Hourly fee	**$2**
20/20 plan	**$20/month**
(includes 20 hours,	
5 Mb disk space)	
disk space	**$5/Mb/month**

Supports mail, USENET, Internet chat, Gopher, WAIS, ClariNet, ftp and telnet. World also offers

discounts for BMUG and BCS members and volunteers.

Software Tool & Die; 1330 Beacon St., Suite 215, Brookline, MA 02146; (617)739-0202, fax: (617)739-0914, email: staff@world.std.com

Maryland

Express Access Online Communications Service

Full Internet service	**$25/month**
Mail/news dialup only	**$15/month**

Digital Express Group, Inc.; 6006 Greenbelt Rd. #228, Greenbelt, MD 20770; (301)220-2020, dial-in: (301)220-0462, (410)766-1855, login: **new**, email: info@digex.com

New Jersey

JVNCNet

Dialup SLIP maintenance	**$19/month**
Dialup SLIP setup	**$36**
SLIP Hourly fee	**$10**
dedicated SLIP	**$99/month**
SLIP + shell	**$120/month**
SLIP setup	**$99**

JVNCNet; (800)35-TIGER, (609)258-2400, email: info@jvnc.net

New York

Echo

First 30 hours	**$19.95/month**
First 30 hours, student	**$13.75/month**
Additional access	**$1/hour**
Internet access	**$9/month**
Unlimited use	**$49.95/month**
Student unlimited	**$43.75/month**
WON & WAC only	**$6.95/month**

Supports Caucus and UUCP mail. telnet, ftp, and USENET access are planned.

Echo Communications Group, Inc.; 97 Perry St., Suite 13, New York, NY 10014; (212)255-3839, online signup: (212)989-8411, (2400-8-N-1), email: echo!horn@panix.com

MindVox

Unlimited use	**$15/month**

MindVox offers full Internet access as well as local conferences on Cyberspace, Virtual Reality, Legal Issues, Security and Viruses, health and alternative medicine, and beauty. MindVox uses Waffle as its BBS software. New members get two weeks of free use. Many of the world's foremost security experts are online at MindVox.

Phantom Access; 1562 First Avenue, Suite 351, New York, NY 10028, (212)989-2418, dialin: (212)989-4141, info@phantom.com

PANIX Public Access Internet

Basic service	$10/month
Discount for yearly service	$20
Internet Service addon	$27/quarter
Internet startup fee	$40
UUCP/USENET	
(to 2 Mb/day)	$5/month
High-speed access	$15 one-time fee
SLIP/PPP dedicated 19.2	$300/month

Panix Public Access Internet, Public Access Networks Corporation, Suite 8F; 110 Riverside Dr., New York, NY 10024; (212)877-4854, dial-in: (212)787-3100, email: info@panix.com

North Carolina

Rock, Research Triangle, North Carolina

Installation	$200
Unlimited use	$25/month

Supports `ftp`, `telnet`, USENET, mail. 56 Kbps and T1 Internet connections are available. Rock is reachable via PC-Pursuit. There are no hourly charges, but disk quotas are enforced.

Rock; email: sellers@concert.net, dorcas@concert.net

Ohio

APK

Unlimited use	$35/month
Registration fee	$20

Akademia Pana Kleksa (APK) offers full Shell Internet access, as well as UniBoard BBS access (`login: bbs`), UUCP/USENET feeds.

APK; 197909 Mohican Ave., Cleveland, OH 44119; dialin: (216)481-9445, `telnet` **wariat.wariat.org,** email: info@wariat.org

Pennsylvania

Telerama

Monthly minimum	$6
(includes 10 hours online time)	
Hourly fees	$0.60
Monthly maximum bill	$30
(unlimited use)	

Telerama offers full Internet access, including ClariNet/UPI newsgroups. Telerama, email: sysop@telerama.pgh.pa.us

Rhode Island

Anomaly

One hr/day (commercial)	$30/month
One hr/day (educational)	$15/month
Extra hour/day	$10/month
UUCP/USENET	$2/hr
Yearly prepayment (commercial)	$200
Yearly prepayment (educational)	$120

Anomaly offers a menu-driven system with dial-in access. They also offer UUCP/USENET, Domain Name Service.

Small Business Systems, Inc.; Anomaly Systems Administration, 33 Moorland Ave., Providence, RI 02908; (401)273-4669, dial-in: (401)455-0347, (401)331-3706

IDS World Network

Dialup Service	$12.50/month
Yearly prepayment	$100

IDS offers full access to Internet in addition to offering RIME conferences.

IDS; (401)884-7856, dialin: (401)884-9002, (401)884-7564, email: sysadmin@ids.net

Texas

Texas Metronet

Dedicated SLIP/PPP	$150/month
SLIP/PPP setup fees	$40
UUCP/USENET feeds	$50/month
UUCP setup fees	$40

Texas Metronet offers Internet access as well as UUCP/USENET feeds and SLIP/PPP connections.

Texas Metronet; (214)705-2900, fax: (214)401-2802, dial-in: (214)705-2902, email: info@metronet.com

Sugarland UNIX

NeoSoft; 3918 Panorama, Missouri City, TX 77459; (713)438-8964, email: info@nesoft.com

Virginia

Grebyn

Dialup Service	**$30/month**
(includes 25 hrs/mo)	
Extra hours	**$1.20/hour**
Disk space	**$2/Mb per month**
(1 Mb included with dialup account)	
Setup fee	**$30**

Grebyn; P.O. Box 497, Vienna, VA 22183-0497; (703)281-2194, telnet grebyn.com

Washington

Eskimo North
Dialup service	**$10/mo**
12-month prepayment	**$96/yr**

Eskimo offers shell access to the Internet. The first two weeks are free. To create an account, telnet or dial-in, login: **new**

Dialin: (206)367-3837, email: nanook@eskimo.com

Halcyon
Startup fee	**$10**
Annual prepayment	**$200**

Halcyon offers UNIX shell accounts with Internet access.

Halcyon; (206)955-1050, dialup: (206)382-6245, login: **new**, email: info@halcyon.com

Seattle Online

2318 2nd Ave., #45, Seattle, WA 98121; (206)328-2412, email: info@online.com

Wisconsin

Milwaukee Internet X

Mix Communications; P.O. Box 17166, Milwaukee, WI 53217; (414)962-8172, email: sysop@mixcom.com

U.S. regional networks

These regional networks concentrate on offering dedicated connections to educational and research institutions.

BARRNET (San Francisco Bay Area)

Pine Hall, Room 115, Stanford University, Stanford, CA 94305; (415)725-1790, fax: (415)723-0010, email: info@nic.barrnet.net, Contact: Paul Baer, baer@jessica.stanford.edu

CERFNet (Southern California)

3550 General Atomics St., San Diego, CA 92121-1194; (619)455-3900, fax: (619)455-3990, email: help@cerf.net

CICNet (Midwest)

ITI Building, 2901 Hubbard, Ann Arbor, MI 48109; (313)998-6103, fax: (313)998-6105, info@cic.net;

Colorado SuperNet (Colorado)

P.O. Box 39, Golden, CO; (303)273-3471, fax: (303)273-3475, email: Kharmon@csn.org

CONCERT (North Carolina)

P.O. Box 12889, 3021 Cornwallis Rd., Research Trinagle Park, NC 27709; (919)248-1404, fax: (919)248-1405, email: info@concert.net

CREN

1112 16th St. NW, Washington, D.C. 20036; (202)872-4200, fax: (202)872-4318, email: conklin@bitnic.bitnet

CSUNET

Information Resources and Technology; P.O. Box 3842, Seal Beach, CA 90740-7842; (213)985-9669, fax: (213)985-9400, email: chris@calstate.edu

FARNET

100 5th Ave., 4th Floor, Waltham, MA 02154; (617)890-5117, fax: (617)890-5117, email: breeden@farnet.org

Appendix B: Choice Products

INet (Indiana)

Wrubel Computing Center, Indiana University; 750 N. State Rd. 46, Bloomington, IN 47405; (812)855-4240, email: ellis@ucs.indiana.edu

Los Nettos (Los Angeles)

Los Nettos Associates

64 Kbps install	**$2000**
1.5 Mbps install	**$4000**
Yearly	**$5000**

Full membership (T1 only)

Install	**$25,000**
Yearly	**$25,000**

Equipment costs

Cisco router	**$3006.50**
Extra memory	**$560**
Cisco V.35 cable	**$100**
Datatel 3081 DSU/CSU	
	$1113
Tax @ 8.25%	**$394.31**

Los Nettos; caters to universities and research laboratories, although the associates programs is open to commercial firms. Prices do not include costs of routers and CSU/DSUs, listed above. Associates membership does not include phone system costs. Los Nettos does not provide dialup service. It may be used for commercial purposes.

Los Nettos; 4676 Admiralty Way, Floor 10, Suite 1001, Marina Del Rey, CA 92092; (310)822-1511, fax: (310)823-6714, email: los-nettos-request@isi.edu, Contact: Ann Westine Cooper, (310)822-1511, email: cooper@isi.edu

MERIT/MichNet (Michigan)

MERIT; 2901 Hubbard, Pod G, Ann Arbor, MI 48105; (313)764-9430, fax: (313)747-3185, email: jogden@merit.edu

MIDnet (Nebraska)

MIDnet; 501 Building 113.1, Lincoln, NE 68588; (402)472-8971, fax: (402)472-8486

MRNet (Minnesota)

MRNet offers dedicated 56 Kbps and T1 access, as well as dialup SLIP access, toll free in the Twin-Cities area.

MRNet, 511 11th Ave., Box 212 South, Minneapolis, MN 55415; (612)342-2570, fax: (612)344-1716, email: info@mr.net

MSEN (Michigan)

Maintenance	**$5/month**
Hourly fee	**$2**
20/20 plan	**$20/month**

MSEN offers shell and SLIP access.

MSEN, Inc.; 628 Brooks St., Ann Arbor, MI 48103; email: (313)998-4562, info@msen.com

NCAR

NCAR; P.O. Box 3000, Boulder, CO; 80307-3000; (303)497-1222, fax: (303)497-1137, email: choy@ncar.ucar.edu

NEARnet (ME, NH, VT, CT, RI, MA)

NEARnet; BB, 10 Moulton St., Cambridge, MA 02138; (617)873-8730, fax: (617)873-5620, email: NEARNet-staff@nic.near.net

NETillinois (Illinois)

NETillinois; 1501 W. Bradley Ave., Peoria, IL 61625, (309)677-3100, fax: (309)677-3092, email: joel@bradley.edu

New Mexico Technet (NM)

Technet; 4100 Osuna Boulevard, NE, Suite 103, Albuquerque, NM 87109; (505)345-6555, email: reynolds@technet.nm.org

NevadaNet (NV)

NevadaNet; 4505 Maryland Pkwy., Las Vegas, NV 89154; (702)597-4500, fax: (702)739-3791, email: greyfox@nevada.edu

NorthWestNet (AK, ID, MT, ND, OR, WA, WY)

NorthWestNet; 15400 S.E. 30th Pl., Suite 202, Bellvue, WA 98007; (206)562-3000, (206)562-4822, email: ehood@nwnet.net

NSFNet

NSFNet, Bolt Beranek and Newman, Inc.; 10 Moulton St., Cambridge, MA 02174; (617)873-3087, fax: (617)873-5620, email: ccarroll@nnsc.nsf.net

NYSERNet (New York)

NYSERNet; 111 College Place, Suite 3-211, Syracuse, NY 13244; (315)443-4120, fax: (315)425-7518, email: `info@nysernet.org`

OARnet (Ohio)

Shared line

Install	$100
Monthly minimum	$40
Dialup hourly rate	$4
950 service hourly	$10
800 number hourly	$12

Dedicated line

Installation	$500
Monthly fee	$330
Support hourly	$100

Research & engineering Leased Line

Unbundled 56 Kbps	$11,500/year
Full service 56 Kbps	$13,000/year
T1, 1.5 Mbps	$31,000/year

Unrestricted leased line

Unbundled 56 Kbps	$1200/year
Full service 56 Kbps	$13,500/year
T1, 1.5 Mbps	$32,000/year

OARNet concentrates on serving local firms and educational institutions. It allows unrestricted commercial traffic on its statewide T1 backbone network. They offer SLIP and PPP connections over voice-grade lines, in addition to leased line service.

OARnet; 1224 Kinnear Rd., Columbus, OH 43212-1163; (614)292-8100, fax: (614)292-7168, email: `nic@oar.net`, tech support: (800)686-1510 or (614)292-6277, Contact: Demetris C. Socli, `demetris@oar.net`

PACCOM

University of Hawaii, Department of ICS; 2565 The Mall, Honolulu, HI 96822; (808)949-6395, `torben@foralie.ics.hawaii.edu`

PREPnet (Pennsylvania)

PREPnet; 305 S. Craig St., Second Floor, Pittsburgh, PA 15213; (412)268-7870, fax: (412)268-7875, email: `prepnet@andrew.cmu.edu`

PSCnet (PE, OH, WV)

PSCnet is for supercomputing access only.

Pittsburgh Supercomputing Ctr.; 4400 5th Ave., Pittsburgh, PA 15213; (412)268-4960, fax: (412)268-5832, email: `hastings@psc.edu`

Intelecom Data Systems World Network (formerly RISCNet)

IntelliCom Data Systems; 11 Franklin Rd., East Greenwich, RI 02818; (401)885-6855, email: `info@ids.com`

SDSCnet (San Diego)

SDSCnet is for supercomputing access.

SDSCnet; San Diego Supercomputing Ctr., P.O. Box 85608, San Diego, CA 92186-9784; (619)534-5043, fax: (619)514-5152, email: `loveep@sdsc.edu`

Sesquinet (Texas)

Sesquinet; P.O. Box 1892, Houston, TX 77251; (713)527-6038, fax: (713)527-6099, email: `gerbode@rice.edu`

Sprint International

Sprint International; 13221 Woodland Park Dr., Herndon, VA 22071; (703)904-2167, fax: (703)904-2680, email: `rdoyle@icm1.icp.net`

SURAnet (Southeastern US)

SURAnet; 8400 Baltimore Blvd., Suite 101, College Park, MD 20740; (301)982-4600, fax: (301)982-4605, email: `mtaranto@sura.net`

THENet (Texas)

THENet, Office of Telecommunications Services; Service Bldg. Rm 319, Austin, TX 78712; (512)471-2444, fax: (512)471-2449, email: `info@nic.the.net`

VERnet (Virginia)

VERnet; Gilmer Hall, B008, University of Virginia, Charlottesville, VA 22903; (804)924-0616, fax: (804)982-4715, email: `jaj@virginia.edu`

Westnet (AZ, CO, ID, NM, UT, WY)

Westnet; 601 S. Howes, 6th Fl. South, Colorado State University, Ft. Collins, CO 80523; (303)491-7260, fax: (303)491-1055, email: `pburns@yuma.acns.colostate.edu`

WiscNet (Wisconsin)

WiscNet; 1210 W. Dayton St., Madison, WI 53706; (608)262-8874, fax: (608)262-4679, email: dorl@macc.wisc.edu

WVNET (West Virginia)

WVNET; 837 Chestnut Ridge Rd., Morgantown, WV 26505; (304)293-5192, (304)293-5540, email: cc011041@wvnvms.wvnet.edu

Chapter 9 – Electronic Mail

Suggestion
QuickMail v2.5

1 user	$190
5 users	$340
10 users	$500
50 users	$2300

QuickMail's newest release now includes software for the PC and the Mac in the same package, as well as greatly improved remote access software. Although I do not recommend QuickMail for use in large installations (use of a UNIX-based mail server will be both less expensive and more reliable), for small work groups it gets the nod. Make sure you have the latest version of the Apple Modem Tool; problems have been reported with earlier versions.

CE Software; 1854 Fuller Rd., P.O. Box 65580, West Des Moines, IA 50265; (800)523-7638

Downright Speculation
Rapport

Rapport integrates word processing, spreadsheets, and charting with email and fax support. The product supports X.500 directory service and can convert a variety of PC, Mac, and UNIX file formats. It is available for Hewlett-Packard, DEC, IBM, Silicon Graphics, and Sun workstations.

Clarity Software Inc.; 2700 Garcia Ave., Mountain View, CA 94043; (415)691-0320, fax: (415)964-4383

Downright Speculation
BeyondMail v1.1

While other email vendors are still trying to send files and messages back and forth between platforms, BeyondMail has started down the road of creating a personal electronic assistant. BeyondMail gives users the power to screen, forward, and automatically take actions based on their mail. BeyondMail supports Novell MHS and Banyan

VINES. The company has also recently introduced Macintosh and Windows versions.

Beyond, Inc.; 17 New England Executive Park, Burlington, MA 01803; (617)229-0006, fax: (617)229-1114.

POP Software – Macintosh

Recommendation

Eudora v1.3	**Free**
Eudora v2.0	**$50**

Eudora is a popmail reader that can send and receive files too. It is compatible with TCP/IP, UUCP, and serial communications, and in serial mode is supported by Holonet and Netcom. Available via `ftp sumex-aim.stanford.edu, cd /info-mac/comm, or ftp.qualcomm.com, cd /mac/eudora`. Insanely great!

Recommendation

PCEudora v1.0	**Free**
PCEudora v2.0 (commercial)	**$50**

PCEudora is a Windows Sockets compatible version of the Eudora POP3 and SMTP mail package written by Qualcomm. The interface and reliability of Mac Eudora is legendary; PCEudora is in every way the equal of the Mac version.

Available via `sunsite.unc.edu, get /pub/micro/pc-stuff/ms-windows/winsock/apps/pce11a10.exe`

Qualcomm; 10555 Sorrento Valley Road, San Diego, CA 92121-1617; (619)597-5103, fax: (619)587-8276, email: jwn2@qualcommm.com

Other Clients

TechMail	`net-dist.mit.edu, cd /pub/TechMail, cd /pub/TechNotify`
MacPOP	`lilac.berkeley.edu, cd /pub`
MailCall	`boombox.micro.umn.edu, cd /pub/POPmail/macintosh/MailCall`

Servers

MailStop (POP2)	`boombox.micro.umn.edu, cd /pub/POPmail/macintosh`

POP Software – PC

Clients

POPmail	`boombox.micro.umn.edu, cd /pub/pc`

UCDmail `ucdavis.ucdavis.edu,`
`cd /dist`

PCPOP `trident.arc.nasa.gov`

POP software – UNIX

Clients

Popper `lilac.berkeley.edu, cd`
`/pub/mh`
imapd `ics.uci.edu, cd /pub/mh`
ipop3d `ftphost.cac.washington.edu,`
`cd /local/etc.next1.0, cd`
`/local/etc.pmax4.0`

Servers

SCO POP `anomaly.sbs.risc.net`
POP3 `ftp.uu.net`

Mail software – alternate character sets

Kanji `ucdavis.ucdavis.edu, cd`
`/pub/Kanji`

IMAP2 Software

Mac POPMail

`ftp sumex-aim.stanford.edu, cd imap`

PC Pine

`ftp ftp.cac.washington.edu, cd /mail,`
`get pcpine_n.zip` (Novell LWP),
`pcpine_f.zip` (FTP PC/TCP version),
`pcpine_p.zip` (WATTCP version)

BINHEX

PC `ftp boombox.micro.umn.edu,`
`cd /pub/binhex/MSDOS`
Mac `ftp boombox.micro.umn.edu,`
`cd /pub/binhex/Mac`

Finger

Suggestion
MacFinger, MacTalk   **Free**

These applications let you talk to other Internet
users, as well as finger users (and be fingered).

Available via `ftp sumex-aim.stanford.edu,`
`cd /info-mac/comm.`

Recommendation
Finger v3.1   **Free**

This is a Windows Sockets version of finger.

Available via `sunsite.unc.edu, get`
`/pub/micro/pc-stuff/ms-`
`windows/winsock/apps/finger31.zip`

Ph documentation

General `ftp ftp.acns.nwu.edu`
`cd /pub/ph/mac`

Ph clients

Mac `ftp ftp.acns.nwu.edu`
`cd /pub/ph/mac`
NeXT `ftp boombox.micro.umn.edu`
`cd /pub/gopher/NeXT`
UNIX `ftp uxc.cso.uiuc.edu`
`get /pub/ph-6.2.tar.Z`

Ph servers

UNIX `ftp uxc.cso.uiuc.edu`
`get /pub/qi-2.1.tar.Z`

Hint for NeXT users trying to build the QI server:
Remove the include of unistd.h from ph.c, and it will
compile just fine.

Mailing list software

The Unix LISTSERV Program (TULP):
`ftp grasp1.univ-lyon1.fr, cd`
`/pub/unix/mail/tulp`
`ftp to lut.fi, cd /pub/tulp`

LISTSERV mailing list program:
`ftp cs.bu.edu, cd /pub/listserv`

Almanac Mail Server (requires root access):
`ftp oes.orst.edu, mget /pub/almanac-`
`*.tar.Z`, contact: `almanac-admin@oes.orst.edu.`

Various mailing list and mail servers:
`ftp gatekeeper.dec.com, cd`
`/.8/mail/srv`

Squirrel Mail Server:
`mail mail-server@nluug.nl`, with the
following commands in the body:
`begin`
`send mail-server`
`end`

Chapter 10 – FTP and Archie

Recommendation
Fetch v2.1
Nonprofits **Free**
Commercial use **$25**

Fetch is a Macintosh FTP client by Jim Matthews of Dartmouth. Available via `ftp sumex-aim.stanford.edu, cd /info-mac/comm.`

Software Sales, Dartmouth College; 6028 Kiewit Computation Center, Hanover, NH 03755-3523; email: fetch@dartmouth.edu

Recommendation
FTPd v2.1
Shareware **$5**

FTPd is a shareware Macintosh FTP server that can handle mulitple simultaneous sessions.

Available by `ftp sumex-aim.stanford.edu, cd /info-mac/comm.`

Peter Lewis; 10 Earlston Way, Booragoon, Perth, WA 6154, Australia; peter@cujo.curtin.ed.au

Suggestion
FTPShare
TCPPack tools

FTPShare is the first multisession background FTP server for Macintosh OS. FTPShare uses MacTCP, and works with any physical connection, including Ethernet, LocalTalk, Token Ring, and SLIP. FTPShare supports up to 20 simultaneous FTP sessions. Administration is maintained through a graphical interface similar to System 7 file sharing, with individual passwords and privilege levels (read-only, write-only, and read-write) available.

Advanced Software Concepts also offers the TCPPack tools which includes a `telnet` tool.

Advanced Software Concepts, Dominique Ducasse; 9551, rue de Saint Laurent du Var, F-06610 La Gaude, France; voice: (33) 93 24 76 00, fax: (33) 93 24 76 06; email, ADV.SOFT@applelink.apple.com

Root Int'l, Paul Lucero; 10601 S. de Anza Blvd., Suite 103, Cupertino, CA 95014; (408)864-0695, fax: (408)864-0694; email: HELIOS.USA@applelink.apple.com

Sysnet Corp., Majid Matinrazm; 5301 Wisconsin Ave., NW, Suite 640, Washington, D.C. 20015; (202)686-5515, fax: (202)686-6992

Downright Speculation
FTP daemon **Free**

This is an FTP daemon for Windows NT.

Available via **sunsite.unc.edu**, `get /pub/micro/pc-stuff/ms-windows/winsock/apps/nt-ftpd.zip`

Archie

Macintosh Archie client (MacArchie) :
`ftp sumex-aim.stanford.edu, cd /info-mac/comm`

NeXT Archie client:
`ftp cs.orst.edu, cd /pub/next/binaries/wide-area-info/`

DOS Archie client:
`ftp omnigate.clarkson.edu, get /pub/cutcp/archie.zip`

UNIX Prospero:
`ftp june.cs.washington.edu, get /pub/prospero.tar.Z.`

Chapter 11 – Telnet

Suggestion
WinQVT/Net **Free**

This is a Windows Sockets compatible version of FTP and Telnet.

Available via `ftp biochemistry.bioc.cwru.edu, cd /pub/qvtnet`

Downright Speculation
WinTel **Free**

WinTel is a version of Telnet for Windows. It is available in a version supporting Windows Sockets, as well as one using the NCSA TCP/IP windows library.

Available via `ftp ftp.ncsa.uiuc.edu, cd /Telnet/windows/executables/ wtel1b1.zip`

Available via `sunsite.unc.edu`, `cd /pub/micro/pc-stuff/ms-windows/winsock/apps`

Recommendation
NCSA/BYU Telnet v2.5   **Free**

NCSA Telnet is a `telnet` and FTP implementation. Multiple sessions can be open simultaneously.

Available by `ftp sumex-aim.stanford.edu`, `cd /info-mac/comm`, or `ftp ftp.ncsa.uiuc.edu`, `cd /mac/telnet`; to retrieve files by mail, `mail archive-server@ncsa.uiuc.edu`

NCSA Software Development; 152 Computing Applications Bldg., 605 East Springfield Ave., Champaign, IL 61820.

NCSA Telnet for DOS:
`ftp merit.edu`, `cd /pub/ppp/ncsappp.zip`, or `ftp ftp.ncsa.uiuc.edu`, `cd /pc/telnet`

Mac version of tn3270:
`ftp ftp.ncsa.uiuc.edu`, `cd /mac/telnet/contributions/tn3270`

Mac version of Hytelnet:
`ftp access.usask.ca`, `cd /pub/hytelnet/mac`

PC version of Hytelnet:
`ftp access.usask.ca`, `cd /pub/hytelnet/pc`

UNIX Hytelnet client:
`ftp access.usask.ca`, `cd /pub/hytelnet/unix`

Catalist:
`ftp ftp.cso.uiuc.edu`, `cd /net-nav/library/catalist`, and `/net-nav/library/internet`

Chapter 12 – USENET

Recommendation
NewsWatcher v2.0   **Free**

NewsWatcher is a graphical news reader for the Macintosh implementing NNTP.

Available via `ftp acns.nwu.edu`, `cd /pub/newswatcher`

John Norstad, Academic Computing and Network Services Northwestern University; email: `j-norstad@nwu.edu`

Suggestion
Nuntius v1.1.7   **Free**

Nuntius is a graphical NNTP newsreader for the Macintosh that looks a lot like System 7's hierarchical browser.

Available by `ftp sumex-aim.stanford.edu`, `cd /info-mac/comm`.

To subscribe to the Nuntius LISTSERV, `mail LISTSERV@CORNELL.EDU`, body: `SUB NUNTIUS-L <Your Name>`

Peter Speck; email: `speck@dat.ruc.dk`

Recommendation
InterNews v1.0
Shareware   **$25**

InterNews gets my recommendation as the best Macintosh NNTP newsreader. It is a hierarchical reader like Nuntius, but also supports creating your own groupings and associated icons. It was created by Dartmouth, and is available via `ftp ftp.dartmouth.edu`, `mget /pub/mac/InterNews*.*`.

Recommendation
Windows Trumpet v1.0   **Free**

Windows Trumpet is a Windows Sockets compatible version of the Trumpet newsreader.

Available via `ftp ftp.utas.edu.au`, `cd /pc/trumpet`

Recommendation
WinVN v0.80   **Free**

WinVN is another Windows Sockets compatible newsreader.

Available via `ftp titan.ksc.nasa.gov`, `cd /pub/win3/winvn`

Available via `sunsite.unc.edu`, `cd /pub/micro/pc-stuff/ms-windows/winsock/apps/winvnstd080.zip`

Chapter 13 – IRC and MUDs

IRC clients

Recommendation
Homer v0.9

Homer is a very nice Macintosh version of IRC that also allows for collaborative graphics via a special "Homerpnt" channel. Available via `ftp sumex-aim.stanford.edu, cd /info-mac/comm`.

Downright Speculation
Ircle v1.26   Free

A Mac version of IRC. Available via `ftp sumex-aim.stanford.edu, cd /info-mac/comm`.

Olaf Titz; email: s_titz@iravcl.ira.uka.de

Other IRC clients

An MS–DOS clients are in `/irc/clients/ms-dos`. A VMS client is available in `/irc/clients/vms`. Other IRC client software is also available via `ftp cs.bu.edu, cd directory /irc/clients`.

IRC servers

IRC server software is available via `ftp cs.bu.edu, cd /irc/servers`.

MUD clients

While `telnet` works fine for connecting to MUDs, there are a number of MUD client programs that add features such as automatically logging your character on, or triggering actions in response to certain actions, such as saying hello whenever a new player enters the room. Client packages include:

Downright Speculation
MUDDweller v1.0   Free

A Macintosh interface for the MUD role-playing games. MUDDweller contains an ordinary terminal emulation mode, but when it connects to MUDs it supports additional features. These include command history, a session log, and MTP (a file transfer protocols used in many MUDs).

Available via `ftp rudolf.ethz.ch` (129.132.57.10), `cd /pub/mud`. email: maquelin@tik.ethz.ch

Downright Speculation
TinyTalk   Free

TinyTalk. A replacement for `telnet` during MUD sessions, Tinytalk has a number of features, such as macro support and command history.

Available via `ftp piggy.ucsb.edu, cd /pub/mud/clients`.

A more complete list of clients is available in the MUD FAQ.

Chapter 14 – WAIS, Gopher, WWW

WAIS

Recommendation
EINET WAIS Clients $35

PC and Macintosh WAIS clients developed by The Enterprise Integration Network are available via `ftp ftp.einet.net, get /einet/mac/macwais*.*` and `/einet/pc/eiwais*.zip`.

Microelectronic and Computer Technology Corp; 3500 W. Balcones Center Drive, Austin, TX 78759-6509; (512)343-0978, fax: (512)338-3897.

Recommendation
WAIS, Inc. client   free

A freeware WAIS, Inc. developed client is also available via `ftp think.com, get /wais/wais-for-mac-1.1.sea.hqx`

Harry Morris, WAIS, Inc.; 1040 Noel Drive, Menlo Park, CA 94025, (415)327-WAIS, fax:(415)327-6513, email: frontdesk@wais.com

Downright Speculation
HyperWAIS

HyperWais v1.7 is an implementation of Z39.50 for Hypercard v2.1. It is available via `ftp mendel.welch.jhu.edu, get /pub/fs/HyperWais.sea.hqx`; for source code, `get /pub/fs/HyperWais.src.sea.hqx`.

Downright Speculation
WinWAIS   **Free**

Windows WAIS is a Windows Sockets compatible version of WAIS that supports relevance feedback and a toolbar interface.

Available via **cnidr.org, cd /pub/NIDR.tools/wais/pc/windows/ waisman3.zip**

Available via **sunsite.unc.edu, get /pub/micro/pc-stuff/ms-windows/winsock/apps/waisman3.zip**

There is also a Novell LAN Workplace Z39.50 client available via **ftp sunsite.unc.edu, get /pub/WAIS/Windows/wwais103.zip**.

Jim Fullton, UNC Office of Information Technology, Computing Systems Development Group; (919)962-9107, email: **fullton@samba.oit.unc.edu**.

Downright Speculation
PCWAIS

PCWAIS, a DOS Z39.50 client which uses the Crynwr drivers is available by **ftp sunsite.unc.edu, get /pub/WAIS/DOS/pcdist.zip**. OACWAIS, a DOS Z39.50 client that requires the PC/TCP software from FTP Software, is available via **ftp oac.hsc.uth.tmc.edu (129.106.30.1), get /public/dos/misc/oacwais.exe**.

Steven E. Newton, Office of Academic Computing, University of Texas Health Science Center, Houston; email: **snewton@oac.hsc.uth.tmc.edu**.

Downright Speculation
UNIX and NeXT clients

The NeXT client is available via
ftp think.com, get /wais/WAIStation-NeXT-1.9.6.tar.Z
A Sun OpenLook client is available via
ftp sunsite.unc.edu, get /pub/wais/openlook-wais.tar.Z

A Motif client is available via
ftp think.com, get /wais/motif-a1.tar.Z. (Requires xwais source code.)

Downright Speculation
DinoWAIS

The USGS has developed a WAIS client for IBM MVS, which runs under TSO.

Tim Gauslin, USGS; email: **tgauslin@isdres.er.usgs.gov**

Downright Speculation
UNIX and NeXT servers

The freeWAIS distribution is available via **ftp ftp.cnidr.org, mget /pub/NIDR.tools/freeWAIS*.*** This version includes support for boolean operators.

The last publicly distributable Thinking Machines server code is available via **ftp think.com, cd /wais/wais-8-b5.1.tar.Z**. This distribution includes X Window, Emacs, and tty clients as well as the server.

Z39.50 directory of servers
/wais/wais-sources.tar.Z

Downright Speculation
Two-month trial   **$5,000**
WAIS Workstation for UNIX   **$10,000**
Source Code License   **$40,000**

Currently supported platforms include Sun 4.1.x, Sun Solaris 2.1, NeXTSTEP v3.0; Ports are underway to DEC Alpha, IBM RS 6000, HP Unix, and other Unix platforms.

WAIS, Inc., 1040 Noel Dr., Menlo Park, CA 94025, (415)327-WAIS, fax:(415)327-6513, email: **frontdesk@wais.com**

Gopher

Gopher clients

Recommendation
TurboGopher v1.3   **Free**

An accelerated version of the Gopher Internet front-end from the University of Minnesota. Insanely great.

Available by **ftp sumex-aim.stanford.edu, cd /info-mac/comm**.

Bugs and comments to:
gopher@boombox.micro.umn.edu

Recommendation
HGopher v1.0   Free

HGopher is a Gopher client, available in Windows Sockets and PC NFS compatible versions.

Available via `ftp lister.cc.ic.ac.uk, get /pub/wingopher/hgopher.exe` (Winsock version), or `hngopher.exe` (PC NFS version).

Available via `sunsite.unc.edu, get /pub/micro/pc-stuff/ms-windows/winsock/apps/hgopher.zip`

Recommendation
GopherBook   Free

GopherBook is a Toolbook and Windows sockets-based Gopher client for Windows.

Available via `sunsite.unc.edu, get /pub/micro/pc-stuff/ms-windows/winsock/apps/gophbook.zip`

Other Gopher clients

Gopher clients for UNIX, DOS, and NeXT are available via `ftp boombox.micro.umn.edu (134.84.132.2), cd /pub/gopher`. Below is a listing of the clients and file names:

DOS (needs Clarkson Drivers):
/pub/gopher/PC_client/

UNIX Curses & Emacs Gopher:
/pub/gopher/Unix/gopher1.02.tar.Z

X-Windows Gopher:
/pub/gopher/Unix/xgopher1.1a.tar.Z

Macintosh:
/pub/gopher/Mac-TurboGopher/

MS-Windows:
/pub/gopher/Windows/

NeXT Gopher:
/pub/gopher/NeXT/

OS/2 2.0:
/pub/gopher/os2/

VM/CMS:
/pub/gopher/Rice_CMS

VMS:
/pub/gopher/VMS/

Gopher servers

Gopher server software is also available via `ftp boombox.micro.umn.edu, cd /pub/gopher`. Here's where the servers are:

DOS: /pub/gopher/PC_server/hamburg

DOS KA9Q Gopher server:
/pub/gopher/PC_server/ka9q

UNIX: /pub/gopher/Unix/gopherxx.tar.Z

X-Windows Gopher:
/pub/gopher/Unix/xgopher1.1a.tar.Z

Macintosh: /pub/gopher/Mac_server/

VM/CMS: /pub/gopher/Rice_CMS

VMS: /pub/gopher/mvs/

Once you've got your server set up, you can publish it as part of the "Other Gophers" hierarchy by sending mail to gopher@boombox.micro.umn.edu.

World Wide Web

World Wide Web clients

Recommendation
MacWWW v1.02   Free

This is a Macintosh version of World Wide Web.

Available via `ftp info.cern.ch, cd /pub/www/bin/mac`

Downright Speculation
MacMosaic   free

MacMosaic an enhanced version of W3 that supports hypertext links, as well as embedded pictures (PICTs and GIFs), movies (QuickTime and MPEG), and sounds (.au files). It is available via `ftp ftp.ncsa.uiuc.edu, cd /Mac/Mosaic`.

Downright Speculation
Windows Cello   Free

This is a Windows Sockets compatible version of World Wide Web.

Available via `ftp fatty.law.cornell.edu, cd /pub/LII/Cello`

Other clients

Client list:
http://info.cern.ch/hypertext/WWW/Clients.html

XMosaic:
//info.cern.ch:/pub/www/bin

MacMosaic client:
//ftp.ncsa.uiuc.edu:/pub/www

Line mode browser for UNIX:
binaries: **//info.cern.ch:/pub/www/bin**
sources:
/pub/www/src/WWWLibrary_v.vv.tar.Z,
/pub/www/src/WWWLineMode_v.vv.tar.Z
/pub/www/src/WWWLineModeDefaults_v.vv.
tar.Z (documentation for line mode browser). The
line mode browser requires the library to compile.

Server information:
http://info.cern.ch/hypertext/WWW/Daemon/
Overview.html

Hypertext editor for NeXT:
ftp info.cern.ch, cd /pub/www/bin/next
for binaries,
/pub/www/src/WWWNextStepEditor.tar.Z

UNIX W3 Server:
//info.cern.ch:
/pub/www/src/WWWDaemon_v.vv.tar.Z.

PostScript documentation:
//info.cern.ch:
/pub/www/doc/WWWBook.tar.Z

Chapter 15 – TCP/IP

Dialup routers

Downright Speculation
Slip On A Stick (SOAS)

Slip On A Stick is a low-cost dialup IP router
supporting SLIP, Compressed SLIP, and PPP at
speeds up to 100 Kbps. It supports both dedicated
connections and on-demand applications. SOAS
includes a 16 MHz 80C186 processor with 1 Mb of
RAM, and 256K EPROM, and is based on a port of the
networking portion of the BSD v4.3 kernel. SOAS
supports SNMP.

Cogwheel, Inc.; 1705 14th St., Suite 308, Boulder, CO
80302; (303)444-1338, fax: 0018523581477, email:
info@cogwheel.com

SLIP/PPP support

Suggestion
Portmaster2e
10 serial ports, expandable	**$2695**
20 serial ports, expandable	**$3295**
30 serial ports, expandable	**$3750**

PortMaster terminal servers offer support for
graphical administration via X-Windows, and
supports RIP, PPP, SLIP & CSLIP, ICMP, UDP, ARP,
Telnet, and Rlogin.

Livingston Enterprises, Inc.; 6920 Koll Center
Parkway #220, Pleasanton, CA 94566, (510)426-0770
(800)458-9966, fax: (510)426-8951, email:
sales@livingston.com.

Suggestion
Morningstar PPP   **$795**

The Morningstar implementation of PPP for UNIX is
one of the most solid around, and their support is
"amazing."

Morningstar; email: sales@morningstar.com.

TCP/IP on the PC

With new versions and applications arriving so
rapidly, no static TCP/IP product listing could
possibly be adequate. For a more complete and
regularly updated listing, **ftp**
netcom1.netcom.com, get
/pub/mailcom/IBMTCP/ibmtcp.zip.

Suggestion
SuperTCP v3.0   **$495**

Frontier offers the most complete TCP/IP
implementation for Windows. This package offers
DOS support via a TSR, and the NFS option offers
server as well as client capabilities. Frontier also
offers support for SLIP, ODI, PPP (option), NDIS,
NetBIOS, packet drivers, SMTP, POP2, POP3, SNMP,
BOOTP, RARP, TN3270, Telnet, NNTP, FTP client
and server, NFS client and server, Finger, Ping,
BIND, rcp, rsh, rexec, and talk. It also offers support
for Int 14h redirection.

Frontier Technologies; 10201 North Port
Washington Road, Mequon, WI 53092; (414)241-
4555, fax: (414)241-7084, email:
tcp@frontiertech.com

Recommendation
Chameleon NFS v3.1   **$400**

Chameleon is a Windows-only product that offers
an NFS option. There is no DOS support, and this
includes being unable to view mounted NFS
volumes within DOS sessions running under
Windows. However, Chameleon does offer support
for SLIP, NDIS, SMTP, ping, POP2, SNMP, BOOTP,
TN3270, Telnet, FTP client and server, NFS client,
Finger, Ping, BIND, and Whois. An NNTP client was
in beta test as of this writing.

NetManage, Inc.; 20823 Stevens Creek Blvd.,
Cupertino, CA 95014; (408)973-7171, fax: (408)257-
6405, email: support@netmanage.com

PCTCP v2.2   **$400**
K210 Protocol Stack Only   **$200**

PCTCP is the most complete implementation of
TCP/IP for DOS and the software itself is very solid,
but the documentation and implementation is
intimidating because there are so many options.
This package also offers only minimal Windows
support. PCTCP supports packet drivers, ODI, NDIS,
SLIP, PPP, BOOTP, BIND, NetBIOS, Int 14h
redirection, Telnet (DOS and WIndows), TN3270,
FTP client (DOS and Windows), FTP server (DOS),
SMTP, POP2, POP3, NNTP client, SNMP, NFS client
(Windows and DOS), ping, lpr, finger, whois,
setclock, rcp, and rsh. Routing is not supported.

FTP Software; 2 High St., North Andover, MA 01845;
(508)685-4000, (800)282-4387, support: (800)382-
4387, fax: (508)794-4477; email: sales@ftp.com

TCP/IP on the Macintosh

Recommendation
MacTCP v2.0   **$49**

Version 2.0 of MacTCP is compatible with System
7.1.

APDA; (800)282-2732

Recommendation
MacSLIP   **$49.95**

MacSLIP is an extension for applications using
MacTCP. Features include auto-dialing, compressed
IP headers, static or bootp IP addressing, and a full
scripting language that can handle navigation
through almost anything. Throughputs are very
good, frequently reaching 1500 cps or higher on a
V.32*bis*/V.42*bis* connection.

TriSoft; 1825 E. 38 1/2 St., Austin, Texas 78722;
(512)472-0744; fax: (512)473-2122

Recommendation
MacPPP v1.13   **Free**

MacPPP is an extension for connecting a Macintosh
to the Internet using the Point to Point Protocol
(PPP) and MacTCP.

Available via `ftp merit.com, cd /pub/ppp`

Suggestion
InterSLIP   **Free**

InterSLIP is a free SLIP extension for MacTCP,
provided by Intercon.

Available via `ftp ftp.intercon.com, cd
/intercon/sales.`

Suggestion
MPing   **Free**

The Mac version of Ping (MPing) is none too stable,
but the source code may be useful as a programming
example. Use the ping in MacTCP Watcher instead.
Available via `ftp ftp.apple.com, get
/dts/mac/netcomm/mactcp-1-1-
examples.hqx.`

Recommendation
MacTCP Watcher   **Free**

MacTCP Watcher by Peter Lewis combines multiple
diagnostic functions, including ping, and tests of
TCP, UDP, and DNS.

Available via `ftp sumex-aim.stanford.edu,
cd /info-mac/comm`

Downright Speculation
Collage v1.0   **Free**

Collage is a collaborative environment that lets you
edit text and graphics, as well as share screens with
other Internet users.

NCSA Software Development; 152 Computing Applications Bldg., 605 East Springfield Ave., Champaign, IL 61820; email: softdev@ncsa.uiuc.edu, report bugs to: bugs@ncsa.uiuc.edu

Downright Speculation
TCP/Connect II

Basic version	**$195**
Extended version	**$495**
Tools & Toys	**$149**

TCP/Connect II supports both a hardwired TCP/IP connection, as well as serial-line IP (SLIP). With the extended version you can be logged in to multiple UNIX hosts in separate windows; do FTP; send mail and read USENET with a Macintosh interface; emulate DEC VT, IBM 327X, and Tektronix 4014 terminals; and execute macros. The Cadillac of Internet software for the Macintosh. Quantity discounts are available.

InterCon also makes a Telenet Driver that allows users of VersaTerm-Pro and MicroPhone II to open terminal sessions via TCP/IP. Check it out.

Tools & Toys is a package of TCP/IP utilities. Support for SLIP is due in the next version.

InterCon Systems Corporation; 950 Herndon Parkway, Suite 420, Herndon, VA 22070; (703)709-9890, fax: (703)709-5555; email: comment@intercon.com or D1988@applelink.apple.com

Recommendation

VersaTerm v4.6	**$87**
VersaTerm-PRO v3.62	**$173**
VersaTerm-Link	**$145**

VersaTerm seems to be first at almost everything in Macintosh communications. They had VT100 emulation put to rest before anyone else had a clue; they were first with KERMIT support, high-speed performance, and Comm Toolbox support. Now they support MacTCP. The scrolling of VersaTerm in very high speed connections (hardwired 38.4 Kbps) must be seen to be believed. The latest version supports VT220, VT100, and Tektronix 4105 and 4014 emulation.

VersaTerm now allows you to dial in to TCP/IP networks via Serial Line IP (SLIP). Since SLIP capability is provided as an extension that requires MacTCP, you can also use it with other applications that support MacTCP such as NCSA Telnet, or Eudora. VersaTerm SLIP is the simplest SLIP to set up but is not as versatile as MacSLIP since it does not offer a scripting language. It also is not as fast as

MacSLIP, with transfer rates running as much as 20 to 30% slower. VersaTerm supports Telnet, FTP (client and server), and Time client, and comes with tools for SLIP and Telnet, among others.

VersaTerm-Link is a complete graphical Internet client, offering file transfer, mail, news, and directory support via the SMTP, POP, NNTP, Finger, Whois, and Ph protocols.

Synergy Software; 2457 Perkiomen Ave., Reading, PA 19606; (215)779-0522, fax: (215)370-0548

Recommendation
The Guide

Educational Price	**$45**

The Graphical User Interface Designed For Education (The Guide) is a complete interface to the Internet, available for Mac and Windows. It is bundled with the Adobe Acrobat Reader, and supports SMTP/POP3, SLIP, NNTP, Telnet, CSO/Ph and Gopher as well as a validation daemon which allows use by multiple people on the same machine. The software was designed by Mark Resmer & Keith Vogt and implemented by Microsoft Consulting. The authentication server, available for Sun, allows for user authorization, newsflash dissemination, and license renewal. A complete 486-based hardware and software server package is in the works.

California Technology Project; P.O. Box 3842, Seal Beach, CA 90740-7842; (310)985-9631, fax: (310)985-9400

TCP/IP packet radio software

It is possible to run TCP/IP over the AX25 packet radio protocol using a Macintosh. This is pretty neat, since it lets you use the Internet without having to pay any phone bills, albeit at slow speed (1200/2400 bps).

Downright Speculation
Virtuoso v1.4

Shareware	**$20**

Virtuoso is a packet terminal program for the Mac which features adjustable split windows with all the usual Mac features (scrolling, cut and paste, print, etc.). Also scripting and selectable fonts. Available via `ftp ucsd.edu, cd /hamradio/packet/misc` as well as from AOL, GEnie, and CompuServe.

Downright Speculation
Net/Mac
Educational use   **Free**

This is a port of KA9Q to the Macintosh, but with only a minimal Mac interface. Since this is a complete TCP/IP implementation, including SLIP and PPP, you won't need MacTCP, MacSLIP, or MacPPP if you run this. I haven't had time to play with it much, so I don't know whether it's reliable enough to use as an FTP, SLIP, or PPP server, or what the performance is like. Net/Mac also allows you to run TCP/IP over the AX25 packet radio protocol. It can handle multiple sessions, each in their own window. For radio use, should be used alongside the SMTP mailer IMI/Mac 1.0b25b and the configuration and accessories collection called "radio-config" available from the /info-mac/radio directory.

Available via `ftp sumex-aim.stanford.edu`, `cd /info-mac/comm`.

Downright Speculation
SoftKiss v1.2.2   **Free**

SoftKiss is an init/cdev/driver that allows a Mac to do packet using only a "poor man's packet" modem. It is available by `ftp akutaktak.andrew.cmu.edu` (128.2.35.1), `cd /aw0g`, as well as from the Compuserve hamnet forum (library 9). Requires NET/Mac.

Mac Xware

Suggestion
MacX

MacX allows you to run X applications under Mac OS. The X apps reside on the desktop within Macintosh windows. If you are planning on doing any substantial work with X, it is recommended that you purchase an Ethernet card, rather than relying on an Ethernet-AppleTalk gateway, in order to increase the speed.

Apple Computer, Inc.; 20525 Mariani Ave., Cupertino, CA 95014; (408)996-1010

Downright Speculation
Planet X

Planet X allows the Mac to act as an X Window client. Using the software, any user on the network can pull up a Macintosh application and run it under

X Windows. You can even do this over the Internet from half a world away. Amazing!

InterCon Systems Corporation; 950 Herndon Parkway, Suite 420, Herndon VA, 22070; (703)709-9890, fax: (703)709-5555; email: `comment@intercon.com` or `D1988@applelink.apple.com`

Chapter 16 – UUCP

UUCP/USENET software for the Mac

Recommendation
uConnect   **$300**
uConnect LITE   **$200**

uConnect is the premier Macintosh UUCP/USENET implementation. It comes in two versions. The LITE version cannot forward or distribute mail and news; the full version can. uConnect can handle batching as well as 12-, 14-, and 16-bit compression, it can automatically send and receive, it includes a scheduler, can forward and distribute mail and news, and it can send and receive files (including BINHEX 4.0 translation). However, it cannot do "smart routing" using the Paths database. uConnect supports the comm toolbox and includes a terminal emulator called UATerm. It only supports the UUCP-g protocol.

InterCon Systems Corporation; 950 Herndon Parkway, Suite 420, Herndon VA, 22070; (703)709-9890, fax: (703)709-5555

ICE Engineering, Inc., 8840 Main St., Whitmore Lake, MI 48189; (313)449-8288, fax: (313)449-9208

Downright Speculation
UUPC v3.0   **Free**

UUPC, which was developed by a group lead by Dave Platt, supports the UUCP-f and g protocols and is compatible along with front-end software such as Eudora (for mail and file transfer), Toadnews (a compression and batching utility), and rnmac, a publicly distributable newsreader. It is available on sumex-aim.stanford.edu, in directory /info-mac/comm.

Dave Platt; email: `dplatt@snulbug.mtview.ca.us`, available via `ftp sumex-aim.stanford.edu`, `cd /info-mac/comm`.

UUCP/USENET software for the PC

Recommendation
UFGATE v1.03
Noncommercial	**Free**
Commercial	**$195**

UFGATE is a group of programs that allows a system to gate between FidoNet and UUCP/USENET mail and EchoMail (newsgroups). UFGATE still has a few bugs left, and it is complex to set up, but if someone has found a better way, we don't know about it.

Available via `ftp zeus.ieee.org`, get `/fidonet/ufgate/ufg_103.arc`.

Late Night Software Co.; 671 28th St., San Francisco, CA 94131; UFGATE is available from the SDS or `zeus.ieee.org` as `UFG_103.ARC`.

Suggestion
FredGate **Free**

Since UFGATE imports and exports from *.MSG format, it is difficult to interface to BBS software that uses a monolithic message base (such as Maximus, TBBS, QuickBBS, and Remote Access). FredGate gets around the problem by doing the importing and exporting to FidoNet *.PKT format instead. Those looking to add UUCP support to TBBS will also want the PIMP software from Boardwatch.

Available via `ftp zeus.ieee.org`, get `/fidonet/ufgate/fred19n6.arj`.

Suggestion
Waffle v1.65
Binaries, Shareware	**$30**
Source Code	**$120**

Waffle is a very complete UUCP and USENET implementation, supporting scheduling, UUX, compression and batching, mail aliases, address routing, and feeding of other sites. It can be run stand-alone or as a complete BBS package. Version 1.65 also has a mailing list program available for it, called VMAIL-SERVER, as well as a QMAIL reader. For more information on Waffle add-ons, check `alt.bbs.waffle`. Waffle's UUCICO is used in a number of gateways, including FredGate, uuPCB, and PCBUUCP. The package also supports NNTP, and is compatible with the HellDiver Windows front-end.

Available by `ftp zeus.ieee.org`, get `/fidonet/ufgate/waf165.zip`.

Thomas E. Dell; P.O. Box 4436, Mountain View, CA 94040; (408)245-SPAM (demo system, 300/1200/2400), email: `dell@vox.darkside.com`.

Downright Speculation
uuPCB
Multiline version **$49/3 lines**

uuPCB gives PCBoard full USENET and UUCP capability. It imports and exports directly from the PCBoard message base. It supports domain-style addressing; distribution limitation (world, country, state, etc.); compressed, batched news; and moderated newsgroups (outgoing messages are sent as UUCP mail to the moderator). uuPCB can also handle subject entries longer than the PCBoard 25-character limit. uuPCB uses the Waffle UUCICO software for transport.

Ed Hopper; BBS: (404)446-9465, (404)446-9462, email: `ed.hopper@ehbbs.gwinnett.com`

Suggestion
PCBUUCP

This package handles UUCP mail and USENET news, file attachments, newsgroup or mailing-list creation, LISTSERV capability, pass through to other systems, archiving of newsgroups, support for moderation, and more.

Merlin Systems, Inc.; P.O. Box 3042, Station C, Ottawa, Ontario, Canada K1Y 4J3; (613)236-1138, fax/BBS: (613)236-1481, email: `info@merlin-systems.on.ca`, FidoNet: 1:163/509, MHS: `info@merlin`

Downright Speculation
Personal Internet Mail Processor (PIMP)
Option Module for
TBBS v2.2 **$179**

PIMP imports and exports UUCP messages from TBBS. It supports either Waffle or FSUUCP UUCICO for mail transport.

Boardwatch; 8500 W. Bowles Ave., Suite 210, Littleton, CO 80123; (303)973-6038, fax: (303)973-3731, BBS: (303)973-4222, email: `jack.rickard@boardwatch.com`.

Downright Speculation
FSUUCP v1.4
Shareware **$35**

Available via `anonymous ftp` to `polyslo.calpoly.edu`, or `simtel20.army.mil`. Current naming convention is `fsuu[VV]r[R].zip`, where VV is the version number in V.V format, and R is the release number. This is the UUCP transport that is used with the PIMP TBBS gateway, as well as PCBUUCP.

Chris Ambler, Fubar Systems; 1720 Diablo Drive, San Luis Obispo, CA 93405-4710; (805)782-8000, fax: (805)543-7376, BBS: (805)54-FUBAR, info: `finger info@toys.fubarsys.com`, email: `support@toys.fubarsys.com`

Stand-alone packages

Downright Speculation
UULINK $335

Includes cron scheduling, uuencode and uudecode, and support for both mail and news. This is the UUCP transport used with the UUCP/USENET gateway for Major BBS.

Vortex Technology; 23241 Ventura Blvd., Suite 208, Woodland Hills, CA 91364; (818)225-2800, fax: (818)225-7203

Suggestion
UUPlus

UUPlus comes in versions for every budget, with the high-end product (UUNode) providing very complete UUCP/USENET capabilities. The capability of storing messages in dBASE format allows for fast retrieval, and can save a great deal more disk space than a one-file-per-message approach. UUPlus is available in three versions: UULight, UULeaf, and UUNode. All versions of the software can handle batching as well as 12-, 14-, and 16-bit compression, Internet or dBASE file formats, and the ZMODEM protocol for faster transfers. The Light version includes mail and news readers but can only manually call out, not take incoming calls. The UULeaf version adds automatic send and receive, and includes a scheduler. Finally, the UUNode version adds to the UULeaf capabilities by including forwarding and distribution of mail and news, and "smart routing" using the Paths database. UUNode is therefore nearly a full UUCP/USENET implementation.

UUPlus; P.O. Box 8, Camarillo, CA 93011; (805)485-0057, email: `info@uuplus.com`

Downright Speculation
RamNet/UUCP $198

RamNet/UUCP is a TSR that handles both UUCP and USENET news, as well as file transfer. The news reading program is an rn implementation.

Software Concepts Design; P.O. Box 191, New Kingston, NY 12459; (914)586-2023, fax: (914)586-2024, email: ramnet@ramnet.com

Chapter 18 – FidoNet

Mac FidoNet utilities

Recommendation
MacWoof v1.53
Shareware $25
(BMUG Disk: Telecom A1)

MacWoof is the only integrated point mailer for the Macintosh. This means that MacWoof is a single application, as opposed to a set of cooperating applications, which is how Copernicus or COUNTERPoint works. This makes MacWoof easier to install, and less threatening to the beginning user. MacWoof can handle File Requests as well as messaging. MacWoof has a 30-day evaluation period, and many sysops will disconnect you if you don't pay the shareware fee after that period.

Craig Vaughan; P.O. Box 2932, Merrifield, VA 22016; BBS: (703)241-5492

BMUG; 1442A Walnut St. #62, Berkeley, CA 94709-1496; (510)549-BMUG, fax: (510)849-9026

Recommendation
COUNTERPoint v2.13 $45
(requires Copernicus, Tabby or F1)

COUNTERPoint v2.13 is a combination point mailer/message reader. Rather than creating a complete point system, Mike Lininger has created a replacement for the reader portion of Copernicus. This means that you still need to purchase Copernicus, Tabby, or F1 in order to use COUNTERPoint, but you'll be rewarded with a very nice user interface. In version 2.1, COUNTERPoint has added QWK support, and the nice interface and extra features of COUNTERPoint make it an attractive QWK reader. COUNTERPoint is shareware and is supported within the MacPoint conference on FidoNet.

Mike Lininger, Lininger Technology; 385 Bowling Green Place, Gahanna, OH 43230; AOL: `Michael86`, email: `Mike.Lininger@cmhgate.fidonet.org`, available via `ftp sumex-aim.stanford.edu, cd /info-mac/comm.`

Downright Speculation
Copernicus II   **$59.95**

Copernicus was the first Macintosh point mailer, and offers several innovative features such as filtering.

Dennis Thieme, Silver City Software; P.O. Box 1661, Sparks, NV 89432-1661; (702)828-2929, email: FidoNet 1:213/777

For Copernicus mailer engine support, contact:

Michael Connick, M. E. Connick and Company; P.O. Box 307, Bradley Beach, NJ 07720; (201)988-0706 (Castle Tabby BBS, FidoNet 1:107/412, 1200/2400/9600 HST)

Downright Speculation
Tabby v3.0   **$80**

Tabby is a program that allows BBSes such as WWIV, Mansion, Second Sight, FirstClass, and Hermes to connect to the FidoNet. Version 3.0 supports file echoing, FirstClass gatewaying, and GroupMail. However, you had better purchase it before November 23, 1993 since after that time Tabby will no longer be sold, although it will continue to be supported.

Michael Connick, M. E. Connick and Company, P.O. Box 307, Bradley Beach, NJ 07720; (908)988-0706 (Castle Tabby BBS, 1200/2400/9600 HST, FidoNet 1:107/412)

Downright Speculation
AutoNodes   **$10**

AutoNodes is an automatic Nodelist compiler for Tabby. It will unARC incoming Nodediff's, create a new Nodelist, and compile the Tabby nodes file, all unattended. It is available either on floppy disk or as a File Attachment.

Chriss Koch; 5325 Red Sky Dr., Colorado Springs, CO 80915; Scorpion BBS: (719)637-1458, 12/24/9600 HST; FidoNet: 1:128/46.

Downright Speculation
Areafix for Mac/FF   **$25**

Areafix for Mac allows systems to automatically add or remove links to Tabby systems. Although not as sophisticated as its DOS cousin, it still gets the job done.

FF is a program that forwards Private Messages that are sent to Second Sight/Tabby systems.

Mac Wizards; 718 East Campbell Ave., Gilbert, AZ 85234; (602)553-8966

Downright Speculation
MacTick   **$35**

MacTick is a Tabby add-on that allows Tabby systems to send and receive .TIC files, the same format that is used by the DOS version of Tick.

Mac Wizards; 718 East Campbell Ave., Gilbert, AZ 85234; (602)553-8966.

Downright Speculation
Formula One
Zip Extract   **$7**
(Shareware registration only)
Mailed copy + registration   **$10**

Formula One is a Tabby-compatible FidoNet mailer for Macintosh that supports Zed Zap (ZMODEM). Zip Extract is a Tabby (as well as a Copernicus and COUNTERPoint) add-on that decompresses ZIPmail archives, allowing point software to process them.

Massimo Senna; via Calchi, 527100 Pavia, Italy; FidoNet 2:331/313, email: `msenna@bix.com`, `71531.32@compuserve.com`, .

Downright Speculation
Darwin
Shareware   **$5**

Darwin is an origin line customizer that works with Copernicus, COUNTERPoint, and Tabby.

Michael S. Taylor; 6101 Tullis Blvd., Apt. 161, New Orleans, LA 70131. Darwin can be FREQed from 1:396/69 as DARWIN.SIT or downloaded from (504)394-3498 on the first call.

MS-DOS FidoNet utilities

Recommendation
BinkleyTerm v2.55
Non-commercial use   **Free**
Commercial use   **Call for license**

BinkleyTerm is the most powerful FidoNet mailer software. It includes full domain, EMSI, and Janus support (a bidirectional protocol). However, it is also the hardest to configure, requiring the aysop to specify hundreds of options in lengthy control, event, and batch files. The easiest way to get started with BinkleyTerm is to copy someone else's setup and then modify it.

Vince Perriello, Bob Hartman, and Alan Bryant. BinkleyTerm is available via File Request from the FidoNet Software Distribution System (SDS) as BNKB_255.ZIP. Documentation is available as BDOC_250.LZH. An OS/2 version is available over the Internet as BNKBP255.ZOO via `ftp luga.latrobe.edu.au.`

Bit Bucket Software; P.O. Box 460398, Aurora, CO 80046; (303)693-4317, FidoNet 1:104/501

Downright Speculation
Wildmail v3.01   **$65**

Wildmail provides FidoNet mail utilites for Wildcat.

Online Computer Resources; 2036 Columbus Parkway #405, Benicia, CA 94510; (707)552-1122, BBS: (707)552-0602, FidoNet 1:161/123

Downright Speculation
Intermail   **$99**

Interzone Software; 9050 Pines Blvd., Suite 430, Pembroke Pines, FL 33024; (305)436-1587, fax: (305)436-5587, BBS: (305)436-1884, FidoNet 1:1/133

Downright Speculation
Fido

For those who are intimidated by setting up a FidoNet system for the first time (who wouldn't be?) Fido offers comfort, doing most of the work for you.

Fido Software; P.O. Box 77731, San Francisco, CA 94107; (415)863-2739, FidoNet 1:125/111

Downright Speculation
D'Bridge   **$139**

Installing D'Bridge is as easy as typing DB.EXE. The program has a graphical interface in which the user scrolls through the configuration menu, and D'Bridge responds by giving a short, comprehensive explanation. In addition, tables and diagrams are presented when necessary. Finally, if the user gets stuck at any point, typing `<F1>` displays a help screen. D'Bridge includes a built-in Nodelist compiler, Areafix clone, message editor, and fax support.

Chris Irwin; Mosaic Press, 358 Oliver Rd., Cincinnati, OH 45215; (513)761-5977, (800)932-4044. An evaluation copy is available for FREQ at 1:1/168 as DBRIDGE.

Downright Speculation
Front Door v2.02
Noncommercial	**Free**
Enhanced version (commercial)	**$295**
Enhanced version (hobbyists)	**$179**

FrontDoor includes a mailer, Nodelist compiler, and editor all in one package. While remote maintenance is also possible under D'Bridge and BinkleyTerm, FrontDoor's remote maintenance option is more powerful and easier to use. Front Door also includes a flexible scripting language.

FrontDoor's interface is also a great improvement over most mailers. FrontDoor uses a menu-driven system, removing much of the complexity.

Online Communications, Inc., 22 State St., Bangor, ME 04401; (207)941-1110, BBS (207)990-3511, FidoNet 1:132/300. The vanilla (hobbyist) version of FrontDoor is available by File Request from the FidoNet Software Distribution System as FD202.ARJ. The enhanced edition includes a printed manual, the TosScan EchoMail processor, custom video support, enhanced security, and other features.

Recommendation
Squish v1.01   **Free**

Squish is the most powerful EchoMail processor available. Features include complete zone/point support, pass-through areas, kludged domain support, .MSG and Squish message format support, and accounting support (useful for Echo coordinators looking to charge back costs to connecting nodes).

Scott Dudley. Squish is available by FidoNet File Request from SDS systems as SQSH_101.LZH. An OS/2 version is available over the Internet as SQSHP101.ZOO via `ftp luga.latrobe.edu.au.`

Recommendation
X00 v1.23
Noncommercial	**Free**
Commercial	**$100**

X00 is a FOSSIL driver, interfacing between a mailer (such as BinkleyTerm or Front Door) and the communications port. X00 runs on a wide variety of hardware, letting machines without standard hardware run FOSSIL-compliant software.

Raymond L. Gwinn; 12469 Cavalier Dr., Woodbridge, VA 22192. X00 is available over the Internet via `ftp wdsrv.edvz.univie.ac.at`, `get /pc/dos/fossil/X00V123.ZIP.`

Recommendation
Xlaxnode v2.53 $15

Xlaxnode is a Nodelist compiler that will compile a variety of Nodelist formats (including Version6, Version7, and SEAdog). It also has flexible and powerful dial and cost entry commands, and it supports PCPursuit.

Scott Samet, (305)595-8833, FidoNet 1:135/990. A crippled version is available by FREQ from the SDS as XLAX_253.LZH; to fully enable the software, you will need to obtain a key from the author.

Downright Speculation
Sysnl v3.14   Free

Sysnl doesn't offer as many features as Xlaxnode but it's free. In addition, it works perfectly and is extremely fast.

Luke Kolin and Jim Nikolich, (416)483-0566, FidoNet 1:250/714. Sysnl is available by File Request from the FidoNet SDS as SYSNL314.ZIP.

Recommendation
Tick v2.10   Free

Tick allows files to be sent to other BBSes and added to their file libraries automatically. Tick supports a variety of security measures so that unauthorized systems cannot spread files throughout the network.

Barry Geller, (609)482-8604, FidoNet 1:266/12. Tick is available from the FidoNet SDS by File Request or as TICK210.ARJ over the Internet via **ftp zeus.ieee.org**. An OS/2 version is available as TICKP210.ZOO by **ftp luga.latrobe.edu.au**.

Recommendation
Areafix v1.30   Free

Areafix allows systems to add and remove EchoMail links from a host's machine without the host having to manually change his or her control file. Areafix works with a variety of formats, including Qmail, QuickBBS, and OMMM. Systems can be assigned security levels and flags restricting access to the EchoMail areas. Areafix can also be set up to forward requests, create new echos upon request, and return a list of available echos.

Greg Dawson, (717)657-7097, 1:270/101 and George Peace, 1:1/1. Areafix is available as AF_130.LZH by File Request from the FidoNet SDS or by **ftp** on the Internet from **zeus.ieee.org**. An OS/2 version is available as AFP_120.ZOO by **ftp luga.latrobe.edu.au**.

FidoNet software for UNIX

Downright Speculation
rfmail v1.03

rfmail will unpack Fido *.PKT files and convert them into USENET-style messages. It only handles FTSC-0001 sessions and therefore can't do ZedZap. Those who have worked with the rfmail code say that getting it to work is only for the intrepid.

Available by anonymous **ftp zeus.ieee.org, cd /pub/mail**.

Downright Speculation
NIXMAIL

NIXMAIL is a Posix-compatible EMSI FidoNet mailer by Anthony Rumble, email: arumble@extro.ucc.su.oz.au.

Available by anonymous **ftp sunsite.unc.edu, mget /pub/Linux/system/BBS/nxm***.

Downright Speculation
UNIX FidoNet Utilities

BinkleyTerm is here, along with UNIX ports of other FidoNet utilities such as UNZIP, ARC, MSGED, PARSELST, OMMM, VPURGE, MSGLNK, MSGREN, OMAIL, LHARC, and ZOO.

Available via **ftp tsx-11.mit.edu, mget /pub/linux/sources/bt*.tar.gz** (use unpack to decompress).

For information, contact: Jon Hogan-Duran 3:711/909, Willy Paine 1:343/15, or Eddy van Loo, 2:285/406.

Chapter 19 – Message Readers

Macintosh reader software

Suggestion
Freddie v1.3
Shareware $15
(BMUG Disk: Telecom A2)

This software is a message reader, which means that it is only used to read messages, rather than being a complete telecommunications package. To use it, you log on to your favorite BBS (which must support QWK packet format), then download the latest messages in compressed QWK form. This saves money and time, avoiding the complexity of setting up a point system. You can use Freddie with any BBS that supports the QWK format; these include TBBS, Maximus, PCBoard, and Remote Access, among others.

Kem Tekinay; c/o Mondore, 75–05 64th Place, Glendale, NY 11357; AOL: KemT; FidoNet: 1:2603/204.

Suggestion
Alice v2.14
Shareware   **$25**
(BMUG Disk: Telecom A1)

The latest version of Alice supports both the XRS and QWK message formats. The XRS format is supported by BBS software such as QuickBBS, and Remote Access, while QWK is supported by PC–Board, TBBS, Maximus, and other software. In a version 2.2, Alice will also serve as a Point, making it an all-purpose offline reader.

Michael Keller, Mine Design; Voglersheck 15, D–6349 Greifenstein 5, Germany.

UnZip v2.0   **Free**
(BMUG Disk: Telecom A1)

This program is used to decompress .ZIP archives created by PKZIP 1.93 on the PC.

A.P. Maika, email: peter.maika@canrem.com

DOS QMail (QWK) readers

QMail Deluxe   **$50**

Mark Herring, Sparkware; P.O. Box 386, Hendersonville, TN 37077; (615)230-6245, BBS: (615)230-8822

MegaMail Reader v2.1

Kip Compton; P.O. Box 206, MIT Branch, Cambridge, MA 02139; BBS: (617)494-1366

KingQWK v1.05

Mike King; P.O. Box 4020, Alameda, CA 94501; BBS: (510)865-7115

Windows QMail (QWK) readers

Recommendation
WinQWK v2.0
Shareware   **$30**

WinQWK is a QWK message reader for Windows. It is capable of packing or unpacking packets in .ZIP, .ARC, .ZOO, or .LZH formats.

Doug Crocker; 1630 228th St. SE #D107, Bothell, WA 98021; FidoNet email: 1:343/105.

EXEC-PC; P.O. Box 57, Elm Grove, WI 53122; (414)789-4200, BBS: (414)789-4210

UNIX QMail (QWK) readers

ATP v1.3

Thomas McWilliams; P.O. Box 7545, Arlington, VA 22207; BBS: (202)686-9086

UQWK

This is a QWK format message packer for UNIX systems by Steve Belczyk., seb3@gte.com. Available via **ftp ftp.gte.com, get /pub/uqwk/uqwk1.3.tar.Z.**

SLNR

Silly Little News Reader (SLNR) is a new message reader standard for USENET. For more information, check out the alt.usenet.offline-reader newsgroup. The FAQ for the group is posted regularly to news.answers. For information on the state of SLNR development, contact Philippe Goujard, pgoujard@infocom.co.uk.

Chapter 22 – File Transfer

Reading PC diskettes on a Mac

Recommendation

AccessPC	**$85**
Macdisk	**$99.95**

If you have a Macintosh with a SuperDrive and you need to read 3.5" PC floppies, you should purchase a copy of AccessPC. If you don't, when you insert a 3.5" PC floppy and you're not running Apple File Exchange, you'll get the message "This disk is unreadable." With AccessPC, you insert the disk and it mounts on the desktop. AccessPC also allows for formatting of DOS 1.44 Mb and 720K diskettes. Aside from mounting DOS floppies on your desktop on SuperDrive machines, it allows you to open various Mac applications based on the extensions of PC files. It is particularly nice when used alongside SoftPC, allowing you to mount and manipulate SoftPC volumes under Mac OS. Macdisk allows PCs running DOS or Windows to see, open, edit, create, save and delete files on Mac disks.

Insignia Solutions Inc.; 1300 Charleston Rd., Mountain View, CA 94043; (415)694-7600, fax: (415)694-3705

File transfer and conversion

Recommendation

LapLink Mac III	**$93**

If you don't have a SuperDrive, LapLink Mac is the way to go. LapLink Mac comes with a four-headed cable that will connect a Mac to either brand of PC serial port. Plus, it works over a modem, AppleTalk, and the SCSI port. It can transfer whole directories, including subdirectories, selections of files, etc. It's fast, too – works at speeds up to 115,200 bps Mac to PC, or 750,000 bps Mac to Mac. Comes with file translators.

Traveling Software; 18702 North Creek Parkway, Bothell, WA 98011-8026; (206)483-8088, (800)343-8080, fax: (206)487-1284

Recommendation

MacLinkPlus/PC v6.0	**$199**
MacLinkPlus/Translators v6.0	**$169.55**

The DataViz translators have become the standard for translation software and are now included with several other products. The latest version includes more than 100 translators and it can translate in batch mode (a godsend when you've got a hard disk worth of files to do). MacLinkPlus/PC includes the translators as well as a cable and program to transfer files. MacLinkPlus/Translators includes just the translators.

DataViz; 55 Corporate Dr., Trumbull, Connecticut 06611; (203)268-0030, fax: (203)268-4345.

UNIX transfer tools

Recommendation

BinHex 4.0	**Free**
(BMUG Disk: Telecom D1)	

This program converts and creates .HQX files, which can be sent using Internet mail.

Yves Lempereur, Mainstay; 28611B Canwood St., Agoura Hills, CA 91301; (818)991-6540

Recommendation

BinHQX DA	**Shareware, $5**
(BMUG Disk: Telecom D1)	

This program will decode .HQX files.

Rainbow Software; 1233-A 7th Ave., Honolulu, HI, 96816

Recommendation

UUTool v2.3	**Free**
(BMUG Disk: Telecom D1)	

This program allows you to decode UNIX UUencoded files and to encode files for decoding by UNIX UUdecode.

Bernhard S. Wieser, Octavian Micro Development; 10516 Bradbury Dr. S.W., Calgary, Alberta, Canada T2W 1A6; (403)259-4907

Recommendation

MacTAR	**Free**
(BMUG Disk: Telecom D1)	

This program allows you to decode UNIX tar archives.

Craig Ruff; cruff@ncar.ucar.edu

Remote Control Software

Recommendation
Timbuktu Remote v5.0   **$199/$139**

For the number of features provided, Timbuktu Remote has to be one of the easiest telecommunications programs ever written. It allows you to control another Mac's screen in color, as well as transfer files. Timbuktu Remote was meant to be used with a high-speed modem, preferably V.32*bis*.

Version 5.0 of Timbuktu (which runs over AppleTalk) now supports remote control of PC's running Windows. Macs supporting color can view the Windows machine in color, but Windows machines connecting to a color Mac will only see the Mac screen in black and white.

Farallon Computing; 2470 Mariner Square Loop, Alameda, CA 94501; (510)814-5100 (main office), (510)814-5000 (customer service), fax: (510)814-5020

Recommendation
PC MacTerm II   **$195**
PC Anywhere

Making the PC look like a Mac, PC MacTerm II lets you control and transfer files with a PC over a modem, a direct serial connection, or AppleTalk.

Dynamic Microprocessor Associates (DMA); 1776 E. Jericho Turnpike, Huntington, NY 11743; (516)462-0440, PC Support: (310)449-4900, Mac Support: (310)449-4990, Customer service: (800)441-7234

Reading other disk formats

Suggestion
MacToDOS v3.0   **$179**

Provided you've got a 1.44 Mb 3.5" diskette drive on your PC, MacToDOS will let your PC read, write, and format Macintosh 1.44 Mb diskettes, as well as copy files to your PC's hard drive. However, it does not allow the Mac disks to be read directly from DOS and can only transfer files one at a time. Version 3.0 supports the mouse, is much faster, and supports PLI's cross-platform removable drives, including both Syquest and optical media.

Peripheral Land Inc.; 47421 Bayside Parkway, Fremont, CA 94538; (800)288-8754, (510)657-2211, fax: (510)683-9713

Recommendation
Mac-In-DOS v1.2   **$99/$59**
Mac-In-DOS for Windows   **$129/$99**
Common-Link

Mac-in-DOS allows a PC to read and write Macintosh-formatted diskettes without additional hardware. A nice way to transfer files from your Toshiba Laptop, loaded with Windows applications, to your Macintosh, since it can handle batch transfers. Mac-in-DOS also supports the mouse, automatiallly adds or removes line feeds from text files as required, and allows you to access both forks of Mac files. Common-Link allows UNIX workstations to read, write, and format Mac and PC diskettes.

Pacific Microelectronics, 201 San Antonio Circle, C250, Mountain View, CA 94040, (415)948-6200, (800)628-3475, fax: (415)948-6296

Recommendation
MacSEE v3.0   **$79.95**

MacSEE can read, copy, and format high density Macintosh floppy disks on a PC. It comes with versions for DOS as well as Windows. v2.2 is Shareware, available via `ftp oak.oakland.edu`, `get /pub/msdos/dskutl/macsee22.zip`.

REEVEsoft, P.O. Box 1884, Clemson, SC 29633, (803)654-7378, email: `71521.2200@compuserve.com`, GEnie: REEVE.SOFT

Recommendation
MAC-ETTE v1.0   **Shareware,$20**

MAC-ETTE is a DOS program that can read, format and copy Macintosh high-density floppy disks. Available via `ftp oak.oakland.edu, get /pub/msdos/dskutl/mac-ette.zip`.

Acute Systems, P.O. Box 37, Algonquin, IL 60102

Downright Speculation
Media Master   **$49.95**
Media Master Plus   **$69.95**

Media Master allows an IBM PC to read CP/M-formatted diskettes. Media Master Plus includes a CP/M emulator (ZP/EM), which emulates both 8080 and Z80 processors.

Using Media Master you can read diskettes from the Chameleon, Columbia, Cromemco, Delta XOR

CP/M, Epson QX-10, Kaypro, Morrow, NewBrain, Osborne, TRS-80, Wang, Altos, DECMATE II CP/M, Eagle, Monroe, Otrona, Pied Piper, and TI Pro, among others.
Available for the IBM PC, Zenith Z-100, Sanyo 555, DEC Rainbow, Osborne 01/Executive, and Kaypro CP/M.

Intersecting Concepts; 30851 Agoura Rd., Suite 200, Agoura Hills, CA 91301; (818)879-0086, fax: (818)879-0623

Other file transfer

Suggestion
DOSTransfer v2.2
With PLI Syquest drive   Free

This control-panel device allows you to read PC-formatted Syquest cartridges on your Macintosh. It's probably the best way to transfer tens of megabytes from the PC to the Macintosh.

Peripheral Land, Inc.; 47421 Bayside Parkway, Fremont, CA 94538; (800)288-8754, (510)657-2211, fax: (510)683-9713

Suggestion
PLI SCSI adapter card $129

This SCSI adapter card for the PC will allow you to mount Syquest, CD-ROM or 128 Mb magneto-optical drives on a PC. Since PLI includes the DOSTransfer utility with their drives, it is possible to mount DOS formatted Syquest cartridges on the Mac. Be aware that the SCSI drivers may not interact well with QEMM, the memory manager from Quarterdeck, and that there are no drivers for UNIX. If you are looking to run under UNIX, or want the optimum transfer rate, you should probably look at other cards, such as those by Adaptec.

Peripheral Land Inc.; 47421 Bayside Parkway, Fremont, CA 94538; (800)288-8754, (510)657-2211, fax: (510)683-9713

Downright Speculation
Adaptec EZ-SCSI 1.2 for Windows $75

This board supports CD–ROM drives, magneto-optical drives, Syquest removal cartridges, and fixed drive units. Drivers are also available for UNIX.

Adaptec; 691 South Milpitas Blvd., Milpitas, CA 95035; (800)959-SCSI, (408)945-8600, fax: (408)262-2533

Downright Speculation
Drivers

Trantor offers drivers that let SCSI devices be used on Macs, PCs, and NeXT machines.

Trantor Systems, Ltd.; 5415 Randall Place, Fremont, CA 94538-3151; (510)770-1400, fax: (510)770-9910

Recommendation

SoftPC $252
EGA/AT module $125 extra

If you can't beat 'em, join 'em. SoftPC lets you emulate a PC/XT with CGA, or if you purchase the EGA/AT module, a 286 machine with a coprocessor as well. The emulation is surprisingly good. In fact, SoftPC is more compatible with DOS applications than Windows is! One thing that I can never get over is that with a CD-ROM drive and the ISO drivers, SoftPC lets you access PC CD-ROMs using their native access software. It's also MultiFinder aware, so you can run PC and Mac applications at the same time. Be aware that you need at least 4 Mb of RAM to run this puppy, and 5 Mb or more doesn't hurt.

Insignia Solutions, Inc.; 1300 Charleston Rd., Mountain View, CA 94043; (415)694-7600, fax: (415)694-3705

Utilities

Recommendation
ON-Location v2.0 $129.95/$75

This is a product I didn't know I needed until I had it. Now I can't give it up. Writing this book would have been much more tedious without it. Well, what does it do? Imagine being able to open a slew of word processing and graphics documents at the click of a mouse. Then imagine being able to search those documents by a keyword, to find the one you're looking for. Great for researchers who have a million pieces of information in a million little places. However, I still have my boxes full of manilla folders for my articles.

ON Technology, Inc.; One Cambridge Center, Cambridge, MA 02142; (617)374-1400, fax: (617)374-1433

Chapter 23 – File Conversion

Macintosh conversion tools

Recommendation
FileTyper v1.01   **Free**

This software lets you change file types and creators, as well as Finder Flags.

Daniel Azuma, Homestead High Computer Lab; 21370 Homestead Rd., Cupertino, CA 95014-0292

Recommendation
TrueType Converter   **Shareware, $10**

This software converts TrueType fonts from Macintosh to Windows.

Chris Reed; 3409 Clearview Dr., San Angelo, Texas 76904–8108; email: chrisreed@aol.com.

Downright Speculation
Mac2NeXT v0.40   **Free**

This converts from 4-bit TIFF to the 2-bit TIFF used on the NeXT machine.

Albert Lunde, lunde@nuacc.acns.nwu.edu

Downright Speculation
Claris Graphics Translator   **$299**

Converts files to and from IGES v3.0 or v4.0, DXF release 9 or 10, Claris CAD, MacDraw II, MacDraw 1.9 (input file type only), or PICT. IGES and DXF file formats do not support features such as fill patterns and text styling.

Claris; 5201 Patrick Henry Dr., Box 58168, Santa Clara, CA 95052-8168; (408)727-8227

Suggestion
deBabelizer v1.5	**$299**
CD-I format converter	**$150**
Digital/Video F/X	**$199**

Converts MacPaint, PhotoShop, PICS Animation, PICT, PixelPaint (read only), QuickTime movies and stills, RIFF (read only), SCRN, TGA, TIFF, Thunderscan, ANM (Deluxe Paint animation), BMP, Dr. Halo, FLI & FLC (AutoDesk Animator), IFF, IMG, PIC (read only), MSP, PCC and PCP, PCX, TGA, TIFF, WPG (read only), Abekas (write only), BOB, GIF, Pixar, Apple II Paintworks, Atari ST, Commodore 64 (read only), Amiga IFF, Silicon Graphics, Sun Raster, and X-Windows screen-dump (read only) formats.

Can handle batch conversions via menus or scripting. Supports Adobe Photoshop filters.

Equilibrium Technologies; 475 Gate Five Rd., Suite 225, Sausalito, CA 94965; (415)332-4343, (800)524-8651, fax: (415)332-4433

Recommendation
MacBinary AFE translator   Free
(BMUG Disk: Telecom A1)

This program allows you to convert a file to and from MacBinary format using Apple File Exchange. The MacBinary format, which is also created by BinHex 5.0, is useful if you want to store Macintosh files on an IBM-PC. You'd want to do this if you were running a PC BBS oriented toward Macintosh owners.

Recommendation
MacLink Plus v7.02   **$169**

Can do numerous word processing translations in addition to translating DXF, CGM, BMP, GEM, and PCX formats into Mac PICT. Supports Easy Open.

DataViz; 55 Corporate Dr., Trumbull, Connecticut 06611; (203)268-0030, fax: (203)268-4345

Recommendation
GraphicConverter v1.6.2
Shareware   **$30**

Includes an editor, special effects, conversions to and from Mac and PC formats, and more. A must have.

Thorsten Lemke; Insterburger Str. 6, W-3150 Peine, Germany

Recommendation
McSink v7.0   **Shareware $45**
(BMUG Disk: Telecom E1)

This program has an endless number of uses in converting files from the PC to the Macintosh. You can't even imagine how many things this baby can do until you get started! Version 7.0 can even load Vantage VCMD's.

Preferred Software, Inc.; 5100 Poplar Ave., Suite 617, Memphis, TN 38137

Recommendation
GIFConverter   **Shareware $40**
(BMUG Disk: Telecom E1)

Can convert GIF (CompuServe Graphics) to EPSF, MacPaint, PICT, RIFF, RLE, Startup Screen, or TIFF format.

Kevin Mitchell; P.O. Box 803066, Chicago, IL 60680-3066

Suggestion
Giffer $20 shareware
(BMUG Disk: Telecom E1)

Converts GIF (CompuServe Graphics) to or from PICT format. This is useful because a GIF can be easily transferred to the IBM-PC, and, once there, can be converted by Hijaak to almost any PC format.

Steve Blackstock, Random Dot Software; 40 Bartlett Ave., Lexington, MA 02173

Recommendation
PICTure This v2.0

Converts Windows BMP, OS/2 BMP, Silicon Graphics RGB, Apollo GPR, PC EPS, Adobe PhotoShop, Amiga IFF, Amiga RIFF, CGM, Dr. Halo CUT, EPSF, Gem Image (IMG), GIF, Lotus PIC, Lotus RLE/BIT, MacPaint, PCX, RIFF, RIX, PCPaint PIC, RLE, Sun Raster File, Targa, TIFF, and X11 Bitmap files to PICT. Also includes utilities that can export from PICT to PCX, Sun, Targa, and XWD formats. PICTure This handles batch translation and 32-bit color.

FGM; 131 Elden St., Suite 108, Herndon, VA 22070; (703)478-9881, technical support: (800)783-7428, fax: (703)478-9883

Downright Speculation
Transverter Pro $249

Transverter's claim to fame is its ability to convert to and from Postscript.

TechPool Software, Inc.;1463 Warrensville Center Road, Cleveland, OH 44121-2676; (216)291-1922, (800)925-6998, fax: (216)382-1915

Downright Speculation
MetaPICT $179

Translates from CGM format to PICT.

GTC Associates, Inc.; 2304 Artesia Blvd., Suite 201, Redondo Beach, CA 90278; (310)379-2113, fax: (310)379-1649

Downright Speculation
PowerDraw Translator v3.0 $275

Engineered Software; 615 Guilford Jamestown Rd., Greensboro, NC 27489; (919)299-4843; fax: (919)852-2867

Suggestion
Adobe Photoshop $895/$575

Can import or export files in EPSF, TIFF, PICT Amiga IFF/ILBM, GIFF, Paint, PIXAR, PixelPaint, Scitex CT, Targa, and Thunderscan formats.

Adobe Systems, Inc.; 1585 Charleston Rd., Mountain View, CA 94039; (415)961-4400, fax: (415)961-3769

Downright Speculation
CAD Mover $495

Translates IGES, DXF, CGM, PICT, Adobe Illustrator and HP-GL files.

Kandu Software Corp., 131 Great Falls St., Suite 100, Falls Church, VA 22205; (703)532-0213, fax: (703)533-0291

Suggestion
PowerDraw Translator v3.0 $275
PowerDraw Externals $249

These translators are offered separately as well as an external for PowerDraw CAD. It exports and imports PowerDraw, DXF, Illustrator and PICT, as well as importing HP-GL, MacDraw II, and Claris CAD.

Engineered Software; 615 Guilford-Jamestown Road, Greesnboro, NC 27419; (919)299-4843, fax: (919)852-2067

Recommendation
Imagery v1.8 Free
(BMUG Disk: Telecom E1)

This software converts Atari ST, Amiga, GIF, IMG, BMP, RLE, Targa, RIX, UNIX (Sun, X-Windows, and many others), and Apple IIgs formats into TIFF, PICT, and GIF files. It also includes a program to convert GIF files to and from JPEG/JFIF format.

Jeff Lewis, email: 76217.2241@compuserve.com

Downright Speculation
FontMonger v1.5.7 $149.95

Ares Software Corp.; 565 Pilgrim Drive, Suite A, Foster City, CA 94404; (415)578-9090, (800)783-2737, fax: (415)378-8999

Downright Speculation
ARTery $99.95

Running on the Macintosh, ARTery translates Adobe Illustrator to FrameMaker Interchange Format (MIF).

Docu-Net, Inc.; 120 Bishops Way, Suite 165, Brookfield, WI 53005; (414)782-0007

PC conversion tools

Downright Speculation
Clip'n Save

Clip'n Save is a flexible Windows screen-capture program. It can save in .BMP, DIB, TIF, PCX, GIF, and EPS formats. The shareware capture programs usually don't have format support.

Dynalink Technologies; P.O. Box 593, Beaconsfield, Quebec, Canada H9W 5V3; (514)489-3007, (800)522-4624

Recommendation
Paint Shop Pro v2.0   Shareware, $49

Paint Shop Pro can import BMP, DIB, GIF, IMG, JAS, MAC, MSP, PCX, PIC, RAS, RLE, TGA, TIF, and WPG files, and can export to BMP, DIB, GIF, PCX, PIC, RAS, RLE, TGA, compressed and uncompressed TIFF, and WPG formats. It runs under Windows and is relatively fast. If Paint Shop Pro can handle the conversions you're looking for, then it's the program to get.

JASC; 17743 Evener Way, Eden Prairie, MN 55346; (612)934-7117

EXEC-PC; P.O. Box 57, Elm Grove, WI 53122; (414)789-4200, BBS: (414)789-4210

Suggestion
PictureEze v2.0 $45

PictureEze is a Windows graphics file converter that includes the CaptureEze screen-capture utilities. The screen capture utility can capture the active window, the client area, or the entire screen. PictureEze can import from BBM, BMP, CUT, DIB, EPS, GIF, IFF, IMG, LBM, MAC, MSP, PCX, PIC, PZI, SC?, TGA, TIF, VMG, WIN, and WPG formats, and can export to Ami Professional, Amiga IFF, AutoDesk Animator, Applause II, Artline, A&L, Autumn, Charisma, ColoRIX, Corel Draw, Cricket Presents, Crystal 3D, Deluxe Paint, Micrografx Designer, Dr. Halo, Energraphics, Express Publisher, Finesse, Freelance Plus, Gallery Collection, Grasp, Gray F/X, Harvard Graphics, Illustrator, Legend, Lumena, MacPaint, Microsoft Paint, Mirage, PageMaker EPS, PageMaker 3.0, PageMaker 4.0, PC Paintbrush, Pictor, Picture Pub.+, Pizazz Plus, Powerpoint, Publish It!, RIO, Show Partner F/X, Slide Write Plus, Storyboard Live, Springboard Publisher, TEMPRA, TIPS, TOPAS,

TrueArt, Venture Publisher, Windows Paintbrush, Wingz, Word, Microsoft Word for Windows, WordPerfect, and Xerox Presents formats. However, it's quite a bit slower than Paint Shop Pro, so this is only recommended if it has a conversion that you can't get elsewhere.

Application Techniques, Inc.; 10 Lomar Park Dr., Pepperell, MA 01463; (800)433-5201, (508)433-5201

Suggestion
JPEG v2.0   Free

These programs (which come with source code) can compress GIF, Targa, RLE, PPM, and PGM format files and produce a JPEG/JFIF file. It can also decompress to PPM, GIF, Targa, or (if the URT library is available) RLE format. It was created by the Independent JPEG Group.

EXEC-PC; P.O. Box 57, Elm Grove, WI 53122; (414)789-4200, BBS: (414)789-4210

Suggestion
GIF2JPG and JPG2GIF v1.41   Shareware, $20

These programs also convert between GIF and JFIF formats.

Handmade Software, Inc.; 15951 Los Gatos Blvd., Suite 7, Los Gatos, CA 95032; (408)358-1292, fax: (408)356-4143, email: hsi@netcom.com, 71330.3136@compuserve.com.

EXEC-PC; P.O. Box 57, Elm Grove, WI 53122; (414)789-4200, BBS: (414)789-4210

Downright Speculation
Graphic Workshop v5.0   Shareware, $35

Running under DOS, this program can view GIF, PCX, or IMG files as well as convert to MacPaint, GEM/IMG, PCX, GIF, TIFF, PostScript (EPS), WordPerfect (WPG), MSP Paint (MSP), Deluxe Paint (IFF), Windows 3 BMP, and PIC files.

Alchemy Mindworks, Inc.; P.O. Box 500, Beeton, Ontario, Canada L0G 1A0

EXEC-PC; P.O. Box 57, Elm Grove, WI 53122; (414)789-4200, BBS: (414)789-4210

Downright Speculation
MetaScan   Shareware, $25

MetaScan converts simple bit-mapped graphics images in TIFF format to Computer Graphics Metafile (vector) format. It does so by tracing lines.

William J. Hinkle; 420 E Boston Mills Rd., Hudson, OH 44236-1111

EXEC-PC; P.O. Box 57, Elm Grove, WI 53122; (414)789-4200, BBS: (414)789-4210

Downright Speculation
GIFDXF   **Shareware, $15**

This software can generate a 3D representation of a GIF image, for use in AutoCAD.

Kamyan Software; 1228 Robin Dr., Carol Stream, IL 60188

EXEC-PC; P.O. Box 57, Elm Grove, WI 53122; (414)789-4200, BBS: (414)789-4210

Downright Speculation
HPGL2DXF   **Shareware, $15**

This program converts plotter files in HPGL format into AutoDesk DXF files. Supports a subset of HPGL.

Quantum Diagnostics, Inc.; 420 Apollo Ste. C, Brea, CA 92621, (714)990-5020

EXEC-PC; P.O. Box 57, Elm Grove, WI 53122; (414)789-4200, BBS: (414)789-4210

Downright Speculation
HPGL2PS   **Shareware, $15**

This program converts plotter files in HPGL format into Adobe PostScript files. Supports a subset of HPGL.

Don McCormick, CSIRO, Division of Applied Physics; P.O. 218 Lindfield, N.S.W., 2070 Australia

EXEC-PC; P.O. Box 57, Elm Grove, WI 53122; (414)789-4200, BBS: (414)789-4210

Downright Speculation
GIF to BMP converter   **Free**

By Graham Welland. Runs under DOS.

EXEC-PC; P.O. Box 57, Elm Grove, WI 53122; (414)789-4200, BBS: (414)789-4210

Downright Speculation
CVTGIF v1.5   **Free**

This utility can convert PIC or PCX files to GIF. Written by John Bridges.

EXEC-PC; P.O. Box 57, Elm Grove, WI 53122; (414)789-4200, BBS: (414)789-4210

Suggestion
Image Alchemy v1.7   **$79.95/DOS**
                                  $199.95/SPARC

Image Alchemy specializes in translating graphics formats between a PC and UNIX workstations. A demo version of the DOS product is available for download on EXEC-PC.

Handmade Software; 15951 Los Gatos Blvd., Suite 17, Los Gatos, CA 95032; (408)358-1292, fax: (408)358-2694

Downright Speculation
Conversion Artist   **$149.95**

Conversion Artist, which runs under Windows, can import files in TIF (compressed and uncompressed), PCX, TGA, WMF, IMG, and CUT formats as well as export in these formats plus EPSF. It can view images; do screen captures, handle 24- and 32-bit color, optimize color palettes, convert from color to gray scale, and operate in batch mode. Future add-on modules will do filtering and color separations.

North Coast Software; P.O. Box 459, Barrington, NH 03825; (603)664-7871, fax: (603)664-7872

Downright Speculation
Juggler   **$149.95**

This software allows you to combine, resize, rotate, and overlay images from different formats. It can import and export images in TIFF, PCX, BMP, GIF, IMB and Windows SC capture mode. It also handles 24-bit color.

Jewell Technologies; 27 New St., Waddersdon, Aylesbury, Bucks HP 180LR, United Kingdom, +011 44 0296658790; (206)937-1081, fax: (206)935-0788

Recommendation
Collage Complete   **$150**

Incredible as it may sound, Collage Complete has dethroned Hijaak as the screen capture/conversion/cataloging program of choice. This program is a kitchen sink of screen capture, cataloging, and conversion tools. The manual is written in English, and the program is a joy to use. Features include support for both DOS and Windows, thumbnails, batch conversions, resizing, rotation, support for drag and drop in windows, video slide shows, photo CD support, preview prior to screen capture, countdown timers, edit and cleanup. Handles TIFF, PCX, GIFF, TGA, BMP, WPG, WMF, DCX, JPEG, and PICT formats.

Inner Media, Inc.; 60 Plain Rd., Hollis, New Hampshire 03049; (603)465-3216

Suggestion

Hijaak version 2.1	**$125**
Hijaak version 2.0 (Windows)	**$140**
PostScript Translation v2.1	**$349**
ColorSep 2.1	**$695**

Hijaak will convert the following source file formats to the following destination file formats:

Source Files	Extension	Destination Files	Extension
Amiga ILBM	IFF	Amiga ILBM	IFFF
ASCII Text	TXT	AT&T Group 4	ATT
AT&T Group 4	ATT	CALS Raster	CAL
AutoCAD DXF	DXF	DataBeam	DBX
CALS Raster	CAL	CompuServe	GIF
CompuServe	GIF	Fax Type	001
Dr. Halo	CUT	GEM Image	IMG
Fax Type	001, FAX	HP LaserJet	PCL
GEM Image	IMG	Inset Systems	IGF
GEM Metafile	GEM	Inset Systems	PIX
HP LaserJet	PCL	KoFax Group 4	KFX
HP Plotter	PGL	Lotus	PIC
Inset Systems	IGF	MS Windows	WMF
Inset Systems	PIX	MacPaint	MAC
Kofax Group 4	KFX	Mac PICT	PCT
Lotus	PIC	Metafile	CGM
MacPaint	MAC	Microsoft Paint	MSP
MacPICT	PCT	PC Paintbrush	PCX
MS Windows	WMF	PM Metafile	MET
Metafile	CGM	PostScript	EPS
Micrografx Draw	DRW	TARGA	TGA
Microsoft Paint	MSP	TIFF	TIF
PC Paintbrush	PCX	Wicat	GED
Storyboard	SBP	Win3-OS/2 Bitmap	BMP
Tek Plot 10	P10	WordPerfect	WPG
TIFF	TIF		
Truevision	TGA		
Tektronix Plot 10	P10		
Wicat	GED		
Win3-OS2 Bitmap	BMP		
Win Metafile	WMF		
WordPerfect	WPG		

Hijaak's Postscript Translation software will convert PostScript to 26 different fax formats. The ColorSep software offers color conversion from Hijaak, PageMaker, and Ventura to Linotronic and Compugraphic typesetters. However, be aware that Hijaak has its share of bugs and that some of the conversions have problems.

INSET Systems, Inc.; 71 Commerce Dr., Brookfield, CT 06804-3405; (203)740-2400, (800)828-8088, fax: (203)775-5634

Chapter 24 – Compression

Macintosh

Recommendation
Compact Pro version 1.33	**$25**
Extractor version 1.2	**Free**
SitToCPT	**Free**
(BMUG Disk: Telecom A1)	

Compact Pro has also improved significantly in version 1.33, but it no longer holds the lead over StuffIt in archive size and speed. However, the price is reasonable, and Compact Pro has been able to make the improvements without changing its archive format, (unlike StuffIt). Make sure to get SitToCPT if you need to convert StuffIt v2.1 archives to Compact Pro archives. Version 1.33 will also convert to and from BinHex 4.0 format (used to communicate with UNIX systems). To use the encryption feature, you must pay the shareware fee.

Extractor decompresses Compact Pro archives.

Bill Goodman; Cyclos, P.O. Box 31417, San Francisco, CA 94131-0417, GEnie: B.GOODMAN5; CompuServe: 71101, 204; email: 71101.204@compuserve.com

Recommendation
StuffIt Deluxe version 3.03	**$65**

StuffIt Deluxe v3.0 is now faster than v2.1, and produces smaller archives. Version 3.0 can decompress files created by ARC v6.2, PKARC v3.6, PKZIP v1.1, Compact Pro, tar, and PackIt III; it can encode and decode files in .HQX format; the StuffIt Engine can be called by HyperCard and MicroPhone XCMD's; operation under script control is supported. StuffIt Deluxe version 3.0 is a must-have for every serious telecommunicator. An unstuffer is now available for the PC.

Aladdin Systems; 165 Westridge Dr., Watsonville, CA 95076; (408)761-6200, fax: (408)761-6206, CIS: 75300,1666, GEnie: ALADDINSYS, Internet: aladdin@well.sf.ca.us, AOL: Aladdin

StuffIt LITE	**$25**
Shareware (BMUG Disk: Telecom C1)	

StuffIt LITE can compress and decompress StuffIt Deluxe v3.0 archives, as well as StuffIt Deluxe v2.0 archives and version 1.51 archives. It can also encode or decode BinHex 4.0 files. To distinguish itself from StuffIt Deluxe, StuffIt LITE does not offer scripting capability or decompression of foreign archives such as .ARC or .ZIP files.

Aladdin Systems; 165 Westridge Dr., Watsonville, CA 95076; (408)761-6200, fax: (408)761-6206, CIS: 75300,1666, GEnie: ALADDINSYS, Internet: aladdin@well.sf.ca.us, AOL: Aladdin

Decompressing PC and UNIX archives on the Macintosh

ArcPop version 1.3	**Free**
(BMUG Disk: Telecom B1)	

This program decompresses .ARC archives created by ARC v6.02 or earlier on the PC, or by PKARC version 3.6 or earlier.

D. G. Gilbert, dogStar Software; P.O. Box 302, Bloomington, IN 47402

MacLHA v2.0	**Free**
(BMUG Disk: Telecom B1)	

LHARC v0.33 can decompress files compressed with LHARC 1.13c on the PC, or UNIX LHARC. It can also compress Macintosh files, either in MacBinary mode (for applications or documents with resource forks), or normal mode (for PC compatibility). MacLHA 2.0 is by the same author and is compatible with PC LHA.

Kazuaki Ishizaki; email: ishiz@muraok.waseda.ac.jp; CompuServe: 74340,13

MacCompress version 3.2	**Free**
(BMUG Disk: Telecom D1)	

In UNIX compress mode, MacCompress will decompress .Z archives created by COMPRESS on the PC, or compress under UNIX. In UNIX compress mode, if used on TEXT files, it will also create .Z archives that can be uncompressed by UNCOMPRESS on the PC, or uncompress under UNIX. Compressing applications or data files with resource forks will result in files that can be uncompressed under UNIX or on the PC but will not be usable (these uncompressed files have MacBinary headers).

Lloyd L. Chambers; P.O. Box 3442, Stanford, CA 94309; email: lloyd@monk.stanford.edu, lloyd@bean.stanford.edu, lloyd@self.stanford.edu

MacBooz version 2.1 **Free**
(BMUG Disk: Telecom B1)

This program is used to decompress .ZOO archives created by ZOO v2.01 on the PC. More than a little slow, however.

Michael Niehaus; Rural Route 1, Box 369, Ferdinand, IN 47532; email: `mithomas@bsu-cs.bsu.edu`

MacZip v1.0 **Free**
(BMUG Disk: Telecom A1)

This program lets the Mac compress .ZIP archives in PKZIP v1.1 format.

Mark Adler, Richard B. Wales, and Jean-loup Gailly.

ZipIt v1.1 **Shareware, $10**

ZipIt is an AppleEvent aware package for the Macintosh that can work alongside message packers such as Tabby, or readers such as Freddie. It supports ZIP compression and expansion.

Tommy Brown, 110-45 Queens Blvd. Apt. 716, Forest Hills, NY 11375.

unZip version 2.0 **Free**
(BMUG Disk: Telecom A1)

This program is used to decompress .ZIP archives created by PKZIP 1.93 on the PC.

A.P. Maika, `peter.maika@canrem.com`

Compression on the PC

Compression software for the PC is available via `ftp oak.oakland.edu, cd /pub/msdos/archivers`, and `cd /pub/msdos/compress`.

Arc+Plus version 7.12 **$89.95**

Arc+Plus is the successor to the popular shareware ARC utilities.

SEA Inc.; P.O. Box 949, Nassawadox, VA 23413; (804)442-5865

ARJ version 2.30 **$40**

Available via `ftp oak.oakland.edu, cd /pub/msdos/archivers/arj230ng.exe`.

Robert K. Jung; 2606 Village Rd. W., Norwood, MA 02062; (617)769-5999

Hpack v0.78 **Free**

Available via `ftp oak.oakland.edu, get /pub/msdos/archivers/hpack078.zip`.

Recommendation
PKZIP v2.04
Shareware **$47**

PKZIP is the king of the PC compression hill – it's faster than ARC, and more efficient as well. Note that only v1.93 archives can be decompressed on the Macintosh by unZIP v2.0.

Available via `ftp oak.oakland.edu, cd /pub/msdos/zip`.

PKWARE, Inc.; 9025 N. Deerwood Dr., Brown Deer, WI 53223; (414)354-8699, fax: (414)354-8559

PC LHA **Free**

LHARC v1.13c can compress and decompress archives in the format used by LHARC v0.33 on the Macintosh, in "normal" mode. However, if Mac LHARC v0.33 is used to compress files with two forks, then the PC LHARC will not be able to decompress them. PC LHA is the latest version of LHARC, and is compatible with MacLHA v2.0.

Available via `ftp oak.oakland.edu, cd /pub/msdos/archivers/lha213.exe`

Squeeze v1.083 **Free**

Available via `ftp oak.oakland.edu, get /pub/msdos/archivers/sqz1083e.exe`.

ZOO **Free**

Available via `ftp oak.oakland.edu, cd /pub/msdos/zoo`

Info Zip v1.9 **Free**

Available via `ftp oak.oakland.edu, get /pub/msdos/zip/zip19p1x.zip`

GNU Zip v1.1.1 **Free**

Available via `ftp oak.oakland.edu, get /pub/msdos/compress/gzip111.zip`

Decompressing Macintosh and UNIX archives on the PC

unPACKIT version 1.0   **Free**

This program is used to decompress .PIT archives created by PackIt I/II on the Macintosh, or by PackIt III if encryption is not used.

R. (Scott) McGinnis; P.O. Box 3607 Mdse. Mart, Chicago, IL 60654-0607

EXEC-PC; P.O. Box 57, Elm Grove, WI 53122; (414)789-4200, BBS: (414)789-4210

UNSTUFF v1.0   **Free**

This program is used to decompress .SIT archives created by StuffIt v1.5.1 to StuffIt Deluxe v3.03. It can handle files with or without a MacBinary header.

Aladdin Systems; 165 Westridge Dr., Watsonville, CA 95076; (408)761-6200, fax: (408)761-6206, CIS: 75300,1666, GEnie: ALADDINSYS, email: aladdin@well.sf.ca.us, AOL: Aladdin

Compress   **Free**

This program is used to create .Z archives under MS–DOS. The Uncompress utility can decompress .Z archives created by MacCompress in UNIX mode. MacCompress archives created in MacCompress mode cannot be decompressed.

Available via `ftp oak.oakland.edu, get /pub/msdos/compress/comp430d.zip`

ExtractorPC   **Free**

This product extracts Compact Pro archives created on the Mac. Since Compact Pro archives do not contain useful information in their resource fork, you can just copy the Compact Pro archive to a PC diskette before extracting it (such as via Apple File Exchange, AccessPC, DOS Mounter, etc.). Alternatively, you can MacBinary the file. ExtractorPC will work in either case.

Bill Goodman; Cyclos, P.O. Box 31417, San Francisco, CA 94131-0417, GEnie: B.GOODMAN5; CompuServe: 71101, 204

Tar   **Free**

This program is used to create and expand .tar archives under MS–DOS.

Available via `ftp oak.oakland.edu, get /pub/msdos/filut1/tar4dos.zip`

UUENCODE   **Free**

This program is used to encode and decode .uu archives under DOS.

Available via `ftp oak.oakland.edu, get /pub/msdos/filut1/uuexe521.zip`.

Compression under UNIX

Recommendation
arc, sit, lharc, unsit, zip, unzip, zoo
         free

UNIX versions of these utilities are available via `ftp world.std.com, cd /src/archivers`.

Software Tool and Die; 1330 Beacon St., Suite 215, Brookline, MA 02146; (617)739-0202, (617)739-9753 (data, 1200/2400/9600 bps, 7 bits, even parity, 1 stop bit), fax: (617)739-0914, email: office@world.std.com, uunet!world!office

Uni-Zip   **$149**

This product will compress or decompress .ZIP archives under UNIX.

Precise Electronics; 31 Englewood Ave., Brookline, MA 02146; (617)566-6867

Chapter 26 – Education Networks

Telecomputing in Education

Suggestion
FrEdMail   **$80**
FrEdNews quarterly   **$10/year**
TeleSensations Educators Handbook   **$34**
T'nT Comprehensive Syllabus   **$249**

FrEdMail is an educational network of Apple II computers that was created by Al Rodgers, "Mr. FrEd." Al is now working with the FrEdMail

Foundation (a California 501c3 nonprofit) full time to advance the cause of telecomputing in education. Since FrEdMail was created by teachers for teachers, the FrEdMail Foundation not only provides software, but also handbooks (TeleSensations) and complete educational resources (T 'n T) to integrate telecomputing into the curriculum.

Since the FrEdMail foundation has more experience with telecommunications and education than anybody, educators are well advised to purchase these materials, even if they don't intend to use FrEdMail in their curriculum.

Al Rogers, FrEdMail Foundation; P.O. Box 243, Bonita, CA 91908; (619)475-4852

Chapter 27 – Home Control

Recommendation
Complete Answering Machine
$299/$199

This product was the first inexpensive voicemail board with its own processor on the market. This was a stroke of genius because it allowed the board to unobtrusively answer calls and record in the background while the user worked on something else. Today the Complete Answering Machine (CAM) is still the only single-line board with its own processor. While perfectly suited for home use, the CAM board is not designed for use in an office environment. Using more than one board in a machine at a time to handle multiple lines is somewhat awkward; the software is not very flexible, and no multiline card or development kit is available to adapt the CAM to business needs.

Be aware that this board is not compatible with full-featured phones that draw too much current, such as those with speakers and multiple lines. This is also a problem with the BigMouth board.

The Complete PC, Inc.; 1983 Concourse Dr., San Jose, CA 95131; (408)434-0145

Voicemail Products – Multiline

Downright Speculation
PowerLine 2 $895

If you've outgrown the CAM board, the two-line PowerLine board is the way to go. The original PowerLine, known as BigMouth, first came out in 1987, and won *PC Magazine's* Editors' Choice award.

However, the board never made it into retail stores because it was packaged with a photo copied manual and shipped in a zip-lock bag. These cosmetic problems and the need for a dedicated PC (the BigMouth card didn't have its own processor) limited its usefulness in the home.

Well, now marketing has its act together, and the PowerLine packaging is as slick as the rest of them. The hardware is improved as well, since the PowerLine 2 board has a processor on it. BigMouth's software always had plenty of flexibility and power (although the somewhat dense manual had to be gone over a few times); this software has been brought over to the PowerLine 2 and updated, as Voice Ranger. You can put up to eight Powerline 2 cards into one PC for up to 16 lines per computer, and a developer's kit, known as Commando, is also available. Talking Technology has also recently introduced FaxMouth, a combined voice/fax application. Talking Technologies' strong developer program has resulted in numerous third-party applications.

Talking Technology; 1125 Atlantic Ave., Alameda, CA 94501; (510)522-3800, fax: (510)522-5556

Downright Speculation
SigmaTech Voice/Fax
4 line hw + software $950

This product integrates fax and voicemail hardware to support Fax-on-Demand, party/chat lines, talking yellow pages, call processing, and other applications. Software supports up to 24 voice lines and 8 fax lines. Supports Rhetorex, New Voice, Dialogic, TTI, and Intel voice and fax hardware.

SigmaTech Software; 10801 Bismarck Ave., Northridge, CA 91326; (818)368-6132, fax: (818)368-7859, demo: (818)368-4566 or (818)386-8848

Downright Speculation
PhonePro hardware $599

The PhonePro hardware does fax, data, and voicemail, and features a scripting language to make it all work together. Using a connect-the-icons approach reminiscent of Design Scope, PhonePro lets you build phone systems that combine fax, data, and voice with more conventional database and mail applications. For example, you could implement a service in which a person calls in, and by a series of voicemail menus, chooses a product specification to be faxed to himself. The fax transmission can begin while the caller is on the line so that your firm doesn't have to pay for the call. Selections can go into a database or can be mailed along with received messages or faxes via Microsoft Mail or QuickMail.

Cypress Research Corp.; 240 E. Carribean Dr., Sunnyvale, CA 94089; (408)752-2700, fax: (408)752-2735

Recommendation
Complete Communicator Gold
9600 bps version   **$699/$520**
2400 bps version   **$499/$319**

The Complete Communicator Gold is a modem, Fax modem, voicemail system, and scanner interface, all on a single board and controlled by a Windows interface. It allows your computer to receive messages by modem, voice, and fax on the same phone line; to send a fax or voice message to an array of callers at scheduled times; and to set up voice and/or fax mailboxes. If you want to scan a document to send, it interfaces with the Complete Half Page scanner. You can also send a fax from within any Windows application. Since it includes its own processsor and memory, it can work in the background and not slow down your machine while answering a call. All Complete needs to do now is to bring out software allowing people to write their own custom applications.

The Complete PC, Inc.; 1983 Concourse Dr., San Jose, CA 95131; (408)434-0145, fax: (408)434-1048

Home control movers and shakers

Radiant

Radiant Enterprises, Inc.; 1714 Stockton St., San Francisco, CA 94133; (415)296-8040, fax: (415)362-3528

CEBUS Specifications

Electronic Industries Association; 2001 Pennsylvania Ave., Washington, DC 20006; (202)457-4975

LON Interface Chips

Echelon Corp.; 4015 Miranda Ave., Palo Alto, CA 94304; (415)855-7400, fax: (415)856-6153

X-10 products

X-10 products are sold under the X-10 label as well as under the Radio Shack Plug 'n' Power label. Keep your eyes peeled for Radio Shack sales on X-10 equipment.
X-10 Home Controls, Inc.; 1200 Aerowood Dr., Unit 20, Mississauga, Ontario, Canada L4W 2S7; (905)624-4446, fax: (905)625-8480

X-10 (USA) Inc.; 91 Ruckman Rd.,,Closter, NJ 07624-0420; (201)784-9700, fax: (201)784-9464

Radiant Products

Common Sense/CNX   **$395**
Low cost temperature sensor $20

The Common Sense AppleTalk Sense and Control Node offers 8 programmable digital input/outputs, 4 analog inputs, and 4 power relay outputs, and it comes with Macintosh applications software to allow control of any of the functions over AppleTalk.

Radiant Enterprises, Inc.; 1714 Stockton St., San Francisco, CA 94133; (415)296-8040, fax: (415)392-6860

CommonSense CAM kit   **$2995**

The Common Sense CAM kit is a camera control system compatible with Apple's Navigable Movie Tookit. This is what was used to make the Navigable Movies included on the developer and QuickTime CDs. The kit includes a camera pan and tilt head, camera motion controller, power supply, and cables.

Radiant Enterprises, Inc.; 1714 Stockton St., San Francisco, CA 94133; (415)296-8040, fax: (415)392-6860

PowerSwitch LT   **$199**

The PowerSwitch LT is a programmable power supply controllable over AppleTalk. It can be programmed to turn off or on anything that's plugged into it. Once programmed, events remain in the parameter RAM, able to execute without further instruction from a computer. The PowerSwitch can be turned on and off from the Chooser, or it can be left in Auto mode, in which case it will sense AppleTalk network Name Binding Protocol (NBP) lookups to the device it is controlling. In this mode it could be used to turn off a LaserWriter after an hour of inactivity and power it on again when a user prints to it. Since laser printers draw power (and lots of it!) even when they aren't doing anything, the PowerSwitch LT typically pays for itself in saved electricity.

Radiant Enterprises, Inc.; 1714 Stockton St., San Francisco, CA 94133; (415)296-8040, fax: (415)392-6860

X-10 Products

Unless otherwise stated, all of the products below are available from X-10 (USA) Inc.

Catalogs, Books, and Associations

How to Automate Your Home $29.95

If this article piqued your interest, then you might want to check this out. The book is an overview of different types of home automation, from security to energy-saving devices.

Home Automation, USA; P.O. Box 22536, Oklahoma City, OK 73123; fax: (405)842-3419

Home Automation by Heath

This is a catalog of Heath products for home automation that concentrates mainly on X-10 technology.

Heath Company; Dept. 350-056, Benton Harbor, MI 49022; (800)444-3284, (616)982-5950, fax: (616)982-5577

Home Automation Laboratories Catalog

If you're interested in home control, and want a complete catalog of X-10 products, you can get it from Home Automation Laboratories of Atlanta, Georgia. They've got stuff in there you wouldn't believe, like an automatic indoor plant-watering system, developed by NASA. They offer a 30-day money-back guarantee, and guarantee the lowest prices on everything.

Home Automation Laboratories; 5500 Highlands Parkway, Suite 450, Atlanta, GA 30082; Orders: (800)466-3522, Catalog requests: (800)935-4425, tech support: (404)319-6000, fax: (404)438-2835

Home Automation Association

If you are in the Home Automation business, you may wish to join the Home Automation Association, which sponsors various trade shows and seminars.

Home Automation Association; 808 17th Street, N.W., Suite 200, Washington, DC 20006; (202)333-8579, fax: (202)223-9569

An Installer's Guide to CEBus
Home Automation $149

For those in the construction business, Parks Associates sells an installer's guide to the CEBUS, which gives you an idea of what can be done. Be aware that the specs are not done yet, so quite a bit of the material will be speculative.

Parks Associates; 5310 Harvest Hill Rd., Suite 235, LB162, Dallas, TX 75230-5805; (214)490-1113, fax: (214)490-1133

Software

X10Utils
Shareware $10

This set of utilities allows you to build a flexible and powerful home control network, stringing the individual utilities together into an event loop using DOS batch script.

EXEC-PC; P.O. Box 57, Elm Grove, WI 53122; (414)789-4200, BBS: (414)789-4210

Tom Salzman; 1008 Castalia Dr., Cary, NC 27513; email: tom@ramona.Cary.NC.US; BBS: (919)481-3787, login: X10, password: X10.

X-10 TW523 Developer's Kit

This kit is for IBM-PC developers, but with a bunch of phone calls, the vendor might be persuaded to port the code to Think C. Code is provided in Microsoft or Turbo C.

Baran-Harper Group; Toronto, Ontario, Canada (416)294-6473, fax: (416)471-6776

Computer interface kits

Model CP290
X-10 Macintosh Interface Kit $49.95
PC Interface Kit $49.95

The CP290 controller is capable of remembering events that are to be triggered at specific times during the week. The software that comes with the CP290 kit allows you to set up events and download them to the CP290. You can also send the CP290 commands in real time. Based on these commands, it sends events to the X-10 appliance modules. The CP290 is only capable of sending events; it cannot receive X-10 events.

X-10 (USA) Inc.; 91 Ruckman Rd.,,Closter, NJ 07624-0420; (201)784-9700, fax: (201)784-9464

Gateway modules

X-10 Model TR551
Telephone Responder $74.95

This unit allows you to control up to ten items from your touch-tone phone. The problem is, it isn't compatible with your answering machine, so you need a line just for it. Yuck!

X-10 Model IR543
Infrared Gateway/Controller

This unit receives infrared signals and then retransmits them over the house wiring. However, it doesn't work the other way, since it can't listen for X-10 signals.

X-10 Model PL513
Power Line Interface

This unit allows a device designed to send X-10 events (typically created by OEMs) to do so without having to couple to the power line.

X-10 Model TW523 $24.95
Two-Way Power Line Interface

This unit allows a device to send as well as receive X-10 events without having to couple to the power line. For example, it could be used to connect your Macintosh to the X-10 system.

Control modules

X-10 Model RC5000
Remote Controlled Security System $39.95

This allows you to manually control up to 16 devices (2 banks of 8 devices) remotely. You can turn your lights on or off, etc.

X-10 Model MC460
Mini Controller $10.95

This unit can control up to eight modules from outside the home (two banks of four).

Sensor modules
(Sends events only)

X-10 Model MT522
Timer Module and Clock $29.95

This module can send events by itself according to the time of day, without having to be programmed by computer. It also has a clock on it.

X-10 Model SD533
Sun Downer $19.95

This is an MC460 with a built-in photocell to turn off up to four devices at a time. It can control up to eight devices (two banks of four).

Appliance modules
(Receives events only)

X-10 Model UM506
Universal Module $18.95

This module activates a relay, and so can be used to turn on sprinklers, open or close drapes, or turn thermostats on or off.

X-10 Model TH2807
Thermostat controller $19.95

This device receives events and is placed underneath a thermostat to turn it on or off.

X-10 Model AM466
Appliance Module $14.95

This module can turn an appliance on or off.

X-10 Model WS467
Wall Dimmer Module $14.95

This module replaces a wall switch and is capable of receiving dimming commands in addition to on or off events.

X-10 Model SR227
Split Receptacle $19.95

This module replaces your wall outlet and can receive on or off events.

X-10 Model LM 465
Lamp Module $12.95

This is an external module that plugs into your wall and can receiving dimming commands in addition to on or off events. This module should not be used with major appliances, since it isn't made to handle the current.

X-10 Model WS477
3 Way Wall Dimmer $19.95

Home security modules (send events only).

X-10 Model DW534
Wireless Door/Window Sensor   **$14.99**

This module sends an event if two magnets become separated.

X-10 Model HT544
Remote Control   **$19.95**

This module can arm or disarm the home security system.

X-10 Model KF574
Miniature Remote Control   **$19.95**

A miniature version of the HT544, it's small enough to place on a key chain. Can operate with the SS5400 security system.

X-10 Model PH508
Power Line Siren   **$49.95**

This little baby can put out 105 decibels when sent an event by a motion sensor or window sensor.

X-10 Model SP554
Wireless Supervised Passive Infrared Motion Detector   **$59.95**

This works with the SS5400 security system, sending an event when motion is detected.

Voicemail cards for the PC

BigMouth	**$199.95**
Programmer's Toolkit	**$79**
SpeakEasy	**$79**

BigMouth is a highly programmable voicemail card for IBM-PC compatibles. Since a developer's kit and an interpreted development language (SpeakEasy) are available, many third-party applications have been written for this card and its two-line sibling, PowerLine. Since it does not have a processor onboard, it requires a dedicated computer. This fact and the large third-party application base make it most popular in business environments. However, BigMouth also has a built in alarm jack that will automatically dial out if your alarm system is tripped. Be aware that version 3.0 of BigMouth is buggy and less stable than version 2.1. I purchased the upgrade, but have never been able to use it due to a myriad of problems.

Talking Technology; 1125 Atlantic Ave., Alameda, CA 94501; (510)522-3800, fax: (510)522-5556

Complete Communicator   **$499/$329**
Complete Fax   **$399/$229**

The Complete Communicator combines a voicemail card, modem, and fax all on one board, while the Complete Fax is just a fax board. Most important for the discussion in this chapter, these boards have a processor on them so that they can run in the background. Even though they are both voicemail cards, the Complete Communicator will not conflict with the BigMouth, provided one of the boards is set to an address other than 3E0 (which is the default for both boards), and the BigMouth is set to pick up on one ring, and the Communicator is set to pick up on two or more rings. Both the Complete Communicator and the Complete Fax can deliver an outgoing fax spooled to the Fax Queue while BigMouth is running in the foreground.

The Complete PC, Inc.; 1983 Concourse Dr., San Jose, CA 95131; (408)434-0145

Automated gardening systems

Suggestion
ACU-DRIP System

The ACU-DRIP System includes everything from tubing to pressure regulators, vacuum breakers, filters, fertilizer applicators, drip emitters, sprayers, and other accessories. For information on their full line of products, request a free Planning Guide for the Wade Rain ACU-DRIP Watering System.

Wade Manufacturing Company; 3081 East Hamilton Ave., Fresno, CA 93721

Suggestion
Rain Bird Calm Shell Hose Repair 1/2 inch (Male end)

To my delight, I found that this hose repair clam shell (with re-usable 1/2 inch male end) fits an Alhambra 2.5 gallon water container perfectly.

Rain Bird National Sales Corporation; 970 West Sierra Madre, City of Azuza, CA 91702; (818)963-9311

Home Security Bundles

X-10 Model SS5400
Protector Plus Home Security System   **$99.95**

This bundle includes:

Number	Model	Description	Price if sold separately
1	LM465	Lamp module	$12.95
1	DW534	Wireless door/window sensor	$14.99
1	BR521	Base receiver	
1	HT544	Remote control unit	$19.95

X-10 (USA) Inc.; 91 Ruckman Rd.,,Closter, NJ 07624-0420; (201)784-9700, fax: (201)784-9464

X-10 Model HS9000
Deluxe Protector Plus Home Security System   **$219.99**

This bundle includes:

Number	Model	Description	Price if sold separately
1	LM465	Lamp module	$12.95
3	DW534	Wireless door/window sensor	$14.99
1	BR521	Base receiver	
1	HT544	Remote control unit	$19.95
1	RT504	Remote control (up to 16)	$39.95
1	PH508	Remote siren	$49.95
1	SP544	Motion sensor	$59.95

X-10 (USA) Inc.; 91 Ruckman Rd.,,Closter, NJ 07624-0420; (201)784-9700, fax: (201)784-9464

Appendix F – UNIX

Downright Speculation
COHERENT v4.0   **$99.95**

COHERENT v4.0 includes a large model C compiler, UUCP networking, and compatibility with many SCO binary applications. Future versions will add features such as support for TCP/IP and X. However, there is no support for DOS under UNIX. BBS software vendors are beginning to take a look at COHERENT, and CocoNet computing has already announced support for the operating system.

Mark Williams Company; 60 Revere Dr., Northbrook, IL 60062; (800)627-5967, (708)291-6700, fax: (708)291-6750

Downright Speculation
Linux v0.98   **Free**

Linux is a Posix-compatible operating system completely free of USL code that supports TCP/IP and X Windows. Available via `ftp` `nic.funet.fi, cd /pub/OS/Linux`.

Suggestion
386BSD v0.1   **Free**
NetBSD v0.9   **Free**
NetBSD, 386BSD, & Linux CD **$40**

386BSD and NetBSD are working versions of the Net/2 tape for the 386, including full TCP/IP and X Windows support, and versions of Tex, ed, make, ispell, emacs, lisp, prolog, and netrek. NetBSD is a version of 386BSD with many of the bugs removed. Tim Pozar installed NetBSD on BMUG's old 386 TBBS machine and it has been sitting on the Internet for almost six months now, with no major problems. Routing performance is 10% to 20% better than KA9Q, and a version of SLIP is available. The drawback is that driver support is only fair; multiport boards such as Digiboard are not yet supported, nor are SCC cards or synchronous PPP. Versions of NetBSD, 386BSD, and Linux are available from the Austin Code Works on a single CD, as well as via `ftp agate.berkeley.edu, cd /pub/386BSD,` and `/pub/NetBSD`

The Austin Code Works; 11100 Leafwood Lane, Austin, TX 78750-3587; (512)258-0785, fax: (512)258-1342, email: info@acw.com.

APPENDIX C: ONLINE RESOURCES

Where to find it

Agricultural

Name: PENpages
Net: Internet
What: A service of the College of Agricultural Sciences, Penn State, offering access to more than 13,000 documents. Includes AgSat (Agricultural Satellite) and databases on food & nutrition, Pennsylvania agriculture, and the grain market.
How: `telnet psupen.psu.edu`, `(128.118.36.4)`, login: **PNOTPA**
Email: Not accessible
Fees: None
Contact: Diann Hunsinger, Training and Support Specialist, PENpages Coordinator, College of Agricultural Sciences, Penn State University; 405 Ag .Admin .Bldg. University Park, PA 16802; (814)863-3449 email: ppmenu@psupen.psu.edu

Name: Agricultural LIbrary Forum
Net: None
What: National Agricultural LIbrary BBS; many agricultural files, including a list of agricultural BBSes.
How: `(301)504-6510`
Email: None
Fees: Free
Contact: Karl Schneider, (301)504-5113

Name: Clemson University Forestry and Agricultural Network (CUFAN)
Net: Internet
What: Requires PF1 on keyboard.
How: `telnet eureka.clemson.edu` `(130.127.8.3)`, login: **PUBLIC**
Email: Not accessible
Fees: Free

Name: Agricultural Services List
Net: Internet
What: List of agricultural Internet services
How: `ftp ftp.sura.net` `(128.167.254.179)` `login: anonymous, get /pub/nic/agricultural.list`
Email: Via FTPmail (see FTP entry)
Fees: Free

Name: CompuFarm BBS
Net: Not connected
What: BBS of the Alberta Farm Business Management Branch; info on agricultural software.
How: (403)556-4104
Email: Not accessible
Fees: Free
Contact: (403)556-4240 (help)

Name: Agricultural Market News
Net: Internet
What: Contains 1200 agricultural commodity market reports compiled by the Agricultural Market News Service of the U.S. Department of Agriculture, most of them updated daily.
How: Accessible via WAIS
Email: Not accessible
WAIS: agricultural-market-news.src
Contact: wais@oes.orst.edu

Name: Research Results Database (RRDB)
Net: Internet
What: Short summaries of research results from the Agricultural Research Service (ARS) and Economic Research Service of the U.S. Dept. of Agriculture. Updated monthly or bimonthly.
How: Accessible via WAIS
Email: Not accessible
WAIS: usda-rrdb.src
Contact: wais@esusda.gov

Name: Almanac Mail Server
Net: Internet
What: Project Gutenberg (online books) and agricultural information.
How: Accessible via email
Email: `mail almanac@oes.orst.edu`, body: `send guide`, or `send topic catalog`, also
`mail almanac@esusda.gov`
`mail almanac@ecn.purdue.edu`
`mail almanac@ces.ncsu.edu`
`mail almanac@silo.ucdavis.edu`
`mail almanac@joe.uwex.edu`
`mail almanac@wisplan.uwex.edu`
Fees: free

Name: QUERRI
Net: Internet
What: Bibliographic database on agriculture
How: `telnet isn.rdns.iastate.edu`, `[129.186.99.26]` DIAL: `querri`
Email: None
Fees: Free
Contact: North Central Region Educational Materials Project
B-10 Curtiss Hall
Iowa State University
Ames, IA 50011
(515)294-8802
fax: (515)294-4517

Archaeology

Name: Archaeological Computing Database
Net: Internet
What: Articles on archaeological computing.
How: Accessible via WAIS
Email: Not accessible
Fees: Free
WAIS: archaeological_computing.src

Archie

Name: Archie
Net: Internet
What: Global file directory.
How: Europe: `telnet archie.funet.fi` (128.214.6.100)
Australia/New Zealand: `telnet archie.au` (139.130.4.6)
Israel: `telnet archie.cs.huji.ac.il` (132.65.6.5)
UK/Ireland: `telnet archie.doc.ic.ac.uk` (146.169.11.3)
Far East:
`telnet archie.ncu.edu.tw`
Maryland: `telnet archie.sura.net` (128.167.254.179)
Nevada: `telnet archie.unl.edu` (129.93.1.14)
New York: `telnet archie.ans.net` (147.225.1.2)
New Jersey: `telnet archie.rutgers.edu` (128.6.18.15)
Sweden: `telnet archie.luth.se` (130.240.18.4)
Email: `mail archie@<address>`, Subject: `help`
WAIS: archie-orst.edu.src
Fees: Free
Contact: Corrections/additions:
archie-admin@archie.rutgers.edu
Bug reports:
archie-l@archie.rutgers.edu

Artificial Intelligence

Name: Machine learning database
Net: Internet
What: Database on learning algorithms
How: `ftp ics.uci.edu`, `[128.195.1.1]`
`cd /pub/machine-learning-databases`
Email: `mail archive-server@ics.uci.edu`, body: `help`
Fees: Free
Contact: Patrick M. Murphy
Department of Information and Computer Science
University of California, Irvine
Irvine, CA 92717-3425
(714)856-5011
email: ml-repository@ics.uci.edu

Name: Lido
Net: Internet
What: Bibliographic database on artificial intelligence
How: mail server
Email: `mail lido@cs.uni-sb.de` [134.96.252.31] subject: `lidosearch info englis`
Fees: Free
Contact: Dr. Alfred Kobsa
Department of Information Science
University of Konstanz
D-W-7750 Konstanz 1
Germany
+49 75 31 88 1
email: bib-1@cs.uni-sb.de

Astronomy

Name: Auroral Activity
Net: Internet
What: Information on activity of Aurora Borealis; updated hourly.
How: `finger aurora@xi.uleth.ca` (142.66.3.29)
Email: Not accessible
Fees: Free

Name: Lunar/Planetary Institute
Net: Internet
What: Information services for the lunar and planetary researcher, including a Lunar and Planetary Bibliography with over 28,000 references. Photos from planetary missions are available, including data from Ranger, Surveyor, Lunar Orbiter, Gemini, Apollo, Skylab, Viking, Voyager, Space Shuttle, Magellan, and Galileo.
How: `telnet lpi.jsc.nasa.gov` (192.101.147.11), login: `lpi`
Email: Not accessible
Fees: Free

Name: NASA Headline News
Net: Internet
What: Daily NASA press releases.
How: `finger nasanews@space.mit.edu` (18.75.0.10)
Email: Not accessible; audio service at (202)755-1788
Fees: Free

Name: NASA SpaceLink
Net: Internet
What: NASA news including shuttle and satellite news, and space history.
How: `telnet spacelink.msfc.nasa.gov` (192.149.89.61), or `ftp` `192.149.89.61`, login: **anonymous** or **(205)895-0028**, Username: **NEWUSER**, Password: **NEWUSER**
Email: Not accessible
Fees: Free

Name: NED
Net: Internet
What: Cross-identifications for 200,000 galaxies, quasars, infrared and radio sources, etc. NED gives positions, names, and basic data, as well as bibliographic references.
How: `telnet ned.ipac.caltech.edu` (134.4.10.118), login: `ned`
Email: Not accessible
Fees: Free
Contact: ned@ipac.caltech.edu, G. Helou, B. Madore, or M. Schmitz at (818)397-9594

Name: NODIS
Net: Internet
What: National Space Science Data Center archive, for space and earth science researchers.
How: `telnet nssdc.gsfc.nasa.gov` (128.183.36.25)
`telnet nssdca.gsfc.nasa.gov` (128.183.36.23), login: `nodis`
Email: Not accessible
Fees: Free
Contact: Angelia Bland; (301)513-1687

Name: Spacemet
Net: Internet, FidoNet
What: Space Science BBS, Department of Physics and Astronomy, University of Massachusetts, Amherst. Maximus BBS on Internet.
How: `telnet spacemet.phast.umass.edu` `(128.119.50.48)`
Also accessible as FidoNet (1:321/110)
Email: Not accessible, modem access:
Boston (617)287-4100, (617)287-4200
`Server>`
`C GEMINI` `Username>` `SPACEMET`
Boston: (617)727-5920, 3 dots (. . .),
`SPACEMET`
Westfield (413)562-5270, (413)562-5279
Boston
`. . ., SPACEMET`
Amherst (413)545-5345,
`SPACEMET.PHAST.UMASS.EDU`
(413)545-8801
Lowell (508)934-2400 `UMLowell>`
`C Woods` `Username>` `SPACEMET`
Worcester (508)856-8990 `login:`
`spacemet,` `password:` `space1`
(lower case only)
SpaceMet South, Holyoke
(413)536-7526, (413)536-9717
SpaceMet North, Greenfield
(413)772-2038, (413)772-2030, (413)772-1020
SpaceMet Central/The Physics Forum,
UMass/Amherst (413)545-1959, (413)545-4453
Fees: Free
Contact: Helen Sternheim
Department of Physics and Astronomy,
Lederle Graduate Research Center 426,
University of Massachusetts
Amherst, MA 01003
(413)545-1908
(413)545-3697

Australia

Name: Australian National University Databases
Net: Internet
What: WAIS databases on aboriginal studies and ethnic groups of Southeast Asia.
How: Accessible via WAIS
WAIS: ANU-aboriginal-studies.src
ANU-Thai-Yunnan.src
Fees: Free

Aviation

Name: GTE Contel DUAT System
Net: Internet
What: Aviation weather reports for pilots.
How: `telnet duat.gtefsd.com` `(131.131.7.105)` (certified pilots),
`telnet duats.gtefsd.com` `(131.131.7.106)` (uncertified pilots)
Email: Not accessible
Fees: Free

Name: Aeronautics archive
Net: Internet
What: Database on aeronautics.
How: Accessible via WAIS
Email: Not accessible
WAIS: archive.orst.edu.src
Fees: Free

BBSes

Name: BBS Lists
Net: Internet
What: Lists of BBSes worldwide
How: `ftp wuarchive.wustl.edu, get` `/mirrors/msdos/bbslists/usbbs95` `.zip`
`ftp vector.intercon.com, cd` `/pub/BBS`
Email: Via FTPmail (see entry under FTP)
Fees: Free
USENET: `alt.bbs.lists`

Name: Endless Forest BBS
Net: Internet
What: Bulletin board running decent software
How: `telnet forest.unomaha.edu` `(137.48.1.5)` **2001**
Email: Not accessible
Fees: Free

BikeLab reports

Name: BEHEMOTH Archive
Net: Internet
What: Reports from the hi-tech nomad, Steve Roberts.
How: `ftp ftp.telebit.com,` login: `anonymous, cd /pub/nomad`
Email: Not accessible
Fees: Free
Contact: Steve.Roberts@Corp.Sun.COM

Biology

Name: GenBank
Net: Internet
What: Gene-sequence information. IntelliGenetics offers interactive access on its commercial online service. Email queries are handled by NCBI mail-servers.
How: Accessible via email
Email: `mail blast@ncbi.nlm.nih.gov,` body: `help`
`mail retrieve@ncbi.nlm.nih.gov,` body: `help`
`mail gene-server@bchs.uh.edu`
Fees: Free for mail server; fees apply for interactive access.
WAIS: bionic-genbank-software.src
bionic-sequence-bibliography.src
Contact: NCBI: info@ncbi.nlm.nih.gov, (301)496-2475, IG timesharing service: consult@presto.ig.com, (415)962-7300; include your mailing address with request.

Name: Gene-Server
Net: Internet
What: Genetics database
How: **Mail server**
Email: `mail gene-server@bchs.uh.edu,` body: `send help`
Fees: free

Name: MBCRR
Net: Internet
What: Archive of UNIX DNA analysis software
How: `ftp mbcrr.harvard.edu`
`[134.174.79.60]`
`cd /MBCRR-Package`
Email: FTPmail (see FTP entry)
Fees: free

Name: NCBI
Net: Internet
What: National Center for Biotechnology Information
How: `ftp ncbi.nlm.nih.gov`
`[130.14.25.1]`
Enzyme dictionary:
`cd /repository/enzyme`
Protein site dictionary:
`cd /repository/prosite`
DNA sequence analysis bibliography:
`cd /repository/seqanalref`
Swiss protein sequence databank:
`cd /repository/swiss-prot`
Email: **Enzyme dictionary:**
`mail netserv@embl-heidelberg.de,` body: `help`
General: use FTPmail (see FTP entry)
Fees: Free
Contact: National Center for Biotechnology Information
National Library of Medicine
Bldg. 38A, NIH
8600 Rockville Pike
Bethesda, MD 20894
(301)496-2475
email: repository@ncbi.nlm.nih.gov

Name: TAXACOM BBS
Net: Internet, BITNET
What: Buffalo Museum Botany BBS; information in environment, NY flora, ornithology, mycology, biodiversity, phylogenetics, etc.
How: (716)896-7581, login: **GUEST,** or
`ftp herbarium.bpp.msu.edu,`
`login: anonymous` or **TAXACOM-NET**
on **BITNET**
Email: Not accessible
Fees: Free
Contact: Buffalo Museum of Science; 1020 Humboldt Parkway; Buffalo, NY 14211

Name: Theoretical population genetics archive
Net: Internet
What: Archive of material on population genetics, including bibliography of articles before 1980, teaching materials, etc.
How: `ftp evolution.genetics.washington.edu` [128.95.12.41]
cd /pub/bible for population genetics bibliography
/pub/phylib for PHYLIB package
/pub/pogen for population genetics teaching material
Email: FTPmail (see FTP entry)
Fees: Free
Contact: Joe Felsenstein
Department of Genetics SK-50
University of Washington
Seattle, WA 98195
(206)543-0150
fax: (206)543-0754
email: joe@genetics.washington.edu

Name: LiMB
Net: Internet
What: Listing of databases in molecular biology
How: Mail server
Email: **mail bioserve@life.lanl.gov** [128.165.24.152] body: **limb-data**
Fees: Free
WAIS: bionic-directory-of-servers.src
Contact: LiMB
Theoretical Biology and Biophysics Group
T-10, Mail Stop K710
Los Alamas National Laboratory
Los Alamos, NM 87545
(505)667-7510
email: limb@life.lanl.gov

Bird watching

Name: Bird Info Network
Net: FidoNet 1:104/234, Internet: bird.com
What: BBS for birders.
How: **(303)423-9775**
Email: Not accessible
Fees: $5/month
Contact: Terry Rune; P.O. Box 632, Arvada, CO 80001; fax: (303)422-6529

Books online

Name: Online book stores
Net: Internet
What: Stores selling books online
How: Electronic mail
Email: Quantum books ordering:
mail quanbook@world.std.com
Quantum books mailing list:
mail quanlist@world.std.com
Computer Literacy information:
mail info@clbooks.com
Computer Literacy ordering:
mail orders@clbooks.com
Computer Literacy ordering problems:
mail service@clbooks.com
CompuBooks ordering:
mail 70007.1333@compuserve.com
Fees: No fees for orders

Name: CPET
Net: Internet
What: Catalog of electronic text archives
How: **telnet guvax3.georgetown.edu** [141.161.1.3] username: **CPET**
Email: None
Fees: Free
Contact: Maragaret Friedman
Project Assistant
The Center for Text and Technology
Academic Computer Center
238 Reiss Science Building
Georgetown University
Washington, DC 20057
email: mfriedman@guvax.georgtown.edu

Name: Online Book Initiative
Net: Internet
What: Text of books in electronic form.
How: **ftp world.std.com,** login: **anonymous,**
cd /obi
Email: Via FTPmail (see entry for FTP)
Fees: Free

Name: Project Gutenberg
Net: Internet
What: Archive of online books.
How: `ftp mrcnext.cso.uiuc.edu`
`(128.174.201.12)`, login: **anonymous**,
`cd etext`
`ftp quake.think.com`, login:
anonymous, `cd /pub/etxt`
`ftp oes.orst.edu`, login:
anonymous, `cd`
`/pub/almanac/guten`
Email: `mail almanac@oes.orst.edu`, body:
send guide, or **send gutten**
<filename>
LISTSERV: **mail**
listserv%uiucvmd.bitnet@uiucvm.
uic.edu, body: **subscribe**
gutnberg <your name>
WAIS: proj-gutenberg.src
Fees: Free
Contact: Michael S. Hart; Project Gutenberg Director
405 West Elm St.; Email:
hart@vmd.cso.uiuc.edu

Name: Book BBS
Net: None
What: Business and Computer Bookstore; CD–
ROMs.
How: (215)657-6130
Email: Not accessible
Fees: Free
Contact: 213 N. Easton Rd., Willow Grove, PA,
(800)233-0233, (215)657-8300

Name: Advantage Foundation
Net: None
What: Archive of online books.
How: BBS: (713)977-9505
Email: Not accessible
Fees: Membership is $24.95, plus charges for each
book.
Contact: Advantage Foundation; P.O. Box 773425
Houston, TX 77215; fax/voice: (713)977-
1719

Name: Dante Project
Net: Internet
What: Material on *The Divine Comedy,* funded by
the National Endowment for the Humanities.
How: `telnet library.dartmouth.edu`
`(129.170.16.11)`, login: **connect**
dante
Email: Not accessible
Fees: Free

Name: Aesop's Fables Archive
Net: Internet
What: Archive of *Aesop's Fables.*
How: Accessible via WAIS
Email: Not accessible
WAIS: Aesop-Fables.src
Fees: Free

Name: Poetry and Shakespeare Server
Net: Internet
What: Small collection of poems by Bronte, Burns,
T. S. Eliot, and Yeats. Works by Shakespeare.
How: `ftp ocf.berkeley.edu`,
`cd /pub/Library/Poetry` or
`cd /pub/Library/Shakespeare`
Email: Accessible via FTPmail
WAIS: poetry.src
Fees: Free

Business

Name: Kimberly BBS
Net: None
What: Minneapolis Federal Reserve Bank BBS,
Economic data, such as economic forecasts
and results of treasury auctions.
How: (612)340-2489
Email: Not accessible
Fees: Free

Name: ABI/Inform
Net: Internet
What: Extensive database of business periodical
literature.
How: `tn3270 GMUIBM.GMU.EDU`, select
`XLIBRIS`, select **PERI**, select **ABII**
Email: Not accessible
Fees: Free

Name: Dow Jones New Retrieval
Net: Internet
What: Extensive business online service.
How: `telnet djnr.dowjones.com`,
SERVICE: **dowjones** or **djnr**
Email: Not accessible
Fees: Off-peak access (8 PM –6 AM) fixed fees:
Tier 1: News & Quotes: $25/month
Tier 2: Forecasts & Analyses: $25/month
Tier 3: General Interest: $12.95/month
Tiers 1 and 2: $45/month
Tiers 1 and 3: $35/month
Tiers 2 and 3: $35/month
Tiers 1,2, and 3: $49.95/month
Contact: Doris Runyon; (609)520-4649 ext. 165

Name: BIX
Net: Internet
What: Hobbyist/Programmer online service.
How: `telnet bos2a.genvid.com`, or `telnet x25.bix.com`, login: `BIX`
Email: Not accessible
Fees: $1/hour above normal BIX rates

Name: Internet Business Pages
Net: Internet
What: Directory of vendors on Internet
How: `ftp ftp.msen.com, get /pub/vendor/msen/ibp` for application form
Email: `mail ibp-info@msen.com`, subject: `send description` or `send form`
Fees: Free

Name: CompuServe
Net: Internet
What: A zillion databases.
How: `telnet hermes.merit.edu`, which host? `compuserve`
Email: Not accessible
Fees: Fixed-fee access available; most database services additional

Name: Dialog
Net: Internet
What: 450 databases including TRW Credit, Moody's, Disclosure, and D&B Donnelly.
How: `telnet dialog.com`
Email: Not accessible
Fees: $45 startup fee, plus $35 annual fee and costs of $1.40 to $1.60/minute.
Contact: (800)334-2564

Name: Nexis
Net: Internet
What: More than 1000 databases, including S&P, Disclosure, Investex, and Predicasts.
How: `telnet lexis.meaddata.com`
Email: Not accessible
Fees: $50/month plus $0.65/minute and $6 to $50 per file.
Contact: Mead Data Central, Inc., (800)227-4908, (800)227-8379 (Ohio)

Name: Wall Street Journal
Net: Internet
What: Full text index of sample of *Wall Street Journal*.
How: Accessible via WAIS
Email: Not accessible
Fees: Free (full version available for sale)
WAIS: wall-street-journal-sample.src

Name: ClariNet Newswires
Net: Internet
What: API, UPI, Newsbytes, many other newswires, including stock market reports.
How: Accessible via NNTP (USENET)
Email: Not accessible
Fees: University site licenses available (see Appendix B: Choice Products)

Name: Stock market Report
Net: Internet
What: Brief summary of market activity; access to QuoteServer.
How: `telnet a2i.rahul.net`, (192.160.13.1) login: `guest`, `select m Market report`, `telnet bolero.rahul.net`, login: `guest`, `select m for market report` `telnet freenet-in-a.cwru.edu`, login: `visitor, select Business & Industrial Park, select USA Today: Headline Business News`
Email: Not accessible
Fees: Free

Name: New England Economic Data Center
Net: Internet
What: Unemployment, housing, and energy statistics from the Bureau of Economic Analysis and the Federal Reserve Bank of Boston.
How: `ftp neeedc.umesbs.maine.edu`, login: `anonymous, cd /bea or cd /frbb` Trade database (on CD-ROM) available by phone only.
Email: Via FTPmail (see FTP entry); telephone access: (207)581-1867
Fees: Free
Contact: email: BREECE@MAINE.MAINE.EDU

Name: Small Business Administration BBS
Net: None
What: BBS for small business people
How: (800)697-4636
Email: Not accessible
Fees: Free
Contact: Small Business Administration, (800)827-5722

CCITT

Name: TeleDoc Auto-Answering Mailbox (TAM)
Net: Internet
What: International Telecommunication Union document retrieval system.
How: Accessible by mail
Email: `mail teledoc@itu.arcom.ch`, in body of message: `help`
Fees: Free
Contact: International Telecommunication Union; Place des Nations, 1211 Geneva 20, Switzerland; voice: +41 22 730 5554, 41 22 730 5338 fax: +41 22 730 5337

Census

Name: 1990 Census
Net: Internet
What: Summaries of tape file from the 1990 U.S. Census.
How: `telnet una.hh.lib.umich.edu`, login: `gopher`, select `Social Science Data`, select `1990 census` `ftp mrcnext.cso.uiuc.edu`, `cd etext/etext92`, `get uscen901.xxx`, `uscen902.xxx` `telnet hermes.merit.edu`, host: `um-ulibrary`, login: `gopher`, select `4 Social Science Data`, select `1. 1990 Census`
Email: Not accessible
Fees: Free

Chatting

Name: Internet Relay Chat
Net: Internet
What: A global party line.
How: `telnet bradenville.andrew.cmu.edu` `(128.2.54.2) telnet ara.kaist.ac.kr (143.248.1.53)`, `telnet santafe.santafe.edu` `(192.12.12.2)`, login: `irc`, `telnet rcserver.itc.univie.ac.at 6668`
Email: Not accessible
Fees: Free
Contact: Tom.Kovar@itc.univie.ac.at

Commodore 64

Name: Commodore 64 Archive Server
Net: Internet
What: Archive of commodore 64 software.
How: Mail-server access only
Email: `mail twtick@corral.uwyo.edu` Subject: `Mail-Archive-Request` Text: `help <CR> end`
Fees: Free

Desktop Publishing

Name: FreeBoard BBS
Net: FidoNet, 1:264/212
What: Desktop publishing BBS.
How: `(804)744-0797`
Email: Not accessible
Fees: Donation for full access
Contact: Bill Hunter, InnerFaces; P.O. Box 1715, Midlothian, VA 23113

Dictionary

Name: Concise Oxford English Dictionary, Oxford Thesaurus, Oxford Dictionary of Quotations
Net: Internet
What: Dictionary, thesaurus, quations, in English.
How: `telnet info.rutgers.edu` `(128.6.26.25)`, choose `library`, then `reference`
Email: Not accessible
Fees: Free

Name: Webster
Net: Internet
What: Online Webster's dictionary.
How: `telnet moose.cs.indiana.edu` `(129.79.254.191) 2627`, `HELP` for info.
Email: Not accessible
Fees: Free

Name: Roget's Thesaurus
Net: Internet
What: Online determination of alternative words.
How: Via WAIS (see entry under WAIS)
Email: Not accessible
WAIS: roget-thesaurus.src
Fees: Free

Education

Name: National Education BBS
Net: Internet
What: BBS for educators.
How: `telnet nebbs.nersc.gov`
`(128.55.160.162)`, login: **guest**
Email: Not accessible
Fees: Free

Name: California Online Resources for Education (CORE)
Net: Internet
What: Online access to educational resources.
How: `telnet liberty.uc.wlu.edu`
`(137.113.10.35)`, login: **lawlib**,
select databases/indexes (5), select
database 65
Email: Not accessible
Fees: Free

Name: International Center for Distance Learning
Net: Internet
What: Open University
How: `telnet sun.nsf.ac.uk`
`(128.86.8.7)`, login: **janet** Hostname:
uk.ac.open.acs.vax Username:
icdl
For information,
`ftp acsvax.open.ac.uk`
`(137.108.48.8)`,
login: **FTP**, password: **FTP**,
get icdlinfo
Email: `mail`
`listserv%psuvm.bitnet@cunyvm.cu`
`ny.edu`
body: **SUB DEOS <your name>**, to
cancel: **UNSUB DEOS <your name>**
Fees: Free
Contact: International Centre for Distance Learning,
The Open University; Walton Hall,
Milton Keynes, MK7 6AA United Kingdom;
+44 908 653537, fax: +44 908 654173,
email: n.ismail@open.ac.uk

Name: MOLIS and FEDIX
Net: Internet
What: Minority OnLine Information Service (MOLIS)
Federal Agencies Opportunities (Fedix, for
scholarship information).
How: `telnet fedix.fie.com`
`(192.111.228.33)`, login: **fedix**
also reachable by **telnet**
info.rutgers.edu
`(128.6.26.25)`, choose **library**, then
federal
Email: Not accessible; (800)783-3349
Fees: Free

Name: ERIC database
Net: Internet
What: Educational database
How: `tn3270 GMUIBM.GMU.EDU`, select
XLIBRIS, select **PERI**, select **ERIC**
`telnet pac.carl.org`
`(192.54.81.128)`
Email: Not accessible
Fees: Free
WAIS: ERIC-archive.src
eric-digest.src
Contact: CARL; 3801 E. Florida St., Suite 300, Denver,
CO 80210; (303)758-3030, fax: (303)758-
0606, email: help@carl.org

Name: Newton
Net: Internet
What: BBS for science, math, and computer science
educators.
How: `telnet newton.dep.anl.gov`
`(130.202.92.50)`, login: **newton**
Email: Not accessible
Fees: Free

Electronic mail addresses

Name: Knowbot
Net: Internet
What: Email address directory.
How: `telnet nri.reston.va.us 185` or
`telnet sol.bucknell.edu 185`
Email: `mail kis@nri.reston.va.us` or
`mail kis@sol.bucknell.edu`
For discussion group:
`mail kis-user@nri.reston.va.edu`
To subscribe:
`kis-users-`
`request@nri.reston.va.edu`
Fees: Free

Name: USENET Addresses Database
Net: Internet
What: Email address directory.
How: `ftp pit-manager.mit.edu`
`cd/pub/usenet-addresses`
`get addresses.Z` (for entire
database)
Email: `mail mail-server@pit-`
`manager.mit.edu`, body: **send**
usenet-addresses/<name>
Fees: Free
Contact: `mail postmaster@pit-`
`manager.mit.edu`

Name: PSI White Pages
Net: Internet
What: X.500 email directory.
How: `telnet wp.pis.com or sp2.psi.com, login: fred`
Email: Accessible via Knowbot
Fees: Free

Engineering and science

Name: CAD/Engineering Services BBS
Net: FidoNet, 1:116/32, RBBSNet 8:967/108, PCGnet 9:517/332
What: Home of CADNet file echo
How: `(615)451-2872`
Email: Not accessible
Fees: Free

Name: Society of Mechanical Engineers BBS
Net: Not connected (PCBoard)
What: Engineering software and data.
How: (608)233-3378
Email: Not accessible
Fees: For ASME members

Name: Applied Science, Technology & Biology Index
Net: Internet
What: Database of scientific periodicals.
How: `tn3270 GMUIBM.GMU.EDU,` select `XLIBRIS,` select `PERI,` select `ASAB`
Email: Not accessible
Fees: Free

Name: F.A.S.T. News
Net: Internet
What: Newsletter on arts, science, and technology.
How: Mail access only
Email: `mail isast@garnet.berkeley.edu`
Fees: Free

Name: Impact Online
Net: Internet
What: Newsletter about social and ethical concerns of information technology.
How: Mail access only
Email: `mail bcs-ss1@compass.com`
Fees: Free

Name: Engineering BBS List
Net: ILINK
What: List of engineering-related bulletin boards, brought to you by Art Petrzelka of Computer Plumber BBS.
How: Call (319)337-6723
Email: Not accessible
Fees: Free
Contact: 76320.204@compuserve.com

Encryption

Name: Privacy FAQ
Net: Internet
What: Privacy & Anonymity on the Internet FAQ.
How: `ftp pit-manager.mit.edu` (18.172.1.27), `cd /pub/usenet/news.answers/net-privacy`
Email: Via FTPmail (see FTP entry)
Fees: Free

Name: Security FAQ
Net: Internet
What: Commonly asked questions on security.
How: `ftp pit-manager.mit.edu` (18.172.1.27), `get /pub/usenet/news.answers/alt-security-faq`
Email: Via FTPmail (see FTP entry)
Fees: Free

Name: Introduction to Cryptography
Net: Internet
What: Public-key cryptography paper.
How: `ftp csrc.ncsl.nist.gov` (129.6.54.11), login: `anonymous,` get `/pub/nistpubs/800-2.txt`
Email: Not accessible
Fees: Free

Name: Public Keys Directory
Net: Internet
What: Directory of public keys.
How: `ftp tbird.cc.iastate.edu, get /usr/explorer/public-keys.pgp ftp toxicwaste.mit.edu, get /pub/keys/public-keys.pgp ftp phil.utmb.edu, get /pub/pgp/public-keys.pgp, ftp ftp.demon.co.uk, get /pub/pgp/pubring.pgp`
Email: Via FTPmail (see FTP)
Fees: Free

Name: Privacy and Encryption Discussion List
Net: Internet
What: Discussion on privacy.
How: `mail cypherpunks-request@toad.com`
Email: Accessible via email only
Fees: Free
Contact: hughes@toad.com

Name: RIPEM
Net: Internet
What: Privacy enhanced mail implementation.
How: `ftp rpub.cl.msu.edu, get /pub/crypt/GETTING_ACCESS;` for RIPEM FAQ, `ftp pit-manager.mit.edu, get /pub/usenet/news.answers/ripem/faq`
Email: Not accessible
Fees: Free

Name: Rivest, Shamir, Adleman (RSA) Encryption
Net: Internet
What: Information on RSA.
How: `ftp rsa.com, cd /pub/faq`
Email: Via FTPmail (see FTP)
Fees: Free

Energy

Name: Gulf Coast Society of Petroleum Engineers BBS
Net: FidoNet, 1:3803/2
What: Engineering software, data.
How: (318)267-3228
Fees: Membership in SPE required for full access.
Contact: sysop@f2.n3803.z1.fidonet.org

Name: Megawatts
Net: None
What: General purpose DOE fle oriented BBS with some energy information
How: `(202)586-0739`
Email: None
Fees: Free

Name: EPUB BBS
Net: Internet
What: Energy Information Administration Electronic Publishing System; information on fossil and nuclear energy, forecasts, many EIA publications. Petroleum supply figures updated monthly available over WAIS
How: `(202)586-2557`
Email: None
Fees: Free
WAIS: EIA-Petroleum-Supply-Monthly.src

Name: CIPS BBS
Net: None
What: Federal Energy Regulatory Administration Commission Issuance Posting System BBS
How: `(202)208-1781`
Email: None
Fees: Free

Name: Offshore BBS
Net: None
What: Offshore Oil and Gas BBS; information on offshore resources and environmental studies
How: `(703)787-1181`
Email: None
Fees: Free
Contact: Marcia Heimberer, (703)787-1043

Name: Home Power Renewable Energy
Net: None
What: BBS for renewable energy; includes electronic versions of *Home Power* magazine.
How: `(707)822-8640`
Email: Not accessible
Fees: Free
Contact: Redwood Environmental Educational Institute; P.O. Box 293, Arcata, CA 95521; (707)822-7884

Environmental

Name: Clean Up Information BBS (CLU-IN)
Net: None
What: Superfund Information BBS, US EPA Office of Solid Waste and Emergency Response
How: `(301)589-8366`
Email: None
Fees: Free
Contact: Environmental Management Support, (301) 589-8368

Name: PIN BBS
Net: None
What: Pesticide Information Network; offers chemical databases on pesticides, US EPA Office of Pesticide Programs
How: **(703)305-5919, 7E1**
Email: None
Fees: Free
Contact: Leslie Davies-Hilliard, (703)305-7499

Name: PIES, ICPIC, OAIC BBS
Net: none
What: USA EPA BBS for the pollution prevention, cleaner production, and ozone action
How: **(703)506-1025**
Email: None
Fees: Free

Name: ECIX
Net: Internet
What: Environmental archive
How: **ftp igc.org** [192.82.108.1], **cd /pub/ECIX, cd /pub/ECIXfiles**
Email: None
Fees: Free
Contact: The Environmental Exchange
1930 18th St. NW
Suite 24
Washington, DC 20009
(202)387-2182
email: tgray@igc.org

Name: Solid Waste Information Clearing House BBS
Net: None
What: Joint effort of the Solid Waste Association of North America and US EPA
How: **(301)585-0204**
Email: None
Fees: SWANA members or EPA employees only

Name: Greenpeace Environet
Net: None
What: ECONEWS newsletter, information on Greenpeace, Wind Energy, and other environmental BBSes.
How: **(415)512-9108**
Email: Not accessible
Fees: Free
Contact: Dick Dillman; (415)512-9025

Name: Water Quality Database
Net: Internet
What: Articles on water quality.
How: Accessible via WAIS
Email: Not accessible
WAIS: water-quality.src
Fees: Free

Name: National Oceanic and Atmospheric Administration Earth Systems Data Directory
Net: Internet
What: Identification, location, and overview descriptions of Earth Science Data Sets.
How: **telnet nodc.nodc.noaa.gov** (140.90.235.10), login: **NOAADIR**
Email: Not accessible
Fees: Free
Contact: Gerald Barton, NOAA/NESDIS, (202)606-4548

Name: Exposure Assesment Modeling BBS
Net: Not connected
What: Information on dispersion modeling.
How: (706)546-3402
Email: Not accessible
Fees: Free
Contact: Athens Environmental Research Laboratory; 960 College Station Rd., Athens, GA 30613-0801; (706)546-3549

Name: EPA Technology Transfer Network
Net: Not connected
What: Information on dispersion modeling, air-quality standards, Best Available Control Technology, emission measurement, Clean Air Act Amendments, etc.
How: (919)541-5472
Email: Not accessible
Fees: Free
Contact: (919)541-5384

Name: Ocean Information Center
Net: Internet
What: Data sets related to the ocean, maintained by the University of Delaware's College of Marine Studies.
How: **telnet delocn.udel.edu** (128.175.24.1), login: **info**
Email: Not accessible
Fees: Free

Name: Environmental Databases
Net: Internet
What: WAIS databases on the environment.
How: Accessible via WAIS
Email: Not accessible
Fees: Free
WAIS: environment-newsgroups.src
great-lakes-factsheets.src
Gobal_Change_Data_Directory.src
NOAA_national_Environmental_Ref.src
DOE_Climate_Data.src

Ethnic studies

Name: Middle Eastern Database
Net: Internet
What: Database of documents on Middle East.
How: `ftp pit-manager@mit.edu`, login: `anonymous, cd /pub/israel`
Email: Via FTPmail (see FTP entry)
Fees: Free

Fax gateways

Name: FaxGate
Net: Internet
What: Sends a fax via email.
How: Accessible by mail
Email: `mail FaxGate@elvis.sovusa.com,` body: `help`
Fees: $10/registration plus $2.50/page

Name: Fax Gateway
Net: RIME
What: Send a fax via RIME conference mail.
How: Send a message within the FAX conference.
Email: Not accessible from Internet
Fees: Free

FidoNet

Name: FidoNet Nodelist
Net: Internet
What: List of FidoNet systems, updated weekly.
How: Accessible via WAIS
Email: Not accessible
WAIS: fidonet-nodelist.src
Fees: Free

Name: FidoNews
Net: Internet
What: Weekly FidoNet newsletter.
How: On USENET as comp.org.fidonet, also accessible via FTP to `ftp.ieee.org, get ftp/pub/fidonet/fidonews`
Email: Via FTPmail (see entry under FTP)
Fees: Free

Name: FidoNet Information
Net: Internet, FidoNet
What: Information on FidoNet.
How: Accessible via email
Email: `mail fidoinfo@fidoinfo.fidonet.org`
Fees: Free

Name: Filebone Mailing List
Net: Internet, FidoNet
What: Information on files coming in over the FileBone to `ftp.ieee.org`
How: Accessible via email
Email: `mail fidonet-ftp-announce-request@zeus.ieee.org`
Fees: Free

Food

Name: Recipe Archives
Net: Internet
What: Database of recipes.
How: `ftp gatekeeper.dec.com, cd /pub/recipes`
`ftp mthvax.cs.miami.edu, cd /recipes`
Email: Via FTPmail (see entry for FTP)
Fees: Free
WAIS: usenet-cookbook.src
recipes.src

French

Name: ARTFL
Net: Internet
What: Treasury of the French Language
How: `telnet artfl.uchicago.edu` [128.135.12.82] login: **guest**, password: **suggest**
Email: None
Fees: Paying service; guest account for evaluation only
Contact: ARTFL
Department of Romance Languages
University of Chicago
1050 East 59th St.
Chicago, IL 60637
(812)702-8488
email: mark@gide.uchicago.edu

Appendix C: Online Resources

FTP archives

Name: File servers
Net: Internet
What: File access via email.
How: Mail access only
Email: `mail smiley@uiuc.edu`, body:
`Filesend: help <CR> Filesend:`
`list`
Fees: Free

Name: FTPmail
Net: Internet
What: FTP via email.
How: Mail access only
Email: `mail ftpmail@decwrl.dec.com`, or
`mail ftpmail@pa.dec.com`, body:
`help <CR> quit`
Fees: Free
Contact: `mail ftpmail-request@pa.dec.com`

Name: File Servers
Net: BITNET
What: File access via email.
How: For BITNET users only mail from
other networks not accepted.
Email: `mail bitftp@pucc.princeton.edu`,
body: `help` or `ftplist`
Fees: Free

Name: List of FTP Sites
Net: Internet
What: List of anonymous `ftp` sites (discontinued).
How: `ftp pilot.njin.net`, `login:`
`anonymous, get /pub/ftp-`
`list/ftp.list`
Email: `mail odin@pilot.njin.net`,
subject: `listserv-request`, body:
`send help`
WAIS: ftp-list.src
Fees: Free

Games

Name: Backgammon server
Net: Internet
What: Lets you play backgammon with other users.
How: `telnet 134.130.130.46 4321`,
`telnet solana.mps.ohio-`
`state.edu (128.146.37.78) 3200`,
`login: guest`
`type help for assistance`
Email: Not accessible
Fees: Free

Name: Chess Server
Net: Internet
What: Lets you play chess in real time.
How: `telnet valkyries.andrew.cmu.edu`
`(128.2.232.4) 5000, login: guest,`
`password: guest; can also create`
`login name, and password. Type help`
`for assistance`
Email: Not accessible
Fees: Free

Name: Go Server
Net: Internet
What: Lets you play GO in real time.
How: `telnet lacerta.unm.edu`
`(129.24.14.70.6969) 6969,`
`telnet`
`icsib18.icsi.Berkeley.EDU`
`6969, telnet cnam.cnam.fr`
`(192.33.159.6) 6969, login/password:`
`go For short help files, ftp`
`unmvax.cs.unm.edu, cd pub/go`
`For postscript help files, ftp`
`u.washington.edu, get`
`public/go/igs.tex.Z`
Email: Not accessible
Fees: Free

Name: Oracle
Net: Internet
What: Oracle that answers all your questions (well, almost all).
How: Mail access only
Email: `mail`
`oracle@iuvax.cs.indiana.edu`,
subject: `help`
To ask a question, put in the
subject: `Tell me <question>`
Fees: The oracle may ask you a nosy question in return.

Name: Micromuse MUD
Net: Internet
What: Role-playing game.
How: `telnet michael.ai.mit.edu`
`(18.43.0.177), login: guest`
Email: Not accessible
Fees: Free

Name: MUD archive
Net: Internet
What: Archive of information on MUDs
How: `ftp actlab.rtf.utexas.edu`
`(128.83.194.11), login: anonymous`
Email: Via FTPmail (See FTP entry)
Fees: Free

Name: Trade Wars
Net: Internet
What: Role-playing game.
How: `telnet nelsons.cern.ch`
`(128.141.8.248) 2002`
Email: Not accessible
Fees: Free

Genealogy

Name: Genealogy BBS
Net: FidoNet 1:109/302
What: National Genealogical Society BBS, list of genealogical BBSes
How: `(703)528-2612`
Email: Not accessible
Fees: Free
Contact: National Genealogical Society, Computer Interest Group; 4527 Seventeenth St. North Arlington, VA 22207-2399; (703)525-0050

Geography

Name: Geography Server
Net: Internet
What: Information on population, latitude, longitude, and elevation, organized by city or area code.
How: `telnet martini.eecs.umich.edu`
`(141.212.99.9) 3000`, type `help` for assistance
Email: Not accessible
Fees: Free
Contact: Tom Libert; (313)936-0827,
`libert@citi.umich.edu`

Name: Global Land Information System
Net: Internet
What: Info on land-use maps.
How: `telnet glis.cr.usgs.gov`,
login: `guest` (for land use maps)
Email: Not accessible
Fees: Free
Contact: EROS Data Center; Sioux Falls, SD 57198; (800)252-4547, fax: (605)594-6589

Geology

Name: Earthquake Information
Net: Internet
What: Information on recent seismic activity.
How: `finger`
`quake@geophys.washington.edu`
`(128.95.16.50)`
Email: Not accessible
Fees: Free

Name: US Geological Survey BBS
Net: Not connected
What: Geological Survey news releases, geological software, and information on USGS CD-ROMs and publications.
How: (703)648-4168
Email: Not accessible
Fees: Free

Name: USGS Earth Science Directory
Net: Internet
What: Directory of USGS data.
How: Accessible via WAIS
Email: Not accessible
WAIS: USGS_Earth_Science_Data_Directory.src
Fees: Free

Name: GeoNet Kansas
Net: GeoInfo Network (QWK/REP packet network)
What: Kansas Geological Survey BBS
How: (316)265-6457, (316)265-1994 (V.32*bis*)
Email: Not accessible
Contact: Kansas Geological Society; 212 North Market St., Witchita, KS 67202

Gopher

Name: Gopher
Net: Internet
What: Online catalog of Internet resources.
How: `telnet consultant.micro.umn.edu`
        `(134.84.132.4)`
        `telnet panda.uiowa.edu`
        `(128.255.63.234)`
        `telnet gdunix.gd.chalmers.se`
        `(129.16.221.40)` (SWEDISH)
        `telnet gopher.uiuc.edu`
        `(128.174.33.160)`
        `telnet gopher.unt.edu`
        `(129.120.1.42)`
        `telnet tolten.puc.cl`
        `(146.155.1.16)` (CHILE),
        `login: gopher`
Email: Not accessible
Fees: Free
Contact: Internet Gopher Developers; 100 Union St. SE #190, Minneapolis, MN 55455
WAIS: alt.gopher.src

Name: Gopher FAQ
Net: Internet
What: Frequently asked Gopher questions.
How: `ftp pit-manager.mit.edu, get /pub/usenet/news.answers/gopher-faq`
Email: `mail-server@rtfm.mit.edu`, `body: send usenet/news.answers/finding-sources`
Fees: Free

Name: Gopher CSO Phone Book Software
Net: Internet
What: Mounts phone books over Gopher.
How: `ftp uxc.cso.uiuc.edu (128.174.5.50)`, `get /pub/qi.tar.Z` (server software), clients in `/pub/ph.tar.Z`
Email: To join mailing list, `mail info-ph-request@uxc.cso.uiuc.edu`
Fees: Free
Contact: Paul Jones, p-pomes@uiuc.edu

Name: Veronica
Net: Internet
What: Index of Gopher databases (Veronica is to Gopher what Archie is to FTP).
How: `telnet consultant.micro.umn.edu (134.84.132.4)`, `login: gopher`, select other gophers, veronica
Email: Not accessible
Fees: Free
Contact: gophadm@futique.scs.unr.edu

Government

Name: White House
Net: Internet
What: Press releases
How: `ftp sunsite.unc.edu, cd /home3/wais/white-house-papers`
        `ftp cco.caltech.edu, cd /pub/bjmcall`
        `ftp cpsr.org, cd /cpsr/clinton`
        `FedWorld BBS, (703)321-8020`
Email: **For press releases: `mail Clinton-info@campaign92.org`**, subject: Help
        For daily summary of releases: `mail almanac@esusda.gov`, body: `subscribe wh-summary`
Fees: Free

Name: House of Representatives
Net: Internet
What: Pilot constituent communications program
How: Mail server
Email: `mail house.hr.gov`
Fees: Free

Name: Federal Bulletin Board
Net: None
What: U.S. Government Printing Office BBS.
How: `(202)512-1387`
Email: Not accessible
Fees: Free for BBS; purchase of books requires GPO Deposit Account
Contact: (202)512-1524

Name: Fed Whistleblower
Net: Internet
What: Whistleblower's BBS and newsgroup
How: `alt.whistleblower` (USENET)
        BBS: `(202)225-5527`
Email: None
Fees: Free

Name: Food and Drug Administration BBS
Net: Internet
What: News releases, AIDS information, drug information, drug and device approvals, FDA federal register, testimony, speeches of FDA commissioner, meetings, import alerts, etc.
How: `telnet fdabbs.fda.gov` `(150.148.8.48)`, login: `bbs`, type `help` for assistance, direct dial: (800)222-0185, 7E1
Email: Not accessible
Fees: Free
Contact: Support: Parklawn Computer Center (PCC) at (301)443-7318
Articles: Karen Malone, FDA Press Office (301)443-3285

Name: Social Security Administration BBS
Net: Internet
What: Information about social security.
How: `ftp soaf1.ssa.gov`, login: `anonymous, cd pub`; for phone book, `get ssa.phone.book.Z`
Email: `mail info@soaf1.ssa.gov`, body: `send index`
Fees: Free

Name: US Senate Bibliographies
Net: Internet
What: Bibliographies of committee hearings and publications for the 99th –103rd congresses.
How: `ftp ncsuvm.cc.ncsu.edu, cd /senate, get readme.gwp9108`
Email: `mail listserv@ncsuvm.cc.ncsu.edu`, body: `get readme gwp9108 senate`
Fees: Free

Name: FCC BBS
Net: Not connected
What: Information on Federal Communications Commission rule makings, equipment authorization, etc.
How: (301)725-1072
Email: Not accessible
Fees: Free

Name: Export-Import Bank BBS
Net: Not connected
What: BBS of the Export-Import Bank.
How: (202)566-4699
Email: Not accessible
Fees: Free

Name: Government WAIS databases
Net: Internet
What: Government databases on WAIS.
How: Accessible via WAIS
Email: Not accessible
Fees: Free
WAIS: US-Gov-Programs.src
us-judges.src

Name: Politics Archive
Net: Internet
What: Archive of organizations, tracts, and opinions.
How: `ftp ftp.css.itd.umich.edu, cd /poli`
Email: Via FTPmail (see FTP entry)
Fees: Free
Contact: To submit files, `mail pauls@umich.edu`, subject: `FTP` Paul Southworth, Computing Resource Center, 3113 School of Education, University of Michigan, Ann Arbor, MI 48109-1259

Ham radio

Name: Ham Radio Callbooks
Net: Internet
What: Catalog of ham radio call-signs.
How: `telnet callsign.cs.buffalo.edu` `(128.205.32.2) 2000`, `telnet ham.njit.edu` `(128.235.1.10) 2000`, type `help` for assistance
Email: Not accessible
Fees: Free

Name: Association of North American Radio Clubs
Net: None
What: BBS for ham radio operators of 20 clubs; shortwave schedules; and magazines.
How: `(913)345-1978`
Email: Not accessible
Fees: Free

... y Archive

... journals, libraries,
... ies, diaries,
... nd programs related to

... edu, cd
... ory
... entry)

Name: Rec.gardens Database
Net: Internet
What: WAIS database.
How: Accessible via WAIS
Fees: Free
WAIS: rec.gardens.src

IBM-PC

Name: IBM-PC Archives
Net: Internet
What: Archive of IBM-PC software
How: `ftp wuarchive.wustl.edu,`
`ftp oak.oakland.edu,`
`ftp wsmr-simtel20.army.mil,`
`login: anonymous`
Email: Via FTPmail (see entry under FTP);
new entries anounced in
comp.sys.ibm.pc.digest
Fees: Free
WAIS: wuarchive.src

Name: IBM-PC Frequently Asked Questions
Net: Internet
What: WAIS database
How: Accessible via WAIS
Email: Not accessible
Fees: Free
WAIS: ibm.pc.FAQ

Name: IBM-PC Info—PC Mailing List
Net: Internet
What: Moderated mailing list.
How: Accessible via email
Email: `mail LISTSERV@UGA.BITNET`, in
body: `SUBSCRIBE IBMPC-L`
`mail LISTSERV@UIUCVMD.BITNET`,
in body: `SUBSCRIBE I-IBMPC`
Fees: Free

International studies

Name: CIA World Factbook
Net: Internet
What: Facts about countries around the world.
How: `telnet info.rutgers.edu`
`(128.6.26.25)`, choose `library`, then
`reference`
`ftp nic.funet.fi, cd`
`/pub/doc/World_facts`
Email: Via FTPmail (see entry under FTP)
WAIS: world-factbook.src
Fees: Free

Name: GSIS
Net: Internet
What: Bibliographic database on Latin America
How: `telnet sabio.ir.miami.edu`
`[129.171.32.26]`
Email: None
Fees: Commercial database; access by account
only
Contact: North-South Center
1500 Monza, P.O. Box 248014
Coral Gables, FL 33124-3027
(305)284-4442
fax: (305)284-5089
email: `msgctr@sabio.ir.miami.edu`

Commonwealth of Independent States

Name: CIS Sites
Net: Internet
What: Internet sites in the CIS.
How: Accessible via WAIS
Email: Not accessible
Fees: Free
WAIS: cissites.src

Name: Soviet Archives
Net: Internet
What: Newly released archives of Soviet documents.
How:
```
ftp ftp.dra.com, cd /pub/loc,
get README
ftp seq1.loc.gov, cd
/pub/soviet.archive/text.english,
get README
ftp sunsite.unc.edu, cd
/pub/docs/russia/english.txt,
get README
```
Email: Accessible via FTPmail (see FTP entry)
Fees: Free
WAIS: cissites.src

Hungary

Name: Hungarian Groups
Net: Internet
What: Mailing lists and USENET groups in Hungarian.
How: USENET: soc.culture.magyar
Email: `mail listserv@ucsbvm.bitnet`, in body: `subscribe hungary <your name>` Hollosi Information eXchange HIX): `mail gtoth@phoenix.princeton.edu`, Subject: `HIX`, body: `HELP` or `SUBS service-name` or `HELP SENDDOCS`
Fees: Free

Japan

Name: Japan Sources
Net: Internet
What: Sources of information on Japan.
How: Accessible via WAIS
Email: Not accessible
Fees: Free
WAIS: fj.sources

Internet access

Name: Washington University Services
Net: Internet
What: Access to Internet libraries and government information services.
How: `telnet wugate.wustl.edu` (128.252.135.4), login: **services**
Email: Not accessible
Fees: Free
Contact: services@wugate.wustl.edu

Name: Special Internet connections
Net: Internet
What: Listing of Internet services
How: `ftp csd4.csd.uwm.edu` [128.89.7.4] `get /pub/inet.services.txt`
Email: `mail bbslist@au3.augsburg.edu` `mail yanoff@csd4.csd.uwm.edu`, subject: **yan-inet**
Fees: Free
USENET: alt.internet.services

Name: Internet mail guide
Net: Internet
What: Listing of gateways
How: `ftp csd4.csd.uwm.edu`[128.89.7.4] `get /pub/internetwork-mail-guide`
Email: FTPmail (see FTP entry)
Fees: Free

Name: Internet Public Access Dialup List
Net: Internet
What: list of public access Internet sites.
How: Posted regularly to alt.internet.access.wanted
Email: `mail info-deli-server@netcom.com`, body: **send PDIAL**
Fees: Free
USENET: alt.internet.access

Internet information

Name: InterNIC
Net: Internet
What: Internet directory and information system
How: `telnet internic.net`
Email: Not accessible
Fees: Free

Name: Matrix News
Net: Internet
What: Publication about the Internet.
How: Accessible via WAIS
Email: Not accessible
Fees: Free
WAIS: matrix_news.src

Name: MERIT Internet Cruise
Net: Internet
What: Tour of the Internet developed by MERIT.
How: `ftp nic.merit.edu, cd /resources, get merit.cruise2.mac.hqx` (Mac) or `merit.cruise2.win` (Windows)
Email: FTPmail (see FTP entry)
Fees: Free
Contact: cruise2feedback@merit.edu

Name: Internet Resource Guide
Net: Internet
What: Guide to Internet developed by NSF.
How: `ftp nnsc.nsf.net, cd /resource-guide`
Email: `mail resource-guide-request@nnsc.1nsf.net`
Fees: Free

Name: Zen and the Art of the Internet
Net: Internet
What: Short guide to Internet for beginners.
How: `ftp ftp.cs.widener.edu,` login: `anonymous, cd /pub/zen`
Email: Via FTPmail (see FTP entry)
Fees: Free
WAIS: zen-internet-src

Name: NorthWestNet User Service Internet Guide
Net: Internet
What: Long guide to Internet (great!).
How: `ftp ftphost.nwnet.net,` login: `anonymous, cd nic/nwnet/user-guide`
Email: via FTPmail (see FTP entry)
Fees: Free

Name: Internet Training Archive
Net: Internet
What: Archive of information for Internet trainers
How: `ftp nstn.ns.ca` [137.186.128.11] login: `anonymous, cd /pub/netinfo`
Email: via FTPmail (see FTP entry)
Fees: Free
Contact: To submit, `mail ftp@hawk.nstn.ns.ca`

Name: The December Lists
Net: Internet
What: Sources of information on Internet.
How: `ftp ftp.rpi.edu, /pub/communications/internet-cmc`
Email: via FTPmail (see FTP entry)
Fees: Free

Name: NYSERNet New User's Guide
Net: Internet
What: New user's guide to Internet.
How: `ftp nysernet.org, get /pub/resources/guides/ new.user.guide.v2.2.txt`
Email: via FTPmail (see FTP entry)
Fees: Free

Name: Internet Bibliography
Net: Internet
What: Bibliography of material on Internet.
How: `telnet liberty.uc.wlu.edu,` login: `lawlib`, select option 11, then option 47.
`ftp liberty.uc.wlu.edu, get /pub/lawlib/internet.bibl`
`ftp nic.merit.edu,` login: `anonymous`, password: `guest`
`cd introducing.the.internet`
`ftp nnsc.nsf.net, cd resource-guide`
`get resource-guide.txt.tar.Z`
`ftp hydra.uwo.ca, cd /libsoft`
Email: Via FTPmail (see entry for FTP)
Fees: Free
WAIS: comp.internet.library.src

Name: JvNCnet Network Information Center On-Line (NICOL)
Net: Internet
What: Has limited documentation on the Internet, such as information on nternet libraries, and the Internet society.
How: `telnet nisc.jvnc.net` (128.121.50.7), login: `nicol`
Email: Not accessible
Fees: Free

Name: Network Information Center Online Aid System (NICOLAS)
Net: Internet
What: BBS for NASA employees, contractors, and affiliated researchers only.
How: `telnet dftnic.gsfc.nasa.gov` (128.183.10.3), login: `dftnic`
Email: Not accessible
Fees: Free

Name: WAIS Databases of Internet Information
Net: Internet
What: Databases of articles and information on Internet.
How: Accessible via WAIS
Email: Not accessible
Fees: Free
WAIS: internet-documents.src
internet-drafts.src
internet-phonebook.src
internet-resource-guide.src
internet-rfcs.src
internet-standards.src
internet-info.src
internet-services.src
ietf-docs.src
ietf-drafts.src
usenet-FAQ.src

Internet debugging

Name: Domain Name Resolver
Net: Internet
What: Tests whether a site is set up correctly for Domain Name Service.
How: Email access only
Email: `mail resolve@cs.widener.edu`, `mail dns@grasp.insa-lyon.fr`, body: `help`
Fees: Free

Name: BITNET Node Database
Net: Internet
What: Listing of BITNET nodes, useful for debugging bounced mail.
How: Accessible via WAIS
WAIS: bitearn.nodes
Fees: Free

Name: FidoNet nodelist
Net: Internet
What: Listing of FidoNet nodes, useful for debugging bounced mail.
How: Accessible via WAIS
WAIS: fidonet-nodelist.src
Fees: Free

Name: Domain Organizations and Contacts Database
Net: Internet
What: Listing of domain names, useful for debugging bounced mail.
How: Accessible via WAIS
WAIS: domain-organizations.src
domain-contacts.src
Fees: Free

K–12

Name: K12Net Conferences
Net: Internet
What: Conferences for K–12 educators and students.
How: On USENET, as k12.*
Fees: Free

Name: KidsNet
Net: Internet
What: Database of information related to children.
How: Accessible via WAIS
Fees: Free
WAIS: kidsnet.src

Legal

Name: Lexis
Net: Internet
What: More than 1000 databases of court decisions, etc.
How: `telnet` lexis.meaddata.com
Email: Not accessible
Fees: $50/month plus $0.65/minute and $6 to $50 per file.
Contact: Mead Data Central, Inc.; (800)227-4908, (800)227-8379 (Ohio)

Name: Supreme Court Decisions
Net: Internet
What: Online text of recent decisions.
How: `ftp ftp.cwru.edu`, login: anonymous, `telnet info.umd.edu` (128.8.10.29), login: `info telnet freenet-in-a.cwru.edu`, login: `visitor`, pick Courthouse, Courthouse legal information, and Supreme Court Opinions.
Email: Via FTPmail (see entry under FTP)
WAIS: supreme-court.src
Fees: Free

Name: Columbia University Law Library
Net: Internet
What: Online card catalog.
How: `telnet sparc-1.law.columbia.edu`, login: `lawnet`
Email: Not accessible
WAIS: columbia-law-library-catalog.src
Fees: Free

Name: Washington and Lee Law Library
Net: Internet
What: Online access to university law library.
How: `telnet liberty.uc.wlu.edu`
(137.113.10.35), login: `lawlib`,
`ftp liberty.uc.wlu.edu`, login:
`anonymous, cd /pub/lawlib`
Email: Not accessible
Fees: Free

Name: Sidney University Law Archive
Net: Internet
What: An archive of U.S. state and federal laws.
How: `ftp sulaw.law.su.oz.au, cd /pub/law`
Email: Via FTPmail (see entry under FTP)
Fees: Free

Name: Law Employers Database
Net: Internet
What: Database of legal employers.
How: Accessible via WAIS
Email: Not accessible
WAIS: law-employers.src
Fees: Free

Name: Cornell Law Library
Net: Internet
What: Online law library, accessible via Gopher.
How: `telnet fatty.law.cornell.edu`,
login: `gopher`
Email: Not accessible
Fees: Free

Library

Name: Colorado Association of Research Libraries (CARL)
Net: Internet
What: Advanced electronic online catalog catering to other libraries and citizens of Colorado.
How: `telnet pac.carl.org`
[192.54.81.128], Choice> `PAC`
Email: Not accessible
Fees: Limited access without payment of membership fees
Contact: CARL
3801 East Florida St., Suite 300
Denver, Co. 80210
(303)758-3030
fax: (303)758-0606
email: help@carl.org

Name: Hebrew University OPAC
Net: Internet
What: Online catalog capable of display in Hebrew, Arabic, Roman, and Cyrillic alphabets (with special terminals)
How: `telnet ram2.huji.ac.il`
[128.139.4.15] login: `aleph`
Email: None
Fees: Free

Name: Library of Congress Catalog
Net: Internet
What: Access to catalog of the Library of Congress.
How: `telnet dra.com` (192.65.218.43)
Email: Not accessible
Fees: Free
Contact: CATALOG@DRA.COM

Name: LOCIS
Net: Internet
What: Library of Congress Information System
How: `telnet locis.loc.gov`
(140.147.254.3)
Email: Not accessible
Fees: Free
Gopher: `telnet marvel.loc.gov`, login:
`marvel`

Name: Melvyl
Net: Internet
What: University of California OPAC
How: `telnet melvyl.ucop.edu`
[192.35.222.222]
Email: None
Fees: Free

Name: Newspaper Index
Net: Internet
What: Indexes to newspaper articles, including articles from the *Wall St. Journal,*
New York Times, and *Washington Post.*
How: `tn3270 GMUIBM.GMU.EDU`, select
`XLIBRIS`, select `PERI`, select `PAPR`
Email: Not accessible
Fees: Free

Name: OCLC
Net: Internet
What: Online Computer Library Center
How: `telnet oclc.org` [132.174.19.28]
Email: None
Fees: Commercial service. Account required.
Contact: Online Computer Library Center, Inc.
6565 Frantz Road
Dublin, OH 43017-3395
(800)848-5878

Name: Periodical Indices
Net: Internet
What: Indexes to periodical literature.
How: `tn3270 GMUIBM.GMU.EDU`, select `XLIBRIS`, select `PERI`, select `DWIL`
Email: Not accessible
Fees: Free

Name: Readers Guide to Periodical Literature
Net: Internet
What: Access to index of articles in periodicals.
How: `telnet lib.uwstout.edu` (144.13.12.1)
Email: Not accessible
Fees: Access limited to employees or students of UW-Stout

Name: RLIN
Net: Internet
What: Catalog of resources at other online libraries.
How: `telnet rlg.stanford.edu`
Email: For info, bl.ric@rlg.stanford.edu.
Fees: Access by registration only; fees required

Name: Meckler's Electronic Publishing
Net: Internet
What: Information on services from Meckler Publishing.
How: `telnet nisc.jvnc.net` (128.121.50.7), login: `nicol`; menu entry MC(2); `ftp ftp.jvnc.net`, login: `anonymous, cd meckler`
Email: Via FTPmail (see entry under FTP)
Fees: Free

Name: New York Public Library
Net: Internet
What: Dance collection catalog, other topics.
How: `telnet nyplgate.nypl.org` (192.94.250.2), login: `nypl`
Email: Not accessible
Fees: Free

Name: Library of Congress Cataloging in Publication (CIP) Program.
Net: Internet
What: Information on new books.
How: `telnet liberty.uc.wlu.edu` (137.113.10.35), login: `lawlib`
Email: Not accessible
Fees: Free

Name: University of North Carolina BBS
Net: Internet
What: Access to Library of Congress and other Internet Libraries.
How: `telnet bbs.oit.unc.edu` [152.2.22.80] login: `launch`, or `bbs`
Email: None
Fees: Free
Contact: help@launchpad.unc.edu

Library Software and Guides

Name: Hy**telnet** Server
Net: Internet
What: Access to online public-access catalogs worldwide.
How: `telnet access.usask.ca` (128.233.3.1), `telnet nctucca.edu.tw` (140.111.3.21), login: `hytelnet telnet liberty.uc.wlu.edu`, login: `lawlib`, select option 8
Email: Not accessible
Fees: Free

Name: Library list
Net: Internet
What: Listing of online public-access catalogs.
How: `ftp ariel.unm.edu, cd library, get internet.library`
Email: `mail listserv@umnvma.bitnet,` body: `get library package,` Via FTPmail (see entry under FTP)
WAIS: online-libraries-st-george.src inet-libraries.src
Fees: Free

Name: Automated Library Info eXchange
Net: None
What: Federal Library and Information Center BBS; lots of useful information on library automation, and the Internet
How: (202)707-4888
Email: None
Fees: Free

Name: Library Resources lists
Net: Internet
What: Information on libraries on Internet
How: `ftp dla.ucop.edu`
`(128.48.108.25), cd`
`/pub/internet/Libcat-guide`
`ftp unt.edu (129.120.1.1),`
`cd /pub/library/libcat-guide`
`ftp hydra.uwo.ca (129.100.2.13),`
`cd /libsoft/internet.com`
Email: Via FTPmail (see FTP entry)
Fees: Free

Name: Librarian's Guide
Net: Internet
What: Librarian's Guide to Dial-Up Internet Access
How: `ftp dla.ucop.edu,cd /pub/docs/`
Email: Via FTPmail (see FTP entry)
Fees: Free

Name: Internet libraries archive
Net: Internet
What: Archive of information and software on libraries
How: `ftp ftp.unt.edu [129.120.1.1]`
`cd /pub/library`
For guide by Dana Noonan:
`get metlib2.txt`
For libtell:
`mget libtel*.*`
Email: FTPmail (see FTP entry)
Fees: Free

Name: UNT Bibliographic database
Net: Internet
What: List of online bibligraphic databases.
How: `ftp ftp.unt.edu,` login:
`anonymous,`
`cd library`
Email: Via FTPmail (see entry under FTP); for info:
billey@unt.edu
Fees: Free

Name: Catalist software
Net: Internet
What: MS Windows catalog of OPACs
How: `ftp ftp.unt.edu [129.120.1.1], cd`
`/pub/library/catalist`
Email: FTPmail (see FTP entry)
Fees: Free

Name: Hytelnet archive
Net: Internet
What: Hytelnet software for Mac, Amiga, PC, UNIX, and VMS platforms
How: `ftp access.usask.ca [128.233.3.1]`
`cd /pub/hytelnet`
Email: FTPmail (see FTP entry)
Fees: Free

Macintosh

Name: University of Michigan Mac Archive
Net: Internet
What: Archive of publicly distributable Mac software.
How: `ftp mac.archive.umich.edu`
`(141.211.165.41),` login: **anonymous**
Email: Via FTPmail (see FTP entry)
Fees: Free
Name: Info-Mac Archive
Net: Internet
What: Best archive of publicly distributable Macintosh software, including all Internet software discussed in this guide (in directory /info-mac/comm).
How: `ftp sumex-aim.stanford.edu,`
`cd /info-mac`
USENET: Additions described in comp.sys.mac.digest
Fees: Free; CD–ROM also available from Walnut Creek CD–ROM
WAIS: info-mac.src

Name: Tidbits
Net: Internet
What: Archive of Macintosh tidbits
How: Accessible via WAIS
Email: Not accessible
WAIS: machintosh-tidbits.src
Fees: Free

Name: Macintosh Frequently Asked Questions
Net: Internet
What: File of questions and answers for Mac.
How: Accessible via WAIS
Email: Not accessible
WAIS: mac.FAQ.src
Fees: Free

Name: Macintosh Mailing List
Net: Internet
What: Moderated mailing list.
How: Accessible via email
Email: `mail LISTSERV@UIUCVMD.BITNET,`
in body: `SUBSCRIBE INFO-MAC`
`mail LISTSERV@YALEV1.BITNET,` in
body: `SUBSCRIBE MAC-L`
Fees: Free

Mailing lists

Name: Electronic Journals Listing
Net: Internet
What: List of journals and newsletters.
How: Accessible via email only
Email: `mail`
`listserv@acadvm1.uottawa.ca,`
body: `get ejournl1 directry <CR>`
`get ejournl2 directry`
Fees: Free

Name: List of Mailing Lists
Net: Internet
What: List of Internet mailing lists.
How: `ftp ftp.nisc.sri.com`
`(192.33.33.22),`
`cd /netinfo/interest-groups`
Email: `mail mail-server@nisc.sri.com,`
in body: `Send netinfo/interest-`
`groups`
`mail info@vm1.nodak.edu`
(subscribes to new mailing lists
mailing list)
`mail LISTSERV@vm1.NoDak.EDU,` in
body of the message `LIST GLOBAL`
To search for a mailing list on a
topic, `mail`
`LISTSERV@VM1.NODAK.EDU,` in body:
INFO DATABASE for information.
Example search body:
`//DBlook JOB Echo=No`
`Database Search DD=Rules`
`//Rules DD *`
`Select <keyword> in lists`
`index`
`Select <keyword> in intgroup`
`index`
`Select <keyword> in new-list`
Fees: Free
WAIS: mailing-lists.src
lists.src

Mathematics

Name: E-Math
Net: Internet
What: American Math Society BBS, including
software and reviews.
How: `telnet e-math.ams.com`
`(130.44.1.100),` login/password:
`e-math`
Email: Not accessible
Fees: Free

Name: Euromath Network
Net: Internet
What: Network of European mathematicians.
How: `telnet concise.funet.fi,` login:
`concise`
Email: Not accessible

Medical

Name: CHAT
Net: Internet
What: Information on AIDS.
How: `telnet debra.dgbt.doc.ca`
`(142.92.36.15)`
Email: Not accessible
Fees: Free

Name: Carpal Tunnel Archive
Net: Internet
What: Archive of info on Carpal Tunnel Syndrome.
How: `ftp soda.berkeley.edu,` login:
`anonymous, cd /pub/typing-`
`injury`
Email: Via FTPmail (see FTP entry)
Fees: Free

Name: History and Analysis of Disabilities
Net: BITNET
What: Newsletter on the historial study of
disabilities.
How: Mail access only
Email: `mail fcty7310%ryerson.bitnet@`
`cunyvmn.cuny.edu`
Fees: Free

Name: CRS-BBS
Net: None
What: Justice Department Civil Rights Division BBS; information on Americans with Disabilities Act
How: **(202)514-6193**
Email: None
Fees: Free
Contact: Daniel A. Searing, (202)307-2215

Name: Handicap Database and Digest
Net: Internet, FidoNet 1:151/420
What: Software and medical information for the handicapped.
How: `ftp handicap.shel.isc-br.com` (129.189.4.184), login: **anonymous**
Email: `mail wtm@bunker.shelp.isc-br.com`, or direct: (203)337-1607, 73170.1064@compuserve.com
Fees: Free

Name: CancerNet
Net: Internet
What: Information on Cancer
How: Mail access only
Email: `mail cancernet@icicb.nci.nih.gov`, body: **help** or **spanish**
Fees: Free

Name: FireNet
Net: FidoNet, 1:128/16
What: Information on fire fighting and emergency medical care.
How: (719)591-7415
Email: Not accessible
Fees: Free
Contact: `sysop@f16.n128.z1.fidonet.org`

Name: Medical Educational Technology Network
Net: Internet
What: Information on audio-visual technology, digital imaging, and computer-aided instruction in medicine.
How: `telnet etnet.nlm.nih.giv` (130.14.10.123), login: **etnet**
Email: Not accessible
Fees: Free

Name: MEDLINE
Net: Internet
What: Medical literature search.
How: `telnet melvyl.ucop.edu` (192.35.222.222) `telnet lib.dartmouth.edu` (129.170.16.11) `telnet library.umdnj.edu` (130.219.2.100), login: **LIBRARY** `telnet utmem1.utmem.edu` (132.192.1.1), login: **HARVEY** `telnet mcclb0.med.nyu.edu` (128.122.135.4) login: **INFORMATION**
Email: Not accessible
Fees: Free

Name: Medical Resource List
Net: Internet
What: List of medical resources on Internet.
How: `ftp ftp.sura.net` (128.167.254.179) login: **anonymous, get /pub/nic/medical.resources.x-y**
Email: Via FTPmail (see FTP entry)
Fees: Free
Contact: Lee Hancock, Educational Technologist, Educational Techology, A Division of Dykes Library, University of Kansas Medical Center Le07144@Ukanvm.cc.ukans.edu

Movies

Name: Movie Lists and Reviews
Net: Internet
What: Listings and reviews of movies.
How: `ftp lcs.mit.edu, cd /common/movie-reviews`
Email: Via FTPmail (see FTP entry)
WAIS: movie-lists.src, movie-reviews.src
Fees: Free

Music

Name: Audiophile Network BBS
Net: None
What: BBS for audio/video
How: **(818)988-0452**
Email: Not accessible
Fees: $24/year
Contact: 14155 Kittridge St., Van Nuys, CA 91405; voice: (818)782-1676, fax (818)780-6260

Name: Billboard Charts
Net: Internet
What: Top singles, updated weekly.
How: `finger buckmr@rpi.edu`
Email: Not accessible
Fees: Free

Name: Guitar Chords
Net: Internet
What: Chords for the guitar.
How: `ftp ftp.nevada.edu`
`(131.216.1.11),`
`cd /pub/guitar`
`ftp clouso.crim.ca, cd`
`/pub/guitar`
Email: Via FTPmail (see entry under FTP)
Fees: Free

Name: Lyrics Server
Net: Internet
What: Archive of lyrics and music pictures.
How: `ftp ftp.uwp.edu`
`ftp ftp.iastate.edu, cd`
`/pub/lyrics, or cd/pub/music,`
contributions to
`/pub/tmp/incoming`
Email: Via FTPmail (see entry under FTP)
Fees: Free

Name: Music Mailing List Listing
Net: Internet
What: A listing of mailing lists about music.
How: Mail access only
Email: `mail mlol-request@wariat.org`
Fees: Free

Name: Music Newsletter
Net: Internet
What: Reviews of recent releases and interviews.
How: Accessible by mail only
Email: `mail listserv@vm.marist.edu`,
(Internet) or `mail`
`listserv@marist` (bitnet), body:
`SUBSCRIBE UPNEWS <your name>`
Fees: Free

Name: NetJam
Net: Internet
What: MIDI archive
How: `ftp xcf.berkeley.edu`
`[128.32.138.1]`
`cd /misc/netjam`
Email: FTPmail (see FTP entry)
Fees: Free
WAIS: midi.src

Name: Sid's Music Server
Net: Internet
What: Lists of rare recordings, CDs.
How: Accessible by mail only
Email: `mail`
`mwilkenf@silver.ucs.indiana.edu`
subject: `BOOTHELP`
Fees: Free

Name: Used Music Server
Net: Internet
What: For sale/wanted listings.
How: Accessible by mail only
Email: `mail Used-Music-Server`
`@cs.ucsb.edu`, subject: `help`
Fees: Free

News

Name: USA Today Headline News
Net: Internet
What: News, updated daily.
How: `telnet freenet-in-`
`[a,b,c].cwru.edu (129.22.8.47)`, or
`telnet yfn.ysu.edu`
`(192.55.234.27) login: visitor`
Email: Not accessible
Fees: Free

NeXT

Name: NeXT FAQ
Net: Internet
What: File of NeXT frequently asked questions.
How: Accessible via WAIS
Email: Not accessible
WAIS: NeXT.FAQ.src
Fees: Free

Name: NeXT Nugget Digest
Net: Internet
What: NeXT newsletter.
How: Mailing list
Email: `mail cgeiger@next.com`
Fees: Free

Name: NeXT FTP Sites
Net: Internet
What: Archives of NeXT software.
How: `ftp sonata.cc.purdue.edu`, `login: anonymous`, `cd /pub/next`
`ftp cs.orst.edu`, `cd /pub/next`
`ftp etlport.etl.go.jp` (Japan)
`ftp pellns.alleg.edu`, `cd /pub` (academic apps)
`ftp otter.stanford.edu` (mathematica)
`ftp src.doc.ic.ac.uk` (UK) (mirror of nova/sonata)
Email: Via FTPmail (see FTP entry)
Fees: Free

Numerical methods

Name: Maple FTP Archives
Net: Internet
What: Archive of tools for Maple mathematical software.
How: `ftp 129.132.101.33`, (Switzerland)
`ftp 129.97.128.58` (Canada)
Email: Via FTPmail (see entry for FTP)
Fees: Free

Name: Matlab
Net: Internet
What: Matlab matrix manipulation software library and digest.
How: `ftp research.att.com`, `login: netlib`
`telnet research.att.com`, `login: walk`,
or (908)582-1238, `login: walk`
Email: For Matlab digest, `mail matlab-users-request@mcs.anl.gov`
`mail netlib@ornl.gov`
Body: `send index from matlab`
WAIS: netlib-index.src
Fee: Free

Name: Mathematica FTP Archives
Net: Internet
What: Archive of tools for Mathematica mathematical software.
How: `ftp otter.stanford.edu`, or
`ftp ftp.ncsa.uiuc.edu`, or
`ftp nic.funet.fi`, or
`ftp fenris.claremont.edu`, or
`ftp siam.unibe.ch`, or
`ftp vax.eedsp.gatech.edu`, `login: anonymous`
Email: Via FTPmail (see entry for FTP)
Fees: Free

Name: NetLib
Net: Internet
What: Library of Numerical methods software.
How: `ftp research.att.com`, `login: netlib`
`telnet research.att.com`, `login: walk`,
or (908)582-1238, `login: walk`
Email: `mail netlib@ornl.gov`, or
`mail netlib@research.att.com`, or
`mail netlib@uunet.uu.net`
Body: `send index`
WAIS: netlib-index.src
Fee: Free

Panda

Name: Panda
Net: Internet
What: PAN campus Data Access network, a Gopher-like service for University of Iowa.
How: `telnet panda.uiowa.edu`
Email: Not accessible
Fees: Free
Contact: isca@umaxc.weeg.uiowa.edu

Philosophy

Name: American Philosophical Association
Net: Internet
What: APA BBS
How: `telnet atl.calstate.edu`
(130.150.102.33), `login: apa`,
`password: apa`
Email: Not accessible
Fees: Free
Contact: Saul Traiger, traiger@oxy.edu

Phone books

Name: University Phone Directories
Net: Internet
What: Searchable phone directories at universities.
How: `telnet consultant.micro.umn.edu,` login: `gopher,` select phone books `telnet liberty.uc.wlu.edu,` login: `lawlib,` select campus information systems
Email: Not accessible
Fees: Free

Physics

Name: Physics Information Network (PINET)
Net: Internet
What: Abstracts, bibliographic databases, jobs, and so on, related to Physics.
How: `telnet pinet.aip.org`
Email: Not accessible
Fees: Free

Name: Nuclear Data Center
Net: Internet
What: Nuclear data.
How: `telnet bnlnd2.dne.bnl.gov` `(130.199.112.132),` login: `nndc`
Email: Not accessible
Fees: Free

Name: SPAN
Net: Internet
What: Space physics analysis network.
How: `telnet nssdca.gsfc.nasa.gov` `(128.183.36.23),` login: `SPAN_NIC`
Email: Not accessible
Fees: Free

Postal Service gateways

Name: PaperGate
Net: Internet
What: Gateway from Internet to Postal Service.
How: Access via mail
Email: `mail PaperGate@elvis.sovusa.com,` body: `help`
Fees: $10/registration plus $2.50/page

Religion

Name: Bible Resources List
Net: Internet
What: List of biblical resources on Internet.
How: `ftp ftp.sura.net (128.167.254.179)` `login: anonymous, get` `/pub/nic/bible.resources`
Email: Via FTPmail (see FTP entry)
Fees: Free
Contact: Michael Strangelove, Department of Religious Studies, University of Ottawa; BITNET: `441495@Uottawa,` Internet: `441495@Acadvm1.Uottawa.CA,` S-Mail: 177 Waller, Ottawa, Ontario, K1N 6N5 CANADA (613)747-0642, fax: (613)564-6641

Name: King James Bible
Net: Internet
What: Online access to King James Bible.
How: `ftp wuarchive.wustl.edu,` login: `anonymous, cd pub/bible`
Email: Via FTPmail (see entry under FTP)
WAIS: bible.src
Fees: Free

Name: Book of Mormon
Net: Internet
What: Online access to the Book of Mormon
How: Accessible via WAIS
Email: Not accessible
WAIS: Book_of_Mormon.src
Fees: Free

Name: Holocaust Archives
Net: Internet
What: Documents relating to the Holocaust.
How: `ftp ftp.sura.net (128.167.254.179)` `login: anonymous, get` `/pub/nic/holocaust.archive`
Email: `mail listserv@oneb.almanac.bc.ca` in body: `index holocaust,` to get a file: `get holocaust <filename><part>`
Fees: Free

Name: Religion Bibliographies
Net: Internet
What: Information on religion-related material on Internet, and the Electric Mystic's Guide to Internet.
How: `ftp panda1.uottawa.ca, cd /pub/religion,` `get jewish.txt` (Jewish electronic sources) `psychology-biblio.txt` (Psych bibliog)
Email: Via FTPmail (see FTP)
Fees: Free

Name: Koran
Net: Internet
What: Online access to the Koran.
How: Accessible via WAIS
Email: Not accessible
WAIS: Quaran.src
Fees: Free

Science

Name: High Wierdness by Email (HWbE)
Net: Internet
What: Magazine on fringe science, UFO's, etc.
How: `ftp ftp.css.itd.umich.edu, cd /poli/Resources/weirdness`
Email: Via FTPmail (see FTP)
Fees: Free
Contact: mporter@nyx.cs.du.edu

Name: Science and Technology Information System (STIS)
Net: Internet
What: Electronic access to NSF publications.
How: `telnet stis.nsf.gov`, login: `public`
Email: Not accessible
Fees: Free

Scuba diving

Name: National Association of Cave Diver's BBS
Net: None
What: Scuba Diving BBS, includes dive-site reports, information on equipment for sale, etc.
How: `(912)246-3280`
Email: Not accessible
Fees: Membership in NACD required for full access

SFNet

Name: SFNet
Net: FidoNet: 1:125/824
What: Network of BBSes in coffee houses in San Francisco bay area.
How: `San Francisco: (415)824-8747, (415)589-2194; Burlingame: (415)375-8487; Oakland: (510)450-0155; San Leandro: (510)638-8644; Richmond: (510)215-7732; Sausalito: (415)332-3923; San Rafael: (415)454-4983`
Email: Not accessible
Fees: $7/month, $13/month deluxe

Smithsonian

Name: Smithsonian photo archive
Net: Internet
What: Electronic images of photographs from the Smithsonian collection
How: `ftp photo1.si.edu`, login: `anonymous`
Email: Not accessible
Fees: Free for non-commercial use

Software

Name: ASK
Net: Internet
What: Online software search (in German!).
How: `telnet askhp.ask.uni-karlsruhe.de` (192.67.194.33), login: `ask`
Email: Not accessible
Fees: Free

Name: ZIB Electronic Library
Net: Internet
What: Online software library.
How: `telnet elib.zib-berlin.de` (130.73.108.11), login: `elib`
Email: Not accessible
Fees: Free

Sports

Name: Baseball Scores
Net: Internet
What: Daily major league baseball scores and standings.
How: `finger jtchern@sandstorm.berkeley.edu`
Email: For a subscription, `mail jtchern@sandstorm.berkeley.edu`, Subject: **MLB**
Fees: Free

Name: Sports schedules
Net: Internet
What: Sports schedules for NBA. NHL, MLB, NFL
How: `telnet culine.colorado.edu <port>` (128.138.129.83)
`<port>` = 859 for NBA, 860 for NHL, 862 for MLB, 863 for NFL
Fees: Free

Statistics

Name: Statlib
Net: Internet
What: Statistical software archive.
How: `ftp lib.stat.cmu.edu`, login: `statlib`, password: `<email address>`
Email: `mail statlib@lib.stat.cmu.edu`, body: **send index**
Fees: Free

Supercomputing

Name: HPCWire
Net: Internet
What: Electronic daily news, information, and library service on high-performance computing, run by Tabor Griffin Communications.
How: `telnet hpcwire.ans.net` (147.225.1.51), login: **hpcwire**
Email: Not accessible; modem: (408)428-2565, N81, VT100
Fees: Free
Contact: admin@hpcwire.ans.net, (619)625-0070, fax: (619)625-0088

TCP/IP

Name: Vendor Guide
Net: Internet
What: General guide to TCP/IP hardware and software
How: `ftp nic.ddn.mil` [192.112.36.5], get `/netinfo/vendors-guide.doc`
Email: FTPmail (see FTP entry)
Fees: Free

Name: IBM PC TCP/IP Info
Net: Internet
What: Information on TCP/IP software for IBM PC-compatibles
How: **Publicly distributable packages:** `ftp netcom1.netcom.com` [192.100.81.100] get `/pub/mailcom/IBMTCP/ibmtcp.zip` **Commercial packages:** `ftp ftp.cac.psu.edu` [128.118.58.3] `/pub/dos/info/tcip.packages` **Windows Sockets FAQ:** `ftp sunsite.unc.edu` [152.2.22.81] `cd /pub/micro/pc-stuff/ms-windows/winsock/FAQ` **Windows Sockets archive:** `ftp sunsite.unc.edu, cd /pub/micro/pc-stuff/ms-windows/winsock` **Microsoft TCP/IP archive:** `ftp rhino.microsoft.com` [131.107.1.121]
Email: FTPmail (see FTP entry)
Fees: Free
USENET: alt.winsock (for Windows Sockets apps) comp.protocols.tcp-ip.ibmpc

Travel

Name: State Department Travel Advisories
Net: Internet
What: State Department advice on travel overseas.
How: `ftp nic.stolaf.edu` (130.71.128.8), login: **anonymous, cd /pub/travel-advisories/advisories**
Email: Not accessible
Fees: Free

Name: Travel Information Library
Net: Internet
What: Travel guides and information.
How: `ftp ccu.umanitoba.ca (130.179.16.8)`,login: `anonymous, cd /pub/rec-travel`
Email: Not accessible
Fees: Free

Name: Colorado Travel Bank BBS
Net: None
What: Provides assistance for Colorado visitors.
How: (303)671-7669
Email: Not accessible
Fees: Free
Contact: Jay Melnick; P.O. Box 200594, Denver, CO 80220

Name: Travel Online
Net: UUCP: travel.com, FidoNet 1:100/635, RIME, ILINK, Smartnet, Toadnet, MIDIlink
What: General BBS system with large file system and distinctive travel section
How: `(314)625-3874`
Email: sysop@travel.com
Fees: Subscription BBS

Name: Boundary Waters BBS
Net: None
What: Fishing/canoeing/outdoors BBS, wilderness studies, scenic photographs.
How: `(218)365-6907`
Email: Not accessible
Fees: Free
Contact: InfoNorth; HC 1 Box 2675, Ely, MN 55731; (218)365-4118

Treasure hunting

Name: Computer Garden
Net: None
What: BBS for treasure hunters; also Online mall, including Computer Garden Inc., Smith's Flower Shop, and Ohmega Electronics.
How: `(410)546-1508`
Email: Not accessible
Fees: None
Contact: Milford P. Webster, Computer Garden, Inc.; 100 Celmwood St., Suite C, Salisbury, MD 21801; (410)749-3226

UNIX

Name: UNIX Reference Material
Net: Internet
What: Online manual, reference card, booklist.
How: Reference card:
`ftp ucselx.sdsu.edu`, login: `anonymous, cd /pub/doc/general`
Booklist:
`ftp ftp.rahul.net`, login: `anonymous, cd /pub/mitch/YABL, get yabl.Z`
Email: Via FTPmail (see entry under FTP)
Fees: Free
WAIS: unix-manual.src

USENET

Name: Access to USENET
Net: Internet
What: Access to USENET newsreaders.
How: `telnet liberty.uc.wlu.edu (137.113.10.35)`, login: `lawlib`, select `USENET readers`
Email: Not accessible
Fees: Free

Name: Public Access UNIX
Net: Internet
What: Access to USENET.
How: `telnet nyx.cs.du.edu (130.253.192.68)`, login: `news`
`telnet digex.com (192.55.213.2)`
Email: Not accessible
Fees: Free

Name: USENET Mail Server
Net: Internet
What: Posts to USENET from email.
How: Accessible via email
Email: `mail [newsgroup]@cs.utexas.edu`
Fees: Free

Name: USENET Access
Net: Internet
What: Telnet access to net news.
How: `telnet bbs.oit.unc.edu (152.2.22.80)`, login: `launch`
Email: Not accessible
Fees: Free

Name: NNTP News Servers
Net: Internet
What: Telnet access to net news.
How: `telnet sol.ctr.columbia.edu`
(128.59.64.40) **119**
`telnet rusmv1.rus.uni-`
`stuttgart.de` (129.69.1.12) **119**
`telnet news.fu-berlin.de`
(130.133.4.250 119) **119**
Email: `mail [newsgroup]@cs.utexas.edu`
Fees: Free

Name: FAQ server
Net: Internet
What: Archive of frequently asked questions for
USENET newsgroups.
How: `ftp pit-manager.mit.edu`
(130.133.4.250 119), `cd`
`/pub/usenet`
Email: Via FTPmail (see FTP entry)
Fees: Free
WAIS: news.answers-faqs.src (FAQs from
news.answers group)
jik-usenet.src (documents on USENET)

UUCP Maps

Name: UUCP Map database
Net: Internet
What: Map entries for registered UUCP sites.
How: available by email, WAIS
Email: `mail dns@grasp.insa-lyon.fr`,
in body: `uucp <site>` to retrieve
the map; `help` for information
Fees: Free
WAIS: uumaps.src

WAIS

Name: Wide Area Information Server
Net: Internet
What: Full text search of online databases.
How: `telnet quake.think.com`,
(192.31.181.1),
`telnet nnsc.nsf.net`
(128.89.1.178)
`telnet wais.funet.fi`
(128.214.6.100)
login: `wais`
`ftp think.com`, login: `anonymous`
for info
Email: Not accessible
Fees: Free
WAIS: alt.wais.src
wais-discussion-archives.src
wais-docs.src
wais-talk-archives.src

Weather

Name: Weather Forecasts
Net: Internet
What: Weather and ski-condition forecasts
for U.S. cities and states.
How: `telnet downwind.sprl.umich.edu`
(141.212.196.177) **3000**
Email: Not accessible
WAIS: midwest-weather.src (for Midwest),
weather.src
Fees: Free

Name: WeatherBank BBS
Net: None
What: Weather forecasts, fire alerts, and radar
data.
How: **(801)530-3188**
Email: Not accessible
Fees: Payment required
Contact: WeatherBank; 5 Triad Center, Suite 315,
Salt Lake, UT 84180; (801)530-3181,
fax: (801)530-3174

Name: Weather Maps
Net: Internet
What: Infrared satellite photos, updated hourly.
How: `ftp vmd.cso.uiuc.edu, login: anonymous, cd wx`
Email: Via FTPmail (see entry under FTP)
Fees: Free

Name: Tropical Storm Forecasts
Net: Internet
What: Seasonal forecasts for Atlantic ocean.
How: `finger forecast@typhoon.atmos.colostat e.edu (129.82.107.24)`
Email: Not accessible
Fees: Free

Whois

Name: Whois Service List
Net: Internet
What: List of Whois services
How: `ftp sipb.mit.edu, cd pub/whois/whois-servers.list`
Email: Via FTPmail (see entry for FTP)
WAIS: whois.src
Fees: Free

Name: Whois Service
Net: Internet
What: Find someone's address on Internet.
How: `telnet nic.ddn.mil (192.112.36.5)`
Email: Not accessible
Fees: Free

Windows

Name: CICA Windows Archive
Net: Internet
What: Archive of Windows 3.0 software.
How: `ftp ftp.cica.indiana.edu, login: anonymous`
Email: Via FTPmail (see entry for FTP)
WAIS: cica-win3.src
Fees: Free

Women

Name: Bay Area Women in Telecom
Net: Internet
What: Mailing list for women interested in telecommunications.
How: Mail access only
Email: `mail bawitrequest@igc.apc.org`
Fees: Free

World Wide Web

Name: World Wide Web (WWW)
Net: Internet
What: Hypertextual catalog of Internet services.
How: `telnet info.cern.ch` (128.141.201.74)(SWISS)
`telnet eies2.njit.edu` (128.235.1.43) (USA [NJ])
`telnet vms.huji.ac.il` (128.139.4.3) (ISRAEL)
`telnet info.funet.fi` (128.214.6.100) (FINLAND), login: `www`
Email: `mail listserv@info.cerh.ch,` `HELP` in body
Fees: Free
Contact: Tim Berners-Lee, WorldWideWeb Project, CERN; 1211 Geneva 23, Switzerland; +41(22)767-3755, fax: +41(22)767-7155 email: tbl@cernvax.cern.ch

WWIV BBSes

Name: WWIV Support BBS
Net: WWIVNet
What: Support BBS for WWIV software.
How: (310)798-9993
Email: Not accessible
Fees: Free

APPENDIX D:
CABLE COMPENDIUM

If you want something done right, do it yourself

Computer serial ports (DTE) – IBM-PC

(As seen from the male connector)

IBM-PC XT Serial Port (DB-25)

```
1   2   3   4   5   6   7   8   9   10  11  12  13
  14  15  16  17  18  19  20  21  22  23  24  25
```

Pin	Abbreviation	Name
1	FG	Frame Ground
2	TD	Transmit Data
3	RD	Receive Data
4	RTS	Ready to Send
5	CTS	Clear to Send
6	DSR	Data Set Ready
7	SG	Signal Ground
8	DCD	Data Carrier Detect
20	DTR	Data Terminal Ready
22	RI	Ring Indicator

IBM-PC AT serial port (DB-9)

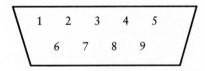

Pin	Function	Name
1	DCD	Data Carrier Detect
2	RD	Receive Data
3	TD	Transmit Data
4	DTR	Data Terminal Ready
5	SG	Signal Ground
6	DSR	Data Set Ready
7	RTS	Ready to Send
8	CTS	Clear to Send
9	RI	Ring Indicator

Computer serial ports

(DTE) – Apple II

Super Serial Card – DB-25

Pin	Function	Name
1	FG	Frame Ground
2	TD	Transmit Data
3	RD	Receive Data
4	RTS	Request to Send
5	CTS	Clear to Send
6	DSR	Data Set Ready
7	SG	Signal Ground
8	DCD	Data Carrier Detect
19	SCTS	Secondary Clear to Send
20	DTR	Data Terminal Ready

Apple IIc Serial Ports – DIN-5

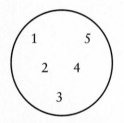

Pin	Function	Name
1	DTR	Data Terminal Ready
2	TD	Transmit Data
3	SG	Signal Ground
4	RD	Receive Data
5	DSR	Data Set Ready

Computer serial ports

(DTE) – Macintosh & NeXT

(Macintosh 128K, 512K, and

512Ke DB-9 connectors

Macintosh 128K, 512K

Pin	Function	Name
1	FG	Frame Ground
2	+5 V	
3	SG	Signal Ground
4	TxD+	Transmit Data +
5	TxD-	Transmit Data -
6	+12 V	
7	HSKin/ External Clock	Handshake In
8	RxD+	Receive Data +
9	RxD-	Receive Data -

Note: Pin 5 is connected to SC RTS; Pin 7 is connected to SCC CTS and Transmit/Receive clock.

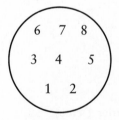

Macintosh and NeXT DIN-8 connector

Macintosh Plus, Classic, LC, VX

Pin	Function	Name
1	HSKout	Handshake Out
2	HSKin	Handshake In
3	TxD-	Transmit Data -
4	SG	Signal Ground
5	RxD-	Receive Data -
6	TxD+	Transmit Data +
7	None	
8	RxD+	Receive Data +

Mac Plus Note: Pin 1 is connected to SCC DTR; pin 2 is connected to SCC CTS and Transmit/Receive clock; pin 6 is connected to SCC RTS.

Macintosh SE, SE/30

Pin	Function	Name
1	HSKout	Handshake Out
2	HSKin	Handshake In
3	TxD-	Transmit Data -
4	SG	Signal Ground
5	RxD-	Receive Data -
6	TxD+	Transmit Data +
7	GPi	General Purpose Input
8	RxD+	Receive Data +

Note: Pin 1 is connected to SCC RTS; pin 2 is connected to SCC CTS and Transmit/Receive clock; pin 7 is connected to SCC DCD. Pin 7 on the modem port is only capable of synchronous communications and will be connected to Receive/Transmit clock if VIA PA3 signal is high)

NeXT 68040 machines

Pin	Function	Name
1	DTR	Data Terminal Ready
2	DCD	Carrier Detect
3	TxD-	Transmit Data -
4	SG	Signal Ground
5	RxD-	Receive Data -
6	RTS	Ready to Send
7	RTXC	
8	CTS	Clear To Send

Macintosh II, IIx, IIfx, Quadra

Pin	Function	Name
1	HSKout	Handshake Out
2	HSKin	Handshake In
3	TxD-	Transmit Data -
4	SG	Signal Ground
5	RxD-	Receive Data -
6	TxD+	Transmit Data +
7	GPi	General Purpose Input
8	RxD+	Receive Data +

Mac II Note: Pin 1 is connected to SCC RTS; pin 2 is connected to SCC CTS and Transmit/Receive clock; pin 7 is connected to SCC DCD. Pin 7 on the modem port is only connected to Receive/Transmit clock if VIA 1 SYNC is high, thus allowing for connection to synchronous modems.

Peripherals

Apple Modem 300/1200 – DB-9 (DCE)

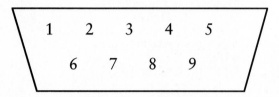

Pin	Function	Name
2	DSR	Data Set Ready
3	SG	Signal Ground
5	RD	Receive Data
6	DTR	Data Terminal Ready
7	DCD	Data Carrier Detect
8	FG	Frame Ground
9	TD	Transmit Data

Apple Personal Modem – DIN-8 (DCE)

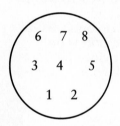

Pin	Function	Name
1	DSR	Data Set Ready
2	DTR	Data Terminal Ready
3	RD	Receive Data
4	SG	Signal Ground
5	TD	Transmit Data
6	SG	Signal Ground
7	DCD	Data Carrier Detect

LaserWriter – DB-25 (DTE)

1	FG	Frame Ground
2	TD	Transmit Data
3	RD	Receive Data
4	RTS	Ready to Send
7	SG	Signal Ground
20	DTR	Data Terminal Ready

ImageWriter I – DB-25

1	FG	Frame Ground
2	TD	Transmit Data
3	RD	Receive Data
4	RTS	Request to Send
7	SG	Signal Ground
14	Fault	Fault
20	DTR	Data Terminal Ready

Apple Scribe Printer – DB-25

1	FG	Frame Ground
2	TD	Transmit Data
3	RD	Receive Data
4	RTS	Request to Send
7	SG	Signal Ground
20	DTR	Data Terminal Ready

Apple Daisywheel Printer – DB-25

1	FG	Frame Ground
2	TD	Transmit Data
3	RD	Receive Data
4	RTS	Request to Send
5	CTS	Clear to Send
6	DSR	Data Set Ready
7	SG	Signal Ground
8	DCD	Data Carrier Detect
20	DTR	Data Terminal Ready

ImageWriter II – DIN-8

1	DTR	Data Terminal Ready
2	DSR	Data Set Ready
3	TXD-	Transmit Data Minus
4	SG	Signal Ground
5	RXD-	Receive Data Minus
6	TXD+	Transmit Data Plus
8	RXD+	Receive Data Plus

LaserWriter – DB-9 (DTE)

```
   1   2   3   4   5

     6   7   8   9
```

1	GND	Ground
3	GND	Ground
4	TXD+	Transmit Data
5	TXD-	Transmit Data
8	RXD+	Receive Data
9	RXD-	Receive Data

Macintosh SCSI port – DB-25

1	REQ-	Request
2	MSG-	Message
3	I/O-	Input/Output
4	RST-	Reset
5	ACK-	Acknowledge
6	BSY-	Busy
7	GND	Ground
8	DB0-	Data Line 0
9	GND	Ground
10	DB3-	Data Line 3
11	DB5-	Data Line 5
12	DB6-	Data Line 6
13	DB7-	Data Line 7
14	GND	Ground (GND)
15	CD-	Carrier Detect
16	GND	Ground
17	ATN-	Attention
18	GND	Ground
19	SEL-	Select
20	DBP-	Parity
21	DB1-	Data Line 1
22	DB2-	Data Line 2
23	DB4-	Data Line 4
24	GND	Ground

Note: Minus in the signal indicates negative logic levels.

Null modem cables

(DTE to DTE)

IBM DB-25 to IBM DB-25

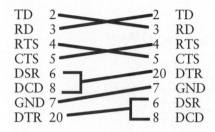

IBM-PC DB-9 to IBM DB-25

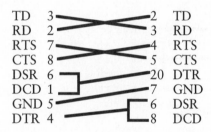

IBM DB-9 to IBM DB-9

Mac DB-9 to Mac DB-9

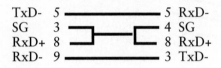

```
FG     1 ————————————— 1 FG
TxD-   5 ————————————— 3 RxD-
SG     3 ——┐   ┌——————— 3 SG
RxD+   8 ——┘   └——————— 8 RxD+
RxD-   9 ————————————— 5 TxD-
```

Mac DB–9 to Mac DIN-8

```
TxD-   5 ————————————— 5 RxD-
SG     3 ——┐   ┌——————— 4 SG
RxD+   8 ——┘   └——————— 8 RxD+
RxD-   9 ————————————— 3 TxD-
```

Mac DB-9 to IBM DB-25

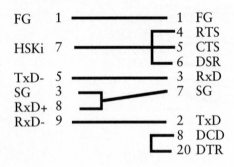

```
FG     1 ————————————— 1 FG
                    ┌—— 4 RTS
HSKi   7 ————————————┤  5 CTS
                    └—— 6 DSR
TxD-   5 ————————————— 3 RxD
SG     3 ——┐       ┌——— 7 SG
RxD+   8 ——┘
RxD-   9 ————————————— 2 TxD
                    ┌—— 8 DCD
                    └—— 20 DTR
```

Mac DB-9 to IBM DB-9

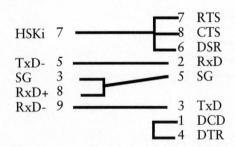

```
                    ┌—— 7 RTS
HSKi   7 ————————————┤  8 CTS
                    └—— 6 DSR
TxD-   5 ————————————— 2 RxD
SG     3 ——┐       ┌——— 5 SG
RxD+   8 ——┘
RxD-   9 ————————————— 3 TxD
                    ┌—— 1 DCD
                    └—— 4 DTR
```

Mac DIN-8 to Mac DIN-8 (Hardware handshake)

```
HSKi   2 ————————————— 1 HSKo
HSKo   1 ————————————— 2 HSKi
TxD-   3 ————————————— 5 RxD-
SG     4 ——┐   ┌——————— 4 SG
RxD+   8 ——┘   └——————— 8 RxD+
RxD-   5 ————————————— 3 TxD-
```

Mac DIN-8 to IBM DB-25

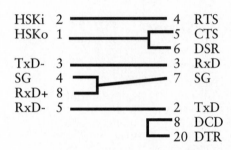

```
HSKi   2 ————————————— 4 RTS
                    ┌—— 5 CTS
HSKo   1 ————————————┤  6 DSR
TxD-   3 ————————————— 3 RxD
SG     4 ——┐       ┌——— 7 SG
RxD+   8 ——┘
RxD-   5 ————————————— 2 TxD
                    ┌—— 8 DCD
                    └—— 20 DTR
```

Mac DIN-8 to IBM DB-9

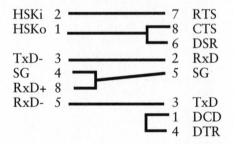

```
HSKi   2 ————————————— 7 RTS
                    ┌—— 8 CTS
HSKo   1 ————————————┤  6 DSR
TxD-   3 ————————————— 2 RxD
SG     4 ——┐       ┌——— 5 SG
RxD+   8 ——┘
RxD-   5 ————————————— 3 TxD
                    ┌—— 1 DCD
                    └—— 4 DTR
```

NeXT DIN-8 to DIN-8 with RTS/CTS flow control

```
DTR   1 ──────────── 2   DCD
DCD   2 ──────────── 1   DTR
TXD   3 ──────────── 5   RXD
GND   4 ──────────── 4   GND
RXD   5 ──────────── 3   TXD
RTS   6 ──────────── 8   CTS
CTS   8 ──────────── 6   RTS
```

NeXT DIN-8 to IBM DB-25 with RTS/CTS flow control

```
DTR   1 ──────────── 8    DCD
DCD   2 ──────────── 20   DTR
TXD   3 ──────────── 3    RXD
GND   4 ──────────── 7    GND
RXD   5 ──────────── 2    TXD
RTS   6 ──────────── 5    CTS
CTS   8 ──────────── 4    RTS
```

NeXT DIN-8 to IBM-25 with DTR flow control

```
DTR   1 ──────────── 8    DCD
DCD   2 ──────────── 5    CTS
TXD   3 ──────────── 3    RXD
GND   4 ──────────── 7    GND
RXD   5 ──────────── 2    TXD
RTS   6 ──────────── 20   DTR
CTS   8 ──────────── 4    RTS
```

Modem cables (DTE to DCE)

IBM DB-25 to Modem

```
FG     1 ──────────── 1    FG
TxD    2 ──────────── 2    TxD
RxD    3 ──────────── 3    RxD
RTS    4 ──────────── 4    RTS
CTS    5 ──────────── 5    CTS
DSR    6 ──────────── 6    DSR
SG     7 ──────────── 7    SG
DCD    8 ──────────── 8    DCD
DTR   20 ──────────── 20   DTR
```

IBM DB-9 to Modem

```
TxD    3 ──────────── 2    TxD
RxD    2 ──────────── 3    RxD
RTS    7 ──────────── 4    RTS
CTS    8 ──────────── 5    CTS
DSR    6 ──────────── 6    DSR
SG     5 ──────────── 7    SG
DCD    1 ──────────── 8    DCD
DTR    4 ──────────── 20   DTR
```

Apple IIGS to Modem

```
HSKout   1 ──────────── 20   DTR
HSKin    2 ──────────── 8    DCD
TxD-     3 ──────────── 2    TD
SG       4 ──┐      ┌─── 7    SG
RxD+     8 ──┘     ╱
RxD-     5 ──────────── 3    RD
```

Macintosh Modem Cables

The Macintosh II and Quadra series serial ports have two handshaking inputs – HSKin and GPi – and one handshaking output – HSKout. This is in contrast to the Macintosh Plus, Classic, VX, and LC machines, which only have one handshaking input – HSKin. The addition of the GPi input on the II and Quadra series machines allows for both hardware handshaking and sensing of Carrier Detect. This is accomplished by using HSKin and HSKout to do CTS/RTS handshaking, and GPi to sense DCD. Since no more handshaking outputs are available, hang-up of the phone is handled by software. Since DTR cannot be lowered, the modem would be requested, via the &D<n> command, to ignore the state of DTR.

BBS software packages such as FirstClass and Hermes use the GPi input to sense DCD. For software that doesn't use GPi, but which must sense loss of carrier (such as BBS software, or programs such as Timbuktu Remote or Carbon Copy), use a cable with Carrier Detect (DCD) tied to HSKin, and Data Terminal Ready (DTR) tied to HSKout.

If your machine does not have the GPi pin and you do not need to sense carrier loss, use a cable that ties Clear to Send (CTS) to HSKin. As for HSKout, Software Ventures has developed a cable that either can do hardware handshake (if you instruct the modem to ignore DTR via &D<n>), or can hang up the phone (if you instruct the modem to ignore RTS/CTS and enable DTR hangup). The company accomplished this by connecting both RTS and DTR to HSKout. Here are the pin arrangements of both types of modem cables:

BBS/Remote Dial-In Modem Cable for Mac without GPi

(For use with 2400 bps modems)

HSKout	1	———	20	DTR
HSKin	2	———	8	DCD
TxD-	3	———	2	TD
SG	4		7	SG
RxD+	8			
RxD-	5	———	3	RD

Software Ventures HW/HS Cable

Macintosh to Modem

HSKout	1	———	4	RTS
			20	DTR
HSKin	2	———	5	CTS
TxD-	3	———	2	TD
SG	4		7	SG
RxD+	8			
RxD-	5	———	3	RD

Hermes BBS Hardware Handshake and Carrier Detect Cable

(For Mac SE, SE/30, II, and Quadra series machines only)

Macintosh to Modem

HSKout	1	———	4	RTS
			20	DTR
HSKin	2	———	5	CTS
TxD-	3	———	2	TD
SG	4		7	SG
RxD+	8			
RxD-	5	———	3	RD
GPi	7	———	8	DCD

NeXT DIN-8 to IBM DB-25

DTR	1	———	20	DTR
DCD	2	———	8	DCD
TXD	3	———	2	TXD
GND	4	———	7	GND
RXD	5	———	3	RXD
RTS	6	———	4	RTS
CTS	8	———	5	CTS

Modem settings for use with BBS cables

Modem nonvolatile RAM settings are specific to the particular software package and modem you are using, and so it is not possible to give general recommendations. If you know you are going be using a particular software package before purchasing your modem, it is best to call the software firm and get a recommendation on what kind of modem to purchase. Be aware that you may have to set the dip switches or parameter RAM settings in your modem so that it will work correctly with your software and modem cable. Consult your software's manual on how to do this. Most software companies cannot afford to test their software against all available modems, and as a result, many modems will not operate satisfactorily with all software packages. This is just one good reason to purchase a well-respected modem.

There are only two brands of modems that I can recommend without reservation for any usage – those made by Hayes and US Robotics. For 1200 or 2400 bps modems, both US Robotics and Hayes modems should satisfy either commercial or hobbyist users. For high-speed modems, however, the US Robotics HST or HST Dual Standard modems are generally preferred by hobbyists, since they are widely used by bulletin board systems. Commercial users often prefer the Hayes modems, particularly the V.32/V.42 *bis* modems, since they are easier to set up than the US Robotics modems. Telebit modems are superior for use with UUCP communications but have not been widely adopted for other purposes.

Unfortunately, few telecommunications software firms give adequate instruction on how to set up modems to work with their software. Many do not even cover setup for well-respected modems such as those from Hayes, US Robotics, or Telebit. This inexcusable behavior virtually guarantees that setup of their software with high-speed modems will be an ordeal. While I cannot hope to make a dent in this callous attitude, we present below a few recommendations for setting up US Robotics modems with selected software packages.

US Robotics 14400 dual-standard V.32/V.42*bis* and Hermes

Dip switch settings

```
QUAD    1 2 3 4 5 6 7 8 9 10
u       u u d u d u u d u u
```

NRAM Settings
(Type ATI4 to get this)

```
B0      C1       E1           F1     M1    Q0
V1      X1
BAUD=38400       PARITY=N     WORDLEN=8
DIAL=TONE        ON HOOK      TIMER

&A3     &B1      &C1          &D2    &G0   &H2    &I0
&J0     &K3      &L0          &M4    &N0   &P0    &R1
&S0     &X0      &Y1

S00=000          S01=000      S02=043       S03=013
S04=010          S05=008      S06=002       S07=060
S08=002          S09=006      S10=007       S11=050
S12=050          S13=000      S14=001       S15=000
S16=000          S17=000      S18=000       S19=000
S20=000          S21=010      S22=017       S23=019
S24=150          S25=000      S26=000       S27=000
S28=008          S38=000
```

HW handshake modem settings

US Robotics Courier 9600 and ZTerm
Dip switch settings

```
QUAD    1 2 3 4 5 6 7 8 9 10
u       d u d u d u u d u u
```

NRAM settings
(Type ATI4 to get this)

```
B1      C1       E1           F1     M1    Q0    V1    X4
BAUD=19200       PARITY=N     WORDLEN=8
DIAL=HUNT        ON HOOK      TIMER

&A1     &B1      &G0          &H1    &I0   &K1
&M4     &N0      &P0          &R2    &S0   &Y1

S00=000          S01=000      S02=043       S03=013
S04=010          S05=008      S06=002       S07=030
S08=002          S09=006      S10=007       S11=070
S12=050          S13=000      S14=001       S15=008
S16=000          S17=000      S18=000       S19=005
S20=002          S21=010      S22=017       S23=019
S24=005          S38=000
```

US Robotics Courier 9600 and OPUS

Dip switch settings

```
QUAD   1 2 3 4 5 6 7 8 9 10
d        d d u d d d d u u d
```

NRAM Settings
(Type ATI5 to get this)

```
DIAL=TONE        M=0         X=7   F=1    B=1
BAUD=19200       PARITY=N    WORDLEN=8

&A1    &B1       &G0    &H1   &I0    &K0
&M4    &N0       &P0    &R2   &S1    &Y1

S02=255          S03=013    S04=010    S05=008
S06=002          S07=030    S08=002    S09=003
S10=007          S11=050    S12=050    S13=004
S15=008          S19=010    S21=010    S22=017
S23=019
```

Telebit WorldBlazer UUCP setup
(see Chapter 16: UUCP for L.sys settings)

```
AT&V
WorldBlazer - SA - Version LA5.00W - Active Configuration
 B1  E1  L2  M1  P   Q0  V1  X1  Y0
&C1 &D3 &G0 &J0 &L0 &Q0 &R0 &S0 &T4 &X0
S000=0   S001=0   S002:128 S003=13  S004=10  S005=8
S006=2   S007:60
S008=2   S009=6   S010=14  S011=70  S012=50  S018=0
S025=5   S026=1
S038=0   S041=0   S045=0   S046=0   S047=4   S048=0
S050=0   S051:254
S056=17  S057=19  S058:2   S059=0   S060=0   S061:0
S062=15  S063=0
S064=0   S068:2   S069=0   S090=0   S092=0   S093=8
S094=1   S100=0
S104=0   S105=1   S111:30  S112=1   S151=4   S155=0
S180=2   S181=1
S183=25  S190=1   S191=7   S253=10  S254=255 S255=255
OK
```

Handshaking behavior of various software

Macintosh

ZTerm v0.90 brings HSKo high on entry and drops it low on exit. If this is connected to DTR, it will cause hangup on exiting the program. Asking ZTerm to hang up will only bring Hsko low if you have set the hardware hangup option, available by selecting **Modem Preferences...** under the **Settings** menu. ZTerm can be set to do hardware handshaking, (see **Connection...** under the **Settings** menu), which is what you should use if you have a high-speed modem and a hardware handshaking cable. White Knight v11.0 has multitudinous ways to manipulate HSKo, in **Serial Port...** under the **Local** menu. You

can drop HSKo on exit; leave it low all the time; do hardware handshaking; or invert DTR for one second.

VersaTerm and VersaTerm PRO bring HSKo high on entry. Whether it drops HSKo on exit depends on whether you have checked the Lower DTR on exit box in the **Extras...** selection under the Settings menu. If **Comm Port DTR handshake** is selected, VersaTerm will attempt HSKo-HSKi handshaking. Make sure you have a hardware handshake cable when you use this, or else DTR really will be lowered and your modem will disconnect. MicroPhone II v4.0 brings HSKo high on entry, and lowers it on exit. Requesting hangup will not lower HSKo; software hangup is attempted instead. Hardware handshaking can be set with **Communications...** under the **Settings** menu.

MacKermit v0.9(40) also brings HSKo high on entry and lowers it on exit. No hardware handshaking is available.

PC

PC Kermit brings RTS and DTR high on entering the program, and leaves RTS and DTR high on exit. This means that you will remain connected unless you hang up or turn off your modem. No hardware handshaking is available.

On entering Telix SE v1.0, or Telix v3.21, RTS and DTR are brought high. On exiting Telix, RTS and DTR will be left as they were found on entering. That is, if both were high on entry, they will be left high. If they were low, they will be left low. Hardware handshaking is not available.

On entry, Procomm Plus v1.0 brings RTS and DTR high. On exit, it will bring RTS and DTR low. Hardware handshaking is not available.

Since bringing DTR down will cause your modem to hang up unless it is set to ignore DTR, if you want to leave these terminal programs temporarily, you should use the software's DOS shell functions. This will leave RTS and DTR high.

APPENDIX E:
NETWORK APPLICATION FORMS

The RelayNet (RIME) application form

Complete and return to: Bonnie Anthony, M.D.; 6901 Whittier Blvd., Bethesda, MD 20817; (301)229-7028, (301)229-7244, fax: (301)229-7244
Membership fee = $25, Node software = $30, Hub software = $60

Sysop's name:_____

Mailing address:_____

City:_____ State:_____ Zip:_____

Voice telephone:_____[ ] home   [ ] business

If a member of the steering committee needs to contact you via a voice

call, what is best time to call (wherever possible please provide a home phone

number)?_____

BBS name:_____

BBS telephone:_____

Number of nodes:_____ Maximum bps rate:_____

Number of years BBS in operation:_____

BBS specialty (if any):_____

BBS software:_____

Node ID desired:_____

Serial number:_____

Are you applying for: [ ] Hub status   [ ] Node status

Hub to Relay with:_____

Where did you hear about RIME?_____
Have you read a copy of the network bylaws?   [ ] Yes   [ ] no
Do you agree to accept the network's bylaws?   [ ] Yes   [ ] no

Signature:_____ Date:_____

The FrEdMail application form

```
************************************************************************
**                FrEdMail Foundation Order Form                    **
**                                                                  **
** Your name:_____       **
**                                                                  **
** School:_____       **
**                                                                  **
** District:_____       **
**                                                                  **
** Mailing address:_____       **
**                                                                  **
** City/state/zip:_____       **
**                                                                  **
** Position/grade level:_____       **
**                                                                  **
** FrEdMail Software:    ____ copies @ $80.00 each = $_____     **
**                                                                  **
** Modem Cable Adapter  ____        @ $18.00 each = $_____      **
**                                                                  **
** FrEdMail Simulation  ____ copies @ $30.00 each = $_____      **
**                                                                  **
** TeleSensations:      ____ copies @ $34.00 each = $_____      **
**                                                                  **
** T 'n T Syllabus:     ____ copies @ $249.00 each = $_____     **
**                                                                  **
** FrEdMail Newsletter  ____ copies @ $10.00 each = $_____      **
**                                                                  **
**                                  Subtotal = $_____           **
**                                                                  **
** CA tax (7.25% San Diego Coounty; 6.25% elsewhere = $_____    **
**                                                                  **
**     Shipping ($3.00 or 3%, whichever is more) = $_____       **
**        (foreign shipping = $10.00 or 10%)                        **
**                                    Total = $_____            **
** Mail this form with a check or purchase order to:                **
**                    FrEdMail Foundation                           **
**                       P.O. Box 243                               **
**                     Bonita, CA 91908                             **
************************************************************************
```

FrEdMail Software for Apple II (includes Simulation) $80.00
Modem Cable Adapter (for external modem) $18.00
FrEdMail Simulation $30.00
TeleSensations: The Educators' Handbook to TeleComputing: $34.00
    The perfect how-to book for planning, integrating, and using
    telecomputing across the curriculum.
T 'n T: Teachers and TeleComputing. Comprehensive $249.00
    instructor's syllabus includes everything needed (three VIS videos,
    overheads, handouts, simulations) to teach a district telecomputing
    workshop for teachers. Written by experts to make your job easier.
FrEdNews: Quarterly newsletters filled with successful telecomputing $10.00
    project summaries, classroom management strategies, sysop insights,
    and the latest Network Map.

MSDN submission form

Each piece of software must have it's own form

Name of author: Date (DD-MMM-YYYY):
Password of author:

File/product name: Version:
Shareware? PD?:   Shareware fee:
Files:

MSDN Area: Keywords:

Product description:

Long description:

Requirements to use the files:

Comments:

The above-named person gives MSDN permission to distribute the above files
via the MSDN network.

Key

The **password** is secret and is used to ensure that the files are truly from you.

The **files** line should list the names of the files that you send us. This is mostly for security
reasons and when you send us the files on disk so that the hatcher knows which files belong to
which product. Note that we will distribute the files in the "8.3" naming format because
operating systems such as MS-DOS do not support more than 8 characters a dot followed by 3
characters. Files are distributed in MacBinary format so the files inside the MacBinary
"envelope" have normal (long) names. If you send the files with normal names, we will shorten
them to the proper length for the MacBinary distribution format. If you have a preference for
what names should be used, you can put that in the **comments** field. **Keywords** are used for
systems that allow keyword searches of their files.

The **Area** indicates which of the MSDN Areas you want the files posted in.

The **descriptions** are a descriptive abstract of your files. This will be distributed with your files.
MSDN sysops can then post these into local areas to make their users aware of new files. The
hatchers may also post these abstracts into the MacFiles echo (or another suitable medium) to
make the new announcement internationally known.

UUCP map entry

```
#N              UUCP name of the machine
#S              Computer, operating system, and version
#O              Organization
#C              Person responsible for the machine
#E              Email address of the postmaster
#T              Phone number of the machine
#P              U.S. Mail address of the organization
#L              Coordinates of the machine (latitude/longitude)
#R              Remarks about the machine
#U              UUCP host
#W              Person who edited the map, and the date
#
site=           alias1, alias2
site            host(polling frequency), host2(polling frequency)
```

Examples

```
#N              bmug, f445.n161.z1.fidonet.org
#S              IBM-PC AT; MS-DOS 5.0
#O              private - FidoNet
#C              Bernard Aboba
#E              bmug!postmaster
#T              (510)849-9118
#P              1442A Walnut St. #62, Berkeley, CA 94709
#L              37 33 N / 122 17 W city
#U              apple
#R              Fido 1:161/445 running UFGATE
#R              this is a FidoNet <-> UUCP gateway site serving Mac BBSes only
#W              merlin@ns.fidonet.org (Burt Juda); Sun Oct 27 15:00:00 EST 1991
#
#               Approved by ddodell@stjhmc.fidonet.org
#               Administrator, fidonet.org
#
bmug=           bmug.fidonet.org, f445.n161.z1.fidonet.org
bmug            apple(DAILY)


#N              fidosw,f111.n125.z1.fidonet.org
#S              '386 Clone, PC-DOS 4.01
#O              Fido Software
#C              Tom Jennings
#E              fidosw!Tom.Jennings
#T              (415)552 8156
#P              Box 77731, San Francisco, CA 94107
#L              37 47 01 N / 122 24 11 W
#R              The system's fido zone:net/number is 1:125/111.
#U              kumr
#W              stjhmc!ddodell (David Dodell); Mon Jun 3 20:45:00 MST 1991
#
#               Approved by ddodell@stjhmc.fidonet.org
#               Administrator, fidonet.org
#
fidosw =        fidosw.fidonet.org, f111.n125.z1.fidonet.org
fidosw          kumr(DAILY/24)
```

APPENDIX F:
UNIX TIPS AND TRICKS

Copyright © 1993 MailCom. All rights reserved. Reprinted by permission.

Brief overview of UNIX

Case sensitivity

Under UNIX, almost everything is case-sensitive. Login names are case-sensitive; passwords are case-sensitive; commands in editors are case sensitive. This means that a ROSE is not a Rose is not a rose. One exception is in the domain portion of a mail address, so bob@dog.COM is equivalent to bob@DOG.com. Note that this is only true for domain-style addressing; UUCP-style addresses are case-sensitive, so dog!bob is NOT the same as Dog!bob. Also, user names are case sensitive so that dog!bob is not equivalent to dog!BOB. Got it?

Background processes

UNIX allows you to accomplish several things at the same time. If you don't want to wait until a command completes, you can execute it in the background by putting a & after the command. You can also string UNIX commands together, separated by a ;. To compress a file in the background, type:

```
% compress foo &
```

To compress a file and then list current processes, type:

```
% compress foo ; ps -g
```

Input and output

The input and output of UNIX programs can be redirected to a file. Normally the input stream (known in UNIX lingo as "stdin", and pronounced standard input) defaults to reading input from your keyboard, and the output stream (known in the lingo as "stdout", and pronounced standard output) defaults to printing output on your screen. However, instead of reading output on your screen, you can send it to a file, and instead of taking input from your terminal, you can have the program take input from a file. The symbol for redirecting input is <. The symbol for redirecting output is >. It is also possible to append output to the end of a file, using the >> symbol. How is this useful? **ls** is the command for printing a directory. If you want to save a directory listing to the file **lsfile**, you can execute the command:

```
% ls >lsfile

% cat lsfile
Mail
NEW.C
News
README
TRANSFER
attach
christ.txt
edonline
```

Piping and batching

The output of one UNIX command can also be used as the input of another command. This is done by stringing commands together, separated by "|". Below, I create a directory listing, sort it, compress it, and download it to my computer using ZMODEM (**sz** is a UNIX ZMODEM implementation):

```
% ls -l | sort | compress >foo.Z | sz -b -
sz: 1 file 564 bytes 0.1 minutes
*
### Receive (Z) foo.Z: 564 bytes, 0:03 elapsed, 160 cps, 66%
```

Here the **-b** option tells **sz** that the file is binary; the extra – tells **sz** that input is coming from a pipe. To compress all files in a directory ending in **.txt** (using zip) and then download the archive to your personal computer, type:

```
zip -m foo.zip *.txt ; sz -b foo.zip
```

To upload a file using ZMODEM , uncompress it, sort it, eliminate duplicated lines, compress it, and download it again with ZMODEM:

```
rz ; uncompress foo ; sort foo  | uniq -q | compress >foo ; sz -b foo.Z
```

Piping can also sometimes be done **within** an application program.

For example, the **ftp** program is a program to transfer files from one machine to another, and **sz** is a program that uploads files via ZMODEM. Using piping, you can tell **ftp** to get a file from a remote site and then download it to your system by sending the commands:

```
ftp> binary
ftp> get big.zip "|sz -b -"
```

Here the pipe asks **ftp** to pipe the output to **sz**. The binary mode in **ftp** and the **-b** flag (binary) in **sz** is used here since it is assumed that big.zip is a binary file. In both **ftp** and **sz** the default file type is text.

Wild cards

With UNIX, you can specify operations on batches of files at the same time. This can be done in very complex ways, but most of the time you will use * to demote a wild card. For example *.txt refers to all files ending in .txt; *.* refers to all files with a "." in the middle; * refers to all files without a ".".

To list all files in a directory with an extension, type:

```
% ls *.*
```

To list all files without an extension, type:

```
% ls *
```

Aspects of C shell

The following features are not handled similarly in all versions of UNIX, but since the majority of commercial Internet sites now use Berkeley System Distribution (BSD) UNIX, we will focus on C shell commands. The C shell is the most commonly used shell on BSD UNIX systems.

Appendix F: UNIX Tips and Tricks

Suspending processes

Suppose you get stuck in a program and can't figure out how to quit; or you decide in the middle of something that you'd like to send mail; or you just want to rest for a while. Just type (CTRL)Z, and your current process will be suspended. You will be able to resume the process later, by typing **%n**, where *n* is the number of the job to resume. You can also resume by typing **%name, assuming that name is a unique substring.**

Job control

Once you've executed commands in the background, or suspended processes, you can view and, if necessary, kill the processes. Each process can be referred to in two ways: as **%n**, where *n* is the number of the job, or by a process-ID number assigned by UNIX. To find out the process-ID number, you can give the command **ps -g**:

```
% ps -g
  PID TT STAT  TIME COMMAND
 6367 pd S     0:00 -csh (csh)
 6385 pd R     0:00 ps -g
```

Here are some of the job-control commands available in C shell:

Command	What it does
jobs	Tells you what jobs are running.
bg %n	Places job *n* in the background.
fg %n	Places job *n* in the foreground.
kill %n	Kills job *n*. You can also substitute process-ID for **%n**.
stop %n	Stops job *n*.
ctrl-Z	Suspends the current process.
%n	Resumes job *n*, bringing it up on your console.

Example

In the session below, I start the mail program, suspend it, ask for a jobs listing, go back into mail, suspend it again, and finally kill the process.

```
% mail
Mail version SMI 4.0 Wed Oct 23 10:38:28 PDT 1991  Type ? for help.
"/usr/spool/mail/aboba": 9 messages 1 new
    1 gary@dreyfuss.portal.com Wed Sep  2 17:22   40/1600  An idea
    2 bhooper@holonet.net Sun Sep  6 08:28   44/1824  Re: BMUG Guide to B.B. &
    3 vwright          Sun Sep  6 14:44   84/3513  Suggestions for BMUG Guid
    4 emv@msen.com     Sun Sep  6 21:14   23/792   Re: your mail
    5 sac@apple.com    Sun Sep  6 23:35   21/753   Re: Is BBS the correct na
    6 ddern            Mon Sep  7 14:08   28/817   SF-local Internet access.
& ^Z
Stopped
% jobs
[1]  + Stopped                 mail
% %1
mail
& ^Z
Stopped
% kill %1
```

History

C shell remembers the last n commands you executed. You can set *n* via the command:

set savehist=n

For example, **set savehist=100** saves the last 100 commands. This is useful, because if you then type:

!<command number>

715

The C shell will reexecute command number *n* in your history. Just typing history will show you a list of the previous commands you typed:

```
% history
   1  pine
   2  ls
   3  compress mactv
   4  uncompress foo.Z | zip -m foo.zip ; sz foo.zip
   5  mv mactv.Z foo.Z
```

An aside: The C shell's history command is the reason that you can't use a ! symbol in any other context without first using a \ before it. Otherwise, the C shell will think you are referring to something in the history file. Since the C shell uses \ to indicate a special symbol, it interprets \! to mean the character ! instead of the command.

Example

In the example below, I reexecute two commands in the history. On my first attempt, I try !k, but this gets me the **kill** command; I need to specify !ke to uniquely determine the command.

```
% history
   1  cd ..
   2  ls
   3  kermit
   4  mail
   5  jobs
   6  %1
   7  kill %1
   8  history
% !k
kill %1
kill: No such job.
% !ke
kermit
C-Kermit, 4E(068) 24 Jan 88, 4.2 BSD
Type ? for help
C-Kermit>quit
```

Shell scripts

A shell script is a file of commands that are executed in batch mode. The .login file is such a script, as is the .cshrc file we will be discussing later on. Scripts are used to automate frequently performed tasks. Part of the difficulty in using the Internet comes from having to remember how to do something. Do I send mail to **dogowner@nit-manager.alpo.com** with a subject of **HELPME** to search for the dog lover's mailing list, or was that **dog-server@mailman.bite.com** with **SEND INFO** in the body of the message? Using shell scripts masks this complexity.

To create a directory for your scripts, do a **mkdir bin** within your home directory, and change directories to it. You can then create scripts with **pico, vi,** or your favorite editor, or even the **cat** command, if you prefer. To grant permission to execute the scripts, please type the command:

```
chmod +x <script-name>
```

Assuming that the directory /bin is within your path (more on this later), you should be able to execute the scripts just by typing their names.

Other useful commands

alias

alias lets you make up nicknames for frequently executed commands. For example:

```
alias femail "mail mail-server@pit-manager.mit.edu"
```

will execute a mail command every time I type **femail** at the shell.

Aliases can make UNIX easier to use, and you will probably want to make a list of aliases available each time you invoke the shell. This is usually put in an .alias file within your home directory. To execute this file every time you invoke the C shell, you will want to put the following statement at the end of your .cshrc file:

source $HOME/.alias

ls

ls shows you the contents of the directory you're in. For example:

```
% ls
Mail            TRANSFER       fda            ka9q           ufgate.txt
NEW.C           attach         gifblast       mactv          vwreview
News            christ.txt     jb.txt         mail
README          edonline       job            mbox
```

The **ls** command also has several options. Some of these are:

-a   Shows all files, including "invisible" ones
-l   Shows file permissions, owner, sizes, and creation date and time

An example of the -l option is:

```
% ls -l
total 127
drwx------   2 aboba        512 Nov 16  1991 Mail
-rw-------   1 aboba       7309 Jun 18 12:09 NEW.C
drwx------   3 aboba        512 Aug 25 22:35 News
-rw-------   1 aboba       7356 Sep  7 13:15 vwreview
```

cat

cat is used to type or to create a file. Here is the syntax:

Example	What it does
cat filename	Types filename
cat >filename	Takes keyboard input; outputs it to filename
cat >>filename	Takes keyboard input; if filename exists, appends to it

When using **cat** to take keyboard input, you stop entering input by typing (CTRL)D, which signifies end-of-file in UNIX.

more

more is a program to display the contents of a file. However, unlike **cat**, which puts the entire file out on your screen without stopping, **more** pauses at the end of each page.

more reads from the standard input, so you need to use redirection in order to get it to show a file. The syntax of more is: **more < file**

Example

```
% more <what.is.nptn.txt

           NPTN AND COMMUNITY COMPUTING

The National Public Telecomputing Network (NPTN)

   The concept behind NPTN is not new.  You are probably familiar
with National Public Radio and Public Broadcasting on T.V.  To
understand NPTN, simply substitute community computer systems for
radio or television stations, and you have the core of what we
hope to accomplish--with two important differences.  First, unlike
NPR or PBS, we are NOT subsidized by the government; and second,
unlike radio and television, our medium, telecomputing, is not yet
as well established.

--More--
```

At the More prompt, you can hit **<space>** if you want to see the next page, or type **q** or **Q** to exit. **b** brings you back one page.

zcat, zmore

These are versions of the **cat** and **more** utilities that operate on files compressed with the **compress** program. This means that you can view a compressed file without uncompressing it.

pwd

pwd tells you where you are in the directory structure. For example:

```
% pwd
/users/aboba
```

cd

cd moves to another directory. For example:

```
% cd /usr/bin
% pwd
/usr/bin
```

telnet and tn3270

telnet allows remote login to another machine on the network; **tn3270** is for remote logins to IBM mainframes supporting the 3270 terminal. The syntax is: **telnet <machine name> <port#>**. The port # is optional and has a default of 23 for **telnet**, 25 for SMTP (mail), and 119 for NNTP (network news). For a listing of common port numbers, please consult Chapter 15: TCP/IP.

After you give the command, you will be greeted by the login prompt of the remote system or you will see a "trying" message without visible signs of success (if this happens, just hit (CTRL) C or (CTRL)] to get out of it). Alternatively, you may receive an error message like this one:

```
% telnet haas.berkeley.edu
Trying 128.32.162.100...
telnet: Unable to connect to remote host: Network is unreachable
```

This error message does not necessarily imply that there is something permanently wrong with the network. Network connections can go down and then up again within an hour. However, if the problem persists you should talk to your system administrator. Here is an example of a successful **telnet** invocation:

```
% telnet sumex-aim.stanford.edu
Trying 36.44.0.6...
Connected to sumex-aim.stanford.edu.
Escape character is '^]'.
SunOS UNIX (SUMEX-AIM)
login:
```

To allow you to suspend a session, **telnet** supports an escape character (default is (CTRL)]. Typing this character brings you back to the telnet> prompt. To set the escape character, type **set escape <character>.** To denote control characters, you can use ^, or type (CTRL) instead. If after giving the telnet command nothing you type appears on the screen, type the command **set echo** to the telnet> prompt. This turns echoing on or off.

rlogin

Early versions of **telnet** did not transmit the user's terminal emulation and login ID to the remote system. Therefore **rlogin** was created as part of the BSD UNIX distribution to address these deficiencies. Note that in the example, **rlogin** is set to default to my current user ID on the remote system, so that it only needs to ask my password:

```
% rlogin bozo.podunk.edu
Password:
```

Setting up your account

Depending on the savvy of your system administrator, you may have a lot of difficulty getting your account set up correctly—or none at all. While World offers good technical support and a wide range of utilities, most Internet services are not strong in technical support and lack one or more of the basic programs described in this chapter. This means that you will have to bug the system administrator to fix the problems and install a fuller menu of utilities; in most cases, you will not have the privileges to do the installation yourself.

You would think that most services would set up accounts with defaults, including VT100 emulation, support of the backspace key, and access protection for user files, but often this is not the case. Users have complained about problems from disabling of the backspace key to unpredictable terminal emulation to default privileges that leave files open to reading by other users.

To correctly configure your account, there are some critical files that you must set up correctly. The most important of these are the .login file and the .cshrc file.

.cshrc file

The .cshrc file is run for every invocation of the C shell, and therefore it is executed prior to the .login script. Since you can have multiple shells running at the same time (such as when using MacLayers), the .cshrc file is used to set up the shell environment, such as the default permissions on your files, your aliases, and your default editor, rather than doing the one-time tasks you'll need on login (such as looking for new mail and printing out system messages).

On the next page is my .cshrc file. The first thing it does is set up default paths to UNIX commands so the shell can find them. Since this is different on every system, you should not blindly copy what is in the example to your .cshrc file. Next, the script sets up the **history** command to save up to 50 commands in the buffer. This is useful if you want to reexecute a command later. Next, it sets up the shell to notify me of new mail.

The next command sets the default file permissions so that other users cannot read my files. This is **very** important! On some Internet services files are readable by default! (This is what happens when **umask** is left at 022 instead of 077). Next, it sets the default editor to **pico**. This is important because several programs (such as **nn**) call on a default editor. The default is often **emacs,** which beginners will find unintelligible. They probably won't even be able to figure out how to leave it!

pico is about as easy to use as UNIX editors get, since there is a menu of commands at the bottom of the screen.

The .login file

Commands stored in the .login file are executed when you log on. The difference between the .login file and the .cshrc file is that the .login file is only executed on login, **NOT** every time you spawn a shell. However, if you ever want to reexecute the .login file, just type **source .login**. In contrast, the .cshrc file **IS** executed for each shell. Things like aliases (nicknames for more complicated commands, which will need to be accessible from each shell) should be put in the .cshrc file, not the .login file.

Many problems are due to improper setup of initialization scripts. If you find that the backspace key doesn't work, or that your default editor is one you're unfamiliar with, or that UNIX thinks you are using a TTY instead of a VT100, then your .login or .cshrc file is probably to blame.

Of course, if your initialization scripts are really messed up, then they are difficult to fix because they will affect almost everything you do, including operating an editor to clean them up!

My advice in this case is to type in some of the basic commands listed on the next page by hand, such as setting terminal emulation, the backspace key, and the default editor. If you do this, you will then have your setup corrected to the point where you can edit the initialization scripts and fix them permanently.

On the following page is my .login file. If you are having troubles with the setup on your system, I recommend you save your old .login file somewhere, replace it with this one, and see if things improve.

It sets up my terminal emulation as a default of VT100 and enables the correct operation of the backspace key.

Transfer protocols

Once you've got your account functioning normally, you need to learn to use (or if necessary, get your system administrator to install) file-transfer programs like ZMODEM.

For some reason, many systems do not have ZMODEM installed yet—only KERMIT and XMODEM. Since ZMODEM is faster than these other protocols, you should try to convince your system administrator to install it.

rx, sx

rx and **sx** are the UNIX commands for receiving and sending via XMODEM. To receive a file, just type **rx**, and send it from your terminal program. To send a file, type:

Command	What it does
sx filename	Sends a text file
sx -b filename	Sends a binary file

.login file

```
# Enable cntrl-H as backspace key
#
stty erase ^H
# Set up vt100 emulation
set term=vt100
#
# set IRC nickname (please change this!)
set IRCNICK=bozobrain
```

.cshrc file

```
# set up path in which to search for commands
set path=(/usr/ucb /usr/unsupported/bin /bin /usr/bin /usr/local/bin /usr/games)
# Set number of command to save to 50
set history=50
#
# Cause files to be created such that no one else can read them.
umask 077
#
# Default editor is pico, since it's easier to use than vi
setenv EDITOR pico
setenv VISUAL $EDITOR
setenv ORGANIZATION "MailCom"
#
# Invoke alias file
source $HOME/.alias
```

.alias file

```
# invoke pine
alias    male    pine
```

rz, sz

rz and **sz** are the UNIX commands for receiving and sending via ZMODEM. They are invoked similarly to XMODEM:

Command	What it does
sz filename	Sends a text file
sz -b filename	Sends a binary file

To see the rest of the **sz** options, just type **sz** at the command line.

After invoking the **sz** command, you will usually not have to do anything, because your terminal program should auto-receive. If for some reason this doesn't happen, or you can't transfer the file, you may have a problem with control characters. Try:

Command	What it does
sz -eb filename	Sends a binary file, escaping control characters.

kermit

kermit is an interactive program for sending and receiving files via the KERMIT protocol. To receive a file via **kermit**, type **receive** at the prompt, and then ask your program to send via **kermit**.

```
% kermit
C-Kermit, 4E(068) 24 Jan 88, 4.2 BSD
Type ? for help
C-Kermit>receive
Escape back to your local system and give a SEND command...
```

To send a file via **kermit**, type **send filename** at the KERMIT prompt, and then ask your **kermit** to receive. You can issue shell commands from within **kermit** by typing:

! <space> <shell command>

For a further listing of KERMIT commands, type **help** at the prompt.

rdist

rdist is an advanced UNIX command that it is useful to know about, although most people will never use it. It is the equivalent to TICK on FidoNet. It moves files from one machine to another in an automated way and can be used for creating mirrored FTP archives. **cron** is often used to schedule the transfers. The form of the **rdist** command is:

rdist -f [-b][-y][-R] <distribution command file>

The **-b** option does a binary comparison between files in the source and destination. Copies will only occur if the files are different. The **-y** option causes files to be copied only if the source files are newer than the destination files. The **-R** option makes the source and destination archives identical; extraneous files in the destination are removed. The **-f** option tells **rdist** to look for distribution commands in the filename that follows. Legal commands in the distribution command file include:

```
<variable name>  =  <list>
[ label: ]  <source list>  ->  <destination list>  <command list>
install    <options>  ;
notify     (user1@domain1 user2@domain2)    ;
except     <name list>   ;
except_pat       <pattern list>;
```

The **=** command is used in order to make the succeeding commands easier to read. The **->** command is used to do a copy. By default, files in the destination list will be overwritten if their creation date and size disagree, even if the destination file is newer than the source file (unless overidden by the **-b** or **-y** options). The **install** command copies directories recursively and causes a copy to occur only if the destination files are older than the source files of the same name. The **notify** command sends mail to the specified users about the transfer; the **except** command exempts the specified files from the source list from being copied; **except_pat** allows files to be excluded via a regular expression.

Example

```
HOSTS1 = ( nu.roo.com foo.roo.com)
   FILES1 = ( /ufgate )
   HOSTS2 = ( planet.com foo.roo.com)
   FILES2 = ( /msdn )
   ${FILES1} -> ${HOSTS1}
           install -R ;
   ${FILES2} -> ${HOSTS2}
           notify Bernard.Aboba@f445.n161.z1.fidonet.org ;
```

Compression programs

Once you've figured out how to get files on and off your machine, you will need to know how to compress and uncompress them, and use other translation programs. UNIX now has a full suite of compression utilities available that are compatible with popular DOS and Macintosh compression programs such as PKZIP, ARC, and StuffIt.

arc

arc is a UNIX version of System Enhancement Associates' PC-compatible ARC program. Most of the time all you will want to do is to create a .arc archive, or extract one. To create an archive, type:

Command	What it does
arc -a <archive> <files>	Compresses files and stores them as an archive.
arc -m <archive> <files>	Compresses files, stores them as an archive, then deletes them.

To extract an archive, type:

    arc -e <archive>

For the full list of **arc** options, just type **arc** at the prompt.

Example

Here I archive a single file, and then extract it:

```
% arc -a ed.arc edonline
Creating new archive: ed.arc
Adding file:    edonline      analyzing, crunched, done. (32%)
% arc -e ed.arc
Extracting file: edonline
WARNING: File edonline already exists!  Overwrite it (y/n)? y
```

lharc

lharc is a UNIX version of the PC-compatible program lharc. As with **arc**, you will typically either create a .lha archive, or extract one. To create an archive, type:

Command	What it does
lharc a <archive> <files>	Compresses files and stores them as an archive.
lharc m <archive> <files>	Compresses files, stores them as an archive, then deletes them.

To extract an archive, type:

    lharc e <archive>

Example

Here I archive a single file, and then extract it:

```
% lharc a ed.lzh edonline
edonline       - Frozen(58%)
% lharc e ed.lzh
edonline OverWrite ?(Yes/No/All) y
edonline       - Melted
```

For a full list of lharc options, type **lharc** at the prompt.

compress

compress and **uncompress** are UNIX compression utilities. Although they are quick, the compression is not very good, and often versions for other operating systems (MS-DOS, Mac) are buggy; so **compress** should not be used if you are intending to transport the file to a non-UNIX machine. Use **zip** instead (see below). **compress** operates by replacing the uncompressed file with a compressed version with a .Z extension.

zip, unzip

zip and **unzip** let you create and expand archives in the popular PKZIP format. .ZIP files can be expanded on the Macintosh and PC, **zip** compression is better than **compress**, and PC and Mac **unzip** utilities are more reliable than versions of **compress** for these machines. As a result, my advice is to use **uncompress** and then **zip** a file before downloading it. This is particularly useful for Internet documentation, which is often stored as compressed PostScript files, with a .ps.Z extension. The following example shows how to translate a file in .Z format into a **zip** archive, and then download it:

```
% uncompress foo.Z ; zip -m foo.zip foo; sz foo.zip
adding foo (imploded 42%)
sz: 1 file 1688 bytes 0.1 minutes
*
### Receive (Z) foo.zip: 1688 bytes, 0:02 elapsed, 713 cps, 49%
```

Be aware that **unzip** will only extract from archives created with PKZIP v1.1 or earlier. The simplest application of **zip** is just to pack a file or files into an archive, and then extract them:

```
% zip ed.zip edonline
adding edonline (imploded 41%)
% unzip ed.zip
replace edonline? [y]es, [n]o, [A]ll, [N]one, [r]ename: y
  Exploding: edonline
```

For a list of all the zip options, just type **zip** at the command line.

sh

sh extracts files included as part of UNIX .shar archives.

tar

tar is a popular backup utility. One of the reasons that it is popular is that you can backup entire directory structures. Very often you will see software with names like foo.tar.Z being distributed on the Internet. This means that the archive foo.tar has been compressed with UNIX **compress.** To extract the archive, you will need to execute the UNIX commands:

```
uncompress  foo.tar.Z
tar  -xf  foo.tar
```

Conversion utilities

To transfer files between the Mac, PC, and UNIX, you will need conversion utilities.

uuencode, uudecode

UNIX cannot enclose binary data within mail. This is because the **sendmail** program interprets control characters as commands.

Therefore you must translate binary data to ASCII before sending a file. Of course, the receiver must then translate back. This is what **uuencode** and **uudecode** do. They are popular because there are versions of these programs for the PC and the Macintosh, as well as for UNIX.

To **uuencode** the file `ed.lzh` as `ed.uu`, so that when it is uudecoded it will end up as `edonline.lzh,` type:

```
% uuencode ed.lzh edonline.lzh >ed.uu
```

To **uudecode** `ed.uu`:

```
% uudecode ed.uu
% ls
ed.lzh
ed.uu
edonline.lzh
```

StuffIt v3.0 includes **uuencode** and **uudecode** translators.

atob, btoa

These programs operate similarly to **uuencode** and **uudecode** in that they translate back and forth between binary and ASCII formats. **atob** stands for ASCII to binary, and **btoa** is binary to ASCII. However, **btoa** is more efficient than **uuencode**, and therefore you may prefer it. StuffIt v3.0 includes **atob/btoa** translators as part of the package.

mcvert

mcvert, which stands for Macintosh Convert, is a program that converts files that have been run through BinHex 4.0 (`.Hqx` extension) to MacBinary format. This is useful because `.hqx` files take up extra space, so if you run **mcvert** on them first before downloading you will save time.

```
% mcvert european-phone-connections.hqx
Converting      Traveling_&_Phones.cpt          type = "PACT", author = "CPCT"
% ls
Traveling_&Phones.cpt.bin
```

Other **mcvert** options include:

`-x`	Translates .hqx files to MacBinary
`-u`	Translates text files to MacBinary
`-d`	.data to MacBinary
`-r`	.rsrc to MacBinary
`-b`	Both .data and .rsrc to MacBinary
`-D`	Download; other to MacBinary
`-U`	Upload; MacBinary to other
`-t`	translate end-of-line chars (useful with -b)
`-s`	silent
`-S`	Silent about "Converting ..." lines too
`-v`	verbose
`-V`	Verbose, includes debugging information
`-H`	disable skip-legal-but-suspect-lines Heuristic

Special directories and files

/tmp

This directory is a place where you can store files temporarily. For example, if you are out of disk space, you can switch to this directory, create another directory with your login name (say `/tmp/aboba`), and then transfer into the newly created directory. You can then do a file transfer into the new directory, download the files to your personal computer, and erase the mess you make by typing: **rm -rf /tmp/aboba** to the shell. This will remove everything in the `/tmp/aboba` directory—even directories within that directory. Please keep in mind that the `/tmp` directory is usually cleaned up on a regular basis, so you should not use it as a permanent storage area.

/usr/bin

The `/usr/bin` directory is one place where UNIX commands are stored. Others are `/usr/local/bin, /bin, and /usr/lib`. If you change directories to one of these and do an **ls**, you will get a listing of commands.

```
% cd /usr/bin
% ls
X11                 hostid              roffbib
[                   hostname            rpcgen
acctcom             hostrfs             screenblank
       .
       .
       .
graph               rmdir               ypwhich
grep                rnews               zsh
```

/etc/hosts

The `/etc/hosts` file contains information on some of the local network connections of your host. Unlike on FidoNet, Internet hosts no longer use a centralized list of network addresses, but instead use a decentralized mechanism known as Domain Name Service (DNS). Nevertheless, it is useful to have a short list of systems available, in case other name-resolution mechanisms are not available. Here is what the `/etc/hosts` file looks like on world:

```
% more </etc/hosts
#
# Sun Host Database
#
# If the NIS is running, this file is only consulted when booting
#
127.0.0.1        localhost
#
192.74.137.5     world.std.com world loghost
192.74.137.9     ussr.std.com ussr
192.74.137.31    ares.std.com ares
```

Pine

Pine, which stands for Pine Is Nearly Elm, is a full-screen mail reader for UNIX. **pine** is the easiest UNIX mail program to use because it supports cursor key positioning, is menu driven, offers context-sensitive help, and has a friendly full-screen editor called **pico** built in. Although **pine** is now one of the most popular UNIX mail readers, no other books provide coverage on it, so it seemed appropriate to provide an overview of it here.

Understanding pine

Everywhere you go in **pine**, the commands you can type are displayed at the bottom of the screen. Since this doesn't leave room for that many commands, there is often an **Other** command that will bring up an alternate menu of commands. However, **pine** is a modal program; when you are in the alternate menu, the commands on the standard menu are no longer available to you.

Within **pine**, using (CTRL) Z to suspend processes will not work. There is also no way to send a command to the shell. Therefore, if you want to do something else, your only alternative is to quit. By the way, commands in pine are **NOT** case sensitive, which is unusual for UNIX.

Appendix F: UNIX Tips and Tricks

Main menu

To enter **pine**, just type **pine** at the UNIX prompt. You will then be greeted by the main menu:

```
PINE 3.05        MAIN MENU      Folder:inbox  44 Messages


        ?   HELP         - Get help using Pine
        C   COMPOSE      - Compose and send a message
        I   MAIL INDEX   - Read mail in current folder
        F   FOLDERS      - Open a different mail folder
        A   ADDRESSES    - Update your address book
        O   OTHER        - Use other functions
        Q   QUIT         - Exit the Pine mail program

    Note: In Pine 3.0 we are encouraging folks to use the MAIL INDEX to read mail instead of
VIEW MAIL, so it is no longer on the main menu. Once in the mail index, it is available as
usual as the "V" command.

? Help      Q Quit      F Folders     O Other
C Compose   I Mail Index A Addresses
```

Pine operates on folder and address books metaphors. Folders contain messages and include the **inbox** folder, which contains your incoming messages; the **sent-mail** folder, which contains outgoing messages; and any other folders you create yourself. Address books contain nicknames, full names, and email addresses of people you want to keep track of. You can copy addresses from incoming mail, or delete or edit the address book.

On entry to **pine**, your default mailbox is **inbox**, the mailbox containing your incoming mail. Usually you will want to type **I** for Mail Index if you have mail in order to view the contents of **inbox**. You can also type **C** for compose if you want to send a message.

The help system

Wherever you are, **pine** offers context-sensitive help. Unfortunately, the command to get help changes depending on where you are in **pine**. In many menus the command for help is a **?**; in others it is (CTRL) G. Here is what the help system looks like if called from the Main Menu:

```
PINE 3.05         HELP FOR MAIN MENU       page 1 of 26

    HELP TEXT FOR MAIN MENU                                      Page 1
Contents: 1. Whom to Call for More Help................ 2
          2. Main Menu Commands    ................... 3
             Frequently Asked Questions:
          3. Printing on PCs and Macs................. 6
          4. Stuck in Read-only mode.................. 7
          5. If ^C Doesn't Work on a Mac.............. 8
          6. Block deletes and paste in the composer... 9
          7. Signature files........................ 10
          8. What is MIME?.......................... 11
          9. Alternate editor for composing messages.. 12
         10. Dialing in with Pine.................. ... 13
         11. Giving Commands in Pine.......... ...... 14
         12. Notes on Pine Screens.................. 17
         13. History and Origin of Pine.............. 18
         14. Pine 3.0 update....................... 23
         15. Pine contributors...................... 24
         16. Copyright notice....................... 25

M Main Menu   E Exit Help                 - Prev Page
L Print       SPACE Next Page             W Where is
```

Typing **W** for "Where is" allows you to find a reference to a particular function within the help system.

Other main menu

Typing **o** brings up the Other Main Menu:

```
PINE 3.05          OTHER          Folder:inbox  44 Messages

?   HELP        - Information on your options at this point
N   NEWS        - News about Pine changes
K   LOCK        - Lock this keyboard against others using it
M   MAIN MENU   - Go back to the main menu
P   PASSWORD    - Change the password you use to login
L   PRINTER     - Choose printer or print command
                  Current printer:attached-to-ansi
D    DISK       - Show space used by mail folders and free space

? Help       K Lock Kbd   P Password    D Disk
N News       M Main Menu  L Printer
```

The Other Main Menu commands are not very useful, which is why they're shunted off to the side. Since the **L** command will print on the host, not on your machine, you probably won't need to use it. I have had problems with the **K** command (it locked me out and, even though I typed my password, wouldn't let me back), so I advise against using it. To go back to the Main menu, type **M**.

Composing a message

Selecting **C** for Compose from the Main Menu puts you into the **pico** editor:

```
PINE 3.05  COMPOSE MESSAGE      Folder:inbox  44 Messages

To      : bozo@clown.harvard.edu
Cc      : wgravy@ocf.berkeley.edu
Attchmnt: 1. /users/aboba/edonline (2.2 KB) ""
Subject : Clown reuni
----- Message Text -----

Bozos of the world unite!

^G Help ^C Cancel ^R Read File^Y Prev Pg   ^K Del Line ^O Postpone
^X Send ^J Justify^W Where is ^V Next Pg   ^U UnDel Lin^T To Spell
```

You can then fill in the To:, cc: (to send copies), Attachment (to enclose a file), and Subject fields in the message. If you make a mistake, you can just maneuver back to the place where you made the error, using the arrow keys on your keyboard. To erase, just use the delete key. You then maneuver down into the message area, also with the cursor keys. Messages that are composed and sent are automatically saved to the **sent-mail** folder.

Spell checking

Typing (CTRL)**T** for spell checking will check the spelling on your message. If the spell checker finds a mistake, the word will be highlighted, and you will be able to change it:

```
PINE 3.05  COMPOSE MESSAGE      Folder:inbox  44 Messages

To      : bozo@clown.harvard.edu
Cc      : wgravy@ocf.berkeley.edu
Attchmnt: 1. /users/aboba/edonline (2.2 KB) ""
Subject : Clown reunion
----- Message Text -----

Bosos of the world unite!


Edit a replacement: Bosos
^G Get Help ^C Cancel
```

Appendix F: UNIX Tips and Tricks

Mail Index

From the main menu, you can also select **I** for Mail Index. This gives you a view of your incoming messages:

```
PINE 3.05  MAIL INDEX      Folder:inbox  Message 42 of 44

   39  Nov  4 Bozo D. Clown   (1,204) Re: Clown reunion
   40  Nov  5 Mr. O. Zone     (1,301) O3 for sale
   41  Nov  6 Joe BMUG        (1,650) BBB: Guide or Desert?
N  42  Nov  7 beaver clever    (553) Email: Bah humbug!
N  43  Nov  7 Elvis Presley    (902) Heartbreak Hotel
N  44  Nov  7 Babe Ruth      (14,799) How to hit home runs


? HelpM      Main Menu    P Prev Msg - Prev Page    F Forward    D Delete
O OTHER CMDS V View Mail  N Next Msg SPACE Next Page R Reply     S Save
```

The status of each message is denoted by a letter preceding the message. A space means that you've already read the message, but have not yet deleted it from the inbox folder; N denotes New Mail; a D denotes a message marked for deletion. In this particular example, there is only one new message, message number 9. The rest of the messages have already been read but not disposed of by deleting them or saving them to a folder. By using your up and down cursor keys, you can select individual mail messages, and then perform operations on them. These operations are:

Command	What it does
F	Forward the message to someone else.
R	Reply to the message.
D	Delete the message.
S	Save a message to a folder.

In addition, there are commands for navigating around the message index and going to other menus:

Command	What it does
?	Get help.
M	Go to the main menu.
P	Go to the previous message.
N	Go to the next message.
-	Show the previous page of messages.
<space>	Show the next page of messages.
O	Show other commands.

Saving to a folder

I have found it useful to store received messages in folders based on their subject matter. To save a message to a folder, select **s** from the Index menu:

```
PINE 3.05  MAIL INDEX      Folder:inbox  Message 42 of 44

   39  Nov  4 Bozo D. Clown   (1,204) Re: Clown reunion
   40  Nov  5 Mr. O. Zone     (1,301) O3 for sale
   41  Nov  6 Joe BMUG        (1,650) BBB: Guide or Desert?
N  42  Nov  7 beaver clever    (553) Email: Bah humbug!
N  43  Nov  7 Elvis Presley    (902) Heartbreak Hotel
N  44  Nov  7 Babe Ruth      (14,799) How to hit home runs


Folder to save message in ["saved-messages"] : bozo-messages
^G Help       ^C Abort
RETURN Enter  ^T To Fldrs
```

You will then be asked which folder you want to save the message in (the default is the folder called "saved-messages"). If you want to select another folder, you can either type its name, or you can browse the existing folder by typing (CTRL)T:

```
PINE 3.05      SAVE MESSAGE      Folder:inbox  Message 42 of 44

inbox          sent-mail        saved-messages  gas-liquid
interrupted-mail                mail.Z          mailcom
ong            sent-mail-oct-1992               supernet

? Help     C Cancel    - Prev Page      A Add         D Delete
S Save     L Print     SPACE Next Page   R Rename      W Where is
```

Using your cursor keys, you can select a folder and then perform various commands on it:

Command	What it does
A	Add a folder.
R	Rename a folder.
C	Cancel the save to folder command.
D	Delete a folder.
L	Print the folder.
S	Save the message in the folder (and mark it for deletion).
W	Find a string in a folder.

Replying to messages

By typing **R** from the Index menu, you can reply to a message:

```
PINE 3.05  MAIL INDEX     Folder:inbox  Message 42 of 44

  39  Nov  4 Bozo D. Clown   (1,204) Re: Clown reunion
  40  Nov  5 Mr. O. Zone     (1,301) O3 for sale
  41  Nov  6 Joe BMUG        (1,650) BBB: Guide or Desert?
N 42  Nov  7 beaver clever    (553) Email: Bah humbug!
N 43  Nov  7 Elvis Presley    (902) Heartbreak Hotel
N 44  Nov  7 Babe Ruth      (14,799) How to hit home runs

Include original message in Reply? (y/n) [n]:
? Help E Export Msg C Compose U Undelete T Take Addr  G Go to Fldr
O OTHER CMDS Z Sort Folder L Print X eXpunge  J Jump  W Where is
```

By typing **yes** to answer the prompt asking whether you want to include the message in your reply, you can quote from the sender's original message:

```
PINE 3.05   COMPOSE MESSAGE   Folder:inbox  44 Messages

To      : bozo@clown.harvard.edu
Cc      :
Attchmnt:
Subject : Re: Clown pictures for book!
----- Message Text -----

On Sat, 7 Nov 1992 bozo@clown.harvard.edu wrote:

> >I'd like your opinions about how to improve the book
> >
>     How about including a portfolio of clown pictures?
> Bozo D. Clown

Not so sure that most people could relate to that, sorry.

^G Get Help ^C Cancel ^R Read File ^Y Prev Pg  ^K Del Line
^O Postpone ^X Send   ^J Justify    ^W Where is ^V Next Pg
^U UnDel Lin^T To Spell
```

The following commands are available within the reply menu:

Command	What it does
(CTRL) C	Cancel the reply.
(CTRL) K	Delete a line.
(CTRL) O	Postpone the reply (do something else within **pine**).
(CTRL) R	Enclose a file with the reply.
(CTRL) T	Spell check the reply.
(CTRL) U	Undelete a line.
(CTRL) W	Search the message for a string.
(CTRL) Y	Go to the previous page of the message.
(CTRL) V	Go to the next page of the message.
(CTRL) X	Send the reply.

Replies to messages are automatically saved to the **sent-mail** folder.

Forwarding messages

By typing **F** from the Index menu, you can forward a message:

```
PINE 3.05  COMPOSE MESSAGE    Folder:inbox  44 Messages

To     : aboba@foo.com
Cc     : Bernard.Aboba@f445.n161.z1.fidonet.org
Attchmnt:
Subject : Suggestions for BBB (fwd)
----- Message Text -----
---------- Forwarded message ----------
Date: Sat, 7 Nov 92 14:31:12 EST
From: Bozo <Bozo@clown.harvard.edu>
To: aboba@world.std.com
Subject: Suggestions for BBB

I think the book would be greatly improved by adding pictures of clowns. I have some
beautiful 4 color clown photographs that would enhance the book immensely.

^G Get Help ^C Cancel    ^R Read File^Y Prev Pg  ^K Del Line
^O Postpone ^X Send      ^J Justify  ^W Where is ^V Next Pg
^U UnDel Lin^T To Spell
```

If you like, you can attach a file to the forwarded message, move addresses into the address book, or delete characters or entire lines.

Other Index Menu

As with the Main Menu, the Index Menu also has an alternate set of commands. You can view these by typing **o** for Other:

```
PINE 3.05  MAIL INDEX     Folder:inbox  Message 42 of 44

   39 Nov  4 Bozo D. Clown  (1,204) Re: Clown reunion
   40 Nov  5 Mr. O. Zone    (1,301) O3 for sale
   41 Nov  6 Joe BMUG       (1,650) BBB: Guide or Desert?
 N 42 Nov  7 beaver clever! (553) Email: Bah humbug!
 N 43 Nov  7 Elvis Presley  (902) Heartbreak Hotel
 N 44 Nov  7 Babe Ruth      (14,799) How to hit home runs

? Help  E Export Msg  C Compose   U Undelete   T Take Addr
G Go to Fldr          O OTHER CMDS Z Sort Folder L Print
X eXpunge             J Jump       W Where is
```

By using your up and down cursor keys, you can select individual mail messages, and then perform operations on them, as with the regular Index menu. These operations are:

Command	What it does
E	Export a message to a file.
L	Print the message.
U	Undelete a message marked for deletion.
W	Find a word within the message.

There are also other commands that you can use:

Command	What it does
?	Context-sensitive help
C	Start a new message (instead of replying).
T	Add address to address book.
J	Jump to another message.
G	Examine another mail folder.
Z	Sort the messages.

Searching a message

Within a long message, it can be useful to be able to search for a given string. This can be done by selecting **W** from the Other Index menu:

```
PINE 3.05  MAIL INDEX     Folder:inbox  Message 42 of 44

     39  Nov  4 Bozo D. Clown  (1,204) Re: Clown reunion
     40  Nov  5 Mr. O. Zone    (1,301) O3 for sale
     41  Nov  6 Joe BMUG       (1,650) BBB: Guide or Desert?
  N  42  Nov  7 beaver clever  (553) Email: Bah humbug!
  N  43  Nov  7 Elvis Presley  (902) Heartbreak Hotel
  N  44  Nov  7 Babe Ruth      (14,799) How to hit home runs

Word to search for [] :
^G Help         ^C Abort
RETURN Enter
```

Operating on folders

Pine operates on mail folders. These folders include the **inbox**, which is the folder that includes incoming mail, the **sent-mail** folder, which includes messages that you send, and any other folders that you create with the **Save** command. To read the messages in one of the folders into **pine**, select **G** from the **Other Index** menu. You will then be given a menu of folders to open:

Address books

Pine can save addresses into an address book. To do this, first select a message, then type **T**:

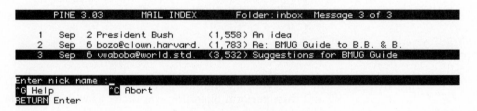

UNIX Q&A

How come UNIX gurus all seem to have long hair and beards?

Prior to learning UNIX, many of these individuals sported crew cuts and were clean shaven. This indicates that UNIX may have potential as an antibaldness remedy. Rumor has it that Novell is planning to play up this angle in its marketing efforts against Windows NT.

I just found out that my UNIX host was letting my files be read by other users. How do I put a stop to this?

If you insert the command **umask 077** in your .cshrc file, you will no longer be creating files with the wrong default. However, you will still have to change the permissions on your old files. You'll need the **chmod** command for this.

chmod

The form of the **chmod** command is:

```
chmod <privilege mask>
```

What the @#$@#% is a privilege mask? The UNIX world divides users into owners, members of your group, and others. Within a corporation, a group might be defined as members of a workgroup, and other users might be anyone in the company.

The privilege mask is constructed of three digits, specifying the privilege level for owners, group members, and others, from left to right. The levels of access implied by the various digits are:

Mask	Privileges implied
1	Execute privileges.
2	Write privileges.
4	Read privileges.
5	Read and Execute privileges.
6	Read and Write privileges.
7	Read, Write, and Execute privileges.

You must have privilege level 1, 5, or 7 set if you wish to execute a binary file or shell script. Levels 4 and 5 will let you read a file, but not modify it. Here are some examples of possible masks, and what they do:

Mask	What it does
700	Allows owner to read, write, and execute; doesn't let anyone else do anything to it (for executable binaries or shell scripts).
710	Allows owner to read, write, and execute; lets members of the group execute, but nothing else.
711	Lets owner read, write, and execute; lets group or anyone else execute.
600	Allows owner to read and write; doesn't let anyone else do anything to it.
640	Allows owner to read and write; lets group read the file; others can't get access.
660	Allows owner to read and write; lets group read and write; others can't get access.

In addition to ensuring proper permissions on individual files and directories, make sure that the execute right on your parent directory is disabled for groups and others to prevent people from getting any information on your files.

My Internet service provider gave me SLIP access, but I can't get access to an NNTP or POP server, and no one else seems to be able to reach my node. What's going on?

Serial Line Internet Protocol (SLIP) access is virtually useless unless your system is entered into routing tables so that other sites can send packets to you. If you intend to access sites outside of your local or regional network, then you will need to be cleared for routing over the NSFNet backbone, or a commercial backbone such as CIX. Before your node can be entered into the NSFNet routing tables, your regional network must forward your IP address onto NSFNet, indicating that you are cleared under the NSFNet Acceptable Use Policy (AUP). You may need to request access to NNTP and POP, possibly for an additional fee. If your provider won't give you access, get another provider.

How can you find out whether your site offers NNTP, or whether there is a problem with your newsreader? As we discuss on the next page, you can use the `telnet` command to connect to your site's NNTP server.

Help! We can't get sendmail to work. What should we do?

Like many other things in telecommunications, the way to get **sendmail** to work is to find someone who's got it working, and copy them. Two `sendmail.cf` files were included in BBB2, the second update to the first edition of this book. BBB2 is available on CompuServe, AOL, and the Internet (**ftp sumex-aim.stanford.edu, /info-mac/reports**). One file was written for a UUCP-only connection, where the local host's name is within the provider's domain; the other for a TCP/IP connection with its own domain name.

For more information

USENET newsgroups

comp.unix.bsd	BSD UNIX for Vax, PC, Sun, DEC, etc.
comp.unix.pc-clone	Versions of UNIX running on PC-compatible hardware
comp.unix.msdos	DOS under UNIX
comp.unix.aux	Apple's A/UX
comp.unix.aix	IBM's AIX
comp.unix.questions	UNIX questions
comp.unix.shell	UNIX shell programming
comp.unix.sys5.r3	System VR3
comp.unix.sys5.r4	System VR4
comp.unix.sys5.misc	Miscellaneous System V material
comp.unix.ultrix	DEC Ultrix

APPENDIX G:
GRAPHICAL BBSES

The house that GUI built

ONENET BBSES

As of June 17, 1993

BBS	Location	Phone Number	Sysop
Electronic Pen	Harrington Park,NJ,USA	(201)767-6337	Maria Langer
Foggy Bottom	Washington DC,USA	(202)337-2368	Rob Albriton
Kamilche Mac BBS	Shelton,WA,USA	(206)426-3262	Kevin & Cindy Carney
DBug ExChange	Seattle,WA,USA	(206)624-8783	Joseph McAllister
MacAct	Univ. of Maine,Orono,ME,USA	(207)381-6114	James M. Gray II
Slice of the Apple	New York,NY,USA	(212)722-7788	J.P. Flaherty
MacRoMouse	Dallas,TX,USA	(214)739-0645	Bob Winingham
Panther Tracks	Midlothian,TX,USA	(214)775-1757	Morris Watson
Starline	Philidelphia,PA,USA	(215)635-2341	Jason Erlich
Feats Imagic	Highland,IN,USA	(219)923-6804	Robert R. Reed
Rad Insp	Rockville,MD,USA	(301)309-1808	Steve Schulin
OneNet Boulder	Boulder,CO,USA	(303)444-7569	Chuck Polisher
Acme Acres	Denver CO,USA	(303)740-7429	
Magic Denver	Denver CO, USA	(303)791-8732	Steve Sande
Black Gold BBS	Gillette,WY,USA	(307)686-7213	Malcolm Shepard
Servant Christian	Redondo Beach,CA,USA	(310)371-2770	Douglas Wade
South Bay	Redondo Beach,CA,USA	(310)376-2150	Kirk Crawford
Mac-HACers	Torrence,CA,USA	(310)549-9640	Bud Grove
Middle Earth	Anaheim,CA,USA	(310)865-4189	Eric Azarcon
Chicago Machine	Chicago,IL,USA	(312)233-9607	Bob Wagner
Insane Domain	Chicago,IL,USA	(312)274-9515	Susan & Aaron Yelton
TROU	Chicago,Il,USA	(312)871-2177	Michael Zastrow
L'AISON	Beverly Hills,MI,USA	(313)647-2634	Jim Hebert
UltraMac	St. Louis,MO,USA	(314)965-0119	Gerry McManama
HCN	Wichita,KS,USA	(316)683-5211	Robert Sporleder
MacPac	Anderson,IN,USA	(317)640-1248	Dave Benit
BayouMac	Shreveport,LA,USA	(318)797-9946	Norris Carden
OMUG Online	Omaha,NE,USA	(402)293-8021	Pete Bates
Lime BBS	Lincoln,NE,USA	(402)435-7378	Patrick Benner
Pathways	Atlant,Ga,USA	(404)920-6571	Vann Baker
Crumal's Dimension	Santa Clara,CA,USA	(408)246-7854	Great Crumal
Positive Image	San Jose,CA,USA	(408)270-8916	John A. Kraenkel
City Connection	San Jose,CA,USA	(408)272-4185	Robert A Kim
Digital Café	Campbell,CA,USA	(408)364-2234	Bruce Gay
Casa Del Cyborg	Santa Cruz,CA,USA	(408)457-2595	Curtis Feigel
IGUANA	Sunnyvale,CA,USA	(408)733-8626	Hank Mollenauer
CyberMac BBS	Baltimore,MD,USA	(410)668-3903	Tim Waire
Laughing Dragon	Columbia,MD,USA	(410)730-5846	Chris Ott
Mac for the Mind	Pittsburgh,PA,USA	(412)661-6120	Davin Flateau
NetRunner	Milwaukee,WI,USA	(414)332-5910	John Hirsch
Metropolis	Milwaukee,WI,USA	(414)783-7667	Peter Flesses
D-Mac	Milwaukee,WI,USA	(414)962-3622	Jim Macak
Global Village	Mountain View,CA,USA	(415)390-8334	John MacWilliamson
OneNet LosAltos	Los Altos,CA,Usa	(415)948-1349	Scott Converse
Public BBS	Half Moon Bay,CA,USA	(415)948-1349	Leonard Chung
Dead Dog Party	Mountain View,CA,USA	(415)968-7919	Nick Chinn
MAGIC	Toronto,ON,Can	(416)288-1767	Mark S. Windrim
The Newsroom	Toronto,ON	(416)444-3361	
CMAC	Toronto,ON,Can	(416)462-2922	Mike Shales
SoftArcOnline	Scarborough,ON,Can	(416)609-2250	SoftArc INC.

BBS	Location	Phone Number	Sysop
CNCI BBS	Toronto,ON,Can	(416)761-1894	Greg Agostinelli
Deep Blue	Richmond Hills,ON,Can	(416)883-9670	Robert Matthews
Voice in the Wilderness	Portland,OR,USA	(503)239-5958	Doug Dumont
MacUniverse	Portland,OR,USA	(503)240-1022	Andrea Scasso
Network 23	Portland,OR, USA	(503)246-1711	Jeff Nichols
Excelsior	Eugene,OR,USA	(503)343-1591	Casey Pilkenton
BendNet/COMUG	Bend,OR,USA	(503)385-3332	Spencer Dahl
Headquarters	Salem,OR,USA	(503)588-6528	Al McMahen
Mac Aloha	Aloha,OR,USA	(503)591-5695	George Clark
Borderline BBS	Springfield,OR,USA	(503)746-5021	Bob Haggin
GreyLand	Springfield,OR,USA	(503)747-6098	Steve Ebener
The Safe House	Ontario,OR,USA	(503)881-1733	Pat Plummer
MCW BBS	New Orleans,LA,USA	(504-837-7984	Bob Nordling
Conspiracy BBS	Hopedale,MA,USA	(508)478-1714	Paul Brady
North Shore Mac	Beverly,MA,USA	(508)921-4716	Johnathan Gourd
MACS BBS	Spokane,WA,USA	(509)326-9307	Darrell McDowell
VIZability	Walnut Creek,CA,USA	(510)210-0800	Dan Schwam
Macrocosm	Livermore,CA,USA	(510)449-1648	Randy Syester
Planet BMUG	Berkeley,CA,USA	(510)849-2684	Steve Costa
DesignLink	Walnut Creek,CA,USA	(510)933-9676	Ash Mehta
Productivity Online	Cincinnati,OH,USA	(513)723-4444	Rick Derringer
IAMUG Info Server	Des Moines,IA,USA	(515)274-9309	Mike Pester
Ender BBS	Great Neck,NY,USA	(516)829-1620	Tim Dillof
MNS Online	Schenectedy,NY,USA	(518)381-4430	Don Rittner
Nexus	London,On,Can	(519)473-7584	Brian Wiltshire
MVCUG	Sierra Vista,AZ,USA	(602)458-9560	John Buono
Falcon's Nest	Phoenix,AZ,USA	(602)581-7827	Gary McSpadden
Tucson Apple Corps	Tucson,AZ,USA	(602)882-2945	Lee Steffeck
AMUG OnNet	Phoenix AZ, USA	(602)946-3780	Alan Heflich
Gate City Striders	Nashua,NH,USA	(603)888-5477	Allan Rube
Community Memory	Vancouver,BC,Can	(604)278-1849	Dann Porter
Breez	Vancouver,BC,Canada	(604)682-8884	Dom Giovanangelli
The Revelation	North Vancouver,BC,Canada	(604)929-1615	Chris Holmes
Sunshine	Tswassen,BC,Canada	(604)943-1612	Bob Cotter
EdgeWays!	North Vancouver,BC,Canada	(604)984-2777	Bob M. Grahame
Autobahn	Ithaca,NY,USA	(607)256-7595	
Memory Alpha	Ithaca,NY,USA	(607)257-5822	Mark H. Anbinder
Information Electronics	Hammondsport,NY,USA	(607)868-3393	Jeff Parker
MacLine	Madison,WI,USA	(608)233-9487	John Allen
The Graphic Building	Minneapolis, MN, USA	(612)425-5265	Robert Jacobs
Allegro	St Paul,MN,USA	(612)487-0947	
Twin City Mac	Minneapolis,MN,USA	(612)822-4122	Richard Potter
Free Thought	Minneapolis,MN, USA	(612)827-6715	Stewart DeVaan
MacFred's	Battle Creek,MI	(616)964-1594	Fred Rainer
4th Dimension	Cambridge,MA,USA	(617)494-0565	
Reflections	Swampscott,MA,USA	(617)593-7228	Bill Reed
BMUG Boston	Boston,MA,USA	(617)721-5840	
RTJ Corp	Waltham,MA,USA	(617)890-8968	Franco Ruggeri
A1EZOK BBS	San Diego CA, USA	(619)693-1575	
Winter Tree	Fargo,ND,USA	(701)234-9420	Robert Wade
SoundNiche	Fairfax,VA,USA	(703)631-5892	Scott D. Cherkofsky
Digital Nation	Alexandria,VA,USA	(703)642-0453	Scot Mandel
Multum In Parvo	Centervile,VA,USA	(703)803-8714	Ted Lesley
Smuggler's BBS	Eureka,CA,USA	(707)445-5962	Paul Reinauer
Byte of the Apple	Benecia,CA,USA	(707)747-0306	Greg Phillips
Terra-X	Sebastapol,CA,USA	(707)823-0416	Rich Mathes
INNOVATORS' BBS	Vernon Hills,IL,USA	(708)918-1231	Winston Tsao
MacLair	Houston,TX,USA	(713)286-5866	Jordan Bean
Mac Central	Houston TX, USA	(713)452-2193	John Dial
Byte Brothers	Mission Viejo,CA,USA	(714)582-5966	Rick R. Vink
ImagiNet	Irvine,CA,USA	(714)660-7738	Doug Nottage
Phoenix Rising	Rochester,NY,USA	(716)429-7635	Ed Reppert
Tyrell	Rochester,NY,USA	(716)461-1301	JF Sebastian
MacGallery	Wrightsville,PA,USA	(717)252-3227	Wayne C. Jaeschke
Malacandra	Colorado Springs,CO,USA	(719)522-0461	Karl Armstrong
Adrenaline Online	Charlotte,VT,USA	(802-)425-2332	
MacInternational	Columbia,SC,USA	(803-798-3755	Ralph Yount
Foundation:Network	Newhall,CA,USA	(805)255-7237	Rölf Quam
CVMUG	Simi Valley,CA, USA	(805)584-0122	Ken Sedlacek
MacMagic	Santa Barbara,CA,USA	(805)682-1737	Ron Luna
ROLNET	Lancaster,CA,USA	(805)948-4900	Wayne Walker

BBS	Location	Phone Number	Sysop
MacDaze	Santa Barbara,CA,USA	(805)964-6320	Bob Murrow
Gooey BBS	Simi Valley,CA,USA	(805)986-1216	Dave Burns
MauiLink	Wailuku,HI,USA	(808)877-6028	Keola Donaghy
BerMug	Pembroke,Bermuda	(809)292-2405	Rolf C. Martin
Crabbs	Pembroke,Bermuda	(809)295-2953	Richard K. (Dick) Butz
Meridian	Sarasota,FL,USA	(813-359-8077	Stuart Andrews
Tropical Bytes BBS	Bartow,FL,USA	(813)667-2025	Dan Smart
The NET	Rockford,IL,USA	(815)968-4729	Chris Weickert
Rainforest	Kansas City,MO,USA	(816)761-0582	Jeff Justice
AppleCorpsDallas	Dallas,TX,USA	(817)355-9363	
LoneStar Mac	Ft Worth,TX,USA	(817)370-2827	Henry Wolanski
SanGabriel Valley MUG	La Cañada,CA,USA	(818)790-3037	Bob Langdon
MacValley OnLine	Burbank,CA,USA	(818)840-0518	Paul W. Hampton
ENet	La Cañada,CA,USA	(818)952-0322	Jim Morrissett
The Drawing Board	Hacienda Heights,CA,USA	(818)965-6241	Char Rice
PowerBoard	Gainesville,FL,USA	(904)336-9501	Alan Lara
Chatterbox	Pensacola,FL,USA	(904)455-7194	Mark Pappas
Mosquito Coast	Ft .Walton Beach,FL,USA	(904)651-3227	Ed A. Sullivan
MacPUBB	Anchorage,AK,USA	(907)563-4735	Richard Mehner
NJMUG	Clark,NJ,USA	(908)388-1676	Mike Bielen
UltraFlight	Somerset,NJ,USA	(908)545-5255	Doug Vetter
Castle Tabby	Bradley Beach,NJ,USA	(908)988-0706	Michael Connick
Gentle Rain	Claremont,CA,USA	(909)593-6144	Richard Truit
Guerilla Symbiotics	La Verne,CA,USA	(909)593-6862	Marvin Price
The Alternative	Topeka,KS,USA	(913)233-1576	Matt Garlinghouse
Mosaic	New York, NY, USA	(914)896-5547	Bob Iannucci
MacShasta	Mt. Shasta,CA,USA	(916)926-4854	Rich Renouf
Native Voices Online	Tulsa,OK,USA	(918)660-0677	Al Webster
Creates Online	Fuji City,Japan	+81-545-53-01618	Fumihide Uchino
SWITCH Online	Lausanne,Switzerland	41211564321	Dian Cuendet-Lewis
Mactivity Venlo	Venlo,Netherlands	+31 (0)77-544384	Henk Hodiamont
Mactivity Büllingen	Bullingen,Belgium	+32 80 647 363	Joe Savelberg
Ellis	Paris, France	+33 147745777	Bruno Dassas
SoloMac Barcelona	Barcelona,Spain	+34 38126172	Alberto Lozano
TransEurope Express	Coimbra,Portugal	+351 39 721 932	
PEBA Graphics Box	Helsinki,Finland	+358 0739989	Peter Björknäs
ON-MAC	Eugendorf,Austria	+43 622589220	Oliver Dick
MacTel_HQ_Iconex	Iconex,UK	+44 602 455417	David Nicholson Cole
MacTel_Metro	London,UK	+44 81 5438019	
The Publishing Shop	Newcastle-upon-Tyne,UK	+44 91 2615228	Roger Booth
Mac-On-Line Denmark	Aalborg,Danmark	+45 98110098	Steen Hestehave
MacForum	Oslo,Norway	+47 2 460213	
Tordensoft Mac BBS	Spikkestad,Norway	+47 31284305	Johnny Gledden
MacInSand	Kristiansand,Norway	+47 4225573	Christian Bjørnerud
INTERZONE	Bochum,Germany	+49 23 4 431150	Fritze von Berswordt
PDMacS_Berlin	Berlin,Germany	+49 30 2625908	Peter Richter
NightMail BBS	Kiel,Germany	+49 43 1 665899	Jens Wallenhorst
DISCUSS	Oldenburg,Germany	+49 44 1 884090	Christian Vollheide
PDMacS_Freiburg	Freiburg,Germany	+49 7633 500040	Daniel Richardy
ChatWorks_MUC	Munich,Germany	+49 89496041	Christoph Henkel
PDMacS_Wuerzburg	Wuerzburg,Germany	+49 931783919	Klaus Scheuerecker
MacAsean	Ukay Heights,Malaysia	+60 3 452 6196	Chunhung Wan
MOOV	Tokyo, Japan	+81 3 5485-7582	Keiki Usui
J-Link	Toyohashi City, Japan	+81 5 3255-7773	John Keegan
Uptown 411	Wanchai,Hong Kong	+852 527 6361	Gilbert Chan
Mackey Mouse	Taipei,Taiwan	+886-2-3627273	Chester Lin
BMUG/OneNet Boston (R,G)	Braintree,MA,USA	Gateway Only	
Bradley Group	Hollywood,CA,USA	not open yet	Lance Mazmanian
BreadNet	Middlebury,VT,USA	Private	David Herren
Color Magic	Mt .View,CA,USA	Private	Brian M. Monroe
Electric Sheep	Portland,OR,USA	Private	Jeff Thorns
FC Slime	Mountain View,CA,USA	Private	Steve Fransen
IR/PS BBS	UC SanDiego,CA,USA	private	Gary Hoffman
Orent Graphics	Omaha,NE,USA	Private	Dave Caplinger
The Purple Shirt	Jackson,MI,USA	Private	Shawn Fitzgerald
The Turnaroud Team	Westfield,NJ,USA	Private	Mike Bielen
WonderNet	Vancouver,BC,Canada	private	Martin L'Heureux
RALPH	Calgary,AB,Can		Rus Hathaway
SoloMac Madrid	Madrid,Spain		
The BOARD BBS	Troy,MI,USA		

TELEFINDER BBSES

As of January 19, 1993

BBS	Sysop	Phone number	Modem requirements
NJ MacLaw BBS	Stuart Kurtzer	(201)235-0121	2400 bps
EssexLink BBS	Ed Edell	(201)773-1177	14,400 bps Hayes Optima
V M E G B B S	Evette Ogden	(209)732-8634	2400 bps
Avalon Mac BBS FidoNet 1:233/14	Santi Zorzopulos	(217)337-0764	2400 bps
Narnia BBS FidoNet 1:233/11	Russ Jacobson	(217)384-3128	14,400 bps V.32/V.32*bis* V.42*bis*
MAGIC BBS	Steven Sande	(303)791-8732	9600 bps V.32/V.42*bis*
Mikie's	Mike Savu	(313)477-9652	9600 bps USR DS
MacGroup-Detroit BBS	Terry White	(313)557-0759 (313)557-2229	9600 bps V.32
MacLinjat BBS (Finland)	Jyrki Nuotio	358-0-5072752	
M.O.U.S.E.	Ken Manke	(403)430-0774	9600 bps USR DS
Mac Asylum BBS	Michael Moore	(405)943-6154 (405)943-6156	2400 bps
PBMUG BBS	Norm Argus	(407)642-6972	9600 bps
The French Connection FidoNet 1:143/227	Barry Dryden	(408)266-8702	Intel14.400EX V.32/V.42*bis*
Baltimore Color Plate	Randy Dorman	(410)391-2029	9600 bps V.32
BayView MUG BBS	Mark Fleming	(410)893-9881	9600 bps V.32/V.42/ V.42*bis*
Club Mac of Kentuckiana	Bill Pittman	(502)458-7666	2400 and 9600 HST
Electronic CMUG	Charles Kuttner	(503)752-4835	
WMUG BBS FidoNet 1:322/115	Chris Silverberg	(508)832-5844	9600 bps, V.32*bis*?
Mid Columbia MUG	Larry Syverson	(509)943-6174	9600 V.32/V.42*bis*

Appendix G: Graphical BBSes

The Peanut Gallery BBS	Mike Sugarbaker	(510)525-6667	2400 bps
WORLDVIEW BBS	Bill Gram-Reefer	(510)676-2919	2-line 14,400 and CSP
Rehabilitation BBS	Tom Hinson	(513)429-4096	2400 and 9600 HST
Iowa Macintosh BBS	Nurudin S. Javeri	(515)225-0003	
Mississippi Online 6 PM - 7 AM CT weekdays	Jerry Salley 24 hours, weekends	(601)627-9029	2400 bps
The Garden Under **the Bridge**	Jason Leach	(604)376-7254	2400 bps
Byte Powerline	Rolf Drommer	(606)738-1302	
Club Mac of Australia FidoNet 3:712/406	John Agapitos	(612)314-1322	9600 bps 4 lines
DTP Exchange FidoNet 1:282/61	Chuck Bjorgen	(612)633-8406	14,400 bps V.32*bis*-PEP
M.O.B. Scene	Michael L. Hale	(616)949-8783	2400 bps
MACaroni! BBS	Brian Spence	(619)592-9026	2400 bps
ASTEC BBS	Rod Paine	(703)338-6025	9600 bps Hayes Ultra
NCMUG BBS	David Fowler	(707)792-1871	9600 bps Hayes Ultra
Beezodog's Place BBS FidoNet 1:115/668	Eric Vann	(708)668-8287	14,400 bps V.32*bis* 14,400 bps Hayes Ultra
Spider Island	Rusty Tucker	(714)730-5785	9600 and 14,400 bps?
The Library BBS 24 hours	Frank English Guest Access	(717)566-1699 CD-ROM access ($15/year)	2400 bps soon V.32
The Veil of Illusion	Don Mayer	(802)496-9330	
The Sand Box (TARMac BBS), FidoNet 1:275/29	Rod McCormack	(804)490-1426	2400 bps
The Caribbean Breeze FidoNet: 1:367/12; RBBS Net 8:999/8 (6 PM to 8:30 AM weekdays; 24 hours weekends and holidays)	Doug Canton	(809)773-0195 (809)773-3784	24 hours ,v.32*bis* 9600 bps Hayes Ultra
Florida OnLine	Robert F. Donahue	(813)586-2084	
TAMU BBS	Rodney Hendricks	(903)597-6560	HST-V.32-V42*bis*-MNP
Texarkana Apple Byters	Greg Saulsburg	(903)832-6836	9600 bps Hayes Ultra
1st Coast BBS	Doug Rowe	(904)388-5275	2400 bps
Sacramento TeleFinder FidoNet 1:203/932	Bill Davies	(916)452-4844	14,400 bps V.32*bis*
MacNexus Main BBS FidoNet 1:203/933	Stan Lunetta 5 lines	(916)455-3726	14,400 bps V.32*bis*
Tulsa Users of Mac Society FidoNet 1:170/404	David Down (6 CDs online)	(918)234-5000	9600 bps, V.32,42*bis*

AppleSeeds (RMUG) 24 hours FidoNet 1:151/152	Paul Lemieux	(919)481-4896 (919)469-5867	US Robotics HST Dual Std. 2400 bps max.
SPIDER (Delft, Holland)	Roel Wigboldus and Hans Haakman	+31 15 158300 (multiline)	14,400 bps max.DTE 57.6
Mastermind BBS (Japan)	Glenn Wright	0292-48-6836	9600 bps
MiC MAC LiNK (France)	Michel Coste	+33-140-910505	9600 bps Hayes Ultra
Theseus Telefinder BBS (France)	Tim Stellery	+33-929-45165	
Apple Domain Board (Milan, Italy)	Gianluca Sordiglioni	+39-2-861858	HST DS
Box 4 Modems reachable only inside Switzerland on ISDN (using LeoTalk/TheLink and NetConect)	Andreas Fink	156 35 25 +41 32 50 12 50	14,400 bps 64K
FrameWORX TF Host	John Woolley	+44-624-663759	38,400 bps V.42*bis*,
Mac-On-Line (4 lines)	Steen Hestehave	+45-98-110098	14,400 bps
Dansk MacUserserService Bulletin Board System FidoNet 2:230/121 (Denmark)	Willy Gronhoj +45-86-915202	+45-86-915080 9600 Hayes Ultra	USR HST
Mac Exchange BBS FidoNet 2:203/211 (Sweden)	Mikael Fredriksson +46-031-948295	+46-031-948290	5 lines V.32/V.32*bis*
MacCity BBS	Hamish Bowly	+61 2 660 2027	
MacConnection Sydney, Australia FidoNet 3:714/914	Brian Macdonald 3 lines	+612-907-9198	PSI COMstation 5 14,400 V.32*bis*
MacInTouch BBS (Sydney, Australia)	Jason Haines	011-61-2-743-5997	14,400 bps V.32*bis*
ADB - rseau (France)	Thierry Liotard	+76 62 73 06	
TransSoft BBS (Belgium)		(091) 20-49-49	

APPENDIX H:
NETWORK BBSES

EchoMac Nodes as of July 23, 1993

FidoNet node #	MacList node #	Phone #	Speed	BBS name	MSDN node
1:2606/203		(201)293-7778	9600	Shadow Spawn BBS,Montague,NJ	
1:2606/202		(201)398-1133	9600	Microcosm BBS,Hopatcong,NJ	
1:2604/101		(201)612-0559	9600	The Hourglass BBS,Ridgewood,NJ	MSDN
1:2605/157	6:6001/9	(201)767-6337	9600	The Electronic Pen B,Harrington Park,NJ	MSDN
1:107/839		(201)798-0065	9600	Computer Connections,Hoboken,NJ	
1:2604/369	6:6001/1	(201)941-7778	9600	The Rock Pile BBS,Ridgefield,NJ	
1:320/20		(203)659-4680	9600	MacTropolis BBS,Glastonbury,CT	
1:141/110		(203)663-1147	9600	The Hub,Killingworth,CT	
1:142/500	6:6004/1	(203)763-3485	9600	The Earth Network,Enfield,CT	
1:3625/467		(205)479-2327	9600	The Intrepid BBS,Mobile,AL	
1:343/81		(206)524-4811	9600	Letters RBBS,Seattle,WA	
1:138/131		(206)565-8853	2400	The right place,Tacoma,WA	
1:138/107		(206)582-9393	2400	Techno Mikey's Shop,Steilacoom,WA	
1:343/31	6:6007/3	(206)725-6629	9600	SEA/MAC,Seattle,WA	
1:343/53		(206)771-8420	9600	Bermuda Triangle BBS,Lynwood,WA	
1:352/11		(206)943-1513	9600	Radio Point BBS,Olympia,WA	
1:132/301		(207)942-7803	9600	Bangor ROS,Bangor,ME	
1:347/37		(208)832-1156	9600	Mac's Mess, Mountain Home AFB	
1;396/69	6:6018/3	(210)546-4812	9600	The Lyceum,Brownsville,TX	
1:102/851		(213)256-8371	9600	Central Computer Ban,Los Angeles, CA	
1:102/754		(213)874-0809	9600	CPMacintosh,Los Angeles,CA	
1:124/1208		(214)250-4479	2400	MacSavvy, Dallas, TX	
1:124/4210		(214)522-1336	9600	HARDWIRED,Dallas,TX	
1:273/203		(215)357-5963	9600	SiSystems,Huntingdon Valley,PA	
1:273/907		(215)535-5816	9600	Tower BBS,Philadelphia,PA	
1:273/721	6:6009/5	(215)743-8779	9600	Proteus	
1:2607/403		(215)779-1259	9600	Macatastrophe,Reading,PA	
1:273/702		(215)884-6122	9600	Rydal Board,Rydal,PA	
1:157/511		(216)273-1340	9600	Appleholic's BBS,Hinckley,OH	
1:157/531		(216)453-9595	9600	Massillon TeleNet,Massillon,OH	
1:157/701		(216)869-5750	9600	NEO Apple Akron,Akron,OH	
1:157/700		(216)942-3389	9600	NEO Apple Cleveland,Cleveland,OH	
1:227/2		(219)287-4326	9600	Michiana Computer Ne,South Bend,IN	
1:109/426		(301)258-7763	2400	Coffee Club BB,Germantown,MD	
1:261/1053		(410)315-8532	2400	CRABBS,Annapolis,MD	
1:109/519		(301)924-0398	9600	Perspectives BBS,Greenbelt,MD	
1:109/716	6:6022/1	(301)946-3070	9600	The Twilight Clone,Rockville,MD	
1:104/207		(303)449-7274	9600	Chidvilas,Boulder,CO	
1:104/236		(303)526-2141	9600	MacCircles,Genesee,CO	
1:104/204		(303)753-9710	2400	Microlink-2,Denver,CO	
1:104/617	6:6020/2	(303)755-1004	9600	Fort Mac.Aurora,CO	
1:104/318		(303)973-1002	9600	Computer Consulting,Littleton,CO	
1:135/92	6:6032/1	(305)378-6828	9600	Sunshine Online Serv,Miami,FL	MSDN
1:369/35		(305)436-1085	9600	The InterZone Cafe,Pembroke Pines,F	
1:369/34		(305)572-7060	9600	Gammatown,Sunrise,FL	
1:369/15		(305)964-1896	9600	PROMEON,Hollywood,FL	
1:369/37		(305)987-7873	9600	Midnight BBS,Pembroke Pines,FL	
1:140/20		(306)777-4493	9600	Regina FIDO,Regina,Saskatchewan	
1:232/44		(309)745-5209	9600	Mac's Place,Peoria,IL	
1:102/132	6:6028/5	(310)376-2150	9600	Kirks BBS,Hermosa Beach,CA	

FidoNet node #	MacList node #	Phone #	Speed	BBS name	MSDN node
1:102/522		(310)391-1351	9600	MicroSource,Mar Vista,CA	
1:115/689		(312)935-6809	9600	BIT WIZ Opus,Chicago,IL	
1:2240/173		(313)239-8004	9600	The Association Mac,Grand Blanc,MI	
1:2240/175		(313)695-6744	9600	The Association Mac,Grand Blanc,MI	
1:2240/174		(313)695-6955	9600	The Association Mac,Grand Blanc,MI	
1:100/490		(314)776-6711	9600	Big Mac Attack][, Creve Coeur, MO	
1:260/615		(315)597-3439	9600	Scolasticom,Palmyra,NY	
1:260/328	6:6030/2	(315)695-4436	9600	Galaxia!,Phoenix,NY	
1:231/480		(317)290-1762	9600	MacConnections,Indianapolis,IN	
1:231/760		(317)640-1248	9600	MacPack BBS, Anderson, IN	
1:283/657		(319)337-9878	9600	Icarus,Iowa City,IA	
1:363/1701		(407)249-1701	9600	NCC-1701,Orlando,FL	
1:374/3		(407)269-2169	9600	Space Coast BBS,Titusville,FL	
1:363/77		(407)323-0025	2400	411 The Information,Sanford,FL	
1:374/73		(407)383-9372	9600	The Bear's Cave,Titusville,FL	
1:363/7		(407)699-1358	2400	Abacus Info Center,Altamonte Spgs.,FL	
1:143/207		(408)738-1119	9600	Sunnyvale Fido Conne,Sunnyvale,CA	
1:261/1047		(410)536-1935	2400	MD State Fireman's A,Catonsville,MD	
1:261/1044		(410)866-8613	9600	The Fire Station,Baltimore,MD	
1:129/120		(412)661-6120	9600	Mac For The Mind,Pittsburgh,PA	
1:321/218		(413)443-6725	9600	K12Net Mail Server,Lanesboro,MA	
1:321/307	6:6002/8	(413)532-1387	9600	The SPA,Springfield,MA	MSDN
1:321/302		(413)536-7526	2400	SpaceMet South 1,Holyoke,MA	
1:321/110		(413)545-4453	9600	Physics Forum,Amherst,MA	
1:321/301		(413)746-4772	9600	Apollo Systems TBBS,Springfield,MA	
1:321/152		(413)772-2030	2400	SpaceMet North 0,Greenfield,MA	
1:154/414		(414)352-6176	9600	Radio Free,Milwaukee,WI	
1:125/77		(415)467-8966	9600	Harv's Hideout,San Francisco,CA	
1:125/110		(415)589-5411	9600	Swizzle Stick,San Bruno, CA	
1:125/222	6:6005/4	(415)621-0567	9600	Macademe/Emma	MSDN
1:125/777		(415)765-0571	2400	NCFCC-KKSF,San Francisco,CA	
1:143/226		(415)961-4313	9600	Rabbits Foot BBS,Sunnyvale,CA	
1:250/210		(416)236-3125	9600	SomethingELSE,Etobicoke,ON	
1:250/416		(416)286-6191	9600	EGS/Philo,Toronto,ON	
1:250/250		(416)299-5380	9600	SoftArc Online, Scarborough, ON	
1:229/436		(416)436-2606	9600	The Daily Planet,Oshawa,ON	
1:284/29		(417)862-6976	9600	The Computer Matrix,Springfield,MO	
1:240/1		(418)523-3117	9600	SQUARE-HEADs,QuebecCity,PQ	
1:240/507		(418)648-9590	9600	Bab-O-Manie,Quebec,PQ	
1:105/67		(503)241-9641	2400	PMUG BBS, Portland, OR	
1:105/44		(503)286-2802	9600	Sea Breeze BBS II,Portland,OR	
1:152/102		(503)474-2354	9600	Public Data Network,Grants Pass,OR	
1:105/378		(503)591-5695	9600	Mac Aloha, Aloha, OR	
1:105/333		(503)648-6462	9600	Outlet BBS,Cornelius,OR	
1:396/5		(504)244-1417	9600	Pontchippi,New Orleans,LA	
1:301/4	6:6013/1	(505)891-3840	9600	The Call,Albuquerque,NM	
1:322/540		(508)393-5346	2400	Northway,Northborough,MA	
1:322/360		(508)429-8857	9600	Cul De Sac,Holliston,MA	
1:322/14		(508)481-7147	9600	WayStar,Marlborough,MA	
1:324/276		(508)694-9593	9600	Macintosh Realm BBS,Tewksbury,MA	
1:322/115	6:6002/6	(508)832-5844	9600	WMUG BBS,Auburn,MA	
1:346/6		(509)924-5364	9600	Macs BBS,Spokane,WA	
1:347/12		(509)966-8555	2400	Acey BBS,Yakima,WA	
1:161/42		(510)426-0793	9600	Records Department,Pleasanton,CA	
1:204/555		(510)795-8862	9600	MacInfo,Newark,CA	
1:161/703	6:6005/12	(510)831-8436	2400	Dear Theophilus	
1:382/12		(512)258-8831	9600	Austin Code Works,Austin,TX	
1:382/1		(512)335-7949	9600	Crystal Palace,Lake Travis,TX	
1:382/18		(512)471-7584	2400	UT School of Nursing,Austin,TX	
1:382/19		(512)835-4848	9600	Middle Earth,Austin,TX	
1:110/430	6:6026/1	(513)438-5542	9600	CURRENTS,Dayton,OH	MSDN
1:110/10		(513)439-9217	9600	Decker's Board	
1:108/89		(513)762-1115	9600	KIC-BBS,Cincinnati,OH	
1:167/290		(514)355-0091	9600	HexaCom Info Service,Montreal,PQ	
1:167/182	6:6033/1	(514)486-2536	2400	Quebec Online,Montreal,PQ	MSDN
1:167/165		(514)937-9984	9600	Electronic Image,Montreal,PQ	
1:290/2	6:6019/1	(515)279-3073	9600	The ZOO System,Des Moines,IA	
1:2619/244		(516)243-2953	9600	MacEcho BBS, Bayshore, NY	
1:159/950		(517)321-0788	9600	The Lighthouse BBS	
1:239/1004		(517)631-3481	9600	Wolverine,Midland,MI	

Appendix H: Network BBSes

FidoNet node #	MacList node #	Phone #	Speed	BBS name	MSDN node
1:221/109	6:6031/1	(519)672-7661	9600	Zynx Corporation,London,ON	
1:361/13		(601)634-1625	9600	The Southern Belle,Vicksburg,MS	
1:3632/6	6:6017/1	(601)992-9459	9600	MacHaven,Brandon,MS	
1:114/73		(602)241-0256	9600	Mac's Place,Phoenix,AZ	
1:114/56	6:6008/3	(602)553-0749	9600	AZ MAC UG,Phoenix,AZ	MSDN
1:114/18		(602)789-5088	9600	Iasd Eng BBS,Phoenix,AZ	
1:114/110	6:6008/6	(602)829-7522	2400	Kitty's Sandbox,Tempe,AZ	MSDN
1:114/20		(602)894-8762	9600	Construction Net 1,Phoenix,AZ	
1:114/53	6:6008/5	(602)947-0587	2400	AZ MAC UG 2,Scottsdale,AZ	MSDN
1:114/27	6:6008/1	(602)992-9879	9600	The Tiger's Den,Phoenix,AZ	MSDN
1:132/131		(603)228-0705	9600	Easy Does It,Bow,NH	
1:340/64		(604)388-4183	2400	Macintosh Way BBS, Victoria, BC	
1:153/915		(604)536-5889	9600	Deep Cove BBS,Surrey,BC	
1:153/104		(604)584-9811	9600	Basic'ly HST,Surrey,BC	
1:153/928		(604)948-0272	9600	Hoggs Hollow,Tsawwassen,BC	
1:121/6		(608)244-0852	2400	The Buyer's Review,Madison,WI	
1:282/24	6:6010/2	(612)426-6687	9600	MacRefuge,St. Paul,MN	
1:282/30		(612)537-8659	9600	The O-Zone BBS,New Hope,MN	
1:282/32		(612)624-4318	9600	University Of Minn.,Minneapolis,MN	
1:282/61		(612)636-7580	9600	DTP Exchange BBS,New Brighton,MN	
1:282/341		(612)721-8967	9600	Terraboard,Minneapolis,MN	
1:282/105	6:6010/1	(612)546-2490	9600	Walk In The Shadows,New Hope,MN	
1:282/37		(612)934-2982	2400	Beg Borrow Or Steal,St Louis Park,MN	
1:282/31		(612)938-8924	9600	Dark Knight's Table,Minnetonka,MN	
1:226/20		(614)475-0295	9600	cmhGate UF Gateway,Columbus,OH	
1:116/19		(615)383-0727	2400	The Nashville Exchange,Nashville,TN	
1:362/122		(615)843-3105	2400	MacChatter Mail System,Chattanooga,TN	
1:101/640		(617)356-0109	9600	BMUG Boston OneNet, Braintree, MA	
1:101/206		(617)472-8612	9600	Photo Talk BBS,Squantum,MA	
1:101/121		(617)621-0882	9600	BCS Info Center,Cambridge,MA	
1:101/470	6:6002/5	(617)698-8734	9600	Tom's BBS,Milton,MA	
1:101/312	6:6002/4	(617)965-6467	9600	BCS Mail Server,Newton,MA	
1:2222/528	6:6015/3	(618)549-1129	9600	Mac UnderGround Head,Carbondale,IL	MSDN
1:2222/530		(618)549-2005	2400	Mac UnderGround,Carbondale,IL	
1:2222/529		(618)549-6918	9600	Mac UnderGround,Carbondale,IL	
1:213/777		(702)359-6979	9600	Nevada Mac,Sparks,NV	
1:109/342	6:6012/4	(703)532-0317	9600	Craig's Place	
1:109/337		(703)264-9698	9600	Board on Boards,Reston,VA	
1:109/305		(703)323-3321	9600	NOVA BBS,Annandale,VA	
1:109/301		(703)323-7654	9600	The Systems Exchange,Fairfax,VA	
1:109/306		(703)358-9112	9600	Sara's Outpost,Arlington,VA	
1:109/302		(703)528-2522	9600	NGS/CIG,Arlington,VA	
1:109/303		(703)620-2827	2400	Scorpio Rising II,Reston,VA	
1:125/7		(707)545-0785	9600	Sonoma Online,Santa Rosa,CA	
1:115/295		(708)295-6926	9600	MACropedia BBS,Lake Forest,IL	
1:115/352	6:6015/5	(708)352-9282	9600	Mac-I-Nations,LaGrange,IL	
1:115/729	6:6015/1	(708)657-1113	9600	Spectrum MACInfo,Glenview,IL	
1:115/767		(708)980-1613	9600	ChicAAgo Hangar,Schaumburg,IL	
1:106/6268		(713)640-1298	9600	MacEndeavour,Houston,TX	MSDN
1:2613/256		(716)247-9056	2400	Mac's Last Stand,Rochester,NY	
1:260/228		(716)442-8144	9600	Concours Decouvertes,Rochester,NY	
1:260/620		(716)526-6495	9600	W-FL Teacher Resource,Stanley,NY	
1:260/204		(716)889-2016	9600	Flower City Central,Chili,NY	
1:278/706		(718)729-6101	9600	Dorsai Diplomatic Mission,Brooklyn,NY	
1:2603/204	6:6003/3	(718)997-1189	9600	Not Even Odd,Forrest Hills,NY	MSDN
1:325/202		(802)388-0025	9600	ACSU BBS,Middlebury,VT	
1:325/124	6:6023/2	(802)425-2332	2400	Adrenaline Online,Charlotte,VT	
1:325/107		(802)656-1182	9600	VT Education System,Hinesburg,VT	
1:360/1		(803)279-5006	9600	Augusta Forum North,Augusta,SC	
1:376/24	6:6014/1	(803)548-0900	9600	Fort Mill BBS,Fort Mill,SC	
1:372/13		(803)764-4917	9600	Steve,Goose Creek,SC	
1:372/100		(803)769-4922	9600	Ashley Oaks BBS,Charleston, SC	
1:372/11		(803)875-3020	9600	Randy's House,Summerville,SC	
1:275/17		(804)471-0736	9600	Computer Forum,Virginia Beach,VA	
1:271/270		(804)877-3562	9600	Virginia Data Exchange,Newport News,VA	
1:345/7		(808)732-6909	9600	The Magic Castle,Honolulu,HI	
1:371/1302		(813)574-4707	9600	CSPI-TWP,Cape Coral,FL	
1:130/33		(817)244-7136	9600	The Bone Box,Fort Worth,TX	
1:130/917		(817)367-2712	9600	KloneZone Mac BBS, Fort Worth, TX	
1:130/1003		(817)421-2293	9600	Mac Exchange, Grapevine, TX	

FidoNet node #	MacList node #	Phone #	Speed	BBS name	MSDN node
1:130/14		(817)641-4842	9600	Cleburne BBS,Cleburne,TX	
1:103/602		(818)965-7220	9600	House Atreides,Rowland Heights,CA	
1:102/895		(818)969-9170	9600	Azusa Pacific BBS,Azusa,CA	
1:123/29		(901)386-1760	9600	The Full Moon BBS,Memphis,TN	
1:3801/1		(903)534-1918	9600	Texas Open Forum!,Tyler,TX	
1:3608/121		(904)769-9688	2400	The BEJUE BBS,Panama City,FL	
1:3608/12		(904)286-5125	9600	The Flame,Tyndall AFB,FL	
1:3608/1		(904)871-6536	9600	221B Baker St.,Panama City,FL	
1:2605/620	6:6001/10	(908)294-0659	9600	Shockwave Rider,Freehold,NJ	MSDN
1:/468		(908)449-6289	9600	The Other BBS,Wall Twp,PA	
1:2605/611	6:6001/5	(908)469-4603	9600	MACnetic BBS,Bound Brook,NJ	
1:107/412	6:6001/6	(908)988-0706	9600	Castle Tabby,Bradley Beach,NJ	
1:207/111		(909)593-6144	9600	Gentle Rain Forum,Claremont,CA	
1:280/108		(913)841-9446	9600	The MacRocosm BBS,Lawrence,KS	
1:272/60		(914)783-2455	9600	Particle Board III,Monroe,NY	
1:381/61		(915)590-9798	9600	Health Professions,El Paso,TX	
1:203/933		(916)455-3728	9600	MacNexus,Main	
1:203/34	6:6005/1	(916)962-1952	9600	Now and Zen Opus,Fair Oaks,CA	
1:151/152		(919)481-4896	9600	AppleSeeds (RMUG),Cary,NC	
1:151/102		(919)779-6674	9600	Micro Message Servic,Raleigh,NC	
2:512/36		31-71-232-577	9600	Cyberdyne Systems,Leiden,Holland	
2:512/114	6:62/2	31-71-318678	9600	OutSide Vamp,Leiden,Holland	
2:362/6	6:62/5	351-61-314336	9600	MSMac,Torres Vedras,	
2:253/200		44-602-455417	9600	MacTel HQ,Nottingham,UK	
2:253/201		44-602-455444	9600	MacTel HQ,Nottingham,UK	
2:253/202		44-81-543-8017	9600	MacTel Metro,London,UK	
2:200/306	6:62/4	46-480-32393	9600	Lanthandein,Kalmar	
2:242/91	6:62/3	49-2191-590872	2400	KokomikoS D-5630,Remscheid,	
2:243/100	6:62/1	49-6101-41471	9600	Rhein-Main Macintosh BBS, Frankfurt	MSDN
3:712/502		61-2-597-7477	2400	Paragon TBBS,Rockdale,NSW	
3:712/707		61-2-745-3500	9600	Eagle Two BBS,Burwood,NSW	
3:713/304		61-47-36-4165	9600	ABCOM dataLINK,Penrith,NSW	
3:680/803		61-8-234-0244	9600	PC Information Excha,Flinders Park,A	
3:680/804		61-8-234-0791	2400	Oracle PC-Network,Flinders Park,A	

RIME MACINTOSH BBSes

BBS name	RIME node	Location	Phone number
CT Department of Revenue Services BBS	AJJJR	Hartford, CT	(203)297-5907
Aardvark BBS	AARDVARK	New York, NY	(212)496-8324
The NYPC BBS	NYPC	New York, NY	(212)679-6972/73
Lunatic Fringe BBS	LUNATIC	Richardson, TX	(214)235-5288
Collector's Edition	EDITION	Dallas, TX	(214)351-9859/9871
TNE BBS	NEWEXPRESS		(215)943-6806
The Dock BBS	THEDOCK	Bristol, IN	(219)848-7200
Port-Of-Call BBS	PORTOFCALL	Bowie, MD	(301)249-4193
Hollywood Information Systems	HOLLYWOOD		(301)373-2150 /3530/5965
Main Frame BBS	MAINFRAM		(301)654-2554
Ruby's Joint	RUBYSJOINT	Miami, FL	(305)856-4897
Sudden Impact	IMPACT	Kokomo, IN	(317)457-5957
Arc Light	ARCLIGHT	Indianapolis, IN	(317)575-8800
The Dew Drop Inn	DEWDROP	Library, PA	(412)854-0619
Space BBS	SPACE	Palo Alto, CA	(415)323-4193
Toad Hall	TOADHALL	San Carlos, CA	(415)595-2427
Canada Remote Systems	CRS	Toronto, CA	(416)629-7000
Chemeketa Online	CHEMEK	Salem, OR	(503)393-5580
Whalers Walk	WHALERS	Martha's Vinyard, MA	(508)627-3285
Sigma Iotia II RBBS	SIGMAIOTIA	Yakima, WA	(509)966-2023/2049
The Web BBS	THEWEB		(513)436-9036
The Union Lake BBS	UNION		(609)327-5553
Holly City BBS	HOLLY	Millville, NJ	(609)825-1621
T.C.N.	COMMUNICATOR	Newark, OH	(614)366-2584
Vanderbilt School of Medicine	MEDCAT		(615)343-8172
Channel 1	CHANNEL1	Cambridge, MA	(617)354-7077
The Garden Spot	GARDEN	Scituate, MA	(617)545-6239
West Coast Connection	WCC	San Diego, CA	(619)449-8333
NOHO BBS	NOHO		(619)949-4021 /4025/4026
Struppi's BBS	STRUPPI	Fairfax, VA	(703)591-9380
The Virginia Connection	VIRGINIA	Washington, DC	(703)648-1841
The GoverNet BBS	AYRISTA	Chicago, IL	(708)837-7552
CommLink	SCCM	Anaheim, CA	(714)282-6055
Lancaster Area Bulletin Board	LABB		(717)394-1357
Bits 'N Bytes BBS	BITBYTES	Hellam, PA	(717)757-4141/9445
New York Running Board	RUNNINGB		(718)519-1791
The Brass Cannon	BRASS	Orem, Utah	(801)226-8310
Edge of the Century	CENTURY	Bountiful, UT	(801)295-1698
The Computer Forum	CFORUM	Va Beach, VA	(804)471-3360
TBBS	TABBFL	Tampa, FL	(813)961-6242
Magnetic Bottle	MAGNET	State College, PA	(814)237-3825
Visions InfoLine	INFOLINE	Plainfield, NJ	(908)769-1779
Apple-Wize BBS	APPLEWIZ		(914)793-1168
Hudson Valley BBS	HVBBS		(914)876-1450
The Ham Radio Emporium	EMPORIUM		(918)272-4327
Clavius Educational	CLAVIUS	Madrid, Spain	341-3112371
The Mail House	MAILHOUSE	Lisboa, Portugal	351-1-9881183
MSmac BBS	MSMAC	Portugal	011-351-61-312935
Skyship BBS	SKYSHIP	Lisbon	011-3511-3527623 /3151435/31514360

ILINK MACINTOSH BBSES

BBS	Location	Phone number
Winnipeg PC UG BBS	Winnipeg, Man.	(204)338-0272
The MATRIX	Birmingham, AL	(205)323-2016/6016
PUBLISHERS' PARADISE	Huntsville, AL	(205)882-6886
Invention Factory BBS	New York, NY	(212)274-8110
The BCS BBS	Los Angeles, CA	(213)962-9202
DSC	Ivyland, PA	(215)443-9434
After Five BBS	Elkhart, IN	(219)262-1370
The Dock BBS	Bristol, IN	(219)848-7200
The Wichita State Univ. BBS	Wichita, KS	(316)689-3779
Eagle's Nest Communications	Prov, RI	(401)732-5290
The Right Place (tm)	Atlanta, GA	(404)476-2607
The Data Dimension	Norcross, GA	(404)921-1186
Higher Powered BBS	Sunnyvale, CA	(408)737-7040
The PC GFX Exchange	San Francisco, CA	(415)337-5416
FUTURETRON	Toronto, ON	(416)868-1888
Compu-Data	Turnersville, NJ	(609)232-1245
Alpha Omega BBS	Vineland, NJ	(609)692-9366
EHV Precision	Ridgecrest, CA	(619)371-1665
EHV Precision	Ridgecrest, CA	(619)371-1665
CHIPS+ Connection	Newport Beach, CA	(714)556-3208
The Kandy Shack	Garden Grove, CA	(714)636-2667
Hackers' Haven	Orem, UT	(801)224-4031
Graphics Connection	Salt Lake City, UT	(801)264-1191
DayDreamer Service	Taipei, Taiwan	
Galway On-Line	Ireland	353 91 27454
EDKX BBS	Stockholm, Sweden	46 8 6812222

INTELLEC MACINTOSH BBSES

As of April 9, 1993

BBS	Location	Phone number
SailBoard BBS	Ringwood, NJ	(201)831-8152
Phantasia	Boise, ID	(208)939-1350
Lunatic Fringe	Richardson, TX	(214)235-5288
The Mad House BBS	Conneaut, OH	(216)593-4438
The Data Hut		(217)875-7114
DZ-Info Service		(309)786-2096
The French Flyer	Long Beach, CA	(310)597-2235
4D BBS		(312)284-7133
Sammy's Litter Box	Waterloo, IA	(319)232-5627
Flying Dutchman	San Jose, CA	(408)294-3065
The PC GFX Exchange	San Francisco, CA	(415)337-5416
The Network 2000	San Francisco, CA	(415)474-4523
Hints BBS	San Mateo, CA	(415)572-8219
Rose Media	Hamilton, ON	(416)575-5363
Canada Remote Systems	Toronto, ON	(416)798-4713
Night Magic BBS	Albuquerque, NM	(505)899-9282
KanonTech		(510)235-6839
Late Nite Diversions	Sarnia, ON	(519)332-0241
Academia BBS	Northfield, NJ	(609)383-9400
Holly City BBS		(609)825-1621
The Outpost!		(612)252-1116
Granite BBS	St. Cloud, MN	(612)654-8372
A-Mega BBS	Houston, TX	(713)488-6077
CHIPS+ Connection	Newport Beach, CA	(714)556-3208

BBS	Location	Phone number
The Crystal Palace	Rochester, NY	(716)264-9383
Taste BBS	Brooklyn, NY	(718)252-4529
MoonDog BBS	Brooklyn, NY	(718)692-2498
The Late Show!	Bakersfield, CA	(805)832-6173
The Seaside	Santa Barbara, CA	(805)964-4766
Mercury Opus	St. Petersburg, FL	(813)321-0734
NetMail PC-Help!	Tampa, FL	(813)949-4993
Bandit BBS	Tampa, FL	(813)977-5600/978-3400
Compuphile	Meadville, PA	(814)337-0501
Darby Research Systems	Erie, PA	(814)825-7905
Metrolink		(818)441-2625
We are from the Continuum		
Panasia BBS	Glendale, CA	(818)569-3740
Synapse BBS	Gatineau, PQ	(819)561-4321
Bill's Board	Sackville, NS	(902)864-5394
Craig's DATA Exchange	Eustis, FL	(904)483-2498
Arakis BBS	NJ	(908)730-7328
Potpourri	Kingsland, GA	(912)729-6184
Dark side of the Moon	Mahopac	(914)621-2865
Bit Stream	Corning, CA	(916)824-1939
Skyship BBS		011-511-3527623

FrEdMail BBSes

As of 9/13/92

Zip Code	Location	System	Node	Phone/bps
	Sydney, Australia	Cabramatta E.R.C.	CABRA	+26072986/24
			CHAMP	(217)351-4345/12
	Guilford County, NC	Guilford County	GUILFRD	(919)271-0649/12
	Sydney, Australia A	Normanhurst B.H.S.	HORNSBY	+24897785/12
			ILEAGLE	(618)532-8894/96
	Kankakee, IL	Kennedy Elementary	KKK111	(815)932-7980
	Onslow, NC		ONSLOW	(991)455-8705
			RENC5	(517)875-5132
	Rialto, CA	Rialto School Dist	RIALTO	(714)820-6865/24
	San Diego, CA	FrEdMail Central	SDCOE	(619)587-7993/96
	Sydney, Australia	Australia FrEdMail	SYDNEY	+26075286/24
00830	St. Thomas, USVI	Caribbean CUE	VIRGINI	(809)777-4026/12
00931	University of Puert	Orillas en Puerto Rico	ORILLAS	(809)763-3925/24
06483	New Haven, CT	New Haven, CT	NWHAVEN	(203)777-5008/24
07031	North Arlington, NJ	North Arlington Schools	NORTHAR	(201)955-6050/24
07081	Springfield, NJ	Springfield Public Schools	SPRING	(201)376-9025/24
07111	Irvington, NJ	Irvington Public Schools	IRVBOE	(201)371-1247/24
07205	Newarrk, NJ	Newark School District	NEWARK1	(201)705-3787/24
07922	Berkeley Heights, N	Berkeley Heights Schools	BHPS	(908)464-8929
08648	Larenceville, NJ	Lawrence Township Schools	LAWRENC	(609)538-1347/24
08733	Lakehurst, NJ	Manchester Schools	MNCHSTR	(908)657-8883/24
10583	Scarsdale, NY	Scarsdale Middle School	SCARSDA	(914)721-2653/12
11217	Brooklyn, NY	Brooklyn BBS	BROOKLN	(718)783-6723p24
11501	Mineola, NY	Nassau BOCES	NASSAU	(516)877-1095/12
11732	Wyong, Australia	Wyong High School	WYONG	+043511093/24
17520	East Petersburg, PA	Lancaster/Lebanon IU	LANLEB	(717)569-9289/24
17520	East Petersburg, PA	Lancaster/Lebanon IU	LEBANON	(717)270-2942
18301	Pocono Mts., PA	Pocono Area Educator's Tec	POCONO	(717)424-3226/24
19118	Philadelphia, PA	Philadelphia	PHILLY	(215)233-0240p12
19520	Reading, PA	Reading	READING	(215)926-8540/24
19803	Wilmington, DE	St. Marks HIgh School	STMARKS	(302)738-0572/96
21030	Hunt Valley, MD		MERC	(410)666-2811-24
22201	Arlington, VA	Long Branch School	LBRANCH	(703)841-9598/12
27104	Winston-Salem, NC	Forsyth Cnty Bd Educ	WSALEM	(919)727-2213/12
27203	Asheboro, NC	Asheboro City Schools	ASHBORO	(919)625-3520/24
27215	Burlington, NC	Micro-5 Users Gp	MICRO5	(919)222-9348/24
27261	High Point, NC	High Point Schools	HIPOINT	(919)888-2561/24
27293	Davidson Co, NC	Davidson Co Bd Ed	DAVIDSN	(704)956-1254/24
27330	Sanford, NC	Lee County School District	LEE	(919)776-7135/24
27555	Micro, NC	Johnston County Schools	JOHNSTN	(919)284-4736/24

Zip Code	Location	System	Node	Phone/bps
27573	Roxboro, NC	Person Co Schools	PERSON	(919)597-8528/24
27611	Raleigh, NC	Wake Co Schools	WAKE	(919)850-8951
27712	Durham, NC	Durham Public Schls	DURHAM	(919)560-3815/12
27858	Greenville, NC	East Carolina University	ECU	(919)757-4154/24
27885	Swan Quarter, NC	Hyde County Bd of Ed	HYDE	(919)926-0953/12
27889	Washington, NC	Washington City Schools	WCS	(919)946-4934/24
27893	Wilson, NC	Wilson Co BdofEduc	WILSON	(919)243-1601/96
28092	Lincoln County, NC	Lincoln County Schools	LINCALL	(919)
28112	Monroe, NC	Union County Schools	UNION	(704)283-3538/12
28133	Wadesboro, NC	Wadesboro MS	ANSON	(704)694-4523/24
28145	Rowan, NC	Rowan-Salisbury Schools	ROWAN	(704)639-3068/24
28203	Charlotte, NC	Charlotte-Mecklenburg Scho	CHARLOT	(704)343-5366
28327	Carthage, NC	Board of Educ	MOORE	(919)947-3954/24
28337	Bladen County, NC	Bladen County Schools	BLADEN	(919)862-8998/24
28379	Rockingham, NC	Rockingham Jr. Hi	RICHMON	(919)895-1416/12
28602	Hickory, NC	Catawba Co Bd Ed	CATAWBA	(704)256-8136/24
28607	Boone, NC	Appalachian State Univ	ASUED	(704)262-3094/24
28681	Taylorsville, NC	Alexander County Schools	ALEXAND	(704)495-8806/12
28713	Bryson City, NC	Swain Co Schools	SWAIN	(704)488-2290/24
28806	Asheville, NC	Buncombe Cnty Schls	BCOMBE	(704)255-5992/12
29407	Charleston, SC	Morningside Middle School	CHARLES	(803)566-1812
30263	Newnan, GA	Heritage School	HERITGE	(404)251-4904/24
32177	Palatka, FL	Jenkins Middle School	EAGLES	(904)329-0627
37909	Knoxville, TN	Knoxville Ed Computing	KECLINK	(615)539-6252/24
38801	Tupelo, MS	Tupelo Public Sch. Dist.	TUPELO	(601)841-8857/24
41537	Jenkins, KY	Jenkins High School	JENKY	(606)832-2185/24
46166	Paragon, IN	Martinsville School Distri	PARAGON	(317)537-2277/24
48043	Mt Clemens, MI	Mt. Clemens Comm. School	MTCLEM	(313)469-5805
48050	Novi, MI	Novi Woods Community Schoo	NOVI	(313)344-8870/24
48067	Pontiac, MI	Oakland County Schls	OAKSCHL	(313)858-1873/12
48859	Mt. Pleasant, MI	Central Mich Univ	CHPCHAT	(517)774-7704/96
48875	Portland, MI	Oakwood Elementary	RAIDERS	(517)647-7474/96
48883	Michigan		BLUEJAY	(517)828-5521/24
49401	Allendale,MI (G.R.)	Grand Valley State Univ	GVSU	(616)895-3202
50613	Cedar Falls, IA	Area Education Agncy 7	AEA7	(319)273-8248/12
55082	Bayport, MN	Stillwater High School	STILWTR	(612)439-1064/24
55123	Eagan, MN	Rosemount/Apple Vally/Eaga	RAVE	(612)683-6832/24
55413	Minneapolis, MN	Minneapolis School Dist	MPLS	(612)627-2170/24
55426	Minneapolis, MN	St Louis Park Schools	SLP	(612)
56501	Detroit Lakes, MN	Detroit Lakes JHS	DLJHS	(218)847-9509/24
61550	Morton, IL	Morton Unit School Distric	MORTON	(309)263-2168/12
61625	Peoria, IL	Bradley University	BRADLEY	(309)667-3686/24
61801	Urbana, IL	Urbana School Dist	URBANA	(217)384-3554/24
61820	Champaign, IL	Univ of Illinois	UIUCED	(217)333-2246/12
61820	Chamgaign, IL	University of Illinois	UIUCED2	(217)244-3368/96
61832	Danville, IL	Danville High School	DANVILLE	(217)431-5885
62026	Edwardsville, IL	SOILED Net (So. IL Educ Ne	EVILLE	(618)692-3595/24
62515	Springfield, IL	Springfield District	SPFLD	(217)525-3349/24
62999	Zeigler,IL		TORNADO	(310)391-4299
63033	Florissant, MO	T.E.N.(Technology Educ. Ne	FLOMO	(314)831-7368/24
63125	St. Louis, MO	Regional Consortium	STLOUIS	(314)894-5592p24
64063	Lee's Summit, MO	R-7 Lee's Summit Schools	LEESUMT	(816)524-5239/12
65201	Columbia, MO	Columbia Public Schools	CPSIMS	(314)886-2784/24
65802	Springfield, MO	Southwest Missouri Consort	SWMO	(417)895-2721
66046	Lawrence, Kansas	Unified School Dist 497	LAWRENC	(913)
67460	McPherson, KS	McPherson USD #418	MCPHRSN	(316)241-1250/96
68506	Lincoln, NE	Lincoln Public Schls	LINCOLN	(402)436-1416/12
68507	Lincoln, NE	Pershing Elementary School	PERSHIN	(402)436-1471/12
70663	Sulphur, LA	JJSouthwest Louisiana	SOWELA	(318)625-3440/24
71656	Monticello, AR	Univ of Arkansas	MONARK	(501)460-1965/24
72204	Little Rock, AR	Univ of Arkansas	UALRED	(501)569-3268/24
80918	Colorado Springs	Rocky Mt. Ed. Computing Co	RMECCO	(719)593-1914/24
82002	Cheyenne WY	Wyoming Dept Educ	WYOMING	(307)777-5945/24
89014	Las Vegas, NV	Las Vegas CUE	VEGAS	(702)898-8552/96
90066	Los Angeles, CA	Los Angeles Unified	FREELA	(310)391-4299
90505	Torrance, CA	Torrance Unified District	TORRANC	(310)542-5378/12
90620	Centralia, CA	Centralia School Dist	CSD	(714)562-9211/24
90627	Anaheim, CA	Anaheim UHSD	ANAHEIM	(714)220-4088/12
90630	Cypress, CA	Lexington JHS	LEX	(714)761-8949/12
91709	Pomona, CA	Cal Poly Univ	CALPOLY	(714)869-2328/12
91710	Chino, CA	Chino High School	CHINO	(714)591-1329/24
91711	Claremont, CA	Claremont High School	CLAREMONT	(714)621-2310/24
91720	Corona, CA	Corona-Norco USD	CNUSD	(714)588-3020/12
91723	Glendora, CA	Charter Oak	CHTROAK	(818)963-2095/12
91761	Ontario, CA	Ontario Montclair SD	OMSD	(714)986-9890/12
91908	Bonita, CA	FrEdMail Central	BONITA	(619)475-4852/24
92009	Encinitas, CA	LaCosta Hts Elem	LACOSTA	(619)944-4383/24
92009	Encinitas, CA	Mission Estancia Elem	ME	(619)943-2012/24
92009	Oceanside, CA	Jefferson JHS	OCNSIDE	(619)757-3180/24
92019	Lakeside, CA	Lakeside MS	LAKESID	(619)390-2689/24

```
Zip
Code  Location            System                     Node       Phone/bps
-----  -------------------  -------------------------  ----------  ----------------
92020 El Cajon, CA         Cajon Valley USD           CVUSD      (619)588-0948/12
92024 Encinitas, CA        Park Dale Lane Elementary  PDL        (619)944-4398/12
92024 Encinitas, CA        Encinitas Union            ENCINIT    (619)944-4316/24
92027 Escondido, CA        Escondido Union            ESCUSD     (619)432-2420/12
92030 Los Angeles, CA      Pepperdine Univ            PEPPER     (213)568-5551/12
92069 San Marcos, CA       San Marcos Unified         SANMARC    (619)774-8547
92075 Ramona, CA           Ramona School District     RAMONA     (619)788-5082/12
92103 San Diego, CA        San Diego USD              SDUSD      (619)295-9591p24
92117 San Diego, CA        Pacific Beach MS           PBMS       (619)483-2097/24
92120 San Diego, CA        San Diego State Univ       SDSU       (619)594-3428p12
92131 San Diego, CA        US Internat'l Univ         USIU       (619)693-4582p12
92243 Imperial Valley CA   El Centro USD              ELCNTR     (619)339-6401
92253 Indio, CA            Desert Sands USD           DESERT     (619)564-6142/12
92330 Lake Elsinor, CA     Lake Elsinore Unified SD   ELSINOR    (714)245-0408/24
92373 Redlands, CA         Redlands Unified School Di RUSD       (714)793-9858/24
92395 Elsinor, CA          Elsinore School District   WILDOM     (714)678-9395/12
92408 San Bernardino,CA    Azusa Pacific              APUSB      (714)888-0047/
92411 San Bernardino, CA   San Bernardino City Unifie SBCUSD     (714)888-1573/24
92544 Hemet, CA            Hemet FrEdMail Center       HEMET      (714)925-0836
92553 Moreno Valley, CA    Vista Heights Middle Schoo MOVAL      (909)485-5550/24
92621 Fullerton, CA        Sunny Hills HS             SHHS       (714)870-3423p96
92626 Newport Beach CA     Newport Mesa USD           NEWPORT    (714)556-3177/24
92628 Orange County, CA    Orange County Office Ed    OCDE1      (714)966-4313/12
92628 Orange County, CA    Orange County Office Ed    OCDE2      (714)966-4313/12
92631 Norwalk, CA          Norwalk-La Mirada USD      NORWALK    (213)868-4773/12
92633 Fullerton CA         Fullerton Elem             FULLRTN    (714)447-7496/12
92645 Garden Grove, CA     Pacifica High School       PHSOC      (714)663-6064
92666 Orange, CA           Orange USD                 ORNGUSD    (714)997-6387/12
92691 Mission Viejo, CA    Saddleback Valley Unified  SDLBACK    (714)586-6297p24
93637 Madera, CA           Alpha Elem                 MADERA     (209)674-4801/24
93706 Fresno, CA           Fresno Unified School Dist FRESNO     (209)237-2839/24
94509 Antioch, CA          Antioch District           ANTIOCH    (510)778-2722
94523 Pleasant Hill, CA    Contra Costa County Office CCCOE      (510)934-5041
94533 Solano County, CA    Solano County Office Educ  SOLCO      (707)427-1268
94550 Livermore, CA        LawrLivrLabSciEd           SECLLNL    (415)373-1231/12
94577 San Leandro, CA      San Leandro USD            SNLNDRO    (510)895-1785/96
94606 Oakland, CA          Oakland USD                OAKLAND    (510)834-2636p24
94965 Sausalito, CA        Autodesk Foundation        MARIN      (415)721-0680/24
95014 Cupertino, CA        Cupertino Unified          CPRTINO    (408)253-5385/12
95116 San Jose, CA         Morrill MS                 CHALK      (408)942-1425/24
95116 San Jose, CA         Berryessa USD              SANJOSE    (408)946-7325/24
95132 San Jose, CA         Piedmont Middle School     NEST       (408)259-6855/24
Austr Bargo, Australia     Wirrimbirra F.S.C._        BARGO      +46841701/24
Irela Dublin, Ireland      FrEd Dublin                DUBLIN     +353-1-597343/2
```

INFOLINK BBSES

As of 7/1/93

BBS	Phone number	Lines
Stray Light	(203)966-3667	1
Gropu Health Cooperative Online Info	(206)448-2179, 6518	2
The Mackie AFter Hours BBS	(206)488-4586	1
Twilight	(206)692-0983	1
BECS-Mac	(206)859-0982	1
Fantasy Land BBS	(217)566-3775,3700,3776	3
The Shadow Network	(306)244-3952	3
Avanti Tech Support System	(310)294-7451	1
ButlerBBS	(313)528-1065	1
MaxMac	(313)747-8352	2
Life, The Universe, and Everything	(403)425-3039	1
Execugraphics	(416)637-7131	2
Exact Imaging	(503)231-2586	2
The Leader IS	(503)255-2513	1
NetLink Services	(503)345-7993	3
HMM BBS	(508)655-8927	2
Split Screens	(514)729-9966	1
the MACS	(517)655-3508	1

BBS	Phone number	Lines
Maclink	(613)837-6080,6750	3
Autocomp	(619)450-6521	14
The Banks of Fergussi	(703)271-4080	2
Colloquial Exchange	(703)825-7533	1
Media Solutions	(708)697-1087	2
NovaCentral	(714)379-9004,9006	11
NY NovaLink	(718)771-3641	1
Sports Spectrum Ltd.	(802)434-2229	4
Blue Oyster Bar	(804)397-5326	2
CFS ResourceNet	(813)974-6137	2
Through the Wire	(818)841-1021	5
Heart of the North BBS	(906)774-3260	2
Power User's Macintosh Association	(909)792-4902	1
Blue Dolphin Press Inc.	(916)265-6968	1
Fun BBS (Switzerland)	0041.22.364.6200	2
Mac In the BoX	"+49-241-48655"	1

APPENDIX I:
FidoNet Organization and Help Nodes

For North America, as of July 23, 1993

FidoNet zones and regions

ZONE 1	**North America**			
	REGION	10	Calif Nevada	CA NV
	REGION	11	MARDUK Region Operat	IL IN KY MI OH WI
	REGION	12	Eastern Canada	ON QC NB NS NF PI
	REGION	13	Mid Atlantic	DC DE MD NJ NY PA VI
	REGION	14	Mid West	IA.KS.MN.MO.NE.ND.SD
	REGION	15	Mountain	AZ CO NM UT WY
	REGION	16	New England	CT ME MA NH RI VT
	REGION	17	North West	AK ALB BC HI ID MAN
	REGION	18	SouthEast/Caribbean	AL FL GA MS NC SC T
	REGION	19	TexArkOkLa	AR.LA.OK.TX
ZONE 2	**Europe**	**EUR**		
	REGION	20	Sweden	S
	REGION	21	Norway	N
	REGION	22	Finland	SF
	REGION	23	Denmark	DK
	REGION	24	West Germany	FRG
	REGION	25	British Isles	UK
	REGION	28	Holland	Utrecht
	REGION	29	Belgium	B
	REGION	30	Switzerland	CH
	REGION	31	Austria	A
	REGION	33	Italy	I
	REGION	34	Spain	Catalunya
	REGION	35	Bulgaria	BG
	REGION	40	Israel	IL
	REGION	41	Greece	Thessaloniki, Greece
	REGION	42	Czechoslovakia	CSFR
	REGION	48	Poland	PL
	REGION	49	Estonia	Tallinn, Estonia
	REGION	50	The Court Of The Crimea	Novosibirsk, USSR
ZONE 3	**Oceania**	**Trans-Tasman**		
	REGION	50	Australia	Melbourne, Austral.
	REGION	54	Western Pacific	Sydney, NSW
	REGION	55	West and North Austral.	Perth W. Austral.
	REGION	57	New Zealand	Christchurch, NZ
ZONE 4	**America Latina**	**Latin America**		
	REGION	80	Rede, Brasil	Brasil
	REGION	90	Red Provincias Unida	Argentina

ZONE 5	**AFRICA**		**Port Elizabeth RSA**	
	REGION	49	South Africa	RSA
	REGION	72	Zimbabwe	Harare, Zimbabwe
	REGION	73	Kenya	Nairobi, Kenya
ZONE 6	**ASIA**		**Taipei Taiwan**	
	REGION	53	Hong Kong and Macau	NT Hong Kong
	REGION	56	Taiwan Net	Taipei, Taiwan
	REGION	58	FidoNet-Japan	Tokyo Japan

FidoNet administration and help nodes

Address	Service	Phone #	Location	Speed
1:1/20	Fido Technical Standards	(604)589-8561	Relay System	9600
1:1/23	FidoNews	(519)570-4176	FidoNews Editor	9600
1:1/30	Inter-Network Coord.	(415)695-0759	San Francisco ,CA	2400
1:1/31	fidonet.org	(908)981-9190	Piscataway, NJ	9600
1:1/101	FrontDoor Help USA	(918)254-6618	Tulsa, OK	9600
1:1/102	BinkleyTerm Help	(713)980-9671	Sugar Land,TX	9600
1:1/103	TBBS Info/Help	(919)772-7806	Raleigh, NC	9600
1:1/104	RBBS-PC Help	(714)381-6013	Colton, CA	9600
1:1/105	PCBoard Help	(201)471-6391	Passaic, NJ	9600
1:1/109	Amiga Help	(613)230-2282	Ottawa, ON	9600
1:1/111	SEAdog HELP	(201)283-1806	Butler,NJ	9600
1:1/112	XRS Help	(803)853-6690	Charleston, SC	9600
1:1/113	OPUS Info	(407)383-1372	Titusville,FL	9600
1:1/114	Quick BBS Help	(504)851-4230	Houma, LA	9600
1:1/116	Dutchie Help	(201)934-0861	Mahwah, NJ	9600
1:1/117	Fido V12 Help	(703)222-0180	Centreville, VA	9600
1:1/118	Qtach2/QNX Support	(215)491-0919	Jamison ,PA	9600
1:1/119	Maximus Help	(705)494-9329	North Bay, ON	9600
1:1/120	RemoteAccess Help US	(918)254-6618	Tulsa, OK	9600
1:1/122	TIMS Help	(303)973-9454	Littleton, CO	9600
1:1/124	GSBBS Help	(716)657-7443	Holcomb, NY	9600
1:1/130	Armadillo Help	(519)672-7661	London, ON	9600
1:1/133	InterMail Help	(305)436-1884	Pembroke Pines, FL	9600
1:1/137	EzyCom Help	(214)641-1136	Dallas, TX	9600
1:1/138	RoboBoard Help	(613)592-9054	Kanata, ON	9600
1:1/139	WPL Language Support	(613)230-2282	Ottawa, ON	9600
1:1/140	GBBS Help	(412)937-9498	Pittsburgh, PA	9600
1:1/141	WME Help	(916)483-8486	Sacramento, CA	9600
1:1/168	D'Bridge Help	(904)372-7408	Gainesville, FL	9600
1:1/201	EchoList Coordinator	(908)506-0472	Toms River, NJ	9600
1:116/29	FileBone List Coordinator	(615)385-4268	Nashville, TN	9600

Appendix I: FidoNet Help Nodes and Coordinators

Echo coordinators

Address	Region	Phone #	Location	Speed
1:1/210	10	(714)838-6539	Tustin, CA	9600
1:1/211	11	(414)384-1701	Milwaukee, WI	9600
1:1/212	12	(613)739-8634	Ottawa, ON	9600
1:1/213	13	(703)620-3947	Oakton, VA	9600
1:1/214	14	(319)337-**9878**	Iowa City, IA	9600
1:1/215	15	(602)780-9180	Phoenix, AZ	9600
1:1/216	16	(617)551-0495	Westwood, MA	9600
1:1/217	17	(604)683-0422	Vancouver, BC	9600
1:1/218	18	(901)876-3270	Millington, TN	9600
1:1/219	19	(918)254-6618	Tulsa, OK	9600

FidoNet/UUCP gateways

Zone 1

Gateway	FidoNet address	Zone gated
puddle	1:105/42	2
puddle	1:105/42	4
puddle	1:105/42	5
puddle	1:105/42	6
zorro9	1:16/390	16
busker	1:105/14	17
busker	1:105/14	40
zorro9	1:16/390	101
mcws	1:102/851	102
mcws	1:102/851	103
paranet	1:104/422	104
busker	1:105/14	105
newport	1:107/390	107
blkcat	1:109/401	109
afitamy	1:110/300	110
fidogate	1:125/777	125
gisatl	1:133/411	133
branch	1:369/11	135
memco	1:139/610	139
klbbs	1:141/370	141
lansend	1:143/3	143
kennel	1:143/8	143
ohiont	1:157/512	157
clubzen	1:161/148	161
jadpc2	1:202/723	202
ccfcc	1:205/42	205
mcws	1:102/851	206
mcws	1:102/851	207
cmhgate	1:226/20	226
royaljok	1:231/510	231
ehsnet	1:233/13	233
egsgate	1:250/98	250

Gateway	FidoNet address	Zone gated
rochgte	1:260/222	260
newport	1:107/930	278
kcufgat	1:280/500	280
terrabit	1:282/341	282
emdisle	1:300/14	300
zorro9	1:16/390	322
buscard	1:324/1	324
wsyd	1:325/2	325
busker	1:105/14	345
kisbbs	1:3624/6	360
branch	1:369/11	369
umagic	1:373/12	373
psycho	1:3603/75	377
mdf	1:382/39	382
nwark	1:391/1060	391
psycho	1:3603/75	3603
branch	1:369/11	3609
kisbbs	1:3624/6	3624
stjhmc	1:1/31	default for zone 1

Zone 2

Gateway	FidoNet address	Zone gated
gnfido	2:254/70	2:25
casino	2:220/801	2:220
casino	2:220/801	2:221
casino	2:220/801	2:222
casino	2:220/801	2:227
gnfido	2:254/70	2:254
casino	2:220/801	2:490

Zone 3

Gateway	FidoNet address	Zone gated
csource	3:632/348	default for zone 3

APPENDIX J:
CONFERENCE LISTINGS

Store-and-forward networks

Conferences on the FidoNet Backbone as of March 19,1993
(FIDONET.NA file, available from the Echo Coordinators)

Conference	Subject
12_STEPS	12 Steps Discussion
4DOS	4DOS ECHO
60S_70S_PROGROCK	60's/70's Progressive Rock Music Echo
80XXX	Assembly language programming (Intel CPUs mainly)
ABLED	disABLED Users Information Exchange
ABLED_ATHLETE	Abled Athletes
ABLENEWS	Disability news, resources, referrals
AD&D	Advanced Dungeons and Dragons
ADAM	Adam International Computer Conference
ADHD	Attention Deficit Hyperactivity Disorders
ADLIB	Adlib and Compatible Sound Cards Discussion
ADOPTEES	Adoptees Information Exchange
ADS_ANNOUNCE	Amiga Distribution System Announcement & Chat Echo
AI	Artificial Intelligence forum
AIDS-HIV	AIDS-HIV Discussion Echo
AIDS/ARC	AIDS/ARC
AIRGUN	Airgunners' Information Exchange
AMATEUR_RADIO	Amateur Radio Conference
AMIGA	Amiga International Echo
AMIGAGAMES	Amiga Gaming
AMIGASALE	Amiga Non-commercial Items for Sale
AMIGA_CDROM	AmigaCDROM & CDTV Discussion/Sales
AMIGA_COMMS	Amiga Communications Software and Hardware Discussions
AMIGA_INT	Amiga Worldwide
AMIGA_LC	Amiga Language C programming & SAS/C Conference
AMIGA_MUSIC	Amiga music/sound topics
AMIGA_NET_DEV	Amiga Network Developers
AMIGA_OS&EM	Amiga Operating Systems and Emulators
AMIGA_PDREVIEW	Amiga Public Domain & Requests
AMIGA_PROG	Amiga Programming Discussions
AMIGA_SYSOP	Amiga sysop general discussions
AMIGA_VIDEO	Amiga video/Graphics and Desktop Video echo
AMPUTEE	Amputee Support
AMY_POINT	Amiga FidoNet Point and Node Software Support
AMY_TECH	Amiga Technical
ANEWS	News of the U.S. and World
ANIMAL_RIGHTS	Animal Rights Conference
ANIME	Japanese Animation Conference
ANIMED	Animal Medicine
APPLE	International Apple Echo
AQUARIUM	Fishkeeping, fresh and marine tanks
ARJ	ARJ Support Echo
ASIAN_LINK	International chat echo - Asia/North America/Europe
ASKACOP	Ask law enforcement professionals about their work
ASKACOP2	Ask a cop
ASK_A_NURSE	Ask a nurse
ASP	ASP (Association of Shareware Professionals)
ASTRONOMY	Observational Astronomy Echo Conference
AT&T	AT&T PC Support Conference
ATARI	Atari 8-bit computers topic
ATARI_ST	Atari ST Echo
AUTOMOTIVE	For the Automotive Enthusiast

Conference	Subject
AUTORACE	Auto Racing
AVIATION	International Aviation Echo
AVICULTURE	Captive Propagation of Birds
A_CAD	International AutoCAD/CAD Conference
A_THEIST	A_Theism Education and Enlightenment Echo
BAMA	Odyssey UFO Echo
BASIC7	PDS and VB/DOS Discussions
BATPOWER	Batch Languages Programming
BATTERED	Family Violence
BB-CARDS	Baseball Card Conference
BBSLAW	Bulletin Board Legal Issues Conference
BBSL_DISC	BBSLIST Discussions
BBS_ADS	Bulletin Board Advertising - To Promote your BBS!
BBS_CARNIVAL	BBS Software & Related Utility Chatter
BIBLE	International Bible Conference
BIKENET	Bicycling and human powered vehicles
BIMODEM	Bimodem Technical Support
BINKLEY	BinkleyTerm Support Conference
BIOMED	Biomedical and Clinical Engineering Topics
BLINDTLK	Blindness-related topics and discussions
BLINKTALK	Visual Disabilities Echo
BLUEWAVE	Blue Wave Reader and Door Support Echo
BOATING	Boating
BODYWORK	Bodywork & Massage Therapy Forum
BRIT_CAR	British Car Echo
BUSINESS	Business Echo
CAD-CAM	Computer Aided Design/Drafting, Computer Aided Manufacturing
CALLNY	New York Interests
CANACHAT	Canada chatter
CANADA	Canada Sysop Echo
CANPOL	Canadian Policics Conference
CARCINOMA	Cancer Survivors
CARE_GIVER	Care Giver
CBM	Commodore Computer Conference
CBM-128	CBM C-128 Computer Conference
CDROM	CD–ROM Discussion and Information
CD_ECHO	Compact Disc Echo
CELLULAR	Cellular Telephone Discussions
CFORSALE	Commercial For Sale Message Area
CFS	Chronic Fatigue Syndrome
CHAMELEON	Reptile, Amphibian & Exotic Pets Discussion Area
CHAOS_LANDING	Chaos_landing
CHATTER	Mindless Chatter Conference
CHEKFREE	Checkfree Software Support Conference
CHESS	International Chess Echo
CHILD_ABUSE	Child Abuse Information and Recovery
CHRONIC_PAIN	Chronic Pain Discussion Area
CIVIL_WAR	Civil War
CIVLIB	Civil Liberties
CLARION	Clarion Developers Echo
CLASSIFIEDS	Classified Advertising Echo
CLIPPER	CLIPPER
CNET	CNet Amiga BBS Software Support For CNet SysOps
COCO	Tandy Color Computer Conference
COFFEE_KLATSCH	A gossip and chit-chat echo with household overtones
COLLEGE	College Echo
COMICS	Comics Echo
COMM	Communications Echo
COMPRESS	Compression Software Discussion
COMPUSALE	Computer related Buy/Sell Echo
CONSULTING	Consulting
CONSUMER_REPORT	Consumer Report
CONTROV	Controversial
COOKING	National Cooking Echo
CPALSY	Cerebral Palsy
CPMTECH	CP/M Technical Echoconference
CRAFTING	Craft and Needlework Hobbies of All Kinds
CRASH	EmergNet Operation & Mission Discussion
CSPSYSOP	International CSP Sysop Echo
CUSS	Computer Users in the Social Sciences
CXL	C programming Routines
C_ADVOCAT	Consumer Advocate

Conference	Subject
C_ECHO	The International C Echo
DADS	Dads
DBASE	Database topics, techniques, and advice
DBRIDGE	D'Bridge Official Support Echo
DBTECH	D'Bridge Email Technical Support.
DB_NOVICE	D'Bridge Novice User Support
DEADHEAD	Grateful Dead Topics
DEBATE	Debate Conference
DESQVIEW	DESQview Tech Conference
DIABETES	Diabetes discussions and support
DIETING	Dieting
DIRTY_DOZEN	Piracy/Hacks/Trojan horses/Virus alerts
DISASTERS	Disaster Info/Relief/Recovery
DLG_INFO	DLG Professional Information
DMNGATES	Domain-Gating Support Conference
DND	Dungeons & Dragons Discussion Base
DOGHOUSE	Dog Lovers' Discussion
DOORGAMES	Door Games Discussion Echo
DOORWARE	Support Echo and General Door Development Forum
DR_DEBUG	Doctor Debug's Laboratory
ECHODOR	EchoDor Users
ECHO_REQ	Echo Requests
ECOLOGY	Ecology, problems and potential solutions
ECONET	Ecology Network
ECPROG	East Coast Programmer's Echo
EC_DEV	Ezycom Development Echo
EC_SUPPORT	Ezycom Support Echo
EDUCATOR	Educator's conference
ELECTRONICS	Home Electronics and Appliances Discussions
EMS	Emergency Medical Services
ENTREPRENEUR	Entrepreneur conference
ENVIRON	Environmental Issues
EQUUS	Horse discussion echo
EVOLUTION	Evolutionary Mechanism Theory Discussion
EXOTIC_BIRDS	Exotic Birds Echo
FALCON_CBCS	Falcon CBCS Amiga BBS Support
FCC	Radio and Data Telecommunications Regulation
FDECHO	FrontDoor/TosScan Support Conference
FEMINISM	Feminism and Gender Issues
FE_HELP	FastEcho Mail Tosser Help/Support Echo
FIDO	FidoBBS Topics
FIDOBILL	FIDOBILL Software Support
FIDODOOR	FIDOdoor & Utility Discussions
FIDOPCB	Support Echo for the FidoPCB, PCBoard<-->Fido interface
FILE_REQ	File Distribution Networks Files, Info, and Links
FILK	Science Fiction Fannish Folksongs
FILM	Film & Movie Review
FIREARMS	Firearms technical discussion echo
FIRENET	Fire and Emergency Medical related topics
FISHING	Fishing discussions of all kinds
FLAME	National Flame! Echo
FMAIL_HELP	Fmail Support Echo
FN_SYSOP	International FidoNet sysop echo
FOR-SALE	National For Sale Echo
FOXPRO	FoxPro & Fox Database Products
FRANCAIS	French echo
FREEMAIL	Support for the FreeMail EchoMail tosser
FS	Flight Simulators
FUNNY	Funny Stories and Jokes
GAMING	International Personal Computer Gaming
GAYLINK	Gaylink - Discussion of Gay Topics
GAYNEWS	Gays/Lesbians News Echo
GAYTEEN	Gay Teenager Forum
GECHO_HELP	GEcho/MBUTIL Support Conference
GENDATA	Genealogy Database
GENDER	Gender Dysphoria Information and Support Echo
GENEALOGY	National Genealogical Conference
GENEALOGY.EUR	Genealogy and Family History international
GENSOFT	Genealogy Software
GENSYSOP	Genealogy Sysop Echo
GEOWORKS	GeoWorks Ensemble Help Echo
GOLDED	GoldED Help & Information Conference

Conference	Subject
GOURMET	Gourmet Cooking
GRAND_ROUNDS	Grand Rounds medical information conference
GREEN.029	The international environment conference
GUITAR	Guitar Topics
GVP_ECHO	Great Valley Products (GVP)
HAM	Amateur Radio Interest
HAM-SALE	Ham Radio equipment sale, swap and buy
HAM_REQ	Amateur Radio File Announcements & File Requests
HAM_TECH	Amateur (Ham) Radio Technology Conference
HANDY.SYSOP	Sysops interested in disability advances
HERBS-N-SUCH	Herbal Delights For Anyone
HERMES_SYSOPS	Hermes Sysops Support
HISTORIA	History Topics in Spanish
HISTORY	International History Echo
HOBBIES	All Hobbies
HOCKEY	North American Hockey Echo
HOLYSMOKE	Religion Debate Echo
HOLY_BIBLE	Wholly Bible Related Discussions.HOME-N-GRDN The Home and Garden Echo
HOMEPOWR	Alternative Energy Systems and Homemade Power
HOMESCHL	Homeschooling support
HOME_OFFICE	Home Office Echo
HOME_REPAIR	The Home Repair Echo
HP	Hewlett-Packard Computer Users support echo
HST	HST Modems from US Robotics
HST-SALE	High Speed Transfer Modems 4-Sale
HS_MODEMS	High Speed Modems
HUMOR	G-Rated Humor: Puns, Jokes, Limericks, Poems, Quotes
ICGAL	Issues Concerning Gays and Lesbians
IEEE	Institute of Electrical and Electronics Engineers
INDIAN_AFFAIRS	Indian_Affairs
INTEL_MODEMS	Intel Modems
INTERCOOK	International Cooking
INTERMAIL	InterMail Support Echo
INTERNET	For discussion of the Internet from a user's perspective
INTERUSER	International communication
INVEST	International Investor's Forum
IN_COUNTRY	In Country
IVS	Interactive Video Support Systems
JAZZ	Jazz music
JOBS	Employment and Job Conference
JOBS-NOW	Job & Employment offerings ONLY
JOURNAL	Pioneer Journals and Diaries
JR-MSG	PCjr Conference
JUDAICA	Jewish Discussions
K9COPS	Conference on Police Dogs
KATTY_KORNER	Cat Conference
KIDS	International Kids Conference
LANTASTI	Lantastic Network Conference
LAPTOP	Laptop Computer Echo
LASERPUB	Laser Publishing
LATINO	Spanish International Conference
LAW	Legal issues conference
LAW_DISORDER	"Law and Disorder" Discussion Area
LIBRARY	Information Power!
LINUX	Linux software discussions
LNXMANAGE	LNXNET Management Echoid
LV_GAMBLER	Las Vegas Gambler and Information
MAC4SALE	Macintosh items for sale/wanted
MACCOMM	Macintosh Telecommunications and Networking Echo
MACDEV	Macintosh Development
MACFSALE	Macintosh For Sale/Wanted
MACHW	Macintosh Hardware
MACHYPE	Macintosh HyperCard
MACSW	Macintosh Software
MACSYSOP	Macintosh Sysop Discussion Forum
MAC_GAMES	Macintosh Entertainment & Education Echo
MAC_TELEFINDER	Macintosh Telefinder BBS Forum
MAINFRAME	Mainframe Computing Technical Topics
MANSION	Mansion BBS & Copernicus Support Echo
MAXDEV	Maximus Developers Conference
MDF	Main Distribution Frame (MDF) - Telecommunications Topics
MEADOW	Meadow Opus Sysops Conference

Conference	Subject
MEBBS	MEBBS Support Echo
MECCA	Maximus MECCA Language Conference
MED_RAYS	Radiology (X-Ray, Ultrasound, Nuclear Med. & Rad. Therapy)
MELEE	MELEE
MEMORIES	Nostalgia
MENSA	Mensa, intelligence, education, other hi-IQ groups, etc.
MENS_ISSUES	Men's Issues
MENTAL_HEALTH	Mental Health
MIDI-NET	MIDI-NET(tm) * International MIDI Conference *
MIDI-PROGRAMMING	MIDI Software Programmer's Conference
MIDRANGE	Midrange Systems
MILITARY_PEOPLE	Military issues of all kinds
MISSING	National Missing Persons Echo
MISSING_CHILD	National Missing Children Echo
ML-BASEBALL	Major League Baseball
MLM	Multi-Level Marketing conference
MM1_TECH	MM1_TECH
MOD1000	Tandy Model 1000 Personal Computer Users Conference
MODERATOR	Moderator's Echo
MODULA-2	Modula-2 Programming Language
MONTE	Monty Python Conference
MOTORCYCLE	An International Motorcycle Conference
MS_WORD	Microsoft Word Echo
MTASK	Multi-TASKing products and problems
MUFFIN	Maximus-CBCS SysOp Conference
MULT-SCLEROSIS	Multiple Sclerosis
MUSIC	MUSIC
MUSICIAN'S_SERVICES	Musician's Classified Conference
MUSIC_COMP_101	Music Composition Conference
MW_GENE	Midwest Genealogy Echo
MYSTERY	Mystery fiction
M_P_D	Multiple Personality Disorder
NET-POL	FidoNet & Net Problem Discussion Area
NEURAL_NET	Artificial Neural Network (ANN) Discussion Echo
NEWOPUS	New Opus Sysop Echo
NEWSCHAT	FidoNet News Chat Conference
NEW_AGE_ECHO	New Age Open Discussion
NFB-TALK	National Federation of the Blind news/discussion
NFL	National Football League
NON_TRAD_STU	Non Traditional Student
NOPIRACY	Piracy and Computer Crime Prevention Forum
NORML	Electronic Media Venture Marijuana Info
NURSES_NETWORK	NurseNet International
NUTRITION	Nutrition
OASIS	OAsis for compulsive overeaters
OFFLINE	Offline Mail (Readers, Doors, Utils., etc.)
OKILLERS	Operation: Overkill II Player Discussion
OLDCARS	Old Cars and related topics
ON_LINE_GAMES	Online Games
OOII	Operation: Overkill II Sysop/Technical Discussion
OPEN_BIBLE	FidoNet International Open Bible Conference
OPTOMETRY	Optometry/Eyecare Topics
OS-DEBATE	Operating System Debate
OS2	OS/2 Conference
OS2BBS	OS/2 BBS'ing
OS2DOSBBS	BBS Software Running in OS/2 DOS Boxes
OS2HW	OS/2 Hardware
OS2LAN	Networking and OS/2
OS2PROG	OS/2 Programming Echo
OS9	OS-9 Operating System conference
OTHERNETS	OtherNets: Information on Networks other than FidoNet
PACKET	Amateur Radio Packet Echo
PARENTS	Parents Echo
PARROTS	Parrots/Hookbill Conference
PASCAL	Pascal
PASCAL_LESSONS	Pascal Programming Lessons
PCBNET	PCBoard Sysops Conference
PCBOARD	Clark Development PCBOARD Support
PCTOOLS	PC-Tools
PCUG	PC User Groups
PCWRITE	MS-DOS to CBM-DOS porting + CBM Publications
PC_ADDICT	Computer Addicts Conference

Conference	Subject
PC_CONSULT	PC Consultants Echo
PDNECHO	Programmers Distribution Network Echo
PDP-11	National DEC PDP-11 Echo
PDREVIEW	Public Domain and Shareware software chatter
PEP	TeleBit Modem & PEP Topics
PERFECT	WordPerfect Corporation Products Basic Echo
PERFECT_MACRO	WordPerfect Corporation Products Advanced Echo
PEROT	Perot & Political Change
PHIL	Philosophy
PHONES	A Telephone Industry Watchdog Conference
PHYSICS	Physics conference
PKEY_DROP	Public-Key Distribution Echo
PLEASE	Stopping the cycle of child abuse (Support & Info)
POINTS	Point usage discussion
POLICY_5	Policy 5 assimilation, discussion, and implementation
POLISH	Poland and Polish related topics
POLITICS	Politics
POST_POLIO	International Post-Polio Survivors Forum
PPI_MODEMS	Practical Peripherals Modem Support
PROBLEM_CHILD	Problem Children
PROBOARD	PROBOARD BBS Support echo
PROWRITE	The Business of Writing
PRO_AUDIO	Professional Audio
PRO_VIDEO	Professional Video
PUBLIC_KEYS	Public-Key Encryption and Distribution Echo
PUBLIC_PSYCH	Public Psychology Support Conference and Discussion Group
PYRO	National Pyrotechnic Echo
P_NEWS	Progressive News & Views
QEDIT	QEdit Echo
QMODEM	QMODEM Support Conference
QMODEM_USER	Qmodem Users Conference
QNX	Quantum Software Systems LTD QNX OS
QTACH2	QTACH2 multi-user, multitasking BBS and utilities
QUICKBBS	QuickBBS Support
QUICKEN	Quicken Software Help conference
QUICKPRO	QuickBBS Professional Sysop's Forum
QUIK_BAS	Quick Basic Programming Echo
QUOTES_2	Quotes_2 General Quotes and Puns
RAILFANS	Railfans, Train Watching, Prototype Railroads
RAINBOW	DEC RAINBOW conference on Digital's Personal Computer
RARE_CONDITION	Rare Diseases
RA_MULTI	Remote Access Multi-Node Sysops Echo
RA_SUPPORT	Remote Access Support Echo
RA_UTIL	Remote Access Utilities Echo
RCM	Radio Controlled Models
RC_MODEL	Radio Controlled Modeling
REAL	The Real Estate Discussion Echo
RECFRP	Role Playing Games
RECOVERY	Recovery (International 12-Step Oriented)
REVIEWS	REVIEWS of almost anything
RIGHTS	Men's Rights/Equality issues
ROBO	RoboBoard EGA/VGA BBS Support Echo
ROBOTIX	Robotix and related discussions
RTKBA	2nd Amendment discussion conference
RTTY	RTTY, SITOR, FAX, CW over radio
SAILING	Sailing
SAR	Search & Rescue
SB-E/N/L	Space Base's Electronic Space Related Newsletters
SB-NASA_NEWS	Space Base NASA News And Press Releases
SB-NASA_TECH	Space Base Technical News & Deep Space Probe Reports
SB-QUESTIONS	Space Base Discussion and Q&A Echo
SB-SAT_TRACK	Amateur Satellite Tracking Discussion & Information
SB-SOLAR_RPT	Space Base's Solar Flare Activity Alerts & Reports
SB-SYSOPS	Space Base Sysops Only Confrence
SB-WORLD_NWS	Space Base's Rest Of The World In Space
SCANRADIO	Scanner & Frequency Discussion-General
SCI&TECH	Science and Technology Conference
SCIENCE	National Science Echo
SCIFOR	VortexNet software & recovering programmer abuse
SCOUTING	International SCOUTING Conference
SCUBA	Scuba diving
SEARCHLIGHT	Searchlight BBS Support Echo

Conference	Subject
SE_GENEALOGY	South Eastern US Genealogy Conference
SF	Science Fiction and Fantasy Literature
SFFAN	Science Fiction and Fandom
SHAREWRE	Shareware Products Discussion Forum
SIERRAN	Sierra Club (Environment)
SILENTTALK	Conference for the Deaf and Hard of Hearing
SIP_AA	Alcoholism & Recovery
SIP_ACA	Adult Children of Alcoholics
SIP_INCEST	Survivor's of Incest & Childhood Sexual Abuse
SIP_MPD	Singleness in Purpose - Multiple Personality Disorder
SIP_NA	Narcotics Anonymous Echo
SIP_SAA	12-Step Recovery from Sexual Addiction
SIRIUS	Sirius Support
SKEPTIC	Skeptical Inquiry Echo
SKYDIVE	Skydiving, Parachuting, and Paragliding
SPACE	Space Development Conference
SPANISH.GEN	Spanish Genealogy
SPINAL_INJURY	Spinal Cord Injury Topics
SPITFIRE	Spitfire Bulletin Board System Support
SPORTS	Sports
SRGAMES	Solar Realms Support Echo
STARWARS	Star Wars Echo
STDSN	Star Trek: Deep Space Nine
STOCK_MARKET	Stock Market
STRESS_MGMT	Learn About Your Mental Powers & Eliminate Stress
STTNG	Star Trek: The Next Generation
STUDIO_101	Studio and Live Music Performance Conference
SUPERBBS	SuperBBS Support Conference
SUPRAFAX	Suprafax Modem Conference
SURVIVOR	Cancer/Leukemia/blood & immune system/coping with adversity
SUST_AG	Sustainable Agriculture
SYS4SALE	SysOp For Sale Echo
SYSOP	International Sysop Conference (the original one)
SYSTEM7	Macintosh System 7 Support
S_KING	Stephen King Discussion - International
TAG	T.A.G. BBS Support Echo
TAGLINES	Taglines
TAGMULTI	T.A.G. BBS (Multinode) Support Echo
TAND2000	Tandy Model 2000 EchoMail Conference
TBBS	TBBS SysOps Support
TECH	National General Technical Discussion Conference
TEEN	International Teenagers' Echo
TELIX	Telix Users Information Exchange
THI_CVA	Brain Injuries
TI-ECHO	Texas Instruments Topics
TOONS	TOONS, cartoon/animation echo
TOTT	Tott Echo [See Elist]
TOTT_SYSOP	TOTT Sysop Echo [See Elist]
TPBOARD	TPBoard BBS Echo
TPWTECH	Turbo Pascal For Windows (Borland) Technical/Programming
TRADE_WARS	Trade Wars
TRAINS	Trains
TRAPDOOR	TrapDoor Support Echo
TREK	Star Trek
TREKTECH	Star Trek technical discussions
TRIBBS	TRIBBS Software Support Conference
TRS-MOD134	Tandy TRS-80 Conference
TUB	SquishMail Users
TVRO	Satellite Television Echo
UFGATE	Usenet-FidoNet Gating Conference
UFO	UFO Topics
UNIX	*N*X (UNIX, XENIX, MINIX, QNX, COHERENT, etc.)
USASA	US and Africa Inter-continent discussion
USA_EURLINK	USA-Europe Link
USS_LIBERTY	USS Liberty (AGTR-5) Incident of June 8, 1967
VAX	VAX conference for users and managers of Digital's VAX.
VBBS	VBBS Support Forum
VFALSAC	Victims of False Accusations of Abuse
VIDEO	Video Making! Video Toaster, and home and semi-pro video
VID_GAME	Videogame System Discussion Echo
VIETNAM_VETS	Vietnam veterans
VIN_MAISON	Home Wine Makers' Conference

Conference	Subject
VIRUS_INFO	Virus Information Conference
VISUAL_BASIC	Visual Basic Programming Echo
WARNINGS	Warnings of Public Interest
WC_TECH	Wildcat Technical Echo
WELFARE	Welfare Conference
WELMAT	Welmat Support Echo
WGW	Genealogy Forum: "Who's Got What" (WGW)
WILDCAT	WILDCAT! BBS Sysops Conference
WILDRNSS	Wilderness Experience
WIN32	Windows/NT and Win32 Discussions Echo
WINDOWS	Microsoft Windows
WORDSTAR	International Wordstar Users Forum
WORLDTLK	World Talk Conference & United Nations News
WP-CRAFT	Wordperfect WRITERS support for anyone!
WP-TOOLS	Wordperfect TOOL development support for anyone!
WRITING	Writing
WUNDERMENT	Sf, fantasy, filk, fen, Faire, pagan, anarchy, anachrony
X00_USER	X00 FOSSIL Users' EchoMail Conference
XPRESS_SUPPORT	Xpress Off-line Mail System Support Confernce
XPRESS_SYSOP	Silver Xpress Sysop Support Conference
YALEBBS_SUPPORT	YaleBBS advanced graphic-style BBS support + YES emulation
YOUNG_ADULT	Young Adult Forum
Z1_ELECTION	Zone 1 Election Echo
ZEC	Zone 1 EchoMail Coordinator Echo Conference
ZMAIL	ZMail Support Conference
ZMODEM	Zmodem Help
ZYMURGY	Beer Homebrewing
ZYXEL	Zyxel Modem Echo
{COMMO}	{Commo} Comms Program

Conferences in other networks

Alternet (Zone 7) echoes

Conference	Subject
ALTERMAC	Alternative Macintosh conference
5_RINGS	

SIGnet (Zones 24–29, 34) echoes

ECHO	SIGnet <gated> "The Network" Echo
FIDO-SIG	
GUYS_N_GALS-ST	SIGnet Guy/Gal Chat Echo
NETWORKS_1201	SIGnet Network 1201 Conference
PUBLIC_PSYCH	
SIG.ADMIN	SIGnet Administration
SIG.BBSAD	SIGnet BBS Ads
SIG.ECHO	SIGnet EchoMail Topics
SIG.JOKE	SIGnet Humor Echo
SIG.OP	SIGnet Operations
SIG.TECH	SIGnet Tech Support
Z26_JUNK	SIGnet Zone 26 General Conference

Vervan's gaming network (Zone 45) echoes

AD&D_CHAT	[GEN]	AD&D Discussions	Ralph Merritt
AD&D_GAMER.GER	[GEN]	AD&D Discussions [in German]	
BATTLE_TECH	[WAR]	Battle Tech	John Sanchez
BLOODSTONE	[RPG]	AD&D Edition 2 Campaign	John Schnaubelt
CAR_WARS	[WAR]	Car Wars	John Bowlin
CYBERPUNK	[RPG]	Cyperpunk RPG	Will Nourse
HARNLINE	[GEN]	Columbia Games Conference	Michael Matson
IMPERIUM	[GEN]	Imperium Support Echo	Chris King
MELEE	[IND]	Melee Door Support Conference	Kevin Higgins
PAINT_BALL	[IND]	Paintball Players Forum	David Nolan
PARANOIA	[RPG]	Paranoia Module	Tom Hazel
ROLEPLAY.GER	[RPG]	RPG in German (From Germany)	Juergen Otte
SEATTLE_SPRAWL	[RPG]	Shadowrun RPG	Lancer
SF-BATTLES	[WAR]	Star Fleet Battles	George Crain
SHADOWRUN	[RPG]	Shadowrun	Edward Branley
TM_LIST	[IND]	Traveller Mailing List	Chuck McKnight
TRAVELLER	[RPG]	Traveller	Edward Branley
TRIAD	[RPG]	AD&D Edition 2 variant RPG	Wayne Shaw
TWIL_2000	[RPG]	Twilight 2000 RPG	Ron Marosko
V-LIBRARY	[GEN]	SF&F book reviews	Chris King
V-TREK	[RPG]	Star Trek RPG	Scott Royall
V_1889	[RPG]	Space 1889 RPG	Doc Urizen
V_BOARD	[GEN]	Boardgames Discussions	Nancy Feldman
V_CHESS	[WAR]	Play-by-Mail Chess	Ken Thierfelder
V_COMPGAME	[GEN]	RPG Computer Game Forum	Neal Feldman
V_CRYPT	[RPG]	Crystal Crypt RPG	John Blankenship
V_DAWN	[RPG]	Twilight of Dawn (AD&D2)	Mark Cleveland
V_GAMECOCK	[RPG]	AD&D Beginner's Game (1st Ed.)	David Nolan
V_GAMER	[GEN]	General Forum for RPG's	Nancy Feldman
V_GM	[GEN]	DM Discussion Forum	Nancy Feldman
V_GURPS	[RPG]	Generic Universal RPG	Neal Feldman
V_HERO	[RPG]	Champions Campaign	Game Knight
V_NETBIZ	[GEN]	VNET Network Business	Ron Lahti
V_RPG	[GEN]	VNET Game System Development	Jeff Freeman
V_STORY	[RPG]	Interactive Story Board	Neal Feldman
V_SYSOPS	[SYS]	General Forum for V-NET SYSOPS	Ron Lahti
V_THEGAME	[RPG]	AD&D 1st Edition RPG	David Nolan
V_TORG	[RPG]	Role Playing in the Multiverse Game Knight	
V_TORG_SD	[RPG]	Living Land Torg RPG	
V_VAMPIRE	[RPG]	White Wolf's Vampire RPG	John Boydston
V_WILLOW	[RPG]	Willowbrook Saga (Ars Magica)	Frank Lazar

Key

[FRP]	Fantasy Role-Playing Game
[GEN]	General Conference
IND]	Independant Echo carried on V-NET Backbone
[RES]	Restricted (VNET Coordinator must approve links)
[RPG]	Role-Playing Game
[SYS]	Sysop-Only Conference
[WAR]	War Game

EchoNet (Zone 50) echoes

ALL_TREK	EchoNet Star Trek (all types) Discussions
ECHO50	EchoNet General Conference
MOVIES_&_TV	EchoNet Movies & Television Discussions
RECIPE_CORNER	EchoNet Cooking/Recipes
STARC_ECHO	EchoNet *C/*EC Conference
WRITERS	EchoNet Writer's Forum

Treknet/Starfleet (Zone 87) echoes

FLEET_7	Starfleet Region 7 Conference
SF_ACAD	Starfleet Academy
SF_COMM	Starfleet Communications
SF_FAN	Starfleet Fans
SF_OPS	Starfleet Operations
SF_RECREATION	Starfleet Chatter Echo
SF_SCIENCE	Starfleet Science
SF_TREK	Starfleet on Star Trek (TOS/STTNG)
STARFLEET	TrekNet Starfleet Conference
STARFLEET_NET	Starfleet Members-Only General Conference
TREK_ORG	Treknet Organization
WARP_SPEED	Treknet General Conference

Eggnet (Zone 99) echoes

E_ADMIN	Eggnet READ ONLY Admin. Conference
E_SYSOP	Eggnet General Sysop-only Conference

FrEdMail Conferences

Subgroup: CALL Teachers' Classroom Projects and Calls for Collaboration. Most are moderated. No discussions or questions may be posted. This area is reserved exclusively for teachers who are looking for partners for their own projects. FrEdmail will provide personalized assistance and resources for teachers who are trying to manage their own collaborative learning projects.

call.partners	Requests for partner classes
call.general	General requests for project partners
call.ideas	Calls for cross- disciplinary projects (moderated)
call.mathsci	Math and science projects (moderated)
call.socsci	Geography, history, culture, surveys (moderated)
call.english	Language arts (moderated)
call.orillas	de Orilla a Orilla: en espanol y francais (moderated)

Subgroup: NEWS News and information

news.general	General news on many subjects; moderated forum where teachers can post news of a general nature which may appeal to a cross- section of users.
news.reportcard	America 2000 Daily Report Card (read only)
news.cnn	CNN Newsroom Daily Lesson Plans (read only)
news.cnndia	CNN Democracy in America Series (read only)
news.admin	Administrative Announcements for Schl.net newsgroups
news.newuser	Information and FAQ's for new users, posted by FrEdMail Foundation on a bi-weekly basis

Subgroup: SIG Special Interest Groups: General Discussion Forums. These are topics of general interest for teachers to discuss. More topics will be added as demand dictates.

sig.bridges	Adult mentors of differently abled students
sig.cosn	Consortium on School Networking (moderated)
sig.kidsnet	Kidsnet Discussions from U. of Pittsburgh (moderated)
sig.telemedia	Library & Media Specialists
sig.ibteacher	International Baccalaureate Teachers (moderated)
sig.video	Video, laser disks, CDROM

Subgroup CURR Curriculum Interest Groups: General Discussion Forums. These are similar to SIG's but are specific to curricular themes.

curr.art	Music, art, dance, drama
curr.logo	Logo & logowriter
curr.math	Math topics & discussions
curr.science	Science topics & discussions
curr.socsci	Social science topics & discussions
curr.sped	Special education
curr.tag	Talented and gifted
curr.tech	Computer science & technology

Subgroup: PROJ Current and Recent Classroom Projects write access: teachers/student assistants. Ongoing projects will be conducted in this area, so that all participants may "peek" at the progress of a topic and new participants may choose to join.

proj.fieldtrips	Field Trip Project (moderated)
proj.gala	Global Authors' Literary Anthology (moderated)
proj.geogame	Geogame Project (moderated)
proj.newsday	Semesterly NEWSDAY Newswire Service (moderated)
proj.hivaids	Jenkins Middle School HIV- AIDS Project

Subgroup: PUB Publish Student Writing. Electronic publishing of student work. Some topics are organized (GALA,NEWSDAY), others are open-ended. Teachers supervise the selection and posting of only the BEST of student work.

pub.fyi	Internet How-To's and FAQ's (moderated)
pub.hilites	Only the Best: Project Highlights (moderated)
pub.newsletter	Assorted Internet Periodicals & Newsletters (read only)
pub.student	General Student Writing Projects

Subgroup: STU Various student topics/exchanges. This is the place for students to correspond with one another. This should be the ONLY place where students are given free access. Every other area is under the specific guidance of a teacher. Students are expected, of course, to observe net etiquette. Other topics will be added as required.

stu.high   High school forum
stu.jrhi   Grades 7-9 forum
stu.elem   Elementary forum
stu.ibstudent   International Baccalaureate Conference
stu.projects   Student-organized projects & research

BITNET/USENET CONFERENCES

As of March 1, 1993

Conference	What it's about
bit.admin	bit Newsgroups Discussions.
bit.general	Discussions Relating to BitNet/Usenet.
bit.listserv.advanc-l	Geac Advanced Integrated Library System Users.
bit.listserv.advise-l	User Services List.
bit.listserv.aix-l	IBM AIX Discussion List.
bit.listserv.allmusic	Discussions on all forms of Music.
bit.listserv.appc-l	APPC Discussion List.
bit.listserv.apple2-l	Apple II List.
bit.listserv.applicat	Applications under BITNET.
bit.listserv.ashe-l	Higher Ed Policy and Research.
bit.listserv.asm370	IBM 370 Assembly Programming Discussions.
bit.listserv.autism	Autism and Developmental Disability List.
bit.listserv.banyan-l	Banyan Vines Network Software Discussions.
bit.listserv.big-lan	Campus-Size LAN Discussion Group (Moderated)
bit.listserv.billing	Chargeback of computer resources.
bit.listserv.biosph-l	Biosphere, ecology, Discussion List.
bit.listserv.bitnews	BITNET News.
bit.listserv.buslib-l	Business Libraries List.
bit.listserv.c+health	Computer and Health Discussion List.
bit.listserv.candle-l	Ca.dle Products Discussion List.
bit.listserv.catholic	Free Catholics Mailing List.
bit.listserv.cdromlan	CD-ROM on Local Area Networks.
bit.listserv.christia	Practical Christian Life (Moderated)
bit.listserv.cfs.newsletter	Chronic Fatigue Syndrome Newsletter (Moderated)
bit.listserv.cics-l	CICS Discussion List.
bit.listserv.cinema-l	Discussions on all forms of Cinema.
bit.listserv.circplus	Circulation Reserve and Related Library Issues.
bit.listserv.cmspip-l	VM/SP CMS Pipelines Discussion List.
bit.listserv.commed	Communication education.
bit.listserv.csg-l	Control System Group Network.
bit.listserv.cumrec-l	CUMREC-L Administrative computer use.
bit.listserv.cw-email	Campus-Wide E-mail Disussion List.
bit.listserv.cwis-l	Campus-Wide Information Systems.
bit.listserv.cyber-l	CDC Computer Discussion.
bit.listserv.c18-l	18th Century Interdisciplinary Discussion.
bit.listserv.c370-l	C/370 Discussion List.
bit.listserv.dasig	Database Administration.
bit.listserv.dbase-l	Discussion on the use of the dBase IV.
bit.listserv.db2-l	DB2 Data Base Discussion List.
bit.listserv.deaf-l	Deaf List.
bit.listserv.decnews	Digital Equipment Corporation News List.
bit.listserv.dectei-l	DECUS Education Software Library Discussions.
bit.listserv.devel-l	Technology Transfer in International Development.
bit.listserv.disarm-l	Disarmament Discussion List.
bit.listserv.domain-l	Domains Discussion Group.
bit.listserv.earntech	EARN Technical Group.
bit.listserv.edi-l	Electronic Data Interchange Issues.
bit.listserv.edpolyan	Professionals and Students Discuss Education.
bit.listserv.edstat-l	Statistics Education Discussion List.
bit.listserv.edtech	EDTECH - Educational Technology (Moderated)

Conference	What it's about
bit.listserv.edusig-l	EDUSIG Discussions.
bit.listserv.emusic-l	Electronic Music Discussion List.
bit.listserv.envbeh-l	Forum on Environment and Human Behavior.
bit.listserv.erl-l	Educational Research List.
bit.listserv.ethics-l	Discussion of Ethics in Computing.
bit.listserv.ethology	Ethology List.
bit.listserv.euearn-l	Eastern Europe List.
bit.listserv.film-l	Film making and reviews List.
bit.listserv.fnord-l	New Ways of Thinking List.
bit.listserv.free-l	Fathers Rights and Equality Discussion List.
bit.listserv.frac-l	FRACTAL Discussion List.
bit.listserv.games-l	Computer Games List.
bit.listserv.gaynet	GayNet Discussion List (Moderated)
bit.listserv.gddm-l	The GDDM Discussion List
bit.listserv.geodesic	List for the Discussion of Buckminster Fuller.
bit.listserv.gguide	BITNIC GGUIDE List.
bit.listserv.govdoc-l	Discussion of Government Document Issues.
bit.listserv.gutnberg	GUTNBERG Discussion List.
bit.listserv.hellas	The Hellenic Discussion List (Moderated)
bit.listserv.history	History List.
bit.listserv.i-amiga	Info-Amiga List.
bit.listserv.ibm-hesc	IBM Higher Education Consortium.
bit.listserv.ibm-main	IBM Mainframe Discussion List.
bit.listserv.ibm-nets	BITNIC IBM-NETS List.
bit.listserv.ibmtcp-l	IBM TCP/IP List.
bit.listserv.ibm7171	Protocol Converter List.
bit.listserv.india-d	India Interest Group (Moderated)
bit.listserv.info-gcg	INFO-GCG: GCG Genetics Software Discussion.
bit.listserv.infonets	Infonets Redistribution.
bit.listserv.ingrafx	Information Graphics.
bit.listserv.innopac	Innovative Interfaces Online Public Access.
bit.listserv.ioob-l	Industrial Psychology.
bit.listserv.isn	ISN Data Switch Technical Discussion Group.
bit.listserv.jes2-l	JES2 Discussion group.
bit.listserv.jnet-l	BITNIC JNET-L List.
bit.listserv.l-hcap	Handicap List (Moderated)
bit.listserv.l-vmctr	VMCENTER Components Discussion List.
bit.listserv.lawsch-l	Law School Discussion List.
bit.listserv.liaison	BITNIC LIAISON.
bit.listserv.libref-l	Library Reference Issues.
bit.listserv.libres	Library and Information Science Research (Moderated)
bit.listserv.license	Software Licensing List.
bit.listserv.linkfail	Link failure announcements.
bit.listserv.literary	Discussions about Literature.
bit.listserv.lstsrv-l	Forum on LISTSERV.
bit.listserv.mail-l	BITNIC MAIL-L List.
bit.listserv.mailbook	MAIL/MAILBOOK subscription List.
bit.listserv.mba-l	MBA Student curriculum Discussion.
bit.listserv.mbu-l	Megabyte University - Computers and Writing.
bit.listserv.mdphd-l	Dual Degree Programs Discussion List.
bit.listserv.medlib-l	Medical Libraries Discussion List.
bit.listserv.mednews	Health Info-Com Network Newsletter (Moderated)
bit.listserv.mideur-l	Middle Europe Discussion List.
bit.listserv.netnws-l	NETNWS-L Netnews List.
bit.listserv.nettrain	Network Trainers List.
bit.listserv.new-list	NEW-LIST - New List Announcements (Moderated)
bit.listserv.next-l	NeXT Computer List.
bit.listserv.nodmgt-l	Node Management.
bit.listserv.notis-l	NOTIS/DOBIS Discussion group List.
bit.listserv.notabene	Nota Bene List.
bit.listserv.novell	Novell LAN Interest Group.
bit.listserv.omrscan	OMR Scanner Discussion.
bit.listserv.ozone	OZONE Discussion List.
bit.listserv.pacs-l	Public-Access Computer System Forum (Moderated)
bit.listserv.page-l	IBM 3812/3820 Tips and Problems Discussion List.
bit.listserv.pagemakr	PageMaker for Desktop Publishers.
bit.listserv.pmdf-l	PMDF Distribution List.
bit.listserv.politics	Forum for the Discussion of Politics.
bit.listserv.power-l	POWER-L IBM RS/6000 POWER Family.
bit.listserv.psycgrad	Psychology Grad Student Discussions.
bit.listserv.qualrs-l	Qualitative Research of the Human Sciences.

Conference	What it's about
bit.listserv.relusr-l	Relay Users Forum.
bit.listserv.rhetoric	Rhetoric, social movements, persuasion.
bit.listserv.rscs-l	VM/RSCS Mailing List.
bit.listserv.rscsmods	The RSCS modifications List.
bit.listserv.s-comput	SuperComputers List.
bit.listserv.sas-l	SAS Discussion.
bit.listserv.script-l	IBM vs Waterloo SCRIPT Discussion Group.
bit.listserv.scuba-l	Scuba diving Discussion List.
bit.listserv.seasia-l	Southeast Asia Discussion List.
bit.listserv.seds-l	Interchapter SEDS Communications.
bit.listserv.sfs-l	VM Shared File System Discussion List.
bit.listserv.sganet	Student Government Global Mail Network.
bit.listserv.simula	The SIMULA Language List.
bit.listserv.slart-l	SLA Research and Teaching.
bit.listserv.slovak-l	Slovak Discussion List.
bit.listserv.snamgt-l	SNA Network Management Discussion.
bit.listserv.sos-data	Social Science Data List.
bit.listserv.spires-l	SPIRES Conference List.
bit.listserv.sportpsy	Exercise and Sports Psychology.
bit.listserv.spssx-l	SPSSX Discussion.
bit.listserv.sqlinfo	Forum for SQL/DS and Related Topics.
bit.listserv.stat-l	STATISTICAL CONSULTING.
bit.listserv.tech-l	BITNIC TECH-L List.
bit.listserv.test	Test Newsgroup.
bit.listserv.tex-l	The TeXnical topics List.
bit.listserv.tn3270-l	tn3270 protocol Discussion List.
bit.listserv.toolb-l	Asymetrix Toolbook List.
bit.listserv.trans-l	BITNIC TRANS-L List.
bit.listserv.travel-l	Tourism Discussions.
bit.listserv.ucp-l	University Computing Project Mailing List.
bit.listserv.ug-l	Usage Guidelines.
bit.listserv.uigis-l	User Interface for Geographical Info Systems.
bit.listserv.urep-l	UREP-L Mailing List.
bit.listserv.usrdir-l	User Directory List.
bit.listserv.valert-l	Virus Alert List (Moderated)
bit.listserv.vfort-l	VS-Fortran Discussion List.
bit.listserv.vm-util	VM Utilities Discussion List.
bit.listserv.vmesa-l	VM/ESA Mailing List.
bit.listserv.vmslsv-l	VAX/VMS LISTSERV Discussion List.
bit.listserv.vmxa-l	VM/XA Discussion List.
bit.listserv.vnews-l	VNEWS Discussion List.
bit.listserv.vpiej-l	Electronic Publishing Discussion List.
bit.listserv.win3-l	Microsoft Windows Version 3 Forum.
bit.listserv.words-l	English Language Discussion Group.
bit.listserv.wpwin-l	WordPerfect for Windows.
bit.listserv.wpcorp-l	WordPerfect Corporation Products Discussions.
bit.listserv.xcult-l	International Intercultural Newsletter.
bit.listserv.xedit-l	VM System Editor List.
bit.listserv.xerox-l	The Xerox Discussion List.
bit.listserv.xmailer	Crosswell Mailer.
bit.listserv.xtropy-l	Extopian List.
bit.listserv.x400-l	x.400 Protocol List.
bit.listserv.9370-l	IBM 9370 and VM/IS specific topics List.
bit.listserv.3com-l	3Com Products Discussion List.
bit.mailserv.word-mac	Word Processing on the Macintosh.
bit.mailserv.word-pc	Word Processing on the IBM PC.

ONENET CONFERENCES

Conference	Location	Conference	Location
ArtNet	ArtNet-main conf	Español	International-sub
ArtGrants	ArtNet-sub	EuroTalk	International-sub
Spaces For Art	ArtNet-sub	Français	International-sub
ARTs Networking	ArtNet-sub	Francophonie	International-sub
ARTs Info	ArtNet-sub	Japan Talk	International-sub
ArtPublications	ArtNet-sub	Lingua Latina	International-sub
ArtTalk	ArtNet-sub	Nihongo	International-sub
Computer Equip.	Classifieds-sub	Reference & News	International-sub
Transportation	Classifieds-sub	New Questions	Life-Dear Darla-sub
Property	Classifieds-sub	Darla Replies	Life-Dear Darla-sub-read
Commercial	Classifieds-sub	History	Life-Education-sub
Misc. Classifieds	Classifieds-sub	Math	Life-Education-sub
Jobs Offered	Classifieds-sub	Sciences	Life-Education-sub
Audio&Video	Classifieds-sub	Computer Sciences	Life-Education-sub
Photography	Classifieds-sub	English	Life-Education-sub
Help Offered	Classifieds-sub	Foreign Language	Life-Education-sub
Romance & Friendship	Classifieds-sub	Study Skills	Life-Education-sub
Book Ends	Entertainment-Books-sub	EMSInfo	Life-Medical-sub
Readers Choice	Entertainment-Books-sub	Medical Library	Life-Medical-sub-files
ReidTHIS	Entertainment-Books-sub	Medical Software	Life-Medical-sub-files
Book Reviews	Entertainment-Books-sub	MD's Only	Life-Medical-sub-Private/MD's
Movie Reviews	Entertainment-Film-sub	RUSH!	Life-Politics-sub
AD&D	Entertainment-Gaming-sub	Politics, USA	Life-Politics-sub
JokeHeap	Entertainment-Humor-sub	Dear Darla	Life-sub
Oracle Digests	Entertainment-Humor-sub	Medical	Life-sub
Political Jokes	Entertainment-Humor-sub	Environment	Life-sub
Stories/Accounts	Entertainment-Humor-sub	Edu-Tech	Life-sub
Top Ten Lists	Entertainment-Humor-sub	Careers	Life-sub
Jokes	Entertainment-Humor-sub	Politics	Life-sub
Armor Alley	Entertainment-Modem Game-sub	Education	Life-sub
Bolo	Entertainment-Modem Game-sub	Religion	Life-sub
Falcon	Entertainment-Modem Game-sub	VoxPopuli	Life-sub
Minotaur	Entertainment-Modem Game-sub	Interactive Media	Life-sub
Robosport	Entertainment-Modem Game-sub	Teen Talk	Life-sub-Private/Teen's only
Auto Racing/RC	Entertainment-Sports-sub	Teen Talk Dating	Life-T Talk-sub-Teen's only
Characters	Entertainment-Star Trek-STIAS	Teen Talk Music	Life-T Talk-sub-Teen's only
Deep Space Nine	Entertainment-Star Trek-sub	Teen Talk Discussion	Life-T Talk-sub-Teen's only
Lynch Reviews	Entertainment-Star Trek-sub	Teen Talk Computers	Life-T Talk-sub-Teen's only
ST:IAS	Entertainment-Star Trek-sub	System Seven	Mac Technical-sub
STARNET	Entertainment-Star Trek-sub	Mac Programming	Mac Technical-sub
Comics	Entertainment-sub	Ask Apple	Mac Technical-sub
Pro Wrestling	Entertainment-sub	Graphics & Animation	Mac Technical-sub
Dancing	Entertainment-sub	QuickTime	Mac Technical-sub
Books	Entertainment-sub	Mac Software	Mac Technical-sub
Sports	Entertainment-sub	MultiMedia	Mac Technical-sub
Star Trek	Entertainment-sub	Musicians & MIDI	Mac Technical-sub
Television	Entertainment-sub	Mac Hardware	Mac Technical-sub
Mind Puzzles	Entertainment-sub	Publishing/PrePress	Mac Technical-sub
Sci Fi	Entertainment-sub	PowerBook	Mac Technical-sub
Modem Games	Entertainment-sub	Online Services	Mac Technical-sub
Gaming	Entertainment-sub	Modems	Mac Technical-sub
Theater	Entertainment-sub	HyperCard	Mac Technical-sub
Audio/Video	Entertainment-sub	PowerPC's	Mac Technical-sub
Music	Entertainment-sub	Apple Answers	Mac Technical-sub-read
FirstClass Suggestions	FirstClass-sub	Apple Press Releases	News-sub
FirstClass News	FirstClass-sub	NuBytes	News-sub
FirstClass Support	FirstClass-sub	OneNet feedback	OneNet Comments-sub
BulkRate	FirstClass-sub	OneNet Member	Private-Admin's only
FirstClass Systems	FirstClass-sub	FirstClass Admins	Private-Admin's only
Your Privacy	General Discussion-sub	Admins Wish List	Private-FC Admins-sub
OneNet Friends	General Discussion-sub	Latest FC Software	Private-FC Admins-sub
Beschuit	International-sub	OneNet Logo/Artwork	Private-FC Admins-sub
Deutsch	International-sub	Tools/Resources	Private-FC Admins-sub
English!	International-sub	Admin Tips	Private-ON Member-sub

Conference	Location
Euro Admins	Private-ON Member-sub
OneNet Alerts	Private-ON Member-sub
New On OneNet	Private-ON Member-sub
NASA Daily News	Science-Space News-sub
Mars Observer Reports	Science-Space News-sub
Galileo Reports	Science-Space News-sub
HST Reports	Science-Space News-sub
Magellan Reports	Science-Space News-sub
GRO Reports	Science-Space News-sub
Russian Space News	Science-Space News-sub
Shuttle Mission Reports	Science-Space News-sub
ESA Reports	Science-Space News-sub
Shuttle Status Reports	Science-Space News-sub
NASA Press Releases	Science-Space News-sub
Announcements	Science-Space News-sub
Space Periodicals	Science-Space News-sub
Scientific Satellites	Science-Space news-sub
Physics	Science-sub
Biotechnology	Science-sub
Chemistry	Science-sub
Computer Science	Science-sub
Astronomy & Space	Science-sub
ScienceTalk	Science-sub
AutoPix	Special Int-Autotalk-sub-file
AutoText	Special Int-Autotalk-sub-file
HamRadio	Special Int-Ham-sub
Ham For Sale	Special Int-Ham-sub
SWL & Scanners	Special Int-Ham-sub
HAMlet	Special Int-Ham-sub
HamRadioFiles	Special Int-Ham-sub-file
CUE	Special Int-Misc-sub
Flix'n'Pix	Special Int-Misc-sub
in St.Louis	Special Int-Misc-sub
Isaac Newton?	Special Int-Misc-sub
MNS Reviews	Special Int-Misc-sub
Tips&Trix	Special Int-Misc-sub
Consumer Action	Special Int-Product Watch-sub
Soft/HardwareReviews	Special Int-Product Watch-sub
Claris S.I.G.	Special Int-Software-sub
4DDeveloper	Special Int-Software-sub
Prograph	Special Int-Software-sub
Script Frontier	Special Int-Software-sub
JFK Assassination	Special Int-SPYNET-sub
King Assassination	Special Int-SPYNET-sub
RFK Assassination	Special Int-SPYNET-sub
Conspiracies and Beyond	Special Int-SPYNET-sub
USA Intelligence	Special Int-SPYNET-sub
Recommended Books	Special Int-SPYNET-sub
Recommended Magazines	Special Int-SPYNET-sub
MIDI	Special Int-sub
AutoTalk	Special Int-sub
Anti-Virus	Special Int-sub
Model/Railfanning	Special Int-sub
BMUG International	Special Int-sub
Aviation	Special Int-sub
Kids Software Forum	Special Int-sub
UFO Watchers	Special Int-sub
A32	Special Int-sub
AskDR.PostScript	Special Int-sub
Bike Shop	Special Int-sub
ChipMUG	Special Int-sub
CyberLawOneNet	Special Int-sub
Earthquake Awareness	Special Int-sub
GraphicArtistsGuild	Special Int-sub
Skiing	Special Int-sub
Abortion	Special Int-sub
Virtual Reality	Special Int-sub
SMUG	Special Int-sub
Journalism	Special Int-sub
Law & Order	Special Int-sub
Fire Fighting	Special Int-sub

Conference	Location
SPYNET	Special Int-sub
Los Altos Law	Special Int-sub
IMG Online Issues	Vendor-IMG-sub
IMG Poll Results	Vendor-IMG-sub
OB Tech. Support	Vendor-Perfit-sub
OB Computers For Sale	Vendor-Perfit-sub
OB Sales/Upgrade Info.	Vendor-PerFit-sub-read
OB Tech. Notes	Vendor-PerFit-sub-read
OB Software to Download	Vendor-PerFit-sub-read-files
Broderbund	Vendor-sub
MacWEEK Q&A	Vendor-sub
Sigma Design Associates	Vendor-sub
Alias Research	Vendor-sub
Connectix	Vendor-sub
Wired Magazine	Vendor-sub
IMG Online Magazine	Vendor-sub
Berkley Systems	Vendor-sub
Global Village Support	Vendor-sub
PLI	Vendor-sub
Ask I.E.	Vendor-sub
PerFit	Vendor-sub
Windows Tech Forum	Windows-Master conf

Appendix K: Glossary

Common terms and what they mean

3270
An IBM terminal capable of limited graphics that is used to connect to IBM mainframe computers. These terminals transmit blocks of data at a time, rather than single characters. 3270-emulation hardware and software is now available for most personal computers, including the Macintosh and IBM-PCs.

Address
In the FidoNet address 1:161/445.2, 445 is the node number; 161 is the network number (East Bay); and 1 is the zone number (North America).

In a TCP/IP address of the form 192.187.134.3, the division of the network and node numbers is determined by the address class. With the Internet on the verge of exhausting its class B address space, alternative addressing schemes are under examination.

ACK
The character ACK (ASCII 06) is used in several transmission protocols to acknowledge correct receipt of a packet.

Address Resolution Protocol (ARP)
ARP, covered in RFC 826, allows a node to find another system's physical address, given its TCP/IP address. ARP is not part of the Internet layer, but rather is included in the Network Access Layer. It may only be used on networks that allow broadcasting of messages to all nodes on the physical network. The table of physical addresses built via ARP requests is called the ARP table and may be examined via the `arp` command.

alias
A nickname for a longer string that is used to make it easier to type email addresses or UNIX commands. **Command aliases are usually contained in a startup script, such as the .login or .cshrc file, or for electronic mail, in the .mailrc file, where they can be used to create outbound mailing lists.** `alias` commands may also be used within the /etc/sendmail/aliases or equivalent file in order to create mail exploders or inbound mailing

lists. However, modifying these files requires root access.

ARJ
Currently the tighest compression format on the PC; it can be decompressed using unArjMac. If you run a PC-based BBS and are looking to save disk space and transmission time, you may wish to consider compressing outgoing packets with ARJ.

Alternet
An Internet service provided by UUNET. Also the name of an (unrelated) alternative network to FidoNet, started in 1987 by Thom Henderson of Systems Enhancement Associates (SEA). Alternet currently adheres to FidoNet Technical Specifications, although there is no guarantee that it will continue to. The major distinction between Alternet and FidoNet is the concept of chivalry. Alternet has a decidedly medieval flavor, which permeates its terminology. (For instance, Alternet region hosts refer to themselves as Dukes.) Also, Alternet has adopted standards of politeness and manners that are to govern behavior; in practice, however, relations are only slightly more polite or mature on Alternet than on FidoNet. The Fido Alternet is not to be confused with the service from UUNET, Inc., of the same name, which provides Internet connectivity services. Currently, Alternet is approximately 10% of the size of FidoNet.

Amplitude Shift Keying (ASK)
A simple form of modulation in which a carrier frequency is turned on and off to represent the presence or absence of a logic 1 signal. ASK is only useful for transmitting in a single direction (simplex), or in one direction at a time (half-duplex), because it does not divide the channel into multiple frequencies (frequency division multiplexing).

ANSI Graphics
American National Standards Institute graphics characters. This refers to ANSI standard X3.64-1979, which allows for adding additional functions to terminal emulators and other devices. For example, the sequence (ESC) E means Next Line. Thus, a series of characters performs a single function. Using ANSI

X3.64 sequences, it is possible to produce fairly elaborate color displays. Many BBSes use ANSI graphics, and so it is useful to have a terminal emulator that can display ANSI graphics in color.

Apple File Exchange (AFE)

A utility from Apple that allows for transfer and subsequent conversion of a PC or Apple II file to Macintosh format. Third-party vendors such as DataViz supply their translators as AFE add-in modules.

ARC

A compression program developed by Systems Enhancement Associates (SEA) that is still the most frequently used compression utility for FidoNet systems. ARC was formerly shareware but as of version 7.0 is now commercial. The most recent shareware version of ARC is version 6.1.

ARCmail

This refers to FidoNet mail packets that have been compressed using the ARC utility from Systems Enhancement Associates (SEA).

AREAS.BBS

A file used under SEAdog, BinkleyTerm, and TBBS (and many others) which lists the conferences that are being received and transmitted on a given FidoNet system.

AREAFIX

A utility that allows updating the AREAS.BBS or ECHO.CTL file via NetMail. This allows point mailers or other network connections to update the echoes they are receiving without sysop intervention. A must-have. The documentation states that AREAFIX is compatible with QUICKBBS, Fido, and OPUS; however, I have used it with TBBS without a hitch.

ARQ

Automatic ReQuest for repeat, an error detection and correction technology that involves waiting for positive (ACK) or negative acknowledgment before sending another block of data.

ASCII

Stands for ANSI Standard (x3.4-1977, revised 1983) Code for Information Interchange. ASCII is a 7-bit code, thus allowing the 8th bit to be used for other purposes. ASCII characters thus go from 0 to 127.

Asynchronous communications

In asynchronous communications, characters do not need to be transmitted constantly. The start and end of a character therefore needs to be set off by use of a start bit and one or more stop bits.

Acceptable Use Policy (AUP)

The policy that governs acceptable uses of a network. Such policies are different for each network and may even differ between regions within a network. For example, the National Science Foundation AUP only applies to use of the NSFNet backbone; many regional networks have adopted less-restrictive policies. Controversies over AUPs and network governance are two common factors driving the creation of new networks.

Archie

A program that catalogs files on hundreds of anonymous FTP sites worldwide and allows users to search against this database by interactive connection, email, or a protocol known as Prospero.

Auto-Answer

A modem set up to answer the phone when called is said to be set to auto-answer.

Auto-dialer

Software that repeatedly dials a phone number, until it gets through. An early Macintosh example was Leo Laporté's QDial. Useful for dialing busy single-line bulletin boards. Make sure you've got the right number before using one of these!

Backbone

A high-capacity series of links that carries a large volume of network traffic. On the Internet the term usually refers to the NSFNet, a National Science Foundation–funded series of links operating at 22 mbps. On the FidoNet, many of the larger FidoNet conferences are carried across the country on a series of links known as the FileBone (for files) or Echo Backbone (for conferences). Each region within FidoNet contains Echo coordinators and may contain a FileBone coordinator that receives and distributes backbone conferences and files. In order to economize, all backbone nodes utilize high speed USR HST modems operating at 16,800 bps. Before PC Pursuit changed its billing policies, the backbone had utilized its service, but is not now utilizing packet-switching services. In order for a conference to reside on the backbone, it needs to have sufficient volume, and it also needs to agree to conform to established distribution policy, known as ECHOPOL. Not all conferences are distributed over the backbone.

Bandwidth

The range of frequencies that can be passed over a given channel. The public-access phone system has a bandwidth of approximately 3 KHz. The greater the range, the more information that can be transmitted.

Baud

In the popular lingo, baud is indistinguishable from bits per second (bps). However, technically these terms are not synonymous. The baud rate is the frequency of the carrier that is used in transmitting information with a modem. A 300 bps modem transmits at 300 baud, or using a 300 Hz carrier frequency. It uses Frequency Shift Keying (FSK), which transmits 1 bit for each baud transition. A 1200 bps modem also transmits with a 300 Hz carrier, but gets 4 bits per baud. A 2400 bps modem uses 8 bits per transition, also with a 300 Hz carrier.

Berkeley Software Distribution (BSD)

A version of UNIX developed by the University of California, Berkeley, which is now the subject of a lawsuit by Unix Systems Laboratories (USL). BSD derived ports to the 80386 include 386BSD, BSDI, and NetBSD. It is possible that BSD-derived products will be the basis for many Internet BBSes.

Bimodem

A telecommunications protocol that allows for transmission of data in both directions at once. Bimodem can be usefully implemented only with full-duplex modems that are capable of transmitting and receiving at the same time, at equal rates. Pseudo-full-duplex modems can transmit and receive at the same time, but one channel is much faster than the other. Such modems are not appropriate for use with Bimodem.

BinHex 4.0

A Macintosh program that converts a Mac application or document with both a data fork and a resource fork into an ASCII text file. These files can be sent over 7-bit channels, such as Internet mail. BinHex 4.0 encoding and decoding is also available within StuffIt Deluxe v.3.0.

BinHex 5.0

A Macintosh program that converts a Mac application or document with a data fork and a resource fork into a single-fork binary-file format also known as MacBinary. These files can be transmitted to PC-based bulletin board systems and subsequently downloaded without difficulty by Mac users using MacBinary reception.

BinkleyTerm

A complex FidoNet external mailer for the IBM-PC written by Vince Perriello and Bob Hartman of Bit Bucket Software. BinkleyTerm can be used to construct a point system on the PC as an external mailer for a compatible BBS system such as Fido, TBBS, OPUS, or WildCat, or even as a terminal emulator used to call BBSes in the FidoNet Nodelist.

Bisync

Stands for Binary Synchronous Communications. Introduced by IBM in 1968 to allow for communication with batch and video terminals. Bisync uses packet headers and CRCs when transmitting EBCDIC characters in order to provide error detection and retransmission.

BITNET

Because It's Time NETwork, a network communicating via the Remote Job Entry (RJE) protocols that communicates over serial lines as well as TCP/IP. BITNET mail is sent via a gateway to the Internet by the CUNYVM machine and others. BITNET machines are capable of performing various server functions for which they are notorious on the network. Among these are LISTSERVs, which can mail conferences to individuals.

Bit

A single binary digit of information. A bit can be on (1) or off (0). No maybe's!

Bits per second

A measure of the rate of data transmission. Typically, these rates do not include the transmission of stop and start bits, which do not provide useful information. Thus, a rate of 2400 bits per second only provides for transmission of 240 bytes or characters of data per second.

BIX

Byte Information eXchange. A commercial online service owned by DELPHI.

BLocked ASynchronous Transmission (BLAST)

A proprietary file transfer-protocol developed by Communications Research Group that is capable of sending and receiving simultaneously. BLAST is available for the Macintosh, the PC, UNIX machines, and IBM mainframes.

Boardwatch

A magazine that covers BBSes and other aspects of telecommunications. This magazine is written from the point of view of the user, rather than the vendors of telecommunications hardware and software.

Bulletin board system (BBS)

A BBS is a software program that accepts connections and provides services such as email, distributed conferencing, database access, file transfer, and online chatting. BBSes have traditionally been part of store and forward networks such as UUCP and FidoNet but are now making their presence felt on the Internet.

Break character
A sequence of bits with a start bit, eight 0s, and instead of stop bits, zero bits. The improper framing of the break character allows it to be distinguished from a normal character.

Bridge
A device that connects network segments at the datalink layer. On TCP/IP networks, both sides of the bridge have the same network ID. Bridges are often used to isolate heavy traffic areas of the network to avoid congestion. Collision rates above 5% (collected from the `netstat` command) indicate the possible need for a bridge.

Brouter
A device that combines the functions of a bridge (datalink layer) and a router (network layer); it performs a combination of both functions depending on how it is configured.

Buffer
A sequence of bytes, used to hold characters as they are received or before they are transmitted. Use of a buffer allows for the handling of incoming or outgoing serial data without each character having to be individually handled, which would waste processing power.

Byte
A single character of data, 8 bits long.

Capture
A feature of most telecommunications programs that allows the user to save incoming and outgoing characters to disk. This allows you to review the session after the fact.

Carrier Detect (DCD)
A line on the RS-232 standard that is brought high when a modem establishes a connection. This allows telecommunications software to respond appropriately, such as by sending a greeting to the caller, or, when carrier detect fails, by hanging up the modem. In the DB-25 connector for RS-232, DCD is pin 8.

Castle Tabby
The home of the author of Tabby, Michael Connick, node 1:107/412, (908)988-0706.

CBCS
Computer Based Conversation System. Equivalent to BBS. First coined by Wynn Wagner III to describe the OPUS BBS software.

Characters per second
A measure of the rate of data transmission. These rates adjust for the transmission of stop and start bits and therefore give a more realistic measure of transfer rates than bits per second. With a 9600 bps modem, transfer rates of 850 characters per second are typical. With V.32*bis* or HST/DS modems, rates of 1700 characters per second are possible.

Chatting
An activity on a bulletin board system in which people type messages to each other. Usually, chatting is popular on systems with eight or more lines. Chatting simulates talking on a party line.

Checksum
A mechanism for error detection used in protocols such as XMODEM and KERMIT. The Checksum method is not as foolproof as the Cyclic Redundancy Check (CRC), so CRC should be used instead whenever possible.

Clear To Send (CTS)
When this RS-232 signal is asserted, it means that the modem is ready to accept data from the computer.

Comité Consultatif Internationale de Télégraphie et Téléphonie (CCITT)
The International Telegraph and Telephone Consultative Committee. CCITT is a committee that sets international standards such as the V.22*bis*, V.32, and V.42 modem standards.

Confmail
A mail tosser compatible with Fido and OPUS BBSes, written by Bob Hartman. This program has been superseded by software such as QMAIL and SQUISH.

Continuous Mail
The ability of a FidoNet system to receive mail at any time. The ability to receive continuous mail is useful because, due to delays and other mishaps, it is rare for all mail to arrive during the National Mail Hour. If this period is missed, then the mail will have to wait until the next day. The ability to receive mail around the clock therefore improves the overall mail transit time.

Most single-line BBS software now offers continuous mail by use of a mailer program. When you call up the BBS system, some sequence of characters (such as the double-ESC of FrontDoor) is required to cause the mailer to transfer control to the BBS software.

Copernicus
The first Macintosh point mailer, written by Michael Pester and Michael Connick.

Corporation for Research and Educational Networking (CREN)
The nonprofit organization that runs the U.S. portion of BITNET. The Canadian equivalent of CREN is NetNorth; the European equivalent is EARN.

COUNTERPoint
Shareware point system for the Macintosh that requires addition of an external mailer such as Copernicus II, Formula 1 or Tabby.

Crash mail
Crash mail is mail that must be delivered immediately, rather than during normally scheduled mail periods. Since mail may be delivered when phone rates are high, crash mail is inherently more expensive than normal mail.

CompuServe Information Service (CIS)
One of the first, and still one of the most extensive, commercial online services. CompuServe Information Service (CIS) has also been a pioneer in the data communications field, authoring the QuickB communications protocol, and the Graphics Interchange Format (GIF) graphics standard, among others. CompuServe offers an incredible array of services, from online airline reservations to trademark and patent searches. Through the CompuServe Information Manager (CIM) many of these services are available via a graphical user interface. Now owned by H&R Block.

CPS
Characters per second. A measure of the data transmission rate. For high-speed modems, speeds of up to 2000 characters per second have been reported, while speeds of 1300 characters per second are more typical.

CPU (Central Processing Unit)
The heart of a computer, which includes the arithmetic logic unit, the control unit, etc.

CRC
Cyclic Redundancy Check. Several types of CRC's are available, including CRC-16, CRC-32, and CRC-CCIT.

CRT
Cathode Ray Tube. The technology underlying most computer displays.

Cypherpunks
Individuals passionately devoted to privacy. Cypherpunk resources include mailing lists (cypherpunks-request@toad.com, info-pgp-request@lucpul.it.luc.edu on the Pretty Good Privacy program); archives (`ftp rsa.com,`

`get /pub/faq.ps.Z` for an RSA FAQ, `ftp soda.berkeley.edu, cd /pub/cypherpunks`).

D'Bridge
A commercial FidoNet external mailer developed by Chris Irwin that includes a number of nice features such as a built-in tosser as well as menu-based operation. I recommend subscribing to the D'BRIDGE echo for a while to see what it's like before purchasing it.

DASNet
A commercial service based on QNX that connects disparate networks. Some commercial online services utilize DASNet to connect their systems to the Internet.

Data Bits
The number of bits within a byte that are used to represent data. If 7 bits are used (as is the case with many UNIX systems), the 8th bit is used for parity, and your telecommunications software must be set accordingly. If all 8 bits are available for use, then usually no parity bit is sent. Note that it is not possible to send a binary file across a 7-bit channel without some kind of translation taking place. Such translation is performed by KERMIT; it also can be accomplished by running the file through BinHex 4.0.

Data Encryption Standard (DES)
A U.S. government standard for encryption, vulnerable to brute-force attack by supercomputers.

datagram
The smallest independent entity within the Internet layer of the TCP/IP protocols. Within the Network Access Layer of TCP/IP, such an entity is referred to as a *frame*; within the transport layer of TCP it is known as a *segment*, and within UDP, as a *packet*.

Data Set Ready (DSR)
A signal under the RS-232 standard that is asserted by data communications equipment (DCE) such as a modem to signify that the DCE is ready to communicate.

Data Terminal Ready (DTR)
A signal under the RS-232 standard that is asserted by the data terminal equipment (DTE) to signify that it is ready to communicate. DTR is de-asserted to cause the modem to hang up.

DCE
Data Communications Equipment.

Default route
The default path by which datagrams are to be forwarded when the other alternatives in the routing table do not apply. Typically with a BBS, the default route will be over a SLIP or PPP link to an Internet provider and will be configured using the `route` statement at bootup, via insertion of a command in the /etc/rc.local file, for example. The default route and other routing table entries may be checked via the `netstat` command.

Deluxe
The version of a product containing mostly unecessary features in addition to one or two critical additions, for which the customer is expected to pay 200% of the price of the low-end package.

DIALOG
A commercial online service specializing in bibliographic databases.

dig
Software that provides Domain Name Service information (such as mail and address records) for Internet sites in a slightly more flexible way than nslookup. See also nslookup.

Domain
A portion of a network. Domain Name Service (DNS) refers to a decentralized system used by the Internet for resolving machine names to IP addresses. In FidoNet, a not yet commonly adopted method for integrating nodelist processing from disparate networks.

Doors
External programs that are written to add functionality to a bulletin board. Most doors are written for single-line bulletin boards, because MS-DOS does not support multitasking or the shared interrupts of multiport serial port boards.

Dow Jones News Retrieval
An online service oriented toward business information, Dow Jones is a good place to get quarterly reports on firms you may be tracking for investment purposes. Also one of the more expensive online services.

Dupes
Slang for duplicate messages. On FidoNet, dupes occur when a closed loop occurs somewhere within the network topology. This can happen, for example, when node 1:161/444 sends mail to node 1:203/34 as well as to node 1:161/84 while nodes 1:203/34 and 1:161/84 both send the mail to node 1:203/1. As a result, node 1:203/1 will receive two copies of each message in the misrouted conference. This makes echo moderators very angry! To prevent duplicates,

most BBSes now include a dupe checker, which maintains a record of recently handled messages. Duplicate incoming messages are automatically discarded. To cut down on duplicates and debug the network topology, policies like Echo Pol have been instituted.

Dutchie
One of the first point mail systems, written by Hank Weavers of the Netherlands.

EBCDIC
A data interchange format rivaling ASCII that was created by IBM and is rarely used outside the world of IBM mainframes.

Echo
FidoNet term for a shared public conference. Also, the name of a USENET-connected conferencing system in New York.

ECHO.CTL
The equivalent of AREAS.BBS, for OPUS.

EchoMail
A FidoNet conferencing implementation based on NetMail, developed by Jeff Rush in 1986. EchoMail is today the most popular means of implementing conferencing on the FidoNet. Under FidoNet, EchoMail is sent as a NetMail message, with an AREA designation contained within the message. In addition, a SEENBY list is tacked on the end of the message, providing for limited debugging of network topology.

Echo Pol
The policy governing the distribution of echo conferences. Since echoes are one of the prime services of FidoNet, the issuance of new Echo Policies by the regional coordinators of FidoNet is regularly the cause of wailing and rending of garments by sysops. After a suitable mourning period, the previously issued policies are forgotten, and life goes on as before. However, certain misguided individuals (see Echo Facist) take a reverential approach to the Echo Policies, attempting to enforce them to the letter. Those people are generally scorned.

Echo Fascist
An individual who attempts to enforce the Echo Policy to the letter of the law.

Echo Sniffers
A program that scans the From: field of incoming messages, looking for messages from an "excessively annoying" individual. These messages are then discarded.

EGGnet

An alternative network similar to Alternet that purports to be more democratic than FidoNet, encouraging members to be "good eggs." Sociologically, EGGnet members eschew the affectations of royalty such as titles, preferring to envision themselves as operating in a vintage 1830 Jeffersonian democracy.

Electronic Frontier Foundation (EFF)

An organization founded to guide the development of cyberspace into a civilized medium, but all too often portrayed by the press as a group of do-gooders out to defend recalcitrant cyberpunks.

Email address

The address at which people believe they can receive mail. Whether or not this is the case depends on the sender's understanding of mail addressing syntax, the proper functioning of host machines, and the degree to which Domain Name Service, mail user agents and mail transport agents are properly configured.

Emoticons

Characters, mostly consisting of punctuation, that are meant to be viewed sideways and which are supposed to give information on the writer's emotional state. Not very effective at reducing "flames."

EMSI

A FidoNet protocol that allows mailers to exchange mail for two FidoNet addresses at once, allowing a node to simultaneously use an RBBS-Net and a FidoNet address, for example.

eSoft

Publishers of TBBS. Reachable at 15200 E. Girard Ave., Suite 2550, Aurora, CO 80014; (303)699-6565.

Ethernet

A networking standard running at a maximum speed of 10 mbps for which hardware is now available at reasonable prices. Note that Ethernet connections, even between only two hosts, require use of tees and terminators for proper operation. Naturally these are not included with most networking cards, forcing another trip to the electronics store. Since Ethernet uses the Carrier Sense Multiple Access with Collision Detection (CSMA/CD) access method, heavy traffic levels can result in an excessive number of collisions and degraded network performance. System operators should therefore monitor the collision frequency using the `netstat` command to determine whether a bridge is needed.

European Academic and Research Network (EARN)

The European arm of BITNET.

Excessively Annoying

Since so many individuals on the FidoNet are annoying, a phrase had to be developed for those sufficiently annoying to be punished. Echo moderators determine who is "excessively annoying" within a given conference after first asking the individual to "cease and desist." A participating FidoNet sysop then has the option of either denying the sanctioned individual access to the echo in question, or of dropping the conference entirely. In the rare instance that the sanction does not work, ECHO SNIFFERs can be employed to purge the network of messages from the offending person.

External Modem

A modem that rests outside your computer, with its own power supply. External modems are usually a better investment than internal ones unless you need to use many of them at once, in which case, rack-mounted internal modems make more sense. External modems are easier to resell than internal models because they can generally be used on any make of computer.

Event

In FidoNet lingo, a specified time at which some task will take place. For example, a sysop could decide that the BBS will shut down and check its hard disk on the third Sunday of each month at 3 AM. The sysop therefore sets a FidoNet event to occur at this time and writes scripts to handle the desired actions. At the specified time, the BBS program will transfer control to the sysop's scripts, which if written correctly will restart the BBS when they are done. On DOS machines, the batch scripts are written in DOS batch language; under UNIX, they are written in shell script; on the Mac they are handled using information stored in files according to a standard developed for Tabby. With the release of AppleScript, this may become somewhat more straightforward.

Fax (Facsimile)

A method for sending images over telephone lines. Most current Fax machines obey the Group III standard, which allows for sending 200-dot-per-inch images in black and white. Group IV fax machines are just beginning to be produced, even though the standard was adopted in 1984. Group IV machines can send data at up to 64 kbps over leased lines or the Integrated Services Digital Network (ISDN), and offer resolutions up to 400 dots per inch, plus gray-scale.

Fax Modem

A computer peripheral supporting the Group III fax standard, including V.29 modulation. Fax modems are great at sending data, but not so great at receiving. They tend to slow your machine to a crawl while receiving and take up large amounts of disk space per fax. The faxes are difficult to view because they are so large. If you do a lot of receiving, but not much sending, don't buy a fax modem, get a fax machine.

Fiber Distributed Data Interface (FDDI)

A high-speed (100 Mb/second) local area networking standard that requires very fast computers to utilize its full capacity.

Fido

Now in version 13, this is the original FidoNet BBS software, invented by Tom Jennings in 1984. Available from Fido Software, Inc.; 164 Shipley, San Francisco, CA 94107.

FidoNet

The network of systems capable of communicating via the FidoNet protocols. FidoNet currently boasts over 22,000 publicly listed nodes.

FidoNet Protocol

Usually synonymous with FSC0001, which is the basic FidoNet technical standard. In transmitting data, FidoNet nodes sometimes use a variant of XMODEM (Diet IFNA), sometimes SEAlink, and sometimes a ZMODEM variant (ZEDZAP).

FidoNews

The weekly publication for FidoNet nodes. The FidoNews is compiled automatically via a newsletter program and sent over the backbone to the regional coordinators and network hubs. Submissions may be sent to node 1:1/1, but must follow a rigidly defined format in order to be properly incorporated.

FILES

A "magic name" that when requested from a properly functioning Software Distribution Network (SDN) node, will result in a list of requestable files on the node. Note that the list of files may not actually be called FILES on the SDN system.

File Attach

A basic feature of the FidoNet protocols whereby a file is transmitted to another system.

File Request

A basic feature of the FidoNet protocols whereby a file is requested from another system. The FTS-0001 standard defined the BARK style of File Request, which is the most basic File Request service;

subsequent revisions have defined the WAZOO method, which is more advanced.

For the request to succeed, the node receiving the request must allow File Requests; the file requested must be designated as available for request; and the request must occur at a date and time that is acceptable to the node receiving the request. By convention, nodes allowing File Requests make a list of the files available for request under the name FILES. File Requests can be done using Macintosh point mailers such as Copernicus and MacWoof.

File section

The part of a bulletin board system where the files available for downloading are kept. Could also be called a file library.

Firewall

A multihomed host that does not route packets from one network to another. Firewalls function as security enhancement devices and have their packet-gatewaying facilities disabled with the intent of protecting internal networks from intrusion by unauthorized personnel.

Flaming

An overly critical, angry, or otherwise irrational online tirade. USENET pioneered the concept of flaming and still leads in the generation of flames.

Flow Control

A means of controlling the flow of characters. For example, at high speeds the computer may send characters to the modem faster than the modem can send them down the line. The modem therefore needs to signal the sending computer to stop while it processes the inventory of incoming bytes. Hardware handshaking is typically accomplished by using the RTS and CTS pins of the RS-232 standard. XON/XOFF handshaking is accomplished by sending the (CTRL) S and (CTRL) Q characters to stop and restart the communications transfer, respectively.

Framing

To distinguish incoming bytes from one another, they are framed by stop and start bits. A normal character is framed by one start bit (a transition from 1 to 0) at the beginning, and 1 or more stop bits (which are always 1) at the end. If one stop bit is used, to send 8 bits of data (one byte), a modem will need to send 10 bits, including the stop and start bits, wasting 20% of all bits sent. This is why, to convert characters per second (cps) to bits per second (commonly but incorrectly referred to as *baud rate*), you need to multiply by ten. Therefore a 2400 bps modem will transmit 240 characters per second if it is operating at 100% efficiency (which it won't).

FrontDoor

A FidoNet external mailer for the PC, written by Joaquim Homrighausen.

FOSSIL Driver

A set of interface routines written for the IBM-PC's serial port, in order to compensate for the lack of decent ROM BIOS support for serial communications on the IBM-PC. Stands for "Fido/Opus/SEAdog Standard Interface Layer." Popular FOSSIL drivers include OPUSCOMM by Bob Hartman and X00 by Ray Gwinn. The latest versions are typically kept on the nodes of the Software Distribution System (SDS).

Frequency Shift Keying (FSK)

A form of modulation used in 300 bps modems.

FTP

File Transfer Protocol. FTP is a machine- and operating system-independent protocol for exchange of files that is very popular among machines connected to the Internet. FTP requires that machines be directly connected to the Internet in order to use it; it will not store requests and forward them later. This means that you cannot use FTP to request files from UUCP sites. You need to use anonymous UUCP instead.

FTS-0001

The FidoNet Technical Standard, subsequently rewritten by Randy Bush. This standard defines the most basic level of FidoNet compatibility that a node must satisfy in order to be part of the network. Prior to adoption as a standard, FTS-0001 was put down in writing as a proposal known as FSC0001, and the methods defined there were given the nickname "Diet IFNA."

Full-duplex

A full-duplex connection is one in which both sides can transmit at the same time; in contrast, a half-duplex connection can only transmit in one direction at a time. Early 9600 bps modems were of the "pseudo half-duplex" variety. This meant that they could transmit rapidly in one direction, but only slowly (300 bps) in the other direction. When the direction of flow reversed, a substantial delay would result. In contrast, the V.32 and V.32*bis* modem standards are full-duplex. Since most transfer protocols (with the exception of Bimodem) only support file transfer in one direction at a time, your computer may not be able to take full advantage of full-duplex modems during a BBS session. However, with network gateways, full-duplex operation can be critical, because packets are often flowing in both directions at the same time,

and pseudo-half-duplex turnaround times can slow the network to a crawl.

If you have ever connected two computers to each other by hooking a null modem cable between their serial ports, you may have noticed that when you are in full-duplex mode and you type on one of the computers, the characters appear on the screen on the other end, but not on your screen. This is because in full-duplex mode your terminal program depends on the other machine to echo the characters you type, rather than putting them up on your screen itself, as it does in half-duplex mode. If the other machine is already echoing characters and you are in half-duplex mode, you will notice that characters will appear twice.

gateway

A gateway is a system that communicates using two protocols (for example, AppleTalk and TCP/IP), and translates services between them. For example, a mail gateway translates mail sent from one network into mail messages traveling over another network. The functionality of a gateway is limited by the degree to which the services provided by the two protocols differ; where there is no equivalent service on one of the networks, gatewaying of that service will not be possible. In TCP/IP usage, *gateway* is sometimes used synonymously with *router,* and refers to a system with interfaces on two or more heterogeneous physical networks (for example, SLIP and Ethernet) that links the network layers by routing packets between them.

gated

A dynamic routing package, known as the "Gate Daemon." More sophisticated than routed, it supports multiple routing protocols, but is not needed in simple situations where there is only one route from the host to the Internet.

GEnie

General Electric's online service, which offers email.vendor forums, weather reports, and other services.

Gopher

A protocol developed at the University of Minnesota that provides for unified presentation of Internet services such as WAIS, Telnet, and FTP. Gopher servers are free for educational use only. With Gopher servers proliferating, VERONICA was created to allow for searching of "Gopher Space." The advent of gopher has spawned verbs such as "to gopherize," which means to make accessible via gopher. For example, ClariNet API newswires have recently been gopherized at world.std.com, making them searchable by keywords, a very interesting use for Gopher.

Group III

Currently the most popular fax standard, it allows for sending of faxes at 9600 bps and 200 dots per inch (dpi).

Group IV

The future fax standard. It will run over ISDN, offer color, and brew your coffee in the morning. Don't hold your breath!

GroupMail

An alternative conferencing system for FidoNet, developed by Thom Henderson of Systems Enhancement Associates (SEA). GroupMail requires a star topology, with a central node feeding the conference to all other nodes. This arrangement is therefore potentially more secure (assuming the connections are passworded) and will have lower transit times than traditional EchoMail distribution methods.

Half-duplex

A connection in which data flows in only one direction at a time. In order for the line to be "turned around," some method must be provided for accomplishing the turnaround. If text data is being transmitted, special characters can be used; if the data is in binary form, a protocol must be created to allow for the turnaround. Group III fax transmissions are an example of half-duplex transmission. Since the transmission is half-duplex, no acknowledgment characters are sent, and no flow control is possible.

Handshaking

A method for controlling the flow of data. Hardware handshaking controls the flow via electrical signals. Software handshaking controls the flow via special characters or commands. For example, in XON/XOFF handshaking, the characters `CTRL` Q and `CTRL` S turn flow on and off, respectively.

Hangup

Termination of a telephone conversation. This can be accomplished under the Hayes Command Set by the command **ATH+++.** Alternatively, hangup can be achieved by lowering the DTR signal on the modem's RS-232 port.

Hayes Command Set

A series of commands for controlling a modem that were introduced with the Hayes Smartmodem 300. These commands have become standardized.

Hayes-compatible

A "Hayes-compatible" modem is one that implements the Hayes Command Set. Recent court cases have established the patentability of the Hayes

hangup sequence. As a result, other modem makers have had to license the patent from Hayes.

Hayes Series V

A 9600 bps modem marketed by Hayes that implements a proprietary high-speed protocol.

Help nodes

These are nodes that agree to respond to questions relating to a particular topic. For example, the BinkleyTerm help node is 1:1/102. Usually the help nodes specialize in something narrower than How to Use the Macintosh Computer—such as how to use BinkleyTerm.

HOLD

Mail or files on hold are kept in storage until the designated system calls to pick them up. A normally operating FidoNet system should not call out to deliver mail with hold priority, but sometimes it happens anyway.

HST

A proprietary high-speed pseudo-full-duplex modem standard created by US Robotics that is very popular among FidoNet systems.

HST/DS

A new line of modems from US Robotics that supports both the older HST standard and the new V.32 and V.32*bis* standards. These modems are therefore known as Dual Standard, or DS, modems.

HUB

A network hub is a BBS that receives EchoMail from the backbone or files from the filebone. If a network is geographically dispersed, it may have several hubs to lessen the costs of mail delivery.

Hunt group

A group of phone lines that can be accessed by calling a single phone number. When one line is busy, the call is automatically passed to the next available line.

Internet Control Message Protocol (ICMP)

ICMP, which is part of the Internet Layer of TCP/IP, provides for error messages, redirection of routes, flow control (source quench), and other remedies. ICMP is exploited by traceroute in order to simulate the path of a packet, since expiration of a packet's Time To Live (TTL) entry will generate an ICMP error message.

InterFace Configure (ifconfig)

Software that is used to configure and give information on individual interfaces, such as the subnet mask and broadcast address.

IFNA
The history of the International FidoNet Association (IFNA) is a tale of intrigue worthy of its own book. At one time, IFNA held the copyrights to the Nodelist and the FidoNet Technical Standards. These are now held by Tom Jennings and the original authors.

Initialization string
The sequence of characters sent to a modem in order to set it up for subsequent communications.

Intel 8250
The UART chip in the original IBM-PC.

Intel 16450
The UART chip used in the IBM-PC/AT, pin compatible with the 8250.

Intel 16550
The recommended UART chip for use with high-speed modems in IBM-PC-compatible systems, the 16550 is pin compatible with the 8250 and 16450. This means that you can remove 8250 chips from your serial port board (if they're socketed) and replace them with 16550s. The 16550 is more appropriate for high-speed communications, because it contains a 16-byte buffer, as opposed to the 8250's 1-byte buffer.

Internal modem
A modem that resides inside the computer.

internet
A network of networks, interconnected by routers.

Internet
The world's largest computer network. When used as an adjective (for instance, Internet router), it adds 300% to the retail price of the item that it is describing. See Deluxe.

Internet Cooperative
A form of organization, pioneered by Tim Pozar and Tom Jennings, in which system operators cooperate on the purchase of a high-speed Internet connection and then fractionate it among themselves, bringing down the cost of Internet connections. Also called a ToasterNet. See also Regional Network.

ISDN
Integrated Services Digital Network. A new form of telephone service that promises markedly increased throughput, as well as other features, assuming that it is ever offered at attractive rates.

KA9Q
A remarkable and very complete TCP/IP implementation by Phil Karn, KA9Q. Originally developed to support TCP/IP over packet radio,

KA9Q is free for educational use. Many versions of it exist, including versions offering lpd, gopher server, and NNTP server capability. For sample setup files, see `comp.protocols.tcp-ip.ibmpc`.

KERMIT
A communications protocol that was developed to allow communications among otherwise incompatible computers. If you cannot get other communications protocols to work, KERMIT is your best bet.

Kilobyte (K)
1024 bytes of data.

Knowbot
A user agent that is able to intelligently gather information. Also, a specific address directory front-end that redirects queries to basic sources such as whois, white pages, X.500, etc.

LHARC
The most efficient archiving program available, written by Haruyasu Yoshizaki. Currently at version 2.13.

LISTSERV
Combination mail-server and mailing-list software operating on the BITNET network; it responds to commands in the body of messages sent by users on BITNET and other networks. Sysops often hate LISTSERVs since inconsiderate users can easily turn on a torrent of messages before tiring of the system, leaving the poor sysop to figure out how to turn off the flow.

Local Area Network (LAN)
Short-distance networks that operate at relatively high speeds.

MacBinary
A specification for how the portions of a Macintosh file (such as the data and resource forks, as well as icon and creator bit information) are to be combined into a single file for transmission over a modem. Most Macintosh communications software has MacBinary built in.

MacBone
This is not an alternative backbone, but rather a periodic listing of Macintosh-oriented bulletin boards receiving one or more of the Macintosh-related backbone conferences. Since only a small fraction of the nodes receiving Macintosh conferences are included in the MACLIST, MACBONE is the most complete listing of Macintosh-related bulletin boards on FidoNet. Unfortunately, MACBONE does not include a list of the system's phone numbers, making it difficult for

ordinary users to utilize it. MACBONE is posted periodically to ECHOMAC, currently by Bob Nordling of New Orleans MUG BBS, 1:396/13, (504)837-8118.

Mail servers
Software that takes actions based on the addressee, subject, or body of a mail message. Mail-server software is available that can carry out this function with or without root permission.

Mailer
FidoNet software that implements the communications portion of the FidoNet specification.

Mailing-list software
Software that provides for sending of mail to a list of individuals. Mailing lists can be generated for outbound mail, or for inbound mail, in which case they are known as "mail exploders." Creation of mail exploders generally requires root permission, since improper use of this facility could generate mail loops.

Major BBS
One of the most popular multiline BBSes, running under DOS, that also supports FidoNet and UUCP via external mailers. Galacticomm, Inc.; 4101 S.W. 47th Ave., Suite 101, Ft. Lauderdale, FL 33314.

Matrix
A term that refers to all networks reachable by mail from the Internet. This includes the Internet, UUCP, FidoNet, BITNET, RBBS-Net, WWIVNet, OneNet, and FrEdMail. Originally used in the book *Neuromancer* and applied to global networks by Wynn Wagner III with the OPUS CBCS, *The Matrix* is also the title of a book by John S. Quarterman.

Maximum Message Size (MMS)
The largest message that can be passed over a particular network. Note that the MMS is determined as much by the weakest link in the network software chain as by network standards. In theory the FidoNet MMS is infinite, but in practice it can be as small as 8K. The BITNET MMS is set at 300K. Note also that the MMS of a particular BBS or network implementation limits the effectiveness of gateways, since satisfying the MMS constraints may require heroic levels of message splitting.

Maximum Transmission Unit (MTU)
The largest packet that can be transferred by a particular networking technology. If IP packets are larger than a network's MTU, then they will need to be fragmented and subsequently reassembled.

MCI Mail
A popular email service sponsored by MCI that only charges for messages sent, not for connect time.

MCS
Multichannel Communications Sytem. Software for the Macintosh written by Yves Lempereur of Mainstay. Allows you to send a file on your Mac while typing in a message window at the same time. Currently in version 1.1.

Megabyte (Mb)
1,048,576 bytes of data.

Message reader
A program capable of reading and creating message packets in a format such as that produced by the QMS/XRS system for QuickBBS or Remote Access. Jabberwocky is an example of a message reader.

Message section
A portion of a BBS that is devoted to a particular topic, such as HyperCard.

Minitel
An online service that is immensely popular in France.

MNP
MicroCom Networking Protocol.

MNP-4
An error detection and retransmission protocol created by MicroCom.

MNP-5
A compression standard created by MicroCom that should be used with care since it tends to expand files that have already been compressed. MNP-5 was frequently adopted for use in early V.32 modems.

MNP-10
An error detection and retransmission protocol developed by MicroCom for use with cellular modems. These modems must contend with dropout of the signal when passing from one cell to another. The modem must not disconnect when this occurs.

Modem
Stands for MOdulator/DEModulator. A modem is used to transmit digital data over an analog channel, usually a phone line. This is necessary because purely digital transmission would require a higher bandwidth than ordinary telephone lines can handle. Although a modem is most commonly used to transmit data over the telephone system, this need not be so. There are radio-frequency modems, for example.

Modem cable
A cable connecting a computer to a modem.

Modem registers
Locations in memory within a modem that contain configuration information. These registers may be volatile, in which case, turning the modem off will erase them, or nonvolatile, in which case the modem will remember them from use to use. Setting these registers correctly (particularly for high-speed modems) can be one of the biggest headaches of communications.

Moderator
Codependent individual who agrees to screen messages in a distributed conference or mailing list to enhance the signal/noise ratio.

MSDN
The Macintosh Software Distribution Network. MSDN is the mechanism for distributing newly released shareware files on the FidoNet. To get their new releases out on the network, shareware authors send the files to one of the MSDN regional coordinators, either by File Attach or by uploading them.

Multihomed Host
A system residing on more than one network, but which does not gateway between them. The lack of gatewaying can be due to security (firewalls), choice (demands on CPU power), or lack of capability (gateway software is harder to write).

Multipurpose Internet Mail Extensions (MIME)
A protocol defined in RFC 1341 that allows inclusion of multiple parts within a message which provides for multi-media enclosures.

Multi User Dungeon (MUD)
An Internet role-playing game in which tens of thousands of graduate students prolong their adolescence while taking up network bandwidth at government and parental expense.

MultiXfer
Software for the Macintosh that allows sending of a file from the Mac while typing in a message window. Similar to MCS.

NAK
Negative Acknowledgment.

National Mail Hour
See Zone Mail Hour.

NetMail
Person-to-person mail sent via FidoNet. Although NetMail messages may be classified as PRIVATE, privacy is not assured. Normal users will not be able to read it, but any number of sysops and assistant sysops may be given access. NetMail (or any FidoNet mail) is not usually encrypted.

Net Police
USENET vigilantes who take it upon themselves to lecture unsuspecting mortals on the nature of The USENET Way. Unfortunately, few Net Police can agree on much of anything, other than that the offender has commited an act of unparalleled stupidity and should be made to grovel.

Netstat
Software that is used to gain information on the state of the routing tables and interfaces. Can also be used to monitor collision levels on ethernet networks.

Network Information Center (NIC)
A site or series of sites agreeing to serve as an information resource for individuals connected to, or looking to join, the network. On FidoNet, the NIC consists of help nodes listed in the weekly Nodelist; on BITNET the NIC function is carried out by BITNIC. The successful advertisement of the NIC address and services is critical to its effectiveness, since otherwise only those in the know (who are usually in the least need of help) will be able to make use of its services.

Network Number
In the address 1:161/445.2 (the address of my point), 161 is the network number for the East Bay Network. Each network has an echo coordinator and a network coordinator, who may be different individuals. The duty of the network administrator is to ensure that network participants receive the weekly NodeDiff's, in addition to the FidoNews.

Network News Transfer Protocol (NNTP)
NNTP v1.0 is a nonauthenticating transport agent for network news that supports 7-bit noncompressed transfers. NNTP v2.0 promises various improvements, including support for 8-bit transfers and authentication.

Network Operations Center (NOC)
A site or series of sites that utilize network diagnostic tools, preferably under automated control, to monitor the operation of the network. The effectiveness of a network NOC is proportional to the power of the tools available to them. Networks such as FidoNet have been notoriously ineffective in diagnosing network problems due to lack of effective diagnostic tools (prior to

implementation of the PATH line). At a minimum, message history functions must be provided for tracking down topology problems; and duplicate elimination facilities are necessary to keep things from getting out of control before intervention can occur.

On FidoNet, NOC functions are often handled on a per conference basis by the moderator, who may generate a regular traffic summary or topology map. This is not always a desirable arrangement since it combines operational (NOC), social (moderator), and informational (NIC) functions in one individual. It also often results in a duplication of effort in the development of appropriate network diagnostic tools. It can speed up burnout in the moderator.

NodeDiff
The weekly difference file describing changes to the FidoNet Nodelist. To compile the NodeDiff you will need the previous copy of the Nodelist. The most recent version of the NodeDiff files is available weekly from network hosts such as 1:125/125.

Nodelist
Put out on a weekly basis for use by all FidoNet nodes, the Nodelist is a list of all public nodes on the FidoNet, which currently number over 10,000. This file is now over 1 Mb in size, and complete compilation and use is beginning to stretch DOS memory limitations for some BBS systems. For this reason, some systems only compile parts of the Nodelist. Nodelist compilation utilities include XLAXNODE, PARSELIST, XLATLIST, and NODECOMP. A copy of the Nodelist is available every week from network hosts.

Node
A single computer system within the FidoNet. Within the hierarchy, the node number differentiates FidoNet systems within a given network. For example, in the address 1:161/445, 445 is the node number and 161 is the network number (East Bay).

Node Number
In the address 1:161/445.2, 445 is the node number within the East Bay Network; 161 is the network number (East Bay), and 1 is the zone number (North America). To send mail to FidoNet from a site on the Internet, mail would be sent to:
Bernard.Aboba@f445.n161.z1.fidonet.org

nslookup
Software that provides information on Domain Name Service information (such as mail and address records) for Internet sites. See dig.

Null Modem Cable
A cable allowing transfer of data between two pieces of data terminal equipment (DTE), for example, between two computers.

OAG
Online Airline Guide. An online service on CompuServe and other online networks that allows you to browse airline schedules and make reservations.

Object-Oriented Technology
Technology facilitating software reusability and encapsulation. Also, technology that increases the value of a firm's stock price when it is announced that they are using it. See Deluxe.

Offline
The state of a computer when it is not connected to another machine via modem. A program that allows the user to read and reply to messages without being connected is known as an Offline Reader.

Online
The state of a computer when it is connected to another machine via modem.

Online Public Access Catalog (OPAC)
An online library catalog, usually situated at a university. While not offering many online books, many OPACs now offer abstracts of articles from periodicals.

OPUS-CBCS
The first of a string of successors to Fido. Originally written by Wynn Wagner III with help from many others, the project has now passed on to other hands. One of the nice features of OPUS is that it includes integrated compression, tossing, unpacking, packing, and message editing, making it compact and (as these things go) simple. OPUS also integrates well with the FidoNet/UUCP gateway software UFGATE, as does Fido. Last time we checked, OPUS was at version 1.73a, with a "major upgrade" to v.2.0 in the works.

OSI Model
A frequently referred to seven-layer model computer network architecture. Networks such as FidoNet and TCP/IP do not implement all the layers of the OSI model.

Outbound area
A directory in which outgoing FidoNet mail packets (which may be compressed) are stored.

Packer

A FidoNet system program that takes files in `*.MSG` format and brings them together into a bundle called a *packet* that usually has a `.PKT` extension.

Packet

A series of bytes communicated in sequence that conform to a particular format. Packets include fields for things like error detection, packet size, and packet type.

Packet switching network (PSN)

A network of computers that communicates via a defined packet format. Packet switching networks are capable of utilizing a single communications line for multiple conversations.

PAK

A compression program along the lines of ARC and ZIP.

Parity

A primitive technique for error detection that utilizes an extra bit per character.

PEP

Packetized Ensemble Protocol. A proprietary high-speed modulation and error-correction protocol developed by Telebit.

Packet INternet Groper (PING)

Software that is used to debug the data link and network layers of an Internet connection. Note that since PING does not utilize TCP packets, it is not affected by the presence or absence of Van Jacobson compression; successful PING attempts do not imply successful negotiation of a SLIP connection.

PKARC

A compression program upwardly compatible with ARC, written by Phil Katz. It should be noted, however, that files compressed with PKARC cannot be unARCed by ARC, or by Macintosh programs such as MacArc or ArcPop. Its use for archiving in Macintosh service should therefore be avoided.

PKZIP

Currently the most popular archiving method for the PC. Not as efficient as ARJ or LHARC, but it comes with a wealth of utilities and documentation. Mac users should use UNZIP or ZipPop to decompress ZIP files.

Point

A series of programs that together allow for the exchange of mail and files between a full-fledged FidoNet host system and an individual user (point). Points differ from full-fledged FidoNet implementations in that they typically lack one or more of the following features: ability to compile or utilize the Nodelist, user passwording, ability to handle incoming calls, and file sections or other typical BBS features. A point should be thought of as a substitute for a terminal program rather than as a BBS. Points get their name from their FidoNet address, for example, 1:161/445.2. Popular point systems include EZPoint, Copernicus, MacWoof, and COUNTERPoint (which requires a mailer).

Point of Presence (POP)

Term used to denote the location of a switching or dial-in facility, usually for an Internet or communications service provider such as Netcom or Sprint.

Point to Point Protocol (PPP)

A multiprotocol standard defined in RFC 1171 which provides for transmission of packets over serial lines. Since PPP defines a data link layer with a protocol field, it can be used with other protocols such as Novell IPX or AppleTalk, in addition to the Internet Protocol. PPP also includes support for error correction via a dialect of HDLC, header or data compression, and link characteristic negotiation. Since PPP is more complex than SLIP, it has not been as widely implemented and is just being added to terminal servers. PPP implementations are available for the PC (KA9Q), the Macintosh (MacPPP), and UNIX (Morningstar PPP, SunOS PPP).

Polling

Part of the mail delivery process in which a bulletin board calls another system on a regular basis to pick up and transmit mail. Both FidoNet and UUCP support polling.

Port number

A 2-byte field that identifies the process to which a particular transport-level protocol should deliver a packet. Note that both the port number and the protocol number are needed to uniquely identify a process.

Postmaster

The individual who is responsible for maintenance of the mailer at a particular site, and to whom complaints should be directed if something goes wrong. Mail sent to `postmaster@host.domain` should generally reach that individual.

Post Office Protocol (POP)

A client/server protocol designed to allow clients to pick up their mail from the server. This is particularly convenient for individuals with dialup IP connections who may not be available for SMTP mail delivery. Instead, their mail is directed to a POP server from which they can pick it up at their leisure. The latest version, POP3, is not compatible with earlier versions.

Privacy Enhanced Mail (PEM)
Internet mail software which offers enhancements such as authentication and encryption. Note that while extremely secure algorithms can be used for authentication purposes, lesser algorithms are used for encryption to allow for surveillance by law enforcement.

Procomm
Commercial communications software for the IBM-PC.

PRODIGY
A controversial commercial online service jointly owned by IBM and Sears.

Protocol
A specification for communications between two computers.

Protocol number
A 1-byte field that identifies the transport-level protocol to receive the IP datagram.

Qmail
A mail tosser for OPUS and Fido BBS systems, which we used to run on the BMUG Mail Hub.

QuickB
A proprietary transfer protocol developed by CompuServe.

QuickBBS
Originally a single-line, now a multiline, BBS program styled after TBBS that allows for custom menus, doors, and quite a few other nice features. QuickBBS stores messages in a single file like TBBS, rather than in *.MSG files like OPUS or Fido. This saves disk space and increases speed, although at the cost of increased complexity. Originally written by Adam Hudson with advice from Phil Becker, this program has now passed on to commercial releases by other authors. The mantle of the militantly public-domain BBS has now passed to Remote Access.

RBBS-PC
Remote Bulletin Board System-PC is a popular bulletin board system for the IBM PC distributed by the Capital PC User Group. RBBS-PC can handle multiple lines, unlimited message sections, custom menus, FidoNet mail, external programs (doors), and many other features. RBBS-PC systems linked together by FidoNet mail form their own network called RBBSNet.

The latest version of this program is available for $8 from the Capitol PC Software Exchange; P.O. Box 6128, Silver Springs, MD 20906. Alternatively, you may contact the authors: Thomas Mac at (203)268-5315 or (203)268-0129 (both data); Jon Martin at (510)689-2090 (data); or Ken Goosens at (703)978-6360 (data).

RBBSNet
The network of RBBS-PC nodes. This network runs FidoNet mailers such as BinkleyTerm in front of the multiline RBBS-PC software.

Red Ryder
Written by Scott Watson and now called White Knight, Red Ryder was the first capable telecommunications software for the Macintosh. Initially distributed as shareware, from version 10.0 onward it has been distributed commercially.

Red Ryder Host
Written by Scott Watson and now called Second Sight, this is the most popular bulletin board software for the Macintosh. It allows for custom menus, like TBBS, and is compatible with Tabby.

Region
A subdivision of the FidoNet that includes several networks. For example, FidoNet systems in California and Nevada form Region 10. A given region generally has a primary source for the incoming backbone echoes, which are then distributed to the network hubs in the region.

Regional Coordinator
The individual responsible for ensuring that a FidoNet region maintains access to the backbone. The regional coordinator receives the backbone conferences requested by the network coordinator, who in turn distributes them to the network hosts. The hosts in turn distribute them to the nodes. The regional coordinator must therefore process an enormous volume of mail, and as a result receives a large phone bill every month. This bill is paid for by semivoluntary (in other words, coerced) contributions by the nodes within the region.

Regional Network
Providers of networking services to research and educational institutions and commercial businesses, which are now in the process of being weaned from government subsidies and establishing themselves as self-supporting businesses.

Remote Access
A BBS package for the PC offered in commercial and shareware versions. Remote Access supports doors and custom menus, making it equivalent in features to TBBS single-line.

Request To Send (RTS).
When this RS-232 signal is asserted, it means that the computer is ready to accept incoming data from the modem.

Reverse Address Resolution Protocol (RARP)
RARP, covered in RFC 903, is typically used by diskless workstations needing to determine their TCP/IP address at bootup, but knowing only their Ethernet address, which is stored on the network card. RARP only works on LANs supporting broadcast.

RIME
RIME is the largest network of bulletin boards running the PostLink software.

Router
A device that connects two or more networks at the network layer, also formerly called a gateway in TCP/IP terminology. Routers typically have a TCP/IP address for each physical medium to which they are linked. A router connected to a SLIP link as well as an Ethernet would have two TCP/IP addresses. Routers function based on information in their routing tables, which can be configured statically (common for BBSes) or dynamically via routing protocols. Also, an expensive device manufactured by hi tech firms with inflated stock prices.

RS-232
A serial wiring standard connecting data terminal equipment (DTE) to data communications equipment (DCE).

RS-422
A serial wiring standard implementing positive and negative wires for transmission and reception. This makes RS-422 more noise-immune than RS-232.

Scan
Part of the process of FidoNet mail processing wherein messages meant for other systems are bundled into packets.

Script
A program written to perform a telecommunications function, such as logging on to a remote system, downloading files, or sending mail. Most sophisticated commercial telecommunications programs such as MicroPhone II, ProComm Plus, and TELIX support scripting.

SDN
Software Distribution Network. This is a way for software authors to publicly distribute their handiwork over the FidoNet. The files travel to and are incorporated into the file systems of BBSes that are configured to receive them. There is an SDN for Macintosh files called MSDN.

SEAdog
The first commercial FidoNet mailer, written by Systems Enhancement Associates (SEA). SEAdog implements a bevy of features, generally in its own way, and has maintained a cult of adherents and another cult of naysayers since the beginning. True to form, SEAdog utilizes the SEAlink protocol, a windowing version of XMODEM, in order to transfer files. It also supports FTS-0001.

SEAlink
A windowing protocol based on XMODEM, developed by Thom Henderson of Systems Enhancement Associates (SEA), that doubled the transfer speed of FidoNet mail overnight when it was introduced.

Second Sight
The current name for the former Red Ryder Host BBS software.

SEENBYs
Fields attached to the bottom of messages that list all the nodes to which a given EchoMail message has been transmitted. The use of SEENBYs prevents the sending of a message to a node that has already received it via the current routing history; however, it does not prevent duplication of messages traveling by an independent route.

sendmail
The most popular Mail Transport Agent (MTA), sendmail routes mail but with the exception of mail delivered by SMTP (which it delivers itself) passes it on to other Delivery Agents. Correctly configuring the sendmail.cf file is probably the most difficult step in getting UNIX mail to work. As with many other tasks in system operation, it is usually best to borrow someone else's working sendmail.cf, rather than attempting to write your own.

Serial Line Internet Protocol (SLIP)
SLIP is a simple "nonstandard" for transmission of Internet Protocol datagrams over serial lines. Since SLIP specifies mechanisms for framing and header compression and little else, it is easy to implement and widely available. It does not provide error correction or negotiation of connection characteristics; such features are provided for in Point-to-Point Protocol (PPP), which will eventually replace SLIP in wide usage.

Serial Port
An output port of a computer that communicates by using transmission and reception lines, plus additional handshaking lines.

Simple Mail Transfer Protocol (SMTP)
A simple mail transport protocol used to transport mail over the Internet.

Sliding Windows
Protocols such as XMODEM wait for acknowledgment that a sent block has been correctly received before sending the next block of characters. At speeds of 2400 bps or higher when using long-distance phone lines or packet-switching services, this method is inefficient, because the round-trip time can be 500 milliseconds or more. To increase efficiency, a protocol implementing sliding windows will not pause to wait for acknowledgment on a given block until it and the next n-1 blocks are pending acknowledgment, where n is the window size. This means that a protocol such as XMODEM will pause for acknowledgment n times more frequently than a sliding windows protocol. Sliding windows protocols include SEAlink, and SuperKermit.

Software
Computer-related products with a very low marginal cost of production, but a high initial development cost. Also, products that will eventually be developed, bought, or sold by Microsoft.

SPAZ
A PC utility that determines whether an incoming mail packet was compressed by PKZIP, ARC, or some other compression utility. Indispensable in these days of fragmented compression standards.

SQUISH
A FidoNet mail tosser/packer.

Stop Bits
Bits that come after the end of a byte of data during transmission to signify the end of the character.

Subnet mask
A 4-byte field that is AND'd with the TCP/IP address to differentiate the network portion of the address from the host address. Although the 1's in the subnet mask do not all need to be contiguous, they almost always are.

Synchronous communications
Serial communications that occurs at regular intervals.

Sysop
Slang for SYStem OPerator.

Tabby
The first FidoNet mailer for the Macintosh, written by Michael Connick of Castle Tabby.

Tag Line (Tear Line)
A line affixed to the end of an EchoMail message listing the name, network address, and possibly the phone number of the system that generated the message. Tag lines maintain a sense of who remains connected to an echo and can be used to analyze the echo traffic via utilities such as AWK.

TDBS
A multiuser implementation of a subset of dBASE III+, written as an add-on module for TBBS and distributed by eSoft.

TBBS
One of the most popular multiline BBS software packages, written by Phil Becker of eSoft. TBBS supports up to 64 lines, with integrated NetMail (TIMS), dBASE III+ (TDBS), and sysop maintenance (SYSOM) add-on modules available. Since its appearance on the TRS-80 computer in 1981, TBBS has accumulated a series of firsts: first multiline BBS running under DOS; first multiline continuous mailer under DOS; first multiline BBS supporting dBASE.

TELIX
Soon-to-be commercial communications software for the IBM-PC, running under DOS.

Telebit
A manufacturer of modems that are very popular in the UNIX community.

Terminal emulation
A process by which communications software emulates the operation of a terminal such as the VT100 or IBM 3270. This is what telecommunications software, such as ZTerm and MicroPhone II, does. Terminal emulation allows microcomputers to be used with programs that were written for these terminals.

Terminal servers
Created to allow for simultaneous logins to a TCP/IP-based network, terminal servers have become increasingly sophisticated devices, recently adding support for SLIP and PPP. Most terminal servers do not yet allow for fully flexible routing (attachment of dialup networks via SLIP/PPP, not just individual hosts), but this is coming. Along with UNIX clones, terminal servers may make possible a new general of Internet BBSes. Popular terminal servers include the Xylogics Annex series of products, the Livingston Portmaster, and products from Emulex.

TGROUP
Software for TBBS that supports GroupMail.

Thread
A series of messages on a given subject, including the original message and the subsequent replies.

Time To Live (TTL)
A field in the Internet Protocol Header that indicates the maximum number of hops that the packet should be allowed to take before it expires and an ICMP error message is generated. Incrementing the TTL field from 1 allows for generation of the traceroute table.

TIMS
The TBBS Integrated Mail System is a multiline mailer that allows continuous reception of incoming mail. The latest version of TIMS can now make outgoing calls. TIMS is written by Bob Hartman.

TMAIL
A former alternative mail processor for TBBS that was recently purchased by eSoft and has been incorporated into the latest version of the TBBS mail utilities.

TMM
An alternate message system for TBBS, written in the dBASE III+ language of TDBS. TMM offers several additional features, such as full text search.

Tosser
A program that separates incoming packets into individual messages and segregates them into different message sections or files according to echo. Examples are CONFMAIL, QMAIL, SQUISH, and WildMail!

Traceroute
Software for simulating the route of a packet going from site A to site B. Traceroute works by generating ICMP error messages through incrementing of the Time To Live field. It merely simulates, but does not actually track, the progress of an individual packet, whose route may not even be identical between successive attempts. With each successive addition to the TTL parameter, three packets are sent out. Since each successive attempt produces independent measurements, traceroute measurements need not necessarily increase from origin to destination; nor do other laws of logic necessarily apply. The most important statistics to check are therefore the reachability and round-trip times for the final destination.

Transport protocol
The protocol by which a service is delivered. For mail on the Internet this is usually SMTP, POP, or UUCP; for news, it is NNTP or UUCP. The most popular TCP/IP Mail Transport Agent (MTA) is sendmail.

Trojan horse
A dangerous program that pretends to be useful software but performs a mischevious function, such as reformatting your hard drive.

TTY
Abbreviation for TeleTYpe. The TTY is the simplest form of terminal, since it does not support cursor positioning or graphics characters.

Tunneling
Use of TCP/IP as a data link layer for another protocol such as FidoNet or UUCP. Tunneling can be particularly inefficient if there is no provision for negotiation of a non-error-correcting version of the protocol to be tunneled; in such a case, error correction will be applied twice.

TYMNET
A commercial packet-switching network.

UART
Universal Asynchronous Receiver Transmitter. The UART is a chip that is interfaced to a microprocessor in order to conduct serial communications. The Intel 8250, 16450, and 16550 chips are examples of UART's.

UFGATE
The FidoNet/UUCP gateway software for the PC written by T. Pozar, G. Paxinos, J. Gilmore, and J. Galvin. Currently in version 1.03, this software is the favored method for gatewaying between FidoNet and USENET systems. Information about UFGATE is available in the UFGATE conference carried over the FidoNet backbone.

UFGATE was designed to work with OPUS, Fido, and other `*.MSG` format BBSes. It does not interface easily with QuickBBS or TBBS, but it can be done (don't ask me how, though). UFGATE can be File Requested from node 1:125/555.

umodem
A UNIX version of XMODEM.

Undialable
To be characterized as undialable, a FidoNet node must pick up the phone and then fail to respond in an intelligible way. If this occurs repeatedly, the node is marked down as "undialable," and until this determination is cleared, mail for this node will pile up and calls to it will not be initiated.

Unpacker
Software that separates incoming mail packets into individual messages in `*.MSG` format.

Update Request
A type of file request in which a node requests a file only if the creation date is more recent than its current copy. This is the mechanism by which GroupMail operates.

USART
Universal Synchronous-Asynchronous Receiver Transmitter. The USART is a chip that can conduct serial communications in either synchronous or asynchronous modes. The Zilog 8530 chip used on the Macintosh is a USART.

USENET
The collection of machines running a variety of operating systems and hardware that participate in a huge distributed conferencing system. USENET messages are transmitted predominantly by UUCP and NNTP protocols. The USENET network has more than 3000 newsgroups, over 70,000 nodes, and a population of readers numbering over 2 million.

US Robotics
The vendor of the current high-speed modem of choice for FidoNet sysops, the HST. Although sysops get special pricing, ordinary folks can get a good deal from US Robotics as well. Under a little-known program, ordinary users can get reconditioned HST or Courier modems for rock-bottom prices.

US Robotics; 8100 North McCormick Blvd., Skokie, IL, 60076; voice: (800)DIAL-USR.

Unix to Unix Copy Protocol (UUCP)
A protocol for transferring files, news, and mail and executing remote commands between machines.

User Agent (UA)
The user interface used to read mail or news. The choice of user agent is important to the end-user experience, and so the relative merits of various user agents is a subject for passionate discussion on USENET.

UUNET
A nonprofit Internet service provider. Their Internet service is called Alternet, not to be confused with the FidoNet network of the same name.

Van Jacobson compression
The means used to compress TCP headers in order to decrease round-trip times with SLIP. Versions of SLIP implementing Van Jacobson compression are referred to as Compressed SLIP or CSLIP.

V.17
A recent half-duplex 14,400 bps modulation standard for fax transmission.

V.21
300 bps modem standard created by CCITT.

V.22
A 1200 bps full-duplex modem standard created by CCITT.

V.22bis
A 2400 bps standard that is an extension of V.22.

V.27ter
A 4800 bps fax modulation standard.

V.29
The half-duplex 9600 bps modulation standard for Group III fax transmission. Group III includes not only modulation but also error correction and compression, although these latter two specifications are not part of V.29.

V.32
A 9600 bps full-duplex modulation standard put forward by CCITT.

V.32bis
A 14,400 bps full-duplex modulation standard put forward by CCITT.

V.42
This CCITT standard defines a method of negotiating between two possible error-correcting standards: MicroCom's MNP-4 and Hayes' LAPM. LAPM is the preferred method; MNP-4 is used only if one of the modems is not compatible with LAPM.

V.42bis
A CCITT standard covering compression on the fly. V.42*bis* has a nice feature: it will not expand files that have already been compressed prior to transmission.

V.FAST
A 28.8 kbps full duplex modulation standard under development from CCITT.

Virus
A software contagion that propagates from machine to machine, possibly damaging the contents of the hard drive or disrupting operation of the computer.

VT100
A popular terminal from Digital Equipment Corporation for which a great deal of software has been written. Today's microcomputer communications software generally provides VT100 emulation.

WAZOO
A negotiation protocol first implemented by the OPUS CBCS. File-transfer methods supported under WAZOO include ZedZap, a variant of ZMODEM, and DietIFNA, which utilizes SEAlink.

Waffle
Bulletin-board software is available under MS-DOS and UNIX that supports UUCP and USENET. On the PC, the software comes with an implementation of UUCP, allowing PCs to connect to UUCP hosts and receive USENET conferences.

The WELL
A Internet online service based in Sausalito, California, that is a gathering place for people knowledgeable about telecommunications. Although the user interface is terrible, this system has the best online atmosphere of any commercial online service.

Well-Known Port
a port number that is statically assigned to an application.

White Knight
Macintosh communications software written by Scott Watson and originally called Red Ryder.

Whois
A program that allows you to query the identify of another individual.

Wide Area Information Servers (WAIS)
A collection of programs implementing a variant of the Z39.50 protocol for information retrieval, alongside indexing a variety of data formats, with widely implemented client software. WAIS research databases are easy to use, making it easy for researchers worldwide to collaborate. Practical information such as domain organization listings, BITNET Nodelists, FidoNet Nodelists, and UUCP map data can be put at every Internet user's fingertips. WAIS databases are also accessible via Gopher and World Wide Web (W3).

Wildcat
Commercial BBS software published by Mustang Software that is network-aware and can import and export mail to FidoNet (using WildMail!), provided that you use an external mailer. If your firm is already using email over a Novell or other network, Wildcat is probably the BBS software to purchase for connecting to the outside.

Mustang Software, Inc.; 3125 19th St., Suite 162, Bakersfield, CA 93301; voice: (805)395-0223, data: (805)395-0650

World Wide Web (W3)
A hypertext representation of Internet, originating at CERN, in Switzerland.

WWIV
Bulletin board software available for the PC or the Macintosh. The Macintosh version was developed by Terry Teague.

X.25
An aging packet-switching standard with error correction built in to multiple levels of the protocol X.25 is the basis for many of today's packet-switching networks, such as TYMNET.

X.400
An email exchange standard that is part of the Open Systems Interconnect (OSI) standard.

X.500
An email address directory standard that is part of the Open Systems Interconnect (OSI) standard.

xmosaic
A W3 client from NCSA which runs under X Windows and supports embedded pictures, sounds, and movies, in addition to kitchen sink support of other protocols. Mosaic is the most comprehensive Internet navigation tool developed to date. Ports to the Macintosh and Windows are in development, and available from `ftp.ncsa.uiuc.edu`.

XMODEM
The first microcomputer transfer protocol, created by Ward Christensen in 1977 for CP/M. The classic XMODEM utilizes an 8-bit checksum for error detection and 128-byte blocks.

XMODEM-1K
A variant of XMODEM that utilizes 1K blocks. This protocol is sometimes mistakenly referred to as YMODEM.

XOFF
The (CTRL) S character, used to stop flow of characters during data transmission.

XON
The (CTRL) Q character, used to resume flow of characters.

YMODEM
A protocol invented by Chuck Forsberg, of Omen Technology, that uses 1K blocks and can handle batch file transfers.

Zilog 8530 SCC
A 40-pin, two-port serial chip used in the Macintosh that supports both synchronous and asynchronous operations. In synchronous mode, it supports automatic CRC generation and checking.

ZipMail
FidoNet mail packets that have been compressed using Phil Katz's PKZIP.

ZMODEM
A highly efficient transfer protocol created by Chuck Forsberg of Omen Technology. Unique features of ZMODEM include adaptive block size, recovery from broken connections, auto-receive, and *streaming* (a technique that effectively offers infinite window size).

Zone
A zone, which originally was intended to refer to a continent, encompasses several regions. For example, in the address 1:161/445.2, the 1 is the zone, which signifies North America. However, several networks have taken it upon themselves to appropriate zone IDs. Examples include MACLIST (Zone 6), and RBBS-NET (Zone 8). Many FidoNet BBS mailers do not support zones correctly. This means that the Nodelist entry for node 1:161/445 could be overwritten by the Nodelist entry for 2:161/445 should such a node exist. Fortunately, measures have been taken to ensure that this doesn't happen; nodelist compilers generally only compile entries for one zone; mail to other zones is sent via zone gateways.

Zone Gateway
A Zone Gateway is a FidoNet node that connects two zones, such as the connection between RBBS-NET and FidoNet. The Zone Gateway thus receives mail from FidoNet bound for RBBS-NET and sends outgoing mail bound for FidoNet from RBBS-Net nodes.

Zone Mail Hour (ZMH)
Zone Mail Hour, defined as 2 PM Greenwich Mean Time (GMT), is the time where FidoNet systems within a specific zone must be available to receive mail. On the West Coast, Zone Mail Hour occurs from 1 AM to 2 AM, Pacific Standard Time.

ZOO
Yet another PC compression program; its files are signified by the .ZOO extension. .ZOO files can be unZOO'd by the Macintosh utility MACBOOZ.

Glossary of software authors

Becker, Phil
The author of TBBS, and one of the best telecommunications programmers around.

Bryant, Alan
Currently at eSoft, he's a regular columnist for Boardwatch and also is the author of the manuals for BinkleyTerm and TIMS, two good sources for information on FidoNet.

Bush, Randy
Author of several of the FidoNet Technical Standards.

Connick, Michael
The author of Tabby, the first Macintosh mailer, and co-author of Copernicus, the first point mailer. Also an Alternet Duke. For those who remember such things, Michael was also the author of Mouse Exchange, the first Mac BBS. No relation to Harry Connick.

Hartman, Bob
The co-author of BinkleyTerm and author of Confmail, Renumber, and several other FidoNet utilities, in addition to TIMS, the continuous mailer for TBBS.

Henderson, Thom
The author of ARC and SEAdog and the founding father of Alternet.

Jennings, Tom
The father of the FidoNet, author of the Fido BBS program, and manager of the Little Garden Internet Cooperative.

Katz, Phil
The author of PKARC and PKZIP. PKZIP is currently the most popular compression scheme for general PC use, and it has found a considerable number of adherents within FidoNet, since it is more efficient than ARC.

Pester, Michael
Author of the Copernicus point reader, the first point reader for the Macintosh; also the author of the Mansion BBS.

Pozar, Tim; Garry Paxinos, John Galvin, and John Gilmore
Authors of UFGATE.

Wagner, Wynn III
Author of the first release of OPUS-CBCS.

APPENDIX L: INDEX

Index

Index

Index

Index

Index

About the Author

Bernard Aboba has been involved with computers since learning to program in IBM 370 assembly language in high school. He has a B.A. in Engineering and Applied Sciences from Harvard College, an M.S. in Thermosciences (Nuclear Engineering, Fluid Mechanics, Thermodynamics) from Stanford, an MBA from the University of California, Berkeley, and a Ph.D. in Petroleum Engineering from Stanford University, in numerical simulation. He presently holds a part-time appointment as a Senior Research Associate at the University of California, Berkeley.

In 1987, Bernard founded MailCom, a consulting firm specializing in electronic publishing and scientific and engineering data management. Clients include biotech firms, engineering firms, universities, professional societies, and software companies. Software development projects have included a simulation toolkit and the statistics package of Quattro Pro for Windows v5.0. Consulting studies have included numerical simulations for private clients, and development of marketing programs and business plans for more than half a dozen online services and electronic publishing programs, including an online business school deployed by the University of California, Berkeley, and several CD-ROMs.

Prior to founding his own company, Bernard spent more than a decade working as a consultant to the Rand Corporation on energy technology, and as a Senior Engineer for Failure Analysis Associates, working on hardware and software development, and numerical simulation of process plant accidents.

It was at Stanford that Bernard first became a system administrator, on a Vax 750 running BSD UNIX 4.2. After he got a Macintosh in 1985, he became interested in trying to get it to communicate with PC compatibles and the school's TCP/IP network. Around the same time, he learned about a store and forward network called FidoNet, and became interested in bulletin boards. Since 1988 he has been a sysop of the BMUG BBS in Berkeley, and he served on the BMUG Board of Directors from 1988 to 1990.

Bernard has been writing articles on communications since 1987, and credits include pieces in *MacWeek, InfoWorld, Computer Currents, MicroTimes, Boardwatch, MacWorld,* and other publications. Work on *The Online User's Encyclopedia* began as a series of articles that eventually grew into *The BMUG Guide to Bulletin Boards and Beyond,* published by BMUG, Inc., in 1992. This book is the successor to *Bulletin Boards and Beyond.*

Colophon

The Online User's Encyclopedia was designed and produced on Macintosh computers running System 7.1. Storage media included a 40-Mb internal hard drive from Quantum, a 300 Mb external drive from APS, and a 128-Mb magneto-optical removable cartridge drive from Peripheral Land. Type is from Adobe's Stone family of type faces. The book was produced using Microsoft Word 5.1 for layout, MacDraw II from Claris for illustrations, Mainstay's Capture for taking Mac screen shots, and Hijaak for Windows for PC screen shots. The book was proofed on a NEC Silentwriter 95 printer. Final copy was output directly to film.

The cover of *The Online User's Encyclopedia* was designed with Adobe Illustrator 3.0.

Plug into the Internet!

HoloNet links you to the **Internet** - the world's largest and fastest growing interactive network. To have *full* access to the **Internet,** all you need is a modem and HoloNet membership.

HoloNet membership can provide you with a wealth of information and possibilities. HoloNet is accessible from a local modem call in over 850 cities nationwide and includes:

- Internet e-mail, USENET news, FTP, IRC, Telenet, MUDs, Go & Chess.
- Eudora Support.
- UUCP Feeds.
- QWK Support.
- Online Publications.

One Month Free!

New HoloNet members can receive a free month of HoloNet membership ($6.00 value). Simply mail in this coupon and mention Bernard Aboba's name when you join HoloNet. To find the access number closest to you modem to 1-800-NET-HOLO (8N1)

Member Account Name: _____

For a **free** demo modem to
510-704-1058 (8N1)

HoloNet is a servicemark of Information Access Technologies, Inc. • 46 Shattuck Square, Suite 11 • Berkeley, CA 94704 • voice 510-704-0160 • © 1993 Information Access Technologies, Inc.

 WATERMARK VOICE MAIL™

WaterMark Voice Mail™ turns a Macintosh computer into a complete voice mail and message processing center. Callers may leave recorded messages, and, when using a Touchtone® telephone, follow easy-to-understand verbal prompts to enter a return telephone number and best time for a call back. Users may access and listen to recorded messages directly from the Macintosh by double-clicking on a message icon, or remotely, by using a standard Touchtone® phone. After listening to a message, users can record a response on the phone that the Macintosh will automatically send back to the caller's number at any user-designated time. High Tide's Insta-Return™ feature is ideal for personal use or sales-driven answering services that need to streamline customer or client support.

All of WaterMark Voice Mail's verbal prompts and messages are stored using state-of-the-art compression techniques, and provide high-clarity on all types of telephones. Additional features include a Calling Log that tracks all incoming and outgoing calls, a time-entry system for scheduling callbacks, a hold feature to enable personal contact during outgoing calls, and support for non-touch-tone telephone users, automatic retry on busy lines, and the ability to select and save, archive or discard message files.

High Tide Software
■ *leaders in innovative telephone applications* ■

2112A McKinley Avenue, Berkeley, CA 94703

Phone: 510/704-9927 ■ FAX: 510/704-9933

MENTION THIS BOOK WHEN YOU ORDER TO GET A FREE UPGRADE FOR SIX MONTHS!

Online registration

To be entitled to special offers and updates to *The Online Users Encyclopedia*, you must register electronically. A copy of the registration form can be obtained by `mail aboba@world.std.com,` subject: `form`. To submit the form, `mail aboba@world.std.com,` subject: `register`.

Suggestions

This guide is what it is mostly because of the suggestions of dozens of readers. If you have an idea to make this guide better, or disagree with the product recommendations, please don't hesitate to send us mail. To submit your suggestions, `mail aboba@world.std.com,` subject: `suggestions`.

Think the Unthinkable!

As detailed in the Memories and Visions section of this book, even the founders of global networks have been surprised by their evolution. Since the future of global networks appears to be unthinkable, we'd like to encourage you to send us your most unthinkable thoughts on the future of the Internet, via `mail aboba@world.std.com,` subject: `unthinkable`.

Filter contest

If my mailbox gets any fuller, I'm going to throw my modem off a cliff. Something must be done, and fast! To spur development of better filters, we will be awarding a $250 prize for the best filter program. Rules for the filter contest can be obtained via `mail aboba@world.std.com,` subject: `contest`.

The Internet Companion
0-201-62224-6

The Internet Companion Plus
0-201-62719-1

Want to Learn More About the Internet?

Check out Addison-Wesley's International Bestsellers:
The Internet Companion and *The Internet Companion Plus*!

Welcome to the Internet, the global web of computer networks reaching millions of people all over the world. From the mundane to the technical, from the humorous to the scientific, the Internet is an open door to the latest information on medicine, environmentalism, sports, politics, social issues, education, and much more. *The Internet Companion* and *The Internet Companion Plus* are your open door to the intricacies and the unique culture of the Internet.

The Internet Companion introduces you to the worldwide community on the Internet, teaching you how to tap into university research databases, online archives, and vast networks of up-to-date information.

The Internet Companion Plus gives you all of the same expert coverage with a plus! Access is the plus. *The Internet Companion Plus* comes bundled with the acclaimed WorldLink Software package which provides a simple and workable interface for Internet access.

Both books are available through booksellers everywhere, or call 1-800-822-6339